NETTLEFOLDS *Cricket Spikes*

Supplied complete with awl and spanner in boxed sets carrying the 'Castle' and 'Imperial' Brand trade marks.

GUEST KEEN & NETTLEFOLDS (MIDLANDS) LTD

Screw Division, Box 24, Heath Street, Birmingham, 18

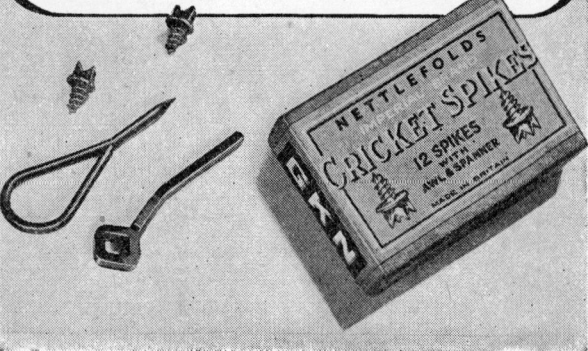

S/CS/2701

TABLE OF MAIN CONTENTS

(A complete Index appears on the following pages)

BRYLCREEM

—all your hair needs
for health and appearance

There's no substitute for Brylcreem, the world's
largest-selling hairdressing. It gives day-long
smartness and lasting hair health. No wonder
Brylcreem is preferred by sportsmen in the
public eye. Give *your* hair the benefit of
Brylcreem. Available in tubs or handy tubes.

the perfect hairdressing

royds 2

INDEX

NOTE:—r. = runs; w. = wickets; * signifies "Not out."

B

THE QUEEN MEETS THE CHAMPIONS

[*Central Press*

The Queen paid her first visit to Kennington Oval when the South Africans played Surrey. Both teams and officials were presented to her. Here Her Majesty is shaking hands with A. J. McIntyre, the Surrey wicket-keeper. Also in the picture are W. S. Surridge, the Surrey captain, P. B. H. May, the Surrey vice-captain and England captain, and Alec Bedser.

SURREY—COUNTY CHAMPIONS, 1955

[*Central Press*

R. C. E. Pratt, D. F. Cox, P. J. Loader, T. H. Clark, G. A. R. Lock, D. G. W. Fletcher, K. Barrington, M. D. Willett, B. Constable. *Front Row:* M. J. Stewart, E. A. Bedser, A. J. McIntyre, P. B. H. May (vice-captain), W. S. Surridge (captain), A. V. Bedser, J. C. Laker, R. Swetman.

SOUTH AFRICANS IN ENGLAND, 1955

[*Sport and General*

V. I. Smith, H. J. Keith, T. L. Goddard, P. L. Winslow, P. Heine, N. A. T. Adcock, C. A. R. Duckworth, E. R. H. Fuller, M. McLennan (scorer). *Front Row*: P. N. F. Mansell, R. A. McLean, W. R. Endean, J. E. Cheetham (captain), K. G. Viljoen (manager), D. J. McGlew (vice-captain), H. J. Tayfield, J. H. B. Waite, A. R. A. Murray.

M.C.C. AUSTRALASIAN TEAM, 1954–55

[*Allan Studios, Melbourne*

G. Duckworth (scorer), K. V. Andrew, P. J. Loader, T. W. Graveney, F. H. Tyson, H. Dalton (masseur). *Middle Row:* J. H. Wardle, R. T. Simpson, J. V. Wilson, R. Appleyard, J. E. McConnon, J. B. Statham, M. C. Cowdrey, G. Howard (manager). *Front Row:* T. E. Bailey, W. J. Edrich, P. B. H. May (vice-captain), L. Hutton (captain), D. Compton, A. V. Bedser, T. G. Evans.

WORLD'S SMALLEST TEST SCORE

[*Star, Auckland*

England finished their tour of the Antipodes by dismissing New Zealand at Auckland for 26, the lowest total in the history of Test cricket. The match was over when this picture was taken, but the wickets tumbled so quickly that the score board workers never completed their job. Statham's bowling should read 3 wickets for 9 runs. The last New Zealand batsman was Hayes, 0

VITAL TEST CATCH FOR SOUTH AFRICA

A feature of the 1955 season was the keen and brilliant fielding of the South African team. Here P. F. Mansell takes a fine slip catch from M. C. Cowdrey off the bowling of H. J. Tayfield in England's first innings of the third Test at Manchester. D. C. S. Compton is the other batsman; W. R. Endean is at silly mid-on; T. L. Goddard is second slip and the umpire is Dai Davies.

[*Central Press*

IMPERIAL CRICKET CONFERENCE

[*Sport and General*]

Delegates to the Imperial Cricket Conference attended a meeting at Lord's in July. *Back Row*: R. W. V. Robins (Australia), R. Aird (Secretary, M.C.C.), H. S. Altham (M.C.C.), A. H. H. Gilligan (New Zealand), K. G. Viljoen (South Africa), Col. R. S. Rait Kerr (M.C.C.). *Front Row*: Group Captain M. M. A. Cheema (Pakistan), The Maharaj Kumar Sir Vijaya Ananda of Vizianagram (India), Harold Bushby (Australia), Viscount Cobham (President of M.C.C., Chairman), A. H. Coy (South Africa), Sir Allan Colymore (West Indies) and Sir Arthur Sims (New Zealand).

FIVE CRICKETERS OF THE YEAR

[*Central Press*

D. J. INSOLE (Essex)

FIVE CRICKETERS OF THE YEAR

[*P.A.—Reuter*

F. H. TYSON (Northamptonshire)

[*P.A.—Reuter*

D. J. McGLEW (South Africa)

FIVE CRICKETERS OF THE YEAR

H. J. TAYFIELD (South Africa)   *[Sport and General*

M. C. COWDREY (Kent)

FIVE CRICKETERS OF THE YEAR

M. C. COWDREY

From the moment he was born at Bangalore in Southern India on Christmas Eve, 1932, MICHAEL COLIN COWDREY was destined for cricket. In naming him, his father gave him his "initial" start, M. C. C. Some sons disappoint their fathers by not adhering to their appointed course, but happily for the Cowdrey family, Colin always possessed cricket ability and a few days after celebrating his 22nd birthday with M.C.C. in Australia he hit his first Test hundred for England.

Unfortunately his father, E. A. Cowdrey, did not live to see his son reach the summit. Colin lunched with his parents on board the Orient liner *Orsova* before bidding them farewell; three weeks later, when M.C.C. arrived at Fremantle, came the sad news of his father's death. In his day, Mr. Cowdrey senior was a capable batsman, but tea-planting claimed most of his time. He played some cricket and when Arthur Gilligan's M.C.C. Team toured India in 1926–27 he made top score, 48, for the Europeans against them at Madras. Opposed to him were those two fine bowlers, M. W. Tate and W. E. Astill, who later as coaches at Tonbridge School helped to fashion young Colin's career.

From the age of four Colin used to play with his father and one of the native servants at their home at Bangalore, but soon he was on his way to England, where from five and a half until thirteen he lived at Homefield Preparatory School at Sutton in Surrey. There, Cowdrey says, he really learned cricket from the headmaster, Mr. C. Walford, whom he describes as a cricket fanatic. In the summer, Sunday was the only rest-day. Mr. Walford coached the boys four days a week and the other two were devoted to matches.

When only seven, Cowdrey made 93 against another school. This won him a Jack Hobbs bat and an inspiring letter from the Surrey idol. Colin says that letter fired his ambition. He put it in a frame and it hangs in his bedroom to this day. Even in those tender years, Cowdrey hit plenty of hundreds and although he used to bowl leg-breaks at the nets, he kept wicket until he was eleven. Then his headmaster told him the time was ripe for him to bowl in matches and already he could send down a googly.

Small wonder that when Cowdrey went to Tonbridge School in 1946 at the age of thirteen he jumped straight into the first team, though not as a batsman. He began in May at number eleven, gaining his place as a bowler, but soon his batting talent was recognised and when the team went to Lord's in July to meet Clifton he had advanced to number three in the order.

He was the youngest player to appear in a Public Schools match at Lord's, but already the steel-nerve which characterised his batting in Australia was evident. He scored 75 and 44 and at the crisis claimed the last five Clifton wickets, thus snatching a thrilling victory for Tonbridge by two runs. For five years, the last two as captain, Cowdrey dominated Tonbridge cricket; he scored 2,894 runs and took 216 wickets. He finished his school career as the Public Schools captain at Lord's, marking his departure with scores of 126 and 55 in the annual match with Combined Services.

It was on August 19, 1950, that Cowdrey began his first-class career for Kent at Derby. His side were overwhelmed but he scored 15 and 26 and *Wisden* commented: *Cowdrey, the Tonbridge School captain, made a promising debut for Kent*. Cowdrey remained at Tonbridge until the following April and then he spent a full season with Kent, gaining his County cap during the Hampshire match at the Canterbury Festival. Earlier that summer he hit his first first-class hundred, 143 for Free Foresters against Oxford University in the Parks, and he wound up a memorable summer by hitting the only century of the Scarborough Festival—106 for Gentlemen against Players. In October he entered Brasenose College, Oxford.

By then his reputation was growing and when the cricket season came round again P. D. S. Blake, the Oxford captain, needed only three matches to make up his mind to award Cowdrey his Blue. That was on May 16, 1952. His only hundred that year was for Kent against India at Canterbury, but in 1953 he left all his other performances behind, scoring 1,917 runs including four centuries.

He chose Lord's for some of his best displays, for he hit 116 against Cambridge and at the end of August he played two grand innings of 50 and 57 for Gentlemen of England against the Australians. In that match he came under the full fire of Lindwall and Miller. They gave him a thorough test, bumpers and everything; he met them with the calm of a matured batsman.

Everyone who saw those displays, including the Australians themselves, knew that England had produced a batsman far above the ordinary. They compared him with W. R. Hammond, whom he resembles so much in confidence, build and method. Cowdrey has the same height, the same massive shoulders, and the same quality in his straight and off drives.

It was with some disappointment that Cowdrey found himself passed over at that time for the M.C.C. Tour of West Indies. The season of 1954 saw him captain of Oxford and he left no doubts as to his flair for leadership. It was a wet summer and for various reasons, including examinations, Cowdrey did not quite approach his best form. Both his aggregate and average fell. Happily for England the selectors had not lost faith in him. They gave him a place in Len Hutton's team for Australia and soon the wisdom of this decision became manifest.

Cowdrey realised this was his great opportunity. If he did

well, a life of cricket was at hand and throughout the tour he proved to be one of only two dependable batsmen in the side. The other was Peter May, with whom he shared a cabin on the ship and with whom he was usually seen in company both off the field and at the crease. The full details of that wonderful tour and the part Cowdrey played can be found elsewhere in this book. Hutton considered May and Cowdrey the two best batsmen in the world under twenty-five.

Australian sunshine and fast Australia pitches brought out the best in Cowdrey. On his first appearance at Sydney he hit two centuries, 110 and 103, against New South Wales, being easily the youngest English cricketer to accomplish this feat. Such was Hutton's problem over finding someone to open the innings with him in the Tests that Cowdrey, for the first time in his career, went in first in that second venture. His success sorely tempted Hutton to promote him permanently, but after one more trial the shrewd captain preferred Cowdrey to occupy his normal position.

Cowdrey returned to England in April 1955 ready for his two years' National Service in the Royal Air Force. For years his feet had given him considerable trouble, but he never mentioned it to the authorities. Never did he expect they would become front-page news and lead to questions in Parliament. He suffers from stiffening of the joints in both big toes and when playing cricket always wears specially made boots.

When sixteen he underwent a manipulative operation and spent the whole of the Easter term in the Tonbridge School sanitorium with both legs completely encased in plaster. That brought about a distinct improvement, but he knew that at some time another operation would be essential to break down the joints. He hopes to put off that operation until he is twenty-five and although no permanent cure can be guaranteed, he thinks there is a sporting chance that his feet will last him through his cricket career until, perhaps, he is forty.

Most people would expect that a young athlete returning from a triumphant cricket tour of Australia could fulfil his initial Forces training without question. Hence the doctors who received him prior to his call up passed him one to the other. This is Cowdrey the cricketer; he's all right, they said.

It was on the day he joined the R.A.F. that the medicos raised the first query. At once they spotted the state of his feet. In Cowdrey's own words, they were scared of allowing him to go before a drill sergeant. Permanent injury and a life pension might have resulted. So they put him in the sick bay far away from the drill sergeants and telephoned Whitehall with their problem. In a few weeks Cowdrey was a civilian again.

So he rejoined the Kent team. He hit his first Championship

century, 139 against Northamptonshire at Tunbridge Wells, and later he repeated his Sydney feat at the expense of the Essex bowlers, 115 and 103, both not out, at Gillingham. A very badly damaged finger, injured when playing against South Africa in the Manchester Test, kept him idle for some weeks and gave England the chance to experiment.

During his first two years at Oxford, Cowdrey played Association and Rugby Football, but because of his troublesome feet he was compelled to give up those winter pastimes. He still plays golf, squash, tennis and rackets. Indeed, he won his Blue for rackets and in 1953 was runner-up in the English Rackets Championship at Queen's Club, falling only to Geoffrey Atkins, the World Champion.

As he had taken up a business appointment with an emporium in Kent whose managing director is another who lives for cricket, Cowdrey should find scope to continue for some years to please his admirers.—N.P.

F. H. TYSON

Not for a long time has a star burst upon the cricket firmament with such startling suddenness as has been the case with FRANK HOLMES TYSON, the Northamptonshire and England fast bowler.

Born at Farnworth, Bolton, on June 6, 1930, Tyson played his first cricket on the "rough backs" near his home at about the age of four, progressing to school cricket of a more serious nature some six years later. Even in those early days he cherished the idea of becoming a fast bowler of class without realising the fame which was eventually to come, and, benefiting from the help of Alf Cassley, a former Middleton Club professional, he did well enough to gain a place in the Middleton second eleven when fourteen. After a year at Fleetwood Grammar School, he moved to Middleton Queen Elizabeth Grammar School, where he stayed till eighteen, captaining first the under-fourteen team and later the first eleven.

By the time Tyson was sixteen he appeared in the Middleton first team and though, in his first match, he took four cheap Royton wickets, he achieved nothing spectacular afterwards. In 1947, upon the recommendation of one of the two brothers Kay who played for Middleton, he went for a trial at Old Trafford, playing for Manchester Schoolboys and in the early county trials of 1948. By now seventeen, he was sitting for his higher school certificate and looking for a place at a University. In 1948, he was called up for the Army, in whose representative matches he appeared without special distinction. When his National Service ended in 1950, Lancashire's interest in him had evaporated, particularly as he was suffering from a strained back-muscle. He therefore approached Northamptonshire with more encouraging results and commenced qualification by residence.

Meanwhile Tyson began studying at Durham University for the B.A. degree which, at the second attempt, he gained soon after the end of last summer. In 1950 he turned out again for Middleton and the following season, by taking close upon 100 wickets, he helped Knypersley to carry off the North Staffordshire League Second Division Championship. At length, in 1952, he made his first-class debut, against the India touring team. In his first over he took a wicket, that of P. Roy, and though that was the extent of his success, his 21 overs cost only 47 runs.

By this time he was acknowledged as the fastest modern bowler if not of all time, a view to which F. R. Brown, the Northamptonshire captain, fully subscribed. Next year he led Durham University to the Universities Athletic Union Championship and at the same time made twelve appearances in County Championship matches for Northamptonshire. Bowling with a run of seventeen measured paces, he dismissed 26 men at an average cost of 25.80. Though he took four wickets for 26 against Derbyshire and four for 59 against Surrey, the performance which earned most distinction was that for his county in the match with the Australians.

When the touring team were sent in to bat at Northampton, Tyson inflicted a shock upon them by disposing of C. C. McDonald and G. B. Hole with the second and fourth deliveries of his opening over, and though he took no other wickets he established himself in the public eye. In the winter which followed he put in a spell of tree-felling to improve his physique and Northamptonshire sent him to the London indoor cricket school run by Alf Gover, the former Surrey and England fast bowler.

Here began a great improvement. Gover says he did not alter Tyson's style, but he eradicated certain faults. For instance, Tyson used to drag the outside of his right foot as the right arm came up to deliver the ball, causing his left side to turn towards cover-point so that at the moment of release his right side pointed towards the batsman. The result of this was that he was almost solely an arm-bowler. In order that he should use his body as well, he was persuaded to take up his left arm later and to drag on the inside of his right foot.

Next summer Tyson established himself as a regular member of the county team; he increased his wickets to 78, reduced their cost to 21.38 and also showed improvement as a batsmen. That year, too, began his notable partnership as opening bowler for England with Statham, of Lancashire, for Tyson was chosen to play in the final Test match with Pakistan in which he distinguished himself by taking four wickets for 35 runs in the first innings. Four times in county engagements he disposed of five batsmen in an innings. Even so his choice as a member of the M.C.C. Team to tour Australia during the winter came as something of a surprise.

In the first Test match in Australia, Tyson took only one wicket and that at a cost of 160 runs, and it looked as though the selectors had made a mistake in choosing him. Then he shortened his run by three or four yards with remarkable results. In the second Test at Sydney he took four wickets for 45 and six for 85, and in the third at Melbourne achieved his best performance by dismissing seven men for 27 runs in the second innings. His place in the England side was thus assured, and, including the two matches with New Zealand, his Test record for the tour read: 39 wickets, average 17.25. Such was his pace that Australian journalists gave him the pseudonym of "Typhoon Tyson." Towards the end of the tour he developed foot trouble which limited his cricket last summer and kept him out of all but the first and third Test matches with South Africa. In these, however, he again showed himself a telling force, particularly in the opening game of the series at Trent Bridge. Here, in taking six wickets for 28 runs in the second innings, he brought about the dismissal of South Africa for 201 and paved the way to victory in an innings with five runs to spare.

Essentially a quiet and modest man, whose thinning hair makes him look older than his twenty-five years, Tyson owes his triumphs to perseverance. Whether in League cricket or when playing in the Army he went on learning all the time. He discovered that fast bowling was a question not so much of strength as of rhythm. When finding himself engaged in three-day matches, he considered a longer run would help to conserve energy; yet in Australia he owed his success to the fact that he returned to the methods he employed earlier in his career. The career of a fast bowler is often notoriously short. Hence Tyson's concentration upon studies, for he always wanted to become a teacher.—E. E.

D. J. McGLEW

Whatever Time's devouring hand wrests from the memory of the South Africans' visit to England in the golden summer of 1955 it will not be the name of Derrick John McGlew. His batting achievements and leadership in the two Test matches which the Springboks won, ensure that.

To England's bowlers he became a solid, unflinching and likeable opponent with a bat which looked uncommonly broad. The terse comment "McGlew's still there" was sufficient to encourage hope or temper enthusiasm, according to whichever camp allegiance lay.

In tenacity of purpose McGlew follows very much the approach of two other distinguished South African opening batsmen, Bruce Mitchell and Eric Rowan. McGlew, too, has equanimity, in cricket a quality of rare value. Symptomatic of his temperament was the way in which he hit hundreds in the Tests at Manchester and Leeds after "bagging a pair" in the Lord's game. He possesses no especial mannerisms at the crease, yet you cannot watch him for long without sensing his individuality.

At the age of four the summer game had already caught his fancy. There is a photograph at his mother's home showing a determined little figure in cricket pads clutching a bat some sizes too big.

When he went to Merchiston Preparatory School in Pietermaritzburg, McGlew held a place in the first XI from the time he entered Standard III until he moved on to Maritzburg College after reaching Standard VI. He captained the team during his last two years at Merchiston and was also vice-captain of the Rugby XV, a middle distance runner and a useful high jumper.

Just as McGlew was developing his talents in the field of sport an attack of diphtheria laid him low and threatened to put an end to his athletic career. He was unable to take part in any physical recreation during his first year at Maritzburg but made such a recovery that he ended his College days captain both of the cricket and rugby teams. Here, indeed, was an early example of his courage when things looked gloomy.

Subsequently, McGlew represented Natal as a fly-half and he also turned out on the wing for the Wanderers, a hockey club in Pietermaritzburg. Further distinction came his way when he was invited to captain Natal Schools in his first Nuffield Week. In that team were Goddard, McLean, Waite, Melle and Arthur Tayfield, a brother of H. J. Tayfield. A year later, in 1948, he led the South African Schools' XI against Natal.

About this period the Provincial selectors chose him to open for Natal against Orange Free State. He made 25 before being run out and followed this by scoring 69 against North-Eastern Transvaal at the end of February.

All the time McGlew was improving and increasing his range of strokes. He did not satisfy those who insist upon the straightest of bats in defence—he still moves too far across the wicket for the purist—but he made runs just the same and in 1951 he realised a boyhood ambition to play for his country. He visited England under the leadership of A. D. Nourse, junior; played in the first two Tests, scored 1,002 runs in all matches at an average of 38.53 and hit centuries against Hampshire and Glamorgan.

When he returned home McGlew succeeded Nourse as captain of Natal and under his guidance the Currie Cup was regained. Next came his selection as vice-captain for the tour of Australasia where he was soon able to demonstrate afresh his natural powers of leadership, for Cheetham strained a groin in the second game against South Australia. Because of a hand injury, McGlew himself missed the fifth Test which South Africa won to share the rubber. He was back in the side for the first Test against New Zealand at Wellington in March, 1953, and set up a seventh wicket Test record of 246 with Anton Murray. McGlew's 255 was the highest individual Test score made by a South African, surpassing Eric Rowan's 236 in the fourth Test against England at Leeds in 1951.

And so in 1955 to a second tour of England where his concentration and physical endurance at the wicket became an integral part of the Springboks' cricket. Attrition is not a popular method of progress. McGlew himself has not always batted this way, but circumstances wrought the change of style.

South Africa depended so much on his performances that he found it necessary to curb those strokes which were charged with risk. The course was justified. McGlew rarely failed his country last summer. When Cheetham was hurt, he took over the captaincy and led the team to their splendid victories in the third and fourth Tests which brought the series level. At Headingley, he and Goddard established a fresh record for a South African side in England by scoring 176 together for the first wicket.

In the field he was the very essence of energy, chasing everything in an arc from cover to mid-off. Only the fittest of men could have projected such vitality. McGlew exercises assiduously every day of his life. It is such thoroughness in all that he does which assures McGlew of a place among the great names of South African cricket. Posterity may rank him alongside a wider company of the game's élite. He is, after all, only twenty-seven years of age.—R. C. S.

H. J. TAYFIELD

In the renaissance of South African cricket since 1951 no role has been more vital, nor more successfully accomplished, than that of HUGH JOSEPH TAYFIELD. To the dark, slimly-built Natal off-break bowler fell the task of shouldering, almost single-handed, the burden formerly shared by those two great spin bowlers, A. M. B. Rowan and the late N. B. F. Mann.

Figures tell eloquently of the splendid manner in which Tayfield responded to that call and the great part he has played in one of the most glorious chapters in South Africa's cricket history. In the seventeen Tests played by South Africa from 1952 to the end of the 1955 tour of England, J. F. Cheetham's spin bowlers accounted for 109 batsmen. Of these, no fewer than 87 fell to the guileful, tenacious Tayfield, an average of four out of every five. His place in the annals of the game became assured when, by dismissing T. W. Graveney in the fifth Test at Kennington Oval last summer, Tayfield claimed his hundredth Test victim. This honour eluded even such famous Springboks as C. L. Vincent

(84) and G. A. Faulkner (82), both of whom appeared in twenty-five Tests compared with Tayfield's twenty-two.

Cricket was in Tayfield's blood when he was born in Durban on January 30, 1929. His uncle, S. H. Martin, played for Worcestershire with considerable success as an all-rounder in the 1930's and later helped to develop his nephew's cricket as a fellow-member of the Natal and Rhodesia sides.

Tayfield's father was also a keen cricketer in his youth and remains among the most demanding critics of Hugh and his younger brothers, Arthur and Cyril, both of whom now play for their adopted province of Transvaal.

As a boy, Hugh bowled out of the back of his hand and though his batting and fielding were sufficient to keep him in the Durban High School XI his opportunities with the ball were limited. The turning-point in Tayfield's career occurred when the school captain, also a leg-break bowler, suggested that Tayfield should try his hand at off-breaks. At his first attempt Hugh took two or three good wickets and promptly resolved to concentrate on his new-found art. Tayfield cannot recall being coached or modelling his technique on that of any other bowler, but he progressed so rapidly that soon after his seventeenth birthday he made his first-class debut for Natal. The following season, 1946–47, he helped Natal to win the revived Currie Cup competition and attracted special attention by taking six for 27 and six for 46 in friendly matches against Rhodesia and Transvaal respectively.

For the next two years Tayfield was lost to Natal through Army service in Rhodesia, where he joined Martin and another former Worcestershire player, A. P. Singleton, in the provincial side. With them he gained his first taste of international cricket against F. G. Mann's 1948–49 M.C.C. team and, though he took only two wickets in the two games, bowled well enough to persuade several English players that they had met a worthy successor to Rowan, then acknowledged as the world's best off-spin bowler.

The following season Rowan broke down with knee trouble a fortnight before the first Test against Australia and Tayfield, back with Natal, replaced him in all five Tests. The first two brought him only five wickets for 234 runs but in the third, on his home ground at Kingsmead, Durban, he became a national hero. Australia, trapped on a "sticky dog," were shot out for 75—their lowest score against South Africa—and Tayfield's analysis read 8.4—1—23—7. Even that performance was not enough to bring about Australia's first post-war defeat, but it established Tayfield as a bowler of Test class.

He finished the series as South Africa's leading wicket-taker with seventeen. Then just as he seemed to be launched securely on his Test career, came a period of setbacks. In the winter of

1950 he damaged his right shoulder playing Rugby football for Durban High School Old Boys. Treatment by a Durban osteopath, Mr. Walley, dispelled fears that Tayfield's bowling might be affected, but the injury left him unable to play tennis or squash, two of his favourite recreations. A bigger disappointment followed when he was omitted from the team to tour England under A. D. Nourse in 1951. Rowan, fit again, was preferred and the Selectors decided against choosing two bowlers of similar style. A few weeks after the tour began, however, they reversed this policy in order to ease the strain on Rowan and Tayfield flew to England. He arrived with high hopes but, with Rowan remaining fit, Tayfield alone of the party did not find a place in any of the Tests, and in all first-class games he took only twenty-nine wickets at an average cost of 36.55 each.

He returned home, however, a much-improved bowler and with the retirement of Rowan had no serious challenger to his place in the side chosen for the memorable tour of Australia in 1952–53. South African suprised the cricket-world by drawing the rubber and Tayfield equalled A. V. Bedser's two-year-old record of thirty wickets in an Australian series. With thirteen in the second Test at Melbourne he beat all previous performances for South Africa and his seventy wickets in all games established a new record for a touring bowler in Australia. From Australia, where he met the girl who was to become his wife, Tayfield went on to further success in New Zealand and the following season he helped to overwhelm the New Zealanders in South Africa.

And so Tayfield came to England again last year, not this time as a late reserve but with the reputation of being the best bowler of his type in the world. Revelling in the sunshine and firm pitches, he promptly erased the memory of his failures four years earlier. Although he did not appear to spin the ball as viciously as Rowan in his prime, his control of length and flight was superb. Many eyebrows were raised at his field-placing— two men almost shoulder to shoulder about fifteen yards from the bat at mid-on and a vast, inviting space between mid-off and extra cover. Tayfield, a keen student of tactics, reasoned that by tempting batsmen to hit against the break he stood a good chance of getting them caught in one of the mid-on positions. Moreover, he claimed that strong on-side players like M. C. Cowdrey and P. B. H. May could be tied down by these fielders and that others were likely to come to grief through trying to hit over the heads of the twin sentinels.

These arguments did not satisfy all Tayfield's critics but none could deny his success. Though troubled by strain and loss of sleep towards the end of the tour, he rose to Cheetham's heavy demands magnificently, bowling 1,170 overs and taking 143 wickets in all games. In the Tests he was mastered only at Lord's. He bowled South Africa to victory at Leeds and nearly did so again in the vital struggle at The Oval.

Tayfield insists on giving much of the credit for his achievements to the splendid support he has received in the field, both for South Africa and Natal. While undoubtedly true, this is no more than his deserts for he is himself a brilliant fielder, either to his own bowling or in any of the close positions. As a batsman Tayfield was not seen at his best in 1955, but he has many fine innings to his credit, notably one of 75 against Australia when runs were badly needed. Apart from these talents, Tayfield has contrived to remain a personality in a side which has submerged individuality to a remarkable degree in the common cause. None has submitted more cheerfully nor more loyally to the discipline imposed by J. E. Cheetham and K. G. Viljoen, but he belongs to the breed of cricketers who compel the interest of spectators. His habit of kissing his cap for luck at the start of each over has been criticised as ostentation, but it is characteristic of Tayfield that he should remain quite unmoved in his determination to continue the ritual. It began during the triumphant Melbourne Test of 1952–53. Australia were 84 for no wicket when Tayfield kissed his cap in desperation. Immediately A. R. Morris gave a return catch and the habit was born.

Tayfield has no explanation, however, for the other mannerism that led the Australians to christen him "Toey" at the outset of his Test career. Whether preparing to wheel into his brief, lopsided run or waiting for the next ball to be bowled to him while batting, he taps the toe of each boot firmly on the ground two or three times. Yet such is his intense concentration that he is hardly aware of doing so.—P. L. W.

D. J. INSOLE

With amateur county cricketers nowadays something of a rarity, it was the more refreshing to find one of them, DOUGLAS JOHN INSOLE, of Essex, not only the first to reach the "milestones" of 1,000 and 2,000 runs last season, but the most prolific run-getter in the country. With 2,427 runs, including nine centuries—two of them in the match with Kent at Gillingham—he averaged 42.57.

Born at Clapton, Middlesex, on April 18, 1926, Insole has spent most of his life in the county he now represents, for he moved to Highams Park when four. His early cricket was of the type by which the average small boy learns the rudiments of the game— on the lawn at home with his father, a keen sports enthusiast. By the time he was eight he engaged in games of a more mature nature at Selwyn Avenue Elementary School where he stayed till eleven. From there he went to the Sir George Monoux Grammar

School, Walthamstow, making such progress that when thirteen he appeared for both London Schoolboys and Essex Schoolboys.

Four years of war-time evacuation with the school to Leominster, Herefordshire, from 1939, interfered somewhat with his advance as a player, for what games were possible took place in rather unconventional circumstances. The effect of this did not prove lastingly detrimental and when the school returned to London he turned out for Chingford in club matches in 1943 and 1944, hitting what he terms "the very occasional century." All this he accomplished with the whole-hearted encouragement of his headmaster, Mr. J. F. Elam, himself a cricket devotee, but without any coaching of a serious character.

This did not necessarily tell against him, for Insole considers that had the basic strokes been instilled into him, he might not have been so successful as the essentially on-side batsman which he eventually became. How coaches, themselves possibly slaves to orthodoxy, may be wrong in their judgment of a player's capabilities was illustrated when, after two years' Army service, Insole went up to Cambridge in 1946. Before the start of the 1947 season the University coaches watched him in the nets at Fenner's and informed G. L. Willatt, the University captain, that in their opinion Insole "would not make a run" because he hit across the ball. He confounded his critics by making many runs in the trial games and for the Crusaders and, on the occasion of his first-class debut, he hit 44 from the Yorkshire bowling at Fenner's before being run out. Even so he might not have gained a Blue that year but for the repeated failure of batsmen with more established reputations. In the match with Oxford he scored 38 and 44 and he wound up the season fourth in the University averages, with 161 not out against Hampshire at Portsmouth his highest innings. That summer he began his career with Essex, to whom he had been introduced by his fellow Blue, Trevor Bailey, and he hit 109 not out from the Lancashire bowling at Clacton.

On one occasion when all recognised wicket-keepers at Cambridge were engaged upon examinations, Insole was pressed into service. He acquitted himself so well that next year, with few accredited stumpers available and those unable to make runs, he was given the position behind the stumps for almost the entire season, including the big game at Lord's.

In 1949, his last year at the University, he led Cambridge to a great triumph by seven wickets over Oxford, a performance all against expectations, for the Light Blues fared moderately in the preliminary fixtures whereas their opponents had beaten both Yorkshire and Middlesex, the eventual joint County Champions, and were also the only side to lower the colours of W. A. Hadlee's New Zealand touring team.

Coming down from Cambridge, Insole continued with Essex.

His first innings for them that season was not encouraging, for he was out for a single against Leicestershire. Against Yorkshire in the following engagement, however, he hit 219 not out, which remains his highest. True, fortune favoured him, for he was missed four times, but this big innings not only won for him his Essex cap, but placed him firmly upon his feet in county cricket. Actually he headed the Essex averages with 65.38. In 1950, when joint captain with T. N. Pearce, he scored more runs, 1,592, than any other member of the eleven and was chosen for England in the third Test match with West Indies.

The following summer Insole took over the sole captaincy and has led Essex ever since, scoring over 1,000 runs each year. Last season he played for England in the fourth Test against South Africa and captained Gentlemen v. Players at Lord's and The Rest against The Champion County. His feat of scoring two separate centuries in a match was one he might well have achieved in 1954 against Northamptonshire at Romford where, having hit 156 not out in the first innings and 92 not out in the second, he declared in the interests of the side. As it happened, the sacrifice was in vain, for Northamptonshire won in the last over by three wickets. Insole occasionally puts in a useful spell of medium-pace bowling. Employing the seam skilfully, he specially distinguished himself against Surrey at Ilford last May when he dismissed five of the Champion county's batsmen in seven overs for 22 runs.

Though Denis Compton was his cricketing hero in his schoolboy days, Insole did not attempt to copy his style. He attributes his success rather to a good eye and some natural aptitude for ball games. A fine fieldsman, especially at slip, Insole has definite ideas on tactics. He stands firmly against the idea that it is better to play for a draw than to bring about a result by a declaration on the last day, for he feels that players and crowd usually enjoy a finish.

Aside from his cricketing ability, Insole is also an Association footballer of class. For two years before going up to the University he played for Walthamstow Avenue at inside-right, in which position he represented Cambridge against Oxford in 1946, 1947 and 1948, being captain in the last season when he figured as reserve in an England International Trial. A founder-member of the famous Pegasus F.C., he was the first player to captain them. For the last two winters he has played at outside-right for Corinthian-Casuals. Sporting talent is not a family attribute, but Insole's younger brother captained London Boys at both Association football and cricket at the age of thirteen and looked to have a highly promising future. Unhappily he developed tuberculosis a year later and died last year aged twenty-three.

Douglas Insole is married and has two daughters.—E. E.

NOTES BY THE EDITOR

ENGLAND'S SEARCH FOR OPENING BATSMEN

One would have imagined after the triumphant tour of Len Hutton's team in Australia and New Zealand and the success which attended England against South Africa under Peter May last summer that there would be general satisfaction and confidence in England's ability to retain the Ashes in the forthcoming series with Australia. Judged by recent results, England stands on top of the cricket world, yet the form of some of the players and their methods as well as their approach to the game have received adverse criticism. Moreover, much of this criticism is justified.

Australian Recovery

Complacency could certainly lead to disaster especially in a summer when the Australians are our visitors and we can no longer count on Hutton and probably Compton. Despite their crushing downfalls at the hands of Statham, Tyson and company, the Australians lost no time in rehabilitating themselves. They went to West Indies and made heaps of runs against less hostile bowling on the easy-paced pitches of the Caribbean.

No doubt Australia still have problems, but their players are blessed with natural ability and they usually possess the happy knack of rising to the occasion and blending well as a team during their four and half months of cricket in England. It must be expected that they will prove a much tougher proposition than when M.C.C. visited them eighteen months ago. Indeed, the stage seems to be set for an exciting series which will find the two countries closely matched.

With the retirement of Hutton, England require two opening batsmen. They faced this problem twelve months ago when Hutton, after being given the captaincy for all five Tests against South Africa, stood down through ill health. Here was the opportunity to get ready for Australia. After his scintillating hundred in the final Test at Sydney in March 1955, Graveney was retained for number one and Kenyon, too, received a prolonged trial. This pair opened in the first three Tests, but managed to make only one double figure partnership—91 in the first Test at Trent Bridge. Bailey and Lowson took over at Headingley for the first innings and Graveney replaced Bailey in the second.

At The Oval, the selectors endeavoured to counter the negative leg theory of the tall left-handed South African bowler, Goddard, by picking five left-handed batsmen. These included the two openers, Ikin and Close, whose joint efforts produced stands of 51 and 5. The left-handed theme was retained for the M.C.C. tour of Pakistan where the duties were shared mainly by Close and

Richardson, the new Worcestershire captain. Other candidates are three right-handers, Simpson, and the two youngsters, Stewart, of Surrey, and M. J. K. Smith, whose proposed transfer from Leicestershire to Warwickshire has met with so much opposition. The form of all these men will be closely studied during the month of May.

One suggestion is that Cowdrey should be promoted in the order but such a move would take away some much-needed stiffening lower down. Some of the anxiety would be lessened if Compton were fit, but assuming he will not be available, then surely May and Cowdrey must fill the number three and four places. Similarly, providing Watson, the Yorkshire left-hander, is in form, England should not need to look further for a number five. This is his best position and the one he occupied on his debut against Australia at Lord's three years ago when his 109 on the last day helped so much to save the match.

The rest of the order should sort itself out presuming that Bailey is again chosen as the all-rounder at number six, to be followed by the wicket-keeper (Evans) and four bowlers. Mentioning bowlers, one finds that here, too, the position is far from clear cut for the selectors. Personally I would like to see the three successes in Australia, Statham, Tyson and Appleyard in action again, but time alone will prove whether Tyson's left heel and Appleyard's troublesome muscle in the right arm have mended.

Left-handed Rivals

Again Wardle and Lock will be rivals for one place and Laker, in his benefit year, should be at the top of his form. Whatever happens, Laker and Lock should be seen together at The Oval where they reign supreme as both Australia and South Africa can already testify.

Despite the overwhelming applications for tickets for the Tests many people fear that cricket as it is being played in this second half of the twentieth century is in danger of losing its public appeal. It is argued that Test matches alone command the people's interest because cricket has become too slow. Yet, maybe, it is the thirty-hour Test that has led to the gradual decrease in the rate of scoring in all first-class cricket.

The ambitious English young county batsman, keen to win the highest honours, must prove himself first in the three-day Championship and to do this he must not only produce runs consistently, but must also show himself fitted to play in the highest company. He discovers that the successful Test batsmen are generally those who decline to take the slighest risk—he must follow the methods of, say, Hutton and McGlew—if he is to win the selectors' approval.

Some people would like to see the return of the four-day Test in England, but I think that would be a step in the wrong direction. We do not want a repetition of the 1949 series when New Zealand pursued a safety-first policy and drew all four three-day Tests. The success of the five-day Tests in this country was emphasised only last summer when for the first time in England all five matches ended with definite results.

Slow scoring does not necessarily mean dull cricket, but when wickets do not fall and the batsmen are content to restrict the pace to 30 runs an hour (often this is due to the negative methods of the fielding side such as leg theory), lack of enterprise calls for complaint.

The President Speaks

No less a person than Lord Cobham made the following remarks last summer during his term of office as President of M.C.C.: "I do not think people will follow cricket much longer unless the game is reborn, but reborn it will be, and I think there are signs that the players will again hit the ball hard, high and often. Can we get rid of those awful bores who prod doubtfully at half-volleys and let every long hop pass by? They are the ones who are emptying our cricket grounds. We must get rid of them."

Lord Cobham used not to be a pessimist. In the years before the 1939–45 war he led Worcestershire twice to victory over Yorkshire by his forceful methods. In this same speech, which he made at Worcester's historic Guildhall when welcoming the South Africans, he said he believed that the technical skill of the game was higher now than ever before and may even have got too high. He thought, possibly, that cricket was on the verge of a revolution and a very good one, for there were signs that they were going back to the old days of sheer fast bowling which was very refreshing in these days of so much leg theory.

In September, *The Times*, in a bold and wide top of the page heading, claimed: "All is not well with English Cricket," and at the end of the year Mr. Ronald Aird, M.C.C. secretary, dwelt on the same theme in his annual speech to the County secretaries.

Dull cricket is not confined to England. Many of the four-day Sheffield Shield matches in Australia never reach a definite conclusion and attendances have fallen to an alarming degree. Matters have also come to an unsatisfactory state in India and Pakistan. When these two countries met a year ago in Pakistan both sides batted and bowled in such an unenterprising way that, for the first time in history, all five Tests in one series were drawn.

A more recent example occurred at Lahore only last January when the full strength of Pakistan met the M.C.C. team in the first representative match of the tour which was intended to show the best side of cricket. Pakistan spent twelve hours twenty minutes over a total of 363 for nine declared, and Hanif Mohammad occupied ten and a half hours getting 142 of those runs. We, in England saw enough of Hanif in 1954 to appreciate that he is a most gifted young batsman with an abundance of beautiful strokes. It is little less than a tragedy that when it comes to a representative match and the ground is packed with spectators the crowd is allowed to witness only a boring spectacle by Hanif. Such tactics are to be deplored and the sooner everyone connected with big cricket realises that the game itself is far more important than the result the better it will be for all those who seek enjoyment from playing and watching cricket.

It was in an effort to help the authorities to find a solution to these things that I enlisted the aid of W. E. Bowes. He has been closely linked with the game as a player and critic since he first performed the "hat-trick" against Cambridge University at Lord's in 1928. He has gone fully into the various problems and set forth his opinion together with those of many other notable person-alities in the article which follows these Notes. The numerous views emphasise the difficulties which must face the legislators if they attempt any revision of the laws. I would not be surprised to see a trial given to an extended lbw rule embracing any ball coming from the off which in the opinion of the umpire would hit the stumps.

A Glorious Summer

The summer of 1955 will be remembered chiefly for four things. The weeks of continuous sunshine beginning at Whit-suntide; the arrival of P. B. H. May as England's captain; the grand but unsuccessful fight of South Africa to win the rubber after losing the first two Tests and the tremendous battle between Surrey and Yorkshire which culminated in W. S. Surridge leading Surrey to the top of the Championship for the fourth successive time.

M.C.C., after amending one of their rules, welcomed Hutton from Australia by making him an honorary life member and the selectors took an unprecedented step—at least in modern times—by naming him captain for all five Tests against South Africa. Unfortunately for England, Hutton could not attain the standard of fitness required for an arduous Test series and he took a well-deserved rest from the Test and county scene in the hope of being ready for Australia this year. Prolonged medical treatment failed to bring about a complete remedy and at the comparatively young age of 39 this great player and captain has retired from the active scene.

For some years Hutton was England's batting sheet anchor. He followed in the trail of Hammond and on the decline of Wash-brook and Compton he stood virtually alone until the arrival of May and Cowdrey. Even the responsibility of captaincy made no difference to Hutton, the batsman. One has only to bear in mind how he carried the side in West Indies to appreciate that fact, and judging by the way May shaped and the number of runs he scored against South Africa, he too has the ability to shoulder the dual role.

Something unique in cricket occurred at The Oval during the Surrey and Yorkshire match last summer. Two England captains, May and Hutton, were serving under their official county captains, Surridge and Yardley. No doubt May will eventually succeed Surridge as the Surrey captain, but for the present he is quite content to be the deputy leader. Under Surridge, Surrey have recaptured their old glories of the 1880's and 1890's. During the four years Surridge has held office they have played 112 Championship matches, winning 71 and losing only 15 and they have equalled the feats of Nottinghamshire in 1883–1886 and Yorkshire 1937–46 in winning the title in four successive seasons. Leadership is a vital matter in cricket and Surridge will rank in history as one of the great County captains.

Rise of Hampshire

In these days when there is a tendency among a few Counties to import talent wholesale from outside their own boundaries, it has been most satisfactory to see the success of Hampshire, who in finishing third enjoyed their most successful season during sixty years in the Championship. They owe much to E. D. R. Eagar, the longest reigning county captain. He has led them with much optimism and enthusiasm since the resumption of big cricket in 1946. Many of the fine young players who have recently appeared for Hampshire were discovered by Eagar when tiny schoolboys and nurtured by him to their present status.

Hat-trick Controversy

The term "hat-trick" has for years been accepted in cricket circles as the feat of a bowler in taking three wickets with three consecutive balls. When Lock, the Surrey left-arm slow bowler, removed McMahon and Lobb with the last two balls of the Somerset first innings at Weston-super-Mare last August and then proceeded to account for Angell with his first ball of the follow-on, the legitimacy of this "hat-trick" was raised because it was split not only between two overs but also between two separate innings. In the past similar efforts have been entered in the Records, but in order to try to prevent disputes over these performances I sought guidance from M.C.C. A "hat-trick" is not covered by the laws but the expression has been in use since 1870 at least as a perusal of old *Wisdens* will reveal.

The M.C.C. Sub-Committee replied that in their opinion a "hat-trick" consists of three wickets in three successive balls from the same bowler in one match. True, this means that one batsman could be out twice in the same "hat-trick" and although this interpretation may not meet with universal approval I think it is a fair one under modern conditions. Eighty years ago pitches had not reached their present state of perfection. Bowlers ruled the game and there were only four balls to the over. I imagine that the presentation of a silk hat to a player must have been for something exceptional and that probably he had to take his three wickets in the same over.

Incidentally, Lock repeated his feat early in the M.C.C. tour of Pakistan. At Bahawalpur he took the last wicket of the first innings and later two wickets with his first two deliveries of the second innings.

Three M.B.E.s

The part cricket plays in cementing good relations between the various members of the British Commonwealth of Nations has yet again been recognised in the Queen's Honours. In the Birthday Honours of June 1955 the award of the M.B.E. to George Headley, the West Indies batsman, was announced, and in the last New Year's Honours Ian Johnson, the Australian captain, and Keith Miller, the Australian vice-captain, received similar recognition for their services to sport.

Wilfred Rhodes Trophy

Mr. W. R. Lambert, the Lancashire cricket bat manufacturer and a life-long admirer of Wilfred Rhodes, has given a handsome Trophy in the name of the great Yorkshire all-rounder, for the leading batsman each year in the Minor Counties Competition. The first winner is D. H. Cole, of Devon, who averaged 89 over 12 innings last summer. Cole is a fine upstanding player of six feet four inches and has played for Devon for 10 years. He hit 235 not out against Dorset at Blandford.

M.C.C. and Hutton

M.C.C. have stated that Hutton received a unanimous vote when he was chosen captain of the team for Australia and that the margin was not by a single vote as appeared in these notes a year ago.

GROWING PAINS OF CRICKET

SEEKING A REMEDY

By W. E. BOWES (*Yorkshire and England*)

What is wrong with the modern game of cricket? Anything?

(a) Are you satisfied with the present lbw rule?

(b) Is the present trend of leg-theory bowling excessive and, if so, is it for the good of the game?

(c) Do you agree that there is a general lack of high-class batsmen and that the cover-drive, one of the loveliest strokes in cricket, is disappearing?

(d) Are you completely satisfied that the present-day pitch is the ideal surface on which to see cricket at its best?

These questions were posed to me by the Editor of *Wisden*. My replies brought an invitation to conduct a thorough investigation into the problems confronting the game at the present time, and to assist in this regard, a letter was sent to prominent personalities in the game, the majority of whom played first-class cricket before and after the lbw law was altered, asking their views.

As one who has always regarded *Wisden* as the Textbook of Cricket, I was delighted to be made responsible for the main inquiry; but let me point out this one important feature at the outset: my own findings are opinion not fact. The replies received from famous personalities in the game were expressions of opinion, nothing more, and in fairness to them, especially where we differ, I have given their comments as received.

It is a remarkable thing that away down the years, prominent writers and cricketers have expressed the view that unless there was a new approach to cricket, unless rules were changed and the game made more attractive to the public, cricket would die a natural death. Very fortunately our administrators have not easily panicked. Changes to the Laws have been made only when, as a general principle, the mass of those playing the game demanded it.

No game can stand still. It must go either backward or forward, and to the everlasting credit of M.C.C., no matter how much the County game to-day might depend on football pools and the share-out of Tour profits, cricket has progressed. Always it has been allowed to develop easily, naturally. Progress has been maintained in the natural sequence of bowlers finding a method of getting batsmen out, and batsmen then finding the counter. Curved bats, like hockey sticks, were discarded for the straight bat when bowlers began to bounce the ball, or undulations in the pitch caused the ball to bounce over the curve of the bat.

The art of batsmanship improved considerably as the bowlers, continually looking for something new, introduced spin; with the advent of overarm bowling, speed; and, in later years, swerve, the googly, off-theory, leg-theory; and finally to the point where, using one skill or the other, specialist fieldsmen were employed in cleverly thought-out positions, and bowlers learned to bowl accurately to them.

With each skill in bowling came improvement in the art of batsmanship. In the days of W. G. Grace, P. F. Warner and the Palairets, batsmen used the right leg as a pivot. The left foot was put towards the ball and strokes to the covers were made in abundance. Bowlers replied with off-theory. They found that by bowling at the off-stump, and just outside, that the batsmen were not always "far enough across" to the ball when driving, and slip catches resulted.

The newer school of batsmen, Jack Hobbs, Wilfred Rhodes (with his famous three lines of defence, left foot, bat, right leg swinging across), Mead, Hammond and others came along. Instead of the right foot being used as a pivot, the first movements were to cover up the stumps with the pads. Do you recall that shuffle across of Philip Mead? My own early recollection of first-class cricket, every time I bowled a ball just outside the off-stump, was seeing Jack Hobbs, Sutcliffe and the rest, "shouldering arms." Without playing a shot, they put bat above their heads, pads in front of the stumps, and allowed the bowler to waste his energy.

The leg-break bowler, the out-swinger with speed, became vital necessities in any attack, and when groundsmen prepared a pitch of such excellence that swing and spin was impossible, I was advised by every batsman in the country (particularly when playing with him and not against him) to bowl the bouncer. It was bowled not with the intention of hitting the batsman, but in the hope of moving him away from the stumps, or getting a catch to long leg. I know of no batsman who denied the right of the fast bowler to bowl a bouncer.

Particularly do I contend that, from the beginning of cricket until 1932, the game was allowed to develop on natural lines, the bowlers calling the tune and the batsmen evolving methods that were many times beautiful to watch. Then came the fast leg-theory of Harold Larwood in Australia during the tour of 1932–3 which later became known as "The Bodyline tour of D. R. Jardine."

It is not for me in the scope of this inquiry to discuss the merits or demerits of the attack used. I can only point out that the world's greatest batsman, Don Bradman, in his book (*Farewell to Cricket*, page 71) states, "Bodyline was first used against me in a match on the Melbourne Cricket Ground between the M.C.C. and an

Australian XI. I reported privately to certain cricket administrators that, in my opinion, there would be serious trouble unless the matter was dealt with quickly."

I shall always regret that "The Don," with his great ability, condemned "Bodyline" from the first moment. The "swervers" of George Hirst and the "googlies" invented by Bosanquet had the world's greatest batsmen floundering for a complete season or more, but the batsmen found the answer eventually.

Perhaps the physical danger of "Bodyline" made it different. Sufficient it is to say that the weight of opinion caused this natural development of cricket theory and tactics to stop. After careful deliberation M.C.C. decided to legislate against Bodyline, and I believe, realising that the bowlers must be given something in return and that pitches were of such perfection that batsmen had all the favours, they made experiments with the lbw law and provided earlier opportunity for the new ball to be taken.

It must be remembered that shortly before the advent of "Bodyline" more help had been given to bowlers. In 1927 the circumference of the ball was reduced and in 1931 the wicket was enlarged by making the stumps higher and broader.

D. R. Jardine, the England captain, during the "Bodyline" tour, suggested a yet smaller ball, but this was not tried until last season when it was used in a few non-competitive first-class matches. It did not win much support and has been discarded.

Now, twenty years after the lbw change, we are asked, "Were the measures taken satisfactory? Did they work towards the betterment of cricket?"

Without hesitation my reply is: No. The new lbw rule, good in theory, has worked badly in practice. I believe, with all my love of the first-class game, that the village green is the real home of cricket. For club cricketers the game was hard enough before. Rules should be kept simple and anything which complicates the game should be avoided. If it is necessary to give the bowlers an advantage, well, go the whole way. Make it so that the Law applies to deliveries pitched on either side of the wickets, or at least, make it so that any ball pitching on the off gains the umpire's verdict of "out" if the batsman prevents it hitting his stumps with the pads. Let us not complicate the issue by saying the batsman is out "If, with any part of his person except the hand, which is in a straight line between wicket and wicket, etc. etc."

But I am moving too fast. If the game is to be played with enjoyment on the village green it should be worth the watching when the finest exponents in the world have the ball and bat. The weight of opinion seems to be that the lbw law has not improved the game either in skill or spectacle.

It is all very well to say that the laws are all right; it is the interpretation by the players that is wrong: to point to the splendid scoring feats that are shown on the third day of a match, after a fancy declaration, and ask, "Why cannot we have more of that enterprise on the first day?"

To my mind that very argument proves that the attitude of the present-day cricketer is good. When the occasion demands he can set about the bowling without thought of averages and failure. The real question is this: What manner of batsman is it who does not think himself capable of making a century no matter how much the bowler is being favoured?

I have seen those great left-arm bowlers, Rhodes and Verity, achieve some unbelievable performances on "sticky" wickets. Verity could never have gained an analysis of ten wickets for 10 runs if every batsman in the opposition had gone down the pitch and had a wallop. But, if that had been the attitude of cricketers whenever bowlers were on top, then I would never have seen any magnificent technical fighting innings like those of Hammond, Woolley, Hobbs, Mead, Hearne . . . performances which would send me the length of England if I could see them again.

The Findlay Report of 1937—which is accepted as impartial—suggested that players should have a different approach to the game. No doubt some could adopt a more dynamic attitude, but this in no way changes the argument.

The more help you give the bowler the more defensive must be the attitude of the batsman. It would be wrong otherwise, for no batsman worth his salt would give the bowler best.

The new lbw rule, designed to encourage the batsmen to hit the ball towards the covers, did not do so. Batsmen accepted the extra limitations, and I believe they found that excessive pad-play, or getting pads outside the off-stump, helped them. The need for this exaggerated pad-play, and the necessity of the batsman to play at the ball pitching just outside the off-stump, again in the natural sequence of development, caused the bowlers to search for fresh ideas.

They found that a leg-stump attack to expert short-leg and leg-slip fieldsmen paid dividends. It was discovered that the medium-pace bowlers, swinging or cutting the ball inwards to the batsmen, were as potent as it was hoped Larwood with his extra pace (apart from physical danger) might have been under the old lbw law.

The new lbw rule unwittingly encouraged the use of the leg stump attack and sent the wheel its full cycle. It was found the nearer you bowl to a batsman's legs—with a well-placed field—the more you limit his scoring strokes. During last summer the South African bowler, Goddard, showed that this type of attack could be extended to well outside the leg-stump and still be successful.

The new rule brought an undesirable trend into the game and from the replies to the questionnaire sent out by the Editor of

Wisden it is clear that almost every cricketer deplores the lbw law as it is now framed, or its consequences.

Not for a moment am I prepared to admit we have not the batsmen to-day that we had in years gone by. Leg-theory bowling must close up the game. Bradman fell a victim to Bedser's leg-stump attack three times before he accepted the limitations and began to take four instead of two and a half hours for a century. Bailey at Leeds four years ago prevented an Australian victory against the clock by bowling wide of the leg-stump. South Africa with negative bowling against England almost took the rubber. Hutton, May, Cowdrey, Compton and Graveney have cover drives as beautiful as any seen on a cricket ground, but they are seldom permitted to use the stroke. An attack directed at the legs of the batsman will always close the game.

No alteration in rule can make a batsman score freely from the attack directed at the leg-stump, but maybe an alteration in rule can make a bowler want to bowl straighter. On that point I believe everyone is agreed. Suitable pitches, of course, would make any bowler attack the stumps, but such is the variable nature of soils and pitches throughout the world that any legislation is impossible.

By legislation it strikes me there are only four possible methods:

    (a) *Scrap the present lbw law and go back to the old.*

    (b) *Limit the fieldsmen a bowler may use on the leg-side of the field.*

    (c) *Extend the lbw law further to include both sides of the pitch or provide that any ball pitched between wicket and wicket or to the off is successful if a batsman stops it from hitting the stumps with his pads, etc.*

    (d) *Make any runs scored on the leg-side count double.*

If the old lbw law came back, then, I presume, cricket would soon drift into the type of play which caused the administrators to make changes. The bowlers needed help.

To deny a bowler the right to use his fieldsmen to the best advantage to suit the tactics of the moment or the state of the pitch would, I believe, be another retrograde step, but, just as in football it was necessary to alter the offside law in order to help the attackers, so may it work out in cricket. It would have been interesting to see the results when this idea was first produced by the New South Wales Cricket Association. It was a pity they did not give it a trial.

The extension of the lbw rule to include both sides of the pitch would not be good. I can imagine Tyson, Statham, Trueman and the rest of the fast bowlers moving to round-the-wicket attack.

The physical danger would again become important, and rules would become far more complicated, or the game suffer, if the bowlers' right to deliver over or round-the-wicket was limited. The second alteration of the law seems much more feasible, i.e. to delete the phrase about stopping the ball with a part of the person in a direct line between the stumps.

If the batsman could be out lbw to any ball which, pitching straight or on the off, would hit the stumps, it seems likely that the leg-break-googly bowler would be encouraged, that bowlers would attack, and batsmen would use the bat more. In practice it may well be found that the off-spin bowler would reap tremendous advantage. Certain it is that the batsman scoring a century would deserve his name in the record book! Yet, once accustomed to a new sense of values, it may not be a bad thing to have the run worth more. Good fielding would be most important.

The fourth suggestion about doubling the score would only work if, by trial and error, the bowlers found it was more expensive to attack the batsman's legs. If every run conceded by South Africa's Goddard had been doubled, he would still have been a most economical bowler on last season's performances.

Suggestions that our England cricket suffers because of the staleness of our players through too much cricket, I have ignored. The leg-stump attack is used almost universally now and was not employed by the South Africans because of staleness.

The idea of using a fourth stump similarly does nothing to eliminate bowling at the batsman's legs. It does not follow that the batsman, given more to defend, will take bigger risks. They are likely to be more careful. And bowlers will not change a mode of attack unless in the process of trial and error they find some other type more successful. Time limits and penalties for bowlers or batsmen are a very last resort. Yet something should be tried.

Why not, in the Festival matches at the end of the season, try out the idea of limiting fieldsmen on the leg-side to four? If it makes for better cricket the Festival Committees and the public will be delighted. Why not, in M.C.C. matches at Lord's, try out an extension of the lbw law and make it known that the results do not count in the first-class averages? I am sure the Australian legislators, anxious to brighten and improve the game just as much as we are, would give this idea a trial.

A remedy for the present growing pains of cricket is hard to find. General opinion points to the latest lbw law as the cause, and if that is so, it should be discarded or widened in scope. It must come sooner or later . . . and the sooner the better.

Sir Pelham Warner (*Middlesex and England*): There is little, if anything, wrong with the laws; it is the approach to the game that matters most. I am surprised at the numerous injuries these days. Fifty years ago we had plenty of fast bowlers but one did not hear of broken fingers as we do now. Has the ball become harder?

Certainly batting gloves are not so effective as in my younger days. We used to have open, airy gloves with plenty of rubber on them. We do not want slow easy pitches, but in recent years some pitches, in my opinion, have been unfair and dangerous to batsmen.

There are too many first-class matches. The players become jaded and consequently lose their power of concentration, especially in Test matches. More consideration and encouragement should be given to the players, particularly when they are out of form. To avoid tedious railway journeys and to enable players to get to their destinations at a reasonable hour in the evening we should become more air-minded. The Board of Control should be prepared, if necessary, to charter special planes to move England players about the country.

Sir John Hobbs (*Surrey and England*): The decline in the arts and grace of batsmanship began with "body-line" and later the change in the lbw law further hampered stroke-making. The bat was given to the cricketer to defend his wicket and to hit the ball; it was not intended as a weapon for self-preservation. The modern bowler is no better than those of years ago, but methods have changed. We have at least one great stroke-player in Peter May, but there should be more.

The bumper and leg-theory have caused the batsman to think primarily of defending himself and consequently his first inclination is to go back. More forward play would improve batting, but above everything else it is the spirit of the game which matters most. The off-drive is a simple stroke, but it requires courage and so many modern players are afraid to let the bat go right through with the stroke. The game needs fast, true wickets; then the batsman and the bowler have an even chance.

I do not think you will get the old freedom in batting while the packed leg-side field remains. I am among those who would like to see the on-side restricted possibly to not more than four fielders.

Sir Donald Bradman (*Australia*): You suggest that the lbw rule of 1937 has a tremendous influence on the modern game of cricket. I very much doubt the accuracy of your belief. Furthermore the prevalence of defensive leg-theory bowling is, in my view, in spite of (and not because of) the present lbw law.

Since 1932 I have contended (Harold Larwood agrees with me —see page 59 of *Bodyline*, written by him in 1933) that an extension of the lbw law on the off-side so that a batsman could be given out even though his leg be outside the off-stump, would be the best antidote to leg-theory bowling.

I think leg-theory is used as a policy rather than because of a law. Remember it was often used prior to 1937 when the captain or the bowler saw fit to do so.

The dearth of leg-spinners in England is not easy to explain, but no doubt it is in part just a cycle, in the same way that at certain periods fast bowlers are scarce.

In addition to that, however, I am reliably informed that English coaches have preferred and encouraged the off-spinner type, claiming that leg-spinners are too expensive. I have been told that players' styles have actually been changed by the direction of a coach and if this is true, it becomes again a matter of deliberate policy.

As for the preparation of pitches, I think it fair to say that those prepared for the 1953 Australian Test series gave less cause for complaint that those in the 1934 series. There has recently been a wide variation in Australia due to special causes, but if we come to a discussion on pitches, who is to be the judge as to the ideal pitch anyway?

I have written before and I still contend that the mental outlook of those who play cricket is the most important thing. Players can ruin any game by their wrong interpretation of its character.

However, if the mental approach is sufficiently wrong to cause serious concern about the welfare of the game itself, then I for one see no harm in conducting experiments to see whether some of the undesirable features complained about can be eliminated legislatively.

Take the lbw law. Some say it is the cause of leg-theory and that we should revert to the old law whereby the ball must pitch in line with the stumps. Others say an extension of the lbw law on the off-side would do more than anything else to eliminate leg-theory. And there is certainly a strong body of opinion which favours the limitation of the number of fielders on the leg-side. How you are to know the answers to these theories without trying them I do not know.

Herbert Sutcliffe (*Yorkshire and England*): I have, over the years, expressed my views in no uncertain manner with regard to the lbw law, which is responsible for both negative batting and negative bowling, and indeed the answers to the first three points (*a*), (*b*) and (*c*) are tied up with the lbw rule.

The lbw rule encourages in-swing bowlers and off-spinners, and all bowlers to-day appear to be exploiting this particular theory with a packed leg-side field. Therefore, you will agree it is all against the elementary principles of batsmanship to attempt the glorious cover drive which, without doubt, is the most fascinating stroke in a batsman's repertoire.

There is a dearth of leg-spinners mainly because the off-spinners are given the additional advantage of the new lbw rule, and indeed leg-spinners and out-swing bowlers have, during the last few years, been greatly discouraged, so that there are very few in first-class cricket.

R. W. V. Robins (*Middlesex and England*): It seems the main issue is the desire among some for a change in the lbw law. I do not agree with the present theory, which the majority of cricketers hold, that the game has deteriorated as a result of the new law. My reasons are:—

1. The game in the '20s and early '30s was by no means so wonderful as the old-timers would have us believe now. In those days the then old-timers were deploring the approach to cricket as compared with the game in their day.

2. The present technique of batsmen, bowlers, captains and fielders is merely a natural modern development of the game. There has been no advance in attack since I began in 1925 and all developments (which have been considerable) have been in defence, be it in batting, bowling or fielding. Other games are suffering from a defence complex.

3. Some think that a change-over to the old lbw law will change the tempo of the game. It won't. Neither will it switch the play over to the off-side, because bowlers have now learned a new technique of preventing fast scoring. A batsman takes a greater risk in trying to score quickly on the leg-side compared with the off-side.

4. To go back to the old law would be a retrograde step unless the bowler is given something in return, such as a fourth stump. The suggestion which New South Wales made, to limit the number of fielders on the leg-side, was a far better one than most people imagine. The pity was it was never tried.

L. N. Constantine (*West Indies*): I have always been opposed to the new lbw rule. Not because of any conservatism but for reason of batting aggressiveness.

Before the rule was introduced you could play the off-break bowlers off your back foot, and by jumping to the pitch of the ball range your shots from the extra cover drive, if you got there, to sweeping to square-leg or long-on, if you did not, providing it was pretty safe to do so. Otherwise you just blocked. The top-class bowlers would often lure you and get you. I mean bowlers like Kennedy, Jupp, Parkin and Tom Goddard.

The rule was introduced in my opinion at the wrong time and for the wrong reasons. Pitches were like feather-beds. Players were holding on to safety tactics and, to confirm their intention, they sneered at the batsman who lifted the ball.

Any discussion of the off-break must necessarily include the in-swinger. The off-break bowler for a time came into his own.

But the history books of cricket tell us that every new devastating weapon invented by bowlers is mastered by batsmen in the course of time, and the new lbw rule has travelled the same road. In mastering the dangers pregnant and potential, batsmen have evolved a movement which not only prevents the ball ever getting in line with the wickets, but frustrates any second thoughts of aggressiveness, even when it is discovered that the ball was straight, i.e. "it had nothing in it." So batsman after batsman pushed his left foot down the line, suspicious and afraid. Of course, the process means a longer stay at the wicket, even if runs come by pushes and singles; the then newly-acquired *modus operandi* takes on the garb of a "philosophy of security and industry." I have another name for it—"the Hall-mark of Mediocrity."

Ian Johnson (*Australia*): The lbw rule of 1937 is not so effective in Australia as in England, for the wickets take less spin and the ball swings less in the air. I doubt very much if, in Australia, it has had any appreciable effect on the batsmen or the game, because of this fact. Leg-theory bowling to my mind is, in nearly every case, a curse on the game. It is negative and shows both lack of confidence on the part of the bowler in his ability to beat the batsman and lack of initiative.

The lack of leg-spinners has been noticeable throughout the cricket world. I think it is due more to the new ball rule than to any change in the lbw law. When the new ball came at a set number of overs the spinners fell into the background and rather than risk the luxury of a few possibly expensive overs from a leg-spinner, captains preferred to bowl tight while waiting for the over that would bring the new ball.

Regarding the general lack of high-class batsmen: They probably asked the same question twenty years ago and twenty before that too. Certainly in Australia, though, the pitches are now less reliable than pre-war. The general falling off in the standard of pitches has been attributed to many things, but probably the major factor is the 40-hour week which tends to make a man work by the clock instead of the result. For the most part in Australia there is too little grass on the wickets.

V. M. Merchant (*India*): The lbw rule of 1937, it was felt, would greatly encourage forward play. It has not done so. There is as great a tendency at present to play back as there was before 1937. This rule has only encouraged off-spin and in-swing bowling to the detriment of the game in general. If this rule is to have greater effect on the batsman and the bowler is to be helped, it should be extended to balls pitching outside the leg-stump also. Then there would be less of back and padded play.

Leg-theory bowling on good wickets has come to stay. Mostly

this leg-theory is negative and the bowler is satisfied with keeping the batsman quiet. Most of the glorious off-side strokes have disappeared from the game except in rare cases. The best way to do away with it is to prevent by law the placing of more than four fielders on the on-side and not more than two behind the square-leg umpire. Then only will bowling again be directed to the off-stump and outside it and bring into play the late-cut, square-cut, the off and the cover drives. I am opposed normally to the change of rules, but the outlook of cricketers at present is such that unless they are changed cricket will cease to entertain.

The 65-overs new ball rule dealt a stunning blow to leg-spinners. Fortunately it has now been done away with. Even so, negative leg-theory bowling will prevent leg-spinners being encouraged. Captains do not want attacking bowling these days in preference to economic bowling. My suggestion about limiting the number of fielders on the leg-side might bring back the genuine leg-spinners.

The general lack of high-class batsmen is due more to back play where one has to wait for a certain kind of ball for making strokes. It will be generally agreed that forward play is more attacking and a high-class batsman has to attack and make his runs against good bowling. Anyone with a certain amount of technique and a lot of patience can make big scores on good wickets. Big scores do not constitute high-class batting.

No other country in the world affords as much cricket as England does, and with the present high standard of bowling in England one cannot understand why England lacks young professional batsmen of the highest class. I wonder if this is due to too much cricket in England where batsmen either go stale or make runs against the lower-placed bowlers and feel complacent about their batting.

R. E. S. Wyatt (*Warwickshire, Worcestershire and England*): Ever since lbw(*n*) was introduced in 1935 I have been of the opinion that such a law is not in the best interests of the game because it encourages the types of bowling (in-swing and off-spin) which decrease the most attractive strokes in cricket, such as the off-drive and late-cut. Furthermore, I consider it was a mistake to put a premium on any particular types of bowling. If it were decided that batsmen were using their legs too much as a second line of defence, I think any such law should have applied to the leg-side as well.

I feel that the latest lbw law has over the years had a great influence in slowing the scoring rate of modern cricket and has been very largely responsible for the present on-side attack which, assisted by this law and probably better field-placing, is more economical.

It is difficult to provide the answer, but I do think that fast pitches and a return to the old law with possibly a wider wicket would produce better and more attractive cricket with a greater number of off-side strokes.

I. A. R. Peebles (*Middlesex and England*): With regard to the lbw law it has always been my opinion that it should be carried further and "Bradman's Amendment" adopted. That is to say, that the provision about the legs being between wicket and wicket should be scrapped. It is a complex question, but I feel that this would be an improvement and would not affect off-side play.

Leg-theory to my mind should be kept under close observation during the next season and, should there be any serious recurrence, some form of legislation should be introduced. What about saying that any ball pitched outside the leg-stump is a no-ball when there are more than six fielders on the leg-side? I do not believe in appeals to spirit as this is capable of such wide interpretation. I think the dearth of leg-spinners is a symptom of a utility age and the fact that we play far too much cricket.

The lack of high-class batsmen I would also attribute to the same cause and the gradual disappearance of the cover drive to the prevailing trends in bowling. The lack of young professional batsmen to replace Test players must be due to many contributory causes—possibly finance, to the extent that careers in industry are more attractive from the material point of view, if less glamorous.

The most desirable quality in the preparation of the pitch is surely pace. The worst which can happen is that we get another series of dead, doped pitches for the Test Match series.

W. S. Surridge (*captain of Surrey's Championship team, 1952–55*): Cricket is rarely monotonous when the struggle is even between the batsman and the bowler. The state of the wicket governs the approach to the game. You do not see packed leg-side fields for off-spinners when the pitch is so true that the batsman is completely on top. Under such conditions Jim Laker does not even employ one short leg. In my opinion the game is not standing still, but at the present time I do not think it would benefit from more changes in the laws. Certainly I would not welcome any limitation on the number of leg-side fielders. When the pitch is helping the off-spinner, why shouldn't he exploit the leg trap? Surely, there is nothing more spectacular in cricket than a sizzling catch in that position. As a captain I would like to inquire as to where I am to put the spare fielders if the on-side is restricted to four? Would the spectators appreciate seeing a lot of idle fellows on the off-side? Competition is an important factor that affects the tempo of the game. At certain times batsmen must take extra care, as when the position demands caution in a struggle for the rubber or a battle for Championship points. The first-class game would soon lose its attraction if every match was played in the mood of some Festival Cricket.

Wilfred Wooller (*Glamorgan*): When the alteration to the lbw law in 1935 had given captains and bowlers, by the process of thought and practice, the opportunity to work out its full offensive and defensive possibilities, the trend and line of attack became more varied. Whereas the off-side had dominated the tactics, it now became apparent that the leg-side had equal possibilities. Its ancillary development produced a crop of top-class leg-slip fielders, and the realisation that the leg-side edge of the bat was as vulnerable as the off-side, but it also sparked off the evolution of the leg-side theory of defence now frequently used to control free scoring on easy-paced wickets.

While I in no way defend the results of the change, I am wholly convinced that the knowledge thus gained has been developed to a degree that any alteration of the lbw law would not prevent the use of these defensive tactics in the future when the occasion warranted it. It would also bring back the defensive use of the pads by the batsmen to a delivery pitched outside the line of the off-stump. We would then be left with the worse of two situations, and the added difficulty of removing stubborn and unenterprising batsmen who would use their pads as a weapon, and not as a means of protecting their limbs from injury.

In the matter of runs, the development of a leg-spinner is a highly expensive business. I imagine most Counties, like myself, prefer the better-balanced attack of a slow left-arm and a slow off-spinner as a combination.

I do not agree that there is a general lack of high-class batsmen, although we are going through a phase when there is a shortage of Hammonds, Huttons and Leylands. In the history of cricket run-getting has *never* been as difficult as it is to-day. Bowlers are not such half-wits as to feed the attractive off-drive or any other favourite shot for that matter.

Let us be thankful that groundsmen have at last realised their true art lies in striking an even balance between bat and ball. One seldom sees dull cricket on wickets which give the bowler a reasonable chance.

A. R. Gover (*Surrey and England*): Cricket is a batsman's game. Bowlers are there to provide sport for the batsmen. In general the public pay to watch batsmen. The bowler with the aid of the lbw rule and present-day pitches is dictating the rate of scoring.

The art of batting as practised in the 1930's has disappeared. Stroke-play is almost non-existent against bowling which is principally aimed at the leg-stump and leg-side fielders. Young players brought up under such conditions have no fair chance to

develop strokes. Cricket was designed to be played on the off-side.
Change the lbw law, so that the batsman can be out if his legs, outside the off-stump, prevent the ball from hitting the wicket. Bowlers
attacking on and outside the off-stump will receive encouragement.
The leg-spinner with the googly would then be seen in first-class
cricket.

The genuine off-spin and in-swing bowler would still take
wickets: witness Goddard and Jupp and in-swingers Andrews and
G. H. Pope before 1936. But leave the pitches alone. It would
be a retrograde step to play again on shirt-front pitches of
pre-war days. With the lbw rule amended young batsmen would
have every chance of developing their strokes and would soon
equal the ability of the great pre-war batsmen.

The whole result would see the game played as it always should
be, with the odds slightly in favour of the batsman. I write from
the experience of having played in both the 1930–39 and the post-
war periods.

D. V. P. Wright (*Kent and England*): Leg-theory, that is,
bowling at the leg-stump and placing the majority of fielders on
the leg-side, and endeavouring to get the batsman "out," is, I
think, quite a fair method of attack. It is entirely different from the
method I have seen in County cricket, of bowling outside, well
outside the leg-stump, putting all the fielders on the leg-side, and
hoping the batsman will throw his wicket away. This negative
bowling is one of the causes of slow cricket. You cannot cover drive
if the ball is not up on the off-side.

Regarding the dearth of leg-spinners, it is far easier to be
accurate with off-spinners than with leg-breaks, and since the
new lbw rule—which concerns the ball coming in from the off—
the off-spinner is far more in favour, especially among Northern
Counties, where generally wickets suit that type of bowling.

J. B. Stollmeyer (*West Indies*): There is no doubt that the
present lbw rule subsidises both the in-swing and off-spin bowlers.
These two types of bowling are more easily controllable and require
less effort on the part of the average bowler. They also discourage
to a large extent the more classical off-side strokes of the batsman
as they are very often operated to defensive fields with the majority
of the fielders on the on-side. I can see no reason why out-swing
and leg-spin bowlers should not receive at least equal consideration
from the laws in the matter of lbw. If any bowler should be sub-
sidised, surely he who attempts the most difficult ball should receive
whatever benefits are going. I have not yet seen any valid reason
why the present lbw law should not be amended to include the
leg-side as well as the off-side.

Leg-theory bowling employed as a defensive measure is the

biggest problem of cricket to-day. There is no doubt in my mind that while it can be a most effective defensive tactic and is entirely lawful, it produces a stalemate which could threaten the very existence of the Test game should it become general practice. The answer lies with the captains and the spirit with which they approach the game and also with the curators who should be encouraged to prepare wickets which give bowlers a better chance, and therefore invites a more positive approach.

The leg-spinner is the most difficult ball to bowl and control. The leg-spin bowler receives no encouragement from the lbw law and still less from the majority of wickets, particularly in tropical countries.

M. Leyland (*Yorkshire and England*), replying after a spell in hospital, wrote: Regarding the changed lbw rule, I think it could be discarded. It has not produced the influence its sponsors expected, for it has failed to encourage off-side stroke play. Leg-theory has existed for a long time but they use it more now because it is the easiest stuff to bowl. Conversely, the leg-spinner is the most difficult one to bowl and, from a swing bowler's point of view, the out-swinger is just as hard to produce and few people seem willing to pursue the hard way these days.

The general lack of class batsmen and the less frequent use of the cover drive are the results of leg-theory bowling. Batsmen are restricted to leg-side strokes and therefore do not get the opportunity in matches to practise the other strokes. At the same time *most* batsmen play the ball on the line of the leg-stump as a leg ball, but it is not; it is a straight one. The best player of the leg-stump ball is Peter May; the best on-side player is Norman Yardley.

Finally, a word to the young players: Many of you do not appreciate that this game is like a trade and to become proficient you have to serve an apprenticeship. Ability without constant practice will not take you very far.

Maurice Leyland is one of the two official coaches of the York-shire County Cricket Club.

N.B. The old lbw law was as follows: The striker is out "If, with any part of his person, he stops the ball, which in the opinion of the umpire at the bowler's wicket shall have been pitched in a straight line from it to the striker's wicket and would have hit it: Leg before wicket."

The new Law was tried experimentally in 1935 and was incor-porated in the Laws of the Game in 1937.

LEN HUTTON: THE MASTER

By Neville Cardus

Len Hutton was the only batsman of his period to whom we could apply the term "Old Master," referring in his case not to his number of years but to the style and vintage of his cricket. He followed in the succession of the classic professional batsmen who each went in first for his county and for England: Shrewsbury, Hayward, Hobbs and Sutcliffe—though Sutcliffe wore his classicism with a subtly Sutcliffian difference.

As Old Masters go, Hutton was young enough; the sadness is that physical disability put an end to his career in its prime. He had all the classic points of style when, not much more than 19, he came to Lord's in 1936 and scored fifty-five. I then wrote of him in this strain of Cassandrian prophecy: "Here is a young cricketer who is already old in the head and destined to enliven many a Lancashire and Yorkshire match of the future."

If by means of some Time-machine capable of television we could today see a picture of Hutton batting twenty years ago, and one taken of him during his maturity, we would notice no fundamental difference in technique. We would see that his cricket had grown in experience and finish, that is all. Like the music of Bach, Hutton's batsmanship in its evolution from an early to a late period presented no marked divisions; it was never raw, unprincipled or embryonic. He batted grammatically from the start, choosing his strokes as carefully as a professor of logic his words.

Even when he first played for Yorkshire, beginning with 0, he seemed to begin an innings to a plan, building the shape and the duration of it to a blue-print in his mind, and to a time-table. But once in the greenest of his salad days he fell into error. He opened a Yorkshire innings on Saturday at Bradford with Arthur Mitchell, dourest and most unsmiling of the clan. After a characteristically Yorkshire investigation of the state of the wicket, the state of the opposition bowling, the state of mind the umpires were in, the state of the weather and barometer, and probably the state of the Bank of England itself, Mitchell and Hutton began to score now and then.

Young Hutton was feeling in form, so after he had played himself in he decided to cut a rising ball outside the off-stump. Remember that he was fresh to the Yorkshire scene and policies. He actually lay back and cut hard and swiftly, with cavalier flourish. He cut under the ball by an inch, and it sped bang into the wicket-keeper's gloves. And Mitchell, from the other end of the pitch, looked hard at Hutton and said, "That's no . . . . . . use!" This was probably Hutton's true baptism, cleansing him of all vanity and lusts for insubstantial pageantry and temporal glory.

He observed the classical unities; that is to say, he did not venture beyond reliable and established limitations of batsmanship

LEN HUTTON

learned in the traditional school. Geometrical precision in the application of bat to ball, each movement of the feet considered until the right position was found almost instinctively, not bringing him merely to the ball and, as far as possible and if necessary over it, but also with body at the proper balance.

Never, or hardly ever, did Hutton play a thoughtless innings; his mind usually seemed to move a fraction of time in advance of his most rapid footwork and sudden tensions of limb, sinew and nerve. It is, of course, wrong to suppose that Hutton was at any time a batsman slow in his mental and physical reactions at the crease.

The score-board may have told us that he was not getting runs feverishly, but the vigilance of Hutton was eternal; the concentration in him was so intense that it frequently exhausted his not robust physique much sooner than did the more obvious toil and burden of the day. In the most austerely defensive Hutton innings we could feel a mental alertness; purpose in him suffered no weariness.

And whether or not he was putting into practice his wide repertoire of strokes, he was the stylist always; rarely was he discovered in an awkward position at the crease, rarely was he bustled or hurried. Once at Kennington Oval, Lindwall knocked Hutton's cap off in a Test Match. Such an outrage could be equalled in a cricketer's imagination only by supposing that Alfred Mynn's tall hat was ever likewise rudely removed.

On a bowler's wicket, when the ball's spin was angular and waspish in turn, he could maintain his premeditated technical responses, often using a "dead" bat, the handle held so loosely that when the ball came into contact with the blade's middle it was as though against a drugged cushion: the spin was anaesthetised into harmlessness.

But Hutton was, when grace descended upon him, a versatile and handsome stroke player. Old Trafford will remember that in 1948 he made a century of a brilliance which, in the circumstances —Bank Holiday and a Lancashire v. Yorkshire match—was almost pagan.

He drove Lindwall with Spooneresque charm and panache at Brisbane in December 1950; at Lord's in the Test Match of 1953, he played one of the most regal and most highly pedigreed innings ever seen in an England and Australia Test Match on that hallowed ground. And he has contributed to a festival at Scarborough.

If Hutton had lived and played in the Lord Hawke epoch, when even Test cricketers in England had somehow to adapt themselves and their skill to matches limited to three days, he would have been a different batsman in his tempo and mental approach. But he could not possibly have been greater.

Any artist or master of craft is an organism in an environment;

he is very much what circumstances and atmosphere make of him. His very greatness consists in how fully he can sum up the technique of his day as he finds it, and how representative he is of his day's spirit. MacLaren, lordly and opulent at the crease, was a representative man and cricketer in a lordly opulent period; Hutton's cricket has been as true as MacLaren's to the Zeitgeist, to the feeling, temper and even to the economy of the age which shaped his character and his skill, both conceived as much as in integrity as in joy.

As a captain he was shrewd but courteous; he knew the game's finest points, and though never likely to give anything away, was too proud to take anything not his due. Sometimes he may have allowed thoughtfulness to turn to worry; but this is a natural habit in the part of the world which Hutton comes from.

Hutton certainly showed that a professional cricketer can wear the robes of leadership in the field of play with dignity. At first, no doubt, he appeared at the head of his troops not wearing anything like a Caesarian toga, but rather the uniform of a sergeant-major. But he moved up in rank and prestige until he became worthy of his command and defeated Australia twice in successive rubbers, wresting one from the enemy at the pinch and looting the other after a series of Tests which were, if I may be free with my allusions and metaphors, the Australians' Austerlitz.

One of Hutton's most winning characteristics—and his personality is extremely attractive—is his smile, a smile with a twinkle in it. He had many occasions in his distinguished career on which to indulge this smile, many provocations to it, and he never missed the joke. A Yorkshireman has his own idea of humour, and Hutton, as great or famous as any Yorkshireman contemporary with him, relished his laugh all the more because very often it came last.

LEN HUTTON: A GREAT CAREER

Statistics by GEOFFREY COPINGER

BATTING (All First-Class Matches)

Season	Inns.	Not Outs	Runs	100's	50's	Highest Inns.	Average	Catches
1934	28	2	863	1	5	196	33.19	8
1935	23	3	577	1	1	131	28.85	6
Yorkshire in Jamaica 1936	5	2	123	0	1	59	41.00	0
1936	49	6	1282	1	8	163	29.81	26
1937	58	7	2888	10	12	271*	56.62	26
1938	37	6	1874	6	5	364	60.45	12
M.C.C. in South Africa 1938–9	19	1	1168	5	4	202	64.88	7
1939	52	6	2883	12	8	280*	62.67	38
1945	16	0	782	2	4	188	48.87	3
1946	38	6	1552	4	7	183*	48.50	13
M.C.C. in Australia 1946–7	21	3	1267	3	8	151*	70.38	5
1947	44	4	2585	11	7	270*	64.62	23
M.C.C. in West Indies 1947–8	10	1	578	2	3	138	64.22	6
1948	48	7	2654	10	13	176*	64.73	23
M.C.C. in South Africa 1948–9	21	1	1477	5	7	174	73.85	8
1949	56	6	3429	12	17	269*	68.58	40
1950	40	3	2128	6	11	202*	55.99	24
M.C.C. in Australia and New Zealand 1950–1	25	4	1382	5	7	156*	65.80	18
1951	47	8	2145	7	9	194*	55.00	33
1952	45	3	2567	11	12	189	61.11	31
1953	44	5	2458	8	10	241	63.02	15
M.C.C. in West Indies 1953–4	12	2	780	2	4	205	78.00	3
1954	28	2	912	2	4	163	35.07	7
M.C.C. in Australia and New Zealand 1954–5	25	2	1059	2	6	145*	46.04	7
1955	19	1	537	1	4	194	29.83	5
Totals ...	810	91	39950	129	177	364	55.56	387

Signifies not out.

AGGREGATES

	Inns.	Not Outs	Runs	100's	50's	Highest Inns.	Average
In England	672	75	32116	105	137	364	53.79
In Australia..........	63	9	3425	10	18	156*	63.42
In West Indies	27	5	1481	4	8	205	67.31
In South Africa	40	2	2645	10	11	202	69.60
In New Zealand	8	0	283	0	3	69	35.37
Totals	810	91	39950	129	177	364	55.56

TEST MATCHES

	Tests	Inns.	Not Outs	Runs	100's	50's	Highest Inns.	Average
Australia	27	49	6	2428	5	14	364	56.46
South Africa ...	19	34	4	1564	4	7	158	52.13
New Zealand ...	11	17	0	777	3	4	206	51.51
West Indies	13	24	3	1661	5	6	205	79.09
India...........	7	11	2	522	2	2	150	58.00
Pakistan	2	3	0	19	0	0	14	6.33
Totals	79	138	15	6971	19	33	364	56.67

COUNTY CHAMPIONSHIP MATCHES

	Inns.	Not Outs	Runs	100's	50's	Highest Inns.	Average
1934	25	1	801	1	4	196	33.37
1935	19	3	411	1	0	131	25.68
1936	43	6	1108	1	6	163	29.94
1937	36	5	1728	5	7	271*	55.74
1938	17	3	631	1	3	107	45.07
1939	40	4	2167	9	6	280*	60.19
1946	26	4	1112	3	5	171	50.54
1947	23	1	1551	6	4	270*	70.50
1948	22	5	1565	8	4	176*	92.05
1949	38	5	2098	6	11	269*	63.57
1950	21	2	1125	4	4	156	59.21
1951	26	5	1222	5	4	194*	58.19
1952	26	1	1482	7	6	189	59.28
1953	21	1	1149	4	4	178	57.45
1954	19	2	676	1	4	149*	39.76
1955	18	0	535	1	4	194	29.72
Totals	420	48	19361	63	76	280*	52.04

* *Signifies not out.*

TEST MATCHES

	Inns.	Not Outs	Runs	100's	50's	Highest Inns.	Average
1937 (v. New Zealand) ...	5	0	127	1	0	100	25.40
1938 (v. Australia)	4	0	473	2	0	364	118.25
1938–9 (v. S. Africa)	6	0	265	0	2	92	44.16
1939 (v. West Indies)	6	1	480	2	1	196	96.00
1946 (v. India)	5	1	123	0	1	67	30.75
1946–7 (v. Australia)	9	1	417	1	2	122*	52.12
1947 (v. S. Africa)	10	2	344	1	1	100	43.00
1947–8 (v. West Indies) ..	4	0	171	0	2	60	42.75
1948 (v. Australia)	9	0	342	0	4	81	42.75
1948–9 (v. S. Africa)	8	0	577	2	2	158	64.11
1949 (v. New Zealand) ...	6	0	469	2	2	206	78.16
1950 (v. West Indies)	6	1	333	1	0	202*	66.60
1950–1 (v. Australia)	10	4	533	1	4	156*	88.83
1950–1 (v. New Zealand) .	3	0	114	0	1	57	38.00
1951 (v. S. Africa)	9	2	378	1	2	100	54.00
1952 (v. India)	6	1	399	2	1	150	79.80
1953 (v. Australia)	9	1	443	1	3	145	55.37
1953–4 (v. West Indies) ..	8	1	677	2	3	205	96.71
1954 (v. Pakistan)	3	0	19	0	0	14	6.33
1954–5 (v. Australia)	9	0	220	0	1	80	24.44
1954–5 (v. New Zealand) .	3	0	67	0	1	53	22.33
Totals	138	15	6971	19	33	364	56.67

FOR YORKSHIRE AGAINST TEAMS IN ENGLAND AND JAMAICA

	Inns.	Not Outs	Runs	100's	50's	Highest Inns.	Average
Derbyshire...........	20	3	865	2	4	271*	50.88
Essex	32	4	1802	7	6	197	64.35
Glamorgan	22	2	1063	2	7	197	53.15
Gloucestershire	30	4	927	2	5	110*	35.65
Hampshire...........	25	5	1055	2	3	280*	52.75
Kent	30	1	1592	5	9	189	54.89
Lancashire	44	5	1763	5	5	201	45.20
Leicestershire	22	4	990	3	5	153	55.00
Middlesex	38	3	1608	6	5	133	45.94
Northamptonshire	18	3	1179	4	5	269*	78.60
Nottinghamshire	17	4	948	4	1	194*	72.92
Somerset	17	1	823	3	3	141	51.43
Surrey	28	0	1286	5	4	163	45.92
Sussex	32	5	1942	8	9	177	71.92
Warwickshire	25	2	820	2	3	158	35.65
Worcestershire	22	2	845	4	2	196	42.25
M.C.C...............	39	6	1834	8	8	161	55.57
Oxford University	19	3	698	2	3	141	43.62
Cambridge University	13	1	702	3	2	180	58.50
Australia	9	0	296	0	3	84	32.88
South Africa	3	0	351	2	1	156	117.00
New Zealand	5	0	345	2	0	167	69.00
India................	2	1	189	1	0	183*	189.00
West Indies	4	0	200	1	1	104	50.00
Scotland.............	3	1	270	1	1	146*	135.00
R.A.F. (1945)	2	0	128	0	2	73	64.00
Combined Services....	1	0	163	1	0	163	163.00
Jamaica	5	2	123	0	1	59	41.00
Totals	527	62	24807	85	98	280*	53.34

* *Signifies not out.*

D

FOR OTHER TEAMS IN ENGLAND

	Inns.	Not Outs	Runs	100's	50's	Highest Inns.	Average
M.C.C.	3	1	118	0	2	64	59.00
North	8	0	510	2	4	102	43.50
Rest v. M.C.C. Australian XI	2	0	68	0	1	50	34.00
M.C.C. S. African XI.	2	0	108	0	1	73	54.00
Players	22	3	1070	2	7	241	56.31
England v. Rest	7	1	309	0	2	85	51.50
England v. Australian Services	11	0	422	1	2	104	38.36
England XI v. Glamorgan	2	0	78	0	1	67	39.00
Leveson Gower's XI v. Australians	4	1	109	0	1	73	36.33
Leveson Gower's XI v. M.C.C. Australian XI	2	0	93	0	1	88	46.50
v. New Zealanders	4	0	335	1	2	188	83.75
T. N. Pearce's XI v. South Africans	2	0	111	0	1	91	55.50
v. Indians	2	0	20	0	0	15	10.00
v. Australians	2	0	151	1	0	102	75.50
Totals	73	6	3502	7	25	241	52.26

FOR M.C.C. TOURING TEAMS (EXCLUDING TESTS)

	Inns.	Not Outs	Runs	100's	50's	Highest Inns.	Average
In Australia	35	4	2255	8	11	151*	72.74
In South Africa	25	2	1803	8	7	202	78.39
In West Indies	10	2	510	2	2	138	63.75
In New Zealand	2	0	102	0	1	69	51.00
Totals	72	8	4670	18	21	202	72.96

MODE OF DISMISSAL

Bowled	207
Caught	372
Lbw	94
Run Out	21
Stumped	19
Hit Wicket	5
Obstructing the Field	1
Totals	719

* Signifies not out.

BATTING ON ENGLISH GROUNDS

Ground	Inns.	Not Outs	Runs	100's	50's	Highest Inns.	Average
Bath	1	0	3	0	0	3	3.00
Birmingham	12	3	491	1	2	158	54.55
Bournemouth	13	4	550	1	2	270*	61.11
Bradford	57	3	2824	9	12	183*	52.29
Brentwood	2	0	147	1	0	141	73.50
Bristol	15	2	450	1	2	110*	34.61
Cambridge	13	1	702	3	2	180	58.50
Canterbury	4	0	207	1	1	120	51.75
Cardiff	10	1	321	0	3	90	35.66
Chesterfield	10	2	233	0	2	84	29.12
Clacton	1	0	58	0	1	58	58.00
Colchester	2	1	167	1	0	156	167.00
Dover	7	0	348	1	3	100	49.71
Eastbourne	3	0	164	0	2	87	54.66
Edinburgh	1	0	79	0	1	79	79.00
Gloucester	4	2	87	0	0	35*	43.50
Harrogate	6	0	392	2	1	163	65.33
Hove	13	2	748	4	2	165	68.00
Huddersfield	17	2	775	4	3	141	51.66
Hull	19	3	1012	3	5	171*	63.25
Ilford	5	1	281	1	1	124	70.20
Leeds	62	6	3192	15	10	189	57.00
Leicester	12	2	454	1	3	137	45.40
Lord's	91	9	3302	11	13	196	40.26
Maidstone	2	0	33	0	0	29	16.50
Manchester	40	4	1739	4	10	201	48.30
Newport	2	0	80	0	1	51	40.00
Northampton	7	0	269	0	2	65	38.42
Nottingham	22	3	1153	4	4	194*	60.68
The Oval	34	2	2291	8	7	364	71.59
Oxford	19	3	698	2	3	141	43.62
Portsmouth	1	0	38	0	0	38	38.00
Scarborough	78	8	4190	13	25	241	59.85
Sheffield	56	9	2756	6	10	280*	59.91
Southend	4	0	379	2	0	197	94.75
Stourbridge	5	0	118	1	0	101	29.50
Swansea	2	0	200	1	0	197	100.00
Taunton	3	0	125	0	1	52	41.66
Tonbridge	1	0	136	1	0	136	136.00
Tunbridge Wells	2	0	106	0	1	74	53.00
Wellingborough	1	1	269	1	0	269*	—
Wells	2	0	25	0	0	16	12.50
Westcliff	4	0	216	1	1	103	54.00
Worcester	7	1	308	1	1	196	51.33
Totals	672	75	32116	105	137	364	53.79

BATTING ON AUSTRALIAN GROUNDS

Ground	Inns.	Not Outs	Runs	100's	50's	Highest Inns.	Average
Adelaide	15	2	1103	3	7	156*	84.74
Brisbane	8	2	138	0	1	62*	23.00
Hobart	1	0	15	0	0	15	15.00
Launceston	3	1	133	0	2	61	66.50
Melbourne	16	2	763	2	3	151*	54.50
Perth	2	1	155	1	0	145*	155.00
Sydney	18	1	1118	4	5	150	65.76
Totals	63	9	3425	10	18	156*	63.42

* *Signifies not out.*

BATTING ON SOUTH AFRICAN GROUNDS

Ground	Inns.	Not Outs	Runs	100's	50's	Highest Inns.	Average
Bulawayo	1	0	145	1	0	145	145.00
Bloemfontein	1	0	134	1	0	134	134.00
Capetown	9	1	401	1	2	125	50.12
Durban	9	0	502	1	4	108	55.77
East London	3	0	8	0	0	5	2.66
Johannesburg	9	0	813	4	2	174	90.33
Kimberley	1	0	149	1	0	149	149.00
Pietermaritzburg	2	1	68	0	1	53*	68.00
Port Elizabeth	3	0	280	1	0	202	93.33
Pretoria	1	0	66	0	1	66	66.00
Salisbury	1	0	79	0	1	79	79.00
Totals	40	2	2645	10	11	202	69.60

BATTING ON NEW ZEALAND GROUNDS

Ground	Inns.	Not Outs	Runs	100's	50's	Highest Inns.	Average
Auckland	2	0	122	0	2	69	61.00
Christchurch	2	0	61	0	0	33	30.50
Dunedin	2	0	14	0	0	11	7.00
Wellington	2	0	86	0	1	57	43.00
Totals	8	0	283	0	3	69	35.37

BATTING IN WEST INDIES

Ground	Inns.	Not Outs	Runs	100's	50's	Highest Inns.	Average
Jamaica	15	2	772	2	4	205	59.38
Barbados	4	1	211	0	3	77	70.33
British Guiana	6	1	424	2	1	169	84.80
Trinidad	2	1	74	0	0	44	74.00
Totals	27	5	1481	4	8	205	67.31

FOR M.C.C. TOURING TEAMS IN SOUTH AFRICA

	Inns.	Not Outs	Runs	100's	50's	Highest Inns.	Average
v. Cape Province	2	1	187	1	1	125	187.00
v. Combined Transvaal XI	1	0	148	1	0	148	148.00
v. Border	3	0	8	0	0	5	2.66
v. Eastern Province	1	0	202	1	0	202	202.00
v. Griqualand	1	0	149	1	0	149	149.00
v. Natal	6	1	358	1	3	108	71.60
v. N. E. Transvaal	1	0	66	0	1	66	66.00
v. Orange Free State	1	0	134	1	0	134	134.00
v. Rhodesia	2	0	224	1	1	145	112.00
v. South Africa	15	0	842	2	4	158	56.13
v. Transvaal	3	0	258	1	1	174	86.00
v. Western Province	4	0	69	0	0	38	16.75
Totals	40	2	2645	10	11	202	69.60

* Signifies not out.

FOR M.C.C. TOURING TEAMS IN AUSTRALIA

	Inns.	Not Outs	Runs	100's	50's	Highest Inns.	Average
v. Australia	28	5	1170	2	7	156*	50.86
v. Australian XI	1	0	71	0	1	71	71.00
v. Combined XI	2	0	25	0	0	15	12.50
v. New South Wales ...	10	0	785	3	4	150	78.50
v. Queensland	2	0	44	0	0	42	22.00
v. South Australia	9	1	647	2	4	136	80.87
v. Tasmania	3	1	133	0	2	61	66.50
v. Victoria	7	1	405	2	0	151*	67.50
v. Western Australia ...	1	1	145	1	0	145*	—
Totals	63	9	3425	10	18	156*	63.42

TEST MATCH HUNDREDS (19)

v. Australia (5).
    364   at The Oval, 1938.
    156* at Adelaide, 1950–1.
    145   at Lord's, 1953.
    122* at Sydney, 1946–7.
    100   at Nottingham, 1938.

v. South Africa (4).
    158   at Johannesburg, 1948–9 (SECOND TEST).
    123   at Johannesburg, 1948–9 (FOURTH TEST).
    100   at Leeds, 1947.
    100   at Leeds, 1951.

v. West Indies (5).
    205   at Kingston, 1953–4.
    202* at The Oval, 1950.
    196   at Lord's, 1939.
    169   at Georgetown, 1953–4.
    165* at The Oval, 1939.

v. New Zealand (3).
    206   at The Oval, 1949.
    101   at Leeds, 1949.
    100   at Manchester, 1937.

v. India (2).
    150   at Lord's, 1952.
    104   at Manchester 1952.

FULL LIST OF HUNDREDS—129

1934 (1)
196   Yorkshire v. Worcestershire, at Worcester.

1935 (1)
131   Yorkshire v. Middlesex, at Leeds.

1936 (1)
163   Yorkshire v. Surrey, at Leeds.

Signifies not out.

1937 (10)

271* Yorkshire v. Derbyshire, at Sheffield.
161   Yorkshire v. M.C.C., at Lord's.
153   Yorkshire v. Leicestershire, at Hull.
136   Yorkshire v. Kent, at Tonbridge.
135   Yorkshire v. New Zealanders, at Leeds.
124   Yorkshire v. Essex, at Ilford.
121   Yorkshire v. Middlesex, at The Oval (Challenge Match).
102   North v. South, at Lord's.
101   Yorkshire v. Worcestershire, at Stourbridge.
100   England v. New Zealand, at Manchester (SECOND TEST).

1938 (6)

364   England v. Australia, at The Oval (FIFTH TEST).
180   Yorkshire v. Cambridge University, at Cambridge.
141   Yorkshire v. Oxford University, at Oxford.
107   Yorkshire v. Sussex, at Leeds.
106* Yorkshire v. M.C.C., at Scarborough.
100   England v. Australia, at Nottingham (FIRST TEST).

1938–39 (5)

202   M.C.C. v. East Province, at Port Elizabeth.
149   M.C.C. v. Griqualand West, at Kimberley.
148   M.C.C. v. Combined Transvaal XI, at Johannesburg.
145   M.C.C. v. Rhodesia, at Bulawayo.
108   M.C.C. v. Natal, at Durban.

1939 (12)

280* Yorkshire v. Hampshire, at Sheffield.
196   England v. West Indies, at Lord's (FIRST TEST).
177   Yorkshire v. Sussex, at Scarborough.
165* England v. West Indies, at The Oval (THIRD TEST).
158   Yorkshire v. Warwickshire, at Birmingham.
151   Yorkshire v. Surrey, at Leeds.
144   Yorkshire v. Glamorgan, at Bradford.
109   Yorkshire v. Worcestershire, at Bradford.
105* Yorkshire v. Lancashire, at Leeds.
103   Yorkshire v. Sussex, at Hove.
102   Yorkshire v. Cambridge University, at Cambridge.
100   Yorkshire v. Kent, at Dover.

1945 (2)

188   H. D. G. Leveson Gower's XI v. New Zealanders, at Scarborough.
104   An England XI v. Australian Services, at Lord's.

1946 (4)

183* Yorkshire v. Indians, at Bradford.
171* Yorkshire v. Northamptonshire, at Hull.
111   Yorkshire v. Leicestershire, at Leeds.
101   Yorkshire v. Surrey, at The Oval.

1946–47 (3)

151* M.C.C. v. Victoria, at Melbourne.
136   M.C.C. v. South Australia, at Adelaide.
122* England v. Australia, at Sydney (FIFTH TEST).

Signifies not out.

1947 (11)

270*	Yorkshire v. Hampshire, at Bournemouth.
197 ⎱ 104 ⎰	Yorkshire v. Essex, at Southend.
197	Yorkshire v. Glamorgan, at Swansea.
137	Yorkshire v. Leicestershire, at Leicester.
137	Yorkshire v. South Africans, at Sheffield.
120*	Yorkshire v. Cambridge University, at Cambridge.
107	Yorkshire v. M.C.C., at Scarborough.
106	Yorkshire v. Sussex, at Bradford.
103	Yorkshire v. Oxford University, at Oxford.
100	England v. South Africa, at Leeds (FOURTH TEST).

1947–48 (2)

138	M.C.C. v. British Guiana, at Georgetown.
128	M.C.C. v. Jamaica (second match), at Kingston.

1948 (10)

176*	Yorkshire v. Sussex, at Sheffield.
155	Yorkshire v. Sussex, at Hove.
144*	Yorkshire v. Essex, at Leeds.
133	Yorkshire v. Middlesex, at Lord's.
132*	Players v. Gentlemen, at Lord's.
107*	Yorkshire v. M.C.C., at Scarborough.
104	Yorkshire v. Lancashire, at Manchester.
103	Yorkshire v. Essex, at Westcliff.
100*	Yorkshire v. Northamptonshire, at Huddersfield.
100	Yorkshire v. Lancashire, at Leeds.

1948–49 (5)

174	M.C.C. v. Transvaal, at Johannesburg.
158	England v. South Africa, at Johannesburg (SECOND TEST).
134	M.C.C. v. Orange Free State, at Bloemfontein.
125	M.C.C. v. Cape Province, at Cape Town.
123	England v. South Africa, at Johannesburg (FOURTH TEST).

1949 (12)

269*	Yorkshire v. Northamptonshire, at Wellingborough.
206	England v. New Zealand, at The Oval (FOURTH TEST).
201	Yorkshire v. Lancashire, at Manchester.
167	Yorkshire v. New Zealanders, at Bradford.
165 ⎱ 100 ⎰	Yorkshire v. Sussex, at Hove.
147	Yorkshire v. M.C.C., at Scarborough.
146*	Yorkshire v. Scotland, at Hull.
113	Yorkshire v. Middlesex, at Lord's.
104	Yorkshire v. Northamptonshire, at Bradford.
101	England v. New Zealand, at Leeds (FIRST TEST).
101	North v. South, at Scarborough.

1950 (6)

202*	England v. West Indies at The Oval.
156	Yorkshire v. Essex at Colchester.
153	Yorkshire v. Nottinghamshire, at Nottingham.
141	Yorkshire v. Somerset, at Huddersfield.
107	Yorkshire v. West Indies, at Sheffield.

* Signifies not out.

1950–51 (5)

156* England v. Australia, at Adelaide (FOURTH TEST).
150 M.C.C. v. New South Wales, at Sydney.
128 M.C.C. v. Victoria, at Melbourne.
126 M.C.C. v. South Australia, at Adelaide.
112 M.C.C. v. New South Wales, at Sydney.

1951 (7)

194* Yorkshire v. Nottinghamshire, at Nottingham.
151 Yorkshire v. Surrey, at The Oval.
117 Yorkshire v. Middlesex, at Lord's.
156 Yorkshire v. South Africans, at Sheffield.
141 Yorkshire v. Essex, at Brentwood.
110* Yorkshire v. Gloucestershire, at Bristol.
100 England v. South Africa, at Leeds (FOURTH TEST).

1952 (11)

189 Yorkshire v. Kent, at Leeds.
152 Yorkshire v. Lancashire, at Leeds.
150 England v. India, at Lord's (SECOND TEST).
132 Yorkshire v. Middlesex, at Lord's.
120 Yorkshire v. Kent, at Canterbury.
119 Yorkshire v. Somerset, at Huddersfield.
108 Yorkshire v. Gloucestershire, at Harrogate.
104 England v. India, at Manchester (THIRD TEST).
104 Yorkshire v. Surrey, at The Oval.
103⎫
107⎭ Yorkshire v. M.C.C., at Scarborough.

1953 (8)

241 Players v. Gentlemen, at Scarborough.
178 Yorkshire v. Somerset, at Leeds.
145 England v. Australia, at Lord's (SECOND TEST).
125 Yorkshire v. Warwickshire, at Bradford.
103* Yorkshire v. M.C.C., at Scarborough.
102 T.N. Pearce's XI v. Australians, at Scarborough.
100* Yorkshire v. Kent, at Scarborough.
100 Yorkshire v. Worcestershire, at Huddersfield.

1953–54 (2)

205 England v. West Indies, at Kingston (FIFTH TEST).
169 England v. West Indies, at Georgetown (THIRD TEST).

1954 (2)

163 Yorkshire v. Combined Services, at Harrogate.
149* Yorkshire v. Notinghamshire, at Bradford.

1954–55 (2)

145* M.C.C. v. Western Australia, at Perth.
102 M.C.C. v. New South Wales, at Sydney.

1955 (1)

194 Yorkshire v. Nottinghamshire, at Nottingham.

* Signifies not out.

BOWLING

	Overs	Maidens	Runs	Wickets	Average
1934	103	17	379	11	34.45
1935	22.1	5	79	2	39.50
1935–6	7	0	45	1	45.00
1936	173.3	44	479	21	22.81
1937	315	56	1025	28	36.60
1938	227.1	51	576	20	28.80
1938–9	24	1	108	2	54.00
1939	220.7	38	822	44	18.68
1945	35	0	167	5	33.40
1946	58	11	173	9	19.22
1946–7	18	1	116	2	58.00
1947	109	18	344	12	28.83
1947–8	5	1	20	0	—
1948	26	5	102	0	—
1948–9	1	0	7	0	—
1949	102	29	286	7	40.86
1950	28	5	90	2	45.00
1950–1	3.6	0	11	1	11.00
1951	11	1	44	4	11.00
1952	10	1	43	1	43.00
1953	31	8	129	0	—
1953–4	6	0	43	0	—
1954–5	00.6	0	2	1	2.00
Totals	1293.5	292	5090	173	29.42

and 243.3 eight-ball overs

NOTABLE ACHIEVEMENTS

Leonard Hutton, born on June 23, 1916, at Fulneck, one mile from Pudsey, scored 39,950 runs in first-class cricket before back-trouble compelled him to retire at the age of 39.

Hutton captained England 23 times, more than any other player, and did not lose a rubber; 11 matches were won, 8 drawn and 4 lost. Only W. M. Woodfull (25) and Sir Donald Bradman (24), both Australians, have led their country in more Tests.

Hutton hit 364, the highest individual score in Test cricket, against Australia at The Oval in 1938. He batted for thirteen hours, twenty minutes, the longest innings in first-class cricket.

Altogether Hutton hit 129 centuries in first-class cricket, a figure exceeded by six players. Sir J. B. Hobbs (197), E. Hendren (170), W. R. Hammond (167), C. P. Mead (153), H. Sutcliffe (149), F. E. Woolley (145).

Hutton played in 79 Tests, a figure exceeded only by W. R. Hammond (85). Only Hammond (7,249) and Sir Donald Bradman (6,996) scored more Test runs than Hutton (6,971). Hutton hit 19 Test centuries, compared with 29 by Bradman and 22 by Hammond.

Despite three successive "ducks," 0 v. New Zealand, 0 and 0 v. Worcestershire, Hutton in June 1949 scored 1,294 runs, the highest aggregate by any one batsman in one month. The previous best was 1,281 by W. R. Hammond in August 1936. Hutton also reached 1,050 runs in August 1949, and thus joined such other great players as C. B. Fry, K. S. Ranjitsinhji and H. Sutcliffe, who obtained over 1,000 runs in each of two months in the same season.

Hutton's aggregate of 3,429 runs in 1949 was greater than that of any other Yorkshire batsman in one season. The previous highest was 3,336 by H. Sutcliffe in 1932.

Hutton has twice shared with C. Washbrook in three-figure stands in each innings of a Test against Australia. At Adelaide in 1946–47 they opened with 137 and 100, and at Leeds in 1948 with 168 and 129.

Hutton and Washbrook made the highest opening stand in Test cricket in 1948–49 when they scored 359 together for England against South Africa in the Second Test at Johannesburg. This was beaten in January 1956 by V. Mankad and P. Roy of India, who made 413 against New Zealand in the Fifth Test at Madras.

In 1955, M.C.C. amended their rules in order to make Hutton the first playing professional member of the club.

The batting feats of Hutton since the war were the more remarkable when one bears in mind the fact that in March 1941, while serving as a P.T. Instructor in an Army Gymnasium, he met with a serious accident to his left arm. He underwent three bone-grafting operations and was in hospital for eight months. Parts of his leg were transferred to his arm. The limb was unresponsive to his previous style of play and he was compelled to remodel his technique.

MORLEY

Surely

This Morley sweater is a credit to any cricketer—
warm, well made, and generously full for comfort.
You'll find the same qualities of comfort and
good taste in all other knitted wear that Morley
make for men.

Always look for the name

MORLEY

RAY LINDWALL AND KEITH MILLER

TWO ERAS OF AUSTRALIAN PACE

GREGORY—MCDONALD TO LINDWALL—MILLER

By I. A. R. Peebles

This summer we welcome the Australians again to our shores. Already they have been here twenty-one times since their first visit in 1878. They come as challengers, for England hold the Ashes which were regained at Kennington Oval in 1953. We, in England, regard the Australians as our most formidable opponents and another exciting series of Tests can be expected. Usually the Australians ride rough-shod over the County clubs. Not since 1912 has a County eleven lowered their colours. During that tour the Australians were without some of their leading players and they suffered eight defeats including five by the Counties: Nottinghamshire, Surrey, Lancashire (twice), and Hampshire. The nearest any County has come to mastering them since then was in 1930 when Gloucestershire tied at Bristol. (Editor.)

Barring mishaps, it does seem certain that once again England will see the old firm of Lindwall and Miller in action. In the past there have been premature reports of their impending retirement, and even at the moment of writing when Sheffield Shield cricket in Australia is well under way and the selectors are doubtless studying the individual form of the players with anxious eyes, both have been troubled by injury. Whatever the future may bring, a comparison between Lindwall and Miller and their only rivals as a pair in the present century of Australian cricket, Gregory and McDonald, is fascinating as it is inevitable.

In making any such comparison it is necessary to recognise that fashions and techniques in cricket, as in other matters, have changed with the passing of the generation which separates two distinct eras. It is a wide subject and, as space will allow only the study of certain aspects, these few reflections are perforce confined to the bowlers' point of view, and again largely to that of the pace bowler.

This will be the third Australian team to visit England since the war, and it will embark on the sixth series since that major interruption. In the number of matches and in actual years this period is almost the exact counterpart of that between the end of the first war and the eve of the 1930 tour. There is also a close parallel in the trend of events. In both cases England were out-played in the reopening tour and the return visit, achieved a solitary victory in the third series and won the fourth in each case by a final deciding match at The Oval. The succeeding series, those of

1928–29 and 1954–55, saw England once more in the ascendancy by a good margin.

The similarity in result during these decades was reflected by a close resemblance in the actual play. A period of Australian supremacy, achieved by a combination of powerful batting, devastating fast bowling and much superior fielding, was followed by a gradual English resurgence led by an outstanding fast-medium bowler. Finally, there comes a complete reversal of the balance, largely brought about by a counterblast of fast bowling. Certainly there were many other factors which contributed to the ebb and flow of the tide, some alike and some totally dissimilar, but few cricket cycles can have been so alike in broad outline.

Bradman Intervenes

They were divided by the era of Bradman who made his first appearance in the 1928–29 series and led the triumphant teams of 1946–47 and 1948. Despite the overlap, the division may be regarded as fairly clear, for on the one hand, despite early success, he was still something of an unknown quantity and, on the other, although still a tremendous force, he was scarcely the man who changed the character of international cricket in the 'thirties. In comparing the two eras, it is possible to identify several elements which affected tactics and techniques; but to say for how many of these Bradman was directly or indirectly accountable or to estimate his total influence on the game as a whole is very difficult. What is plain is that the game as played in the post second war years differed considerably in form from that of 1921.

To start with cold, impersonal figures—if indeed cricket figures can ever be cold or impersonal—surely the most pertinent item amongst Mr. Roy Webber's exhaustive figures dealing with these years is the fact that in the 1920–21 and 1921 series England, a well-beaten side, scored forty-nine and fifty runs per hundred balls bowled. Australia were naturally rather more expeditious scoring fifty-three and fifty-six. In the first two post second war series the rates dropped to thirty-seven and thirty-eight for England and fifty and forty-six for Australia. Thereafter the Australian rate dropped farther back. The trend in the intervening years had been a steady decline in the pace of scoring despite a large proportion of runs supplied by Bradman at an exceptionally high personal rate. Even if the 1920–21 and 1921 seasons were abnormal, it hardly calls for the mass of additional evidence available to demonstrate that the play of thirty-five years ago was of a considerably freer character. Whether it was as efficient is another matter.

What is the main reason for this change or deceleration? The broad answer must surely be the transference of the bowlers' focus from the region of the off-stump to that of the leg and the consequent throttling of off-side play but, equally importantly, the

denial of the safe deflecting stroke to leg. The causes of this transference are several and complex, and the credit or responsibility
must be shared between groundsman, bowler and batsman in what
proportion we may later determine. Somewhat unfashionably I
am inclined to exculpate the legislators.

In 1921 the spearhead of the Australian attack, the speed of
Gregory and McDonald, was directed at the stumps and supported
by three slips. The good length ball aimed at the stumps pitched
regularly to the off and it was desirable that any error should be
further in that direction. If the error was to drop the ball outside
the leg-stump the batsman could play boldly in the knowledge that
he had free passage to a distant fine-leg who could, at most, rob
him of three runs.

When Lindwall and Miller bowled the slips had increased in
number and some of them had now migrated to the hitherto
uninhabited regions on the leg-side. For England, Bedser, with his
sharp in-swerver, had perfected the same technique and the impact
on batsmanship must have been as profound as the introduction of
the googly. What had been a safe and attractive scoring shot had
now elements of suicide, for if the ball "moved" a little to the on a
mishit was almost certain to result in a catch. Indeed, a correctly
executed stroke was often fatal, owing to the difficulty of placing
and keeping the ball down in this sector. The dangers of this
situation were clear when Bradman, who seldom repeated a serious
mistake, fell three times in succession to the backward short-leg
position during the 1948 series.

The development of this form of attack is, as I have said,
attributable to several causes. Most are agreed that the glory of
cricket exists on the off-side, the highest art of the bowler to make
the ball go away, and the beauty of batsmanship the variety of
stroke between third-man and mid-off. But with the undoubted
improvement in defensive back-play and the increase of dead,
over-prepared pitches the bowler was given little incentive to
attack, especially on the off-side.

While the old lbw rule prevailed it was extremely hard to dislodge a batsman who made good use of his pads, for under its
terms the ball had to pitch on and hit. Geometrically it is almost
impossible for the faster bowler to drop the ball on a good length
and comply with these requirements, unless he turns the ball from
the leg—a tall order in the circumstances where it is most required.
(In passing, it seems strange that those who advocate the reintro-
duction of the old law, having robbed the bowler of what little
opportunity the present rule affords him in that quarter, expect
thereby a return to off-side play.)

When the bowler was shorn of practically all means of positive
action on the off-side it was not unnatural that he should seek some
line of defence, or at least economy, and the on-side offered decided

advantages in time of stress. It was seen as an area of attack in the 1932–33 series, a state of affairs largely precipitated by the tremendous off-side attacks of Bradman on the paceless pitches of 1930. At the same time O'Reilly dimmed much of Hammond's brilliance by concentrating on his relatively weaker on-side play. From then on much thought was given to the placing and feeding of the close leg-side field.

In the present age the "in-coming" form of attack, so to speak, has been brought to a very fine art and one speculates on the reactions of the great stroke players of the past suddenly confronted with Bedser at his best. On the other side one wonders what additional problems Barnes and Tate might have raised by systematic use of the close leg field.

It is important to distinguish between the legitimate leg stump attack and "leg-theory" applied in a purely negative sense to discourage scoring. That any bowler should be permitted to pack the leg-side field and bowl outside the batsman's legs is deplorable and to be discouraged at all costs. Appeals to the spirit of the game are, to my mind, of dubious value, for the very good reason that the "spirit" is inclined to vary greatly with circumstances and in interpretation. A clear-cut law operates with certainty in all conditions, but the difficulty in this case is, admittedly, to frame such a law without adding further complication to an already intricate code.

My own suggestion to meet this situation has just that disadvantage but seems to have a basis of justice. If, which is perhaps improbable, this form of bowling should ever become widespread, would it not be possible to say that, when five or more fielders were posted to the on, any ball pitching outside the leg stump should be a no-ball? This may be cumbersome but it would exercise restraint where it is needed without interfering with the honest citizen.

The real answer to all cricket problems is, of course, to give the bowler fair incentive and opportunity to attack at all times. In doing so he will get wickets but will be more prone to make mistakes from which the striker can derive benefit and, indeed, in the absence of any guaranteed security, will be anxious to do so. This is hardly the place in which to reopen the discussion as to the best ways and means of achieving this healthy state of affairs, but, as I have implied, a return to the old lbw law is surely not one of them.

The point of these rather rambling reflections is really to say that could the modern spectator be wafted back thirty-five years he would not only see a faster scoring match but one of largely different character. It might or might not be that he would find them more interesting than the battles of attrition to which he has grown accustomed. It might be more accurate to say "had grown accustomed," for it must be borne in mind that the recent series in Australia was the most exciting cricket, whatever its standard. But it was also exceptional.

Much of the action and excitement was due to the fact that the pitches gave considerable, and not always fair, help to the prevailing type of bowling. Their inconsistency occasionally gave the proceedings an air of hit or miss which went beyond the bounds of "glorious uncertainty" and must always detract from an equally balanced and scientific contest. To one who has played on it, the thought constantly recurs that the matting wicket of the old Wanderers ground at Johannesburg, with all its disadvantages, was the one surface which gave both departments full scope for their talents and was at all times a true reflection of merit.

The highlights of each era, Gregory and McDonald attacking Hobbs and Woolley or Lindwall and Miller in action against Compton and Hutton obviously transcended the differences in character to which I have referred and even the one-sided nature of the matches. The chief point in common amongst the batsmen is that they formed a first line of defence with little reserve behind them. The bowlers have much similarity in circumstance and in performance. They reigned supreme at a time when there was a world shortage of fast bowling and batsmen were ill-equipped to meet it.

Which was the finer pair and which the greatest individual must ever be open to argument and is much a matter of opinion. Certainly in span and in the matter of statistics the moderns have a much more impressive record. Gregory and McDonald appeared together in but eleven Test matches, eight against England and three against South Africa. The latter then left the international field at the height of his powers but his senior partner played for another seven years, a total of 24 matches. There is no doubt, however, that his powers declined greatly after the dissolution of the partnership.

Comparison of Figures

Up to the present Lindwall and Miller have appeared together on 46 occasions and have played 49 and 47 Test matches respectively. In his Test career Gregory took 75 wickets at 35.30 runs apiece and McDonald 43 at 35.60 each. So far Lindwall has taken 192 wickets for 21.88 apiece and Miller 147 at 22.99 runs each.

There can be little doubt that McDonald was the most graceful of the quartette and possibly the most perfect cricket machine of all time. In the opinion of many well-qualified judges he could produce a faster ball than anyone within living memory. In his county days he seldom exerted himself to the full; only recently I was given an enthralling eye-witness account of one of his latter bursts of speed, occasioned by the appearance of an amateur who had treated him roughly in a previous match. This apparently irritated him out of his customary impassive calm and the results were spectacular. My informant, who has played most of the fast bowlers of the last thirty years, says it was the fastest bowling he has ever seen and only approached by Lindwall's stupendous three-over burst at Manchester in 1948. It was interesting to hear that the only perceptible increase in effort was that he accelerated in the last five yards of the impeccable run up to a swift gallop. His point established he reverted to the normal cruising speed which carried him through many strenuous seasons.

Gregory was to my mind the most inspiring. One might apply to him the words of a motoring critic who said of a famous make of sports car that others might have gone faster but none had achieved the glorious frenzy of its progress. Estimates as to his maximum speed vary, but it must have been extremely swift especially in the opening overs, and his height and very high arm added greatly to the general hostility of the performance. It might also be said of both Gregory and Miller that, in contrast to the polished craftsmanship of their partners, they were both children of nature.

Lindwall Comes First

A large mass of opinion places Lindwall first of all fast bowlers, a judgement based on pace, variation, control and consummate technique of seam and swerve. In addition he is a wonderfully shrewd and discerning tactician. I have already dwelt on the modern emphasis on the leg stump and the close surrounding field. Lindwall has retained the classical off-side attack but has added to it the cramping assault on the region of the batsman's pads. The so-called "Carmody field," which consists of a cover-point and a short-leg to the fore and the rest of the field spread on either side of the wicket-keeper like the horns of a Zulu Impi, would doubtless appear monstrous and absurd to an eye reopened after thirty years. In the hands of the master it is in fact a formidable instrument. When it is new, the bowler pitches the ball well up, almost to half-volley length, and invites the batsman to drive him into the untenanted foreground. But swinging bat and very late swinging ball are ill met and the mis-hit from either edge means almost certain disaster with the Australian in-field to hand.

Batsmen have told me that Lindwall's low arm gives the ball an awkward angle of flight in addition to the complication of his late and unpredicted dip in either direction. When, as in the last series, the ball came at varying heights from the pitch the skill demanded of the modern opener is such that it is not surprising that few regularly succeed in such circumstances. It may be observed that doped, paceless wickets kill these dangers just as effectively as they obliterate any other point of interest.

Of Miller it might be said that he is the most mercurial but, in the mood, as deadly as any. His careless, almost casual air bears no relation to the power and fire of his action which seems to develop its maximum effort and weight as the arm comes to the downward sector of its swing so that the ball hits the pitch with a resounding thump. Although it may be with less design than in the case of Lindwall, he makes the ball move sharply in either direction.

Miller The Menace

After the splendid performances of our own fast bowlers in Australia in 1954–55 it may seem almost ungrateful to say so but, with Lindwall in at least a temporary decline, Miller was the most menacing bowler of the series with the new ball. He may have lost something of his stamina but his opening assaults at Brisbane, Melbourne and Adelaide were positively hair-raising as seen through the eyes of a visiting supporter. Three balls at the start of the crucial second innings at Adelaide all but wrecked English hopes and remain vividly in the imagination. First there was a ferocious "in-dipper," which appeared to affect Edrich's nervous system as violently as it did his middle and leg stumps. This was followed at uncomfortably short intervals by two very fast balls to Hutton and Cowdrey which left the pitch like leg-breaks and resulted in bullet-like catches, both beautifully picked up in the slips. The challenge was met by magnificent batting by May and Compton, but until the first welcome signs of fatigue appeared the final target of 94 runs seemed immeasurably distant.

Miller has the additional virtue of being a most entertaining bowler, and his impish delight in loosing off googlies and round armers without previous notice must be highly disconcerting, if it does not seem to meet with any great material success.

The Combined Effort

But when all is said and done, which of these great pairs will be given premier place in Australian cricket history in the years to come is a very open question. Gregory and McDonald have one very special niche in all cricket history. At least so far as international cricket is concerned they were the pioneers of all fast opening attack. Since then it has been regarded as the most effective use that can be made of the new ball, and it can well be argued that two fast bowlers, provided they are of quality, have had more influence on the result of a given series than any other factor, with the possible exception of the phenomenal Bradman. In support of this view I would cite Larwood and Voce; Martindale and Constantine in their own country; Lindwall and Miller and finally Statham and Tyson. There have been many fine individual performers during the same time, but it seems that the combined effort is necessary to derive the fullest service from the individual.

K. R. MILLER IN TEST CRICKET
Statistics by Roy Webber

Batting and Fielding

	M.	I.	N.O.	Runs	H.S.	Avge.	100	50	Ct.
1945–46 v. New Zealand	1	1	0	30	30	30.00	0	0	1
1946–47 v. England	5	7	2	384	141*	76.80	1	1	3
1947–48 v. India	5	5	0	185	67	37.00	0	2	5
1948 v. England...........	5	7	0	184	74	28.26	0	2	8
1949–50 v. South Africa......	5	8	2	246	84	41.00	0	2	3
1950–51 v. England	5	9	1	350	145*	43.75	1	1	3
1951–52 v. West Indies	5	10	1	362	129	40.22	1	1	5
1952–53 v. South Africa	4	6	0	153	55	25.50	0	2	3
1953 v. England	5	9	0	223	109	24.77	1	1	2
1954–55 v. England	4	7	0	167	49	23.85	0	0	1
1954–55 v. West Indies	5	6	0	439	147	73.16	3	0	1
Total	49	75	6	2723	147	39.46	7	12	35

Bowling

	Balls	Mds.	Runs	Wkts.	Avge.	5 w I
1945–46 v. New Zealand	36	2	6	2	3.00	0
1946–47 v. England	979	15	334	16	20.87	1
1947–48 v. India	576	14	223	9	24.77	0
1948 v. England	829	43	301	13	23.15	0
1949–50 v. South Africa	1080	18	390	17	22.94	1
1950–51 v. England	854	23	301	17	17.70	0
1951–52 v. West Indies	1027	16	398	20	19.90	2
1952–53 v. South Africa	728	17	241	13	18.53	0
1953 v. England	1116	72	303	10	30.30	0
1954–55 v. England	708	28	243	10	24.30	0
1954–55 v. West Indies	1136	37	640	20	32.00	1
Total	9069	285	3380	147	22.99	5

* Signifies not out. 5 w I denotes 5 wickets in one innings.

K. R. Miller completed the Test "double" of 1,000 runs and 100 wickets in his 33rd Test match, and now has the best all-round record for any Test player, surpassing the record of W. Rhodes (England) who scored 2,325 runs (av. 30.19) and took 127 wickets (av. 26.96) in 58 Test matches.

R. R. LINDWALL IN TEST CRICKET

Batting and Fielding

	M.	I.	N.O.	Runs	H.S.	Avge.	100	50	Ct.
1945–46 v. New Zealand	1	1	0	0	0	0.00	0	0	0
1946–47 v. England	4	5	0	160	100	32.00	1	0	2
1947–48 v. India	5	5	0	70	35	14.00	0	0	2
1948 v. England	5	6	0	191	77	31.83	0	1	3
1949–50 v. South Africa	4	4	1	41	21	13.66	0	0	0
1950–51 v. England	5	9	1	124	41	15.50	0	0	4
1951–52 v. West Indies	5	9	1	211	61	26.37	0	1	1
1952–53 v. South Africa	4	6	1	66	38*	13.20	0	0	3
1953 v. England	5	9	0	159	62	17.66	0	2	2
1954–55 v. England	4	6	2	106	64*	26.50	0	1	2
1954–55 v. West Indies	5	6	1	187	118	37.40	1	0	1
Total	47	66	7	1315	118	22.28	2	5	20

* Signifies not out.

Bowling

	Balls	Mdns.	Runs	Wkts.	Avge.	5 w I
1945–46 v. New Zealand	102	4	29	2	14.50	0
1946–47 v. Australia	977	20	367	18	20.38	1
1947–48 v. India	908	23	304	18	16.88	1
1948 v. England	1337	57	530	27	19.62	2
1949–50 v. South Africa	756	13	248	12	20.66	1
1950–51 v. England	795	11	344	15	22.93	0
1951–52 v. West Indies	1232	19	484	21	23.04	1
1952–53 v. South Africa	1079	18	383	19	20.15	1
1953 v. England	1444	62	490	26	18.84	3
1954–55 v. England	1046	28	381	14	27.21	0
1954–55 v. West Indies	1056	25	643	20	32.15	1
Total	10732	280	4203	192	21.80	11

ENGLAND BATTING AGAINST AUSTRALIA

(Qualification: 7 innings, average 10)

	Period	Tests	Inns.	Not Outs	Runs	100's	Highest Inns.	Average
R. Abel	1888–1902	11	19	1	555	1	132*	30.83
G. O. Allen	1930–36	13	21	1	479	0	68	23.95
L. E. G. Ames	1932–38	17	27	2	675	1	120	27.00
E. G. Arnold	1903–05	8	12	3	144	0	40	16.00
W. Attewell	1884–91	10	15	6	150	0	43*	16.66
T. E. Bailey	1950–	14	23	3	558	0	88	27.90
R. G. Barlow	1881–91	17	30	4	591	0	62	22.73
W. Barnes	1880–90	21	33	2	725	1	134	23.38
C. J. Barnett	1936–48	9	16	0	624	2	129	39.00
W. Bates	1881–86	15	26	2	656	0	64	27.33
A. V. Bedser	1946–	21	35	9	373	0	79	14.34
Hon. Ivo Bligh	1882–83	4	7	1	62	0	19	10.33
B. J. T. Bosanquet	1903–05	7	14	3	145	0	27	13.18
L. C. Braund	1901–07	20	36	3	834	2	103*	25.27
J. Briggs	1884–99	31	48	5	809	1	121	18.81
W. Brockwell	1893–99	7	12	0	202	0	49	16.83
F. R. Brown	1950–53	6	10	0	260	0	79	26.00
J. T. Brown	1894–99	8	16	3	470	1	140	36.15
A. P. F. Chapman	1924–30	16	25	3	784	1	121	35.63
D. C. S. Compton	1938–	27	49	7	1713	5	184	40.78
M. C. Cowdrey	1954–	5	9	0	319	1	102	35.44
J. N. Crawford	1907–08	5	10	1	162	0	62	18.00
J. W. H. T. Douglas	1911–24	17	28	2	696	0	75	26.76
N. F. Druce	1897–98	5	9	0	252	0	64	28.00
G. Duckworth	1928–30	10	17	6	163	0	39*	14.81
K. S. Duleepsinhji	1930	4	7	0	416	1	173	59.42
W. J. Edrich	1938–	21	39	1	1184	2	119	31.15
T. Emmett	1876–81	7	13	1	160	0	48	13.93
T. G. Evans	1946–	23	40	8	641	0	50	20.03
F. L. Fane	1907–08	4	8	0	192	0	50	24.00
P. G. H. Fender	1920–21	5	9	1	198	0	59	24.75
A. Fielder	1903–07	6	12	5	78	0	20	11.14
W. Flowers	1884–93	8	14	0	254	0	56	18.14
F. G. J. Ford	1894–95	5	9	0	168	0	48	18.66
F. R. Foster	1911–12	8	11	1	281	0	71	28.10
R. E. Foster	1903–04	5	9	1	486	1	287	60.75
C. B. Fry	1899–1912	18	29	3	825	1	144	31.73
G. Geary	1926–34	9	15	2	202	0	66	15.53
W. G. Grace	1880–99	22	36	2	1098	2	170	32.29

Signifies not out.

	Period	Tests	Inns.	Not Outs	Runs	100's	Highest Inns.	Average
T. W. Graveney ..	1953–	7	10	0	301	1	111	30.10
G. Gunn	1907–11	11	21	1	844	2	122*	42.20
J. Gunn	1901–05	6	10	2	85	0	24	10.62
W. Gunn	1886–99	11	20	2	392	1	102*	21.77
W. R. Hammond ..	1928–46	33	58	3	2852	9	251	51.85
J. Hardstaff	1907–08	5	10	0	311	0	72	31.10
J. Hardstaff, jr. ..	1936–48	9	16	1	559	1	169*	37.26
T. Hayward	1896–1909	29	51	2	1747	2	137	35.65
J. W. Hearne	1911–26	16	24	2	554	1	114	25.18
E. Hendren	1920–34	28	48	4	1740	3	169	39.54
G. H. Hirst	1897–1909	21	33	3	746	0	85	24.86
J. W. Hitch	1911–21	6	9	2	103	0	51*	14.71
J. B. Hobbs	1907–30	41	71	4	3636	12	187	54.26
J. Hunter	1884–85	5	7	2	93	0	39*	18.60
K. L. Hutchings .	1907–09	7	12	0	341	1	126	28.41
L. Hutton	1938–	27	49	6	2428	5	364	56.46
J. T. Ikin	1946–	5	10	0	184	0	60	18.40
F. S. Jackson ...	1893–1905	20	33	4	1412	5	144*	48.68
D. R. Jardine	1928–32	10	18	1	540	1	98	31.76
G. L. Jessop	1899–1909	13	18	0	433	1	104	24.05
A. O. Jones	1899–1909	12	21	0	291	0	34	13.85
R. Kilner	1924–26	7	7	1	174	0	74	29.00
J. C. Laker	1948–	6	10	1	178	0	63	19.77
H. Larwood	1926–32	15	22	2	386	0	98	19.30
C. F. H. Leslie ..	1882–83	4	7	0	106	0	54	15.14
M. Leyland	1928–36	20	34	4	1705	7	187	56.83
A. A. Lilley	1896–1909	32	47	7	800	0	84	20.00
W. H. Lockwood .	1893–1902	12	16	3	235	0	52	18.07
G. A. Lohmann ..	1886–96	15	22	2	203	0	62*	10.15
A. P. Lucas	1878–84	5	9	1	157	0	55	19.62
Hon. A. Lyttelton	1880–84	4	7	1	94	0	31	15.66
G. MacGregor ...	1890–93	8	11	3	96	0	31	12.00
A. C. MacLaren..	1894–1909	35	61	4	1931	5	140	33.87
H. Makepeace ...	1920–21	4	8	0	279	1	117	34.87
J. R. Mason	1897	5	10	0	129	0	32	12.90
P. B. H. May	1953–	7	12	0	436	1	104	36.33
C. P. Mead	1911–28	7	10	2	415	1	182*	51.87
W. E. Midwinter..	1881–82	4	7	0	95	0	36	13.57
C. H. Parkin	1920–21	9	15	2	152	1	36	11.69
E. Paynter	1932–38	7	11	4	591	1	216*	84.42
E. Peate	1881–86	9	14	8	70	0	13	11.66
R. Peel	1884–96	20	33	4	427	0	83	14.72
W. G. Quaife	1899–1901	7	13	1	228	0	68	19.00
K. S. Rantitsinhji.	1896–1902	15	26	4	985	2	175	44.77
J. M. Read	1882–93	15	26	2	447	0	57	18.62
W. W. Read	1882–93	17	26	1	680	1	117	27.20
W. Rhodes	1899–1926	41	69	14	1706	1	179	31.01
T. Richardson....	1893–97	14	24	8	177	0	25*	11.06
R. W. V. Robins ..	1930–36	6	10	2	183	0	61	22.87
A. C. Russell	1920–21	6	11	2	474	3	135*	52.66
W. H. Scotton ...	1881–86	15	25	2	510	0	90	22.17
J. Selby	1876–81	6	12	1	256	0	70	23.27
A. Shaw	1876–81	7	12	1	111	0	40	10.09
A. Shrewsbury ...	1881–93	23	40	4	1277	3	164	35.47
R. T. Simpson ...	1950–	9	17	2	434	1	156*	28.93
R. H. Spooner ...	1905–12	7	11	0	233	0	79	21.18
J. B. Statham	1953–	6	8	2	84	0	35	14.00
A. G. Steel	1880–88	13	20	3	600	2	148	35.29
A. E. Stoddart ...	1887–97	16	30	2	996	2	173	35.57

* Signifies not out.

	Period	Tests	Inns.	Not Outs	Runs	100's	Highest Inns.	Average
W. Storer.........	1897–99	6	11	0	215	0	51	19.54
C. T. Studd	1882–83	5	9	1	160	0	48	20.00
H. Sutcliffe	1924–32	27	46	5	2741	8	194	66.85
M. W. Tate	1924–30	20	30	1	578	0	54	19.93
E. Tyldesley	1921–26	5	7	1	257	0	81	42.83
J. T. Tyldesley ..	1899–1909	26	46	1	1389	3	138	30.86
E. F. S. Tylecote..	1882–86	6	9	1	152	0	66	19.00
F. H. Tyson	1954–	5	7	1	66	0	37*	11.00
G. Ulyett	1876–90	23	36	0	901	1	149	25.02
H. Verity	1932–38	18	27	8	344	0	60*	18.10
E. Wainwright ...	1893–97	5	9	0	132	0	49	14.66
A. Ward	1893–94	7	13	0	487	1	117	37.46
C. F. Walters ...	1934	5	9	1	401	0	82	50.12
J. H. Wardle	1953–	7	10	3	166	0	38	23.71
P. F. Warner.....	1903–12	7	13	1	287	0	79	23.91
C. Washbrook ...	1946–	14	28	1	892	2	143	33.03
J. C. White	1921–30	7	12	6	110	0	29	18.33
W. W. Whysall ..	1924–30	4	7	0	209	0	76	29.85
F. E. Woolley ...	1909–34	32	51	1	1664	2	133*	33.28
R. E. S. Wyatt ...	1930–36	12	21	2	633	0	78	33.31
N. W. D. Yardley	1946–48	10	19	2	402	0	61	23.64

* Signifies not out.

ENGLAND BOWLING AGAINST AUSTRALIA

(Qualification: 10 wickets)

	Period	Tests	Balls	Maidens	Runs	Wickets	Average
G. O. Allen	1930–36	13	2782	58	1603	43	37.27
R. Appleyard	1954–	4	632	22	224	11	20.36
E. G. Arnold	1903–05	8	1365	47	689	25	27.56
W. Attewell	1884–91	10	2850	326	626	27	23.18
T. E. Bailey	1950–	14	2047	59	891	32	27.84
R. G. Barlow	1881–91	17	2456	315	767	35	21.91
S. F. Barnes	1901–12	20	5749	264	2288	106	21.58
W. Barnes........	1880–90	21	2285	271	793	51	15.54
W. Bates	1881–86	15	2362	282	821	49	16.75
A. V. Bedser	1946–	21	7065	205	2859	104	27.49
C. Blythe	1901–09	9	1977	99	877	41	21.39
B. J. T. Bosanquet..	1903–05	7	989	10	604	25	24.16
W. E. Bowes	1932–38	6	1459	41	741	30	24.70
L. C. Braund	1901–07	20	3561	140	1769	46	38.45
W. Brearley	1905–09	3	669	23	355	17	20.88
J. Briggs.........	1884–99	31	4959	338	1993	97	20.54
F. R. Brown	1950–53	6	1184	23	524	22	23.81
J. N. Crawford ..	1907–08	5	1426	36	742	30	24.73
J. W. H. T. Douglas	1911–24	17	2318	53	1227	35	35.05
W. J. Edrich	1938–	21	1477	22	888	16	55.50
K. Farnes	1934–38	8	2153	58	1065	38	28.05
P. G. H. Fender..	1920–21	5	806	16	522	14	37.28
A. Fielder	1903–07	6	1485	42	711	26	27.34
W. Flowers	1884–93	8	858	92	296	14	21.14
F. R. Foster	1911–12	8	1888	76	742	34	21.82
G. Geary	1926–34	9	2628	112	963	27	35.66
A. E. R. Gilligan..	1924–25	5	1088	15	519	10	51.90
J. Gunn.........	1901–05	6	903	54	387	18	21.50
W. R. Hammond.	1928–46	33	3958	135	1612	36	44.77
T. Hayward......	1896–1909	29	843	38	486	12	40.50
J. T. Hearne	1896–99	11	2936	209	1070	48	22.29
J. W. Hearne	1911–26	16	2098	34	1026	16	64.12

	Period	Tests	Balls	Maidens	Runs	Wickets	Average
G. H. Hirst	1897–1909	21	3457	118	1585	49	32.34
F. S. Jackson	1893–1905	20	1587	77	799	24	33.29
G. L. Jessop	1899–1909	13	660	28	346	10	34.60
R. Kilner	1924–26	7	2163	66	675	24	28.12
J. C. Laker	1948–	6	1285	48	684	18	38.55
H. Larwood	1926–32	15	4053	120	1916	64	29.93
W. H. Lockwood .	1893–1902	12	2029	100	844	43	20.55
G. A. Lohmann ..	1886–96	15	3301	326	1002	77	13.01
F. Martin	1890	1	287	21	102	12	8.50
W. E. Midwinter .	1881–82	4	776	79	272	10	27.20
F. Morley	1880–82	4	972	124	296	16	18.50
C. H. Parkin	1920–21	9	1999	50	1090	32	34.06
E. Peate	1881–86	9	2096	260	683	31	22.03
R. Peel	1884–96	20	5336	444	1715	102	16.81
W. Rhodes	1899–1926	41	5785	237	2616	109	24.00
T. Richardson ...	1893–97	14	4555	191	2220	88	25.22
R. W. V. Robins .	1930–36	6	960	10	558	14	39.85
J. W. Sharpe ...	1890–91	3	975	61	305	11	27.72
A. Shaw	1876–81	7	1099	155	285	12	23.75
J. B. Statham	1953–	6	1405	26	587	20	29.35
A. G. Steel	1880–88	13	1402	108	605	29	20.86
M. W. Tate	1924–30	20	7686	330	2536	83	30.55
F. H. Tyson	1954–	5	1208	16	583	28	20.82
H. Verity	1932–38	18	4930	257	1656	59	28.06
W. Voce........	1932–46	11	2450	55	1128	41	27.51
G. Ulyett	1876–90	23	2523	286	992	49	20.24
J. H. Wardle	1953–	7	1499	73	573	23	24.91
J. C. White	1921–30	7	2974	148	1033	31	33.32
F. E. Woolley ...	1909–34	32	3590	129	1555	43	36.16
D. V. P. Wright .	1938–	14	3709	61	2039	48	42.47
N. W. D. Yardley .	1946–48	10	1416	37	576	19	30.31
H. Young	1899	2	551	39	262	12	21.83

AUSTRALIA BATTING AGAINST ENGLAND

(Qualification: 7 innings, average 10)

	Period	Tests	Inns.	Not Outs	Runs	100's	Highest Inns.	Average
T. J. E. Andrews .	1921–26	13	19	0	541	0	94	28.47
R. G. Archer	1953–	7	12	1	212	0	49	19.27
W. W. Armstrong.	1901–21	42	71	9	2172	4	158	35.03
C. L. Badcock ..	1936–38	7	12	1	160	1	118	14.54
A. C. Bannerman.	1878–93	28	50	2	1108	0	94	23.08
W. Bardsley	1909–26	30	49	4	1487	3	193*	33.04
S. G. Barnes	1938–48	9	14	2	846	2	234	70.50
B. A. Barnett ...	1938	4	8	1	195	0	57	27.85
R. Benaud	1953–	8	14	0	163	0	34	11.64
J. McC. Blackham	1876–94	35	62	11	800	0	74	15.68
G. J. Bonnor ...	1880–88	17	30	0	512	1	128	17.06
H. F. Boyle	1878–84	12	16	4	153	0	36*	12.75
J. W. Burke......	1950–	4	8	1	206	1	101*	29.42
D. G. Bradman ..	1928–48	37	63	7	5028	19	334	89.78
W. A. Brown	1934–48	13	24	1	980	3	206*	42.60
W. Bruce	1884–94	14	26	2	702	0	80	29.25
H. Carter	1907–21	21	35	4	776	0	72	25.03
A. G. Chipperfield	1934–38	9	15	3	356	0	99	29.66
H. L. Collins.....	1920–26	16	26	0	1012	3	162	38.92
A. Cotter	1903–11	16	29	1	377	0	45	13.46
J. Darling.......	1894–1905	31	55	2	1632	3	178	30.79

* Signifies not out.

	Period	Tests	Inns.	Not Outs	Runs	100's	Highest Inns.	Average
L. S. Darling....	1932–36	7	12	0	245	0	85	20.41
A. K. Davidson ..	1953–	8	15	2	253	0	76	19.46
R. A. Duff.......	1901–05	19	34	1	1079	2	146	32.69
E. Evans	1881–86	6	10	2	82	0	33	10.25
L. Favell	1954–	4	7	0	130	0	30	18.57
J. H. Fingleton ..	1932–38	12	21	0	671	2	136	31.95
T. W. Garrett ...	1876–87	19	33	6	339	0	51*	12.55
G. Giffen	1881–96	31	53	0	1238	1	161	23.35
H. Graham	1893–96	6	10	0	301	2	107	30.10
J. M. Gregory....	1920–28	21	30	3	941	1	100	34.85
S. E. Gregory ...	1890–1912	52	92	7	2193	4	201	25.80
C. V. Grimmett ..	1924–34	22	34	6	366	0	50	13.07
R. N. Harvey ...	1948–	17	31	2	1195	3	162	41.20
A. L. Hassett ...	1938–53	24	42	1	1572	4	137	38.34
G. R. Hazlitt ...	1907–12	6	9	3	87	0	34*	14.50
H. L. Hendry ...	1921–28	9	15	2	284	1	112	21.84
C. Hill	1896–1911	41	76	1	2660	4	188	35.46
G. B. Hole	1950–	9	17	0	439	0	66	25.82
A. J. Hopkins ...	1901–09	17	28	2	434	0	43	16.69
T. Horan	1876–84	15	27	2	471	1	124	18.84
H. V. Hordern ..	1911–12	5	10	2	173	0	49*	21.62
P. M. Hornibrook	1928–30	6	7	1	60	0	26	10.00
F. A. Iredale ...	1894–99	14	23	1	807	2	140	36.68
†A. A. Jackson ..	1928–30	4	6	0	350	1	164	58.33
A. H. Jarvis	1884–94	11	21	3	303	0	82	16.83
I. W. Johnson ...	1946–	17	26	5	424	0	77	20.19
W. A. Johnston ..	1946–	17	25	12	138	0	29	10.61
S. P. Jones.......	1881–87	12	24	4	428	0	87	21.40
C. Kelleway	1911–28	18	30	2	874	1	147	31.21
J. J. Kelly	1896–1905	33	52	17	613	0	46*	17.51
A. F. Kippax	1924–34	13	23	1	753	1	100	34.22
F. J. Laver	1899–1909	15	23	6	196	0	45	11.52
R. R. Lindwall ..	1946–	23	35	3	740	1	100	23.12
S. J. E. Loxton ..	1948–	6	8	0	210	0	93	27.37
J. J. Lyons.......	1886–97	14	27	0	731	1	134	27.07
C. G. Macartney ..	1907–26	26	42	4	1640	5	170	43.15
E. A. McDonald ..	1920–21	8	9	4	101	0	36	20.20
A. A. Mailey....	1920–26	18	25	8	201	0	46*	11.82
T. J. Matthews ..	1911–12	5	7	0	74	0	53	10.57
H. H. Massie ...	1881–84	9	16	0	249	0	55	15.56
P. A. McAlister ..	1903–09	8	16	1	252	0	41	16.80
S. J. McCabe ...	1930–38	24	43	3	1931	4	232	48.27
C. L. McCool ...	1946–	5	7	2	272	1	104*	54.40
P. S. McDonnell ..	1880–88	19	34	1	958	3	147	29.03
T. R. McKibbin ..	1894–97	5	8	2	88	0	28*	14.66
C. E. McLeod....	1894–1905	17	29	5	573	1	112	23.87
R. W. McLeod ..	1891–93	6	11	0	146	0	31	13.27
W. E. Midwinter ..	1876–86	8	14	1	174	0	37	13.38
R. B. Minnett ...	1911–12	6	12	0	309	0	90	25.75
K. R. Miller	1946–	24	39	3	1308	3	145*	36.33
A. R. Morris	1946–	24	43	2	2080	8	206	50.73
H. Moses	1886–94	6	10	0	197	0	33	19.70
W. L. Murdoch ..	1876–90	18	33	5	896	2	211	32.00
M. A. Noble	1897–1909	39	68	6	1905	1	133	30.72
J. A. O'Connor ..	1907–09	4	8	1	86	0	20	12.28
W. A. Oldfield...	1920–36	38	62	14	1116	1	65*	23.25
W. J. O'Reilly ...	1932–38	19	32	6	277	0	42	10.65
G. E. Palmer.....	1880–86	17	25	4	296	0	48	14.09

† A. A. Jackson died at the age of 23.
Signifies not out.

	Period	Tests	Inns.	Not Outs	Runs	100's	Highest Inns.	Average
C. E. Pellew	1920–21	9	13	1	478	2	116	39.83
W. H. Ponsford ..	1924–34	20	35	2	1558	5	266	47.21
V. S. Ransford ...	1907–11	15	29	6	893	1	143*	38.82
A. J. Richardson .	1924–26	9	13	0	403	1	100	31.00
V. Y. Richardson.	1924–32	14	25	0	622	1	138	24.88
J. S. Ryder	1920–28	17	28	4	1060	2	201*	44.16
H. J. H. Scott ...	1884–86	8	14	1	359	1	102	27.61
D. Tallon........	1946–53	15	20	2	340	0	92	18.88
J. M. Taylor	1920–26	18	25	0	957	1	108	38.28
E. R. H. Toshack.	1946–48	9	9	5	65	0	20*	16.25
G. H. S. Trott ...	1888–97	24	42	0	921	1	143	21.92
H. Trumble	1890–1903	31	55	13	838	0	70	19.95
J. W. Trumble ...	1884–86	7	13	1	243	0	59	20.25
V. T. Trumper ...	1899–1911	40	74	5	2263	6	185*	32.79
C. T. B. Turner ..	1886–94	17	32	4	323	0	29	11.53
W. M. Woodfull ..	1926–34	25	41	3	1675	6	155	44.07
J. Worrall	1884–99	11	22	3	478	0	76	25.15

* *Signifies not out.*

AUSTRALIA BOWLING AGAINST ENGLAND
(Qualification: 10 wickets)

	Period	Tests	Balls	Maidens	Runs	Wickets	Average
R. G. Archer	1953–	7	1199	59	310	17	18.23
W. W. Armstrong.	1901–21	13	6806	360	2288	74	30.91
R. Benaud	1953–	8	1343	42	551	12	45.91
D. J. Blackie	1928	3	1260	51	444	14	31.71
H. F. Boyle	1878–84	12	1732	173	641	32	20.03
W. Bruce	1884–94	14	954	71	440	12	36.66
A. Cotter	1903–11	16	3464	63	1916	67	28.59
A. K. Davidson ..	1953–	8	1319	58	432	11	39.27
A. Fairfax	1928–30	5	1010	38	439	14	31.35
J. J. Ferris	1886–90	8	2030	224	684	48	14.25
L. B. Fleetwood-Smith	1936–38	7	2359	54	1190	33	36.06
T. W. Garrett ...	1876–87	19	2708	297	970	36	26.94
G. Giffen	1881–96	31	6325	434	2791	103	27.09
J. M. Gregory....	1920–28	21	4887	109	2364	70	33.77
C. V. Grimmett ..	1924–34	22	9224	427	3439	106	32.44
G. R. Hazlitt	1907–12	6	1107	49	433	16	27.68
H. L. Hendry	1921–28	9	1430	65	504	14	36.00
A. J. Hopkins ...	1901–09	17	1183	47	581	21	27.66
T. Horan	1876–84	15	373	45	143	11	13.00
H. V. Hordern ...	1911–12	5	1664	43	780	32	24.37
P. M. Hornibrook	1928–30	6	1579	63	664	17	39.05
W. P. Howell	1897–1903	16	3508	229	1245	35	35.57
H. Ironmonger ..	1928–32	6	2445	155	711	21	33.85
J. Iverson........	1951–	5	1108	29	320	21	15.23
I. W. Johnson ...	1946–	17	3878	155	1287	36	35.75
W. A. Johnston ..	1946–	17	5263	224	1818	75	24.24
E. Jones	1894–1902	18	3586	153	1757	60	29.28
C. Kelleway	1911–28	18	3340	108	1155	37	31.21
T. Kendall	1876	2	563	56	215	14	15.35
F. J. Laver	1899–1909	15	2367	122	961	37	25.97
R. R. Lindwall ..	1946–	23	5591	178	2112	100	21.12
C. G. Macartney .	1907–26	26	2633	120	908	33	27.51
A. A. Mailey.....	1920–26	18	5199	91	2935	86	34.12
S. J. McCabe	1930–38	24	2585	84	1076	21	51.23
C. L. McCool ...	1946–	5	1456	27	491	18	27.27

	Period	Tests	Balls	Maidens	Runs	Wickets	Average
E. L. McCormick.	1936–38	7	1356	26	661	21	31.47
E. A. McDonald .	1920–21	8	1991	42	1060	33	32.12
T. R. McKibbin .	1894–97	5	1032	41	496	17	29.17
C. E. McLeod....	1894–1905	17	3374	172	1325	33	40.15
R. W. McLeod ..	1891–93	6	1089	67	384	12	32.00
W. E. Midwinter..	1876–86	8	949	102	333	14	23.78
K. R. Miller	1946–	24	4486	180	1482	66	22.45
M. A. Noble	1897–1909	39	6845	353	2862	115	24.88
J. A. O'Connor ..	1907–09	4	692	24	340	13	26.15
W. J. O'Reilly...	1932–38	19	7864	439	2587	102	25.36
G. E. Palmer.....	1880–86	17	4519	452	1678	78	21.51
A. J. Richardson..	1924–26	9	1812	91	521	12	43.41
J. S. Ryder	1920–28	17	1531	54	630	13	48.46
J. V. Saunders ...	1901–07	12	3268	108	1621	64	25.32
F. R. Spofforth...	1876–86	18	4185	419	1731	94	18.41
E. R. H. Toshack.	1946–48	9	2469	119	801	28	28.60
G. H. S. Trott ...	1888–97	24	1890	47	1019	29	35.13
H. Trumble	1890–1903	31	7895	447	2945	141	20.88
J. W. Trumble ...	1884–86	7	600	59	222	10	22.20
C. T. B. Turner ..	1886–94	17	5179	457	1670	101	16.53
T. W. Wall	1928–34	25	3821	115	1663	43	38.67
F. A. Ward	1936–38	4	1268	30	574	11	52.18
W. J. Whitty	1909–12	6	1302	71	498	15	33.20

For results and other personal achievements in England–Australia Tests see pages 179–187.

THE ASHES

The Ashes were originated in 1882 when, on August 29, Australia defeated the full strength of England on English soil for the first time. The Australians won by the narrow margin of seven runs, and the following day the *Sporting Times* printed a mock obituary notice, written by Shirley Brooks, son of an editor of *Punch*, which read:

"In affectionate remembrance of English Cricket which died at The Oval, 29th August, 1882. Deeply lamented by a large circle of sorrowing friends and acquaintances. R.I.P. N.B. The body will be cremated and the Ashes taken to Australia."

The following winter the Hon. Ivo Bligh, afterwards Lord Darnley, set out to Australia to recover these mythical Ashes. Australia won the first match by nine wickets, but England won the next two, and the real ashes came into being when some Melbourne women burnt a stump used in the third game and presented the ashes in an urn to Ivo Bligh.

When Lord Darnley died in 1927, the urn, by a bequest in his will, was given to M.C.C., and it held a place of honour in the Long Room at Lord's until early 1953 when, with other cricket treasures, it was moved to the newly built Imperial Cricket Memorial near the pavilion. There it stands permanently, together with the velvet bag in which the urn was originally given to Lord Darnley and the score card of the 1882 match.

CENTENARY OF FREE FORESTERS

By Colonel K. B. Stanley

(*Honorary Secretary since* 1936)

Cricket's famous wandering side, the Free Foresters, celebrate their centenary this summer. Behind this bare announcement lies the story of the rise and progress of a club which has become a by-word of sportsmanship and good company wherever the game is played.

It is fitting that the Free Foresters enjoy such a reputation, for their founder, the Rev. W. K. R. Bedford, always envisaged a club which would embody the highest traditions. Bedford, the local squarson, had his own cricket ground at Sutton Coldfield rectory and was assisted in the formation of the club by a trio of brothers well known at Oxford, W. G., H. S. and J. R. Armitstead, and the families of Charles and Robert Garnett who resided in the neighbourhood of Tamworth.

Recording the purpose of the club, Bedford wrote: "The composition of the club was intended to have a Midland county character—not to be a provincial I. Zingari, because we did not propose to exact that unlimited fealty to our colours which the queen-mother of amateur wandering elevens so rigidly requires, but to imitate that unrivalled club in dispensing altogether with the hired assistance without which some of the strongest local clubs of gentlemen then imagined themselves unable to play matches.

"This was the meaning of the motto we adopted 'United though Untied' which I borrowed from an epigram I met with in some book of the period and adapted it to a heraldic design called the Hastings knot, a cord loosely entwined connecting a sickle and a wheatsheaf for which we substituted two capital F's. . . ."

The title was derived from the fact that all Bedford's eleven were from the precincts of the Forest of Arden in Warwickshire, or Needwood in Staffordshire.

Yet, as Bedford explained, "my castles in the air would have been swallowed up by night" had he not renewed acquaintance with the brothers Armitstead. They promised to bring an eleven to inaugurate his new ground at Sutton rectory, and it was on this occasion that the Free Foresters first entered the pages of the sporting chronicles.

The match was played on July 20, 1856, the opposition bearing the picturesque title of the "Pilgrims of the Dee." The Free Foresters made scores of 65 and 57 and the Pilgrims obtained totals of 38 and 66. The obvious dominance of ball over bat in the country games of those days was due to a variety of factors, several of which a friend quoted to Bedford when they discussed the matter some 40 years later. "Scores were generally small," recalled this associate of the sporting parson. "There were no boundaries, no cane-handled bats and the wicket was mown with a scythe at 3 a.m. on the morning of the match and the rest of the ground only fed sheep."

The fixture was repeated the following year and the Free Foresters played four other matches at Rugby, Leamington and Manchester. "The Rubicon then was crossed, but what next and next?" commented the Rev. Bedford when he discussed those early days in a book he published toward the end of the last century. "Were we to join the 'swarm of butterflies, grasshoppers, chrysalis wasps and other ephemeral bodies that quicken in the summertime under the genial influence of cricket,' consider the lawn match our metier, and a pretty ribbon and a pleasant autumn the objects of our ambition; or fling down the gauntlet of higher pretensions in the recognised centres of cricket?

"In either event we required some kind of organisation; so when we met at Oxford on June 1, 1858, we at once proceeded to appoint a secretary and a committee, the first office falling to my share, and four cricketers being selected from our ranks as committee men representing the various interests bound up in our welfare.

"One of the most prominent of these was a man hardly less instrumental in raising our club to the proud position it eventually attained than were Armitstead or Goodrich—Arthur Faber, Fellow of New College, who a few years later became headmaster of the newly founded school at Malvern . . . a player who ought to be remembered as having held the premier place in the batting averages of amateur cricket in the year immediately preceding the rise of Mr. W. G. Grace."

Goodrich, who first played for the club in 1857 when he took 13 wickets against the Western club, Manchester, had already established such a reputation that it was written of him: "Over the early grave of many a younger cricketer shall it be written 'Frightened to death by the slow bowling of Goodrich'."

At their meeting in Oxford the Free Foresters not only settled upon a motto but also decided that the colours would be crimson, green and white. These colours occasioned some opposition on the part of the older members who recalled that they were similar to those of the Chartists of 1848, but this appears to have been only a passing criticism. The same three shades are still worn to-day, a living symbol to the influence and standing of the club.

The meeting also decreed that members elected from the families (entail male) of Armitstead, Bedford and Garnett should be honoured with the title of "Founders Kin."

No rules were evolved or printed until 1866. Meanwhile the Rev. Bedford ensured the success of the Free Foresters by the gradual expansion and improvement of fixtures, and the careful selection of promising young players, especially bowlers, from the public schools.

In the rules the club's policy was "to play against County, University, College, Regimental elevens and with recognised clubs in desirable localities"; except for Counties this policy holds good to-day, though the club now play cricket wherever the interests of the game can be encouraged and assisted.

With this in mind Free Foresters make tours a feature of their fixture list. They have travelled to Scotland, the Channel Islands, Ireland, Holland, Germany, Egypt, India and Singapore. The list has steadily increased from fifteen matches in 1858, fifty in 1900, to a maximum of one hundred and twelve in 1938. After the second world war, through force of circumstances, the number of fixtures had to be reduced to between sixty and seventy.

The Free Foresters are perhaps unique in that they have no president or chairman. The affairs of the club remain, as they began, in the hands of a secretary, who is helped by a treasurer, match secretary and fifteen members of committee. An entrance fee of five guineas is the sole subscription. Each match has to pay for itself, the players being responsible for their individual travel and hotel expenses, and they share other costs such as purchase of balls and umpires' fees.

In conclusion, an incident which is responsible for umpires to-day being supplied with white coats, is worth recording. It occurred during a match at Eccles in 1861 when the United England XI were beaten by Sixteen Free Foresters. W. G. Armitstead, the old Oxford Blue to whom reference was made earlier in this article, complained that he could not see the hand of G. Atkinson, a Yorkshire professional bowler, against the umpire's body. After a short delay a white garment, possibly a night shirt, was produced for the umpire to wear. It was the first time in cricket history that an umpire had been so invested.

Many of the greatest names in cricket have represented the club. All can bear witness to the comradeship which springs from being a Free Forester. "United though Untied."

TEST CRICKETERS

FULL LIST FROM 1877 TO AUGUST 1955

Here is a complete record of all appearances by cricketers in Test matches. The following lists have been compiled on a home and abroad basis, appearances abroad being printed in *italics*.

Abbreviations.—E: England. A: Australia. SA: South Africa. WI: West Indies. NZ: New Zealand. In: India. P: Pakistan.

All appearances are placed in this order of seniority. Hence, any England cricketer playing against Australia in England has that achievement recorded first and the remainder of his appearances at home (if any) are set down before passing to matches abroad. To denote English professionals, initials are given in brackets. The figures immediately following each name represent the total number of appearances in *all* Tests.

Where the season embraces two different years, the first year is given, i.e. 1876 indicates 1876–77.

ENGLAND

Abel (R.) 13: v A 1888 (3) 1896 (3) 1902 (2); *v A 1891 (3)*; *v SA 1888 (2)*
Absolom C. 1: *v A 1878*
Allen, G. O. 25: v A 1930 (1) 1934 (2); v WI 1933 (1); v NZ 1931 (3); v In 1936 (3); *v A 1932 (5) 1936 (5)*; *v WI 1947 (3)*; *v NZ 1932 (2)*
Allom, M. J. C. 5: *v SA 1930 (1)*; *v NZ 1929 (4)*
Ames (L. E. G.) 47: v A 1934 (5) 1938 (2); v SA 1929 (1) 1935 (4); v WI 1933 (3); v NZ 1931 (3) 1937 (3); v In 1932 (1); *v A 1932 (5) 1936 (5)*; *v SA 1938 (5)*; *v WI 1929 (4)*; *1934 (4)*; *v NZ 1932 (2)*
Andrew (K. V.) 1: *v A 1954*
Appleyard (R.) 8: v SA 1955 (1); v P 1954 (1); *v A 1954 (4)*; *v NZ 1954 (2)*.
Archer A. G. 1: *v SA 1898*
Armitage (T) 2: *v A 1876 (2)*
Arnold (E. G.) 10: v A 1905 (4); v SA 1907 (2); *v A 1903 (4)*
Arnold (J.) 1: v NZ 1931
Astill (W. E.) 9: *v SA 1927 (5)*; *v WI 1929 (4)*
Attewell (W.) 10: v A 1890 (1); *v A 1884 (5) 1887 (1) 1891 (3)*

Bailey, T. E. 39: v A 1953 (5); v SA 1951 (2) 1955 (5); v WI 1950 (2); v NZ 1949 (4); v P 1954 (3); *v A 1950 (4) 1954 (5)*; *v WI 1953 (5)*; *v NZ 1950 (2) 1954 (2)*
Bakewell (A. H.) 6: v SA 1935 (2); v WI 1933 (1); v NZ 1931 (2); *v In 1933 (1)*
Barber (W.) 2: v SA 1935 (2)
Barlow (R. G.) 17: v A 1882 (1) 1884 (3) 1886 (3); *v A 1881 (4) 1882 (4) 1886 (2)*
Barnes (S. F.) 27: v A 1902 (1) 1909 (3) 1912 (3); v SA 1912 (3); *v A 1901 (3) 1907 (5) 1911 (5)*; *v SA 1913 (4)*
Barnes (W.) 21: v A 1880 (1) 1882 (1) 1884 (2) 1886 (2) 1888 (3) 1890 (2); *v A 1882 (4) 1884 (5) 1886 (1)*
Barnett (C. J.) 20: v A 1938 (3); 1948 (1); v SA 1947 (3); v WI 1933 (1); v NZ 1937 (3); v In 1936 (1); *v A 1936 (5)*; *v In 1933 (3)*
Barratt (F.) 5: v SA 1929 (1); *v NZ 1929 (4)*
Barrington (K.) 2: v SA 1955 (2)
Barton (V.) 1: *v SA 1891*
Bates (W.) 15: *v A 1881 (4) 1882 (4) 1884 (5) 1886 (2)*
Bean (G.) 3: *v A 1891 (3)*
Bedser (A. V) 51: v A 1948 (5) 1953 (5); v SA 1947 (2) 1951 (5) 1955 (1); v WI 1950 (2); v NZ 1949 (2); v In 1946 (3) 1952 (4); v P 1954 (2); *v A 1946 (5) 1950 (5) 1954 (1)*; *v SA 1948 (5)*; *v NZ 1947 (1) 1950 (2)*
Berry (R) 2: v WI 1950 (2)

Bird, M. C. 10: v *SA 1909 (5) 1913 (5)*
Bligh, Hon. Ivo. 4: v *A 1882 (4)*
Blythe (C.) 19: v A 1905 (1) 1909 (2); v SA 1907 (3); v *A 1901 (5) 1907 (1)*; v *SA 1905 (5) 1909 (2)*
Board (J. H.) 6: v *SA 1898 (2) 1905 (4)*
Booth (M. W.) 2: v *SA 1913 (2)*
Bosanquet, B. J. T. 7: v A 1905 (3); v *A 1903 (4)*
Bowden, M. P. 2: v *SA 1888 (2)*
Bowes (W. E.) 15: v A 1934 (3) 1938 (2); v SA 1935 (4); v WI 1939 (2); v In 1932 (1); 1946 (1); v *A 1932 (1)*; v *NZ 1932 (1)*
Bowley (E. H.) 5: v SA 1929 (2); v *NZ 1929 (3)*
Bradley, W. M. 2: v A 1899 (2)
Braund (L. C.) 23: v A 1902 (5); v SA 1907 (3); v *A 1901 (5) 1903 (5) 1907 (5)*
Brearley, W. 4: v A 1905 (2) 1909 (1); v SA 1912 (1)
Brennan, D. V. 2: v SA 1951 (2)
Briggs (John) 33: v A 1886 (3) 1888 (3) 1893 (2) 1896 (1) 1899 (1); v *A 1884 (5) 1886 (2) 1887 (1) 1891 (3) 1894 (5)*; *1897 (5)*; v *SA 1888 (2)*
Brockwell (W.) 7: v A 1893 (1) 1899 (1); v *A 1894 (5)*
Bromley-Davenport, R. H. 4: v *SA 1895 (3) 1898 (1)*
Brookes, (D.) 1: v *WI 1947*
Brown, F. R. 22: v A 1953 (1); v SA 1951 (5); v WI 1950 (1); v NZ 1931 (2) 1937 (1) 1949 (2); v In 1932 (1); v *A 1950 (5)*; v *NZ 1932 (2) 1950 (2)*
Brown (G.) 7: v A 1921 (3); v *SA 1922 (4)*
Brown (J. T.) 8: v A 1896 (2) 1899 (1); v *A 1894 (5)*
Buckenham (C. P.) 4: v *SA 1909 (4)*
Butler (H. J.) 2: v SA 1947 (1); v *WI 1947 (1)*
Butt (H. R.) 3: v *SA 1895 (3)*

Calthorpe, Hon. F. S. G. 4: v *WI 1929 (4)*
Carr, A. W. 11: v A 1926 (4); v SA 1929 (2); v *SA 1922 (5)*
Carr, D. B. 2: v *In 1951 (2)*
Carr, D. W. 1: v A 1909
Chapman, A. P. F. 26: v A 1926 (4) 1930 (4); v SA 1924 (2); v WI 1928 (3); v *A 1924 (4) 1928 (4)*; v *SA 1930 (5)*
Charlwood (H.) 2: v *A 1876 (2)*
Chatterton (W.) 1: v *SA 1891*
Christopherson, S. 1: v A 1884
Clark (E. W.) 8: v A 1934 (2); v SA 1929 (1); v WI 1933 (2); v *In 1933 (3)*
Clay, J. C. 1: v SA 1935
Close (D. B.) 3: v SA 1955 (1); v NZ 1949 (1); v *A 1950 (1)*
Compton (D.) 72: v. A 1938 (4) 1948 (5) 1953 (5); v SA 1947 (5) 1951 (4) 1955 (5); v WI 1939 (3) 1950 (1); v NZ 1937 (1) 1949 (4); v In 1946 (3) 1952 (2); v P 1954 (4); v *A 1946 (5) 1950 (4) 1954 (4)*; v *SA 1948 (5)*; v *WI 1953 (5)*; v *NZ 1947 (1) 1950 (2)*
Cook (C.) 1: v SA 1947
Copson (W.) 3: v SA 1947 (1); v WI 1939 (2)
Cornford (W.) 4: v *NZ 1929 (4)*
Coventry, Hon. C. J. 2: v *SA 1888 (2)*
Cowdrey, M. C. 8: v SA 1955 (1); v *A 1954 (5)*; v *NZ 1954 (2)*
Coxon (A.) 1: v A 1948
Cranston, J. 1: v A 1890
Cranston, K. 8: v A 1948 (1); v SA 1947 (3); v *WI 1947 (1)*
Crapp (J. F.) 7: v A 1948 (3); v *SA 1948 (4)*
Crawford, J. N. 12: v SA 1907 (2); v *A 1907 (5)*; v *SA 1905 (5)*
Cuttell, (W. R.) 2: v *SA 1898 (2)*

Dawson, E. W. 5: v *SA 1927 (1)*; v *NZ 1929 (4)*
Dean (H.) 3: v A 1912 (2); v SA 1912 (1)
Denton (D.) 11: v A 1905 (1); v *SA 1905 (5) 1909 (5)*
Dewes, J. G. 5: v A 1948 (1); v WI 1950 (2); v *A 1950 (2)*
Dipper (A. E.) 1: v A 1921
Doggart, G. H. G. 2: v WI 1950 (2)
Dollery (H. E.) 4: v A 1948 (2); v SA 1947; v WI 1950 (1)

Dolphin (A.) 1: *v A 1920*

Douglas, J. W. H. T. 23: v A 1912 (1) 1921 (5); v SA 1924 (1); *v A 1911 (5) 1920 (5) 1924 (1); v SA 1913 (5)*

Druce, N. F. 5: *v A 1897 (5)*

Ducat (A.) 1: v A 1921

Duckworth (G.) 24: v A 1930 (5); v SA 1924 (1) 1929 (4) 1935 (1); v WI 1928 (1); v In 1936 (3); *v A 1928 (5); v SA 1930 (3); v NZ 1932 (1)*

Duleepsinhji, K. S. 12: v A 1930 (4); v SA 1929 (1); v NZ 1931 (3); *v NZ 1929 (4)*

Durston (T. J.) 1: v A 1921

Edrich, W. J. 39: v A 1938 (4) 1948 (5) 1953 (3); v SA 1947 (4); v WI 1950 (2); v NZ 1949 (4); v In 1946 (1); v P 1954 (1); *v A 1946 (5) 1954 (4); v SA 1938 (5); v NZ 1947 (1)*

Elliott (H.) 4: v WI 1928 (1); *v SA 1927 (1); v In 1933 (2)*

Emmett, (G. M.) 1: v A 1948

Emmett (T.) 7: *v A 1876 (2) 1878 (1) 1881 (4)*

Evans, A. J. 1: v A 1921

Evans (T. G.) 66: v A 1948 (5) 1953 (5); v SA 1947 (5) 1951 (3) 1955 (3); v WI 1950 (3); v NZ 1949 (4); v In 1946 (1) 1952 (4); v P 1954 (1); *v A 1946 (4) 1950 (5) 1954 (4); v SA 1948 (3); v WI 1947 (4) 1953 (4); v NZ 1947 (1) 1950 (2) 1954 (2)*

Fagg (A. E.) 5: v WI 1939 (1); v In 1936 (2); *v A 1936 (2)*

Fane, F. L. 14: *v A 1907 (4); v SA 1905 (5) 1909 (5)*

Farnes, K. 15: v A 1934 (2) 1938 (4); *v A 1936 (2); v SA 1938 (5); v WI 1934 (2)*

Farrimond (W.) 4: v A 1935 (1); *v SA 1930 (2); v WI 1934 (1)*

Fender, P. G. H. 13: v A 1921 (2); v SA 1924 (2) 1929 (1); *v A 1920 (3); v SA 1922 (2)*

Ferris, J. J. 1: *v SA 1891*

Fielder, (A.) 6: *v A 1903 (2) 1907 (4)*

Fishlock (L. B.) 4: v In 1936 (2) 1946 (1); *v A 1946 (1)*

Flowers (W.) 8: v A 1893 (1); *v A 1884 (5) 1886 (2)*

Ford, F. G. J. 5: *v A 1894 (5)*

Foster, F. R. 11: v A 1912 (3); v SA 1912 (3); *v A 1911 (5)*

Foster, R. E. 8: v SA 1907 (3); *v A 1903 (5)*

Fothergill (A. J.) 2: *v SA 1888 (2)*

Freeman (A. P.) 12: v SA 1929 (3); v WI 1928 (3); *v A 1924 (2); v SA 1927 (4)*

Fry, C. B. 26: v A 1899 (5) 1902 (5) 1905 (4) 1909 (3) 1912 (3); v SA 1907 (3) 1912 (3); *v SA 1895 (2)*

Gay, L. H. 1: *v A 1894*

Geary (G.) 14: v A 1926 (2) 1930 (1) 1934 (2); v SA 1924 (1) 1929 (2); *v A 1928 (4); v SA 1927 (2)*

Gibb, P. A. 8: v In 1946 (2); *v A 1946 (1); v SA 1938 (5)*

Gilligan, A. E. R. 11: v SA 1924 (4); *v A 1924 (5); v SA 1922 (2)*

Gilligan, A. H. H. 4: *v NZ 1929 (4)*

Gimblett (H.) 3: v WI 1939 (1); v In 1936 (2)

Gladwin (C.) 8: v SA 1947 (1); v NZ 1949 (1); *v SA 1948 (5)*

Goddard (T. W.) 8: v A 1930 (1); v NZ 1937 (2); *v SA 1938 (3)*

Gover (A. R.) 4: v NZ 1937 (2); v In 1936 (1) 1946 (1)

Grace, E. M. 1: v A 1880

Grace, G. F. 1: v A 1880

Grace, W. G. 22: v A 1880 (1) 1882 (1) 1884 (3) 1886 (3) 1888 (3) 1890 (2) 1893 (2) 1896 (3) 1899 (1); *v A 1891 (3)*

Graveney (T. W.) 31: v A 1953 (5); v SA 1951 (1) 1955 (5); v In 1952 (4); v P 1954 (3); *v A 1954 (2); v In 1951 (4); v WI 1953 (5); v NZ 1954 (2)*

Greenwood (A.) 2: *v A 1876 (2)*

Grieve, B. A. F. 2: *v SA 1888 (2)*

Griffith, S. C. 3: *v SA 1948 (2); v WI 1947 (1)*

Gunn (G.) 15: v A 1909 (1); *v A 1907 (5) 1911 (5); v WI 1929 (4)*

Gunn (J.) 6: v A 1905 (1); *v A 1901 (5)*

Gunn (W.) 11: v A 1888 (2) 1890 (2) 1893 (3) 1896 (1) 1899 (1); *v A 1886 (2)*

Haig, N. E. 5: v A 1921 (1); *v WI 1929 (4)*

Haigh (S.) 11: v A 1905 (2) 1909 (1); 1912 (1); *v SA 1898 (2) 1905 (5)*

Hallows (C.) 2: v A 1921 (1); v WI 1928 (1)

Hammond, W. R. 85: v A 1930 (5) 1934 (5) 1938 (4); v SA 1929 (4) 1935 **(5)**; v WI 1928 (3) 1933 (3) 1939 (3); v NZ 1931 (3) 1937 (3); v In 1932 (1) 1936 **(2)** 1946 (3); *v A 1928 (5) 1932 (5) 1936 (5) 1946 (4); v SA 1927 (5) 1930 (5) 1938 (5); v NZ 1932 (2) 1947 (1); v WI 1934 (4)*

Hardinge (H. T. W.) 1: v A 1921

Hardstaff (J.) 5: *v A 1907 (5)*

Hardstaff (J., Jnr.) 23: v A 1938 (2) 1948 (1); v SA 1935 (1); v WI 1939 (3); v NZ 1937 (3); v In 1936 (2) 1946 (2); *v A 1936 (5) 1946 (1); v WI 1947 (3)*

Harris, Lord 4: v A 1880 (1) 1884 (2); *v A 1878 (1)*

Hartley, J. C. 2: *v SA 1905 (2)*

Hawke, Lord 5: *v SA 1895 (3) 1898 (2)*

Hayes (E. G.) 5: v A 1909 (1); v SA 1912 (1); *v SA 1905 (3)*

Hayward (T. W.) 35: v A 1896 (2) 1899 (5) 1902 (1) 1905 (5) 1909 (1); v SA 1907 (3); *v A 1897 (5) 1901 (5); 1903 (5) v SA 1895 (3)*

Hearne (A.) 1: *v SA 1891*

Hearne (F.) 2: *v SA 1888 (2)*

Hearne (G. C.) 1: *v SA 1891*

Hearne (J. T.) 12: v A 1896 (3) 1899 (3); *v A 1897 (5); v SA 1891 (1)*

Hearne (J. W.) 24: v A 1912 (3) 1921 (1) 1926 (1); v SA 1912 (2) 1924 (3); *v A 1911 (5) 1920 (2) 1924 (4); v SA 1913 (3)*

Hendren (E.) 51: v A 1921 (2) 1926 (5) 1930 (2) 1934 (4); v SA 1924 (5) 1929 (4) v WI 1928 (1); *v A 1920 (5) 1924 (5) 1928 (5); v SA 1930 (5); v WI 1929 (4) 1934 (4)*

Heseltine, C. 2: *v SA 1895 (2)*

Hill (A.) 2: *v A 1876 (2)*

Hill, A. J. L. 3: *v SA 1895 (3)*

Hilton (M. J.) 4: v SA 1951 (1); v WI 1950 (1); *v In 1951 (2)*

Hirst (G. H.) 24: v A 1899 (1) 1902 (4) 1905 (3) 1909 (4); v SA 1907 (3); *v A 1897 (4) 1903 (5)*

Hitch (J. W.) 7: v A 1912 (1) 1921 (1); v SA 1912 (1); *v A 1911 (3) 1920 (1)*

Hobbs (J. B.) 61: v A 1909 (3) 1912 (3) 1921 (1) 1926 (5) 1930 (5); v SA 1912 (3) 1924 (5) 1929 (1); v WI 1928 (2**)**; *v A 1907 (4) 1911 (5) 1920 (5) 1924 (5) 1928 (5); v SA 1909 (5) 1913 (5)*

Hollies (E.) 13: v A 1948 (1); v SA 1947 (3); v WI 1950 (2); v NZ 1949 (4); *v WI 1934 (3)*

Holmes, E. R. T. 5: v SA 1935 (1); *v WI 1934 (4)*

Holmes (P.) 7: v A 1921 (1); v In 1932 (1); *v SA 1927 (5)*

Hone, L. 1: *v A 1878*

Hopwood (J. L.) 2: v A 1934 (2)

Hornby, A. N. 3: v A 1882 (1) 1884 (1); *v A 1878 (1)*

Howard, N. D. 4: *v In 1951 (4)*

Howorth (R.) 5: v SA 1947; *v WI 1947 (4)*

Howell (H.) 5: v A 1921 (1); v SA 1924 (1); *v A 1920 (3)*

Humphries (J.) 3: *v A 1907 (3)*

Hunter (J.) 5: *v A 1884 (5)*

Hutchings, K. L. 7: v A 1909 (2); *v A 1907 (5)*

Hutton (L.) 79: v A 1938 (3) 1948 (4) 1953 (5); v SA 1947 (5) 1951 (5); v WI 1939 (3) 1950 (3); v NZ 1937 (3) 1949 (4); v In 1946 (3) 1952 (4); v P 1954 (2); *v A 1946 (5) 1950 (5) 1954 (5); v SA 1938 (4) 1948 (5); v WI 1947 (2**)** 1953 (5); v NZ 1950 (2) 1954 (2)*

Iddon (J.) 5: v SA 1935 (1); *v WI 1934 (4)*

Ikin (J. T.) 18: v SA 1951 (3) 1954 (1); v In 1946 (2); 1952 (2); *v A 1946 (5); v NZ 1947 (1); v WI 1947 (4)*

Insole, D. J. 2: v SA 1955 (1); v WI 1950 (1)

Jackson, (L.) 1: v NZ 1949

Jackson, Rt. Hon. Sir F. S. 20: v A 1893 (2) 1896 (3) 1899 (5) 1902 (5) 1905 (5)

Jardine, D. R. 22: v WI 1928 (2) 1933 (2); v NZ 1931 (3); v In 1932 (1); *v A 1928 (5) 1932 (5); v NZ 1932 (1); v In 1933 (3)*

Jenkins (R. O.) 9: v WI 1950 (2); v In 1952 (2); *v SA 1948 (5)*
Jessop, G. L. 18: v A 1899 (1) 1902 (4) 1905 (1) 1909 (2); v SA 1907 (3) 1912 **(2)**; *v A 1901 (5)*
Jones, A. O. 12: v A 1899 (1) 1905 (2) 1909 (2); *v A 1901 (5) 1907 (2)*
Jupp (H.) 2: *v A 1876 (2)*
Jupp, V. W. C. 8: v A 1921 (2); v WI 1928 (2); *v SA 1922 (4)*

Keeton (W. W.) 2: v A 1934 (1); v WI 1939 (1)
Kennedy (A. S.) 5: *v SA 1922 (5)*
Kenyon (D.) 8: v A 1953 (2); v SA 1955 (3); *v In 1951 (3)*.
Killick, E. T. 2: v SA 1929 (2)
Kilner (R.) 9: v A 1926 (4); v SA 1924 (2); *v A 1924 (3)*
King (J. H.) 1: v A 1909
Kinneir (S. P.) 1: *v A 1911*
Knight (A. E.) 3: *v A 1903 (3)*
Knight, D. J. 2: v A 1921 (2)
Knox, N. A. 2: v SA 1907 (2)

Laker (J. C.) 24: v A 1948 (3) 1953 (3); v SA 1951 (2) 1955 (1); v WI 1950 (1); v NZ 1949 (1); v In 1952 (4); v P 1954 (1); *v WI 1947 (4) 1953 (4)*
Langridge (James) 8: v A 1935 (1); v WI 1933 (2); v In 1936 (1) 1946 (1); *v In 1933 (3)*
Larwood (H.) 21: v A 1926 (2) 1930 (3); v SA 1929 (3); v WI 1928 (2); v NZ 1931 (1); *v A 1928 (5) 1932 (5)*
Leadbeater (E) 2: *v In 1951 (2)*
Lee (H. W.) 1: *v SA 1930*
Lees (W.) 5: *v SA 1905 (5)*
Legge, G. B. 5: *v SA 1927 (I)*; *v NZ 1929 (4)*
Leslie, C. F. H. 4: *v A 1882 (4)*
Leveson Gower, H. D. G. 3: *v SA 1909 (3)*
Levett, W. H. V. 1: *v In 1933*
Leyland (M.) 41: v A 1930 (3) 1934 (5) 1938 (1); v SA 1929 (5) 1935 (4); v WI 1928 (1) 1933 (1); v In 1936 (2); *v A 1928 (I) 1932 (5) 1936 (5)*; *v SA 1930 (5); v WI 1934 (3)*
Lilley (A. A.) 35: v A 1896 (3) 1899 (4) 1902 (5) 1905 (5) 1909 (5); v SA 1907 (3); *v A 1901 (5) 1903 (5)*
Lillywhite (Jas. Jnr.) 2: *v A 1876 (2)*
Loader (P. J.) 2: v SA 1955 (1); v P 1954 (1)
Lock (G. A. R.) 12: v A 1953 (2); v SA 1955 (3); v In 1952 (2); *v WI 1953 (5)*
Lockwood (W. H.) 12: v A 1893 (2) 1899 (1) 1902 (4); *v A 1894 (5)*
Lohmann (G.) 18: v A 1886 (3) 1888 (3) 1890 (2) 1896 (1); *v A 1886* **(2)** *1887 (I) 1891 (3) : v SA 1895 (3)*
Lowson (F. A.) 7: v SA 1951 (2) 1955 (1); *v In 1951 (4)*
Lucas, A. P. 5: v A 1880 (1) 1882 (1) 1884 (2); *v A 1878 (I)*
Lyttelton, Rt. Hon. A. 4: v A 1880 (1) 1882 (1) 1884 (2)

Macaulay (G. G.) 8: v A 1926 (1); v SA 1924 (1); v WI 1933 (2); *v SA 1922 (4)*
MacBryan, J. C. W. 1: v SA 1924
McConnon (J.) 2: v P 1954 (2)
McGahey, C. P. 2: *v A 1901 (2)*
MacGregor, G. 8: v A 1890 (2) 1893 (3): *v A 1891 (3)*
McIntyre (A. J.) 3: v SA 1955 (1); v WI 1950 (1); *v A 1950 (I)*
MacKinnon, F. A. 1: *v A 1878*
MacLaren, A. C. 35: v A 1896 (2) 1899 (4) 1902 (5) 1905 (4) 1909 (5); *v A 1894 (5) 1897 (5) 1901 (5)*
McMaster, J. E. P. 1: *v SA 1888*
Makepeace (H.) 4: *v A 1920 (4)*
Mann, F. G. 7: v NZ 1949 (2); *v SA 1948 (5)*
Mann, F. T. 5: *v SA 1922 (5)*
Marriott, C. S. 1: v WI 1933
Martin (F.) 2: v A 1890 (1); *v SA 1891 (I)*
Martin, J. W. 1: v SA 1947
Mason, J. R. 5: *v A 1897 (5)*

Matthews (A. D. G.) 1: v NZ 1937
May, P. B. H. 29: v A 1953 (2); v SA 1951 (2) 1955 (5); v In 1952 (4); v P 1954 (4); *v A 1954 (5)*; *v WI 1953 (5)*; *v NZ 1954 (2)*
Mead (C. P.) 17: v A 1921 (2); *v A 1911 (4) 1928 (1)*; *v SA 1913 (5) 1922 (5)*
Mead (W.) 1: v A 1899
Midwinter (W. E.) 4: *v A 1881 (4)*
Miller, A. M. 1: *v SA 1895*
Milligan, F. W. 2: *v SA 1898 (2)*
Mitchell (A.) 6: v SA 1935 (2); v In 1936 (1); *v In 1933 (3)*
Mitchell, F. 2: *v SA 1898 (2)*
Mitchell (T. B.) 5: v A 1934 (2); v SA 1935 (1) *v A 1932 (1)*; *v NZ 1932 (1)*
Mitchell-Innes, N. S. 1: v SA 1935
Mold (A.) 3: v A 1893 (3)
Moon, L. J. 4: *v SA 1905 (4)*
Morley (F.) 4: v A 1880 (1); *v A 1882 (3)*
Moss (A. E.) 1: *v WI 1953*
Murdoch, W. L. 1: *v SA 1891*

Newham (W.) 1: *v A 1887*
Nichols (M. S.) 14: v A 1930 (1); v SA 1935 (4); v WI 1933 (1) 1939 (1) *v NZ 1929 (4)*; *v In 1933 (3)*

O'Brien, Sir T. C. 5: v A 1884 (1) 1888 (1); *v SA 1895 (3)*
O'Connor (J.) 4: v SA 1929 (1); *v WI 1929 (3)*
Oldfield (N.) 1: v WI 1939

Paine (G. A. E.) 4: *v WI 1934 (4)*
Palairet, L. C. H. 2: v A 1902 (2)
Palmer, C. H. 1: *v WI 1953*
Parker (C. W. L.) 1: v A 1921
Parkhouse (W. G. A.) 5: v WI 1950 (2); *v A 1950 (2)*; *v NZ 1950 (1)*
Parkin (C. H.) 10: v A 1921 (4); v SA 1924 (1); *v A 1920 (5)*
Parks (J. H.) 1: v NZ 1937
Parks (J. M.) 1: v P 1954
Pataudi, Nawab of 3: v A 1934 (1); *v A 1932 (2)*
Paynter (E.) 20: v A 1938 (4); v WI 1939 (2); v NZ 1931 (1) 1937 (2); v In 1932 (1); *v A 1932 (3)*; *v SA 1938 (5)*; *v NZ 1932 (2)*
Peate (E.) 9: v A 1882 (1) 1884 (1) 1886 (1); *v A 1881 (4)*
Peebles, I. A. R. 13: v A 1930 (2); v NZ 1931 (3); *v SA 1927 (4) 1930 (4)*
Peel (R.) 20: v A 1888 (3) 1890 (1) 1893 (1) 1896 (1); *v A 1884 (5) 1887 (1) 1891 (3) 1894 (5)*
Penn, F. 1: v A 1880
Perks (R. T. D.) 2: v WI 1939 (1); *v SA 1938 (1)*
Philipson, H. 5: *v A 1891 (1) 1894 (4)*
Pilling (R.) 8: v A 1884 (1) 1886 (1) 1888 (1); *v A 1881 (4) 1887 (1)*
Place (W.) 3: *v WI 1947 (3)*
Pollard (R.) 4: v A 1948 (2); v In 1946 (1); *v NZ 1947 (1)*
Poole (C. J.) 3: *v In 1951 (3)*
Pope (G. H.) 1: v SA 1947
Pougher (A. D.) 1: *v SA 1891*
Price (W. F.) 1: v A 1938

Quaife (W. G.) 7: v A 1899 (2); *v A 1901 (5)*

Ranjitsinhji, K. S. 15: v A 1896 (2) 1899 (5) 1902 (3); *v A 1897 (5)*
Read, H. D. 1: v SA 1935
Read (J. M.) 17: v A 1882 (1) 1890 (2) 1893 (1); *v A 1884 (5) 1886 (2) 1887 (1) 1891 (1)*; *v SA 1888 (2)*
Read, W. W. 18: v A 1884 (2) 1886 (3) 1888 (3) 1890 (2) 1893 (2); *v A 1882 (4) 1887 (1)*; *v SA 1891 (1)*
Relf (A. E.) 13: v A 1909 (1); *v A 1903 (2)*; *v SA 1905 (5) 1913 (5)*
Rhodes (W.) 58: v A 1899 (3) 1902 (5) 1905 (4) 1909 (4) 1912 (3) 1921 (1) 1926 (1); v SA 1912 (3); *v A 1903 (5) 1907 (5) 1911 (5) 1920 (5)*; *v SA 1909 (5) 1913 (5)*; *v WI 1929 (4)*

Richardson (T.) 14: v A 1893 (1) 1896 (3); *v A 1894 (5) 1897 (5)*
Richmond (T. L.) 1: v A 1921
Ridgway (F.) 5: *v In 1951(5)*
Robertson (J. D.) 11: v SA 1947 (1); v NZ 1949 (1); *v WI 1947 (4); v In 1951 (5)*
Robins, R. W. V. 19: v A 1930 (2); v SA 1929 (1) 1935 (3); v WI 1933 (2);
    v NZ 1931 (1) 1937 (3); v In 1932 (1) 1936 (2); *v A 1936 (4)*
Root (C. F.) 3: v A 1926 (3)
Royle, V. P. F. A. 1: *v A 1878*
Russell (A. C.) 10: v A. 1921 (2); *v A 1920 (4); v SA 1922 (4)*

Sandham (A.) 14: v A 1921 (1); v SA 1924 (2); *v A 1924 (2); v SA 1922 (5);*
    v WI 1929 (4)
Schultz, S. S. 1: *v A 1878*
Scotton (W. H.) 15: v A 1884 (1) 1886 (3); *v A 1881 (4) 1884 (5) 1886 (2)*
Selby (J.) 6: *v A 1876 (2) 1881 (4)*
Shackleton (D.) 3: v SA 1951 (1); v WI 1950 (1); *v In 1951 (1)*
Sharp (J.) 3: v A 1909 (3)
Sharpe (J. W.) 3: v A 1890 (1); *v A 1891 (2)*
Shaw (A.) 7: v A 1880 (1); *v A 1876 (2) 1881 (4)*
Sheppard, D. S. 8: v WI 1950 (1); v In 1952 (2); v P 1954 (2); *v A 1950 (2);*
    v NZ 1950 (1)
Sherwin (M.) 3: v A 1888 (1); *v A 1886 (2)*
Shrewsbury (A.) 23: v A 1884 (3) 1886 (3) 1890 (3) 1893 (3); *v A 1881 (4)*
    1884 (5) 1886 (2) 1887 (1)
Shuter, J. 1: v A 1888
Sims (J. M.) 4: v SA 1935 (1); v In 1936 (1); *v A 1936 (2)*
Simpson, R. T. 27: v A 1953 (3); v SA 1951 (3); v WI 1950 (3); v NZ 1949 (2);
    v In 1952 (2); v P 1954 (2); *v A 1950 (5) 1954 (1); v SA 1948 (1); v NZ 1950 (2)*
    1954 (2)
Simpson-Hayward, G. H. 5: *v SA 1909 (5)*
Sinfield (R. A.) 1: v A 1938
Smailes (T. F.) 1: v In 1946 (1)
Smith, C. A. 1: *v SA 1888*
Smith (C. I. J.) 5: v NZ 1937 (1); *v WI 1934 (4)*
Smith (D.) 2: v SA 1935 (2)
Smith (E. J.) 11: v A 1912 (3); v SA 1912 (3); *v A 1911 (4); v SA 1913 (1)*
Smith (H.) 1: v WI 1928
Smith (T. P. B.) 4: v In 1946 (1); *v A 1946 (2); v NZ 1947 (1)*
Smithson (G. A.) 2: *v WI 1947 (2)*
Southerton (J.) 2: *v A 1876 (2)*
Spooner, R. H. 10: v A 1905 (2) 1909 (2) 1912 (3); v SA 1912 (3)
Spooner (R. T.) 7: v SA 1955 (1); *v In 1951 (5); v WI 1953 (1)*
Stanyforth, R. T. 4: *v SA 1927 (4)*
Staples (S. J.) 3: *v SA 1927 (3)*
Statham (J. B.) 28: v A 1953 (1); v SA 1951 (2) 1955 (4); v P 1954 (4); *v A 1954*
    (5); v NZ 1950 (1) 1954 (2); v WI 1953 (4); v In 1951 (5)
Steel, A. G. 13: v A 1880 (1) 1882 (1) 1884 (3) 1886 (3) 1888 (1); *v A 1882 (4)*
Stevens, G. T. S. 10: v A 1926 (2); *v SA 1922 (1) 1927 (5); v WI 1929 (2)*
Stoddart, A. E. 16: v A 1893 (3) 1896 (2); *v A 1887 (1) 1891 (3) 1894 (5) 1897 (2)*
Storer (W.) 6: v A 1899 (1); *v A 1897 (5)*
Street (G.) 1: *v SA 1922*
Strudwick (H.) 28: v A 1921 (2) 1926 (5); v SA 1924 (1); *v A 1911 (1) 1920 (4)*
    1924 (5); v SA 1909 (5) 1913 (5)
Studd, C. T. 5: v A 1882 (1); *v A 1882 (4)*
Studd, G. B. 4: *v A 1882 (4)*
Sugg (F. H.) 2: v A 1888 (2)
Sutcliffe (H.) 54: v A 1926 (5) 1930 (4) 1934 (4); v SA 1924 (5) 1929 (5) 1935 (2);
    v WI 1928 (3) 1933 (2); v NZ 1931 (2); v In 1932 (1); *v A 1924 (5) 1928 (4)*
    1932 (5); v SA 1927 (5); v NZ 1932 (2)

Tate (F. W.) 1: v A 1902 (1)
Tate (M. W.) 39: v A 1926 (5) 1930 (5); v SA 1924 (5) 1929 (3) 1935 (1); v WI
    1928 (3); v NZ 1931 (1); *v A 1924 (5) 1928 (5); v SA 1930 (5); v NZ 1932 (1)*

Tattersall (R.) 16: v A 1953 (1); v SA 1951 (5); v P 1954 (1); *v A 1950* (*2*); *v NZ 1950* (*2*); *v In 1951* (*5*)
Tennyson, Lord, 9: v A 1921 (4); *v SA 1913* (*5*)
Thompson (G. J.) 6: v A 1909 (1); *v SA 1909* (5)
Titmus (F. J.) 2: v SA 1955 (2)
Townsend, C. L. 2: v A 1899 (2)
Townsend, D. C. H. 3: *v WI 1934* (*3*)
Townsend (L. F.) 4: *v WI 1929* (*1*); *v In 1933* (*3*)
Tremlett (M. F.) 3: *v WI 1947* (*3*)
Trott (A. E.) 2: *v SA 1898* (*2*)
Trueman (F. S.) 9: v A 1953 (1); v SA 1955 (1); v In 1952 (4); *v WI 1953* (*3*)
Tuſnell, N. C. 1: *v SA 1909*
Turnbull, M. J. 9: v WI 1933 (2); v In 1936 (1); *v SA 1930* (*5*); *v NZ 1929* (*1*)
Tyldesley (E.) 14: v A 1921 (3) 1926 (1); v SA 1924 (1); v WI 198 2(3); *v A 1928* (*1*); *v SA 1927* (5)
Tyldesley (J. T.) 31: v A 1899 (2) 1902 (5) 1905 (5) 1909 (4); v SA 1907 (3); *v A 1901* (*5*) *1903* (*5*); *v SA 1898* (*2*)
Tyldesley (R.) 7: v A 1930 (2); v SA 1924 (4); *v A 1924* (*1*)
Tylecote, E. F. S. 6: v A 1886 (2); *v A 1882* (*4*)
Tyler (E. J.) 1: *v SA 1895*
Tyson (F. H.) 10: v SA 1955 (2); v P 1954 (1); *v A 1954* (*5*); *v NZ 1954* (2)

Ulyett (G.) 25: v A 1882 (1) 1884 (3) 1886 (3) 1888 (2) 1890 (1); *v A 1876* (*2*) *1878* (*1*) *1881* (*4*) *1884* (*5*) *1887* (*1*); *v SA 1888* (*2*)

Valentine, B. H. 7: *v SA 1938* (*5*); *v In 1933* (2)
Verity (H.) 40: **v** A 1934 (5) 1938 (4); v SA 1935 (4); v WI 1933 (2) 1939 (1); **v** NZ 1931 (2) 1937 (1); v In 1936 (3); *v A 1932* (*4*) *1936* (*5*); *v SA 1938* (*5*); *v NZ 1932* (*1*); *v In 1933* (*3*)
Vernon G. F. 1: *v A 1882*
Vine (J.) 2: *v A 1911* (*2*)
Voce (W.) 27: v NZ 1931 (1) 1937 (1); v In 1932 (1) 1936 (1) 1946 (1); *v A 1932* (*4*) *1936* (*5*) *1946* (2); *v SA 1930* (*5*); *v NZ 1932* (*1*); *v WI 1929* (4)

Waddington (A.) 2: *v A 1920* (*2*)
Wainwright (E.) 5: v A 1893 (1); *v A 1897* (*4*)
Walters, C. F. 11: v A 1934 (5); v WI 1933 (3); *v In 1933* (*3*)
Ward (A.) 7: v A 1893 (2); *v A 1894* (*5*)
Wardle (J. H.) 22: v A 1953 (3); v SA 1951 (2) 1955 (3); v WI 1950 (1); v P 1954 (4); *v A 1954* (*4*); *v WI 1947* (*1*) *1953* (2); *v NZ 1954* (2)
Warner, Sir Pelham, 15: v A 1909 (1); 1912 (1); v SA 1912 (1); *v A 1903* (*5*); *v SA 1898* (2) *1905* (*5*)
Warr, J. J. 2: *v A 1950* (2)
Warren, (A. R.) 1: v A 1905
Washbrook (C.) 34: v A 1948 (4); v SA 1947 (5); v WI 1950 (2); v NZ 1937 (1) 1949 (2); v In 1946 (3); *v A 1946* (*5*) *1951* (*5*); *v SA 1948* (*5*); *v NZ 1947* (*1*) *1951* (*1*)
Watkins (A.) 15: v A 1948 (1); v NZ 1949 (1); v In 1952 (3); *v SA 1948* (*5*); *v In 1951* (5)
Watson (W.) 15: v A 1953 (3); v SA 1951 (5) 1955 (1); v In 1952 (1); *v WI 1953* (*5*)
Webbe, A. J. 1: *v A 1878*
Wellard (A. W.) 2: v A 1938 (1); v NZ 1937 (1)
Wharton (A.) 1: v NZ 1949
White, J. C. 15: v A 1921 (1) 1930 (1); v SA 1929 (3); v WI 1928 (1); *v A 1928* (*5*); *v SA 1930* (*4*)
Whysall (W. W.) 4: v A 1930 (1); *v A 1924* (*3*)
Wilkinson (L. L.) 3: *v SA 1938* (*3*)
Wilson, C. E. M. 2: *v SA 1898* (2)
Wilson, E. R. 1: *v A 1920*
Wood (A.) 4: v A 1938 (1); v WI 1939 (3)
Wood, G. E. C. 3: v SA 1924 (3)
Wood (H.) 4: v A 1888 (1); *v SA 1888* (*2*) *1891* (*1*)
Wood (R.) 1: *v A 1886*

Woods, S. M. J. 3: v *SA 1895 (3)*
Woolley (F. E.) 64: v A 1909 (1) 1912 (3) 1921 (5) 1926 (5) 1930 (2) 1934 (1);
 v SA 1912 (3) 1924 (5) 1929 (3); v NZ 1931 (1); v In 1932 (1); *v A 1911 (5)
 1920 (5) 1924 (5); v SA 1909 (5) 1913 (5) 1922 (5); v NZ 1929 (4)*
Worthington (T. S.) 9: v In 1936 (2); *v A 1936 (3); v NZ 1929 (4)*
Wright, C. W. 3: v *SA 1895 (3)*
Wright (D. V. P.) 34: v A 1938 (3) 1948 (1); v SA 1947 (4); v WI 1939 (3) 1950 (1);
 v NZ 1949 (1); v In 1946 (2); *v A 1946 (5) 1950 (5); v SA 1938 (3) 1948 (3);
 v NZ 1947 (1) 1950 (2)*
Wynyard, E. G. 3: v A 1896 (1); *v SA 190*5 (2)
Wyatt, R. E. S. 40: v A 1930 (1) 1934 (4); v SA 1929 (2) 1935 (5); v WI 1933 (2);
 v In 1936 (1); *v A 1932 (5) 1936 (2); v SA 1927 (5) 1930 (5); v NZ 1932 (2);
 v WI 1929 (2) 1934 (4)*

Yardley, N. W. D. 20: v A 1948 (5); v SA 1947 (5); v WI 1950 (3); *v A 1946 (5);
 v SA 1938 (1); v NZ 1947 (1)*
Young (H.) 2: v A 1899 (2)
Young (J. A.) 8: v A 1948 (3); v SA 1947 (1); v NZ 1949 (2); *v SA 1948 (2)*
Young, R. A. 2: *v A 1907 (2)*

AUSTRALIA

a'Beckett, E. L. 4: v E 1928 (2) v SA 1931 (1); *v E 1930 (1)*
Alexander, G. 2: v E 1884 (1); *v E 1880 (1)*
Alexander, H. H. 1: v E 1932
Allan, F. E. 1: v E 1878
Allen, R. 1: v E 1886
Andrews, T. J. E. 16: v E 1924 (3); *v E 1921 (5) 1926 (5); v SA 1921 (3)*
Archer, K. A. 5: v E 1950 (3); v WI 1951 (2)
Archer, R. G. 13: v E 1954 (4); v SA 1952 (1); *v E 1953 (3); v WI 1955 (5)*
Armstrong, W. W. 50: v E 1901 (4) 1903 (3) 1907 (5) 1911 (5) 1920 (5); **v SA**
 1910 (5); *v E 1902 (5) 1905 (5) 1909 (5) 1921 (5); v SA 1902 (3)*

Badcock, C. L. 7: v E 1936 (3); *v E 1938 (4)*
Bannerman, A. C. 28: v E 1878 (1) 1881 (3) 1882 (4) 1884 (4) 1886 (1) 1887 (1)
 1891 (3); *v E 1880 (1) 1882 (1) 1884 (3) 1888 (3) 1893 (3)*
Bannerman, C. 3: v E 1876 (2) 1878 (1)
Bardsley, W. 41: v E 1911 (4) 1920 (5) 1924 (3); v SA 1910 (5); *v E 1909 (5)
 1912 (3) 1921 (5) 1926 (5); v SA 1912 (3) 1921 (3)*
Barnes, S. G. 13: v E 1946 (4); v In 1947 (3); *v E 1938 (1) 1948 (4); v NZ 1946 (1)*
Barnett, B. A. 4: *v E 1938 (4)*
Barrett, J. E. 2: *v E 1890 (2)*
Benaud, R. 18: v E 1954 (5); v SA 1952 (4); v WI 1951 (1); *v E 1953 (3); v WI
 1955 (5)*
Blackham, J. McC. 35: v E 1876 (2) 1878 (1) 1881 (4) 1882 (4) 1884 (2) 1886 (1)
 1887 (1) 1891 (3) 1894 (1); *v E 1880 (1) 1882 (1) 1884 (3) 1886 (3) 1888 (3)
 1890 (2) 1893 (3)*
Blackie, D. J. 3: v E 1928 (3)
Bonnor, G. J. 17: v E 1882 (4) 1884 (3); *v E 1880 (1) 1882 (1) 1884 (3) 1886 (2)
 1888 (3)*
Boyle, H. F. 12: v E 1878 (1) 1881 (4) 1882 (1) 1884 (1); *v E 1880 (1) 1882 (1)
 1884 (3)*
Bradman, D. G. 52: v E 1928 (4) 1932 (4) 1936 (5) 1946 (5); v SA 1931 (5);
 v WI 1930 (5); v In 1947 (5); *v E 1930 (5) 1934 (5) 1938 (4) 1948 (5)*
Bromley, E. H. 2: v E 1932 (1); *v E 1934 (1)*
Brown, W. A. 22: v E 1936 (2); **v In** 1947 (3); *v E 1934 (5) 1938 (4) 1948 (2);
 v SA 1935 (5); v NZ 1946 (1)*
Bruce, W. 14: v E 1884 (2) 1891 (3) 1894 (4); *v E 1886 (2) 1893 (3)*
Burn, K. E. 2: *v E 1890 (2)*
Burge, P. 2: v E 1954 (1); *v WI 1955 (1)*
Burke, J. 5: v E 1950 (2) 1954 (2); v WI 1951 (1)
Burton, F. J. 2: v E 1886 (1) 1887 (1)

Callaway, S. T. 3: v E 1891 (2) 1894 (1)
Carkeek, W. 6: v E 1912 (3); v SA 1912 (3)
Carter, H. 28: v E 1907 (5) 1911 (5) 1920 (2); v SA 1910 (5); *v E 1909 (5) 1921 (4); v SA 1921 (2)*
Charlton, P. C. 2: *v E 1890 (2)*
Chipperfield, A. G. 14: v E 1936 (3); *v E 1934 (5) 1938 (1)*; *v SA 1935 (5)*
Collins, H. L. 19: v E 1920 (5) 1924 (5); *v E 1921 (3) 1926 (3)*; *v SA 1921 (3)*
Coningham, A. 1: v E 1894
Cooper, B. B. 1: v E 1876
Cooper, W. H. 2: v E 1881 (1) 1884 (1)
Cottam, J. 1: v E 1886
Cotter, A. 21: v E 1903 (2) 1907 (2) 1911 (4); v SA 1910 (5); *v E 1905 (3) 1909 (5)*
Coulthard, G. 1: v E 1881
Craig, I. D. 1: v SA 1952

Darling, J. 34: v E 1894 (5) 1897 (5) 1901 (3); *v E 1896 (3) 1899 (5) 1902 (5) 1905 (5)*; *v SA 1902 (3)*
Darling, L. S. 12: v E 1932 (2) 1936 (1); *v E 1934 (4)*; *v SA 1935 (5)*
Davidson, A. K. (8): v E 1954 (3); *v E 1953 (5)*
de Courcy, J. H. 3: *v E 1953 (3)*
Donnan, H. 5: v E 1891 (2); *v E 1896 (3)*
Dooland, B. 3: v E 1946 (2); v In 1947 (1)
Duff, R. A. 22: v E 1901 (4) 1903 (5); *v E 1902 (5) 1905 (5)*; *v SA 1902 (3)*

Eady, C. J. 2: v E 1901 (1); *v E 1896 (1)*
Ebeling, H. I. 1: *v E 1934*
Edwards, J. D. 3: *v E 1888 (3)*
Emery, S. H. 4: *v E 1912 (2)*; *v SA 1912 (2)*
Evans, E. 6: v E 1881 (2) 1882 (1) 1884 (1); *v E 1886 (2)*

Fairfax, A. 10: v E 1928 (1); v WI 1930 (5); *v E 1930 (4)*
Favell, L. 6: v E 1954 (4); *v WI 1955 (2)*
Fingleton, J. H. 18: v E 1932 (3) 1936 (5); v SA 1931 (1); *v E 1938 (4)*; *v SA 1935 (5)*
Fleetwood-Smith, L. O.'B. 10: v E 1936 (3); *v E 1938 (4)*; *v SA 1935 (3)*
Freer, F. 1: v E 1946

Garrett, T. W. 19: v E 1876 (2) 1878 (1) 1881 (3) 1882 (3) 1884 (3) 1886 (2) 1887 (1); *v E 1882 (1) 1886 (3)*
Gehrs, D. R. A. 6: v E 1903 (1); v SA 1910 (4); *v E 1905 (1)*
Giffen, G. 31: v E 1881 (3) 1882 (4) 1884 (3) 1891 (3) 1894 (5); *v E 1882 (1) 1884 (3) 1886 (3) 1893 (3) 1896 (3)*
Giffen, W. F. 3: v E 1886 (1) 1891 (2)
Graham, H. 6: v E 1894 (2); *v E 1893 (3) 1896 (1)*
Gregory, D. W. 3: v E 1876 (2) 1878 (1)
Gregory, E. J. 1: v E 1876
Gregory, J. M. 24: v E 1920 (5) 1924 (5) 1928 (1); *v E 1921 (5) 1926 (5)*; *v SA 1921 (3)*
Gregory, R. 2: v E 1936 (2)
Gregory, S. E. 58: v E 1891 (1) 1894 (5) 1897 (5) 1901 (5) 1903 (4) 1907 (2) 1911 (1); *v E 1890 (2) 1893 (3) 1896 (3) 1899 (5) 1902 (5) 1905 (3) 1909 (5) 1912 (3)*; *v SA 1902 (3) 1912 (3)*
Grimmett, C. V. 37: v E 1924 (1) 1928 (5) 1932 (3); v SA 1931 (5); v WI 1930 (5); *v E 1926 (3) 1930 (5) 1934 (5)*; *v SA 1935 (5)*
Groube, T. U. 1: *v E 1880*

Hamence, R. A. 3: v E 1946 (1); v In 1947 (2)
Harry, J. 1: v E 1894
Hartigan, R. J. 2: v E 1907 (2)
Hartkopf, A. E. V. 1: v E 1924
Harvey, M. 1: v E 1946
Harvey, R. N. 39: v E 1950 (5) 1954 (5); v SA 1952 (5); v WI 1951 (5); v In 1947 (2); *v E 1948 (2) 1953 (5)*; *v SA 1949 (5)*; *v WI 1955 (5)*

Hassett, A. L. 43: v E 1946 (5) 1950 (5); v SA 1952 (5); v WI 1951 (4); v In 1947 (4); *v E 1938 (4) 1948 (5) 1953 (5); v SA 1949 (5); v NZ 1946 (1)*
Hazlitt, G. 9: v E 1907 (2) 1911 (1); *v E 1912 (3); v SA 1912 (3)*
Hendry, H. L. 11: v E 1924 (1) 1928 (4); *v E 1921 (4); v SA1912 (2)*
Hill, Clem, 49: v E 1897 (5) 1901 (5) 1903 (5) 1907 (5) 1911 (5); v SA 1910 (5); *v E 1896 (3) 1899 (3) 1902 (5) 1905 (5); v SA 1902 (3)*
Hill, J. C. 3: *v E 1953 (2); v WI 1955 (1)*
Hodges, J. 2: v E 1876 (2)
Hole, G. 18: v E 1950 (1) 1954 (3); v SA 1952 (4); v WI 1951 (5); *v E 1953 (5)*
Hopkins, A. J. 20: v E 1901 (2) 1903 (5); *v E 1902 (5) 1905 (3) 1909 (2); v SA 1902 (3)*
Horan, T. 15: v E 1876 (1) 1878 (1) 1881 (4) 1882 (4) 1884 (4); *v E 1882 (1)*
Hordern, H. V. 7: v E 1911 (5); v SA 1910 (5)
Hornibrook, P. M. 6: v E 1928 (1); *v E 1930 (5)*
Howell, W. P. 18: v E 1897 (3) 1901 (4) 1903 (3); *v E 1899 (5) 1902 (1); v SA 1902 (2)*
Hunt, W. A. 1: v SA 1931
Hurwood, A. 2: v WI 1930 (2)

Iredale, F. A. 14: v E 1894 (5) 1897 (4); *v E 1896 (2) 1899 (3)*
Ironmonger, H. 14: v E 1928 (2) 1932 (4); v SA 1931 (4); v WI 1930 (4)
Iverson, J. 5: v E 1950 (5)

Jackson, A. A. 8: v E 1928 (2); v WI 1930 (4); *v E 1930 (2)*
Jarvis, A. H. 11: v E 1884 (3) 1894 (4); *v E 1886 (2) 1888 (2)*
Jennings, C. B. 6: *v E 1912 (3); v SA 1912 (3)*
Johnson, I. W. 37: v E 1946 (4) 1950 (5) 1954 (4); v SA 1952 (1); v WI 1951 (4); v In 1947 (4); *v E 1958 (4); v SA 1949 (5); v WI 1955 (5); v NZ 1946 (1)*
Johnson, L. 1: v In 1947
Johnston, W. A. 40: v E 1950 (5) 1954 (4); v SA 1952 (5); v WI 1951 (5); v In 1947 (4); *v E 1948 (5) 1953 (3); v SA 1949 (5); v WI 1955 (4)*
Jones, E. 19: v E 1894 (1) 1897 (5) 1901 (2); *v E 1896 (3) 1899 (5) 1902(2); v SA 1902 (1)*
Jones, S. P. 12: v E 1881 (2) 1884 (4) 1886 (1) 1887 (1); *v E 1882 (1) 1886 (3)*

Kelleway, C. E. 26: v E 1911 (4) 1920 (5) 1924 (5) 1928 (1); v SA 1910 (5); *v E 1912 (3); v SA 1912 (3)*
Kelly, J. J. 36: v E 1897 (5) 1901 (5) 1903 (5); *v E 1896 (3) 1899 (5) 1902 (5) 1905 (5); v SA 1902 (3)*
Kelly, T. J. D. 2: v E 1876 (1) 1878 (1)
Kendall, T. 2: v E 1876 (2)
Kippax, A. F. 22: v E 1924 (1) 1928 (5) 1932 (1); v SA 1931 (4); v WI 1930 (5); *v E 1930 (5) 1934 (1)*

Laver, F. 15: v E 1901 (1) 1903 (1); *v E 1899 (4) 1905 (5) 1909 (4)*
Langley, G. 20: v E 1954 (2); v SA 1952 (5); v WI 1951 (5); *v E 1953 (4); v WI 1955 (4)*
Lee, P. K. 2: v E 1932 (1); v SA 1931 (1)
Lindwall, R. 47: v E 1946 (4) 1950 (5) 1954 (4); v SA 1952 (4); v WI 1951 (5); v In 1947 (5); *v E 1948 (5) 1953 (5); v SA 1949 (4); v WI 1955 (5); v NZ 1946 (1)*
Love, H. S. 1: v E 1932
Loxton, S. J. 12: v E 1950 (3); v In 1947 (1); *v E 1948 (3); v SA 1949 (5)*
Lyons, J. J. 14: v E 1886 (1) 1891 (3) 1894 (3) 1897 (1); *v E 1888 (1) 1890 (2) 1893 (3)*

Macartney, C. G. 35: v E 1907 (5) 1911 (1) 1920 (2); v SA 1910 (4); *v E 1909 (5) 1912 (3) 1921 (5) 1926 (5); v SA 1912 (3) 1921 (2)*
Maddocks, L. 4: v E 1954 (3); *v WI 1955 (1).*
Mailey, A. A. 21: v E 1920 (5) 1924 (5); *v E 1921 (3) 1926 (5); v SA 1921 (3)*
Marr, P. 1: v E 1884
Massie, H. H. 9: v E 1881 (4) 1882 (3) 1884 (1); *v E 1882 (1)*
Matthews, T. J. 8: v E 1911 (2); *v E 1912 (3); v SA 1912 (3)*

Mayne, E. R. 4: v *E 1912 (1)*; v *SA 1912 (1) 1921 (2)*
McAlister, P. A. 8: v E 1903 (2) 1907 (4); v *E 1909 (2)*
McCabe, S. J. 39: v E 1932 (5) 1936 (5); v SA 1931 (5); v WI 1930 (5); v *E 1930 (5) 1934 (5) 1938 (4)*; v *SA 1935 (5)*
McCool, C. 14: v E 1946 (5); v In 1947 (3); v *SA 1949 (5)*; v *NZ 1946 (1)*
McCormick, E. L. 12: v E 1936 (4); v *E 1938 (3)*; v *SA 1935 (5)*
McDonald, C. 13: v E 1954 (2); v SA 1952 (5); v WI 1951 (1); v *WI 1955 (5)*
McDonald, E. A. 11: v E 1920 (3); v *E 1921 (5)*; v *SA 1921 (3)*
McDonnell, P. S. 19: v E 1881 (4) 1882 (3) 1884 (2) 1886 (2) 1887 (1); v *E 1880 (1) 1884 (3) 1888 (3)*
McLaren, J. W. 1: v E 1911
McLeod, C. E. 17: v E 1894 (1) 1897 (5) 1901 (2) 1903 (3); v *E 1899 (1) 1905 (5)*
McLeod, R. W. 6: v E 1891 (3); v *E 1893 (3)*
Meuleman, K. 1: v *NZ 1946*
Midwinter, W. E. 8: v E 1876 (2) 1882 (1) 1886 (2); v *E 1884 (3)*
Miller, K. R. 49: v E 1946 (5) 1950 (5) 1954 (4); v SA 1952 (4); v WI 1951 (5); v In 1947 (5); v *E 1948 (5) 1953 (5)*; v *SA 1949 (5)*; v *WI 1955 (5)*; v *NZ 1946 (1)*
M'Ilwraith, J. 1: v *E 1886*
Minnett, R. B. 9: v E 1911 (5); v *E 1912 (1)*; v *SA 1912 (3)*
M'Kibbin, T. R. 5: v E 1894 (1) 1897 (2); v *E 1896 (2)*
Moroney, J. 7: v E 1950 (1); v WI 1951 (1); v *SA 1949 (5)*
Morris, A. R. 46: v E 1946 (5) 1950 (5) 1954 (4); v SA 1952 (5); v WI 1951 (4); v In 1947 (4); v *E 1948 (5) 1953 (5)*; v *SA 1949 (5)*; v *WI 1955 (4).*
Morris, S. 1: v E 1884
Moses, H. 6: v E 1886 (2) 1887 (1) 1891 (2) 1894 (1)
Moule, W. H. 1: v *E 1880*
M'Shane, P. G. 3: v E 1884 (1) 1886 (1) 1887 (1)
Murdoch, W. L. 18: v E 1876 (1) 1878 (1) 1881 (4) 1882 (4) 1884 (1); v *E 1880 (1) 1882 (1) 1884 (3) 1890 (2*
Musgrove, H. 1: v E 1884

Nagel, L. E. 1: v E 1932
Nash, L. J. 2: v E 1936 (1); v SA 1931 (1)
Nitschke, H. C. 2: v SA 1931 (2)
Noble, M. A. 42: v E 1897 (4) 1901 (5) 1903 (5) 1907 (5); v *E 1899 (5) 1902 (5) 1905 (5) 1909 (5)*; v *SA 1902 (3)*
Noblet, G. 3: v SA 1952 (1); v WI 1951 (1); v *SA 1949 (1)*
Nothling, O. E. 1: v E 1928

O'Brien, L. P. 5: v E 1932 (2) 1936 (1); v *SA 1935 (2)*
O'Connor, J. A. 4: v E 1907 (3); v *E 1909 (1)*
Oldfield, W. A. 54: v E 1920 (3) 1924 (5) 1928 (5) 1932 (4) 1936 (5); v SA 1931 (5); v WI 1930 (5); v *E 1921 (1) 1926 (5) 1930 (5) 1934 (5)*; v *SA 1921 (1) 1935 (5)*
O'Reilly, W. J. 27: v E 1932 (5) 1936 (5); v SA 1931 (2); v *E 1934 (5) 1938 (4)*; v *SA 1935 (5)*; v *NZ 1946 (1)*
Oxenham, R. K. 7: v E 1928 (3); v SA 1931 (1); v WI 1930 (3)

Palmer, G. E. 17: v E 1881 (4) 1882 (4) 1884 (2); v *E 1880 (1) 1884 (3) 1886 (3)*
Park, R. L. 1: v E 1920
Pellew, C. E. 10: v E 1920 (4); v *E 1921 (5)*; v *SA 1921 (1)*
Ponsford, W. H. 29: v E 1924 (5) 1928 (2) 1932 (3); v SA 1931 (4); v WI 1930 (5); v *E 1926 (2) 1930 (4) 1934 (4)*
Pope, R. 1: v E 1884

Ransford, V. S. 20: v E 1907 (5) 1911 (5); v SA 1910 (5); v *E 1909 (5)*
Reedman, J. C. 1: v E 1894
Richardson, A. J. 9: v E 1924 (4); v *E 1926 (5)*
Richardson, V. Y. 19: v E 1924 (3) 1928 (2) 1932 (5); v *E 1930 (4)*; v *SA 1935 (5)*
Rigg, K. E. 8: v E 1936 (3); v SA 1931 (4); v WI 1930 (1)
Ring, D. 13: v SA 1952 (5); v WI 1951 (5); v In 1947 (1); v *E 1948 (1) 1953 (1)*
Robertson, W. R. 1: v E 1884
Robinson, R. 1: v E 1936
Ryder, J. S. 20: v E 1920 (5) 1924 (3) 1928 (5); v *E 1926 (4)*; v *SA 1921 (3)*

Saggers, R. A. 6: *v E 1948 (1)*; *v SA 1949 (5)*
Saunders, J. V. 14: v E 1901 (1) 1903 (2) 1907 (5); *v E 1902 (4)*; *v SA 1902 (2)*
Scott, H. J. H. 8: v E 1884 (2); *v E 1884 (3) 1886 (3)*
Sievers, M. 3: v E 1936 (3)
Slight, J. 1: *v E 1880*
Smith, D. 2: *v E 1912 (2)*
Spofforth, F. R. 18: v E 1876 (1) 1878 (1) 1881 (1) 1882 (4) 1884 (3) 1886 (1);
    v E 1882 (1) 1884 (3) 1886 (3)

Tallon, D. 21: v E 1946 (5) 1950 (5); v In 1947 (5); *v E 1948 (4) 1953 (1)*;
    v NZ 1946 (1)
Taylor, J. M. 20: v E 1920 (5) 1924 (5); *v E 1921 (5) 1926 (3)*; *v SA 1921 (2)*
Thompson, N. 2: v E 1876 (2)
Thoms, G. 1: v WI 1951
Thurlow, H. M. 1: v SA 1931
Toshack, E. 12: v E 1946 (5); v In 1947 (2); *v E 1948 (4)*; *v NZ 1946 (1)*
Travers, J. F. 1: v E 1901
Tribe, G. 3: v E 1946 (3)
Trott, A. E. 3: v E 1894 (3)
Trott, G. H. S. 24: v E 1891 (3) 1894 (5) 1897 (5); *v E 1888 (3) 1890 (2) 1893 (3)*
    1896 (3)
Trumble, H. 32: v E 1894 (1) 1897 (5) 1901 (5) 1903 (4); *v E 1890 (2) 1893 (3)*
    1896 (3) 1899 (5) 1902 (3); *v SA 1902 (1)*
Trumble, J. W. 7: v E 1884 (4); *v E 1886 (3)*
Trumper, V. T. 48: v E 1901 (5) 1903 (5) 1907 (5) 1911 (5); v SA 1910 (5);
    v E 1899 (5) 1902 (5) 1905 (5) 1909 (5); *v SA 1902 (3)*
Turner, C. T. B. 17: v E 1886 (2) 1887 (1) 1891 (3) 1894 (3); *v E 1888 (3) 1890 (2)*
    1893 (3)

Waite, M. G. 2: *v E 1938 (2)*
Wall, T. W. 18: v E 1928 (1) 1932 (4); v SA 1931 (3); v WI 1930 (1); *v E 1930 (5)*
    1934 (4)
Walters, F. H. 1: v E 1884
Ward, F. 4: v E 1936 (3); *v E 1938 (1)*
Watson, W. 4: v E 1954 (1); *v WI 1955 (3)*
Whitty, W. J. 14: v E 1911 (2); v SA 1910 (5); *v E 1909 (1) 1912 (3)*; *v SA 1912 (3)*
Woodfull, W. M. 35: v E 1928 (5) 1932 (5); v SA 1931 (5); v WI 1930 (5);
    v E 1926 (5) 1930 (5) 1934 (5)
Woods, S. M. J. 3: *v E 1888 (3)*
Worrall, J 11: v E 1884 (1) 1887 (1) 1894 (1) 1897 (1); *v E 1888 (3) 1899 (4)*

SOUTH AFRICA

Adcock, N. 9: v NZ 1953 (5); *v E 1955 (4)*
Anderson, J. H. 1: v A 1902
Ashley, W. H. 1: v E 1888

Balaskas, X. C. 9: v E 1930 (2) 1938 (1); v A 1935 (3); *v E 1935 (1)*; *v NZ 1931 (2)*
Baumgartner, H. V. 1: v E 1913
Beaumont, R. 5: v E 1913 (2); *v E 1912 (1)*; *v A 1912 (2)*
Begbie, D. W. 5: v E 1948 (3); v A 1949 (2)
Bell, A. J. 16: v E 1930 (3); *v E 1929 (3) 1935 (3)*; *v A 1931 (5)*; *v NZ 1931 (2)*
Bisset, M. 3: v E 1898 (2) 1909 (1)
Bissett, G. F. 4: v E 1927 (4)
Blanckenberg, J. M. 18: v E 1913 (5) 1922 (5); v A 1921 (3); *v E 1924 (5)*
Bock, E. G. 1: v A 1935
Bond, G. E. 1: v E 1938
Brann, W. H. 3: v E 1922 (3)
Briscoe, A. W. 2: v E 1938 (1); v A 1935 (1)
Brown, L. S. 2: *v A 1931 (1)*; *v NZ 1931 (1)*
Buys, I. D. 1: v E 1922

Cameron, H. B. 26: v E 1927 (5) 1930 (5); *v E 1929 (4) 1935 (5)*; *v A 1931 (5)*: *v NZ 1931 (2)*
Campbell, T. 5: v E 1909 (4); *v E 1912 (1)*
Carter, C. P. 10: v E 1913 (2); v A 1921 (3); *v E 1912 (2) 1924 (3)*
Catterall, R. H. 24: v E 1922 (5) 1927 (5) 1930 (4); *v E 1924 (5) 1929 (5)*
Chapman, H. W. 2: v E 1913 (1); v A 1921 (1)
Cheetham J. E. 24: v E 1948 (1); v A 1949 (3); v NZ 1953 (5); *v E 1951 (5) 1955 (3)*; *v A 1952 (5); v NZ 1952 (2)*
Christy, J. A. J. 10: v E 1930 (1); *v E 1929 (2)*; *v A 1931 (5)*; *v NZ 1931 (2)*
Chubb, G. W. A. 5: *v E 1951 (5)*
Cochran, J. A. K. 1: v E 1930
Coen, S. K. 2: v E 1927 (2)
Commaille, J. M. 12: v E 1909 (5) 1927 (2); *v E 1924 (5)*
Conyngham, D. P. 1: v E 1922
Cook, F. J. 1: v E 1895
Cooper, A. H. C. 1: v E 1913
Cox, J. L. 3: v E 1913 (3)
Cripps, G. 1: v E 1891
Curnow, S. H. 7: v E 1930 (3); *v A 1931 (4)*
Crisp, R. J. 9: v A 1935 (4); *v E 1935 (5)*

Dalton, E. L .15: v E 1930 (1) 1938 (4); v A 1935 (1); *v E 1929 (1) 1935 (4)*; *v A 1931 (2); v NZ 1931 (2)*
Davies, E. Q. 5: v E 1938 (3); v A 1935 (2)
Dawson, O. C. 9: v E 1948 (4); *v E 1947 (5)*
Deane, H. G. 17: v E 1927 (5) 1930 (2); *v E 1924 (5) 1929 (5)*
Dixon, C. D. 1: v E 1913
Dower, R. R. 1: v E 1898
Draper, R. 2; v A 1949 (2)
Duminy, J. P. 3: v E 1927 (2); *v E 1929 (1)*
Dunell, O. R. 2: v E 1888 (2)
Du Toit, J. F. 1: v E 1891
Dyer, D. V. 3: *v E 1947 (3)*

Endean, W. R. 18: v NZ 1953 (5); *v E 1951 (1) 1955 (5)*; *v A 1952 (5);   v NZ 1952 (2)*

Faulkner, G. A. 25: v E 1905 (5) 1909 (5); *v E 1907 (3) 1912 (3) 1924 (1)*; *v A 1910 (5) 1912 (3)*
Fichardt, C. G. 2: v E 1891 (1) 1895 (1)
Finlason, C. E. 1: v E 1888
Floquet, C. E. 1: v E 1909
Francis, H. H. 2: v E 1898 (2)
Francois, C. M. 5: v E 1922 (5)
Frank, C. N. 3: v A 1921 (3)
Frank, W. H. B. 1: v E 1895
Fuller, E. R. H. 6: *v E 1955 (2)*; *v A 1952 (2)*; *v NZ 1952 (2)*
Fullerton, G. M. 7: v A 1949 (2); *v E 1947 (2) 1951 (3)*
Funston, K. G. 10: v NZ 1953 (3); *v A 1952 (5); v NZ 1952 (2)*

Gleeson, R. A. 1: v E 1895
Glover, G. K. 1: v E 1895
Goddard, T. L. 5: *v E 1955 (5)*
Gordon, N. 5: v E 1938 (5)
Graham, R. 2: v E 1898 (2)
Grieveson, R. E. 2: v E 1938 (2)

Hall, A. E. 7: v E 1922 (4) 1927 (2) 1930 (1)
Halliwell, E. A. 8: v E 1891 (1) 1895 (3) 1898 (1); v A 1902 (3)
Hands, P. A. M. 7: v E 1913 (5); v A 1921 (1); *v E 1924 (1)*
Hands, R. H. M. 1: v E 1913
Hanley, M. A. 1: v E 1948
Harris, T. A. 3: v E 1948 (1); *v E 1947 (2)*

Hartigan, G. P. D. 5: v E 1912 (3); *v E 1912 (1)*; *v A 1912 (1)*
Harvey, R. L. 2: v A 1935 (2)
Hathorn, M. 12: v E 1905 (5); v A 1902 (3); *v E 1907 (3)*; *v A 1910 (1)*
Hearne, F. 4: v E 1891 (1) 1895 (3)
Hearne, G. A. L. 3: v E 1922 (2); *v E 1924 (1)*
Heine, P. 4: *v E 1955 (4)*
Hime, C. F. W. 1: v E 1895
Hutchinson, P. 2: v E 1888 (2)

Innes, A. R. 2: v E 1888 (2)
Ironside, D. E. J. 3: v NZ 1953 (3)

Johnson, C. L. 1: v E 1895
Jones, P. S. T. 1: v A 1902

Keith, H. J. 5: *v E 1955 (4)*; *v A 1952 (1)*
Kempis, G. A. 1: v E 1888
Kotze, J. J. 3: v A 1902 (2) *v E 1907 (1)*
Kuys, F. 1: v E 1898

Langton, A. B. C. 15: v E 1938 (5); v A 1935 (5); *v E 1935 (5)*
Le Roux, F. le S. 1: v E 1913
Lewis, P. T. 1: v E 1913
Lindsay, J. D. 3: *v E 1947 (3)*
Lindsay, N. V. 1: v A 1921
Ling, W. V. S. 6: v E 1922 (3); v A 1921 (3)
Llewellyn, C. B. 15: v E 1895 (1) 1898 (1); v A 1902 (3); *v E 1912 (3)*; *v A 1910 (5) 1912 (2)*
Lundie, E. B. 1: v E 1913

Mann, N. B. F. 19: v E 1948 (5); v A 1949 (5); *v E 1947 (5) 1951 (4)*
Mansell, P. N. F. 13: *v E 1951 (2) 1955 (4)*; *v A 1952 (5)*; *v NZ 1952 (2)*
Markham, L. A. 1: v E 1948
Marx, W. F. E. 3: v A 1921 (3)
McCarthy, C. N. 15: v E 1948 (5); v A 1949 (5); *v E 1951 (5)*
McGlew, D. J. 18: v NZ 1953 (5); *v E 1951 (2) 1955 (5)*; *v A 1952 (4)*; *v NZ 1952 (2)*
McLean, R. A. 19: v NZ 1953 (4); *v E 1951 (3) 1955 (5)*; *v A 1952 (5)*; *v NZ 1952 (2)*
McMillan, Q. 13: v E 1930 (5); *v E 1929 (2)*; *v A 1931 (4)*; *v NZ 1931 (2)*
Meintjes, D. J. 2: v E 1922 (2)
Melle, M. G. 7: v A 1949 (2); *v E 1951 (1)*; *v A 1952 (4)*
Melville, A. 11: v E 1938 (5) 1948 (1); *v E 1947 (5)*
Middleton, J. 6: v E 1895 (2) 1898 (2) ; v A 1902 (2)
Mills, C. 1: v E 1891
Milton, W. H. 3: v E 1888 (2) 1891 (1)
Mitchell, B. 42: v E 1930 (5) 1938 (5) 1948 (5); v A 1935 (5); *v E 1929 (5) 1935 (5) 1947 (5)*; *v A 1931 (5)*; *v NZ 1931 (2)*
Mitchell, F. 3: *v E 1912 (1)*; *v A 1912 (2)*
Morkel, D. P. B. 16: v E 1927 (5); *v E 1929 (5)*; *v A 1931 (5)*: *v NZ 1931 (1)*
Murray, A. R. A. 10: v NZ 1953 (4); *v A 1952 (4)*; *v NZ 1952 (2)*

Nel, J. 5: v A 1949 (5)
Newberry, C. 4: v E 1913 (4)
Newson, E. S. 3: v E 1930 (1) 1938 (2)
Nicholson, F. 4: v A 1935 (4)
Nicolson, J. F. W. 3: v E 1927 (3)
Norton, N. O. 1: v E 1909
Nourse, A. D. 45: v E 1905 (5) 1909 (5) 1913 (5) 1922 (5); v A 1902 (3) 1921 (3); *v E 1907 (3) 1912 (3) 1924 (5)*; *v A 1910 (5) 1912 (3)*
Nourse, Jnr., A. D. 34: v E 1938 (5) 1948 (5); v A 1935 (5) 1949 (5); *v E 1935 (4) 1947 (5) 1951 (5)*
Nupen, E. P. 17: v E 1922 (4) 1927 (5) 1930 (3); v A 1921 (2) 1935 (1); *v E 1924 (2)*

Ochse, A. E. 2: v E 1888 (2)
Ochse, A. L. 3: v E 1927 (1); *v E 1929* (2)
Owen-Smith, H. G. 5: *v E 1929* (5)

Palm, A. W. 1: v E 1927
Parker, G. M. 2: *v E 1924* (2)
Parkin, D. C. 1: v E 1891
Pearse, O. C. 3: *v A 1910* (3)
Pegler, S. J. 16: v E 1909 (1); *v E 1912* (3) *1924* (5); *v A 1910* (4) *1912* (3)
Plimsoll, J. B. 1: *v E 1947*
Poore, R. M. 3: v E 1895 (3)
Powell, A. W. 1: v E 1898
Prince, C. F. 1: v E 1898
Promnitz, H. L. E. 2: v E 1927 (2)

Quinn, N. A. 12: v E 1930 (1); *v E 1929* (4); *v A 1931* (5); *v NZ 1931* (2)

Reid, N. 1: v A 1921
Richards, A. 1: v E 1895
Richards, W. H. 1: v E 1888
Robertson, J. B. 3: v A 1935 (3)
Routledge, T. 4: v E 1891 (1) 1895 (3)
Rowan, A. M. B. 15: v E 1948 (5); *v E 1947* (5) *1951* (5)
Rowan, E. A. B. 26: v E 1938 (4) 1948 (4); v A 1935 (3) 1949 (5); *v E 1935* (5) *1951* (5)
Rowe, G. A. 5: v E 1895 (2) 1898 (2); v A 1902 (1)

Samuelson, S. V. 1: v E 1909
Schwarz, R. O. 20: v E 1905 (5) 1909 (4); *v E 1907* (3) *1912* (1): *v A 1910* (5) *1912* (2)
Seccull, A. W. 1: v E 1895
Shalders, W. A. 12: v E 1898 (1) 1905 (5); v A 1902 (3); *v E 1907* (3)
Shepstone, G. H. 2: v E 1895 (1) 1898 (1)
Sherwell, P. W. 13: v E 1905 (5); *v E 1907* (3); *v A 1910* (5)
Siedle, I. J. 18: v E 1927 (1) 1930 (5); v A 1935 (5); *v E 1929* (3) *1935* (4)
Sinclair, J. H. 25: v E 1895 (3) 1898 (2) 1905 (5) 1909 (4); v A 1902 (3); *v E 1907* (3); *v A 1910* (5)
Smith, C. J. E. 3; v A 1902 (3)
Smith, F. W. 3: v E 1888 (2) 1895 (1)
Smith, V. I. 8: v A 1949 (3); *v E 1947* (4) *1955* (1)
Snooke, S. D. 1: v E 1907
Snooke, S. J. 26: v E 1905 (5) 1909 (5) 1922 (3); *v E 1907* (3) *1912* (3); *v A 1910* (5) *1912* (2)
Solomon, W. R. 1: v E 1898
Stewart, R. B. 1: v E 1888
Stricker, L. A. 13: v E 1909 (4); *v E 1912* (2); *v A 1910* (5) *1912* (2)
Susskind, M. J. 5: *v E 1924* (5)

Taberer, H. M. 1: v A 1902
Tancred, A. B. 2: v E 1888 (2)
Tancred, L. J. 14: v E 1905 (5) 1913 (1); v A 1902 (3); *v E 1907* (1) *1912* (2); *v A 1912* (2)
Tancred, V. M. 1: v E 1898
Tapscott, L. E. 2: v E 1922 (2)
Tapscott, L. G. 1: v E 1913
Tayfield, H. J. 22: v A 1949 (5); v NZ 1953 (5); *v E 1955* (5); *v A 1952* (5); *v NZ 1952* (2)
Taylor, D. 2: v E 1913 (2)
Taylor, H. W. 42: v E 1913 (5) 1922 (5) 1927 (5) 1930 (4); v A 1921 (3); *v E 1912* (3) *1924* (5) *1929* (3); *v A 1912* (3) *1931* (5); *v NZ 1931* (1)
Theunissen, N. H. 1: v E 1888
Thornton, G. 1: v A 1902
Tomlinson, D. S. 1: *v E 1935*

Tuckett, L. 9: v E 1948 (4); *v E 1947 (5)*
Tuckett, L. R. 1: v E 1913

Van der Bijl, P. G. 5: v E 1938 (5)
Van der Merwe, E. A. 2: v A 1935 (1); *v E 1929 (1)*
Van Ryneveld, C. B. 10: v NZ 1953 (5); *v E 1951 (5)*
Viljoen, K. G. 27: v E 1930 (3) 1938 (4) 1948 (2); v A 1935 **(4)**; *v E 1935* **(4)**
    1947 (5); v A 1931 (4); v NZ 1931 (1)
Vincent, C. L. 25: v E 1927 (5) 1930 (5); *v E 1929 (4); 1935 (4);* **v** *A 1931 (5);*
    v NZ 1931 (2)
Vintcent, C. H. 3: v E 1888 (2) 1891 (1)
Vogler, A. E. 15: v E 1905 (5) 1909 (5); *v E 1907 (3); v A 1910 (2)*

Wade, H. F. 10: v A 1935 (5); *v E 1935 (5)*
Wade, W. W .11: v E 1938 (3) 1948 (5); v A 1949 (3)
Waite, J. H. B. 21: v NZ 1953 (5); *v E 1951 (4) 1955 (5);* v A 1952 (5); *v NZ
    1952 (2)*
Ward, T. A. 23: v E 1913 (5) 1922 (5); v A 1921 (3); *v E 1912 (2) 1924 (5);
    v A 1912 (3)*
Watkins, J. C. 13: v A 1949 (3); v NZ 1953 (3); *v A 1952 (5); v NZ 1952 (2)*
Westcott, R. J. 3: v NZ 1953 (3)
White, G. C. 17: v E 1905 (5) 1909 (4); *v E 1907 (3) 1912 (2); v A 1912 (3)*
Willoughby, J. T. I. 2: v E 1895 (2)
Wimble, C. S. 1: v E 1891
Winslow, P. 5: v A 1949 (2); *v E 1955 (3)*
Wynne, O. E. 6: v E 1948 (3); v A 1949 (3)

Zulch, J. W. 16: v E 1909 (5) 1913 (3); v A 1921 (3); *v A 1910 (5)*

WEST INDIES

Achong, E. 6: v E 1929 (1) 1934 (2): *v E 1933 (3)*
Atkinson, D. 15: v E 1953 (4); v A 1955 (4); *v A 1951 (2); v NZ 1951 (1); v In
    1948 (4)*

Barrow, I. 11: v E 1929 (1) 1934 (1); *v E 1933 (3) 1939 (1); v A 1930 (5)*
Bartlett, E. L. 5: *v E 1928 (1); v A 1930 (4)*
Betancourt, N. 1: v E 1929
Binns, A. P. 2: v A 1955 (1); v In 1952 (1)
Birkett, L. S. 4: *v A 1930 (4)*
Browne, C. R. 4: v E 1929 (2); *v E 1928 (2)*
Butler, L. 1: v A 1955

Caires, F. I. de 3: v E 1929 (3)
Cameron, F. J. 5: *v In 1948 (5)*
Cameron, J. H. 2: *v E 1939 (2)*
Carew, G. 4: v E 1934 (1) 1947 (2); *v In 1948 (1)*
Challenor, G. 3: *v E 1928 (3)*
Christiani, C. M. 4: v E 1934 (4)
Christiani, R. J. 22: v E 1947 (4) 1953 (1); v In 1952 (2); *v E 1950 (4); v A
    1951 (5); v NZ 1951 (1); v In 1948 (5)*
Clarke, C. B. 3: *v E 1939 (3)*
Constantine, L. N. 18: v E 1929 (3) 1934 (3); *v E 1928 (3) 1933 (1) 1939 (3);
    v A 1930 (5)*
Cosra, O. C. da, 5: v E 1929 (1) 1934 (1); *v E 1933 (3)*

Depeiza, C. 3: v A 1955 (3)
Dewdney, T. 2: v A 1955 (2)

Ferguson, W. 8: v E 1947 (4) 1953 (1); *v In 1948 (3)*
Fernandes, M. P. 2: v E 1929 (1); *v E 1928 (1)*
Francis, G. N. 10: v E 1929 (1); *v E 1928 (3) 1933 (1); v A 1930 (5)*

Frederick, M. 1: v E 1953
Fuller, R. L. 1: v E 1934
Furlonge, H. 1: v A 1955

Ganteaume, A. 1: v E 1947
Gaskin, B. 2: v E 1947 (2)
Gibbs, G. 1: v A 1955
Gladstone, G. 1: v E 1929
Goddard, J. D. 19: v E 1947 (4); *v E 1950 (4)*; *v A 1951 (4)*; *v NZ 1951 (2)*; *v In 1948 (5)*
Gomez, G. E. 29: v E 1947 (4) 1953 (4); v In 1952 (4); *v E 1939 (2) 1950 (4)*; *v A 1951 (5)*; *v NZ 1951 (1)*; *v In 1948 (5)*
Grant, G. C. 12: v E 1934 (4); *v E 1933 (3)*; *v A 1930 (5)*
Grant, R. S. 7: v E 1934 (4); *v E 1939 (3)*
Grell, M. 1: v E 1929
Griffith, H. C. 13: v E 1929 (3); *v E 1928 (3) 1933 (2)*; *v A 1930 (5)*
Guillen, S. 5: *v A 1951 (3)*; *v NZ 1951 (2)*

Headley, G. 22: v E 1929 (4) 1934 (4) 1947 (1) 1953 (1); *v E 1933 (3) 1939 (3)*; *v A 1930 (5)*; *v In 1948 (1)*
Hoad. E. L. G. 4: v E 1929 (1); *v E 1928 (1) 1933 (2)*
Holt, J. K. 10: v E 1953 (5); v A 1955 (5)
Hunte, E. 2: v E 1929 (2)
Hunte, R. L. 1: v E 1929
Hylton, L. G. 6: v E 1934 (4); *v E 1939 (2)*

Johnson, H. H. 3: v E 1947 (1); *v E 1950 (2)*
Johnson, T. 1: *v E 1939*
Jones, C. M. 4: v E 1929 (1) 1934 (3)
Jones, P. E. 9: v E 1947 (1); *v E 1950 (2)*; *v A 1951 (1)*; *v In 1948 (5)*

Kentish, E. 2: v E 1947 (1) 1953 (1)
King, F. 12: v E 1953 (3); v A 1955 (4); v In 1952 (5)

Legall, R. 4: v In 1952 (4)

McWatt, C. A. 6: v E 1953 (5), v A 1955 (1)
Marshall, N. 1: v A 1955
Marshall, R. E. 4: *v A 1951 (2)*; *v NZ 1951 (2)*
Martin, F. R. 9: v E 1929 (1); *v E 1928 (3)*; *v A 1930 (5)*
Martindale, E. A. 10: v E 1934 (4); *v E 1933 (3) 1939 (3)*
Merry, C. A. 2: *v E 1933 (2)*
Miller, R. 1: v In 1952
Moodie, G. H. 1: v E 1934

Neblett, J. 1: v E 1934
Nunes, R. K. 4: v E 1929 (1); *v E 1928 (3)*

Pairaudeau, B. H. 7: v E 1953 (2); v In 1952 (5)
Passalaique, C. 1: v E 1929
Pierre, L. R. 1: v E 1947

Rae, A. F. 15: v In 1952 (2); *v E 1950 (4)*; *v A 1951 (3)*; *v NZ 1951 (1)*; *v In 1948 (5)*
Ramadhin, S. 24: v E 1953 (5); v A 1955 (4); v In 1952 (4); *v E 1950 (4) v A 1951 (5)*; *v NZ 1951 (2)*
Rickards, K. 2: v E 1947 (1); *v A 1951 (1)*
Roach, C. A. 16: v E 1929 (4) 1934 (1); *v E 1928 (3) 1933 (3)*; *v A 1930 (5)*

St. Hill, E. 2: v E 1929 (2)
St. Hill, W. H. 3: v E 1929 (1); *v E 1928 (2)*
Scott, A. P. H. 1: v In 1952
Scott, O. C. 8: v E 1929 (1); *v E 1928 (2)*; *v A 1930 (5)*

Sealey, B. J. 1: v *E 1933*
Sealy, J. E. D. 11: v E 1929 (2) 1934 (4); v *A 1939 (3)*; v *A 1930 (2)*
Small, J. A. 3: v E 1929 (1); v *E 1928 (2)*
Smith, C. 4: v A 1955 (4)
Sobers, G. 5: v E 1953 (1); v A 1955 (4)
Stollmeyer, J. B. 32: v E 1947 (2) 1953 (5); v A 1955 (2); v In 1952 (5); v *E 1939
    (3) 1950 (4)*; v *A 1951 (5)*; v *NZ 1951* (2); v *In 1948* (4)
Stollmeyer, V. H. 1: v *E 1939*

Trim, J. 4: v E 1947 (1); v *A 1951 (1)*; v *In 1948* (2)

Valentine, A. L. 22: v E 1953 (3); v A 1955 (3); v In 1952 (5); v *E 1950* (4); v
    A 1951 (5); v *NZ 1951* (2)
Valentine, V. A. 2: v *E 1933* (2)

Walcott, C. L. 33: v E 1947 (4) 1953 (5); v A 1955 (5); v In 1952 (5); v *E 1950* (4);
    v *A 1951* (3); v *NZ 1951* (2); v *In 1948* (5)
Walcott, L. A. 1: v E 1929
Weekes, E. 34: v E 1947 (4) 1953 (4); v A 1955 (5); v In 1952 (5); v *E 1950* (4);
    v *A 1951* (5); v *NZ 1951* (2); v *In 1948* (5)
Weekes, K. H. 2: v *E 1939* (2)
Wight, C. V. 2: v E 1929 (*1*); v *E 1928* (*1*)
Wight, L. 1: v In 1952
Wiles, C. A. 1: v *E 1933*
Williams, E. A. V. 4: v E 1947 (3); v *E 1939*
Wishart, K. L. 1: v E 1934
Worrell, F. M. 27: v E 1947 (3) 1953 (4); v A 1955 (4); v In 1952 (5); v *1950* (4);
    v *A 1951* (5); v *NZ 1951* (2)

NEW ZEALAND

Allcott, C. F. W. 6: v E 1929 (2); v SA 1931 (1); v *E 1931* (3)
Anderson, W. M. 1: v A 1946

Badcock, F. T. 7: v E 1929 (3) 1932 (2); v SA 1931 (2)
Beard, D. D. 2: v WI 1951 (2)
Beck, J. E. F. 4: v *SA 1953* (4)
Bell, W. 2: v *SA 1953* (2)
Blair, R. W. 7: v E 1955 (1); v SA 1952 (2); v *SA 1953* (4)
Blunt, R. C. 9: v E 1929 (4); v SA 1931 (2); v *E 1931* (3)
Burke, C. C. 1: v A 1946
Burtt, T. B. 10: v E 1947 (1) 1950 (2); v SA 1952 (1); v WI 1951 (2); v *E 1949* (4)
Butterfield, L. A. 1: v A 1946

Cave, H. B. 6: v E 1955 (2); v *E 1949* (4)
Chapple, M. E. 7: v E 1955 (1); v SA 1952 (1); v *SA 1953* (5)
Cleverley, D. C. 2: v SA 1931 (1); v A 1946 (1)
Colquhoun, I. A. 2: v E 1955 (2)
Cowie, J. 9: v E 1947 (1); v A 1946 (1); v *E 1937* (3) *1949* (4)
Cresswell, G. F. 3: v E 1950 (2); v *E 1949* (*1*)
Cromb, I. B. 5: v SA 1931 (2); v *E 1931* (3)

Dempster, C. S. 10: v E 1929 (4) 1932 (2); v SA 1931 (2); v *E 1931* (2)
Dempster, E. W. 5: v SA 1952 (1); v *SA 1953* (4)
Dickinson, G. R. 3: v E 1929 (2); v SA 1931 (1)
Dunning, J. A. 4: v E 1932 (1); v *E 1937* (3)
Donnelly, M. P. 7: v *E 1937* (3) *1949* (4)

Emery, R. W. G. 2: v WI 1951 (2)

Fisher, F. E. 1: v SA 1952
Foley, H. 1: v E 1929

Freeman, D. L. 2: v E 1932 (2)

Gallichan, N. M. 1: *v E 1937*

Hadlee, W. A. 11: v E 1947 (1) 1950 (2): v A 1946 (1); *v E 1937 (3) 1949 (4)*
Hayes, J. A. 5: v E 1950 (2) 1955 (1); v WI 1951 (2)
Henderson, M. 1; v E 1929

James, K. C. 11: v E 1929 (4) 1932 (2); v SA 1931 (2); *v E 1931 (3)*

Kerr, J. L. 7: v E 1932 (2); v SA 1931 (1); *v E 1931 (2) 1937 (2)*

Leggat, I. B. 1: *v SA 1953*
Leggatt, J. G. 3: v E 1955 (1); v SA 1952 (1); v WI 1951 (1)
Lowry, T. C. 7: v E 1929 (4); *v E 1931 (3)*

MacGibbon, A. R. 10: v E 1950 (2) 1955 (2); v SA 1952 (1); *v SA 1953 (5)*
McGirr, H. M 2: v E 1929 (2)
McGregor, S. N. 2: v E 1955 (2)
McLeod, E. A. 1: v E 1929
McRae, D. A. N. 1: v A 1946
Maloney, D. A. R. 3: *v E 1937 (3)*
Matheson, A. M. 2: v E 1929 (1): *v E 1931 (1)*
Merritt, W. E. 6: v E 1929 (4); *v E 1931 (2)*
Meuli, E. M. 1: v SA 1952
Miller, L. S. M. 6: v SA 1952 (2); *v SA 1953 (4)*
Mills, J. W. E. 7: v E 1929 (3) 1932 (1); *v E 1931 (3)*
Moir, A. M. 7: v E 1950 (2) 1955 (2); v SA 1952 (1); v WI 1951 (2)
Mooney, F. L. H. 14: v E 1950 (2); v SA 1952 (2); v WI 1951 (2); *v E 1949 (3); v SA 1953 (5)*

Newman, J. 3: v E 1932 (2); v SA 1931 (1)

Overton, G. W. F. 3: *v SA 1953 (3)*

Page, M. L. 14: v E 1929 (4) 1932 (2): v SA 1931 (2): *v E 1931 (3) 1937 (3)*
Poore, M. B. 7: v E 1955 (1); v SA 1952 (1); *v SA 1953 (5)*

Rabone, G. O. 12: v E 1955 (2); v SA 1952 (1); v WI (1951 (2); *v E 1949 (4); v SA 1953 (3)*
Reid, J. R. 15: v E 1950 (2) 1955 (2); v SA 1952 (2); v WI 1951 (2); *v E 1949 (2); v SA 1953 (5)*
Roberts, A. W. 5: v E 1929 (1); v SA 1931 (2); *v E 1937 (2)*
Rowe, C. G. 1: v A 1946

Scott, R. H. 1: v E 1947
Scott, V. J. 10: v E 1947 (1) 1950 (2); v A 1946 (1); v WI 1951 (2); *v E 1949 (4)*
Smith, D. 1: v E 1932
Smith, F. B. 4: v E 1947 (1); v WI 1951 (1); *v E 1949 (2)*
Snedden, C. A. 1: v E 1947
Sutcliffe, B. 18: v E 1947 (1) 1950 (2) 1955 (2); v SA 1952 (2); v WI 1951 (2); *v E 1949 (4); v SA 1953 (5)*

Taylor, D. D. 1: v E 1947
Tindill, E. W. 5: v E 1947 (1); v A 1946 (1); *v E 1937 (3)*

Vivian. H. G. 7: v E 1932 (1); v SA 1931 (1); *v E 1931 (2) 1937 (3)*

Wallace, W. M. 13: v E 1947 (1) 1950 (2); v A 1946 (1); v SA 1952 (2); *v E 1937 (3) 1949 (4)*
Watt, L. A. 1: v E 1955
Weir, G. L. 11: v E 1929 (3) 1932 (2); v SA 1931 (2); *v E 1931 (3) 1937 (1)*
Whitelaw, D. 2: v E 1932 (2)

INDIA

Adhikari, H. R. 18: v E 1951 (3); v WI 1948 (5); v P 1952 (2); *v E 1952 (3)*;
v A 1947 (5)
Ali, S. Nazir, 2: v E 1933 (1); *v E 1932 (1)*
Ali, S. Wazir, 7: v E 1933 (3); *v E 1932 (1) 1936 (3)*
Amarnath, L. 24: v E 1933 (3) 1951 (3); v WI 1948 (5); v P 1952 (5); *v E 1946 (3)*;
v A 1947 (5)
Amar Singh 7: v E 1933 (3); *v E 1932 (1) 1936 (3)*
Amir Elahi 1: *v A 1947*
Apte, M. L. 7: v P 1952 (2); *v WI 1952 (5)*

Banerjee, S. N. 1: v WI 1948
Banerjee, Sunil, 1: v WI 1948
Bhandari, P. 1: *v P 1954*

Chowdhury, N. 2: v E 1951 (1); v WI 1948 (1)
Colah, S. H. M. 2: v E 1933 (1); *v E 1932 (1)*

Dani, H. T. 1: v P 1952
Divecha, R. V. 5: v E 1951 (2); v P 1952 (1); *v E 1952 (2)*

Gadkari, C. V. 6: *v WI 1952 (3)*; *v P 1954 (3)*
Gaekwad, D. K. 5: v P 1952 (2); *v E 1952 (1)*; *v WI 1952 (2)*
Gaekwad, H. G. 1: v P 1952
Ghorpade, J. M. 2: *v WI 1952 (2)*
Ghulam Ahmed 17: v E 1951 (2); v WI 1948 (3); v P 1952 (4); *v E 1952 (4)*;
v P 1954 (4)
Gopalan, M. 1: v E 1933
Gopinath, C. D. 7: v E 1951 (3); v P. 1952 (1); *v E 1952 (1)*; *v P 1954 (2)*
Gupte, S. P. 13: v E 1951 (1); v P 1952 (2); *v WI 1952 (5)*; *v P 1954 (5)*

Hafeez, A. 3: *v E 1946 (3)*
Hazare, V. S. 30: v E 1951 (5); v WI 1948 (5); v P 1952 (3); *v E 1946 (3) 1952 (4)*;
v A 1947 (5); *v WI 1952 (5)*
Hindlekar, D. D. 4: *v E 1936 (1) 1946 (3)*
Hussain, Dilawar, 3: v E 1933 (2); *v E 1936 (1)*

Ibrahim, K. C. 4: v WI 1948 (4)
Irani, J. K. 2: *v A 1947 (2)*

Jai, L. P. 1: v E 1933
Jamshedji, R. J. 1: v E 1933
Jahangir Khan, M. 4: *v E 1932 (1) 1936 (3)*
Jilani, M. Baqa, 1: *v E 1936*
Joshi, P. G. 6: v E 1951 (2); v P 1952 (1); *v WI 1952 (3)*

Kardar, A. H., *see* Hafeez
Kishenchand, G. 5: v P 1952 (1); *v A 1947 (4)*

Lall Singh 1: *v E 1932*

Maka, E. S. 2: v P 1952 (1); *v WI 1952 (1)*
Mankad V. 35: v E 1951 (5): v WI 1948 (5); v P 1952 (4); *v E 1946 (3) 1952 (3)*;
v A 1947 (5); *v WI 1952 (5)*; *v P 1954 (5)*
Manjrekar, V. L. 18: v E 1951 (2); v P 1952 (3); *v E 1952 (4)*; *v WI 1952 (4)*;
v P 1954 (5)
Mantri, M. K. 4: v E 1951 (1); *v E 1952 (2)*; *v P 1954 (1)*
Meherhomji, K. R. 1: *v E 1936*
Merchant, V. M. 10; v E 1933 (3) 1951 (1); *v E 1936 (3) 1946 (3)*
Modi, R. S. 10: v E 1951 (1); v WI 1948 (5); v P 1952 (1); *v E 1946 (3)*
Mushtaq Ali 11: v E 1933 (2) 1951 (1); v WI 1948 (3); *v E 1936 (3) 1946 (2)*

Naoomal Jeoomal 3: v E 1933 (2); *v E 1932 (1)*
Navle, J. G. 2: v E 1933 (1); *v E 1932 (1)*
Nayudu, C. K. 7: v E 1933 (3); *v E 1932 (1) 1936 (3)*
Nayudu, C. S. 11: v E 1933 (2) 1951 (1); *v E 1936 (2) 1946 (2); v A 1947 (4)*
Nissar, Mahomed 6: v E 1933 (2); *v E 1932 (1) 1936 (3)*
Nyalchand, K. 1: v P 1952

Palia, P. E. 2: *v E 1932 (1) 1936 (1)*
Pataudi, Nawab of, 3: *v E 1946 (3)*
Patel, J. S. 1: *v P 1954.*
Patiala, Yuvraj of, 1: v E 1933
Phadkar, D. G. 25: v E 1951 (4); v WI 1948 (4); v P 1952 (2);*v E 1952 (4); v A 1947 (4); v WI 1952 (4); v P 1954 (3)*
Punjabi, P. L. 5: *v P 1954 (5)*

Rai Singh 1: *v A 1947*
Rajindernath, V. 1: v P 1952
Ramaswami, C. 2: *v E 1936 (2)*
Ramchand, G. S. 17: v P 1952 (3); *v E 1952 (4); v WI 1952 (5); v P 1954 (5)*
Ramji, L. 1: v E 1933
Rangachari, C. 4: v WI 1948 (2); *v A 1947 (2)*
Rangnekar, K. M. 3: *v A 1947 (3)*
Rege, M. 1: v WI 1948
Roy, P. 21: v E 1951 (5); v P 1952 (3); *v E 1952 (4); v WI 1952 (4); v P 1954 (5)*

Sarwate, C. T. 9: v E 1951 (1); v WI 1948 (2); *v E 1946 (1); v A 1947 (5)*
Sen, P. 14: v E 1951 (2); v WI 1948 (5); v P 1952 (2); *v E 1952 (2); v A 1947 (3)*
Shinde, S. G. 7: v E 1951 (3) v WI 1948 (1); *v E 1946 (1) 1952 (2)*
Shodhan, D. H. 3: v P 1952 (1); *v WI 1952 (2)*
Sohoni, S. W. 4: v E 1951 (1); *v E 1946 (2); v A 1947 (1)*

Tamhane, N S. 5: *v P 1954*(5)
Tarpore, K. 1: v WI 1948

Umrigar, P. R. 25: v E 1951 (5); v WI 1948 (1); v P 1952 (5); *v E 1952 (4); v WI 1952 (5); v P 1954 (5)*

Vizianagram, Maharaj Sir Vijaya, 3: *v E 1936 (3)*

Note.—Hafeez, on going later to Oxford University, took his correct name, Kardar.

PAKISTAN

Alim-ud-Din 8: v In 1954 (5); *v E 1954 (3)*
Amir Elahi 5: *v In 1952 (5)*
Anwar Hussain 4: *v In 1952 (4)*

Fazal Mahmood 13: v In 1954 (4); *v E 1954 (4); v In 1952 (5)*

Ghazali, M. E. Z. 2: *v E 1954 (2)*

Hanif Mohammad 14: v In 1954 (5); *v E 1954 (4); v In 1952 (5)*

Imtiaz Ahmed 14: v In 1954 (5); *v E 1954 (4); v In 1952 (5)*
Israr Ali 2: *v In 1952 (2)*

Kardar, A. H. 14: v In 1954 (5); *v E 1954 (4); v In 1952 (5)*
Khalid Hassan 1: *v E 1954*
Khalid Wazir 2: *v E 1954 (2)*
Khan Mohammad 7: v In 1954 (4); *v E 1954 (2); v In 1952 (1)*

Mahmood Hussain 11: v In 1954 (5); *v E 1954* (2); *v In 1952* (4)
Maqsood Ahmed 14: v In 1954 (5); *v E 1954* (4); *v In 1952* (5)
Miran Bux 2: v In 1954 (2)
Mohammad Aslam 1: *v E 1954*

Nazar Mohammad 5: *v In 1952* (5)

Shuja-ud-Din 8: v In 1954 (5); *v E 1954* (3)

Waqar Hassan 14: v In 1954 (5); *v E 1954* (4); *v In 1952* (5)
Wazir Mohammad 8: v In 1954 (5); *v E 1954* (2); *v In 1952* (1)

Zulfiqar Ahmed 5: *v E 1954* (2); *v In 1952* (3)

Ten cricketers have appeared for two countries in Test Matches, namely:

W. E. Midwinter, for England v. Australia and for Australia v. England;
J. J. Ferris, W. L. Murdoch, A. E. Trott and S. M. J. Woods, for Australia
v. England and for England v. South Africa. F. Mitchell played for England
v. South Africa and for South Africa v. England and v. Australia; F. Hearne
played for England v. South Africa and for South Africa v. England; Nawab of
Pataudi played for England v. Australia and for India v. England; A. H. Kardar
(Hafeez) played for India v. England and for Pakistan v. England and v. India;
Amir Elahi played for India v. Australia and for Pakistan v. India.

CRICKET RECORDS

AMENDED BY G. A. COPINGER TO SEPTEMBER 30, 1955

Unless otherwise stated, all records, apart from Throwing the Cricket Ball, apply only to first-class cricket.

* denotes "not out" or an unfinished partnership.

(A), (S.A.), (W.I.), (N.Z.), or (I) indicates either the nationality of the player, or the country in which the record was made.

INDEX

BATTING

BOWLING AND FIELDING

THE SIDES

TEST MATCH RECORDS

VARIA

INDIVIDUAL SCORES OF 300 OR MORE

452*	D. G. Bradman, New South Wales v. Queensland, at Sydney	1929–30
443*	B. B. Nimbalkar, Maharashtra v. Western India States, at Poona	1948–49
437	W. H. Ponsford, Victoria v. Queensland, at Melbourne	1927–28
429	W. H. Ponsford, Victoria v. Tasmania, at Melbourne	1922–23
424	A. C. MacLaren, Lancashire v. Somerset, at Taunton	1895
385	B. Sutcliffe, Otago v. Canterbury, at Christchurch	1952–53
383	C. W. Gregory, New South Wales v. Queensland, at Brisbane	1906–07
369	D. G. Bradman, South Australia v. Tasmania, at Adelaide	1935–36
365*	C. Hill, South Australia v. New South Wales, at Adelaide	1900–01
364†	Hutton (L.), England v. Australia, at The Oval	1938
359*	V. M. Merchant, Bombay v. Maharashtra, at Bombay	1943–44
357*	Abel (R.), Surrey v. Somerset, at The Oval	1899
357	D. G. Bradman, South Australia v. Victoria, at Melbourne	1935–36
355	B. Sutcliffe, Otago v. Auckland, at Dunedin	1949–50
352	W. H. Ponsford, Victoria v. New South Wales, at Melbourne	1926–27
345	C. G. Macartney, Australia v. Nottinghamshire, at Nottingham	1921
344*	G. Headley, All Jamaica v. Lord Tennyson's Team, at Kingston	1931–32
344	W. G. Grace, M.C.C. v. Kent, at Canterbury	1876
343*	P. A. Perrin, Essex v. Derbyshire, at Chesterfield	1904
341	Hirst (G. H.), Yorkshire v. Leicestershire, at Leicester	1905
340*	D. G. Bradman, New South Wales v. Victoria, at Sydney	1928–29
338*	R. C. Blunt, Otago v. Canterbury, at Canterbury	1931–32
338	W. W. Read, Surrey v. Oxford University, at The Oval	1888
336	W. H. Ponsford, Victoria v. New South Wales, at Melbourne	1927–28
336*	Hammond (W. R.), England v. New Zealand, at Auckland	1932–33
334	D. G. Bradman, Australia v. England, at Leeds	1930
333	K. S. Duleepsinhji, Sussex v. Northamptonshire, at Hove	1930
332	Ashdown (W. H.), Kent v. Essex, at Brentwood	1934

† Hutton batted 13 hours 20 minutes—the longest innings in first-class cricket.

331* Robertson (J. D.), Middlesex v. Worcestershire, at Worcester ..		1949
325* H. L. Hendry, Victoria v. New Zealand, at Melbourne		1925–26
325 C. L. Badcock, South Australia v. Victoria, at Adelaide		1935–36
325 Sandham (A.), England v. West Indies, at Kingston ..		1929–30
324 J. B. Stollmeyer, Trinidad v. British Guiana, at Port of Spain ..		1946–47
322 Paynter (E.), Lancashire v. Sussex, at Hove		1937
321 W. L. Murdoch, New South Wales v. Victoria, at Sydney ..		1881–82
319 Gul Mahomed, Baroda v. Holkar, at Baroda		1946–7
318* W. G. Grace, Gloucestershire v. Yorkshire, at Cheltenham ..		1876
317 Hammond (W. R.), Gloucestershire v. Notts, at Gloucester		1936
316* V. S. Hazare, Maharashtra v. Baroda, at Poona		1939–40
316* Hobbs (J. B.), Surrey v. Middlesex, at Lord's ..		1926
316 R. H. Moore, Hampshire v. Warwickshire, at Bournemouth ..		1937
315* Hayward (T.), Surrey v. Lancashire, at The Oval		1898
315* Holmes (P.), Yorkshire v. Middlesex, at Lord's ..		1925
315* A. F. Kippax, New South Wales v. Queensland, at Sydney ..		1927–28
314* C. L. Walcott, Barbados v. Trinidad, at Port of Spain ..		1945–46
313 Sutcliffe (H.), Yorkshire v. Essex, at Leyton		1932
312* Keeton (W. W.), Nottinghamshire v. Middlesex, at The Oval‡ ..		1939
311 Brown (J. T.), Yorkshire v. Sussex, at Sheffield		1897
310 Gimblett (H.), Somerset v. Sussex, at Eastbourne ..		1948
309 V. S. Hazare, The Rest v. Hindus, at Brabourne Stadium ..		1943–44
308* F. M. Worrell, Barbados v. Trinidad, at Bridgetown ..		1943–44
306* Ducat (A.), Surrey v. Oxford University, at The Oval ..		1919
306* E. A. B. Rowan, Transvaal v. Natal, at Johannesburg ..		1939–40
305* Woolley (F. E.), M.C.C. v. Tasmania, at Hobart		1911–12
305* F. R. Foster, Warwickshire v. Worcestershire, at Dudley ..		1914
305* Ashdown (W. H.), Kent v. Derbyshire, at Dover ..		1935
304* P. H. Tarilton, Barbados v. Trinidad, at Kensington (Barbados)		1919–20
304* A. D. Nourse, sen., Natal v. Transvaal, at Johannesburg ..		1919–20
304* E. D. Weekes, West Indies v. Cambridge University, at Cambridge		1950
304 R. M. Poore, Hampshire v. Somerset, at Taunton		1899
304 D. G. Bradman, Australia v. England, at Leeds		1934
303* W. W. Armstrong, Australia v. Somerset, at Bath		1905
302* Holmes (P.), Yorkshire v. Hampshire, at Portsmouth ..		1920
302* Hammond (W. R.), Gloucestershire v. Glamorgan, at Bristol ..		1934
302 W. R. Hammond, Gloucestershire v. Glamorgan, at Newport ..		1939
301 W. G. Grace, Gloucestershire v. Sussex, at Bristol ..		1896
301* Hendren (E.), Middlesex v. Worcestershire, at Dudley ..		1933
300* Imtiaz Ahmed, Prime Minister's XI v. Commonwealth XI, at Bombay		1950–51
300* V. T. Trumper, Australia v. Sussex, at Hove		1899
300* Watson (F.), Lancashire v. Surrey, at Manchester.. ..		1928
300 Brown (J. T.), Yorkshire v. Derbyshire, at Chesterfield ..		1898
300 Compton (D. C. S.). M.C.C. v. N.E. Transvaal, at Benoni ' ..		1948–49

HIGHEST FOR TEAMS

INDIVIDUAL SCORES

For English Teams in Australia

305* Woolley (F. E.), M.C.C. v. Tasmania, at Hobart		1911–12
287 R. E. Foster, England v. Australia, at Sydney		1903–04

Against Australians in England

364 Hutton (L.), for England v. Australia, at The Oval (in any match)		1938
219 Sandham (A.), for Surrey, at The Oval (record for any county)..		1934

For Australian Teams in England

345 C. G. Macartney, v. Nottinghamshire, at Nottingham		1921
334 D. G. Bradman, Australia v. England, at Leeds		1930

AGAINST ENGLISH TEAMS IN AUSTRALIA

280 A. J. Richardson, South Australia v. M.C.C., at Adelaide   .. 1922–23
270 D. G. Bradman, Australia v. England, at Melbourne (in any
     home Test) 1936–37

FOR EACH FIRST-CLASS COUNTY

Derbyshire	..	274 Davidson (G.), v. Lancashire, at Manchester ..	1896
Essex	..	343* P. A. Perrin, v. Derbyshire, at Chesterfield ..	1904
Glamorgan	..	287* Davies (E.), v. Gloucestershire, at Newport ..	1939
Gloucestershire	..	318* W. G. Grace, v. Yorkshire, at Cheltenham ..	1876
Hampshire	..	316 R. H. Moore, v. Warwickshire, at Bournemouth	1937
Kent	..	332 Ashdown (W. H.), v. Essex, at Brentwood ..	1934
Lancashire	..	424 A. C. MacLaren, v. Somerset, at Taunton ..	1895
Leicestershire	..	252* Coe (S.), v. Northamptonshire, at Leicester ..	1914
Middlesex	..	331* Robertson (J. D.), v. Worcestershire, at Worcester	1949
Northamptonshire		260* R. Subba Row, v. Lancashire, at Northampton	1955
Nottinghamshire..		312* Keeton (W. W.), v. Middlesex, at The Oval‡	1939
Somerset ..		310 Gimblett (H.), v. Sussex, at Eastbourne ..	1948
Surrey	..	357* Abel (R.), v. Somerset, at The Oval ..	1899
Sussex	..	333 K. S. Duleepsinhji, v. Northants, at Hove ..	1930
Warwickshire	..	305* F. R. Foster, v. Worcestershire, at Dudley	1914
Worcestershire	..	276 Bowley (F. L.), v. Hampshire, at Dudley	1914
Yorkshire	..	341 Hirst (G. H.), v. Leicestershire, at Leicester	1905

‡ On this date Eton played Harrow at Lord's.

HIGHEST IN A MINOR COUNTY MATCH

323* F. E. Lacey, Hampshire v. Norfolk, at Southampton 1887

HIGHEST IN MINOR COUNTIES CHAMPIONSHIP

282 F. Garnet, Berkshire v. Wiltshire, at Reading   1908
254 H. E. Morgan, Glamorgan v. Monmouthshire, at Cardiff .. 1901
253* G. J. Whittaker, Surrey II v. Gloucestershire II, at The Oval .. 1950
253 A. Booth, Lancashire II v. Lincolnshire II, at Grimsby .. 1950
252 J. A. Deed, Kent II v. Surrey II, at The Oval   1924

HIGHEST IN AN IMPORTANT SCHOOL MATCH IN ENGLAND

278 J. L. Guise, Winchester v. Eton, at Eton 1921

HIGHEST IN OTHER MATCHES

628* A. E. J. Collins, Clarke's House v. North Town, at Clifton College.
     (A Junior House match. His innings of 6 hours 50 minutes was
     spread over five afternoons)   1899
566 C. J. Eady, Break-o'-Day v. Wellington, at Hobart 1901–02
506* J. C. Sharp, Melbourne G.S. v. Geelong Coll., at Melbourne .. 1914–15
485 A. E. Stoddart, Hampstead v. Stoics, at Hampstead 1886
466* G. T. S. Stevens, Beta v. Lambda (University College School House
     Match), at Neasden   1919
459 J. A. Prout, Wesley Coll. v. Geelong Coll., at Geelong 1908–09
438 W. W. Armstrong, Melbourne v. Melbourne University, at
     Melbourne   1903–04
419* J. S. Carrick, West of Scotland v. Priory Park, at Chichester .. 1885
417* J. Worrall, Carlton v. Melbourne University   1895–96
415* W. N. Roe, Emmanuel College, L.V.C. v. Caius College L.V.C.,
     at Cambridge   1881
412* M. I. Yusef, Government Indian School v. Star Club, at Bulawayo 1936–37
404* E. F. S. Tylecote, Classical v. Modern, at Clifton College .. 1868
402* A. H. Du Boulay, School of Military Engineering v. Royal Navy
     and Royal Marines, at Chatham 1907

HUNDRED ON DEBUT IN ENGLAND

(The following list does not include instances of players who have previously appeared in first-class cricket outside England.)

114	Bacon (F. H.), Hampshire v. Warwickshire, at Birmingham	..	1894
107*	G. Barker, Essex v. Canadians, at Clacton	..	1954
116*	B. L. Bisgood, Somerset v. Worcestershire, at Worcester	..	1907
107*	H. O. Bloomfield, Surrey v. Northamptonshire, at Northampton	..	1921
124	G. J. Bryan, Kent v. Nottinghamshire, at Nottingham	..	†1920
100	J. F. Byrne, Warwickshire v. Leicestershire, at Birmingham		1897
118	A. P. F. Chapman, Cambridge University v. Essex, at Cambridge		1920
101*	S. H. Day, Kent v. Gloucestershire, at Cheltenham	..	†1897
176	F. C. de Saram, Oxford University v. Gloucestershire, at Oxford	..	1934
108	E. W. Dillon, London County v. Worcestershire, at Crystal Palace		1900
215*	G. H. G. Doggart, Cambridge University v. Lancashire, at Cambridge		1948
137	C. H. M. Ebden, Camb. U. v. Leveson Gower's XI, at Cambridge		1902
108	A. Fairbairn, Middlesex v. Somerset, at Taunton	..	††‡1947
123	Gimblett (H.), Somerset v. Essex, at Frome	..	1935
101	P. M. Hall, Oxford University v. Free Foresters, at Oxford		1919
121	C. P. Hamilton, Army v. West Indies, at Aldershot		1933
156	M. N. Harbottle, Army v. Oxford University, at Camberley		1938
124	Hearn (P.), Kent v. Warwickshire, at Gillingham	..	1947
101	K. A. Higgs, Sussex v. Worcestershire, at Hove	..	1920
103*	A. L. Hilder, Kent v. Essex, at Gravesend	..	†1924
158*	J. H. Human, Camb. U. v. Leveson Gower's XI, at Eastbourne	..	1932
111*	C. F. H. Leslie, Oxford U., v. M.C.C. and Ground, at Oxford	..	1881
108	A. C. MacLaren, Lancashire v. Sussex, at Hove	..	1890
144	Marlow (F. W.), Sussex v. M.C.C. and Ground, at Lord's		1891
124	N. Miller, Surrey v. Sussex, at Hove	..	1899
100*	W. Murray Wood, Oxford University v. Gloucestershire, at Oxford		1936
164	Nichol (M.), Worcestershire v. West Indies, at Worcester	..	1928
101	C. A. L. Payne, M.C.C. and Ground v. Derbyshire, at Lord's	..	1905
138*	F. B. Pinch, Glamorgan v. Worcestershire, at Swansea	..	1921
124	H. C. Pretty, Surrey v. Nottinghamshire, at The Oval	..	1899
149	H. R. J. Rhys, Free Foresters v. Cambridge U., at Cambridge		1929
195*	Ricketts (J.), Lancashire v. Surrey, at The Oval		1867
137	J. G. C. Scott, Sussex v. Oxford University, at Eastbourne		1907
135	J. K. E. Slack, Cambridge University v. Middlesex, at Cambridge	..	1954
114	Stocks (F. W.), Nottinghamshire v. Kent, at Nottingham	..	1946
110	Hon. L. H. Tennyson, M.C.C. and Ground v. Oxford U., at Lord's		†1913
103	A. H. Trevor, Sussex v. Kent, at Hove	..	†1880
125	G. S. Tuck, Royal Navy v. New Zealanders, at Portsmouth		1927
100*	Tyson (C.), Yorkshire v. Hampshire, at Southampton	..	1921
102	I. D. Walker, Middlesex v. Surrey at The Oval	..	1862
131*	Whitehead (R.), Lancashire v. Nottinghamshire, at Manchester		1908
117*	E. R. Wilson, A. J. Webbe's XI v. Cambridge U., at Cambridge	..	1899
124	L. Winslow, Sussex v. Gloucestershire, at Hove	..	1875

A number of players abroad have also made a century on a first appearance.

The highest innings on debut was hit by W. F. E. Marx when he made 240 for Transvaal against Griqualand West at Johannesburg in 1920-21.

The following feats stand alone for a cricketer making two separate hundreds on debut: A. R. Morris, New South Wales, 148 and 111 against Queensland in 1940-41, and N. J. Contractor, Gujerat, 152 and 102 not out against Baroda in 1952-53.

† In second innings. S. H. Day, schoolboy at Malvern, aged 18.

‡ A. Fairbairn (Middlesex) in 1947 scored centuries in the second innings of his first two matches in first-class cricket: 108 Middlesex v. Somerset, at Taunton; 110* Middlesex v. Nottinghamshire, at Nottingham.

INDIVIDUAL HUNDREDS

(35 OR MORE)

	Hundreds Total	Abr'd	100th 100		Hundreds Total	Abr'd	100th 100
J. B. Hobbs ...	197	22	1923	W. G. Grace ..	126	1	1895
E. Hendren	170	19	1928	D. G. Bradman	117	76	1947–8
W. R. Hammond	167	33	1935	D. C. S. Compton	115	28	1952
C. P. Mead	153	8	1927	A. Sandham ..	107	20	1935
H. Sutcliffe	149	14	1932	T. Hayward ...	104	4	1913
F. E. Woolley..	145	10	1929	L. E. G. Ames ..	102	13	1950
L. Hutton	129	24	1934	E. Tyldesley ..	102	8	1934

J. W. Hearne ...	96	James Seymour ...	53	H. W. Parks ...	42
C. B. Fry	94	E. H. Bowley	52	T. F. Shepherd ...	42
J. T. Tyldesley ...	86	A. Ducat	52	V. T. Trumper ...	42
R. E. S. Wyatt ...	85	R. T. Simpson ...	52	J. Gunn	41
W. J. Edrich	83	W. W. Whysall ...	51	D. Kenyon	41
J. Hardstaff, junr. .	83	H. E. Dollery ...	50	A. D. Nourse, junr.	41
M. Leyland	80	H. Gimblett	50	J. H. Parks	41
John Langridge ...	76	V. S. Hazare	50	W. H. Ashdown ...	39
H. T. W. Hardinge	75	F. Watson	50	W. A. Brown ...	39
C. Washbrook	75	G. Cox, junr.	49	R. J. Gregory ...	39
R. Abel	74	K. S. Duleepsinhji.	49	W. R. D. Payton..	39
J. O'Connor	72	W. M. Woodfull ..	49	F. Bowley	38
W. G. Quaife ...	72	C. J. Barnett	48	A. D. Nourse, senr.	38
K. S. Ranjitsinhji. .	72	W. Gunn	48	N. Oldfield	38
A. C. Russell	71	E. G. Hayes	48	Rev. J. H. Parsons..	38
D. Denton	69	C. G. Macartney ..	48	W. W. Read	38
P. Holmes	67	T. W. Graveney ..	47	J. Sharp	38
P. A. Perrin	66	A. C. MacLaren ..	47	L. J. Todd	38
G. Gunn	62	P. B. H. May	47	J. Arnold	37
J. D. Robertson ..	61	W. H. Ponsford ...	47	G. Brown	37
G. H. Hirst	60	J. Iddon	46	J. F. Crapp	37
P. F. Warner	60	A. R. Morris	46	R. N. Harvey	37
D. Brookes	59	W. W. Armstrong .	45	H. W. Lee	37
A. L. Hassett ...	59	L. G. Berry	45	M. A. Noble	37
A. Shrewsbury ...	59	A. W. Carr	45	E. Oldroyd	37
A. E. Fagg	58	C. Hill	45	H. S. Squires......	37
W. Rhodes	58	E. Paynter	45	C. J. B. Wood ...	37
L. B. Fishlock	56	H. H. I. Gibbons .	44	N. F. Armstrong ..	36
C. Hallows	55	A. Mitchell	44	K. R. Miller	36
W. W. Keeton ...	54	A. F. Kippax	43	W. Place	36
W. Bardsley	53	H. Makepeace ...	43	Rev. D. S. Sheppard	36
A. E. Dipper.....	53	V. M. Merchant ..	43	C. S. Dempster....	35
G. L. Jessop	53	James Langridge ..	42	D. R. Jardine	35
				B. H. Valentine	35

In all cricket J. B. Hobbs hit 244 hundreds and W. G. Grace hit 217.

TWO SEPARATE HUNDREDS IN A MATCH

Seven Times: W. R. HAMMOND.

Six Times: J. B. HOBBS.

Five Times: C. B. FRY.

Four Times: D. G. BRADMAN, L. B. FISHLOCK, H. T. W. HARDINGE, E. HENDREN, G. L. JESSOP, P. A. PERRIN, B. SUTCLIFFE, H. SUTCLIFFE.

Three Times: L. E. G. AMES, D. C. S. COMPTON, D. DENTON, K. S. DULEEPSINHJI, R. E. FOSTER, W. G. GRACE, G. GUNN, T. HAYWARD, V. S. HAZARE, L. HUTTON, C. P. MEAD, A. C. RUSSELL, J. T. TYLDESLEY.

Twice: B. J. T. BOSANQUET, M. C. COWDREY, C. C. DACRE, G. M. EMMETT, A. E. FAGG, H. GIMBLETT, C. HALLOWS, R. HAMENCE, A. L. HASSETT, G. HEADLEY, J. H. KING, A. F. KIPPAX, JOHN LANGRIDGE, H. W. LEE, E. LESTER, G. C. B. LLEWELLYN, C. G. MACARTNEY, P. B. H. MAY, A. R. MORRIS, E. PAYNTER, W. RHODES, JAS. SEYMOUR, E. TYLDESLEY, C. L. WALCOTT, W. W. WHYSALL.

W. Lambert scored 107 and 157 for Sussex v. Epsom at Lord's in 1817 and it was not until W. G. Grace made 130 and 102* for South of the Thames v. North of the Thames at Canterbury in 1868 that the feat was repeated.

A. E. Fagg alone has scored two double hundreds in the same match; 244 and 202* for Kent v. Essex at Colchester, 1938.

W. L. Foster, 140 and 172*, and R. E. Foster, 134 and 101*, at Worcester against Hampshire in July 1899, set up a record by brothers both scoring two separate hundreds in the same first-class match. This remains unequalled.

G. Gunn, 183 and G. V. Gunn, 100* for Notts. v. Warwickshire at Birmingham in 1931, provide the only instance of father and son each hitting a century in the same innings of a first-class match.

Most Recent Instances

In 1954:—

140	and 105	G. H. G. Doggart	Sussex v. Oxford University, at Oxford.

In 1954–55:—

110	and 103	M. C. Cowdrey	M.C.C. v. New South Wales, at Sydney.
126	and 110	C. L. Walcott	West Indies v. Australia, at Trinidad.
155	and 110	C. L. Walcott	West Indies v. Australia, at Kingston.

In 1955:—

121*	and 105	J. M. Allan	Kent v. Northamptonshire, at Northampton.
115*	and 103*	M. C. Cowdrey	Kent v. Essex, at Gillingham.
111	and 118	D. J. Insole	Essex v. Kent, at Gillingham.
121	and 117*	D. M. Young	Gloucestershire v. Northamptonshire, at Kettering.

TWO SEPARATE HUNDREDS IN A TEST MATCH

Twice in one Series: C. L. Walcott v. Australia (1954–55).

Twice: H. Sutcliffe v. Australia (1924–25), South Africa (1929).
       G. Headley v. England (1929–30 and 1939).

Once: W. Bardsley v. England (1909).
      A. C. Russell v. South Africa (1922–23).
      W. R. Hammond v. Australia (1928–29).
      E. Paynter v. South Africa (1938–39).
      D. C. S. Compton v. Australia (1946–47).
      A. R. Morris v. England (1946–47).
      A. Melville v. England (1947).
      B. Mitchell v. England (1947).
      D. G. Bradman v. India (1947–48).
      V. S. Hazare v. Australia (1947–48).
      E. Weekes v. India (1948–49).
      J. R. Moroney v. South Africa (1949–50).

BATSMEN WHO HAVE SCORED 30,000 RUNS

	Career	Runs	Inns.	Times Not Out	Highest Inns.	100's	Average.
J. B. Hobbs	1905–34	61237	1315	106	316*	197	50.65
F. E. Woolley	1906–38	58969	1532	85	305*	145	40.75
E. Hendren	1907–38	57610	1300	166	301*	170	50.81
C. P. Mead	1905–36	55060	1335	185	280*	153	47.67
W. G. Grace	1865–1908	54896	1493	105	344	126	39.55
W. R. Hammond ..	1920–51	50493	1004	104	336*	167	56.10
H. Sutcliffe	1919–45	50135	1087	123	313	149	52.00
T. Hayward........	1893–1914	43518	1137	96	315	104	41.80
A. Sandham	1911–37	41284	1002	81	325	107	44.82
L. Hutton	1934–55	39950	810	91	364	129	55.56
W. Rhodes	1898–1930	39797	1532	236	267*	58	30.71
R. E. S. Wyatt	1923–55	39353	1137	157	232	85	40.15
E. Tyldesley	1909–36	38874	961	106	256*	102	45.46
J. T. Tyldesley	1895–1923	37809	991	62	295*	86	40.69
J. W. Hearne	1909–35	37250	1024	116	285	96	41.02
L. E. G. Ames	1926–51	37245	950	95	295	102	43.56
D. Denton	1894–1920	36520	1164	70	221	69	33.38
G. H. Hirst	1889–1929	36203	1215	152	341	60	34.05
W. G. Quaife	1894–1928	36050	1204	186	255*	72	35.41
D. C. S. Compton .	1936–55	35213	731	85	300	115	54.50
G. Gunn	1902–32	35190	1062	82	220	62	35.90
John Langridge	1928–55	34380	984	66	250*	76	37.45
M. Leyland	1920–48	33660	932	101	263	80	40.51
H. T. W. Hardinge .	1902–33	33519	1021	103	263*	75	36.51
W. J. Edrich	1934–55	33283	822	84	267*	83	45.09
R. Abel	1881–1904	32621	991	73	357*	74	35.53
J. Hardstaff, junr. ..	1930–55	31841	812	94	266	83	44.34
James Langridge....	1924–53	31716	1058	157	167	42	35.20
C. B. Fry	1892–1921	30886	658	43	258	94	50.22
P. Holmes	1913–35	30574	810	84	315	67	42.11
L. G. Berry	1924–51	30188	1048	57	232	45	30.46

1,000 RUNS IN A SEASON

(OVERSEAS TOURS INCLUDED)

28 Times: W. G. GRACE 2,000 (6); F. E. WOOLLEY 3,000 (1), 2,000 (12).

27 Times: C. P. MEAD 3,000 (2), 2,000 (9).

26 Times: J. B. HOBBS 3,000 (1), 2,000 (16).

25 Times: E. HENDREN 3,000 (3), 2,000 (12); W. G. QUAIFE 2,000 (1).

24 Times: H. SUTCLIFFE 3,000 (3), 2,000 (12).

21 Times: D. DENTON 2,000 (5); W. R. HAMMOND 3,000 (3), 2,000 (9); W. RHODES 2,000 (2).

20 Times: G. GUNN; T. HAYWARD 3,000 (2), 2,000 (8); James LANGRIDGE 2,000 (1); A. SANDHAM 2,000 (8).

19 Times: J. W. HEARNE 2,000 (4); G. H. HIRST 3,000 (1); E. TYLDESLEY 3,000 (1), 2,000 (5); J. T. TYLDESLEY 3,000 (1), 2,000 (4).

18 Times: L. G. BERRY 2,000 (1); H. T. W. HARDINGE 2,000 (4); P. A. PERRIN; C. WASHBROOK 2,000 (2); R. E. S. WYATT 2,000 (5).

17 Times: L. E. G. AMES 3,000 (1), 2,000 (5); L. HUTTON 3,000 (1), 2,000 (8); JOHN LANGRIDGE 2,000 (11); M. LEYLAND 2,000 (3).

16 Times: D. G. BRADMAN 2,000 (4); D. C. S. COMPTON 3,000 (1), 2,000 (5); EMRYS DAVIES 2,000 (1); E. G. HAYES 2,000 (2); J. O'CONNOR 2,000 (4); JAMES SEYMOUR 2,000 (1).

15 Times: E. H. BOWLEY 2,000 (4); A. E. DIPPER 2,000 (5); H. E. DOLLERY 2,000 (2); P. HOLMES 2,000 (7).

FOUR HUNDREDS OR MORE IN SUCCESSION
Six in Succession

C. B. FRY: in 1901.   D. G. BRADMAN: in 1938–39.

Four in Succession

J. B. HOBBS: 1920, 1925.   JOHN LANGRIDGE: 1949.
H. SUTCLIFFE: 1931, 1939.   C. G. MACARTNEY: 1921.
D. G. BRADMAN: 1931–32 (A.).   V. M. MERCHANT: 1941–42
D. C. S. COMPTON: 1946–47.   A. MITCHELL: 1933.
K. S. DULEEPSINHJI: 1931.   NAWAB OF PATAUDI: 1931.
C. B. FRY: 1911.   E. TYLDESLEY: 1926.
W. R. HAMMOND: 1936–37.   W. W. WHYSALL: 1930.
T. HAYWARD: 1906.   F. E. WOOLLEY: 1929
H. T. W. HARDINGE: 1913.

Five Hundreds in Successive Test Innings

E. Weekes (West Indies), 141 v. England, 1947–48; 128, 194, 162 and 101 v. India, 1948–49.

Four Hundreds in Successive Test Innings

J. H. Fingleton (Australia), 112, 108, 118 in South Africa, 1935–36, and 100 v. England in Australia, 1936–37.

A. Melville (South Africa), 103 v. England in South Africa, 1938–39, 189, 104* and 117 in England, 1947.

MOST HUNDREDS IN A SEASON

Eighteen: D. C. S. Compton, in 1947. These included six centuries against the South Africans in which matches his average was 84.78. His aggregate for the season was 3,816, also a record.

Sixteen: J. B. Hobbs, in 1925, when aged 42, played 16 three-figure innings in first-class matches. It was during this season that he exceeded the number of hundreds obtained in first-class cricket by W. G. Grace.

Fifteen: W. R. Hammond, in 1938.

Fourteen: H. Sutcliffe, in 1932.

Thirteen: D. G. Bradman in 1938, C. B. Fry in 1901, W. R. Hammond in 1933 and 1937, T. Hayward in 1906, E. Hendren in 1923, 1927 and 1928, C. P. Mead in 1928, and H. Sutcliffe in 1928 and 1931.

FAST SCORING

E. Alletson, for Notts v. Sussex, at Brighton, in 1911, scored 189 out of 227 runs obtained whilst at the wicket in ninety minutes.

D. Compton, for M.C.C. v. N.E. Transvaal, at Benoni, in 1948–49, scored 300 out of 399 in 181 minutes.

P. G. H. Fender, for Surrey v. Northamptonshire, at Northampton, in 1920, scored 113* out of 171 in forty-two minutes. He reached 50 in nineteen minutes and 100 in thirty-five minutes. Fender and H. A. Peach added 171 in forty-two minutes.

G. L. Jessop, for Gloucestershire v. Yorkshire, at Harrogate, in 1897, scored 101 out of 118 in forty minutes.

G. L. Jessop, for Gentlemen of South v. Players of South, at Hastings, in 1907, scored 191 runs out of 234 in ninety minutes. He reached 50 in twenty-four minutes, 100 in forty-two, and 150 in sixty-three.

C. I. J. Smith, in June 1938, made 69 in twenty minutes for Middlesex against Sussex at Lord's, and ten days later against Gloucestershire at Bristol he scored 66 in eighteen minutes—the first 50 coming in the record time of eleven minutes.

For Auckland v. Otago, at Dunedin in 1936–37, P. E. Whitelaw and W. N. Carson added 445 runs for the third wicket in 268 minutes—a world's record.

Worcestershire, set to make 131 in forty minutes against Nottinghamshire at Worcester in 1951, hit off the runs in thirty-five minutes for the loss of D. Kenyon's wicket. The other batsmen were G. Dews and R. O. Jenkins.

Kent scored 219 in seventy-one minutes when beating Gloucestershire at Dover, 1937. They averaged nine runs an over.

F. R. Santall (201) scored 173 out of 230 in 116 minutes before lunch on the third day for Warwickshire v. Northants at Northampton, 1933.

F. R. Brown made 168 out of 206 in 125 minutes for Surrey v. Kent, Blackheath, 1932. He advanced from 100 to 150 in fifteen minutes.

H. Sutcliffe (194) and M. Leyland (45) hit 102 off six consecutive overs for Yorkshire v. Essex, Scarborough, 1932.

J. B. Hobbs (47) and J. N. Crawford (48) made 98 without loss in thirty-two minutes at The Oval, 1919, after Kent left Surrey to get 95 in forty-two minutes.

RECORD HIT

The Rev. W. Fellows, while at practice on the Christchurch Ground at Oxford in 1856, drove a ball bowled by Charles Rogers 175 yards from hit to pitch.

MOST PERSONAL SIXES IN AN INNINGS

11	C. K. Nayudu (153)	Hindus v. M.C.C., at Bombay	1926–27
11	C. J. Barnett (194)	Gloucestershire v. Somerset, at Bath ..	1934
11	R. Benaud (135)	Australians v. T. N. Pearce's XI, at Scarborough	1953

MOST RUNS SCORED OFF ONE OVER

34	Alletson (E.)	off Killick (E. H.), Notts v. Sussex, at Hove .. (including two no-balls)	1911
32	Smart (C.)	off Hill (G.), Glamorgan v. Hampshire, at Cardiff ..	1935
31	Wellard (A. W.)	off Woolley (F. E.), Somerset v. Kent, at Wells .. (including five 6's)	1938
30	D. G. Bradman	off Freeman (A. P.), Australians v. England XI, at Folkestone	1934
30	H. B. Cameron	off Verity (H.), South Africans v. Yorkshire, at Sheffield	1935
30	Wellard (A. W.)	off Armstrong (T. R.), Somerset v. Derbyshire, at Wells (five 6's)	1936
30	P. L. Winslow	off Ikin (J. T.), South Africans v. Lancashire, at Manchester	1955
28	J. H. de Courcy	off Greensmith (W. T.), Australians v. Essex, at Southend	1953
28	Hazell (H. L.)	off Verity (H.), Somerset v. Yorkshire, at Bath ..	1936
28	G. L. Jessop	off Braund (L. C.), Gloucestershire v. Somerset, at Bristol	1904
28	G. L. Jessop	off Burrows (R. D.), Gloucestershire v. Worcestershire, at Stourbridge	1910
28	McConnon (J. E.)	off Thomson (N. I.), Glamorgan v. Sussex, at Cardiff	1955

(All the above instances refer to six-ball overs.)

300 RUNS IN ONE DAY

345	C. G. Macartney	Australians v. Notts.	Nottingham	1921
338*	R. C. Blunt	Otago v. Canterbury	Canterbury	1931–32
334	W. H. Ponsford	Victoria v. New South Wales	Melbourne	1926–27
333	K. S. Duleepsinhji	Sussex v. Northamptonshire	Hove	1930
331*	Robertson (J. D.)	Middlesex v. Worcestershire	Worcester	1949
322	Paynter (E.)	Lancashire v. Sussex	Hove	1937
318	C. W. Gregory	New South Wales v. Queensland (completed innings 383)	Brisbane	1906–7

F

316	R. H. Moore	Hampshire v. Warwickshire	Bournemouth	1937
309	D. G. Bradman	Australia v. England (completed innings 334)	Leeds	1930
307	Ashdown (W. H.)	Kent v. Essex (completed innings 332)	Brentwood	1934
306	Ducat (A.)	Surrey v. Oxford University	The Oval	1919
305	F. R. Foster	Warwickshire v. Worcestershire	Dudley	1914

HIGHEST PARTNERSHIPS

577 V. Hazare (288) and Gul Mahomed (319), fourth wicket for Baroda v. Holkar, at Baroda 1946–47

574 F. M. Worrell (255*) and C. L. Walcott (314*), fourth wicket for Barbados v. Trinidad, at Port of Spain 1945–46

555 Holmes (P.) (224*) and Sutcliffe (H.) (313), first wicket, Yorkshire v. Essex, at Leyton 1932

554 Brown (J. T.) (300) and Tunnicliffe (J.) (243), first wicket, Yorkshire v. Derbyshire, at Chesterfield 1898

502 F. M. Worrell (308*) and J. D. Goddard (218*), fourth wicket, Barbados v. Trinidad, at Bridgetown 1943–44

490 Bowley (E. H.) (283) and Langridge (John) (195), first wicket, Sussex v. Middlesex, at Hove 1933

487 G. Headley (344*) and C. C. Passailaigue (261*), sixth wicket, Jamaica v. Lord Tennyson's XI, at Kingston 1931–32

456 E. R. Mayne (209) and W. H. Ponsford (248), first wicket, Victoria v. Queensland, at Melbourne 1923–24

455 B. B. Nimbalkar (443*) and K. V. Bhandarkar (205), second wicket for Maharashtra v. Western India States, at Poona .. 1948–49

451 D. G. Bradman (244) and W. H. Ponsford (266), second wicket, 5th Test, Australia v. England, at Kennington Oval .. 1934

PARTNERSHIPS FOR FIRST WICKET

555 Holmes (P.) and Sutcliffe (H.), Yorkshire v. Essex, at Leyton .. 1932

554 Brown (J. T.) and Tunnicliffe (J.), Yorkshire v. Derbyshire, at Chesterfield 1898

490 Bowley (E. H.) and Langridge (John), Sussex v. Middlesex, at Hove 1933

456 E. R. Mayne and W. H. Ponsford, Victoria v. Queensland, at Melbourne 1923–24

428 Hobbs (J. B.) and Sandham (A.), Surrey v. Oxford U., at Oval .. 1926

424 J. F. W. Nicolson and I. J. Siedle, Natal v. Orange Free State, at Bloemfontein 1926–27

391 A. O. Jones and Shrewsbury (A.), Notts v. Glos., at Bristol .. 1899

390 L. Wight and G. Gibbs, British Guiana v. Barbados, at Georgetown 1951–52

380 Whitehead (H.) and C. J. B. Wood, Leicestershire v. Worcestershire, at Worcester 1906

379 Abel (R.) and Brockwell (W.), Surrey v. Hampshire, at The Oval 1897

378 Brown (J. T.) and Tunnicliffe (J.), Yorkshire v. Sussex, at Sheffield 1897

375 W. H. Ponsford and W. M. Woodfull, Victoria v. New South Wales, at Melbourne 1926–27

373 B. Sutcliffe and L. A. Watt, Otago v. Auckland, at Auckland .. 1950–51

368 A. C. MacLaren and R. H. Spooner, Lancashire v. Gloucestershire, at Liverpool 1903

368 Bowley (E. H.) and Parks (J. H.), Sussex v. Glos., at Hove .. 1929

364 Abel (R.) and D. L. A. Jephson, Surrey v. Derbyshire, at The Oval 1900

361 Oldfield (N.) and Broderick (V.), Northamptonshire v. Scotland, at Peterborough 1953

359 Hutton (L.) and Washbrook (C.), England v. South Africa, at Johannesburg 1948–49

355 A. F. Rae and J. B. Stollmeyer, West Indies v. Sussex, at Hove .. 1950

352 Hayward (T.) and Hobbs (J. B.), Surrey v. Warwickshire, at The
Oval 1909
350 Washbrook (C.) and Place (W.), Lancashire v. Sussex, at Manchester (unbroken) 1947

FIRST-WICKET HUNDREDS IN BOTH INNINGS

B. Sutcliffe and D. D. Taylor, for Auckland v. Canterbury in 1948–49, scored
for the first wicket 220 in the first innings and 286 in the second innings. This
is the only instance of two double century opening stands in the same match.

Hayward (T.) and Hobbs (J. B.) in 1907 accomplished a performance without parallel by scoring over 100 together for the first wicket of Surrey four times
in one week: 106 and 125 v. Cambridge University, at The Oval, and 147 and
105 v. Middlesex, at Lord's.

Hutton (L.) and Washbrook (C.), in three consecutive innings which they
opened together for England in Test Matches with Australia in 1946–47, made
138 in the second innings at Melbourne, and 137 and 100 at Adelaide. They
also opened with 168 and 129 at Leeds in 1948.

Hobbs (J. B.) and Sutcliffe (H.), in three consecutive innings which they
opened together for England in Test matches with Australia in 1924–25, made
157 and 110 at Sydney and 283 at Melbourne. On 26 occasions—15 times in
Test matches—Hobbs and Sutcliffe took part in a three-figure first wicket partnership. Seven of these stands exceeded 200.

Holmes (P.) and Sutcliffe (H.) made 100 or more runs for the first wicket of
Yorkshire on sixty-nine occasions; Hobbs (J. B.) and Sandham (A.) of Surrey on
sixty-three; Keeton (W. W.) and Harris (C. B.) of Notts on forty-six;
Hayward (T.) and Hobbs (J. B.) of Surrey on forty; Gunn (G.) and Whysall
(W. W.) of Notts on forty; C. B. Fry and Vine (J.) of Sussex on thirty-three;
E. Davies and A. H. Dyson of Glamorgan on thirty-two; and A. O. Jones and
Iremonger (J.) of Notts on twenty-four.

J. Douglas and A. E. Stoddart in 1896 scored over 150 runs for the first
wicket of Middlesex three times within a fortnight. In 1901, Iremonger (J.) and
A. O. Jones obtained over 100 for the first wicket of Nottinghamshire four times
within eight days, scoring 134 and 144* v. Surrey at The Oval, 238 v. Essex at
Leyton, and 119 v. Derbyshire at Welbeck.

Lee (J. W.) and Lee (F. S.), brothers, in 1934, for Somerset, scored over
100 runs thrice in succession in the County Championship.

W. G. Grace and A. E. Stoddart in three consecutive innings against the
Australians in 1893 made over 100 runs for each opening partnership.

In consecutive innings for Lancashire in 1928 Hallows (C.) and Watson (F.)
opened with 200, 202, 107, 118; reached three figures twelve times, 200 four times.

Hobbs (J. B.) during his career, which extended from 1905 to 1934, helped
to make 100 or more for the first wicket in first-class cricket 166 times—15 of
them in 1926, when in consecutive innings he helped to make 428, 182, 106 and
123 before a wicket fell. As many as 117 of the 166 stands were made for Surrey.

In the period 1919–1939 inclusive, Sutcliffe (H.) shared in 145 first wicket
partnerships of 100 runs or more.

WICKET RECORDS FOR ALL COUNTRIES

Best First Wicket Stands

English	..	555	Holmes (P.) (224*) and Sutcliffe (H.) (313), Yorkshire v. Essex, at Leyton	1932
Australian	..	456	W. H. Ponsford (248) and E. R. Mayne (209), Victoria v. Queensland, at Melbourne	1923–24
South African	..	424	J. F. W. Nicolson (252*) and I. J. Siedle (174), Natal v. Orange Free State, at Bloemfontein	1926–27
West Indian	..	390	L. Wight (262*) and G. Gibbs (216), British Guiana v. Barbados, at Georgetown ..	1951–52
New Zealand	..	373	B. Sutcliffe (275) and L. A. Watt (96), Otago v. Auckland, at Auckland ..	1950–51
Indian	..	293	V. M. Merchant (205) and V. Mankad (105), Indians v. Sussex, at Hove	1946

Best Second Wicket Stands

Indian ..	.. 455	B. B. Nimbalkar (443*) and K. V. Bhandakar (205), Maharashtra v. W.I. States, at Poona	1948–49
Australian	.. 451	D. G. Bradman (244) and W. H. Ponsford (266), Australia v. England, at The Oval ..	1934
English..	.. 429	J. G. Dewes (204*) and G. H. G. Doggart (219*), Cambridge U. v. Essex, at Cambridge	1949
South African	305	S. K. Coen (165) and J. M. M. Commaille (186), Orange Free State v. Natal, at Bloemfontein	1926–27
New Zealand ..	301	C. S. Dempster (180) and C. F. W. Allcott (131), N. Z'drs. v. Warwicks., at Birmingham	1927
West Indian ..	295	J. B. Stollmeyer (261) and K. B. Trestrail (161) Trinidad v. Jamaica, at Port of Spain ..	1949–50

Best Third Wicket Stands

New Zealand ..	445	P. E. Whitelaw (195) and W. N. Carson (290), Auckland v. Otago, at Dunedin	1936–37
West Indian ..	434	J. B. Stollmeyer (324) and G. E. Gomez (190), Trinidad v. British Guiana, at Port of Spain	1946–47
English..	.. 424	Compton (D. C. S.) (252*) and W. J. Edrich (168*), Middlesex v. Somerset, at Lord's ..	1948
Indian ..	.. 410	L. Amarnath (262) and R. S. Modi (156), Indians v. The Rest, at Calcutta	1946–47
Australian	.. 389	S. J. McCabe (192) and W. H. Ponsford (281*), Australians v. M.C.C., at Lord's ..	1934
South African ..	319	A. Melville (189) and A. D. Nourse, junr. (149), South Africa v. England, at Nottingham ..	1947

Best Fourth Wicket Stands

Indian ..	.. 577	V. S. Hazare (288) and Gul Mahomed (319), Baroda v. Holkar, at Baroda	1946–47
West Indian ..	574	F. M. Worrell (255*) and C. L. Walcott (314*), Barbados v. Trinidad, at Port of Spain	1945–46
English..	.. 448	Abel (R.) (193) and Hayward (T.) (273), Surrey v. Yorkshire, at The Oval ..	1899
Australian	.. 424	I. S. Lee (258) and S. O. Quin (210), Victoria v. Tasmania, at Melbourne	1933–34
South African..	342	E. A. B. Rowan (196) and P. J. M. Gibb (203), Transvaal v. N.E. Transvaal, at Johannesburg	1952–53
New Zealand ..	324	W. M. Wallace (197) and J. R. Reid (188*), N. Z'drs. v. Camb. U., at Cambridge ..	1949

Best Fifth Wicket Stands

Australian	.. 405	D. G. Bradman (234) and S. G. Barnes (234), Australia v. England, at Sydney	1946–47
English..	.. 393	Arnold (E. G.) (200*) and W. B. Burns (196), Worcs. v. Warwicks., at Birmingham ..	1909
Indian ..	.. 360	Uday Merchant (217) and M. N. Raiji (170), Bombay v. Hyderabad, at Bombay ..	1947–48
South African ..	327	A. W. Briscoe (191) and H. B. Cameron (182), Transvaal v. Griqualand West, at Jo'burg..	1934–35
New Zealand ..	266	B. Sutcliffe (355) and W. S. Haig (67), Otago v. Auckland, at Dunedin	1949–50
West Indian ..	283	N. L. Bonitto (207) and A. P. Binns (157), Jamaica v. British Guiana, at Georgetown..	1951–52

Best Sixth Wicket Stands

West Indian ..	487	G. Headley (344*) and C. C. Passailaigue (261*), Jamaica v. Lord Tennyson's XI, at Kingston	1931–32

Australian	..	428	W. W. Armstrong (172*) and M. A. Noble (284), Australians v. Sussex, at Hove	1902
English..	..	411	R. M. Poore (304) and E. G. Wynyard (225), Hampshire v. Somerset, at Taunton ..	1899
Indian ..	..	371	V. M. Merchant (359*) and R. S. Modi (168), Bombay v. Maharashtra, at Bombay ..	1943–44
South African ..		244	J. M. M. Commaille (132*) and A. W. Palm (106*), Western Province v. Griqualand West, at Johannesburg ..	1923–24
New Zealand	..	184	D. C. Collins (85) and H. M. McGirr (117), Wellington v. Otago, at Dunedin ..	1923–24

Best Seventh Wicket Stands

West Indian	..	348	D. Atkinson (219) and C. Depeiza (112), West Indies v. Australia, at Bridgetown ..	1954–55
English..	..	344	K. S. Ranjitsinhji (230) and W. Newham (153), Sussex v. Essex, at Leyton ..	1902
Australian	..	335	C. W. Andrews (253) and E. C. Bensted (155), Queensland v. New South Wales, at Sydney	1934–35
South African ..		299	B. Mitchell (159) and A. Melville (153), Transvaal v. Griqualand West, at Kimberley	1946–47
Indian ..	..	274	K. C. Ibrahim (250) and K. M. Rangnekar (138), Bijapur XI v. Bengal XI, at Bombay..	1942–43
New Zealand	..	265	J. L. Powell (164) and N. Doreen (105*), Canterbury v. Otago, at Christchurch ..	1929–30

Best Eighth Wicket Stands

Australian	..	433	A. Sims (184*) and V. T. Trumper (293), An Australian XI v. Canterbury, at Christchurch ..	1913–14
English..	..	292	Lord Hawke (166) and Peel (R.) (210*), Yorkshire v. Warwickshire, at Birmingham ..	1896
West Indian	..	255	E. A. V. Williams (131*) and E. A. Martindale (134), Barbados v. Trinidad, at Bridgetown	1935–36
Indian ..	..	236	C. T. Sarwate (235) and R. P. Singh (88), Holkar v. Delhi and Dis., at New Delhi ..	1949–50
South African ..		222	D. P. B. Morkel (114) and S. S. L. Steyn (261*), Western Province v. Border, at Cape Town	1929–30
New Zealand	..	190	J. E. Mills (104*) and C. F. W. Allcott (102*), New Zealanders v. Civil Service, at Chiswick	1927

Best Ninth Wicket Stands

English..	..	283	J. Chapman (165) and Warren (A. R.) (123), Derbyshire v. Warwickshire, at Blackwell ..	1910
Indian ..	..	245	V. S. Hazare (316*) and N. D. Nagarwalla (98), Maharashtra v. Baroda, at Poona ..	1939–40
New Zealand	..	239	H. B. Cave (118) and I. B. Leggat (142*), Central Districts v. Otago, at Dunedin ..	1952–53
Australian	..	232	C. Hill (365*) and E. Walkley (53), South Australia v. N.S.W., at Adelaide ..	1900–01
South African ..		221	N. V. Lindsay (160*) and G. R. McCubbin (97), Transvaal v. Rhodesia, at Bulawayo ..	1922–23
West Indian	..	106	E. Constantine (55) and R. Tang Choon (72), Trinidad v. Barbados, at Georgetown ..	1931–32
			R. J. Christiani (107) and D. Atkinson (45), West Indies v. India, at New Delhi ..	1948–49

Best Tenth Wicket Stands

| Australian | .. | 307 | A. F. Kippax (260*), and J. E. H. Hooker (62) New South Wales v. Victoria, at Melbourne | 1928–29 |
| Indian .. | .. | 249 | C. T. Sarwate (124*) and S. N. Banerjee (121), Indians v. Surrey, at The Oval .. .. | 1946 |

English..	..	235	Fielder (A.) (112*) and Woolley (F. E.) (185), Kent v. Worcestershire, at Stourbridge	..	1909
New Zealand		184	R. C. Blunt (338*) and W. Hawkesworth (21), Otago v. Canterbury, at Christchurch		1931–32
West Indian	..	138	E. L. G. Hoad (149*) and H. C. Griffith (84), West Indies v. Sussex, at Hove		1933
South African	..	129	F. Caulfield (56*) and L. R. Tuckett (70), Orange Free State v. Western Province, at Bloemfontein	..	1925–26

(All the English record wicket partnerships were made in the County Championship with the exception of the second, for which the best county stand is: 398, Gunn (W.) (196) and Shrewsbury (A.) (267), Notts v. Sussex, at Nottingham, 1890.)

HIGHEST AGGREGATES IN A SEASON: OVER 3,000

		Inns.		Times Not Out		Runs		Highest Score		No. of 100's		Average
1947	Compton (D. C. S.)	50	..	8	..	3816	..	246	..	18	..	90.85
1947	W. J. Edrich	52	..	8	..	3539	..	267*	..	12	..	80.43
1906	Hayward (T.)	61	..	8	..	3518	..	219	..	13	..	66.37
1949	Hutton (L.)	56	..	6	..	3429	..	269*	..	12	..	68.58
1928	Woolley (F. E.)	59	..	4	..	3352	..	198	..	12	..	60.94
1932	Sutcliffe (H.)	52	..	7	..	3336	..	313	..	14	..	74.13
1933	Hammond (W. R.)	54	..	5	..	3323	..	264	..	13	..	67.81
1928	Hendren (E.)	54	..	7	..	3311	..	209*	..	13	..	70.44
1901	Abel (R.)	68	..	8	..	3309	..	247	..	7	..	55.15
1937	Hammond (W.R.)	55	..	5	..	3252	..	217	..	13	..	65.04
1933	Hendren (E.)	65	..	9	..	3186	..	301*	..	11	..	56.89
1921	Mead (C. P.)	52	..	6	..	3179	..	280*	..	10	..	69.10
1904	Hayward (T.)	63	..	5	..	3170	..	205	..	11	..	54.65
1899	K. S. Ranjitsinhji	58	..	8	..	3159	..	197	..	8	..	63.18
1901	C. B. Fry	43	..	3	..	3147	..	244	..	13	..	78.67
1900	K. S. Ranjitsinhji	40	..	5	..	3065	..	275	..	11	..	87.57
1933	Ames (L. E. G.)	57	..	5	..	3058	..	295	..	9	..	58.80
1901	Tyldesley (J. T.)	60	..	5	..	3041	..	221	..	9	..	55.29
1928	Mead (C. P.)	50	..	10	..	3027	..	180	..	13	..	75.67
1925	Hobbs (J. B.)	48	..	5	..	3024	..	266*	..	16	..	70.32
1928	Tyldesley (E.)	48	..	10	..	3024	..	242	..	10	..	79.57
1938	W. R. Hammond	42	..	2	..	3011	..	271	..	15	..	75.27
1923	Hendren (E.)	51	..	12	..	3010	..	200*	..	13	..	77.17
1931	Sutcliffe (H.)	42	..	11	..	3006	..	230	..	13	..	96.96
1937	Parks (J. H.)	63	..	4	..	3003	..	168	..	11	..	50.89
1928	Sutcliffe (H.)	44	..	5	..	3002	..	228	..	13	..	76.97

W. G. Grace scored 2,739 runs in 1871 when every stroke was run out. He made ten centuries and twice exceeded 200, with an average of 78·25; all first-class matches and the over was four balls.

LARGEST AGGREGATES OUTSIDE ENGLAND

		Inns.	Not out	Runs	Highest Score	No. of 100's	Average
IN AUSTRALIA 1928–29	D. G. Bradman	24	6	1690	340*	7	93.88
IN SOUTH AFRICA 1948–49	Compton (D. C. S.)	26	5	1781	300	8	84.80
IN WEST INDIES 1929–30	Hendren (E.)	18	5	1765	254	6	135.76
IN INDIA 1926–27	Sandham (A.	33	4	1977	150	8	68.17

1,000 RUNS IN MAY

Three batsmen have scored 1,000 runs in May, and three others—D. G. Bradman twice—have made 1,000 runs before June. Their innings-by-innings records are as follows:—

	Runs	Average

W. G. GRACE, May 9 to May 30, 1895 (22 days):
13, 103, 18, 25, 288, 52, 257, 73*, 18, 169 .. .. 1016 112.88
"W.G." was within two months of completing his 47th year.

W. R. HAMMOND, May 7 to May 31, 1927 (25 days):
27, 135, 108, 128, 17, 11, 99, 187, 4, 30, 83, 7, 192, 14 .. 1042 74.42
Hammond scored his 1,000th run on May 28, thus equalling "W.G.'s" record of 22 days.

HALLOWS (C.), May 5 to May 31, 1928 (27 days):
100, 101, 51*, 123, 101*, 22, 74, 104, 58, 34*, 232 .. .. 1000 125.00

HAYWARD (T.), April 16 to May 31, 1900:
120*, 55, 108, 131*, 55, 193, 120, 5, 6, 3, 40, 146, 92 .. 1074 97.63
Hayward scored 120 not out on April 16.

D. G. BRADMAN, April 30 to May 31, 1930:
236, 185*, 78, 9, 48*, 66, 4, 44, 252*, 32, 47* 1001 143.00
On April 30 Bradman scored 75 not out.

D. G. BRADMAN, April 30 to May 31, 1938:
258, 58, 137, 278, 2, 143, 145*, 5, 30* 1056 150.85
Bradman scored 258 on April 30, and his 1,000th run on May 27.

EDRICH (W. J.), April 30 to May 31, 1938:
104, 37, 115, 63, 20*, 182, 71, 31, 53*, 45, 15, 245, 0, 9, 20*. 1010 84.16
Edrich scored 21 not out on April 30. All his runs were scored at Lord's.

1,000 RUNS IN TWO SEPARATE MONTHS

Hutton (L.), by scoring 1,294 in June 1949, made more runs in a single month than anyone else. The previous best was by Hammond (W. R.), 1,281, in August 1936. Hutton also made 1,050 in August 1949, and thus joined C. B. Fry, K. S. Ranjitsinhji and H. Sutcliffe, who scored over 1,000 in each of two months in the same season.

BOWLING AND FIELDING RECORDS

Four Wickets With Consecutive Balls

Wells (J.) Kent v. Sussex, at Brighton	1862
Ulyett (G.), England v. New South Wales, at Sydney	1878–79
Nash (G.), Lancashire v. Somerset, at Manchester	1882
Hide (J. B.), Sussex v. M.C.C. and Ground, at Lord's	1890
Shacklock (F.), Notts v. Somerset, at Nottingham	1893
A. Downes, Otago v. Auckland, at Dunedin	1893–94
Martin (F.), M.C.C. and Ground v. Derbyshire, at Lord's	1895
Mold (A.), Lancashire v. Notts, at Nottingham	1895
W. Brearley, Lancashire v. Somerset, at Manchester	1905
(Not all in same innings)	
Haigh (S.), M.C.C. v. Army XI, at Pretoria	1905–06
†Trott (A. E.), Middlesex v. Somerset, at Lord's	1907
(It was Trott's benefit match and he did the hat-trick also in the same innings)	
Tarrant (F. A.), Middlesex v. Gloucestershire, at Bristol	1907
Drake (A.), Yorkshire v. Derbyshire, at Chesterfield	1914
S. G. Smith, Northamptonshire v. Warwickshire, at Edgbaston ..	1914
Peach (H. A.), Surrey v. Sussex, at The Oval	1924
A. F. Borland, Natal v. Griqualand West, at Kimberley	1926–27
J. E. H. Hooker, New South Wales v. Victoria, at Sydney	1928–29
(Not all in same innings)	

Tyldesley (R.), Lancashire v. Derbyshire, at Derby 1929
(Not all in same innings)
R. J. Crisp, Western Province v. Griqualand West, at Johannesburg .. 1931–32
R. J. Crisp, Western Province v. Natal, at Durban 1933–34
Gover (A. R.), Surrey v. Worcestershire, at Worcester 1935
Copson (W. H.), Derbyshire v. Warwickshire, at Derby 1937
W. A. Henderson, North-Eastern Transvaal v. Orange Free State at
Bloemfontein 1937–38
Ridgway (F.), Kent v. Derbyshire, at Folkestone 1951

Trott's double performance is without parallel in important cricket.

In their match with England at The Oval in 1863, Surrey lost four wickets in the course of a four-ball over from Bennett (G.). From his first Stephenson (H. H.) was stumped, from his second Caffyn (W.) was run out, E. Dowson was bowled by his third, and Griffiths (G.) was caught off his fourth.

Double Hat-Trick

Besides Trott's performance, which is given in the preceding section, the following instances are recorded of players having performed the hat-trick twice in the same match:—

Shaw (A.), Notts v. Gloucestershire, at Trent Bridge, 1884.
T. J. Matthews, Australia v. South Africa, at Manchester, 1912.
Parker (C. W. L.), Gloucestershire v. Middlesex, at Bristol, 1924.
Jenkins (R. O.), Worcestershire v. Surrey, at Worcester, 1949.

Most Hat-Tricks

SEVEN TIMES	FOUR TIMES	J. W. Hearne.
D. V. P. Wright.	J. T. Hearne.	A. Hill.
	J. C. Laker.	R. O. Jenkins.
SIX TIMES	G. G. Macaulay.	A. S. Kennedy.
T. W. Goddard.		W. H. Lockwood.
C. W. L. Parker.		E. A. McDonald.
	THREE TIMES	T. J. Matthews.
	H. J. Butler.	T. L. Pritchard.
FIVE TIMES	W. H. Copson.	T. Richardson.
S. Haigh.	R. J. Crisp.	A. Shaw.
V. W. C. Jupp.	J. W. H. T. Douglas.	F. R. Spofforth.
A. E. G. Rhodes.	A. P. Freeman.	M. W. Tate.
F. A. Tarrant.	G. Giffen.	H. Trumble.

TEN WICKETS IN ONE INNINGS

O. M. R.

	O.	M.	R.		
W. Clarke (Notts.)				v. Leicester., at Nottingham	1845
E. Hinkly (Kent)				v. England, at Lord's	1848
J. Wisden (North)				v. South, at Lord's	1850
V. E. Walker (England)	43		74	v. Surrey, at The Oval	1859
E. M. Grace (M.C.C.).....				v. Gents. of Kent, at Canter-	
				bury.................	1862
V. E. Walker (Middlesex) ..	44.2		104	v. Lancashire, at Manchester	1865
G. Wootton (All England) ..				v. Yorkshire, at Sheffield...	1865
W. Hickton (Lancashire) ...	36.2	19	46	v. Hampshire, at Manchester	1870
S. E. Butler (Oxford)	24.1	11	38	v. Cambridge, at Lord's....	1871
Jas. Lillywhite (South)	60.2	22	129	v. North, at Canterbury....	1872
A. Shaw (M.C.C.)	36.2	8	73	v. North, at Lord's	1874
E. Barratt (Players)	29	11	43	v. Australians, at The Oval	1878
G. Giffen (Fourth Aust. XI)	26	10	66	v. The Rest, at Sydney ...1883–84	
W. G. Grace (M.C.C.)	36.2	17	49	v. Oxford U., at Oxford....	1886
G. Burton (Middlesex)	52.3	25	59	v. Surrey, at The Oval	1888
A. E. Moss (Canterbury) ...	21.3		28	v. Wellington, at Christ-	
				church 1889–90	

	O.	M.	R.		
S. M. J. Woods (Cambridge U.)	31	6	69	v. Thornton's XI, at Cambridge	1890
T. Richardson (Surrey)	15.3	3	45	v. Essex, at The Oval	1894
H. Pickett (Essex)	27	11	32	v. Leicester., at Leyton ...	1895
E. J. Tyler (Somerset)	34.3	15	49	v. Surrey, at Taunton	1895
W. P. Howell (Australians)..	23.2	14	28	v. Surrey, at The Oval	1899
C. H. G. Bland (Sussex)	25.2	0	48	v. Kent, at Tonbridge	1899
J. Briggs (Lancashire) .:....	28.5	7	55	v. Worcester., at Manchester	1900
A. E. Trott (Middlesex)	14.2	5	42	v. Somerset, at Taunton	1900
A. Fielder (Players)	24.5	1	90	v. Gentlemen, at Lord's ...	1906
G. Dennett (Gloucester.)....	19.4	7	40	v. Essex, at Bristol	1906
A. E. E. Vogler (Eastern Prov.)	12	2	26	v. Griq. West, at Johannesburg	1906–07
C. Blythe (Kent)...........	16	7	30	v. Northants, at Northampton	1907
A. Drake (Yorkshire).......	8.5	0	35	v. Somerset, at Weston	1914
W. Bestwick (Derbyshire) ..	19	2	40	v. Glamorgan, at Cardiff ..	1921
A. A. Mailey (Australians)..	28.4	5	66	v. Glos., at Cheltenham ...	1921
C. W. L. Parker (Gloucester.)	40.3	13	79	v. Somerset, at Bristol	1921
T. Rushby (Surrey)	17.5	4	43	v. Somerset, at Taunton ...	1921
J. C. White (Somerset)	42.2	11	76	v. Worcester., at Worcester.	1921
G. C. Collins (Kent)	19.3	4	65	v. Notts., at Dover	1922
H. Howell (Warwicks.)	25.1	5	51	v. Yorkshire, at Birmingham	1923
A. S. Kennedy (Players)	22.4	10	37	v. Gentlemen, at The Oval .	1927
G. O. Allen (Middlesex)	25.3	10	40	v. Lancashire, at Lord's ...	1929
A. P. Freeman (Kent)	42	9	131	v. Lancashire, at Maidstone	1929
G. Geary (Leicester.)	16.2	8	18	v. Glamorgan, at Pontypridd	1929
C. V. Grimmett (Australians)	22.3	8	37	v. Yorkshire, at Sheffield..	1930
A. P. Freeman (Kent)	30.4	8	53	v. Essex, at Southend	1930
H. Verity (Yorkshire)	18.4	6	36	v. Warwicks., at Leeds	1931
A. P. Freeman (Kent)	36.1	9	79	v. Lancashire, at Manchester	1931
V. W. C. Jupp (Northants) ..	39	6	127	v. Kent, at Tunbridge Wells	1932
H. Verity (Yorkshire)	19.4	16	10	v. Notts., at Leeds	1932
T. W. Wall (Sth. Australia)..	12.4	2	36	v. N.S.W., at Sydney	1932–33
T. B. Mitchell (Derbyshire)..	19.1	4	64	v. Leicester., at Leicester ...	1935
J. Mercer (Glamorgan)	26	10	51	v. Worcester., at Worcester.	1936
T. W. Goddard (Gloucester.)	28.4	4	113	v. Worcester., at Cheltenham	1937
T. F. Smailes (Yorkshire) ..	17.1	5	47	v. Derbyshire, at Sheffield..	1939
E. A. Watts (Surrey)	24.1	8	67	v. Warwicks., at Birmingham	1939
W. E. Hollies (Warwicks.)..	20.4	4	49	v. Notts., at Birmingham...	1946
J. M. Sims (East)	18.4	2	90	v. West, at Kingston	1948
T. E. Bailey (Essex)	39.4	9	90	v. Lancs., at Clacton	1949
J. K. Graveney (Gloucester.)	18.4	2	66	v. Derby., at Chesterfield..	1949
R. Berry (Lancashire)	36.2	9	102	v. Worcester., at Blackpool	1953
S. Gupte (Bombay)	24.2	7	78	v. Comb.XI, at Bahawalpur	1954–5

SEVENTEEN WICKETS IN A MATCH

Fenner (F. P.), Cambridge Town Club v. The University, at Cambridge	1844
Mycroft (W.), for 103 runs, Derbyshire v. Hampshire, at Southampton	1876
W. G. Grace, for 89 runs, Gloucestershire v. Notts., at Cheltenham ..	1877
G. Giffen, for 201 runs, South Australia v. Victoria, at Adelaide ..	1885–86
C. T. B. Turner, for 50 runs, Australians v. An England Eleven, at Hastings	1888
Mead (W.), for 205 runs, Essex v. Australians, at Leyton	1893
Mead (W.), for 119 runs, Essex v. Hampshire, at Southampton	1895
W. P. Howell, for 54 runs, Australians v. Western Province, at Cape Town	1902–03
W. Brearley, for 137 runs, Lancashire v. Somerset, at Manchester	1905
Blythe (C.), for 48 runs, Kent v. Northants, at Northampton	1907

Dean (H.), for 91 runs, Lancashire v. Yorkshire, at Liverpool ..,   ..   1913
Barnes (S. F.), for 159 runs, England v. South Africa, at Johannesburg   1913–14
Freeman (A. P.), for 67 runs, Kent v. Sussex, at Brighton   ..   1922
Matthews (F. C. L.), for 89 runs, Notts v. Northants, at Nottingham ..   1923
Parker (C. W. L.), for 56 runs, Gloucestershire v. Essex, at Gloucester   1925
Cox (G. R.), for 106 runs, Sussex v. Warwickshire, at Horsham   ..   1926
Freeman (A. P.), for 92 runs, Kent v. Warwickshire, at Folkestone   ..   1932
Verity (H.), for 91 runs, Yorkshire v. Essex, at Leyton   1933
J. C. Clay, for 212 runs, Glamorgan v. Worcestershire, at Swansea   ..   1937
Goddard (T. W.), for 106 runs, Gloucestershire v. Kent, at Bristol   ..   1939

REMARKABLE ANALYSES

(Also see TEN WICKETS IN ONE INNINGS on preceding pages.)

	O.	M.	R.	W.		
H. Verity (Yorkshire)	19.4	16	10	10 v. Notts, at Leeds		1932
G. Geary (Leicestershire) ...	16.2	8	18	10 v. Glamorgan, at Pontypridd		1929
A. E. Vogler (Eastern Province)	12	2	26	10 v. Griqualand West, at Johannesburg		1906
A. P. Freeman (Kent)	10	4	11	9 v. Sussex, at Brighton ..		1922
H. Verity (Yorkshire)	6.3	3	12	9 v. Kent, at Sheffield		1936
C. T. B. Turner (Australia) .	17.1	10	15	9 v. An England XI, at Stoke		1888
F. R. Spofforth (Australia) ..	15.2	7	18	9 v. Oxford University, at Oxford		1886
A. Rowan (Transvaal)......	15.4	7	19	9 v. Australians, at Johannesburg..........		1949–50
W. G. Grace (M.C.C.)	35.1	25	20	9 v. Notts, at Lord's		1885
J. C. Laker (England)	14	12	2	8 v. The Rest, at Bradford		1950
D. Shackleton (Hampshire) .	11.1	7	4	8 v. Somerset, at Weston.		1955
E. Peate (Yorkshire)	16	11	5	8 v. Surrey, at Holbeck ..		1883
G. A. Lohmann (England) ..	9.4	5	7	8 v. South Africa, at Port Elizabeth		1896
C. H. Palmer (Leic.)	14	12	7	8 v. Surrey, at Leicester...		1955
J. E. D. Sealy (Barbados) ..	6.7	2	8	8 v. Trinidad, at Bridgetown		1942
M. G. Melle (Transvaal)....	12	7	8	8 v. Griqualand West, at Johannesburg.....		1950–51
G. Dennett (Gloucestershire)	6	1	9	8 v. Northants, at Gloucester		1907
J. Briggs (English XI)	14.2	5	11	8 v. South Africa XI, at Cape Town		1889
A. Kennedy (Hampshire) ...	13	7	11	8 v. Glamorgan, at Cardiff		1921
W. Copson (Derbyshire) ...	8.2	2	11	8 v. Warwickshire, at Derby		1937
R. Peel (Yorkshire)	20.2	13	12	8 v. Notts, at Sheffield....		1888
R. W. Norden (Transvaal) ..	12	8	12	8 v. Rhodesia, at Johannesburg		1905
C. W. L. Parker (Gloucestershire)	17	10	12	8 v. Essex, at Gloucester..		1925
W. H. R. Andrews (Somerset)	6.4	2	12	8 v. Surrey, at The Oval...		1937
F. R. Spofforth (Australia)..	8.3	6	3	7 v. An England XI, at Birmingham.........		1884
W. A. Henderson (N.E. Transvaal)	9.3	7	4	7 v. Orange Free State, at Bloemfontein ...	1937–38	
F. Morley (M.C.C.)	22	18	6	7 v. Oxford University, at Oxford		1877
A. Waddington (Yorkshire) .	7	4	6	7 v. Sussex, at Hull		1922
R. Tyldesley (Lancashire) ...	14	12	6	7 v. Northants, at Liverpool		1924

	O.	M.	R.	W.		
F. Morley (Notts)	10.2	7	7	7 v. Derbyshire, at Nottingham..............	1879
A. Shaw (Notts)	41.2	36	7	7 v. M.C.C., at Lord's....	1875
L. T. Driffield (Cambridge)..	6.4	3	7	7 v. M.C.C., at Cambridge	1900
J. Bailey (Hampshire)	7	3	7	7 v. Notts, at Southampton	1932
G. Geary (Leicestershire) ...13.3		8	7	7 v. Warwickshire, at Hinckley..........	1936
L. Cook (Lancashire)	14	9	8	7 v. Derbyshire, at Chesterfield	1920
G. R. Cox (Sussex)	16	9	8	7 v. Derbyshire, at Hove..	1920
A. Kennedy (Hampshire) ...	10	7	8	7 v. Warwickshire, at Portsmouth	1927
James Langridge (Sussex) ..	11.5	7	8	7 v. Gloucestershire, at Cheltenham	1932
C. Blythe (Kent)	7.5	3	9	7 v. Leicestershire, at Leicester	1912
T. Emmett (Yorkshire)	9.3	6	9	7 v. Sussex, at Hove	1878
G. G. Macaulay (Yorkshire).	14	7	9	7 v. Northants, at Kettering	1933
F. Morley (Notts)	22	15	9	7 v. Kent, at Town Malling	1878
F. Morley (Notts)	19.2	12	9	7 v. Surrey, at The Oval ..	1880
H. Verity (Yorkshire)	6	1	9	7 v. Sussex, at Hove	1939
F. E. Woolley (Kent)	6.3	3	9	7 v. Surrey, at The Oval ..	1911
V. I. Smith (South Africans).	4.5	3	1	6 v. Derbyshire, at Derby.	1947
S. Cosstick (Victoria)	21.1	20	1	6 v. Tasmania, at Melbourne	1868–69
F. E. Field (Warwickshire)..	8.4	7	2	6 v. Worcestershire, at Dudley	1914
T. Wass (Notts)	4.4	3	3	6 v. M.C.C., at Lord's....	1907
A. Penn (Kent)	13.3	11	3	6 v. Sussex, at Tunbridge Wells	1878
R. G. Barlow (Lancashire)..	10.1	9	3	6 v. Derbyshire, at Derby.	1881
G. G. Macaulay (Yorkshire).	7	4	3	6 v. Derbyshire, at Hull ..	1921
J. Cowie (New Zealand) ...	8	5	3	6 v. Ireland, at Dublin ...	1937
A. D. Pougher (M.C.C.) ...	3	3	0	5 v. Australians, at Lord's.	1896
G. R. Cox (Sussex)	6	6	0	5 v. Somerset, at Weston-super-Mare	1921
R. Tyldesley (Lancashire) ...	4	4	0	5 v. Leicestershire, at Manchester	1924
P. T. Mills (Gloucestershire).	6.4	6	0	5 v. Somerset, at Bristol....	1928
F. W. Tate (Sussex)	4	3	1	5 v. Kent, at Tonbridge...	1888
D. Ashby (Canterbury)	15.2	13	2	5 v. Auckland, at Auckland	1877–78
E. H. Killick (Sussex)	6.1	4	2	5 v. Hampshire, at Chichester	1907
E. R. H. Toshack (Australia)	2.3	1	2	5 v. India, at Brisbane ..	1947–48
G. A. R. Lock (Surrey).....	5.3	4	2	5 v. Worcestershire, at The Oval	1954

Sixteen or More Wickets in a Day

17	Blythe (C.), Kent v. Northants, at Northampton (for 48 runs) ..	1907
17	Verity (H.), Yorkshire v. Essex, at Leyton (for 91 runs)	1933
17	Goddard (T. W.), Gloucestershire v. Kent, at Bristol (for 106 runs)	1939
16	Emmett (T.), Yorkshire v. Cambridgeshire, at Hunslet (for 38 runs)	1869
16	Southerton (J.), South v. North, at Lord's (for 52 runs)	1875
16	Wass (T.), Nottinghamshire v. Lancashire, at Liverpool (for 69 runs)	1906
16	Vogler (A. E. E.), Eastern Province v. Griqualand West, at Johannesburg (for 38 runs)	1906
16	Wass (T.), Nottinghamshire v. Essex, at Nottingham (for 103 runs)	1908
16	J. C. White, Somerset v. Worcestershire, at Bath (for 83 runs) ..	1919

200 OR MORE WICKETS IN A SEASON

		Overs	Maidens	Runs	Wickets	Average
	1928	Freeman (A. P.)...	1976.1	423	5489	304	18.05
	1933	Freeman (A. P.)...	2039	651	4549	298	15.26
(2)	1895	Richardson (T.) ..	1690.1	463	4170	290	14.37
(1)	1888	C. T. B. Turner**..	2427.2	1127	3307	283	11.68
	1931	Freeman (A. P.)...	1618	360	4307	276	15.60
	1930	Freeman (A. P.)...	1914.3	472	4632	275	16.84
(2)	1897	Richardson (T.) ..	1603.4	495	3945	273	14.45
	1929	Freeman (A. P.)...	1670.5	381	4879	267	18.27
	1900	Rhodes (W.)......	1553	455	3606	261	13.81
(2)	1896	Hearne (J. T.)	2003.1	818	3670	257	14.28
	1932	Freeman (A. P.)...	1565.5	404	4149	253	16.39
	1901	Rhodes (W.)	1565	505	3797	251	15.12
	1937	Goddard (T. W.) .	1478.1	359	4158	248	16.76
	1910	Smith (W. C.)	1423.3	420	3225	247	13.05
(2)	1896	Richardson (T.) ..	1656.2	526	4015	246	16.32
(2)	1899	Trott (A. E.)......	1772.4	587	4086	239	17.09
	1947	Goddard (T. W.)..	1451.2	344	4119	238	17.30
	1925	Tate (M. W.)	1694.3	472	3415	228	14.97
(2)	1898	Hearne (J. T.)	1802.2	781	3120	222	14.05
	1925	Parker (C. W. L.) .	1512.3	478	3311	222	14.91
(2)	1890	Lohmann (H. A.) .	1759.1	737	2998	220	13.62
	1923	Tate (M. W.)	1608.5	331	3061	219	13.97
	1925	Root (C. F.)	1493.2	416	3770	219	17.21
	1931	Parker (C. W. L.) .	1320.4	386	3125	219	14.26
(1)	1884	F. R. Spofforth***	1625	672	2732	218	12.53
	1936	Verity (H.)	1289.3	463	2847	216	13.18
	1955	Lock (G. A. R.)...	1408.4	497	3109	216	14.39
	1909	Blythe (C)	1273.5	343	3128	215	14.54
(1)	1882	Peate (E)	1853.1	868	2466	214	11.52
(2)	1895	Mold (A.)	1629	598	3400	213	15.96
	1902	Rhodes (W.)	1306.3	405	2801	213	13.15
	1926	Parker (C. W. L.) .	1739.5	556	3920	213	18.40
(2)	1893	Hearne (J. T.)	1741.4	667	3492	212	16.47
	1935	Freeman (A. P.)...	1503.2	320	4562	212	21.51
	1900	Trott (A. E.)......	1547.1	363	4923	211	23.33
	1925	Macaulay (G. G.) .	1338.2	307	3268	211	15.48
	1935	Verity (H.)	1279.2	453	3032	211	14.36
(1)	1870	Southerton (J.) ...	1863.2	696	3069	210	14.61
(1)	1888	Lohmann (G. A.) .	1649.1	783	2280	209	10.90
	1923	Parkin (C. H.)	1356.2	356	3543	209	16.94
	1906	Hirst (G. H.)	1306.1	271	3434	208	16.50
(2)	1894	Mold (A)	1288.3	456	2548	207	12.30
	1922	Parker (C. W. L.) .	1294.5	445	2712	206	13.16
	1922	Kennedy (A.)	1346.4	366	3444	205	16.80
	1924	Tate (M. W.)	1469.5	465	2818	205	13.74
	1925	McDonald (E. A.)	1249.4	282	3828	205	18.67
	1934	Freeman (A. P.)...	1744.4	440	4753	205	23.18
	1924	Parker (C. W. L.) .	1303.5	411	2913	204	14.27
(2)	1889	Lohmann (G. A.) .	1614.1	646	2714	202	13.43
	1937	Verity (H.)	1386.2	487	3168	202	15.68
(1)	1878	Shaw (A.)	2630	—	2203	201	10.96
	1907	Dennett (G. E.) ...	1216.2	305	3227	201	16.05
	1937	Gover (A. R.)	1219.4	191	3816	201	18.98

(1) *Indicates 4-ball;* (2) *5-ball; and* (3) *8-ball overs. All others were 6-ball overs.*

** Exclusive of matches not reckoned as first-class.

*** Including Smokers v. Non-Smokers, at Lord's, and all matches of the Australians' tour.

		Overs	Maidens	Runs	Wickets	Average
1924	Parkin (C. H.)	1162.5	357	2735	200	13.67
1935	Goddard (T. W.) .	1553	384	4073	200	20.36
1936	Gover (A. R.)	1159.2	185	3547	200	17.73
(3) 1939	Goddard (T. W.) .	819	139	2973	200	14.86
1951	Appleyard (R)	1313.2	391	2829	200	14.14

(1) *Indicates* 4-*ball;* (2) 5-*ball: and* (3) 8-*ball overs. All others were* 6-*ball overs.*

In four consecutive seasons (1928-31), Freeman (A. P.) took 1,122 wickets, and in eight consecutive seasons (1928–35), 2,090 wickets. In each of these eight seasons he took over 200 wickets.

Richardson (T.) took 1,005 wickets in four consecutive seasons (1894–97).

In 1896, Hearne (J. T.) took his 100th wicket as early as June 12th. In 1931, Parker (C. W. L.) did the same and Freeman (A. P.) obtained his 100th wicket a day later.

BOWLERS WHO HAVE TAKEN 2,000 WICKETS

	Career	Wickets	Runs	Average
Rhodes (W.)	1898–1930	4188	69986	16.71
Freeman (A. P.)	1914–36	3775	69579	18.43
Parker (C. W. L.)	1903–35	3274	63805	19.48
Hearne (J. T.)	1888–1923	3055	54278	17.76
Goddard (T. W.)..............	1922–52	2979	59116	19.84
Kennedy (A. S.)	1907–36	2877	59044	20.52
W. G. Grace	1865–1908	2876	51545	17.92
Tate (M. W.)	1912–37	2784	50567	18.12
Hirst (G. H.)...............	1889–1929	2727	51209	18.77
Blythe (C.)	1899–1914	2506	42136	16.81
Astill (W. E.)	1906–39	2432	57836	23.78
J. C. White	1909–37	2358	43778	18.56
Perks (R. T. D.)	1930–55	2233	53770	24.07
Briggs (J.)	1879–1900	2200	35430	16.10
Dennett (G.)	1903–26	2147	42568	19.82
Hollies (W. E.).............	1932–55	2109	44220	20.96
Richardson (T.)	1892–1905	2105	38794	18.42
Shaw (A.)	1864–97	2072	24827	11.97
Woolley (F. E.)	1906–38	2068	41075	19.86
Geary (G.)	1912–39	2063	41246	20.15
Newman (J.)	1906–30	2032	51211	25.20
Haigh (S.)	1895–1913	2012	32091	15.94

BOWLERS WHO HAVE TAKEN 100 WICKETS IN A SEASON EIGHT TIMES OR MORE

23 Times: W. RHODES 200 wickets (3).

17 Times: A. P. FREEMAN 300 wickets (1), 200 wickets (7).

16 Times: T. W. GODDARD 200 wickets (4); C. W. L. PARKER 200 wickets (5); R. T. D. PERKS.

15 Times: J. T. HEARNE 200 wickets (3); G. H. HIRST 200 wickets (1); A. S. KENNEDY 200 wickets (1).

14 Times: C. BLYTHE 200 wickets (1); M. W. TATE 200 wickets (3); J. C. WHITE.

13 Times: W. E. HOLLIES.

12 Times: J. BRIGGS; G. DENNETT 200 wickets (1).

11 Times: G. GEARY; S. HAIGH; M. S. NICHOLS; A. E. RELF.

10 Times: W. ATTEWELL; A. V. BEDSER, W. G. GRACE; V. W. C. JUPP; G. MACAULAY 200 wickets (1); W. MEAD; T. B. MITCHELL; T. RICHARDSON 200 wickets (3); R. TYLDESLEY; T. WASS; D. V. P. WRIGHT.

9 Times: W. E. ASTILL; W. E. BOWES; C GLADWIN; R HOWORTH; J. MERCER; A. MOLD 200 wickets (2); J. NEWMAN, C. F. ROOT 200 wickets (1); J. SOUTHERTON 200 wickets (1); H. VERITY 200 wickets (3).

8 Times: H. DEAN; A. R. GOVER 200 wickets (2); J. C. LAKER; H. LARWOOD; G. A. LOHMANN 200 wickets (3); R. PEEL; A. SHAW, J. M. SIMS; F. A. TARRANT; G. J. THOMPSON; J. H. WARDLE; A. W. WELLARD; F. E. WOOLEY; J. A. YOUNG.

ALL-ROUND CRICKET

2,000 RUNS AND 200 WICKETS IN A SEASON

1906   G. H. Hirst   2,385 runs and 208 wickets

3,000 RUNS AND 100 WICKETS IN A SEASON

1937   J. H. Parks   3,003 runs and 101 wickets.

2,000 RUNS AND 100 WICKETS IN A SEASON

		Runs	Wickets			Runs	Wickets
1873	W. G. Grace	2139	106	1914	J. W. Hearne	2116	123
1876	W. G. Grace	2622	129	1914	F. E. Woolley	2272	125
1899	C. L. Townsend	2440	101	1920	J. W. Hearne	2148	142
1900	G. L. Jessop	2210	104	1921	V. W. C. Jupp	2169	121
1904	G. H. Hirst	2501	132	1921	F. E. Woolley	2101	167
1905	G. H. Hirst	2266	110	1922	F. E. Woolley	2022	163
1909	W. Rhodes	2094	141	1923	F. E. Woolley	2091	101
1911	W. Rhodes	2261	117	1933	L. Townsend	2268	100
1911	F. A. Tarrant	2030	111	1937	E. Davies	2012	103
1913	J. W. Hearne	2036	124	1937	Jas. Langridge	2082	101

1,000 RUNS AND 200 WICKETS IN A SEASON

1899	A. E. Trott	1175	239	1923	M. W. Tate	1168	219
1900	A. E. Trott	1337	211	1924	M. W. Tate	1419	205
1922	A. S. Kennedy	1129	205	1925	M. W. Tate	1290	228

The double feat of scoring 1,000 runs and taking 100 wickets in one season of first-class cricket has been accomplished 258 times as follows:—

SIXTEEN
Rhodes (W.)

FOURTEEN
Hirst (G. H.)

TEN
V. W. C. JUPP

NINE
Astill (W. E.)

EIGHT
W. G. Grace
Nichols (M. S.)
Relf (A. E.)
Tarrant (F. A.)
Tate (M. W.)
Woolley (F. E.)

SIX
P. G. H. Fender
Langridge (Jas.)

FIVE
J. W. H. T. Douglas
Hearne (J. W.)
Kennedy (A. S.)
Newman (J.)

FOUR
Arnold (E. G.)
Gunn (J.)
Kilner (R.)
Tribe (G. E.)

THREE
W. W. Armstrong (Australia)
T. E. Bailey
Braund (L. C.)
G. Giffen (Australia)
N. E. Haig
Howorth (R.)
Llewellyn (C. B.)
Smith (Ray)
S. G. Smith
Townsend (L.)
Wellard (A. W.)

TWO
Andrews (W. H. R.)
F. R. Brown
Close (D. B.)
J. N. Crawford
Davies (E.)

F. R. Foster
Hopwood (J. L.)
Jenkins (R. O.)
G. L. Jessop
Lockwood (W. H.)
Martin (S. H.)
Parks (J. H.)
Pope (G. H.)
Sinfield (R. A.
C. T. Studd
Thompson (G. J.)
C. L. Townsend
Trott (A. E.)
Watkins (A. J.)
J. C. White

ONE
Bailey (J.)
Barratt (F.)
Booth (M. W.)
B. J. T. Bosanquet
Brockwell (W.)
Broderick (V.)
Hon. F. S. G. Calthorpe
H. L. Collins (Australia)

L. N. Constantine (West Indies)	Hallows (J.)	R. W. V. Robins
Cuffe (J. A.)	Hayward (T.)	Root (C. F.)
Cuttell (W. R.)	Horton (M. J.)	H. L. Simms
Davidson (G.)	F. S. Jackson	Smailes (T. F.)
Dooland (B.)	Jackson (V. E.)	Smith (T. P. B.)
Drake (A.)	Killick (E. H.)	Titmus (F. J.).
G. A. Faulkner (South Africa)	King (J. H.)	Todd (L. J.)
	V. Mankad (India)	H. Trumble (Australia)
Flowers (W.)	J. R. Mason	Vine (J.)
A. E. R. Gilligan	Muncer (B. L.)	Wainwright (E.)
G. Goonesena	G. E. Palmer (Australia)	Walsh (J. E.)
J. M. Gregory (Australia)	Pearson (F.)	Wensley (A. F.)
Haigh (S.)	Peel (R.)	W. Wooller

G. Goonesena, Horton (M. J.), Jackson (V. E.), Titmus (F. J.), Tribe (G. E.), and Watkins (A. J.) accomplished this feat in 1955.

Ames (L. E. G.), in 1928 scored 1,919 runs and obtained 121 wickets while keeping wicket. In 1929 his aggregates were 1,795 runs and 127 wickets, and in 1932, 2,482 runs and 100 wickets.

CENTURY AND HAT-TRICK

1885 W. E. Roller, Surrey v. Sussex, at The Oval, 204 and 4 for 28 including hat-trick.

1927 R. E. S. Wyatt, M.C.C. v. Ceylon, at Colombo, 124 and 5 for 39 including hat-trick.

1928 L. N. Constantine, West Indies v. Northamptonshire, at Northampton, 7 for 45 including hat-trick, 107 (five 6's) and 6 for 67.

1937 Emrys Davies, Glamorgan v. Leicestershire, at Leicester, 139 and 4 for 27 and 3 for 31 including hat-trick.

(There may be other instances.)

WICKET-KEEPING FEATS

Most Dismissals:	H. Strudwick (1902–27)	1,493
Most Catches:	H. Strudwick (1902–27)	1,235
Most Stumpings:	L. E. G. Ames (1926–38)	413

12 wickets in match, ct. 8, st. 4, Pooley (E.), Surrey v. Sussex, at The Oval	1868
12 wickets in match, ct. 9, st. 3, D. Tallon, Queensland v. New South Wales, at Sydney ..	1938–39
10 wickets in match, all ct., Wilson (A. E.), Gloucestershire v. Hampshire, at Portsmouth	1953
10 wickets in match, ct. 5, st. 5, Phillips (H.),Sussex v. Surrey, at The Oval	1872
10 wickets in match, ct. 2, st. 8, Pooley (E.), Surrey v. Kent, at The Oval	1878
10 wickets in match, ct. 9, st. 1, Oates (T. W.), Nottinghamshire v. Middlesex, at Nottingham ..	1906
10 wickets in match, ct. 1, st. 9, Huish (F. H.), Kent v. Surrey, at The Oval	1911
10 wickets in match, ct. 9, st. 1, Hubble (J. C.), Kent v. Gloucestershire, at Cheltenham	1923
10 wickets in match, ct. 8, st. 2, Elliott (H.), Derbyshire v. Lancashire, at Manchester ..	1935
10 wickets in match, ct. 7, st. 3, Corrall (P.), Leicestershire v. Sussex, at Hove ..	1936
7 wickets in innings, ct. 4, st. 3, Smith (E. J.), Warwickshire v. Derbyshire, at Edgbaston	1926
7 wickets in innings, ct. 6, st. 1, Farrimond (W.), Lancashire v. Kent, at Manchester	1930
7 wickets in innings, ct. 7, Price (W. F.), Middlesex v. Yorkshire, at Lord's ..	1937
7 wickets in innings, ct. 3, st. 4, D. Tallon, Queensland v. Victoria, at Brisbane ..	1938–39

7 wickets in innings, ct. 7, R. Saggers, N.S.W. v. Queensland and
Victoria Combined, at Brisbane **1940–41**
7 wickets in innings, ct. 1, st. 6, Yarnold (H.), Worcestershire v. Scot-   **1951**
land, at Broughty Ferry .. ..

Three men stumped off successive balls, W. H. Brain, Gloucestershire
v. Somerset, at Cheltenham, 1893. (The bowler thus credited with the hat-trick
was C. L. Townsend.)

Wood (A.) kept wicket for Yorkshire in 222 consecutive County Championship matches (1928–1935).

127 wickets in a season, ct. 79, st. 48, Ames (L. E. G.), of Kent 1929
121 wickets in a season, ct. 69, st. 52, Ames (L. E. G.), of Kent .. 1928
110 wickets in a season, ct. 62, st. 48, Yarnold (H.), of Worcestershire 1949
107 wickets in a season, ct. 77, st. 30, Duckworth (G.), of Lancashire .. 1928
102 wickets in a season, ct. 70, st. 32, Huish (F. H.), of Kent 1913
100 wickets in a season, ct. 36, st. 64, Ames (L. E. G.), of Kent .. 1932
100 wickets in a season, ct. 62, st. 38, Huish (F. H.), of Kent .. 1911

MOST CATCHES

In a Career

913   F. E. Woolley   871 W. G. Grace

In a Season

78   W. R. Hammond   1928   65   J. Tunnicliffe   1895
70   J. Tunnicliffe   1901   64   J. Tunnicliffe   1904
69   John Langridge.........   1955   63   K. Grieves   1950
65   W. R. Hammond   1925

In a Match

10   W. R. Hammond, Gloucestershire v. Surrey, Cheltenham   1928
8   W. B. Burns, Worcestershire v. Yorkshire, Bradford   1907
8   A. H. Bakewell, Northamptonshire v. Essex, Leyton   1928
8   W. R. Hammond, Gloucestershire v. Worcestershire, Cheltenham ..   1932
8   K. Grieves, Lancashire v. Sussex, Manchester..   1951
8   C. A. Milton, Gloucestershire v. Sussex, Hove..   1952

THROWING THE CRICKET BALL

140 yards 2 feet, R. Percival, on the Durham Sand Racecourse   ..   1884
140 yards 9 inches, Ross Mackenzie, at Toronto **1872**

W. F. Forbes, on March 16th, 1876, threw 132 yards at the Eton College
Sports. He was then 18 years of age.

William Yardley, while a boy at Rugby, threw 100 yards with his
right hand and 78 with his left.

Charles Arnold, of Cambridge, once threw 112 yards with the wind and 108
against.   W. H. Game, at The Oval, in 1875, threw the ball 111 yards and then
back the same distance.   W. G. Grace threw 109 yards one way and back 105,
and George Millyard 108 with the wind and 103 against.   At The Oval in 1868,
W. G. Grace made three successive throws of 116, 117 and 118 yards, and then
threw back over a hundred yards.   D. G. Foster (Warwickshire) has thrown
133 yards, and in 1930 he made a Danish record with 120.1 metres—about
130 yards.

GREAT TOTALS

1107	Victoria v. New South Wales, at Melbourne	1926–27
1059	Victoria v. Tasmania, at Melbourne	1922–23
918	New South Wales v. South Australia, at Sydney	1900–01
912	(eight wkts., dec.), Holkar v. Mysore, at Indore	1945–46
903	(seven wkts.), England v. Australia, at The Oval.. ..	1938
887	Yorkshire v. Warwickshire, at Edgbaston	1896
849	England v. West Indies, at Kingston	1929–30
843	Australians v. Oxford and Cambridge Universities Past and Present, at Portsmouth	1893

HIGHEST FOR EACH FIRST-CLASS COUNTY

Derbyshire	.. 645 v. Hampshire, at Derby	1898
Essex	.. 692 v. Somerset, at Taunton	1895
Glamorgan	.. 587 (eight wickets) v. Derbyshire, at Cardiff ..	1951
Gloucestershire	.. 653 (six wickets) v. Glamorgan, at Bristol ..	1928
Hampshire	.. 672 (seven wickets) v. Somerset, at Taunton	1899
Kent	.. 803 (four wickets) v. Essex, at Brentwood ..	1934
Lancashire..	.. 801 v. Somerset, at Taunton	1895
Leicestershire	.. 701 (four wickets) v. Worcestershire, at Worcester..	1906
Middlesex ..	.. 642 (three wickets) v. Hampshire, at Southampton..	1923
Northamptonshire	557 (six wickets) v. Sussex, at Hove	1914
Nottinghamshire ..	739 (seven wickets) v. Leicestershire, at Nottingham	1903
Somerset ..	.. 675 (nine wickets) v. Hampshire, at Bath	1924
Surrey	.. 811 v. Somerset, at The Oval	1899
Sussex	.. 705 (eight wickets) v. Surrey, at Hastings ..	1902
Warwickshire	.. 657 (six wickets), v. Hampshire, at Edgbaston ..	1899
Worcestershire	.. 633 v. Warwickshire, at Worcester	1906
Yorkshire	.. 887 v. Warwickshire, at Edgbaston	1896

SMALL TOTALS

12	Oxford University v. M.C.C. and Ground, at Oxford	†1877
12	Northamptonshire v. Gloucestershire, at Gloucester	1907
13	Nottinghamshire v. Yorkshire, at Nottingham	1901
15	M.C.C. v. Surrey, at Lord's	1839
15	Victoria v. M.C.C., at Melbourne	†1903–04
15	Northamptonshire v. Yorkshire, at Northampton	†1908
15	Hampshire v. Warwickshire, at Edgbaston	1922
	(Following-on, Hampshire scored 521 and won by 155 runs)	
16	M.C.C. and Ground v. Surrey, at Lord's	1872
16	Derbyshire v. Notts, at Nottingham	1879
16	Surrey v. Nottinghamshire, at the Oval	1880
16	Warwickshire v. Kent, at Tonbridge	1913
16	Trinidad v. Barbados, at Bridgetown	1941–42
17	Derbyshire v. Lancashire, at Manchester	1888
17	Gloucestershire v. Australians, at Cheltenham	1896
18	Kent v. Sussex, at Gravesend	†1867
18	Australians v. M.C.C. and Ground, at Lord's	†1896
19	Sussex v. Surrey, at Godalming	1830
19	Sussex v. Nottinghamshire, at Hove	†1873
19	M.C.C. and Ground v. Australians, at Lord's	1878

† Signifies that one man was absent.

LOWEST FOR EACH COUNTY

Derbyshire	.. ..	16 v. Nottinghamshire, at Nottingham	 1879
Essex ..	.. ..	30 v. Yorkshire, at Leyton	 1901
Glamorgan	..	22 v. Lancashire, at Liverpool	 1924
Gloucestershire		17 v. Australians, at Cheltenham ..	 1896
Hampshire	..	15 v. Warwickshire, at Birmingham	 1922
Kent ..	..	18 v. Sussex, at Gravesend ..	 1867
Lancashire	..	25 v. Derbyshire, at Manchester ..	 1871
Leicestershire	..	25 v. Kent, at Leicester ..	 1912
Middlesex	..	20 v. M.C.C., at Lord's	 1864
Northamptonshire	..	12 v. Gloucestershire, at Gloucester	 1907
Nottinghamshire		13 v. Yorkshire, at Nottingham	 1901
Somerset	..	25 v. Gloucestershire, at Bristol ..	 1947
Surrey	..	16 v. Nottinghamshire, at The Oval	 1880
Sussex	..	19 v. Nottinghamshire, at Hove ..	 1873
Warwickshire	..	16 v. Kent, at Tonbridge ..	 1913
Worcestershire	..	24 v. Yorkshire, at Huddersfield ..	 1903
Yorkshire	..	26 v. Surrey, at The Oval	 1909

HIGHEST AGGREGATES

2376 for 38 wickets, Maharashtra v. Bombay, at Poona	1948–49
2078 for 40 wickets, Bombay v. Holkar, a Bombay	1944–45
1981 for 35 wickets, England v. South Africa, at Durban ..	1938–39
1929 for 39 wickets, New South Wales v. South Australia, at Sydney..	1925–26

In England

1723 for 31 wickets, England v. Australia, at Leeds	1948
1601 for 29 wickets, England v. Australia, at Lord's	1930
1502 for 28 wickets, M.C.C. v. New Zealand, at Lord's ..	1927
1496 for 24 wickets, England v. Australia, at Nottingham ..	1938
1494 for 37 wickets, England v. Australia, at The Oval.. ..	1934
1492 for 33 wickets, Worcestershire v. Oxford University, at Worcester	1904
1477 for 32 wickets, Hampshire v. Oxford University, at Southampton	1913
1477 for 33 wickets, England v. South Africa, at The Oval ..	1947
1475 for 27 wickets, Northamptonshire v. Surrey, at Northampton ..	1920

HEAVY SCORING IN FOURTH INNINGS

654 (five wickets), England v. South Africa, at Durban	1938–39
(After being set 696 to win. The match was left drawn on the tenth day.)	
604 Maharashtra v. Bombay, at Poona	1948–49
576 (eight wickets), Trinidad v. Barbados, at Port of Spain	1946
(After being set 672 to win. Match drawn on fifth day.)	
572 New South Wales v. South Australia, at Sydney	1907–08
(After being set 593 to win)	
518 Victoria v. Queensland, at Brisbane	1926–27
(When set 753 to win)	
507 (seven wickets), Cambridge University v. M.C.C. and Ground, at Lord's	1896
502 (six wickets), Middlesex v. Nottinghamshire, at Trent Bridge ..	1925
(Game won by an unfinished stand of 271: county record)	
502 (eight wickets), Players v. Gentlemen, at Lord's	1900

(Unless otherwise stated, the side making the runs won the match.)

BIGGEST VICTORIES

Yorkshire (555 for one wkt., dec.) beat Essex at Leyton on June 15, 16, 17, 1932, by an innings and 313 runs. Holmes and Sutcliffe made 555, the world's highest first-wicket partnership.

Middlesex (464 for one wkt., dec.) beat Essex at Leyton on May 23, 25, 26, 1914, by an innings and 56 runs.

Victoria (1,059) beat Tasmania by an innings and 666 runs at Melbourne, 1922–23.

Victoria (1,107) beat New South Wales by an innings and 656 runs at Melbourne, 1926–27.

New South Wales (918) beat South Australia by an innings and 605 runs at Sydney, 1900–01.

England (903 for seven wkts., dec.) beat Australia by an innings and 579 runs at The Oval in 1938.

England (521 and 342 for eight wkts., dec.) beat Australia by 675 runs at Brisbane in 1928–29.

Surrey (698) beat Sussex by an innings and 485 runs at The Oval in 1888.

Australians (675) beat Nottinghamshire by an innings and 517 runs at Nottingham in 1921. In their previous game they defeated Northamptonshire by an innings and 484 runs.

SCORERS OF 1,500 RUNS IN TESTS

ENGLAND

	Tests	Inns.	Not Outs	Runs	Highest Score	100's	Average
W. R. Hammond ..	85	140	16	7249	336*	22	58.45
L. Hutton	79	138	15	6971	364	19	56.67
D. C. S. Compton ..	72	119	14	5436	278	17	51.77
J. B. Hobbs	61	102	7	5410	211	15	56.94
H. Sutcliffe	54	84	9	4555	194	16	60.73
E. Hendren	51	83	9	3525	205*	7	47.63
F. E. Woolley	64	98	7	3283	154	5	36.07
M. Leyland	41	65	5	2764	187	9	46.06
C. Washbrook	34	63	6	2465	195	6	43.24
W. J. Edrich	39	63	2	2440	219	6	40.00
L. E. G. Ames	47	72	12	2434	149	8	40.56
W. Rhodes	58	98	21	2325	179	2	30.19
P. B. H. May	29	48	2	2000	138	5	43.47
T. Hayward	35	60	2	1999	137	3	34.46
A. C. Maclaren	35	61	4	1931	140	5	33.87
R. E. S. Wyatt	40	64	6	1839	149	2	31.70
T. G. Evans	66	97	11	1831	104	2	21.29
T. E. Bailey	39	58	11	1670	134*	1	35.53
J. T. Tyldesley ...	31	55	1	1661	138	4	30.75
J. Hardstaff, junr. ..	23	38	3	1636	205*	4	46.74
T. W. Graveney	31	50	7	1590	175	2	36.97
E. Paynter	20	31	5	1540	243	4	59.23

AUSTRALIA

D. G. Bradman	52	80	10	6996	334	29	99.94
R. N. Harvey	39	67	6	3766	205	15	61.73
A. R. Morris.......	47	79	3	3533	206	12	46.48
C. Hill	49	89	3	3402	191	7	39.55
V. Trumper	48	89	8	3163	214*	8	39.04
A. L. Hassett	43	69	3	3073	198*	10	46.56

* Signifies not out.

	Tests	Inns.	Not Outs	Runs	Highest Score	100's	Average
W. W. Armstrong ..	50	84	10	2873	159*	6	38.82
S. J. McCabe	39	62	5	2748	232	6	48.21
K. R. Miller	49	75	6	2723	147	7	39.46
W. Bardsley	41	66	5	2469	193*	6	40.47
W. M. Woodfull ...	35	54	4	2300	161	7	46.00
S. E. Gregory	58	100	7	2282	201	4	24.53
C. G. Macartney ...	35	55	4	2132	170	7	41.80
W. H. Ponsford ...	29	48	4	2122	266	7	48.22
M. A. Noble	42	73	7	1997	133	1	30.25
J. Darling	34	60	2	1657	178	3	28.56
W. A. Brown	22	35	1	1592	206*	4	46.82

SOUTH AFRICA

	Tests	Inns.	Not Outs	Runs	Highest Score	100's	Average
B. Mitchell	42	80	9	3471	189*	8	48.88
A. D. Nourse, junr.	34	52	7	2960	231	9	53.81
H. W. Taylor	42	76	4	2936	176	7	40.77
A. D. Nourse, senr.	45	83	8	2234	111	1	29.78
E. A. B. Rowan ...	26	50	5	1965	236	3	43.66
G. A. Faulkner	25	47	4	1754	204	4	40.79
R. H. Catterall	24	43	2	1555	120	3	37.92

WEST INDIES

	Tests	Inns.	Not Outs	Runs	Highest Score	100's	Average
E. Weekes	34	58	4	3387	297	11	62.72
C. L. Walcott	33	56	5	3082	220	14	60.43
F. M. Worrell	27	47	4	2341	261	7	54.44
G. A. Headley	22	40	4	2190	270	10	60.83
J. B. Stollmeyer	32	56	5	2159	160	4	42.33

INDIA

	Tests	Inns.	Not Outs	Runs	Highest Score	100's	Average
V. S. Hazare	30	52	6	2192	164*	8	47.65

* *Signifies not out.*

BOWLERS WITH 75 WICKETS IN TESTS

ENGLAND

	Tests	Runs	Wickets	Average
A. V. Bedser	51	5876	236	24.89
S. F. Barnes	27	3106	189	16.43
M. W. Tate	39	4051	155	26.13
H. Verity	40	3510	144	24.37
W. Rhodes	58	3425	127	26.96
J. Briggs..................	33	2094	118	17.74
G. A. Lohmann	18	1205	112	10.75
D. V. P. Wright	34	4224	108	39.11
R. Peel	20	1715	102	16.81
C. Blythe	19	1863	100	18.63
W. Voce...................	27	2733	98	27.88
J. B. Statham	28	2128	89	23.91
T. Richardson.............	14	2220	88	25.22
J. C. Laker	24	2394	86	27.83
T. E. Bailey	39	2772	84	33.00
W. R. Hammond	85	3127	83	37.67
F. E. Woolley	64	2815	83	33.91
G. O. Allen	25	2379	81	29.37
H. Larwood	21	2216	78	28.41

AUSTRALIA

	Tests	Runs	Wickets	Average
C. V. Grimmett	37	5231	216	24.21
R. R. Lindwall	47	4203	192	21.89
W. A. Johnston	40	3825	160	23.90
K. R. Miller	49	3380	147	22.99
W. J. O'Reilly.............	27	3254	144	22.59
H. Trumble	32	3072	141	21.78
M. A. Noble	42	3027	121	25.01
G. Giffen	31	2791	103	27.09
C. T. B. Turner	17	1670	101	16.53
A. A. Mailey...............	21	3358	99	33.91
F. R. Spofforth............	18	1731	94	18.41
A. Cotter	21	2549	89	28.64
W. W. Armstrong	50	2923	87	33.59
J. M. Gregory.............	24	2648	85	31.15
J. V. Saunders	14	1797	79	22.74
G. E. Palmer...............	17	1678	78	21.51

SOUTH AFRICA

H. J. Tayfield	22	2676	104	25.73
C. L. Vincent	25	2631	84	31.32
G. A. Faulkner.............	25	2180	82	26.58

WEST INDIES

A. L. Valentine.............	22	3073	105	29.26
S. Ramadhin	24	2873	93	30.98

INDIA

V. Mankad	35	4332	135	32.08

MOST WICKETS IN A TEST

17/159	S. F. Barnes, England v. South Africa, Johannesburg	1913–14
15/28	J. Briggs, England v. South Africa, Cape Town	1888–89
15/45	G. A. Lohmann, England v. South Africa, Port Elizabeth ..	1895–96
15/99	C. Blythe, England v. South Africa, Leeds	1907
15/104	H. Verity, England v. Australia, Lord's	1934
15/124	W. Rhodes, England v. Australia, Melbourne	1903–04
14/90	F. R. Spofforth, Australia v. England, Oval	1882
14/99	A. V. Bedser, England v. Australia, Nottingham	1953
14/144	S. F. Barnes, England v. South Africa, Durban	1913–14
14/199	C. V. Grimmett, Australia v. South Africa, Adelaide	1931–32

The best for South Africa is 13/165 by H. Tayfield against Australia at Melbourne, 1952–53.

SLOW TEST INNINGS

18 in 180 minutes—G. O. Rabone, New Zealand v. England, Dunedin.	1954–55
19 not out in 150 minutes—W. L. Murdoch, Aust. v. Engl., Melbourne	1882–83
34 in 225 minutes—W. H. Scotton, England v. Australia, Oval ..	1886
38 in 260 minutes—T. E. Bailey, England v. Australia, Leeds ..	1953
41 in 240 minutes—A. C. Bannerman, Australia v. England, Melbourne	1891–92
40 in 295 minutes—H. L. Collins, Australia v. England, Manchester ..	1921
71 in 255 minutes—T. E. Bailey, England v. Australia, Lord's	1953
82 in 360 minutes—W. H. Scotton, England v. Australia, Adelaide ..	1884–85

ENGLAND v. AUSTRALIA

SUMMARY OF RESULTS

Season	Visiting Captain	Won by England	Won by Australia	Drawn	Total
1876–77	J. Lillywhite .... (E.)	1	1	0	2
1878–79	Lord Harris .... (E.)	0	1	0	1
1880	W. L. Murdoch ..... (A.)	1	0	0	1
1881–82	A. Shaw .... (E.)	0	2	2	4
1882	W. L. Murdoch ..... (A.)	0	1	0	1
1882–83	Hon. Ivo. Bligh ... (E.)	2	2	0	4
1884	W. L. Murdoch ..... (A.)	1	0	2	3
1884–85	A. Shrewsbury ...... (E.)	3	2	0	5
1886	H. J. H. Scott ..... (A.)	3	0	0	3
1886–87	A. Shrewsbury ...... (E.)	2	0	0	2
1887–88	W. W. Read .... (E.)	1	0	0	1
1888	P. S. McDonnell .... (A.)	2	1	0	3
1890*	W. L. Murdoch ..... (A.)	2	0	0	2
1891–92	W. G. Grace .... (E.)	1	2	0	3
1893	J. McC. Blackham ... (A.)	1	0	2	3
1894–95	A. E. Stoddart ...... (E.)	3	2	0	5
1896	G. H. S. Trott ...... (A.)	2	1	0	3
1897–98	A. E. Stoddart ...... (E.)	1	4	0	5
1899	J. Darling .... (A.)	0	1	4	5
1901–2	A. C. MacLaren ..... (E.)	1	4	0	5
1902	J. Darling .... (A.)	1	2	2	5
1903–4	P. E. Warner .... (E.)	3	2	0	5
1905	J. Darling .... (A.)	2	0	3	5
1907–8	A. O. Jones .... (E.)	1	4	0	5
1909	M. A. Noble .... (A.)	1	2	2	5
1911–12	J. W. H. T. Douglas.. (E.)	4	1	0	5
1912	S. E. Gregory ...... (A.)	1	0	2	3
1920–21	J. W. H. T. Douglas.. (E.)	0	5	0	5
1921	W. W. Armstrong ...(A.)	0	3	2	5
1924–25	A. E. R. Gilligan ... (E.)	1	4	0	5
1926	H. L. Collins .... (A.)	1	0	4	5
928–29	A. P. F. Chapman ...(E.)	4	1	0	5
1930	W. M. Woodfull ..... (A.)	1	2	2	5
1932–33	D. R. Jardine........ (E.)	4	1	0	5
1934	W. M. Woodfull ..... (A.)	1	2	2	5
1936–37	G. O. Allen .... (E.)	2	3	0	5
1938*	D. G. Bradman ..... (A.)	1	1	2	4
1946–47	W. R. Hammond ..... (E.)	0	3	2	5
1948	D. G. Bradman ..... (A.)	0	4	1	5
1950–51	F. R. Brown......... (E.)	1	4	0	5
1953	A. L. Hassett .... (A.)	1	0	4	5
1954–55	L. Hutton .... (E.)	3	1	1	5
	In Australia	38	49	5	92
	In England	22	20	34	76
	Totals	60	69	39	168

* The match at Manchester was abandoned without a ball bowled.

HIGHEST TOTALS FOR AN INNINGS

By England		
903	(7 wkts.), The Oval ..	1938
658	(8 wkts.), Nottingham	1938
636	.. Sydney	1928–29
627	(9 wkts.), Manchester	1934

By Australia		
729	(6 wkts.), Lord's	1930
701	.. The Oval	1934
695	.. The Oval	1930
659	(8 wkts.), Sydney	1946–47
645	.. Brisbane	1946–47
604	.. Melbourne	1936–37
601	(8 wkts.), Brisbane ...	1954–55

SMALLEST TOTALS FOR AN INNINGS

36 .. Australia .. Edgbaston 1902	44 .. Australia .. The Oval 1896
42 .. Australia .. Sydney 1887–88	45 .. England .. Sydney 1886–87

RECORD PARTNERSHIP FOR EACH WICKET

By England

323 for 1st	J. B. Hobbs and W. Rhodes, at Melbourne	1911–12
382 for 2nd	L. Hutton and M. Leyland, at The Oval ..	1938
262 for 3rd	W. R. Hammond and D. R. Jardine, at Adelaide	1928–29
222 for 4th	W. R. Hammond and E. Paynter, at Lord's	1938
206 for 5th	E. Paynter and D. Compton, at Nottingham	1938
215 for 6th	L. Hutton and J. Hardstaff, at The Oval ..	1938
143 for 7th	J. Vine and F. E. Woolley, at Sydney	1911–12
124 for 8th	E. Hendren and H. Larwood, at Brisbane	1928–29
151 for 9th	W. W. Read and W. H. Scotton, at The Oval	1884
130 for 10th	R. E. Foster and W. Rhodes, at Sydney ..	1903–04

By Australia

180 for 1st	W. Bardsley and S. E. Gregory, at The Oval	1909
451 for 2nd	W. H. Ponsford and D. G. Bradman, at The Oval	1934
276 for 3rd	D. G. Bradman and A. L. Hassett, at Brisbane ..	1946–47
388 for 4th	W. H. Ponsford and D. G. Bradman, at Leeds ..	1934
405 for 5th	S. G. Barnes and D. G. Bradman, at Sydney	1946–47
346 for 6th	D. G. Bradman and J. H. Fingleton, at Melbourne	1936–37
165 for 7th	C. Hill and H. Trumble, at Melbourne ..	1897–98
243 for 8th	C. Hill and R. J. Hartigan, at Adelaide ..	1907–08
154 for 9th	J. McC. Blackham and S. E. Gregory, at Sydney	1894–95
127 for 10th	J. M. Taylor and A. A. Mailey, at Sydney	1924–25

HUNDRED ON DEBUT IN ENGLAND–AUSTRALIA TESTS

For England

152	W.G.Grace,atThe Oval	1880
154*	K. S. Ranjitsinhji,Manchester	1896
287	R. E. Foster, Sydney..	1903–04
119	G. Gunn, Sydney 1907–08
115	H. Sutcliffe, Sydney ..	1924–25
137	M. Leyland, Melbourne	1928–29

173	K. S. Duleepsinhji, Lord's	1930
102	Nawab of Pataudi, Sydney	1932–33
100	L. Hutton, Nottingham	1938
102	D. C. S. Compton, Nottingham	1938
109	W. Watson, Lord's	1953

For Australia

165*	C. Bannerman, Melbourne (Retired.) ..	1876–77
107	H. Graham, Lord's ..	1893
104	R. A. Duff, Melbourne	1901–02
116	R. J. Hartigan, Adelaide	1907–08

104	H. L. Collins, Sydney..	1920–21
110	W. H. Ponsford, Sydney	1924–25
164	A. A. Jackson, Adelaide	1928–29
112	R. N. Harvey, Leeds..	1948
101*	J. Burke, Adelaide ..	1950–51

* Signifies not out.

INDIVIDUAL HUNDREDS IN THE MATCHES 1876–1955

For England (118)

132*	R. Abel, Sydney	1891–2
120	L. E. G. Ames, Lord's..	1934
134	W. Barnes, Adelaide....	1884–5
129	C. J. Barnett, Adelaide..	1936–7
126	C. J. Barnett, Nottingham	1938
103*	L. C. Braund, Adelaide..	1901–2
102	L. C. Braund, Sydney ..	1903–4
121	J. Briggs, Melbourne ...	1884–5
140	J. T. Brown, Melbourne	1894–5
121	A. P. F. Chapman, Lord's	1930
102	D. C. S. Compton, Nottingham	1938
147 103*	} D. C. S. Compton, Adelaide	1946–7
184	D. C. S. Compton, Nottingham	1948
145*	D. C. S. Compton, Manchester	1948
102	M. C. Cowdrey, Melbourne	1954–5
173	K. S. Duleepsinhji, Lord's	1930
119	W. J. Edrich, Sydney...	1946–7
111	W. J. Edrich, Leeds	1948
287	R. E. Foster, Sydney...	1903–4
144	C. B. Fry, The Oval ..	1905
152	W. G. Grace, The Oval..	1880
170	W. G. Grace, The Oval..	1886
111	T. W. Graveney, Sydney	1954–5
119	G. Gunn, Sydney	1907–8
122*	G. Gunn, Sydney	1907–8
102*	W. Gunn, Manchester ..	1893
251	W. R. Hammond, Sydney	1928–9
200	W. R. Hammond, Melbourne	1928–9
119* 177	} W. R. Hammond, Adelaide	1928–9
113	W. R. Hammond, Leeds	1930
112	W. R. Hammond, Sydney	1932–3
101	W. R. Hammond, Sydney	1932–3
231*	W. R. Hammond, Sydney	1936–7
240	W. R. Hammond, Lord's	1938
169*	J. Hardstaff, junr., The Oval	1938
130	T. Hayward, Manchester	1899
137	T. Hayward, The Oval..	1899
114	J. W. Hearne, Melbourne	1911–12
127*	E. Hendren, Lord's......	1926
169	E. Hendren, Brisbane...	1928–9
132	E. Hendren, Manchester	1934
126*	J. B. Hobbs, Melbourne.	1911–12
187	J. B. Hobbs, Melbourne.	1911–12
178	J. B. Hobbs, Melbourne.	1911–12
107	J. B. Hobbs, Lord's	1912
122	J. B. Hobbs, Melbourne.	1920–1
123	J. B. Hobbs, Adelaide ..	1920–1
115	J. B. Hobbs, Sydney ...	1924–5
154	J. B. Hobbs, Melbourne.	1924–5
119	J. B. Hobbs, Adelaide ..	1924–5

119	J. B. Hobbs, Lord's	1926
100	J. B. Hobbs, The Oval..	1926
142	J. B. Hobbs, Melbourne.	1928–9
126	K. L. Hutchings, Melbourne......	1907–8
100	L. Hutton, Nottingham .	1938
364	L. Hutton, The Oval....	1938
122*	L. Hutton, Sydney	1946–7
156*	L. Hutton, Adelaide....	1950–1
145	L. Hutton, Lord's	1953
103	Hon. F. S. Jackson, The Oval	1893
118	Hon. F. S. Jackson, The Oval	1899
128	Hon. F. S. Jackson, Manchester	1902
144*	Hon. F. S. Jackson, Leeds	1905
113	Hon. F. S. Jackson, Manchester	1905
104	G. L. Jessop, The Oval..	1902
137	M. Leyland, Melbourne.	1928–9
109	M. Leyland, Lord's.....	1934
153	M. Leyland, Manchester	1934
110	M. Leyland, The Oval..	1934
126	M. Leyland, Brisbane...	1936–7
111*	M. Leyland, Melbourne.	1936–7
187	M. Leyland, The Oval ..	1938
130	A. C. MacLaren, Melbourne	1894–5
109	A. C. MacLaren, Sydney	1897–8
124	A. C. MacLaren, Adelaide	1897–8
116	A. C. MacLaren, Sydney	1901–2
140	A. C. MacLaren, Nottingham	1905
117	H. Makepeace, Melbourne	1920–1
102	P. B. H. May, Sydney..	1954–5
182*	C. P. Mead, The Oval...	1921
102	Nawab of Pataudi, Sydney	1932–3
216*	E. Paynter, Nottingham.	1938
154*	K. S. Ranjitsinhji, Manchester	1896
175	K. S. Ranjitsinhji, Sydney	1897–8
117	W. W. Read, The Oval..	1884
179	W. Rhodes, Melbourne .	1911–12
135*	A. C. Russell, Adelaide..	1920–1
101	A. C. Russell, Manchester	1921
102*	A. C. Russell, The Oval.	1921
105	J. Sharp, The Oval	1909
105*	A. Shrewsbury, Melbourne	1884–5
164	A. Shrewsbury, Lord's..	1886
106	A. Shrewsbury, Lord's..	1893
156*	R. T. Simpson, Melbourne	1950–1
135*	A. G. Steel, Sydney.....	1882–3

* Signifies not out.

148	A. G. Steel, Lord's	1884
134	A. E. Stoddart, Adelaide	1891–2
173	A. E. Stoddart, Melbourne	1894–5
115	H. Sutcliffe, Sydney ...	1924–5
176 127 }	H. Sutcliffe, Melbourne.	1924–5
143	H. Sutcliffe, Melbourne.	1924–5
161	H. Sutcliffe, The Oval ..	1926
135	H. Sutcliffe, Melbourne.	1928–9
161	H. Sutcliffe, The Oval ..	1930
194	H. Sutcliffe, Sydney	1932–3

138	J. T. Tyldesley, Edgbaston	1902
100	J. T. Tyldesley, Leeds...	1905
112*	J. T. Tyldesley, The Oval	1905
149	G. Ulyett, Melbourne ...	1881–2
117	A. Ward, Sydney	1894–5
109	W. Watson, Lord's	1953
112	C. Washbrook, Melbourne	1946–7
143	C. Washbrook, Leeds...	1948
133*	F. E. Woolley, Sydney .	1911–12
123	F. E. Woolley, Sydney..	1924–5

Note.—In consecutive innings in 1928–29 W. R. Hammond scored 251 at Sydney, 200 and 32 at Melbourne, and 119* and 177 at Adelaide.

For Australia (129)

133*	W. W. Armstrong, Melbourne	1907–8
158	W. W. Armstrong, Sydney.................	1920–1
121	W. W. Armstrong, Adelaide	1920–1
123*	W. W. Armstrong, Melbourne	1920–1
118	C. L. Badcock, Melbourne	1936–7
165*	C. Bannerman, Melbourne	1876–7
136 130 }	W. Bardsley, The Oval..	1909
193*	W. Bardsley, Lord's	1926
234	S. G. Barnes, Sydney...	1946–7
141	S. G. Barnes, Lord's...	1948
128	G. J. Bonnor, Sydney...	1884–5
112	D. G. Bradman, Melbourne	1928–9
123	D. G. Bradman, Melbourne	1928–9
131	D. G. Bradman, Nottingham	1930
254	D. G. Bradman, Lord's.	1930
334	D. G. Bradman, Leeds..	1930
232	D. G. Bradman, The Oval	1930
103*	D. G. Bradman, Melbourne	1932–3
304	D. G. Bradman, Leeds..	1934
244	D. G. Bradman, The Oval	1934
270	D. G. Bradman, Melbourne	1936–7
212	D. G. Bradman, Adelaide	1936–7
169	D. G. Bradman, Melbourne	1936–7
144*	D. G. Bradman, Nottingham	1938
102*	D. G. Bradman, Lord's..	1938
103	D. G. Bradman, Leeds..	1938
187	D. G. Bradman, Brisbane	1946–7
234	D. G. Bradman, Sydney.	1946–7
138	D. G. Bradman, Nottingham	1948

173*	D. G. Bradman, Leeds..	1948
105	W. A. Brown, Lord's...	1934
133	W. A. Brown, Nottingham	1938
206*	W. A. Brown, Lord's...	1938
101*	J. Burke, Adelaide	1950–1
104	H. L. Collins, Sydney...	1920–1
162	H. L. Collins, Adelaide..	1920–1
114	H. L. Collins, Sydney...	1924–5
101	J. Darling, Sydney	1897–8
178	J. Darling, Adelaide	1897–8
160	J. Darling, Sydney	1897–8
104	R. A. Duff, Melbourne..	1901–2
146	R. A. Duff, The Oval....	1905
100	J. H. Fingleton, Brisbane	1936–7
136	J. H. Fingleton, Melbourne	1936–7
161	G. Giffen, Sydney	1894–5
107	H. Graham, Lord's.....	1893
105	H. Graham, Sydney	1894–5
100	J. M. Gregory, Melbourne	1920–1
201	S. E. Gregory, Sydney..	1894–5
103	S. E. Gregory, Lord's...	1896
117	S. E. Gregory, The Oval	1899
112	S. E. Gregory, Adelaide.	1903–4
116	R. J. Hartigan, Adelaide	1907–8
112	R. N. Harvey, Leeds....	1948
122	R. N. Harvey, Manchester	1953
162	R. N. Harvey, Brisbane.	1954–5
128	A. L. Hassett, Brisbane.	1946–7
137	A. L. Hassett, Nottingham	1948
115	A. L. Hassett, Nottingham	1953
104	A. L. Hassett, Lord's ..	1953
112	H. L. Hendry, Sydney..	1928–9
188	C. Hill, Melbourne	1897–8
135	C. Hill, Lord's	1899
119	C. Hill, Sheffield	1902
160	C. Hill, Adelaide	1907–8
124	T. Horan, Melbourne ...	1881–2
140	F. A. Iredale, Adelaide..	1894–5
108	F. A. Iredale, Manchester	1896

* *Signifies not out.*

164	A. A. Jackson, Adelaide.	1928–9		153*	W. L. Murdoch, The Oval	1880
147	C. Kelleway, Adelaide..	1920–1		211	W. L. Murdoch, The Oval	1884
100	A. F. Kippax, Melbourne	1928–9		133	M. A. Noble, Sydney...	1903–4
100	R. Lindwall, Melbourne.	1946–7		116	C. E. Pellew, Melbourne	1920–1
134	J. J. Lyons, Sydney.....	1891–2		104	C. E. Pellew, Adelaide..	1920–1
170	C. G. Macartney, Sydney	1920–1		110	W. H. Ponsford, Sydney	1924–5
115	C. G. Macartney, Leeds.	1921		128	W. H. Ponsford, Melbourne	1924–5
133*	C. G. Macartney, Lord's	1926				
151	C. G. Macartney, Leeds.	1926		110	W. H. Ponsford, The Oval	1930
109	C. G. Macartney, Manchester..............	1926		181	W. H. Ponsford, Leeds..	1934
				266	W. H. Ponsford, The Oval	1934
187*	S. J. McCabe, Sydney...	1932–3		143*	V. S. Ransford, Lord's..	1909
137	S. J. McCabe, Manchester..............	1934		100	A. J. Richardson, Leeds.	1926
				138	V. Y. Richardson, Melbourne	1924–5
232	S. J. McCabe, Melbourne	1936–7				
	S. J. McCabe, Nottingham	1938		201*	J. Ryder, Adelaide	1924–5
				112	J. Ryder, Melbourne ...	1928–9
104*	C. McCool, Melbourne.	1946–7		102	H. J. H. Scott, The Oval	1884
147	P. S. McDonnell, Sydney	1881–2		108	J. M. Taylor, Sydney...	1924–5
103	P. S. McDonnell, The Oval	1884		143	G. H. S. Trott, Lord's..	1896
				135*	V. T. Trumper, Lord's..	1899
124	P. S. McDonnell, Adelaide	1884–5		104	V. T. Trumper, Manchester..............	1902
				185*	V. T. Trumper, Sydney..	1903–4
112	C. E. McLeod, Melbourne	1897–8		113	V. T. Trumper, Adelaide	1903–14
				166	V. T. Trumper, Sydney..	1907–8
141*	K. R. Miller, Adelaide..	1946–7		113	V. T. Trumper, Sydney..	1911–12
145*	K. R. Miller, Sydney...	1950–1		141	W. M. Woodfull, Leeds.	1926
109	K. R. Miller, Lord's ...	1953		117	W. M. Woodfull, Manchester..............	1926
155	A. R. Morris, Melbourne	1946–7				
122	} A. R. Morris, Adelaide	1946–7		111	W. M. Woodfull, Sydney	1928–9
124*				107	W. M. Woodfull, Melbourne..............	1928–9
105	A. R. Morris, Lord's ...	1948				
182	A. R. Morris, Leeds....	1948		102	W. M. Woodfull, Melbourne..............	1928–9
196	A. R. Morris, The Oval.	1948				
206	A. R. Morris, Adelaide..	1950–1		155	W. M. Woodfull, Lord's	1930
153	A. R. Morris, Brisbane..	1954–5				

D. G. Bradman's scores in 1930 were 8 and 131 at Nottingham, 254 and 1 at Lord's, 334 at Leeds, 14 at Manchester, and 232 at The Oval.

D. G. Bradman scored a hundred in six consecutive Test Matches v. England —three in 1936–37 and three in 1938.

No right-handed batsman has obtained two 100's for Australia in a Test Match against England. H. Sutcliffe, in his first two games for England, scored 59 and 115 at Sydney and 176 and 127 at Melbourne in 1924–25. In the latter match, which lasted into the seventh day, he was on the field throughout except for 86 minutes, namely 27 hours 52 minutes.

C. Hill made 98 and 97 at Adelaide in 1901–02, and F. E. Woolley 95 and 93 at Lord's in 1921.

C. G. Macartney in 1926, Sutcliffe (H.) in 1924–25 and A. Morris in 1946–47 made three hundreds in consecutive innings.

J. B. Hobbs and H. Sutcliffe shared in eleven first-wicket three-figure partnerships.

L. Hutton and C. Washbrook have twice made three-figure stands in each innings, at Adelaide in 1946–47 and at Leeds in 1948.

H. Sutcliffe, during his highest score of 194, v. Australia in 1932–33, took part in three stands each exceeding 100, viz. 112 with R. E. S. Wyatt for the first wicket, 188 with W. R. Hammond for the second wicket, and 123 with

* Signifies not out.

the Nawab of Pataudi for the third wicket. In 1903–04 R. E. Foster, in his historic innings of 287, added 192 for the fifth wicket with L. C. Braund, 115 for the ninth with A. E. Relf, and 130 for the tenth with W. Rhodes.

When L. Hutton scored 364 at The Oval in 1938 he added 382 for the second wicket with M. Leyland and 215 for the sixth wicket with J. Hardstaff, junr.

D. C. S. Compton and A. Morris at Adelaide in 1946–47 provide the only instance of a player on each side hitting two separate hundreds in a Test match.

MOST RUNS IN A RUBBER

For England—905, average 113.12, by W. R. Hammond, 1928–29.
For Australia—974, average 139.14, by D. G. Bradman, 1930.

MOST WICKETS IN A RUBBER

For England—39, for 17.48 runs each, in 1953, by A. V. Bedser.
For England—38, for 23.18 runs each, in 1924–25, by M. W. Tate.
For Australia—36, for 26.27 runs each, in 1920–21, by A. A. Mailey.

MOST WICKETS IN A MATCH

For England—15, for 124 runs, W. Rhodes, at Melbourne, 1903–04.
For England—15, for 104 runs, H. Verity, at Lord's, 1934.
For Australia—14, for 90 runs, F. R. Spofforth, at The Oval, 1882.

THE HAT TRICK

For England		For Australia	
W. Bates	Melbourne 1882–83	F. R. Spofforth	Melbourne 1878–79
J. Briggs	Sydney ... 1891–92	H. Trumble	Melbourne 1901–02
J. T. Hearne	Leeds..... 1899	H. Trumble	Melbourne 1903–04

W. A. Oldfield in Tests v. England dismissed 90 men: 59 caught, 31 stumped. He created another Test record at Melbourne in February 1925 by dismissing five men in one innings.

A. A. Lilley dismissed 84.

SCORERS OF OVER 2,000 RUNS

	Innings		Not out		Runs		Highest Innings		Average
D. G. Bradman	63	..	7	..	5028	..	334	..	89.78
J. B. Hobbs	71	..	4	..	3636	..	187	..	54.26
W. R. Hammond	58	..	3	..	2852	..	251	..	51.85
H. Sutcliffe	46	..	5	..	2741	..	194	..	66.85
C. Hill	76	..	1	..	2660	..	188	..	35.46
L. Hutton	49	..	6	..	2428	..	364	..	56.46
V. T. Trumper	74	..	5	..	2263	..	185*	..	32.79
S. E. Gregory	92	..	7	..	2193	..	201	..	25.80
W. W. Armstrong	71	..	9	..	2172	..	158	..	35.03

Signifies not out.

ENGLAND v. SOUTH AFRICA
SUMMARY OF RESULTS

Season	Visiting Captain	Won by England	Won by South Africa	Drawn	Total
1888–89	C. A. Smith ....(E.)	2	0	0	2
1891–92	W. W. Read ....(E.)	1	0	0	1
1895–96	Lord Hawke ....(E.)	3	0	0	3
1898–99	Lord Hawke ....(E.)	2	0	0	2
1905–06	P. F. Warner ....(E.)	1	4	0	5
1907	P. W. Sherwell ....(S.A.)	1	0	2	3
1909–10	H. D. G. Leveson Gower (E.)	2	3	0	5
1912	F. Mitchell ....(S.A.)	3	0	0	3
1913–14	J. W. H. T. Douglas ....(E.)	4	0	1	5
1922–23	F. T. Mann ....(E.)	2	1	2	5
1924	H. W. Taylor ....(S.A.)	3	0	2	5
1927–28	Capt. R. T. Stanyforth..(E.)	2	2	1	5
1929	H. G. Deane ....(S.A.)	2	0	3	5
1930–31	A. P. F. Chapman ......(E.)	0	1	4	5
1935	H. F. Wade ....(S.A.)	0	1	4	5
1938–39	W. R. Hammond ....(E.)	1	0	4	5
1947	A. Melville ....(S.A.)	3	0	2	5
1948–49	F. G. Mann ....(E.)	2	0	3	5
1951	A. D. Nourse ....(S.A.)	3	1	1	5
1955	J. E. Cheetham ......(S.A.)	3	2	0	5
	In South Africa	22	11	15	48
	In England	18	4	14	36
	Totals	40	15	29	84

HIGHEST TOTALS

By England		By South Africa	
654 for 5 Durban	1938–39	538 .. Leeds............	1951
608 .. Johannesburg....	1948–49	533 .. Nottingham......	1947
559 for 9 dec. Cape Town ..	1938–39	530 .. Durban	1938–39
554 for 8 Lord's	1947	521 for 8 Manchester......	1955
551 .. Nottingham......	1947	513 for 8 Cape Town......	1930–31
534 for 6 The Oval	1935	500 .. Leeds	1955
531 for 2 Lord's..........	1924	492 for 8 The Oval........	1929

SMALLEST TOTALS

By England		By South Africa	
76 .. Leeds...........	1907	30 .. Port Elizabeth	1895–96
		30 .. Edgbaston	1924
		35 .. Cape Town.......	1898–99

RECORD PARTNERSHIPS FOR EACH WICKET
By England

359 for 1st	L. Hutton and C. Washbrook, at Johannesburg	1948–49
280 for 2nd	P. A. Gibb and W. J. Edrich, at Durban	1938–39
370 for 3rd	W. J. Edrich and D. C. S. Compton, at Lord's ..	1947
197 for 4th	W. R. Hammond and L. E. G. Ames, at Cape Town ..	1938–39
237 for 5th	D. C. S. Compton and N. W. D. Yardley, at Nottingham..	1947
156 for 6th	C. P. Mead and F. T. Mann, at Durban	1922–23
115 for 7th	M. C. Bird and J. W. H. T. Douglas, at Durban	1913–14
154 for 8th	H. R. Bromley-Davenport and C. W. Wright, at Johannesburg	1895–96
71 for 9th	H. Wood and J. T. Hearne, at Cape Town	1891–92
92 for 10th	A. C. Russell and A. E. R. Gilligan, at Durban	1922–23

By South Africa

260 for 1st	I. J. Siedle and B. Mitchell, at Cape Town	1930–31
198 for 2nd	E. A. B. Rowan and C. B. van Ryneveld, at Leeds	1951
319 for 3rd	A. Melville and A. D. Nourse, junr., at Nottingham ..	1947
214 for 4th	H. W. Taylor and H. G. Deane, at The Oval ..	1929
136 for 5th	H. B. Cameron and R. H. Catterall, at Durban ..	1927–28
99 for 6th	G. A. Faulkner and S. J. Snooke, at Johannesburg ..	1909–10
123 for 7th	H. G. Deane and E. P. Nupen, at Durban	1927–28
109 for 8th	B. Mitchell and L. Tuckett, at The Oval	1947
137 for 9th	E. L. Dalton and A. B. C. Langton, at The Oval	1935
103 for 10th	H. G. Owen-Smith and A. J. Bell, at Leeds	1929

HUNDRED ON DEBUT IN ENGLAND–S. AFRICA TESTS

For England

104	L. C. Braund	Lord's	1907	
163‡	D. C. S. Compton	Nottingham	1947	
119	J.W.H.T.Douglas	Durban	1913–14	
106	P. A. Gibb	Jo'burg	1938–39	

138	P. B. H. May	Leeds	1951	
117 and 100	E. Paynter	Jo'burg	1938–39	
119	R. H. Spooner	Lord's	1912	
132†	P. F. Warner	Jo'burg	1898–99	

‡ Second innings.   † Carried his bat through the second innings.

No instance for South Africa. The highest scores by South African batsmen in the series are as follows: 93* by A. D. Nourse, sen., at Johannesburg in 1905–06 and 90 by P. N. F. Mansell at Leeds, 1951.

INDIVIDUAL HUNDREDS IN THE MATCHES

For England (74)

120	R. Abel, Cape Town	1888–9
148*	L. E. G. Ames, The Oval	1935
115	L. E. G. Ames, Cape Town	1938–9
104	L. C. Braund, Lord's...	1907
208	D. C. S. Compton, Lord's	1947
163	D. C. S. Compton, Nottingham	1947
115	D. C. S. Compton, Manchester	1947
113	D. C. S. Compton, The Oval	1947
114	D. C. S. Compton, Johannesburg	1948–9
114	D. C. S. Compton, Nottingham	1951
158	D. C. S. Compton, Manchester	1955
104	D. Denton, Johannesburg	1909–10
119	J. W. H. T. Douglas, Durban	1913–14
219	W. J. Edrich, Durban	1938–9
191	W. J. Edrich, Manchester	1947
189	W. J. Edrich, Lord's	1947
143	F. L. Fane, Johannesburg	1905–6
129	C. B. Fry, The Oval	1907
106	P. A. Gibb, Johannesburg	1938–9
120	P. A. Gibb, Durban	1938–9

138*	W. R. Hammond, Birmingham	1929
136*	W. R. Hammond, Durban	1930–1
101*	W. R. Hammond, The Oval	1929
181	W. R. Hammond, Cape Town	1938–9
120	W. R. Hammond, Durban	1938–9
140	W. R. Hammond, Durban	1938–9
122	T. Hayward, Johannesburg	1895–6
132	E. Hendren, Leeds	1924
142	E. Hendren, The Oval	1924
124	A. J. L. Hill, Cape Town	1895–6
187	J. B. Hobbs, Cape Town	1909–10
211	J. B. Hobbs, Lord's	1924
100	L. Hutton, Leeds	1947
158	L. Hutton, Johannesburg	1948–9
123	L. Hutton, Johannesburg	1948–9
100	L. Hutton, Leeds	1951
102	M. Leyland, Lord's	1929
161	M. Leyland, The Oval	1935
136*	F. G. Mann, Port Elizabeth	1948–9
138	P. B. H. May, Leeds	1951
112	P. B. H. May, Lord's	1955
117	P. B. H. May, Manchester	1955

* Signifies not out.

102	C. P. Mead, Johannesburgh	1913–14
117	C. P. Mead, Port Elizabeth	1913–14
181	C. P. Mead, Durban...	1922–3
117 / 100 }	E. Paynter, Johannesburg	1938–9
243	E. Paynter, Durban....	1938–9
152	W. Rhodes, Johannesburg	1913–14
108	R. W. V. Robins, Manchester	1935
140 / 111 }	A. C. Russell, Durban..	1922–3
137	R. T. Simpson, Nottingham	1951
119	R. H. Spooner, Lord's..	1912
122	H. Sutcliffe, Lord's.....	1924
102	H. Sutcliffe, Johannesburg	1927–8
114	H. Sutcliffe, Birmingham	1929
100	H. Sutcliffe, Lord's.....	1929
104 / 109* }	H. Sutcliffe, The Oval..	1929
100*	M. W. Tate, Lord's	1929

122	E. Tyldesley, Johannesburg	1927–8
100	E. Tyldesley, Johannesburg	1927–8
112	J. T. Tyldesley, Cape Town	1898–9
112	B. H. Valentine, Cape Town	1938–9
132*	P. F. Warner, Johannesburg	1898–9
195	C. Washbrook, Johannesburg	1948–9
111	A. Watkins, Johannesburg	1948–9
134*	H. Wood, Cape Town..	1891–2
115*	F. E. Woolley, Johannesburg	1922–3
134*	F. E. Woolley, Lord's...	1924
154	F. E. Woolley, Manchester	1929
113	R. E. S. Wyatt, Manchester	1929
149	R. E. S. Wyatt, Nottingham	1935

FOR SOUTH AFRICA (49)

125	P. G. Van der Byl, Durban	1938–9
120	R. H. Catterall, Birmingham	1924
120	R. H. Catterall, Lord's..	1924
119	R. H. Catterall, Durban	1927–8
117	E. L. Dalton, The Oval..	1935
102	E. L. Dalton, Johannesburg	1938–9
116*	W. R. Endean, Leeds...	1955
123	G. A. Faulkner, Johannesburg	1909–10
102	M. Hathorn, Johannesburg	1905–6
104*	D. J. McGlew, Manchester	1955
133	D. J. McGlew, Leeds....	1955
142	R. A. McLean, Lord's..	1955
103	A. Melville, Durban....	1938–9
189 / 104* }	A. Melville, Nottingham	1947
117	A. Melville, Lord's	1947
123	B. Mitchell, Cape Town	1930–1
164*	B. Mitchell, Lord's....	1935
128	B. Mitchell, The Oval...	1935
109	B. Mitchell, Durban....	1938–9
120 / 189* }	B. Mitchell, The Oval..	1947
120	B. Mitchell, Cape Town.	1948–9
120	A. D. Nourse, junr., Cape Town	1938–9
103	A. D. Nourse, junr., Durban	1938–9

149	A. D. Nourse, junr., Nottingham	1947
115	A. D. Nourse, junr., Manchester	1947
129*	A. D. Nourse, junr., Johannesburg	1948–9
112	A. D. Nourse, junr., Cape Town	1948–9
208	A. D. Nourse, junr., Nottingham	1951
129	H. G. Owen-Smith, Leeds	1929
156*	E. A. B. Rowan, Johannesburg	1948–9
236	E. A. B. Rowan, Leeds..	1951
115	P. W. Sherwell, Lord's..	1907
141	I. J. Siedle, Cape Town.	1930–1
106	J. H. Sinclair, Cape Town	1898–9
109	H. W. Taylor, Durban..	1913–14
176	H. W. Taylor, Johannesburg	1922–3
101	H. W. Taylor, Johannesburg	1922–3
102	H. W. Taylor, Durban..	1922–3
101	H. W. Taylor, Johannesburg	1927–8
121	H. W. Taylor, The Oval	1929
117	H. W. Taylor, Cape Town	1930–1
124	K. J. Viljoen, Manchester	1935
125	W. W. Wade, Port Elizabeth	1948–9

* *Signifies not out.*

113	J. H. B. Waite, Man-		118	G. C. White, Durban...1909–10
	chester...............	1955	108	P. L. Winslow, Man-
147	G. C. White, Johannes-			chester............. 1955
	burg...............	1905–6		

A. Melville, B. Mitchell, E. Paynter, A. C. Russell and H. Sutcliffe are the only players who have made two separate hundreds in a match in these Tests.

HIGHEST RUN AGGREGATES BY A BATSMAN IN A RUBBER

England in England	753 (av. 94.12) D. C. S. Compton ...	1947
England in South Africa	653 (av. 81.62) E. Paynter	1938–39
South Africa in England	621 (av. 69.00) A. D. Nourse, junr...	1947
South Africa in South Africa..	582 (av. 64.66) H. W. Taylor	1922–23

HIGHEST WICKET AGGREGATES BY A BOWLER IN A RUBBER

England in England	34 (av. 8.29) S. F. Barnes	1912
England in South Africa	49 (av. 10.93) S. F. Barnes	1913–14
South Africa in England	26 (av. 21.84) H. J. Tayfield	1955
South Africa in South Africa..	36 (av. 21.75) A. E. E. Vogler	1909–10

HIGHEST MATCH AGGREGATES

1,981 for 35 wkts., at Durban	..	..	..	1938–39
1,477 for 33 wkts., at The Oval	..	..	..	1947
1,458 for 31 wkts., at Nottingham	..	..	..	1947

LOWEST MATCH AGGREGATES

| 378 for 30 wkts., at The Oval .. | .. | .. | .. | 1912 |
| 382 for 30 wkts., at Cape Town | .. | .. | .. | 1888–89 |

HAT-TRICK

| G. A. Lohmann | | T. W. Goddard |
| Port Elizabeth | 1895–96 | Johannesburg 1938–39 |

At Leeds in 1947 K. Cranston finished South Africa's second innings by taking 4 wickets in one over of six balls for no runs, but this did not include the hat-trick.

ENGLAND v. WEST INDIES

	Date of First Match		Won by England		Won by West Indies		Drawn		Total
In England	1928	..	7	..	3	..	3	..	13
In West Indies	1929	..	4	..	7	..	6	..	17
Totals			11	..	10	..	9	..	30

HIGHEST TOTALS FOR AN INNINGS

By ENGLAND				By WEST INDIES		
849	..	Kingston...........	1930	681	..	(8 wkts.), Port of Spain	1954
537	..	Port of Spain	1954	558	..	Nottingham	1950
				535	..	(7 wkts.), Kingston..	1935
				503	..	The Oval	1950

LOWEST TOTALS FOR AN INNINGS

By ENGLAND				By WEST INDIES		
103	..	Kingston...........1935		97	..	Lord's	1933
103	..	The Oval 1950					

INDIVIDUAL HUNDREDS IN THE MATCHES

For England (27)

105	L. E. G. Ames, Port of Spain	1930
146	L. E. G. Ames, Kingston	1930
126	L. E. G. Ames, Kingston	1935
107†	A. H. Bakewell, The Oval	1933
120†	D. C. S. Compton, Lord's	1939
133	D. C. S. Compton, Port of Spain	1954
104	T. G. Evans, Manchester	1950
140†	S. C. Griffith, Port of Spain	1948
138	W. R. Hammond, The Oval	1939
205*	E. Hendren, Port of Spain	1930
123	E. Hendren, Georgetown	1930
159	J. B. Hobbs, The Oval	1928
196†	L. Hutton, Lord's	1939
165*	L. Hutton, The Oval	1939
202*	L. Hutton, The Oval	1950
169	L. Hutton, Georgetown	1954
205	L. Hutton, Kingston	1954
127	D. R. Jardine, Manchester	1933
135	P. B. H. May, Port of Spain	1954
107	W. Place, Kingston	1948
133	J. D. Robertson, Port of Spain	1948
152†	A. Sandham, Bridgetown	1930
325	A. Sandham, Kingston	1930
122†	E. Tyldesley, Lord's	1928
114†	C. Washbrook, Lord's	1950
102	C. Washbrook, Nottingham	1950
116†	W. Watson, Kingston	1954

For West Indies (28)

105	I. Barrow, Manchester	1933
107	G. Carew, Port of Spain	1948
112†	A. Ganteaume, Port of Spain	1948
176†	G. A. Headley, Bridgetown	1930
114 }	G. A. Headley, Georgetown	1930
112 }		
223	G. A. Headley, Kingston	1930
169*	G. A. Headley, Manchester	1933
270*	G. A. Headley, Kingston	1935
106 }	G. A. Headley, Lord's	1939
107 }		
166	J. K. Holt, Bridgetown	1954
106	A. F. Rae, Lord's	1950
109	A. F. Rae, The Oval	1950
122	C. A. Roach, Bridgetown	1930
209	C. A. Roach, Georgetown	1930
168*	C. L. Walcott, Lord's	1950
220	C. L. Walcott, Bridgetown	1954
124	C. L. Walcott, Port of Spain	1954
116	C. L. Walcott, Kingston	1954
141	E. Weekes, Kingston	1948
129	E. Weekes, Nottingham	1950
206	E. Weekes, Port of Spain	1954
137	K. H. Weekes, The Oval	1939
131*	F. M. Worrell, Georgetown	1948
261	F. M. Worrell, Nottingham	1950
138	F. M. Worrell, The Oval	1950
167	F. M. Worrell, Port of Spain	1954

† *Signifies hundred on debut in England–West Indies Test. S. C. Griffith provides the only instance of a player hitting his maiden century in first-class cricket in his FIRST Test.*

ENGLAND v. NEW ZEALAND

	Date of First Match	Won by England	Won by New Zealand	Drawn	Total
In New Zealand	1929–30	4	0	7	11
In England	1931	2	0	8	10
Totals		6	0	15	21

HIGHEST TOTALS FOR AN INNINGS

By England

560	(8 wkts., dec.) Christchurch	1932–33
550	Christchurch	1950–51
548	(7 wkts., dec.), Auckland	1932–33
540	Auckland	1929–30

By New Zealand

484	Lord's	1949
469	(9 wkts., dec.), Lord's	1931
440	Wellington	1920–30

LOWEST TOTALS FOR AN INNINGS

By England

181	Christchurch	1929–30

By New Zealand

26	Auckland	1954–55
112	Christchurch	1929–30

* *Signifies not out.*

INDIVIDUAL HUNDREDS IN THE MATCHES

FOR ENGLAND (22)

122†	G. O. Allen, Lord's	1931
137†	L. E. G. Ames, Lord's	1931
103	L. E. G. Ames, Christchurch	1933
134*	T. E. Bailey, Christchurch	1951
109	E. H. Bowley, Auckland	1930
114	D. C. S. Compton, Leeds	1949
116	D. C. S. Compton, Lord's	1949
117	K. S. Duleepsinhji, Auckland	1930
109	K. S. Duleepsinhji, The Oval	1931
100	W. J. Edrich, The Oval	1949
100*	W. R. Hammond, The Oval	1931
227	W. R. Hammond, Christchurch	1933

336*	W. R. Hammond, Auckland	1933
140	W. R. Hammond, Lord's	1937
114†	J. Hardstaff, Lord's	1937
103	J. Hardstaff, The Oval	1937
100	L. Hutton, Manchester	1937
101	L. Hutton, Leeds	1949
206	L. Hutton, The Oval	1949
196	G. B. Legge, Auckland	1930
121†	J. D. Robertson, Lord's	1949
103†	R. T. Simpson, Manchester	1949
117†	H. Sutcliffe, The Oval	1931
109*	H. Sutcliffe, Manchester	1931
103*	C. Washbrook, Leeds	1949

FOR NEW ZEALAND (8)

136	C. S. Dempster, Wellington	1930
120	C. S. Dempster, Lord's	1931
206	M. P. Donnelly, Lord's	1949
116	W. A. Hadlee, Christchurch	1947

117†	J. W. E. Mills, Wellington	1930
101	M. L. Page, Lord's	1931
101	B. Sutcliffe, Manchester	1949
116	B. Sutcliffe, Christchurch	1951

† *Signifies hundred on first appearance in England–N.Z. Tests.*

HAT-TRICK

M. J. C. Allom, in his first Test match, England v. New Zealand at Christchurch in 1929–30, dismissed T. C. Lowry, K. C. James and F. T. Badcock with consecutive balls and took four wickets in five balls.

ENGLAND v. INDIA

	Date of First Match		Won by England		Won by India		Drawn		Total
In England	1932	..	7	..	0	..	4	..	11
In India	1933–34	..	3	..	1	..	4	..	8
Totals			10		1		8		19

HIGHEST TOTALS FOR AN INNINGS

BY ENGLAND

571	.. (8 wkts.), Manchester	1936
537	.. Lord's	1952
471	.. (8 wkts.), The Oval	1936
456	.. Bombay	1951–52
438	.. Bombay	1933–34

BY INDIA

485	.. Bombay	1951–52
457	.. (9 wkts.), Madras	1951–52
418	.. New Delhi	1951–52

LOWEST TOTALS FOR AN INNINGS

BY ENGLAND

134	.. Lord's	1936

BY INDIA

58	.. Manchester	1952
82	.. Manchester	1952
93	.. Lord's	1936
98	.. The Oval	1952

* *Signifies not out.*

G

INDIVIDUAL HUNDREDS IN THE MATCHES

For England (12)

104	T. G. Evans, Lord's	1952
175†	T. W. Graveney, Bombay	1951–2
167	W. R. Hammond, Manchester.............	1936
217	W. R. Hammond, The Oval	1936
205*	J. Hardstaff, junr., Lord's	1946
150	L. Hutton, Lord's	1952
104	L. Hutton, Manchester..	1952
119	D. S. Sheppard, The Oval	1952
136†	B. H. Valentine, Bombay	1933–4
102	C. F. Walters, Madras..	1933–4
138*†	A. J. Watkins, New Delhi	1951–2
128	T. S. Worthington, The Oval	1936

For India (13)

118†	L. Amarnath, Bombay..	1933–4
164*	V. S. Hazare, New Delhi	1951–2
155	V. S. Hazare, Bombay..	1951–2
114	V. M. Merchant, Manchester.............	1936
128	V. M. Merchant, The Oval	1946
154	V. M. Merchant, New Delhi	1951–2
133	V. L. Manjrekar, Leeds..	1952
184	V. Mankad, Lord's	1952
112	Mushtaq Ali, Manchester	1936
115	D. G. Phadkar, Calcutta	1951–2
140	P. Roy, Bombay	1951–2
111	P. Roy, Madras........	1951–2
130*	P. R. Umrigar, Madras..	1951–2

† *Signifies hundred on debut in England–India Tests.*

ENGLAND v. PAKISTAN

	Date of First Match	Won by England	Won by Pakistan	Drawn	Total
In England	1954	1	1	2	4

HIGHEST TOTALS:—England, 558 for 6, Nottingham, 1954.
Pakistan, 272, Nottingham, 1954.

LOWEST TOTALS:—England, 130, The Oval, 1954.
Pakistan, 87, Lord's, 1954.

INDIVIDUAL HUNDREDS IN THE MATCHES

For England (2)

278	D. C. S. Compton, Nottingham	..	..	1954
101	R. T. Simpson, Nottingham	..	..	1954

AUSTRALIA v. SOUTH AFRICA

	Date of First Match		Won by Australia		Won by S. Africa		Drawn		Total
In South Africa ..	1902–03	..	11	..	0	..	5	..	16
In Australia	1910–11	..	11	..	3	..	1	..	15
In England	1912	..	2	..	0	..	1	..	3
			—		—		—		—
	Totals		24	..	3	..	7	..	34

HIGHEST TOTALS FOR AN INNINGS

By Australia

578	.. Melbourne.......	1910–11
554	.. Melbourne.......	1931–32
549 for 7	Port Elizabeth ...	1949–50
530	.. Adelaide	1952–53
528	.. Sydney	1910–11
526 for 7	Cape Town	1949–50
520	.. Melbourne.......	1952–53
513	.. Adelaide	1931–32

By South Africa

506	.. Melbourne	1910–11
491	.. Johannesburg....	1935–36
482	.. Adelaide	1910–11
472 for 8	Johannesburg	1921–22

* *Signifies not out.*

SMALLEST TOTALS FOR AN INNINGS

By Australia		By South Africa	
75 .. Durban	1949–50	36 & 45† Melbourne	1931–32
153 .. Melbourne	1931–32	80 .. Melbourne	1910–11
175 .. Johannesburg	1902–03	85 .. Johannesburg.....	1902–03

† The aggregate of 81 (12 extras) for two innings is the smallest in Test cricket.

INDIVIDUAL HUNDREDS IN THE MATCHES

For Australia (47)

159* W. W. Armstrong, Johannesburg 1902–3
132 W. W. Armstrong, Melbourne............... 1910–11
132 W. Bardsley, Sydney....1910–11
121 W. Bardsley, Manchester 1912
164 W. Bardsley, Lord's.... 1912
226 D. G. Bradman, Brisbane 1931–2
112 D. G. Bradman, Sydney 1931–2
167 D. G. Bradman, Melbourne 1931–2
299* D. G. Bradman, Adelaide 1931–2
121 W. A. Brown, Cape Town.............. 1935–6
109 A. G. Chipperfield, Durban 1935–6
203 H. L. Collins, Johannesburg................ 1921–2
112 J. H. Fingleton Cape Town.............. 1935–6
108 J. H. Fingleton, Johannesburg 1935–6
118 J. H. Fingleton, Durban 1935–6
119 J. M. Gregory, Johannesburg................ 1921–2
178 R. N. Harvey, Cape Town.............1949–50
151 R. N. Harvey, Durban..1949–50
116 R. N. Harvey, Port Elizabeth 1949–50
100 R. N. Harvey, Johannesburg..................1949–50
109 R. N. Harvey, Brisbane.1952–53
190 R. N. Harvey, Sydney..1952–53
116 R. N. Harvey, Adelaide.1952–53

205 R. N. Harvey, Melbourne 1952–53
112 A. L. Hassett, Johannesburg................1949–50
167 A. L. Hassett, Port Elizabeth 1949–50
163 A. L. Hassett, Adelaide.1952–53
142 C. Hill, Johannesburg... 1902–3
191 C. Hill, Sydney 1910–11
100 C. Hill, Melbourne....1910–11
114 C. E. Kelleway, Manchester.............. 1912
102 C. E. Kelleway, Lord's.. 1912
101 S. J. Loxton, Johannesburg................1949–50
137 C. G. Macartney, Sydney1910–11
116 C. G. Macartney, Durban 1921–2
149 S. J. McCabe, Durban.. 1935–6
189* S. J. McCabe, Johannesburg................ 1935–6
154 C. McDonald, Adelaide 1952–53
111 A. R. Morris, Johannesburg................1949–50
157 A. R. Morris, Port Elizabeth 1949–50
118 ⎱ J. R. Moroney, Johannesburg 1949–50
101* ⎰
127 K. E. Rigg, Sydney..... 1931–2
142 J. S. Ryder, Cape Town 1921–2
159 V. T. Trumper, Melbourne 1910–11
214* V. T. Trumper, Adelaide 1910–11
161 W. M. Woodfull, Melbourne.............. 1931–2

For South Africa (15)

162* W. R. Endean, Melbourne 1952–53
204 G. A. Faulkner, Melbourne...............1910–11
115 G. A. Faulkner, Adelaide..............1910–11
122* G. A. Faulkner, Manchester............. 1912
152 C. N. Frank, Johannesburg................ 1921–2
111 A. D. Nourse, senr., Johannesburg........ 1921–2

231 A. D. Nourse, junr., Johannesburg........ 1935–6
114 A. D. Nourse, junr., Cape Town..........1949–50
143 E. A. B. Rowan, Durban 1949–50
101 J. H. Sinclair, Johannesburg................ 1902–3
104 J. H. Sinclair, Cape Town 1902–3
103 S. J. Snooke, Adelaide..1910–11
111 K. G. Viljoen, Melbourne 1931–2
105 J. W. Zulch, Adelaide..1910–11
150 J. W. Zulch, Sydney....1910–11

* Signifies not out.

HUNDRED ON DEBUT IN AUSTRALIA–S. AFRICA TESTS

142 ..	C. Hill, Johannesburg 1902–03		127 ..	K. E. Rigg, Sydney.. 1931–32
132 ..	W. Bardsley, Sydney 1910–11		109 ..	A. G. Chipperfield,
226 ..	D. G. Bradman,			Durban 1935–36
	Brisbane 1931–32		112 ..	A. L. Hassett,
				Johannesburg...... 1949–50
			101 ..	S. J. Loxton
				Johannesburg..... 1949–50

No instance for South Africa.

MOST WICKETS IN A RUBBER

44, for 14.59 runs each, by C. V. Grimmett for Australia in 1935–36.
30, for 28.10 runs each, by H. Tayfield for South Africa in 1952–53.

AUSTRALIA v. NEW ZEALAND

One match has been played, at Wellington, where Australia beat New Zealand by an innings and 103 runs in March 1946. No centuries were scored.

AUSTRALIA v. WEST INDIES

	Date of First Match	Won by Australia	Won by West Indies	Drawn	Total
In Australia.......	1930–31	8	2	0	10
In West Indies	1954–55	3	0	2	5
Totals		11	2	2	15

HIGHEST TOTALS FOR AN INNINGS

By Australia			By West Indies		
758–8	Kingston............	1954–5	510	Bridgetown..........	1954–5
668	Bridgetown..........	1954–5			
600–9	Port of Spain	1954–5			
558	Brisbane	1930–1			
515–9	Kingston............	1954–5			

INDIVIDUAL HUNDREDS IN THE MATCHES

For Australia (19)

128	R. G. Archer, Kingston.	1954–5	110	C. C. McDonald, Port of Spain	1954–5
121	R. Benaud, Kingston ...	1954–5			
223	D. G. Bradman, Brisbane	1930–1	127	C. C. McDonald, Kingston	1954–5
152	D. G. Bradman, Melbourne	1930–1	129	K. R. Miller, Sydney....	1951–2
133	R. N. Harvey, Kingston.	1954–5	147	K. R. Miller, Kingston..	1954–5
133	R. N. Harvey, Port of Spain	1954–5	137	K. R. Miller, Bridgetown	1954–5
			109	K. R. Miller, Kingston..	1954–5
204	R. N. Harvey, Kingston.	1954–5	111	A. R. Morris, Port of Spain	1954–5
132	A. L. Hassett, Sydney...	1951–2			
102	A. L. Hassett, Melbourne	1951–2	183	W. H. Ponsford, Sydney	1930–1
146†	A. F. Kippax, Adelaide.	1930–1	109	W. H. Ponsford, Brisbane	1930–1
118	R. R. Lindwall, Bridgetown	1954–5			

† Signifies hundred on debut in Australia–W. Indies Tests.

For West Indies (14)

219	D. Atkinson, Bridgetown	1954–5
122	C. Depeiza, Bridgetown.	1954–5
102*	G. A. Headley, Brisbane	1930–1
105	G. A. Headley, Sydney..	1930–1
123†	F. R. Martin, Sydney...	1930–1
104†	C. Smith, Kingston.....	1954–5
104	J. B. Stollmeyer, Sydney	1951–2
108	C. L. Walcott, Kingston	1954–5

126 \	C. L. Walcott, Port of	
110 /	Spain	1954–5
155 \	C. L. Walcott, Kingston	1954–5
110 /		
139	E. Weekes, Port of Spain	1954–5
108	F. M. Worrell, Melbourne	1951–2

† *Signifies hundred on debut in Australia–W. Indies Tests.*

AUSTRALIA v. INDIA

	Date of First Match	Won by Australia	Won by India	Drawn	Total
In Australia.......	1947–8	.. 4	.. 0	.. 1	.. 5

HIGHEST TOTALS FOR AN INNINGS

By Australia		By India	
674 Adelaide	1947–48	381 Adelaide	1947–48
575 (8 wkts., dec.), Melbourne	1947–48		

LOWEST TOTALS FOR AN INNINGS

By Australia		By India	
107 Sydney	1947–48	58 Brisbane	1947–48
		67 Melbourne	1947–48

INDIVIDUAL HUNDREDS IN THE MATCHES

For Australia (8)		For India (5)	
112 S. G. Barnes, Adelaide..	1947–8	145 \ V. S. Hazare, Adelaide..	1947–8
201 D. G. Bradman, Adelaide	1947–8	116 /	
185† D. G. Bradman, Brisbane	1947–8	116 V. Mankad, Melbourne.	1947–8
132 \ D. G. Bradman, Melbourne	1947–8	111 V. Mankad, Melbourne.	1948–8
127* /		123 D. Phadkar, Adelaide...	1947–8
153 R. N. Harvey, Melbourne	1947–8		
198* A. L. Hassett, Adelaide.	1947–8		
100* A. R. Morris, Melbourne	1947–8		

† *Signifies hundred on debut in Australia–India Tests.*

SOUTH AFRICA v. NEW ZEALAND

	Date of First Match	Won by South Africa	Won by New Zealand	Drawn	Total
In New Zealand ..	1931–32	3	0	1	4
In South Africa ...	1953–54	4	0	1	5
Totals		7	0	2	9

Highest Totals:—South Africa, 524 for 8, Wellington, 1952–53.
New Zealand, 505, Cape Town, 1953–54.

Lowest Totals:—South Africa, 146, Johannesburg, 1953–54.
New Zealand, 79, Johannesburg, 1953–54.

* *Signifies not out.*

INDIVIDUAL HUNDREDS IN THE MATCHES

For South Africa (7)

122* X. Balaskas, Wellington 1931–2
103† J. A. J. Christy, Christchurch 1931–2
116 W. R. Endean, Auckland 1952–3
255*†D. J. McGlew, Wellington 1952–3
101 R. A. McLean, Durban. 1953–4
113† B. Mitchell, Christ-
church 1931–2
109† A. R. A. Murray, Wellington 1952–3

For New Zealand (3)

107 G. O. Rabone, Durban.. 1953–4
135 J. R. Reid, Cape Town.. 1953–4
100† H. G. Vivian, Wellington 1931–2

† *Signifies hundred on debut in South Africa–New Zealand Tests.*

D. J. McGlew provides the only instance of a player being on the field throughout a Test.

WEST INDIES v. NEW ZEALAND

	Date of First Match	Won by West Indies	Won by New Zealand	Drawn	Totals
In New Zealand ..	1951–52	1	0	1	2

HIGHEST TOTALS FOR AN INNINGS

By West Indies
546 for 6 Auckland 1951–52

By New Zealand
236 Christchurch......... 1951–52

J. B. Stollmeyer (152), C. L. Walcott (115) and F. M. Worrell (100) have scored hundreds for West Indies. No instance for N.Z.

WEST INDIES v. INDIA

	Date of First Match	Won by India	Won by West Indies	Drawn	Total
In India	1948–49	0	1	4	5
In West Indies....	1952–53	0	1	4	5
Totals		0	2	8	10

Highest Totals:—India, 454, at New Delhi, 1948; 444 at Kingston, 1953. West Indies, 631, at New Delhi, 1948; 629 (for six wickets, dec.), at Bombay, 1948.

Lowest Totals:—India, 129, at Bridgetown, 1953; West Indies, 228, at Bridgetown, 1953.

INDIVIDUAL HUNDREDS IN THE MATCHES

For India (10)

114*†H. R. Adhikari, New
Delhi 1948–9
163* M. L. Apte, Port of
Spain 1952–3
134* V. S. Hazare, Bombay.. 1948–9
122 V. S. Hazare, Bombay.. 1948–9
118 V. L. Manjrekar, Kingston 1952–3

112 R. S. Modi, Bombay... 1948–9
106† Mushtaq Ali, Calcutta.. 1948–9
150 P. Roy, Kingston 1952–3
130 P. R. Umrigar, Port of
Spain 1952–3
117 P. R. Umrigar, Kingston 1952–3

* *Signifies not out.*

FOR WEST INDIES (19)

107† R. J. Christiani, New Delhi 1948–9	108 C. L. Walcott, Calcutta.. 1948–9
101† G. E. Gomez, New Delhi 1948–9	125 C. L. Walcott, Georgetown 1952–3
115† B. Pairaudeau, Port of Spain 1952–3	118 C. L. Walcott, Kingston 1952–3
104 A. F. Rae, Bombay 1948–9	128† E. Weekes, New Delhi .. 1948–9
109 A. F. Rae, Madras..... 1948–9	194 E. Weekes, Bombay 1948–9
160 J. B. Stollmeyer, Madras 1948–9	162 \ E. Weekes, Calcutta 1948–9
104* J. B. Stollmeyer, Port of Spain 1952–3	101 /
	207 E. Weekes, Port of Spain 1952–3
	161 E. Weekes, Port of Spain 1952–3
152† C. L. Walcott, New Delhi 1948–9	109 E. Weekes, Kingston ... 1952–3
	237 F. M. Worrell, Kingston 1952–3

† *Signifies hundred on debut in West Indies–India Tests.*

INDIA v. PAKISTAN

	Date of First Match	Won by India	Won by Pakistan	Drawn	Total
In India	1952–53	2	1	2	5
In Pakistan	1954–55	0	0	5	5
Totals		2	1	7	10

HIGHEST TOTALS:—India, 397, Calcutta, 1952–53. Pakistan, 344, Madras, 1952–53.

LOWEST TOTALS:—India, 106, Lucknow, 1952–53. Pakistan, 150, Delhi, 1952–53.

INDIVIDUAL HUNDREDS IN THE MATCHES

FOR INDIA (4)

146* V. S. Hazare, Bombay..	1952–3
110† D. S. Shodhan, Calcutta	1952–3
102 P. R. Umrigar, Bombay	1952–3
108 P. R. Umrigar, Peshawar	1954–5

FOR PAKISTAN (3)

103* Alim-ud-Din, Karachi..	1945–5
142 Hanif Mohammad, Bahawalpur..............	1954–5
124* Nazar Mohammed, Lucknow	1952–3

† *Signifies hundred on debut in India v. Pakistan Tests.*

* *Signifies not out.*

YOUNGEST TEST PLAYERS

16 years 352 days	Khalid Hassan	Pakistan v. England, at Nottingham. 1954.
17 years 122 days	J. E. D. Sealy	West Indies v. England, at Kensington Oval, Barbados, 1929–30.
17 years 239 days	I. D. Craig	Australia v. South Africa, at Melbourne, 1952–53.
17 years 245 days	G. Sobers	West Indies v. England, at Kingston, 1953–54.
17 years 300 days	Hanif Mohammed	Pakistan v. India, at New Delhi, 1952–53
18 years 44 days	Khalid Wazir	Pakistan v. England, at Lord's, 1954.
18 years 105 days	J. B. Stollmeyer	West Indies v. England, at Lord's, 1939.
18 years 149 days	Close (D. B.)	England v. New Zealand, at Manchester, 1949.

18 years 197 days	D. L. Freeman	New Zealand v. England, at Christchurch, 1932–33
18 years 232 days	T. W. Garrett	Australia v. England, at Melbourne, 1876–77.
18 years 267 days	H. G. Vivian	New Zealand v. England, at Manchester, 1931.

OLDEST PLAYERS ON TEST DEBUT

49 years 119 days	J. Southerton	England v. Australia, Melbourne, 1876–77.
46 years 273 days	D. J. Blackie	Australia v. England, Sydney, 1928–29.
41 years 337 days	E. R. Wilson	England v. Australia, Sydney, 1920–21.
41 years 275 days	H. Ironmonger	Australia v. England, Sydney, 1928–29.
41 years 28 days	R. J. Jamshedji	India v. England, Bombay, 1933.
40 years 346 days	C. A. Wiles	West Indies v. England, Manchester, 1933.
40 years 110 days	Lee (H. W.)	England v. South Africa, Johannesburg, 1930–31.
40 years 56 days	G. W. A. Chubb	South Africa v. England, Nottingham, 1951.
40 years 37 days	G. Ramaswami	India v. England, Manchester, 1936.
39 years 361 days	G. Challoner	West Indies v. England, Lord's, 1928.
39 years 360 days	Wood (A.)	England v. Australia, The Oval, 1938.

WICKET-KEEPING FEATS

MOST VICTIMS IN A TEST SERIES

23 (16 c 7 s)	J. H. Waite	South Africa v. New Zealand	..	1953–54
21 (16 c 5 s)	G. R. Langley	Australia v. West Indies	..	1951–52
21 (13 c 8 s)	R. A. Saggers	Australia v. South Africa	..	1949–50
21 (15 c 6 s)	H. Strudwick	England v. South Africa	..	1913–14

MOST BALLS BOWLED IN A TEST MATCH

A. L. Valentine (West Indies) sent down 92 overs, 552 balls, in the second innings against England in the Third Test Match at Nottingham, 1950. This is the highest number of balls bowled in one innings in Test cricket.

GENTLEMEN v. PLAYERS

The highest individual scores are:—

266*..	Hobbs (J. B.)	Scarboro'	1925	215 ..	W. G. Grace	The Oval	1870
247 ..	Abel (R.)	The Oval	1901	203 ..	Hayward (T.)	The Oval	1904
241 ..	Hutton (L.)	Scarboro'	1953	201 ..	Ames (L.E.G.)	Folkestone	1933
232*..	C. B. Fry	Lord's..	1903	195 ..	Abel (R.)	The Oval	1899
223 ..	Mead (C. P.)	Scarboro'	1911	194*..	Hendren (E.)	The Oval	1932
217 ..	W. G. Grace	Brighton	1871				

W. G. Grace played no fewer than fifteen three-figure innings for Gentlemen v. Players. On his fifty-eighth birthday—at The Oval in July 1906—he scored 74.

Hobbs (J. B.) in all matches under this title scored 16 three-figure innings and had an aggregate of 4,052 runs with an average of 54.75.

The match dates back to 1806.

* *Signifies not out.*

OXFORD v. CAMBRIDGE

Largest totals

503	..	Oxford	....	1900	432‡	..	Cambridge	....	1936
457	..	Oxford	....	1946	431	..	Cambridge	....	1932
453†	..	Oxford	....	1931	425	..	Cambridge	....	1938

† For eight wickets.   ‡ For nine wickets.

Smallest totals

32	..	Oxford	....	1878	42	..	Oxford	....	1890
39	..	Cambridge	....	1858	47	..	Cambridge	....	1838

Highest individual scores

238*	..	Nawab of Pataudi (O.) 1931	172*	..	J. F. Marsh (C.)	1904
201*	..	M. J. K. Smith (O.).. 1954	171	..	R. E. Foster (O.)....	1900
201	..	A. Ratcliffe (C.) ..	1931	170	..	M. Howell (O.)	1919
193	..	D.C.H. Townsend (O.) 1934				

A. P. F. Chapman and M. P. Donnelly enjoy the following distinction: Chapman scored a century at Lord's in the University match (102*, 1922); for Gentlemen v. Players (160, 1922); 108, 1926); and for England v. Australia (121, 1930). M. P. Donnelly scored a century at Lord's in the University match (142, 1946); for Gentlemen v. Players (162*, 1947); and for New Zealand v. England (206, 1949).

A. Ratcliffe's 201 for Cambridge remained a record for the match for only one day, being beaten by the Nawab of Pataudi's 238* for Oxford next day.

The following players have scored two hundreds: W. Yardley (Cambridge) 100 in 1870 and 130 in 1872; H. J. Enthoven (Cambridge) 104 in 1924 and 129 in 1925; The Nawab of Pataudi (Oxford) 106 in 1929 and 238 not out in 1931: A. Ratcliffe (Cambridge) 201 in 1931 124 in 1932; D. R. W. Silk (Cambridge) 116* in 1953 and 118 in 1954, and M. J. K. Smith (Oxford) 201* in 1954 and 104 in 1955.

F. C. Cobden, in the Oxford and Cambridge match in 1870, performed the hat-trick by taking the last three wickets and won an extraordinary game for Cambridge by two runs. The feat is without parallel in first-class cricket. Cobden obtained the last three wickets of Oxford in each innings—a curious coincidence. Other hat-tricks, all for Cambridge, have been credited to A. G. Steel (1879), P. H. Morton (1880), J. F. Ireland (1911), and R. G. H. Lowe (1926).

S. E. Butler, in the 1871 match, took all ten wickets in the Cambridge first innings. The feat is unique in University matches. He bowled 24 overs and a ball. In the follow-on he took 5 wickets for 57, making 15 for 95 runs in the match.

P. R. Le Couteur scored 160 and took eleven Cambridge wickets for 66 runs in 1910—the best all-round performance in the history of the match.

Of the 111 matches played, Cambridge have won 48 and Oxford 42. The remaining twenty-one games have been drawn. The match dates back to 1827.

* Signifies not out.

TIE MATCHES IN FIRST-CLASS CRICKET

There have been sixteen since the first World War:—

Somerset v. Sussex, at Taunton 1919
   (The last Sussex batsman not allowed to bat under Law 45.)
Orange Free State v. Eastern Province, at Bloemfontein 1925–26
   (Eastern Province had two wickets to fall.)
Essex v. Somerset, at Chelmsford 1926
   (Essex had one man to go in, and the M.C.C. ruled that the game should rank as a tie. The ninth wicket fell half a minute before time.)
Gloucestershire v. Australians, at Bristol 1930

Victoria v. M.C.C., at Melbourne   1932–33
    (Victoria's third wicket fell to the last ball of the match when one
    run was needed to win.)
Somerset v. Worcestershire, at Kidderminster   1939
Southern Punjab v. Baroda, at Patiala   1945–46
Essex v. Northamptonshire, at Ilford   1947
Hampshire v. Lancashire, at Bournemouth   1947
D. G. Bradman's XI v. A. L. Hassett's XI, at Melbourne (Bradman's
    Testimonial)   1948–49
Hampshire v. Kent, at Southampton   1950
Sussex v. Warwickshire, at Hove   1952
Essex v. Lancashire, at Brentwood   1952
Northamptonshire v. Middlesex, at Peterborough   1953
Yorkshire v. Leicestershire, at Huddersfield   1954
Sussex v. Hampshire, Eastbourne   1955

    Note.—Beginning in 1948 a tie has been recognised only when the scores
are level with all the wickets down in the fourth innings. This ruling applies to
all grades of Cricket, and in the case of a one-day match to the second innings,
provided that the match has not been brought to a further conclusion.

FIRST-CLASS MATCHES BEGUN AND FINISHED IN ONE DAY

The most notable instances during the nineteenth and present centuries are:—

The B's v. England, at Lord's, June 13   1831
Cambridge University v. M.C.C. and Ground, at Cambridge, May 18   1837
M.C.C. and Ground v. Cambridge University, at Lord's, June 19   ..   1848
Gentlemen of Kent v. Gentlemen of England, at Lord's, July 1   ..   1850
North v. South, at Lord's, July 15   1850
M.C.C. and Ground v. Sussex, at Lord's, June 2   1856
Surrey v. Sussex, at The Oval, July 16   1857
Kent v. England, at Lord's, July 5   1858
M.C.C. and Ground v. Oxford University, at Lord's, June 18   1863
North of Thames v. South of Thames, at Lord's, July 8   1863
M.C.C. and Ground v. Surrey, at Lord's, May 14   1872
Middlesex v. Oxford University, at Prince's, June 18   1874
North v. South, at Lord's, May 17   1875
M.C.C. and Ground v. Oxford University, at Oxford, May 24   ..   1877
M.C.C. and Ground v. Australians, at Lord's, May 27   1878
M.C.C. and Ground v. Oxford University, at Oxford, May 28   ..   1880
An England XI v. Australians, at Aston Lower Grounds, Birmingham,
    May 26   1884
M.C.C. and Ground v. Lancashire, at Lord's, May 18   1886
North v. South, at Lord's, May 30   1887
Lancashire v. Surrey, at Manchester, August 2   1888
M.C.C. and Ground v. Notts, at Lord's, June 1   1891
Lancashire v. Somerset, at Old Trafford, August 9   1892
M.C.C. and Ground v. Sussex, at Lord's, May 2   1894
Lancashire v. Somerset, at Old Trafford, July 17   1894
Yorkshire v. Somerset, at Huddersfield, July 19   1894
Leicestershire v. Surrey, at Leicester, June 10   1897
Hampshire v. Yorkshire, at Southampton, May 27 (H. Baldwin's benefit)   1898
Middlesex v. Somerset, at Lord's, May 23 (W. Flower's benefit)   ..   1899
Yorkshire v. Worcestershire, at Bradford, May 7   1900
M.C.C. and Ground v. London County, at Lord's, May 20   1903
Transvaal v. Orange Free State, at Johannesburg   1906
Middlesex v. Gentlemen of Philadelphia, at Lord's, July 20   1908
Gloucestershire v. Middlesex, at Bristol, August 26   1909
Kent v. Sussex, at Tonbridge, June 21   1919
Lancashire v. Somerset, at Manchester, May 21   1925
Madras v. Mysore, at Madras, November 4   1934

Ireland v. New Zealanders, at Dublin, September 11 1937
Derbyshire v. Somerset, at Chesterfield, June 11 1947
Lancashire v. Sussex, at Manchester, July 12 1950
Surrey v. Warwickshire, at The Oval, May 16 1953
Somerset v. Lancashire, at Bath, June 6 (H. T. F. Buse's benefit) .. 1953

LARGE ATTENDANCES AND GATE RECEIPTS

933,513 persons (exclusive of about 10,000 who watched the last day's play of the Fifth Test free of charge) were present at the five Test matches between England and Australia in 1936–37, receipts amounting to £A90,909. The Third Test at Melbourne broke the records for attendances and receipts 350,534 persons were present, and the receipts amounted to £A30,124. In this match, the records for one day's play were also broken—87,798 and £A7,405 on January 4th.

£200,194, record receipts for any series, was paid by the 549,650 people who attended the five Tests between England and Australia in England, 1953.

£57,716 is the largest sum of money taken at any cricket match in the world when England met Australia at Lord's, 1953.

With increased prices for admission after the 1939–45 war, the Third Test at Melbourne in 1946–47 established a new Australian record for receipts— £A44,063. The attendance figures were 343,675. The full figures for the five Tests in 1946–47 were 846,263; receipts £A115,858.

£A47,933 is the largest sum of money taken at any match in Australia when England played at Melbourne in the Third Test, 1954–55. The attendance at that match was 300,270. The full figures for the five Tests in 1954–55 were 707,510; receipts, £A119,059.

Over 158,000 persons were present during the five days of the England v. Australia match at Leeds, and the total receipts were £34,000   1948

132,000 people paid £43,000 for admission during the five days in the England v. Australia match at Lord's   1948

116,000 people (receipts £26,000) were present during the four days of the England v. South Africa Test at Leeds. Both the attendance and receipts were records for any Test between the two countries   1951

£31,032, which was taken at Leeds in the five days, constituted a new record for receipts for any match between England and South Africa. The total attendance was 113,500   ..   1955

Just under 115,000 persons were present during the four days of the England v. Australia match, at Lord's   1930

99,614 people were present at the Fourth Test Match at Leeds (over in three days). (75,614 paid: receipts £14,189)   1938

Over 80,000 persons watched the play, Surrey v. Yorkshire, at The Oval, (Lees' benefit—£2,300—66,923 paid for admission) .. July 1906

78,792 persons watched the play, Yorkshire v. Lancashire, at Leeds, (Hirst's benefit—£3,703)   ..   ..   ..   August, 1904

78,617 persons were present at the match between Lancashire and Yorkshire, at Manchester   1926

About 76,000 watched the play in the Surrey v. Kent match at The Oval   1920

BEST BENEFITS

£14,000   C. Washbrook. Lancashire v. Australians   1948
£12,866   A. V. Bedser, Surrey v. Yorkshire   1953
£12,200   D. C. S. Compton, Middlesex v. Sussex   1949
£9,713   L. Hutton, Yorkshire v. Middlesex   1950
£8,083   W. E. Bowes, Yorkshire v. Middlesex   1947
£8,000   R. Pollard, Lancashire v. Derbyshire   1949

The following figures were records at the respective date of each match:

£4,016   R. Kilner, Yorkshire v. Middlesex   1925
£3,703   G. H. Hirst, Yorkshire v. Lancashire   1904

Sir Donald Bradman received £A10,000 from his Testimonial match, D. G. Bradman's XI v. A. L. Hassett's XI, 1948–49.

W. G. Grace was given three Testimonials which raised £1,458, £2,377 and £5,000, a total of £8,835.

Hedley Verity's Memorial Fund in 1945 yielded £8,233.

COUNTY CHAMPIONSHIP

Since the institution of the Championship in 1873 it has been won outright as follows:—Yorkshire 22 times, Surrey 12, Lancashire 8, Nottinghamshire 8, Middlesex 5, Kent 4, Derbyshire 2, Gloucestershire 2, Warwickshire 2, Glamorgan 1.

Six times, 1873, 1879, 1882, 1889, 1949, 1950, the Championship was shared as follows: Nottinghamshire 4, Lancashire 4, Gloucestershire 1, Middlesex 1, Surrey 2, Yorkshire 3.

Yorkshire, champions in 1946, finished first in the three seasons and seven times in the nine seasons immediately preceding the 1939–45 war.

LORD'S CRICKET GROUND

Lord's and the M.C.C. were founded in 1787. The Club has enjoyed an uninterrupted career since that date, but there have been three grounds known as Lord's. The first (1787–1810) was situated where Dorset Square now is; the second (1809–13), at North Bank, had to be abandoned owing to the cutting of the Regent's Canal; and the third, opened in 1814, is that where the game is played to-day. It was not until 1886 that the freehold of Lord's was secured by the M.C.C. The present pavilion was erected in 1890 at a cost of £21,000.

THE LARGEST INDIVIDUAL SCORES MADE AT LORD'S ARE:—

316*	Hobbs (J. B.), Surrey v. Middlesex	1926
315*	Holmes (P.), Yorkshire v. Middlesex	1925
281*	W. H. Ponsford, Australians v. M.C.C.	1934
278	W. Ward, M.C.C. v. Norfolk (with E. H. Budd, T. Vigne and F. Ladbroke)	1820
278	D. G. Bradman, Australians v. M.C.C.	1938
277*	Hendren (E.), Middlesex v. Kent	1922

THE GREATEST TOTALS OBTAINED THERE ARE:—

FIRST-CLASS MATCHES

729	(six wickets), Australia v. England	1930
665	West Indies v. Middlesex	1939
612	(eight wickets), Middlesex v. Nottinghamshire	1921
609	(eight wickets), Cambridge University v. M.C.C. and Ground ..	1913
608	(seven wickets), Middlesex v. Hampshire	1919
607	M.C.C. and Ground v. Cambridge University	1902

MINOR MATCH

735	(nine wickets), M.C.C. and Ground v. Wiltshire	1888

* Signifies not out.

BIGGEST HIT AT LORD'S

The only known instance of a batsman hitting a ball over the present pavilion at Lord's occurred when A. E. Trott, appearing for M.C.C. against Australians at Lord's, July 31, August 1, 2, 1899, drove M. A. Noble so far and high that the ball struck a chimney pot and fell behind the building.

CHAMPION COUNTY SINCE INSTITUTION OF CHAMPIONSHIP

1873 {	Gloucestershire	1897	Lancashire	1927	Lancashire
	Nottinghamshire	1898	Yorkshire	1928	Lancashire
1874	Derbyshire	1899	Surrey	1929	Nottinghamshire
1875	Nottinghamshire	1900	Yorkshire	1930	Lancashire
1876	Gloucestershire	1901	Yorkshire	1931	Yorkshire
1877	Gloucestershire	1902	Yorkshire	1932	Yorkshire
1878	Middlesex	1903	Middlesex	1933	Yorkshire
1879 {	Nottinghamshire	1904	Lancashire	1934	Lancashire
	Lancashire	1905	Yorkshire	1935	Yorkshire
1880	Nottinghamshire	1906	Kent	1936	Derbyshire
1881	Lancashire	1907	Nottinghamshire	1937	Yorkshire
1882 {	Nottinghamshire	1908	Yorkshire	1938	Yorkshire
	Lancashire	1909	Kent	1939	Yorkshire
1883	Nottinghamshire	1910	Kent	1940 {	No competition
1884	Nottinghamshire	1911	Warwickshire	to	owing to the
1885	Nottinghamshire	1912	Yorkshire	1945	War
1886	Nottinghamshire	1913	Kent	1946	Yorkshire
1887	Surrey	1914	Surrey	1947	Middlesex
1888	Surrey	1915 {	No competition	1948	Glamorgan
	Surrey	to	owing to the	1949 {	Middlesex
1889 {	Lancashire	1918	War		Yorkshire
	Nottinghamshire	1919	Yorkshire	1950 {	Lancashire
1890	Surrey	1920	Middlesex		Surrey
1891	Surrey	1921	Middlesex	1951	Warwickshire
1892	Surrey	1922	Yorkshire	1952	Surrey
1893	Yorkshire	1923	Yorkshire	1953	Surrey
1894	Surrey	1924	Yorkshire	1954	Surrey
1895	Surrey	1925	Yorkshire	1955	Surrey
1896	Yorkshire	1926	Lancashire		

POINTS GAINED BY CHAMPIONS FROM 1946

Year	Champions	Played	Won	Points
1946	Yorkshire	26	17	216
1947	Middlesex	26	19	236
1948	Glamorgan	26	13	172
1949 {	Middlesex	26	14	192
	Yorkshire	26	14	192
1950 {	Lancashire	28	16	220
	Surrey	28	17	220
1951	Warwickshire	28	16	216
1952	Surrey	28	20	256
1953	Surrey	28	13	184
1954	Surrey	28	15	208
1955	Surrey	28	23	284

Note: Yorkshire hold the record number of wins in one season, i.e. 25 out of 32 Championship matches in 1923.

MATCH RESULTS IN THE COUNTY CHAMPIONSHIP

	Won	Lost	Drawn	Tie	Total
Derbyshire	323	534	397	0	1254
Essex	324	412	486	3	1225
Glamorgan	155	286	301	0	742
Gloucestershire	468	595	434	0	1497
Hampshire	318	489	452	3	1262
Kent	631	496	415	2	1544
Lancashire	732	293	620	3	1648
Leicestershire	241	511	436	1	1189
Middlesex	546	368	452	2	1368
Northamptonshire	189	436	330	2	957
Nottinghamshire	527	332	614	0	1473
Somerset	265	582	347	3	1197
Surrey	726	364	571	3	1664
Sussex	479	565	548	3	1595
Warwickshire	321	370	500	1	1192
Worcestershire	241	505	386	1	1133
Yorkshire	895	243	589	1	1728
	7381	7381	7878	28	22668

11,334 matches have been played in the County Championship of which 7,395 have been finished and 3,939 unfinished.

DATES OF FORMATION OF COUNTY CLUBS NOW FIRST-CLASS

Derbyshire, 1870; Essex, 1864–65 (dissolved in 1866) and re-formed in 1876 and 1886; Glamorgan, 1888–89; Gloucestershire, 1871; Hampshire, 1863; Kent, 1859 and re-formed 1870; Lancashire, 1864; Leicestershire, 1873; Middlesex, 1864; Northamptonshire, about 1843 and re-formed 1878; Nottinghamshire, 1859; Somerset, 1875 and re-organised 1885; Surrey, 1845; Sussex, 1836 and re-formed 1839 and 1857; Warwickshire, 1863–64 and re-formed 1882; Worcestershire, 1865; and Yorkshire, 1863.

CONSTITUTION OF COUNTY CHAMPIONSHIP

When the County Championship was first formed in 1873—the authorities in April having agreed that no cricketer should play for more than one county during the same season—the following counties were considered first-class:—Derbyshire, Gloucestershire, Kent, Lancashire, Middlesex, Notts, Surrey, Sussex and Yorkshire. In 1887 Derbyshire fell out. For 1891 Somerset were promoted. There was a further extension in 1895, as Essex, Derbyshire, Hampshire, Leicestershire and Warwickshire were admitted to the group. Worcestershire, who came in for 1899, have since played regularly except for 1919, the first season after the First World War. Northamptonshire were raised for 1905 and Glamorgan were adopted in 1921.

THE MINOR COUNTIES CHAMPIONSHIP

1895	Norfolk Durham Worcestershire	1923	Buckinghamshire
		1924	Berkshire
		1925	Buckinghamshire
1896	Worcestershire	1926	Durham
1897	Worcestershire	1927	Staffordshire
1898	Worcestershire	1928	Berkshire
1899	Northamptonshire Buckinghamshire	1929	Oxfordshire
		1930	Durham
1900	Glamorgan Durham Northamptonshire	1931	Leicestershire Second XI
		1932	Buckinghamshire
		1933	Undecided
1901	Durham	1934	Lancashire Second XI
1902	Wiltshire	1935	Middlesex Second XI
1903	Northamptonshire	1936	Hertfordshire
1904	Northamptonshire	1937	Lancashire Second XI
1905	Norfolk	1938	Buckinghamshire
1906	Staffordshire	1939	Surrey Second XI
1907	Lancashire Second XI	1946	Suffolk
1908	Staffordshire	1947	Yorkshire Second XI
1909	Wiltshire	1948	Lancashire Second XI
1910	Norfolk	1949	Lancashire Second XI
1911	Staffordshire	1950	Surrey Second XI
1912	In abeyance	1951	Kent Second XI
1913	Norfolk	1952	Buckinghamshire
1920	Staffordshire	1953	Berkshire
1921	Staffordshire	1954	Surrey Second XI
1922	Buckinghamshire	1955	Surrey Second XI

FEATURES OF 1955

Double Hundreds

260* R. Subba Row (Northamptonshire v. Lancashire, at Northampton).
227 A. Hamer (Derbyshire v. Nottinghamshire, at Nottingham).
214* W. Watson (Yorkshire v. Worcestershire, at Worcester).
205* J. M. Parks (Sussex v. Somerset, at Hove).

Two Hundreds in a Match

121* and 105 J. M. Allan (Kent v. Northamptonshire, at Northampton).
115* and 103* M. C. Cowdrey (Kent v. Essex, at Gillingham).
111 and 118 D. J. Insole (Essex v. Kent, at Gillingham).
121 and 117* D. M. Young (Gloucestershire v. Northamptonshire, at Kettering)

Signifies not out.

First to 1,000 Runs

D. J. Insole (Essex), June 28.

First to 2,000 Runs

D. J. Insole (Essex), August 23.

Stand Over 250

281 for third wicket by L. Livingston and R. Subba Row (Northamptonshire v. Nottinghamshire, at Nottingham).

The Double

G. Goonesena (Cambridge Univ. and Notts.), 1,380 runs; 134 wickets.
M. J. Horton (Worcestershire), 1,296 runs; 103 wickets.
V. E. Jackson (Leicestershire), 1,582 runs; 112 wickets.
F. J. Titmus (Middlesex), 1,235 runs; 191 wickets.
G. E. Tribe (Northamptonshire), 1,127 runs; 176 wickets.
A. J. Watkins (Glamorgan), 1,160 runs; 114 wickets.

First to 100 Wickets

G. A. R. Lock, Surrey, July 2.

200 Wickets

G. A. R. Lock, Surrey, September 6.

Nine Wickets in an Innings

J. Flavell (Worcestershire v. Kent, at Dover), 9 for 30.
J. D. Bannister (Warwickshire v. Yorkshire, at Sheffield), 9 for 35.
G. E. Tribe (Northamptonshire v. Yorkshire, at Bradford), 9 for 45.
R. G. Marlar (Sussex v. Lancashire, at Hove), 9 for 46.
E. Smith (Derbyshire v. Scotland, at Edinburgh), 9 for 46.
M. J. Horton (Worcestershire v. South Africans, at Worcester), 9 for 56.
A. E. James (Sussex v. Yorkshire, at Hove), 9 for 60.

Two Exceptional Bowling Feats

D. Shackleton (Hampshire v. Somerset, at Weston-super-Mare), 8 for 4.
C. H. Palmer (Leicestershire v. Surrey, at Leicester), 8 for 7.

Hat-Tricks

J. D. Bannister (Warwickshire v. Yorkshire, at Sheffield).
J. Hilton (Somerset v. Hampshire, at Weston-super-Mare).
G. A. R. Lock (Surrey v. Somerset, at Weston-super-Mare).
K. Smales (Nottingham v. Lancashire, at Nottingham).
F. S. Trueman (Yorkshire v. Nottinghamshire, at Scarborough).

Totals of 500 and Over

521 for 8 dec., South Africa v. England, at Manchester.
517 for 9 dec., Northamptonshire v. Lancashire, at Northampton.
503 for 4 dec., South Africans v. Essex, at Colchester.
500   South Africa v. England, at Leeds.

Totals Under 75

36   Somerset v. Surrey, at Weston-super-Mare.
37   Somerset v. Hampshire, at Weston-super-Mare.
40   Nottinghamshire v. Surrey, at The Oval.
42   Leicestershire v. Lancashire, at Hinckley.
47   Gloucestershire v. Derbyshire, at Derby.
47   Worcestershire v. Cambridge University, at Worcester.
50   Kent v. Worcestershire, at Dover.
51   Gloucestershire v. Yorkshire, at Bristol.
56   Glamorgan v. Surrey, at The Oval.
59   Northamptonshire v. Yorkshire, at Bradford.
60   Northamptonshire v. Kent, at Tunbridge Wells.
61   Hampshire v. Middlesex, at Lord's.
61   Northamptonshire v. Yorkshire, at Bradford.
62   Yorkshire v. Hampshire, at Bradford.
64   Glamorgan v. South Africans, at Swansea.
66   Kent v. Sussex, at Hastings.
67   Cambridge University v. South Africans, at Cambridge.
68   Glamorgan v. Hampshire, at Southampton.
68   Somerset v. South Africans, at Taunton.
70   Lancashire v. Warwickshire, at Manchester.
70   Worcestershire v. Middlesex, at Lord's.
73   Yorkshire v. Warwickshire, at Sheffield.

Note: Lancashire declared at 48 for nine v. Hampshire, at Portsmouth.

Record Number of "Extras"

A record number of extras in first-class cricket was conceded by Kent against Northamptonshire, at Northampton on August 22. The total of 73 extras comprised 48 byes, 23 leg-byes and 2 wides. A. W. Catt, the wicket-keeper, was subsequently found to be suffering from sun-stroke.

The "County" Cups

(*Excluding Festival Matches*)

Batting: Fastest Hundred—R. Smith (Essex v. Northamptonshire, at Wellingborough), in 73 minutes.
Bowling: Best Figures in an Innings—J. Flavell (Worcestershire v. Kent, at Dover), nine for 30.
Fielding: Most Catches—John Langridge (Sussex), 69 in season.
Wicket-keeping: Most victims in Season—A. J. McIntyre (Surrey), 85 (65 catches, 20 stumpings).
Special Award for Best Performance of Season—To the South African touring team for their cricket during the season.

FIRST-CLASS AVERAGES, 1955

BATTING

(Qualification: 8 innings, average 10.00)

† *Denotes a left-handed batsman.*   * *Signifies not out.*

	Innings	Not Outs	Runs	Highest Innings	Average
P. B. H. May (*Surrey*)	42	5	1902	125	51.40
M. C. Cowdrey (*Kent*)	25	4	1038	139	49.42
†J. G. Dewes (*Middlesex*)	16	2	673	117	48.07
†W. Watson (*Yorkshire*)	48	14	1623	214*	47.73
T. W. Graveney (*Gloucestershire*)	51	2	2117	159	43.20
D. J. Insole (*Essex*)	62	5	2427	142	42.57
K. Grieves (*Lancashire*)	35	6	1232	137	42.48
J. M. Parks (*Sussex*)	63	8	2314	205*	42.07
†L. Livingston (*Northants*)	58	5	2172	172*	40.98
C. Washbrook (*Lancashire*)	46	3	1743	170	40.53
†G. L. Willatt (*Derbyshire*)	11	1	401	133	40.10
†P. E. Richardson (*Worcester.*)	26	3	905	91*	39.34
†R. Subba Row (*Northants*)	41	5	1384	260*	38.44
D. Brookes (*Northants*)	58	5	2012	177	37.96
R. E. Marshall (*Hampshire*)	60	4	2115	110*	37.76
D. Kenyon (*Worcestershire*)	64	3	2296	131	37.63
T. E. Bailey (*Essex*)	50	12	1429	152*	37.60
D. S. Sheppard (*Sussex*)	18	1	637	104	37.47
M. Tompkin (*Leicestershire*)	62	3	2190	131	37.11
J. Baker (*Somerset*)	8	2	221	91*	36.83
†J. V. Wilson (*Yorkshire*)	58	4	1948	132*	36.07
H. E. Dollery (*Warwickshire*)	52	2	1783	156	35.66
†J. T. Ikin (*Lancashire*)	53	2	1814	114	35.56
D. W. Barrick (*Northants*)	45	7	1339	139	35.23
R. J. Giles (*Nottinghamshire*)	40	3	1293	142	34.94
R. Illingworth (*Yorkshire*)	36	6	1040	138	34.66
†R. E. Hitchcock (*Warwickshire*)	55	6	1695	128	34.59
D. C. S. Compton (*Middlesex*)	36	1	1209	158	34.54
A. V. Wolton (*Warwickshire*)	58	5	1809	136	34.13
D. M. Young (*Gloucestershire*)	63	1	2106	170	33.96
†F. W. Stocks (*Nottinghamshire*)	37	3	1153	99	33.91
†C. J. Poole (*Nottinghamshire*)	50	3	1572	122	33.44
W. H. H. Sutcliffe (*Yorkshire*)	41	3	1261	161*	33.18
K. Barrington (*Surrey*)	55	7	1580	135*	32.91
A. Hamer (*Derbyshire*)	55	1	1755	227	32.50
J. D. Robertson (*Middlesex*)	64	0	2070	137	32.34
J. Hardstaff (*Nottinghamshire*)	23	0	741	134	32.21
C. H. Palmer (*Leicestershire*)	59	1	1857	154	32.01
M. F. Tremlett (*Somerset*)	59	1	1850	153	31.89
H. Horton (*Hampshire*)	42	3	1231	139	31.56
R. T. Simpson (*Nottinghamshire*)	49	0	1541	105	31.44
†A. Wharton (*Lancashire*)	49	2	1477	123	31.42
D. B. Carr (*Derbyshire*)	55	2	1659	146	31.30
C. C. P. Williams (*Essex*)	41	2	1219	120	31.25
M. J. K. Smith (*Leicestershire*)	58	2	1740	118	31.07
†R. C. Wilson (*Kent*)	44	4	1241	107	31.02
P. Arnold (*Northamptonshire*)	57	2	1699	122	30.89
†J. F. Crapp (*Gloucestershire*)	62	4	1732	101	29.86
L. Hutton (*Yorkshire*)	19	1	537	194	29.83
W. G. A. Parkhouse (*Glamorgan*)	52	3	1461	143	29.81
L. Outschoorn (*Worcestershire*)	54	2	1535	150*	29.51
†S. Singh (*Camb. Univ.*)	25	1	707	94	29.45
C. A. Milton (*Gloucestershire*)	64	2	1821	150	29.37

	Innings	Not Outs	Runs	Highest Innings	Average
M. J. Stewart (*Surrey*)	42	5	1085	118	29.32
V. E. Jackson (*Leicestershire*)	59	5	1582	121	29.29
G. Goonesena (*Nottinghamshire*)	54	6	1380	118	28.75
†K. G. Suttle (*Sussex*)	55	4	1466	104	28.74
F. C. Gardner (*Warwickshire*)	55	4	1459	167	28.60
V. R. Lumsden (*Camb. Univ.*)	22	0	627	99	28.50
J. Pettiford (*Kent*)	55	8	1336	90	28.42
W. J. Edrich (*Middlesex*)	63	5	1642	133	28.31
†R. T. Spooner (*Warwickshire*)	59	7	1467	125	28.21
J. M. Allan (*Kent*)	52	3	1369	121*	27.93
J. P. Fellows-Smith (*Oxford U.*)	18	2	445	58	27.81
†D. B. Close (*Yorkshire*)	53	5	1330	143	27.70
A. A. K. Lawrence (*Sussex*)	12	2	277	63*	27.70
G. Barker (*Essex*)	58	4	1494	106	27.66
H. P. Sharp (*Middlesex*)	13	4	249	68*	27.66
G. M. Emmett (*Gloucestershire*)	61	4	1568	122	27.50
R. G. Broadbent (*Worcester.*)	59	3	1531	146	27.33
D. E. V. Padgett (*Yorkshire*)	22	1	571	115	27.19
†W. E. Jones (*Glamorgan*)	55	5	1355	112*	27.10
N. F. Horner (*Warwickshire*)	46	0	1239	119	26.93
A. S. M. Oakman (*Sussex*)	57	3	1412	102	26.14
J. D. Clay (*Nottinghamshire*)	53	2	1323	127	25.94
N. H. Rogers (*Hampshire*)	47	3	1137	121*	25.84
G. A. Edrich (*Lancashire*)	43	4	994	117	25.48
M. R. Hallam (*Leicestershire*)	43	1	1068	86	25.42
D. G. W. Fletcher (*Surrey*)	36	3	836	84	25.33
F. A. Lowson (*Yorkshire*)	45	2	1087	116	25.27
B. Constable (*Surrey*)	54	6	1208	132	25.16
D. F. Cox (*Surrey*)	9	1	201	57	25.12
A. C. Shirreff (*Hampshire*)	25	1	603	77	25.12
A. J. McIntyre (*Surrey*)	43	6	927	110	25.05
†G. E. Tribe (*Northamptonshire*)	51	6	1127	80*	25.04
P. B. Wight (*Somerset*)	56	3	1326	106	25.01
A. E. Fagg (*Kent*)	56	1	1375	106	25.00
†D. W. Richardson (*Worcester.*)	38	4	848	126	24.94
F. J. Titmus (*Middlesex*)	64	14	1235	104	24.70
†J. Kelly (*Nottinghamshire*)	10	3	172	41	24.57
A. C. Revill (*Derbyshire*)	53	4	1199	79	24.46
T. C. Dodds (*Essex*)	57	1	1364	94	24.35
E. A. Bedser (*Surrey*)	36	4	776	79	24.25
†A. J. Watkins (*Glamorgan*)	52	4	1160	111	24.16
N. W. D. Yardley (*Yorkshire*)	44	6	917	100*	24.13
G. Cox (*Sussex*)	50	3	1133	79	24.10
John Langridge (*Sussex*)	54	1	1276	153	24.07
B. L. Reynolds (*Northants*)	20	3	403	64*	23.70
J. Lister (*Worcestershire*)	26	2	567	99	23.62
A. H. Phebey (*Kent*)	45	2	1014	122	23.58
W. T. Greensmith (*Essex*)	47	17	698	63*	23.26
†J. F. Pretlove (*Kent*)	37	4	762	114	23.09
P. A. Gibb (*Essex*)	58	5	1223	77	23.07
J. Dyson (*Lancashire*)	29	3	599	84	23.03
G. P. S. Delisle (*Middlesex*)	55	3	1185	113	22.78
M. J. Horton (*Worcestershire*)	62	5	1296	103	22.73
S. M. Brown (*Middlesex*)	47	2	1016	83	22.57
B. Dooland (*Nottinghamshire*)	45	3	948	91	22.57
†G. G. Tordoff (*Somerset*)	57	4	1196	145*	22.56
†P. Hearn (*Kent*)	33	4	654	87*	22.55
J. R. Gray (*Hampshire*)	56	3	1189	98	22.43
G. Dews (*Worcestershire*)	47	1	1021	105	22.19
A. D. Buckingham (*Camb. Univ.*)	8	1	155	52*	22.14
E. J. Martin (*Nottinghamshire*)	35	4	686	76	22.12

	Innings	Not Outs	Runs	Highest Innings	Average
J. Lawrence (*Somerset*)	52	1	1128	122	22.11
J. C. Laker (*Surrey*)	38	6	706	78*	22.06
D. Bennett (*Middlesex*)	58	6	1144	99	22.00
R. A. Diment (*Leicestershire*)	18	1	374	71	22.00
†D. V. Smith (*Sussex*)	55	2	1163	90	21.94
A. C. Walton (*Oxford Univ.*)	28	0	612	68	21.85
G. Lester (*Leicestershire*)	57	3	1178	143	21.81
J. Kelly (*Derbyshire*)	53	2	1110	72	21.76
R. Swetman (*Surrey*)	8	1	152	36	21.71
E. G. Witherden (*Kent*)	10	2	171	69	21.37
J. G. Lomax (*Somerset*)	48	6	892	71	21.23
H. W. Stephenson (*Somerset*)	56	5	1082	85*	21.21
H. M. Barnard (*Hampshire*)	48	5	908	116	21.11
I. Gibson (*Oxford Univ.*)	25	3	464	52*	21.09
J. Pleass (*Glamorgan*)	37	3	713	102*	20.97
W. Wooller (*Glamorgan*)	43	2	860	128	20.97
G. A. R. Lock (*Surrey*)	41	9	669	55	20.90
J. G. Binks (*Yorkshire*)	20	11	186	42*	20.66
†V. Broderick (*Northants.*)	43	6	761	68	20.56
R. O'Brien (*Cambridge Univ.*)	26	2	486	49	20.25
A. W. H. Rayment (*Hampshire*)	40	4	719	104	19.97
J. Mortimore (*Gloucestershire*)	58	11	935	120	19.89
A. Townsend (*Warwickshire*)	53	7	898	84	19.52
T. H. Clark (*Surrey*)	42	1	798	113	19.46
† R. C. E. Pratt (*Surrey*)	23	0	447	59	19.43
J. E. McConnon (*Glamorgan*)	25	5	388	52	19.40
A. W. Catt (*Kent*)	12	4	155	88*	19.37
K. R. Dollery (*Warwickshire*)	27	9	347	38	19.27
D. G. Greasley (*Northants.*)	12	1	210	63	19.09
K. J. Poole (*Nottinghamshire*)	21	2	362	58	19.05
G. O. Dawkes (*Leicestershire*)	52	7	853	86	18.95
W. J. Stewart (*Warwickshire*)	10	3	131	33*	18.71
E. Lester (*Yorkshire*)	22	0	410	54	18.63
L. N. Devereux (*Worcestershire*)	20	0	372	59	18.60
D. J. Green (*Derbyshire*)	11	1	185	49	18.50
R. Collins (*Lancashire*)	23	3	365	52*	18.25
F. L. Angell (*Somerset*)	32	0	578	90	18.06
B. Hedges (*Glamorgan*)	41	2	703	87	18.02
D. C. Morgan (*Derbyshire*)	49	6	775	109*	18.02
G. E. Lambert (*Gloucestershire*)	56	8	861	100*	17.93
J. Pressdee (*Glamorgan*)	50	5	803	67	17.84
A. B. D. Parsons (*Camb. Univ.*)	24	2	391	46	17.77
J. P. Whitehead (*Worcester.*)	15	4	190	51*	17.27
A. P. Walshe (*Oxford Univ.*)	24	3	361	77	17.19
R. Horsfall (*Essex*)	45	3	721	69	17.16
R. O. Jenkins (*Worcestershire*)	40	8	549	54*	17.15
P. F. Harvey (*Nottinghamshire*)	30	4	444	54*	17.07
T. W. Cartwright (*Warwicks.*)	14	1	221	58	17.00
C. Gladwin (*Derbyshire*)	44	13	520	67	16.77
P. J. Loader (*Surrey*)	36	11	418	81	16.72
Yawar Saeed (*Somerset*)	46	2	731	64	16.61
G. Potter (*Sussex*)	20	3	282	48*	16.58
J. E. Firth (*Leicestershire*)	40	16	396	51	16.50
H. L. Johnson (*Derbyshire*)	45	2	703	52	16.34
D. R. W. Silk (*Cam. Univ.*)	26	0	425	63	16.34
R. T. Webb (*Sussex*)	43	16	439	49*	16.25
C. S. Smith (*Cambridge Univ.*)	29	5	388	40*	16.16
†N. Knightley-Smith (*Gloucs.*)	32	3	464	95	16.00
K. Smales (*Nottinghamshire*)	44	16	447	41	15.96
M. Walker (*Somerset*)	15	0	239	100	15.93
R. Ralph (*Essex*)	26	5	329	53*	15.66

	Innings	Not Outs	Runs	Highest Innings	Average
B. E. Disbury (*Kent*)	9	2	109	26*	15.57
P. J. Sainsbury (*Hampshire*) ...	45	7	586	73*	15.42
†B. Taylor (*Essex*)	35	2	508	75	15.39
†R. W. Barber (*Lancashire*)	23	6	260	53	15.29
†V. Munden (*Leicestershire*).....	56	5	777	61	15.23
Ray Smith (*Essex*)	50	4	685	101*	14.89
G. H. G. Doggart (*Sussex*)	18	0	267	84	14.83
A. Jepson (*Nottinghamshire*) ...	41	6	519	52*	14.82
†B. R. Edrich (*Glamorgan*)	24	2	326	43	14.81
C. F. Davey (*Somerset*)........	10	1	132	46	14.66
H. G. Davies (*Glamorgan*)	43	8	512	77*	14.62
N. I. Thomson (*Sussex*)	43	10	473	35*	14.33
M. E. L. Melluish (*Camb. Univ.*)	20	6	197	36	14.07
†J. E. Walsh (*Leicestershire*)	35	2	464	59	14.06
W. Place (*Lancashire*)	14	1	179	52	13.76
E. D. R. Eagar (*Hampshire*)....	37	1	488	53	13.55
†D. G. Ufton (*Kent*)	23	2	282	36	13.42
†G. A. Smithson (*Leicestershire*) ..	41	3	509	55	13.39
†M. Bear (*Essex*)	11	3	106	53	13.25
S. Smith (*Lancashire*)..........	15	1	185	54*	13.21
M. Heath (*Hampshire*)	11	6	66	33	13.20
G. Smith (*Essex*)	9	2	92	29*	13.14
D. Shackleton (*Hampshire*)	47	7	525	50	13.12
F. S. Trueman (*Yorkshire*)	38	8	391	74	13.03
P. D. Croft (*Cambridge Univ.*) .	20	1	246	47*	12.94
R. Booth (*Yorkshire*)..........	17	4	166	48	12.76
A. L. Dixon (*Kent*)	22	0	279	63	12.68
J. Hilton (*Somerset*)...........	39	8	390	61*	12.58
R. B. Nicholls (*Gloucestershire*).	19	2	213	63	12.52
L. Harrison (*Hampshire*).......	50	6	548	43	12.45
†J. H. Wardle (*Yorkshire*)	47	1	571	74	12.41
M. J. Hilton (*Lancashire*)	37	2	432	100*	12.34
F. H. Tyson (*Northamptonshire*)	25	4	257	72	12.23
D. V. P. Wright (*Kent*)	45	13	389	66*	12.15
†J. V. C. Griffiths (*Gloucs.*)	14	4	120	27*	12.00
L. Jackson (*Derbyshire*)	17	5	143	20*	11.91
K. V. Andrew (*Northants*)	41	12	345	32	11.89
P. B. Clift (*Glamorgan*)	18	1	202	45	11.88
D. O. Baldry (*Middlesex*)	27	2	295	26	11.80
E. Smith (*Derbyshire*)	41	11	350	57	11.66
R. G. Marlar (*Sussex*).........	46	8	439	39	11.55
C. T. Spencer (*Leicestershire*)..	47	12	404	75	11.54
K. H. Lewis (*Glamorgan*)	11	4	80	18*	11.42
E. B. Lewis (*Warwickshire*)	13	2	124	29	11.27
V. H. D. Cannings (*Hampshire*).	35	16	212	43*	11.15
T. G. Evans (*Kent*)	19	0	209	40	11.00
F. Ridgway (*Kent*)	11	2	99	26	11.00
C. Lee (*Derbyshire*)	29	1	305	63	10.89
A. F. Brazier (*Kent*)..........	27	2	272	51*	10.88
†J. B. Statham (*Lancashire*)	29	5	260	62	10.83
J. J. Warr (*Middlesex*).........	52	5	509	51	10.82
K. C. Preston (*Essex*)	35	13	238	30*	10.81
D. J. Shepherd (*Glamorgan*) ...	35	8	291	48	10.77
†R. W. Clarke (*Northants*)	31	14	182	27*	10.70
G. Smith (*Kent*)	16	3	138	38	10.61
W. S. Surridge (*Surrey*)........	37	5	330	33	10.31

BOWLING

(Qualification: 10 wickets)

† *Denotes a left-arm bowler.*

	Overs	Maidens	Runs	Wickets	Average
D. F. Cox (*Surrey*)	76.5	21	169	14	12.07
R. Appleyard (*Yorkshire*) ...	558	185	1106	85	13.01
D. Shackleton (*Hampshire*)...	1220.2	438	2183	159	13.72
L. Jackson (*Derbyshire*)	469.1	153	914	64	14.28
†G. A. R. Lock (*Surrey*)......	1408.4	497	3109	216	14.39
J. B. Statham (*Lancashire*) ...	754.5	216	1573	108	14.56
H. R. A. Kelleher (*Surrey*) ..	74	15	179	12	14.91
R. E. Marshall (*Hampshire*) .	188.4	69	439	28	15.67
F. S. Trueman (*Yorkshire*) ..	995.5	214	2454	153	16.03
†J. H. Wardle (*Yorkshire*)	1495.4	572	3149	195	16.14
C. Gladwin (*Derbyshire*)	1163.5	434	2383	147	16.21
F. J. Titmus (*Middlesex*).....	1449.5	523	3117	191	16.31
M. Kerrigan (*Scotland*)	88.2	27	188	11	17.09
D. V. P. Wright (*Kent*)	739	193	2185	127	17.20
V. H. D. Cannings (*Hampshire*)	788.1	263	1659	94	17.64
P. J. Loader (*Surrey*)	718.2	178	1695	96	17.65
E. Smith (*Derbyshire*)	878.2	320	1854	105	17.65
W. E. Hollies (*Warwicks.*) ...	1053.1	400	2035	115	17.69
N. W. D. Yardley (*Yorkshire*)	137.3	58	213	12	17.75
J. C. Laker (*Surrey*).........	1086.1	362	2382	133	17.90
†D. V. Smith (*Sussex*)	657.4	240	1345	73	18.42
†P. J. Sainsbury (*Hampshire*)..	942.5	381	1887	102	18.50
F. Goodwin (*Lancashire*)	161	29	484	26	18.61
†J. V. C. Griffiths (*Gloucs.*)	84.5	24	245	13	18.84
†C. Cook (*Gloucestershire*)	899	374	1662	88	18.88
C. H. Palmer (*Leicestershire*) .	447.1	187	914	48	19.04
†J. Pressdee (*Glamorgan*)	592.2	181	1374	72	19.08
R. G. Carter (*Warwickshire*) .	66	12	191	10	19.10
A. V. Bedser (*Surrey*)	1146.3	296	2752	144	19.11
†G. E. Tribe (*Northants*)	1289	345	3366	176	19.12
F. Ridgway (*Kent*)	159.1	33	441	23	19.17
F. H. Tyson (*Northants*)	587.5	126	1445	75	19.26
J. T. Ikin (*Lancashire*)	305	89	756	39	19.38
A. E. Moss (*Middlesex*)	754	148	2059	105	19.60
J. E. McConnon (*Glamorgan*) .	426	122	966	48	20.12
M. Heath (*Hampshire*)	265.5	57	675	33	20.45
†A. J. Watkins (*Glamorgan*) ...	983.3	270	2336	114	20.49
J. R. Gray (*Hampshire*)......	505.3	178	1025	50	20.50
M. Ryan (*Yorkshire*)	124.5	25	330	16	20.62
†J. A. Young (*Middlesex*).....	875.3	322	1944	94	20.68
†M. J. Hilton (*Lancashire*)	1030.4	391	2162	104	20.78
D. Ward (*Glamorgan*)	177.1	38	478	23	20.78
†M. J. Cowan (*Yorkshire*)	346	72	894	43	20.79
B. D. Wells (*Gloucestershire*) .	1167.4	414	2540	122	20.81
G. Goonesena (*Notts.*)	1039.5	254	2822	134	21.05
E. A. Bedser (*Surrey*)	367.2	104	893	42	21.26
A. E. James (*Sussex*)	1112.5	397	2366	111	21.31
R. G. Thompson (*Warwicks.*)	788.4	182	1967	92	21.38
R. G. Marlar (*Sussex*)........	1187.2	356	2996	139	21.55
V. E. Jackson (*Leicestershire*).	1075.2	414	2432	112	21.71
M. D. Burden (*Hampshire*) ...	644.2	195	1523	70	21.75
T. H. Clark (*Surrey*)	165.2	42	392	18	21.77
R. E. Hitchcock (*Warwicks.*)..	383.1	111	983	45	21.84
R. Tattersall (*Lancashire*)	1241.4	426	2709	124	21.84
†D. B. Carr (*Derbyshire*)	337.2	86	1001	45	22.24
†J. M. Allan (*Kent*)	872.3	287	2147	95	22.60
N. I. Thomson (*Sussex*)	1163.2	301	2675	118	22.66

	Overs	Maidens	Runs	Wickets	Average
J. D. Bannister (*Warwickshire*)	912	209	2272	100	22.72
†R. J. Hurst (*Middlesex*)	186.5	82	387	17	22.76
C. S. Smith (*Lancashire*)	453.5	103	1173	51	23.00
B. Dooland (*Nottinghamshire*)	1245.3	327	3452	150	23.01
D. L. Bates (*Sussex*)	139.1	31	348	15	23.20
D. B. Close (*Yorkshire*)	872.4	257	2274	97	23.44
G. H. Chesterton (*Worcester.*)	225.4	72	587	25	23.48
D. Bennett (*Middlesex*)	322.5	54	824	35	23.54
†V. Munden (*Leicestershire*)...	923.1	350	2048	87	23.54
J. J. Warr (*Middlesex*).......	769	176	1864	79	23.59
L. Coldwell (*Worcester.*)	95.4	21	308	13	23.69
R. O. Jenkins (*Worcester.*)..	518.5	96	1712	72	23.77
R. V. C. Robins (*Middlesex*).	128.5	24	428	18	23.77
T. E. Bailey (*Essex*)	835.3	198	2129	89	23.92
D. A. Bick (*Middlesex*)	73.3	16	240	10	24.00
S. Singh (*Cambridge Univ.*) .	416.3	107	1032	43	24.00
K. Smales (*Nottinghamshire*) .	1160.1	385	2823	117	24.12
R. T. D. Perks (*Worcester.*)..	877	209	2468	102	24.19
†R. Berry (*Worcestershire*) ...	850.4	327	1697	68	24.95
K. C. Preston (*Essex*)	868	185	2348	94	24.97
B. Lobb (*Somerset*)	780.3	159	2273	90	25.25
A. L. Dixon (*Kent*)	130.1	25	457	18	25.38
R. Collins (*Lancashire*)	273.2	106	585	23	25.43
J. Mortimore (*Gloucestershire*)	724.3	218	1659	65	25.52
J. C. T. Page (*Kent*)	485.2	114	1526	58	26.31
†J. E. Walsh (*Leicestershire*) ..	455.1	98	1450	55	26.36
D. Hall (*Derbyshire*)	210.1	42	634	24	26.41
†J. F. Pretlove (*Kent*)	109.4	27	317	12	26.41
W. T. Greensmith (*Essex*)....	735.3	158	2220	84	26.42
K. H. Lewis (*Glamorgan*)	216.1	36	558	21	26.57
F. P. McHugh (*Gloucs.*)	868.5	206	2017	75	26.89
A. Lightfoot (*Northants*)	125.5	31	296	11	26.90
J. Lawrence (*Somerset*)	609.5	114	1917	71	27.00
M. J. Horton (*Worcestershire*)	910.1	213	2821	103	27.38
M. Walker (*Somerset*)	85	15	329	12	27.41
G. Smith (*Kent*)	354.5	101	852	31	27.48
T. C. Dodds (*Essex*)	84.5	14	330	12	27.50
G. Lester (*Leicestershire*)	258.4	59	881	32	27.53
W. Wooller (*Glamorgan*)	598.1	177	1519	55	27.61
Ray Smith (*Essex*)	815.5	174	2211	79	27.98
J. A. Arenhold (*Oxford U.*) ..	147	26	452	16	28.25
R. Illingworth (*Yorkshire*) ...	589	198	1358	48	28.29
J. Hilton (*Somerset*)....	368.1	88	1019	36	28.30
J. Flavell (*Worcestershire*) ...	494.3	86	1648	58	28.41
D. C. Morgan (*Derbyshire*) ..	700.2	180	1886	66	28.57
T. Greenhough (*Lancashire*)..	179.5	51	430	15	28.66
D. C. P. R. Jowett (*Oxford U.*)	286.3	71	774	27	28.66
†J. W. McMahon (*Somerset*) ..	814.3	225	2158	75	28.77
J. Pettiford (*Kent*)	368.2	110	1100	38	28.94
D. J. Smith (*Cambridge U.*) ..	439	90	1220	42	29.04
A. C. Revill (*Derbyshire*)	134.4	39	381	13	29.30
G. E. Lambert (*Gloucs.*).....	805.3	148	2360	80	29.50
R. Ralph (*Essex*)	359	72	1063	36	29.52
R. Subba Row (*Northants*) ..	131.4	26	446	15	29.73
†V. Broderick (*Northants*)	902.5	323	2143	72	29.76
H. D. Davies (*Glamorgan*) ...	260	62	804	27	29.77
W. S. Surridge (*Surrey*)	311.4	73	783	26	30.11
A. Jepson (*Nottinghamshire*)..	799.5	216	1925	63	30.55
†R. T. Weeks (*Warwickshire*) .	207.1	69	490	16	30.62
K. R. Dollery (*Warwickshire*).	390.3	59	1173	38	30.86
J. B. Phillips (*Kent*)	492.5	114	1390	45	30.88
†J. Goodwin (*Leicestershire*) ..	279.2	50	930	30	31.00

	Overs	Maidens	Runs	Wickets	Average
D. J. Shepherd (*Glamorgan*)..	714.4	166	1937	62	31.24
K. B. Standring (*Lancashire*) .	113	26	316	10	31.60
A. Wharton (*Lancashire*)	273	71	674	21	32.09
D. J. Insole (*Essex*)	241.5	45	771	24	32.12
C. T. Spencer (*Leics.*)	819	161	2600	80	32.50
D. K. Fasken (*Oxford U.*) ...	121	21	367	11	33.36
A. S. M. Oakman (*Sussex*)...	600.1	194	1373	41	33.48
J. P. Fellows-Smith (*Oxf. U.*)	180.4	44	503	15	33.53
T. W. Graveney (*Gloucs.*)....	105.3	22	374	11	34.00
Yawar Saeed (*Somerset*)	407.3	54	1464	43	34.04
J. Spanswick (*Kent*)	318.4	52	1065	31	34.35
A. Townsend (*Warwickshire*).	194.1	30	598	17	35.17
A. C. Shirreff (*Kent*)	410.4	99	1163	32	36.34
B. Boshier (*Leicestershire*) ...	196.5	36	607	16	37.93
F. W. Moore (*Lancashire*) ...	290.3	74	844	22	38.36
J. A. Bailey (*Essex*)	333	74	850	21	40.47
J. Webster (*Northants*)	233.2	64	617	15	41.13
S. Starkie (*Northants*)	228.1	69	557	13	42.84
†R. W. Clarke (*Northants*) ...	616.1	110	1714	38	45.10
P. F. Harvey (*Notts.*).........	331.1	101	860	19	45.26
J. Wild (*Northants*)	223.3	48	748	14	53.42
J. G. Lomax (*Somerset*)	376	78	1073	19	56.47

FIELDING STATISTICS IN 1955

Except in the case of a wicket-keeper, identified by (s) indicating stumpings, the figures apply to catches.

85 A. J. McIntyre (65 c, 20 s)	40 D. B. Carr	26 F. S. Trueman
82 H. G. Davies (59 c, 23 s)	40 F. J. Titmus	26 D. G. Ufton (19 c, 7 s)
76 H. W. Stephenson (53 c, 23 s)	39 R. Broadbent	26 A. J. Watkins
	38 J. G. Binks (32 c, 6 s)	26 W. Wooller
	38 D. B. Close	25 G. Dews
71 K. Andrew (42 c, 29 s)	37 A. E. Fagg	25 G. Goonesena
69 G. O. Dawkes (54 c, 15 s)	35 A. Townsend	25 J. G. Lomax
	34 K Grieves (33 c, 1 s)	25 K. C. Preston
69 J. Langridge	34 M. E. L. Melluish (25 c, 9 s)	25 K. G. Suttle
66 H. Yarnold (52 c, 14 s)	34 P. J. Sainsbury	24 J. D. Bannister
65 R. T. Spooner (51c, 14 s)	33 H. M. Barnard	24 B. Dooland
	33 J. D. Clay	24 J. R. Gray
65 R. T. Webb (41 c, 24 s)	33 P. B. H. May	24 R. Illingworth
	33 R. E. Marshall	24 J. Jordan (20 c, 4 s)
63 P. A. Gibb (52 c, 11 s)	32 A. S. M. Oakman	23 A. E. Moss
62 L. H. Compton (56 c, 6 s)	32 C. T. Spencer	23 J. D. Robertson
	31 T. W. Graveney	22 G. M. Emmett
61 J. V. Wilson	30 J. M. Allan	22 J. Pettiford
60 P. Rochford (48 c, 12 s)	30 J. T. Ikin	22 C. J. Poole
	30 D. J. Insole	22 N. H. Rogers
56 W. S. Surridge	29 G. A. Edrich	22 G. A. Smithson
55 L. Harrison (45 c, 10 s)	29 M. F. Tremlett	22 G. G. Tordoff
	28 W. J. Edrich	21 K. Barrington
52 M. J. Stewart	28 A. C. Revill	21 R. W. Clarke
49 E. Rowe (37 c, 12 s)	28 B. Taylor (25 c, 3 s)	21 T. G. Evans (17 c, 4 s)
48 G. A. R. Lock	28 G. E. Tribe	21 E. B. Lewis (15 c, 6 s)
46 C. A. Milton	28 W. Watson	21 F. A. Lowson
43 J. Firth (34 c, 9 s)	27 F. C. Gardner	21 D. V. Smith
43 D. C. Morgan	26 R. Booth (24 c, 2 s)	21 A. Wharton
43 A. E. Wilson (32 c, 11 s)	26 E. D. R. Eagar	21 C. C. P. Williams
	26 M. J. Hilton	20 G. E. Lambert
42 J. Pressdee	26 J. C. Laker	20 C. H. Palmer
41 M. R. Hallam	26 F. W. Stocks	20 J. M. Parks

INDIVIDUAL SCORES OF 100 AND OVER

There were 231 individual three-figure innings in first-class cricket in 1955, the same number as in 1954. The list includes 173 hit in County Championship matches and 41 in other first-class games, but not the 17 by members of the South African team which can be found in their own section.

D. J. Insole (9):
142 Essex v. Yorks: Bradford
129 Essex v. S. Africans: Colchester.
119 Essex v. Yorks: Southend
117* Essex v. Glos: Westcliff.
114* Essex v. Notts: Southend.
111 }
118 } Essex v. Kent: Gillingham.
109 Essex v. Leics: Leicester.
104 Essex v Derby: Chesterfield.

T. W. Graveney (5):
159 Pearce's XI v. S. Africans: Scarborough.
128 Glos. v. Worcs: Worcester.
104 Glos. v. Somerset: Taunton.
101 Glos. v. Northants: Kettering.
101 M.C.C. v. Yorks: Scarborough.

D. Kenyon (5):
131 Worcs. v. Leics: Leicester.
129 Worcs. v. Leics: Dudley
117 An Eng. XI v. Comm. XI: Torquay.
108 Worcs. v. Glos: Worcester.
103* Worcs. v. Hants: Bournemouth.

L. Livingston (5):
172* Northants v. Essex: Wellingboro.
170 Northants v. Notts: Nottm.
107 Northants v. Worcs: Stourbridge
105 Northants v. Leics :Northampton.
101 Northants v. War: Northampton.

P. B. H. May (5):
125 Champ. Cty. v. Rest: Oval.
122* Surrey v. Lancs: Oval.
117 Eng. v. S. Africa: Manchester.
112 Eng. v. S. Africa: Lord's.
102 Surrey v. Kent: Blackheath.

J. M. Parks (5):
205* Sussex v. Somerset: Hove.
175* Sussex v. Camb. U.: Horsham.
118 Sussex v. S. Africans: Hove.
117 Sussex v. Notts: Hove.
101* Sussex v. Derby: Hove.

M. C. Cowdrey (4):
139 Kent v. Northants: Tun. Wells.
115* }
103* } Kent v. Essex: Gillingham.
101 M.C.C. v. Oxford U.: Lord's.

H. E. Dollery (4):
156 War. v. Essex: Westcliff.
151 War. v. Notts: Birmingham.
106 War. v. Leics: Hinckley.
105 War. v. Somerset: Birmingham.

R. E. Hitchcock (4):
128 War. v. Essex: Birmingham.
123* War. v. Surrey: Coventry.
121 War. v. Leics: Hinckley.
110 War. v. Derby: Derby.

V. E. Jackson (4):
121 Leics. v. Essex: Leicester.
114 Leics. v. Worcs.: Leicester.
105 Leics. v. Glam: Cardiff.
100 Leics. v. Derby: Ashby.

C. H. Palmer (4):
154 Gents. v. Players: Lord's.
128 Leics. v. Notts: Nottingham.
126 Leics. v. War: Birmingham.
102 Leics v. Northants: Leicester

R. Subba Row (4):
260* Northants v. Lancs: Nottm.
132 Northants v. Notts: Nottm.
112 Northants v. Surrey: Guildford.
102 Northants v. Worcs: Stourbdge.

C. Washbrook (4):
170 Lancs. v. Worcs: Manchester.
166 Lancs. v. Comb. Ser.: Manchr.
131 Lancs. v. Glam: Manchester.
102 Lancs. v. Glam: Swansea.

W. Watson (4):
214* Yorks. v. Worcs: Worcester.
174 Yorks. v. Lancs: Sheffield.
163 Yorks. v. Sussex: Sheffield.
105 Yorks. v. Essex: Bradford.

J. V. Wilson (4):
132* Yorks. v. War: Birmingham.
132 Yorks. v. Essex: Bradford.
110 Yorks. v. Camb. U.: Cambridge.
109* Yorks. v. Som: Taunton.

D. M. Young (4):
170 Glos. v. Oxford U.: Oxford.
137 Glos. v. Kent: Canterbury.
121 }
117* } Glos. v. Northants: Kettering.

* *Signifies not out.*

J. M. Allan (3):
121* } Kent v. Northants: Northn.
105 }
105   Kent v. Glos: Canterbury.

P. Arnold (3):
122   Northants v. Som: Taunton.
118   Northants v. Kent: Tun. Wells.
113   Northants v. Glam: Northn.

T. E. Bailey (3):
152* Essex v. Kent: Clacton.
114* Essex v. Notts: Southend.
107   Essex v. S. Africans: Colchester.

R. G. Broadbent (3):
146   Worcs. v. Som: Worcester.
108   Worcs. v. Lancs: Manchester.
106   Worcs. v. Scotland: Glasgow.

D. Brookes (3)
177   Northants v. Som: Taunton.
117   Northants v. Leics: Leicester.
102* Northants v. Glam: Northn.

D. B. Carr (3):
146   Derby. v. Leics: Ashby.
139   Derby. v. Glos: Derby.
131   An Eng. XI v. Com. XI: Hastns.

R. J. Giles (3):
142   Notts. v. Yorks: Nottm.
121   Notts. v. Lancs: Manchester.
115   Notts. v. Lancs: Nottm.

H. Horton (3):
139   Hants v. Leics: Leicester.
109   Hants v. Surrey: Brnmth.
104* Hants v. Sussex: Portsmouth.

J. T. Ikin (3):
114   Lancs. v. Notts: Nottingham.
109   Lancs. v. Surrey: Manchester.
107   Lancs. v. Glam: Manchester.

R. E. Marshall (3):
110* Hants. v. Oxford U.: Brnmth.
106   Hants. v. Middx: Brnmth.
105   Hants. v. Notts: Nottingham.

M. J. K. Smith (3):
118   Oxford U. v. M.C.C.: Lord's.
104   Oxford U. v. Camb. U.: Lord's
100   Oxford U. v. Sussex: Hove.

W. H. H. Sutcliffe (3):
161* Yorks. v. Glam: Harrogate.
133   Yorks. v. Derby: Bradford.
107   Yorks. v. Kent: Hull.

M. Tompkin (3):
131   Leics. v. Worcs: Dudley.
121   Leics. v. Middx: Lord's.
115   Players v. Gents: Lord's.

A. V. Wolton (3):
136   War. v. Comb. Serv.: Bham.
107   War. v. Yorks: Birmingham.
105* War. v. Oxford U.: Oxford.

G. Barker (2):
106   Essex v. War.: Birmingham.
104   Essex v. Notts: Nottingham.

D. W. Barrick (2):
139   Northants. v. Middx: Lord's.
105* Northants. v. Derby: Chesterd.

K. Barrington (2):
135* Surrey v Lancs: Oval.
126   Surrey v. Notts: Nottingham.

J. D. Clay (2):
127   Notts. v. Som: Taunton.
102   Notts. v. Essex: Nottingham.

D. B. Close (2):
143   Yorks. v. Som: Taunton.
114   Yorks. v. Camb. U.: Cambridge.

D. C. S. Compton (2):
158   Eng. v. S. Africa: Manchester.
150   Middx. v. Sussex: Lord's.

B. Constable (2):
132   Surrey v Worcs: Worcester.
104   Surrey v. Leics: Oval.

J. F. Crapp (2):
101   Glos. v. Sussex: Eastbourne.
100* Glos. v. War: Birmingham.

G. P. Delisle (2):
113   Oxford U. v. Glos: Oxford.
105   Middx. v. Notts: Nottingham.

J. G. Dewes (2):
117   Middx. v. Sussex: Hove.
101* Middx. v. Surrey: Oval.

G. A. Edrich (2):
117   Lancs. v. Middx: Liverpool.
103   Lancs. v. Kent: Manchester.

W. J. Edrich (2):
133   Gents. v. Players: Scarborough.
125* Middx. v. War: Birmingham.

G. M. Emmett (2):
122   Glos. v. Northants: Gloucester.
113   Glos. v. War: Birmingham.

G. Goonesena (2):
118   Camb. U. v. War: Birmingham.
107* Notts. v. Northants: Nottm.

K. Grieves (2)
137   Lancs. v. Derby: Manchester.
119   Lancs. v. Kent: Maidstone.

* Signifies not out.

A. Hamer (2):
227 Derby. v. Notts: Nottm.
111* Derby. v. Glam: Derby.

R. Illingworth (2):
138 Yorks. v. M.C.C.: Scarborough.
116 Yorks. v. Essex: Southend.

J. Langridge (2):
153 Sussex v. Oxford U.: Hove.
101 Sussex v. Essex: Chelmsford.

G. Lester (2):
143 Leics. v. Surrey: Oval.
109 Leics. v. War: Birmingham.

C. A. Milton (2):
150 Glos. v. Worcs: Gloucester.
138 Glos. v. Som: Taunton.

L. Outschoorn (2):
150* Worcs. v. Essex: Chelmsford.
106 Worcs. v. Northants: Stourbdge.

C. J. Poole (2):
122 Notts. v. Derby: Ilkeston.
108 Notts. v. Lancs: Manchester.

J. F. Pretlove (2):
114 Camb. U. v. Oxf. U.: Lord's.
110 Camb. U. v. Middx: Cambridge.

N. H. Rogers (2):
121* Hants. v. Oxford U.: Brnmth.
103* Hants. v. Kent: Canterbury.

R. T. Simpson (2):
105 Notts. v. Kent: Nottingham.
100 Notts. v. Surrey: Nottingham.

M. J. Stewart (2):
118 Surrey v. Kent: Blackheath.
105 Surrey v. Leics: Oval.

M. F. Tremlett (2)
153 Som. v. Northants: Taunton.
120 Som. v. Notts: Taunton.

A. J. Watkins (2):
111 Glam. v. Notts: Llanelly.
107* Glam. v. Worcs: Swansea.

A. Wharton (2):
123 Lancs. v. Som: Manchester.
108* Lancs. v. Glos: Blackpool.

C. C. P. Williams (2):
120 Oxford U. v. Glos: Oxford.
119 Essex v. Leics: Leicester.

The following thirty-eight each played one three-figure innings:—

H. M. Barnard, 116, Hants. v. Leics., Bournemouth.
T. H. Clark, 113, Surrey v. Oxford U., Guildford.
G. Dews, 105, Worcs. v. Scotland, Glasgow.
A. E. Fagg, 106, Kent v. Sussex, Tunbridge Wells.
F. C. Gardner, 167, War. v. Som., Bath.
J. Hardstaff, 134, Notts. v. Yorks., Nottingham; M. J. Hilton, 100*, Lancs. v.
Northants., Northampton; N. F. Horner, 119, War. v. Glos., Bristol; M. J.
Horton, 103, Worcs. v. Leics., Leicester; L. Hutton, 194, Yorks. v. Notts.,
Nottingham.
W. E. Jones, 112*, Glam. v. Som., Newport.
G. E. Lambert, 100*, Glos. v. Worcs., Worcester; J. Lawrence, 122, Som. v.
Worcs., Worcester; F. A. Lowson, 116, Yorks. v Middx., Lord's.
A. J. McIntyre, 110, Surrey v Notts., Nottingham; D. C. Morgan; 109*, Derby. v.
Kent, Gravesend; J. Mortimore, 120, Glos. v. Oxford U., Oxford.
A. S. M. Oakman, 102, Sussex v. Derby., Hove.
D. E. V. Padgett, 115, Yorks. v. War., Birmingham; W. G. A. Parkhouse, 143,
Glam. v. Lancs., Manchester; A. H. Phebey, 122, Kent v Northants, North-
ampton; J. Pleass, 102*, Glam. v. Yorks., Harrogate.
A. W. H. Rayment, 104, Hants. v. Som., Weston; D. W. Richardson, 126, Worcs.
v. Glos., Worcester; J. D. Robertson, 137, Middx. v. Som., Lord's.
D. S. Sheppard, 104, Sussex v. S. Africans, Hove; R. Smith, 101* Essex v.
Northants, Wellingbro.; R. T. Spooner, 125, War. v. Leics., Birmingham;
K. G. Suttle, 104, Sussex v. Glos., Eastbourne.
F. J. Titmus, 104, Middx. v. Hants., Bournemouth; G. G. Tordoff, 145*, Som. v.
Glos., Taunton.
M. Walker, 100, Som. v. Essex, Romford; P. B. Wight, 106, Som. v. Worcs.,
Taunton; G. L. Willatt, 133, Derby. v. Scotland, Edinburgh; R. C. Wilson,
107, Kent v Middx., Folkestone; W. Wooller, 128, Glam. v. War., Neath;
F. M. Worrell, 100, Comm. XI v. Eng. XI, Torquay.
N. W. D. Yardley, 100*, Yorks. v. Glos., Bristol.

* *Signifies not out.*

SOUTH AFRICANS IN ENGLAND, 1955

Although they narrowly failed to win the rubber, the South African cricketers who toured England in 1955 under the captaincy of J. E. Cheetham went home knowing they had done better than any of their predecessors. Never before had South Africa won two Tests in a tour in England as they did at Old Trafford and Headingley; in fact their only other victories were at Lord's in 1935 and at Nottingham in 1951.

England should have been prepared for a serious challenge, for they were fully aware of the way South Africa shared the Test honours in Australia in 1952–53 when each country won two matches. As many as ten of that combination came to England last summer and, more important, the two key-men—K. G. Viljoen, the manager, and Cheetham—were again in charge. They disciplined the team with the same thoroughness as they did in Australia, insisting upon a high standard of physical fitness, which produced an exceptionally brilliant fielding combination and kept the men fresh throughout a long and arduous tour. By the end of June the South Africans could show only four wins, against M.C.C., Oxford, Somerset, and Sussex, but afterwards their first-class victories numbered eleven, including two over England, and only one more match was lost—the final Test at The Oval.

Considering their adversities in May and June, the South Africans deserved the highest praise for finishing the summer with flying colours. Few touring teams have begun so discouragingly and yet arrived at The Oval in August with the rubber still at stake. Bitterly cold weather in May produced conditions entirely foreign to the majority of the side, and not only were they beaten in the very first match at Worcester, but they lost the first two Tests at Trent Bridge and Lord's. On those occasions the pace of Tyson and Statham in turn brought about their undoing; but when the sun shone warmly they went to Old Trafford resolved to meet the fast bowling unflinchingly, and their positive approach was rewarded with a total of 521 and victory by a margin of three wickets.

This success came early in July when the team struck such excellent form that, besides going on to win the fourth Test at Headingley, they mastered the two strongest counties, Yorkshire at Sheffield by 193 runs and Surrey at The Oval by 82. While England could point to injuries disturbing the composition of the side, no one would say that these detracted from the merit of South Africa's wonderful recovery and everybody was prepared for a hard and close contest in the final match. Thanks almost entirely to a not out innings of 89 by their captain, May, and accurate and persistent spin bowling by Lock and Laker, England gained the verdict in a match which drew 100,000 spectators in four days.

That South Africa did not achieve their ambition to win the rubber was due almost entirely to inconsistent batting. D. J. McGlew, their vice-captain, was the only really dependable batsman, and even he failed in both innings at Lord's; otherwise he enjoyed a successful tour with easily the highest aggregate and average. Much will be found about McGlew and Tayfield in their biographies in the *Five Cricketers of the Year*, but here one would emphasise that besides his ability as a run-maker McGlew was outstanding at cover in a set of brilliant fielders, and in addition he proved himself a most capable understudy to Cheetham when the captain was away. Indeed, the South Africans' two Test victories were achieved under McGlew's leadership.

A valuable ally to McGlew as a batsman, and especially in the Tests, was Goddard, who besides scoring 1,163 runs in the first-class matches also took 60 wickets. Standing six feet two inches, Goddard was new to Test matches. Left-handed in batting as well as bowling and a capable slip fielder, he was the best all-rounder. In most of his work Goddard showed himself to be a defensive cricketer. When batting, survival at the crease was his main consideration, and when bowling (left arm over the wicket at medium pace) he pegged down the opposition by aiming persistently at or outside the leg-stump to a field set suitably for these tactics. As he was only 23, much more may be yet heard of Goddard who was obviously a cricketer of great possibilities.

By far the most attractive batsman—apart from the sheer hitters—was McLean. He visited England first in 1951 when only twenty, and on this his second tour he gave many fine exhibitions of clean stylish stroke play. His purposeful driving was an absolute delight. Most notable were his devastating 142 in the Lord's Test and a simply superb innings of 151 out of a total of 242 against Surrey at The Oval. Unfortunately for South Africa, McLean in the vital Oval Test made only a single in two innings. Endean and the left-handed Keith also failed badly in that match. After taking a long time to settle down, Endean found his best form in the fourth Test at Headingley where he made 116 not out, but considering his experience in big cricket he should have made more than 1,242 runs during the whole tour.

On his day, Waite, the wicket-keeper, looked a better batsman than his modest aggregate would suggest. He seized one of the big occasions to hit his only century of the tour—113 in the Manchester Test—and he alone really challenged Laker and Lock when they were carrying all before them in the deciding game of the rubber. As Waite served his side splendidly in his arduous duties behind the stumps, he could be excused any shortcomings with the bat.

Much was expected from Winslow, a tall (six feet three inches), lean player with a reputation for big hitting. He reserved his two best displays for the Old Trafford ground. On his first visit, when he faced the Lancashire bowlers, Winslow scored 40 in the course of eight successive balls that he received, punishing Ikin for 30 in an over and following with 4 and 6 off Goodwin. Then a month later he drove with such power in the Third Test that he hit three 6's and thirteen 4's while making 108 in an innings worthy almost of Jessop himself. Moreover, Winslow and Waite engaged in a memorable partnership that day which produced 171, a new South African Test record for the sixth wicket.

South Africa's real strength was their well-equipped attack and the grand fielding that gave all possible support. There were eight first-class bowlers in a party of sixteen players and standing above them all was Tayfield, the renowned off-spinner. Altogether, he took 143 wickets at 15.75 runs each and between them Tayfield, Goddard and Heine claimed 72 of the 90 England wickets which fell to bowlers in the five Tests. Tayfield's success was expected, but Heine and Goddard came without experience of Test cricket.

Apparently the South Africans themselves did not at first appreciate the worth of Heine, for they left him out of the Trent Bridge Test. One of many splendidly-built cricketers in this very popular team, Heine was the tallest of them all, six feet four inches, and he could be extremely hostile with the new ball which he moved each way. Also when he desired he bounced the ball nastily. Adcock was the fastest member of the attack, but his length was poor and he never achieved the number of victims his admirers anticipated. Indeed, he gave way in the end to Fuller, a spirited bowler of fast-medium pace. Murray made the fifth "seamer" in the side, but like Duckworth, the reserve wicket-keeper, no room could be found for him in the representative matches.

There were three spin bowlers, Tayfield (off) and Smith and Mansell (leg), but with Tayfield showing no decline in his powers there were not many opportunities for the other two and each claimed only one wicket in the Tests.

Both on and off the field Cheetham showed himself a talented and determined leader but he accomplished little with the bat in the Tests, scoring only 96 runs in the three matches in which he played. When Cheetham might well have run into form he received a blow on the left elbow from the very last ball sent down on the Saturday evening of the Lord's Test. The bone was chipped and Cheetham remained out of cricket for a whole month, but when he returned he eventually found his form and hit his only century against Kent at Canterbury.

Wherever the South Africans went they were most agreeable companions and foes. They will always be remembered for their superb fielding. In such a team where all were so alert in the field, it is somewhat invidious to single out individuals, but besides McGlew whose prowess at cover has already been noted, one particularly recalls McLean in the deep, Mansell, Goddard, Heine and Tayfield close to the wicket and, last but not least, Cheetham himself, always setting a grand example at mid-on.

To hold England for so long was a great performance, and no doubt when the M.C.C. visit South Africa in the coming winter they will find these talented Springboks even more formidable on their native Veld.

N. P.

SOUTH AFRICAN RESULTS

Test Matches.—Played 5, Won 2, Lost 3.

First-Class Matches.—Played 28, Won 15, Lost 4, Drawn 9.

All Matches.—Played 31, Won 16, Lost 4, Drawn 11.

Wins.—England (2), M.C.C., Oxford University, Somerset, Sussex, Yorkshire, Surrey, Glamorgan, Warwickshire, Leicestershire, Hampshire, Kent, Middlesex, Durham, T. N. Pearce's XI.

Draws—Derbyshire, Nottinghamshire, Cambridge University, Glamorgan, Essex, Lancashire, Northamptonshire, Minor Counties, Gloucestershire, An England XI, Cumberland and Westmorland.

Losses.—England (3), Worcestershire.

TEST MATCH AVERAGES

ENGLAND

BATTING

	Matches	Inns.	Not Outs	Runs	Highest Inns.	Average
P. B. H. May	5	9	0	582	117	72.75
D. C. S. Compton	5	9	0	492	158	54.66
T. W. Graveney	5	9	0	219	60	24.33
T. E. Bailey	5	9	1	184	49	23.00
D. Kenyon	3	5	0	96	87	19.20
K. Barrington	2	3	0	52	34	17.33
T. G. Evans	3	5	0	82	36	16.40
G. A. R. Lock	3	6	1	79	19*	15.80
J. H. Wardle	3	5	0	71	24	14.20
F. J. Titmus	2	4	0	39	19	9.75
J. B. Statham	4	7	1	42	20	7.00
F. H. Tyson	2	3	0	10	8	3.33

Also batted: R. Appleyard 0*; A. V. Bedser 1 and 3; D. B. Close 32 and 15; M. C. Cowdrey 1 and 50; J. T. Ikin 17 and 0; D. J. Insole 3 and 47; J. C. Laker 2 and 12; P. J. Loader 0* and 0*; F. A. Lowson 5 and 0; A. J. McIntyre 3 and 4; R. T. Spooner 0 and 0; F. S. Trueman 2* and 6*; W. Watson 25 and 3.

* *Signifies not out.*

BOWLING

	Overs	Maidens	Runs	Wickets	Average
J. H. Wardle	165.4	77	273	15	18.20
F. H. Tyson	103	19	258	14	18.42
J. B. Statham	177.2	54	363	17	21.35
G. A. R. Lock	164	65	353	13	27.15
T. E. Bailey	142.5	40	328	9	36.44

Also bowled: R. Appleyard 47—13—78—2; A. V. Bedser 41—3—153—4; J. C. Laker 60.4—31—84—7; P. J. Loader 48—16—119—4; F. J. Titmus 33—10—101—1; F. S. Trueman 35—4—112—2.

SOUTH AFRICA

BATTING

	Matches	Inns.	Not Outs	Runs	Highest Inns.	Average
D. J. McGlew	5	10	1	476	133	52.88
J. H. B. Waite	5	10	1	265	113	29.44
R. A. McLean	5	10	0	277	142	27.70
W. R. Endean............	5	10	1	246	116*	27.33
P. L. Winslow............	3	6	0	156	108	26.00
J. E. Cheetham	3	6	2	96	54	24.00
T. L. Goddard	5	10	0	235	74	23.50
H. J. Keith	4	8	0	178	73	22.25
H. J. Tayfield	5	10	3	117	28	16.71
P. Heine................	4	7	1	74	22*	12.33
E. R. H. Fuller	2	4	0	42	16	10.50
P. N. F. Mansell	4	8	0	45	16	5.62
N. A. T. Adcock	4	6	3	13	6	4.33

Also batted: V. I. Smith 0 and 2*.

BOWLING

	Overs	Maidens	Runs	Wickets	Average
E. R. H. Fuller	76	19	126	6	21.00
T. L. Goddard	315.4	148	528	25	21.12
H. J. Tayfield	313.3	124	568	26	21.84
P. Heine................	199.5	46	494	21	23.52
N. A. T. Adcock	126	37	252	10	25.20
P. N. F. Mansell	48	7	130	1	130.00

Also bowled: H. J. Keith 6—1—19—0; V. I. Smith 30—9—62—1.

The following hundreds were hit in the Test Matches:—

FOR ENGLAND (3):

P. B. H. May (2): 117 at Manchester (Third Test).
112 at Lord's (Second Test).
D. C. S. Compton: 158 at Manchester (Third Test).

FOR SOUTH AFRICA (6):

D. J. McGlew (2): 133 at Leeds (Fourth Test).
104* at Manchester (Third Test).
W. R. Endean: 116* at Leeds (Fourth Test).
R. A. McLean: 142 at Lord's (Second Test).
J. H. B. Waite: 113 at Manchester (Third Test).
P. L. Winslow: 108 at Manchester (Third Test).

* Signifies not out.

SOUTH AFRICANS—FIRST-CLASS AVERAGES

BATTING

† *Denotes left-handed batsman.*

	Matches	Inns.	Not Outs	Runs	Highest Inns.	Average
D. J. McGlew	22	34	2	1871	161	58.46
R. A. McLean	25	41	3	1448	151	38.10
J. E. Cheetham	19	30	8	765	112	34.77
W. R. Endean.......	24	40	4	1242	138*	34.50
†T. L. Goddard	23	39	1	1163	121	30.60
J. H. B. Waite	24	39	3	930	113	25.83
P. N. F. Mansell	19	27	3	611	99	25.45
†H. J. Keith	19	29	1	682	100	24.35
C. A. R. Duckworth ..	13	19	4	362	158	24.13
P. L. Winslow........	22	34	2	758	108	23.68
P. Heine............	17	25	6	361	58	19.00
A. R. A. Murray	14	20	3	275	51	16.17
H. J. Tayfield	23	35	9	392	65	15.07
E. R. H. Fuller	16	23	2	223	38	10.61
V. I. Smith	15	15	8	44	10	6.28
N. A. T. Adcock	13	11	5	18	6	3.00

BOWLING

† *Denotes left-arm bowler.*

	Overs	Maidens	Runs	Wickets	Average
H. J. Tayfield	1170.5	461	2253	143	15.75
A. R. A. Murray	321.4	150	575	31	18.54
E. R. H. Fuller	486.1	145	956	49	19.51
P. Heine............	653.1	175	1470	74	19.86
V. I. Smith	383.3	111	1030	49	21.02
†T. L. Goddard	810	352	1311	60	21.85
P. N. F. Mansell	336.4	95	771	29	26.58
N. A. T. Adcock	364	84	914	34	26.88
†H. J. Keith	138	60	276	8	34.50

Also bowled: J. E. Cheetham 1—0—3—0; W. R. Endean 1—0—1—1; D. J. McGlew 1—0—4—0; R. A. McLean 2—0—2—0.

SOUTH AFRICANS—HUNDREDS

The following twenty three-figure innings were played by the South Africans, three not being first-class:—

D. J. McGlew (5):
  161   v. Kent at Canterbury.
  161   v. Leicestershire at Leicester.
  133   v. England at Leeds (Fourth Test).
  118   v. Essex at Colchester.
  104*   v. England at Manchester (Third Test).

R. A. McLean (4):
  151   v. Surrey at The Oval.
  142   v. England at Lord's (Second Test).
  129   v. Sussex at Hove.
  101*   v. Essex at Colchester.

W. R. Endean (2):
  138*   v. T. N. Pearce's XI at Scarborough.
  116*   v. England at Leeds (Fourth Test).

Signifies not out.

H

P. L. Winslow (2):
    133   v. Durham at Sunderland†.
    108   v. England at Manchester (Third Test).

J. E. Cheetham (1):
    112   v. Kent at Canterbury.

C. A. R. Duckworth (1):
    158   v. Northamptonshire at Northampton.

T. L. Goddard (1):
    12₁   v. Oxford University at Oxford.

H. J. Keith (1):
    100   v. Leicestershire at Leicester.

P. N. F. Mansell (1):
    148   v. Durham at Sunderland†.

A. R. A. Murray (1):
    100   v. Minor Counties at Stoke-on-Trent†.

J. H. B. Waite (1):
    113   v. England at Manchester (Third Test).

* Signifies not out. † Not First-Class.*

The following eight three-figure innings were played against the South Africans in all matches:—

P. B. H. May (2):
    117 for England at Manchester (Third Test).
    112 for England at Lord's (Second Test).

T. E. Bailey (1):
    107 for Essex at Colchester.

D. C. S. Compton (1):
    158 for England at Manchester (Third Test).

T. W. Graveney (1):
    159 for T. N. Pearce's XI at Scarborough.

D. J. Insole (1):
    129 for Essex at Colchester.

J. M. Parks (1):
    118 for Sussex at Hove.

D. S. Sheppard (1):
    104 for Sussex at Hove.

SOUTH AFRICANS—FIELDING

J. H. B. Waite (55 caught, 10 stumped) 65, P. N. F. Mansell 27, C. A. R. Duckworth (16 caught, 5 stumped) 21, T. L. Goddard 21, H. J. Tayfield 21, R. A. McLean 18, H. J. Keith 17, W. R. Endean 16, P. L. Winslow 15, P. Heine 14, J. E. Cheetham 13, E. R. H. Fuller 11, A. R. A. Murray 8, N. A. T. Adcock 6, D. J. McGlew 4, V. I. Smith 2.

WORCESTERSHIRE v. SOUTH AFRICANS

At Worcester, May 7, 9 10. Worcestershire won by 117 runs. In repeating their success of 1947, the county gave a fine display when for the first time they were under the official captaincy of Perks. A second wicket stand of 113 by Kenyon and Outschoorn ensured confidence, and later Perks (three 6's and three 4's) hit all 41 runs added for the ninth wicket while Jenkins unselfishly played only three balls. Fielding errors handicapped the South Africans but Tayfield bowled up to his reputation. At no time was the South African batting inspiring and when they were left to make 261 in three hours forty minutes heavy showers made the pitch wet. When Perks moved Berry to the Diglis end he fortunately provided ideal conditions for Horton, who, bowling from the New Road end, so completely bewildered the opposition with his off-spinners that he finished the match with this analysis: 12.5 overs, 4 maidens, 25 runs, 8 wickets, taking nine for 56 in the innings—easily the best performance of his short career.

Worcestershire

D. Kenyon lbw b Heine	58 —	lbw b Tayfield 32
P. E. Richardson b Heine............	0 —	lbw b Tayfield 12
L. Outschoorn c Cheetham b Tayfield ..	80 —	lbw b Tayfield 3
G. Dews c Goddard b Murray	39 —	lbw b Tayfield 52
R. G. Broadbent st Waite b Tayfield	4 —	c Goddard b Tayfield 10
M. J. Horton b Tayfield	0 —	run out 4
J. P. Whitehead c Heine b Tayfield	7 —	not out 51
R. O. Jenkins c Tayfield b Murray	10 —	c Waite b Mansell........ 16
H. Yarnold c Endean b Murray	1 —	c Tayfield b Heine 1
R. T. D. Perks lbw b Tayfield	41 —	b Heine 16
R. Berry not out	0 —	b Heine 0
B 9, l-b 11	20 —	B 8, l-b 3, w 1 12

1/7 2/120 3/187 4/198 5/198 6/205   260   1/28 2/38 3/55 4/69   209
7/218 8/219 9/260   5/74 6/155 7/180 8/199 9/209

South Africans

D. J. McGlew lbw b Perks	0 —	b Horton 46
T. L. Goddard c Yarnold b Berry	47 —	b Horton 23
J. H. B. Waite b Berry	36 —	b Berry 3
W. R. Endean c Yarnold b Jenkins	32 —	c Jenkins b Horton 17
R. A. McLean c and b Horton	13 —	lbw b Horton............ 4
J. E. Cheetham c Yarnold b Berry	4 —	lbw b Horton............ 13
P. L. Winslow b Berry	37 —	c Dews b Horton 0
A. R. A. Murray b Horton	3 —	b Horton 9
P. N. F. Mansell not out	14 —	lbw b Horton............ 11
H. J. Tayfield c Kenyon b Berry	5 —	b Horton 6
P. Heine c Horton b Jenkins	14 —	not out 1
L-b 3, n-b 1	4	B 4, l-b 3, n-b 3........ 10

1/0 2/85 3/88 4/117 5/122 6/154   209   1/56 2/65 3/96 4/100   143
7/176 8/180 9/190   5/100 6/105 7/121 8/136 9/142

South Africans Bowling

	O.	M.	R.	W.		O.	M.	R.	W.
Heine	16	6	37	2	....	17.5	3	45	3
Goddard	18	11	17	0	....	19	11	32	0
Tayfield	37	10	93	5	....	30	9	81	5
Murray	38.5	20	60	3	....	8	3	15	0
Mansell	17	6	33	0	....	12	5	24	1

Worcestershire Bowling

	O.	M.	R.	W.		O.	M.	R.	W.
Perks	11	4	32	1	....	5	0	18	0
Whitehead ...	8	1	21	0	....	4	1	17	0
Jenkins	22.4	2	65	2	....	6	3	15	0
Berry	30	11	60	5	....	20	11	27	1
Horton	7	1	27	2	....	21.5	6	56	9
			Outschoorn ...			1	1	0	0

Umpires: D. Davies and L. H. Gray.

DERBYSHIRE v. SOUTH AFRICANS

At Derby, May 11, 12, 13. Drawn. The South Africans were again made to struggle, but their disappointing cricket could be excused because of the bitterly cold weather. The reorganised Derby ground was officially opened by the President, the Duke of Devonshire, before the match. On an easy-paced pitch, Derbyshire began with a stand of 76 by Hamer and Kelly, but despite numerous dropped catches few of the others did much. Against accurate bowling the South Africans were not prepared to take risks and in two hours between the start of the second day and lunch they scored only 37. Their caution did not help them and Derbyshire led by 66. This they increased to 166 with six wickets left before heavy overnight rain prevented cricket on the last day.

Derbyshire

A. Hamer st Waite b Tayfield	47	— c Waite b Adcock 24
J. Kelly lbw b Goddard	24	— not out 35
C Lee b Goddard	2	— b Adcock 0
A. C. Revill b Adcock	22	— c Winslow b Heine 7
D. B. Carr b Heine	19	— c Waite b Adcock 0
H. L. Johnson b Adcock	3	— not out 30
D. C. Morgan b Heine	1	
G. O. Dawkes b Tayfield	19	
C. Gladwin not out	12	
E Smith b Tayfield	0	
L. Jackson c Duckworth b Tayfield	20	
B 2, l-b 7, n-b 1	10	B 3 ,w 1 4

1/76 2/78 3/82 4/113 5/125 6/127   179   1/42 2/42 3/53   (4 wkts.) 100
7/128 8/159 9/159   4/54

South Africans

D. J. McGlew c Dawkes b Morgan	23	P. L. Winslow c Lee b Gladwin .. 13
T. L. Goddard c Carr b Morgan...	5	P. Heine lbw b Jackson.......... 3
J. H. B. Waite lbw b Jackson	19	N. A. T. Adcock c Morgan b
H. J. Tayfield b Jackson	6	Gladwin 1
W. R. Endean c Dawkes b Morgan	15	N-b 2 2
R. A. McLean run out	6	
C. A. R. Duckworth not out	14	1/17 2/41 3/50 4/55 5/62 6/85 113
H. J. Keith c Carr b Gladwin	6	7/94 8/108 9/112

South Africans Bowling

	O.	M.	R.	W.		O.	M.	R.	W.
Heine	24	6	50	2	....	12	3	24	1
Adcock	17	4	39	2	....	11	4	20	3
Tayfield	26.2	8	61	4	....	16	5	23	0
Goddard	15	6	19	2	....	10	3	18	0
Keith						11	4	11	0

Derbyshire Bowling

	O.	M.	R.	W.
Jackson	24	8	37	3
Gladwin	26.3	12	26	3
Morgan	19	6	40	3
Smith	5	1	8	0

Umpires: T. Spencer and T. J. Bartley.

NOTTINGHAMSHIRE v. SOUTH AFRICANS

Nottingham, May 14, 16, 17. Drawn, rain preventing play on the final day.
The South Africans improved on earlier displays, notably in the support given by
Smith, the leg-spin bowler, to Tayfield. On a slow pitch, Smith's bowling compared
favourably with that of the Australian Dooland, who did not approach his usual
form until late in the South African innings. On a cold first day he and Harvey
presented McGlew, Waite and Endean with many easy runs through erratic
length so that despite a general lack of enterprise the touring side reached 229
for five. The last five men fell in fifty minutes, Dooland dismissing four for 21.
The South Africans again fielded below their reputed standard and both Simpson
and Stocks were badly missed.

South Africans

D. J. McGlew c Rowe b Smales	88	— not out 24
T. L. Goddard b Dooland	12	— not out 24
J. H. B. Waite c and b Harvey	30	
W. R. Endean b Smales	78	
R. A. McLean b Smales	0	
J. E. Cheetham lbw b Jepson	22	
H. J. Keith b Dooland	8	
E. R. H. Fuller b Dooland	0	
H. J. Tayfield c Jepson b Dooland	10	
V. I. Smith c Martin b Dooland	9	
N. A. T. Adcock not out	1	
B 10, l-b 3, w 1	14	B 3 l-b 3 6

1/53 2/138 3/138 4/138 5/223   272   (No wkt.) 54
6/252 7/252 8/252 9/268

Nottinghamshire

R. T. Simpson c Goddard b Smith	57	K. Smales lbw b Smith 14
J. D. Clay c and b Tayfield	15	A Jepson c Keith b Smith 23
C. J. Poole, c Waite b Smith	25	E. J. Rowe not out 0
J. Hardstaff b Smith	9	B 2, l-b 3, n-b 2 7
E. J. Martin lbw b Tayfield	14	
F. W. Stocks lbw b Tayfield	54	
P. F. Harvey b Tayfield	1	1/52 2/84 3/102 4/119 5/129 231
B. Dooland, c Goddard b Tayfield	12	6/131 7/153 8/202 9/210

Nottinghamshire Bowling

	O.	M.	R.	W.	O.	M.	R.	W.
Jepson	28	11	50	1	 5	2	14	0
Smales	40	18	55	3	 8	2	11	0
Dooland	33.2	8	94	5	 9	3	23	0
Harvey	24	12	52	1				
Stocks	4	1	7	0				

South Africans Bowling

	O.	M.	R.	W.
Adcock	12	5	24	0
Fuller	6	2	14	0
Goddard	4	1	5	0
Keith	7	2	16	0
Tayfield	39	14	95	5
Smith	27.5	7	70	5

Umpires: Harry Elliott (Derbyshire) and H. Elliott (Lancashire).

CAMBRIDGE UNIVERSITY v. SOUTH AFRICANS

At Cambridge, May 18, 19, 20. Drawn. The South Africans looked like gaining their first victory when Cambridge at the close of the second day had lost two second innings wickets and still required 125 runs to save defeat. Rain, however, reduced play to three hours on Friday, when Silk, striving to regain his form, spent three hours over fifty. The South Africans began with their first century opening partnership—137 between McGlew and Waite—and throughout the innings was marked by splendid running between the wickets. The University would have been well advised to learn from this, for bad calling deprived them of many runs and caused the dismissal of Singh, their heaviest scorer. The South Africans gave nothing away in supporting the accurate leg-breaks of Smith and the off-breaks of Tayfield. The Cambridge first innings total of 67 was their lowest against any South African team, and although their batting later showed more solidity it remained unconvincing.

South Africans

D. J. McGlew b Singh	85	A. R. A. Murray b D. Smith	5
J. H. B. Waite c Parsons b Singh	78	E. R. H. Fuller c O'Brien b Singh	7
C. A. R. Duckworth st Melluish b Goonesena	15	H. J. Tayfield b Singh	1
		V. I. Smith not out	4
W. R. Endean c Parsons b C. Smith	24	P. Heine b Singh	12
P. L. Winslow st Melluish b Goonesena	0	B 4, l-b 6, w 1, n-b 3	14
J. E. Cheetham c Pretlove b C. Smith	23		**268**

1/137 2/180 3/188 4/190
5/228 6/239 7/251 8/251 9/252

Cambridge University

D. R. W. Silk b Smith	15	— c Cheetham b Fuller	54
R. O'Brien st Duckworth b Smith	25	— c Waite b Tayfield	0
A. B. D. Parsons c Waite b Smith	1	— c Cheetham b Tayfield	11
S. Singh run out	0	— c Waite b Fuller	20
V. R. Lumsden c and b Tayfield	9	— b Tayfield	5
W. Knightley-Smith c Heine b Tayfield	6	— b Fuller	5
J. F. Pretlove b Tayfield	0	— not out	19
C. S. Smith b Heine	1	— c Heine b Smith	7
G. Goonesena lbw b Heine	8	— lbw b Tayfield	31
M. E. L. Melluish b Tayfield	0	— not out	0
D. J. Smith not out	0		
L-b	2	L-b 2	2
	67	**(8 wkts.)**	**154**

1/35 2/41 3/41 4/42 5/56 6/56
7/57 8/65 9/67

1/10 2/70 3/86 (8 wkts.) 154
4/116 5/120 6/123 7/131 8/153

Cambridge University Bowling

	O.	M.	R.	W.	O.	M.	R.	W.
C Smith	22	11	36	2				
D. Smith	19	3	50	1				
Singh	28.4	6	73	5				
Goonesena	24	2	74	2				
Pretlove	2	0	21	0				

South Africans Bowling

	O.	M.	R.	W.	O.	M.	R.	W.
Heine	17	8	17	2	20	10	32	0
Fuller	9	5	8	0	21	12	24	3
Tayfield	22.2	8	31	4	44	23	51	4
Smith	12	6	9	3	17	7	33	1
Murray					11	6	12	0

Umpires: H. Palmer and F. S. Lee.

M.C.C. v. SOUTH AFRICANS

At Lord's, May 21, 23, 24. South Africans won by 93 runs. This was a most auspicious occasion for the touring team to gain their first victory, and it was achieved mainly by sound bowling supported by excellent fielding. The task was made easier owing to Hutton, the M.C.C. captain, taking no part in the match after the opening day because of an attack of lumbago. In his absence the M.C.C. batting proved woefully weak and that of the South Africans was no better until the second afternoon when McLean in a dazzling display of pulling and driving hit one 6 and fourteen 4's. Although holding a substantial lead, the South Africans could add only eight runs while losing their last five wickets on the third morning. They broke down completely in face of really splendid off-spin bowling by Titmus who took those five wickets in seven overs and one ball while conceding only three runs. Titmus's analysis of eight wickets for 43 runs was the best of his career.

South Africans

T. L. Goddard b Titmus	19	—	c Andrew b Bailey	1
J. H. B. Waite c Close b Titmus	16	—	b Titmus	27
H. J. Keith c Berry b Loader	21	—	c Titmus b Bailey	22
W. R. Endean st Andrew b Berry	20	—	b Titmus	4
R. A. McLean lbw b Loader	4	—	lbw b Titmus	85
J. E. Cheetham c Graveney b Berry	38	—	c Andrew b Titmus	29
P. L. Winslow c Andrew b Close	25	—	c Andrew b Titmus	11
A. R. A. Murray c Andrew b Bailey	9	—	b Titmus	0
E. R. H. Fuller c Graveney b Bailey	5	—	c and b Titmus	0
H. J. Tayfield not out	20	—	b Titmus	0
V. I. Smith did not bat		—	not out	1
B 4, l-b 3, n-b 1	8		B 1, l-b 3	4

1/23 2/38 3/83 4/83   (9 wkts., dec.) 185   1/1 2/25 3/35 4/100   184
5/90 6/121 7/140 8/154 9/185   5/154 6/177 7/177 8/177 9/179

M.C.C.

L. Hutton retired ill	2	—	absent ill	0
T. W. Graveney c Winslow b Murray	1	—	c Goddard b Smith	34
J. M. Parks c Fuller b Goddard	15	—	c Keith b Smith	30
K. Barrington lbw b Goddard	3	—	lbw b Goddard	27
D. C. S. Compton c Endean b Smith	25	—	run out	20
D. B. Close b Fuller	0	—	c Waite b Fuller	13
T. E. Bailey c McLean b Smith	19	—	c Murray b Tayfield	14
F. J. Titmus lbw b Tayfield	1	—	lbw b Tayfield	3
K. V. Andrew b Tayfield	7	—	c Waite b Smith	4
P. J. Loader c Endean b Smith	3	—	not out	29
R. Berry not out	2	—	c Waite b Smith	8
B 7, l-b 2	9		B 3, l-b 2, w 1, n-b 1	7

1/3 2/8 3/39 4/39 5/56 6/65 7/82   1/19 2/68 3/95 4/105   189
8/85   5/141 6/144 7/145 8/163
                                          9/189

M.C.C. Bowling

	O.	M.	R.	W.		O.	M.	R.	W.
Loader	20	8	45	2	....	14	5	32	0
Bailey	13	4	29	2	....	14	6	28	2
Titmus	20	11	27	2	....	23.1	7	43	8
Berry	23.5	10	28	2	....	23	10	43	0
Close	19	6	48	1	....	8	0	24	0
Compton						1	0	10	0

South Africans Bowling

	O.	M.	R.	W.		O.	M.	R.	W.
Fuller	9	2	20	1	....	10	6	12	1
Goddard	12	5	19	2	....	16	4	40	1
Tayfield	16.2	9	13	2	....	29	10	54	2
Murray	3	1	5	1					
Smith	16	6	21	3	....	23.4	4	76	4

Umpires: F. S. Lee and F. Chester.

OXFORD UNIVERSITY v. SOUTH AFRICANS

At Oxford (Christ Church ground), May 25, 26, 27. South Africans won by an innings and 137 runs. The tourists followed their good showing against M.C.C. with another improved display of batting and bowling. Goddard made watchfulness his main concern during a stay of five and a quarter hours, but McGlew, McLean, Winslow—a powerful on-driver—and Murray all batted light-heartedly. Winslow and Murray each hit three 6's. Oxford failed badly in their first innings against the fast outswingers of Heine, but although the University batsmen gave a more determined exhibition after following on 344 behind they never mastered a well-balanced attack. Oxford were 154 for five on the last day when play on a damp pitch was resumed at one o'clock, and the tourists beat further rain in finishing the match at half-past three.

South Africans

D. J. McGlew c Smith b Allan....	66	A. R. A. Murray not out	36
T. L. Goddard c Williams b Jowett	121	P. Heine not out	18
J. H. B. Waite run out	13		
H. J. Keith c Walton b Jowett.....	19	B 3, l-b 6, n-b 1.............	10
R. A. McLean b Phillips..........	67		
C. A. R. Duckworth b Phillips....	0	1/110 2/127 3/158 (8 wkts dec.)	434
P. L. Winslow c Jowett b Phillips .	60	4/256 5/256 6/338 7/359 8/380	
J. E. Cheetham b Gibson b Jowett .	24	V. I. Smith did not bat.	

Oxford University

M. J. K. Smith b Goddard	4	— c Murray b Keith	33
J. M. Allan c Waite by Heine	3	— c Keith b Murray	10
A. C. Walton c Duckworth b Heine.....	22	— c Winslow b Keith	21
C. C. P. Williams b Heine	0	— b Smith	19
G. P. S. Delisle c Duckworth b Heine ...	13	— run out	32
I. Gibson, c Goddard b Heine..........	0	— c Waite b Goddard	14
J. P. Fellows-Smith c Cheetham b Smith.	28	— lbw b Keith	40
A. P. Walshe b Murray	11	— c Duckworth b Heine......	20
J. A. Arenhold st Duckworth b Smith ..	2	— c Waite b Keith..........	6
D. C. P. R. Jowett b Smith	0	— c Keith b Goddard	9
J. B. Phillips not out	0	— not out	1
B 4, l-b 3	7	L-b 1, n-b 1	2

1/5 2/21 3/21 4/36 5/36 6/57 7/84   90   1/18 2/59 3/70 4/108   207
8/86 9/90   5/119 6/171 7/171 8/186 9/202

Oxford University Bowling

	O.	M.	R.	W.
Arenhold	12	2	28	0
Phillips	25	2	87	3
Fellows-Smith .	20	3	86	0
Jowett	33	9	101	3
Allan	27	7	89	1
Gibson	6		33	0

South Africans Bowling

	O.	M.	R.	W.	O.	M.	R.	W.
Heine	17	9	31	5	29	13	52	1
Goddard	7	4	11	1	18.2	7	27	2
McGlew	1	0	4	0				
Murray	12.5	2	24	1	13	10	15	1
Smith	4	1	13	3	24	10	51	1
			Keith		41	24	60	4

Umpires: D. Hendren and J. S. Buller.

GLAMORGAN v. SOUTH AFRICANS

At Cardiff, May 28, 30, 31. Drawn. As rain prevented any cricket on the first day there never seemed any likelihood of a definite result. When cricket was possible Glamorgan batted with the utmost restraint, four hours of play before tea yielding only 169 runs for the loss of three wickets. Afterwards Glamorgan changed their policy and the Bank Holiday crowd saw them sacrifice their seven remaining wickets for 65 in a bold attempt to force the pace against some accurate fast bowling by Adcock and Fuller. The South Africans, in their turn, also exercised caution but as in 1951 when McConnon caused their downfall and brought victory to Glamorgan he again broke through after a defiant opening stand of 84 by McGlew and Goddard. McConnon took six wickets for 49 with his well-controlled flight and off-spin and only some daring hitting by Winslow (one 6, five 4's) prevented him gaining an even better analysis.

Glamorgan

W. G. A. Parkhouse c Waite b Fuller	62	— not out 29
W. E. Jones c Adcock b Tayfield	27	— b Fuller................................ 0
B. Hedges st Waite b Mansell	58	
J. Pressdee lbw b Fuller	1	— b Fuller................................ 8
A. J. Watkins b Mansell	37	— b Fuller................................ 20
W. Wooller, c Mansell b Keith	2	
P. B. Clift b Fuller	13	— not out 6
D. Ward c Tayfield b Adcock	14	— c and b Adcock 4
J. E. McConnon b Adcock	0	
D. J. Shepherd not out	13	
H. G. Davies b Fuller	0	
L-b 7	7	B 1, l-b 5 6

1/50 2/135 3/135 4/190 5/191   234   1/0 2/14 3/29   (4 wkts.) 73
6/197 7/219 8/219 9/231   4/56

South Africans

D. J. McGlew b Watkins	53	E. R. H. Fuller c McConnon b
T. L. Goddard lbw b McConnon	26	Pressdee 1
J. H. B. Waite c Watkins b McConnon	4	H. J. Tayfield c Hedges b McConnon ... 3
W. R. Endean lbw b Watkins	0	N. A. T. Adcock b McConnon ... 1
P. L. Winslow b McConnon	36	
H. J. Keith st Davies b Pressdee	11	B 8, l-b 1 9
J. E. Cheetham not out	12	
P. N. F. Mansell c Wooller b McConnon	0	1/84 2/84 3/84 4/104 5/139 156
		6/143 7/146 8/147 9/150

South Africans Bowling

	O.	M.	R.	W.		O.	M.	R.	W.
Adcock	17	3	47	2	....	10	3	33	1
Fuller	19.3	4	46	4	....	14	6	27	3
Goddard	9	5	18	0	....	3	0	6	0
Mansell	16	6	27	2	....	2	1	1	0
Tayfield	28	8	56	1					
Keith	12	6	33	1					

Glamorgan Bowling

	O.	M.	R.	W.
Shepherd	12	4	34	0
Wooller	11	4	20	0
McConnon	24.5	8	49	6
Pressdee	13	5	27	2
Watkins	11	5	17	2

Umpires: D. Davies and J. S. Buller.

ESSEX v. SOUTH AFRICANS

At Colchester, June 1, 2, 3. Drawn. Fortunate to gain first use of a fast, true pitch, the South Africans scored readily against moderate bowling. McGlew, specially good in cutting, hit thirteen 4's, sharing an opening stand of 137 with Endean. Keith (sixteen 4's) and Mansell (fifteen 4's) drove hard during a partnership of 110, and McLean, strong all round, obtained 101 inside two hours, with one 6 and eleven 4's among his figures. Facing the biggest total registered against them by a South African team, Essex lost four men for 81, but Insole and Bailey stayed together for three and a half hours and added 184. Hard drives brought each batsman fifteen 4's and Insole also hit a 6. Then the batting breakdown recommenced and Essex followed on 153 behind. They stood in danger when half the side were out for 67, but again Insole and Bailey filled the breach.

South Africans

D. J. McGlew c Smith b Preston	.118	P. L. Winslow not out	20
W. R. Endean lbw b Greensmith	64	B 5, l-b 2	7
H. J. Keith c and b Smith	94		
P. N. F. Mansell b T. Bailey	99	1/137 2/221 3/331 (4 wkts., dec.) 503	
R. A. McLean not out	101	4/456	

C. A. R. Duckworth, A. R. A. Murray, P. Heine, V. I. Smith and N A. T. Adcock did not bat.

Essex

T. C. Dodds run out	8	— run out	21
P. A. Gibb b Adcock	12	— c Heine b Smith	4
G. Barker lbw b Smith	4	— c Endean b Murray	5
R. Horsfall c Mansell b Murray	42	— c Duckworth b Mansell	12
D. J. Insole b Smith	129	— not out	22
T. E. Bailey b Murray	107	— not out	11
B. Knight c and b Smith	0	— run out	13
R. Smith c Endean b Adcock	24		
W. T. Greensmith c Adcock b Heine	4		
K. C. Preston not out	4		
J. A. Bailey c Endean b Mansell	4		
B 5, l-b 7	12	L-b 1	1

1/12 2/20 3/30 4/81 5/265 6/267   350   1/25 2/25 3/43 (5 wkts.) 89
7/302 8/332 9/345   4/43 5/67

Essex Bowling

	O.	M.	R.	W.	O	M.	R.	W.
T. Bailey	32	3	102	1				
Preston	25	2	83	1				
Smith	27	5	83	1				
J. Bailey	32	4	117	0				
Greensmith	20	1	70	1				
Insole	6	0	41	0				

South Africans Bowling

Adcock	28	8	58	2	 10	2	21	0
Heine	26	4	49	1	 5	2	13	0
Smith	38	10	138	3	 6	1	22	1
Murray	30	11	65	2	 11	7	14	1
Keith	9	5	13	0				
Mansell	9.5	4	14	1	 9	5	18	1
McLean	1	0	1	0				

Umpires: E. Cooke and J. J. Hills.

LANCASHIRE v. SOUTH AFRICANS

At Manchester, June 4, 6, 7. Drawn. Exceptional hitting by Winslow dwarfed everything else in this match. The South Africans had lost seven men for 81 when Winslow arrived. He began unsteadily against the slow bowlers and then hit Ikin for 30 in one over—4–4–6–6–4–6. The next two balls he received (from Goodwin) he punished for 4 and 6, making 40 off eight successive balls. Altogether Winslow hit five 6's and six 4's in his 61, which came in forty-two minutes. With Fuller, Winslow put on 56 in a quarter of an hour for the eighth wicket, Winslow's share being 53. In spite of his great effort, South Africans made only 154, Lancashire finishing the opening day at 64 for three. On Monday, Adcock bowled with marked hostility and accuracy, but no one could make any impression on Jordan, the week-end "watchman." He batted two hours for 29, helping Grieves to add 53. Dyson was out first ball but Collins not only prevented Tayfield achieving a hat-trick, but stayed an hour with Grieves while the stand realised 61. Grieves, last out, cut splendidly during a stay of two hours. He hit fifteen 4's and saw Lancashire gain a lead of 47. The tourists fared much better with the bat at their second attempt but with the game in a most interesting position rain prevented any cricket on the last day.

South Africans

W. R. Endean c Grieves b Wharton.....	13	— c Edrich b Goodwin	51
T. L. Goddard c Grieves b Wharton	0	— lbw b Goodwin	14
J. H. B. Waite b Wharton	17		
J. E. Cheetham lbw b Wharton	0	— c Jordan b Goodwin	45
R. A. McLean run out	35	— not out	34
P. N. F. Mansell c Goodwin b Ikin	8	— c Grieves b Collins	79
P. L. Winslow c Hilton b Goodwin	61		
H. J. Tayfield st Jordan b Hilton	0	— not out	9
E. H. R. Fuller c Collins b Hilton	15		
V. I. Smith not out	5		
N. A. T. Adcock b Hilton	0		

1/4 2/19 3/19 4/65 5/65 6/80   154   1/21 2/92   (4 wkts.) 232
7/81 8/137 9/153   3/183 4/205

Lancashire

J. T. Ikin lbw b Goddard	35	R. Collins c Adcock b Goddard	..	17
W. Place b Goddard	13	M. J. Hilton c Winslow b Tayfield	.	1
G. A Edrich c Winslow b Adcock	3	F. Goodwin not out		0
C. Washbrook c Fuller b Adcock	14			
J. Jordan c Waite b Tayfield	29	B 4, l-b 4		8
A Wharton c Waite b Adcock	4			
K. Grieves b Tayfield	77	1/41 2/46 3/62 4/69 5/75 6/128		201
J. Dyson c Mansell b Tayfield	0	7/128 8/189 9/194		

Lancashire Bowling

	O.	M.	R.	W.		O.	M.	R.	W.
Goodwin	11	2	42	1	....	16	3	47	3
Wharton	13	3	26	4	....	11	3	17	0
Ikin	7	3	51	1	....	8	0	29	0
Collins	2	1	8	0	....	17	6	41	1
Hilton	15	5	27	3	....	13	4	36	0
Dyson						8	1	38	0
Grieves						9	2	24	0

South Africans Bowling

	O.	M.	R.	W.
Adcock	22	3	53	3
Goddard	29	15	41	3
Fuller	19	4	48	0
Smith	5	0	24	0
Tayfield	11.5	6	27	4

Umpires: W. T. Jones and N. Oldfield.

ENGLAND v. SOUTH AFRICA

First Test Match

At Nottingham, June 9, 10, 11, 13. England won by an innings and five runs with one day to spare. For the most part, this was an unsatisfactory game in which the South Africans and Bailey overdid defensive methods. In the end the sheer pace of Tyson, who took six wickets for 28 runs, carried England to a comfortable victory.

It was also a triumph for May, the new Captain, given the leadership the previous Sunday when Hutton, originally chosen for all five games, stood down because of lumbago. The Selectors announced that, as Cowdrey had not taken part in any first-class cricket at that stage of the summer, he was not considered. They named Milton, of Gloucestershire, twelfth man, but an injury compelled him to withdraw on the eve of the match, when the Selectors not only replaced him by calling on Lock, the Surrey left-arm slow bowler, but decided to choose the team from twelve, including Lock. This move was prompted by the saturated state of the ground; there was a question whether the pitch would be of any use to Tyson.

Just before the captains went out to toss came the announcement that the original eleven would be left undisturbed which, as events turned out, proved to be a happy decision. Lock was released to play for Surrey during the latter part of the game, when Morgan, of Derbyshire, acted as twelfth man.

The match began on a soft easy pitch and, despite the absence of Hutton, England, on May winning the toss, began satisfactorily. Their new opening pair, Kenyon and Graveney, made a stand of 91. Disaster might have overtaken Kenyon in Adcock's second over when he was only one, but Tayfield, standing three yards from the bat at silly mid-on, could not hold a very hard drive. During the early overs, Adcock, Goddard and Fuller caused the batsmen some anxiety, for a cross wind helped them to swing the ball awkwardly. The first hour yielded only 29, but when they accustomed themselves to the peculiar light and pace of the pitch, Kenyon and Graveney added 50 in the second hour. Kenyon, undisturbed by his escape, appeared very sure in defence and he excelled with an occasional cover drive and leg glance.

By the time May arrived the sun shone, providing a perfect light, and when he settled down he indulged in powerful driving. In ninety-five minutes Kenyon and May added 75 before Kenyon, trying to force Goddard away to leg, was lbw, having made 87 out of 166 in just under four hours. He hit ten 4's. Compton in his early minutes at the crease shaped well, but he lost his touch after some grand strokes had been cut off by a set of brilliant fielders, of whom McLean was outstanding at cover. All the time the South Africans pursued negative tactics which did not change even when Adcock and Fuller took the new ball at 204. Compton spent one hour forty minutes at the wicket and could not manage one boundary.

Twenty minutes of the first day remained when Barrington, the only new cap in the England team, joined May. He survived no more than three balls and a keen but not an exhilarating day's cricket ended with England 244 for four, representing an average of 41 an hour. On Friday England were all out for 334, having taken nine hours over the task. In a dreary performance completely devoid of enterprise, Bailey maintained his dour reputation by occupying three and a quarter hours over 49. True, South Africa, possibly discouraged by the state of the pitch, bowled and fielded defensively. They waited for the England batsmen to get themselves out and all except Bailey fell in attempting forcing strokes. May, 81 overnight, added only two more runs, his 83 (eight 4's) taking him three hours fifty-five minutes. Statham alone showed initiative and drove well, but England needed three hours to add the last 90 runs.

South Africa broke down against Tyson and Statham, half their wickets falling for 55. Waite was run out by a superb return by Statham from third man. In both innings McGlew saved South Africa from complete rout. In all he defied the England bowlers for nine and a quarter hours. His first innings of 68 occupied five hours five minutes, during which Cheetham helped him to put on 94 in just over three hours. The only other notable stand for South Africa came immediately after May enforced the follow-on, when Goddard stayed with McGlew for just over three hours and then only the quickness of Statham at mid-wicket caused him to be run out.

Meanwhile several hours of torrential rain soaked the ground following the close of play on Saturday, when South Africa were 46 for no wicket. Nothing could be done until one o'clock on Monday and then England finished the match in three hours twenty minutes of actual cricket. The turf was so soft at the Trent Bridge end that Statham attempted only two overs, the second with a very shortened run. Neither Wardle, who had bowled 40 overs for 31 runs and four wickets, nor Appleyard were accurate, but from the pavilion end Tyson and Bailey took eight of the ten wickets.

During a spell of forty minutes Tyson accounted for Waite, caught off a glove in the leg trap at 83. Next Bailey put in a good effort lasting nearly an hour in which he removed first Endean and then beat McGlew with a ball that lifted, May taking the catch in the gully.

The total was 131 for four wickets when Tyson returned just after four o'clock and his pace, even with a ball already used for 82 overs, proved too great for the opposition. In ten minutes before tea McLean, brilliantly caught low at first slip, and Cheetham who played on, fell to Tyson and subsequently Tyson hit the stumps in removing Tayfield, Winslow and Adcock. In addition Fuller was dropped by Evans, who soon afterwards caught him at the other end. Tyson's figures in his final spell were: 7.3 overs, 3 maidens, 5 runs and 5 wickets.

This feat gave Tyson 52 wickets in nine Tests in his first ten months as an England cricketer. For once, Tyson wrought havoc without the help of Statham. He was just as impressive as earlier in the year at Sydney, Melbourne and Adelaide, but the situation was different for on this occasion England were not sorely pressed like they were on all three occasions in Australia. Sheer pace coupled with astute judgment in mixing the odd bouncer with the more valuable yorker were features of Tyson's bowling.

The match also brought distinction to Evans who, when he caught Fuller, claimed his 150th victim in Test cricket—112 caught, 38 stumped.

The national railway strike must have kept many people away from the match, but it did not wholly account for the disappointing attendances on three of the four days. On Saturday, when South Africa made only 144 runs in five and three-quarter hours, the patient crowd of 25,000 resorted towards the end of the day to a mild form of slow hand-clapping. This slow play was comparable with England's 128 in five hours against West Indies in Barbados in January 1954 and New Zealand's 125 in four hours fifty-two minutes against England at Dunedin in March 1955.

N. P.

England

D. Kenyon lbw b Goddard	87	F. H. Tyson c McLean b Tayfield	0
T. W. Graveney c Waite b Adcock	42	J. B. Statham c Waite b Fuller	20
P. B. H. May c McGlew b Smith	83	R. Appleyard not out	0
D. C. S. Compton lbw b Adcock	27		
K. Barrington c Waite b Fuller	0	B 6, l-b 6	12
T. E. Bailey lbw b Goddard	49		—
T. G. Evans c Goddard b Fuller	12	1/91 2/166 3/228 4/233 5/252	334
J. H. Wardle lbw b Tayfield	2	6/285 7/294 8/298 9/334	

South Africa

D. J. McGlew c Evans b Wardle	68	— c May b Bailey	51
T. L. Goddard lbw b Statham	12	— run out	32
J. H. B. Waite run out	0	— c Compton b Tyson	3
W. R. Endean lbw b Tyson	0	— c Graveney b Bailey	6
R. A. McLean b Tyson	13	— c Graveney b Tyson	16
P. L. Winslow c May b Appleyard	2	— b Tyson	3
J. E. Cheetham c Graveney b Wardle	54	— b Tyson	5
H. J. Tayfield c Bailey b Appleyard	11	— b Tyson	0
E. R. H. Fuller b Wardle	15	— c Evans b Wardle	6
V. I. Smith c May b Wardle	0	— not out	2
N. A. T. Adcock not out	1	— b Tyson	6
B 1, l-b 2, n-b 2	5	B 8, l-b 4, w 4, n-b 2	18

1/15 2/17 3/19 4/35 5/55 6/149   181   1/73 2/83 3/101 4/108   148
7/156 8/174 9/180   5/131 6/132 7/132 8/135 9/141

South Africa Bowling

	O.	M.	R.	W.	O.	M.	R.	W.
Adcock	36	9	74	2				
Goddard	36.4	18	61	2				
Fuller	29	5	59	3				
Tayfield	37	11	66	2				
Smith	30	9	62	1				

England Bowling

	O.	M.	R.	W.		O.	M.	R.	W.
Statham	25	5	47	1	....	10	4	16	0
Tyson	24	5	51	2	....	21.3	7	28	6
Bailey	5	2	8	0	....	17	8	21	2
Appleyard	28	9	46	2	....	19	4	32	0
Wardle	32	23	24	4	....	29	17	33	1

Umpires: F. S. Lee and T. J. Bartley.

SOMERSET v. SOUTH AFRICANS

At Taunton, June 15, 16, 17. South Africans won by an innings and 32 runs Somerset could find no answer to the pace and hostility of Heine, whose performance in this match did much to earn him a place in the team for the Second Test. Heine began by sending back the first three batsmen for six runs on a "green" pitch and was even more devastating in the second innings when, with the help of several ill-judged strokes, he gained the best figures by any member of the touring side thus far. Saeed batted with commendable determination in each innings and Tordoff, although handicapped by a badly bruised elbow, helped to show up the South African bowling in a truer and less formidable light when he made a belated second innings appearance. Saeed also bowled well and with Lobb caused the touring batsmen such trouble that six were out for 94. Dogged batting by Waite and Cheetham restored the South Africans' advantage.

Somerset

G. G. Tordoff c Goddard b Heine	0	— not out	41
H. W. Stephenson c Waite b Heine	3	— c Duckworth b Heine	15
J. Lawrence lbw b Murray	14	— b Heine	13
P. B. Wight b Heine	1	— c Mansell b Heine	2
M. F. Tremlett run out	6	— c Waite b Heine	2
J. G. Lomax c Keith b Goddard	6	— c Murray b Mansell	18
G. M. Tripp c Heine b Murray	2	— c Duckworth b Heine	13
Yawar Saeed c Endean b Tayfield	24	— c Duckworth b Heine	43
J. Hilton b Goddard	0	— c Waite b Heine	2
J. W. McMahon c Heine b Tayfield	6	— lbw b Tayfield	9
B. Lobb not out	1	— b Tayfield	1
B 1, 1-b 3, n-b 1	5	— B 11	11

1/0 2/5 3/7 4/25 5/34 6/34 7/43   68   1/17 2/19 3/29 4/32 5/54   170
8/46 9/67   6/80 7/84 8/141 9/162

South Africans

W. R. Endean lbw b Lobb	7	J. H. B. Waite c Stephenson b Lobb	42
T. L. Goddard c Stephenson b Lobb	5	J, E. Cheetham not out	87
H. J. Keith c Stephenson b Yawar Saeed	49	A. R. A. Murray b Yawar Saeed	1
R. A. McLean c Hilton b Yawar Saeed	16	H. J. Tayfield c Stephenson b Lobb	44
C. A. R. Duckworth b Yawar Saeed	7	P. Heine not out	0
P. N. F. Mansell c Stephenson b Yawar Saeed	8	B 3, w 1	4

1/11 2/14 3/41   (9 wkts., dec.) 270
4/55 5/93 6/94 7/172 8/173 9/260

South Africans Bowling

	O.	M.	R.	W.		O.	M.	R.	W.
Heine	17	5	33	3	....	31	11	58	7
Goddard	17	8	16	2	....	20	10	30	0
Murray	9	4	10	2	....	10	3	21	0
Tayfield	5	2	4	2	....	37.2	15	32	2
					Mansell	20	13	18	1

Somerset Bowling

	O.	M.	R.	W.
Lobb	26.3	7	72	4
Lomax	14	1	42	0
Yawar Saeed	22	4	61	5
Lawrence	15	1	62	0
MaMahon	14	2	29	0

Umpires: A. E. Pothecary and W. F. Price.

SUSSEX v. SOUTH AFRICANS

At Hove, June 18, 20, 21. South Africans won by nine wickets. They well deserved success, with McLean and Fuller taking honours for fine batting and bowling. Parks and Sheppard, both excelling in off-side play, rallied Sussex in the first innings with a stand of 195 in three hours and ten minutes which created a record for the fourth-wicket against a South African side in England. McGlew, acting captain as Cheetham rested, stayed four hours and twenty minutes for 69, but McLean, driving magnificently, made 129, including twenty 4's and a 6, in three hours. McGlew, although behind, declared on the second evening to get Sussex in for the closing half-hour, and gained three wickets for 21 runs. Fuller, moving the ball deceptively at medium-fast pace, completed the rout next morning and Endean and Waite, with a sound opening partnership of 96, put the tourists well on the way to scoring the 142 wanted for victory.

Sussex

J. Langridge c Waite b Fuller	16	— b Fuller	14
D. V. Smith lbw b Fuller	14	— c Endean b Fuller	4
A. S. M. Oakman b Fuller	25	— c sub b Tayfield	0
J. M. Parks c Endean b Tayfield	118	— b Keith	45
D. S. Sheppard c Waite b Adcock	104	— c and b Fuller	0
K. G. Suttle not out	44	— lbw b Fuller	14
G. Cox lbw b Tayfield	23	— lbw b Fuller	0
R. G. Marlar did not bat		— c Winslow b Fuller	0
R. T. Webb did not bat		— b Fuller	17
N. I. Thomson did not bat		— c Mansell b Keith	0
A. E. James did not bat		— not out	0
L-b 8	8	B 3	3

1/25 2/52 3/59 4/254   (6 wkts., dec.) 352
5/308 6/352

1/11 2/16 3/16 4/31 5/31   97
6/45 7/45 8/93 9/95

South Africans

D. J. McGlew c Langridge b Thomson	69		
H. J. Tayfield run out	4		
H. J. Keith c Oakman b James	0	— not out	10
P. L. Winslow c Sheppard b James	21		
R. A. McLean lbw b Marlar	129		
W R. Endean not out	38	— not out	73
J. H. B. Waite hit wkt b James	13	— run out	53
E. R. H. Fuller c James b Thomson	20		
B 14	14	B 4, l-b 3	7

1/9 2/12 3/38 4/220   (7 wkts., dec.) 308
5/240 6/279 7/308

1/96   (1 wkt.) 143

P. N. F. Mansell, V. I. Smith and N. A. T. Adcock did not bat.

South Africans Bowling

	O.	M.	R.	W.		O.	M.	R.	W.
Adcock	20	2	67	1					
Fuller	31	6	86	3	....	22	6	61	7
Mansell	5	2	20	0					
Tayfield	33.3	8	119	2	....	6	2	7	1
Smith	11	0	39	0					
Keith	3	1	13	0	....	15	8	26	2

Sussex Bowling

	O.	M.	R.	W.		O.	M.	R.	W.
Thomson	31	7	70	2	....	8	2	33	0
James	35	12	95	3	....	2	0	8	0
Marlar	27	6	65	1	....	13	3	35	0
Oakman	12	4	52	0	....	10	3	30	0
Smith	8	2	12	0	....	14	8	16	0
					Parks	3.2	0	14	0

Umpires: A. J. B. Fowler and E. A. Roberts.

ENGLAND v. SOUTH AFRICA

Second Test Match

At Lord's, June 23, 24, 25, 27. England won by 71 runs. In contrast to the dismal match at Trent Bridge, the second Test produced an exhilarating struggle, with both sides going all out for victory from the first ball. For this a good deal of credit must be given to Swannell, the chief groundsman, who, in charge of the preparations of a Test ground for the first time, provided a pitch upon which attacking cricket could be played. Again the South Africans failed against fast bowling, but their display won them many admirers and until the fourth and final day they looked like winning.

In the absence of Tyson and Appleyard, both unfit, England brought in Trueman and Titmus, who at the age of 22 made his Test debut. South Africa included Mansell, Heine and Keith for Smith, Fuller and Winslow and these changes strengthened the side. Heine, in particular, made a creditable Test debut.

When May won the toss, he must have been doubtful about batting, for the "green" and well-grassed pitch seemed almost certain to help bowlers. So it proved, the England batsmen being most uncomfortable against the awkward, lifting ball. Heine, 6 ft. 4½ in., made the most of his height and frequently brought the ball up nastily from just short of a length. May and Compton were caught when unable to avoid "kickers." Barrington, top scorer with 34, stayed just over an hour and a half, but he never looked comfortable and a number of his hooks fell just clear of fieldsmen.

The persistent Goddard upset the later batsmen with accurate left-arm medium-paced bowling on or outside the leg stump. Wardle hit him for two 6's off successive balls, but England were all out in three hours ten minutes for 133.

When McGlew snicked the first ball of the innings to Evans and the other opening batsman, Goddard, also edged a catch to the wicket-keeper without scoring, South Africa looked like collapsing just as badly. Then after tea the pitch lost its viciousness and, although for the rest of the match bowlers always enjoyed encouragement, the conditions provided a more even fight between bat and ball.

South Africa's recovery began when Cheetham and Endean, both missed before tea, added 44. Endean and McLean followed with 50 for the fourth wicket and South Africa went ahead for the loss of four batsmen. McLean gave a dashing display of fierce driving, particularly on the second morning when he made the most of a number of dropped catches. Eventually bowled by the last ball before lunch—the only success for England all morning—McLean batted just over three and a half hours for 142 which included one 6 and twenty-one 4's. He dominated the cricket and made his 142 out of 196. Keith, a left-hander, played a valuable defensive role in helping to add 109, a new sixth wicket record for South Africa. Ninth out, Keith stayed three hours twenty minutes.

South Africa led by 171 and when England, at nine, lost Kenyon, lbw without offering a stroke, an easy victory seemed possible for the touring team. From that moment the situation changed.

Graveney and May took complete command and they carried the score to 108 by the close of the second day. Both reached 50 in the last over. Graveney did not stay long on Saturday morning, but his innings, which lasted three hours twenty minutes, helped to swing the match. This second wicket stand added 132 and May found another splendid partner in Compton. In a spirited eighty-five minutes they added 96 before May overbalanced and kicked down his wicket. Crisp off-drives and powerful square cuts featured May's splendid 112, which occupied four and a half hours and contained fifteen 4's. When 102 he offered a return catch to Mansell, but that was his only error and he earned the distinction of scoring a century on his first appearance as captain at Lord's.

During his innings Compton completed 5,000 runs in Test Cricket, a feat accomplished by only four other batsmen—Hammond, Hutton, Hobbs and Bradman. Between lunch and tea the game again turned in favour of South Africa, five wickets falling for 82. Compton batted two and a half hours for 69, but the later batsmen were troubled by Tayfield's off-breaks. When he took his fifth wicket, Tayfield set up a new Test record for any South African bowler, beating the 84 wickets of C. L. Vincent, who played in 25 Tests. Tayfield was taking part in his 19th game for South Africa.

When South Africa went in to get 183 to win, Statham struck two valuable blows in the last half-hour before the close, sending back the opening pair, McGlew and Goddard. McGlew received only three balls in the match and was dismissed without scoring in either innings. The last ball by Trueman on Saturday struck Cheetham on the left elbow and chipped a bone. The South African captain could not resume on Monday and this was a severe set-back. No one faced Statham confidently, although he gained only one success in the first hour. Then fate proved kind to England, for bad light held up play from 12.30 p.m. until 2.30 p.m. This break of two hours enabled Statham to come back refreshed and he won the match by sending back McLean, Endean, Waite and Keith at a personal cost of 17 runs. He took the first seven wickets in 22 overs for 31 runs and by five o'clock the match was over.

Statham bowled unchanged throughout an innings which lasted three and three-quarter hours. Even allowing for his rest, this feat of endurance was a magnificent effort and undoubtedly brought victory to England. His seven wickets for 39 runs was the best performance of his career.

The 103,000 who watched the game must have been well satisfied with the entertainment, for every day produced exciting and splendid cricket.　　　L. S.

England

D. Kenyon b Adcock	1	— lbw b Goddard	2
T. W. Graveney c Waite b Heine	15	— c Heine b Goddard	60
P. B. H. May c Tayfield b Heine	0	— hit wkt b Heine	112
D. C. S. Compton c Keith b Heine	20	— c Mansell b Goddard	69
K. Barrington b Heine	34	— c McLean b Tayfield	18
T. E. Bailey lbw b Goddard	13	— c Adcock b Tayfield	22
T. G. Evans c Waite b Heine	20	— c and b Tayfield	14
F. T. Titmus lbw b Goddard	4	— c Waite b Adcock	16
J. H. Wardle c Tayfield b Goddard	20	— c Heine b Tayfield	4
J. B. Statham c McLean b Goddard	0	— b Tayfield	11
F. S. Trueman not out	2	— not out	6
B 2, l-b 2	4	B 15, l-b 2, n-b 2	19

1/7 2/8 3/30 4/45 5/82 6/98 7/111　　　**133**
8/111 9/111

1/9 2/141 3/237 4/277　　　**353**
5/285 6/302 7/306 8/336 9/336

South Africa

D. J. McGlew c Evans b Statham	0	— lbw b Statham	0
T. L. Goddard c Evans b Trueman	0	— c Evans b Statham	10
J. E. Cheetham lbw b Bailey	13	— retired hurt	3
W. R. Endean lbw b Wardle	48	— c Evans b Statham	28
R. A. McLean b Statham	142	— b Statham	8
J. H. B. Waite c Evans b Trueman	5	— lbw b Statham	9
H. J. Keith c Titmus b Wardle	57	— c Graveney b Statham	5
P. N F. Mansell c Graveney b Wardle	2	— c Kenyon b Wardle	16
H J. Tayfield b Titmus	21	— c Evans b Statham	3
P. Heine st Evans b Wardle	0	— c Kenyon b Wardle	14
N. A. T. Adcock not out	0	— not out	0
B 6 l-b 1, n-b 4	11	B 9, l-b 5, n-b 1	15

1/0 2/7 3/51 4/101 5/138 6/247　　　**304**
7/259 6/302 9/304

1/0 2/17 3/40 4/54　　　**111**
5/63 6/75 7/78 8/111 9/111

South Africa Bowling

	O.	M.	R.	W.		O.	M.	R.	W.
Heine	25	7	60	5	….	29	5	87	1
Adcock	8	3	10	1	….	25	5	64	1
Goddard	21.2	8	59	4	….	55	23	96	3
Tayfield						38.5	12	80	5
Mansell						2	0	7	0

England Bowling

	O.	M.	R.	W.		O.	M.	R.	W.
Statham	27	9	49	2	....	29	12	39	7
Trueman	16	2	73	2	....	19	2	39	0
Bailey	16	2	56	1					
Wardle	29	10	65	4	....	9.4	4	18	2
Titmus	14	3	50	1					

Umpires: F. Chester and L. H. Gray.

NORTHAMPTONSHIRE v. SOUTH AFRICANS

At Northampton, June 29, 30, July 1. Drawn. The South Africans, though much the stronger side, could not force victory. Duckworth, the young wicket-keeper, made his first century and the best score by any South African to that point of the tour when he scored 158. He hit twenty-six 4's in a capable innings marked by sound defence and strong driving and pulling. Goddard helped in an opening stand of 129 and with Mansell added 138 for the third wicket. Despite a useful opening stand by Brooks and Arnold, Northamptonshire were in danger of following-on, but Subba Row batted carefully for three hours twenty minutes. McGlew surprised by declaring quickly and setting Northamptonshire to get 219 in 180 minutes. After the loss of two wickets for nine, Northamptonshire fell well behind the clock. Subba Row again batted steadily.

South Africans

T. L. Goddard c Tribe b Broderick	70		
C. A. R. Duckworth lbw b Tribe	158	— not out	30
H. J. Keith lbw b Barrick	24		
P. N. F. Mansell run out	88		
R. A. McLean st Andrew b Tribe	4		
A. R. A. Murray lbw b Clarke	12	— b Clarke	46
P. L. Winslow c Broderick b Tribe	1		
E. R. H. Fuller c Andrew b Clarke	22		
D. J. McGlew b Tribe	18		
V. I. Smith c and b Tribe	4		
N. A. T. Adcock not out	2		
B 2, l-b 3, n-b 1	6	L-b 4	4

1/129 2/193 3/331 4/341 5/360   6/361 7/361 8/397 9/401   **409**   1/80   (1 wkt., dec.)   **80**

Northamptonshire

D. Brookes c and b Murray	64	— not out	20
P. Arnold c Keith b Adcock	23	— lbw b Adcock	1
L. Livingston c Keith b Adcock	5	— c Goddard b Adcock	8
D. Barrick b Adcock	42		
R. Subba Row c Duckworth b Goddard	70	— lbw b Keith	59
B. Reynolds b Fuller	3	— run out	17
G. E. Tribe c Duckworth b Goddard	19	— not out	24
V. Broderick c Duckworth b Goddard	0		
J. Manning c Mansell b Smith	10		
K. V. Andrew not out	23		
R. W. Clarke c Fuller b Goddard	0		
B 7, l-b 3, n-b 2	12	L-b 4	4

1/60 2/72 3/116 4/151 5/160 6/199   7/201 8/226 9/269   **271**   1/4 2/9 3/56   (4 wkts.)   **133**   4/91

Northamptonshire Bowling

	O.	M.	R.	W.		O.	M.	R.	W.
Clarke	31	5	91	2	....	10.1	1	30	1
Barrick	18	3	67	1					
Manning	23	5	73	0	....	7	1	21	0
Tribe	33.5	11	81	5	....	9	3	15	0
Broderick......	25	9	72	1	....	6	2	10	0
Subba Row	4	0	19	0					

South Africans Bowling

	O.	M.	R.	W.		O.	M.	R.	W.
Fuller	21	6	51	1	....	4	0	16	0
Adcock	27	4	90	3	....	12	2	30	2
Keith	10	5	20	0	....	12	0	35	1
Murray	15	10	18	1					
Smith	26	6	59	1	....	3	0	15	0
McLean	1	0	1	0					
Goddard	19.4	11	20	4	....	17	2	33	0

Umpires: A. E. Pothecary and N. Oldfield.

YORKSHIRE v. SOUTH AFRICANS

At Sheffield, July 2, 4, 5. South Africans won by 193 runs. Although Yorkshire were without Hutton, Appleyard and Trueman, the touring team must have found encouragement for the third Test from the convincing nature of their win. McGlew and Goddard began the match brightly with a stand of 92 but later wickets fell rapidly on a pitch of easy pace to the left-arm slows of Wardle and the off-breaks of Illingworth. After a shaky start, Lowson and Watson made 94 for the first Yorkshire wicket, but following rain at the week-end the county collapsed against the pace of Heine and the off-spin of Tayfield. When they lost five second innings wickets for 130, the South Africans appeared to be in trouble, but the later batsmen, especially Winslow and Tayfield, made runs readily. Three lbw's in the course of seven balls put the total stood at 13 put Yorkshire into difficulties and they never looked like saving the game although Wardle enlivened the closing stages with terrific hitting. In half an hour he made 74, including six 6's and seven 4's, after reaching 51 in eighteen minutes.

South Africans

D. J. McGlew c Hodgson b Wardle	 51	— c Lowson b Close	 47
T. L. Goddard b Wardle	 42	— c Watson b Wardle	 22
C. A. R. Duckworth b Hodgson	 5	— b Close	 35
W. R. Endean c Wilson b Wardle	 2	— c and b Close	 16
R. A. McLean c Hodgson b Close	 41	— c Close b Wardle	 4
J. H. B. Waite b Illingworth	 19	— c Watson b Wardle	 39
P. L. Winslow c Close b Illingworth	 19	— b Wardle	 51
H. J. Tayfield lbw b Illingworth	 4	— c Lester b Illingworth	 65
E. R. H. Fuller c Illingworth b Wardle..	5	— b Illingworth	 38
P. Heine c and b Illingworth	 8	— not out	 16
V. I. Smith not out	 0	— b Wardle	 7
B 5, l-b 7, n-b 1	 13	B 10, l-b 9, w 1	 20

1/92 2/105 3/105 4/119 5/173 6/173   209

7/184 8/201 9/208

1/36 2/95 3/121 4/124   360

5/130 6/194 7/255 8/327

9/334

Yorkshire

F. A. Lowson c Goddard b Heine	50	— lbw b Goddard	5
W. Watson c Heine b Smith	51	— lbw b Fuller	8
J. V. Wilson st Waite b Tayfield	23	— c Tayfield b Goddard	19
E. Lester b Heine	10	— lbw b Goddard	0
D. B. Close b Heine	9	— c McLean b Tayfield	29
N. W. D. Yardley b Tayfield	4	— b Tayfield	14
R. Illingworth c McLean b Tayfield	11	— c Waite b Smith	17
J. H. Wardle c and b Tayfield	9	— b Tayfield	74
J. G. Binks not out	18	— b Tayfield	2
P. Hodgson b Goddard	6	— c sub b Smith	0
M. J. Cowan run out	0	— not out	0
B 6, l-b 1	7	B 8, l-b 2	10

1/94 2/115 3/127 4/139 5/145 6/150   198   1/13 2/13 3/13 4/61   178
7/174 8/175 9/197   5/61 6/93 7/97 8/121 9/152

Yorkshire Bowling

	O.	M.	R.	W.		O.	M.	R.	W.
Cowan	15	3	40	0	....	17	3	57	0
Hodgson	11	0	39	1	....	12	3	34	0
Wardle	28	6	72	4	....	32.5	7	105	5
Close	13	5	24	1	....	35	10	67	3
Illingworth	4.2	1	21	4	....	27	9	77	2

South Africans Bowling

	O.	M.	R.	W.		O.	M.	R.	W.
Heine	27	4	60	3					
Goddard	17	9	19	1	....	21	6	32	3
Tayfield	37.3	13	94	4	....	21.4	11	58	4
Fuller	4	1	7	0	....	9	0	22	1
Smith	4	1	11	1	....	9	1	56	2

Umpires: A. Skelding and G. S. Mobey.

ENGLAND v. SOUTH AFRICA

Third Test Match

At Manchester, July 7, 8, 9, 11, 12. South Africa won by three wickets and kept the series alive by gaining an exciting victory with three minutes to spare. As at Lord's the South Africans built up a commanding position and this time they did not allow their advantage to slip. England fought hard, but once more poor catching proved their biggest weakness and they were deservedly beaten at Old Trafford for the first time in any Test since 1902. South Africa gained their third victory in England and their first at Old Trafford.

The game will be remembered for the astonishing number of mishaps to players on both sides, due largely to the fast, lively pitch which caused the ball to rise knuckle high throughout. Hand injuries were frequent, the worst being to Evans, who fractured the little finger of his right hand in two places while keeping wicket in the first innings. Graveney, who deputised behind the stumps, hurt a thumb while taking Tyson, and Compton, May and Cowdrey (England) and McGlew, Tayfield and Waite (South Africa) were others with hand troubles. In addition strains and mishaps worried Bailey and Tyson (England) and Heine and Keith (South Africa). Glorious sunshine on all five days provided Old Trafford with its best Test weather for many years, and the attendance of nearly 90,000 was the second highest in the history of the ground.

Alec Bedser returned to Test cricket, being brought in for Statham, who failed to pass a test on his strained stomach muscles the day before the match began. The selectors made three other changes from the Lord's side, including

Cowdrey, Lock and Tyson (recovered from a heel injury) for Barrington, Wardle and Trueman. So not a Yorkshire or Lancashire player found a place in the team. South Africa were without their captain, Cheetham, recovering from the chipped elbow bone suffered in the second Test. Winslow replaced him and McGlew led the Test side for the first time.

When May won the toss for the third successive match England looked to have gained a big advantage, but as at Lord's the pitch first thing was a "green top" and they were soon struggling. In Adcock's second over Graveney fell to a catch at backward short leg and Kenyon, who never settled down, touched an outswinger to the wicket-keeper at 22. May showed splendid form from the start, but Compton began shakily and he almost gave catches off his first two scoring strokes. The third pair added 48 in an hour before May left and when Cowdrey followed five runs later England were 75 for four. Then Compton found his touch and with Bailey playing his usual reliable supporting game 144 runs came for the fifth wicket before Bailey, who batted for three hours, edged a catch shortly after Adcock took the new ball.

Only Lock of the other batsmen gave Compton much support. Compton, 155 at the end of the day, added only three more next morning. Batting five and a half hours he hit twenty-two 4's in his 158—a splendid fighting innings although not one of his best. Apart from the shaky start he offered chances when 58 and 115. The unevenness of England's innings can be seen from the score, seven batsmen making only nine runs between them. South Africa did well to dismiss England for under 300 and batting under somewhat easier conditions they built a substantial lead.

McGlew and Goddard led the way with an opening stand of 147, but the partnership should have been broken much earlier for both batsmen were missed, Goddard when 24 and McGlew when 68. England waited three and a quarter hours for their first success, but between tea and the close they captured four wickets. Shortly after Goddard left, McGlew, when 77, retired with a damaged right hand and Mansell, Endean and McLean were soon out.

Dropped catches proved disastrous to England. Keith, missed when eight, stayed to the close of the second day when South Africa with six wickets left, were 85 behind. First thing next morning Waite (then 15) offered a slip catch. Keith and Waite added 63 and then followed a stand of 171 between Waite and Winslow. Both men scored their first Test centuries and they set up a new South African record for the sixth wicket.

Winslow, who at times drove with great power, was dropped when 64 and he reached his hundred with a mighty straight hit for 6 over the sightscreen. Altogether he obtained three 6's and thirteen 4's while scoring 108 in three hours ten minutes. Waite took just over five and a half hours over his patient 113 which included twelve 4's. McGlew resumed his innings at the fall of the seventh wicket and at the close of the third day South Africa were 198 on with three wickets left. They increased their lead to 237 before declaring. Their total of 521 for eight was only 17 short of their best in all Tests. McGlew, who became the third man in the innings to reach a century, batted four hours forty minutes for his not out 104. Lock bowled extremely well without luck, but the others were completely mastered.

England's second innings again began disastrously, the opening pair, Kenyon and Graveney, both being out at two. Then a glorious stand by May and Compton halted South Africa's progress. Both showed their best form in adding 124 in 105 minutes. Compton, batting as well as he had ever done in his most successful days, hit twelve 4's in 71 and twenty-one boundaries came during this partnership. Cowdrey, missed at slip when 6, helped May in another good stand of 108. May hit his second century in successive Tests and his 117, made in four and a half hours, included sixteen 4's.

When the final day began England, with six wickets left, stood 13 ahead. The remaining batsmen tried their best to play for time until the last pair came together. Cowdrey defended resolutely for just over four hours for 50, Lock, sent in as overnight stop gap, stayed an hour and a quarter and Bailey again showed stern defence. Even so, South African looked like gaining an easy victory when the ninth wicket fell at 333. Then Evans, with his fractured finger in plaster, joined Bailey and there followed a thrilling last stand of 48 of which Evans made 36. Despite his injury he hit powerfully and two of his seven 4's were almost 6's. Bailey remained unbeaten for nearly three hours.

South Africa needed 145 to win in two and a quarter hours and the excitement continued. They went for the runs from the start and after two wickets had fallen for 23, McGlew and McLean hit 72 in fifty minutes, McLean's share being 50 which contained one 6 and seven 4's. England continued to fight well and four more wickets, including that of McGlew, were soon captured. South Africa wanted 10 with three wickets left. Waite, cover-driving Tyson for 4, made the winning hit off the third ball of what must have been the last over but one.

L. S.

England

D. Kenyon c Waite b Heine	....	5	— c Waite b Heine	....	1
T. W. Graveney c Tayfield b Adcock	....	0	— b Adcock	....	1
P. B. H. May c Mansell b Goddard	....	34	— b Mansell	....	117
D. C. S. Compton c Waite b Adcock	....	158	— c Mansell b Heine	....	71
M. C. Cowdrey c Mansell b Tayfield	....	1	— c Goddard b Heine	....	50
T. E. Bailey c Waite b Adcock	....	44	— not out	....	38
F. J. Titmus lbw b Heine	....	0	— c Mansell b Adcock	....	19
T. G. Evans c Keith b Heine	....	0	— c McLean b Tayfield	....	36
G. A. R. Lock not out	....	19	— c McGlew b Adcock	....	17
F. H. Tyson b Goddard	....	2	— b Heine	....	8
A. V. Bedser lbw b Goddard	....	1	— c Waite b Heine	....	3
B 13, l-b 6, w 1	....	20	B 13, l-b 5, w 2	....	20

1/2 2/22 3/70 4/75 5/219 6/234   **284**
7/242 8/271 9/280

1/2 2/2 3/126 4/234   **381**
5/270 6/274 7/304 8/325
9/333

South Africa

D. J. McGlew not out	....	104	— b Tyson	....	48
T. L. Goddard c Graveney b Tyson	....	62	— c May b Bedser	....	8
H. J. Keith c Graveney b Bailey	....	38	— b Bedser	....	0
P. N. F. Mansell lbw b Lock	....	7	— lbw b Tyson	....	4
W. R. Endean c Evans b Lock	....	5	— c Titmus b Lock	....	2
R. A. McLean b Tyson	....	3	— run out	....	50
J. H. B. Waite c Kenyon b Bedser	....	113	— not out	....	10
P. L. Winslow lbw b Bedser	....	108	— b Tyson	....	16
H. J. Tayfield b Tyson	....	28	— not out	....	1
P. Heine not out	....	22			
B 15, l-b 12, w 1, n-b 3	....	31	B 2, l-b 2, w 1, n-b 1	..	6

1/147 2/171 3/179   (8 wkts., dec.) **521**
4/182 5/245 6/416 7/457 8/494

1/18 2/23 3/95   (7 wkts.) **145**
4/112 5/129 6/132 7/135

N. A. T. Adcock did not bat.

South Africa Bowling

	O.	M.	R.	W.		O.	M.	R.	W.
Heine	24	4	71	3	....	32	8	86	5
Adcock	25	5	52	3	....	28	12	48	5
Tayfield	35	15	57	1	....	51.5	21	102	1
Goddard	27	10	52	3	....	47	21	92	0
Mansell	6	2	13	0	....	15	3	33	1
Keith	6	1	19	0					

England Bowling

	O.	M.	R.	W.		O.	M.	R.	W.
Bedser	31	2	92	2	....	10	1	61	2
Tyson	44	5	124	3	....	13.3	2	55	3
Bailey	37	8	102	1					
Lock	64	24	121	2	....	7	2	23	1
Titmus	19	7	51	0					

Umpires: F. S. Lee and D. Davies.

SURREY v. SOUTH AFRICANS

At The Oval, July 16, 18, 19. South Africans won by 82 runs. In a match graced by the presence of the Queen on the second afternoon, McLean, for his dashing century, and Tayfield, for skilful off-spin bowling which brought him 13 wickets for 98 runs, were notable personalities. McLean, in a magnificent display, hit 151 out of 199 in three and a half hours. As the fortunes of his side fluctuated after Endean, acting captain, won the toss, McLean adapted his mood to the situation and showed himself a master of defensive cricket as well as forcing play. He hit twenty 4's before falling to the new ball after tea. Loader, lively and accurate, took the bowling honours for Surrey who lost Clark and Stewart for 66 before the close. On the second day Tayfield and Laker showed their capabilities. May was quite comfortable in carrying his Saturday score of 28 to 62 but Tayfield routed his colleagues. He came on at 115 for three, and in forty-five minutes the last seven wickets went for 25 runs, five to Tayfield in eight overs for 13 runs. The South Africans, 104 in front, were troubled by Laker's off-spin and with Loader in hostile form they were out soon after five o'clock. Surrey needed 275 to win. In an hour they scored 34 for the loss of Stewart, and on the last day looked to have a good chance at lunch when 139 for three, but Tayfield finished the match soon after half-past three. Clark and May, partners in a second-wicket stand of 86, batted confidently enough, but Tayfield, turning the ball judiciously on a dusty pitch and cleverly varying flight and pace, beat them both and between lunch and the end he sent back six men for 37 runs. Tayfield fittingly finished the match by dismissing Barrington and Loader in three deliveries.

South Africans

W. R. Endean c McIntyre b Loader	32	—	lbw b A. Bedser		0
T. L. Goddard c Stewart b Loader	9	—	c McIntyre b Loader		17
H. J. Keith c McIntyre b A. Bedser	16	—	c Stewart b Loader		11
C. A. R. Duckworth c Surridge b Loader	0	—	lbw b Laker		20
R. A. McLean c McIntyre b Loader	151	—	c Stewart b Laker		15
J. H. B. Waite lbw b Laker	0	—	c McIntyre b Loader		41
P. L. Winslow c Laker b A. Bedser	13	—	c May b Laker		4
P. N. F. Mansell b E. Bedser	14	—	c E. Bedser b Laker		20
E. R. H. Fuller c Stewart b E. Bedser	0	—	run out		7
H. J. Tayfield st McIntyre b A. Bedser	6	—	not out		14
V. I. Smith not out	0	—	c E. Bedser b Laker		10
L-b 3	3		B 6, l-b 1, n-b 4		11

1/17 2/42 3/45 4/112 5/115 6/160   244   1/1 2/24 3/49 4/71 5/72   170
7/213 8/213 9/244   6/86 7/120 8/142 9/148

Surrey

T. H. Clark b Fuller	2	—	c McLean b Tayfield		58
M. J. Stewart b Fuller	8	—	hit wkt b Smith		13
P. B. H. May lbw b Tayfield	62	—	c Mansell b Tayfield		43
B. Constable st Duckworth b Mansell	34	—	c Keith b Tayfield		16
K. Barrington lbw b Tayfield	5	—	c Winslow b Tayfield		34
E. A. Bedser c Waite b Goddard	0	—	c Winslow b Tayfield		1
A. J. McIntyre c Fuller b Tayfield	9	—	b Tayfield		7
J. C. Laker c Mansell b Goddard	7	—	c Keith b Tayfield		0
W. S. Surridge b Tayfield	2	—	c Mansell b Fuller		1
P. J. Loader c Endean b Tayfield	4	—	b Tayfield		14
A. V. Bedser not out	0	—	not out		0
B 4, l-b 3	7		B 3, l-b 2		5

1/7 2/26 3/83 4/115 5/118 6/118   140   1/21 2/107 3/120 4/149   192
7/132 8/136 9/137   5/151 6/171 7/171 8/176
                                       9/192

Surrey Bowling

	O.	M.	R.	W.		O.	M.	R.	W.
A. Bedser......	15.5	2	48	3	....	10	1	21	1
Surridge	7	2	31	0					
Loader	16	3	46	4	....	17	3	58	3
Laker	28	9	71	1	....	18	3	56	5
E. Bedser	13	3	37	2	....	10	2	24	0
Clark	4	1	8	0					

South Africans Bowling

	O.	M.	R.	W.		O.	M.	R.	W.
Goddard	20	2	32	2	....	23	9	39	0
Fuller	17	7	23	2	....	24	8	42	1
Smith	8	5	24	0	....	7	3	14	1
Tayfield	12.2	4	22	5	....	51.3	26	76	8
Mansell	13	3	32	1	....	9	4	16	0

Umpires: H. G. Baldwin and E. A. Roberts.

ENGLAND v. SOUTH AFRICA

Fouth Test Match

At Leeds, July 21, 22, 23, 25, 26. South African won by 224 runs with two hours to spare. Theirs was a remarkable triumph, for on winning the toss half their wickets fell for 38 and seven were down for 98. England appeared to have gained a tremendous advantage when they batted on an easy-paced pitch and Adcock, after sending down only four overs, retired with a broken bone in the left foot. It was at that stage when victory for England seemed almost a foregone conclusion that South Africa proceeded to make their glorious recovery.

Admirable bowling by Heine, Goddard and Tayfield, of which more will be written later, was splendidly supported in the field and throughout McGlew, the deputy captain, excelled in field placing as well as in the splendid example he set his men by his enthusiastic run-saving and determined batting. Not only was this the first victory by South Africa at Headingley but never before had they won two matches in the same series in England. Fuller, the twelfth man, fielded splendidly.

Whereas injury in the Lord's Test still deprived South Africa of their captain, Cheetham, England could not call on Cowdrey, Evans, Tyson or Appleyard and Watson, the Yorkshire left-hander, preferred as opener to Kenyon, withdrew through injury, being replaced by Lowson. As Titmus had not fulfilled expectations in the two previous Tests, England played the two left-arm slow bowlers, Wardle and Lock, and went into the match without a right-handed spinner which proved a big handicap judged by Tayfield's nine wickets for South Africa.

As at Old Trafford, grand weather favoured the match. The sun shone powerfully all five days and, with increased accommodation, the total attendance of 113,500 and receipts £31,032 were both records for any match between the two countries. On the fourth day, Monday, the gates were closed at midday with 36,000 present.

This was the only time South Africa won the toss in this series and they retained their winning team of the previous Test at Manchester. Dews, of Worcestershire, was twelfth man for England. May used his fast bowlers, Statham, Loader and Bailey in short spells and it was when Loader crossed to Statham's Kirkstall end with 26 runs scored in an hour that he struck the early blows for England. For seventy-five minutes the South African first pair remained together before Loader, who varied his pace and angle of attack skilfully, disposed of McGlew, Keith and Goddard and Bailey accounted for Mansell who played on. At lunch South Africa were 37 for four and immediately afterwards the left-handed Wardle, running from cover, ran out Waite, making 38 for five.

By clean hitting McLean improved the position until splendidly caught low to the left by May at cover; but Endean, sent in late owing to his previous lack of success, played well for an hour and fifty minutes until Statham yorked his middle stump. South Africa were all out in four hours forty minutes, a most disappointing performance, the honours going to the three seam bowlers, Loader, Statham and Bailey. Compared with Manchester, England's fielding showed much improvement, McIntyre making a worthy deputy for Evans.

England, left with seventy minutes at the crease at the end of the first day, lost their opening pair for 23. The decision of the selectors to use Bailey as a number one batsman not only proved a failure but it left the side without any stiffening in the middle of the order.

Next day an X-ray revealed the extent of Adcock's foot injury and with only three recognised bowlers at his disposal McGlew set his field deep giving England the task of fighting for runs. Lock had joined May overnight and altogether he lasted 50 minutes. May and Compton put on 64, both batting attractively before May, trying to drive Tayfield, was bowled by an offbreak. Compton drove and hooked well, but when at 152 he was caught at slip, England even found difficulty in gaining the lead. Wardle alone attacked the bowling; he helped himself to 24 from six strokes against Tayfield, including two drives for 6 into the top balcony of the football stand. Insole, back to Test cricket after five years, stayed an hour being last out, but he never looked comfortable.

Although in the field from 11.30 a.m. till 3.55 p.m. South Africa made only two bowling changes. Heine, fast and hostile, bowled till 12.20 when he was relieved at 60 by Tayfield who proceeded to bowl his off-breaks from the pavilion end till the innings closed. Goddard, attacking the leg stump, began with a spell of one hour fifty minutes, after which Heine from 1.20 p.m. shared the attack with Tayfield. Considering that at lunch England needed only 43 for the lead with six wickets left, South Africa accomplished a fine performance in restricting their advantage to 20. As many as six of the England team were lbw, an indication of their faulty methods in preferring pads to bat.

McGlew showed a keen sense in resting Goddard on the boundary after lunch for he needed him to open the innings. Having bowled themselves out of trouble the South Africans continued to show initiative. The diminutive McGlew and the tall left-handed Goddard sought runs. McGlew, quick on his feet, drove the pitched-up ball or cut or pulled the shorter one and Goddard, who was content with nine runs in an hour and fifty minutes in the first innings, now became more active. Statham beat both batsmen but nightfall found South Africa 107 for no wicket; McGlew 59; Goddard 46.

By exercising more caution and batting to the pattern now accepted by Test crowds South Africa extracted 234 runs in six hours from the England bowlers on the fourth day (Saturday) while losing five wickets. Loader could not repeat his deadly work of Thursday but he put in a good spell before lunch when his bouncer caused McGlew, then in the "nineties," some concern. Statham, unable to use the Kirkstall end because of the deep foothold which brought about Adcock's injury and later prevented Heine from bowling, seemed to lack inspiration in the absence of Tyson.

England toiled for four and a quarter hours before Goddard, flicking outside the off stump when playing back, fell to the first ball after lunch. The stand of 176 was South Africa's best for the first wicket in England beating the 171 by R. H. Catterall and B. Mitchell at Birmingham in 1929. A feature of the partnership was the quick running; not a run was wasted and some were stolen cheekily.

McGlew reached his hundred in four and a half hours and two more hours passed before at 265 he pulled a simple catch to his rival captain at mid wicket. He hit thirteen 4's. Keith, like Goddard left-handed, stayed three hours twenty minutes, his boundaries numbering eleven, and at the end of the day South Africa were 341 for five wickets and two days remained.

Monday provided a triumph for Endean, who batting just over four hours, hit his first Test century against England. He received valuable help from Waite, who stayed one hundred minutes while 76 were added, and Tayfield, Heine and even Adcock, who came without a runner, all played their part in swelling the total to a round 500. Very watchful Endean batted almost without fault and hit sixteen 4's. Altogether the innings lasted eleven hours fifty minutes.

England needed 481 in eight hours twenty minutes, an average of one a minute and this time Graveney opened with Lowson, Bailey batting at number six. At once disaster overtook England, Lowson falling to a ball that kept low, but generally the pitch did not favour the bowlers. It lasted remarkably well. Graveney shaped well only to fall to a fine catch at mid-off. McLean took the ball low and cleanly and Graveney set a splendid example for all Test cricketers by merely asking McLean whether it was a catch and then walking to the pavilion without waiting for an appeal to the umpires.

An unfinished stand of 56 by May and Insole left England with a fighting chance on the last day when with eight wickets in hand they wanted 366 in the last six hours. Thanks to the two Cambridge Blues, England held their own almost till lunch time. Insole stayed another seventy-five minutes, the stand realising 47, and Compton, having been held back for the final effort, shaped splendidly, but May fell to the fourth ball of the last over before the interval when playing back and his dismissal at that vital period proved to be the final turning-point. May batted four hours, hitting thirteen 4's.

Here tribute must be paid to the South African bowlers. Heine was entrusted with the first over of the day, but in his trial run from the Kirkstall end he found the foothold too awkward and dangerous and consequently he did not bowl at all on this last day. Instead, the tall left-handed Goddard bowled over the wicket without relief from 11.30 a.m. until the match was won at 4.12 p.m. A glance at the analysis for both innings reveals the wonderful part Goddard and Tayfield played. Mansell, too, contributed an important part for he bowled steadily from 11.30 until 1.5 p.m. keeping Tayfield fresh for the final effort and that was the only change when the total was 180 for three.

In the circumstances, South Africa did not claim the new ball and Tayfield and Goddard took the last six wickets in two hours after the interval for the addition of 52 runs. Bailey resisted for those two hours being last out to a smart low return catch by Tayfield. South Africa thoroughly merited their win and with the rubber level the issue depended on the final Test at The Oval.   N. P.

South Africa

D. J. McGlew c McIntyre b Loader	23	— c May b Wardle	133
T. L. Goddard b Loader	9	— c McIntyre b Wardle	74
H. J. Keith c McIntyre b Loader	0	— b Wardle	73
P. N. F. Mansell b Bailey	0	— lbw b Bailey	1
R. A. McLean c May b Loader	41	— c Lowson b Wardle	3
J. H. B. Waite run out	2	— c McIntyre b Lock	32
P. L. Winslow b Statham	8	— c Lock b Statham	19
W. R. Endean b Statham	41	— not out	116
H. J. Tayfield not out	25	— lbw b Statham	14
P. Heine b Lock	14	— b Bailey	10
N. A. T. Adcock lbw b Statham	0	— b Bailey	6
L-b 4, n-b 4	8	B 8, l-b 6, w.1, n-b 4	19

1/33 2/33 3/34 4/34 5/38 6/63   171   1/176 2/265 3/269 4/303   500
7/98 8/154 9/170   5/311 6/387 7/400 8/439
                                                      9/468

England

T. E. Bailey lbw b Heine	9	— c and b Tayfield	8
F. A. Lowson lbw b Goddard	5	— b Goddard	0
P. B. H. May b Tayfield	47	— lbw b Tayfield	97
G. A. R. Lock lbw b Goddard	17	— c Mansell b Goddard	7
D. C. S. Compton c Mansell b Tayfield	61	— c Waite b Goddard	26
T. W. Graveney lbw b Heine	10	— c McLean b Tayfield	36
D. J. Insole lbw b Heine	3	— c Keith b Goddard	47
A. J. McIntyre lbw b Heine	3	— c Heine b Tayfield	4
J. H. Wardle c Goddard b Tayfield	24	— c Heine b Tayfield	21
J. B. Statham b Tayfield	4	— hit wkt b Goddard	3
P. J. Loader not out	0	— not out	0
B 5, l-b 2, w 1	8	B 1, l-b 6	7

1/15 2/23 3/53 4/117 5/152 6/152   191   1/3 2/59 3/160 4/204   256
7/161 8/186 9/191   5/210 6/215 7/239 8/246
                                                      9/256

England Bowling

	O.	M.	R.	W.		O.	M.	R.	W.
Statham	20.2	7	35	3	....	40	10	129	2
Loader	19	7	52	4	....	29	9	67	0
Bailey	16	7	23	1	....	40.5	11	97	3
Wardle	9	1	33	0	....	57	22	100	4
Lock .	6	1	20	1	....	32	13	88	1

South Africa Bowling

	O.	M.	R.	W.		O.	M.	R.	W.
Heine	29.5	11	70	4	....	14	2	33	0
Adcock	4	3	4	0					
Goddard	25	12	39	2	....	62	37	69	5
Tayfield	31	14	70	4	....	47.1	15	94	5
		Mansell				19	2	53	0

Umpires: F. Chester and T. J. Bartley.

MINOR COUNTIES v. SOUTH AFRICANS

At Stoke-on-Trent, July 27, 28. Drawn. After three Yorkshiremen, Taylor, Padgett and Leadbeater had helped Minor Counties to record a commendable total, Murray, batting for the first time since injuring a thumb at the beginning of the month, hit his only century of the tour. He stayed three hours ten minutes for exactly 100, which included sixteen 4's. Endean completed an unusual but nevertheless successful opening combination for South Africa. The pair put on 99 runs in seventy-five minutes. Just over three hours remained when Minor Counties began their second innings 69 runs behind. On a dusty pitch Tayfield and Smith looked capable of causing a collapse but Padgett stood in their way with another splendid example of skilful batting against good spin bowling.

Minor Counties

K. Taylor c Duckworth b Smith	57	— c Murray b Tayfield	32
G. Walton b Fuller	2	— c and b Smith	17
D. E. V. Padgett b Smith	33	— b Fuller..................	59
H. D. Fairclough c Winslow b Tayfield .	38	— c Cheetham b Smith	11
R. Gautrey lbw b Tayfield	9	— c Waite b Smith	8
R. Collins c Winslow b Smith	6	— c Fuller b Smith	7
D. M. Haynes c Keith b Smith	2	— lbw b Fuller	12
D. J. Smith c McGlew b Tayfield	39	— not out	2
E. Leadbeater not out	30	— b Tayfield	7
F. Taylor c Murray b Tayfield	7	— not out	11
H. B. Henderson b Smith	4		
L-b 6	6	B 14..................	14

1/5 2/64 3/123 4/132 5/145 6/150   233   1/50 2/56 3/98   (8 wkts.) 180
7/150 8/226 9/226   4/103 5/119 6/132 7/163
                                               8/164

South Africans

W. R. Endean c K. Taylor b F. Taylor	66	J. H. B. Waite c Walton b Collins..	37
A. R. A. Murray c Henderson b F. Taylor	100	E. R. H. Fuller b Fairclough	19
		D. J. McGlew run out	6
H. J. Keith c Fairclough b F. Taylor	6	H. J. Tayfield b Collins	5
C. A. R. Duckworth b F. Taylor .	0	V. I. Smith not out	1
P. L. Winslow c Haynes b Leadbeater	40	B 1, l-b 3	4
J. E. Cheetham c and b Smith	18		

1/99 2/111 3/111 4/180 5/224   302
6/234 7/267 8/294 9/301

South Africans Bowling

	O.	M.	R.	W.	O.	M.	R.	W.
Fuller	14	2	37	1	11	5	17	2
Murray	15	4	42	0	7	5	11	0
McGlew	2	0	6	0				
Tayfield	30	9	71	4	25	10	53	2
Smith	24.5	8	71	5	17	3	51	4
Keith					10	5	23	0
Waite					2	0	11	0

Minor Counties Bowling

	O.	M.	R.	W.
F. Taylor	29	9	88	4
Smith	17	1	66	1
Collins	17.4	5	57	2
Fairclough	12	1	37	1
Leadbeater	4	0	34	1
K. Taylor	4	0	16	0

Umpires: T. McMurray and A. Barrett.

GLAMORGAN v. SOUTH AFRICANS

At Swansea, July 30, August 1, 2. South Africans won by 226 runs. The bowling of Heine and Tayfield proved too much for the county who did well in the early stages when Hugh Davies, a 24-year-old medium pace bowler, was mainly responsible for the first six wickets falling for 132. When Davies tired, he was not adequately replaced and Cheetham and Mansell seized the chance to add 63 in brisk style. Before the close on Saturday Glamorgan lost four men for 45 and on the Bank Holiday the remaining six wickets went for 19, Heine's figures being 8.1—1—11—5. Cheetham preferred not to enforce the follow-on and this time the first six wickets fell for 92. Carelessness caused this breakdown, but Waite and Mansell left little to chance and their deliberate methods resulted in a stand of 71. Mansell drove strongly, hitting eight 4's. Heine, who hit two 6's in the first innings, pleased the 20,000 crowd by hitting another 6 and three 4's before Glamorgan found themselves wanting 392 to win. In the absence of McConnon, who contributed largely to their defeat in 1951, the South Africans gained revenge. Glamorgan were baffled by the off-spin of Tayfield and only a fourth wicket stand by the left-handers Jones and Watkins gave the tourists any trouble.

South Africans

D. J. McGlew c Watkins b H. D. Davies	36	— b Watkins	11
A. R. A. Murray c Pressdee b H. D. Davies	19	— b Watkins	17
H. J. Keith lbw b H. D. Davies	2	— b Watkins	14
C. A. R. Duckworth c H. G. Davies b Ward	32	— b Ward	24
R. A. McLean c H. G. Davies b H. D. Davies	18	— c Pressdee b Ward	4
J. E. Cheetham b Watkins	46	— st H. G. Davies b Pressdee	18
J. H. B. Waite lbw b Pressdee	12	— c H. G. Davies b Watkins	31
P. N. F. Mansell lbw b Watkins	29	— c Wooller b Pressdee	61
H. J. Tayfield not out	9	— st H. G. Davies b Pressdee	15
E. R. H. Fuller c H. D. Davies b Ward	4	— c H. G. Davies b Pressdee	5
P. Heine c H. G. Davies b H. D. Davies	12	— not out	26
B 5, n-b 1	6	L-b 4	4

1/48 2/50 3/84 4/107 5/111 6/132   225
7/195 8/204 9/209

1/11 2/39 3/44 4/57   230
5/88 6/92 7/163 8/185 9/197

Glamorgan

W. G. A. Parkhouse b Fuller	13	— b Heine	4
P. B. Clift run out	16	— b Heine	21
J. Pleass c Murray b Tayfield	14	— c Waite b Fuller	1
W. E. Jones lbw b Fuller	2	— c Cheetham b Murray	50
A. J. Watkins c Waite b Heine	8	— c Cheetham b Tayfield	23
J. Pressdee c Waite b Heine	3	— c Keith b Tayfield	18
B. R. Edrich c Waite b Heine	4	— c McLean b Tayfield	18
D. J. Ward b Heine	0	— not out	10
W. Wooller run out	1	— b Tayfield	0
H. G. Davies b Heine	1	— lbw b Tayfield	14
H. D. Davies not out	0	— c Cheetham b Tayfield	2
L-b 2	2	B 1, l-b 3	4

1/25 2/31 3/45 4/45 5/56 6/57　　64
7/57 8/62 9/64

1/13 2/22 3/46 4/102　　165
5/102 6/134 7/145 8/147
9/163

Glamorgan Bowling

	O.	M.	R.	W.		O.	M.	R.	W.
Watkins	14	2	41	2	....	28	6	73	4
H. D. Davies	20.4	8	35	5	....	12	6	29	0
Wooller	13	4	43	0	....	5	1	15	0
Ward	19	4	71	2	....	27	6	63	2
Pressdee	5	1	15	1	....	16.1	3	46	4
Clift	3	0	14	0					

South Africans Bowling

	O.	M.	R.	W.		O.	M.	R.	W.
Heine	18.1	5	26	5	....	19	5	34	2
Fuller	21	12	20	2	....	13	3	37	1
Tayfield	16	12	16	1	....	25	11	35	6
Murray						13	6	25	1
Mansell						9	2	30	0

Umpires: H. G. Baldwin and E. A. Roberts.

WARWICKSHIRE v. SOUTH AFRICANS

At Birmingham, August 3, 4, 5. South Africans won by ten wickets and thoroughly deserved their success for they were much the better side. A laborious display by Gardner who occupied the first three and a half hours for 58 surrendered the initiative to the touring team and they never relaxed their grip. Fuller achieved his best bowling performance of the tour by taking seven wickets for 60 and then by consistently sound batting the South Africans gained a lead of 194. Their opening pair, McGlew and Goddard, took their stand to 146 and Goddard, third out, batted three and three-quarter hours. In a lively stand Endean and McLean added 95, the latter hitting one 6 and eight 4's. Endean (fourteen 4's) was smartly caught at the wicket when trying a powerful cut to complete a hundred. Hollies bowled admirably on a dusty pitch which encouraged spin and Spooner gave such a fine display behind the stumps that it helped to earn him a place in the final Test. After Fuller and Goddard had exploited the new ball and dismissed the first three Warwickshire batsmen, the two leg-spinners, Mansell and Smith, carried all before them. When two were needed to avert an innings defeat, Smith disposed of Townsend and Thompson with successive deliveries. Hollies prevented the hat-trick, but the South Africans needed only eight runs for victory.

Warwickshire

F. C. Gardner c Mansell b Smith	58	— b Fuller	11
N. F. Horner c Winslow b Heine	26	— c Endean b Goddard	26
A. V. Wolton c and b Fuller	2	— c Winslow b Fuller	33
R. T. Spooner c Duckworth b Fuller	2	— c McLean b Mansell	28
H. E. Dollery b Fuller	33	— lbw b Mansell	4
R. E. Hitchcock c Winslow b Fuller	29	— b Mansell	22
A. Townsend not out	12	— c Endean b Smith	36
K. R. Dollery c Mansell b Smith	4	— lbw b Smith	8
I. M. King b Fuller	6	— b Mansell	11
R. G. Thompson b Fuller	0	— st Duckworth b Smith	0
W. E. Hollies b Fuller	0	— not out	2
B 10, l-b 6	16	L-b 20	20

1/33 2/40 3/52 4/112 5/160 6/160   188
7/167 8/186 9/188

1/35 2/55 3/102 4/102   201
5/118 6/149 7/175 8/192
9/192

South Africans

D. J. McGlew lbw b Townsend	84		
T. L. Goddard c Townsend b Hollies	71		
C. A. R. Duckworth c Spooner b King	9	— not out	0
W. R. Endean c Spooner b Thompson	98		
R. A. McLean c and b Thompson	64		
J. E. Cheetham c and b Hollies	17		
P. L. Winslow st Spooner b Hollies	8	— not out	8
P. N. F. Mansell not out	13		
E. R. H. Fuller st Spooner b Hollies	9		
P. Heine c Spooner b Thompson	6		
L-b 3	3		

1/146 2/160 3/178   (9 wkts., dec.) 382   (No wkt.) 8
4/273 5/333 6/351 7/353 8/371 9/382

V. I. Smith did not bat.

South Africans Bowling

	O.	M.	R.	W.	O.	M.	R.	W.
Heine	21	9	36	1	8	2	20	0
Goddard	10	2	19	0	17	10	23	1
Fuller	29.4	6	60	7	32	10	47	2
Smith	23	7	57	2	11.1	2	39	3
Mansell					18	3	52	4

Warwickshire Bowling

	O.	M.	R.	W.
Thompson	22.5	4	67	3
K. Dollery	21	3	76	0
Hollies	51	16	100	4
King	26	6	83	1
Hitchcock	8	1	35	0
Townsend	7	1	18	1
Gardner	1	0	5	0
Horner	0.1	0	3	0

Umpires: P. Corrall and E. Davies.

GLOUCESTERSHIRE v. SOUTH AFRICANS

At Cheltenham, August 6, 8, 9. Drawn. Rain spoilt the prospects of an interesting finish after the South Africans had been set to get 214 runs to win on a pitch showing signs of wear. When Murray and Goddard were dismissed with only five scored there were visions of Gloucestershire repeating the notable victory they achieved over H. F. Wade's team 20 years previously. Play continued for a further forty minutes in a persistent drizzle before the players sought shelter and when the game was resumed nearly two hours later conditions were much easier for batting. The Gloucestershire batsmen, apart from Milton, gave a sorry display on the first day against Smith's leg-breaks and the South Africans, after a fine start by Murray and Goddard, came within one of the county's total with only three men gone. Then the course of their innings completely changed when the young off-break bowlers, Mortimore and Wells, in two remarkable overs took five wickets while the total remained at 183. In the end the lead was restricted to 13. Graveney, curbing his natural desire to attack, dominated Gloucestershire's second innings and it was a pity that hat, with everything set for an enthralling final day, the weather made its untimely intervention.

Gloucestershire

D. M. Young c Mansell b Smith	26	—	b Goddard		1
C. A. Milton c Fuller b Smith	58	—	c and b Fuller		4
T. W. Graveney c Mansell b Smith	0	—	c Duckworth b Fuller		98
J. F. Crapp b Smith	28	—	b Fuller		46
G. M. Emmett c Cheetham b Smith	0	—	c Cheetham b Fuller		12
G. E. Lambert b Goddard	9	—	c McLean b Smith		10
J. Mortimore not out	26	—	b Goddard		15
J. V. C. Griffiths c and b Murray	12	—	not out		8
P. Rochford c Duckworth b Mansell	3	—	st Duckworth b Smith		6
B. D. Wells c McLean b Murray	1	—	b Goddard		5
F. P. McHugh b Murray	0	—	c Duckworth b Murray		12
B 15, l-b 6	21		B 2, l-b 7		9

1/57 2/57 3/100 4/100 5/123 6/143   184   1/4 2/12 3/104 4/124   226
7/180 8/184 9/184   5/149 6/187 7/193 8/205
                                                            9/210

South Africans

A. R. A. Murray lbw b Griffiths	51	—	lbw b McHugh		1
T. L. Goddard c Milton b Mortimore	93	—	hit wkt b Lambert		1
H. J. Keith b Griffiths	1				
W. R. Endean b Mortimore	28	—	c Milton b Mortimore		17
R. A. McLean b Wells	3	—	not out		50
P. N. F. Mansell c Lambert b Mortimore	0				
P. L. Winslow c Wells b Mortimore	2				
C. A. R. Duckworth lbw b Wells	0				
J. E. Cheetham lbw b Wells	0	—	not out		36
E. R. H. Fuller not out	11				
V. I. Smith c Graveney b Wells	1		L-b 3		3
B 4, l-b 3	7				

1/116 2/120 3/176 4/183 5/183 6/183   197   1/1 2/5 3/52   (3 wkts.) 108
7/183 8/183 9/185

South Africans Bowling

	O.	M.	R.	W.	O.	M.	R.	W.
Goddard	21	8	33	1	24	7	33	3
Fuller	17	4	27	0	31	11	60	4
Murray	21.3	12	22	3	7.3	6	2	1
Smith	28	8	75	5	21	7	62	2
Mansell	5	2	6	1	11	1	30	0
Keith					12	4	30	0

Gloucestershire Bowling

	O.	M.	R.	W.		O.	M.	R.	W.
Lambert	8	3	16	0	....	12	2	30	1
McHugh	19	4	30	0	....	14	7	33	1
Wells	15	5	39	4	....	5	1	16	0
Mortimore	18	5	42	4	....	8	3	20	1
Graveney	2	0	12	0					
Griffiths	11	2	51	2					
					Milton	1	0	6	0

Umpires: J. J. Hills and A. Skelding.

LEICESTERSHIRE v. SOUTH AFRICANS

At Leicester, August 10, 11, 12. South Africans won by an innings and 117 runs. Their vice-captain, McGlew, hit 161, the highest score of the tour, which he later equalled against Kent. Leicestershire paid dearly for missing McGlew at slip when 12. He made no other mistake in a fine innings which lasted four and three-quarter hours and included twenty-two 4's. Goddard shared an opening stand of 101 and Keith helped McGlew add 224 in 170 minutes for the second wicket. Leicestershire were made to struggle on a good pitch because of accurate bowling supported by grand fielding. Palmer tried hard and Diment gave him useful support, but Tayfield worried nearly all the batsmen. Following on 255 behind, Leicestershire started with an opening stand of 69 between Lester and Smith, but collapsed badly before the spin of Mansell and Tayfield. The South Africans won with two hours to spare.

South Africans

D. J. McGlew b Munden 161	J. E. Cheetham not out 18
T. L. Goddard b Palmer 61	P. N. F. Mansell not out 53
H. J. Keith c Tompkin b Munden.100	
W. R. Endean b Spencer 41	L-b 4, w 1, n-b 7 12
P. L. Winslow c Goodwin b Jack-son.................... 1	1/101 2/325 (6 wkts., dec.) 463
J. H. B. Waite st Firth b Munden.. 16	3/329 4/334 5/388 6/390

A. R. A. Murray, H. J. Tayfield and N. A. T. Adcock did not bat.

Leicestershire

G. Lester c Mansell b Adcock 29	— st Waite b Tayfield 36
M. J. K. Smith c McGlew b Murray 36	— b Tayfield 28
M. Tompkin lbw b Adcock 5	— lbw b Mansell 7
C. H. Palmer lbw b Mansell 68	— c Endean b Tayfield 14
V. E. Jackson c Adcock b Tayfield 11	— st Waite b Mansell 1
R. A. Diment c Winslow b Tayfield 31	— run out 4
V. S. Munden c Cheetham b Mansell ... 3	— c Keith b Mansell 2
J. E. Walsh c Waite b Tayfield 1	— lbw b Mansell 2
J. Firth not out 7	— c Waite b Mansell......... 0
C. T. Spencer c Waite b Tayfield 5	— c Tayfield b Mansell 15
J. Goodwin c Murray b Tayfield........ 0	— not out 11
B 9, l-b 1, w 1, n-b 1 12	B 10, l-b 6, n-b 2...... 18

1/46 2/62 3/81 4/113 5/175 6/183   208
7/186 8/197 9/206

1/69 2/78 3/78 4/81   138
5/94 6/104 7/104 8/110
9/120

I

Leicestershire Bowling

	O.	M.	R.	W.	O.	M.	R.	W.
Spencer	30	2	124	1				
Goodwin	19	3	69	0				
Jackson	35	11	91	1				
Walsh	13	2	51	0				
Munden	30	12	83	3				
Palmer	9	1	33	1				

South Africans Bowling

	O.	M.	R.	W.		O.	M.	R.	W.
Adcock	15	2	55	2	....	6	1	27	0
Goddard	6	3	6	0	....	6	4	2	0
Murray	22	10	37	1	....	5	1	11	0
Tayfield	39.1	21	56	5	....	23	11	28	3
Mansell	25	10	42	2	....	23	8	52	6

Umpires: K. McCanlis and W. F. Price.

ENGLAND v. SOUTH AFRICA
Fifth Test Match

At The Oval, August 13, 15, 16, 17. England won by 92 runs at a quarter past five on the fourth day with a day to spare. For the first time in the history of cricket in England all five Tests were brought to a definite conclusion, England winning the rubber in this deciding contest. The victory was a triumph for three Surrey players. Peter May, the captain, besides leading his side skilfully, made the highest score, 89 not out, and the two spin bowlers, Laker and Lock, took fifteen of the eighteen wickets that fell to bowlers in the two South African innings.

For South Africa, who have never won a rubber in England, the result was a bitter disappointment. They were badly let down by three of their early batsmen as between them Keith, Endean and McLean made only six runs, all being dismissed for nought in the second innings, while Endean, like Spooner, the England wicket-keeper, went for "a pair."

The match was memorable for some grand off-spin bowling by Tayfield. On the third day he bowled from half past twelve until the close, five hours of cricket time, without relief, his figures during this spell being: 52 overs, 29 maidens, 54 runs, four wickets. This sustained effort was considered to be without parallel in Test cricket.

England again lacked the help of Evans, Cowdrey and Tyson. The last two were chosen only to be pronounced unfit the day prior to the match; their places were filled by Graveney and Bailey. In an effort to counter Goddard's leg theory bowling England included five left-handed batsmen, Ikin, Close, Watson, Spooner and Statham, but the plan failed. Indeed, in the second innings these five mustered only 18 runs between them. South Africa showed two changes from Leeds, Cheetham and Fuller coming in for Winslow and Adcock.

As no team had up to that stage of the summer made 200 runs in the fourth innings at The Oval, it was realised before the start that winning the toss might play an important part and May, by succeeding in this respect for the fourth time in the series, gained England an important advantage.

The match began under a leaden sky and soon after lunch on the opening day rain set in, stopping the cricket which amounted to only two and a half hours while England scored 70 for the loss of their first three batsmen. These three men contributed towards the opening stand of 51, Ikin having retired sick after 43 had been made in seventy minutes through being struck in the solar plexus from a ball delivered by Heine who had previously caused him much pain from bouncers.

The heavy atmosphere suited the seam bowlers and both Fuller and Heine were menacing. May never settled down, being first to leave, caught at second slip, and in the last over before lunch Close, who had batted confidently, fell to a fine right-handed catch, Mansell at first slip holding the ball with his right hand high above his head. Ikin resumed his innings after the interval but, deflecting Heine, he was splendidly taken by Waite, the wicket-keeper, low with the right hand on the leg-side.

Then came the downpour which lasted for twelve hours and although most of Sunday was fine the pitch was soft when Compton and Watson resumed batting in brilliant sunshine promptly to time on Monday. All day the bowlers held the mastery, 17 wickets falling for 193 runs, and England gained a valuable lead of 39. First thing South Africa toiled for seventy-five minutes without reward before disposing of Compton who in each innings was dismissed for the same score by precisely the same stroke—a leg sweep which presented a catch to the wicket-keeper. After Compton left, Tayfield disposed of Watson, Bailey and Spooner in five overs for a single, England's total at lunch being 122 for seven wickets.

Goddard, left arm over the wicket, and bowling at or outside the leg-stump, soon removed Laker, Graveney and Lock and finished with five wickets for 31 runs. Whereas England batted for nearly five hours they needed only three and a half hours to dismiss the whole of the South African team. It soon became clear that the soft turf was of no use to Statham, but at 22 Bailey deceived Goddard, the ball keeping low, and then, while Laker sent down a succession of maiden overs from the Vauxhall end, Lock bowled Keith playing forward, trapped Endean in the gully and knocked back the middle stump when McLean lashed out wildly.

For a time Waite stayed with McGlew, their stand yielding 44 before Lock, rolling over, caught Waite in the leg-trap. Next, McGlew, having defended valiantly for two and a half hours, paid the penalty for flashing at Statham, and although Cheetham resisted for nearly an hour none could stay with him, Statham, returning for the second time, finishing the tail.

The third day found the pitch reasonably docile. The rain of Saturday seemed to have bound it together and there was little evidence of dust, but England soon ran into trouble for they lost Ikin in the third over. Close lasted seventy minutes until Goddard disturbed his off-bail, and then May began his important innings which enabled his side to make the highest total of this low-scoring struggle. Graveney, owing to Compton being lame, had been promoted to number three and he and May proceeded to make the best stand of the match, the pair adding 65 in seventy-five minutes. Graveney played really well, but May when only four survived an appeal by Tayfield for lbw. It must have been close. The only time the batsmen showed any freedom was immediately after lunch (61 for two wickets) when they scored 23 off four overs from Mansell.

South Africa badly needed another reliable slow bowler; instead Cheetham was compelled to rely on Heine who maintained a hostile attack for one and three-quarter hours in conjunction with the persistent Tayfield. After Graveney left, May and Compton added only 26 runs in eighty minutes before tea, and Compton when 10 was dropped in the gully by Keith off Heine.

Despite severe pain from his swollen knee and his inability to move freely, Compton by staying two and a quarter hours while the fourth wicket added 62, gave his captain valuable assistance. This was appreciated later for after Compton left England lost four wickets in the last hour for only 38 more runs. So the end of the third day found England 195 for eight, the outcome of six hours at the crease, and next morning South Africa disposed of Lock and Statham, both lbw, for nine more runs. May took out his bat for 89, having defied the opposition for five hours; he hit ten 4's. In each of his four second innings in this series—England batted only once at Trent Bridge—May had carried his side with scores of 112 at Lord's, 117 at Manchester, 97 at Leeds and 89 not out at The Oval.

As England used the heavy roller first thing, Cheetham preferred to have the pitch only swept before South Africa began their task of scoring 244 to win. Compton, who had no runner when batting, could not field and Morgan (Derbyshire) acted as substitute. At the end of half an hour Close missed Goddard off Bailey at first slip and England took fifty-five minutes to separate the opening pair by which time Laker and Lock were in charge of the attack.

The whole outlook changed when in the course of eighteen balls England gained four wickets. South Africa's collapse began in Lock's third over when Goddard was caught at first slip and May when off a forward short-leg held a hot catch from Keith at the third attempt. These sudden reverses may have accounted for the panic methods adopted by Endean and McLean; both tried to sweep Laker and were lbw. In marked contrast, Waite arrived cool and collected and using his feet he displayed the value of the forward stroke down the line of the ball.

As McGlew was still there, South Africa were not yet without hope, but soon after lunch (57 for four) McGlew went right back on his wicket and was lbw, and, well as Waite continued to play, England's success now appeared to be only a matter of time. Three more missed catches prolonged the issue. A partnership between Waite and Mansell lasted eighty minutes, but after a brief rest Lock and Laker changed ends, and in quick succession Mansell lofted a drive to cover and Waite, with nine boundaries in a splendid innings of two and a half hours, was surprised by a turning ball which just nudged his off stump. Then came a few bold hits by Fuller and Heine before this splendidly-fought match ended with Graveney taking a skier from Heine on the long-on boundary.

So Laker and Lock repeated their success of 1953 when they wrested the Ashes from Australia on this familiar Oval pitch. As on that occasion the turf never crumbled, nor did the ball lift. Laker turned the ball only slightly, much the same as Tayfield, but Lock moved it sharply from leg. Altogether 100,000 people attended during the four days.   N. P.

England

J. T. Ikin c Waite b Heine	17	— c Goddard b Heine	0
D. B. Close c Mansell b Goddard	32	— b Goddard	15
P. B. H. May c Goddard b Fuller	3	— not out	89
D. C. S. Compton c Waite b Goddard	30	— c Waite b Fuller	30
W. Watson c Mansell b Tayfield	25	— b Fuller	3
T. W. Graveney c Fuller b Goddard	13	— b Tayfield	42
T. E. Bailey c Heine b Tayfield	0	— lbw b Tayfield	1
R. T. Spooner b Tayfield	0	— b Tayfield	0
J. C. Laker c and b Goddard	2	— b Tayfield	12
G. A. R. Lock c McLean b Goddard	18	— lbw b Heine	1
J. B. Statham not out	4	— lbw b Tayfield	0
B 2, l-b 5	7	B 4, l-b 6, n-b 1	11

1/51 2/59 3/69 4/105 5/117 6/117   151   1/5 2/30 3/95 4/157 5/165   204
7/118 8/123 9/130   6/166 7/170 8/188 9/197

South Africa

D. J. McGlew c Spooner b Statham	30	— lbw b Lock	19
T. L. Goddard lbw b Bailey	8	— c Graveney b Lock	20
H. J. Keith b Lock	5	— c May b Lock	0
W. R. Endean c Ikin b Lock	0	— lbw b Laker	0
R. A. McLean b Lock	1	— lbw b Laker	0
J. H. B. Waite c Lock b Laker	28	— b Laker	60
J. E. Cheetham not out	12	— lbw b Laker	9
P. N. F. Mansell lbw b Laker	6	— c Watson b Lock	9
H. J. Tayfield b Statham	4	— not out	10
E. R. H. Fuller c Spooner b Lock	5	— run out	16
P. Heine run out	5	— c Graveney b Laker	7
L-b 7, n-b 1	8	L-b 1	1

1/22 2/29 3/31 4/33 5/77 6/77 7/86   112   1/28 2/28 3/29 4/33 5/59   151
8/91 9/98   6/88 7/118 8/118 9/144

South Africa Bowling

	O.	M.	R.	W.		O.	M.	R.	W.
Heine	21	3	43	1	....	25	6	44	2
Goddard	22.4	9	31	5	....	19	10	29	1
Fuller	27	11	31	1	....	20	3	36	2
Tayfield	19	7	39	3	....	53.4	29	60	5
Mansell						6	0	24	0

England Bowling

	O.	M.	R.	W.		O.	M.	R.	W.
Statham	15	3	31	2	....	11	4	17	0
Bailey	5	1	6	1	....	6	1	15	0
Lock	22	11	39	4	....	33	14	62	4
Laker	23	13	28	2	....	37.4	18	56	5

Umpires: D. Davies and T. J. Bartley.

HAMPSHIRE v. SOUTH AFRICANS

At Southampton, August 20, 22, 23. South Africans won by 275 runs. This was a splendid match and, although beaten, Hampshire, thanks to some fine all-round cricket by Shackleton, at times extended the touring team, but in the end the splendid off-spin bowling of Tayfield left the visitors undisputed winners. Taking eight wickets for 40—his best performance of the tour—Tayfield saw the South Africans safely home before lunch on the third day. His full match analysis was 14 wickets for 126. As many as thirteen 6's were hit on Monday, when Shackleton drove Tayfield three times over the boundary in one over. The South Africans scored 302 in three and a half hours, Winslow getting 87 in sixty-seven minutes with five 6's and ten 4's as his chief strokes. Heine, whose first innings 58 contained two 6's and nine 4's, hit 54 in the last half-hour.

South Africans

D. J. McGlew b Burden	81	— b Shackleton	8
T. L. Goddard c Rogers b Cannings	0	— lbw b Shackleton	77
W. R. Endean b Shackleton	7	— c Rayment b Sainsbury	46
C. A. R. Duckworth lbw b Shackleton	0	— not out	2
R. A. McLean c Cannings b Burden	75	— b Sainsbury	22
J. H. B. Waite c Harrison b Burden	1		
A. R. A. Murray b Sainsbury	14	— c Sainsbury b Gray	0
P. L. Winslow c and b Shackleton	13	— c Rogers b Sainsbury	87
H. J. Tayfield c Sainsbury b Burden	5		
P. Heine b Shackleton	58	— b Gray	54
V. I. Smith not out	1		
B 4	4	B 2, 1-b 4	6
	259	(7 wkts., dec.)	302

1/0 2/19 3/19 4/127 5/141 6/182 7/182 8/195 9/230

1/10 2/94 3/216 4/242 5/291 6/292 7/302

Hampshire

J. R. Gray b Heine	0	— b Tayfield	15
R. E. Marshall c Waite b Tayfield	37	— b Tayfield	38
H. Horton run out	2	— b Tayfield	2
A. W. H. Rayment lbw b Smith	11	— c Waite b Goddard	0
N. H. Rogers c Duckworth b Heine	2	— c and b Tayfield	7
H. M. Barnard b Tayfield	1	— b Tayfield	29
L. Harrison c McLean b Tayfield	43	— not out	17
P. J. Sainsbury c Goddard b Tayfield	1	— c Goddard b Tayfield	0
D. Shackleton c and b Tayfield	50	— b Tayfield	3
V. H. D. Cannings b Tayfield	4	— b Tayfield	2
M. D. Burden not out	10	— b Smith	0
B 3, 1-b 2	5	B 5, 1-b 2	7
	166		120

1/1 2/9 3/40 4/55 5/55 6/63 7/67 8/131 9/149

1/45 2/54 3/57 4/59 5/76 6/99 7/99 8/113 9/115

Hampshire Bowling

	O.	M.	R.	W.		O.	M.	R.	W.
Shackleton	21.3	4	66	4	....	19	3	61	2
Cannings	20	6	69	1	....	1	1	0	0
Gray	9	6	6	0	....	11.3	2	26	2
Sainsbury	22	12	46	1	....	23	4	111	3
Burden	28	12	68	4	....	11	2	52	0
					Marshall	8	1	46	0

South Africans Bowling

	O.	M.	R.	W.		O.	M.	R.	W.
Heine	20	5	47	2	....	4	1	12	0
Goddard	10	5	13	0	....	18	5	44	1
Tayfield	29.1	10	86	6	....	19	9	40	8
Smith	6	0	15	1	....	4.4	1	17	1

Umpires: F. S. Lee and A. E. Pothecary.

KENT v. SOUTH AFRICANS

At Canterbury, August 24, 25, 26. South Africans won by eight wickets with ten minutes to spare, after being given a much harder fight than at one time seemed likely. Fine weather and a fast, true pitch made conditions ideal for batting throughout the three days, and on the first the South Africans took full advantage by averaging nearly 80 runs an hour. McGlew completely mastered Kent's moderate bowling for four and a quarter hours in equalling his highest score of the summer, and Cheetham completed his only century of the tour. At times, Dixon bowled off-breaks well, but generally Kent's work in the field was below standard. Apart from Wilson, who played delightfully, their first innings also disappointed. After following-on 292 behind, however, they gave a much more determined display. Fagg and Phebey both scored freely off the erratic Adcock, and shared the first century opening-partnership against the touring team. After their dismissals at the same score Hearn led Kent's resistance bravely and in the end the South Africans were left only thirty-three minutes in which to score 23 for victory.

South Africans

D. J. McGlew c Catt b Dixon	161		
J. H. B. Waite c and b Dixon	41	— not out	9
H. J. Keith c Catt b Spanswick	12	— c and b Allan	0
R. A. McLean c Fagg b Dixon	14		
J. E. Cheetham lbw b Disbury	112		
P. L. Winslow c Fagg b Allan	57	— c and b Dixon	3
P. N. F. Mansell lbw b Disbury	12		
A. R. A. Murray not out	19	— not out	10
H. J. Tayfield b Dixon	10		
E. R. H. Fuller not out	13		
B 9, l-b 7	16	B 3	3

1/99 2/139 3/165 4/318 (8 wkts., dec.) 467 1/6 2/9 (2 wkts.) 25
5/409 6/417 7/424 8/448

N. A. T. Adcock did not bat.

Kent

A. E. Fagg c Waite b Adcock	20	— c Mansell b Murray	64
A. H. Phebey c Waite b Murray	21	— b Tayfield	48
R. C. Wilson c Cheetham b Mansell	70	— b Murray	19
J. M. Allan c Winslow b Adcock	17	— c Fuller b Tayfield	0
J. Pettiford c Waite b Adcock	5	— c and b Tayfield	35
P. Hearn c Waite b Mansell	16	— c McLean b Mansell	79
B. E. Disbury c Cheetham b Tayfield	4	— b Murray	15
A. Dixon st Waite b Mansell	5	— b Mansell	6
A. W. Catt not out	8	— not out	19
J. Spanswick c Winslow b Tayfield	2	— lbw b Tayfield	19
D. V. P. Wright lbw b Mansell	0	— c and b Tayfield	4
L-b 4, w 1, n-b 2	7	B 4, l-b 2	6

1/34 2/59 3/99 4/116 5/143 6/160   175
7/160 8/166 9/175

1/114 2/114 3/121 4/137   314
5/196 6/248 7/259 8/274
9/306

Kent Bowling

	O.	M.	R.	W.	O.	M.	R.	W.
Spanswick	18	1	84	1				
Disbury	15	0	76	2				
Wright	13	3	40	0				
Allan	35	7	100	1	3.2	0	10	1
Dixon	25	4	122	4	4	0	12	1
Pettiford	5	0	29	0				

South Africans Bowling

	O.	M.	R.	W.	O.	M.	R.	W.
Adcock	16	3	39	3	15	1	59	0
Fuller	5	0	18	0	22	5	54	0
Tayfield	23	9	56	2	43.5	20	76	5
Murray	9	5	15	1	31	15	50	3
Mansell	20.5	5	40	4	27	6	69	2

Umpires: F. Chester and K. McCanlis.

MIDDLESEX v. SOUTH AFRICANS

At Lord's, August 27, 29, 30. South Africans won by 235 runs, after Middlesex collapsed against the pace of Heine and the leg-spin of Smith. On their last appearance at Lord's, the South Africans faded away after a sound, rather than brilliant opening partnership of 128 between Endean and Goddard, the later batsmen falling to the sustained accuracy of Titmus, who bowled off-breaks steadily from half an hour before lunch until the close of the innings at 5.35 p.m. Middlesex scored 32 without loss before the close, but their fortunes slumped against the devastating pace of Heine before lunch on Monday. In 12.2 overs Heine captured seven wickets at a cost of 48 runs and Middlesex narrowly avoided following on, the South Africans beginning their second innings 146 ahead. Once again Titmus proved the county's most successful bowler, and when he captured Cheetham's wicket he established a new bowling record for Middlesex, surpassing A. E. Trott's 154 in 1900. McLean provided the only innings of note in this second venture, hitting nine 4's in an attractive display. Middlesex, left to get 334 to win in seven hours, never looked like accomplishing the task. Few of the batsmen shaped confidently against the accurate leg spin of Smith, and the match ended soon after lunch on the third day.

South Africans

W. R. Endean b Titmus	75	— b Titmus	39
T. L. Goddard c L. Compton b Titmus..	56	— c Edrich b Warr	0
C. A. R. Duckworth b Titmus	1	— b Moss	10
J. H. B. Waite lbw b Young	24	— c and b Titmus	12
R. A. McLean run out	26	— c Warr b Young	58
P. L. Winslow b Young	11	— c D. Compton b Titmus	6
J. E. Cheetham b Titmus	1	— c Robertson b Titmus	5
H. J. Tayfield lbw b Titmus	14	— not out	13
P. Heine c Robertson b Young	30	— c sub b Titmus	10
E. R. H. Fuller b Titmus	4	— st L. Compton b Young	15
V. I. Smith not out	0	— c L. Compton b Young	0
B 6, l-b 5, w 1	12	B 11, l-b 6, n-b 2	19

1/128 2/134 3/147 4/193 5/196 6/205   **254**
7/207 8/236 9/254

1/4 2/26 3/58 4/79   **187**
5/119 6/133 7/141 8/163
9/187

Middlesex

J. D. Robertson c Fuller b Heine	44	— c Tayfield b Heine	9
J. G. Dewes hit wkt b Heine	17	— c Tayfield b Smith	12
W. J. Edrich c Tayfield b Heine	16	— c Waite b Heine	25
D. C. S. Compton st Waite b Tayfield ..	8	— b Smith	20
G. P. S. Delisle c Smith b Heine	0	— c Cheetham b Smith	0
F. J. Titmus run out	0	— c Goddard b Tayfield	7
H. W. Tilly c Tayfield b Heine	0	— st Waite b Smith	0
L. H. Compton c Waite b Heine	4	— b Tayfield	1
J. J. Warr b Tayfield	6	— b Tayfield	6
J. A. Young b Heine	10	— not out	9
A. E. Moss not out	0	— c Winslow b Smith	5
B 1, l-b 1	2	B 1, l-b 2, n-b 1	4

1/36 2/70 3/84 4/86 5/87 6/88   **108**
7/88 8/94 9/106

1/27 2/45 3/52 4/60 5/77   **98**
6/77 7/77 8/82 9/85

Middlesex Bowling

	O.	M.	R.	W.		O.	M.	R.	W.
Moss	12	1	36	0	....	9	1	22	1
Warr	11	2	28	0	....	7	2	14	1
Tilly	18	3	51	0	....	5	0	16	0
Titmus	38	18	65	6	....	24	9	54	5
Young	21.1	7	62	3	....	18	3	62	3

South Africans Bowling

	O.	M.	R.	W.		O.	M.	R.	W.
Heine	18.2	3	60	7	....	17	6	36	2
Goddard	7	3	13	0	....	20	15	12	0
Tayfield	14	3	32	2	....	12	5	19	3
Smith	3	2	1	0	....	15.4	7	27	5

Umpires: L. H. Gray and A. Skelding.

AN ENGLAND XI v. SOUTH AFRICANS

At Hastings, August 31, September 1, 2. Drawn. The South Africans batted moderately in the first innings on a well-grassed pitch. Young began so freely for the England team that his 45 contained nine 4's, but five wickets were down for 117. Then Spooner, with cuts and drives, attacked the bowling freely for an hour and Wooller defended stubbornly, so that the South Africans went in again 53 behind. They cleared the arrears without loss, and on the last day

McLean played a dashing innings, scoring 79, including one 6 and thirteen 4's, out of 110 in seventy-five minutes. Cheetham delayed the declaration so long that the England side, set 235 to get, were in no real danger, though several wickets were thrown away by careless strokes.

South Africans

D. J. McGlew b Wooller	20	— c Gardner b Wooller	47
T. L. Goddard run out	7	— b Statham	32
H. J. Keith run out	60	— lbw b Statham	24
W. R. Endean c Spooner b Wooller	7	— c Parkhouse b Wooller	13
R. A. McLean c Wooller b Tyson	30	— lbw b Statham	79
J. H. B. Waite b Tyson	1	— b Statham	12
J. E. Cheetham b Statham	7	— not out	41
P. N. F. Mansell lbw b Wooller	17	— b Tyson	19
A. R. A. Murray b Wooller	3	— b Mortimore	10
H. J. Tayfield not out	3	— b Mortimore	4
P. Heine c Statham b Tattersall	1		
B 5, l-b 4	9	B 6	6

1/11 2/37 3/49 4/81 5/83 6/107   165   1/72 2/99   (9 wkts., dec.) 287
7/149 8/161 9/164   3/106 4/120 5/189 6/216
                                                 7/252 8/275 9/287

An England XI

D. M. Young c Keith b Heine	45	— c Goddard b Tayfield	26
F. C. Gardner c Waite b Tayfield	15	— run out	16
W. G. A. Parkhouse run out	5	— c Goddard b Murray	1
C. A. Milton b Mansell	26	— c Mansell b Murray	0
D. Barrick c Keith b Tayfield	13	— c Endean b Murray	11
R. T. Spooner b Heine	50	— c Keith b Tayfield	5
W. Wooller c McLean b Tayfield	31	— b Endean	4
J. Mortimore b Murray	25	— not out	6
F. H. Tyson c Heine b Murray	0	— not out	3
J. B. Statham b Tayfield	0		
R. Tattersall not out	3		
B 2, l-b 3	5	L-b 5	5

1/61 2/63 3/69 4/107 5/117 6/166   218   1/46 2/47 3/47   (7 wkts.) 77
7/212 8/212 9/213   4/52 5/62 6/68 7/73

An England XI Bowling

	O.	M.	R.	W.		O.	M.	R.	W.
Tyson	15	4	29	2	....	22	3	66	1
Statham	14	2	27	1	....	15	2	43	4
Wooller	16	4	38	4	....	13	2	74	2
Tattersall	18.2	9	30	1	....	16	4	60	0
Mortimore	12	3	32	0	....	9.3	1	28	2
Barrick						2	0	10	0

South Africans Bowling

	O.	M.	R.	W.		O.	M.	R.	W.
Heine	26	4	62	2	....	10	1	31	0
Goddard	3	0	20	0	....	11	7	9	0
Murray	8	3	29	2	....	11	4	19	3
Tayfield	38.3	14	68	4	....	10	5	9	2
Mansell	14	0	34	1					
Endean						1	0	1	1
Cheetham					....	1	0	3	0

Umpires: A. E. Pothecary and K. McCanlis.

DURHAM v. SOUTH AFRICANS

At Sunderland, September 3, 5. South Africans won by an innings and 324 runs. As expected, Durham were outclassed, but the local enthusiasts thoroughly enjoyed the entertaining cricket of the first day when 621 runs were scored in five hours. After taking twenty minutes over his first three runs, Winslow reached 100 in ninety minutes and his 133 included seven 6's and thirteen 4's. Mansell was almost as powerful with his driving, and he rarely lifted the ball. He occupied only two hours and five minutes over 148, hitting one 6 and eighteen 4's. South Africans needed no more than three and a half hours to capture 15 Durham wickets on the second day, Smith causing much destruction with his accurate leg spinners.

South Africans

T. L. Goddard b K. Williamson ..	9	D. J. McGlew b K. Williamson ..	21
C. A. R. Duckworth run out	33	E. R. H. Fuller b J. Williamson ..	1
H. J. Keith run out	65	V. I. Smith c Hardy b K. Williamson	16
P. L. Winslow c Fairley b K.		N. A. T. Adcock not out	12
Williamson 133		B 4, l-b 4	8
A. R. A. Murray b Scott	36		
P. N. F. Mansell run out........148		1/31 2/53 3/120 4/204 5/308	543
W. R. Endean c Keeler b Scott ...	61	6/432 7/506 8/513 9/527	

Durham

J. G. Keeler b Adcock	2	— c Mansell b Smith.........	8
H. D. Bell c and b Smith	28	— b Murray	7
G. C. Lamb b Murray.................	1	— b Murray	10
G. M. Crawford b Adcock.............	0	— c Mansell b Smith.........	6
D. W. Hardy c Duckworth b Murray ...	45	— c Mansell b Smith.........	23
M. E. Scott c Goddard b Smith	0	— c Mansell b Goddard	16
R. Aspinall lbw b Smith	28	— c Mansell b Smith.........	9
G. F. Fairley c Mansell b Murray	1	— not out	9
K. Williamson c Winslow b Smith	1	— c Duckworth b Goddard ...	1
J. G. Williamson st Duckworth b Smith .	0	— c Adcock b Smith	2
J. G. Fox not out.....................	0	— lbw b Keith	11
B 2, l-b 3	5	B 3, l-b 3	6
			—
1/14 2/23 3/24 4/59 5/75 6/93 7/107	111	1/7 2/19 3/35 4/41 5/69	108
8/108 9/108		6/85 7/85 8/88 9/91	

Durham Bowling

	O.	M.	R.	W.	O.	M.	R.	W.
J. Williamson ..	17	2	122	1				
K. Williamson .	23.1	3	99	4				
Hardy.........	11	2	66	0				
Scott	22	3	111	2				
Aspinall	16	0	126	0				
Crawford	2	0	11	0				

South Africans Bowling

	O.	M.	R.	W.		O.	M.	R.	W.
Murray	20	11	36	3	....	13	6	20	2
Adcock	8	1	28	2	....	6	0	13	0
Fuller	2	1	6	0					
Smith	14.1	9	29	5	....	16	1	44	5
Keith	1	1	0	0	....	2	1	4	1
Goddard	1	0	7	0	....	7	4	10	2
					Winslow	3	0	11	0

Umpires: G. W. F. Reeves and A. Mitchison.

T. N. PEARCE'S XI v. SOUTH AFRICANS

At Scarborough, September 7, 8, 9. South Africans won by four wickets. They finished the tour in grand style, Cheetham, the captain, making the winning hit almost on the stroke of time with only one ball to spare. The visitors wanted 211 in two hours twenty minutes, and McGlew and Goddard set a good pace by scoring 105 in seventy-five minutes, but a collapse occurred. When McGlew, who was sixth out, left at 174, only thirteen minutes remained with 37 still needed. Cheetham and Waite turned the scales by punishing Close for 20 in one over. Earlier on the last day Graveney played brilliantly for three and a half hours, hitting one 6 and twenty-four 4's in his 159, which raised his aggregate for the Festival to 460 runs in six innings, once not out. The match also produced a splendid not out innings of 138 by Endean. He hit with great power for nearly three hours, and among his strokes were two 6's and twenty 4's. The South Africans thoroughly merited their victory if only for their grand fielding which was vastly superior to that of the opposition.

T. N. Pearce's XI

R. T. Simpson b Tayfield	17	— b Heine	5
D. B. Close c Endean b Goddard	33	— b Mansell	45
T. W. Graveney c Heine b Tayfield	37	— c McLean b Murray	159
D. C. S. Compton c Endean b Murray	27	— st Waite b Tayfield	27
W. J. Edrich c Waite b Murray	42	— b Heine	0
J. V. Wilson c Murray b Goddard	34	— c Mansell b Tayfield	4
T. E. Bailey c Mansell b Murray	16	— c and b Goddard	37
J. H. Wardle c McGlew b Goddard	17	— b Tayfield	28
G. O. Dawkes b Goddard	6	— not out	10
F. S. Trueman not out	3	— b Tayfield	0
A. V. Bedser lbw b Goddard	0	— not out	2
L-b 4	4	B 9, l-b 2	11

1/48 2/51 3/114 4/114 5/175 6/203   236   1/10 2/79   (9 wkts., dec.) 328
7/227 8/227 9/236   3/90 4/93 5/142 6/248
                                                                 7/316 8/318 9/318

South Africans

D. J. McGlew c Dawkes b Trueman	23	— b Close	75
T. L. Goddard lbw b Bedser	29	— run out	44
J. H. B. Waite b Close	20	— not out	36
W. R. Endean not out	138	— c Edrich b Trueman	1
R. A. McLean c and b Close	11	— b Close	8
P. L. Winslow c Dawkes b Close	22	— c Wardle b Close	12
J. E. Cheetham b Trueman	52	— not out	19
P. N. F. Mansell lbw b Bailey	21		
A. R. A. Murray b Bailey	10		
H. J. Tayfield b Wardle	5		
P. Heine st Dawkes b Wardle	11	— c Simpson b Wardle	7
B 12	12	B 7, l-b 2	9

1/48 2/66 3/95 4/119 5/157 6/243   354   1/105 2/106 3/123   (6 wkts.) 211
7/289 8/309 9/336   4/132 5/139 6/174

South Africans Bowling

	O.	M.	R.	W.		O.	M.	R.	W.
Heine	14	2	43	0	....	19	2	65	2
Goddard	13.2	3	30	5	....	13	3	55	1
Mansell	10	1	32	0	....	13	1	51	1
Tayfield	32	11	74	2	....	28	5	93	4
Murray	22	9	53	3	....	10	2	53	1

T. N. Pearce's XI Bowling

	O.	M.	R.	W.		O.	M.	R.	W.
Trueman	17	2	59	2	....	9	1	46	1
Bedser	20	4	79	1	....	6	0	27	0
Wardle	18.4	3	76	2	....	10.5	0	53	1
Close	16	2	94	3	....	13	2	58	3
Bailey	6	1	34	2	....	6	1	18	0

Umpires: H. G. Baldwin and Harry Elliott (Derbyshire).

CUMBERLAND AND WESTMORLAND v. SOUTH AFRICANS

At Carlisle, September 10. Drawn. South Africans 332 (R. A. McLean 83, H. J. Keith 63); Cumberland and Westmorland 104 for eight (J. Dennis 44).

THE MARYLEBONE CRICKET CLUB

PATRON—HER MAJESTY THE QUEEN

President—VISCOUNT COBHAM

President-Designate—FIELD MARSHAL EARL ALEXANDER OF TUNIS

Treasurer—H. S. ALTHAM

Secretary—R. AIRD, Lord's Cricket Ground, St. John's Wood, N.W.8

Assistant Secretaries—J. G. DUNBAR and S. C. GRIFFITH

Trustees—SIR PELHAM WARNER, CAPTAIN LORD CORNWALLIS, R. H. TWINING, LT.-COL. R. T. STANYFORTH

Committee—THE EARL OF ROSEBERY, G. C. NEWMAN, COL. SIR WILLIAM WORSLEY, Bt., M. J. C. ALLOM, G. O. SHELMERDINE, THE DUKE OF BEAUFORT, F. G. MANN, MAJOR M. F. S. JEWELL, G. O. ALLEN, E. R. T. HOLMES, COL. R. S. RAIT KERR, R. W. V. ROBINS, F. R. BROWN, A. G. DOGGART, VISCOUNT COBHAM.

M.C.C. held their 168th Annual Meeting at Lord's on May 4, when Field Marshal Earl Alexander of Tunis was nominated President-Designate in succession to Viscount Cobham, the appointment to take effect from October 1, 1955.

Col. Sir Eric Gore Brown, R. A. Boddington, Gen. Sir Ronald Adam, Bt., Hubert Ashton, W. W. Hill-Wood and Lt.-Col. Sir Terence Nugent, who retired from the Committee by rotation, were replaced by the retiring President, F. R. Brown, A. G. Doggart, Col. R. S. Rait Kerr and R. W. V. Robins.

The deaths of 154 members occurred during the preceding year, the report making special mention of Sir Henry D. G. Leveson Gower, who was knighted for his services to cricket in 1953, G. Brann, N. F. Druce, Sir George Robey, C. D. McIver, G. H. Hirst, one of the greatest all-round cricketers in history, and R. C. N. Palairet.

Membership

On December 31, 1954, the Club consisted of 7,900 members, including 37 Honorary Life Members and 314 Life Members. Members paying the Abroad List subscription numbered 385.

Honorary Life Membership

The Committee elected the Rt. Hon. R. G. Menzies, C.H., Q.C., an Honorary Life Member of the Club. L. Hutton, who captained England in Australasia, was elected an Honorary Life Member following a Special General Meeting which revised certain rules of the M.C.C. One alteration, to Rule XII (*a*), was: "That each such candidate shall be an English Professional Cricketer who has throughout his career rendered outstanding service to the game, and to the M.C.C. in particular. Save in exceptional circumstances such candidate shall have retired from First Class Cricket."

Election of Candidates

The Committee reported that they had been gravely concerned at the ever-increasing "waiting period" between a candidate's nomination and his election. With the "build up" of candidates increasing each year the period of waiting might before long extend to over forty years.

To meet the serious problem the Committee reported that they had decided to reconstruct "A" Stand as a Pavilion extension, and that they felt such provision would justify an increase of 3,000 in the membership of the Club. This would substantially reduce the "waiting period" for existing candidates. To prevent a similar "build up" on the Register in future, the Committee proposed that for an experimental period a certain restriction be placed on the nomination of candidates. For a period, a member would only be entitled to propose one candidate and second one candidate in any year. Such candidates would not be nominated before their seventeenth birthday, and proposers and seconders, in every case, would have to send with the Candidates' Forms letters testifying the candidates' active interest in the game. Approval was sought by the Committee to increase the membership of the Club from 8,000 to 11,000 and for the additional 3,000 members to be elected as soon as possible after the new Pavilion was constructed. The Committee undertook to submit a definite proposal after giving the matter further consideration.

Finance

The accounts for the year ended December 31, 1954, showed an excess of expenditure over revenue of £1,286.

Secretary's Visit to Australia

At the invitation of the New Zealand Cricket Council the Secretary paid a goodwill visit lasting two months to Australasia during the winter of 1954/5, and he reported on the high regard in which the prestige of M.C.C. was held in all the countries through which he travelled.

Youth Cricket Association

The report stated that the work of the Association continued to expand. There were thirty-four Area Youth Associations or similar bodies actively engaged in all the first-class counties, sixteen other counties and in Scotland. Since its start, nearly 7,000 school-masters and others had attended at least one coaching course. The Committee felt that the long-term impact upon the boy cricketers of the country would be considerable. Tribute was paid to the work of the Youth Council and its Secretary, Vice-Admiral E. G. N. Rushbrooke.

Arts and Library

The paid attendance in the Memorial Gallery in 1954 totalled 11,700—an increase of 1,200 on 1953. The Memorial Appeal Fund altogether realised £5,229. The Committee decided to mark the bi-centenary of the birth of Thomas Lord at Thirsk, Yorkshire, by presenting a plaque to be placed in the Thirsk Cricket Club pavilion.

M.C.C. Staff

It was reported that A. Martin, Head Groundsman at Lord's since 1936, had left the service of the Club to take up another appointment. He was succeeded by E. C. Swannell who had been at Lord's since 1923.

M.C.C. RESULTS

First-Class Matches—Played 6, *Won* 1, *Drawn* 2, *Lost* 3

Other Matches—Played 137, *Won* 77, *Drawn* 41, *Lost* 13, *Abandoned* 6

| April 27, 28 Wisbech | Wisbech Town C.C. | 132 and 172 for 8* | Drawn |
| | M.C.C. | 199 for 8* and 69 for 4 | |

* Innings declared closed.

M.C.C. v. YORKSHIRE

At Lord's, April 30, May 2, 3. Yorkshire won by an innings and 15 runs. Wilson, recovering his best form after setbacks in Australia, gave a fine display of driving and pulling. Fourteen thousand people watched his splendid batting on the opening day, and they saw Trueman, just before the close, knock out Richardson's middle stump with a very fast ball. Despite rain, Wardle and Appleyard proved too much for their rivals and their skilful spin bowling did most to finish the match by just after three o'clock on the third day. M.C.C. were well served in the closing stages by Ikin and Titmus, but Yorkshire were too strong. For the first time the experimental smaller ball was used in a match.

Yorkshire

F. A. Lowson b Warr	48	R. Booth not out	9
W. H. H. Sutcliffe lbw b Watkins	44	F. S. Trueman b Bennett	10
J. V. Wilson c Watkins b Titmus	89	R. Appleyard not out	4
D. B. Close c Andrew b Marlar	27	B 5, l-b 6	11
W. Watson b Bennett	12		
E. Lester c Parks b Warr	14	1/87 2/107 3/166 (9 wkts., dec.) 285	
N. W. D. Yardley c Parks b Titmus	17	4/199 5/216 6/256 7/258 8/262	
J. H. Wardle c Ikin b Titmus	0	9/277	

M.C.C.

D. Kenyon lbw b Wardle	14	— c Wilson b Wardle	21
P. E. Richardson b Trueman	1	— c Trueman b Wardle	3
K. V. Andrew b Wardle	13	— c Wilson b Wardle	10
J. T. Ikin c Wilson b Appleyard	27	— c Wardle b Appleyard	41
J. M. Parks lbw b Trueman	3	— b Close	2
A. J. Watkins c and b Wardle	27	— b Appleyard	19
D. B. Carr c Wilson b Appleyard	2	— c Yardley b Wardle	12
D. Bennett b Wardle	7	— b Appleyard	4
F. J. Titmus not out	3	— b Trueman	23
J. J. Warr c Wilson b Wardle	2	— b Wardle	2
R. G. Marlar c Trueman b Appleyard	1	— not out	11
B 8, l-b 1, n-b 1	10	B 8, l-b 1, n-b 3	12

1/3 2/24 3/41 4/54 5/85 6/87   110   1/23 2/24 3/33 4/76   160
7/96 8/105 9/109   5/97 6/113 7/113 8/122 9/146

M.C.C. Bowling

	O.	M.	R.	W.	O.	M.	R.	W.
Warr	22	3	50	2				
Bennett	24	5	49	2				
Watkins	25	6	66	1				
Marlar	15	2	57	1				
Titmus	22	9	49	3				
Ikin	3	0	3	0				

Yorkshire Bowling

	O.	M.	R.	W.	O.	M.	R.	W.
Trueman	18	7	34	2	8.5	1	25	1
Appleyard	20.2	6	32	3	20	9	28	3
Wardle	28	13	34	5	31	14	70	5
Close					9	2	25	1

Umpires: E. G. Canning and G. Morton.

M.C.C. v. SURREY

At Lord's, May 4, 5, 6. Surrey won by seven wickets. The experimental smaller ball was again employed, but as in the previous game, against Yorkshire, bowlers thought it made little difference to their effectiveness. The spin bowlers, particularly Laker and Lock, took their opportunities on damp turf, but both owed a good deal to smart catching. May played the best innings. He met the rising ball surely and excelled with a flashing square-drive. Surrey raced the rain on the last day and won before lunch. Wardle pulled a ball from Bedser over the Tavern score box and out into the road, but Laker took the four remaining M.C.C. wickets for eight runs out of 27, and Surrey hit off the 54 runs wanted in an hour. Laker had match figures of 11 for 67.

M.C.C.

R. T. Simpson c McIntyre b Lock	18	— b Bedser	19
P. E. Richardson b Bedser	0	— c McIntyre b Laker	2
C. A. Milton b Bedser	19	— c Clark b Laker	3
J. M. Parks c McIntyre b Laker	9	— c and b Lock	5
C. H. Palmer c Fletcher b Lock	0	— c May b Lock	12
D. J. Insole b Lock	3	— b Laker	12
A. S. M. Oakman c and b Laker	0	— c Surridge b Lock	0
L. Harrison b Laker	23	— b Laker	12
D. C. Morgan b Laker	41	— c Surridge b Laker	0
J. H. Wardle c Barrington b Laker	0	— c Bedser b Laker	15
J. D. Bannister not out	1	— not out	2
B 5, l-b 7, n-b 3	15	B 1	1

1/1 2/40 3/54 4/56 5/65 6/65   129   1/22 2/24 3/26 4/41   83
7/65 8/127 9/127   5/42 6/42 7/57 8/58 9/77

Surrey

T. H. Clark b Morgan	4	— not out	21
D. G. W. Fletcher c Simpson b Palmer	33	— c Palmer b Bannister	12
P. B. H. May c Parks b Wardle	71	— c Palmer b Bannister	1
B. Constable lbw b Wardle	10	— lbw b Wardle	6
K. Barrington b Bannister	14	— not out	15
A. J. McIntyre b Wardle	7		
J. C. Laker c Harrison b Bannister	0		
W. S. Surridge c Harrison b Bannister	2		
G. A. R. Lock, c Milton b Bannister	1		
A. V. Bedser b Wardle	1		
P. J. Loader not out	8		
B 8	8		

1/11 2/57 3/90 4/131 5/142 6/143   159   1/17 2/19 3/26   (3 wkts.) 55
7/143 8/144 9/151

Surrey Bowling

	O.	M.	R.	W.		O.	M.	R.	W.
Bedser	19	9	37	2	....	13	5	34	1
Loader	4	2	9	0	....	3	0	10	0
Lock	12	3	29	3	....	9	5	10	3
Laker	12.4	1	39	5	....	18.3	6	28	6

M.C.C. Bowling

	O.	M.	R.	W.		O.	M.	R.	W.
Bannister	14	4	26	4	....	10	4	35	2
Morgan	10	4	22	1	....	2	0	4	0
Oakman	12	2	51	0					
Wardle	23.4	7	50	4	....	8	4	10	1
Palmer	2	1	2	1					
Parks						0.2	0	6	0

Umpires: E. G. Canning and W. Harrington.

May 7 Motspur Park	B.B.C. Club M.C.C.	166 167 for 3	Won by seven wickets
May 14 Motspur Park	Univ. of London C.C. M.C.C.	234 127 for 6	Drawn
May 18 Chigwell	M.C.C. Chigwell School	135 105	Won by 30 runs

M.C.C. v. CLUB CRICKET CONFERENCE

At Lord's, May 18, 19. Drawn. M.C.C. 116 for seven wickets, declared, and 177 for three wickets, declared (R. Subba Row 77, C. J. Poole 60 not out); Club Cricket Conference 163 for eight wickets, declared (G. Downton 52 not out, D. Bennett four for 44) and 85 for six wickets. Tyson, of Northamptonshire, playing for M.C.C., took two wickets for 18 in 14 overs and one for 25 in seven overs.

May 19 Repton	M.C.C. Repton School	159 for 4* 124 for 5	Drawn

At Lord's, May 21, 23, 24. M.C.C. lost to SOUTH AFRICANS by 93 runs. (See SOUTH AFRICAN section.)

May 21 Framlingham	M.C.C. Framlingham College	— —	Abandoned (rain)
May 21 Rugby	Rugby School M.C.C.	98 99 for 6	Won by four wickets

* Innings declared closed.

May 24 Malvern	Malvern College M.C.C.	130 131 for 0	Won by ten wickets
May 24 Cricklewood	M.C.C. University College Sch.	172 for 8* 53	Won by 119 runs
May 24 Winchester	M.C.C. Winchester College	230 for 6* 159	Won by 71 runs

M.C.C. v. R.M.A. (Sandhurst)

At Lord's May 25, 26. Drawn. M.C.C. 214 (S. T. Smail six for 71) and 196 for five wickets declared (M. J. Hardy 72 not out, A. G. Skinner 58); R.M.A. Sandhurst 222 (J. G. Willcox 58) and 117 for seven wickets.

May 25 Highgate	Highgate School M.C.C.	80 81 for 3	Won by seven wickets
May 25 Croydon	Whitgift School M.C.C.	147 153 for 5	Won by five wickets
May 26 Eastbourne	M.C.C. Eastbourne College	221 for 6* 171 for 6	Drawn
May 26 Harrow	M.C.C. Harrow School	222 for 10* (12-a-side) 179 for 6	Drawn
May 27 Brentwood	M.C.C. Brentwood School	— —	Abandoned (rain)
May 27 Wellington	M.C.C. Wrekin College	169 for 5* 60	Won by 109 runs
May 28 Berkhamsted	M.C.C. Berkhamsted School	—	Abandoned (rain)
May 28 Cheltenham	Cheltenham College M.C.C.	117 119 for 4	Won by six wickets
May 28 Radley	M.C.C. Radley College	— —	Abandoned (rain)
May 28 Shrewsbury	M.C.C. Shrewsbury School	— —	Abandoned (rain)
May 28 Cambridge	M.C.C. The Leys School	206 for 5* 92	Won by 114 runs
May 30 Old Windsor	Beaumont College M.C.C.	136 140 for 5	Won by five wickets
May 31 Canterbury	M.C.C. King's School	229 for 7* 117 for 8	Drawn
May 31 Shoreham	Lancing College M.C.C.	195 196 for 8	Won by two wickets
May 31 Oxford	M.C.C. St. Edward's School	245 for 5* 163 for 6	Drawn
June 1 Northwood	M.C.C. Merchant Taylors' Sch.	235 for 3* 99	Won by 136 runs
June 1 Monkton Combe	M.C.C. Monkton Combe Sch.	187 for 6* 53	Won by 134 runs
June 1 Catford	St. Dunstan's College M.C.C.	140 141 for 9	Won by one wicket
June 1 Stonyhurst	Stonyhurst College M.C.C.	179 181 for 6	Won by four wickets

* Innings declared closed.

M.C.C. v. GLOUCESTERSHIRE

At Lord's, June 1, 2, 3. M.C.C. won by eight wickets, thanks to a fine innings of 92 by H. E. Dollery and some capable spin bowling by Illingworth, Clarke of West Indies, and Card. The last named was making his first appearance in first-class cricket. Three splendid return catches also helped to check Gloucestershire on the first day and on Thursday, Dollery, with three 6's and eight 4's, gave a grand display. He made his runs in just over two hours, a fine stand with Illingworth yielding 106 in seventy minutes. Facing a deficit of 94, Gloucestershire lost half their wickets before the close for 128, but on Friday Mortimore hit freely, the sixth wicket adding 48 before the tail fell to the left arm slows of Card whose match analysis was six for 43. M.C.C. wanted only 108 and Sharp, who batted with a runner because of lameness, hit ten 4's in a brisk innings which provided an entertaining finish.

Gloucestershire

D. M. Young	c and b Clarke	56	— c Moss b Bannister		12
C. A. Milton	c and b Illingworth	31	— c Illingworth b Moss		39
T. W. Graveney	b Illingworth	20	— b Bannister		2
J. F. Crapp	c and b Card	45	— c Dollery b Card		42
R. B. Nicholls	c Horner b Card	12	— c and b Illingworth		3
J. Mortimore	b Clarke	0	— c Thompson b Illingworth		43
G. E. Lambert	b Clarke	6	— b Illingworth		17
P. Rochford	not out	15	— c Dollery b Card		10
C. Cook	c and b Clarke	1	— not out		10
B. D. Wells	b Bannister	19	— c Thompson b Card		13
F. P. McHugh	b Moss	0	— c Moss b Card		0
	B 4, l-b 3, n-b 1	8	B 3, l-b 5 n-b 2		10

1/52 2/83 3/143 4/157 5/158 6/168   213   1/18 2/43 3/91 4/102   201
7/172 8/177 9/211   5/116 6/164 7/167 8/177
                                             9/201

M.C.C.

N. F. Horner	c Rochford b McHugh	47			
H. P. Sharp	lbw b Cook	27	— not out		68
A. Thompson	c Milton b Mortimore	3	— b McHugh		2
R. E. Bird	lbw b Cook	52	— not out		21
H. E. Dollery	c Nicholls b Wells	92			
R. Illingworth	c Milton b Mortimore	39			
H. W. Stephenson	c Cook b Mortimore	7			
A. J. Card	not out	15	— c Milton b Wells		10
C. B. Clarke	b Cook	6			
A. E. Moss	not out	6			
	B 8, l-b 4, n-b 1	13	B 6, l-b 3		9

1/49 2/58 3/108 4/164   (8 wkts., dec.) 307   1/4 2/34   (2 wkts.) 110
5/270 6/271 7/282 8/301

J. D. Bannister did not bat.

M.C.C. Bowling

	O.	M.	R.	W.	O.	M.	R.	W.
Bannister	13	2	32	1	18	4	39	2
Moss	15.4	1	50	1	15	2	50	1
Illingworth	18	9	30	2	11	3	30	3
Clarke	35	2	76	4	8	1	46	0
Card	12	2	17	2	4.4	1	26	4

Gloucestershire Bowling

	O.	M.	R.	W.	O.	M.	R.	W.
Lambert	20	1	79	0	9	2	19	0
McHugh	21	2	58	1	11	1	30	1
Mortimore.....	19.1	3	53	3	1	0	4	0
Cook	28	7	60	3	3	0	11	0
Wells	18	3	44	1	9	4	20	1
Graveney					3.4	0	17	0

Umpires: E. G. Canning and G. Morton.

June 2 Godalming	Charterhouse School M.C.C.	160 161 for 7	Won by three wickets
June 2 Stratton-on-Fosse	M.C.C. Downside School	166 170 for 5	Lost by five wickets
June 2 Mill Hill	M.C.C. Mill Hill School	163 for 7* 107 for 7	Drawn
June 4 Elstree	Aldenham School M.C.C.	137 111	Lost by 26 runs
June 4 Felsted	M.C.C. Felsted School	206 180 for 7	Drawn
June 4 Hertford	Haileybury & I.S.C. M.C.C.	120 124 for 7	Won by three wickets
June 4 Oundle	Oundle School M.C.C.	55 56 for 1	Won by nine wickets
June 4 Buckingham	M.C.C. Stowe School	136 105	Won by 31 runs
June 6 Dulwich	Alleyn's School M.C.C.	128 131 for 2	Won by eight wickets
June 6 Devizes	Dauntsey's School M.C.C.	98 99 for 1	Won by nine wickets
June 7 Sherborne	M.C.C. Sherborne School	199 142 for 9	Drawn
June 8 Wellington	M.C.C. Wellington School	146 121	Won by 25 runs
June 9 Blandford	M.C.C. Bryanston School	180 for 7* 107 for 7	Drawn
June 10 Taunton	M.C.C. Queen's College	200 for 7* 152	Won by 48 runs
June 11 Bath	Prior Park College M.C.C.	142 12 for 0	Drawn (rain)
June 7 Bishop's Stortford	M.C.C. Bishop's Stortford Coll.	137 for 7* 75 for 5	Drawn
June 7 Cranleigh	M.C.C. Cranleigh School	132 for 6* 134 for 5	Lost by five wickets
June 8 Horsham	Christ's Hospital M.C.C.	101 102 for 1	Won by nine wickets
June 9 Sedbergh	M.C.C. Sedbergh School	195 123 for 9	Drawn
June 9 Vincent Square	M.C.C. Westminster School	133 for 6* 127 for 8	Drawn

* Innings declared closed.

June 10 Weybridge	St. George's College M.C.C.	207 208 for 5	Won by five wickets
June 11 Dulwich	Dulwich College M.C.C.	214 for 3* 180	Lost by 34 runs
June 11 Eton	M.C.C. Eton College	222 for 5* 208 for 6	Drawn
June 11 Holt	Gresham's School M.C.C.	222 for 9* 169 for 9	Drawn
June 13 Beddington Park	Beddington C.C. M.C.C.	243 for 8* 124 for 8	Drawn
June 14 Ampleforth	M.C.C. Ampleforth College	— —	Abandoned (rain)
June 14 Banbury	M.C.C. Bloxham School	118 (12-a-side) 90 for 10	Drawn
June 14 Crouch End	M.C.C. Hornsey C.C.	169 103	Won by 66 runs
June 15 Lee	M.C.C. City of London School	193 for 7* 51	Won by 142 runs
June 15 Mill Hill	M.C.C. Haberdashers' School	181 for 7* 57	Won by 124 runs
June 15 York	St. Peter's School M.C.C.	202 83	Lost by 119 runs

* Innings declared closed.

M.C.C. v. OXFORD UNIVERSITY

At Lord's, June 15, 16, 17. Drawn. The finish was disappointing with Oxford unable to score 276 for victory in three and three-quarter hours, but much of the cricket proved of high interest. Cowdrey, on his first first-class appearance of the season, looked as good as ever, and his match aggregate reached 148. He drove and cut superbly while making his century in three hours. Bennett and Tilly added 106 for M.C.C.'s tenth wicket on the first day and both bowled well at medium-fast pace. Allan showed good all-round form for the University and in the first innings he and Smith, who drove forcefully for a splendid 118, began with a partnership of 167.

M.C.C.

D. E. Blake c and b Arenhold	14 —	c Allen b Phillips 21
B. H. Lock b Arenhold.................	10 —	c Walshe b Phillips 0
A. L. Dowding c Walton b Allan	38 —	c Metcalfe b Phillips....... 2
M. C. Cowdrey c Walton b Allan.......	47 —	b Allan 101
W. Murray Wood b Jowett	1 —	b Phillips 8
D. Bennett c Walshe b Fellows-Smith ...	84 —	c Allan b Phillips 31
F. J. Titmus c Gibson b Allan..........	0 —	not out 25
P. Cranmer c Walton b Allan	0 —	st Walshe b Allan 45
R. V. C. Robins b Allan...............	17 —	st Walshe b Jowett 1
J. D. P. Tanner c Fellows-Smith b Jowett	3	
H. W. Tilly not out	49 —	c Walshe b Allan ...., 19
B 4, l-b 6, w 1	11	B 14, l-b 5 19

1/24 2/25 3/97 4/100 5/118 6/118   274   1/2 2/20 3/31 (9 wkts., dec.)272
7/118 8/157 9/168   4/61 5/154 6/192 7/205
                                             8/265 9/272

Oxford University

M. J. K. Smith b Bennett	118	—	b Bennett	14
J. M. Allan b Titmus	47	—	c Tanner b Bennett	59
S. G. Metcalfe b Bennett	0	—	b Bennett	0
A. C. Walton c Lock b Titmus	4	—	c Titmus b Bennett	46
G. P. S. Delisle b Bennett	2	—	c Lock b Robins	35
I. Gibson c Tanner b Tilly	33	—	not out	52
J. P. Fellows-Smith lbw b Tilly	52	—	st Tanner b Titmus	5
J. A. Arenhold b Tilly	9			
A. P. Walshe lbw b Tilly	0	—	not out	15
D. C. P. R. Jowett lbw b Titmus	1			
J. B. Phillips not out	1			
(L-b 3, w 1)	4		B 9, l-b 3	12

1/167 2/167 3/167 4/173 5/175 6/248　　271　　　1/18 2/18 3/115　(6 wkts.) 238
7/268 8/268 9/269　　　　　　　　　　　　　　　4/140 5/149 6/182

Oxford University Bowling

	O.	M.	R.	W.		O.	M.	R.	W.
Arenhold	15	2	58	2	....	13	2	38	0
Phillips	18	6	57	0	....	25	7	62	5
Fellows-Smith	16.2	5	43	1	....	12	4	30	0
Allan	34	15	51	5	....	25	4	83	3
Jowett	18	7	40	2	....	12	2	40	1
Gibson	4	1	14	0					

M.C.C. Bowling

Bennett	23	3	67	3	....	21	5	50	4
Tilly	24	6	49	4	....	16	1	56	0
Titmus	37	10	101	3	....	20	7	59	1
Robins	6	0	36	0	....	12	2	37	1
Murray Wood	5	2	14	0	....	8	1	17	0
					Cowdrey	1	0	7	0

Umpires: E. G. Canning and W. Harrington.

June 16 Bedford	M.C.C. Bedford School	168 for 7* 86 for 5	Drawn
June 16 Giggleswick	Giggleswick School M.C.C.	88 48	Lost by 40 runs
June 18 Wimborne	M.C.C. Canford School	165 for 6* 116	Won by 49 runs
June 18 Weybridge	Oatlands Park C.C. M.C.C.	224 for 8* 225 for 2	Won by eight wickets
June 18 Richmond	Richmond C.C. M.C.C.	62 63 for 3	Won by seven wickets
June 18 Wellingborough	M.C.C. Wellingborough School	242 for 6* 179	Won by 63 runs
June 20 Oxted	M.C.C. Oxted C.C.	208 for 3* 69	Won by 139 runs
June 21 Clifton	M.C.C. Clifton College	171 for 8* 176 for 6	Lost by four wickets
June 21 Woodford	M.C.C. Woodford Wells C.C.	255 for 6* 197	Won by 58 runs
June 22 Burton Court	Household Bde. C.C. M.C.C.	240 for 8* 244 for 5	Won by five wickets

* Innings declared closed.

| June 22 | M.C.C. | 200 for 4* | Drawn |
| Woodcote | Oratory School | 174 for 6 | |

| June 22 | Streatham C.C. | 93 | Won by nine |
| Thornton Heath | M.C.C. | 97 for 1 | wickets |

* Innings declared closed.

M.C.C. v. CAMBRIDGE UNIVERSITY

At Lord's, June 29, 30, July 1. Drawn. Cambridge saved the game with their last batsmen together. Sent in, M.C.C. did not find the pitch unduly helpful to bowlers and Dowding hit skilfully. A partnership of 59 by Lumsden and Pretlove put Cambridge in a good position, but Spencer, the Leicestershire fast-medium bowler, caused a collapse, the last five wickets falling after lunch on the second day for 33 runs. Missed chances proved expensive to Cambridge when M.C.C. batted again 22 ahead, and a partnership of 91 by Davies and Stevenson left the University 269 to get. Davies hit very hard, his 87 in two hours ten minutes containing fourteen 4's. Though Goonesena and Lumsden added 95, eight Cambridge wickets fell for 182, but Croft and Melluish held out for fifty minutes and D. Smith survived the remaining three balls.

M.C.C.

K. P. A. Matthews lbw b C. Smith	41	— lbw b C. Smith	10
D. E. Blake c Melluish b D. Smith	8	— b D. Smith	40
A. C. Shirreff b C. Smith	10	— b C. Smith	4
J. F. Crapp c Silk b Singh	25	— b Singh	18
V. S. Munden b Goonesena	25	— c Croft b Goonesena	4
A. L. Dowding c Melluish b C. Smith	57	— b Goonesena	22
W. R. Coldwell lbw b Singh	8	— b C. Smith	7
M. H. Stevenson c and b Goonesena	1	— c Singh b C. Smith	37
J. G. W. Davies st Melluish b Goonesena	0	— b D. Smith	87
B. D. Wells b Goonesena	8	— not out	1
C. T. Spencer not out	0	— b D. Smith	2
B 3, l-b 1, n-b 1	5	B 10, l-b 1, n-b 3	14

1/13 2/34 3/73 4/105 5/125 6/154   188
7/157 8/165 9/182

1/30 2/34 3/34 4/80   246
5/91 6/112 7/151 8/242
9/244

Cambridge University

D. R. W. Silk c Blake b Spencer	0	— c Blake b Spencer	4
R. O'Brien c Munden b Shirreff	27	— b Spencer	3
G. Goonesena c Stevenson b Spencer	11	— c Crapp b Davies	55
V. R. Lumsden c Blake b Spencer	55	— c Munden b Davies	44
J. F. Pretlove st Blake b Wells	26	— c Blake b Spencer	4
S. Singh b Wells	0	— lbw b Wells	21
A. B. D. Parsons st Blake b Wells	16	— st Blake b Wells	18
P. D. Croft lbw b Spencer	0	— not out	47
C. S. Smith b Spencer	0	— lbw b Munden	5
M. E. L. Melluish c Munden b Spencer	14	— b Spencer	6
D. J. Smith not out	1	— not out	0
B 8, l-b 5	13	B 4, l-b 2	6

1/0 2/42 3/42 4/101 5/107 6/144   166
7/148 8/148 9/153

1/9 2/12 3/107   (9 wkts.) 213
4/112 5/112 6/146 7/151
8/182 9/213

Cambridge University Bowling

	O.	M.	R.	W.	O.	M.	R.	W.
C. Smith	22	5	60	3	27	2	90	4
D. Smith	19	4	53	1	19.5	3	63	3
Singh	19	7	26	2	13	6	28	1
Goonesena	19	7	44	4	18	8	42	2
Pretlove					4	1	9	0

M.C.C. Bowling

	O.	M.	R.	W.	O.	M.	R.	W.
Spencer	27.5	9	58	6	21	5	55	4
Shirreff	18	6	37	1	21	5	68	0
Munden	12	6	21	0	15	6	24	1
Wells	17	5	37	3	21	9	35	2
Davies					9	2	25	2

Umpires: E. G. Canning and G. Morton.

June 30 Cranbrook	M.C.C. Cranbrook School	166 for 6* 101	Won by 65 runs
June 30 Snaresbrook	M.C.C. Forest School	213 83	Won by 130 runs
July 2 Bushey	M.C.C. Bushey C.C.	213 214 for 5	Lost by five wickets
July 2 Woolhampton	M.C.C. Douai School	236 for 6* 131	Won by 105 runs
July 2 Winchmore Hill	M.C.C. Winchmore Hill C.C.	176 for 9* 131	Won by 45 runs
July 2 Worksop	M.C.C. Worksop College	186 189 for 6	Lost by four wickets
July 5 Chiswick	Civil Service Crusaders C.C. M.C.C.	239 for 6* 122 for 7	Drawn
July 5 Sutton Valence	M.C.C. Sutton Valence School	250 for 4* 101	Won by 149 runs
July 6 Beckenham	M.C.C. Cyphers Club	233 for 8* 184	Won by 49 runs
July 6 Epsom	Epsom College M.C.C.	219 220 for 4	Won by six wickets
July 6 Fleetwood	M.C.C. Rossall School	215 for 5* 132 for 9	Drawn
July 7 Bradfield	Bradfield College M.C.C.	220 for 4* 221 for 8	Won by two wickets
July 7 Uttoxeter	Denstone College M.C.C.	206 154 for 8	Drawn
July 7 New Beckenham	M.C.C. Nat. Prov. Bank C.C.	214 for 3* 147 for 6	Drawn
July 8 Southgate	M.C.C. Southgate C.C.	227 for 7* 154	Won by 73 runs
July 9 Dover	M.C.C. Dover College	184 for 7* 114	Won by 70 runs
July 9 Cranwell	M.C.C. R.A.F. College	224 for 4* 139	Won by 85 runs

* Innings declared closed.

July 9 Chislehurst	M.C.C. West Kent C.C.	245 for 6* 218 for 3	Drawn
July 11 Beckenham	Beckenham C.C. M.C.C.	156 119	Lost by 37 runs
July 11 New Eltham	Nigerian C.A. XI M.C.C.	179 180 for 5	Won by five wickets
July 12 Leatherhead	M.C.C. St. John's School	185 for 2* 119	Won by 66 runs
July 12 Sutton	M.C.C. Sutton C.C.	249 for 9* 154	Won by 95 runs
July 13 Woodford	M.C.C. Bancroft's School	211 124	Won by 87 runs
July 14 Bushey Park	Hampton Wick Royal C.C. M.C.C.	123 82	Lost by 41 runs
July 15, 16 Aldershot	Aldershot Services C.C. M.C.C.	94 for 9* and 312 for 8* 263 for 8* and 131 for 5	Drawn
July 16 Wimbledon	M.C.C. King's College School	222 for 5* 214 for 8	Drawn
July 16 Oakham	Oakham School M.C.C.	278 for 3* 255 for 6	Drawn
July 16 W. Kensington	St. Paul's School M.C.C.	152 (12-a-side) 154 for 5	Won by six wickets
July 19 Roehampton	M.C.C. Bank of England C.C.	152 153 for 5	Lost by five wickets
July 19 Brighton	M.C.C. Brighton College	287 for 5* 116	Won by 171 runs
July 19 Kingston-on- Thames	M.C.C. Kingston Grammar School	215 for 6* 146 for 5	Drawn
July 20 Reading	Reading School M.C.C.	268 for 9* 188 for 3	Drawn
July 20 Colwyn Bay	M.C.C. Rydal School	262 for 6* 144	Won by 118 runs
July 21 Tonbridge	M.C.C. Tonbridge School	218 219 for 4	Lost by six wickets
July 21 Liverpool	M.C.C. Liverpool College	226 for 8* 80	Won by 146 runs
July 23 Bexley	M.C.C. Bexley C.C.	247 232 for 9	Drawn
July 23 Hove	M.C.C. Brighton & Hove C.C.	182 for 9* 152	Won by 30 runs
July 23 Marlborough	M.C.C. Marlborough College	243 for 6* 111	Won by 132 runs
July 23 Bestwood Park	M.C.C. Notts. Amateur C.C.	183 180	Won by 3 runs
July 23 Crowthorne	M.C.C. Wellington College	219 167 for 8	Drawn

* Innings declared closed.

July 26 Hurlingham Club	M.C.C. Lords & Commons C.C.	227 for 5* 170	Won by 57
July 27 Twickenham	M.C.C. Exiles C.C.	239 for 6* 183	Won by 56 runs
July 27 Guildford	Guildford C.C. M.C.C.	222 for 7* 223 for 4	Won by six wickets
July 27 Maldon	M.C.C. Maldon C.C.	264 for 9* 164 for 7	Drawn
July 30 Buxton	Buxton C.C. M.C.C.	104 106 for 5	Won by five wickets
July 30 Haywards Heath	M.C.C. Lindfield C.C.	220 for 2* 135	Won by 85 runs
August 1 Sevenoaks	Sevenoaks Vine C.C. M.C.C.	140 142 for 9	Won by one wicket
August 1 Wimbledon Park	Wimbledon C.C. M.C.C.	272 for 7* 167 for 4	Drawn
August 2 Ashford	Ashford C.C. M.C.C.	161 165 for 9	Won by one wicket
August 3 Chichester	M.C.C. Chichester Priory Park C.C.	202 for 9* 174	Won by 28 runs
August 4 East Grinstead	M.C.C. East Grinstead C.C.	256 177	Won by 79 runs
August 5 Thames Ditton	Thames Ditton C.C. M.C.C.	147 148 for 4	Won by six wickets
August 6 Banstead	Banstead C.C. M.C.C.	164 165 for 3	Won by seven wickets
August 6 Blackheath	Blackheath C.C. M.C.C.	211 for 7* 213 for 2	Won by eight wickets
August 6 West Meon	M.C.C. West Meon and Warnford C.C.	215 for 7* 73	Won by 142 runs
August 8 Horsham	M.C.C. Horsham C.C.	188 for 9* 157	Won by 31 runs
August 12 Buckhurst Hill	M.C.C. Buckhurst Hill C.C.	268 for 5* 116	Won by 152 runs
August 13 City Road	M.C.C. Hon. Artillery Coy. C.C. —	161 for 6	Drawn (rain)
August 13 Rugby	Rugby C.C. M.C.C.	253 for 8* 244 for 4	Drawn

M.C.C. v. DE FLAMINGOS

At Lord's, August 16. M.C.C. won by 95 runs. M.C.C. 243 for five wickets declared (J. A. R. Oliver 83 not out, B. H. Lock 42 not out); De Flamingos 148 (W. C. Van Manen 71; A. W. H. Mallett six for 28).

| August 20 Beaconsfield | M.C.C. Beaconsfield C.C. | 244 for 6* 200 for 9 | Drawn |

* Innings declared closed.

M.C.C. YOUNG PROFESSIONALS v. ENGLISH SCHOOLS C.A.

At Lord's, August 31. M.C.C. Young Professionals won by 52 runs. M.C.C. Young Professionals 194 for four wickets declared (D. Eames 82); English Schools Cricket Association 142 (J. Wills four for 37).

At Scarborough, August 31, September 1, 2. M.C.C. drew with YORKSHIRE. (See YORKSHIRE section.)

M.C.C. YOUNG PROFESSIONALS v. LONDON FEDERATION OF BOYS' CLUBS

At Lord's, September 1. M.C.C. Young Professionals won by 43 runs. M.C.C. Young Professionals 231 for six wickets declared (J. Shaw 61 not out, D. Eames 56); London Federation of Boys' Clubs 188 (A. Tasker six for 55).

M.C.C. v. IRELAND

At Lord's, September 2, 3. M.C.C. won by 184 runs. M.C.C. 250 for nine wickets declared (C. J. M. Kenny five for 57) and 136 for four wickets declared (M. M. Walford 67 not out, Kenny three for 32); Ireland 91 (P. I. Bedford six for 54) and 111 (Bedford five for 54). (Not first-class.)

I ZINGARI MATCHES, 1955

Matches 26, Won 3, Lost 13, Drawn 7, Abandoned 3

April 30	v. Trinity College, Cambridge	Trinity won by four wickets
May 7	v. Charterhouse School	Charterhouse won by 24 runs
May 14	v. R.A.F. College, Cranwell	Drawn
May 14	v. Magdalen College, Oxford	Drawn
May 21	v. R.M.A., Sandhurst	I Zingari won by 78 runs
May 21	v. Magdalene College, Cambridge	Magdalene won by six wickets
May 28	v. Christ Church, Oxford	No play—rain
May 28, 29	v. Royal Artillery	I Zingari won by four wickets
May 29	v. Duke of Norfolk's XI	No play—rain
June 4	v. Royal Engineers	R.E. won by 46 runs
June 4, 5	v. Royal Navy	R.N. won by six wickets
June 8	v. Household Brigade	Abandoned—rain
June 18	v. Wellington College	Wellington won by 40 runs
June 21	v. Winchester College	Winchester won by 106 runs
June 22	v. Middlesex Regiment	Middlesex Regiment won by six wickets
June 25	v Harrow School	Drawn
July 2	v. Eton College 1st XI	Eton won by 81 runs
July 2	v. Eton College 2nd XI	I Zingari won by one wicket
July 9	v. Royal Naval College, Greenwich	Drawn
July 15, 16	v. Green Jackets	Drawn
July 16	v. Sir William Worsley's XI	Worsley's XI won by eight wickets
July 17	v. Ampleforth College	Drawn
July 23	v. Aldershot Services	Drawn
July 30	v. Staff College, Camberley	Staff College won by five wickets
July 30	v. Royal Fusiliers	Royal Fusiliers won by 21 runs
August 6	v. Lord Porchester's XI	Porchester's XI won by 66 runs

OTHER MATCHES AT LORD'S

June 23, 24, 25, 27. ENGLAND beat SOUTH AFRICA in the Second Test Match by 71 runs. (See SOUTH AFRICAN section.)

OXFORD v. CAMBRIDGE

July 2, 4, 5. Drawn. Cambridge held the upper hand for a long time, but they were foiled by the resolution of M. J. K. Smith who equalled the feat of A. Ratcliffe by scoring a double-century and a hundred in successive University matches. Silk, the Cambridge captain, who had made centuries in the two previous University matches, had little chance to score another as he dropped himself to No. 8 in the order because of an injured thumb.

The honours of the first day were shared by Fellows-Smith and Pretlove. The clever variations of Fellows-Smith at medium-pace upset most of the Light Blues, but Pretlove, a crisp cutter and firm driver, stood firm in scoring an attractive 114 in three hours and fifty minutes. Silk, though in pain, helped Pretlove in a seventh wicket stand of 70. Oxford lost their grip after Cambridge were 139 for five, and Allan might have been given more work to do, admirably though Fellows-Smith filled the role of stock bowler.

Cambridge gained a strong position on the second day. Despite fluent driving by Walton and a few big hits by Fellows-Smith, including a pull for 6 on to the Grand Stand balcony off Goonesena, Oxford were out in just over three hours. Batsmen reluctant to use their feet failed against the skilful slow and medium-pace bowling of Goonesena and the bearded and turbanned Singh. Singh, at a cost of 15, took four of the last seven Oxford wickets which fell for 40. Goonesena, with lively stroke-play, showed his all-round ability when Cambridge batted a second time leading by 134, and after a spell of fast and accurate bowling by Fasken, Lumsden hit forcefully. Cambridge, at the close, led by 237 with four wickets left, but they could not command success. Silk waited until just after one o'clock on the last day before declaring.

The task of making 313 for victory in four and a quarter hours did not dismay Oxford. With Smith finding his best driving form from the start and Williams settling down to confident stroke-play the Dark Blues had a chance as long as this pair were together. Their fourth-wicket stand yielded 103 in ninety minutes, but with the catching of Smith at long-on the game swung in favour of Cambridge. Fortunately for Oxford, their captain was unshakable and he kept up his end until Silk, with only ten minutes of the extra half-hour left, gave up his quest for victory.

Cambridge

R. O'Brien (Wellington and Corpus
Christi) b Fellows-Smith .... 34 — b Fasken 24
A. B. D. Parsons (Brighton College and
Corpus Christi) c Allan b Fellows-Smith 31 — lbw b Fasken 0
G. Goonesena (Royal College, Colombo
and Queen's) c Williams b Gibson .... 23 — c and b Fasken 21
V. R. Lumsden (Munro College, Jamaica
and Emmanuel) lbw b Fasken .... 14 — c Smith b Allan 25
J. F. Pretlove (Alleyn's and Caius) c Smith
b Allan ....114 — c Walshe b Fasken 40
S. Singh (Khalsa College, Punjab Univ.
and Christ's) c Williams b Fellows-Smith 2 — c and b Phillips 11
P. D. Croft (Gresham's and Jesus) lbw b
Allan .... 9 — c Fasken b Gibson 1
D. R. W. Silk (Christ's Hospital and
Sidney Sussex) lbw b Fellows-Smith .. 23 — c Gibson b Phillips 6
C. S. Smith (William Hulme Grammar
School and Christ's) run out .... 7 — not out 26
M. E. L. Melluish (Rossall and Caius)
c Allan b Fellows-Smith .... 12 — not out 13
D. J. Smith (Stockport Grammar School
and St. John's) not out 4
B 18, l-b 10, w 1, n-b 2 31   B 8, l-b 3 11

1/56 2/73 3/104 4/122 5/139 6/151   304   1/8 2/41   (8 wkts., dec.) 178
7/221 8/238 9/287   3/46 4/63 5/97 6/103 7/112
                                           8/149

Oxford

M. J. K. Smith (Stamford and St. Edmund
Hall) c Melluish b C. Smith .... 25 — c Singh b Goonesena 104
J. M. Allan (Edinburgh Academy and
Worcester) c Pretlove b D. Smith .... 9 — b Goonesena 11
A. C. Walton (Radley and Lincoln) st
Melluish b Goonesena .... 57 — c Silk b D. Smith 2
C. C. P. Williams (Westminster and Christ
Church) b Goonesena .... 18 — not out 47
A. P. Walshe (Milton, Rhodesia and Wad-
ham) b Singh .... 20 — not out 5
G. P. S. Delisle (Stonyhurst and Lincoln)
c Silk b Goonesena .... 0 — c Melluish b Singh 15
I. Gibson (Manchester Grammar School
and Brasenose) c Pretlove b Singh..... 2 — b D. Smith 8
J. P. Fellows-Smith (Durban H.S. and
Brasenose) not out .... 24 — lbw b C. Smith 23
D. K. Fasken (Wellington and Trinity)
c Lumsden b Goonesena 4
D. C. P. R. Jowett (Sherborne and St.
John's) b Singh.................... 0
J. B. Phillips (King's, Canterbury and St.
Edmund Hall) lbw b Singh 2
B 9 9   B 12, l-b 3 15

1/38 2/42 3/73 4/130 5/135 6/138   170   1/3 2/34 3/72   (6 wkts.) 230
7/138 8/158 9/166   4/175 5/190 6/216

Oxford Bowling

	O.	M.	R.	W.	O.	M.	R.	W·
Phillips	21	3	54	0	 21	4	46	2
Fasken	22	6	39	1	 18	6	38	4
Fellows-Smith .	37	9	83	5	 6	2	20	0
Jowett	9	3	22	0	 10	4	14	0
Allan	14.2	4	36	2	 17	6	21	1
Gibson	13	5	39	1	 6	1	28	1

Cambridge Bowling

	O.	M.	R.	W.	O.	M.	R.	W.
C. Smith.......	18	1	49	1	 23	9	47	1
D. Smith.......	13	3	30	1	 18	5	46	2
Singh	17	7	20	4	 14	2	49	1
Goonesena	21	5	62	4	 18	4	73	2
					Pretlove 3	3	0	0

Umpires: A. E. Pothecary and N. Oldfield.

OXFORD v. CAMBRIDGE

From 1827 to 1954 the Universities played 111 matches, Cambridge winning 48, Oxford 42, and 21 being drawn.

The Universities did not play official matches in the war years 1915 to 1918 and 1940 to 1945. Results since the first world war:—

1919	Oxford won by 45
1920	Drawn
1921	Cambridge won by inns. and 24
1922	Cambridge won by inns. and 100
1923	Oxford won by inns. and 227
1924	Cambridge won by nine wickets
1925	Drawn
1926	Cambridge won by 24
1927	Cambridge won by 116
1928	Drawn
1929	Drawn
1930	Cambridge won by 205
1931	Oxford won by eight wickets
1932	Drawn
1933	Drawn
1934	Drawn
1935	Cambridge won by 195
1936	Cambridge won by eight wickets
1937	Oxford won by seven wickets
1938	Drawn
1939	Oxford won by 45
1940 to 1945	No official matches
1946	Oxford won by six wickets
1947	Drawn
1948	Oxford won by inns. and 8
1949	Cambridge won by seven wickets
1950	Drawn
1951	Oxford won by 21
1952	Drawn
1953	Cambridge won by two wickets
1954	Drawn
1955	Drawn

The highest totals by the sides are:—

OXFORD 503 (in 1900), OXFORD 457 (in 1947), OXFORD 453 eight wickets dec. (in 1931), CAMBRIDGE 431 (in 1932), CAMBRIDGE 425 (in 1938), CAMBRIDGE 422 nine wickets dec. (in 1936), OXFORD 422 (in 1923), CAMBRIDGE 415 eight wickets dec.

(in 1921), OXFORD 415 (in 1934), CAMBRIDGE 409 (in 1925), CAMBRIDGE 408 eight wickets dec. (in 1952), CAMBRIDGE 403 four wickets dec. (in 1922), OXFORD 401 three wickets dec. (in 1954), and CAMBRIDGE 400 (in 1934).

Sixty-five three-figure innings have been played in the University matches. For those scored before 1919 see 1940 *Wisden*. Those subsequent to 1919 include the three highest as shown here:—

238*	..	Nawab of Pataudi	..	1931	Oxford
201*	..	M. J. K. Smith	..	1954	Oxford
201	..	A. T. Ratcliffe	..	1931	Cambridge
193	..	D. C. H. Townsend	..	1934	Oxford
170	..	M. Howell	..	1919	Oxford
167	..	B. W. Hone	..	1932	Oxford
157	..	D. R. Wilcox	..	1932	Cambridge
149	..	J. T. Morgan	..	1929	Cambridge
145*	..	H. E. Webb	..	1948	Oxford
142	..	M. P. Donnelly	..	1946	Oxford
136	..	E. T. Killick	..	1930	Cambridge
135	..	H. A. Pawson	..	1947	Oxford
129	..	H. J. Enthoven	..	1925	Cambridge
127	..	D. S. Sheppard	..	1952	Cambridge
124	..	A. K. Judd	..	1927	Cambridge
124	..	A. T. Ratcliffe	..	1932	Cambridge
122	..	P. A. Gibb	..	1938	Cambridge
121	..	J. N. Grover	..	1937	Oxford
118	..	H. Ashton	..	1921	Cambridge
118	..	D. R. W. Silk	..	1954	Cambridge
116*	..	D. R. W. Silk	..	1953	Cambridge
116	..	M. C. Cowdrey	..	1953	Oxford
115	..	A. W. Allen	..	1934	Cambridge
114	..	J. F. Pretlove	..	1955	Cambridge
113	..	E. R. T. Holmes	..	1927	Oxford
109	..	C. H. Taylor	..	1923	Oxford
108	..	F. G. H. Chalk	..	1934	Oxford
106	..	Nawab of Pataudi	..	1929	Oxford
104	..	H. J. Enthoven	..	1924	Cambridge
104	..	M. J. K. Smith	..	1955	Oxford
102*	..	A. P. F. Chapman	..	1922	Cambridge
101*	..	R. W. V. Robins	..	1928	Cambridge
101	..	N. W. D. Yardley	..	1937	Cambridge
100	..	P. J. Dickinson	..	1939	Cambridge

* Signifies not out.

For other particulars see Records.

ETON v. HARROW

July 8, 9. Eton won by 38 runs. Harrow, overplayed on the first innings, put up a good fight, and Neame, their captain and off-spin bowler, performed the first hat-trick in the match since 1900. Eton owed much for victory to their left-arm bowlers Pennant (medium pace) and Lane-Fox (slow). Gibson, the Eton captain, batted forcefully on the first day when Neame troubled most of his colleagues, and when Harrow went in Neame again took the eye with some attractive strokes. The other Harrow batsmen failed to counter the guile of Lane-Fox and at close of play Eton led by 74 with all their second innings wickets standing. Then, on the second morning, Neame sent back Lane-Fox, Wolfe-Murray and Blofeld with successive deliveries at 115 and Eton, for whom Stoddart played a sound innings, left their rivals to make 223 in four hours and ten minutes. Champniss, a steady left-hander, did his best by staying two and a half hours to give his side a chance of victory, but the clever variations of Pennant, who bowled to a menacing slip field and took seven wickets for 33 runs, settled the issue and Eton won in the extra half-hour. The boisterous scenes witnessed at the finish in some previous games were not repeated.

Eton

C. T. M. Pugh b Miller	24	—	b Champniss	22
D. R. Stoddart c Cable b Maydon	17	—	c Miller b Champniss	38
I. A. C. Sinclair b Miller	0	—	run out	7
C. H. Gibson b Maydon	53	—	b Neame	3
A. R. B. Burrows b Neame	9	—	lbw b Maydon	21
E. J. Lane-Fox b Neame	0	—	c Maydon b Neame	6
A. M. Wolfe-Murray b Neame	18	—	c Miller b Neame	0
H. C. Blofeld c Champniss b Neame	22	—	b Neame	0
A. P. Marsham c Massy b Maydon	1	—	not out	20
D. MacL. Pearson run out	0	—	b Maydon	6
S. D. Pennant not out	0	—	b Champniss	10
B 15, l-b 2	17		B 18, l-b 12, n-b 3	33

1/53 2/53 3/54 4/74 5/74 6/110   161   1/60 2/69 3/74 4/100   166
7/156 8/161 9/161   5/115 6/115 7/115 8/119
                                   9/139

Harrow

J. M. Parker b Pennant	5	—	c and b Pennant	21
A. R. B. Neame c Blofeld b Sinclair	24	—	c Blofeld b Pennant	16
R. S. Miller b Pennant	0	—	c Blofeld b Pennant	0
G. D. Massy b Lane-Fox	14	—	b Pennant	22
A. S. R. de W. Winlaw c Pennant b Lane-Fox	23	—	b Pearson	12
A. J. Champniss b Lane-Fox	0	—	c Sinclair b Pennant	49
A. B. Cable lbw b Lane-Fox	10	—	c Sinclair b Pennant	20
J. C. T. Harvey c Stoddart b Sinclair	9	—	c Gibson b Pennant	2
I. H. Stewart-Brown b Sinclair	0	—	c Burrows b Pearson	4
N. Davies-Barker not out	6	—	lbw b Sinclair	6
M. L. Maydon b Lane-Fox	12	—	not out	9
L-b 2	2		B 17, l-b 4, w 1	22

1/29 2/29 3/29 4/61 5/61 6/77 7/82   105   1/37 2/38 3/39 4/72   184
8/86 9/86   5/84 6/116 7/118 8/123 9/145

Harrow Bowling

	O.	M.	R.	W.		O.	M.	R.	W.
Davies-Barker	7	3	16	0	....	2	1	5	0
Maydon	8.2	1	31	3	....	14	3	45	2
Miller	11	4	20	2	....	1	1	14	0
Champniss	14	7	34	0	....	14.3	3	31	3
Neame	20	6	43	4	....	18	5	38	4

Eton Bowling

	O.	M.	R.	W.		O.	M.	R.	W.
Pennant	11	9	23	2	....	24	12	33	7
Sinclair	18	8	30	3	....	22	8	51	1
Pearson	6	1	17	0	....	20	7	44	2
Lane-Fox	14	5	33	5	....	18	13	21	0
Gibson						1	1	0	0
Burrows						2	0	13	0

Umpires: W. Harrington and L. D'Arcy.

ETON v. HARROW MATCHES

Of the 120 matches played Eton have won 46, Harrow 38 and 36 have been drawn. This is the generally published record, but Harrow men object very strongly to the first game in 1805 being treated as a regular contest between the two schools, contending that it is no more correct to count that one than the fixture in 1857 which has been rejected.

The matches played during the war years 1915–1918 and 1940–1945 are not reckoned as belonging to the regular series.

Results since the first world war:—

1919	Eton won by 202 runs	1934	Drawn
1920	Eton won by nine wickets	1935	Drawn
1921	Eton won by seven wickets	1936	Drawn
1922	Drawn	1937	Eton won by seven wickets
1923	Drawn	1938	Drawn
1924	Drawn	1939	Harrow won by eight wickets
1925	Drawn	1946	Drawn
1926	Drawn	1947	Drawn
1927	Drawn	1948	Drawn
1928	Eton won by 28 runs	1949	Eton won by seven wickets
1929	Drawn	1950	Drawn
1930	Eton won by eight wickets	1951	Drawn
1931	Eton won by inns. and 16 runs	1952	Harrow won by seven wickets
1932	Drawn	1953	Eton won by ten wickets
1933	Drawn	1954	Harrow won by nine wickets.
		1955	Eton won by 38 runs

For other particulars see Records.

Forty three-figure innings have been played in matches between these two schools. Those since 1918:—

159 E. W. Dawson	(in 1923), Eton	104 R. Pulbrook	(in 1932), Harrow
158 I. Akers-Douglas	(in 1928), Eton	103 L. G. Crawley	(in 1921), Harrow
153 N. S. Hotchkin	(in 1931), Eton	103 T. Hare	(in 1947), Eton
135 J. Atkinson-Clark		102*P. H. Stewart-Brown	
	(in 1930), Eton		(in 1923), Harrow
115 E. Crutchley	(in 1939), Harrow	102 R. V. C. Robins	(in 1953), Eton
112 A. W. Allen	(in 1931), Eton	100 R. H. Cobbold	(in 1923), Eton
111 R. A. Holt	(in 1937), Harrow	100*P. V. F. Cazalet	(in 1926), Eton
109 K. F. H. Hale	(in 1929), Eton	100 A. N. A. Boyd	(in 1934), Eton
109 N. S. Hotchkin	(in 1932), Eton	100*P. M. Studd	(in 1935), Harrow
107 W. N. Coles	(in 1946), Eton	100 S. D. D. Sainsbury	
			(in 1947), Eton

In 1904, D. C. Boles of Eton, making 183, set up a new record for the match, beating the 152 obtained in 1841 by Emilius Bayley, afterwards the Rev. Sir John Robert Laurie, Eton. M. C. Bird, Harrow, in 1907, scored 100 not out and 131, the only batsman who has made two 100's in the match. N. S. Hotchkin, Eton played the following innings: 1931, 153; 1932, 109 and 96; 1933, 88 and 12.

* *Signifies not out.*

ROYAL ARTILLERY v. ROYAL ENGINEERS

July 11, 12. Drawn. Royal Artillery 216 for eight wickets declared (Gnr. N. W. Hill 83; Spr. B. James four for 53) and 145 for three wickets declared (Hill 81 not out); Royal Engineers 139 (Lt. R. Proctor 50; 2nd/Lt. T. E. Dickenson six for 46) and 147 for four wickets (Proctor 51).

GENTLEMEN v. PLAYERS

July 13, 14, 15 Players won by 20 runs with five minutes to spare. Injuries ruined the match, for not only were May, the Gentlemen's captain, Bailey, Compton, Graveney, Evans and Statham prevented from appearing, but during the game Cowdrey, Tyson and Lock were also hurt. Bedser captained the Players and as he had been given Watson, a batsman, in place of Statham, he was left at one time with only two fit bowlers, Titmus and himself.

Two Leicestershire cricketers, Tompkin and Palmer, carried off the batting honours, each scoring hundreds. Tompkin's hundred was the first by a Leicestershire professional in this fixture at Lord's since J. H. King made 104 and 109

K

not out in 1904, the only instance of two separate hundreds for the Players. Very sure and driving cleanly, Tompkin hit sixteen 4's in an attractive display and next day when the Gentlemen were handicapped through the retirement of Cowdrey at 57, Palmer, with twenty-four 4's, batted neatly and without mistake until near the end of his long and splendid innings. Insole, who led the Gentlemen, was always resourceful and put on 195 with Palmer.

By the end of the second day, the Players were 16 ahead, having cleared a deficit of 20 and all their wickets were standing. With Kenyon and Watson taking their opening stand to 70, the side looked safe but Goonesena put in a very long spell of bowling from the nursery end. He mixed his spin and kept an excellent length but, thanks to Dollery's skill, the Gentlemen were left to make 201 in two hours thirty-five minutes.

In an hour the left-handed Tordoff, and Smith made 63. Then came a five minutes' break on the field for tea, after which all ten wickets fell in eighty-five minutes for 117 more runs. At one period the Gentlemen were well on terms with the clock. The powerfully built Fellows-Smith hit to leg with such unerring judgment that there were eight 4's and one 6 in his fearless 51 and during his gay innings Warr helped him add 52 in twenty-five minutes. Consequently, 50 more were needed in thirty-five minutes, but Bedser, Titmus and Lock bowled so well and were so splendidly supported in the field that the last four wickets produced only 16 runs. With ten minutes left and 24 still required, Cowdrey came in last only to loft the ball beyond the bowler where Bedser, who had managed his limited resources with much skill, finished the match by holding the catch which brought a thoroughly deserved victory to his side.

Players

D. Kenyon c Barnett b Palmer	32	— c Fellows-Smith b Goonesena 39
W. Watson lbw b Fellows-Smith	2	— c Tordoff b Marlar 29
M. Tompkin c Goonesena b Warr	115	— c Barnett b Goonesena 11
J. M. Parks c Smith b Marlar	35	— c and b Goonesena 8
K. Barrington c Fellows-Smith b Warr	3	— st Barnett b Goonesena 0
H. E. Dollery c Pretlove b Warr	14	— c Goonesena b Marlar 82
F. J. Titmus c Insole b Marlar	40	— lbw b Goonesena 14
L. Harrison c Fellows-Smith b Warr	13	— b Goonesena 20
G. A. R. Lock b Goonesena	28	— not out 9
F. H. Tyson not out	15	— absent hurt 0
A. V. Bedser c Smith b Marlar	2	— lbw b Marlar 0
B 6, l-b 10, w 1	17	B 3, l-b 2, w 2, n-b 1 .. 8

1/4 2/52 3/175 4/178 5/216 6/216   316
7/270 8/283 9/308

1/70 2/72 3/82 4/82   220
5/103 6/138 7/202 8/220
9/220

Gentlemen

M. J. K. Smith lbw b Titmus	17	— c Harrison b Titmus 28
G. G. Tordoff b Lock	20	— c Barrington b Bedser 44
M. C. Cowdrey retired hurt	0	— c Bedser b Titmus 0
C. H. Palmer c Dollery b Bedser	154	— run out 5
D. J. Insole c Tompkin b Titmus	72	— c Titmus b Lock 1
J. P. Fellows-Smith run out	9	— lbw b Lock 51
J. F. Pretlove c Barrington b Bedser	0	— not out 3
G. Goonesena c Barrington b Titmus	13	— c Lock b Titmus 1
B. A. Barnett not out	22	— b Bedser 2
J. J. Warr c sub b Bedser	11	— run out 21
R. G. Marlar (did not bat)		— c Titmus b Bedser 5
B 15, l-b 3	18	B 13, l-b 6 19

1/51 2/51 3/252 4/290   (8 wkts., dec.) 336
5/290 6/291 7/313 8/336

1/63 2/65 3/71 4/76   180
5/112 6/164 7/172 8/172
9/179

Gentlemen Bowling

	O.	M.	R.	W.		O.	M.	R.	W.
Warr	22	5	54	4	....	13	3	38	0
Fellows-Smith	24	6	62	1	....	3	1	11	0
Palmer	13	2	41	1	....	5	1	4	0
Insole	4	0	9	0					
Marlar	21.5	5	61	3	....	24.5	3	76	3
Goonesena	10	0	58	1	....	26	2	83	6
Pretlove	5	1	14	0					

Players Bowling

	O.	M.	R.	W.		O.	M.	R.	W.
Tyson	3	0	7	0					
Bedser	30.4	3	86	3	....	16	4	44	3
Lock	32	10	63	1	....	18	2	77	2
Titmus	40	13	139	3	....	10.4	1	40	3
Parks	10	0	23	0					

Umpires: J. S. Buller and K. McCanlis.

HUNDREDS FOR GENTLEMEN AND PLAYERS AT LORD'S

GENTLEMEN

102*	W. Ward	1825	124	D J. Knight	1919
134*	W. G. Grace	1868	101	P. G. H. Fender	1921
109	W. G. Grace	1870	160	A. P. F. Chapman	1922
112	W. G. Grace	1872	122	G. T. S. Stevens	1923
163	W. G. Grace	1873	120	M. D. Lyon	1923
152	W. G. Grace	1875	129	G. T. S. Stevens	1925
169	W. G. Grace	1876	108	A. P. F. Chapman	1926
103	A. W. Ridley	1876	123	D. R. Jardine	1927
107	A. P. Lucas	1882	125 103* }	K. S. Duleepsinhji	1930
100	C. T. Studd	1882	165	Nawab of Pataudi	1932
107	E. F. S. Tylecote	1883	132	K. S. Duleepsinhji	1932
118	W. G. Grace	1895	104*	R. E. S. Wyatt	1934
104	C. B. Fry	1899	175*	H. T. Bartlett	1938
102* 136 }	R. E. Foster	1900	162*	M. P. Donnelly	1947
126	C. B. Fry	1901	122	F. R. Brown	1950
232*	C. B. Fry	1903	119*	P. B. H. May	1951
168*	A. C. MacLaren	1903	127	C. H. Palmer	1952
121	K. S. Ranjitsinhji	1904	117	R. T. Simpson	1953
114	R. H Spooner	1906	154	C. H. Palmer	1955

PLAYERS

113*	T. Beagley	1821	141	L. C. Braund	1902
100	J. Saunders	1827	100	W. H. Lockwood	1902
132	Thomas Hayward	1860	139	A. E. Knight	1903
112*	Thomas Hayward	1863	104 109* }	J. H. King	1904
122*	Thomas Hearne	1866	123*	T. W. Hayward	1905
102	Richard Daft	1872	146*	T. W. Hayward	1907
111	Arthur Shrewsbury	1887	154*	J. B. Hobbs	1911
130*	W. Barnes	1889	113	J. B. Hobbs	1919
103	W. Gunn	1892	108	C. P. Mead	1921
116*	T. W. Hayward	1896	140	J. B. Hobbs	1922
125	Arthur Shrewsbury	1897	162	A. C. Russell	1922
139	W. Gunn	1898	118	J. B. Hobbs	1924
163	J. T. Brown	1900	113	R. Kilner	1924
111	T. W. Hayward	1900	140	J. B. Hobbs	1925
140	J. T. Tyldesley	1901			

Signifies not out.

163	J. B. Hobbs	1926	105	C. Washbrook	1946
131	E. Tyldesley	1926	101	C. Washbrook	1947
107	H. Sutcliffe	1926	132*	L. Hutton	1948
161*	J. B. Hobbs	1931	123	H. E. Dollery	1950
110	W. R. Hammond	1932	150	D. C. S. Compton	1951
120	A. Mitchell	1934	115	M. Tompkin	1955

* Signifies not out.

RESULTS AT LORD'S

Since 1806, 130 matches have been played at Lord's. Gentlemen have won 41, Players 67, with 22 drawn.
Results since 1919:—

1919	Drawn	1935	Players won by nine wickets
1920	Players won by seven wickets	1936	Drawn
1921	Players won by nine wickets	1937	Players won by eight wickets
1922	Drawn	1938	Gentlemen won by 133 runs
1923	Drawn	1939	Players won by 160 runs
1924	Players won by innings and 231 runs	1946	Players won by innings and 140 runs
1925	Drawn	1947	Drawn
1926	Drawn	1948	Players won by seven wickets
1927	Drawn	1949	Players won by four wickets
1928	Players won by nine wickets	1950	Drawn
1929	Players won by seven wickets	1951	Players won by 21 runs
1930	Drawn	1952	Players won by two runs
1931	Drawn	1953	Gentlemen won by 95 runs
1932	Drawn	1954	Players won by 49 runs.
1933	Players won by ten wickets	1955	Players won by 20 runs
1934	Gentlemen won by seven wickets		

BEAUMONT v. ORATORY

July 23. Drawn. Beaumont 172 (R. S. Nichol four for 61); Oratory 166 for seven wickets (J. N. Moore 76).

CLIFTON v. TONBRIDGE

July 25, 26. Tonbridge won by 82 runs. Splendid off-break bowling by Gracey, the captain, was mainly responsible for their victory. Clifton, set to make 162 to win, were helpless on a wearing pitch against his flighted off-breaks. In 15 overs he took seven wickets for 16 and finished the match just before tea. Linell, of Clifton, played many attractive strokes in scoring the only fifty of the match.

Tonbridge

G. E. Godfrey c Whitty b Mills	37	—	c White b Bernard	15
C. M. Smith lbw b Whitty	12	—	run out	4
C. J. Crang c Mills b Whittaker	2	—	c Carter b Whitty	10
R. M. Prideaux c Linell b Mills	4	—	not out	40
N. Heroys b Whitty	21	—	b Whitty	0
R. M. K. Gracey b Bernard	5	—	c Mills b Whittaker	17
R. Ward b Whitty	14	—	c Whitty b Bernard	1
A. B. E. Hudson c Mathias b Whitty	36	—	c White b Bernard	0
M. H. Foster c Mills b Whitty	10	—	c Bernard b Mills	23
N. R. B. Prowse run out	1	—	c Brain b Mathias	0
P. Meredith not out	2	—	lbw b Bernard	1
B 10, l-b 7	17		B 3, l-b 2	5

1/25 2/39 3/48 4/77 5/93 6/111   161   1/13 2/31 3/33 4/33 5/61   116
7/117 8/145 9/154   6/64 7/64 8/114 9/115

Clifton

J. R. Bernard b Meredith	0	— lbw b Gracey	16
D. J. Carter c Smith b Meredith	0	— lbw b Gracey	1
R. W. Mathias st Smith b Foster	21	— b Meredith	1
D. C. Mills c Foster b Meredith	4	— lbw b Gracey	6
C. A. H. White b Meredith	3	— c Smith b Gracey	7
W. S. Linell not out	54	— b Gracey	1
M. R. Williams b Foster	0	— lbw b Hudson	15
C. J. U. Coates c Heroys b Foster	0	— c Godfrey b Gracey	4
P. A. Brain b Prowse	12	— b Gracey	6
R. H. Whitty b Prowse	2	— not out	9
J. C. M. Whittaker b Prowse	0	— b Prowse	0
B 14, l-b 3, n-b 3	20	B 9, l-b 3, n-b 1	13

1/0 2/7 3/11 4/24 5/29 6/31 7/33   116
8/67 9/98

1/26 2/27 3/40 4/56 5/58   79
6/60 7/64 8/65 9/78

Clifton Bowling

	O.	M.	R.	W.		O.	M.	R.	W.
Whitty	20.4	7	53	5	....	16	2	47	2
Bernard	15	5	38	1	....	18.1	7	38	4
Mills	13	4	32	2	....	7	3	5	1
Whittaker	8	1	21	1	....	7	2	20	1
Mathias					....	2	1	1	1

Tonbridge Bowling

	O.	M.	R.	W.		O.	M.	R.	W.
Foster	5	1	11	3	....	2	1	1	0
Meredith	13	6	19	4	....	14	4	20	1
Prowse	14.5	3	43	3	....	4	0	15	1
Hudson	6	3	13	0	....	4	1	14	1
Gracey	2	0	10	0	....	15	6	16	7

Umpires: R. Routledge and W. Harrington.

Clifton v. Tonbridge Results

First played at Lord's in 1914, Clifton winning by nine wickets.

Of 31 matches played at Lord's from 1919, Tonbridge have won 14, Clifton 7; 9 drawn, one abandoned.

RUGBY v. MARLBOROUGH

July 27, 28. Marlborough won by five wickets. The Centenary year of the meeting of the two schools was marked by a splendid match in which bowlers held the upper hand all through. Coghlan and Sabine each took ten wickets and well deserved their success. Coghlan bowled at a great pace for a schoolboy, and if Sabine was not as fast he enjoyed better control of length. When Marlborough were left to make 95 for victory, the result was far from a foregone conclusion. Three men were out for 41, but Coke Wallis, the Marlborough captain, and Marr, a stylish batsman, scored readily and helped to settle the issue. The catching and ground fielding of both sides reached a high standard and gave much pleasure to the largest crowd which had ever attended the game.

Rugby

E. M. Rose b Roberts	1	— c Gairdner b Coke Wallis ..	9
C. R. B. Neame c and b Slatter	25	— c Marr b Roberts	31
G. D. G. Shaw b Sabine	22	— b Sabine	14
M. A. Oddy b Slatter	2	— c Morris b Coke Wallis	20
T. B. L. Coghlan c and b Sabine	0	— b Sabine	2
P. R. Colville c Gairdner b Slatter	20	— b Sabine	4
H. M. Fox b Sabine	9	— b Roberts	0
W. N. Livingstone b Roberts	10	— c and b Coke Wallis	3
W. S. Black lbw b Sabine	1	— b Sabine	1
M. F. Attenborough not out	7	— not out	2
G. S. Harcourt c Gairdner b Sabine	8	— c Chamberlain b Sabine	0
B 4, l-b 4, n-b 3	11	B 3, l-b 6, w 2	11

1/3 2/40 3/48 4/52 5/52 6/67 7/82   116   1/15 2/15 3/25 4/42   97
8/92 9/105   5/72 6/78 7/82 8/90 9/95

Marlborough

H. M. Stratford lbw b Black	17	— c Livingstone b Coghlan	7
R. C. Coke Wallis c Fox b Coghlan	10	— c Livingstone b Coghlan	28
C. A. Morris b Coghlan	0	— b Coghlan	2
B. A. C. Marr st Fox b Black	34	— not out	22
R. E. Coote b Harcourt	1	— b Harcourt	13
V. Roberts b Coghlan	4	— run out	8
P. R. Chamberlain b Coghlan	0	— not out	4
J. A. C. Gairdner c Attenborough b Coghlan	25		
A. J. B. Sabine c Black b Coghlan	1		
D. M. Slatter c Livingstone b Coghlan	4		
A. J. H. Gardner not out	0		
B 10, l-b 8, w 2, n-b 3	23	B 9, l-b 3, n-b 2	14

1/23 2/27 3/40 4/47 5/59 6/59   119   1/31 2/38 3/41   (5 wkts.)   98
7/101 8/115 9/119   4/74 5/94

Marlborough Bowling

	O.	M.	R.	W.		O.	M.	R.	W.
Coke Wallis	8	1	21	0	....	9	3	16	3
Roberts	7	3	16	2	....	5	2	17	2
Sabine	13	4	32	5	....	11.4	2	21	5
Gardner	7	2	21	0					
Slatter	11	4	13	3	....	15	5	31	0
Morris	1	0	2	0	....	1	0	1	0

Rugby Bowling

	O.	M.	R.	W.		O.	M.	R.	W.
Coghlan	17	5	35	7	....	14.1	4	33	3
Livingstone	5	2	8	0	....	1	0	4	0
Black	14.1	7	23	2	....	3	0	14	0
Harcourt	10	2	18	1	....	14	3	33	1
Attenborough	3	0	12	0					

Umpires: G. Morton and R. Routledge.

RUGBY v. MARLBOROUGH RESULTS

Of 96 matches, Rugby have won 41 and Marlborough 29; 25 drawn, one abandoned. The match was first played in 1855. All matches, excepting the following, were played at Lord's: Oval—1857, 1863, 1867; Middlesex Ground, Islington—1864; Rugby—1868, 1915, 1917; Marlborough—1870, 1916, 1918, 1944. No match took place in 1858, 1859 and 1861 owing to the weakness of Marlborough cricket in those early years, and in 1940 and 1947 when Rugby were unable to play.

CHELTENHAM v. HAILEYBURY AND I.S.C.

July 29, 30. Drawn. After gaining first innings lead with their last pair together, Haileybury had to fight hard to save the game. Stuchbury and Marsden, in an entertaining third-wicket stand of 142, put Cheltenham in a declaring position and Wichers and Benke, with steady spin bowling, came close to forcing victory. Haileybury, who were set to score 223 in three and a quarter hours, lost seven men for 150 before Bagnall-Oakeley and Leighton held out in the extra half-hour.

Cheltenham

T. H. Coke lbw b Smith	4	— c Mitton b Leighton	2
P. W. F. Stuchbury b Smith	29	— c Mitton b Leighton	70
J. A. S. Donald b Smith	0	— b Smith	2
C. D. Marsden c M. Foster b Claxton	6	— b Claxton	69
D. J. G. James c Thompson b Claxton	36	— b Claxton	1
G. J. Cleland b Claxton	1	— b Smith	11
P. F. Ross c Claxton b Smith	39	— lbw b Claxton	6
J. A. Hancock b Smith	2	— not out	13
A. F. Benke not out	7	— run out	4
S. E. Khazzam b Claxton	11	— b Smith	30
J. A. Wichers b Claxton	1		
B 1, l-b 1, w 1, n-b 1	4	B 15, l-b 11, w 1, n-b 2	29

1/22 2/27 3/41 4/41 5/50 6/101   140
7/119 8/121 9/138

1/12 2/19   (9 wkts., dec.) 237
3/161 4/162 5/171 6/183
7/196 8/200 9/237

Haileybury and I.S.C.

D. J. Newsom c Hancock b Wichers	36	— b Benke	23
M. G. P. Foster b Cleland	12	— lbw b James	2
D. L. Stretton Cox st Marsden b Benke	25	— c James b Wichers	50
D. J. E. Foster st Marsden b Benke	1	— c Coke b Benke	0
P. R. Mitton c Cleland b Wichers	3	— b Benke	26
J. R. Thompson c Stuchbury b James	32	— st Marsden b Wichers	22
R. A. B. Hall b Benke	0	— b Wichers	6
H. J. K. Bagnall-Oakeley b Benke	20	— not out	12
C. R. Leighton c Donald b Wichers	3	— not out	8
A. D. N. Smith not out	10		
A. J. Claxton lbw b Wichers	3		
B 7, l-b 3	10	B 16, l-b 6, n-b 1	23

1/38 2/57 3/58 4/74 5/86 6/86   155
7/127 8/139 9/139

1/8 2/53 3/53   (7 wkts.) 172
4/115 5/140 6/143 7/150

Haileybury Bowling

	O.	M.	R.	W.		O.	M.	R.	W.
Smith	17	5	48	5	....	19.3	6	53	3
Leighton	7	1	20	0	....	12	2	56	2
Claxton	16.3	2	45	5	....	19	6	46	3
Bagnall-Oakeley	7	1	23	0	....	6	0	20	0
Hall						7	0	33	0

Cheltenham Bowling

	O.	M.	R.	W.		O.	M.	R.	W.
Khazzam	4	0	22	0	....	5	1	10	0
James	9	3	20	1	....	15	6	31	1
Cleland	10	5	25	1	....	2	0	13	0
Benke	21	7	38	4	....	25	5	45	3
Wichers	17.3	5	40	4	....	21	7	50	3

Umpires: W. Harrington and G. Morton.

Of the 58 matches played from 1893, Haileybury have won 19 and Cheltenham 17; 21 drawn, one abandoned.

SOUTHERN SCHOOLS v. THE REST

August 1, 2. Southern Schools won by 123 runs. Neame excelled for the winners. He captained the side capably, scored 132 by confident stroke-play without losing his wicket and crowned a fine display by taking five wickets for 24 runs. Reed and G. W. Cook also played good innings for Southern Schools. Sharpe, who came to the match with a considerable reputation, did enough for The Rest to demonstrate his quality, particularly in the art of on-driving.

Southern Schools

I. A. Addison (Wellington) b Fletcher	33	lbw b Duck	24
J. A. Lush (Brighton) lbw b Cook	8	b Cook	16
B. L. Reed (Winchester) b Alty	53	b Cook	4
G. W. Cook (Dulwich) c Smith b Alty	52	c Purves b Hurd	8
D. J. Mordaunt (Wellington) st Smith b Langlands	9	c Fletcher b Duck	3
A. R. B. Neame (Harrow) not out	87	not out	45
R. C. Coke Wallis (Marlborough) c Corran b Fletcher	19	b Hurd	8
D. S. Williams (Ottershaw) (did not bat)	—	c Hurd b Cook	0
R. D. Montgomerie (Merchant Taylors') (did not bat)	—	lbw b Duck	0
C. B. Howland (Dulwich) (did not bat)	—	b Cook	1
C. A. A. Black (Winchester) (did not bat)	—	b Alty	0
B 5	5	B 7, l-b 2	9

1/33 2/50 3/103 4/119   (6 wkts., dec.) 266
5/183 6/266

1/27 2/33 3/40 4/45   118
5/49 6/52 7/52 8/75 9/117

The Rest

P. J. Sharpe (Worksop) lbw b Williams	38	c Addison b Neame	30
E. M. Rose (Rugby) b Black	4	run out	10
J. H. Purves (Uppingham) b Black	28	lbw b Black	2
J. A. Corran (Greshams) lbw b Coke Wallis	12	st Howland b Williams	2
M. D. Duck (Wellingborough) run out	13	c Montgomerie b Williams	0
D. M. Alty (Merchant Taylors', Crosby) c Mordaunt b Coke Wallis	3	c Cook b Neame	21
A. C. Smith (King Edward's, Birmingham) st Howland b Montgomerie	4	c Addison b Neame	10
D. R. Cook (Warwick) c Montgomerie b Black	29	c Mordaunt b Coke Wallis	6
H. B. Langlands (Loretto) c Montgomerie b Coke Wallis	11	c Mordaunt b Neame	22
J. R. Fletcher (Repton) c Reed b Black	1	b Neame	1
A. Hurd (Chigwell) not out	1	not out	1
B 3, l-b 6, w 1	10	L-b 1, w 1	2

1/14 2/60 3/84 4/90 5/106 6/109   154
7/130 8/145 9/146

1/27 2/31 3/45 4/45 5/45   107
6/59 7/69 8/104 9/106

The Rest Bowling

	O.	M.	R.	W.		O.	M.	R.	W.
Cook	19	4	40	1	....	12	3	25	4
Corran	12	2	40	0	....	3	0	17	0
Duck	11	4	52	0	....	9	5	21	3
Fletcher	13.2	2	43	2					
Alty	20	6	51	2	....	6.4	0	19	1
Langlands	11	2	35	1					
			Hurd			7	0	27	2

Southern Schools Bowling

	O.	M.	R.	W.		O.	M.	R.	W.
Black	18	4	41	4	....	11	3	19	1
Coke Wallis	15.3	6	24	3	....	11	1	38	1
Mordaunt	10	1	27	0					
Williams	8	1	18	1	....	7	4	8	2
Cook	8	5	10	0					
Montgomerie	6	1	24	1	....	2	1	16	0
			Neame			8.4	1	24	5

Umpires: W. Harrington and R. Routledge.

COMBINED SERVICES v. PUBLIC SCHOOLS

August 3, 4. Drawn. The Schools, sent in to bat after rain, made a good fight and came out of the game with credit. Mordaunt, stylish in driving, carried off their batting honours, and D. R. Cook, left-hand medium-fast, bowled well. Richardson, the Worcestershire left-hander, was much the best batsman for the Services, and Stevens, in the first innings, showed control of length in taking five for 24. The Services wanted 184 in their second innings when two hours twenty minutes remained. They soon lapsed into a lethargic pace, surrendering the initiative to the Schools' bowlers. It was a most disappointing finish to a game which could have produced an exciting climax.

Public Schools

I. A. Addison (Wellington) c Heaton b Shirreff	17	— c Leary b Steer	8
P. J. Sharpe (Worksop) c Ainsworth b Deighton	20	— lbw b Shirreff	7
B. L. Reed (Winchester) c Shirreff b Deighton	5	— c Murray b Steer	2
G. W. Cook (Dulwich) c Murray b Deighton	18	— lbw b Heaton	32
D. J. Mordaunt (Wellington) c Addison b Stevens	25	— c Richardson b Leary	58
A. R. B. Neame (Harrow) lbw b Stevens	6	— b Gale	22
M. D. Duck (Wellingborough) c Ainsworth b Leary	9	— run out	6
D. M. Alty (Merchant Taylors', Crosby) c Shirreff b Stevens	22	— c Richardson b Leary	12
C. B. Howland (Dulwich) b Stevens	7	— st Murray b Leary	23
D. R. Cook (Warwick) st Murray b Stevens	7	— not out	6
C. A. A. Black (Winchester) not out	0	— st Murray b Stevens	10
L-b 3, n-b 1	4	B 27, l-b 1, w 2	30

1/25 2/38 3/51 4/67 5/87 6/94   140   1/12 2/16 3/30 4/101   216
7/120 8/133 9/138   5/133 6/153 7/158 8/199
                                                           9/206

Combined Services

L/Cpl. P. E. Richardson c and b Neame	51	— c Alty b Mordaunt	24
S/Ldr. A. C. Shirreff c Neame b D. Cook	23	— b Duck	0
Lt.-Cdr. M. L. Y. Ainsworth run out	12	— b Duck	32
Cdr. (E) A. L. Thackara lbw b D. Cook	8	— c Sharpe b Neame	24
L/A/C J. T. Murray c Black b D. Cook	2	— b G. Cook	33
A/C S. E. Leary c Howland b Black	27	— c Howland b D. Cook	8
L/Bdr. R. A. Gale not out	25	— b Alty	5
F/O D. Heaton b Black	2	— not out	1
Major J. H. G. Deighton c Duck b Black	3	— not out	2
E/A G. D. Steer c G. Cook b D. Cook	13		
2/Lt. R. G. Stevens b D. Cook	4		
L-b 3	3	L-b 1, n-b 1	2

1/45 2/60 3/81 4/85 5/126 6/126 **173**   1/15 2/49 3/63 (7 wkts.) **131**
7/128 8/136 9/167   4/87 5/103 6/122 7/130

Combined Services Bowling

	O.	M.	R.	W.		O.	M.	R.	W.
Steer	4	1	26	0	....	14	5	31	2
Shirreff	9	3	17	1	....	8	1	22	1
Deighton	18	8	26	3	....	9	1	15	0
Heaton	6	1	17	0	....	5	2	10	1
Gale	5	1	8	0	....	7	3	8	1
Stevens	13.4	6	24	5	....	14	5	41	1
Leary	6	1	18	1	....	20	1	59	3

Public Schools Bowling

	O.	M.	R.	W.		O.	M.	R.	W.
D. Cook	21.2	2	66	5	....	6	0	12	1
Black	18	6	38	3	....	11	2	34	0
Duck	3	0	19	0	....	12	0	32	2
Alty	8	0	35	0	....	3	0	13	1
Neame	8	4	12	1	....	4	1	14	1
Mordaunt					....	3	0	17	1
G. Cook					....	4	0	7	1

Umpires: G. D. Morton and R. Routledge.

ROYAL NAVY v. THE ARMY

August 5, 6. Drawn. Midshipmen Blackshaw and Brown, who roused the crowd in a forceful opening partnership of 121 on the second day, and Cartwright, who batted soundly for the Army, carried off the honours. The Army needed 244 to win in two hours, but against steady bowling found the task beyond them. In the Navy's first innings, Lightfoot, an accurate fast-medium bowler, took the first three wickets before conceding a run.

Royal Navy

Mid. W. Blackshaw c Gale b Lightfoot	1	— c Dickinson b Hawkins	56
Mid. A. Brown b Lightfoot	4	— c Marner b Hawkins	77
Lt.-Cdr. M. L. Y. Ainsworth b Lightfoot	11	— b Dickinson	40
Sub.-Lt. N. Durden-Smith b Hawkins	24	— b Hill	15
Cdr. (E) A. L. Thackara c Richardson b Allsopp	22	— not out	47
Inst./Lt. B. Prentis lbw b Hawkins	0	— c Gale b Lightfoot	16
Lt.-Cdr. J. D. Sayer b Allsopp	35	— b Deighton	0
CPO. G. A. Steer b Hawkins	11	— b Lightfoot	0
2/Lt. R. G. Stevens (R.M.) c Richardson b Allsopp	0	— lbw b Hill	19
Lt. D. Chapman b Hawkins	9	— c Marner b Hawkins	13
Lt.-Cdr. I. Stoop not out	1		
B 5, l-b 8, w 6, n-b 2	21	B 18, w 1, n-b 2	21

1/1 2/11 3/18 4/72 5/77 6/108   139
7/128 8/128 9/130

1/121 2/152 (9 wkts., dec.) 304
3/191 4/205 5/250 6/253
7/258 8/285 9/304

The Army

L/Cpl. P. E. Richardson lbw b Stevens	46	— c Sayer b Chapman	18
L/Bdr. T. W. Cartwright b Steer	56	— not out	62
L/Cpl. P. T. Marner b Chapman	22	— c Stoop b Chapman	2
Gnr. N. W. Hill run out	25	— b Stevens	41
Cpl. D. G. Hawkins b Stevens	1	— not out	27
L/Bdr. R. A. Gale not out	37		
2/Lt. C. Fetherstonhaugh b Sayer	6		
L/Cpl. A. Lightfoot not out	0		
B 5, l-b 1, w 1	7	B 13, w 1, n-b 1	15

1/72 2/116 3/132 4/137   (6 wkts., dec.) 200   1/43 2/45 3/101   (3 wkts.) 165
5/181 6/200

Major J. H. G. Deighton, 2/Lt. T. E. Dickinson and Sgt. R. Allsopp did not bat.

The Army Bowling

	O.	M.	R.	W.	O.	M.	R.	W.
Dickinson	5	0	18	0	10	2	30	1
Lightfoot	9	4	12	3	16	2	43	2
Deighton	11	5	21	0	9	0	32	1
Allsopp	18	8	48	3	17	4	55	0
Hawkins	11.4	3	19	4	22.4	1	87	3
Gale					5	2	13	0
Hill					8	1	23	2

Royal Navy Bowling

	O.	M.	R.	W.	O.	M.	R.	W.
Steer	17	3	66	1	9	1	23	0
Chapman	17	3	45	1	11	2	31	2
Stevens	25	8	49	2	9	2	33	1
Sayer	8	0	33	1	6	1	31	0
Ainsworth					5	0	14	0
Thackara					2	0	6	0
Prentis					2	0	12	0

Umpires: W. Harrington and G. D. Morton.

ROYAL NAVY v. ROYAL AIR FORCE

August 8, 9. Royal Air Force won by ten wickets before lunch on the second day. Junior Technician Cowan, the Yorkshire left-arm fast bowler, and L/A/C Murray, the Middlesex reserve wicket-keeper, were the men of the match. Too fast for his opponents who were baffled by his ability to make the ball move in the air and off the pitch, Cowan took 13 wickets for 82 runs. At one time in the second innings, his figures were six for seven. Murray hit eighteen 4's in his attractive century.

Royal Navy

Mid. W. Blackshaw b Shirreff	64	— c Murray b McKinna	0
Mid. A. Brown c Leary b McKinna	7	— b Cowan	0
Lt.-Cdr. M. L. Y. Ainsworth b Cowan	3	— b Cowan	10
Sub-Lt. N. Durden-Smith b Shirreff	10	— lbw b Cowan	0
Cdr. (E) A. L. Thackara c McKinna b Cowan	43	— b McKinna	1
O/S J. Proctor c Murray b Cowan	33	— b McKinna	0
Lt.-Cdr. J. D. Sayer c Leary b Cowan	5	— not out	16
CPO G. A. Steer c Leary b Cowan	10	— b Cowan	0
2/Lt. R. G. Stevens (R.M.) b Cowan	0	— b Cowan	0
Lt. D. Chapman b Cowan	0	— b Cowan	0
Lt.-Cdr. I. Stoop not out	4	— b Shirreff	18
B 7, l-b 3, n-b 5	15	L-b 1	1

1/23 2/30 3/53 4/103 5/161 6/176   194   1/0 2/10 3/10 4/11 5/11   46
7/183 8/183 9/183   6/11 7/11 8/13 9/17

Royal Air Force

L/A/C J. T. Murray not out	105	— not out	11
Sqdn.-Ldr. A. C. Shirreff c Blackshaw b Steer	14	— not out	27
A/C G. Millman c Stoop b Chapman	10		
A/C S. E. Leary c Stevens b Chapman	45		
A/C W. B. Stott not out	8		
B 7, l-b 9, w 2	18	B 3, w 1	4

1/59 2/86 3/179   (3 wkts., dec.) 200   (No wkt.) 42

L/A/C B. A. Langford, Flt/Lt. E. M. Senior, Flt/Lt. R. Leggett, F/O J. D. Heaton, F/O G. A. McKinna and J/T M. J. Cowan did not bat.

Royal Air Force Bowling

	O.	M.	R.	W.		O.	M.	R.	W.
Cowan	20.3	1	62	7	....	8	2	20	6
McKinna	11	3	31	1	....	8	3	22	3
Leary	7	0	35	0					
Shirreff	11	2	42	2	....	1	0	3	1
Heaton	3	0	6	0					
Langford	2	1	3	0					

Royal Navy Bowling

	O.	M.	R.	W.		O.	M.	R.	W.
Steer	15	2	50	0	....	3	1	2	0
Chapman	15	1	51	2	....	6	2	21	0
Stevens	18	7	51	1	....	4.2	1	14	0
Sayer	5	2	21	0					
Ainsworth	5	2	9	0	....	1	0	1	0

Umpires: W. Harrington and R. Routledge.

THE COUNTY CHAMPIONSHIP
IN 1955

In winning the Championship outright for the fourth year in succession, Surrey equalled the records of Nottinghamshire and Yorkshire, the only other counties to accomplish such a feat. Nottinghamshire were first from 1883 to 1886 inclusive, and as they also shared top place with Lancashire in 1882 their performance is slightly better in figures, although it must be emphasised that competition then was not so keen as nowadays. Yorkshire were Champions from 1922 to 1925 and again in 1937, 1938, 1939 and 1946. No Championship competition took place between 1939 and 1946 because of the war.

The glorious summer, following immediately upon the disastrous season of 1954, enabled most counties to improve their financial situation and it also led to a considerably higher proportion of matches being finished. Indeed, only one game throughout the season ended without a decision on first innings compared with twenty the previous year.

Surrey took advantage of the weather to set up a new record for the number of points in the Championship table since the system of awarding 12 points for a win and 4 for a lead on first innings was introduced in 1938. The previous best was the 260 obtained by Yorkshire in 1939. Then the Championship was decided on average, with counties not being obliged to play the same number of matches. As it happened Yorkshire's 260 points came from 28 games, the same number as all counties now have to play, so the comparison is fair.

Last season Surrey obtained 284 points, winning 23 games and leading on first innings in two of the five matches they lost. Not a single Championship match in which Surrey took part ended in a draw. Such a record will be extremely hard to beat. Yorkshire, themselves, gained 268 points, eight more than their 1939 figure, but even this fine effort was not good enough to wrest the Championship from Surrey.

The struggle for supremacy between these two counties dominated the Championship season and not until late in August could Surrey say they were safe. The two counties began neck and neck and at the end of May each held 100 per cent records through winning their first six matches. Surrey did not drop a point until their tenth game when Yorkshire gained revenge for defeat at The Oval by beating them at Leeds on June 21. Meanwhile Yorkshire had gone through a bad patch, losing three matches in succession early in June. They recovered form and on July 29 went into first place for the only time, leading by eight points, although Surrey, with two games in hand, always appeared likely to overtake them again. Surrey drew level in the next match and although Yorkshire remained equal with them until August 16, Surrey eventually finished 16 points clear.

No other county looked capable of challenging for first place, but an interesting struggle developed between Hampshire, Sussex and Middlesex for third position. This eventually fell to Hampshire who, making the biggest improvement of any county, enjoyed the best season in their history. In 1954 they finished fourteenth. Leicestershire also did exceptionally well, rising from sixteenth to sixth place. The worst decline came from Glamorgan, who dropped from fourth to sixteenth and others who fell away badly were Nottinghamshire, fifth to eleventh, and Derbyshire, third to eighth. The unfortunate Somerset side doubled their victories of the previous year, but even four successes failed to take them away from bottom place, a position they have occupied four seasons running.

FINAL POSITIONS

	Pld.	Won	Lost	Drn.	Tied	No Dcsn.	First Inns. Lead in Match Lost	Drn.	Pts.
Points Awarded	—	12			6	—	4	4	
Surrey (1)	28	23	5	0	0	0	2	0	284
Yorkshire (2)	28	21	5	2	0	0	2	2	268
Hampshire (14)......	28	16	5	6	1	0	0	3	210
Sussex (9)...........	28	13	8	6	1	0	3	5	196
Middlesex (7)	28	14	12	2	0	0	6	0	192
Leicestershire (16) ...	28	11	10	7	0	0	3	2	154
Northamptonshire (7)	28	9	10	9	0	0	3	7	148
Derbyshire (3).......	28	9	10	9	0	0	2	7	146
⎰ Lancashire (10)	28	10	9	8	0	1	2	3	140
⎱ Warwickshire (6)	28	10	9	9	0	0	2	3	140
Nottinghamshire (5) .	28	10	11	7	0	0	1	2	132
Gloucestershire (13) .	28	9	13	6	0	0	2	3	128
Kent (11)	28	8	13	7	0	0	0	2	104
Essex (15)	28	6	15	7	0	0	3	4	100
Worcestershire (11) ..	28	5	17	6	0	0	2	4	84
Glamorgan (4)	28	5	14	8	0	1	2	3	80
Somerset (17)	28	4	17	7	0	0	2	2	64

The Derbyshire and Leicestershire records include two points for a tie on first innings in match drawn.

The Sussex record includes two points for tie on first innings in match lost.

(Figures in parentheses indicate positions in 1954 table.)

SCORING IN THE COUNTY CHAMPIONSHIP

The scheme for scoring in the County Championship was as follows:—

(*a*) Should a match be finished, the winning side to score 12 points.

(*b*) Should a match be finished and the scores be equal (a tie), each side to score 6 points.

(*c*) Should the scores be equal in a drawn match, the side batting in the fourth innings to score 6 points in all (whether or not it has first innings lead) and the opponents to score no points, except they will retain such first innings points as they may already have gained.

(*d*) Should the match be finished, the side which leads on the first innings, if it loses the match, 4 points. If the scores on the first innings be equal, the side which loses the match, 2 points.

(*e*) Should a match not be finished, the side which leads on the first innings, 4 points.

(*f*) Should a match not be finished, and the scores of the first innings be equal, each side 2 points.

(*g*) Every match, even should there be no play for any reason, shall be included in the table of results as a "Match Played," neither side to score points.

(*h*) If there is no play on the first two days of a match and it is not carried to a further conclusion than that of the first innings, the side which leads on the first innings shall score 8 points.

(*i*) The side which has the highest aggregate of points gained at the end of the season shall be Champion County.

COUNTY CHAMPIONSHIP STATISTICS FOR 1955

County	For			Against		
	Runs	Wickets	Average	Runs	Wickets	Average
Derbyshire.......	9521	442	21.53	9371	463	20.23
Essex	10868	454	23.93	11288	422	26.74
Glamorgan	8986	432	20.80	10032	402	24.95
Gloucestershire ..	10392	482	21.56	10005	410	24.40
Hampshire.......	9303	435	21.38	8847	522	16.37
Kent	9966	469	21.24	10338	409	25.27
Lancashire	9763	411	23.75	9407	432	21.77
Leicestershire	10727	449	23.89	11082	420	26.38
Middlesex	9900	470	21.06	9769	472	20.69
Northamptonshire	11422	407	28.06	11760	421	27.93
Nottinghamshire .	12012	461	26.05	11714	430	27.24
Somerset	10341	515	20.07	11100	366	30.32
Surrey	9572	367	26.08	9295	537	17.30
Sussex	10432	437	23.87	10386	489	21.23
Warwickshire	10793	439	24.58	9714	409	23.75
Worcestershire ...	10460	484	21.61	10661	391	27.26
Yorkshire	10231	370	27.65	9920	529	18.75
	174689	7524	23.21	174689	7524	23.21

DERBYSHIRE

President—THE DUKE OF DEVONSHIRE

Secretary—W. T. TAYLOR, County Cricket Ground, Nottingham Road, Derby

Captain—D. B. CARR

| D. B. Carr | County Badge | G. O. Dawkes |

After being third in the County Championship in 1954, Derbyshire began the summer with hopes of making a strong bid for honours, but they finished no higher than eighth. For this disappointing result there were two main causes, a severe shoulder strain which kept that aggressive opening bowler, Jackson, out of the side for thirteen games towards the end of the season, and the inadequate batting of the side as a whole.

In May and June, Gladwin and Jackson fully maintained their reputations of being among the most formidable pairs of opening bowlers in county cricket, and despite his long period of inactivity Jackson headed the bowling averages. When his partner was out of action, Gladwin continued to bowl with that skill and tenacity which has made him such an excellent servant of Derbyshire. More responsibility than usual fell upon Morgan, but he did not make the most of his opportunity. This provided first-team chances for two young pace bowlers, Hall, who stands well over six feet, and H. Rhodes, son of A. E. G. Rhodes, the county's former leg-break bowler. Both showed distinct promise.

The most satisfactory feature of the out-cricket was the big advance of Smith, the off-break bowler, who fulfilled in full measure the hopes held for him. Although many of the prevailing hard pitches afforded him little help, Smith bowled with accuracy and skill, and took more than 100 wickets in all first-class games. In the field, too, Derbyshire did well. Carr, in his first season as captain, Revill and Morgan all excelled close to the wicket, and Dawkes, for whom a testimonial fund was opened in 1956, again did splendid work behind the stumps.

Only late in the season was G. L. Willatt, the former captain, able to play, and the loss of this reliable left-hander at number three formed the main reason for the batting decline. Hamer, who scored more runs than in any previous season for Derbyshire, and Kelly often gave the side a good start and Hamer, who made a magnificent 227 against Nottinghamshire at Trent Bridge, batted with refreshing freedom. When they were parted, however, wickets usually fell quickly, although Carr tried several batsmen at number three. Lee, though always shaping like a batsman of quality, seldom made runs and Johnson, returning to the county after an absence of four years, disappointed. Fortunately Revill again proved his dependability, and Carr showed such improved form that he scored over 600 more runs in Championship games than in 1954. He well earned the honour of leading the M.C.C. team in Pakistan during the winter.

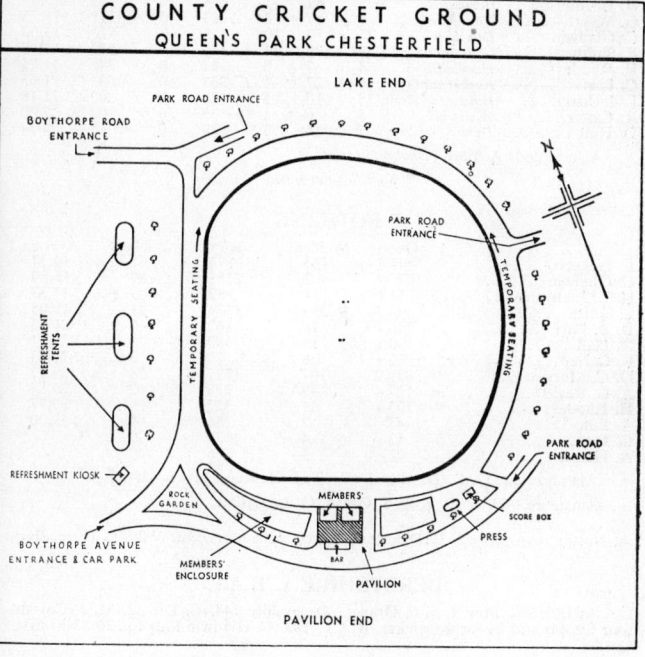

DERBYSHIRE RESULTS

All First-Class Matches—Played 30, *Won* 10, *Lost* 10, *Drawn* 10
County Championship Matches—Played 28, *Won* 9, *Lost* 10,
Drawn 9

COUNTY CHAMPIONSHIP AVERAGES

BATTING

	Birthplace	Mtchs.	Inns.	Not Outs	Runs	100's	Highest Inns.	Aver.
A. Hamer	*Huddersfield*	28	49	1	1509	2	227	31.43
D. B. Carr	*Wiesbaden*	28	48	2	1438	2	146	31.26
G. L. Willatt	*Nottingham*	5	9	0	228	0	68	25.33
A. C. Revill	*Bolsover*	28	49	3	1146	0	79	24.91
J. Kelly	*Bacup*	28	49	1	974	0	72	20.29
G. O. Dawkes	*Leicester*	28	46	6	806	0	86	20.15
D. J. Green	*Burton-on-Trent*	6	11	1	185	0	49	18.50
D. C. Morgan	*Middlesex*	26	43	5	681	1	109*	17.92
H. L. Johnson	*Barbados*	25	42	1	654	0	52	15.95
G. Wyatt	*New Mills*	4	7	3	63	0	31*	15.75
C. Gladwin	*Doe Lea*	27	39	10	435	0	67	15.00
E. Smith	*Grassmoor*	28	39	11	350	0	57	12.50
H. Rhodes	*Hadfield*	4	7	3	47	0	34	11.75
C. Lee	*Rotherham*	16	27	1	303	0	63	11.65
L. Jackson	*Whitwell*	15	16	5	123	0	20*	11.18
R. Carter	*Whitwell*	3	6	1	35	0	10	7.00
D. Hall	*Derby*	7	14	7	29	0	6*	4.14

Also batted: A. Eato (*Duckmanton*) 6, 0.

* Signifies not out.

BOWLING

	Overs	Maidens	Runs	Wickets	Average
L. Jackson	445.1	145	877	61	14.37
C. Gladwin	1075.1	407	2155	139	15.50
H. L. Johnson	13.1	4	52	3	17.33
E. Smith	808.2	293	1734	91	19.05
D. B. Carr	296.1	78	862	40	21.55
D. Hall	190.1	39	580	23	25.21
R. Carter	22	6	79	3	26.33
D. C. Morgan	639.2	164	1727	58	29.77
A. C. Revill	127.4	39	358	62	29.83
H. Rhodes	105.1	21	322	9	35.77
A. Eato	43	7	156	4	39.00
C. Lee	13	4	29	0	—
A. Hamer	22	3	66	0	—

Also bowled: G. O. Dawkes 1—0—9—0; J. Kelly 11—5—25—1.

Amateurs.—D. B. Carr, D. J. Green, G. L. Willatt.

At Nottingham, May 2, 3. DERBYSHIRE drew with NOTTINGHAMSHIRE. (Friendly.)

DERBYSHIRE v. R.A.F.

At Ilkeston, May 4, 5, 6, Drawn. Derbyshire 144 (C. Lee 58, M. J. Cowan four for 44) and 24 for no wicket; R.A.F. 109 (C. Gladwin four for 26). Not first class.

At Lord's, May 7, 9, 10. DERBYSHIRE drew with MIDDLESEX.

At Derby, May 11, 12, 13. DERBYSHIRE drew with SOUTH AFRICANS. (See SOUTH AFRICAN section.)

At Ilford, May 14, 16, 17. DERBYSHIRE drew with ESSEX.

At Gravesend, May 18, 19, 20. DERBYSHIRE beat KENT by an innings and 51 runs.

DERBYSHIRE v. YORKSHIRE

At Chesterfield, May 21, 23, 24. Yorkshire won by 139 runs. Although Derbyshire fought hard throughout, Yorkshire retained the initiative and won worthily. On the first day Derbyshire bowled accurately and restrained the Yorkshire batsmen, but later Wilson and Lester punished them heavily. Derbyshire, too, began well, but could not maintain their early run-getting against the fiery pace of Trueman, and the spin and accuracy of Appleyard and Wardle. Good driving by Yardley, the Yorkshire captain, enabled him to declare soon after lunch on the last day, and Derbyshire again found Appleyard and Wardle too much for them. Appleyard finished the match with ten wickets for 80.

Yorkshire

F. A. Lowson c Dawkes b Morgan	24	—	lbw b Gladwin	7
W. H. H. Sutcliffe b Smith	57	—	b Jackson	15
J. V. Wilson b Gladwin	64	—	b Jackson	11
E. Lester lbw b Carr	54	—	b Jackson	6
W. Watson b Smith	20	—	c and b Smith	33
N. W. D. Yardley c Carr b Jackson	33	—	not out	58
J. H. Wardle st Dawkes b Smith	5	—	lbw b Jackson	6
R. Illingworth b Jackson	1	—	c Lee b Smith	2
R. Booth not out	2			
F. S. Trueman run out	3			
B 1, l-b 7, n-b 1	9		L-b 3	3

1/34 2/130 3/201 4/201   (9 wkts., dec.) 272
5/253 6/263 7/267 8/268 9/272

1/7 2/31   (7 wkts., dec.) 141
3/39 4/40 5/105 6/107 7/141

R. Appleyard did not bat.

Derbyshire

A Hamer c Booth b Appleyard	10	—	c Illingworth b Wardle	35
J. Kelly b Trueman	46	—	c Booth b Wardle	11
C. Lee lbw b Wardle	42	—	b Wardle	6
A. C. Revill b Appleyard	14	—	b Appleyard	2
D. B. Carr c Illingworth b Appleyard	0	—	lbw b Appleyard	0
H. L. Johnson c Wilson b Trueman	13	—	c Lowson b Trueman	2
D. C. Morgan lbw b Appleyard	1	—	c Wilson b Appleyard	2
G. O Dawkes c Booth b Wardle	9	—	b Appleyard	16
C. Gladwin c Trueman b Appleyard	7	—	c Illingworth b Trueman	2
E. Smith c Booth b Wardle	10	—	not out	10
L. Jackson not out	0	—	b Appleyard	0
B 12, l-b 16, n-b 4	32		L-b 2, n-b 3	5

1/27 2/104 3/130 4/130 5/131   184
6/141 7/158 8/160 9/184

1/29 2/47 3/56 4/56   90
5/58 6/60 7/67 8/70 9/90

Derbyshire Bowling

	O.	M.	R.	W.		O.	M.	R.	W.
Jackson	29.2	11	48	2	....	19.1	5	52	4
Gladwin	30	13	57	1	....	15	4	37	1
Morgan	26	6	86	1	....	6	0	21	0
Smith	24	10	44	3	....	6	0	28	2
Hamer	3	0	18	0					
Carr	2	0	10	1					

Yorkshire Bowling

	O.	M.	R.	W.		O.	M.	R.	W.
Trueman	21	4	37	2	....	11	2	25	2
Appleyard	37	17	51	5	....	13.4	4	29	5
Illingworth	11	3	25	0					
Wardle	42.3	25	39	3	....	18	9	31	3

Umpires: N. Oldfield and H. Elliott (Lancashire).

DERBYSHIRE v. KENT

At Derby, May 25, 26. Derbyshire won by an innings and 21 runs. For the second time within a week, Derbyshire beat Kent with an innings to spare. Carr put Kent in to bat on a green topped pitch, and their batsmen found scoring difficult against accurate fast-medium bowling by Jackson, Gladwin and Morgan. Fagg did not score his first run for nearly an hour and only 45 were made in two hours before lunch. Only Evans, who hit well, resisted Jackson effectively. Derbyshire batted consistently, despite good seam bowling by Ridgway and accurate leg-breaks from Wright. Their lead of 143 proved ample, for Jackson and Morgan, aided by excellent catching, brought about another collapse.

Kent

A. E. Fagg c Hamer b Jackson	12	— b Jackson	9
A. H. Phebey c Dawkes b Smith	27	— c Carr b Jackson	21
P. Hearn b Jackson	29	— c Revill b Morgan	45
J. Pettiford c Dawkes b Gladwin	0	— b Gladwin	5
T. G. Evans c Lee b Smith	40	— c Carr b Jackson	7
A. F. Brazier b Jackson	0	— c Hamer b Morgan	4
A. Dixon b Jackson	0	— c Jackson b Morgan	3
E. G. Witherden lbw b Jackson	1	— c Dawkes b Morgan	1
F. Ridgway not out	2	— st Dawkes b Smith	19
D. V. P. Wright b Jackson	0	— absent hurt	0
J. C. T. Page b Smith	2	— not out	2
B 5, n-b 1	6	B 1, l-b 4, n-b 1	6

1/39 2/43 3/49 4/100 5/104 6/104   119   1/18 2/53 3/60 4/73   122
7/114 8/116 9/116   5/96 6/100 7/101 8/110 9/122

Derbyshire

A. Hamer c Witherden b Wright	22	C. Gladwin not out	20
J. Kelly lbw b Wright	35	E. Smith c Pettiford b Ridgway	5
C. Lee st Evans b Wright	13	L. Jackson run out	0
A. C. Revill b Ridgway	24		
D. B. Carr c Evans b Ridgway	53		
H. L. Johnson b Ridgway	13	B 6, l-b 12	18
D. C. Morgan b Wright	12		
G. O. Dawkes c Pettiford b Ridgway	47	1/23 2/59 3/95 4/99 5/126 262

6/154 7/201 8/240 9/258

Derbyshire Bowling

	O.	M.	R.	W.	O.	M.	R.	W.
Jackson	24	8	40	6	 15	1	44	3
Gladwin	22	9	21	1	 16	5	28	1
Morgan	10	1	36	0	 8	0	32	4
Smith	14.3	10	16	3	.... 9.3	4	12	1

Kent Bowling

	O.	M.	R.	W.
Ridgway	33	2	109	5
Brazier	8.4	1	24	0
Wright	23	8	45	4
Page	22	5	64	0
Dixon	1	0	2	0

Umpires: T. J. Bartley and W. T. Jones.

At Birmingham, May 28, 30, 31. Derbyshire drew with Warwickshire.

At Worcester, June 1, 2. Derbyshire beat Worcestershire by 144 runs.

DERBYSHIRE v. LEICESTERSHIRE

At Burton-on-Trent, June 4, 6, 7. Drawn. Derbyshire drew level on the first innings with five wickets standing in the last over on the second day, but rain prevented further play and they had to be content with sharing four points. After careful thought Palmer, the Leicestershire captain, decided to bat on a wet pitch and his side fared badly against Gladwin and Jackson, who made the ball lift. Six wickets fell for 70 runs in a limited first day's play, but Spencer restored respectability to the score with a fiercely hit 75. Kelly, Johnson and Revill all batted brightly for Derbyshire, despite lively fast-medium bowling by Spencer.

Leicestershire

G. Lester lbw b Jackson	10	J. E. Walsh b Gladwin...........	17
M. R. Hallam c Jackson b Gladwin	6	C. T. Spencer b Jackson	75
M. Tompkin c Dawkes b Jackson..	28	R. Julian b Jackson	0
C. H. Palmer c Revill b Gladwin..	22	B. Boshier not out	0
V. E. Jackson c Carr b Jackson ..	0	B 6, l-b 2	8
G. A. Smithson c Dawkes b Gladwin	49	1/16 2/18 3/66 5/68 5/68	215
V. S Munden c Morgan b Gladwin	0	6/68 7/94 8/201 9/202	

Derbyshire

A. Hamer b Spencer.............	0	D. C. Morgan not out	2
J. Kelly c and b Munden........	51		
H. L. Johnson c Tompkin b Walsh	46	B 2, l-b 5, n-b 1.............	8
A. C. Revill b Spencer	79		
D. B. Carr c Julian b Spencer	17	1/0 2/73 3/132 4/193 (5 wkts.) 215
G. Wyatt not out	12	5/200	

G. O. Dawkes, C. Gladwin, E. Smith and L. Jackson did not bat.

Derbyshire Bowling

	O.	M.	R.	W.
Jackson	27.4	9	59	5
Gladwin	29	11	59	5
Morgan	13	4	39	0
Smith	13	6	35	0
Carr	6	1	15	0

Leicestershire Bowling

	O.	M.	R.	W.
Spencer	16	5	39	3
Boshier	12	0	40	0
Palmer	11	6	12	0
Jackson	19	11	25	0
Walsh	9	1	39	1
Munden	9	2	30	1
Lester	5	2	22	0

Umpires: L. H. Gray and D. Davies.

At Bristol, June 8, 9, 10. DERBYSHIRE drew with GLOUCESTERSHIRE.

DERBYSHIRE v. ESSEX

At Chesterfield, June 15, 16, 17. Drawn. Insole, the Essex captain became the first player to score a century against Derbyshire during the summer. Batting with skill and a wide range of strokes, he made 104 in less than three hours and hit twelve 4's. Other batsmen, particularly Bailey and Gibb, scored slowly against a keen attack in which Smith bowled off-breaks with accuracy. After a sound opening stand of 64 between Hamer and Kelly, Derbyshire batted disappointingly against accurate pace bowling by Preston and Bailey and well-controlled leg-breaks by Greensmith and fell 74 behind. Once again Smith's off-breaks brought about an Essex breakdown. After a delay through rain on the last day, Derbyshire were set to make 154 in 97 minutes. They lost three men for seven runs to Bailey's outswingers and then concentrated on saving the game.

Essex

T. C. Dodds c Dawkes b Gladwin	19	— c Carr b Gladwin 11
G. Barker run out	36	— b Gladwin 2
T. E. Bailey c Kelly b Smith	16	— lbw b Gladwin 0
R. Horsfall b Smith	22	— st Dawkes b Smith 7
D. J. Insole lbw b Jackson	104	— lbw b Smith 8
P. A. Gibb c Morgan b Smith	58	— c Carr b Gladwin 19
B. Taylor b Smith	9	— not out 29
R. Smith b Smith	7	
M. Bear b Smith	1	— not out 3
W. T. Greensmith not out	4	
K. C. Preston not out	2	
B 3, l-b 6, w 2	11	

1/23 2/72 3/75 4/110   (9 wkts., dec.) 289   1/13 2/13   (6 wkts., dec.) 79
5/239 6/274 7/274 8/282 9/285   3/24 4/42 5/46 6/48

Derbyshire

A. Hamer c Taylor b Preston	46	— c Gibb b Bailey 3
J. Kelly c Smith b Greensmith	38	— c Dodds b Bailey 2
H. L. Johnson c Horsfall b Preston	0	— c Insole b Bailey 0
A. C. Revill c Bear b Preston	36	— not out 38
D. B. Carr c Bear b Smith	37	— c Gibb b Bailey 9
G. Wyatt run out	3	— not out 6
D. C. Morgan c and b Greensmith	8	
G. O. Dawkes lbw b Bailey	1	
C. Gladwin lbw b Preston	10	
E. Smith b Preston	16	
L. Jackson not out	11	
B 3, l-b 6	9	L-b 2 2

1/64 2/64 3/116 4/138 5/142   215   1/4 2/6 3/7   (4 wkts.) 60
6/155 7/168 8/175 9/202   4/27

Derbyshire Bowling

	O.	M.	R.	W.		O.	M.	R.	W.
Jackson	20	3	52	1	....	12	4	31	0
Gladwin	26	14	42	1	....	17	7	28	3
Morgan	25	8	43	0	....	4	2	6	0
Smith	38	12	69	6	....	8	4	14	3
Carr	17	2	51	0					
Johnson	3	0	21	0					

Essex Bowling

	O.	M.	R.	W.		O.	M.	R.	W.
Bailey	26	7	52	1	....	10	2	25	4
Preston........	29.2	9	61	5	....	6	0	10	0
Smith	13	2	32	1	....	3	0	21	0
Greensmith	35	13	54	2					
Insole	5	2	7	0					
Bear..........						1	0	2	0

Umpires: G. S Mobey and E. Davies.

At Cardiff, June 18, 20, 21. DERBYSHIRE beat GLAMORGAN by 132 runs.

DERBYSHIRE v. LANCASHIRE

At Chesterfield, June 25, 27, 28. Lancashire won by 129 runs on a pitch which gave assistance to spin bowlers for most of the match. They began well when Ikin and Wharton made 78 for the opening stand, and passed 200 with four wickets down, despite accurate off-spin bowling by Smith. Then Jackson and Gladwin, with the new ball, brought about a collapse. On the second day Derbyshire found difficulty in the left-arm slows of Hilton and Tattersall's off-breaks. Apart from Ikin, who again batted soundly, Lancashire struggled in the second innings in face of slow left-arm bowling by Carr, who achieved the best analysis of his career. Against the off-breaks of Collins, Derbyshire never looked like achieving the task of scoring 305.

Lancashire

J. T. Ikin c Johnson b Smith	....	90	— b Carr	56
A. Wharton c Revill b Smith	....	41	— c Gladwin b Smith	27
G. A. Edrich lbw b Jackson	....	24	— c Gladwin b Carr	8
K. Grieves c Johnson b Carr	....	6	— c Lee b Carr	9
J. Dyson c Revill b Gladwin	....	22	— c Morgan b Carr........	31
W. Place lbw b Gladwin	....	19	— st Dawkes b Smith	1
R. Collins b Jackson	....	1	— b Carr	1
J. Jordan c Revill b Jackson	....	1	— lbw b Carr	35
M. J. Hilton b Gladwin	....	14	— c Jackson b Carr	13
R. Tattersall b Jackson	....	7	— not out	5
F. W. Moore not out	....	10	— not out	6
B 4		4	B 3..................	3

1/78 2/131 3/140 4/174 5/205   239   1/53 2/80   (9 wkts., dec.) 195
6/206 7/208 8/208 9/217   3/93 4/100 5/101 6/104
                                                7/118 8/183 9/186

Derbyshire

A. Hamer c Place b Hilton	36	— c Jordan b Tattersall 24
J. Kelly c Edrich b Hilton	7	— c Ikin b Moore 0
H. L. Johnson c Jordan b Hilton	4	— c Place b Hilton 38
A. C. Revill c Grieves b Hilton	5	— c Collins b Ikin........... 30
D. B. Carr c Edrich b Hilton	40	— c Edrich b Collins 9
C. Lee c Moore b Hilton	1	— c Edrich b Collins 0
D. C. Morgan c Grieves b Tattersall	0	— lbw b Collins 16
G. O. Dawkes b Tattersall	16	— b Ikin 14
C. Gladwin c Grieves b Tattersall	2	— not out 10
E. Smith not out	7	— c Grieves b Collins 9
L. Jackson c Place b Tattersall	6	— c Place b Collins 17
B 4, l-b 2	6	B 5, l-b 3 8
	130	**175**

1/32 2/45 3/50 4/59 5/61 6/71   1/3 2/62 3/84 4/107
7/89 8/95 9/119   5/107 6/107 7/131 8/141
                                        9/157

Derbyshire Bowling

	O.	M.	R.	W.	O.	M.	R.	W.
Jackson	27	8	48	4	12	4	27	0
Gladwin	25.2	11	54	3	14	5	33	0
Morgan	17	5	43	0	6	2	12	0
Smith	41	22	52	2	30	11	53	2
Carr	19	9	38	1	19	5	53	7
Hamer					5	0	14	0

Lancashire Bowling

	O.	M.	R.	W.	O.	M.	R.	W.
Moore	4	0	15	0	3	1	14	1
Wharton	5	0	14	0	5	1	12	0
Tattersall	24.4	8	36	4	15	5	29	1
Hilton	23	6	59	6	23	4	59	1
Dyson					1	1	0	0
Ikin					10	4	23	2
Collins					12.5	4	30	5

Umpires: J. S. Buller and E. Davies.

DERBYSHIRE v. GLAMORGAN

At Derby, June 29, 30, July 1. Drawn. Rain rescued Glamorgan from a most unpromising position when, set 282 to get, they collapsed completely against the fast-medium bowling of Gladwin and Jackson. Bowlers were masters for most of the game and only a fifth wicket stand of 88 between Carr and Johnson saved Derbyshire from a first innings failure. Jackson and Gladwin proved too much for the Glamorgan batsmen and Derbyshire led by 98. In the second innings Hamer outshone everybody, reaching three figures in two hours fifty minutes and hitting nine 4's.

Derbyshire

A. Hamer c Watkins b Wooler	....	28	— not out	....	111
J. Kelly c Davies b Wooler	......	15	— c Davies b Lewis	....	22
D. C. Morgan c Davies b Wooler	......	0	— c Parkhouse, b Shepherd	.	32
A. C. Revill c Wooler b Watkins	.....	9	— c Lewis b Shepherd	....	1
D. B. Carr c Edrich b Wooler	......	78			
H. L. Johnson c Davies b Lewis	....	35			
C. Lee b Watkins	....	10	— c Wooler b Shepherd	.....	7
G. O. Dawkes c Pressdee b Wooler	....	18	— not out	....	1
C. Gladwin c Davies b Watkins	....	0			
E. Smith not out	....	12			
L. Jackson c Pressdee b Shepherd	....	12			
B 1, l-b 1, w 1	....	3	B 2, l-b 5, w 2	....	9

1/41 2/43 3/44 4/58 5/146 6/176   220   1/83 2/150   (4 wkts., dec.) 183
7/180 8/180 9/208   3/152 4/176

Glamorgan

B. R. Edrich lbw b Jackson	....	16	— lbw b Gladwin	....	2
W. G. A. Parkhouse b Gladwin	....	7	— c Dawkes b Jackson	......	2
B. Hedges b Gladwin	....	4	— c Kelly b Gladwin	......	1
W. E. Jones c Revill b Jackson	....	0	— c Dawkes b Gladwin	......	3
A. J. Watkins c Dawkes b Jackson	......	1	— lbw b Gladwin	....	2
W. Wooler b Gladwin	....	22	— b Jackson	....	19
J. Pressdee c Dawkes b Jackson	....	22	— not out	....	16
J. E. McConnon b Morgan	....	13	— not out	....	6
H. G. Davies b Jackson	....	5			
K. H. Lewis not out	....	18			
D. J. Shepherd b Gladwin	....	5			
B 5, l-b 4	....	9	L-b 4	....	4

1/7 2/29 3/31 4/32 5/35 6/59   122   1/4 2/5 3/5 4/10   (6 wkts.) 55
7/76 8/89 9/111   5/17 6/45

Glamorgan Bowling

	O.	M.	R.	W.		O.	M.	R.	W.
Lewis	12	2	34	1	....	13	0	54	1
Shepherd	20.1	2	69	1	....	21	2	81	3
Wooler	52	27	64	5	....	12	3	26	0
Watkins	25	3	50	3	....	4	2	8	0
Parkhouse					....	1	0	5	0

Derbyshire Bowling

	O.	M.	R.	W.		O.	M.	R.	W.
Jackson	20	7	39	5	....	17	5	25	2
Gladwin	20.2	8	38	4	....	18.3	10	15	4
Morgan	9	1	28	1	....	5	4	6	0
Smith	2	0	8	0					
Carr					....	3	1	5	0

Umpires: G. S. Mobey and A. Skelding.

At Manchester, July 2, 4, 5. DERBYSHIRE lost to LANCASHIRE by eight wickets.

At Southampton, July 6, 7, 8. DERBYSHIRE beat HAMPSHIRE by 26 runs.

At Ashby-de-la-Zouch, July 9, 11, 12. DERBYSHIRE drew with LEICESTERSHIRE.

At Nottingham, July 13, 14, 15. DERBYSHIRE beat NOTTINGHAMSHIRE by 111 runs.

DERBYSHIRE v. HAMPSHIRE

At Chesterfield, July 16, 18, 19. Hampshire won by 58 runs. Bowlers always held the upper hand. Although Marshall hit hard, most of the early Hampshire batsmen were troubled by Gladwin in their first innings, but the later men retrieved the situation by bold methods. Apart from Revill, Derbyshire could do little against the fast-medium attack of Shackleton, Cannings and Gray, but they hit back when Hampshire batted again. On drying turf, Gladwin and Smith quickly dismissed irresolute batsmen. Derbyshire needed 159 to win, but collapsed against a well-balanced attack in which Sainsbury excelled.

Hampshire

J. R. Gray c Dawkes b Gladwin	2	— b Revill	26
R. E. Marshall c Lee b Hall	55	— b Gladwin	15
H. Horton b Revill	15	— c Revill b Smith	7
L. Harrison c Carr b Gladwin	4	— c Hamer b Smith	0
N. H. Rogers lbw b Gladwin	0	— b Smith	25
H. M. Barnard lbw b Carter	25	— c Hamer b Gladwin	6
E. D. R. Eagar c Revill b Hall	32	— c Dawkes b Gladwin	4
P. J. Sainsbury lbw b Gladwin	36	— c Gladwin b Smith	0
D. Shackleton b Carter	26	— c Johnson b Smith	3
V. H. D. Cannings not out	15	— b Gladwin	0
M. D. Burden b Hall	2	— not out	0
W 1, n-b 1	2	L-b 2, n-b 1	3

1/3 2/33 3/48 4/54 5/81 6/113   214   1/36 2/49 3/51 4/51 5/74   89
7/147 8/181 9/211   6/82 7/82 8/87 9/87

Derbyshire

A. Hamer c Barnard b Shackleton	3	— c Marshall b Cannings	33
J. Kelly lbw b Gray	25	— c Rogers b Sainsbury	7
C. Lee lbw b Cannings	0	— c Harrison b Sainsbury	6
A. C. Revill c Cannings b Gray	47	— c Marshall b Sainsbury	31
D. B. Carr lbw b Shackleton	13	— run out	3
H. L. Johnson c Marshall b Gray	22	— c Harrison b Burden	2
G. O. Dawkes lbw b Shackleton	0	— b Burden	0
C. Gladwin c Eagar b Gray	11	— lbw b Shackleton	4
E. Smith c Harrison b Cannings	7	— c Harrison b Shackleton	0
R. Carter not out	6	— c Harrison b Cannings	5
D. Hall b Cannings	1	— not out	0
B 6, l-b 3, n-b 1	10	L-b 9	9

1/16 2/17 3/44 4/73 5/114 6/114   145   1/13 2/30 3/58 4/59 5/63   100
7/116 8/135 9/139   6/66 7/66 8/88 9/88

Derbyshire Bowling

	O.	M.	R.	W.		O.	M.	R.	W.
Hall	21.4	3	76	3	....	8	1	25	0
Gladwin	18	4	35	4	....	15	9	18	4
Revill	8	2	29	1	....	7	2	12	1
Smith	16	5	36	0	....	11.4	5	22	5
Carr	4	1	12	0	....	2	0	9	0
Carter	9	3	24	2					

Hampshire Bowling

	O.	M.	R.	W.		O.	M.	R.	W.
Shackleton	26	6	40	3	....	13	7	16	2
Cannings	18.5	3	49	3	....	14	7	13	2
Gray	25	14	28	4					
Sainsbury	11	6	17	0	....	34.1	20	47	3
Burden	1	0	1	0	....	14	8	15	2

Umpires: T. J. Bartley and D. Davies.

DERBYSHIRE v. NOTTINGHAMSHIRE

At Ilkeston, July 23, 25, 26. Drawn. Bowlers toiled throughout on an easy pitch in heat-wave conditions and a draw always seemed likely. Nottinghamshire, without the leg-break bowlers, Dooland and Goonesena, were further handicapped by an injury to Jepson on the first day, and did well to dismiss Derbyshire for 278. The young left-arm pace bowler, Matthews, showed splendid stamina. Accurate fast-medium bowling by Gladwin and Morgan gave Derbyshire the first innings points, despite a hard-hit century by the left-hander, Poole, who batted just over three hours and hit twenty 4's. Derbyshire hit boldly before declaring on the third day, but could make little impression on Nottinghamshire, for whom Giles and Clay made 105 for the first wicket.

Derbyshire

A. Hamer lbw b Harvey	84	— b Matthews 0
J. Kelly c Kelly b Smales	15	— c Harvey b Kelly 50
C. Lee c Clay b Kelly	0	— b Smales 6
A. C. Revill b Matthews	18	— c Stocks b Smales 35
D. B. Carr c and b Harvey	20	— c Rowe b Kelly 40
H. L. Johnson c Poole b Matthews	52	— c Stocks b Smales 13
D. C. Morgan c Harvey b Matthews	38	— lbw b Smales 5
G. O. Dawkes b Matthews	34	— not out 53
C. Gladwin b Matthews	5	— c Martin b Smales 0
E. Smith c sub b Matthews	3	— b Smales 8
D. Hall not out	0	— not out 2
B 3, l-b 6	9	B 4, l-b 9 13

1/52 2/56 3/97 4/129 5/142 6/220   278
7/269 8/272 9/277

1/0 2/19   (9 wkts., dec.) 225
3/94 4/104 5/139 6/151
7/155 8/157 9/175

Nottinghamshire

J. D. Clay b Gladwin	19	— c and b Carr 55
R. J. Giles b Gladwin	21	— not out 70
E. J. Martin b Hall	3	— c Dawkes b Gladwin 7
F. W. Stocks c and b Revill	21	— lbw b Carr 0
C. J. Poole c Dawkes b Gladwin	122	— c Dawkes b Gladwin 6
P. F. Harvey b Gladwin	2	— b Carr 12
J. Kelly b Morgan	21	— not out 4
K. Smales not out	15	
A. Jepson c Gladwin b Morgan	12	
C. S. Matthews c Dawkes b Morgan	0	
E. J. Rowe run out	2	
B 8, l-b 3, n-b 3	14	W 1 1

1/41 2/44 3/44 4/122 5/140 6/222   252
7/222 8/241 9/245

1/105 2/112 3/128 (5 wkts.) 155
4/132 5/151

Nottinghamshire Bowling

	O.	M.	R.	W.		O.	M.	R.	W.
Jepson	9	1	31	0					
Matthews	26.1	9	65	6	....	16	4	33	1
Smales	35	6	94	1	....	36.2	9	91	6
Kelly	18	9	37	1	....	29	14	52	2
Harvey	19	8	27	2	....	18	9	36	0
Stocks	5	1	15	0					

Derbyshire Bowling

	O.	M.	R.	W.	O.	M.	R.	W.
Hall	20	5	55	1				
Gladwin	31	8	70	4	12	5	19	2
Morgan	23	7	73	3	10	2	46	0
Smith	14	6	21	0	13	4	34	0
Revlil	9	5	19	1				
Carr..........					17	4	55	3

Umpires: F. S. Lee and N. Oldfield.

DERBYSHIRE v. NORTHAMPTONSHIRE

At Chesterfield, July 27, 28, 29. Northamptonshire won by six wickets. After losing six wickets for 57 runs, Derbyshire recovered well on the opening day largely through the efforts of Green, playing his first game of the season. He shared stands of 77 with Dawkes and 63 with Rhodes. An accurate attack enabled Derbyshire to gain a lead of 22 and when, in the second innings, Hamer and Morgan made a second wicket stand of 101, they seemed to be heading for victory. Then the two left-arm spin bowlers, Tribe and Broderick, met with success, and Northamptonshire completed their recovery by aggressive batting. Barrick, at the crease two hours forty minutes, hit three 6's and fourteen 4's, and he received excellent support from Livingston and Tribe.

Derbyshire

A. Hamer c Barrick b Clarke	12	— lbw b Wild	62
J. Kelly c Livingston b Liddell	3	— c Andrew b Clarke	3
D. C. Morgan lbw b Clarke..........	12	— b Broderick	86
A. C. Revill lbw b Tribe	11	— c Subba Row b Liddell	29
D. B. Carr b Liddell	0	— c Tribe b Broderick	12
H. L. Johnson lbw b Barrick	18	— st Andrew b Broderick.....	0
D. J. Green run out	49	— c Brookes b Tribe	6
G. O. Dawkes b Broderick.............	55	— c and b Tribe	19
H. J. Rhodes c Arnold b Subba Row	34	— not out	8
C. Gladwin c Arnold b Subba Row	8	— st Andrew b Broderick.....	1
E. Smith not out	1	— st Andrew b Tribe	0
L-b 9	9	L-b 5	5

1/12 2/26 3/28 4/28 5/47 6/57   212
7/134 8/197 9/211

1/15 2/116 3/168 4/188   231
5/188 6/197 7/213 8/225
9/230

Northamptonshire

D. Brookes lbw b Gladwin	7	— lbw b Gladwin.............	12
P. Arnold c and b Morgan.............	51	— lbw b Gladwin	20
L. Livingston c Dawkes b Gladwin	48	— c Johnson b Smith	58
D. Barrick c Hamer b Gladwin	1	— not out 105	
R. Subba Row b Carr	23	— lbw b Gladwin	0
G. E. Tribe run out	1	— not out	55
V. Broderick lbw b Rhodes	4		
A. G. Liddell c Revill b Carr..........	29		
K. V. Andrew not out...............	13		
J. Wild c Dawkes b Smith	8		
R. W. Clarke run out	5		
		B 1, l-b 1, w 1, n-b 1 ..	4

1/13 2/101 3/103 4/107 5/112 6/120   190
7/143 8/174 9/183

1/35 2/68 3/115   (4 wkts.) 254
4/119

Northamptonshire Bowling

	O.	M.	R.	W.		O.	M.	R.	W.
Clarke	19	4	45	2	....	17	4	66	1
Liddell	15	3	36	2	....	13	1	32	1
Tribe	15	3	50	1	....	32.4	9	75	3
Barrick	4	1	8	1	....	1	1	0	0
Broderick	18	10	34	1	....	21	7	36	4
Wild	8	1	27	0	....	7	1	17	1
Subba Row	3.3	1	3	2					

Derbyshire Bowling

	O.	M.	R.	W.		O.	M.	R.	W.
Morgan	20	4	43	1	....	8	0	54	0
Gladwin	24	9	41	3	....	21	5	64	3
Rhodes	16	2	49	1	....	10	4	34	0
Smith	29	16	36	1	....	17	4	56	1
Carr	18	12	21	2	....	13	2	40	0
Revill						1	0	2	0

Umpires: H. Elliott (Lancashire) and A. J. B. Fowler.

DERBYSHIRE v. WARWICKSHIRE

At Derby, July 30, August 1, 2. Warwickshire won by 164 runs, after holding the initiative throughout. Derbyshire put them in to bat on a pitch promising to help the faster bowlers, but Warwickshire batted confidently. For the fifth wicket Dollery and Hitchcock added 131 runs and Hitchcock reached his century in 78 minutes, hitting one 6 and sixteen 4's. Afterwards Rhodes, aged 18, brought about a collapse. Hamer and Kelly gave Derbyshire a good start, but the pace of Bannister and spin of Hollies then caused such trouble that only dour batting by Green and Gladwin averted a follow-on. Aggressive batting by Spooner enabled Warwickshire to declare their second innings, and only Dawkes offered much resistance to the pace bowlers, Thompson, Bannister and Keith Dollery when Derbyshire batted a second time.

Warwickshire

F. C. Gardner lbw b Gladwin	18	— b Gladwin ... 14
N. F. Horner c Morgan b Rhodes	38	— lbw b Rhodes ... 24
A. V. Wolton c Revill b Morgan	24	— b Gladwin ... 4
R. T. Spooner c Morgan b Carr	31	— b Morgan ... 77
H. E. Dollery c Dawkes b Morgan	73	— lbw b Revill ... 13
R. E. Hitchcock c Dawkes b Rhodes	110	— not out ... 17
A. Townsend c Hamer b Rhodes	9	
K. R. Dollery c Dawkes b Rhodes	20	— not out ... 34
J. D. Bannister b Rhodes	0	
R. G. Thompson not out	6	
W. E. Hollies c Carr b Rhodes	0	
L-b 1	1	B 12, l-b 3 ... 15

1/53 2/71 3/84 4/149 5/280 6/294   330   1/30 2/42   (5 wkts., dec.) 198
7/308 8/312 9/325   3/52 4/83 5/151

Derbyshire

A. Hamer b K. Dollery	37	—	c Bannister b Thompson	27
J. Kelly c Townsend b Thompson	32	—	b Thompson	24
D. C. Morgan c Townsend b Thompson	0	—	b Bannister	19
A. C. Revill b Bannister	31	—	c Spooner b K. Dollery	2
D. B. Carr b Bannister	21	—	c Spooner b Thompson	5
H. L. Johnson b Hollies	3	—	b K. Dollery	0
D. J. Green c H. Dollery b Bannister	26	—	c Horner b Bannister	4
G. O. Dawkes b Hollies	13	—	not out	45
H. J. Rhodes b Hollies	3	—	b Hollies	1
C. Gladwin b Hitchcock	24	—	c H. Dollery b Bannister	0
E. Smith not out	6	—	c Hitchcock b K. Dollery	16
B 1, l-b 4, n-b 3	8		B 16, n-b 1	17

1/71 2/71 3/76 4/102 5/111 6/141 　　204　　　1/63 2/64 3/64 4/66 5/72 　　160
7/158 8/167 9/181　　　　　　　　　　　　　6/77 7/113 8/127 9/128

Derbyshire Bowling

	O.	M.	R.	W.		O.	M.	R.	W.
Morgan	24	4	95	2	....	12	1	39	1
Gladwin	26	6	64	1	....	18	4	55	2
Rhodes	23.1	3	86	6	....	17	2	49	1
Revill	5	1	13	0	....	9	3	39	1
Smith	17	5	49	0					
Carr	5	2	22	1					
Johnson						0.1	0	1	0

Warwickshire Bowling

	O.	M.	R.	W.		O.	M.	R.	W.
Thompson	22	6	56	2	....	19	6	43	3
Bannister	24	5	62	3	....	17	4	37	3
K. Dollery	17	0	56	1	....	13.4	0	36	3
Hollies	14	7	19	3	....	6	3	17	1
Hitchcock	0.3	0	3	1	....	3	0	10	0

Umpires: F. Chester and D. Davies.

At Edinburgh, August 3, 4, 5. DERBYSHIRE beat SCOTLAND by eight wickets.

At Bradford, August 6, 8. DERBYSHIRE lost to YORKSHIRE by an innings and 94 runs.

DERBYSHIRE v. SUSSEX

At Derby, August 10, 11, 12. Sussex won by 49 runs. Hall, the tall fast-medium bowler, gave Sussex considerable trouble on the first day with his accurate attack, but Derbyshire found James, with his persistent medium-pace bowling, equally difficult to time. Parks, Suttle and Cox all drove strongly when Sussex batted again, but other batsmen fared poorly against the steady bowling of Gladwin. Derbyshire were set to make 283, a task which appeared well within their compass after Hamer and Kelly scored 94 for the first wicket. Despite accurate bowling by Thomson and Smith, the score passed 200 with five wickets down, but these bowlers then brought about a collapse.

Sussex

J. Langridge lbw b Revill	18	— c Lee b Hall		12
D. V. Smith b Hall	41	— c Dawkes b Gladwin		5
A. S. M. Oakman lbw b Morgan	41	— lbw b Gladwin		3
J. M. Parks c Revill b Gladwin	31	— c Dawkes b Morgan		48
K. G. Suttle b Gladwin	0	— b Gladwin		63
D. S. Sheppard c Revill b Morgan	1	— b Gladwin		26
G. H. G. Doggart c Dawkes b Revill	18	— c Carr b Gladwin		0
G. Cox c Hamer b Hall	28	— lbw b Morgan		38
R. T. Webb c Carr b Hall	7	— b Gladwin		0
N. I. Thomson c Dawkes b Hall	0	— c Dawkes b Hall		2
A. E. James not out	0	— not out		1
B 2, l-b 1, n-b 1	4	B 12, l-b 6		18

1/47 2/67 3/117 4/121 5/124 6/137   189   1/5 2/19 3/42 4/91 5/159   216
7/170 8/186 9/186   6/159 7/168 8/168 9/194

Derbyshire

A. Hamer b James	1	— b Thomson		38
J. Kelly lbw b Smith	10	— c Sheppard b Smith		54
C. Lee c Suttle b James	16	— c Oakman b Smith		18
A. C. Revill st Webb b James	42	— b James		33
D. B. Carr b James	26	— st Webb b Thomson		16
H. L. Johnson lbw b James	1	— c Doggart b Smith		46
D. C. Morgan b James	21	— lbw b Thomson		10
G. O. Dawkes c Webb b Smith	1	— c Smith b Thomson		0
C. Gladwin run out	3	— c Doggart b Smith		9
E. Smith c Webb b Thomson	0	— b Smith		0
D. Hall not out	0	— not out		0
L-b 2	2	L-b 8, n-b 1		9

1/5 2/27 3/31 4/88 5/96 6/99   123   1/94 2/94 3/136 4/151   233
7/102 8/119 9/123   5/180 6/206 7/206 8/224
                                        9/228

Derbyshire Bowling

	O.	M.	R.	W.		O.	M.	R.	W.
Hall	20.1	4	57	4	....	18	3	62	2
Gladwin	24	8	53	2	....	21	6	44	6
Morgan	29	6	57	2	....	19.2	7	64	2
Revill	11	5	18	2	....	8	2	23	0
Smith						2	0	5	0

Sussex Bowling

	O.	M.	R.	W.		O.	M.	R.	W.
Thomson	17	4	46	1	....	27	3	72	4
James	25.4	8	56	6	....	28	10	61	1
Smith	9	4	19	2	....	31.3	12	58	5
Oakman						17	5	33	0

Umpires: H. Elliott (Lancashire) and N. Oldfield.

DERBYSHIRE v. WORCESTERSHIRE

At Buxton, August 13, 15, 16. Derbyshire won by seven wickets. After dismissing Worcestershire cheaply on the first day on a pitch which aided seam bowlers, Derbyshire retained the initiative throughout. Jackson, in his first match for six weeks, and Gladwin bowled splendidly when the match began, and Derbyshire consolidated their advantage with hard hitting, particularly by Revill, who scored all but two of his runs in 4's. Worcestershire resisted more strongly when they batted again, and Dews stayed for nearly four hours, but Derbyshire, given a good start by the forceful Hamer, found their second innings task comfortable.

Worcestershire

D. Kenyon lbw b Jackson	7	— run out	41
L. Outschoorn lbw b Morgan	26	— c Dawkes b Smith	20
R. G. Broadbent c Dawkes b Jackson	0	— lbw b Jackson	15
M. J. Horton lbw b Gladwin	5	— c Kelly b Carr	9
G. Dews c Carr b Gladwin	1	— c and b Smith	73
D. W. Jackson c Dawkes b Gladwin	12	— b Carr	8
R. O. Jenkins b Jackson	11	— lbw b Gladwin	46
H. Yarnold c Revill b Gladwin	18	— c and b Morgan	3
G. H. Chesterton b Gladwin	2	— lbw b Morgan	5
R. T. D. Perks not out	14	— c Gladwin b Morgan	4
J. Flavell b Jackson	17	— not out	1
N-b 3	3	B 1, l-b 9, n-b 5	15
	—		—
	116		240

1/9 2/9 3/14 4/17 5/48 6/60
7/83 8/85 9/85

1/63 2/66 3/79 4/98
5/123 6/201 7/220 8/232
9/238

Derbyshire

A. Hamer st Yarnold b Jenkins	36	— b Perks	49
J. Kelly lbw b Flavell	30	— lbw b Flavell	8
G. L. Willatt lbw b Chesterton	3	— c Yarnold b Perks	4
A. C. Revill c Chesterton b Jenkins	50	— not out	22
D. B. Carr c Richardson b Horton	39	— not out	32
H. L. Johnson b Horton	1		
D. C. Morgan not out	35		
G. O. Dawkes c Perks b Horton	0		
C. Gladwin b Jenkins	3		
E. Smith lbw b Perks	11		
L. Jackson run out	14		
L-b 6, n-b 1	7	B 7, l-b 3, w 4	14
	—		—
	229	(3 wkts.)	129

1/57 2/60 3/90 4/147 5/156 6/169
7/169 8/178 9/207

1/32 2/63 3/68   (3 wkts.) 129

Derbyshire Bowling

	O.	M.	R.	W.	O.	M.	R.	W.
Jackson	16.5	4	52	4	13.1	4	47	1
Gladwin	17	9	36	5	26	11	46	1
Morgan	9	4	17	1	23	7	48	3
Smith	6	2	8	0	22.4	8	45	2
Carr					9	2	23	2
Revill					4	1	16	0

Worcestershire Bowling

	O.	M.	R.	W.	O.	M.	R.	W.
Perks	12.1	2	47	1	14	1	37	2
Flavell	15	3	47	1	6	1	17	1
Chesterton	12	8	26	1	5	2	20	0
Jenkins	20	3	57	3	7	1	21	0
Horton	14	2	45	3	6	0	20	0

Umpires: K. McCanlis and W. F. Price.

DERBYSHIRE v. GLOUCESTERSHIRE

At Derby, August 20, 22, 23. Derbyshire won by an innings and 36 runs. Emmett, the Gloucestershire captain, erred in putting Derbyshire in to bat, for the pitch played easily on the first day, and the batsmen scored freely, particularly Carr, who batted stylishly for three hours ten minutes. In heavy atmosphere on the second day, Gladwin and Morgan made the ball swerve late, and bowling unchanged, forced Gloucestershire to follow on 282 behind. Gloucestershire then batted with more spirit, Young showing patience and defensive skill, but on the last day Gladwin produced another deadly spell, and the final five wickets fell for 35 runs.

Derbyshire

A. Hamer lbw b Lambert	17	G. O. Dawkes not out	9
J. Kelly lbw b McHugh	52	H. J. Rhodes not out	0
G. L. Willatt b Wells	37		
A. C. Revill b McHugh	10	B 15, l-b 8	23
D. B. Carr c Emmett b Griffiths	139		
D. J. Green c Rochford b Lambert	30	1/22 2/104 3/133 (7 wkts., dec.)	329
D. C. Morgan c Young b Griffiths	12	4/134 5/226 6/307 7/323	

C. Gladwin and E. Smith did not bat.

Gloucestershire

D. M. Young b Gladwin	3	— c Kelly b Carr	94
C. A. Milton lbw b Gladwin	1	— run out	36
T. W. Graveney b Gladwin	2	— c Dawkes b Smith	33
J. F. Crapp b Morgan	1	— c Morgan b Smith	23
G. M. Emmett b Morgan	15	— c Revill b Morgan	21
G. E. Lambert c Kelly b Morgan	0	— c Dawkes b Gladwin	8
J. V. C. Griffiths not out	11	— c Revill b Carr	0
P. Rochford b Gladwin	2	— not out	16
C. Cook b Gladwin	0	— c Hamer b Gladwin	3
B. D. Wells c Hamer b Gladwin	4	— c Smith b Gladwin	6
F. P. McHugh b Gladwin	8	— b Gladwin	2
		L-b 3, n-b 1	4
1/3 2/4 3/5 4/13 5/18 6/25 7/30	47	1/75 2/141 3/187 4/187	246
8/30 9/34		5/189 6/217 7/217 8/231	
		9/241	

Gloucestershire Bowling

	O.	M.	R.	W.	O.	M.	R.	W.
Lambert	22	2	79	2				
McHugh	23	5	45	2				
Wells	42	15	84	1				
Cook	16	8	46	0				
Graveney	4	2	8	0				
Milton	5	1	15	0				
Griffiths	9	3	29	2				

Derbyshire Bowling

	O.	M.	R.	W.	O.	M.	R.	W.
Morgan	12	2	31	3	26	4	53	1
Gladwin	11.1	4	16	7	25.1	12	30	4
Rhodes					14	3	48	0
Revill					4	0	10	0
Smith					28	7	72	2
Carr					12	4	29	2

Umpires: E. Cooke and E. A. Roberts.

DERBYSHIRE v. SOMERSET

At Chesterfield, August 24, 25, 26. Derbyshire won by 115 runs. Somerset put Derbyshire in to bat, and they seemed to be justified when their opponents were out cheaply, but in the end Derbyshire won comfortably. A "green" pitch influenced the decision, and Lobb took advantage of the conditions, bowling at medium pace with considerable hostility. Only Carr impressed among the Derbyshire batsmen. Somerset found run-getting equally difficult, apart from Tremlett, who drove freely, and they led by only one run. Bright batting by Kelly,

L

Willatt, Carr and Dawkes swung the game in favour of Derbyshire, and Gladwin drove home their advantage with excellent bowling despite another attractive display of strokes by Tremlett.

Derbyshire

A. Hamer b Lobb	1	—	c Lomax b Yawar Saeed	11
J. Kelly c Tremlett b Yawar Saeed	4	—	c Tordoff b McMahon	72
G. L. Willatt c Lomax b Lawrence	27	—	c Stephenson b Lawrence	56
A. C. Revill b Yawar Saeed	1	—	c Stephenson b McMahon	11
D. B. Carr c Angell b Lobb	51	—	b Yawar Saeed	57
D. J. Green st Stephenson b Lawrence	19	—	not out	7
D. C. Morgan lbw b Lobb	7	—	c Lawrence b Yawar Saeed	13
G. O. Dawkes b Lobb	10	—	c Stephenson b Lobb	34
H. J. Rhodes c Stephenson b Lawrence	0	—	not out	1
C. Gladwin lbw b Lobb	12			
E. Smith not out	9			
B 16, n-b 2	18		B 8, l-b 7	15

1/2 2/10 3/15 4/98 5/98 6/109   159   1/12 2/99   (7 wkts., dec.) 277
7/125 8/126 9/149   3/136 4/189 5/251 6/259
                                               7/275

Somerset

G. G. Tordoff c Willatt b Gladwin	17	—	c Carr b Morgan	3
F. L. Angell lbw b Morgan	5	—	b Gladwin	16
J. Lawrence st Dawkes b Carr	19	—	lbw b Gladwin	1
M. F. Tremlett c Smith b Revill	83	—	b Revill	76
P. B. Wight b Carr	0	—	b Gladwin	2
J. G. Lomax c Smith b Carr	1	—	b Rhodes	40
J. Hilton b Gladwin	0	—	not out	14
H. W. Stephenson c Hamer b Smith	24	—	lbw b Revill	0
Yawar Saeed not out	8	—	b Gladwin	0
J. W. McMahon lbw b Smith	0	—	b Gladwin	0
B. Lobb st Dawkes b Smith	0	—	run out	0
B 1, l-b 1, n-b 1	3		B 4, l-b 5	9

1/23 2/25 3/89 4/97 5/99 6/104   160   1/2 2/8 3/15 4/29 5/33   161
7/147 8/160 9/160   6/120 7/130 8/150 9/161

Somerset Bowling

	O.	M.	R.	W.		O.	M.	R.	W.
Yawar Saeed	8	2	14	2	....	17	1	72	3
Lobb	25	10	41	5	....	14	1	50	1
Lomax	6	0	27	0	....	7	1	18	0
Tordoff	6	0	19	0					
Lawrence	18	4	40	3	....	20	4	48	1
McMahon					....	24	6	64	2
Hilton					....	4	1	10	0

Derbyshire Bowling

	O.	M.	R.	W.		O.	M.	R.	W.
Morgan	20	6	43	1	....	10	1	24	1
Gladwin	24	8	45	2	....	13	4	22	5
Rhodes	16	3	30	0	....	9	4	26	1
Smith	4.5	1	14	3	....	11	1	39	0
Carr	9	5	6	3	....	6	1	30	0
Revill	6	0	19	1	....	8	4	11	2

Umpires: E. Cooke and J. J. Hills.

At Hove, August 27, 29, 30 DERBYSHIRE lost to SUSSEX by 94 runs.

At The Oval, August 31, Sept. 1. DERBYSHIRE lost to Surrey by eight wickets.

ESSEX

President—HUBERT ASHTON
Secretary—T. E. BAILEY, 60, London Road, Chelmsford
Captain—D. J. INSOLE

G. Barker

County Badge

K. C. Preston

Essex showed no improvement upon their performances of 1954, for whereas they gained six County Championship victories as against three, they suffered defeat on four more occasions.

Insole, the captain, could in no way be blamed for the lack of success. He managed his limited resources skilfully, set a splendid example in the field and far outshone his colleagues in batting, heading the averages for the second year in succession. Not only was he the first man in the country to reach both 1,000 and 2,000 runs, but his aggregate in all games, 2,427, was the biggest of any player in English first-class cricket and of his career. Including that against the South Africans at Colchester, he reached three-figures on nine occasions, two of his centuries coming in the match with Kent at Gillingham. Furthermore his medium-pace seam bowling proved valuable at times, as when he dismissed five Surrey batsmen for 22 runs at Ilford. Honoured by selection for England in the fourth Test match, he also captained the Gentlemen at Lord's and The Rest against the Champion County.

Despite the calls of the Test matches, T. E. Bailey again demonstrated his all-round value. He and Insole shared in some big stands, notably those of 239 against Nottinghamshire and 184 against the South Africans. The consistency of Barker, the new Yorkshire-born opening batsman, earned him his county cap. His two centuries helped substantially in wins over Nottinghamshire and Warwickshire. Others to exceed 1,000 runs were Gibb, patient as ever, and Dodds, who would have done better but for periodical faulty judgment in running. Williams, after the University match, Greensmith, Taylor, a capable deputy wicket-keeper, and Ray

Smith, who hit the fastest hundred of the season, also did good work in run-getting, but Horsfall fell away so badly that his services, together with those of Cousens, the slow left-arm bowler, were dispensed with at the end of the summer.

The chief feature of the bowling was the advance of Preston. Though he did not attempt to produce his pace of some previous years, he maintained considerable accuracy for long spells and not only increased his number of wickets by 65 compared with 1954, but substantially reduced their cost. Greensmith, with leg-breaks, was another bowler who greatly improved his record, but the lack of another reliable spinner was severely felt. Ray Smith, despite advancing years, got through a lot of hard work with credit and Ralph achieved some good things, but J. A. Bailey, now up at Oxford, lost his effectiveness and was called upon for only ten Championship fixtures.

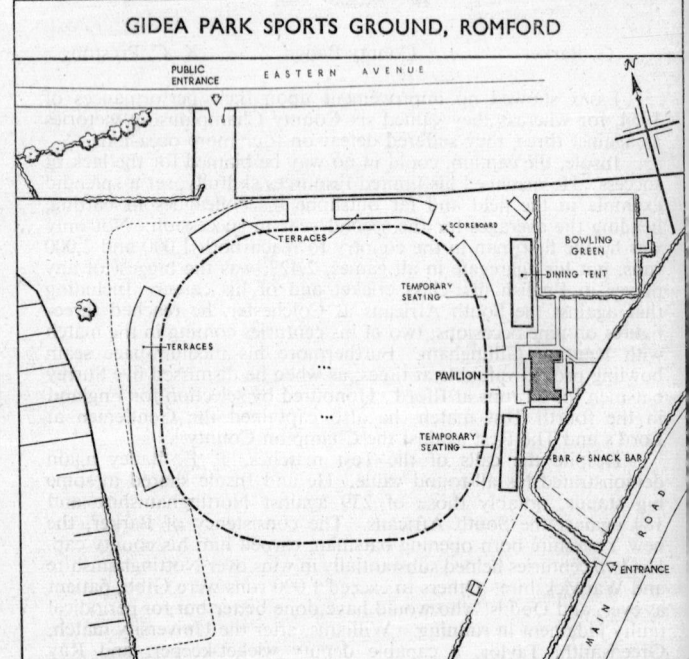

ESSEX RESULTS

All First-Class Matches—Played 30, *Won* 6, *Lost* 15, *Drawn* 9

County Championship Matches—Played 28, *Won* 6, *Lost* 15, *Drawn* 7

COUNTY CHAMPIONSHIP AVERAGES

BATTING

	Birthplace	Mtchs.	Inns.	Not Outs.	Runs	100's	Highest Inns.	Aver.
D. J. Insole ...	*Clapton*	26	47	4	1907	8	142	44.34
T. E. Bailey ...	*Westcliff*	16	28	7	878	2	152*	41.80
G. Barker	*Leeds*	28	54	3	1394	2	106	27.33
C. C. P. Williams	*Oxford*	10	17	0	454	1	119	26.70
P. A. Gibb	*York*	28	52	5	1170	0	77	24.89
T. C. Dodds ...	*Bedford*	28	53	1	1283	0	94	24.67
W. T. Greensmith	*Middlesbrough*	28	45	16	664	0	63*	22.89
R. Horsfall	*Todmorden*	23	41	2	622	0	69	15.94
B. Taylor	*West Ham*	18	34	2	508	0	75	15.87
R. Ralph	*East Ham*	17	26	5	329	0	53*	15.66
Ray Smith	*Boreham*	28	48	4	655	1	101*	14.55
M. Bear	*Brentwood*	6	11	3	106	0	53	13.25
G. Smith	*Braintree*	7	9	2	92	0	29*	13.14
K. C. Preston ..	*Goodmayes*	27	34	12	234	0	30*	10.63
B. Knight	*Chesterfield*	3	4	0	42	0	22	10.50
J. A. Bailey	*Brixton*	10	17	7	43	0	14*	4.30
P. Cousens	*Durban*	4	7	2	19	0	9	3.80

Also batted: R. E. Evans (*East Ham*) 3, 4.

* *Signifies not out.*

BOWLING

	Overs	Maidens	Runs	Wickets	Average
T. E. Bailey	526.3	123	1314	63	20.85
K. C. Preston	843	183	2265	93	24.35
W. T. Greensmith	682.3	151	2055	78	26.34
Ray Smith	759.5	161	2072	76	27.26
T. C. Dodds	84.5	14	330	12	27.50
R. Ralph	359	72	1063	36	29.52
D. J. Insole	229.5	45	711	24	29.62
J. A. Bailey	276	65	677	20	33.85
P. Cousens	79	28	194	5	38.80
G. Barker	5	1	19	0	—
G. Smith	43	19	111	0	—

Also bowled: M. Bear 1.2—0—6—0; C. C. P. Williams 0.1—0—4—0.

Amateurs.—J. A. Bailey, T. E. Bailey, R. E. Evans, D. J. Insole, C. C. P. Williams.

At Cambridge, May 7, 9, 10. ESSEX drew with CAMBRIDGE UNIVERSITY.

At Lord's, May 11, 12, 13. ESSEX lost to MIDDLESEX by 70 runs.

ESSEX v. DERBYSHIRE

At Ilford, May 14, 16, 17. Drawn. Badly dropped off the first ball of the match, Dodds became the only Essex batsman to offer serious resistance to accurate and persistent fast-medium bowling by Gladwin, Jackson and Morgan, although Taylor hit hard in the first innings and Bailey twice defended stubbornly. Showers interfered with play on the first day, and on drying turf Derbyshire also struggled until Dawkes settled down to sound batting. Ably supported by Morgan and Gladwin, he defended watchfully and drove with power for ninety minutes. For a second time Essex struggled, but rain prevented play on the last day and allayed their anxiety.

Essex

T. C. Dodds run out	58	—	c Gladwin b Jackson		2
P. A. Gibb lbw b Jackson	0	—	c Carr b Gladwin		1
G. Barker b Morgan	6	—	c Morgan b Smith		15
R. Horsfall b Jackson	3	—	b Jackson		0
D. J. Insole c Revill b Gladwin	9	—	c Morgan b Gladwin		3
T. E. Bailey c Smith b Gladwin	9	—	not out		15
B. Taylor lbw b Gladwin	28	—	lbw b Smith		0
R. Smith c Kelly b Gladwin	5	—	c Dawkes b Morgan		3
W. T. Greensmith lbw b Jackson	0	—	not out		0
K. C. Preston not out	9				
P. Cousens c Jackson b Gladwin	5				
L-b 3, w 1, n-b 4	8		N-b 7		7

1/3 2/19 3/27 4/83 5/83 6/112   **140**   1/6 2/9 3/11   (7 wkts.) **46**
7/121 8/122 9/128   4/15 5/43 6/43 7/46

Derbyshire

A. Hamer b Bailey	25	C. Gladwin c Gibb b Smith	16
J. Kelly c Barker b Bailey	6	E. Smith c Dodds b Smith	1
C. Lee b Bailey	9	L. Jackson not out	2
A. C. Revill c Gibb b Bailey	7		
D. B. Carr b Preston	0	N-b 5	5
H. L. Johnson c Bailey b Preston	12		
D. C. Morgan lbw b Bailey	13	1/19 2/37 3/45 4/46 5/63 6/63	**149**
G. O. Dawkes c Insole b Smith	53	7/92 8/130 9/144	

Derbyshire Bowling

	O.	M.	R.	W.		O.	M.	R.	W.
Jackson	28	11	51	3	....	10	3	15	2
Gladwin	29.4	18	41	5	....	9	7	8	2
Morgan	9	2	21	1	....	8	3	11	1
Smith	9	4	19	0	....	6	4	5	2

Essex Bowling

	O.	M.	R.	W.
Bailey	21	5	56	5
Smith	13.2	3	43	3
Preston	13	3	31	2
Greensmith	7	2	14	0

Umpires: L. H. Gray and A. J. B. Fowler.

ESSEX v. SURREY

At Ilford, May 18, 19, 20. Surrey won by five wickets just before a heavy storm broke. Lock, left arm, played a big part in the success, taking nine wickets and effecting some superb catches. On rain-damaged turf, Essex lost half their wickets for 27, but Taylor drove fearlessly, his 75 in seventy minutes including one

6 and twelve 4's. Bailey helped him add 93. Surrey went ahead with five wickets standing, but Insole, medium pace, speedily ended the innings. Essex, 53 behind, again began badly, but Horsfall drove hard and he and Bailey put on 95. Lock restored the balance by dismissing four men in four overs without cost and Surrey needed 150. Three wickets fell for 25, but May (nine 4's) and Barrington added 62 before McIntyre (seven 4's), with powerful driving, decided the issue.

Essex

T. C. Dodds c Surridge b Bedser	0	— c Lock b Bedser	6
P. A. Gibb c May b Bedser	0	— c McIntyre b Lock	19
G. Barker c Lock b Loader	3	— st McIntyre b Laker	22
R. Horsfall lbw b Loader	3	— c Surridge b Lock	69
D. J. Insole b Loader	17	— c Lock b Laker	1
T. E. Bailey lbw b Laker..............	21	— not out	48
B. Taylor b Lock	75	— c and b Lock	0
R. Smith c and b Laker	0	— lbw b Lock	0
W. T. Greensmith not out	0	— c May b Lock	0
K. C. Preston lbw b Lock	0	— b Laker.................	5
P. Cousens b Lock...................	0	— b Lock..................	5
B 2, l-b 5	7	B 17, l-b 9, n-b 1......	27

1/0 2/3 3/3 4/14 5/27 6/120   126   1/18 2/61 3/63 4/77   202
7/120 8/126 9/126   5/172 6/172 7/174 8/174
                                             9/183

Surrey

T. H. Clark c Horsfall b Greensmith ...	26	— c Dodds b Preston	20
D. G. W. Fletcher c Barker b Bailey	13	— b Bailey	0
P. B. H. May c and b Greensmith	25	— b Bailey	59
B. Constable run out	4	— lbw b Preston	0
K. Barrington b Insole	39	— lbw b Greensmith	23
A. J. McIntyre st Gibb b Cousens	24	— not out	41
J. C. Laker b Insole.................	11	— not out	2
W. S. Surridge c and b Insole	9		
G. A. R. Lock b Insole................	16		
P. J. Loader not out	3		
A. V. Bedser lbw b Insole	2		
B 4, l-b 2, n-b 1.................	7	B 2, l-b 1, n-b 2........	5

1/38 2/53 3/73 4/73 5/116 6/144   179   1/7 2/25 3/25   (5 wkts.) 150
7/153 8/158 9/177   4/87 5/112

Surrey Bowling

	O.	M.	R.	W.		O.	M.	R.	W.
Bedser	8	0	40	2	....	6	2	14	1
Loader	8	3	23	3	....	5	1	16	0
Lock	9	2	28	3	....	28.5	13	48	6
Laker	8	2	28	2	....	31	11	67	3
Clark						11	1	30	0

Essex Bowling

	O.	M.	R.	W.		O.	M.	R.	W.
Bailey	22	8	46	1	....	15	6	34	2
Smith	2	0	8	0					
Preston........	18	9	33	0	....	15	2	62	2
Cousens	9	3	33	1	....	6	2	23	0
Greensmith	12	5	30	2	....	4	1	6	1
Insole	7	2	22	5	....	5.4	2	20	0

Umpires: L. H. Gray and A. J. B. Fowler.

At Worthing, May 21, 23, 24. ESSEX lost to SUSSEX by six wickets.

At Worcester, May 28, 30, 31. ESSEX drew with WORCESTERSHIRE.

At Colchester, June 1, 2 3. ESSEX drew with SOUTH AFRICANS. (See SOUTH AFRICAN Section.)

ESSEX v. GLAMORGAN

At Colchester, June 4, 6, 7. Drawn. A match marked by much tedious batting never looked like bringing a definite result, particularly as rain delayed the start till after four o'clock. Sent in to bat, Essex displayed caution on a pitch not unduly helpful to bowlers. Insole batted two and three-quarter hours in making top score for them. Glamorgan pursued the policy of passive resistance and though McConnon drove with power and Edrich batted judiciously, Essex gained first innings lead by a single run. Dodds, by hard hitting all round, obtained ten 4's in scoring 52 in just over forty minutes when Essex batted again. Shepherd began the Glamorgan second innings with an extraordinary 6. Trying to hook a rising ball from T. Bailey he edged it high over slips to deep third man, where it bounced out of the hands of Knight over the boundary. Two balls later a repetition of this stroke resulted in him being caught in the same position.

Essex

T. C. Dodds c Wooller b Watkins	37	— c Parkhouse b McConnon.. 52
P. A. Gibb c Davies b Pressdee........	48	— not out 47
G. Barker run out	6	— not out 36
R. Horsfall c Parkhouse b Wooller	3	
D. J. Insole not out	65	
T. E. Bailey c Edrich b Lewis	3	
B. Knight st Davies b McConnon	18	
R. Smith c Shepherd b McConnon......	17	— c Wooller b Pressdee 0
W. T. Greensmith c Watkins b McConnon	2	
J. A. Bailey c Watkins b McConnon	0	
K. C. Preston not out	1	
L-b 9	9	B 4................... 4

1/55 2/63 3/72 4/103   (9 wkts., dec.) 209   1/71 2/71   (2 wkts., dec.) 139
5/116 6/157 7/187 8/196 9/196

Glamorgan

W. G. A. Parkhouse c and b Smith	21	— c Gibb b Preston.......... 1
W. E. Jones lbw b Preston	0	— not out 7
B. Hedges c Gibb b J. Bailey	57	— c Insole b T. Bailey 1
J. Pressdee c Gibb b J. Bailey	5	
A. J. Watkins c Knight b Greensmith ...	8	
W. Wooller c and b J. Bailey...........	15	
B. R. Edrich c Barker b Preston	43	
J. E. McConnon c Insole b Preston	28	
H. G. Davies not out	10	
K. H. Lewis b Preston	2	— c Insole b Preston 0
D. J. Shepherd c Gibb b T. Bailey	8	— c Knight b T. Bailey......... 6
B 3, l-b 7, n-b 1	11	

1/0 2/41 3/48 4/82 5/107 6/110   208   1/6 2/8 3/8   (4 wkts.) 15
7/147 8/195 9/197   4/15

Glamorgan Bowling

	O.	M.	R.	W.		O.	M.	R.	W.
Shepherd	13	4	39	0	....	2	0	12	0
Lewis	20	4	54	1	....	4	1	20	0
Watkins	16	6	37	1					
Wooller	15	8	8	1	....	3	0	10	0
Jones	1	0	5	0					
McConnon	10	1	32	4	....	12	0	46	1
Pressdee	8	1	25	1	....	10	2	40	1
Parkhouse					....	2.4	0	7	0

Essex Bowling

	O.	M.	R.	W.		O.	M.	R.	W.
T. Bailey	14.4	5	24	1	....	3.5	0	14	2
Preston	14	5	25	4	....	3	2	1	2
Smith	14	4	40	1					
J. Bailey	35	7	61	3					
Greensmith	17	5	47	1					

Umpires: E. Cooke and J. J. Hills.

At Southampton, June 8, 9. Essex lost to Hampshire by seven wickets.

At The Oval, June 11, 13, 14. Essex lost to Surrey by 62 runs.

At Chesterfield, June 15, 16, 17. Essex drew with Derbyshire.

ESSEX v. GLOUCESTERSHIRE

At Westcliff, June 18, 20, 21. Essex won by five wickets—their first victory of the season. They owed much to the batting of Insole and the bowling of R. Smith, who in the match took 11 wickets for 96, and Preston. Essex began by losing seven wickets for 174, but Insole found good partners in Greensmith and a newcomer to first-class cricket, G. Smith, who stayed while 101 were added in an unfinished stand. Apart from a chance when 31, Insole batted faultlessly for just over three and a half hours, hitting fifteen 4's, mainly drives and leg-side strokes. Gloucestershire failed in the first innings, but when they followed on 204 behind Milton and Graveney put on 132 and Crapp and Mortimore 65. Essex found unexpected difficulty in scoring 65 to win.

Essex

T. C. Dodds b Lambert	25	— c Rochford b McHugh	1
G. Barker c Rochford b Lambert	44	— st Rochford b Crapp	35
T. E. Bailey c Rochford b McHugh	1	— c Crapp b Lambert	1
R. Horsfall b Lambert	53	— c Rochford b McHugh	5
D. J. Insole not out	117	— c Rochford b Young	10
P. A. Gibb c Graveney b Lambert	0	— not out	0
B. Taylor b McHugh	16	— not out	8
R. Smith c Emmett b McHugh	11		
W. T. Greensmith c Crapp b McHugh	21		
G. Smith not out	27		
L-b 10, n-b 1	11	L-b 4, n-b 2	6

1/40 2/41 3/121 4/132   (8 wkts., dec.) 326
5/132 6/154 7/174 8/225
K. C. Preston did not bat.

1/5 2/19 3/30 4/56 (5 wkts.) 66
5/58

Gloucestershire

D. M. Young b Preston	1	— b Preston	3
C. A. Milton lbw b Preston	17	— lbw b R. Smith	66
T. W. Graveney b Bailey	25	— c Insole b Preston	80
J. F. Crapp b Preston	5	— c Greensmith b R. Smith	61
G. M. Emmett c R. Smith b Bailey	24	— b R. Smith	1
G. E. Lambert c Bailey b Preston	0	— c Insole b R. Smith	4
J. Mortimore b R. Smith	35	— c Insole b Bailey	23
P. Rochford b R. Smith	1	— not out	6
C. Cook c G. Smith b R. Smith	8	— c Dodds b R. Smith	2
B. D. Wells c Insole b R. Smith	2	— b R. Smith	5
F. P. McHugh not out	0	— b R. Smith	4
L-b 4	4	L-b 12, n-b 1	13

1/7 2/42 3/48 4/48 5/59 6/83   122
7/98 8/113 9/120

1/7 2/139 3/160 4/164   268
5/174 6/239 7/253 8/255
9/260

Gloucestershire Bowling

	O.	M.	R.	W.		O.	M.	R.	W.
Lambert	30	6	102	4	....	6	2	23	1
McHugh	35	6	93	4	....	6	3	17	2
Wells	21	3	57	0					
Cook	19	5	49	0					
Graveney	1	0	9	0					
Mortimore	2	0	5	0					
Young						1.5	0	19	1
Crapp						1	0	1	1

Essex Bowling

	O.	M.	R.	W.		O.	M.	R.	W.
Bailey	17	4	40	2	....	31	6	56	1
Preston	16	3	48	4	....	28	4	70	2
R. Smith	6.1	4	16	4	....	36	6	80	7
Insole	6	2	14	0	....	6	0	14	0
Greensmith						5	0	23	0
G. Smith						2	0	12	0

Umpires: F. S. Lee and A. Skelding.

ESSEX v. WARWICKSHIRE

At Westcliff, June 22, 23, 24. Warwickshire won by 142 runs. No such result appeared likely when on the opening day they lost five wickets for 70, but H. Dollery played a splendid innings. For just over four hours he was complete master of the bowling and, in scoring 156 out of 237, hit one 6 and twenty-one 4's, chiefly drives and strokes to leg. Townsend and K. Dollery helped him in stands of 62 and 119. Essex found defensive tactics unprofitable and, though Gibb stayed nearly four hours and a half, faced arrears of 70. A partnership of 111 by Gardner and H. Dollery paved the way to a Warwickshire declaration. Set 275 to get, Essex never looked like succeeding against the leg-breaks of Hollies who, bowling unchanged and exploiting a worn patch, brought his match analysis to 11 wickets for 78 runs.

Warwickshire

F. C. Gardner c Preston b Ralph	12	— c and b Preston	74
T. W. Cartwright c Taylor b R. Smith	30	— b Preston	5
A. V. Wolton b Preston	4	— lbw b Preston	9
R. E. Hitchcock c Barker b R. Smith	1	— c Taylor b Greensmith	12
H. E. Dollery b Ralph	156	— c and b R. Smith	65
R. T. Spooner b Ralph	4	— c Insole b R. Smith	0
A. Townsend lbw b Insole	22	— not out	18
J. D. Bannister c Gibb b Insole	2	— c Ralph b Preston	9
K. R. Dollery b Preston	29	— not out	5
R. G. Thompson not out	1		
W. E. Hollies c Gibb b Ralph	0		
L-b 5, n-b 3	8	B 4, l-b 1, n-b 2	7

1/15 2/24 3/32 4/57 5/70 6/132   269
7/144 8/263 9/269

1/26 2/37 3/54   (7 wkts., dec.) 204
4/165 5/165 6/177 7/189

Essex

T. C. Dodds c Hitchcock b Bannister	4	— c Spooner b Bannister	13
G. Barker lbw b Hollies	14	— c Spooner b Hollies	5
P. A. Gibb c Spooner b K. Dollery	76	— c Townsend b Hollies	16
W. T. Greensmith lbw b Thompson	19	— not out	9
R. Horsfall c Gardner b Bannister	15	— st Spooner b Hollies	9
D. J. Insole c H. Dollery b K. Dollery	11	— c Gardner b Hollies	4
B. Taylor c Hitchcock b Hollies	12	— c Gardner b Hollies	12
R. Ralph b Bannister	10	— c K. Dollery b Townsend	0
R. Smith b K. Dollery	0	— b Hollies	32
G. Smith not out	29	— c Hitchcock b Hollies	8
K. C. Preston c and b Hollies	1	— c Spooner b Hollies	10
B 3, l-b 4, n-b 1	8	B 8, l-b 6	14

1/4 2/37 3/84 4/112 5/132 6/157   199
7/157 8/157 9/198

1/16 2/20 3/32 4/33   132
5/44 6/49 7/88 8/101 9/113

Essex Bowling

	O.	M.	R.	W.		O.	M.	R.	W.
Preston	29	11	46	2	....	23	3	64	4
R. Smith	27	3	88	2	....	16	1	57	2
Ralph	25.4	11	55	4	....	4	0	27	0
Insole	12	3	30	2					
Greensmith	9	2	26	0	....	21	4	49	1
G. Smith	1	0	16	0					

Warwickshire Bowling

	O.	M.	R.	W.		O.	M.	R.	W.
Bannister	24	7	49	3	....	7	3	21	1
Thompson	17	7	32	1	....	2	0	4	0
K. Dollery	23	4	51	3	....	3	2	1	0
Hollies	29.2	17	36	3	....	22.4	11	42	8
Hitchcock	5	1	12	0	....	5	2	17	0
Townsend	3	0	11	0	....	6	0	33	1

Umpires: F. S. Lee and A. Skelding.

At Gillingham, June 25, 27, 28. ESSEX lost to KENT by five wickets.

At Nottingham, July 2, 4, 5. ESSEX beat NOTTINGHAMSHIRE by 95 runs.

ESSEX v. SOMERSET

At Romford, July 6, 7, 8. Essex won by five wickets, despite a maiden century by the 20-year-old Walker who, at the end of an innings lasting three and a quarter hours, was found to be suffering from appendicitis. Promoted to opening batsman, Walker drove splendidly, hitting fifteen 4's. In each innings the fourth wicket was the most productive. Insole figured in partnerships of 160 with the patient Gibb, missed when two, and 93 with Horsfall. In the first Somerset innings Lawrence stayed three hours, he and Wight putting on 88, and Stephenson hit 53 out of 59 in less than fifty minutes. In the second Walker and Wight put on 152 in two and a quarter hours and were chiefly responsible for Essex being set to make 195.

Somerset

G. G. Tordoff b R. Smith	45	— c Taylor b Preston	2
Yawar Saeed c Taylor b R. Smith	1	— b Ralph	20
J. Lawrence b Greensmith	59	— lbw b Ralph	23
M. F. Tremlett b R. Smith	4	— c and b Ralph	8
P. B. Wight b Ralph	47	— c Horsfall b Preston	78
M. Walker lbw b Ralph	1	— b R. Smith	100
H. W. Stephenson c Ralph b R. Smith	53	— c R. Smith b Preston	1
J. Hilton b R. Smith	18	— c Taylor b Ralph	20
K. Palmer b Preston	6	— lbw b Insole	2
J. W. McMahon not out	1	— not out	2
B. Lobb c Preston b R. Smith	0	— c Preston b Ralph	2
B 2, l-b 7	9	B 4, l-b 3, w 1, n-b 1	9

1/4 2/60 3/66 4/154 5/162 6/170   **244**   1/2 2/47 3/57 4/209   **267**
7/229 8/239 9/243   5/217 6/220 7/252 8/259
                                       9/263

Essex

T. C. Dodds c Tremlett b Yawar Saeed	24	— c sub b Lobb	24
G. Barker c Tremlett b Yawar Saeed	17	— c Yawar Saeed b Lobb	43
P. A. Gibb b Lobb	77	— run out	2
R. Horsfall c Tremlett b Lobb	6	— st Stephenson b Lawrence	69
D. J. Insole b Yawar Saeed	94	— not out	52
B. Taylor b McMahon	39	— b Lawrence	4
R. Smith c McMahon b Yawar Saeed	10	— not out	0
W. T. Greensmith b Lobb	38		
G. S. Smith st Stephenson b Lawrence	8		
R. Ralph lbw b Lawrence	0		
K. C. Preston not out	0		
L-b 3, n-b 1	4	L-b 1	1

1/37 2/44 3/55 4/215 5/225 6/242   **317**   1/32 2/47 3/92   (5 wkts.) **195**
7/295 8/317 9/317   4/185 5/193

Essex Bowling

	O.	M.	R.	W.	O.	M.	R.	W.
Preston	20	4	40	1	23	6	58	3
R. Smith	30	8	76	6	33	5	85	1
Ralph	17	4	50	2	19.3	3	64	5
Insole	6	2	17	0	5	2	3	1
Greensmith	14	1	52	1	6	1	15	0
Dodds					2	0	19	0
G. Smith					13	9	14	0

Somerset Bowling

	O.	M.	R.	W.	O.	M.	R.	W.
Lobb	27.4	6	68	3	13	1	54	2
Yawar Saeed	25	1	101	4	11	0	53	0
Tordoff	11	5	25	0	1.1	0	5	0
Palmer	2	0	7	0				
Lawrence	16	3	53	2	6	0	35	2
McMahon	15	3	40	1	10	0	47	0
Hilton	4	0	19	0				

Umpires: W. T. Jones and A. E. Pothecary.

ESSEX v. NORTHAMPTONSHIRE

At Romford, July 9, 11, 12. Northamptonshire won by 124 runs. They began indifferently on a firm pitch, losing five wickets for 74, but Tribe and Broderick, by adding 67, effected a recovery. Essex fared even worse, for despite good work by Gibb eight men were out for 76, and although the later batsmen scored readily, Northamptonshire led by 181. A stand of 104 by Arnold and Livingston followed by a sound innings from Barrick led to a declaration and Essex, set 319 to win, never looked like succeeding in face of accurate left-arm spin bowling by Broderick.

Northamptonshire

D. Brookes run out	15	— lbw b Smith	7
P. Arnold lbw b Smith	1	— c Barker b Preston	70
L. Livingston c Taylor b Preston	13	— lbw b Greensmith	51
D. Barrick c Taylor b Greensmith	32	— not out	70
D. G. Greasley b Greensmith	9	— c Barker b Preston	1
G. E. Tribe c Ralph b Greensmith	64	— c Taylor b Insole	10
V. Broderick b Greensmith	26	— b Preston	15
K. V. Andrew b Ralph	8		
J. Wild c Taylor b Preston	16	— c Smith b Preston	8
J. Webster b Ralph	0		
R. W. Clarke not out	11		
B 16, l-b 7, w 1, n-b 1	25	B 1, l-b 4	5

	220	(7 wkts., dec.)	**237**

1/2 2/28 3/40 4/71 5/74 6/141
7/181 8/183 9/196

1/9 2/113 3/149 4/157 5/186 6/219
7/237

Essex

T. C. Dodds lbw b Clarke	6	— c and b Wild	32
G. Barker c Andrew b Webster	0	— c Clarke b Webster	5
P. A. Gibb lbw b Tribe	38	— c Tribe b Broderick	28
C. C. P. Williams c Livingston b Clarke	0	— c and b Broderick	16
D. J. Insole lbw b Webster	4	— c Andrew b Broderick	33
R. Horsfall run out	3	— lbw b Broderick	13
B. Taylor b Tribe	10	— lbw b Tribe	6
R. Smith b Clarke	5	— lbw b Tribe	5
W. T. Greensmith not out	16	— not out	19
R. Ralph st Andrew b Tribe	20	— lbw b Wild	3
K. C. Preston c Livingston b Broderick	30	— c Tribe b Broderick	25
L-b 7	7	B 5, l-b 4	9

	139		**194**

1/10 2/14 3/14 4/23 5/37 6/65
7/66 8/76 9/102

1/6 2/51 3/77 4/108 5/131
6/134 7/142 8/143 9/159

Essex Bowling

	O.	M.	R.	W.		O.	M.	R.	W.
Preston	15.4	2	35	2	....	27.1	4	64	4
Smith	27	9	64	1	....	19	1	69	1
Ralph	14	7	21	2	....	10	1	30	0
Insole	5	2	9	0	....	11	5	28	1
Greensmith	27	10	66	4	....	11	1	41	1

Northamptonshire Bowling

	O.	M.	R.	W.		O.	M.	R.	W.
Clarke	22	7	47	3	....	11	3	18	0
Webster	17	7	25	2	....	5	1	16	1
Tribe	22	8	47	3	....	20	10	32	2
Broderick	5.4	2	13	1	....	35	15	66	5
Wild						9	1	53	2

Umpires: W. T. Jones and A. E. Pothecary.

At Pontypridd, July 13, 14, 15. ESSEX beat GLAMORGAN by 91 runs.

ESSEX v. LEICESTERSHIRE

At Brentwood, July 23, 25. Leicestershire won by 18 runs. Victory went to the visitors after Essex, at one point 126 for one, looked assured of success. The dramatic turn in the game was due to the clever spin bowling of Munden and Lester, and with nine wickets falling in an hour for 47 runs, Leicestershire won in two days with six minutes of the extra half-hour to spare. Leicestershire owed much to Smith, the Oxford Blue, for two splendid exhibitions of forcing stroke-play. J. A. Bailey, the Essex medium-fast bowler, bowled particularly well in the first innings.

Leicestershire

G. Lester c Ralph b Bailey	26	— c Bailey b Greensmith	32
M. R. Hallam c Ralph b Smith	0	— c Dodds b Smith	7
M. Tompkin c Barker b Bailey	52	— b Ralph	27
M. J. K. Smith c Gibb b Preston	60	— lbw b Bailey	63
C. H. Palmer c Ralph b Bailey	0	— c Bailey b Greensmith	6
V. E. Jackson c Ralph b Bailey	18	— c Williams b Greensmith	5
G. A. Smithson c Barker b Bailey	0	— c Taylor b Greensmith	0
V. S. Munden c Barker b Bailey	2	— c Preston b Greensmith	0
J. Firth st Taylor b Dodds	27	— not out	12
C. T. Spencer b Preston	15	— c Taylor b Bailey	5
J. Goodwin not out	0	— c Dodds b Preston	0
B 5, l-b 1	6	B 6, l-b 5	11

1/0 2/74 3/93 4/97 5/129 6/129   206   1/18 2/62 3/79 4/91   168
7/137 8/182 9/202   5/111 6/111 7/111 8/155
9/167

Essex

T. C. Dodds c Firth b Spencer	0	— b Jackson	39
G. Barker b Jackson	51	— c Palmer b Munden	46
P. A. Gibb b Goodwin	27	— c Spencer b Lester	40
C. C. P. Williams b Palmer	19	— b Palmer	22
R. Horsfall c Munden b Jackson	4	— c Hallam b Lester	8
B. Taylor lbw b Spencer	34	— c Hallam b Munden	1
R. Smith b Jackson	4	— c Spencer b Lester	5
W. T. Greensmith c Spencer b Jackson	32	— c Spencer b Munden	3
R. Ralph c Firth b Palmer	4	— c sub b Munden	0
K. C. Preston b Palmer	4	— b Munden	4
J. A. Bailey not out	0	— not out	0
B 4	4	B 4, w 1	5

1/0 2/27 3/93 4/97 5/108 6/126   183   1/70 2/127 3/130 4/138   173
7/152 8/179 9/183   5/139 6/144 7/155 8/155
9/169

Essex Bowling

	O.	M.	R.	W.		O.	M.	R.	W.
Preston	14.5	4	44	2	....	6.5	1	24	1
Smith	6	1	14	1	....	9	0	38	1
Bailey	24	5	53	6	....	17	8	26	2
Ralph	8	2	20	0	....	9	3	19	1
Dodds	5	0	33	1					
Greensmith	13	3	36	0	....	10	1	50	5

Leicestershire Bowling

	O.	M.	R.	W.	O.	M.	R.	W.
Spencer	21	4	76	2	 5	0	41	0
Goodwin	9	0	34	1				
Palmer	15.3	5	36	3	.... 6.4	1	20	1
Jackson	23	14	33	4	 10	2	36	1
Munden					16	7	29	5
Lester					9	1	42	3

Umpires: E. Cooke and J. J. Hills.

At Bradford, July 27, 28, 29. ESSEX lost to YORKSHIRE by ten wickets.

ESSEX v. WORCESTERSHIRE

At Chelmsford, July 30, August 1, 2. Worcestershire won by 115 runs. The better team in all departments they well deserved the victory they gained with eight minutes to spare. Outschoorn, who batted soundly for five and a quarter hours, Kenyon, P. E. Richardson and Broadbent all played well in helping Worcestershire to their highest total of the season, but few Essex batsmen showed to advantage on an easy-paced pitch. Flavell, the lively fast bowler, Perks and Chesterton were always troublesome to play and when Essex accepted a challenge to make 260 in two hours twenty minutes these bowlers won the game. Barker completed his 1,000 runs in his first full season.

Worcestershire

D. Kenyon b Preston	80	— c and b J. Bailey	1
P. E. Richardson b Preston	75	— not out	51
L. Outschoorn not out	150	— run out	20
R. G. Broadbent c Williams b J. Bailey..	55	— b Smith	19
M. J. Horton st Taylor b Insole	11	— not out	13
D. W. Richardson b Preston	29		
R. O. Jenkins not out	21		
B 14, l-b 12, w 1, n-b 2	29	L-b 6	6

1/145 2/174 3/312 4/326 (5 wkts., dec.) 450   1/1 2/57   (3 wkts., dec.) 110
5/400   3/90

H. Yarnold, G. H. Chesterton, R. T. D. Perks and J. Flavell did not bat.

Essex

T. C. Dodds c P. Richardson b Jenkins..	41	— lbw b Perks	12
G. Barker b Chesterton	64	— st Yarnold b Jenkins	25
P. A. Gibb c Yarnold b Chesterton ..	20	— c Yarnold b Flavell	7
C. C. P. Williams c Broadbent b Perks ..	32	— b Chesterton	8
D. J. Insole c Yarnold b Flavell	54	— c Kenyon b Perks	5
T. E. Bailey not out..................	46	— b Chesterton	9
W. T. Greensmith lbw b Flavell	6	— b Flavell	26
B. Taylor c Yarnold b Flavell	1	— b Flavell	36
R. Smith c D. Richardson b Chesterton .	0	— b Perks	1
K. C. Preston c and b Flavell	15	— c Broadbent b Perks	6
J. A. Bailey not out	1	— not out	8
B 3, l-b 15, n-b 3	21	L-b 1	1

1/101 2/117 3/167   (9 wkts., dec.) 301   1/14 2/21 3/50 4/57 5/67 144
4/183 5/253 6/271 7/273 8/274 9/293   6/69 7/92 8/101 9/125

Essex Bowling

	O.	M.	R.	W.	O.	M.	R.	W.
Preston........	30	9	83	3	7	0	29	0
J. Bailey	31	6	105	1	9	1	31	1
Smith	24	4	82	0	7	1	20	1
Insole	12	2	50	1	5	0	24	0
Greensmith	9	0	40	0				
T. Bailey	23.2	4	61	0				

Worcestershire Bowling

	O.	M.	R.	W.	O.	M.	R.	W.
Perks	32	11	67	1	17	3	48	4
Flavell	29	4	99	4	9.3	1	53	3
Jenkins	7	1	30	1	8	1	31	1
Chesterton	34.4	12	69	3	7	2	11	2
Horton	4	1	15	0				

Umpires: J. S. Buller and G. S. Mobey.

ESSEX v. SUSSEX

At Chemsford, August 3, 4, 5. Drawn. In a dramatic climax, Sussex, set to make 56 in 20 minutes, failed by only two runs, having hit 54 off six overs. For most of the game play ran much in favour of Sussex. On lively turf on the first day, Thomson and James bowled at medium pace with sustained accuracy in long spells, and only Insole of the Essex batsmen looked at all comfortable A marathon innings for Sussex by Langridge, who batted five and three-quarter hours, contrasted strongly with the methods of Parks, who hit one 6 and ten 4's in making 98 before lunch on the second day. Doggart (one 6, eleven 4's) also hit strongly after a slow start. Essex lost six men for 107 in the second innings, but a determined innings of four hours by Bailey prolonged their resistance.

Essex

T. C. Dodds b Thomson	18	— c Langridge b Thomson....	36
G. Barker c Langridge b Thomson	11	— c Doggart b Marlar	9
T. E. Bailey c Marlar b James	3	— not out	63
C. C. P. Williams c Langridge b James ..	21	— c sub b James	10
D. J. Insole c Doggart b James	48	— run out	1
P. A. Gibb b Smith	27	— b James...................	28
W. T. Greensmith c Oakman b Smith ...	9	— b Oakman	3
B. Taylor b Marlar	1	— c Parks b Oakman	15
R. Ralph not out	14	— c Langridge b Thomson ..	39
R. Smith c Webb b Thomson	28	— c Webb b James	4
K. C. Preston b James	3	— c Webb b Smith	9
B 2, l-b 3	5	B 17, l-b 6	23

1/31 2/34 3/34 4/90 5/103 6/139　　　188
7/140 8/140 9/181

1/34 2/64 3/90 4/91　　　240
5/96 6/107 7/131 8/213
9/226

Sussex

J. Langridge c and b Insole		101			
D. V. Smith b Bailey		0	— c Dodds b Preston		9
A. S. M. Oakman c Gibb b Ralph		32	— not out		7
R. T. Webb c Preston b Ralph		2			
J. M. Parks b Ralph		98	— not out		17
K. G. Suttle c Insole b Bailey		15	— b Bailey		17
G. H. G. Doggart c Gibb b Greensmith		84			
G. Cox not out		22	— c Gibb b Bailey		0
R. G. Marlar b Bailey		0			
B 7, l-b 12		19	B 2, l-b 2		4

1/1 2/46 3/48 4/174   (8 wkts., dec.) 373   1/17 2/44 3/44   (3 wkts.) 54
5/207 6/303 7/372 8/373

N. I. Thomson and A. E. James did not bat.

Sussex Bowling

	O.	M.	R.	W.		O.	M.	R.	W.
Thomson	31	6	69	3	....	37	9	59	2
James	28.4	4	72	4	....	27	9	59	3
Smith	13	4	29	2	....	6	4	2	1
Marlar	8	4	9	1	....	21	5	47	1
Oakman	3	1	4	0	....	22	14	29	2
Parks						9	2	21	0

Essex Bowling

	O.	M.	R.	W.		O.	M.	R.	W.
Bailey	38.2	15	86	3	....	3	0	26	2
Preston	21	2	69	0	....	3	0	24	1
Ralph	22	3	69	3					
Smith	18	3	59	0					
Greensmith	5	1	35	1					
Insole	16	2	36	1					

Umpires: J. S. Buller and G. S. Mobey.

At Wellingborough, August 6, 8, 9. ESSEX lost to NORTHAMPTONSHIRE by seven wickets.

ESSEX v. KENT

At Clacton, August 10, 11, 12. Essex won by ten wickets. Dodds and Barker gave them a fine start with a partnership of 91 and Bailey followed with his second century of the season. Taking two hours to reach 50, Bailey got to three figures in three hours twenty-five minutes, and he hit one 6 and twenty-one 4's. Kent collapsed against the pace of Bailey and the leg-spin of Dodds and followed on 237 behind. Despite good batting by Allan, six wickets fell before the deficit was cleared, but a partnership of 84 by Catt and Brazier meant that Essex needed 81 for victory. Catt put together his highest innings in first-class cricket.

Essex

T. C. Dodds c Fagg b Pettiford	62	—	not out		31
G. Barker c Cowdrey b Pettiford	25	—	not out		42
T. E. Bailey not out	152				
C. C. P. Williams c Fagg b Wright	13				
D. J. Insole b Allan	32				
P. A. Gibb st Catt b Wright	17				
R. Horsfall c Catt b Allan	2				
W. T. Greensmith c Wilson b Allan	38				
R. Smith b Allan	7				
R. Ralph not out	17				
B 9, l-b 2	11		B 8		8

1/91 2/98 3/125 4/167 (8 wkts., dec.) 376
5/206 6/217 7/309 8/337

(No wkt.) 81

K. C. Preston did not bat.

Kent

A. E. Fagg c Dodds b Bailey	11	—	lbw b Bailey		11
J. M. Allan lbw b Bailey	15	—	b Greensmith		61
R. C. Wilson c Gibb b Dodds	61	—	c Dodds b Preston		7
M. C. Cowdrey c Williams b Preston	4	—	b Ralph		45
J. Pettiford b Smith	4	—	c Gibb b Bailey		5
J. F. Pretlove b Dodds	12	—	st Gibb b Greensmith		27
A. F. Brazier c Gibb b Bailey	1	—	hit wkt b Smith		50
A. W. Catt c Gibb b Bailey	8	—	not out		88
J. Spanswick c Williams b Dodds	15	—	c Bailey b Greensmith		0
D. V. P. Wright not out	4	—	c Ralph b Bailey		12
J. B. Phillips c Bailey b Dodds	0	—	b Greensmith		0
L-b 3, n-b 1	4		B 5, l-b 3, w 1, n-b 2		11

1/20 2/37 3/44 4/57 5/86 6/97 7/116 139
8/134 9/136

1/20 2/32 3/93 4/107 317
5/149 6/166 7/250 8/285
9/315

Kent Bowling

	O.	M.	R.	W.		O.	M.	R.	W.
Spanswick	16	4	59	0	....	3	0	4	0
Phillips	25	6	69	0	....	5	0	33	0
Wright	24	5	84	2	....	5	1	14	0
Allan	35	16	93	4	....	3	0	17	0
Pettiford	13	3	60	2					
Pretlove						0.2	0	5	0

Essex Bowling

	O.	M.	R.	W.		O.	M.	R.	W.
Bailey	21	3	53	4	....	25	8	52	3
Preston	11	7	13	1	....	29	7	72	1
Smith	7	1	17	1	....	17	9	20	1
Ralph	4	0	18	0	....	14	3	32	1
Dodds	12.3	4	34	4	....	15	2	55	0
Insole						6	1	18	0
Greensmith						26	8	57	4

Umpires: F. Chester and E. A. Roberts.

ESSEX v. LANCASHIRE

At Clacton, August 13, 15, 16. Drawn, the loss of the first day through rain ruling out the possibility of a definite result. Wharton took the batting honours for Lancashire, driving and pulling well for two hours fifty minutes, and he and Washbrook put on 70, but against the leg-breaks of Greensmith the last seven wickets fell for 76. Specially strong on the leg-side, Barker (twelve 4's) stood out for Essex, and the patient Gibb helped him add 83, but not till the last pair of batsmen, Preston and Bailey, put on 43 was the question of the lead settled.

Lancashire

A. Wharton c Horsfall b Ralph	80	— c Gibb b Greensmith 26
J. Dyson run out	13	— retired ill.................. 20
G. A. Edrich c Bailey b Ralph	8	— not out 41
C. Washbrook b Greensmith	20	
G. Pullar st Gibb b Greensmith	39	— c Dodds b Greensmith ... 7
R. W. Barber st Gibb b Greensmith	15	— not out 6
R. Collins c Gibb b Greensmith	18	
M. J. Hilton c Bailey b Greensmith	3	
K. B. Standring not out	0	
A. Wilson c Preston b Greensmith	0	
R. Tattersall c Greensmith b Smith	1	
B 1, l-b 2, n-b 1	4	B 7.................. 7

1/37 2/55 3/125 4/125 5/162 6/188   201   1/44 2/75   (2 wkts.) 107
7/200 8/200 9/200

Essex

T. C. Dodds c and b Wharton	8		R. Ralph run out	10
G. Barker lbw b Collins	92		K. C. Preston not out	30
P. A. Gibb c Dyson b Collins	24		J. A. Bailey c Wilson b Collins ...	9
C. C. P. Williams b Barber	27			
D. J. Insole run out	14		B 12, l-b 1	13
R. Horsfall c Wilson b Tattersall	6			
W. T. Greensmith b Tattersall	0		1/9 2/92 3/135 4/165 5/178	243
R. Smith c Wilson b Collins	10		6/180 7/180 8/200 9/200	

Essex Bowling

	O.	M.	R.	W.		O.	M.	R.	W.
Preston	15	4	48	0	....	9	2	16	0
Smith	15.3	3	29	1					
Bailey	15	3	37	0	....	10	2	25	0
Ralph	15	2	25	2	....	7	2	20	0
Insole	6	1	14	0					
Greensmith	16	3	44	6	....	17	2	39	2

Lancashire Bowling

Wharton	10	4	17	1
Standring	4	0	12	0
Tattersall	39	17	67	2
Hilton	19	11	33	0
Collins	22	6	56	4
Barber	7	1	35	1
Dyson	3	1	10	0

Umpires: F. Chester and E. A. Roberts.

At Leicester, August 17, 18, 19. Essex lost to Leicestershire by 59 runs.

At Birmingham, August 20, 22, 23. Essex beat Warwickshire by 36 runs.

ESSEX v. YORKSHIRE

At Southend, August 24, 25, 26. Yorkshire won by nine wickets. Insole's policy of sending them in on a well-grassed pitch brought disastrous consequences. Yorkshire batted unevenly against accurate fast-medium bowling by Bailey. Lowson, hitting one 4 in three hours, prevented an early breakdown. Illingworth, batting quarter of an hour longer for the second century of his career, obtained twelve boundaries and he received able help from Yardley and Binks in stands of 70 and 52. Apart from Barker and Gibbs, both missed, the Essex batsmen failed before the pace of Trueman, and in the follow-on 200 behind six wickets fell for 149. Insole led a recovery in which the later batsmen gave admirable support, but Yorkshire required only 43 to win. Batting without mistake for his eighth three-figure score of the season, Insole drove specially well, hitting sixteen 4's.

Yorkshire

F. A. Lowson c Greensmith b R. Smith .	56	— not out	17
D. B. Close b Bailey	11	— c Ralph b Bailey	0
J. V. Wilson c Gibb b Bailey	10	— not out	26
D. E. V. Padgett b R. Smith	26		
W. Watson c Gibb b Bailey	13		
R. Illingworth c R. Smith b Insole	116		
N. W. D. Yardley b Bailey	18		
J. H. Wardle c Gibb b Bailey	11		
F. S. Trueman c Ralph b Bailey	3		
J. G. Binks b R. Smith	26		
M. Ryan not out	3		
L-b 3	3	L-b 1	1

1/12 2/36 3/91 4/104 5/142 6/212   296   1/0   (1 wkt.) 44
7/228 8/232 9/284

Essex

T. C. Dodds c Wilson b Trueman	3	— b Trueman	25
G. Barker c Watson b Trueman	30	— lbw b Wardle	14
P. A. Gibb c Binks b Trueman	25	— c Close b Trueman	0
D. J. Insole c Watson b Trueman	0	— b Ryan	119
T. E. Bailey lbw b Yardley	4	— b Ryan	17
M. Bear c Binks b Trueman	1	— b Trueman	10
W. T. Greensmith not out	14	— c Wilson b Wardle	8
G. Smith b Trueman	0	— c Ryan b Wardle	14
R. Smith c Ryan b Wardle	14	— c Wardle b Close	9
R. Ralph c Close b Wardle	1	— c Binks b Ryan	21
K. C. Preston b Ryan	0	— not out	1
L-b 4	4	L-b 4	4

1/17 2/36 3/36 4/43 5/58 6/67 7/67   96   1/38 2/38 3/62 4/95   242
8/92 9/95   5/128 6/149 7/172 8/192
9/233

Essex Bowling

	O.	M.	R.	W.		O.	M.	R.	W.
Bailey	31	6	93	6	....	5	2	18	1
Preston	21	3	45	0	....	4	0	21	0
R. Smith	23	2	68	3					
Ralph	9	1	33	0					
Insole	13.1	4	38	1	......				
Greensmith	4	0	16	0					
Barker						1	1	0	0
Bear						0.2	0	4	0

Yorkshire Bowling

	O.	M.	R.	W.		O.	M.	R.	W.
Trueman	19	4	45	6	....	19	0	68	3
Ryan	10	3	23	1	....	20.2	2	78	3
Yardley	16	8	13	1	....	5	3	11	0
Wardle	2	0	11	2	....	31	9	64	3
					Close	8	2	17	1

Umpires: D. Davies and T. Spencer.

ESSEX v. NOTTINGHAMSHIRE

At Southend, August 27, 29, 30. Nottinghamshire won by two wickets after a remarkable finish in which the winning hit was made from the last ball of the match. Essex, despite a stubborn innings by Bailey, disappointed in their first innings. Bailey followed with a good piece of bowling, but thanks largely to Giles and Goonesena, Nottinghamshire led by 20. An unbroken fourth wicket stand of 239 in three hours by Insole and Bailey led to Essex declaring, and they set Nottinghamshire to score 311 in three and a half hours. Nottinghamshire went for the runs and with an over to go six were wanted. With the sides level Dooland gave a catch off the fifth ball, but Jepson drove the last for four.

Essex

T. C. Dodds c Rowe b Jepson	32	— b Dooland	44
G. Barker lbw b Jepson	2	— c Clay b K. Poole	2
P. A. Gibb run out	2	— c Stocks b Goonesena	40
D. J. Insole lbw b Goonesena	37	— not out	114
T. E. Bailey b Stocks b Dooland	54	— not out	114
M. Bear c Clay b Dooland	0		
W. T. Greensmith lbw b Goonesena	46		
G. Smith c Stocks b Dooland	3		
R. Smith lbw b Dooland	2		
R. Ralph not out	0		
K. C. Preston b Dooland	0		
B 8, l-b 2, w 1, n-b 2	13	B 11, l-b 5	16

1/5 2/36 3/36 4/109 5/114 6/181   191
7/189 8/190 9/191

1/18 2/91   (3 wkts., dec.) 330
3/91

Nottinghamshire

R. T. Simpson c Gibb b Bailey	8	— c Preston b Greensmith	39
J. D. Clay c Bear b Ralph	18	— c Bailey b Preston	6
R. J. Giles c and b Insole	55	— b R. Smith	77
E. J. Rowe b Bailey	4		
F. W. Stocks c Ralph b Bailey	2	— c Ralph b R. Smith	7
C. J. Poole b Bailey	13	— b R. Smith	59
K. J. Poole c Gibb b Bailey	13	— lbw b Preston	58
G. Goonesena not out	66	— st Gibb b Greensmith	5
B. Dooland c Preston b Greensmith	14	— c G. Smith b Preston	35
K. Smales c Barker b Greensmith	6	— not out	0
A. Jepson run out	7	— not out	11
B 3, l-b 1, n-b 1	5	B 6, l-b 9, n-b 2	17

1/22 2/36 3/51 4/65 5/87 6/105   211
7/137 8/187 9/193

1/9 2/88 3/105   (8 wkts.) 314
4/181 5/210 6/227 7/296
8/310

Nottinghamshire Bowling

	O.	M.	R.	W.		O.	M.	R.	W.
Jepson	17	5	30	2	....	26	2	67	0
K. Poole	12	2	44	0	....	14	1	62	1
Smales	16	7	37	0	....	8	2	39	0
Dooland	17.3	4	34	5	....	29	8	92	1
Goonesena	17	6	33	2	....	15	2	54	1

Essex Bowling

	O.	M.	R.	W.		O.	M.	R.	W.
Bailey	31	6	68	5	....	8	0	33	0
Preston........	13	2	32	0	....	11	1	42	3
R. Smith	20	5	34	0	....	26	5	97	3
Ralph	11	2	33	1	....	2	0	14	0
Insole	3	0	9	1	....	8	0	32	0
Greensmith	11.3	2	30	2	....	17	0	79	2

Umpires: D. Davies and T. Spencer.

GLAMORGAN

President—SIR HERBERT MERRETT
Hon. Secretary—J. C. CLAY, 6, High Street, Cardiff.
Captain—WILFRED WOOLLER

A. J. Watkins   County Badge   W. G. A. Parkhouse

After much success since they won the Championship in 1948 the pendulum of fortune receded for Glamorgan, who dropped twelve places and finished last but one in the table. This reversal of form meant six fewer victories and nine more defeats than in 1954. The season proved one of the most disappointing in the history of the club, and even many supporters lost their appetite for the game, receipts in a fine summer declining by £2,000 after a heavy loss the year before.

During the season Glamorgan were criticised for playing negative cricket. They were held to be victims of an inferiority complex by conceding the superiority of their opponents before the match started. Then in an effort to prevent progress by the other side they resorted to short-of-a-length bowling and themselves adopted go-slow methods with the bat. Whatever grounds existed for these strictures, the fact remained that Glamorgan struggled nearly half the season before recording their first victory. This success at the expense of Somerset, usually easy prey for most counties, scarcely suggested they had turned the corner, and the defeat of Yorkshire at Harrogate by four wickets proved a more convincing performance. Yet Glamorgan were on and off the bottom of the table at frequent intervals, and not until August did they really avoid the indignity of the bottom place.

By splendid work behind the wicket Haydn Davies restored a little prestige for the side. The prize for the season went to McIntyre, the Surrey stumper, but Davies, as runner-up, was only four behind with 81 victims. Watkins as an all-rounder stood above his colleagues and completed the "double" for the second successive season. He merited his selection for the M.C.C. Pakistan tour. Wooller stayed over seven hours for 128, the highest score of his career, in the last match of the programme against Warwickshire at Neath, but the all-round powers of this stalwart captain appeared to be on the wane in his 43rd year. The ability of Parkinson to score 1,000 runs in every campaign since he received his county cap in 1948 did not desert him, but, like Jones, he failed to make the advance Glamorgan needed in a lean run-getting period, and Pleass and Hedges frequently disappointed.

Owing to injury McConnon returned home before the rest of the M.C.C. party which toured Australia. Unfortunately Glamorgan were also destined to lose his off-spin bowling in eleven matches, and as Shepherd lacked some of his penetrative skill with the new ball they were seldom strong in attack. Pressdee was the most impressive of the younger players.

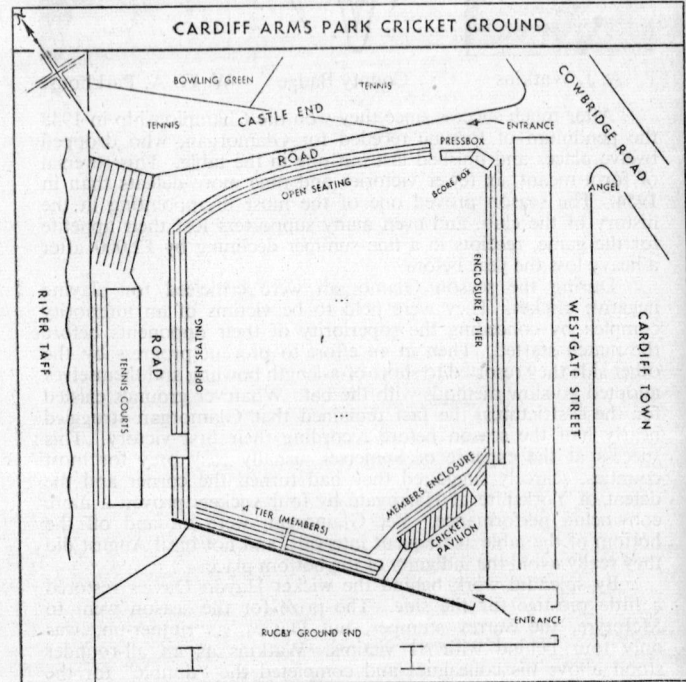

GLAMORGAN RESULTS

All First-Class Matches—Played 30, *Won* 5, *Lost* 15, *Drawn* 10

County Championship Matches—Played 28, *Won* 5, *Lost* 14,
Drawn 8, *No Decision* 1

COUNTY CHAMPIONSHIP AVERAGES
BATTING

	Birthplace	Mtchs.	Inns.	Not Out	Runs	100's	Highest Inns.	Aver.
W. G. A. Parkhouse	*Swansea*	26	46	2	1347	1	143	30.61
W. E. Jones......	*Carmarthen*	28	49	5	1173	1	112*	26.65
A. J. Watkins	*Usk*	28	46	4	1026	2	111	24.42
W. Wooller	*Colwyn Bay*	22	38	2	822	1	128	22.83
J. F. Pleass	*Cardiff*	22	35	3	698	1	102*	21.81
J. E. McConnon..	*Newcastle*	17	24	5	388	0	52	20.42
J. Pressdee	*Swansea*	28	46	5	773	0	67	18.85
B. Hedges	*Pontypridd*	22	40	2	645	0	87	16.97
H. G. Davies ...	*Llanelly*	28	40	8	497	0	77*	15.53
B. R. Edrich	*Cantley*	15	22	2	304	0	43	15.20
K. H. Lewis	*Newtown*	8	11	4	80	0	18*	11.42
D. J. Shepherd ...	*Swansea*	22	32	7	272	0	48	10.88
P. B. Clift	*Usk*	9	14	0	146	0	45	10.42
D. Ward	*Tonypandy*	16	27	4	224	0	35	9.73
A. Lewis	*Neath*	2	3	0	28	0	19	9.33
H. D. Davies ...	*Pembury*	11	16	8	65	0	16	8.12
G. B. Shaw	*Treharris*	3	4	1	1	0	1	0.33

Also batted: A. Rees (*Port Talbot*) 12.

* *Signifies not out.*

BOWLING

	Overs	Maidens	Runs	Wickets	Average
D. Ward	131.1	28	344	19	18.10
J. Pressdee	558.1	172	1286	65	19.78
A. J. Watkins	905.3	251	2139	105	20.37
J. E. McConnon.......	401.1	114	917	42	21.83
K. H. Lewis	216.1	36	558	21	26.57
W. Wooller	540.1	162	1329	49	27.12
D. J. Shepherd	665.4	157	1770	59	30.00
H. D. Davies	227.2	48	740	22	33.63
W. E. Jones...........	82	15	243	6	40.50
G. B. Shaw	69	14	256	6	42.66

Also bowled: P. B. Clift 11—4—19—1; W. G. A. Parkhouse 3.4—0—12—0.

Amateur.—W. Wooller.

At Taunton, April 28, 29. GLAMORGAN drew with SOMERSET. (Friendly.)

At Southampton, May 7, 9, 10. GLAMORGAN lost to HAMPSHIRE by three wickets.

GLAMORGAN v. LANCASHIRE

At Swansea, May 14, 16, 17. Drawn. With Statham achieving his best
analysis and Washbrook hitting a splendid century, Lancashire gained a strong
position before rain, which began after tea on the second day and prevented further
cricket, ruined their chances of victory. Glamorgan showed promise of doing
reasonably well until at 61 Washbrook changed Statham to the other end and the

England fast bowler proceeded to take his last five wickets for nine runs. Grieves helping Washbrook to add 85, Lancashire finished the first day 122 ahead with three wickets left. Washbrook hit one 6 and twelve 4's in his attractive 102 and Lancashire put on 85 more runs. Glamorgan fared better with the bat at the second attempt, thanks to the enterprise of the left-handers, Jones and Watkins, but Statham broke the stand when recalled for another spell. He bowled Watkins with his first ball; then came rain which ended the game.

Glamorgan

W. Wooller c and b Statham	4	— c Wharton b Statham...... 19
W. G. A. Parkhouse c Wilson b Hilton	11	— c Statham b Hilton 8
B. Hedges c Place b Statham	19	— c Grieves b Hilton 15
W. E. Jones c Ikin b Tattersall	22	— not out 34
A. J. Watkins c Hilton b Tattersall	4	— b Statham................. 27
J. Pressdee b Statham	0	— not out 0
J. Pleass c Smith b Statham	0	
B. R. Edrich c Hilton b Tattersall	3	
J. E. McConnon not out	6	
H. G. Davies lbw b Statham	1	
D. Shepherd b Statham	0	
B 6, l-b 1	7	B 4, l-b 5, n-b 3....... 12

1/6 2/35 3/61 4/67 5/67 6/67   77   1/33 2/35 3/67   (4 wkts.) 115
7/68 8/76 9/77   4/109

Lancashire

J. T. Ikin, b Wooller	12	R. Tattersall run out 19
S. Smith b Shepherd	11	A. Wilson not out 19
A. Wharton st Davies b McConnon	35	T. Greenhough c and b Wooller .. 12
C. Washbrook lbw b Shepherd	102	
W. Place b McConnon	0	
K. Grieves c Pleass b Wooller	42	B 3, l-b 18 21
M. J. Hilton b Shepherd	1	
J. B. Statham c Parkhouse b Shepherd	0	1/19 2/51 3/85 4/87 5/172 274
		6/173 7/177 8/219 9/249

Lancashire Bowling

	O.	M.	R.	W.		O.	M.	R.	W.
Statham	14.3	7	17	6	....	15	6	16	2
Wharton	3	2	2	0	....	3	1	4	0
Tattersall	21	11	22	3	....	20	8	32	0
Hilton	11	6	18	1	....	15	7	34	2
Greenhough	2	0	11	0	....	3	0	17	0

Glamorgan Bowling

	O.	M.	R.	W.
Shepherd	18	5	42	4
Wooller	27.5	3	97	3
McConnon	23	11	58	2
Watkins	18	5	27	0
Pressdee	5	0	29	0

Umpires: A. E. Pothecary and K. McCanlis.

GLAMORGAN v. SUSSEX

At Cardiff, May 18, 19, 20. Drawn. Rain also spoiled this match, less than an hour's cricket being possible on the first day when intermittent hail storms alternated with blazing sunshine. At one time hailstones and sleet covered the ground like a white mantle. In gaining first innings points, Glamorgan were mainly indebted to fine all-round cricket by McConnon who, because he con-

sidered himself not quite fit, declined an invitation to appear for M.C.C. against
the South Africans at Lord's the following week-end. After taking five wickets
for 54 runs, McConnon hit three 6's and six 4's while making 50 in forty minutes.
Not usually regarded as a big hitter, McConnon punished Thomson for 28 in one
over: 4, 6, 4, 4, 4, 6. The last six was a gigantic pull, the ball pitching on the
roof of a block of five-storey flats, eighty feet high.

Sussex

J. Langridge b McConnon	55	— c Davies b Pressdee	28
D. V. Smith lbw b McConnon	30	— not out	34
A. S. M. Oakman c Shepherd b McConnon	2	— c and b Pressdee	4
J. M. Parks c Wooller b McConnon	6	— not out	16
K. G. Suttle st Davies b Watkins	6		
G. Cox c Preesdee b Wooller	36		
R. G. Marlar c McConnon b Pressdee	0		
G. Potter b McConnon	1		
N. I. Thomson c Jones b Ward	22		
A. E. James not out	10		
R. T. Webb not out	0		
B 2, n-b 1	3	L-b 4, n-b 1	5

1/49 2/55 3/62 4/69   (9 wkts., dec.) 171   1/46 2/56   (2 wkts.) 87
5/113 6/116 7/121 8/149 9/166

Glamorgan

W. Wooller b Marlar	41	J. E. McConnon c Langridge b Thomson	52
W. G. A. Parkhouse c Smith b James	15	D. Shepherd b Thomson	10
B. Hedges b James	18	H. G. Davies not out	1
W. E. Jones lbw b Marlar	49		
A. J. Watkins c Smith b Oakman	13	B 7, w 1	8
J. Pressdee c James b Thomson	17		
P. B. Clift c Suttle b Oakman	3	1/25 2/67 3/79 4/97 5/119 243
D. Ward b Marlar	16	6/128 7/151 8/219 9/235

Glamorgan Bowling

	O.	M.	R.	W.	O.	M.	R.	W.
Shepherd	7	3	18	0	9	3	16	0
Wooller	9	2	34	1	5	2	7	0
McConnon	20	4	54	5				
Watkins	13	6	23	1	7	4	12	0
Pressdee	8	0	27	1	12	6	25	2
Ward	4	0	12	1	10.4	5	22	0

Sussex Bowling

	O.	M.	R.	W.
Thomson	18	5	74	3
James	40	25	50	2
Oakman	34	15	31	2
Marlar	20.4	5	65	3
Potter	4	1	15	0

Umpires: A. E. Pothecary and K. McCanlis.

At Birmingham, May 21, 23, 34. GLAMORGAN lost to WARWICKSHIRE by six wickets.

At Worthing, May 25, 26, 27. GLAMORGAN drew with SUSSEX.

At Cardiff, May 28, 30, 31. GLAMORGAN drew with SOUTH AFRICANS. (See
SOUTH AFRICAN section.)

At The Oval, June 1, 2, 3. GLAMORGAN lost to SURREY by eight wickets.

At Colchester, June 4, 6, 7. GLAMORGAN drew with ESSEX.

GLAMORGAN v. NOTTINGHAMSHIRE

At Llanelly, June 8, 9, 10. Drawn. A keen struggle for first innings points favoured Nottinghamshire by five runs. Rain restricted play to less than three hours on the opening day, when a sparkling third wicket stand of 117 by Simpson and Hardstaff proved the chief feature. Simpson, Nottinghamshire captain, maintained his reputation as a polished forward stroke player, and Hardstaff, always ready to punish the loose ball, hit four 6's and seven 4's. The Glamorgan batting lacked consistency, but Watkins made a valiant effort. The left-hander, who drove, hooked, and hit to leg in exhilarating style, made a century in two hours twenty minutes with the help of eighteen boundaries. Parkhouse gave him good support, but the rest did little. Smales employed off-spinners effectively for Nottinghamshire.

Nottinghamshire

R. T. Simpson st Davies b Pressdee	....	82	— c Pressdee b Lewis	....	11
J. D. Clay hit wkt b McConnon	....	5	— b Watkins	....	21
C. J. Poole c Shepherd b McConnon	...	3	— c Watkins b Lewis	....	0
J. Hardstaff b Shepherd	....	83	— b Pressdee	....	58
E. J. Martin c Davies b Lewis	....	17	— not out	....	16
R. Giles not out	....	55	— lbw b Pressdee	....	4
P. F. Harvey c Davies b Lewis	....	0	— not out	....	1
B. Dooland c Parkhouse b Watkins	....	19			
K. Smales b Pressdee	....	5			
A. Jepson st Davies b Pressdee	....	13			
E. J. Rowe b Lewis	....	5			
L-b 4	....	4	B 5	....	5

1/20 2/42 3/159 4/177 5/217 6/217   291   1/12 2/12   (5 wkts.) 116
7/254 8/262 9/276   3/58 4/103 5/115

Glamorgan

W. G. A. Parkhouse lbw b Smales	.	84	H. G. Davies b Smales	....	5
W. E. Jones c Harvey b Jepson	...	5	K. H. Lewis c Giles b Smales	....	15
B. Hedges lbw b Jepson	....	9	D. J. Shepherd c Rowe b Jepson	.	4
J. Pressdee b Dooland	....	6			
A. J. Watkins b Harvey	....	111	B 5, l-b 3	....	8
B. R. Edrich b Smales	....	17			
J. Pleass not out	....	22	1/7 2/33 3/74 4/156 5/238		286
J. E. McConnon c Poole b Smales		0	6/238 7/238 8/254 9/282		

Glamorgan Bowling

	O.	M.	R.	W.		O.	M.	R.	W.
Shepherd	30	7	86	1	....	9	2	42	0
Lewis	20.5	3	41	3	....	11	4	22	2
Watkins	25	4	56	1	....	10	3	16	1
McConnon	15	2	63	2	....	9	2	25	0
Pressdee	11	2	41	3	....	7	3	6	2

Nottinghamshire Bowling

Smales	43	18	82	5
Jepson	28.2	7	70	3
Dooland	22	4	92	1
Harvey	16	7	34	1

Umpires: Harry Elliott (Derbyshire) and P. Corrall.

GLAMORGAN v. GLOUCESTERSHIRE

(A. J. Watkins's Benefit)

At Swansea, June 11, 13, 14. Drawn. Unfortunately for the beneficiary, rain seriously interfered, not a ball being bowled on the third day, and the total gate receipts amounted to only £280. Fine seam bowling by Wooller caused most trouble for Gloucestershire. A second wicket stand of 61 by Young and Nicholls was the one redeeming feature in their first innings. In the Glamorgan second innings Wooller and Parkhouse scored 70 for the first wicket, but Cook flighted left-arm slows so cleverly that at one period five men left for the addition of 51. H. Davies hit four 6's, but missed catches helped Glamorgan gain first innings points.

Gloucestershire

G. M. Emmett c Watkins b Wooller	0	— not out	61
D. M. Young c and b Pressdee	46	— c Edrich b Wooller	3
R. B. Nicholls b McConnon	27	— b Watkins	8
J. F. Crapp c Pressdee b Wooller	39	— b McConnon	28
G. E. Lambert c Pleass b Wooller	13	— c H. G. Davies b Pressdee	0
A. E. Wilson c Parkhouse b Wooller	5		
J. Mortimore b Wooller	0	— not out	0
P. Rochford c Edrich b McConnon	3		
C. Cook c Pressdee b McConnon	1		
B. D. Wells c Pressdee b Wooller	15		
F. P. McHugh not out	1		
B 3, l-b 3, w 1	7	L-b 1	1

1/0 2/61 3/79 4/118 5/125 6/125   **157**   1/6 2/25 3/80   (4 wkts.) **101**
7/140 8/140 9/142   4/89

Glamorgan

W. Wooller c and b Cook	33	B. R. Edrich c Cook b Mortimore	19
W. G. A. Parkhouse c Rochford b Cook	39	J. E. McConnon b Wells	20
B. Hedges b Mortimore	0	H. G. Davies b Wells	35
W. E. Jones c and b Mortimore	11	H. D. Davies not out	1
A. J. Watkins c Lambert b Cook	34	B 10, l-b 4	14
J. Pressdee c Nicholls b Cook	0		
J. Pleass c Lambert b Cook	22	1/70 2/71 3/77 4/109 5/121	**228**
		6/122 7/162 8/187 9/209	

Glamorgan Bowling

	O.	M.	R.	W.		O.	M.	R.	W.
Wooller	21.4	10	33	6	....	5	1	11	1
H. D. Davies	7	1	25	0					
Watkins	9	2	30	0	....	14	2	30	1
McConnon	23	11	36	3	....	13	6	30	1
Pressdee	14	9	26	1	....	11	4	25	1
Jones						2	1	4	0

Gloucestershire Bowling

	O.	M.	R.	W.
Lambert	3	1	14	0
McHugh	2	0	15	0
Cook	36	16	68	5
Wells	11	2	34	2
Mortimore	30	9	83	3

Umpires: Harry Elliott (Derbyshire) and P. Corrall.

At Northampton, June 15, 16, 17. GLAMORGAN drew with NORTHAMPTONSHIRE.

GLAMORGAN v. DERBYSHIRE

At Cardiff, June 18, 20, 21. Derbyshire won by 132 runs. Set 265 to win, Glamorgan broke down so badly that eight wickets fell for 27 runs before McConnon and H. Davies (two 6's, five 4's) added 75 in three-quarters of an hour. Carr, Derbyshire captain, laid the foundations of his side's success by sound batting in each innings Although three times hit for six in the match, Gladwin, like Jackson, generally held the upper hand as a pace bowler, and Smith's off-spinners strengthened a Derbyshire attack which remained formidable throughout.

Derbyshire

A. Hamer c Pressdee b McConnon	50	— lbw b Watkins	12
J. Kelly b McConnon	29	— lbw b McConnon	29
H. L. Johnson st Davies b Clift	22	— c Davies b McConnon	2
A. C. Revill run out	4	— b McConnon	6
D. B. Carr b Shepherd	66	— st Davies b Watkins	52
G. Wyatt c Wooller b Pressdee	4	— not out	31
D. C. Morgan lbw b McConnon	5	— b Wooller	13
G. O. Dawkes c Pressdee b McConnon	8	— not out	8
C. Gladwin not out	37		
E. Smith lbw b Wooller	6		
L. Jackson b Wooller	12		
B 4, l-b 6, w 1	11	B 5, l-b 2	7

1/75 2/86 3/90 4/122 5/141 6/154   **254**   1/42 2/42   (6 wkts., dec.) **160**
7/162 8/217 9/230   3/49 4/58 5/123 6/149

Glamorgan

W. Wooller b Gladwin	1	— lbw b Smith	5
P. B. Clift c Dawkes b Jackson	5	— run out	0
B. Hedges b Jackson	0	— lbw b Gladwin	0
W. E. Jones b Jackson	1	— c Dawkes b Morgan	2
A. J. Watkins c Dawkes b Jackson	11	— b Jackson	12
J. Pressdee b Smith	19	— c Morgan b Smith	0
B. R. Edrich c Morgan b Gladwin	42	— c Dawkes b Jackson	5
J. Pleass not out	27	— lbw b Gladwin	1
J. E. McConnon lbw b Smith	22	— not out	37
H. G. Davies b Smith	0	— c Dawkes b Carr	48
D. J. Shepherd c Dawkes b Smith	16	— b Morgan	15
B 5, l-b 1	6	B 4, w 3	7

1/1 2/2 3/4 4/17 5/20 6/74 7/95   **150**   1/1 2/1 3/8 4/10 5/11   **132**
8/124 9/124   6/19 7/27 8/27 9/102

Glamorgan Bowling

	O.	M.	R.	W.		O.	M.	R.	W.
Shepherd	19	6	56	1	....	16	2	49	0
Wooller	17.4	9	31	2	....	16	5	27	1
Watkins	14	2	35	0	....	18	4	45	2
McConnon	28	6	57	4	....	19	5	29	3
Pressdee	29	12	44	1	....	2	0	3	0
Clift	11	4	19	1					
Jones	1	0	1	0					

Derbyshire Bowling

	O.	M.	R.	W.		O.	M.	R.	W.
Jackson	29	15	21	4	....	15	7	21	2
Gladwin	28	13	67	2	....	14	8	25	2
Smith	16	6	34	4	....	12	2	20	2
Morgan	6	0	14	0	....	7.5	1	26	2
Carr	3	1	8	0	....	5	1	33	1

Umpires: H. G. Baldwin and H. Elliott (Lancashire).

GLAMORGAN v. SOMERSET

At Newport, June 22, 23, 24. Glamorgan won by eight wickets. Their first victory of the season came mainly through a stubborn century by Jones and clever bowling by Watkins. Shepherd and Lewis with lively pace bowling struck early blows for Glamorgan, but sound batting by Tremlett and Lomax saved Somerset from collapse. Though Lobb maintained his promise with the new ball, Jones stayed five hours without being beaten. When Somerset batted again 77 behind they lost two wickets for one run. On the third day Hilton stayed two hours, but after lunch deadly bowling by Watkins, who took five wickets for 13, soon ended the match.

Somerset

H. W. Stephenson c Pressdee b Lewis ..	12	— lbw b Lewis	0
Yawar Saeed c McConnon b Shepherd ..	1	— c Davies b Lewis	0
J. Lawrence c Pressdee b Shepherd	7	— c and b Lewis	14
G. G. Tordoff c Davies b Shepherd	1	— c Parkhouse b Watkins	27
P. B. Wight c Pressdee b Lewis	29	— c McConnon b Watkins ...	5
M. F. Tremlett b Shepherd	68	— c Davies b Watkins	4
J. G. Lomax c McConnon b Watkins	68	— c Watkins b Pressdee	19
G. M. Tripp b Watkins	8	— c Shepherd b Pressdee	2
J. Hilton c Davies b Watkins...........	6	— c Davies b Watkins	9
J. W. McMahon not out	2	— lbw b Watkins.............	0
B. Lobb st Davies b Shepherd	5	— not out	0
B 3, l-b 9, n-b 2	14	L-b 2	2
	—		—
	221		82

1/13 2/13 3/14 4/21 5/85 6/152   221
7/187 8/209 9/216

1/0 2/1 3/18 4/42   82
5/57 6/57 7/77 8/81 9/82

Glamorgan

W. G. A. Parkhouse c Stephenson b Lomax	27	— b McMahon.............	0
B. R. Edrich lbw b Yawar Saeed	23	— c Yawar Saeed b Hilton ...	3
B. Hedges lbw b Lomax	0	— not out	0
W. E. Jones not out 112		— not out	2
A. J. Watkins b Lobb	30		
J. Pressdee c Stephenson b Lobb	0		
J. Pleass c Stephenson b Lobb	40		
J. E. McConnon c Stephenson b Lobb ..	15		
H. G. Davies c Wight b McMahon	43		
L-b 2, w 6	8	L-b 1	1
	—		—
	298		6

1/41 2/41 3/71 4/137   (8 wkts., dec.) 298
5/141 6/203 7/229 8/298

1/4 2/4   (2 wkts.) 6

K. H. Lewis and D. J. Shepherd did not bat.

Glamorgan Bowling

	O.	M.	R.	W.		O.	M.	R.	W.
Lewis	17	2	46	2	....	15	5	19	3
Shepherd	30.5	4	92	5	....	9	4	12	0
Watkins	19	5	44	3	....	11	5	13	5
McConnon	7	2	16	0	....	13	5	32	0
Pressdee	3	1	9	0	....	4	2	4	2

Somerset Bowling

	O.	M.	R.	W.		O.	M.	R.	W.
Lobb	32	14	94	4					
Lomax	26	8	68	2					
Hilton	7	3	22	0	....	1	0	1	1
Yawar Saeed	9	4	28	1					
McMahon	15.2	5	42	1	....	2	0	4	1
Lawrence	7	1	27	0					
Tordoff	1	0	9	0					

Umpires: H. G. Baldwin and H. Elliott (Lancashire.

GLAMORGAN v. HAMPSHIRE

At Swansea, June 25, 27, 28. Hampshire won by five wickets. Chiefly through Horton, who batted nearly four and a half hours, they gained a first innings lead of 10 runs. Previously Hedges, Jones and Watkins did so well for Glamorgan that at one time a larger total seemed likely. After a stand of 123 by Watkins and Jones, however, Cannings and Shackleton caused a breakdown with the new ball, the last six wickets falling for 61. When Cannings pulled a muscle Gray seized his chance as a seam bowler in the Glamorgan second innings, achieving his best performance in first-class cricket. Left 141 to win, Hampshire were troubled by the swing bowling of Lewis, but determined batting by Marshall, Rayment and Barnard settled the issue.

Glamorgan

W. G. A. Parkhouse lbw b Cannings	...	6	— lbw b Gray	44
B. R. Edrich b Cannings		29	— c Eagar b Burden	2
B. Hedges c Eagar b Sainsbury		54	— st Harrison b Sainsbury	... 2
W. E. Jones b Shackleton		62	— c and b Gray	55
A. J. Watkins c and b Cannings		75	— c Harrison b Gray	11
W. Wooller c Rayment b Cannings		0	— c Marshall b Gray	10
J. Pleass c Barnard b Shackleton		10	— c Marshall b Shackleton	11
J. Pressdee c Cannings b Shackleton		16	— b Gray	0
J. E. McConnon not out		5	— c Marshall b Gray	5
H. G. Davies c Eagar b Cannings		6	— b Gray	0
K. H. Lewis b Cannings		0	— not out	7
B 1, l-b 7, n-b 2		10	B 2, l-b 1	3

1/9 2/60 3/107 4/230 5/234 6/236   273   1/21 2/24 3/76 4/106   150
7/253 8/266 9/273   5/122 6/131 7/133 8/139 9/139

Hampshire

J. R. Gray c Hedges b McConnon	.....	46	— c Wooller b Lewis	5
R. E. Marshall c Pressdee b Wooller	....	30	— c Wooller b Lewis	31
H. Horton c Edrich b McConnon		89	— b Lewis	0
A. W. H. Rayment lbw b Lewis		12	— not out	35
H. M. Barnard c and b Pressdee		33	— c Hedges b Watkins	52
E. D. R. Eagar c Pleass b Jones		15	— c Wooller b Lewis	16
L. Harrison c Jones b McConnon		28	— not out	1
P. J. Sainsbury c Edrich b McConnon		1		
D. Shackleton not out		17		
V. H. D. Cannings b McConnon		0		
M. D. Burden c Wooller b Watkins	...	2		
B 7, l-b 3		10	B 1	1

1/44 2/114 3/138 4/187 5/222   283   1/18 2/18 3/37   (5 wkts.)   141
6/252 7/258 8/271 9/272   4/112 5/135

Hampshire Bowling

	O.	M.	R.	W.		O.	M.	R.	W.
Shackleton.....	23	8	58	3	....	25	9	63	1
Cannings	27	9	67	6	....	4	1	14	0
Burden	22	8	40	0	....	4	2	8	1
Gray	17	2	37	0	....	21.3	3	52	7
Sainsbury......	15	5	40	1	....	8	7	5	1
Marshall	11	6	19	0	....	5	3	3	0
Barnard	1	0	2	0	....	1	0	2	0

Glamorgan Bowling

	O.	M.	R.	W.		O.	M.	R.	W.
Wooller	19	5	53	1	....	2	0	14	0
Lewis	16	3	36	1	....	14.5	3	51	4
McConnon	34	12	59	5	....	7	1	23	0
Watkins	27.4	9	66	1	....	12	1	40	1
Pressdee	16	4	38	1	....	2	0	12	0
Jones	6	3	21	1					

Umpires: W. T. Jones and G. S. Mobey.

At Derby, June 29, 30, July 1. GLAMORGAN drew with DERBYSHIRE.

At Loughborough, July 2, 4, 5. GLAMORGAN lost to LEICESTERSHIRE by 21 runs.

At Harrogate, July 6, 7, 8. GLAMORGAN beat YORKSHIRE by four wickets.

GLAMORGAN v. ESSEX

At Pontypridd, July 13, 14, 15. Essex won by 91 runs. Ray Smith, their acting captain, struck the winning blows on the third day when he captured eight wickets for 63. A spot at one end of the pitch helped bowlers and there were other triumphs. Dodds exploited leg breaks for Essex, and took three wickets without conceding a run, but Dodds and Barker, the Essex opening pair, fell in their second innings without either scoring. Owing to a fractured finger McConnon retired from the game and did not bat for Glamorgan, who were also handicapped by an injury to Wooller, but Watkins stood out for them by his fine all-round cricket.

Essex

T. C. Dodds c Davies b Shepherd	15	— c Wooller b Watkins	0
G. Barker c Shepherd b Watkins	48	— lbw b Watkins	0
P. A. Gibb lbw b Shaw................	14	— c Davies b Watkins	37
C. C. P. Williams c Watkins b Jones	45	— b Watkins...............	5
R. E. Evans c and b Jones	3	— c sub b Wooller..........	4
R. Horsfall st Davies b Jones	47	— st Davies b Watkins	39
B. Taylor c Hedges b Wooller	57	— c Watkins b Wooller	0
R. Smith c Pressdee b Watkins	5	— c Pleass b Wooller	9
W. T. Greensmith not out	37	— b Watkins...............	16
R. Ralph not out	53	— b Shepherd	15
K. C. Preston (did not bat)		— not out	15
L-b 2, w 1, n-b 2	5	B 2, l-b 1, n-b 1.......	4

1/24 2/60 3/127 4/127   (8 wkts., dec.) 329   1/0 2/1 3/22 4/33 5/63   144
5/132 6/195 7/212 8/249   6/66 7/84 8/105 9/124

M

Glamorgan

W. Wooller c Dodds b Greensmith	43	—	c Evans b Smith	4
W. G. A. Parkhouse c Taylor b Preston	1	—	b Greensmith	19
B. Hedges run out	56	—	c Barker b Smith	4
W. E. Jones not out	64	—	c Preston b Smith	26
A. J. Watkins c Taylor b Greensmith	0	—	c Williams b Smith	55
J. Pleass b Greensmith	18	—	c and b Smith	12
J. Pressdee b Smith	18	—	lbw b Smith	16
H. G. Davies c Greensmith b Dodds	4	—	c Barker b Smith	10
G. B. Shaw b Dodds	0	—	not out	0
D. J. Shepherd c and b Dodds	0	—	c Gibb b Smith	0
J. E. McConnon absent hurt	0	—	absent hurt	0
B 4, l-b 4, n-b 6	14		B 15, l-b 1, w 1, n-b 1	18
	218			164

1/3 2/91 3/117 4/118 5/168 6/195
7/216 8/218 9/218

1/11 2/21 3/43 4/84 5/113
6/146 7/160 8/160 9/164

Glamorgan Bowling

	O.	M.	R.	W.		O.	M.	R.	W.
Shepherd	23	5	60	1	....	7	2	30	1
Watkins	24	6	50	2	....	27	8	57	6
Wooller	13	3	33	1	....	16	3	40	3
Shaw	17	3	91	1					
Jones	25	3	71	3					
Pressdee	5	1	19	0	....	4	0	13	0

Essex Bowling

	O.	M.	R.	W.		O.	M.	R.	W.
Preston	24	5	41	1	....	8	5	11	0
Smith	31	9	45	1	....	25.5	8	63	8
Dodds	3.2	3	0	3	....	9	1	36	0
Ralph	13	3	31	0	....	2	0	9	0
Greensmith	31	7	87	3	....	11	1	27	1

Umpires: N. Oldfield and Harry Elliott (Derbyshire).

GLAMORGAN v. NORTHAMPTONSHIRE

At Cardiff, July 16, 18, 19. Northamptonshire won by four wickets. Glamorgan showed enterprise by twice declaring, but they reckoned without the fighting qualities of their opponents, who in a thrilling struggle got home three minutes before time. Set 204 to win in 135 minutes, Northamptonshire accepted the challenge, and through the enterprise of Brookes and Arnold 116 appeared in an hour with only one man out. Effective off spin bowling by Ward worried the visitors, but Greasley stood firm, and at a critical stage they were helped by two over-throws to the boundary. Jones and Parkhouse were convincing batsmen for Glamorgan, and Pressdee maintained his promising form.

Glamorgan

W. Wooller c Clarke b Barrick	21	— b Broderick 16
W. G. A. Parkhouse c Andrew b Broderick	83	— b Broderick 52
B. Hedges lbw b Tribe	1	— b Broderick 29
W. E. Jones c Andrew b Clarke	95	— lbw b Broderick 16
A. J. Watkins hit wkt b Tribe	7	— c Andrew b Broderick 0
J. Pleass c Livingston b Tribe	4	— lbw b Tribe 10
J. Pressdee not out	52	— not out 15
D. Ward c Arnold b Barrick	35	— not out 14
H. G. Davies c Reynolds b Broderick	29	— b Tribe 2
D. J. Shepherd (did not bat)		— c Tribe b Broderick 35
B 5, l-b 7, w 1	13	B 2, l-b 4 6

1/50 2/78 3/169 4/190   (8 wkts., dec.) 340
5/205 6/228 7/283 8/340

1/56 2/97   (8 wkts., dec.) 195
3/102 4/102 5/119 6/137
7/140 8/172

G. B. Shaw did not bat.

Northamptonshire

D. Brookes c Wooller b Ward	78	— c Pressdee b Wooller 50
P. Arnold lbw b Watkins	4	— c and b Ward 61
L. Livingston c Davies b Shaw	39	— c and b Ward 17
D. Barrick lbw b Shaw	46	— c Pressdee b Ward 17
D. G. Greasley c Watkins b Shaw	17	— not out 45
G. E. Tribe lbw b Ward	0	— c Wooller b Ward 1
V. Broderick c Watkins b Ward	34	— c Davies b Watkins 6
B. Reynolds not out	64	
K. V. Andrew c Pressdee b Wooller	21	
R. W. Clarke hit wkt b Shaw	9	— not out 5
A. L. Wells c Watkins b Ward	1	
B 4, l-b 15	19	B 2, l-b 2, n-b 1....... 5

1/16 2/102 3/176 4/176 5/176 6/218   332
7/238 8/302 9/327

1/81 2/124 3/135   (6 wkts.) 207
4/137 5/171 6/191

Northamptonshire Bowling

	O.	M.	R.	W.		O.	M.	R.	W.
Clarke	25	3	94	1	....	12	3	25	0
Wells	25	9	59	0					
Barrick	16	2	49	2	....	9	6	6	0
Tribe	40	14	86	3	....	26	6	66	2
Broderick......	27.4	9	39	2	....	22	1	86	6
Greasley						3	1	6	0

Glamorgan Bowling

	O.	M.	R.	W.		O.	M.	R.	W.
Shepherd	15	0	38	0	....	6	0	34	0
Watkins	21	7	53	1	....	11	3	41	1
Wooller	20	9	55	1	....	10	0	46	1
Shaw	36	11	76	4	....	6	0	35	0
Pressdee	8	0	44	0					
Jones	3	1	5	0					
Ward	25.2	10	42	4	....	12.1	2	46	4

Umpires: N. Oldfield and Harry Elliott (Derbyshire).

GLAMORGAN v. SURREY

At Swansea, July 20, 21. Surrey won by nine wickets. Haydn Davies captained an all-professional side of Welshmen for the first time in Glamorgan history, but they were scarcely a match for the Champions, who gained a fairly easy victory in two days. Laker's splendid all-round form for Surrey provided the chief feature of the match. Besides taking ten wickets for 121, he scored 53 by bold hitting. Eric Bedser and Barrington also batted well for Surrey, but apart from Parkhouse and Haydn Davies Glamorgan batsmen were disappointing. Davies saved the side from an innings defeat with a courageous not out 77, which fell only three short of his highest score in first-class cricket.

Glamorgan

W. G. A. Parkhouse c Swetman b Laker	54 — lbw b A. Bedser	9
B. Hedges b Laker	23 — c Surridge b Laker	7
J. Pleass hit wkt b Laker	10 — c Surridge b A. Bedser	2
W. E. Jones c Stewart b Laker	0 — st Swetman b Laker	27
A. J. Watkins b A. Bedser	11 — c Swetman b A. Bedser	5
J. Pressdee c Stewart b E. Bedser	2 — c Swetman b A. Bedser	1
D. Ward lbw b E. Bedser	0 — lbw b Laker	9
D. J. Shepherd c Surridge b A. Bedser	20 — c Surridge b Laker	2
H. G. Davies lbw b A. Bedser	18 — not out	77
H. G. Davies not out	14 — c Cox b Laker	16
G. B. Shaw c Surridge b Laker	1 — run out	0
B 12, l-b 5, n-b 1	18 — B 4, l-b 10, n-b 1	15

1/56 2/76 3/76 4/93 5/108 6/108   171   1/20 2/20 3/24 4/52 5/54   170
7/132 8/132 9/162   6/68 7/75 8/145 9/147

Surrey

R. C. E. Pratt c Pressdee b Shaw	23 — c sub b Shepherd	7
M. J. Stewart c H. G. Davies b H. D. Davies	9 — not out	26
B. Constable c H. G. Davies b Watkins	19 — not out	13
K. Barrington b Watkins	59	
T. H. Clark lbw b Pressdee	1	
E. A. Bedser lbw b H. D. Davies	61	
D. F. Cox c Shepherd b Watkins	26	
R. Swetman b H. D. Davies	9	
J. C. Laker c and b Pressdee	53	
W. S. Surridge b H. D. Davies	6	
A. V. Bedser not out	19	
L-b 6, n-b 3	9 — L-b 1, n-b 1	2

1/37 2/37 3/93 4/94 5/127 6/164   294   1/22   (1 wkt.) 48
7/208 8/226 9/240

Surrey Bowling

	O.	M.	R.	W.	O.	M.	R.	W.
A. Bedser	13	2	38	3	25	6	78	4
Surridge	5	0	23	0				
Laker	22.1	8	53	5	27.5	5	68	5
Cox	1	0	3	0				
E. Bedser	14	5	36	2	4	1	9	0

Glamorgan Bowling

Shepherd	14	3	44	0	6	2	26	1
H. D. Davies	23	7	63	4	4	1	8	0
Shaw	10	0	54	1				
Pressdee	30.3	8	64	2				
Ward	1	0	5	0	3.3	0	12	0
Watkins	19	5	37	3				
Jones	3	0	18	0				

Umpires: A. E. Pothecary and J. S. Buller.

At Maidstone, July 23, 25, 26. GLAMORGAN lost to KENT by 63 runs.

GLAMORGAN v. MIDDLESEX

At Cardiff, July 27, 28, 29. Middlesex won by one wicket. The match had
an amazing finish, for the teams had to turn out on the last morning for what
proved to be less than one minute's cricket. The remarkable situation was created
the previous evening. Middlesex needed 145 to win with ample time to finish the
game in two days, but when the extra half-hour was claimed they still required
19 with three wickets to fall. They lost two more men and the last over came with
six runs wanted, but Young could get only two two's and a single. Five hundred
spectators, admitted free next morning, saw Young win the match by driving the
third ball from Watkins to the boundary. Play lasted fifty-two seconds. The
players were properly attired and all the usual procedure was observed. Moss,
Young's partner, whose arm had swollen through an insect bite, had an injection
to relieve pain before he went in, and on returning to London spent the next night
in hospital. All through the game spin bowlers held the upper hand on a dry
pitch.

Glamorgan

W. Wooller c Titmus b Young	9	— c Robertson b Moss		8
W. G. A. Parkhouse b Titmus	21	— run out		22
B. Hedges lbw b Titmus	6	— b Warr		8
W. E. Jones b Titmus	5	— c Robins b Titmus		43
A. J. Watkins c Compton b Young	18	— b Warr		0
J. Pleass c Edrich b Young	11	— lbw b Young		35
J. Pressdee lbw b Young	2	— lbw b Young		10
D. J. Ward c Robertson b Titmus	1	— c Compton b Young		24
H. G. Davies b Titmus	6	— c sub b Young		1
H. D. Davies not out	6	— not out		1
D. J. Shepherd b Young	6	— b Titmus		0
B 6, l-b 6, n-b 1	13	B 12, l-b 4		16

1/31 2/31 3/37 4/50 5/74 6/83   104   1/8 2/37 3/46 4/47 5/100   168
7/84 8/92 9/92   6/118 7/152 8/163 9/167

Middlesex

J. D. Robertson b H. D. Davies	15	— lbw b Pressdee		22
S. M. Brown lbw b H. D. Davies	1	— c Parkhouse b Watkins		4
W. J. Edrich c Parkhouse b Watkins	22	— c H. G. Davies b Watkins		18
G. P. S. Delisle c Pleass b Pressdee	35	— c Watkins b Pressdee		28
D. Bennett b Watkins	10	— c and b Watkins		6
F. J. Titmus c and b Pressdee	23	— c Parkhouse b Pressdee		25
J. J. Warr c Jones b Pressdee	7	— b Watkins		15
L. H. Compton c and b Watkins	4	— lbw b Watkins		13
R. V. C. Robins st H. G. Davies b Watkins	0	— c Wooller b Pressdee		0
J. A. Young b Pressdee	6	— not out		12
A. E. Moss not out	0	— not out		0
L-b 5	5	B 1, l-b 2, w 1, n-b 1		5

1/8 2/25 3/62 4/88 5/88 6/103   128   1/4 2/48 3/48   (9 wkts.) 148
7/118 8/122 9/122   4/59 5/98 6/111 7/126
                             8/127 9/139

Middlesex Bowling

	O.	M.	R.	W.		O.	M.	R.	W.
Moss	5	2	7	0	....	2	0	2	1
Warr	4	0	19	0	....	11	0	34	2
Titmus	24	13	29	5	....	33.3	15	69	2
Young	23.5	11	36	5	....	33	17	47	4

Glamorgan Bowling

	O.	M.	R.	W.		O.	M.	R.	W.
Watkins	22	6	52	4	....	38.3	13	89	5
H. D. Davies	7	1	24	2	....	3	1	7	0
Ward	7	0	12	0					
Pressdee	20.4	10	32	4	....	35	13	47	4
Jones	2	0	3	0					

Umpires: E. A. Roberts and H. G. Baldwin.

At Swansea, July 30, August 1, 2. GLAMORGAN lost to SOUTH AFRICANS by 226 runs. (See SOUTH AFRICAN section.)

GLAMORGAN v. WORCESTERSHIRE

At Swansea, August 3, 4. Glamorgan won by an innings and 23 runs. Following six successive defeats, five in the Championship, they gained an emphatic victory. The captains decided to use a substitute pitch because they considered the original to have been too well prepared to achieve a result in three days. Worcestershire were saved from a rout by Broadbent, whose 51 made in two hours, included ten 4's. Watkins was the mainstay of the Glamorgan innings. He completed a fine century in two and a half hours and followed with lively bowling when Worcestershire batted again 157 behind. The match was over before tea on the second day, the batsmen again failing on a pitch which always gave bowlers help.

Worcestershire

D. Kenyon lbw b Watkins	8	— lbw b Watkins	2
J. Lister lbw b Watkins	2	— c Watkins b Ward	0
L. Outschoorn c H. G. Davies b H. D. Davies	0	— lbw b H. D. Davies	4
R. G. Broadbent c Pleass b Ward	51	— lbw b Ward	23
M. J. Horton lbw b Pressdee	20	— c Parkhouse b H. D. Davies	5
D. W. Richardson b Pressdee	5	— st H. G. Davies b Pressdee	46
R. O. Jenkins c H. G. Davies b Ward	2	— c Clift b Watkins	17
H. Yarnold c and b Ward	0	— c Clift b Pressdee	3
G. H. Chesterton run out	8	— not out	14
R. T. D. Perks b Watkins	4	— b Pressdee	2
J. Flavell not out	0	— b Watkins	10
B 6 l-b 1	7	L-b 8	8
	107		**134**

1/2 2/3 3/13 4/57 5/65 6/86 7/86 8/95 9/99

1/5 2/11 3/16 4/59 5/59 6/97 7/105 8/112 9/131

Glamorgan

W. G. A. Parkhouse c Kenyon b Horton	36	D. Ward b Horton	0
P. B. Clift b Perks	0	W. Wooller c Yarnold b Perks	29
J. Pleass c Horton b Jenkins	36	H. G. Davies b Flavell	2
W. E. Jones b Jenkins	12	H. D. Davies c Broadbent b Perks	12
A. J. Watkins not out	107	B 4, l-b 5, w 1, n-b 7	17
J. Pressdee lbw b Horton	13		**264**
B. R. Edrich c Broadbent b Horton	0		

1/13 2/48 3/87 4/99 5/146 6/154 7/154 8/237 9/243

Glamorgan Bowling

	O.	M.	R.	W.		O.	M.	R.	W.
H. D. Davies ..	10	3	19	1	....	9	3	32	2
Watkins	14	3	32	3	....	20	8	35	3
Wooller	11	6	20	0					
Pressdee	8	3	22	2	....	18.3	6	39	3
Ward	2	0	7	3	....	8	2	20	2

Worcestershire Bowling

	O.	M.	R.	W.
Perks	22.3	3	70	3
Flavell	12	2	47	1
Chesterton	2	1	4	0
Horton	26	3	62	4
Jenkins	18	3	64	2

Umpires: H. Elliott (Lancashire) and J. J. Hills.

At Manchester, August 6, 8, 9. GLAMORGAN drew with LANCASHIRE.

At Cheltenham, August 10, 11, 12. GLAMORGAN lost to Gloucestershire by an innings and 9 runs.

At Weston-super-Mare, August 13, 15, 16. GLAMORGAN beat SOMERSET by an innings and 15 runs.

At Lord's, August 17, 18, 19. GLAMORGAN lost to MIDDLESEX by 164 runs.

GLAMORGAN v. LEICESTERSHIRE

At Cardiff, August 20, 22, 23. Leicestershire won by ten wickets. Glamorgan's batting again disappointed and they went through the season without winning a match at their headquarters. After Parkhouse and Pressdee had shown good form in a second wicket stand Glamorgan collapsed before the slow left arm bowling of Munden and Walsh. An opening partnership of 68 between Lester and Smith gave Leicestershire a steady start, but they owed most to Jackson whose century came out of 135 in two and a half hours and included three 6's and fifteen 4's. Glamorgan, 96 behind, again broke down and Leicestershire needed only 51 to win.

Glamorgan

W. Wooller c Palmer b Spencer	0	— lbw b Walsh..............	23
W. G. A. Parkhouse b Munden	53	— lbw b Goodwin	18
J. Pressdee c Jackson b Walsh	67	— b Spencer	5
W. E. Jones b Munden	0	— b Jackson	26
A. J. Watkins lbw b Munden	33	— run out	27
J. Pleass lbw b Munden	26	— b Spencer	0
A. Lewis lbw b Walsh	0	— c Lester b Munden	9
D. Ward st Firth b Walsh	10	— lbw b Munden	1
H. G. Davies not out	8	— c Palmer b Walsh	23
H. D. Davies b Munden	0	— not out	0
D. J. Shepherd c Palmer b Munden	6	— b Walsh	0
B 6	6	B 12, l-b 1, n-b 1	14

1/0 2/71 3/85 4/151 5/179 6/179   209   1/17 2/17 3/34 4/71   146
7/195 8/195 9/203   5/93 6/107 7/111 8/124
                                                           9/125

Leicestershire

G. Lester c Wooller b Pressdee	33	— not out	12
M. J. K. Smith st H. G. Davies b Pressdee	61	— not out	39
J. Firth c Parkhouse b Pressdee	6		
M. Tompkin st H. G. Davies b Pressdee	11		
C. H. Palmer b Shepherd	9		
V. E. Jackson c Wooller b Watkins	105		
R. A. Diment b Shepherd	6		
V. S. Munden lbw b Pressdee	9		
J. E. Walsh c sub b Ward	35		
C. T. Spencer b Shepherd	18		
J. Goodwin not out	0		
B 5, l-b 5, n-b 2	12	W 1	1

1/68 2/107 3/112 4/119 5/170 6/187   305   (No wkt.) 52
7/227 8/264 9/301

Leicestershire Bowling

	O.	M.	R.	W.		O.	M.	R.	W.
Spencer	12	2	42	1	....	11	4	31	2
Goodwin	5	1	18	0	....	9	1	16	1
Palmer	4	1	6	0					
Munden	36	17	59	6	....	23	8	47	2
Jackson	12	6	26	0	....	7	4	7	1
Walsh	18	3	52	3	....	19.3	8	31	3

Glamorgan Bowling

	O.	M.	R.	W.		O.	M.	R.	W.
Watkins	23	6	64	1	....	5	2	8	0
H. D. Davies	7	0	36	0					
Shepherd	44	15	80	3	....	1.4	0	9	0
Pressdee	39	16	77	5	....	5	0	21	0
Ward	12.3	3	36	1					
Wooller						9	1	13	0

Umpires: T. J. Bartley and W. T. Jones.

GLAMORGAN v. WARWICKSHIRE

At Neath, August 24, 25. Glamorgan won by an innings and 80 runs, ending a disappointing season with an overwhelming success. The match was marked by careful batting on a pitch of varying pace. Warwickshire took just over three hours to score 125. Then Wooller showed unlimited patience in batting seven hours nine minutes. He waited for the ball to punish and he hit fourteen 4's, besides a 6 (4 overthrows) in 128, his highest score in County cricket. Glamorgan declared 178 ahead and they dismissed Warwickshire in an hour and three-quarters. Watkins and Shepherd bowled splendidly, but the batting lacked resolution.

Warwickshire

F. C. Gardner b Shepherd	52	— lbw b Watkins	5
N. F. Horner c Pressdee b Watkins	12	— c Davies b Watkins	9
A. V. Wolton run out	0	— b Shepherd	32
R. T. Spooner c Pressdee b Shepherd	8	— c Jones b Watkins	33
H. E. Dollery b Shepherd	2	— b Watkins	1
R. E. Hitchcock b Watkins	22	— st Davies b Shepherd	8
A. Townsend b Shepherd	2	— c Parkhouse b Watkins	0
J. D. Bannister c Jones b Shepherd	11	— b Shepherd	0
W. B. Bridge c Davies b Watkins	2	— b Shepherd	3
R. G. Thompson c Watkins b Shepherd	1	— c Hedges b Pressdee	2
W. E. Hollies not out	1	— not out	0
B 9, l-b 2, n-b 1	12	B 4, n-b 1	5

1/26 2/26 3/46 4/54 5/85 6/90   125   1/14 2/29 3/29 4/51 5/56   98
7/117 8/120 9/123   6/56 7/56 8/96 9/98

Glamorgan

W. Wooller b Thompson	128
W. G. A. Parkhouse b Hollies	11
J. Pressdee c Townsend b Thompson	28
W. E. Jones b Thompson	0
B. Hedges c Townsend b Hollies	35
A. J. Watkins c Hollies b Bridge	36
J. Pleass run out	5

A. Lewis c Spooner b Hollies	19
D. Ward not out	5
H. G. Davies not out	19
B 12, l-b 2, w 1, n-b 2	17

D. J. Shepherd did not bat.

1/34 2/71 3/71   (8 wkts., dec.) 303
4/148 5/196 6/203 7/275 8/275

Glamorgan Bowling

	O.	M.	R.	W.		O.	M.	R.	W.
Wooller	9	0	32	0					
Watkins	24.4	8	38	3	....	16	5	43	5
Shepherd	22	8	40	6	....	11	2	45	4
Pressdee	1	0	3	0	....	4.4	2	5	1

Warwickshire Bowling

	O.	M.	R.	W.
Bannister	21	8	47	0
Thompson	28	13	59	3
Hollies	51	27	70	3
Bridge	22	6	39	1
Townsend	7	0	33	0
Hitchcock	17	3	38	0

Umpires: T. J. Bartley and W. T. Jones.

GLOUCESTERSHIRE

President—THE DUKE OF BEAUFORT

Secretary—LIEUT.-COL. H. A. HENSON, County Ground, Bristol, 7

Captain—G. M. EMMETT

| D. M. Young | County Badge | B. D. Wells |

With only five batsmen capable of returning an average of over 20 runs during the Championship programme, Gloucestershire once more disappointed their supporters. There were many good individual batting performances and the bowling was dependable enough, but lack of consistency and determination often allowed a game to slip away after an advantage had been gained. In a season which favoured the playing out of matches, four more were won, but losses rose and the club moved only from thirteenth to twelfth place in the table.

The county missed Graveney who was away for the five Test Matches, but even he was not as successful as in 1954. His Championship aggregate fell from 1,626 to 1,283 and average from 73.90 to 44.24. After a brief spell as a first-wicket batsman he soon returned to number three in the order and looked happier there. Young and Milton quickly made the opening positions their own, and Young, in particular, enjoyed a very good season. Sound and consistent, he scored nearly 600 more runs and for the first time passed 2,000 in all matches. He hit two separate hundreds against Northamptonshire at Kettering.

Crapp, relieved of the cares of captaincy, batted vigorously and almost doubled his aggregate. Emmett, who took over the leadership, did not seem as carefree in his stroke-play as in the past, but he carried his responsibilities well. Mortimore, one of the growing band of young all-rounders specialising in off-spin bowling, maintained his promise, but few meritorious displays came from those in the second half of the order. There was one batting curiosity. Not one of the fifteen centuries hit for Gloucestershire in first-class matches was made on the headquarters ground at Bristol.

The attack proved adequate if not specially penetrating. Wells, as anticipated after his clever off-spin bowling in 1954—his first full season—went ahead and took 103 wickets, though Cook, the left-arm spin bowler, surpassed him in average. Illness limited Cook's opportunities. McHugh, the big fast bowler, did best when he reduced his pace, and Lambert, with his lively bowling, took the opportunity in his benefit season to increase his wickets from 51 to 77, and, like Mortimore, he also hit his first hundred. The wicket-keeping of young Rochford deserved commendation, and as usual Milton excelled in fielding.

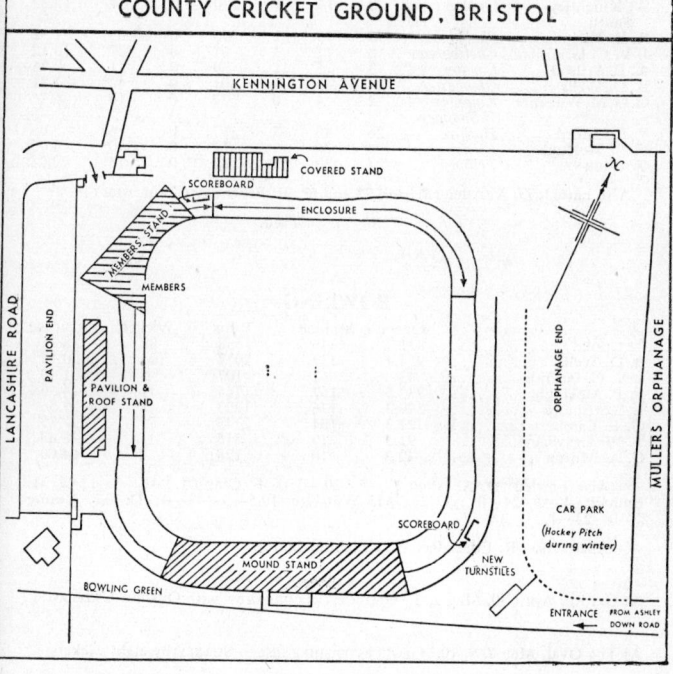

COUNTY CRICKET GROUND, BRISTOL

GLOUCESTERSHIRE RESULTS

All First-Class Matches—Played 32, *Won* 10, *Lost* 14, *Drawn* 8

County Championship Matches—Played 28, *Won* 9, *Lost* 13, *Drawn* 6

COUNTY CHAMPIONSHIP AVERAGES

BATTING

	Birthplace	Mtchs.	Inns.	Not Outs	Runs	100's	Highest Inns	Aver.
T. W. Graveney .	*Riding Mill*	16	30	1	1283	3	128	44.24
D. M. Young ...	*Coalville*	28	54	1	1691	3	137	31.90
C. A. Milton ...	*Bristol*	26	51	2	1495	2	150	30.51
J. F. Crapp	*St. Colomb*	27	51	3	1401	2	101	29.18
G. M. Emmett ...	*Agra (India)*	28	53	3	1418	2	122	28.36
G. E. Lambert ..	*London*	28	51	8	819	1	100*	19.04
J. Mortimore ...	*Bristol*	27	50	9	650	0	73	15.85
W. Knightley-Smith	*London*	8	16	1	200	0	64	13.33
R. B. Nicholls...	*Shapness*	8	15	2	155	0	63	11.92
J. V. C. Griffiths.	*Cheltenham*	6	11	3	81	0	27*	10.12
A. E. Wilson ...	*London*	3	5	1	39	0	21	9.75
B. D. Wells	*Gloucester*	24	43	4	301	0	42*	7.71
G.G.M.Wiltshire	*Chipping Sodbury*	2	4	0	27	0	13	6.75
P. Rochford ...	*Halifax*	26	40	7	167	0	16*	5.06
F. P. McHugh ..	*Leeds*	24	36	19	52	0	10*	3.05
C. Cook	*Tetbury*	24	38	4	81	0	15	2.38

Also batted: D. A. Allen (*Bristol*) 2* and 6*; R. Etheridge (Gloucester) 19, 2.

* Signifies not out.

BOWLING

	Overs	Maidens	Runs	Wickets	Average
C. Cook	831	348	1538	82	18.75
B. D. Wells	954.4	339	2077	103	20.16
J. V. C. Griffiths	43	12	107	5	21.40
F. P. McHugh	733.5	167	1744	71	24.56
J. Mortimore	579.3	176	1323	48	27.56
G. E. Lambert	727.3	134	2145	77	27.85
T. W. Graveney	91.5	19	315	11	28.63
C. A. Milton	42.3	10	128	2	64.00

Also bowled: D. A. Allen 12—5—29—0; J. F. Crapp 1.3—0—5—1; G. M. Emmett 4—0—24—0; G. G. M. Wiltshire 10.5—3—43—0; D. M. Young 2—0—23—1.

Amateurs.—R. Etheridge, W. Knightley-Smith.

At Oxford, April 30, May 2, 3. GLOUCESTERSHIRE drew with OXFORD UNIVERSITY.

At The Oval, May 7, 9, 10. GLOUCESTERSHIRE lost to SURREY by eight wickets.

GLOUCESTERSHIRE v. YORKSHIRE

At Bristol, May 14, 16. Yorkshire won by an innings and 54 runs. Gloucestershire, who again tried Graveney as opening batsman, recovered after a bad first-innings breakdown but could not match their opponents' all-round strength. Close hit boldly and Yardley, who made a century in faultless style, shared in an unbroken stand of 178 with Illingworth. On rain-affected turf, Gloucestershire were twice dismissed in a day. In the first innings Wardle pitched his left-arm spin bowling so accurately that he sent back six men for six runs—a four and a two by Crapp. Appleyard's skilful right-arm medium-pace bowling was the main factor in Gloucestershire's second downfall. An attractive display by Emmett—he hit eleven 4's—redeemed the early failures.

Yorkshire

W. Watson c Rochford b Cook ..	26
W. H. H. Sutcliffe b Cook	21
J. V. Wilson b Lambert	11
D. B. Close c McHugh b Mortimore	72
E. Lester b Wells	42
N. W. D. Yardley not out.......	100

R. Illingworth not out	71
B 4, lb 11	15
	—
1/48 2/49 3/95 (5 wkts., dec.)	358
4/173 5/180	

J. H. Wardle, R. Booth, F. S. Trueman and R. Appleyard did not bat.

Gloucestershire

D. M. Young b Appleyard...........	7	— b Appleyard	27
T. W. Graveney b Wardle	13	— c Booth b Appleyard	27
G. M. Emmett c Watson b Wardle	1	— lbw b Appleyard	89
C. A. Milton c Trueman b Appleyard .	1	— c Booth b Close	5
J. F. Crapp b Wardle	7	— lbw b Appleyard	6
G. E. Lambert c Watson b Wardle......	5	— b Appleyard	54
J. Mortimore c Booth b Appleyard	0	— not out	21
P. Rochford b Appleyard	0	— lbw b Trueman	0
C. Cook not out	5	— b Trueman	3
B. D. Wells b Wardle	1	— b Appleyard	4
F. P. McHugh b Wardle..............	0	— b Trueman	0
B 7, l-b 2, n-b 2	11	B 4, l-b 8, n-b 5.......	17

1/11 2/20 3/25 4/35 5/41 6/42	51	1/47 2/58 3/67 4/100	253
7/43 8/47 9/51		5/203 6/234 7/242 8/246	
		9/252	

Gloucestershire Bowling

	O.	M.	R.	W.	O.	M.	R.	W.
Lambert	21	3	74	1				
McHugh	25	5	58	0				
Cook	27	9	71	2				
Wells	32	7	69	1				
Mortimore.....	16	2	67	1				
Graveney	2	1	4	0				

Yorkshire Bowling

	O.	M.	R.	W.		O.	M.	R.	W.
Trueman	5	3	15	0	....	15.3	3	40	3
Appleyard	13	3	19	4	....	31	6	91	6
Wardle	9.4	7	6	6	....	6	1	26	0
			Close			15	2	54	1
			Illingworth ...			10	3	25	0

Umpire: D. Davies and E. Davies.

GLOUCESTERSHIRE v. LEICESTERSHIRE

At Bristol, May 18, 19, 20. Leicestershire won by two wickets. On a damp pitch the clever spin bowling of Jackson and Munden gave them the advantage against hesitant batsmen. Young and Graveney were sound at the start of each innings, but their colleagues, apart from Crapp who hit powerfully in the second innings, were perplexed by Jackson's variation of flight and pace and the accuracy of Munden's left-arm slows. On the first day Gloucestershire, after an opening partnership of 81, lost their nine remaining wickets in little over an hour for 26. Wells and Cook each took two wickets with consecutive balls on the last day, but Jackson and Walsh made sure of victory for Leicestershire just before a heavy rainstorm broke over the ground.

Gloucestershire

D. M. Young c Spencer b Jackson	40	— b Jackson	39
T. W. Graveney c Hallam b Munden	49	— lbw b Munden	29
G. M. Emmett c Spencer b Jackson	4	— b Munden	8
C. A. Milton c Smithson b Munden	0	— b Jackson	9
J. F. Crapp c Spencer b Jackson	1	— c and b Lester	73
G. E. Lambert b Munden	9	— b Jackson	0
J. Mortimore b Firth b Munden	8	— lbw b Munden	12
P. Rochford c Smithson b Munden	1	— c Tompkin b Jackson	1
C. Cook b Jackson	0	— b Spencer	2
B. D. Wells c Hallam b Jackson	0	— st Firth b Lester	0
F. P. McHugh not out	0	— not out	2
B 1, l-b 2	3	B 8, l-b 1	9
	107		**184**

1/81 2/88 3/89 4/90 5/103 6/103
7/103 8/106 9/106

1/51 2/79 3/103 4/116
5/117 6/133 7/149 8/180
9/182

Leicestershire

G. Lester b Cook	2	— c Rochford b Lambert	2
M. R. Hallam c Milton b Mortimore	22	— b Mortimore	34
M. Tompkin c Emmett b Mortimore	40	— b Wells	27
C. H. Palmer c Emmett b Mortimore	0	— b Cook	9
G. A. Smithson b Mortimore	7	— c Graveney b Wells	0
V. E. Jackson c Cook b Wells	25	— b Cook	23
V. S. Munden c Mortimore b Lambert	17	— c Emmett b Cook	0
J. E. Walsh c Rochford b McHugh	20	— lbw b Mortimore	24
J. Firth b McHugh	5	— not out	2
C. T. Spencer b Lambert	4	— not out	3
B. Boshier not out	0		
B 7, l-b 4	11	B 9, l-b 8	17
	153		**141**

1/2 2/31 3/44 4/45 5/95 6/112
7/125 8/142 9/149

1/6 2/68 3/79   (8 wkts.) 141
4/79 5/91 6/91 7/134 8/138

Leicestershire Bowling

	O.	M.	R.	W.	O.	M.	R.	W.
Boshier	5	2	9	0	2	0	11	0
Spencer	5	1	16	0	8	1	22	1
Jackson	18.3	8	39	5	41	16	63	5
Munden	18	5	40	5	38	11	76	2
Lester					2	0	3	2

Gloucestershire Bowling

	O.	M.	R.	W.	O.	M.	R.	W.
Cook	17	5	45	1	15	8	23	3
Wells	22	10	32	1	17	6	34	2
Mortimore	26	10	41	4	19.4	11	21	2
Lambert	7.2	1	16	2	17	2	36	1
McHugh	5	1	8	2	3	1	10	0

Umpires: D. Davies and E. Davies.

GLOUCESTERSHIRE v. KENT

At Gloucester, May 21, 23, 24. Kent won by eight wickets. They pulled the game round in praiseworthy style after being 69 behind, and most credit went to Wright, Hearn and Phebey for an unexpected success. Gloucestershire, who lost their last five wickets on the opening day for 12 runs, were indebted to the sound, yet stylish, Milton for a moderate total. Kent, troubled by the medium-fast bowling of Lambert, fared even worse, but Wright, with splendidly controlled leg-break and googly bowling, redressed the balance. He took the last six Gloucestershire wickets after tea on the second day for 18 runs. Mortimore, top scorer, hit nine 4's in 43. Kent, left to make 230 to win, scored 23 without loss overnight and then sound stroke-play by Hearn, Phebey, Fagg and Pettiford carried them to victory with nearly an hour to spare. Hearn stayed three hours.

Gloucestershire

D. M. Young c Fagg b Wright	25	— b Ridgway	6
C. A. Milton st Evans b Pettiford	85	— b Wright	41
J. F. Crapp b Wright	7	— c Fagg b Brazier	12
R. B. Nicholls c and b Page	8	— b Ridgway	3
G. M. Emmett b Page	5	— c Brazier b Pettiford	29
G. E. Lambert run out	19	— c Fagg b Wright	3
J. Mortimore c and b Pettiford	1	— c Pettiford b Wright	43
J. V. C. Griffiths b Pettiford	0	— b Wright	0
G. G. M. Wiltshire b Dixon	4	— b Wright	10
P. Rochford not out	2	— not out	0
C. Cook c Hearn b Dixon	3	— b Wright	3
B 2, l-b 4, n-b	7	B 3, l-b 6, n-b 1	10
	—		—
	166		160

1/58 2/70 3/85 4/95 5/154 6/155
7/155 8/156 9/160

1/8 2/41 3/48 4/88
5/100 6/104 7/108 8/150
9/157

Kent

A. E. Fagg lbw b Lambert	11	— lbw b Griffiths	34
A. H. Phebey b Lambert	5	— lbw b Cook	65
P. Hearn lbw b Lambert	13	— not out	87
J. Pettiford b Mortimore	39	— not out	40
J. C. T. Page c Rochford b Lambert	1		
T. G. Evans b Lambert	0		
A. F. Brazier b Mortimore	9		
A. Dixon c Wiltshire b Mortimore	2		
E. C. Witherden not out	2		
F. Ridgway c Rochford b Griffiths	10		
D. V. P. Wright b Lambert	1		
B 1, l-b 3	4	L-b 3, n-b 1	4
	—		—
	97	(2 wkts.)	230

1/12 2/25 3/47 4/50 5/50 6/78
7/83 8/84 9/95

1/80 2/110

Kent Bowling

	O.	M.	R.	W.		O.	M.	R.	W.
Ridgway	4	2	7	0	....	18	7	34	2
Brazier	3	0	7	0	....	12	6	23	1
Page	20	3	50	2	....	2	0	7	0
Wright	21	3	68	2	....	17.1	7	32	6
Dixon	10.1	2	16	2					
Pettiford	9	4	11	3	....	14	3	54	1

Gloucestershire Bowling

	O.	M.	R.	W.	O.	M.	R.	W.
Lambert	23.2	9	33	6	22	3	56	0
Wiltshire	1	0	4	0	9.5	3	39	0
Cook	26	20	8	0	30	18	27	1
Mortimore	28	13	27	3	40	16	62	0
Griffiths	9	3	21	1	17	3	42	1

Umpires: K. McCanlis and E. Cooke.

GLOUCESTERSHIRE v. MIDDLESEX

At Bristol, May 25, 26, 27. Gloucestershire won by 60 runs. They turned a big first innings deficit into a handsome victory in the last minute of the extra half-hour. Middlesex, to their credit, did all they could to ensure a good finish on rain-affected turf. Cricket on the last day could not start until three o'clock. Gloucestershire, 117 in front, lost their three remaining wickets for 40 runs so that Middlesex wanted 158 in 114 minutes. Their first five wickets went for 36. D. Compton, undeterred, scored with audacious strokes, he and Baldry adding 55 in just over half an hour, but after Compton mistimed a cover-drive the last four men left in ten minutes. Crapp, Emmett, Nicholls, and Lambert all batted well at the crisis and Titmus stood out for his fine all-round cricket for Middlesex.

Gloucestershire

D. M. Young b Hurst	7	— lbw b D. Compton	9
C. A. Milton b Titmus	11	— b Titmus	0
T. W. Graveney c and b Hurst	17	— lbw b Titmus	4
J. F. Crapp c Robertson b Titmus	0	— lbw b Warr	80
G. M. Emmett b Titmus	55	— b Hurst	26
J. Mortimore b Titmus	0	— b Warr	47
R. B. Nicholls lbw b Titmus	8	— b Hurst	63
G. E. Lambert c and b Hurst	5	— c Moss b Hurst	28
P. Rochford run out	0	— run out	15
C. Cook b Titmus	2	— c D. Compton b Hurst	1
B. D. Wells not out	1	— not out	2
B 4	4	B 1, n-b 1	2

1/18 2/18 3/18 4/74 5/94 6/94   110   1/0 2/4 3/24 4/82 5/131   277
7/107 8/107 9/109   6/217 7/237 8/270 9/274

Middlesex

J. D. Robertson c Lambert b Mortimore	53	— c Graveney b Lambert	9
A. Thompson b Lambert	2	— c Rochford b Lambert	0
W. J. Edrich b Lambert	0	— b Cook	20
D. C. S. Compton st Rochford b Wells	20	— c Nicholls b Cook	44
D. Bennett lbw b Wells	14	— b Lambert	1
D. O. Baldry b Cook	2	— c Lambert b Wells	18
F. J. Titmus not out	76	— b Lambert	0
J. J. Warr b Lambert	34	— c Wells b Cook	3
L. H. Compton lbw b Wells	11	— c Milton b Cook	0
R. J. Hurst st Rochford b Cook	0	— b Wells	1
A. E. Moss c Graveney b Milton	7	— not out	1
B 10, n-b 1	11		

1/17 2/25 3/68 4/82 5/84 6/104   230   1/0 2/25 3/31 4/34 5/36   97
7/171 8/182 9/207   6/91 7/93 8/95 9/96

Middlesex Bowling

	O.	M.	R.	W.	O.	M.	R.	W
Moss	4	0	14	0	 13	5	21	0
Warr..........	3	2	4	0	 16	7	21	2
Titmus	21	7	45	6	 45	18	75	2
Hurst	20	10	43	3	 39	18	71	4
D. Compton ..					31	6	87	1

Gloucestershire Bowling

	O.	M.	R.	W.	O.	M.	R.	W
Lambert	21	5	46	3	 10	1	32	4
Graveney	5	2	13	0				
Cook	25	9	55	2	 9	0	36	4
Mortimore.....	17	5	41	1				
Wells	36	12	63	3	.... 6.3	0	18	2
Milton	1.5	0	1	1	 2	0	11	0

Umpires: G. S. Mobey and A. J. B. Fowler.

At Taunton, May 28, 30, 31. GLOUCESTERSHIRE drew with SOMERSET.

At Lord's, June 1, 2, 3. GLOUCESTERSHIRE lost to M.C.C. by eight wickets.

At Portsmouth, June 4, 6, 7. GLOUCESTERSHIRE drew with Hampshire.

GLOUCESTERSHIRE v. DERBYSHIRE

At Bristol, June 8, 9, 10. Drawn. Despite rain which allowed only an hour's play on the first day and delayed the start of the second until after lunch, an interesting finish occurred. Carr made a sporting declaration in setting Gloucestershire to score 130 for victory at one a minute. The home team lost eight wickets for 81 when Derbyshire claimed the extra half-hour, but Lambert and Griffiths held out. Gloucestershire were well served by Wells, the slow off-spin bowler, who took 11 wickets for 82. Smith and Gladwin, for Derbyshire, also made good use of soft turf. Top scorer in the match, Hamer, stayed two and a half hours.

Derbyshire

A. Hamer c Emmett b Mortimore	59	—	st Rochford b Cook		8
J. Kelly c Rochford b Wells	6	—	c Mortimore b Wells		3
H. L. Johnson c Emmett b Lambert	0	—	b Wells		4
A. C. Revill lbw b Wells	8	—	b Wells		1
D. B. Carr b Wells	35	—	c Crapp b Cook		1
G. Wyatt b Mortimore	1	—	b Wells		6
D. C. Morgan c Emmett b Wells	3	—	not out		21
G. O. Dawkes c Young b Wells	6	—	b Wells		24
C. Gladwin not out	13	—	not out		8
E. Smith b Wells	5				
L. Jackson st Rochford b Cook	4				
L-b 1	1		L-b 2		2

1/14 2/15 3/36 4/98 5/103 6/108   141   1/10 2/12   (7 wkts., dec.)   78
7/118 8/118 9/136   3/13 4/14 5/34 6/43 7/59

Gloucestershire

D. M. Young c Morgan b Smith	10	— run out	35
A. E. Wilson b Gladwin	9	— st Dawkes b Smith	2
J. F. Crapp c Morgan b Carr	26	— b Smith	10
R. B. Nicholls b Gladwin	18	— b Gladwin	2
G. M. Emmett c Johnson b Gladwin	1	— c Morgan b Jackson	7
J. Mortimore lbw b Smith	10	— c Morgan b Smith	1
P. Rochford c Revill b Smith	6		
G. E. Lambert c Johnson b Gladwin	2	— not out	23
J. V. C. Griffiths lbw b Gladwin	4	— not out	2
C. Cook not out	2	— c Carr b Smith	0
B. D. Wells run out	0	— b Smith	7
B 2	2	B 7, l-b 4	11
	—		—
	90	(8 wkts.)	100

1/14 2/25 3/64 4/65 5/68 6/81
7/82 8/84 9/90

1/18 2/32 3/46 (8 wkts.)
4/51 5/53 6/74 7/81 8/81

Gloucestershire Bowling

	O.	M.	R.	W.		O.	M.	R.	W.
Lambert	13	4	20	1	....	4	1	5	0
Wells	33	12	52	6	....	29	16	30	5
Cook	18.4	9	32	1	....	20	10	27	2
Mortimore	20	6	36	2	....	6	2	14	0

Derbyshire Bowling

	O.	M.	R.	W.		O.	M.	R.	W.
Jackson	5	2	11	0	....	6	0	11	1
Gladwin	24.4	11	28	5	....	17	8	28	1
Morgan	8	5	8	0					
Smith	18	9	29	3	....	18	3	39	5
Carr	5	1	12	1	....	7	2	11	0

Umpires: J. S. Buller and E. A. Roberts.

At Swansea, June 11, 13, 14. GLOUCESTERSHIRE drew with GLAMORGAN.

At Birmingham, June 15, 16, 17. GLOUCESTERSHIRE beat WARWICKSHIRE by seven wickets.

At Westcliff, June 18, 20, 21. GLOUCESTERSHIRE lost to ESSEX by five wickets.

GLOUCESTERSHIRE v. HAMPSHIRE

At Bristol, June 22, 23, 24. Hampshire won by eight wickets. Their bowling strength settled the issue. Cannings, fast and accurate, clean bowled his five victims in the first innings, and Sainsbury, with guileful left-arm spin on drying turf, routed Gloucestershire in the second. Crapp, a hard driver, and Barnard, who hit a 6 and six 4's, played the soundest innings in a match dominated by bowlers. Wells, the off-spinner, gave little away in long spells. Hampshire, left to make 33 for victory, claimed the extra half-hour on the second evening, but scored only 13 for the loss of Marshall, and half an hour's cricket was necessary next morning.

Gloucestershire

D. M. Young b Cannings	11	— c Eagar b Burden	30
C. A. Milton b Cannings	9	— c and b Sainsbury	5
R. B. Nicholls b Cannings	1	— b Sainsbury	0
J. F. Crapp c and b Burden	52	— b Sainsbury	0
G. M. Emmett lbw b Burden	6	— c Shackleton b Burden	10
G. E. Lambert run out	4	— b Marshall	25
J. Mortimore c Barnard b Burden	15	— c and b Sainsbury	9
P. Rochford b Burden	6	— b Sainsbury	1
C. Cook not out	1	— b Sainsbury	0
B. D. Wells b Cannings	5	— c Gray b Shackleton	10
F. P. McHugh b Cannings	0	— not out	0
B 7, l-b 4	11	B 4, l-b 11	15

1/23 2/27 3/28 4/51 5/83 6/91   121
7/110 8/116 9/121

1/31 2/39 3/39 4/39   105
5/60 6/88 7/92 8/94 9/101

Hampshire

J. R. Gray run out	12	— lbw b McHugh	12
R. E. Marshall lbw b Wells	15	— b Lambert	2
H. Horton c Rochford b Wells	12	— not out	12
N. H. Rogers c Rochford b McHugh	23		
H. M. Barnard b Wells	67	— not out	6
E. D. R. Eagar c Rochford b Mortimore	19		
L. Harrison b Wells	28		
P. J. Sainsbury b Lambert	0		
D. Shackleton b Lambert	0		
V. H. D. Cannings b Wells	3		
M. D. Burden not out	1		
B 5, l-b 7, n-b 1	13	L-b 1	1

1/25 2/39 3/43 4/89 5/144 6/169   194
7/174 8/174 9/182

1/7 2/23   (2 wkts.)   33

Hampshire Bowling

	O.	M.	R.	W.		O.	M.	R.	W.
Shackleton	21	13	16	0	....	15	5	21	1
Cannings	20	8	29	5	....	3	0	16	0
Burden	21	4	65	4	....	22	12	13	2
Sainsbury					....	23	9	37	6
Marshall					....	7	5	3	1

Gloucestershire Bowling

	O.	M.	R.	W.		O.	M.	R.	W.
Lambert	16	5	26	2	....	9	2	15	1
McHugh	18	6	32	1	....	8	1	13	1
Cook	26	13	36	0					
Wells	31	19	50	5					
Mortimore	19	6	37	1					
Crapp						0.3	0	4	0

Umpires: T. J. Bartley and D. Davies.

GLOUCESTERSHIRE v. CAMBRIDGE UNIVERSITY

At Bristol, June 25, 27, 28. Gloucestershire won by seven wickets. Cambridge, given a splendid start by Silk who hit two 6's and six 4's by forceful stroke-play, lost their grip, and rain handicapped them in the final stages. Splendid medium-fast bowling by Smith, who with the new ball took three of the last four wickets which fell at the same total, brought the Light Blues an unexpected lead, but then spin upset them. While Gloucestershire were scoring 171 for victory, the University bowlers had to contend with a ball made slippery by continuous drizzle. Young and Milton began with a century partnership and victory came with five minutes of extra time to spare.

Cambridge University

D. R. W. Silk c Wells b Griffiths	63	— b Mortimore	24
R. O'Brien lbw b Wells	45	— lbw b Wiltshire	7
G. Goonesena c Wells b Griffiths	28	— c Griffiths b Mortimore	7
V. R. Lumsden lbw b Wells	8	— c Griffiths b Mortimore	28
J. F. Pretlove lbw b Wells	54	— run out	34
S. Singh b Mortimore	13	— c Milton b Wells	5
A. B. D. Parsons b Milton	22	— b McHugh	9
W. Knightley-Smith not out	11	— c Nicholls b Wells	0
P. D. Croft c Milton b Griffiths	26	— c Milton b Griffiths	11
M. E. L. Melluish st Rochford b Griffiths	0	— c Rochford b Griffiths	6
D. J. Smith (did not bat)		— not out	0
B 11, l-b 8	19	B 6, l-b 3	9

1/100 2/127 3/145 4/163 (9 wkts., dec.) 289
5/195 6/249 7/249 8/288 9/289

1/10 2/31 3/75 4/81 5/95 140
6/100 7/104 8/127 9/137

Gloucestershire

D. M. Young b Smith	29	— c and b Smith	50
C. A. Milton c Croft b Goonesena	28	— st Melluish b Pretlove	54
R. B. Nicholls b Smith	31	— b Pretlove	12
J. F. Crapp c and b Singh	49	— not out	29
J. Mortimore b Smith	50		
J. V. C. Griffths b Smith	19		
G. G. M. Wiltshire c Pretlove b Smith	6		
G. M. Emmett lbw b Singh	21	— not out	22
P. Rochford not out	0		
B. D. Wells b Smith	0		
F. P. McHugh st Melluish b Smith	0		
B 10, l-b 15, w 1	26	L-b 5	5

1/50 2/81 3/151 4/171 5/228 6/234 259
7/259 8/259 9/259

1/102 2/112 (3 wkts.) 172
3/133

Gloucestershire Bowling

	O.	M.	R.	W.		O.	M.	R.	W.
McHugh	15	6	21	0	....	19	8	22	1
Wiltshire	20	4	38	0	....	4	1	8	1
Wells	46	22	77	3	....	22	8	60	2
Griffiths	23.5	6	74	4	....	7	4	13	2
Mortimore	26	11	45	1	....	23	10	28	3
Milton	7	2	15	1					

Cambridge University Bowling

	O.	M.	R.	W.		O.	M.	R.	W.
Smith	31.1	10	55	7	....	13	1	59	1
Singh	42	13	96	2	....	9	0	41	0
Goonesena	26	8	56	1	....	2	0	12	0
Pretlove	11	4	14	0	....	7	0	32	2
Lumsden	4	1	12	0	....	3	0	18	0
			Silk			0.3	0	5	0

Umpires: T. J. Bartley and W. F. Price.

At Kettering, July 2, 4, 5. GLOUCESTERSHIRE beat NORTHAMPTONSHIRE by 154 runs.

At Eastbourne, July 6, 7. GLOUCESTERSHIRE lost to SUSSEX by an innings and 173 runs.

GLOUCESTERSHIRE v. WORCESTERSHIRE

At Gloucester, July 9, 11, 12. Gloucestershire won by 138 runs. Victory, after first innings arrears of 54, was largely due to the forceful batting of Milton and the astute left-arm spin bowling of Cook on a wearing pitch. Worcestershire seemed well placed after clever leg-break bowling by Jenkins on the first day, but Milton, hitting twenty 4's by attractive strokes, turned the fortunes of the game with a splendid 150. Despite excellent off-spin bowling by Horton, who took eight for 124, Worcestershire found themselves needing 263 to win and this was beyond them against a lifting and turning ball which gave eager fielders near the wicket chances they turned to account.

Gloucestershire

D. M. Young lbw b Jenkins	63	—	c Richardson b Horton	64
C. A. Milton b Perks	2	—	c Lister b Berry	150
J. F. Crapp b Perks	3	—	b Horton	12
G. M. Emmett lbw b Perks	0	—	c Yarnold b Horton	31
W. Knightley-Smith b Horton	6	—	c Dews b Horton	0
G. E. Lambert b Jenkins	24	—	b Horton	14
J. Mortimore c Whitehead b Jenkins	23	—	b Horton	6
P. Rochford c Horton b Jenkins	6	—	lbw b Horton	0
C. Cook b Jenkins	1	—	c Jenkins b Berry	0
B. D. Wells st Yarnold b Jenkins	19	—	c Dews b Horton	30
F. P. McHugh not out	0	—	not out	0
L-b 3	3		B 5, l-b 3, n-b 1	9

1/5 2/13 3/13 4/38 5/100 6/107   150
7/130 8/130 9/139

1/125 2/159 3/217 4/217   316
5/256 6/268 7/286
8/286 9/300

Worcestershire

L. Outschoorn b McHugh	12	—	c Milton b Cook	16
J. Lister b Mortimore	46	—	c Cook b Lambert	1
D. W. Richardson b Cook	23	—	c Emmett b Cook	26
M. J. Horton c Lambert b McHugh	37	—	c Wells b Cook	6
G. Dews b McHugh	41	—	c McHugh b Cook	18
R. G. Broadbent not out	17	—	c Milton b Cook	0
J. P. Whitehead c Milton b McHugh	0	—	st Rochford b Cook	4
R. O. Jenkins lbw b Wells	4	—	c Cook b Wells	21
H. Yarnold c McHugh b Cook	6	—	c Crapp b Cook	0
R. T. D. Perks b Lambert	0	—	c Milton b Wells	13
R. Berry c Rochford b Lambert	6	—	not out	7
B 7, l-b 5	12		B 10, l-b 2	12

1/25 2/82 3/84 4/160 5/166 6/170   204
7/177 8/186 9/186

1/11 2/30 3/40 4/60 5/64   124
6/68 7/102 8/104 9/104

Worcestershire Bowling

	O.	M.	R.	W.		O.	M.	R.	W.
Perks	12	3	30	3	....	9	0	28	0
Outschoorn	4	2	8	0	....	4	2	7	0
Whitehead	3	1	11	0					
Horton	16	5	53	1	....	34.1	7	124	8
Jenkins	16.2	4	35	6	....	19	3	66	0
Berry	5	1	10	0	....	24	5	82	2

Gloucestershire Bowling

	O.	M.	R.	W.		O.	M.	R.	W.
Lambert	13.4	4	28	2	....	3	0	23	1
McHugh	26	6	45	4	....	4	1	10	0
Wells	18	5	47	1	....	16.2	9	21	2
Cook	30	16	35	2	....	22	12	41	7
Mortimore	13	3	37	1	....	10	6	17	0

Umpires: D. Davies and J. J. Hills.

GLOUCESTERSHIRE v. NORTHAMPTONSHIRE

At Gloucester, July 13, 14, 15. Gloucestershire won by 40 runs. The winners suffered shocks at the start of each innings, but lively batting by Emmett, Young, Crapp and Lambert, and skilful spin bowling by Cook and Wells well supported in the field earned success. Gloucestershire lost Milton and Knightley-Smith for two runs before two century stands brought relief, and in the second innings their first two wickets fell for three runs. Northamptonshire, in contrast, began confidently in each innings, but despite excellent batting by Brookes the task of making 213 to win proved too much for them. Lightfoot, a 19-year-old medium-fast bowler on leave from the Army, impressed for Northamptonshire in his early spell.

Gloucestershire

D. M. Young c Livingston b Tribe	67	— c Andrew b Lightfoot	3
C. A. Milton c Andrew b Lightfoot	0	— c and b Clarke	0
W. Knightley-Smith b Lightfoot	0	— c Lightfoot b Broderick	0
J. F. Crapp c Lightfoot b Tribe	74	— b Tribe	29
G. M. Emmett c Andrew b Tribe	122	— c and b Broderick	38
G. E. Lambert not out	50	— st Andrew b Tribe	5
J. Mortimore not out	7	— b Broderick	5
P. Rochford (did not bat)		— run out	7
C. Cook (did not bat)		— c Lightfoot b Tribe	0
B. D. Wells (did not bat)		— b Tribe	29
F. P. McHugh (did not bat)		— not out	10
B 1, l-b 5, w 1	7		

1/2 2/2 3/144 4/149   5 wkts., dec.) 327   1/3 2/3 3/70 4/74 5/74   126
5/304   6/80 7/80 8/80 9/114

Northamptonshire

D. Brookes lbw b Wells	57	— lbw b Cook	60
P. Arnold c Wells b Cook	20	— run out	22
L. Livingston c and b Mortimore	63	— b Cook	20
B. Reynolds not out	21	— c Milton b Cook	4
D. G. Greasley lbw b Wells	9	— c Lambert b Mortimore	22
G. E. Tribe c Wells b Cook	13	— c Milton b Wells	7
V. Broderick lbw b Cook	25	— b Wells	0
A. Lightfoot c Milton b Mortimore	1	— run out	17
K. V. Andrew b Cook	3	— c Milton b Cook	2
R. W. Clarke c McHugh b Cook	16	— lbw b Wells	4
J. Wild absent hurt	0	— not out	2
B 11, l-b 2	13	B 8, l-b 4	12

1/46 2/147 3/148 4/158 5/173 6/203   241   1/84 2/86 3/104 4/109   172
7/204 8/219 9/241   5/124 6/124 7/150 8/158
9/167

Northamptonshire Bowling

	O.	M.	R.	W.		O.	M.	R.	W.
Clarke	20	3	55	0	....	7	0	30	1
Lightfoot	20	2	56	2	....	5	1	21	1
Tribe	29	3	99	3	....	9.3	2	32	4
Broderick	24	5	60	0	....	11	2	43	3
Wild	14	4	32	0					
Greasley	5	0	18	0					

Gloucestershire Bowling

	O.	M.	R.	W.		O.	M.	R.	W.
Lambert	7	1	22	0	....	4	0	15	0
McHugh	8	1	22	0	....	3	1	7	0
Cook	38.2	16	59	5	....	28	11	53	4
Wells	32	9	67	2	....	34	16	49	3
Mortimore	23	6	58	2	....	10.3	2	36	1

Umpires: E. Davies and J. J. Hills.

GLOUCESTERSHIRE v. WARWICKSHIRE

At Bristol, July 16, 18, 19. Warwickshire won by an innings and 39 runs. Fine batting in which a double-century opening partnership by Horner and Gardner was the feature, and skilful leg-break bowling brought this convincing victory to the visitors. Horner, a fluent driver, and Gardner were together for three and a quarter hours while making 203, and Wolton supplemented their efforts with some vigorous stroke-play. Milton was out for his third successive duck before the close, and on Monday Gloucestershire lost fourteen wickets, twelve to Hollies and Hitchcock. At the start of the last morning Gloucestershire were 148 for five and they were out in another half an hour. Only Milton, back to form, and Mortimore played the spinners confidently.

Warwickshire

F. C. Gardner lbw b Wells	79	A. Townsend st Rochford b Cook	12
N. F. Horner c Rochford b Wells	119	R. G. Thompson not out	0
A. V. Wolton c Wells b Cook	61	B 8, l-b 3, n-b 1	12
R. E. Hitchcock b Lambert	43		
H. E. Dollery b Mortimore	22	1/203 2/212 3/287 (7 wkts., dec.)	387
R. T. Spooner c Cook b Wells	39	4/329 5/334 6/387 7/387	

I. M. King, W. E. Hollies and K. R. Dollery did not bat.

Gloucestershire

D. M. Young st Spooner b Hollies	15	— lbw b Hollies	19
C. A. Milton b K. Dollery	0	— c Spooner b Hitchcock	58
P. Rochford b Hollies	9	— absent ill	0
J. F. Crapp run out	53	— c Townsend b Hitchcock	8
G. M. Emmett b Hollies	20	— c Spooner b Hitchcock	4
W. Knightley-Smith b Hollies	44	— b King	8
G. E. Lambert lbw b Hitchcock	9	— b Hitchcock	20
J. Mortimore st Spooner b Hollies	0	— b Hitchcock	48
B. D. Wells b Hitchcock	3	— b Hollies	0
C. Cook b Hitchcock	2	— lbw b Hitchcock	2
F. P. McHugh not out	0	— not out	1
B 3, l-b 8, n-b 3	14	B 2, l-b 8, n-b 1	11

1/0 2/25 3/38 4/82 5/144 6/164	169	1/39 2/56 3/64 4/92	179
7/164 8/167 9/167		5/106 6/152 7/157 8/174	

Gloucestershire Bowling

	O.	M.	R.	W.		O.	M.	R.	W.
Lambert	14	0	74	1					
McHugh	22	6	64	0					
Wells	34	9	82	3					
Cook	24.1	8	56	2					
Mortimore.....	28	5	91	1					
Milton	3	1	8	0					

Warwickshire Bowling

	O.	M.	R.	W.		O.	M.	R.	W.
Thompson	16	3	31	0	....	4	1	16	0
K. Dollery	16	3	33	1	....	7	1	17	0
Hollies	22	9	52	5	....	26	9	52	2
King	2	0	16	0	....	14	6	19	1
Townsend	5	1	15	0	....	2	0	6	0
Hitchcock	6	3	8	3	....	27.4	11	58	6

Umpires: W. T. Jones and A. E. Pothecary.

At Nottingham, July 20, 21, 22. GLOUCESTERSHIRE beat NOTTINGHAMSHIRE by 146 runs.

GLOUCESTERSHIRE v. SUSSEX

(J. Lambert's Benefit)

At Bristol, July 23, 25, 26. Gloucestershire won by 16 runs. First there was an exciting duel for first innings lead and later one for victory which fell to Gloucestershire mid-way through the extra half-hour. Emmett set Sussex to score 180 in two hours twenty-five minutes, and the visitors fared well until Langridge was fifth out at 93 made in eighty-five minutes. Then Cook, again in fine form with his skilful left-arm spin bowling, settled the issue. Marlar shone for his wily off-spin bowling. He took his last three wickets in the first innings in four deliveries and his full match analysis was twelve for 138. Good catching contributed to Gloucestershire's success.

Gloucestershire

D. M. Young b Marlar................	71	— b Marlar	27
C. A. Milton b Marlar	35	— c Webb b Smith	40
J. F. Crapp c and b Oakman...........	51	— c Langridge b Marlar	26
G. M. Emmett b Marlar...............	42	— b Marlar	29
W. Knightley-Smith c Oakman b Cox ..	20	— b Smith	7
G. E. Lambert lbw b Smith	8	— c Foreman b Marlar.......	15
J. Mortimore b Marlar	30	— not out	21
P. Rochford lbw b Marlar	4	— c Langridge b Smith	7
C. Cook c Foreman b Marlar	0	— not out	1
B. D. Wells c Oakman b Marlar	0	— b Marlar	1
F. P. McHugh not out	0		
L-b 3	3	B 10................	10

1/89 2/126 3/186 4/220 5/231 6/243   264   1/54 2/86   (8 wkts., dec.) 184
7/263 8/264 9/264   3/100 4/133 5/140 6/149
    7/163 8/176

Sussex

J. Langridge b Cook	28	c Emmett b Cook	35
A. S. M. Oakman c Emmett b Cook	70	st Rochford b Wells	28
D. V. Smith b Wells	5	b Cook	2
J. M. Parks c Milton b Mortimore	10	b Cook	11
K. G. Suttle b Lambert	20	c McHugh b Cook	2
A. A. K. Lawrence lbw b Lambert	6	lbw b Mortimore	4
G. Cox c Lambert b Cook	65	c Lambert b Wells	21
D. J. Foreman lbw b Wells	33	c Lambert b Cook	15
N. I. Thomson c Lambert b Cook	0	c Milton b Cook	20
R. T. Webb not out	3	not out	0
R. G. Marlar b Wells	17	c Wells b Cook	15
B 5, l-b 7	12	B 6, l-b 4	10
	269		**163**

1/63 2/68 3/88 4/120 5/126 6/166 269
7/247 8/247 9/247

1/45 2/48 3/64 4/70 163
5/93 6/117 7/128 8/149
9/163

Sussex Bowling

	O.	M.	R.	W.	O.	M.	R.	W.
Thomson	21	6	35	0	5	2	18	0
Smith	30	12	71	1	21	4	50	3
Oakman	13	2	44	1	10	3	35	0
Parks	9	1	37	0				
Marlar	39.5	11	67	7	29	8	71	5
Cox	6	3	7	1				

Gloucestershire Bowling

	O.	M.	R.	W.	O.	M.	R.	W.
Lambert	19	2	70	2	3	0	15	0
McHugh	15	3	32	0	2	1	4	0
Wells	37.4	18	80	3	13	0	69	2
Cook	48	25	51	4	20.1	8	36	7
Mortimore	13	6	24	1	7	1	29	1

Umpires: Harry Elliott (Derbyshire) and J. S. Buller.

At Blackpool, July 27, 28, 79. GLOUCESTERSHIRE lost to LANCASHIRE by six wickets.

GLOUCESTERSHIRE v. SOMERSET

At Bristol, July 30, August 1, 2. Drawn. When Somerset, set 284 to get, lost nine wickets for 146, Gloucestershire appeared to have victory within their grasp, but Hilton and McMahon doggedly played out the last forty-eight, minutes. Gloucestershire gained a strong position on the opening day when Milton (ten 4's) and Graveney shared a partnership of 125 and Emmett (nine 4's) hit freely for ninety-five minutes. Thanks chiefly to Tremlett and Lawrence, Somerset finished the first innings no more than 78 behind. Young gave Gloucestershire an excellent start when they batted again, joining in stands of 93 and 59 with Milton and Graveney, and though Walker, with off-breaks, caused trouble they were able to declare a second time.

Gloucestershire

D. M. Young c Stephenson b Lomax ...	17	— c Hilton b Walker.........	75
C. A. Milton c Lomax b McMahon	84	— c Angell b McMahon ...	48
T. W. Graveney st Stephenson b McMahon	84	— c Hilton b McMahon	34
J. F. Crapp b Hilton	19	— st Stephenson b Walker ...	1
G. M. Emmett c Tordoff b Hilton	61	— b Walker	14
G. E. Lambert run out	55	— c Hilton b Walker........	8
J. Mortimore c Lawrence b Hilton	0	— b Walker	0
D. A. Allen not out	2	— not out	6
B. D. Wells b McMahon.............	0	— b McMahon.............	8
P. Rochford st Stephenson b Hilton.....	1	— not out	2
B 2, l-b 1	3	B 7, l-b 2	9

1/41 2/166 3/205 4/209   (9 wkts., dec.) 326
5/303 6/310 7/323 8/323 9/326

1/93 2/152   (8 wkts., dec.) 205
3/157 4/170 5/181 6/185
7/188 8/201

C. Cook did not bat.

Somerset

F. L. Angell b Cook	9	— c Graveney b Cook	33
M. Walker lbw b Wells................	14	— b Wells	3
G. G. Tordoff c Lambert b Cook	32	— c Rochford b Lambert	4
J. Lawrence c Allan b Cook	44	— lbw b Cook	5
P. B. Wight b Cook..................	11	— c Rochford b Wells	6
M. F. Tremlett c Cook b Wells........	66	— c Graveney b Cook	10
J. G. Lomax c Milton b Lambert	20	— b Lambert	45
Yawar Saeed b Wells	25	— c Graveney b Wells	2
H. W. Stephenson c Emmett b Mortimore	4	— lbw b Wells	35
J. Hilton not out	1	— not out	7
J. W. McMahon b Mortimore..........	6	— not out	6
B 5, l-b 10, n-b 1	16	B 1, l-b 2	3

1/22 2/46 3/83 4/100 5/154 6/188   248
7/226 8/241 9/241

1/12 2/33 3/51   (9 wkts.) 159
4/58 5/58 6/70 7/76
8/144 9/146

Somerset Bowling

	O.	M.	R.	W.		O.	M.	R.	W.
Yawar Saeed ..	6	1	21	0	....	6	1	24	0
Lomax	19	5	44	1	....	6	0	17	0
Lawrence	29	9	74	0					
Hilton	28.1	5	88	4	....	14	3	49	0
McMahon	36	10	94	3	....	22	6	61	3
Walker	1	0	2	0	....	9	0	45	5

Gloucestershire Bowling

	O.	M.	R.	W.		O.	M.	R.	W.
Lambert	15	2	43	1	....	13	6	11	2
Wells	37	15	64	3	....	31	14	58	4
Cook	42	21	64	4	....	30	11	54	3
Allan	5	1	21	0	....	7	4	8	0
Mortimore	13	5	25	2	....	4	1	8	0
Graveney	2	0	7	0	....	3	1	8	0
Milton	2	1	8	0	....	3	1	9	0

Umpires: A. E. Pothecary and J. J. Hills.

At Canterbury, August 3, 4, 5. GLOUCESTERSHIRE drew with KENT.

At Cheltenham, August 6, 8, 9. GLOUCESTERSHIRE drew with SOUTH AFRICANS.
(See SOUTH AFRICAN section.)

GLOUCESTERSHIRE v. GLAMORGAN

At Cheltenham, August 10, 11, 12. Gloucestershire won by an innings and nine runs. Glamorgan never recovered from a disastrous start when they lost half their side for 32 on a pitch damp on top. Gloucestershire went ahead with only two men out, Milton, Graveney and Emmett showing fine form. Emmett's 62 came in just over an hour. A vigorous 42 in twenty-three minutes by Wells helped Gloucestershire to a lead of 190. Parkhouse retired with a bruised finger in Glamorgan's second innings. The batting once more disappointed and only ninety minutes were needed on the last day.

Glamorgan

W. G. A. Parkhouse run out	22	— retired hurt	0
P. B. Clift c Emmett b Lambert	1	— c Young b Lambert	33
J. Pleass c Lambert b McHugh	1	— c Milton b Griffiths	34
W. E. Jones c Lambert b McHugh	17	— lbw b Graveney	28
A. J. Watkins lbw b McHugh	17	— run out	14
J. Pressdee c Milton b Wells	0	— b Mortimore	17
W. Wooller not out	46	— b Graveney	24
B. R. Edrich c Milton b Mortimore	23	— c Milton b Mortimore	12
D. Ward c Mortimore b Wells	3	— c Milton b Mortimore	0
H. G. Davies run out	20	— lbw b Wells	5
H. D. Davies c Milton b Wells	0	— not out	0
B 2	2	B 4, l-b 10	14

1/4 2/5 3/5 4/31 5/32 6/63 7/103   135   1/71 2/71 3/113 4/116   181
8/112 9/134   5/156 6/174 7/176 8/181
                                              9/181

Gloucestershire

D. M. Young c Clift b Wooller	13	P. Rochford c Pressdee b Wooller	7
C. A. Milton c Parkhouse b Pressdee	58	B. D. Wells not out	42
T. W. Graveney c Jones b H. D. Davies	87	F. P. McHugh st H. G. Davies b Watkins	1
J. F. Crapp c Jones b Ward	16		
G. M. Emmett b Watkins	62		
G. E. Lambert b Watkins	8		
J. Mortimore c Ward b Wooller	17	B 8, l-b 4	12
J. V. C. Griffiths c Pressdee b Watkins	2		

1/28 2/116 3/165 4/212 5/256   325
6/259 7/261 8/274 9/293

Gloucestershire Bowling

	O.	M.	R.	W.		O.	M.	R.	W.
Lambert	13	3	31	1	....	14	5	32	1
McHugh	19	7	43	3	....	8	3	17	0
Wells	10	5	48	3	....	26	15	36	1
Mortimore	11	4	11	1	....	23.3	7	44	3
Griffiths						8	3	15	1
Graveney						11	3	23	2

Glamorgan Bowling

	O.	M.	R.	W.
H. D. Davies	19	6	53	1
Watkins	36	10	110	4
Wooller	12	3	48	3
Pressdee	24	2	66	1
Ward	6	0	22	1
Jones	3	0	14	0

Umpires: A. Skelding and J. S. Buller.

GLOUCESTERSHIRE v. SURREY

At Cheltenham, August 13, 15. Surrey won by 43 runs. Gloucestershire put up a good fight before going down to the Champions. The pitch was always difficult but Surrey, after losing half their side for 39, fought back through a hard-hitting innings by Cox. He took 24 off one over from Wells and altogether he made 57 in fifty-five minutes with the help of three 6's, a 5 and five 4's. Despite a steady innings by Young, Gloucestershire also collapsed. They declared 45 behind and dismissed Surrey in two hours. Although set the reasonable task of scoring 123 on a pitch a little easier, Gloucestershire failed in face of determined bowling and brilliant catching. In the absence of Laker, Clark bowled his off-breaks effectively and A. Bedser, who bowled unchanged, also did extremely well.

Surrey

T. H. Clark lbw b Lambert	4	—	b McHugh		13
M. J. Stewart c Crapp b Lambert	4	—	c Milton b Lambert		2
B. Constable c Rochford b Lambert	7	—	b Wells		5
K. Barrington c Milton b Lambert	12	—	c Crapp b Mortimore		11
R. C. E. Pratt c Milton b Lambert	7	—	c and b Mortimore		18
E. A. Bedser b Mortimore	34	—	lbw b Wells		4
A. J. McIntyre c Rochford b McHugh	20	—	st Rochford b Mortimore		9
D. F. Cox c Lambert b Mortimore	57	—	b Wells		1
W. S. Surridge c Emmett b McHugh	7	—	not out		3
P. J. Loader b Mortimore	8	—	c Knightley-Smith b Wells		4
A. V. Bedser not out	5	—	c Crapp b Wells		0
B 7, l-b 8	15		B 3, l-b 4		7
	180				**77**

1/4 2/15 3/18 4/28 5/39 6/68 7/124
8/165 9/166

1/5 2/13 3/25 4/27 5/45
6/65 7/66 8/68 9/75

Gloucestershire

D. M. Young c Barrington b A. Bedser	42	—	b Loader		9
C. A. Milton b A. Bedser	0	—	c Stewart b A. Bedser		0
J. F. Crapp b Loader	10	—	c Stewart b A. Bedser		0
G. M. Emmett c McIntyre b A. Bedser	0	—	lbw b Clark		28
W. Knightley-Smith c Cox b Loader	0	—	b A. Bedser		0
G. E. Lambert lbw b Loader	0	—	lbw b Clark		15
J. Mortimore c Pratt b A. Bedser	1	—	c Clark b A. Bedser		7
J. V. C. Griffiths not out	27	—	c Surridge b Clark		10
P. Rochford c McIntyre b E. Bedser	8	—	c Stewart b Loader		6
B. D. Wells c A. Bedser b Loader	37	—	c Constable b Clark		0
F. P. McHugh not out	0	—	not out		0
B 4, l-b 3, n-b 3	10		L-b 1, n-b 3		4
	(9 wkts., dec.) **135**				**79**

1/1 2/23 3/27 4/28
5/30 6/31 7/66 8/88 9/135

1/0 2/0 3/13 4/44 5/44
6/44 7/59 8/70 9/79

Gloucestershire Bowling

	O.	M.	R.	W.	O.	M.	R.	W.
Lambert	19	3	42	5	5	1	4	1
McHugh	24	7	49	2	12	3	18	1
Wells	5	0	52	0	13.4	4	29	5
Mortimore	6.5	0	22	3	7	0	19	3

Surrey Bowling

	O.	M.	R.	W.	O.	M.	R.	W.
A. Bedser	21	3	56	4	19.2	6	42	4
Loader	15	3	33	4	10	5	9	2
Surridge	9	1	35	0				
E. Bedser	4	3	1	1				
Clark					9	2	24	4

Umpires: L. H. Gray and H. G. Baldwin.

At Huddersfield, August 17, 18, 19. GLOUCESTERSHIRE lost to YORKSHIRE by 67 runs.

At Derby, August 20, 22, 23. GLOUCESTERSHIRE lost to DERBYSHIRE by an innings and 36 runs.

At Worcester, August 24, 25, 26. GLOUCESTERSHIRE lost to WORCESTERSHIRE by seven wickets.

GLOUCESTERSHIRE v. LANCASHIRE

At Bristol, August 27, 29. Gloucestershire won by 88 runs. The bowling of McHugh (fast) and Wells (off-breaks) played a big part in the success. Between them they took all the Lancashire wickets in the match. On the first day Lambert followed his maiden century of the previous match at Worcestershire with another useful innings and he prevented a Gloucestershire failure. Lancashire looked like taking the lead but lost their last six wickets for 17. Gloucestershire, 73 ahead, again broke down on a worn pitch, but Milton batted throughout the innings for the first time in his career. Lancashire, needing 191, reached 76 before their second wicket fell. Then their last eight fell in forty minutes for another 26 runs.

Gloucestershire

D. M. Young hit wkt b Collins	11	—	c Wilson b C. Smith		4
C. A. Milton c Ikin b Tattersall	12	—	not out		51
T. W. Graveney lbw b Tattersall	22	—	c Edrich b C. Smith		0
J. F. Crapp c and b Collins	30	—	b C. Smith		0
G. M. Emmett c S. Smith b Ikin	33	—	c Edrich b Tattersall		16
J. Mortimore lbw b Tattersall	0	—	c Washbrook b Greenough		7
G. E. Lambert not out	53	—	c Wharton b Greenough		0
R. Etheridge c Wharton b Greenough	19	—	c Collins b Greenough		2
C. Cook b Tattersall	0	—	c S. Smith b Greenough		0
B. D. Wells c Greenough b Tattersall	0	—	b Tattersall		6
F. P. McHugh run out	0	—	run out		5
B 12 l-b 4 n-b 2	18		B 12, l-b 11, n-b 3		26

1/24 2/32 3/79 4/98 5/99 6/134   198
7/166 8/179 9/179

1/4 2/8 3/8 4/36 5/57   117
6/57 7/74 8/84 9/89

Lancashire

J. T. Ikin b McHugh	35	—	c Graveney b McHugh		6
A. Wharton b Wells	9	—	c Etheridge b Wells		57
G. A. Edrich b Wells	22	—	lbw b McHugh		7
C. Washbrook lbw b Wells	11	—	lbw b McHugh		1
R. Collins b McHugh	26	—	c Young b Wells		1
R. W. Barber b McHugh	1	—	b McHugh		3
S. Smith lbw b Wells	2	—	b Wells		16
C. S. Smith c Lambert b Wells	0	—	b McHugh		0
T. Greenough c Etheridge b McHugh	0	—	b McHugh		0
R. Tattersall c Young b Wells	5	—	b Wells		0
A. Wilson not out	2	—	not out		0
B 7 l-b 4 n-b 1	12		B 3 l-b 6 n-b 2		11

1/17 2/50 3/68 4/108 5/109 6/118   125
7/118 8/118 9/119

1/26 2/76 3/80 4/82   102
5/85 6/87 7/94 8/94 9/95

Lancashire Bowling

	O.	M.	R.	W.		O.	M.	R.	W.
C. Smith	4	2	7	0	....	8	1	17	3
Wharton	2	0	5	0					
Collins	32	15	62	2	....	6	4	5	0
Tattersall	35	12	71	5	....	12	3	43	2
Greenhough ...	11	4	16	1	....	9.5	3	26	4
Ikin...........	9	3	19	1					

Gloucestershire Bowling

	O.	M.	R.	W.		O.	M.	R.	W.
Lambert	2	0	5	0	....	4	0	20	0
McHugh	12	6	19	4	....	18	3	36	6
Cook	13	5	27	0	....	3	0	13	0
Wells	22.5	9	34	6	....	13.5	4	22	4
Mortimore.....	8	1	28	0					

Umpires: T. J. Bartley and W. T. Jones.

HAMPSHIRE

President—H. S. ALTHAM

Captain and Secretary—E. D. R. EAGAR, County Ground,
Southampton

| R. E. Marshall | County Badge | D. Shackleton |

Hampshire celebrated the jubilee of the club with the most successful season in their history. They finished third in the county table, higher than ever before during the sixty years they have been in the competition; sixteen Championship fixtures were won, two more than the previous best in 1921, and record crowds were attracted to their grounds.

Victory over Surrey, the champions, at Bournemouth in August set the seal on a wonderful summer, and the spontaneous demonstrations of enthusiasm which followed that success reflected the pride felt throughout the county for E. D. R. Eagar and his team.

The great uprising of spirit coincided with the advance to maturity of the younger players and the availability for Championship games of R. E. Marshall, the West Indies Test all-rounder. To no one did the achievements give more pleasure than Eagar. For most of his ten years as captain he had the frustrating experience of directing an attack which lacked adequate spin bowling resources and preparing a batting order which was notably suspect. At last he found himself with a team of all-round strength—only 14 players were required for Championship games—and under his virile guidance they played with tremendous zest. Hampshire, in the field, were a pleasure to watch.

While the county's accomplishments were essentially a corporate affair, the bowling feats of Shackleton must be singled out. He took 100 wickets for the seventh consecutive season; more than 150 for the first time, and completed 1,000 wickets in his career. On eight occasions he obtained five or more wickets in an innings, including an analysis of eight for four against Somerset at Weston-super-Mare. Cannings, who shared the opening attack, also bowled splendidly. Sainsbury, in his first full season, did so well as a left-arm slow bowler that he was honoured with selection for the M.C.C. tour of Pakistan. Undoubtedly his finest performance was nine wickets for 62 in the match at Bradford where Hampshire gained their first win in Yorkshire for twenty-three years. Burden, justifying expectations with his off-breaks, Gray and Heath also gave strength to the attack.

Marshall brought a dashing note to the batting. Almost invariably he was in search of runs from the start of the innings and he deservedly headed the averages. Horton, making a maiden hundred, showed tenacious defence. Rogers played several splendid innings and successfully deputised as captain in the last six games when Eagar was injured. At the end of the summer he retired to take a business appointment. Harrison again kept wicket efficiently and played for the Players against the Gentlemen at Lord's.

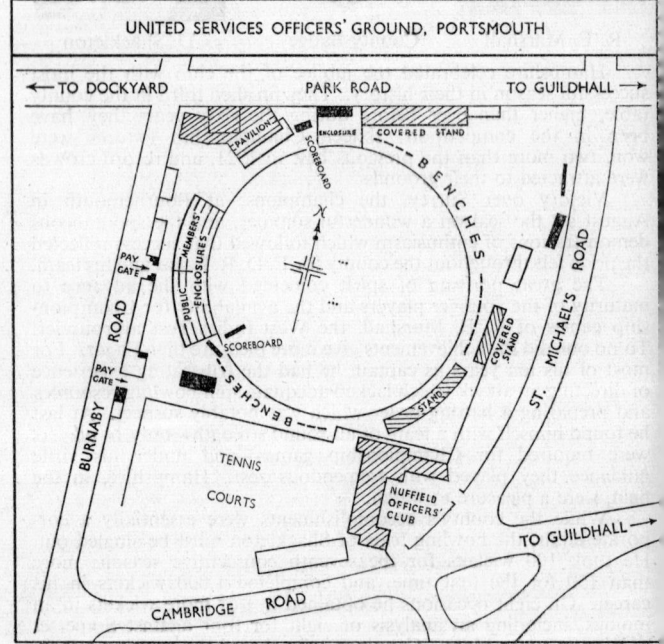

UNITED SERVICES OFFICERS' GROUND, PORTSMOUTH

← TO DOCKYARD   PARK ROAD   TO GUILDHALL →

PAVILION
ENCLOSURE
COVERED STAND
SCOREBOARD
BENCHES
PUBLIC MEMBERS ENCLOSURES
PAY GATE
PAY GATE
SCOREBOARD
BENCHES
STAND
COVERED STAND
ST. MICHAEL'S ROAD
BURNABY ROAD
TENNIS COURTS
NUFFIELD OFFICERS' CLUB
TO GUILDHALL →
CAMBRIDGE ROAD

HAMPSHIRE RESULTS

All First-Class Matches—Played 30, Won 17, Lost 6, Drawn 6, Tied 1

County Championship Matches—Played 28, Won 16, Lost 5, Drawn 6, Tied 1

COUNTY CHAMPIONSHIP AVERAGES

BATTING

	Birthplace	Mtchs.	Inns.	Not Outs	Runs	100's	Highest Inns.	Aver.
R. E. Marshall ..	*West Indies*	28	52	3	1705	2	106	34.79
H. Horton	*Hereford*	21	38	3	1190	3	139	34.00
N. H. Rogers ...	*Oxford*	24	41	2	955	1	103*	24.48
J. R. Gray	*Southampton*	28	52	3	1115	0	98	22.75
H. M. Barnard .	*Portsmouth*	25	44	5	862	1	116	22.10
A. W. H. Rayment	*Finchley*	20	38	4	708	1	104	20.82
P. J. Sainsbury ..	*Southampton*	28	42	7	562	0	73*	16.05
E. D. R. Eagar .	*Cheltenham*	22	35	0	482	0	53	13.77
M. Heath.......	*Bournemouth*	7	10	5	66	0	33	13.20
D. Shackleton ..	*Todmorden*	28	43	7	466	0	47	12.94
V. H. D. Cannings	*Bighton*	24	33	16	206	0	43*	12.11
L. Harrison	*Mudeford*	27	43	5	395	0	35*	10.39
M. D. Burden ..	*Southampton*	25	31	8	97	0	30	4.21

Also batted: A. C. D. Ingleby-Mackenzie (*Devon*) 34.

* *Signifies not out.*

BOWLING

	Overs	Maidens	Runs	Wickets	Average
R. E. Marshall	148.4	59	298	25	11.92
D. Shackleton	1111.5	410	1923	147	13.08
P. J. Sainsbury	850.5	352	1623	96	16.90
V. H. D. Cannings......	767.1	256	1590	93	17.09
M. Heath...............	243.5	48	634	32	19.81
J. R. Gray	462.2	163	938	45	20.84
H. M. Barnard	23	5	66	3	22.00
M. D. Burden	567.3	171	1322	59	22.40

Also bowled: E. D. R. Eagar 1—0—4—0.

Amateurs.—E. D. R. Eagar, A. C. D. Ingleby-Mackenzie.

At Hove, May 2, 3. HAMPSHIRE drew with SUSSEX. (Friendly match.)

HAMPSHIRE v. SOMERSET

At Southampton, May 4, 5. Drawn. Somerset 136 (M. D. Burden four for 44) and 68 for five wickets; Hampshire 229 for eight wickets, declared (E. D. R. Eagar 58; J. W. McMahon four for 47). (Friendly match—twelve a-side.)

HAMPSHIRE v. GLAMORGAN

At Southampton, May 7, 9, 10. Hampshire won by three wickets. Batsmen generally were in difficulties on a rain-affected pitch and Hampshire earned their success because of better spin bowling. Glamorgan, deciding to bat first, were dismissed in two hours twenty-five minutes, Sainsbury, left-arm, and Burden, right-arm off-breaks, causing most trouble. Largely through a fourth wicket partnership of 83 between Rogers and Rayment, Hampshire gained a comfortable lead. Although Glamorgan displayed more resistance in their second innings Sainsbury and Burden again worried the batsmen. Hampshire, not without anxious moments, obtained the 97 runs needed after the third day's play had been restricted considerably by rain.

Glamorgan

W. Wooller c Harrison b Heath	6	— c Rogers b Heath	1
W. G. A. Parkhouse c and b Shackleton	8	— b Burden	18
B. Hedges c Sainsbury b Shackleton	2	— lbw b Sainsbury	10
W. E. Jones c Heath b Burden	16	— b Sainsbury	20
A. J. Watkins b Burden	8	— c Gray b Shackleton	28
J. Pressdee c Gray b Sainsbury	6	— c and b Burden	46
J. Pleass c Harrison b Sainsbury	16	— c Gray b Sainsbury	5
D. Ward c Eager b Sainsbury	1	— lbw b Sainsbury	0
J. E. McConnon b Sainsbury	1	— c Burden b Marshall	9
H. G. Davies c Sainsbury b Burden	0	— c and b Burden	24
D. Shepherd not out	2	— not out	15
B 1, l-b 2	3	B 9, n-b 1	10

1/11 2/17 3/17 4/30 5/37 6/63 7/65   68   1/6 2/29 3/39 4/83   186
8/66 9/66   5/92 6/102 7/102 8/133 9/169

Hampshire

J. R. Gray lbw b McConnon	22	— c Davies b Wooller	10
R. E. Marshall hit wkt b Pressdee	32	— c Davies b Shepherd	4
H. M. Barnard c and b McConnon	6	— b Shepherd	19
E. D. R. Eagar b Pressdee	0	— b Shepherd	0
N. H. Rogers c Davies b Shepherd	45	— b Shepherd	30
A. W. H. Rayment not out	48	— c Pressdee b Watkins	17
L. Harrison c Pressdee b Watkins	1	— b Watkins	0
P. J. Sainsbury b Shepherd	0	— not out	1
D. Shackleton c Parkhouse b Watkins	0	— not out	5
M. Heath run out	0		
M. D. Burden b Shepherd	0		
B 2, l-b 1, n-b 1	4	B 7 l-b 4	11

1/53 2/59 3/60 4/62 5/145 6/146   158   1/6 2/34 3/34   (7 wkts.)   97
7/146 8/149 9/150   4/35 5/82 6/91 7/91

Hampshire Bowling

	O.	M.	R.	W.		O.	M.	R.	W.
Shackleton	11	6	8	2	....	23	13	21	1
Heath	10	2	23	1	....	11	3	29	1
Burden	18	8	15	3	....	34.5	13	63	3
Sainsbury	11.4	5	19	4	....	31	17	37	4
Marshall					....	8	2	26	1

Glamorgan Bowling

	O.	M.	R.	W.		O.	M.	R.	W.
Wooller	5	0	25	0	....	19	4	41	1
Watkins	14	3	37	2	....	6.2	2	6	2
McConnon	16	3	35	2					
Pressdee	14	5	30	2					
Shepherd	8.4	1	27	3	....	25	5	39	4

Umpires: A. J. B. Flower and J. J. Hills.

HAMPSHIRE v. NOTTINGHAMSHIRE

At Portsmouth, May 11, 12, 13. Nottinghamshire won by nine wickets. They displayed all-round superiority. Hampshire, trying to emulate the brisk start given them by Marshall, failed against steady bowling. Nottinghamshire gained the lead for the loss of one wicket and though the middle batting collapsed, a fine display by Dooland ensured that Hampshire had to face formidable arrears. Marshall again hit briskly and Hampshire's prospects improved through an excellent third wicket stand of 127 between Gray and Sainsbury. Thereafter the spin bowlers, Smales and Dooland, took command on a moist pitch and the last seven wickets fell for 40.

Hampshire

J. R. Gray b Smales	6	—	lbw b Dooland	98
R. E. Marshall lbw b Dooland	46	—	c Clay b Smales	37
H. M. Barnard c and b Jepson	4	—	c Clay b Smales	0
E. D. R. Eagar c Rowe b Smales	21	—	c Smales b Dooland	2
N. H. Rogers lbw b Jepson	12	—	c Poole b Smales	2
A. W. H. Rayment c Rowe b Smales	13	—	c Rowe b Smales	24
L. Harrison c Rowe b Dooland	27	—	c Harvey b Smales	3
P. J. Sainsbury c Stocks b Smales	3	—	c Clay b Dooland	49
D. Shackleton c Rowe b Jepson	11	—	c Stocks b Dooland	4
M. Heath not out	0	—	c Simpson b Smales	0
M. D. Burden c Jepson b Dooland	3	—	not out	0
			B 5, l-b 6, w 2	13

1/9 2/28 3/71 4/88 5/92 6/112   146
7/124 8/143 9/143

1/65 2/65 3/192 4/195   232
5/195 6/200 7/214 8/222
9/227

Nottinghamshire

R. T. Simpson c Gray b Sainsbury	42	—	st Harrison b Burden	15
J. D. Clay st Harrison b Gray	83	—	not out	5
C. J. Poole c Harrison b Shackleton	33	—	not out	5
J. Hardstaff b Shackleton	3			
E. J. Martin c Rogers b Gray	11			
F. W. Stocks c Shackleton b Sainsbury	14			
P. F. Harvey b Gray	19			
B. Dooland b Heath	91			
K. Smales c Gray b Burden	5			
A. Jepson c Marshall b Shackleton	27			
E. J. Rowe not out	5			
B 12, l-b 12	24			

1/68 2/161 3/165 4/189 5/200   357
6/208 7/243 8/284 9/326

1/15   (1 wkt.)   25

Nottinghamshire Bowling

	O.	M.	R.	W.		O.	M.	R.	W.
Jepson	18	3	63	3		20	5	51	0
Smales	13	5	34	4		43.3	11	97	6
Harvey	6	1	20	0		6	0	22	0
Dooland	14.	4	29	3		34	16	49	4

Hampshire Bowling

	O.	M.	R.	W.		O.	M.	R.	W.
Shackleton	44	19	76	3					
Heath	34.3	6	112	1		5	0	10	0
Gray	41	18	72	3					
Sainsbury	17	7	40	2					
Burden	9	1	33	1		5.2	0	15	1

Umpires: F. Chester and E. A. Roberts.

At Lord's, May 14, 16.   HAMPSHIRE lost to MIDDLESEX by 55 runs.

At Worcester, May 18, 19, 20.   HAMPSHIRE drew with WORCESTERSHIRE.

At Manchester, May 21, 23, 24.   HAMPSHIRE drew with LANCASHIRE.

ROYAL NAVY v. HAMPSHIRE

At Portsmouth, May 25, 26. Drawn. Royal Navy 135 and 191 for seven wickets, declared (C. A. R. Weston 62; M. Heath four for 57); Hampshire 215 H. M. Barnard 82; G. D. Steer six for 88) and 105 for five (G. D. Steer four for 54).

HAMPSHIRE v. KENT

At Southampton, May 28, 30. 31. Drawn. A stubborn unbroken ninth wicket partnership of 63 between Wright and Witherden prevented Hampshire from winning. Seam bowlers held the upper hand after rain caused a blank first day and the only innings of distinction before Kent's final resistance came from Marshall. Largely through his technical skill Hampshire were able to set their opponents to get 167 runs in almost as many minutes.

Hampshire

J. R. Gray lbw b Smith	1	— b Ridgway	0
R. E. Marshall c Smith b Ridgway	26	— c Hearn b Smith	48
N. H. Rogers c Evans b Smith	5	— b Ridgway	1
A. W. H. Rayment c Evans b Ridgway	16	— lbw b Ridgway	0
H. M. Barnard run out	26	— c Brazier b Wright	2
E. D. R. Eagar c Phebey b Ridgway	8	— b Ridgway	5
L. Harrison c Wright b Ridgway	5	— b Smith	9
P. J. Sainsbury b Ridgway	2	— not out	25
D. Shackleton c Wright b Ridgway	19	— not out	29
V. H. D. Cannings b Wright	4		
M. D. Burden not out	0		
B 7, l-b 2	9	L-b 8	8

1/8 2/26 3/38 4/76 5/78 6/88   121
7/91 8/113 9/117

1/7 2/13 3/13 (7 wkts., dec.) 127
4/47 5/52 6/71 8/72

Kent

A. E. Fagg, b Gray	14	— b Sainsbury	18
A. H. Phebey lbw b Sainsbury	28	— c Harrison b Cannings	0
P. Hearn lbw b Cannings	1	— b Shackleton	1
J. Pettiford b Shackleton	8	— b Cannings	3
T. G. Evans b Shackleton	16	— b Cannings	2
A. F. Brazier b Shackleton	0	— c Rayment b Cannings	2
E. G. Witherden b Sainsbury	1	— not out	46
G. Smith lbw b Sainsbury	2	— c Barnard b Sainsbury	6
F. Ridgway b Shackleton	7	— c Burden b Sainsbury	0
D. V. P. Wright b Shackleton	3	— not out	35
J. C. T. Page not out	1		
L-b 1	1	B 1, l-b 3	4

1/30 2/31 3/44 4/67 5/68 6/69   82
7/69 8/78 9/78

1/0 2/3 3/14   (8 wkts.) 117
4/18 5/20 6/46 7/52 8/54

Kent Bowling

	O.	M.	R.	W.	O.	M.	R.	W.
Ridgway	17.1	3	50	6	15	5	32	4
Smith	10	2	38	2	19	4	43	2
Wright	12	5	24	1	12	2	32	1
Page					6	1	12	0

Hampshire Bowling

	O.	M.	R.	W.	O.	M.	R.	W.
Shackleton	18.1	6	36	5	18	8	37	1
Cannings	10	5	8	1	15	2	29	4
Burden	3	1	5	0	3	0	10	0
Gray	11	5	16	1	5	4	1	0
Sainsbury	18	10	16	3	14	3	36	3

Umpires: F. S. Lee and W. F. Price.

At Peterborough, June 1, 2, 3. HAMPSHIRE beat NORTHAMPTONSHIRE by seven wickets.

HAMPSHIRE v. GLOUCESTERSHIRE

At Portsmouth, June 4, 6, 7. Drawn. Only Milton, Graveney and Emmett coped successfully with the off-breaks of Marshall on a drying pitch. Hampshire, in turn, were unhappy against the fast bowling of McHugh and Lambert and finished 71 runs in arrear. An opening stand of 80 between Young and Milton led to Gloucestershire declaring 213 runs ahead. Hampshire, losing three wickets cheaply, found the task of getting the runs in two hours and three-quarters too much, though Marshall batted splendidly, and shared an unbroken fourth wicket partnership of 101 with Rogers.

Gloucestershire

D. M. Young b Marshall	15	— c Rogers b Shackleton	55
C. A. Milton st Harrison b Marshall	39	— c Eagar b Sainsbury	33
T. W. Graveney c Eagar b Gray	35	— run out	23
J. F. Crapp c and b Sainsbury	4	— c Marshall b Shackleton	0
G. M. Emmett not out	53	— not out	15
R. B. Nicholls b Marshall	5	— not out	0
J. Mortimore c Gray b Marshall	4	— c Barnard b Cannings	4
G. E. Lambert b Marshall	20	— c Gray b Shackleton	1
P. Rochford c Rogers b Marshall	0		
C. Cook run out	0		
F. P. McHugh lbw b Sainsbury	1		
B 3, l-b 1	4	B 6, l-b 5	11

1/28 2/84 3/93 4/101 5/111 6/117   180   1/80 2/114   (6 wkts., dec.) 142
7/169 8/175 9/175   3/119 4/121 5/131 6/133

Hampshire

J. R. Gray b McHugh	13	— c Rochford b McHugh	0
R. E. Marshall c Young b Lambert	34	— not out	80
N. H. Rogers c Mortimore b McHugh	5	— not out	39
A. W. H. Rayment c Rochford b Lambert	23	— c Rochford b McHugh	0
H. M. Barnard lbw b Cook	1		
E. D. R. Eagar b Lambert	9	— c Nicholls b Lambert	3
L. Harrison c Rochford b Lambert	4		
P. J. Sainsbury b McHugh	8		
D. Shackleton c and b McHugh	0		
V. H. D. Cannings not out	4		
M. D. Burden b McHugh	1		
B 1, l-b 6	7	B 1	1

1/40 2/52 3/54 4/55 5/71 6/81   109   1/2 2/15 3/22   (3 wkts.) 123
7/94 8/100 9/106

Hampshire Bowling

	O.	M.	R.	W.		O.	M.	R.	W.
Shackleton	10	4	15	0	....	25	10	41	3
Cannings	11	5	18	0	....	22	8	51	1
Sainsbury	32.3	13	54	2	....	6	3	19	1
Burden	8	2	22	0					
Marshall	31	9	57	6					
Gray	7	2	10	1	....	4	0	12	0
Barnard						2	0	8	0

Gloucestershire Bowling

	O.	M.	R.	W.		O.	M.	R.	W.
Lambert	27	7	62	4	....	6	2	22	1
McHugh	33.2	15	30	5	....	13	2	35	2
Cook	13	10	10	1	....	15	4	39	0
Mortimore					....	10	3	15	0
Graveney					....	2	1	2	0
Emmett					....	1	0	9	0

Umpires: K. McCanlis and W. F. Price.

HAMPSHIRE v. ESSEX

At Southampton, June 8, 9. Hampshire won by seven wickets, the match ending at tea-time on the second day. Their batsmen mastered a tricky pitch better than those of Essex, whose first innings ended an hour after lunch. A technically correct display by Rogers helped Hampshire to a lead of 62 and when Essex batted again they collapsed against the skilful left-arm slow bowling of Sainsbury.

Essex

T. C. Dodds c Burden b Shackleton	47	— c Cannings b Sainsbury	...	17
P. A. Gibb c Harrison b Cannings	0	— lbw b Sainsbury		7
G. Barker c Rayment b Sainsbury	30	— c Eagar b Sainsbury		14
R. Horsfall c and b Shackleton	0	— c Gray b Sainsbury		2
D. J. Insole c Eagar b Burden	16	— lbw b Sainsbury		12
B. Taylor c Marshall b Shackleton	5	— b Burden		9
B. Knight c and b Sainsbury	0	— b Burden		2
R. Smith c Sainsbury b Burden	14	— c Harrison b Sainsbury		0
W. T. Greensmith lbw b Cannings	1	— not out		5
J. A. Bailey c and b Cannings	0	— c Eagar b Burden		4
K. C. Preston not out	0	— b Sainsbury		9
B 6, l-b 5	11	B 1		1

1/10 2/76 3/81 4/81 5/88 6/88   124   1/23 2/37 3/41 4/46   82
7/115 8/120 9/120   5/61 6/63 7/63 8/65 9/69

Hampshire

J. R. Gray c Gibb b Preston	1	— lbw b Bailey		4
R. E. Marshall c Insole b Preston	8	— b Bailey		2
N. H. Rogers lbw b Smith	75	— c Barker b Preston		7
A. W. H. Rayment c Taylor b Preston	0	— not out		6
H. M. Barnard c Horsfall b Preston	19	— not out		0
E. D. R. Eagar b Preston	32			
L. Harrison b Smith	2			
P. J. Sainsbury not out	20			
D. Shackleton c and b Smith	7			
V. H. D. Cannings b Preston	1			
M. D. Burden c Bailey b Greensmith	18			
L-b 2, w 1	3	B 2		2

1/8 2/23 3/23 4/63 5/131 6/138   186   1/4 2/13 3/16   (3 wkts.   21
7/138 8/148 9/149

Hampshire Bowling

	O.	M.	R.	W.	O.	M.	R.	W.
Shackleton	17	4	43	3	 9	2	23	0
Cannings	10	3	10	2	 4	1	6	0
Sainsbury	22	9	30	2	.... 20.4	12	25	7
Burden	8.3	0	24	2	 16	5	27	3
Marshall	2	0	6	0				

Essex Bowling

	O.	M.	R.	W.	O.	M.	R.	W.
Preston	25	7	65	6	.... 5.4	1	15	1
Bailey	12	6	26	0	 5	2	4	2
Smith	23	3	54	3				
Greensmith	3.2	0	22	1				
Insole	3	0	16	0				

Umpires: K. McCanlis and E. Davies.

At Bradford, June 11, 13. HAMPSHIRE beat YORKSHIRE by an innings and 43 runs.

HAMPSHIRE v. THE ARMY

At Southampton, June 15, 16, 17. Hampshire won by eight wickets. The Army 269 (Gunner N. W. Hill 67, Major J. H. G. Deighton 84; M. D. Burden four for 52) and 218 for eight declared (Gunner N. W. Hill 56; H. M. Barnard five for 48); Hampshire 277 for nine, declared (J. R. Gray 124, N. H. Rogers 111 not out; L/Cpl. A. Lightfoot five for 69) and 212 for two (J. R. Gray 78, H. Horton 53).

HAMPSHIRE v. OXFORD UNIVERSITY

At Bournemouth, June 18, 20, 21. Hampshire won by six wickets, after declaring 33 runs behind on first innings. At one period they were in danger of following on, but a sixth wicket partnership of 71 between Rogers and Harrison retrieved their fortunes. The off-breaks of Burden caused the University to collapse on the third morning, six wickets falling to that bowler in less than ten overs at a personal cost of 29. Hampshire, with Marshall playing a characteristically dashing innings, made light of their task, hitting the 171 needed in just over two hours.

Oxford University

J. M. Allan lbw b Shackleton	62	— lbw b Sainsbury 6
M. J. K. Smith b Heath	31	— not out 76
A. C. Walton run out	10	— lbw b Sainsbury 0
C. C. P. Williams b Shackleton	42	— st Harrison b Burden 7
G. P. S. Delisle b Gray	25	— c Barnard b Marshall 15
I. Gibson b Gray	0	— c Heath b Burden 11
J. P. Fellows-Smith st Harrison b Shackleton	30	— c and b Burden 0
A. P. Walshe lbw b Shackleton	0	— b Burden 14
J. A. Arenhold not out	32	— c Sainsbury b Burden 2
D. C. P. R. Jowett c Burden b Gray	24	— c Gray b Burden 0
J. B. Phillips (did not bat)		— c Sainsbury b Burden 0
B 16, l-b 10	26	B 2, l-b 4 6

1/78 2/109 3/117 4/157   (9 wkts., dec.) 282   1/16 2/16 3/35 4/69   137
5/165 6/206 7/208 8/227 9/282   5/93 6/93 7/115 8/131 9/137

Hampshire

J. R. Gray run out	4	—	c Walshe b Allan		35
R. E. Marshall c Williams b Phillips	0	—	not out		110
H. Horton b Jowett	22	—	b Arenhold		15
N. H. Rogers not out	121	—	c and b Allan		0
H. M. Barnard c Arenhold b Allan	8	—	b Arenhold		8
E. D. R. Eagar lbw b Jowett	6	—	not out		0
L. Harrison c Gibson b Phillips	25				
P. J. Sainsbury c Smith b Arenhold	23				
D. Shackleton c Williams b Phillips	6				
M. Heath not out	0				
B 12, l-b 1, n-b 1	14		B 2, n-b 1		3

1/5 2/42 3/53 4/81 5/93 (8 wkts., dec.) 249
6/164 7/232 8/249

1/91 2/154 (4 wkts.) 171
3/155 4/168

M. D. Burden did not bat.

Hampshire Bowling

	O.	M.	R.	W.		O.	M.	R.	W.
Shackleton	27	12	53	4	....	5	2	3	0
Heath	20	7	41	1	....	2	2	0	0
Gray	22.4	7	55	3					
Sainsbury	18	5	43	0	....	29	8	64	2
Burden	13	4	28	0	....	24.5	6	53	7
Barnard	5	1	21	0					
Marshall	4	3	15	0	....	8	5	11	1

Oxford University Bowling

	O.	M.	R.	W.		O.	M.	R.	W.
Arenhold	10	3	25	1	....	9	1	35	2
Phillips	17	4	44	3	....	7	1	16	0
Fellows-Smith	12	3	39	0	....	1	0	4	0
Jowett	23	7	51	2	....	10	1	33	0
Allan	30	9	76	1	....	14	0	62	2
Gibson						2	0	15	0
Williams						0.2	0	3	0

Umpires: W. Homan and G. Dennett.

At Bristol, June 22, 23, 24. HAMPSHIRE beat GLOUCESTERSHIRE by eight wickets.

At Swansea, June 25, 27, 28. HAMPSHIRE beat GLAMORGAN by five wickets.

HAMPSHIRE v. YORKSHIRE

At Bournemouth, June 29, 30. Yorkshire won by 96 runs, avenging a defeat at Bradford earlier in the month. Bowlers were nearly always on top on a wearing pitch. Sent in to bat while the turf was drying, Yorkshire were saved from collapse by the resolute stroke-play of the left-hander, Watson, who hit two sixes off Marshall. Yorkshire, without a fast bowler because of injuries, were further handicapped when Appleyard retired with a pulled leg muscle, but Wardle, in the unaccustomed role of a new ball bowler, and Illingworth, dismissed Hampshire in an hour and three-quarters. Lester, restraining his natural desire to hit, was largely responsible for Hampshire being set to get 228, a task they found beyond them against the wiles of Wardle and Illingworth.

Yorkshire

L. Hutton c Rayment b Shackleton	....	0	— c Harrison b Marshall	2
F. A. Lowson b Sainsbury	....	12	— c and b Marshall..........	32
J. V. Wilson b Sainsbury	....	24	— b Sainsbury	15
E. Lester run out	....	11	— c Rayment b Burden	54
W. Watson b Burden	....	68	— lbw b Shackleton	1
D. B. Close b Marshall	....	3	— lbw b Marshall	0
N. W. D. Yardley c Sainsbury b Burden		34	— c Eagar b Cannings	6
R. Illingworth c Gray b Marshall	......	3	— c Barnard b Burden	15
J. H. Wardle b Marshall	....	0	— lbw b Cannings	11
R. Appleyard c Shackleton b Marshall	..	6	— c Harrison b Shackleton ...	8
J. G. Binks not out	....	0	— not out	13
B 4	....	4	B 4, l-b 4	8
		—		—
		165		165

1/0 2/29 3/48 4/50 5/66 6/119   165
7/136 8/139 9/161

1/4 2/37 3/85 4/93   165
5/93 6/102 7/129 8/134 9/150

Hampshire

J. R. Gray b Appleyard	....	9	— lbw b Wardle	10
R. E. Marshall c Close b Wardle	....	31	— st Binks b Wardle	31
H. Horton run out	....	20	— b Close	11
A. W. H. Rayment c and b Wardle	....	2	— st Binks b Wardle	6
H. M. Barnard lbw b Wardle	....	7	— c Wilson b Close	4
E. D. R. Eagar lbw b Illingworth	.....	19	— b Illingworth	6
L. Harrison c Wilson b Illingworth	....	1	— b Wardle	9
P. J. Sainsbury c Wilson b Illingworth	..	4	— c Wilson b Illingworth	8
D. Shackleton b Wardle	....	4	— c Lowson b Illingworth	17
V. H. D. Cannings not out	....	0	— b Wardle	3
M. D. Burden b Illingworth	....	0	— not out	0
B 2, l-b 4	....	6	B 11, l-b 10, w 5	26
		—		—
		103		131

1/21 2/49 3/55 4/71 5/75 6/76   103
7/88 8/103 9/103

1/30 2/47 3/71 4/78   131
5/88 6/92 7/102 8/124 9/129

Hampshire Bowling

	O.	M.	R.	W.		O.	M.	R.	W.
Shackleton.....	8	4	16	1	....	11.2	6	18	2
Cannings	7	3	10	0	....	22	9	36	2
Sainsbury......	13	3	32	2	....	16	3	42	1
Burden	24	6	52	2	....	10	5	26	2
Marshall	15.4	3	51	4	....	17	6	35	3

Yorkshire Bowling

	O.	M.	R.	W.		O.	M.	R.	W.
Appleyard	8	1	35	1					
Wardle	18	8	26	4	....	30	12	50	5
Close	5	2	21	0	....	11	6	18	2
Illingworth	5.2	1	15	4	....	18.2	6	37	3

Umpires: H. G. Baldwin and J. J. Hills.

At Eastbourne, July, 2, 4, 5. HAMPSHIRE tied with SUSSEX.

HAMPSHIRE v. DERBYSHIRE

At Southampton, July 6, 7, 8. Derbyshire won by 26 runs with three minutes to spare after a well-timed declaration. After losing two wickets in the first over from Cannings, Derbyshire remained in trouble, especially against the left-arm bowling of Sainsbury, who was awarded his county cap. Hampshire's reply came almost entirely from a second wicket stand of 91 between Marshall and Horton, the remaining wickets falling for 62. A stylish innings by their captain,

Carr, enabled Derbyshire to set their opponents to get 252 in three and three-quarter hours. While Marshall batted, Hampshire looked to have a chance, for he hit with fine judgment while making 99 out of 138, but when he left the attack gained control.

Derbyshire

A. Hamer b Sainsbury	49	— lbw b Shackleton 0
J. Kelly c Barnard b Cannings	0	— c Horton b Sainsbury...... 32
D. C. Morgan c Barnard b Cannings	0	— b Shackleton 19
A. C. Revill lbw b Sainsbury	31	— run out 31
D. B. Carr c Barnard b Gray	34	— not out 82
H. L. Johnson c Barnard b Cannings	16	— b Sainsbury 31
C. Lee c Harrison b Sainsbury	6	— run out 21
G. O. Dawkes c Eagar b Sainsbury	4	— c Shackleton b Cannings .. 1
C. Gladwin not out	20	— not out 5
E. Smith c Harrison b Burden	2	
A. Eato lbw b Sainsbury	6	— lbw b Cannings 0
B 3, l-b 9, n-b 1	13	L-b 1 1

1/2 2/2 3/65 4/110 5/128 6/141   181   1/40 2/43   (8 wkts., dec.) 223
7/145 8/161 9/168   3/84 4/86 5/167 6/202
    7/211 8/211

Hampshire

J. R. Gray c Morgan b Gladwin	0	— lbw b Eato 13
R. E. Marshall c and b Morgan	52	— b Smith 99
H. Horton c Morgan b Smith	48	— c Carr b Morgan......... 5
A. W. H. Rayment b Smith	11	— c Dawkes b Gladwin 22
H. M. Barnard lbw b Smith	0	— c Carr b Gladwin 37
E. D. R. Eagar run out	24	— b Gladwin 10
L. Harrison c Carr b Morgan	4	— run out 3
P. J. Sainsbury c Dawkes b Morgan	0	— c Carr b Eato 9
D. Shackleton not out	7	— b Gladwin 2
V. H. D. Cannings b Morgan	4	— not out 16
M. D. Burden b Morgan	0	— c Kelly b Morgan 1
L-b 2, w 1	3	L-b 7, w 1 8

1/0 2/91 3/106 4/106 5/121 6/134   153   1/50 2/53 3/138 4/152   225
7/138 8/149 9/153   5/158 6/182 7/199 8/204
    9/204

Hampshire Bowling

	O.	M.	R.	W.		O.	M.	R.	W.
Shackleton	16	7	17	0	....	21	5	50	2
Cannings	13	1	38	3	....	16	7	32	2
Gray	12	6	15	1	....	6	1	14	0
Sainsbury	44.1	27	45	5	....	38	14	71	2
Burden	29	9	52	1	....	28	12	55	0
Barnard	1	0	1	0					

Derbyshire Bowling

	O.	M.	R.	W.		O.	M.	R.	W.
Eato	10	0	43	0	....	6	3	20	2
Gladwin	14	7	21	1	....	23	4	60	4
Morgan	19	6	41	5	....	18.4	2	71	2
Smith	22	10	31	3	....	14	1	50	1
Carr	9	5	14	0	....	4	0	16	0

Umpires: K. McCanlis and N. Oldfield.

HAMPSHIRE v. SOMERSET

At Portsmouth, July 9, 11, 12. Hampshire won by eight wickets. Their strong array of fast-medium bowlers proved too much for Somerset, the match finishing before lunch on the third day. Hampshire's early batsmen made such good progress that the total reached 211 for three at tea, Gray and Horton putting on 118 for the second wicket. Afterwards the remaining wickets fell for the addition of 48, Lobb taking five of them in 8.3 overs for 13 runs. Somerset, dismissed in three and a half hours, followed on 164 behind. Hampshire fielded splendidly and held twelve catches.

Hampshire

J. R. Gray b McMahon	87			
R. E. Marshall c and b Lomax	33			
H. Horton run out	56	— not out		7
A. W. H. Rayment b Lomax	29	— not out		0
N. H. Rogers c Lomax b Yawar Saeed	11			
H. M. Barnard lbw b Lobb	10			
L. Harrison c Yawar Saeed b Lobb	21			
P. J. Sainsbury c Tremlett b Lomax	2	— lbw b Lawrence		3
D. Shackleton c Tremlett b Lobb	0			
V. H. D. Cannings b Lobb	0			
M. Heath not out	3	— hit wkt b Tremlett		5
B 1, l-b 6	7			

1/52 2/170 3/204 4/217 5/222 6/233   259   1/3 2/11   (2 wkts.) 15
7/256 8/256 9/256

Somerset

G. G. Tordoff b Heath	4	— c Shackleton b Gray		23
J. Lawrence c Barnard b Cannings	11	— c Harrison b Heath		16
J. Hilton c Rogers b Cannings	0	— c and b Shackleton		8
M. F. Tremlett c Harrison b Cannings	16	— run out		0
P. B. Wight c Barnard b Cannings	38	— c Marshall b Heath		38
J. G. Lomax b Shackleton	1	— b Heath		30
G. G. Atkinson b Shackleton	8	— c and b Sainsbury		2
Yawar Saeed lbw b Heath	7	— b Heath		28
H. W. Stephenson c Cannings b Heath	5	— c Barnard b Shackleton		0
J. W. McMahon not out	1	— c Gray b Shackleton		19
B. Lobb b Heath	0	— not out		0
L-b 4	4	B 3, l-b 8		11

1/6 2/7 3/30 4/37 5/38 6/72 7/85   95   1/33 2/37 3/53 4/103   175
8/89 9/95   5/120 6/127 7/132 8/151
                                   9/165

Somerset Bowling

	O.	M.	R.	W.	O.	M.	R.	W.
Lobb	22.3	4	44	5				
Yawar Saeed	10	0	48	1				
Lomax	11	3	29	2				
Tordoff	16	7	22	0				
Lawrence	18	4	61	0	2.3	0	11	1
Hilton	10	1	21	0				
McMahon	11	2	27	1				
Tremlett					3	1	4	1

Hampshire Bowling

	O.	M.	R.	W.		O.	M.	R.	W.
Shackleton	18	6	24	2	....	15.1	5	31	3
Cannings	13	5	26	4	....	14	8	18	0
Heath	18.2	5	38	4	....	20	2	46	4
Sainsbury	1	1	0	0	....	15	6	32	1
Gray	6	4	3	0	....	8	2	33	1
					Barnard	1	0	4	0

Umpires: H. G. Baldwin and G. S. Mobey.

At Birmingham, July 13, 14, 15. HAMPSHIRE drew with WARWICKSHIRE.

At Chesterfield, July 16, 18, 19. HAMPSHIRE beat DERBYSHIRE by 58 runs.

At Leicester, July 20, 21, 22. HAMPSHIRE lost to LEICESTERSHIRE by two wickets.

HAMPSHIRE v. MIDDLESEX

At Bournemouth, July 23, 25, 26. Hampshire won by an innings and six runs. They held the initiative practically throughout the game. Middlesex gave a sorry display on an ideal batting pitch and were dismissed in two hours forty minutes. Shackleton took five of the last six wickets in fifteen balls without conceding a run. Marshall, who dominated a first wicket stand of 137 with Gray, went on to complete his maiden hundred in championship cricket. It was an innings full of well-timed drives and wristy cuts. Rogers and Barnard swelled Hampshire's total by adding 117 for the fifth wicket. Middlesex faced arrears of 247, and Titmus, going in when four wickets fell for 62, batted admirably while recording a maiden century in first-class cricket. Always attractive to watch, he hit eighteen 4's and shared a partnership of 119 with Bennett, but the game ended on the third morning.

Middlesex

J. D. Robertson lbw b Cannings	19	— b Cannings	7
S. M. Brown b Cannings	7	— c Harrison b Burden	25
W. J. Edrich run out	32	— c Harrison b Cannings	3
G. P. S. Delisle b Gray	7	— c Marshall b Burden	20
D. Bennett b Gray	10	— c Barnard b Shackleton	42
F. J. Titmus b Shackleton	0	— b Cannings	104
R. V. C. Robins lbw b Shackleton	0	— b Sainsbury	1
J. J. Warr b Shackleton	0	— not out	16
L. H. Compton c Burden b Shackleton	1	— b Shackleton	1
J. A. Young b Shackleton	3	— b Cannings	8
A. E. Moss not out	0	— lbw b Cannings	4
L-b 9, n-b 1	10	B 6, l-b 4	10

1/14 2/33 3/59 4/81 5/83 6/83   89   1/9 2/27 3/52 4/62 5/181   241
7/85 8/86 9/86   6/188 7/205 8/217 9/227

Hampshire

J. R. Gray b Young	51	D. Shackleton c Robertson b Young	0
R. E. Marshall c and b Young	106	V. H. D. Cannings not out	1
H. Horton b Young	6	M. D. Burden b Young	2
E. D. R. Eagar c Brown b Young	0		
N. H. Rogers c Compton b Robins	59	B 10, l-b 4, w 2, n-b 1	17
H. M. Barnard c and b Robins	75		
L. Harrison b Robins	3	1/137 2/164 3/164 4/171 5/288 336
P. J. Sainsbury c Edrich b Robins	16	6/296 7/331 8/332 9/333

Hampshire Bowling

	O.	M.	R.	W.	O.	M.	R.	W.
Shackleton	19.3	9	26	5	31	3	63	2
Cannings	14	5	27	2	23.3	7	53	5
Gray	15	7	26	2	18	6	38	0
Burden					21	6	47	2
Sainsbury					20	10	30	1

Middlesex Bowling

	O.	M.	R.	W.
Moss	18	2	66	0
Warr	16	2	34	0
Bennett	3	0	17	0
Robins	24	4	91	4
Titmus	11	1	35	0
Young	25.5	6	76	6

Umpires: A. Skelding and E. Davies.

HAMPSHIRE v. LEICESTERSHIRE

At Bournemouth, July 27, 28, 29. Hampshire won by ten wickets in an exciting finish. They were left to score 71 in thirty-four minutes and Marshall hit with such power that the task was accomplished in eight overs and one ball with seven minutes to spare. Horton, awarded his county cap after a painstaking display lasting four hours forty minutes, prevented a complete breakdown in Hampshire's early batting on the first day. Subsequently Barnard, using a wide range of strokes, hit his first hundred in championship matches, helping Horton to increase the total by 162. Leicestershire, routed by the intelligent fast-medium bowling of Shackleton, fought back splendidly and cleared their arrears of 281 through such consistent batting that their first innings collapse was difficult to understand.

Hampshire

J. R. Gray c Hallam b Spencer	2	— not out	15
R. E. Marshall b Pratt	12	— not out	47
H. Horton c Jackson b Munden	139		
E. D. R. Eagar b Spencer	31		
N. H. Rogers c Hallam b Lester	26		
H. M. Barnard run out	116		
L. Harrison lbw b Palmer	13		
P. J. Sainsbury c Hallam b Lester	19		
D. Shackleton not out	4		
M. D. Burden b Palmer	0		
V. H. D. Cannings b Palmer	2		
B 5, l-b 3, w 4, n-b 1	13	B 5, l-b 4	9

1/14 2/14 3/65 4/120 5/282 6/342   377   (No wkt.) 71
7/365 8/372 9/373

Leicestershire

G. Lester run out	16	—	run out	15
M. R. Hallam b Shackleton	2	—	c Harrison b Cannings	20
J. Firth c Sainsbury b Shackleton	0	—	c Eagar b Shackleton	51
M. Tompkin lbw b Shackleton	3	—	c Rogers b Gray	4
M. J. K. Smith lbw b Shackleton	6	—	b Shackleton	32
C. H. Palmer lbw b Cannings	0	—	c Horton b Cannings	65
V. E. Jackson c Eagar b Gray	43	—	b Shackleton	65
G. A. Smithson b Gray	0	—	c Harrison b Cannings	21
V. S. Munden b Shackleton	23	—	c and b Gray	50
C. T. Spencer b Shackleton	0	—	c Barnard b Gray	15
R. L. Pratt not out	0	—	not out	1
B 2, l-b 1	3		B 11, l-b 1	12
	—			—
	96			351

1/3 2/7 3/11 4/27 5/27 6/27 7/38   96
8/76 9/96

1/25 2/38 3/44 4/105   351
5/198 6/224 7/228 8/335
9/335

Leicestershire Bowling

	O.	M.	R.	W.		O.	M.	R.	W.
Spencer	19	5	69	2	....	4.1	0	35	0
Pratt	14	0	64	1					
Jackson	24	7	75	0					
Palmer	18.1	7	35	3	....	4	0	27	0
Munden	24	11	52	1					
Lester	23	7	69	2					

Hampshire Bowling

	O.	M.	R.	W.		O.	M.	R.	W.
Shackleton	18.1	9	24	6	....	47	22	78	3
Cannings	12	5	18	1	....	28	12	74	3
Gray	10	4	25	2	....	35.5	15	81	3
Sainsbury	8	3	19	0	....	36	14	61	0
Burden	4	2	7	0	....	11	1	29	0
Barnard						1	0	10	0
Marshall						2	0	6	0

Umpires: A. Skelding and D. Davies.

At Canterbury, July 30, August 1, 2. HAMPSHIRE beat KENT by 30 runs.

HAMPSHIRE v. SUSSEX

At Portsmouth, August 6, 8, 9. Hampshire won by 151 runs. From the time that Cannings and Heath added 72 runs in just over an hour for the last wicket Hampshire, who had lost nine first innings wickets for 164, gradually took command. Sussex did not consolidate an opening stand of 52 between Langridge and Oakman and were all out in three hours to the bowling of Cannings, Shackleton and Heath. Hampshire, 98 runs ahead, punished the Sussex attack to such purpose that they declared with a lead of 363 after batting for only three hours 40 minutes. Their opponents, after early batting failures, resisted stubbornly, but Hampshire won with more than an hour to spare.

Hampshire

R. E. Marshall c James b Smith	51	— lbw b Thomson	22
J. R. Gray lbw b Smith	24	— b Thomson	59
H. Horton c Doggart b Thomson	16	— not out	104
E. D. R. Eagar c Parks b Smith	29		
N. H. Rogers st Webb b James	9	— c Langridge b Cox	46
H. M. Barnard c Thomson b James	12	— not out	29
L. Harrison c Smith b James	4		
P. J. Sainsbury c Langridge b Smith	0		
D. Shackleton c Webb b Thomson	13		
V. H. D. Cannings not out	43		
M. Heath c Potter b James	33		
L-b 2	2	B 4, l-b 1	5

1/53 2/76 3/104 4/125 5/135 6/140   236
7/145 8/147 9/164

1/32 2/110   (3 wkts., dec.) 265
3/202

Sussex

J. Langridge c Barnard b Cannings	15	— b Shackleton	11
A. S. M. Oakman lbw b Cannings	34	— c Barnard b Shackleton	35
G. H. G. Doggart b Cannings	0	— b Gray	1
J. M. Parks c Barnard b Cannings	7	— lbw b Gray	3
K. G. Suttle lbw b Shackleton	32	— c Marshall b Gray	0
D. V. Smith c Sainsbury b Shackleton	14	— c Sainsbury b Cannings	20
G. Potter c Harrison b Shackleton	3	— c Sainsbury b Shackleton	32
G. Cox c Rogers b Shackleton	5	— b Heath	54
R. T. Webb b Heath	8	— lbw b Sainsbury	8
N. I. Thomson b Heath	9	— not out	24
A. E. James not out	1	— c Harrison b Shackleton	10
B 1, l-b 9	10	B 10, l-b 4	14

1/52 2/58 3/61 4/68 5/92 6/106   138
7/114 8/125 9/133

1/12 2/44 3/75 4/75 5/81   212
6/81 7/139 8/178 9/178

Sussex Bowling

	O.	M.	R.	W.		O.	M.	R.	W.
Thomson	28	7	63	2	....	17	2	60	2
James	29.2	8	105	4	....	22	7	85	0
Smith	28	6	64	4	....	15	2	57	0
Oakman	2	1	2	0	....	10	2	32	0
Cox						5	1	14	1
Parks						3	0	12	0

Hampshire Bowling

	O.	M.	R.	W.		O.	M.	R.	W.
Shackleton	21	7	39	4	....	22.2	8	43	4
Cannings	16	8	34	4	....	16	4	42	1
Heath	17.2	1	55	2	....	23	6	59	1
Gray						19	9	29	3
Sainsbury						6	2	25	1

Umpires: G. S. Mobey and A. J. B. Fowler.

HAMPSHIRE v. LANCASHIRE

At Portsmouth, August 10, 11, 12. Hampshire won by 39 runs after being sent in to bat for the second successive match. Rain which frequently interrupted their first innings made the pitch so difficult on the second day that 22 wickets fell for 184 runs. Heath and Shackleton made the ball lift viciously and Lancashire lost nine men for 48 before Washbrook declared. In similar conditions Hampshire's batting also broke down and before the close Lancashire began their second innings needing 232 to win. They reached 134 with only three wickets down but after Washbrook left, only Collins survived against the fast bowling of Heath who took the last four wickets in nineteen balls for five runs.

Hampshire

J. R. Gray c Wilson b Statham	6	— c Wilson b Statham 0
R. E. Marshall b Wharton	36	— c Ikin b Hilton 17
H. Horton c Wilson b Statham	31	— c Wilson b Hilton 9
A. W. H. Rayment c Wharton b Standring	31	— c Statham b Hilton 27
N. H. Rogers c Edrich b Hilton	7	— c Edrich b Standring 7
H. M. Barnard b Hilton	9	— c Collins b Wharton 10
L. Harrison c Wilson b Statham	17	— c Hilton b Statham 7
P. J. Sainsbury c Wilson b Standring	3	— c Barber b Hilton 12
D. Shackleton c Barber b Hilton	28	— not out 8
V. D. H. Cannings c Wilson b Statham..	3	— b Statham................. 0
M. Heath not out	2	— c Wilson b Hilton 0
B 5, w 1, n-b 1	7	L-b 1, n-b 1 2

1/40 2/44 3/100 4/114 5/122 6/134   180   1/0 2/24 3/29 4/44 5/70   99
7/142 8/160 9/172   6/71 7/85 8/91 9/94

Lancashire

J. T. Ikin c Barnard b Cannings	10	— lbw b Gray 25
J. Dyson c Rogers b Shackleton	2	— c Sainsbury b Shackleton .. 2
G. A. Edrich c Harrison b Heath	10	— c Rogers b Shackleton 38
C. Washbrook c Sainsbury b Heath	0	— c Harrison b Shackleton ... 45
A. Wharton c Sainsbury b Shackleton ..	2	— b Shackleton 23
R. W. Barber c Rogers b Heath	1	— lbw b Cannings 10
R. Collins c Sainsbury b Heath	8	— not out 39
K. B. Standring c Harrison b Heath	0	— c Marshall b Heath 4
M. J. Hilton c Barnard b Shackleton	13	— c Sainsbury b Heath 1
J. B. Statham not out	2	— b Heath 1
A. Wilson (did not bat)		— c Marshall b Heath 2
		B 2.................. 2

1/3 2/15 3/18 4/21   (9 wkts., dec.)   48   1/3 2/43 3/100 4/134   192
5/24 6/29 7/29 8/36 9/48   5/135 6/163 7/182 8/186
                                            9/190

Lancashire Bowling

	O.	M.	R.	W.		O.	M.	R.	W.
Statham	25	10	49	4	....	11	4	15	3
Standring	19	4	61	2	....	6	1	34	1
Wharton	14	4	44	1	....	3	0	9	1
Hilton	11.1	4	19	3	....	15.4	6	39	5

Hampshire Bowling

	O.	M.	R.	W.		O.	M.	R.	W.
Shackleton.....	11	5	24	3	....	26	13	31	4
Cannings	9	5	10	1	....	24	9	43	1
Heath	7	3	14	5	....	25.4	8	63	4
Sainsbury						19	6	36	0
Gray						4	2	17	1

Umpires: G. S. Mobey and A. J. B. Fowler.

At Nottingham, August 13, 15, 16. HAMPSHIRE drew with NOTTINGHAMSHIRE.

At Weston-super-Mare, August 17, 18. HAMPSHIRE beat SOMERSET by 264 runs.

At Southampton, August 20, 22, 23. HAMPSHIRE lost to SOUTH AFRICANS by 275 runs. (See SOUTH AFRICAN section.)

HAMPSHIRE v. SURREY

At Bournemouth, August 27, 29, 30. Hampshire won by 129 runs. This success over the county champions assured them of finishing higher in the Championship than ever before in their history. Hampshire took full advantage of an ideal batting pitch. Gray and Marshall began with a partnership of 102 in less than an hour and a half. Subsequently Horton stayed three hours forty minutes while Hampshire established a commanding position. Surrey were in danger of having to follow-on but an eighth wicket stand of 69 in an hour and a quarter between Laker and Lock saved them from this indignity. Hampshire scored at a brisk rate and set Surrey to get 304 in four hours. Pratt and Stewart kept the champion county ahead of the clock but at 56 Rogers threw out Stewart from mid-wicket and thereafter the only issue was whether Surrey would be dismissed in the time available. Sainsbury, the young left-arm slow bowler, taking four wickets in six overs after tea at a cost of 13 runs, hastened the end. Crowds swarmed in front of the pavilion to applaud the victors and Mr. H. S. Altham, president of the county, described it as a great day for Hampshire cricket.

Hampshire

J. R. Gray c Surridge b Laker 91	— c Surridge b Lock 22
R. E. Marshall c and b Laker 52	— c McIntyre b A. Bedser ... 14
H. Horton c Surridge b A..Bedser ...109	— c Stewart b Laker 22
A. W. H. Rayment lbw b Lock 14	— lbw b E. Bedser 43
N. H. Rogers b A. Bedser 27	— c Lock b E. Bedser 42
H. M. Barnard not out 42	— b E. Bedser 20
D. Shackleton c Constable b A. Bedser . 10	— c Surridge b E. Bedser 4
L. Harrison b Lock 0	— not out 0
B 11, l-b 12 23	B 4, l-b 8, w 1 13

1/102 2/194 3/250 4/302 (7 wkts., dec.) 368   1/43 2/43 (7 wkts., dec.) 180
5/330 6/360 7/368   3/75 4/141 5/176 6/180
7/180

P. J. Sainsbury, M. Heath and M. D. Burden did not bat.

Surrey

R. C. E. Pratt c Barnard b Burden 41	— c Horton b Gray 43
M. J. Stewart b Heath 9	— run out 27
K. Barrington b Shackleton 19	— c Burden b Gray 12
E. A. Bedser c Barnard b Heath 16	— c Marshall b Sainsbury ... 20
T. H. Clark c Heath b Sainsbury 5	— c Sainsbury b Gray....... 0
B. Constable c Marshall b Heath 22	— b Sainsbury 11
A. J. McIntyre c Harrison b Heath 8	— c Barnard b Sainsbury ... 26
J. C. Laker c Rayment b Burden 43	— lbw b Sainsbury 0
G. A. R. Lock not out 51	— c Marshall b Burden 14
W. S. Surridge c Burden b Heath 17	— st Harrison b Sainsbury ... 14
A. V. Bedser b Shackleton 11	— not out 0
L-b 3 3	B 4, l-b 3 7

1/16 2/69 3/70 4/77 5/97 6/109   245   1/56 2/81 3/104 4/109   174
7/126 8/195 9/222   5/109 6/132 7/132 8/159
9/169

Surrey Bowling

	O.	M.	R.	W.		O.	M.	R.	W.
A. Bedser......	23	1	73	3	....	15	4	35	1
Surridge	9	1	42	0	....	3	3	0	0
Lock	36	8	90	2	....	19	11	37	1
Laker	26	8	52	2	....	13	0	65	1
E. Bedser	19	3	37	0	....	5.5	0	30	4
Clark	18	5	51	0					

Hampshire Bowling

	O.	M.	R.	W.		O.	M.	R.	W.
Shackleton.....	26.3	8	63	2	....	9	1	26	0
Heath	27	5	69	5	....	5	0	23	0
Gray	16	6	41	0	....	16	6	48	3
Burden	12	4	34	2	....	7	1	30	1
Sainsbury......	23	12	35	1	....	19.2	9	40	5

Umpires: E. A. Roberts and W. F. Price.

HAMPSHIRE v. WORCESTERSHIRE

At Bournemouth, August 31, September 1, 2. Hampshire won by 79 runs in an exciting finish. Worcestershire, wanting 295 to win, lost nine wickets for 214 and Hampshire took the additional half-hour but almost immediately a drizzle stopped play. Six minutes later it ceased and Shackleton got Berry caught with his fifth ball. Solid batting enabled Hampshire to reach a respectable total. Perks, by taking five wickets, completed 100 wickets for the sixteenth consecutive time. With half their wickets standing Worcestershire required only 76 for the lead but Gray, using the new ball effectively, caused a collapse. Sound innings by H. Horton and Sainsbury, who made his highest score in first-class cricket, enabled Hampshire to declare shortly after lunch. Kenyon, passing 2,000 runs for the sixth successive year, did his best to stave off defeat, but Hampshire's superior all-round play told in the end.

Hampshire

J. R. Gray lbw b Jenkins	34	— lbw b Flavell	7
R. E. Marshall b Jenkins	30	— b Flavell	5
H. Horton b Perks.................	0	— c Kenyon b Horton	84
A. W. H. Rayment b Perks	46	— c Horton b Perks	18
N. H. Rogers lbw b Perks	50	— c Horton b Perks	29
H. M. Barnard b Perks	47	— c Broadbent b Berry	11
L. Harrison b Jenkins	6		
P. J. Sainsbury lbw b Perks	24	— not out	73
D. Shackleton b Jenkins	18	— b Horton b Berry	18
M. Heath not out	20	— not out	3
M. D. Burden c Berry b Jenkins	5		
B 3, l-b 9, w 1, n-b 1	14	B 2, l-b 3, n-b 2........	7

1/44 2/45 3/85 4/166 5/187 6/204   294
7/250 8/259 9/284

1/5 2/25   (7 wkts., dec.) 255
3/51 4/119 5/132 6/192
7/232

Worcestershire

D. Kenyon c Shackleton b Burden	58	— not out 103	
L. Outschoorn c Harrison b Heath......	6	— c Burden b Heath	5
R. G. Broadbent c Marshall b Shackleton	1	— b Heath	11
M. J. Horton c Sainsbury b Burden ...	55	— b Sainsbury	40
G. Dews c Shackleton b Burden	25	— lbw b Sainsbury 9	
J. Lister run out	57	— b Burden	26
R. O. Jenkins lbw b Gray	30	— st Harrison b Burden......	10
H. Yarnold c Burden b Gray.........	5	— c Gray b Heath	2
R. Berry c Sainsbury b Gray	8	— c Harrison b Shackleton ...	0
J. Flavell not out	4	— c Rayment b Burden	0
R. T. D. Perks b Shackleton	0	— b Burden	0
L-b 6	6	B 5, l-b 4	9

1/12 2/15 3/125 4/126 5/158 6/219   255
7/235 8/244 9/254

1/12 2/32 3/84 4/112   215
5/185 6/197 7/211 8/211
9/214

Worcestershire Bowling

	O.	M.	R.	W.		O.	M.	R.	W.
Perks	36	9	79	5	....	28	10	40	2
Flavell	12	2	53	0	....	11	1	34	2
Outschoorn ...	1	0	2	0					
Jenkins	23.1	4	91	5	....	12	0	46	0
Horton	10	4	36	0	....	16	3	68	1
Berry	10	4	19	0	....	22	10	60	2

Hampshire Bowling

	O.	M.	R.	W.		O.	M.	R.	W.
Shackleton.....	29.4	5	65	2	....	13.5	2	30	1
Heath	26	4	60	1	....	14	3	33	3
Sainsbury......	16	8	28	0	....	19	4	80	2
Gray	15	4	38	3					
Burden	15	4	58	3	....	20	4	63	4

Umpires: E. A. Roberts and G. S. Mobey.

KENT

President—Col. A. O. B. Ffrench-Blake

Secretary—Nevill Christopherson, St. Lawrence Ground, Canterbury

Captain—D. V. P. Wright

R. C. Wilson County Badge J. M. Allan

Any team deprived for most of the season of its best batsman, its only bowler of genuine pace and a wicket-keeper of supreme quality may be excused some shortcomings. For that reason Kent should not, perhaps, be judged too harshly on their performance in 1955, when they dropped from 11th to 13th in the table.

Cowdrey, whose cricket was upset first by conscription to the R.A.F. and then, following his medical discharge, by a recurrent hand injury, played in only nine of the twenty-eight Championship games. Illness kept Ridgway idle after six matches, and Evans had appeared for his county only eight times when a broken finger, received in the Third Test, ended his season abruptly. The loss of Cowdrey was probably felt most for it was in the batting that the inspiration of a top-class player was specially needed. Fagg, Phebey, Wilson and Hearn all showed against the South Africans that they were capable of playing attractive forcing strokes against the best bowling. Yet too often they and their colleagues were tied to a niggardly rate of scoring by moderate attacks.

Cowdrey did not come into the side until June, and then it was with a flourish. He hit three centuries, including two against Essex at Gillingham, in his first three games, but his form suffered later when, at the request of the England selectors, he was tried as an opening batsman.

Ironically, Cowdrey was away playing for England when Wright and his team enjoyed their supreme moment—the dramatic defeat of Surrey at The Oval. This totally unexpected victory over the Champions emphasised the value to Kent of the Oxford Blue,

Allan, whose accurate left-arm slow bowling made him an ideal partner to Wright. In match after match he closed one end while his captain, rejoicing in the hard, fast pitches, attacked from the other. He helped Wright to enjoy one of his best seasons.

Allan's batting was notable more for its determination than freedom of stroke play, but he also hit three hundreds for the county and, at Northampton, emulated Cowdrey with one in each innings. He fully earned his county cap. Pretlove, who played against Allan in the University match, joined the county as assistant secretary immediately afterwards and made several appearances as a left-handed batsman. Wilson added to his growing reputation with two excellent innings against Middlesex at Dover. He and Dixon, a young right-handed batsman and off-spin bowler of high promise, stood out in a side that did not earn many tributes for fielding.

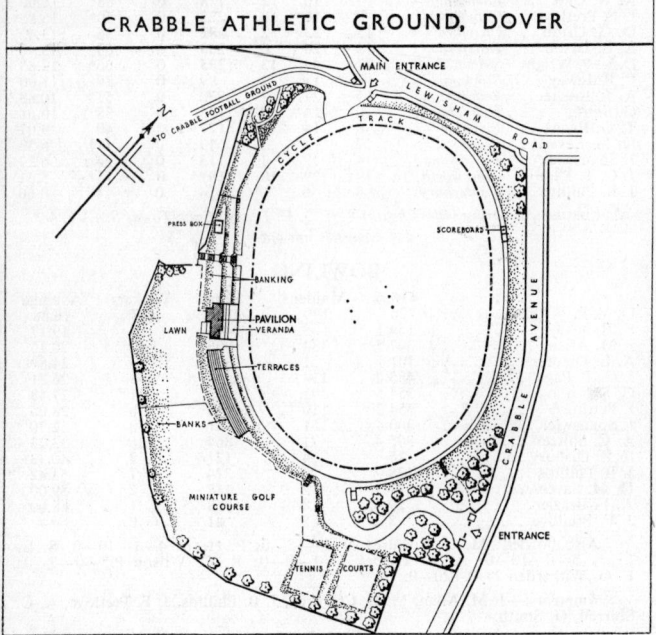

CRABBLE ATHLETIC GROUND, DOVER

KENT RESULTS

All First-Class Matches—Played 29, *Won* 8, *Lost* 14, *Drawn* 7

County Championship Matches—Played 28, *Won* 8, *Lost* 13,
Drawn 7

COUNTY CHAMPIONSHIP AVERAGES
BATTING

	Birthplace	Mtchs.	Inns.	Not Outs	Runs	100's	Highest Inns.	Aver.
M. C. Cowdrey	*Bangalore*	9	16	3	737	3	139	56.69
J. M. Allan ...	*Leeds*	12	21	1	665	3	121*	33.25
R. C. Wilson..	*Bapchild*	22	42	4	1152	1	107	30.31
J. Pettiford ...	*Sydney, N.S.W.*	28	51	8	1197	0	90	27.83
A. C. Shirreff .	*Ealing*	11	19	0	519	0	77	27.31
A. E. Fagg ...	*Chartham*	28	54	1	1291	1	106	24.35
A. H. Phebey .	*Catford*	22	43	2	945	1	122	23.04
E. G. Witherden	*Goudhurst*	6	10	2	171	0	69	21.37
P. Hearn	*Tunbridge Wells*	17	31	4	559	0	87*	20.70
B. E. Disbury .	*Bedford*	5	7	2	90	0	26*	18.00
A. W. Catt ...	*Edenbridge*	7	10	2	128	0	88*	16.00
J. F. Pretlove ..	*Camberwell*	9	16	2	222	0	60*	15.85
D. G. Ufton ..	*Crayford*	13	23	2	282	0	36	13.42
A. L. Dixon ..	*Dartford*	12	20	0	268	0	63	13.40
D. V. P. Wright	*Sidcup*	27	43	13	385	0	66*	12.83
F. Ridgway ..	*Stockport*	6	11	2	99	0	26	11.00
A. F. Brazier..	*Paddington*	15	27	2	272	0	51*	10.88
G. Smith	*Huddersfield*	10	16	3	138	0	38	10.61
T. G. Evans ..	*Finchley*	8	14	0	127	0	40	9.07
D. M. Sayer ..	*Romford*	2	3	1	13	0	11*	6.50
J. Spanswick ..	*Folkestone*	14	19	1	113	0	24	6.27
J. C. T. Page .	*Mereworth*	19	29	10	101	0	15*	5.31
J. B. Phillips ..	*Canterbury*	4	6	0	4	0	4	0.66

Also batted: C. Dring (*Blackheath*) 8, 0; S. E. Leary (*Cape Town, S.A.*) 1, 48*.

* *Signifies not out.*

BOWLING

	Overs	Maidens	Runs	Wickets	Average
D. V. P. Wright	726	190	2145	127	16.88
F. Ridgway	159.1	33	441	23	19.17
J. M. Allan	367.5	134	806	40	20.15
A. L. Dixon	101.1	21	323	13	24.84
J. C. T. Page	485.2	114	1526	58	26.31
G. Smith	354.5	101	852	31	27.48
J. Pettiford	354.2	110	1010	36	28.05
J. Spanswick	300.4	51	981	30	32.70
A. C. Shirreff	305.4	71	864	26	33.23
B. E. Disbury	26	4	121	3	40.33
J. B. Phillips	128	24	374	7	53.42
D. M. Sayer	31	2	118	2	59.00
A. F. Brazier..........	29.4	8	68	1	68.00
J. F. Pretlove	8.2	2	41	0	—

Also bowled: M. C. Cowdrey 4—1—13—0; P. Hearn 4—1—10—0; S. E. Leary 3—0—10—0; A. H. Phebey 1—1—0—0; R. C. Wilson 0.5—0—7—0; E. G. Witherden 2—0—20—0.

Amateurs.—J. M. Allan, M. C. Cowdrey, J. B. Phillips, J. F. Pretlove, A. C. Shirreff, G. Smith.

At Leicester, May 7, 9, 10. KENT drew with LEICESTERSHIRE.

KENT v. LEICESTERSHIRE

At Gravesend, May 14, 16, Leicestershire won by six wickets with forty minutes to spare on the second day. They owed most to the efforts of their Australians, Walsh and Jackson. Kent had no answer to the left-arm "chinamen" and googlies of Walsh in their first innings, but their own spin bowlers failed to make the same use of a drying pitch. Hallam and Jackson, who was caught attempting to complete his century in under two hours with a third six, assured Leicestershire of a commanding lead. Jackson followed with a devastating spell of off-spin bowling. Fagg batted skilfully but Leicestershire needed only 99 to win.

Kent

A. E. Fagg c Palmer b Boshier	8	— b Munden	94
A. H. Phebey b Walsh	36	— c Hallam b Jackson	23
A. C. Shirreff b Walsh	16	— lbw b Walsh	6
R. C. Wilson b Walsh	16	— c Smithson b Jackson	40
J. Pettiford b Lester	1	— c Hallam b Jackson	0
A. F. Brazier b Walsh	0	— c Spencer b Jackson	4
P. Hearn not out	11	— not out	25
T. G. Evans c Spencer b Walsh	5	— c Spencer b Jackson	9
F. Ridgway c Boshier b Lester	14	— b Jackson	26
D. V. P. Wright lbw b Walsh	2	— b Walsh	10
J. C. T. Page lbw b Walsh	0	— c Hallam b Jackson	4
N-b 1	1	B 4, l-b 5	9
	110		250

1/43 2/58 3/69 4/78 5/78 6/78
7/83 8/108 9/110

1/69 2/90 3/167 4/171
5/175 6/176 7/188 8/222
9/245

Leicestershire

G. Lester b Ridgway	1	— b Wright	31
M. R. Hallam b Ridgway	76	— lbw b Ridgway	18
M. Tompkin c Shirreff b Page	39	— c Evans b Ridgway	6
C. H. Palmer lbw b Wright	10	— c Wilson b Page	33
G. A. Smithson c Fagg b Page	2	— not out	1
V. E. Jackson c Shirreff b Page	99	— not out	12
V. Munden b Page	25		
J. E. Walsh c Fagg b Ridgway	1		
J. Firth c and b Page	1		
C. T. Spencer not out	4		
B 1, l-b 2, w 1	4		
	262		101

1/2 2/70 3/95 4/116   (9 wkts., dec.) 262
5/156 6/239 7/246 8/247 9/262

1/29 2/35 3/80   (4 wkts.) 101
4/88

B. Boshier did not bat.

Leicestershire Bowling

	O.	M.	R.	W.		O.	M.	R.	W.
Spencer	7	1	23	0	....	3	0	23	0
Boshier	9	2	18	1	....	3	0	18	0
Walsh	16.3	5	35	7	....	28	6	84	2
Jackson	4	1	4	0	....	32.4	15	62	7
Munden	5	2	9	0	....	20	11	35	1
Lester	5	0	20	2	....	5	2	19	0

Kent Bowling

	O.	M.	R.	W.		O.	M.	R.	W.
Ridgway	18	4	55	3	....	11	1	38	2
Shirreff	6	3	15	0	....	2	0	9	0
Page	24.5	8	99	5	....	12	4	45	1
Pettiford	5	0	34	0					
Wright	10	0	55	1	....	3.4	2	9	1

Umpires: P. Corrall and G. S. Mobey.

KENT v. DERBYSHIRE

At Gravesend, May 18, 19. 20. Derbyshire won by an innings and 51 runs, the match being a personal triumph for their young all-rounder Morgan. After upsetting Kent's first innings with his fast-medium bowling, Morgan arrived at the crease when Derbyshire were struggling on a rain-affected pitch to build a worthwhile lead. In little over two hours he hit his maiden century with the help of sixteen 4's. Kent lost wickets steadily to keen bowling and fielding and when it seemed that an approaching storm might save them from defeat Morgan hastened the end by dismissing the last three men for 12 runs. Kent were unlucky to lose Wilson with a sprained wrist in the second innings.

Kent

A. E. Fagg lbw b Jackson	0	— c Dawkes b Gladwin	0
A. H. Phebey c Dawkes b Morgan	37	— st Dawkes b Smith	8
A. C. Shirreff c Revill b Gladwin	20	— c Morgan b Gladwin	15
R. C. Wilson c Carr b Smith	31	— retired hurt...............	16
J. Pettiford b Morgan	27	— b Morgan	36
A. F. Brazier b Morgan	3	— b Gladwin	3
P. Hearn c and b Smith	1	— c Johnson b Smith	2
T. G. Evans c Dawkes b Morgan	1	— st Dawkes b Smith	14
F. Ridgway not out	9	— b Morgan	4
D. V. P. Wright b Jackson	3	— b Morgan	4
J. C. T. Page c Morgan b Jackson	9	— not out	4
B 1, l b 5	6	L-b 6, n-b 1	7

1/0 2/35 3/74 4/100 5/116 6/121   147   1/1 2/28 3/36 4/52   113
7/123 8/124 9/133   5/59 6/85 7/90 8/100

Derbyshire

A. Hamer c Wilson b Page	35	G. O. Dawkes c Evans b Pettiford	4
J. Kelly b Wright	19	C. Gladwin b Wright	13
C. Lee c Fagg b Wright	11	E. Smith not out	23
A. C. Revill c Pettiford b Page ..	37	B 8, l-b 11, w 1	20
D. B. Carr c Ridgway b Wright ..	5		
H. L. Johnson b Pettiford	35	1/57 2/67 3/100 (8 wkts., dec.) 311
D. C. Morgan not out 109		4/112 5/134 6/201 7/205 8/241

L. Jackson did not bat.

Derbyshire Bowling

	O.	M.	R.	W.		O.	M.	R.	W.
Jackson	17.4	5	33	3	....	10	4	23	0
Gladwin	20	8	42	1	....	22	9	40	3
Morgan	18	8	43	4	....	5.3	2	12	3
Smith	17	8	23	2	....	22	9	31	3

Kent Bowling

	O.	M.	R.	W.
Ridgway	16	2	46	0
Shirreff	5	0	23	0
Page	35	5	123	2
Wright	30	14	74	4
Pettiford	11	3	25	2

Umpires: P. Corrall and G. S. Mobey.

At Gloucester, May 21, 23, 24. KENT beat GLOUCESTERSHIRE by eight wickets.

At Derby, May 25, 26. KENT lost to DERBYSHIRE by an innings and 21 runs.

At Southampton, May 28, 30, 31. KENT drew with HAMPSHIRE.

At Manchester, June 1, 2, 3. KENT lost to LANCASHIRE by 167 runs.

KENT v. NOTTINGHAMSHIRE

At Blackheath, June 4, 6, 7. Drawn. Rain delayed the start by an hour and prevented play on the final day. Except during a brief spell after lunch when Dooland and Smales turned the ball sharply, the pitch dried out too easily to justify Simpson's decision to give Kent first innings. Pettiford batted determinedly during an awkward period, and Dixon and Smith began a complete recovery with 75 runs for the eighth wicket. Nottinghamshire batted with confidence, Poole (thirteen 4's) making strokes all round the wicket for just over two hours, but Pettiford and Wright bowled leg-breaks persistently, and 26 runs were needed for the lead when the eighth wicket fell. Jepson, by bold hitting, made sure of this.

Kent

A. E. Fagg c Dooland b Smales	23	— not out	2
A. H. Phebey c Wood b Dooland	27	— not out	10
P. Hearn lbw b Dooland	0		
J. Pettiford b Jepson	45		
B. E. Disbury lbw b Harvey	14		
E. G. Witherden c Harvey b Jepson	17		
A. Dixon b Jepson	63		
T. G. Evans c Harvey b Jepson	5		
G. Smith b Harvey	38		
D. V. P. Wright c Clay b Wood	31		
J. C. T. Page not out	15		
B 3, l-b 9	12	L-b 1	1
	290	(No wkt.)	13

1/46 2/46 3/62 4/91 5/136 6/139
7/147 8/222 9/258

Nottinghamshire

R. T. Simpson b Pettiford	33	A. Jepson c Evans b Smith	47
J. D. Clay b Pettiford	31	E. J. Rowe lbw b Disbury	16
C. J. Poole c Phebey b Smith	90	M. Wood not out	0
J. Hardstaff b Page	16		
E. J. Martin c Wright b Pettiford	41	B 21, l-b 3, w 1, n-b 4	29
P. F. Harvey c Evans b Pettiford	12		
B. Dooland c Evans b Wright	17	1/54 2/69 3/121 4/212 5/240	339
K. Smales c Fagg b Wright	7	6/245 7/264 8/265 9/335	

Nottinghamshire Bowling

	O.	M.	R.	W.		O.	M.	R.	W.
Jepson	40	8	100	4	....	2	1	5	0
Wood	14.5	2	46	1	....	2	0	7	0
Dooland	41	14	86	2					
Smales	16	8	17	1					
Harvey	14	6	29	2					

Kent Bowling

	O.	M.	R.	W.
Smith	19.2	5	56	2
Disbury	6	0	30	1
Pettiford	37	13	90	4
Wright	27	7	82	2
Page	12	3	40	1
Dixon	5	1	12	0

Umpires: A. J. B. Fowler and G. S. Mobey.

At Lord's, June 8, 9, 10. KENT beat MIDDLESEX by six wickets.

At Yeovil, June 11, 13, 14. KENT lost to SOMERSET by three wickets.

At Hull, June 15, 16, 17. KENT lost to YORKSHIRE by ten wickets.

KENT v. NORTHAMPTONSHIRE

At Tunbridge Wells, June 18, 20, 21. Kent won by 142 runs after a remarkable transformation. Ten minutes after the start of the final day they needed 51 runs to save an innings defeat with six wickets left. Then Cowdrey and Wilson added 227 in three hours twenty minutes. On a pitch helpful to bowlers, Cowdrey, missed before scoring, gave a brilliant display in his first county match of the season. He punished the loose deliveries with such certainty and power that 108 of his 139 runs came from 28 hits—two 6's and twenty-four 4's. Wilson hit fifteen 4's. So Kent set their opponents to score 203, and won with twenty-five minutes in hand. Northamptonshire, who received only limited service from Tyson because of a sore heel, went ahead on the first innings with their opening pair, Brookes and Arnold, still together. Arnold (twelve 4's) equalled his highest score.

Kent

A. E. Fagg c Barrick b Clarke	11	—	c Subba Row b Broderick	34
A. H. Phebey lbw b Tyson	6	—	b Tribe	33
R. C. Wilson b Tribe	57	—	b Starkie	90
M. C. Cowdrey b Clarke	5	—	run out	139
J. Pettiford c Tribe b Tyson	5	—	not out	9
A. Dixon c Andrew b Clarke	0	—	c sub b Subba Row	11
D. G. Ufton b Clarke	36	—	not out	6
G. Smith b Broderick	13			
J. Spanswick b Clarke	0			
D. V. P. Wright not out	18	—	c Starkie b Broderick	0
J. C. T. Page b Broderick	2	—	b Broderick	7
B 4, l-b 4	8		B 5, l-b 4, n-b 1	10

1/17 2/17 3/31 4/64 5/69 6/108   161   1/72 2/72   (7 wkts., dec.) 339
7/139 8/139 9/147   3/72 4/86 5/313 6/313 7/328

Northamptonshire

D. Brookes c Ufton b Pettiford	71	— c Dixon b Spanswick	7
P. Arnold c and b Wright	118	— run out	18
L. Livingston b Pettiford	18	— c Ufton b Spanswick	0
D. Barrick b Smith	21	— run out	3
R. Subba Row not out	35	— c Smith b Spanswick	2
G. E. Tribe c Phebey b Smith	0	— c Phebey b Page	5
V. Broderick c Wilson b Spanswick	6	— not out	14
F. H. Tyson c Phebey b Smith	7	— absent hurt	0
S. Starkie (did not bat)		— b Page	0
R. W. Clarke (did not bat)		— b Page	0
K. V. Andrew (did not bat)		— lbw b Wright	6
B 13, l-b 8, w 1	22	B 4, l-b 1	5

1/166 2/198 3/240   (7 wkts., dec.) 298   1/23 2/23 3/29 4/29   60
4/250 5/252 6/267 7/298   5/34 6/43 7/43 8/43 9/60

Northamptonshire Bowling

	O.	M.	R.	W.	O.	M.	R.	W.
Tyson	14	3	27	2	1	0	10	0
Clarke	25	10	48	5	10	1	37	0
Tribe	19	3	44	1	27	8	75	1
Barrick	5	2	3	0	8	1	26	0
Starkie	11	6	15	0	23	8	68	1
Broderick	12.2	5	16	2	32	14	77	3
Subba Row					7.2	1	36	1

Kent Bowling

	O.	M.	R.	W.	O.	M.	R.	W.
Spanswick	21	3	63	1	9	2	23	3
Smith	26.3	6	56	3	9	4	13	0
Pettiford	18	6	56	2	2	1	4	0
Page	20	3	63	0	5	3	6	3
Dixon	4	1	10	0				
Wright	12	3	28	1	7.5	3	9	1

Umpires: T. Spencer and J. J. Hills.

KENT v. SUSSEX

At Tunbridge Wells, June 22, 23, 24. Kent won by 104 runs with quarter of an hour to spare. They began well, but Smith, left-arm medium, caused trouble, the last seven wickets falling for 94 runs. Despite good batting by Oakman, Sussex lost seven wickets before taking the lead, but Thomson and Webb hit briskly. Facing arrears of 29, Kent did better, thanks in large measure to careful play for four and a half hours by Fagg, and despite accurate off-break bowling by Marlar, Sussex needed 248 to win, a task which proved beyond their powers.

Kent

A. E. Fagg c Suttle b Smith	46	— lbw b Marlar	106
A. H. Phebey b Smith	31	— b Marlar	19
R. C. Wilson lbw b Smith	17	— c Oakman b Marlar	7
M. C. Cowdrey c Cox b Marlar	48	— c Parks b Marlar	44
J. Pettiford lbw b Smith	0	— not out	41
A. C. Shirreff c Webb b Smith	9	— c Sheppard b Marlar	30
A. Dixon b Thomson	14	— c Oakman b Thomson	12
D. G. Ufton c Langridge b Marlar	1	— c Langridge b Marlar	8
J. C. T. Page c Webb b Thomson	6		
D. V. P. Wright run out	15		
D. M. Sayer not out	11		
L-b 6	6	B 5, l-b 4	9

1/56 2/87 3/110 4/110 5/130 6/154   204   1/74 2/94   (7 wkts., dec.) 276
7/162 8/174 9/189   3/161 4/206 5/248 6/267 7/276

Sussex

J. Langridge c Dixon b Sayer	6	— c Phebey b Shirreff 12
D. V. Smith c Ufton b Shirreff	1	— b Pettiford 5
A. S. M. Oakman lbw b Page	53	— b Page 15
J. M. Parks c Wright b Shirreff	35	— lbw b Pettiford 10
D. S. Sheppard lbw b Shirreff	4	— c Fagg b Page 7
K. G. Suttle b Pettiford	26	— c Pettiford b Page 23
G. Cox lbw b Wright	33	— c Fagg b Shirreff 39
N. I. Thomson c Wilson b Pettiford	30	— c Fagg b Wright 7
R. T. Webb not out	30	— lbw b Wright 4
R. G. Marlar c Wilson b Pettiford	0	— b Wright 4
D. J. Wood c Dixon b Pettiford	0	— not out 0
B 8, l-b 6, n-b 1	15	B 12, l-b 2, n-b 3 17
	233	143

1/11 2/17 3/75 4/85 5/128 6/144
7/180 8/220 9/233

1/33 2/72 3/72 4/79
5/102 6/122 7/122 8/136 9/142

Sussex Bowling

	O.	M.	R.	W.		O.	M.	R.	W.
Thomson	21.4	6	46	2	....	19	4	49	1
Wood	8	0	27	0	....	5	1	19	0
Smith	30	18	35	5	....	42	13	80	0
Marlar	36	11	79	2	....	58.5	22	111	6
Oakman	2	0	11	0	....	3	0	8	0

Kent Bowling

	O.	M.	R.	W.		O.	M.	R.	W.
Shirreff	26	8	64	3	....	13	4	34	2
Sayer	12	1	43	1	....	3	0	18	0
Wright	12	4	45	1	....	7.3	3	27	3
Page	13	4	43	1	....	17	7	33	3
Pettiford	11.3	3	23	4	....	8	3	13	2

Umpires: T. Spencer and J. J. Hills.

KENT v. ESSEX

At Gillingham, June 25, 27, 28. Kent won by five wickets with three minutes remaining. The game was rendered memorable by the performances of Insole and Cowdrey. Each hit two separate hundreds in a match for the first time and Insole became the first player to reach 1,000 runs. On an awkward pitch, Insole saved Essex in the first innings, he and Greensmith adding 142 for the eighth wicket. In turn Cowdrey (fourteen 4's) helped Kent to a lead of 35 and a declaration. Then Insole shared with Gibb in a stand of 117 and enabled Essex to declare and leave Kent to get 206 in two and a quarter hours. Despite the loss of three men for 28, Kent kept up with the clock and Cowdrey and Hearn in a partnership of 152 in an hour and a quarter, virtually decided the issue.

Essex

T. C. Dodds c Smith b Spanswick	21	— c Smith b Spanswick ... 25
G. Barker c Ufton b Spanswick	10	— c Fagg b Spanswick 8
P. A. Gibb c Hearn b Page	38	— lbw b Smith 53
R. Ralph c Spanswick b Smith	1	— not out 0
D. J. Insole c Spanswick b Page	111	— c Phebey b Smith 118
R. Horsfall b Page	17	— c Ufton b Spanswick 0
M. Bear c Ufton b Page	0	— not out 19
R. Smith b Smith	8	— c Wilson b Page 12
W. T. Greensmith not out	63	
G. Smith c Cowdrey b Smith	1	
K. C. Preston lbw b Page	11	
B 1, l-b 4	5	L-b 2, w 1 3
	286	(6 wkts., dec.) 240

1/29 2/32 3/33 4/81 5/113 6/113
7/126 8/268 9/269

1/30 2/33   (6 wkts., dec.) 240
3/41 4/158 5/171 6/237

Kent

A. E. Fagg c Gibb b Greensmith	49	— lbw b Preston	15
A. H. Phebey c Insole b R. Smith	0	— b Preston	6
R. C. Wilson b Ralph	52	— c Dodds b R. Smith	7
M. C. Cowdrey not out	115	— not out	103
P. Hearn c Gibb b Ralph	3	— b Preston	60
J. Pettiford run out	30		
A. L. Dixon b R. Smith	32	— b Ralph	10
D. G. Ufton not out	35		
G. Smith (did not bat)		— not out	0
L-b 4, w 1	5	B 2, l-b 6	8

1/0 2/92 3/110 4/114   (6 wkts., dec.) 321   1/9 2/28 3/28   (5 wkts.) 209
5/174 6/270   4/180 5/205

J. Spanswick and J. C. T. Page did not bat.

Kent Bowling

	O.	M.	R.	W.		O.	M.	R.	W.
Spanswick	18	4	48	2	....	18	3	75	3
Smith	33	15	75	3	....	26	4	62	2
Page	41.2	11	110	5	....	21	3	82	1
Pettiford	17	7	39	0					
Dixon	3	1	9	0	....	3	0	9	0
Cowdrey					....	2	0	9	0

Essex Bowling

	O.	M.	R.	W.		O.	M.	R.	W.
Preston	21	4	69	0	....	11.1	1	57	3
R. Smith	22	4	56	2	....	4	0	19	1
Ralph	33	7	80	2	....	8	1	33	1
Insole	5	0	18	0					
Greensmith	27	5	58	1	....	10	1	36	0
G. Smith	16	7	35	0	....	3	0	18	0
Dodds						8	1	38	0

Umpires: H. G. Baldwin and E. Cooke.

KENT v. SURREY

At Blackheath, July 2, 4. Surrey won by an innings and 28 runs. Kent were completely outplayed on the first day which Surrey finished 233 ahead with five wickets down, and although they batted more resolutely in the second innings the result was never in doubt. A crowd of 12,000, the biggest at the Rectory Field for many years, saw Kent collapse on a perfect pitch against Lock, who became the first bowler to take one hundred wickets during the season. Fletcher and Stewart gave Surrey the lead without loss, completing their first century opening stand in eighty minutes, and May and Stewart added 125 in another seventy minutes. Cowdrey led Kent's rally on the second day, powerful drives earning most of his thirteen 4's, but after his stand with Wilson was broken Surrey met with little more resistance.

Kent

A. E. Fagg c McIntyre b Lock	....	49	— lbw b Laker	....	18
A. H. Phebey c Stewart b A. Bedser	....	0	— c McIntyre b Kelleher	....	4
R. C. Wilson b A. Bedser	....	4	— b Lock	....	35
M. C. Cowdrey st McIntyre b Laker	...	3	— b A. Bedser	....	67
J. Pettiford c May b Lock	....	0	— b E. Bedser	....	31
A. Dixon c Stewart b Lock	....	2	— c May b A. Bedser	....	0
T. G. Evans c May b Laker	....	11	— b A. Bedser	....	0
G. Smith lbw b Laker	....	4	— c McIntyre b E. Bedser	....	28
J. Spanswick c Stewart b Lock	....	18	— not out	....	6
D. V. P. Wright c May b Lock	....	3	— c Constable b Lock	....	4
J. C. T. Page not out	....	1	— b E. Bedser	....	4
B 4, l-b 8	....	12	B 2, l-b 6	....	8

1/3 2/21 3/37 4/46 5/60 6/81 7/81   107   1/22 2/25 3/115 4/143   205
8/103 9/103   5/145 6/145 7/190 8/191
                                       9/200

Surrey

D. G. W. Fletcher b Dixon	....	62	A. J. McIntyre not out	....	10
M. J. Stewart c Pettiford b Smith	..	118			
P. B. H. May c Spanswick b Dixon		102	B 4, l-b 6, n-b 3	....	13
B. Constable c Phebey b Dixon	...	30			
K. Barrington not out	....	5	1/118 2/243 3/316 (5 wkts., dec.)		340
E. A. Bedser lbw b Page	....	0	4/325 5/326		

J. C. Laker, G. A. R. Lock, A. V. Bedser and H. R. A. Kelleher did not bat.

Surrey Bowling

	O.	M.	R.	W.	O.	M.	R.	W.
A. Bedser	6	1	12	2	17	5	43	3
Kelleher	4	1	6	0	7	3	6	1
Lock	18.2	8	43	5	29	10	61	2
Laker	17	6	34	3	21	6	52	1
E. Bedser					12.4	6	35	3

Kent Bowling

	O.	M.	R.	W.
Smith	19	4	62	1
Spanswick	16	2	79	0
Page	16	3	61	1
Wright	9	0	54	0
Pettiford	1	0	8	0
Dixon	19	5	63	3

Umpires: F. S. Lee and L. H. Gray.

At Worcester, July 6, 7, 8. KENT lost to WORCESTERSHIRE by 188 runs.

At The Oval, July 9, 11, 12. KENT beat SURREY by 13 runs.

At Hastings, July 16, 18, 19. KENT lost to SUSSEX by nine wickets.

KENT v. LANCASHIRE

At Maidstone, July 20, 21, 22. Drawn. Both sides were to blame for a match which was of no credit to cricket. Its spirit was so far removed from the Festival mood that seventeen and a half hours' play in ideal conditions produced a total of only 805 runs and twenty-three wickets. Kent began the tedium by scoring only 206 for six on the first day and, although Wright brought some colour to the game by his bold batting on the second morning, his surprising declaration left Lancashire with little to play for but first innings points. These were won shortly before lunch on the last day, Grieves batting three hours fifty minutes for his 119.

Kent

A. E. Fagg c Jordan b Moore	14	— lbw b Moore	6
J. M. Allan lbw b Wharton	25	— run out	1
A. C. Shirreff lbw b Ikin	46	— c Standring b Dyson	60
J. F. Pretlove b Hilton	28	— not out	60
J. Pettiford not out	73	— b Hilton	1
A. H. Phebey b Standring	9	— c and b Tattersall	20
A. F. Brazier c Moore b Hilton	36	— not out	8
D. G. Ufton b Standring	5		
J. Spanswick c Grieves b Standring	0		
D. V. P. Wright not out	47		
B 8, l-b 2, n-b 1	11	B 7	7

1/27 2/54 3/111 4/115   (8 wkts., dec.) 294   1/10 2/50   (5 wkts., dec.) 163
5/135 6/199 7/215 8/215   3/127 4/137 5/139

J. C. T. Page did not bat.

Lancashire

J. T. Ikin c Brazier b Shirreff	12	M. J. Hilton c Phebey b Page	22
J. Dyson c Ufton b Page	41	F. W. Moore c Pretlove b Spanswick	0
G. A. Edrich lbw b Shirreff	0	R. Tattersall not out	0
C. Washbrook lbw b Spanswick	63		
A. Wharton c Shirreff b Spanswick	53	B 18, l-b 5	23
K. Grieves c Ufton b Spanswick	119		
K. B. Standring b Wright	13	1/30 2/38 3/101 4/143 5/230	348
J. Jordan c Fagg b Page	2	6/260 7/295 8/345 9/345	

Lancashire Bowling

	O.	M.	R.	W.		O.	M.	R.	W.
Moore	32	11	58	1	....	11	2	19	1
Standring	20	6	44	3	....	5	2	9	0
Tattersall	36	14	82	0	....	14	5	31	1
Wharton	9	4	19	1	....	7	0	8	0
Hilton	45	21	60	2	....	16	6	34	1
Ikin	14	6	20	1	....	6	2	11	0
Dyson						12	3	40	1
Washbrook						1	0	4	0

Kent Bowling

	O.	M.	R.	W.
Shirreff	45	10	113	2
Spanswick	30	3	64	4
Wright	27	5	78	1
Page	23	15	61	3
Allan	9	3	9	0

Umpires: L. H. Gray and G. S. Mobey.

KENT v. GLAMORGAN

At Maidstone, July 23, 25, 26. Kent won by 63 runs. Kent's batting showed some improvement on the previous match but Glamorgan provided the most attractive stroke play. Fagg and Wilson gave Kent a useful start with a second wicket partnership of 128 in just under three hours but the later batsmen struggled against the accurate left-arm medium paced bowling of Watkins. Glamorgan began in enterprising fashion, but a splendid spell of seven overs by Pettiford, in which he took five wickets for 16 runs, left Kent with an advantage of 27. Kent, helped by a solid display from Pettiford, set their opponents to get 229 in three hours fifty minutes, but Glamorgan failed on a wearing pitch against the leg-breaks of Wright.

Kent

A. E. Fagg c Watkins b Wooller	76	—	lbw b Wooller		23
A. C. Shirreff c Wooller b H. D. Davies	2	—	c H. G. Davies b Watkins		32
R. C. Wilson c Pressdee b H. D. Davies	63	—	b Pressdee		28
J. F. Pretlove b H. D. Davies	1	—	lbw b Ward		3
J. Pettiford b Watkins	29	—	c Pressdee b H. D. Davies		47
P. Hearn c H. G. Davies b Watkins	1	—	st H. G. Davies b Ward		4
A. F Brazier lbw b Watkins	2	—	lbw b Pressdee		28
D. G. Ufton c and b Watkins	6	—	c H. G. Davies b Pressdee		7
G. Smith not out	16	—	lbw b Pressdee		8
J. Spanswick c H. G. Davies b Shepherd	5	—	b Pressdee		5
D. V. P. Wright c H. G. Davies b Shepherd	4	—	not out		13
L-b 4, n-b 5	9		B 3		3

1/3 2/131 3/128 4/167 5/168 6/181   214   1/49 2/67 3/106 4/113   201
7/182 8/193 9/210   5/118 6/124 7/135 8/151
                                                             9/163

Glamorgan

W. Wooller lbw b Wright	31	—	c Fagg b Shirreff		7
W. G. A. Parkhouse lbw b Wright	23	—	b Shirreff		19
B. Hedges lbw b Smith	24	—	c Pettiford b Smith		2
W. E. Jones c Ufton b Wright	6	—	run out		11
A. J. Watkins c Wright b Pettiford	40	—	b Wright		10
J. Pleass st Ufton b Pettiford	29	—	c Spanswick b Wright		37
J. Pressdee b Pettiford	3	—	c Brazier b Wright		18
D. J. Ward st Ufton b Wright	7	—	c Brazier b Wright		0
H. G. Davies lbw b Pettiford	12	—	not out		29
H. D. Davies not out	4	—	st Ufton b Wright		0
D. J. Shepherd c Wilson b Pettiford	0	—	b Wright		12
L-b 3, w 4, n-b 1	8		B 12, l-b 2, w 4, n-b 2		20

1/51 2/80 3/90 4/90 5/159 6/164   187   1/26 2/27 3/37 4/50 5/73   165
7/165 8/175 9/187   6/101 7/101 8/136 9/146

Glamorgan Bowling

	O.	M.	R.	W.		O.	M.	R.	W.
H. D. Davies	22	7	52	3	....	11.2	2	34	1
Shepherd	20.5	3	56	2	....	9	3	10	0
Wooller	23	7	45	1	....	12	3	31	1
Watkins	25	9	52	4	....	11	4	24	1
Pressdee						33	16	46	5
Jones						5	2	10	0
Ward						21	4	43	2

Kent Bowling

	O.	M.	R.	W.		O.	M.	R.	W.
Spanswick	4	0	18	0					
Shirreff	13	3	40	0	....	12	6	13	2
Smith	13	1	51	1	....	13	4	33	1
Wright	19	7	48	4	....	17.2	4	63	6
Pettiford	9	3	22	5	....	16	5	36	0

Umpires: L. H. Gray and G. S. Mobey.

KENT v. HAMPSHIRE

At Canterbury, July 30, August 1, 2. Hampshire won by 30 runs. Though excellent bowling by Shackleton and Cannings provided the final thrust, astute captaincy by Eagar did most to make Hampshire's dramatic victory possible. Kent, set to score 253 for victory in four hours, made no attempt to force the pace and when the sixth wicket fell, the extra half-hour was claimed with Kent still needing 75 to win. Leary and Ufton then took advantage of much loose bowling and their vigorous methods raised the total past 200, whereupon Eagar promptly claimed the new ball. Ufton and Brazier were dismissed quickly, but it was not until the last possible ball that Wright was lbw, to give Hampshire the victory they deserved. The best batting of the match came from Rogers in the Hampshire first innings, though Wilson in Kent's first innings and Barnard in Hampshire's second both played attractively. Cowdrey, promoted to open the Kent innings at the request of the Test selectors, made two useful scores, but by methods far removed from his usual freedom and certainty.

Hampshire

R. E. Marshall c Leary b Shirreff	37	— b Smith	31
J. R. Gray c Smith b Allan	61	— lbw b Shirreff	38
H. Horton c Brazier b Smith	29	— run out	8
E. D. R. Eagar c Ufton b Allan	4	— run out	15
N. H. Rogers not out	103	— lbw b Shirreff	2
H. M. Barnard c Cowdrey b Wright	0	— c Fagg b Smith	34
L. Harrison c Ufton b Smith	19	— c Wilson b Shirreff	4
P. J. Sainsbury st Ufton b Shirreff	19	— c Leary b Wright	16
D. Shackleton lbw b Smith	13	— c Leary b Wright	1
V. H. D. Cannings not out	9	— not out	2
B 8, l-b 5, w 1, n-b 1	15	B 8, l-b 1	9

1/78 2/131 3/139 4/156 (8 wkts., dec.) 309
5/157 6/196 7/267 8/284

1/67 2/84 (9 wkts., dec.) 160
3/100 4/102 5/106 6/112
7/149 8/156 9/160

M. D. Burden did not bat.

Kent

A. E. Fagg c Barnard b Shackleton	3	— lbw b Cannings	10
M. C. Cowdrey c Gray b Cannings	45	— c Sainsbury b Gray	67
A. C. Shirreff c Eagar b Gray	72	— c Rogers b Sainsbury	15
J. M. Allan lbw b Shackleton	0	— lbw b Shackleton	5
R. C. Wilson c Harrison b Cannings	72	— b Sainsbury	20
J. Pettiford lbw b Shackleton	8	— c Burden b Sainsbury	26
S. E. Leary st Harrison b Shackleton	1	— not out	48
A. F. Brazier b Cannings	4	— c Rogers b Shackleton	2
D. G. Ufton c Sainsbury b Shackleton	2	— b Shackleton	14
G. Smith not out	0	— c Eagar b Sainsbury	0
D. V. P. Wright lbw b Cannings	1	— lbw b Cannings	5
B 8, l-b 1	9	B 8, w 2	10

1/12 2/77 3/79 4/180 5/209 6/209 217
7/210 8/214 9/216

1/13 2/27 3/49 4/101 222
5/133 6/178 7/178 8/213
9/215

Kent Bowling

	O.	M.	R.	W.		O.	M.	R.	W.
Shirreff	27	5	75	2	....	18	2	60	3
Smith	25	8	67	3	....	15	4	39	2
Wright	21	4	64	1	....	2.5	0	16	2
Leary	3	0	10	0					
Pettiford	12	5	30	0					
Allan	18	4	48	2		8	1	36	0

O

Hampshire Bowling

	O.	M.	R.	W.		O.	M.	R.	W.
Shackleton	27	8	42	5	....	12	2	27	3
Cannings	26	9	51	4	....	19	8	41	2
Gray	22	8	31	1	....	11	2	32	1
Sainsbury	16	4	36	0	....	32	9	81	4
Barnard	1	0	3	0					
Burden	12	4	45	0	....	9	1	27	0
					Eagar	1	0	4	0

Umpires: Harry Elliott (Derbyshire) and W. T. Jones.

KENT v. GLOUCESTERSHIRE

At Canterbury, August 3, 4, 5. Drawn. A determined innings by Young, who held up Kent for five and a quarter hours, did most to save Gloucestershire from defeat. They started the last day 91 behind with nine wickets left and when Wright dismissed Graveney for the addition of a single Kent seemed to be heading for victory. Young stood firm, however, and Crapp helped in a stand of 129. Fine medium-paced bowling by Smith was chiefly responsible for Gloucestershire's cheap first-innings dismissal, although Wright improved his figures by taking the last three wickets without cost. Allan provided the backbone of Kent's highest innings of the season by hitting his maiden Championship century.

Gloucestershire

D. M. Young b Smith	0	— b Allan 137
C. A. Milton c Cowdrey b Wright	50	— c Pettiford b Smith 14
T. W. Graveney c and b Smith	18	— b Wright 34
J. F. Crapp c Smith b Wright	3	— not out 69
G. M. Emmett lbw b Smith	1	— c Pettiford b Allan 22
G. E. Lambert c Ufton b Phillips	7	— not out 8
J. Mortimore c Smith b Phillips	24	
P. Rochford not out	3	
B. D. Wells c Ufton b Wright	26	
C. Cook lbw b Wright	0	
F. P. McHugh c Allan b Wright	0	
B 8, l-b 1, w 1, n-b 2	12	B 16, l-b 5, n-b 3 24

1/0 2/22 3/29 4/30 5/51 6/110   144   1/31 2/126   (4 wkts., dec.) 308
7/113 8/140 9/140   3/255 4/291

Kent

A. E. Fagg c Graveney b Lambert	78		G. Smith c Mortimore b McHugh	14
M. C. Cowdrey b McHugh	5		D. V. P. Wright not out	0
J. M. Allan lbw b McHugh	105			
R. C. Wilson c Lambert b Cook	32		B 12, l-b 4, n-b 3	19
J. Pettiford c McHugh b Wells	71			
J. F. Pretlove c Rochford b McHugh	0		1/20 2/116 3/177 (9 wkts., dec.) 360
A. F. Brazier b Cook	9		4/281 5/289 6/319 7/319 8/360
D. G. Ufton b Lambert	27		9/360

J. B. Phillips did not bat.

Kent Bowling

	O.	M.	R.	W.		O.	M.	R.	W.
Smith	26	13	26	3	....	40	13	56	1
Phillips	27	7	69	2	....	20	2	70	0
Wright	14.4	3	37	5	....	20	4	60	1
Pettiford						9	2	35	0
Allan						18	8	33	2
Pretlove						5	1	26	0
Cowdrey						2	1	4	0

Gloucestershire Bowling

	O.	M.	R.	W.
Lambert	32.3	4	96	2
McHugh	36	9	91	4
Cook	27	8	63	2
Wells	27	7	69	1
Milton	5	0	14	0
Mortimore	3	0	8	0

Umpires: Harry Elliott (Derbyshire) and W. T. Jones.

At Nottingham, August 6, 8, 9. KENT lost to NOTTINGHAMSHIRE by 278 runs.

At Clacton, August 10, 11, 12. KENT lost to ESSEX by ten wickets.

KENT v. WARWICKSHIRE

At Dover, August 13, 15, 16. Drawn. As the first day was washed out entirely, Kent's lead of 104 enabled them to enforce the follow-on—the first time they had been in a position to do so for two years. For this they owed everything to Wright. He dominated a last-wicket stand of 99 in eighty minutes with Phebey, his remarkable 66 not out including two 6's and ten 4's. He also caused most of Warwickshire's troubles with the ball. Having made the gesture of sending their opponents in again, Kent could hope for little more in the limited time available.

Kent

A. E. Fagg c Thompson b Bannister	0	A. F. Brazier c Dollery b Thompson	16
J. M. Allan run out	25	A. W. Catt lbw b Thompson	8
R. C. Wilson b Hollies	9	J. Spanswick run out	1
A. C. Shirreff b Bannister	36	D. V. P. Wright not out	66
J. Pettiford lbw b Thompson	34	B 1, l-b 4, n-b 1	6
A. H. Phebey c Hitchcock b Thompson	49		
J. F. Pretlove c Lewis b Thompson	0	1/1 2/19 3/44 4/86 5/114 6/114	250
		7/134 8/150 9/151	

Warwickshire

F. C. Gardner b Wright	25	— st Catt b Allan	44
N. F. Horner c Pettiford b Spanswick	..	— c Brazier b Shirreff	7
A. Townsend st Catt b Allan	36	— not out	34
T. W. Cartwright c Brazier b Wright	0	— not out	4
R. E. Hitchcock c Allan b Wright	6		
H. E. Dollery c Wilson b Allan	1		
E. B. Lewis c Wright b Shirreff	17		
R. T. Weeks b Shirreff	18		
J. D. Bannister st Catt b Wright	10		
R. G. Thompson b Shirreff	0		
W. E. Hollies not out	7		
B 10, l-b 5, n-b 2	17	L-b 5	5
1/23 2/64 3/64 4/84 5/87 6/92	146	1/22 2/82 (2 wkts.)	94
7/123 8/136 9/136			

Warwickshire Bowling

	O.	M.	R.	W.
Thompson	22.3	8	52	5
Bannister	28	10	39	2
Hollies	25	10	46	1
Weeks	13	3	35	0
Townsend	10	3	31	0
Hitchcock	10	4	41	0

Kent Bowling

	O.	M.	R.	W.	O.	M.	R.	W.
Spanswick	8	4	16	1	4	0	21	0
Shirreff	17	6	38	3	6	2	24	1
Wright	22.5	5	59	4	4	1	17	0
Allan	13	5	16	2	6	3	9	1
Pettiford					8	2	18	0

Umpires: A. E. Pothecary and F. S. Lee.

KENT v. WORCESTERSHIRE

At Dover, August 17, 18, 19. Worcestershire won by 52 runs in a match dominated by two outstanding bowling performances. Wright shattered Worcestershire's first innings on an excellent batting pitch, but even his magnificent effort was surpassed by that of Flavell. Bowling very fast and straight he demoralised the Kent batsmen in taking nine for 30—the best bowling figures of the season. Kent were all out in an hour and three-quarters, but hit back effectively before the first day ended by taking four more wickets for 49 runs. They were checked next morning by Horton and then Flavell celebrated with his highest first-class score in a valuable last-wicket stand.   Kent needed only 256, but their hopes fell when Berry sent back Fagg, Phebey and Allan cheaply. A good innings by Wilson was not enough to prevent Worcestershire achieving the "double" at their expense.

Worcestershire

D. Kenyon lbw b Wright	21	—	c Catt b Smith		28
L. Outschoorn c Phebey b Wright	39	—	c Fagg b Sayer		7
R. G. Broadbent c Sayer b Wright	9	—	b Smith		6
M. J. Horton b Wright	16	—	b Allan		62
G. Dews lbw b Wright	8	—	c Wright b Pettiford		33
D. W. Richardson c Catt b Allan	1	—	c Catt b Smith		0
R. O. Jenkins b Wright	2	—	c Wilson b Wright		1
H. Yarnold not out	0	—	c Pretlove b Allan		0
G. H. Chesterton b Wright	4	—	not out		6
R. Berry b Allan	5	—	b Allan		0
J. Flavell c Sayer b Wright	4	—	c Allan b Wright		29
B 9, l-b 1	10		B 8, l-b 5, w 1		14

1/56 2/70 3/79 4/95 5/100 6/106   119   1/39 2/46 3/47 4/49   186
7/111 8/111 9/115   5/132 6/137 7/145 8/145
9/146

Kent

A. E. Fagg lbw b Flavell	0	—	c Richardson b Berry		14
A. H. Phebey lbw b Flavell	16	—	lbw b Berry		20
R. C. Wilson b Flavell	11	—	c Dews b Flavell		73
J. Pettiford b Flavell	13	—	b Berry		30
J. F. Pretlove c Yarnold b Flavell	0	—	run out		4
J. M. Allan b Flavell	3	—	c Chesterton b Berry		11
A. F. Brazier c Broadbent b Chesterton	4	—	c Broadbent b Chesterton		0
A. W. Catt b Flavell	0	—	not out		17
G. Smith c Yarnold b Flavell	0	—	b Chesterton		5
D. V. P. Wright not out	3	—	c Outschoorn b Chesterton		13
D. M. Sayer b Flavell	0	—	b Flavell		2
			L-b 4		4

1/0 2/20 3/34 4/36 5/42 6/47 7/47   50   1/29 2/34 3/69 4/137   203
8/47 9/50   5/147 6/164 7/164 8/179
9/201

Kent Bowling

	O.	M.	R.	W.		O.	M.	R.	W.
Smith	7	2	25	0	....	22	6	53	3
Sayer	5	0	22	0	....	11	1	35	1
Allan	25	15	26	2	....	25	12	56	3
Wright	21.5	11	36	8	....	11.2	5	21	2
Pettiford						3	1	7	1

Worcestershire Bowling

	O.	M.	R.	W.		O.	M.	R.	W.
Flavell	13.4	3	30	9	....	24	2	78	2
Chesterton	13	6	20	1	....	19	3	61	3
Berry						24	13	40	4
Jenkins						4	1	5	0
Horton						6	3	15	0

Umpires: F. S. Lee and A. E. Pothecary.

At Northampton, August 20, 22, 23. KENT drew with NORTHAMPTONSHIRE.

At Canterbury, August 24, 25, 26. KENT lost to SOUTH AFRICANS by eight wickets.
(See SOUTH AFRICAN section.)

KENT v. MIDDLESEX

At Folkestone, August 31, September 1, 2. Kent won by nine wickets, so ending their season in encouraging fashion by completing the "double" over Middlesex. Their superiority was even more decisive than at Lord's. Wright again bewildered their batsmen with his leg-breaks and googlies and Wilson, whose only previous Championship hundred was in the corresponding match twelve months earlier, again took runs freely off their bowling. Titmus shook Kent's grip for a while on the first day with a valiant innings, during which he achieved the double for the first time, but Wilson, Phebey and Allan assured Kent of a useful lead. Wright replied to suggestions that his declaration was over-ambitious by bowling Middlesex out cheaply again and, with nine wickets standing, Kent needed only 78 to win on the last day. These were obtained in three-quarters of an hour.

Middlesex

J. D. Robertson c Catt b Spanswick	0	— c Pettiford b Wright 25
S. M. Brown lbw b Wright	27	— c Catt b Wright 21
W. J. Edrich b Shirreff	4	— b Shirreff 33
D. C. S. Compton c Wright b Spanswick	1	— lbw b Wright 11
G. P. S. Delisle c Pettiford b Wright	12	— c Hearn b Wright 67
D. Bennett lbw b Shirreff	2	— c Fagg b Wright 24
J. T. Murray c Catt b Spanswick	14	— lbw b Wright 0
F. J. Titmus c and b Shirreff	79	— c Fagg b Allan 8
J. J. Warr c Pettiford b Wright	14	— c Pettiford b Allan 0
J. A. Young c Fagg b Wright	0	— c and b Allan............ 1
A. E. Moss not out	0	— not out 4
B 2, l-b 1, n-b 1	4	B 6, l-b 9, w 1, n-b 1 .. 17

1/0 2/11 3/12 4/39 5/46 6/46 7/67   157

8/157 9/157

1/51 2/60 3/92 4/102   211
5/160 6/165 7/200 8/200
9/205

Kent

A. E. Fagg lbw b Moss	0	— run out	11
A. H. Phebey c and b Compton	39	— not out	26
R. C. Wilson b Titmus	107	— not out	63
J. M. Allan run out	67		
M. C. Cowdrey not out	34		
J. Pettiford c Bennett b Warr	8		
B 3, l-b 5, n-b 3	11	B 3	3

1/0 2/83 3/197 4/243　　(5 wkts., dec.) 266　　1/15　　(1 wkt.) 103
5/266

P. Hearn, A. C. Shirreff, A. W. Catt, J. Spanswick and D. V. P. Wright did not bat.

Kent Bowling

	O.	M.	R.	W.		O.	M.	R.	W.
Spanswick	17	5	40	3	....	5	0	23	0
Shirreff	24.2	6	53	3	....	16	3	60	1
Wright	17	7	33	4	....	24	7	75	6
Allan	10	3	14	0	....	7.4	2	20	3
Pettiford	2	0	13	0	....	5	1	16	0

Middlesex Bowling

	O.	M.	R.	W.		O.	M.	R.	W.
Moss	15	2	41	1					
Warr	15.5	5	41	1	....	9	1	17	0
Titmus	21	5	54	1	....	3	0	14	0
Young	15	3	49	0	....	1	0	13	0
Compton	12	0	36	1	....	4	0	25	0
Bennett	9	0	34	0	....	9	1	30	0
					Edrich	0.1	0	1	0

Umpires: P. Corrall and A. J. B. Fowler.

LANCASHIRE

Patron—HER MAJESTY THE QUEEN

President—Dr. J. BOWLING HOLMES

Secretary—C. G. HOWARD, County Cricket Ground, Old Trafford, Manchester, 16

Captain—CYRIL WASHBROOK

| J. T. Ikin | County Badge | J. B. Statham |

Lancashire in 1955 were still in the process of transition and while their performances again proved only mediocre some encouraging signs for the future were to be found. The development of youth, however, takes time without producing immediate results and for the second successive season the county finished in the middle of the Championship table. Apart from a period in June when four out of five matches were won the side seldom looked like becoming a winning combination.

Many young members did sufficiently well to merit optimism for the future, particularly Dyson, the 20-year-old right-handed batsman. Against Sussex at Liverpool he went in with Ikin when Wharton suffered from stomach trouble and by helping in the first three-figure opening partnership of the season showed that he possesses the right temperament. Barber when home from Cambridge displayed a pleasing style without the satisfaction of big scores and Collins, Pullar and Jordan, the wicket-keeper, gave promise of better things to come.

In pursuing their policy of giving youth every chance, the selectors made frequent team changes and consequently much responsibility fell on the established players. Ikin was a sound opening batsman who played for England again. The captain, Washbrook, three years Ikin's senior at 40, gave evidence that when in form he remained among the leading cricketers. Both reached 1,500 runs, Washbrook exceeding 1,000 for the fifteenth time. Wharton did almost as well and Grieves and Edrich, who helped in a recovery during his benefit match against Derbyshire at Manchester, provided several stimulating displays.

The main problem which confronted Lancashire was to find a suitable pace bowler to open the attack with Statham. Standring, marking his debut in the "Roses" fixture at Old Trafford by bowling Hutton for two; Goodwin and Moore were tried in turn, but they met with only limited success. Statham deserved better support. He did magnificently but with the assistance of genuine pace at the other end would have been even more effective. Tattersall was by no means the bowler of past years, but he and Hilton got through a lot of work and took most wickets. Hilton also hit his maiden century in first-class cricket at Northampton.

The brilliant summer may have lost some of its lustre because of the disappointing form, but the sunshine at least gave supporters a full season.

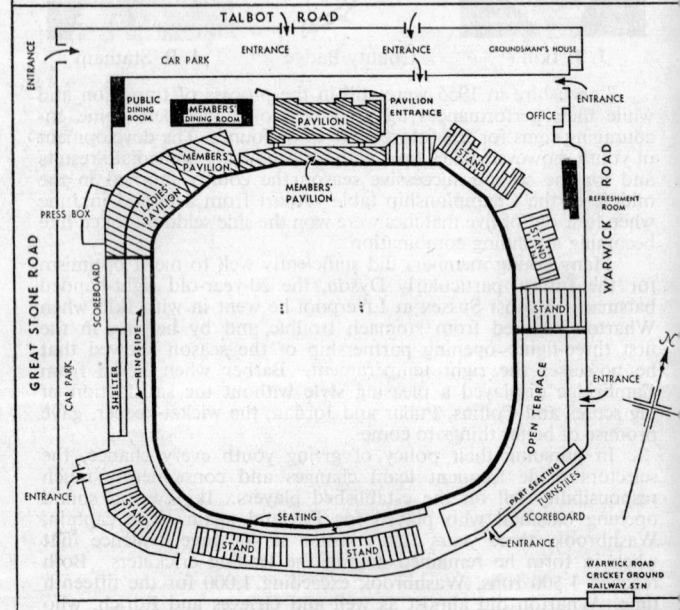

LANCASHIRE RESULTS

All First-Class Matches—Played 33, *Won* 11, *Lost* 9, *Drawn* 13

County Championship Matches—Played 28, *Won* 10, *Lost* 9, *Drawn* 8, *No Decision* 1

COUNTY CHAMPIONSHIP AVERAGES
BATTING

	Birthplace	Mtchs.	Inns.	Not Outs	Runs	100's	Highest Inns.	Aver.
K. Grieves	*Sydney*	21	32	5	1146	2	137	42.44
C. Washbrook .	*Barrow*	26	41	2	1500	3	170	38.46
J. T. Ikin	*Stoke*	26	43	1	1581	3	114	37.64
A. Wharton....	*Heywood*	27	43	2	1400	2	123	34.14
G. Pullar	*Swinton*	3	5	0	138	0	76	27.60
G. A. Edrich ..	*Lingwood*	24	40	3	916	2	117	24.75
J. Dyson	*Oldham*	16	28	3	599	0	84	23.96
R. Collins	*Manchester*	13	20	3	318	0	52*	18.70
C. S. Smith	*Disbury*	4	7	0	101	0	36	14.42
J. B. Statham ..	*Manchester*	14	19	4	199	0	62	13.26
M. J. Hilton ...	*Chadderton*	24	35	2	426	1	100*	12.90
R. W. Barber ..	*Manchester*	7	12	3	93	0	25*	10.33
W. Place	*Rawtenstall*	6	11	0	110	0	19	10.00
F. Goodwin ...	*Heywood*	7	8	3	46	0	21*	9.20
J. D. Bond	*Kearsley*	2	3	0	26	0	25	8.66
S. Smith	*Heywood*	8	12	0	103	0	19	8.58
J. Jordan	*Clough Fold*	14	22	2	171	0	35	8.55
F. W. Moore ..	*Rochdale*	11	16	4	102	0	18	8.50
P. Marner	*Oldham*	3	4	0	29	0	21	7.25
A. Wilson	*Newton-le-Willows*	14	18	7	79	0	19*	7.18
T. Greenhough .	*Rochdale*	6	9	3	37	0	14	6.16
R. Tattersall ...	*Bolton*	26	33	11	123	0	28	5.59
K. B. Standring	*Clitheroe*	6	10	2	28	0	13	3.50

* *Signifies not out.*

BOWLING

	Overs	Maidens	Runs	Wickets	Average
J. B. Statham	489.5	145	1015	79	12.84
F. Goodwin	134	24	395	22	17.95
J. T. Ikin	260	71	646	32	20.18
R. Tattersall	1059	374	2173	105	20.69
M. J. Hilton	910.5	341	1938	91	21.29
T. Greenhough	91.5	24	215	10	21.50
C. S. Smith	71	15	196	9	21.77
R. Collins	209.2	76	449	17	26.41
K. B. Standring	113	26	316	10	31.60
A. Wharton...........	210	56	530	16	33.12
F. W. Moore	267.3	70	771	21	36.71
R. W. Barber	10.4	1	58	1	58.00
J. Dyson	93	30	203	3	67.66
K. Grieves	13	4	37	0	—
P. Marner	22	5	60	0	—

Also bowled: C. Washbrook 1—0—4—0.

Amateurs.—R. W. Barber, J. Jordan, G. Pullar, C. S. Smith, K. B. Standring.

At Oxford, May 4, 5, 6. LANCASHIRE drew with OXFORD UNIVERSITY.

LANCASHIRE v. SCOTLAND

At Manchester, May 7, 9, 10. Drawn. Because of rain play was limited to the opening day of Scotland's first visit to Lancashire for thirty years. Scotland failed against the spin bowling of Hilton and Greenhough and were all out in just over four hours. Cosh alone showed aggression, hitting one 6 and four 4's. Then Ikin and Smith batted freely and Lancashire looked in a strong position when stumps were drawn on Saturday. The county introduced Farrar, a seam bowler, and Jordan, who impressed as wicket-keeper. He helped in four dismissals.

Scotland

R. H. Chisholm b Hilton	39
J. F. Mendl b Wharton	2
J. Aitchison b Hilton	25
K. R. Deas c Jordan b Greenhough	7
W. Nichol lbw b Greenhough	1
S. H. Cosh lbw b Greenhough	28
W. A. Edward st Jordan b Hilton	26
J. Brown c Jordan b Tattersall	6
D. W. Drummond c Jordan b Hilton	12
A. M. Dowell b Ikin	5
G. W. Youngson not out	0
B 4, l-b 6, n-b 3	13
	164

1/11 2/51 3/76 4/78 5/93
6/116 7/135 8/157 9/162

Lancashire

J. T. Ikin not out	55
S. Smith not out	54
L-b 4	4
(No wkt.)	113

A. Wharton, C. Washbrook, W. Place, K. Grieves, M. J. Hilton, J. Jordan, R. Tattersall, T. Greenhough and H. Farrar did not bat.

Lancashire Bowling

	O.	M.	R.	W.
Farrar	13	4	25	0
Wharton	5	2	8	1
Tattersall	20	7	25	1
Greenhough	20	8	32	3
Hilton	23.3	11	45	4
Ikin	12	8	11	1
Grieves	4	1	5	0

Scotland Bowling

	O.	M.	R.	W.
Youngson	14	2	30	0
Dowell	8	3	15	0
Nichol	14	3	35	0
Edward	14	4	22	0
Drummond	5	2	7	0

Umpires: T. J. Bartley and P. Corrall.

LANCASHIRE v. NORTHAMPTONSHIRE
(Friendly Match)

At Manchester, May 11, 12, 13. Drawn. Rain, which froze on the pitch covers overnight, prevented a start until lunch and brought the game to a close one over after the first interval on the second day. In between Lancashire missed a good opportunity of making a favourable start. Brookes was dropped before he scored and Arnold escaped twice. Later the bowlers received better support and Tattersall in one spell of ten overs took four wickets for 18 runs. When Lancashire batted they were soon in trouble against pace and spin.

Northamptonshire

D. Brookes b Tattersall	41	S. Starkie c Grieves b Dyson	0
P. Arnold c Grieves b Tattersall	49	K. V. Andrew b Tattersall	11
L. Livingston b Tattersall	34	R. W. Clarke not out	0
D. Barrick lbw b Statham	37		
R. Subba Row lbw b Tattersall	0	B 3, l-b 2	5
G. E. Tribe c Grieves b Tattersall	1		
V. Broderick b Hilton	1	1/74 2/107 3/128 4/128 5/130	180
F. H. Tyson b Hilton	1	6/131 7/147 8/148 9/174	

Lancashire

J. T. Ikin b Clarke	8	K. Grieves not out	0
S. Smith run out	21		
A. Wharton b Clarke	7	B 4, l-b 2	6
C. Washbrook lbw b Tribe	19		
W. Place not out	4	1/17 2/33 3/40 4/62 (4 wkts.)	65

J. Dyson, M. J. Hilton, A. Wilson, J. B. Statham and R. Tattersall did not bat.

Lancashire Bowling

	O.	M.	R.	W.
Statham	15	6	14	1
Wharton	5	3	2	0
Tattersall	37.2	9	77	6
Hilton	30	7	57	2
Dyson	10	3	25	1

Northamptonshire Bowling

	O.	M.	R.	W.
Tyson	7	3	11	0
Clarke	10	3	17	2
Tribe	9	2	22	1
Starkie	5	0	9	0

Umpires: J. S. Buller and R. E. Cooke.

At Swansea, May 14, 16, 17. LANCASHIRE drew with GLAMORGAN.

LANCASHIRE v. WARWICKSHIRE

At Manchester, May 18, 19, 20. Lancashire won by 72 runs and owed much to Statham, their England fast bowler. He took five wickets for 9 runs when Warwickshire looked reasonably placed for the lead and dismissed the first three batsmen for 11 runs in the second innings. Statham also helped Hilton in the first innings by taking a brilliant catch. Warwickshire, mainly through the skilful bowling of Hollies and Bannister, still held a chance of victory while Gardner and Dollery were together on the final day. Neither looked in trouble on a pitch that had dried. The turning-point came when Gardner was carried off with a suspected slipped disc.

Lancashire

J. T. Ikin c Thompson b Weeks	47	— b Thompson	1
S. Smith st Spooner b Hollies	19	— c Gardner b Hollies	11
A. Wharton c Bannister b Thompson	71	— c and b Bannister	3
C. Washbrook st Spooner b Hollies	8	— c Spooner b Hollies	26
W. Place lbw b Bannister	15	— b Hollies	0
K. Grieves c Townsend b Bannister	37	— b Hollies	9
M. J. Hilton c Dollery b Thompson	18	— b Bannister	11
J. B. Statham b Hollies	18	— c Spooner b Bannister	0
A. Wilson c and b Bannister	1	— not out	9
R. Tattersall c Thompson b Weeks	11	— c Dollery b Bannister	0
T. Greenhough not out	0	— c Gardner b Bannister	0
B 3, l-b 8, n-b 2	13		

1/30 2/90 3/101 4/144 5/208 6/217	258	1/6 2/11 3/23 4/23	70
7/231 8/232 9/258		5/43 6/54 7/55 8/62 9/70	

Warwickshire

F. C. Gardner c Grieves b Hilton	10	— retired hurt	46
N. F. Horner c Grieves b Hilton	37	— b Statham	1
A. V. Wolton c and b Hilton	53	— b Statham	0
R. T. Spooner lbw b Statham	9	— c Wharton b Statham	4
H. E. Dollery st Wilson b Hilton	10	— b Hilton	52
A. Townsend lbw b Statham	0	— lbw b Greenhough	0
R. E. Hitchcock b Statham	2	— lbw b Greenhough	0
R. T. Weeks not out	3	— b Statham	9
J. D. Bannister b Statham	5	— lbw b Statham	0
R. G. Thompson c Statham b Hilton	4	— not out	0
W. E. Hollies b Statham	0	— st Wilson b Hilton	0
B 2, l-b 2, n-b 3	7	B 2, n-b 2	4

1/31 2/67 3/106 4/121 5/121 6/123   **140**   1/3 2/3 3/11 4/87 5/87   **116**
7/128 8/133 9/140   6/116 7/116 8/116

Warwickshire Bowling

	O.	M.	R.	W.		O.	M.	R.	W.
Thompson	24	4	52	2	....	4	0	7	1
Bannister	26	8	61	3	....	8.5	2	16	5
Weeks	22.2	8	62	2	....	10	3	25	0
Hollies	30	12	67	3	....	15	8	22	4
Wolton	5	3	3	0					

Lancashire Bowling

	O.	M.	R.	W.		O.	M.	R.	W.
Statham	20.1	10	27	5	....	15	5	21	5
Wharton	4	2	6	0	....	2	1	3	0
Tattersall	15	4	35	0	....	17	3	34	0
Hilton	23	5	65	5	....	18.4	5	37	2
Greenhough					..	9	2	17	2

Umpires: T. Spencer and J. J. Hills.

LANCASHIRE v. HAMPSHIRE

At Manchester, May 21, 23, 24. Drawn. Only Marshall, the former West Indies batsman, compensated the crowd who braved chilly conditions on the first day. He hit seven 4's in an attractive innings which occupied less than two hours and provided a contrast to Eager, who spent almost as long over 24. Lancashire were just as stolid during the final hour and a half. Rain, which prevented cricket on Monday, livened the turf on Tuesday when Hampshire would have done better but for dropped catches. Wharton was missed three times. Last out after batting nearly two and a half hours, he scored nearly half the Lancashire total.

Hampshire

J. R. Gray c Edrich b Wharton	4	— c Wilson b Hilton	15
R. E. Marshall c Grieves b Statham	71	— b Tattersall	15
H. Horton b Tattersall	2	— c Wilson b Hilton	6
A. W. H. Rayment lbw b Statham	13	— c Ikin b Tattersall	8
N. H. Rogers c Ikin b Greenhough	17	— c Washbrook b Statham	7
E. D. R. Eagar c Washbrook b Hilton	24	— c Edrich b Wharton	15
L. Harrison b Hilton	26	— b Statham	0
P. J. Sainsbury lbw b Hilton	32	— not out	20
D. Shackleton c and b Ikin	6	— not out	1
V. H. D. Cannings not out	0		
M. D. Burden st Wilson b Hilton	0		
B 6, l-b 5, n-b 1	12	B 2, l-b 2, n-b 1	5

1/13 2/37 3/89 4/94 5/128 6/157   **207**   1/17 2/28 3/43 (7 wkts.) **92**
7/194 8/201 9/207   4/55 5/55 6/55 7/90

Lancashire

J. T. Ikin lbw b Cannings	6	A. Wilson c and b Shackleton	12
S. Smith lbw b Shackleton	1	R. Tattersall run out	0
G. A. Edrich c Eagar b Shackleton	24	T. Greenhough not out	0
C. Washbrook c Rogers b Burden	29		
A. Wharton c Marshall b Cannings	73	B 5, l-b 4, n-b 1	10
K. Grieves c Sainsbury b Gray	1		—
M. J. Hilton c Sainsbury b Gray	3	1/7 2/7 3/37 4/96 5/99	167
J. B. Statham c Shackleton b Burden	8	6/111 7/124 8/162 9/164	

Lancashire Bowling

	O.	M.	R.	W.	O.	M.	R.	W.
Statham	18	5	34	2	12	4	19	2
Tattersall	21	10	32	1	17	2	24	2
Wharton	4	1	10	1	2	2	0	1
Greenhough	19	5	46	1	5	1	9	0
Hilton	27	7	58	4	13	3	35	2
Ikin	7	2	15	1				

Hampshire Bowling

	O.	M.	R.	W.
Shackleton	31	10	59	3
Cannings	17.2	5	36	2
Sainsbury	9	6	14	0
Burden	10	1	36	2
Gray	11	4	12	2

Umpires: A. Skelding and W. T. Jones.

At The Oval, May 25, 26, 27. LANCASHIRE lost to SURREY by an innings and 143 runs.

LANCASHIRE v. YORKSHIRE

At Manchester, May 28, 30, 31. Yorkshire won by five wickets and Wardle finished the match with 6, 4, 6 off successive balls from Ikin, an unusually light-hearted climax to this traditionally stern encounter. Despite a magnificent innings lasting two and a half hours by Washbrook, Lancashire enjoyed mixed fortunes at the start, but with Standring, the 20-year-old amateur fast bowler, marking his unexpected debut by dismissing Hutton, and Wilson and Lowson also out they were reasonably placed at the end of the day. The initiative was conceded through missed catches. Watson, top scorer, was dropped twice and Booth and Yardley also received second chances. Grieves, dropped before scoring, played a fine innings and delayed the Yorkshire victory.

Lancashire

W. Place b Cowan	13	— b Appleyard	9
J. T. Ikin c Watson b Appleyard	45	— run out	33
G. A. Edrich lbw b Wardle	0	— c Booth b Appleyard	9
C. Washbrook lbw b Trueman	70	— lbw b Close	20
A. Wharton lbw b Cowan	3	— c Trueman b Wardle	8
K. Grieves c Booth b Cowan	1	— not out	83
K. B. Standring c Watson b Trueman	1	— lbw b Close	2
J. Jordan lbw b Appleyard	23	— c Trueman b Close	0
M. J. Hilton b Trueman	0	— c Watson b Close	11
J. B. Statham not out	36	— c Booth b Trueman	26
R. Tattersall b Appleyard	1	— b Cowan	9
B 1, l-b 5, n-b 5	11	B 10, l-b 4, n-b 6	20
	—		—
1/44 2/45 3/113 4/120 5/122	204	1/30 2/48 3/65 4/88	230
6/133 7/140 8/140 9/196		5/88 6/104 7/104 8/161	
		9/211	

Yorkshire

L. Hutton b Standring	2	—	b Tattersall		17
F. A. Lowson c Wharton b Statham	11	—	c sub b Ikin		63
J. V. Wilson c Hilton b Tattersall	13	—	c and b Hilton		4
R. Booth b Statham	36				
D. B. Close b Tattersall	31	—	b Hilton		0
W. Watson lbw b Statham	94	—	c and b Ikin		46
N. W. D. Yardley c Jordan b Tattersall	25	—	not out		13
J. H. Wardle c Tattersall b Hilton	11	—	not out		16
F. S. Trueman b Tattersall	33				
R. Appleyard not out	6				
M. J. Cowan c Jordan b Tattersall	0				
B 1, l-b 5, n-b 3	9		B 8, l-b 1		9

1/12 2/28 3/28 4/68 5/141 6/188   271   1/56 2/69 3/69   (5 wkts.) 168
7/199 8/265 9/267   4/131 5/152

Yorkshire Bowling

	O.	M.	R.	W.		O.	M.	R.	W.
Trueman	17	4	44	3	....	11	2	44	1
Cowan	26	7	59	3	....	5.4	2	16	1
Appleyard	26	5	41	3	....	24	9	38	2
Wardle	21	4	49	1	....	26	9	59	1
				Close	....	14	4	53	4

Lancashire Bowling

	O.	M.	R.	W.		O.	M.	R.	W.
Statham	30	5	68	3	....	6	2	8	0
Strandring	15	4	52	1	....	4	1	9	0
Tattersall	25.3	7	91	5	....	20	1	57	1
Hilton	12	3	36	1	....	14	3	34	2
Ikin	4	0	15	0	....	6	0	43	2
				Grieves	....	1	0	8	0

Umpires: Harry Elliott (Derbyshire) and L. H. Gray.

LANCASHIRE v. KENT

At Manchester, June 1, 2, 3. Lancashire won by 167 runs. They were given a favourable start by Ikin, who hit fifteen 4's in two and a half hours before treading on his wicket, and, although Fagg and Hearn batted well for Kent, Lancashire established a commanding position on the second day. With a lead of 25 they punished Kent's all-spin attack, hitting 226, including five 6's and thirty-seven 4's, in one period of two hours. Edrich reached his first century of the season in two hours ten minutes. Only Hearn offered resistance when Kent went in to get 307 to win. Ikin, cleverly varying the flight of his leg-breaks, completed a successful match, taking four wickets for 23 runs.

Lancashire

J. T. Ikin hit wkt b Wright	78	—	b Wright		2
W. Place c Fagg b Wright	13	—	b Wright		12
G. A. Edrich b Page	31	—	c Page b Pettiford		103
C. Washbrook lbw b Wright	16	—	c and b Page		64
A. Wharton lbw b Wright	59	—	b Pettiford		45
K. Grieves c Pettiford b Page	35	—	not out		33
R. Collins c Hearn b Page	0	—	not out		20
J. Jordan c Pettiford b Wright	5				
F. Goodwin st Evans b Wright	1				
T. Greenhough not out	11				
R. Tattersall c Pettiford b Wright	0				
L-b 2	2		L-b 1, n-b 1		2

1/41 2/105 3/139 4/140 5/204 6/204   251   1/6 2/17   (5 wkts., dec.) 281
7/209 8/209 9/251   3/122 4/225 5/229

Kent

A. E. Fagg b Greenhough	56	— lbw b Goodwin	9
A. H. Phebey lbw b Greenhough	21	— c Place b Goodwin	0
P. Hearn c Greenhough b Ikin	56	— c Jordan b Tattersall	53
E. G. Witherden lbw b Ikin	17	— c Edrich b Goodwin	11
J. Pettiford b Goodwin	27	— c Tattersall b Ikin	18
T. G. Evans c Jordan b Ikin	0	— c Wharton b Tattersall	17
A. F. Brazier c Jordan b Ikin	3	— c Goodwin b Ikin	6
A. Dixon c Collins b Ikin	26	— c Collins b Ikin	13
C. Dring c Grieves b Goodwin	8	— b Tattersall	0
D. V. P. Wright c Tattersall b Wharton	2	— c Place b Ikin	0
J. C. T. Page not out	1	— not out	6
B 6, l-b 3	9	B 4, n-b 2	6

1/77 2/110 3/148 4/163 5/163   226
6/173 7/209 8/221 9/224

1/3 2/24 3/68 4/86   139
5/100 6/112 7/130 8/131
9/132

Kent Bowling

	O.	M.	R.	W.		O.	M.	R.	W.
Wright	25.4	9	78	7	....	13	3	46	2
Brazier	4	1	7	0	....	2	0	7	0
Page	23	3	71	3	....	18	0	92	1
Dixon	6	2	21	0	....	7	0	51	0
Pettiford	22	7	72	0	....	10	0	63	2
Witherden					....	2	0	20	0

Lancashire Bowling

	O.	M.	R.	W.		O.	M.	R.	W.
Goodwin	13	2	33	2	....	11	1	55	3
Wharton	8	5	14	1	....	8	2	22	0
Tattersall	34	13	74	0	....	13	3	33	3
Greenhough	21	6	39	2					
Collins	10	2	18	0					
Ikin	19	4	39	5	..	8.3	1	23	4

Umpires: Harry Elliott (Derbyshire) and L. H. Gray.

At Manchester, June 4, 6, 7. LANCASHIRE drew with SOUTH AFRICANS. (See SOUTH AFRICAN section.)

At Birmingham, June 8, 9, 10. LANCASHIRE drew with WARWICKSHIRE.

At Lord's, June 11, 13. LANCASHIRE beat MIDDLESEX by an innings and 13 runs.

At Hinckley, June 15, 16. LANCASHIRE beat LEICESTERSHIRE by an innings and 101 runs.

LANCASHIRE v. WORCESTERSHIRE

At Manchester, June 18, 20, 21. Lancashire won by eight wickets. Washbrook dominated the cricket on the first day, batting nearly four hours for 170. He hit one 6 and twenty-three 4's and cleverly "farmed" the bowling in scoring all but five of the 73 added for the last wicket. Ikin gave sound support, as he did again on Monday in taking three brilliant catches to help Statham capture seven wickets for 43 runs. Statham took the first seven wickets on a rain-affected pitch. Conditions changed and Broadbent, defending flawlessly and punishing loose balls with great power, hit three 6's, one 5 and fourteen 4's in his first century of the season. Lancashire, despite their big first-innings lead, won with only ten minutes to spare.

Lancashire

J. T. Ikin c Richardson b Devereux	70	— b Perks	15
A. Wharton c Horton b Flavell	0	— c Dews b Flavell	39
G. A. Edrich c Lister b Perks	28	— not out	30
C. Washbrook c Lister b Berry	170	— not out	5
K. Grieves b Devereux	4		
P. Marner c Yarnold b Devereux	0		
J. B. Statham c Yarnold b Berry.......	0		
M. J. Hilton c Richardson b Perks	23		
A. Wilson c Kenyon b Flavell	1		
F. Goodwin b Perks	10		
R. Tattersall not out	5		
B 4, l-b 12, n-b 1	17	B 1, n-b 1	2

1/0 2/59 3/135 4/153 5/153 6/164   328   1/21 2/81   (2 wkts.) 91
7/230 8/231 9/255

Worcestershire

D. Kenyon c Ikin b Statham	37	— hit wkt b Goodwin	5
J. Lister b Statham	0	— c Wilson b Ikin	12
L. N. Devereux c Grieves b Statham	17	— lbw b Ikin	39
D. W. Richardson c Wharton, b Statham	4	— b Statham.............	16
M. J. Horton c Ikin b Statham	36	— c and b Tattersall	49
R. G. Broadbent b Statham	1	— b Hilton	108
G. Dews c Wharton b Tattersall	25	— st Wilson b Ikin	0
H. Yarnold b Statham	0	— c Edrich b Goodwin	24
R. T. D. Perks c Ikin b Tattersall	4	— c Marner b Goodwin	0
R. Berry not out	2	— not out	10
J. Flavell c Goodwin b Tattersall	7	— b Tattersall.............	11
B 1, n-b 2	3	B 5, l-b 2	7

1/1 2/54 3/60 4/61 5/63 6/118   136   1/9 2/97 3/97 4/97   281
7/118 8/123 9/130   5/139 6/159 7/182 8/220
                                           9/224

Worcestershire Bowling

	O.	M.	R.	W.		O.	M.	R.	W.
Perks	29	6	69	3	....	7	1	30	1
Flavell	22	4	71	2	....	7.4	0	45	1
Horton	10	3	35	0					
Berry	38.5	7	98	2	....	1	0	14	0
Devereux	12	3	38	3					

Lancashire Bowling

	O.	M.	R.	W.		O.	M.	R.	W.
Statham	27	12	43	7	....	25	7	55	1
Goodwin	16	3	38	0	....	9	1	39	3
Tattersall	16.5	7	16	3	....	28	10	69	2
Hilton	9	2	22	0	....	19.5	6	42	1
Ikin...........	4	0	14	0	....	28	9	64	3
				Marner		2	0	5	0

Umpires: G. S. Mobey and E. Cooke.

LANCASHIRE v. NOTTINGHAMSHIRE

At Manchester, June 22, 23, 24. Nottinghamshire won by ten wickets. The Lancashire attack, without Statham, gave little trouble. Giles and Clay began with 91 and then Giles and Poole proceeded to hit their first centuries of the season. Both mixed dogged defence with aggression. Then Dooland, the leg-break bowler, came into his own on a drying pitch and after conceding 30 runs he took eight wickets in 11.5 overs for a further 31. He also held two catches.

Following on 244 behind, Lancashire possessed a chance of saving the game while Grieves and Dyson were together. They added 131 runs in two and a quarter hours for the fifth wicket but Dooland again caused a collapse, taking four wickets for 12 runs. He finished the match with fourteen wickets for 154 runs.

Nottinghamshire

J. D. Clay c Ikin b Hilton	60	— not out	18
R. Giles c Ikin b Moore	121	— not out	2
C. J. Poole b Goodwin	108		
J. Hardstaff c Jordan b Hilton	16		
E. J. Martin c Ikin b Moore	27		
J. Kelly b Tattersall	0		
P. F. Harvey b Moore	31		
B. Dooland run out	2		
A. Jepson not out	20		
K. Smales not out	1		
L-b 2, n-b 1	3		

1/91 2/227 3/257 4/312   (8 wkts., dec.) 389   (no wkt.) 20
5/313 6/365 7/367 8/376

E. J. Rowe did not bat.

Lancashire

J. T. Ikin c Jepson b Dooland	40	— c Harvey b Smales	12
A. Wharrton c Dooland b Jepson	6	— c Harvey b Smales	20
G. A. Edrich lbw b Dooland	26	— c Rowe b Harvey	1
C. Washbrook c Clay b Dooland	16	— c and b Smales	5
K. Grieves c Kelly b Dooland	8	— b Dooland	96
J. Dyson b Dooland	11	— not out	66
J. Jordan c Dooland b Jepson	4	— c Poole b Dooland	0
M. J. Hilton c Kelly b Dooland	15	— c Poole b Dooland	17
F. Goodwin st Rowe b Dooland	4	— c Clay b Dooland	0
F. W. Moore c Clay b Dooland	7	— c Poole b Dooland	18
R. Tattersall not out	0	— c Jepson b Dooland	17
B 6, l-b 1, n-b 1	8	B 4, l-b 6	10

1/16 2/73 3/90 4/90 5/101 6/114   145   1/23 2/32 3/38 4/48   262
7/116 8/130 9/139   5/179 6/179 7/206 8/206
                                     9/232

Lancashire Bowling

	O.	M.	R.	W.	O.	M.	R.	W.
Goodwin	18	3	70	1				
Moore	31	7	96	3	1.1	0	9	0
Tattersall	32	10	74	1				
Hilton	35	14	69	2				
Ikin	12	1	34	0				
Dyson	9	2	25	0				
Wharton	7	1	18	0	1	0	11	0

Nottinghamshire Bowling

	O.	M.	R.	W.	O.	M.	R.	W.
Jepson	19	9	33	2	18	7	25	0
Smales	19	7	43	0	38	15	75	3
Dooland	24	9	61	8	33.4	10	93	6
Harvey					24	6	59	1

Umpires: J. S. Buller and P. Corrall.

At Chesterfield, June 25, 27, 28. LANCASHIRE beat DERBYSHIRE by 129 runs.

LANCASHIRE v. SUSSEX

At Liverpool, June 29, 30, July 1. Drawn. A downpour shortly after three o'clock on the last day prevented further cricket and Lancashire's good recovery brought no reward. Place, the acting captain, was unfortunate in deciding to bat first, for after three overs rain caused a long delay and on a drying pitch Lancashire collapsed. Sussex went ahead with three men out, but despite a good innings from Parks their lead was restricted to 101. With Wharton suffering from stomach trouble, Dyson opened the Lancashire innings with Ikin and he shared a stand of 107, the first opening three-figure partnership of the season for the county. Grieves also showed good form and Lancashire led by 142 with four wickets left when the rain came.

Lancashire

J. T. Ikin c Sheppard b Thomson	4	— c Suttle b Marlar 76
A. Wharton c Webb b Marlar	33	
G. A. Edrich c Smith b Bates	8	— lbw b Bates 0
K. Grieves c and b Bates	7	— not out 57
J. Dyson c Sheppard b Marlar	12	— c Bates b Smith 42
W. Place b Cooper	13	— c Bates b Marlar 15
R. Collins c Smith b Cooper	11	— c Cox b Bates 10
J. Jordan b Cooper	1	— st Webb b Bates 13
M. J. Hilton c Cox b Marlar	0	— not out 11
F. Goodwin run out	2	
R. Tattersall not out	0	
B 3, l-b 2	5	B 9, l-b 10 19
	96	(6 wkts.) 243

1/8 2/25 3/37 4/63 5/66 6/81
7/82 8/83 9/89

1/107 2/108 3/136
4/136 5/191 6/209

Sussex

J. Langridge lbw b Collins	22	R. T. Webb not out	11
D. V. Smith b Goodwin	27	D. L. Bates b Tattersall	0
D. S. Sheppard b Goodwin	27	R. G. Marlar c Grieves b Tattersall	1
J. M. Parks c Hilton b Tattersall	63		
K. G. Suttle run out	28	B 2, l-b 1, n-b 2	5
G. Cox c Collins b Hilton	1		197
G. C. Cooper c Place b Hilton	11		
N. I. Thomson c Hilton b Tattersall	1		

1/38 2/75 3/92 4/135 5/137
6/177 7/184 8/185 9/185

Sussex Bowling

	O.	M.	R.	W.	O.	M.	R.	W.
Thomson	19	5	25	1	31.2	11	61	0
Bates	18	5	28	2	24	7	47	3
Marlar	13	5	25	3	30	10	59	2
Cooper	7.4	3	13	3	14	5	42	0
Smith					11	5	15	1

Lancashire Bowling

	O.	M.	R.	W.
Goodwin	11	1	39	2
Wharrton	2	1	2	0
Tattersall	25.1	11	40	4
Hilton	33	13	62	2
Collins	16	1	49	1

Umpires: E. Davies and P. Corrall.

LANCASHIRE v. DERBYSHIRE
(G. A. Edrich's Benefit)

At Manchester, July 2, 4, 5. Lancashire won by eight wickets. Edrich appropriately helped in a recovery by batting dourly for four hours after two wickets fell for four runs. Grieves, however, took most of the honours with a chanceless innings in which he hit twenty 4's. The limitations of the Derbyshire batsmen were then exposed on a pitch giving bowlers little help, but they did better when following on 168 behind. Kelly defied his former colleagues for over three hours. Even so, Lancashire would have won more comfortably had they not missed three simple catches within the space of five minutes. Gladwin, dropped when 18, scored 67 of the 97 added for the last two wickets. During Lancashire's second innings Kelly bowled only one delivery—a no-ball which Dyson hit to the boundary.

Lancashire

J. T. Ikin b Jackson	0	— c Carr b Revill	10
J. Dyson b Gladwin	4	— not out	46
G. A. Edrich lbw b Smith	56	— lbw b Morgan	2
C. Washbrook c Dawkes b Morgan	22	— not out	33
K. Grieves c and b Morgan	137		
R. Collins c Kelly b Morgan	21		
J. Jordan c Morgan b Gladwin	1		
M. J. Hilton b Smith	30		
J. B. Statham not out	22		
F. Goodwin not out	21		
L-b 6, w 1	7	B 4 n-b 1	5

1/0 2/4 3/46 4/157   (8 wkts., dec.) 321   1/15 2/39   (2 wkts.) 96
5/227 6/234 7/250 8/294

R. Tattersall did not bat.

Derbyshire

A. Hamer c Jordan b Goodwin	14	— c Grieves b Statham	25
J. Kelly lbw b Statham	1	— lbw b Statham	63
D. C. Morgan c Hilton b Ikin	45	— b Hilton	11
A. C. Revill c Jordan b Statham	4	— b Statham	9
H. L. Johnson c Ikin b Tattersall	5	— c Edrich b Hilton	17
D. B. Carr c Edrich b Tattersall	14	— lbw b Hilton	6
C. Lee not out	27	— b Tattersall	16
G. O. Dawkes lbw b Statham	7	— run out	2
C. Gladwin b Statham	5	— lbw b Tattersall	67
E. Smith lbw b Collins	16	— lbw b Ikin	12
L. Jackson b Statham	4	— not out	20
B 5, l-b 6	11	B 10, l-b 2	12

1/19 2/27 3/43 4/52 5/86 6/96   153   1/54 2/76 3/96 4/116   263
7/113 8/123 9/146   5/129 6/150 7/152 8/166
9/191

Derbyshire Bowling

	O.	M.	R.	W.		O.	M.	R.	W.
Jackson	17	9	26	1					
Gladwin	38	10	92	2	....	7	1	14	0
Morgan	35	6	96	3	....	15	7	21	1
Smith	21	6	73	2	....	10	2	25	0
Carr	4	1	27	0					
Revill						3	0	9	1
Lee						3	0	13	0
Hamer						3	0	5	0
Kelly						0	0	4	0

Lancashire Bowling

	O.	M.	R.	W.		O.	M.	R.	W.
Statham	17.1	3	57	5	....	22	7	47	3
Goodwin	7	0	24	1					
Tattersall	12	4	23	2	....	32	8	71	2
Hilton	5	4	1	0	....	33	18	38	3
Collins	14	6	25	1	....	29	13	44	0
Ikin...........	7	3	12	1	....	17	4	50	1
					Grieves	3	2	1	0

Umpires: T. J. Bartley and A. J. B. Fowler.

At Manchester, July 7, 8, 9, 11, 12. SOUTH AFRICA beat ENGLAND (Third Test Match) by three wickets. (See SOUTH AFRICAN section.)

At Nottingham, July 9, 11, 12. LANCASHIRE lost to NOTTINGHAMSHIRE by 32 runs.

LANCASHIRE v. MIDDLESEX

At Liverpool, July 13, 14, 15. Middlesex won by two wickets. G. A. Edrich, hitting two 6's and eleven 4's, celebrated his birthday by helping Lancashire to recover from an indifferent start, but he owed much to his brother, W. J. Edrich, who dropped him when seven and 70. Middlesex began their reply with an opening partnership of 164 in three hours by Robertson and Brown, but their innings was equally untidy against the varied flight of Hilton and the spin of Tattersall. Lancashire, 43 ahead, batted poorly on the final morning when in one spell Young, the left-arm slow bowler, took six wickets for nine runs. Set to score 208 in three and a quarter hours, Middlesex were again given a good start, but only ten minutes remained when Young made the winning hit.

Lancashire

J. T. Ikin b Tilly	17	— b Moss	6
J. Dyson c and b Young	19	— b Moss	35
G. A. Edrich c Compton b Young	117	— lbw b Young	29
C. Washbrook b Young	1	— c Edrich b Young	38
A. Wharton b Young	40	— c Bick b Young	30
K. Grieves c Compton b Moss	42	— c Bick b Young	3
R. Collins b Bennett	6	— lbw b Young	5
C. S. Smith b Tilly..................	9	— c Sharp b Young..........	1
M. J. Hilton c Compton b Tilly	15	— run out	5
A. Wilson not out	6	— not out	1
R. Tattersall c Edrich b Tilly	0	— c Compton b Young	0
B 11, l-b 3, n-b 1	15	B 4, l-b 6, w 1	11

1/32 2/44 3/45 4/113 5/214 6/226	287	1/9 2/59 3/95 4/137	164
7/266 8/266 9/287		5/151 6/152 7/153 8/162
		9/162

Middlesex

J. D. Robertson c Smith b Tattersall	....	79	— c and b Hilton..........	16
S. M. Brown c Grieves b Tattersall	.....	83	— c Grieves b Collins	62
W. J. Edrich c and b Hilton	....	7	— c Washbrook b Hilton	 35
D. Bennett c Ikin b Hilton	....	13	— b Dyson	8
H. P. Sharp c Edrich b Hilton	......	5	— not out	17
D. O. Baldry c Washbrook b Hilton	....	17	— b Tattersall	12
D. A. Bick c Ikin b Hilton	......	2	— c Tattersall b Hilton	 2
L. H. Compton c Grieves b Tattersall	...	16	— b Hilton	16
H. W. Tilly c and b Hilton	....	8	— b Hilton	20
J. A. Young not out	....	4	— not out	4
A. E. Moss c Washbrook b Hilton	....	0		
B 4, l-b 4, w 1, n-b 1	....	10	B 14, l-b 3	17

1/164 2/169 3/183 4/192 5/201 6/214　　244
7/226 8/240 9/244

1/51 2/90 3/120　(8 wkts.) 209
4/130 5/159 6/169 7/184
8/188

Middlesex Bowling

	O.	M.	R.	W.		O.	M.	R.	W.
Moss	17	6	25	1	....	10	1	36	2
Bennett	19	4	40	1	....	1	0	4	0
Young	36	12	100	4	....	23.3	9	45	7
Tilly	33.2	3	68	4	....	23	7	51	0
Bick	9	1	35	0					
Edrich	4	1	4	0					
Robertson						9	1	17	0

Lancashire Bowling

	O.	M.	R.	W.		O.	M.	R.	W.
Smith	9	0	40	0	....	2	0	10	0
Wharton	4	2	7	0	....	2	0	5	0
Tattersall	40	14	71	3	....	31	5	87	1
Ikin..........	8	2	19	0					
Hilton	36.4	17	65	7	....	27.3	10	69	5
Collins	10	3	18	0	....	4	1	15	1
Dyson	5	3	14	0	....	4	0	6	1

Umpires: D. Davies and T. J. Bartley.

LANCASHIRE v. LEICESTERSHIRE

At Manchester, July 16, 18, 19. Lancashire won by an innings and 59 runs. Their captain, Washbrook, played a leading part by completing 1,000 runs in a season for the fifteenth time in his career. He, like the remainder of the batsmen, showed great respect for an accurate, hostile attack on the first day, but the scoring rate soared later through a fierce onslaught by Statham. With two 6's, twelve 4's and two singles he raced to 62 in half an hour. Statham emphasised his stamina by helping to dismiss his opponents cheaply and he claimed the first Leicestershire wicket at three when they followed on 256 behind. Good slow bowling by Hilton and Tattersall completed the success.

Lancashire

J. T. Ikin b Palmer	....	63	F. W. Moore not ou	 6
J. Dyson c Hallam b Jackson	....	26	A. Wilson c Jackson b Munden	.. 0
G. A. Edrich c Smith b Spencer...		12		
C. Washbrook c Hallam b Munden		90	B 2, l-b 6, n-b 1	9
A. Wharton c Firth b Munden....		36		
K. Grieves b Jackson	....	63	1/38 2/62 3/181　(9 wkts., dec.) 389
M. J. Hilton b Spencer	....	22	4/199 5/267 6/307 7/375 8/389
J. B. Statham b Munden	....	62	9/389

R. Tattersall did not bat.

Leicestershire

G. Lester c Wilson b Moore	3	— c Grieves b Hilton	46
M. R. Hallam b Statham	10	— c Wilson b Statham	0
M. Tompkin st Wilson b Hilton	15	— c Moore b Tattersall	67
M. J. K. Smith lbw b Statham	4	— c Grieves b Tattersall	1
C. H. Palmer c Grieves b Tattersall	49	— c Edrich b Hilton	1
V. E. Jackson c Grieves b Statham	24	— c Dyson b Hilton	38
G. A. Smithson c Ikin b Statham	0	— hit wkt b Hilton	5
V. S. Munden st Wilson b Hilton	7	— lbw b Tattersall	9
J. Firth not out	3	— not out	16
C. T. Spencer c Ikin b Tattersall	5	— b Ikin	5
J. Goodwin c Edrich b Hilton	4	— c Statham b Tattersall	6
L-b 9	9	L-b 3	3
	—		—
	133		197

1/13 2/13 3/18 4/40 5/79 6/79
7/112 8/124 9/129

1/3 2/113 3/114 4/115
5/117 6/141 7/160 8/177
9/190

Leicestershire Bowling

	O.	M.	R.	W.	O.	M.	R.	W.
Spencer	23	6	73	2				
Goodwin	28	6	98	0				
Palmer	21	8	44	1				
Jackson	15	4	49	2				
Munden	32	11	101	4				
Lester	3	0	15	0				

Lancashire Bowling

	O.	M.	R.	W.	O.	M.	R.	W.
Statham	13	1	34	4	15	3	32	1
Moore	8	2	21	1	6	2	9	0
Tattersall	16	11	9	2	27.3	9	57	4
Hilton	15	5	51	3	36	13	69	4
Dyson	6	3	9	0	2	0	10	0
Ikin					6	1	17	1

Umpires: T. Spencer and E. Cooke.

At Maidstone, July 20, 21, 22. LANCASHIRE drew with KENT.

At Northampton, July 23, 25, 26. LANCASHIRE drew with NORTHAMPTONSHIRE.

LANCASHIRE v. GLOUCESTERSHIRE

At Blackpool, July 27, 28, 29. Lancashire won by six wickets. The Blackpool pitch maintained its sporting reputation on the first day when both sides completed an innings. Gloucestershire, 46 runs in arrear, did much better on Thursday when they earned reward for enterprise. Graveney produced his best form and Crapp, who hit eighteen 4's, made his strokes fluently despite a badly bruised and swollen left hand. Set to score 257 to win, Lancashire looked in trouble when Graveney, with leg-breaks, dismissed Ikin, Edrich and Washbrook at a personal cost of 20 runs. Wharton hit a fine century in one hour forty minutes, and Grieves helped him to retrieve the situation with an unbroken partnership of 148 runs in ninety minutes.

Gloucestershire

D. M. Young lbw b Statham	22	— b Moore	16
C. A. Milton lbw b Statham	12	— lbw b Wharton	22
T. W. Graveney st Jordan b Moore	49	— b Hilton	46
J. F. Crapp c Hilton b Statham	11	— c Grieves b Moore	98
G. M. Emmett b Statham	0	— c Ikin b Hilton	32
G. E. Lambert run out	1	— lbw b Hilton	28
J. Mortimore b Moore	0	— c Hilton b Tattersall	20
P. Rochford not out	12	— b Tattersall	6
C. Cook b Statham	5	— c Ikin b Moore	6
B. D. Wells c Hilton b Moore	13	— b Tattersall	11
F. P. McHugh run out	0	— not out	1
N-b 5	5	B 6, l-b 7, n-b 3	16

1/23 2/38 3/67 4/67 5/74 6/86   130   1/31 2/45 3/104 4/184   302
7/100 8/105 9/128   5/234 6/260 7/276 8/286
9/288

Lancashire

J. T. Ikin lbw b Wells	39	— c and b Graveney	25
J. Dyson c Graveney b McHugh	8	— c Milton b Wells	6
G. A. Edrich c Rochford b Wells	12	— b Graveney	48
C. Washbrook c Wells b McHugh	8	— lbw b Graveney	12
A. Wharton not out	58	— not out	108
K. Grieves lbw b Lambert	11	— not out	42
M. J. Hilton c Young b Cook	31		
J. Jordan b Cook	0		
J. B. Statham lbw b Wells	0		
F. W. Moore c Milton b Cook	1		
R. Tattersall b Cook	0		
B 2, l-b 5, n-b 1	8	B 3, l-b 10, w 1, n-b 5	19

1/16 2/43 3/64 4/78 5/103 6/162   176   1/25 2/79 3/99   (4 wkts.) 260
7/162 8/163 9/168   4/112

Lancashire Bowling

	O.	M.	R.	W.	O.	M.	R.	W.
Statham	18	4	58	5	26	4	62	0
Moore	17	4	67	3	21	7	55	3
Wharton					6	0	36	1
Tattersall					21	7	67	3
Hilton					20	9	51	3
Ikin					7	4	15	0

Gloucestershire Bowling

	O.	M.	R.	W.	O.	M.	R.	W.
Lambert	14	3	53	1	15	2	68	0
McHugh	22	4	55	2	26	7	53	0
Wells	30	15	38	3	17	7	34	1
Cook	11.3	5	22	4	3	2	5	0
Mortimore					5	2	8	0
Graveney					15	2	61	3
Milton					1	0	8	0
Young					0.1	0	4	0

Umpires: T. Spencer and K. McCanlis.

At Sheffield, July 30, August 1, 2. LANCASHIRE drew with YORKSHIRE.

LANCASHIRE v. SURREY

At Manchester, August 3, 4, 5. Surrey won by seven wickets and were again indebted to the intelligent bowling of Lock. In a spell of 4.1 overs on the first day he took six wickets for ten runs after Ikin, with his second century of the season, helped Lancashire to score 188 for two by tea. On a good pitch, Lock kept a nagging length and was aided by alert fielding close to the wicket. Despite attractive batting by Barrington and a breezy innings, which included eleven 4's, by Laker, Surrey conceded first innings points by 28 runs. Lock again proved troublesome to Lancashire in their second innings, when he completed a match analysis of thirteen wickets for 130 runs, and Surrey had plenty of time in which to score 154 to win. T. Spencer, the umpire, at one stage held up play until a section of the crowd stopped barracking Surrey for their slow scoring. This was an unfortunate incident during an absorbing match.

Lancashire

J. T. Ikin b Lock	109	— c Swetman b Laker	20
J. Dyson c Swetman b Lock	28	— lbw b Lock	5
A. Wharton b Laker	42	— lbw b Laker	22
C. Washbrook lbw b Lock	24	— b Lock	28
J. D. Bond c Stewart b Lock	0	— c and b Lock	1
R. W. Barber not out	4	— not out	25
M. J. Hilton c Barrington b Lock	0	— c sub b E. Bedser	6
J. Jordan c Surridge b Lock	6	— c E. Bedser b Lock	3
J. B. Statham c Surridge b Lock	0	— c Laker b Lock	0
F. W. Moore c Barrington b Lock	6	— c Swetman b Laker	4
R. Tattersall c Lock b Laker	10	— b Laker	0
B 3, l-b 9, w 6, n-b 1	19	B 8, l-b 3, n-b 1	12

1/67 2/188 3/218 4/218 5/220 6/220   248
7/230 8/230 9/236

1/14 2/45 3/50 4/61 5/87   125
6/114 7/119 8/119 9/123

Surrey

E. A. Bedser c Bond b Tattersall	24	— b Tattersall	24
M. J. Stewart c Jordan b Statham	0	— b Statham	17
P. B. H. May b Moore	43	— st Jordan b Tattersall	17
B. Constable c Hilton b Moore	0	— not out	53
K. Barrington c Jordan b Tattersall	54	— not out	38
R. Swetman b Statham	11		
J. C. Laker b Hilton	55		
W. S. Surridge b Tattersall	4		
G. A. R. Lock lbw b Statham	3		
P. J. Loader c Wharton b Moore	17		
A. V. Bedser not out	3		
B 1, l-b 5	6	B 1, l-b 4, n-b 1	6

1/0 2/63 3/63 4/81 5/119 6/193   220
7/197 8/197 9/216

1/38 2/58 3/70   (3 wkts.) 155

Surrey Bowling

	O.	M.	R.	W.		O.	M.	R.	W
A. Bedser	14	2	38	0	....	7	1	14	0
Loader	12	2	38	0	....	3	1	2	0
Laker	30.5	9	54	2	....	16	7	37	4
Surridge	7	1	12	0					
Lock	37	9	82	8	....	25	11	48	5
E. Bedser	4	2	5	0	....	7	2	12	1

Lancashire Bowling

	O.	M.	R.	W.	O.	M.	R.	W.
Statham	24	4	56	3	 17	9	21	1
Moore	16	8	49	3	 3	0	5	0
Tattersall	20	7	55	3	 27	7	46	2
Hilton	21	8	42	1	 33	12	70	0
Ikin..........	2	1	12	0				
Dyson					2	0	3	0
Barber					0.4	0	4	0

Umpires: D. Davies and T. Spencer.

LANCASHIRE v. GLAMORGAN

At Manchester, August 6, 8, 9. Drawn. Rain caused a blank third day and brought about the only no decision match of the season. Ikin, scoring his second successive century, and Washbrook did most towards the big Lancashire total with a partnership of 123 in two hours. Altogether fifty boundaries were hit and of those Washbrook, who was in brilliant form, obtained twenty. All had to be earned against alert fielding. In reply Parkhouse reached three figures for Glamorgan and despite the slowness of his scoring it was a gallant innings. Few of the spectators who showed disapproval realised that he batted throughout five hours forty minutes handicapped by arthritis in the right shoulder.

Lancashire

J. T. Ikin c Pleass b Ward........107	J. Jordan not out 20
J. Dyson lbw b Watkins 0	J. B. Statham c Edrich b H. D.
A. Wharton c Wooller b H. D.	Davies 1
Davies 43	F. W. Moore b Watkins 5
C. Washbrook c H. G. Davies b	L-b 12, n-b 1 13
Wooller......................131	
R. W. Barber b Watkins 16	1/4 2/73 3/196 (9 wkts., dec.) 362
J. D. Bond c Ward b Wooller 25	4/257 5/329 6/333 7/334 8/335
M. J. Hilton c Clift b Wooller 1	9/362

R. Tattersall did not bat.

Glamorgan

W. G. A. Parkhouse lbw b Hilton .143	B. R. Edrich not out 9
P. B. Clift c Jordan b Statham ... 7	D. J. Ward not out.............. 4
J. Pleass lbw b Statham 26	
W. E. Jones c and b Hilton 12	B 15, l-b 2, n-b 1 18
A. J. Watkins c Barber b Tattersall 7	
J. Pressdee b Hilton 4	1/29 2/107 3/124 4/137 (7 wkts.) 271
W. Wooller lbw b Tattersall 41	5/166 6/253 7/267

H. G. Davies and H. D. Davies did not bat.

Glamorgan Bowling

	O.	M.	R.	W.
H. D. Davies .	25	7	65	2
Watkins	28	6	83	3
Wooller.........	33	10	84	3
Ward	18	2	65	1
Pressdee	15	1	52	0

Lancashire Bowling

	O.	M.	R.	W.
Statham	27	10	46	2
Moore	12	2	52	0
Wharton	8	1	24	0
Tattersall	27	18	36	2
Hilton	41	22	64	3
Ikin	10	3	20	0
Barber	2	0	11	0

Umpires: N. Oldfield and W. F. Price.

At Portsmouth, August 10, 11, 12. LANCASHIRE lost to HAMPSHIRE by 39 runs.

At Clacton, August 13, 15, 16. LANCASHIRE drew with ESSEX.

At Hove, August 17, 18, 19. LANCASHIRE lost to SUSSEX by 87 runs.

LANCASHIRE v. SOMERSET

At Manchester, August 20, 22, 23. Lancashire won by an innings and 79 runs. They were helped by poor Somerset fielding. Wharton, who hit one 6 and sixteen 4's in his highest score in championship cricket, was missed four times. Three of the dropped catches were off Lawrence, the leg spinner, whose figures bore little relation to the quality of his bowling. Pullar, the 20-year-old amateur, showed pleasing style in passing fifty for the first time. Somerset were as weak in batting as in fielding. They lost their last six wickets for 47 runs in the first innings and on the final morning, when Smith, the Cambridge Blue, took four wickets for six runs in six overs, the score went from 28 for one to 46 for seven in forty-five minutes.

Lancashire

J. T. Ikin c Stephenson b Lobb ...	11
A. Wharton c Tremlett b Lawrence	123
G. A. Edrich run out	16
C. Washbrook st Stephenson b Lawrence	5
G. Pullar c McMahon b Lawrence	76
R. Collins c Tordoff b Lawrence..	38
R. W. Barber b Lawrence	6
C. S. Smith st Stephenson b Lomax	27

F. W. Moore st Stephenson b Lomax	1
A. Wilson not out	16
R. Tattersall st Stephenson b Lawrence	28
B 2, l-b 5	7

1/26 2/62 3/81 4/196 5/264   354
6/275 7/279 8/282 9/313

Somerset

G. G. Tordoff st Wilson b Collins	34	— c Washbrook b Ikin	9
F. L. Angell b Tattersall	35	— c Wilson b Tattersall	14
J. Lawrence c Edrich b Smith	20	— b Smith	0
M. F. Tremlett b Ikin	26	— c Edrich b Smith	3
P. B. Wight c Edrich b Tattersall	11	— b Tattersall	3
J. G. Lomax lbw b Smith	11	— c Wilson b Smith	0
H. W. Stephenson lbw b Tattersall	7	— not out	45
Yawar Saeed run out	11	— c Edrich b Smith	1
J. Hilton not out	8	— c Wharton b Ikin	7
J. W. McMahon b Ikin	2	— run out	3
B. Lobb c Wilson b Ikin	0	— c Barber b Tattersall	2
B 5, l-b 1	6	B 9, l-b 8	17

1/58 2/72 3/109 4/124 5/134 6/138   171
7/148 8/156 9/171

1/28 2/30 3/36 4/44 5/44   104
6/44 7/46 8/76 9/94

Somerset Bowling

	O.	M.	R.	W.
Lobb	25	9	53	1
Yawar Saeed	24	5	63	0
Hilton	2	0	5	0
Lomax	28	9	69	2
Tordoff	2	0	15	0
Lawrence	40.5	6	142	6

Lancashire Bowling

	O.	M.	R.	W.	O.	M.	R.	W.
Smith	16	6	32	2	13	3	22	4
Wharton	5	1	22	0				
Moore	5	1	20	0	5	3	5	0
Tattersall	26	11	41	3	16.2	6	26	3
Collins	7	1	27	1	4	2	15	0
Ikin	9.2	3	23	3	13	5	19	2

Umpires: Harry Elliott (Derbyshire) and W. F. Price.

LANCASHIRE v. COMBINED SERVICES

At Manchester, August 24, 25, 26. Lancashire won by 107 runs. A strong Combined Services' attack performed creditably in taking the first five Lancashire wickets for 96. Then all the bowlers were punished by Washbrook, who, hitting three 6's and twenty 4's, batted faultlessly for three hours on a fast, true pitch. Barber gave good support in a sixth wicket stand of 176. Richardson, Cartwright and Ainsworth, the captain, did well in reply but with the exception of Richardson and Leary the batsmen failed when the Services went in a second time needing 266 runs in three hours thirty-five minutes to win. Ikin, bowling leg-breaks with admirable control, took five wickets for twelve runs in eight overs.

Lancashire

J. T. Ikin b Lightfoot	10	—	b Lightfoot	22
A. Wharton c Ainsworth b Leary	30	—	c Murray b Cowan	5
G. A. Edrich c Stott b Cowan	0	—	not out	75
G. Pullar lbw b Leary	28			
R. Collins c Ainsworth b Leary	18	—	b Cowan	12
R. W. Barber c and b Marner	53	—	lbw b Shirreff	21
C. Washbrook c Cartwright b Shirreff	166	—	not out	30
C. S. Smith lbw b Shirreff	14			
F. W. Moore c Cartwright b Shirreff	5			
T. Greenhough not out	16			
A. Wilson c Ainsworth b Lightfoot	1			
B 7, l-b 7	14		B 7, l-b 1	8

1/23 2/24 3/64 4/73 5/96 6/272   355   1/15 2/41   (4 wkts., dec.) 173
7/332 8/334 9/343   3/72 4/126

Combined Services

Sgt. P. E. Richardson c and b Greenhough	43	—	lbw b Collins	90
L/Bdr. T. W. Cartwright b Collins	51	—	c and b Ikin	0
L/A/C J. T. Murray c Wilson b Barber	9	—	lbw b Ikin	0
A/C S. E. Leary b Smith	20	—	c Barber b Moore	31
Lt.-Comdr. M. L. Y. Ainsworth c Washbrook b Smith	60	—	c sub b Ikin	12
L/Cpl. P. T. Marner b Collins	13	—	b Collins	4
A/C W. B. Stott lbw b Greenhough	23	—	not out	8
S/Ldr. A. C. Shirreff c Wilson b Smith	10	—	c Ikin b Smith	1
L/Bdr. R. A. Gale b Smith	0	—	c Wilson b Collins	5
L/Cpl. M. A. Lightfoot not out	8	—	st Wilson b Ikin	4
J/T M. J. Cowan b Smith	4	—	st Wilson b Ikin	0
B 14, l-b 7, w 1	22		B 2, l-b 1	3

1/68 2/96 3/134 4/156 5/198 6/223   263   1/9 2/16 3/95 4/141   158
7/245 8/251 9/251   5/141 6/142 7/142 8/149
                                            9/154

Combined Services Bowling

	O.	M.	R.	W.		O.	M.	R.	W.
Cowan	19	3	66	1	....	15	2	38	2
Lightfoot	27.5	5	73	2	....	20	7	41	1
Shirreff	28	9	72	3	....	16	3	44	0
Leary	13	2	64	3	....	2	1	5	0
Gale	11	2	37	0	....	11	3	35	0
Marner........	8	2	29	1	....	2	1	2	0

Lancashire Bowling

	O.	M.	R.	W.		O.	M.	R.	W.
Smith	18.2	6	39	5	....	6	1	17	1
Moore	15	3	40	0	....	8	1	33	1
Greenhough ...	33	9	81	2	....	11	1	58	0
Collins	26	14	55	2	....	19	9	32	3
Barber	4	1	13	1					
Ikin..........	4	3	1	0	....	8	3	12	5
Wharton	2	0	12	0	....	2	0	3	0

Umpires: Harry Elliott (Derbyshire) and N. Oldfield.

At Bristol, August 27, 29. LANCASHIRE lost to GLOUCESTERSHIRE by 88 runs.

LEICESTERSHIRE

President—S. H. B. LIVINGSTON

Captain and Secretary—C. H. PALMER, Spencer Chambers,
4, Market Place, Leicester

| M. Tompkin | County Badge | V. E. Jackson |

Suited by the prevailing dry pitches, Leicestershire experienced a heartening revival of form after their lapse of 1954, and rose ten places in the Championship table, from sixteenth to sixth, gaining 154 points, only two fewer than in 1953, when they finished third, the highest position in their history.

Eleven victories were won in the County Championship, equalling the record number for the county, gained in 1935, and a twelfth success was achieved against Cambridge University. Moreover, Leicestershire set out to provide entertaining cricket under the enterprising captaincy of C. H. Palmer, and only seven championship games were drawn. A number of thrilling finishes added excitement to an enjoyable summer.

From the point of view of individual success, the season will be remembered for the achievement of Jackson, the Australian all-rounder, who performed the "cricketer's double" for the first time in his tenth season with Leicestershire. Jackson also hit more runs, and took more wickets with his well-controlled off-breaks, than in any previous season, and he finished in glorious style with three centuries in the county's last four games. He was granted a benefit to be taken in 1956.

Jackson was the only Leicestershire bowler to reach 100 wickets, but his total runs were exceeded by both Tompkin and Palmer who, like Jackson, batted with enterprise, particularly in their driving. Tompkin exceeded 2,000 runs in all first-class matches for the first time, and gained recognition for the Players against the Gentlemen at Lord's, where he hit a splendid 115. Palmer made 154 for the Gentlemen in the same match. Tompkin was chosen to tour Pakistan with M.C.C.

Apart from his excellent batting, Palmer gained distinction with the ball. Against the Champions, Surrey, at Leicester during May, he took eight wickets before conceding a run with remarkably accurate medium-paced bowling, and finished with an analysis of eight for seven. Thereafter Palmer bowled more than usual and headed the averages. Hallam and Lester also exceeded 1,000 runs, and M. J. K. Smith again lent strength to the batting after he finished playing for Oxford University.

Munden, with left-arm slows, enjoyed his most successful season with the ball, but Spencer, who returned from National Service, did not quite live up to expectations as an opening bowler. Walsh, the Australian left-arm slow bowler, played a less prominent part than in recent years. In the field, Leicestershire did well. Particularly satisfying was the success of Hallam, tried as a slip fielder. He held 41 catches.

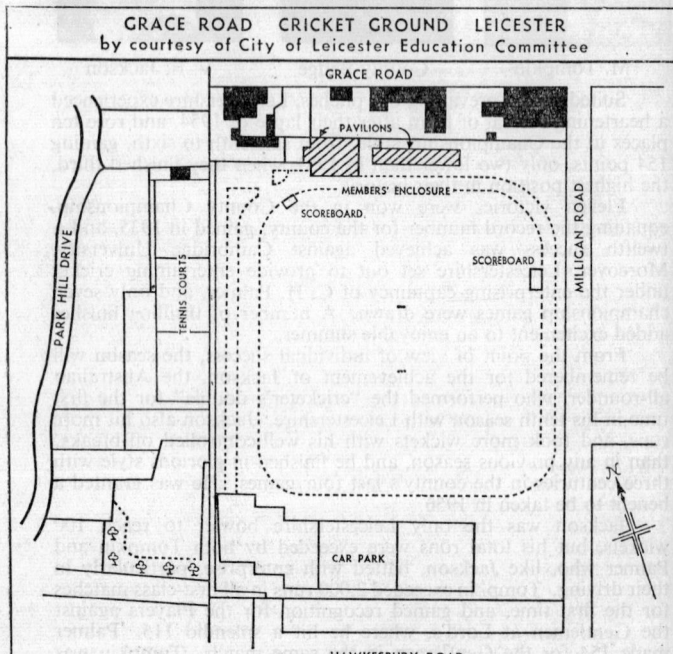

LEICESTERSHIRE RESULTS

All First-Class Matches—Played 31, *Won* 12, *Lost* 11, *Drawn* 8

County Championship Matches—Played 28, *Won* 11, *Lost* 10, *Drawn* 7

COUNTY CHAMPIONSHIP AVERAGES

BATTING

	Birthplace	Mtchs.	Inns.	Not Outs	Runs	100's	Highest Inns.	Aver.
M. Tompkin .	*Countesthorpe*	28	51	3	1865	2	131	38.85
V. E. Jackson .	*Sydney*	28	50	3	1451	4	121	30.87
C. H. Palmer .	*Old Hill*	28	50	1	1474	3	128	30.08
M. J. K. Smith	*Leicester*	14	27	1	688	0	70	26.46
M. R. Hallam	*Leicester*	22	40	1	1014	0	86	26.00
R. A. Diment .	*Tortworth*	9	16	1	339	0	71	22.60
G. Lester	*Long Whatton*	28	52	2	999	2	143	19.98
J. Firth.......	*Cottingley*	24	36	13	369	0	51	16.04
V. S. Munden	*Leicester*	28	46	4	632	0	50	15.04
J. E. Walsh ...	*Sydney*	20	29	2	389	0	57*	14.40
G. A. Smithson	*Harrogate*	22	38	3	473	0	55	13.51
R. Pratt	*Stoney Stanton*	4	5	4	12	0	8*	12.00
C. T. Spencer .	*Leicester*	27	42	11	370	0	75	11.93
J. Goodwin ..	*Audley*	11	16	9	50	0	11*	7.14
B. Boshier	*Leicester*	10	11	8	14	0	13*	4.66
R. Julian	*Cosby*	4	6	1	11	0	9	2.20

Also batted: L. R. Gardner (*Ledbury*) 9*, 14.

* Signifies not out.

BOWLING

	Overs	Maidens	Runs	Wickets	Average
C. H. Palmer	416.1	181	832	45	18.48
V. E. Jackson	971.2	381	2143	106	20.21
V. S. Munden	777.1	286	1750	72	24.30
J. E. Walsh	378.1	92	1127	43	26.20
G. Lester	238.4	56	814	30	27.13
J. Goodwin	252.2	42	853	30	28.43
C. T. Spencer	697	137	2248	67	33.55
R. Pratt	81.4	10	304	8	38.00
B. Boshier	166	24	533	10	53.30

Also bowled: M. Tomkin 1—0—4—0.

Amateurs.—R. A. Diment, C. H. Palmer, M. J. K. Smith.

LEICESTERSHIRE v. WORCESTERSHIRE

At Leicester, May 2, 3. Drawn. Leicestershire 165 for six wickets, declared (M. Tompkin 62); Worcestershire 22 for one wicket. (Friendly match.)

At Northampton, May 4, 5. LEICESTERSHIRE drew with NORTHAMPTONSHIRE (Friendly match.)

LEICESTERSHIRE v. KENT

At Leicester, May 7, 9, 10. Drawn. Jackson, so often a thorn in the side of Kent, upset them by off-break bowling, taking nine wickets for 98 in the match. Well supported by the left-arm slows of Munden, Jackson troubled all the batsmen on the opening day except Brazier, formerly of Surrey, who remained unbeaten after two hours. Lester and Palmer batted confidently for Leicestershire, who went ahead with seven wickets standing. Then they collapsed against good spin bowling by Pettiford and Page. Shirreff, Hearn and Dixon did so well in the second innings that, despite the accuracy of Jackson, Kent were able to set Leicestershire to make 151 in an hour and three-quarters, a task not seriously attempted before bad light and rain ended play 15 minutes early.

Kent

A. E. Fagg c Smithson b Boshier	0	— c Spencer b Walsh	26
A. C. Shirreff c Hallam b Jackson	23	— b Lester	77
R. C. Wilson c Firth b Jackson	16	— b Jackson	0
J. Pettiford run out	1	— lbw b Walsh	3
A. F. Brazier not out	51	— c Firth b Spencer	12
P. Hearn c Hallam b Munden	1	— c and b Jackson	55
A. Dixon b Jackson	24	— b Jackson	40
A. W. Catt lbw b Munden	0	— b Spencer	1
F. Ridgway c Boshier b Jackson	8	— c Palmer b Jackson	0
D. V. P. Wright b Munden	4	— st Firth b Jackson	0
J. C. T. Page run out	3	— not out	2
B 5, n-b 1	6	B 5, l-b 6, w 1, n-b 3	15

1/1 2/40 3/41 4/44 5/63 6/94   137
7/97 8/116 9/129

1/40 2/41 3/56 4/93   231
5/165 6/227 7/229 8/229
9/229

Leicestershire

G. Lester c Catt b Page	63	— not out	19
M. R. Hallam b Shirreff	0	— b Page	24
M. Tompkin b Ridgway	19	— not out	4
C. H. Palmer b Page	58		
G. A. Smithson lbw b Pettiford	13		
V. E. Jackson lbw b Page	20		
V. Munden b Page	13		
J. E. Walsh lbw b Pettiford	4		
J. Firth lbw b Pettiford	11		
C. T. Spencer not out	10		
B. Boshier b Pettiford	0		
B 4, l-b 2, n-b 1	7	B 1	1

1/0 2/41 3/122 4/142 5/171 6/180   218
7/191 8/201 9/218

1/44   (1 wkt.) 48

Leicestershire Bowling

	O.	M.	R.	W.		O.	M.	R.	W.
Spencer	8	3	15	0	....	27	5	47	2
Boshier	5	0	16	1	....	3	0	12	0
Jackson	29	9	51	4	....	32.1	16	47	5
Munden	26.1	11	49	3	....	20	9	22	0
Lester						13	4	31	1
Walsh						24	8	57	2
Palmer						2	2	0	0

Kent Bowling

	O.	M.	R.	W.	O.	M.	R.	W.
Ridgway	19	5	49	1	 8	2	21	0
Shirreff	13	4	31	1	 3	0	16	0
Wright	7	0	23	0				
Page	30	7	60	4	.... 6.3	3	6	1
Pettiford	28.5	12	48	4	 2	0	4	0

Umpires: H. Elliott (Lancashire) and K. McCanlis.

At Cambridge, May 11, 12, 13. LEICESTERSHIRE beat CAMBRIDGE UNIVERSITY by three wickets.

At Gravesend, May 14, 16. LEICESTERSHIRE beat KENT by six wickets.

At Bristol, May 18, 19 20. LEICESTERSHIRE beat GLOUCESTERSHIRE by two wickets.

LEICESTERSHIRE v. SURREY

(J. E. Walsh's Benefit)

At Leicestershire, May 21, 23, 24. Surrey won by seven wickets. Despite remarkable all-round cricket from Palmer, Surrey, although behind on first innings, won comfortably. On drying turf Leicestershire began well on the first day, but the left-arm spin of Lock brought about a collapse. Then Palmer, bowling medium pace with great accuracy and bringing the ball back sharply off the seam, so severely troubled the Surrey batsmen that he took eight wickets before conceding a run. He hit the stumps seven times. Alec Bedser and Lock troubled Leicestershire in their second innings, but Tompkin and Palmer resisted strongly. Palmer, defending skilfully, stayed for four hours, but all his efforts went for nought, for in the last innings May, Clark and Constable carried Surrey to victory. Palmer conceded only one run in thirteen overs in the second innings.

Leicestershire

G. Lester b Clark	22	— b Bedser	4
M. R. Hallam b Laker	39	-- b Bedser	7
M. Tompkin c and b Lock	19	— c McIntyre b Bedser	50
C. H. Palmer c Laker b Clark	1	— b Bedser	64
G. A. Smithson c Stewart b Lock	4	— lbw b Lock	0
V. E. Jackson c Stewart b Lock	2	— c Pratt b Bedser	2
V. S. Munden b Lock	4	— lbw b Bedser	6
J. E. Walsh b Lock	3	— b Lock	20
J. Firth not out	7	— b Lock	0
C. T. Spencer c May b Laker	0	— st McIntyre b Lock	0
B. Boshier c Bedser b Lock	0	— not out	0
B 7, l-b 5, n-b 1	13	B 8, l-b 3, n-b 1	12

1/68 2/74 3/75 4/98 5/99 6/100   114   1/20 2/21 3/98 4/101   165
7/104 8/109 9/114   5/106 6/116 7/151 8/153
                                                      9/165

P

Surrey

T. H. Clark b Spencer	7	— b Spencer		44
D. G. W. Fletcher b Palmer	7	— b Boshier		8
P. B. H. May b Palmer	28	— b Munden		84
B. Constable c Lester b Palmer	0	— not out		49
M. J. Stewart b Palmer	0	— not out		5
R. C. E. Pratt b Palmer	7			
A. J. McIntyre b Palmer	0			
J. C. Laker b Spencer	14			
W. S. Surridge b Palmer	0			
G. A. R. Lock b Palmer	4			
A. V. Bedser not out	2			
L-b 7, n-b 1	8	B 10, l-b 3		13
	77		(3 wkts.)	203

1/10 2/42 3/42 4/42 5/55 6/56   1/18 2/98 3/181
7/61 8/61 9/67

Surrey Bowling

	O.	M.	R.	W.		O.	M.	R.	W.
Bedser	12	6	14	0	....	32	14	53	6
Surridge	6	0	18	0	....	5	1	7	0
Lock	18.2	7	37	6	....	29.2	13	41	4
Laker	22	7	24	2	....	24	9	35	0
Clark	9	5	8	2	....	10	5	17	0

Leicestershire Bowling

	O.	M.	R.	W.		O.	M.	R.	W.
Spencer	11.2	3	19	2	....	26	6	61	1
Boshier	4	0	13	0	....	15	2	44	1
Munden	4	1	15	0	....	16.4	5	35	1
Jackson	4	3	1	0	....	23	8	42	0
Palmer	14	12	7	8	....	13	12	1	0
Walsh	7	3	14	0					
				Lester		1	0	7	0

Umpires: J. S. Buller and J. J. Hills.

At Dudley, May 25, 26, 27. LEICESTERSHIRE drew with WORCESTERSHIRE.

At Northampton, May 28, 30, 31. LEICESTERSHIRE drew with NORTHAMPTONSHIRE.

LEICESTERSHIRE v. NOTTINGHAMSHIRE

At Leicester, June 1, 2, 3. Leicestershire won by three wickets. On a hard pitch Nottinghamshire, apart from a sound display by Martin, batted uncertainly against keen bowling and fielding, Spencer and Palmer, both very accurate, being particularly effective. The spin bowling of Dooland and Smales proved equally troublesome to Leicestershire and only spirited hitting by Walsh, who made all 20 runs for the last wicket, enabled them to lead by three. Martin gave Nottinghamshire a chance of victory with another sound innings, but when Leicestershire batted again four dropped catches allowed them to emerge rather fortunate winners.

Nottinghamshire

R. T. Simpson b Spencer	21	—	b Jackson	23
J. D. Clay lbw b Spencer	0	—	b Spencer	3
C. J. Poole c Smithson b Jackson	33	—	c Spencer b Jackson	30
J. Hardstaff lbw b Jackson	22	—	c Hallam b Munden	19
E. J. Martin c Spencer b Munden	53	—	lbw b Spencer	47
P. F. Harvey c Hallam b Jackson	0	—	c Hallam b Jackson	20
B. Dooland b Palmer	37	—	b Palmer	5
K. Smales lbw b Palmer	2	—	c Smithson b Spencer	2
A. Jepson c Jackson b Munden	10	—	c Walsh b Palmer	22
E. J. Rowe not out	0	—	not out	1
M. Wood b Palmer	0	—	b Palmer	0
L-b 4, n-b 1	5		B 1, l-b 5	6

1/3 2/46 3/68 4/81 5/81 6/169　　183
7/171 8/179 9/183

1/15 2/37 3/64 4/78　　178
5/138 6/150 7/152 8/170
9/178

Leicestershire

G. Lester b Wood	11	—	b Jepson	2
M. R. Hallam b Dooland	39	—	b Dooland	44
M. Tompkin lbw b Dooland	7	—	c Harvey b Dooland	28
C. H. Palmer c and b Smales	20	—	lbw b Jepson	6
V. E. Jackson c Jepson b Dooland	13	—	c Poole b Smales	21
G. A. Smithson b Smales	4	—	c Clay b Dooland	8
V. S. Munden c Jepson b Smales	25	—	c Jepson b Dooland	32
J. E. Walsh b Smales	57	—	not out	15
C. T. Spencer b Dooland	0	—	not out	3
R. Julian b Dooland	0			
B. Boshier not out	0			
B 4, l-b 6	10		B 12, l-b 5	17

1/33 2/59 3/63 4/82 5/94 6/98　　186
7/165 8/166 9/166

1/8 2/61 3/80　　(7 wkts.) 176
4/80 5/94 6/147 7/161

Leicestershire Bowling

	O.	M.	R.	W.		O.	M.	R.	W.
Spencer	12	1	49	2	....	17	4	35	3
Boshier	5	1	24	0	....	4	0	14	0
Jackson	21	11	48	3	....	24	11	41	3
Walsh	14	5	37	0	....	5	1	11	0
Palmer	8.1	5	10	3	....	10.3	5	23	3
Munden	8	4	10	2	....	17	2	48	1

Nottinghamshire Bowling

	O.	M.	R.	W.		O.	M.	R.	W.
Jepson	12	3	39	0	....	15	7	20	2
Wood	8	1	21	1	....	2	0	16	0
Dooland	29	12	68	5	....	26	8	77	4
Smales	25.4	11	48	4	....	16.1	6	46	1

Umpires: T. Spencer and T. J. Bartley.

At Burton-on-Trent, June 4, 6, 7. LEICESTERSHIRE drew with DERBYSHIRE.

At Oxford, June 8, 9, 10. LEICESTERSHIRE drew with OXFORD UNIVERSITY.

LEICESTERSHIRE v. WARWICKSHIRE

At Hinckley, June 11, 13, 14. Warwickshire won by nine wickets. A partnership of 220 for the fourth wicket by Hitchcock and Dollery and the penetrative pace bowling of Thompson were match-winning factors. Bowling with life and accuracy on a helpful pitch on the first day, Thompson worried all the Leicestershire batsmen except Tompkin, who drove boldly. Spencer and Goodwin also proved troublesome when Warwickshire batted, but Dollery and Hitchcock, a left-hander, mastered the attack. Dollery, who hit two 6's and eleven 4's, made his sixth century against Leicestershire in seven seasons, and Hitchcock, with three 6's and fourteen 4's, reached three figures for the first time in first-class cricket. Despite more good batting by Tompkin and determined defence by Munden, Leicestershire set Warwickshire only 50 to get.

Leicestershire

G. Lester b Thompson	4	—	c Spooner b Thompson		12
M. R. Hallam b Bannister	3	—	c Townsend b Hollies		24
M. Tompkin b Thompson	42	—	b Townsend		49
C. H. Palmer c and b King	12	—	c King b Townsend		12
V. E. Jackson b Thompson	13	—	st Spooner b Thompson		33
G. A. Smithson b Thompson	0	—	b Thompson		4
V. S. Munden b Thompson	7	—	not out		33
J. E. Walsh c Spooner b Thompson	17	—	b Townsend		9
C. T. Spencer b Hollies	21	—	c Townsend b Thompson		8
R. Julian not out	2	—	b Hollies		9
J. Goodwin b Hollies	0	—	c Spooner b Hollies		0
B 9, l-b 2	11		B 10, l-b 4, n-b 2		16

1/7 2/13 3/60 4/76 5/76 6/86   **132**
7/101 8/122 9/132

1/21 2/56 3/96 4/119   **209**
5/126 6/145 7/158 8/171
9/209

Warwickshire

F. C. Gardner c Walsh b Spencer	0	—	not out	10
R. T. Spooner lbw b Goodwin	4	—	c Smithson b Goodwin	19
A. V. Wolton c Walsh b Spencer	3	—	not out	19
R. E. Hitchcock b Jackson	121			
H. E. Dollery b Lester	106			
A. Townsend b Lester	11			
W. J. Stewart b Jackson	0			
J. D. Bannister not out	18			
I. M. King c Hallam b Jackson	11			
R. G. Thompson c Palmer b Jackson	10			
W. E. Hollies c Palmer b Lester	0			
B 8	8		B 4	4

1/0 2/4 3/16 4/236 5/236 6/236   **292**   1/28   (1 wkt.) **52**
7/254 8/271 9/291

Warwickshire Bowling

	O.	M.	R.	W.	O.	M.	R.	W.
Bannister	14	5	25	1	12	4	23	0
Thompson	23	9	37	6	23	5	48	4
Hollies	11.4	4	33	2	30.5	15	49	3
King	14	6	26	1	14	7	19	0
Hitchcock					5	2	14	0
Townsend					20	6	40	3

Leicestershire Bowling

	O.	M.	R.	W.	O.	M.	R.	W.
Spencer	14	2	50	2	4	1	13	0
Goodwin	9	2	24	1	3.4	0	35	1
Palmer	11	1	31	0				
Jackson	31	0	84	4				
Munden	9	1	26	0				
Walsh	6	0	33	0				
Lester	9.3	3	36	3				

Umpires: E. Cooke and A. J. B. Fowler.

LEICESTERSHIRE v. LANCASHIRE

At Hinckley, June 15, 16. Lancashire won by an innings and 101 runs. The speed of Statham and Tattersall's sharply turning off-breaks on a pitch which always assisted bowlers proved too much for Leicestershire. Ikin gave Lancashire a good start with a careful innings lasting three and a half hours, and Edrich helped him in a stand of 95. Washbrook, too, batted soundly but the turf became more difficult as it dried, and the spin of Jackson and Munden brought about a collapse. When Leicestershire batted Statham took four wickets in 34 balls, and he remained effective next morning when Tattersall joined in the destruction. Leicestershire followed on 182 behind and fared little better, although Smithson batted doggedly for an hour and a quarter. After further successes for Statham and Tattersall, Hilton with left-arm slows, finished the match.

Lancashire

J. T. Ikin c Tompkin b Spencer	75	J. B. Statham not out	2
A. Wharton st Julian b Walsh	15	A. Wilson b Jackson	0
G. A. Edrich c Palmer b Munden	37	R. Tattersall b Jackson	0
C. Washbrook b Munden	54		
K. Grieves b Jackson	5	B 27, l-b 2	29
S. Smith c Hallam b Munden	2		—
R. Collins b Jackson	1	1/35 2/130 3/170 4/191 5/200	224
M. J. Hilton b Jackson	4	6/203 7/213 8/221 9/222	

Leicestershire

G. Lester b Statham	0	— b Tattersall	9
M. R. Hallam b Statham	0	— b Tattersall	7
M. Tompkin b Statham	5	— c Wilson b Statham	1
C. H. Palmer b Statham	10	— c Statham b Tattersall	18
L. Jackson b Statham	0	— lbw b Statham	0
G. A. Smithson b Tattersall	9	— c Collins b Hilton	20
V. S. Munden b Statham	0	— b Tattersall	6
J. E. Walsh lbw b Tattersall	1	— c Tattersall b Statham	10
C. T. Spencer b Tattersall	0	— c Smith b Hilton	6
R. Julian b Tattersall	0	— c Tattersall b Hilton	0
B. S. Boshier not out	13	— not out	1
B 4	4	B 1, l-b 1, n-b 1	3
	—		—
1/0 2/1 3/10 4/10 5/18 6/18	42	1/14 2/15 3/25 4/30	81
7/25 8/25 9/25		5/36 6/60 7/70 8/80 9/80	

Leicestershire Bowling

	O.	M.	R.	W.	O.	M.	R.	W.
Spencer	13	5	22	1				
Boshier	6	3	7	0				
Walsh	11	3	30	1				
Jackson	25.4	10	48	5				
Munden	32	15	62	3				
Lester	6	2	13	0				
Palmer	12	8	13	0				

Lancashire Bowling

	O.	M.	R.	W.		O.	M.	R.	W.
Statham	14	6	20	6	....	16	1	46	3
Tattersall	9.1	6	12	4	....	17	7	23	4
Hilton	4	1	6	0	....	2.5	0	9	3

Umpires: F. S. Lee and W. T. Jones.

At Nottingham, June 18, 20, 21. LEICESTERSHIRE lost to NOTTINGHAMSHIRE by two wickets.

LEICESTERSHIRE v. MIDDLESEX

At Leicester, June 22, 23, 24. Leicestershire won by six wickets after being 46 behind on first innings. On a pitch of easy pace Middlesex began well, Robertson playing a sound innings. They passed 200 with four wickets down, but Spencer and Pratt, with the new ball, brought about a collapse. Apart from Hallam and Palmer, who both drove well, Leicestershire could do little with the left-arm slows of Young and the off-breaks of Robertson, who maintained his all-round form with another good display in the second innings. When rain held up play for 45 minutes on the last day, it appeared that the task of scoring 228 might be too much for Leicestershire, but bold hitting by Hallam and Tompkin brought victory with fourteen minutes to spare.

Middlesex

J. D. Robertson	lbw b Lester	74	—	c Smithson b Munden	48
S. M. Brown	lbw b Jackson	35	—	lbw b Spencer	8
W. J. Edrich	b Munden	46	—	c Hallam b Jackson	22
A. Thompson	c Firth b Spencer	3	—	c Hallam b Lester	17
D. Bennett	c Firth b Spencer	45	—	c Hallam b Lester	5
D. O. Baldry	b Lester	9	—	lbw b Lester	5
D. Bick	c and b Spencer	29	—	c Firth b Jackson	1
J. J. Warr	b Pratt	0	—	c Firth b Spencer	22
L. H. Compton	b Pratt	7	—	lbw b Jackson	8
J. A. Young	b Pratt	1	—	not out	17
A. E. Moss	not out	0	—	c Smithson b Spencer	16
	B 10, l-b 3	13		B 9, l-b 3	12

1/59 2/129 3/145 4/181 5/202　　　262
6/249 7/250 8/254 9/255

1/14 2/67 3/85 4/107　　　181
5/108 6/109 7/113 8/137
9/159

Leicestershire

G. Lester	c Robertson b Warr	20	—	c Robertson b Young	9
M. R. Hallam	b Bick	56	—	b Moss	83
M. Tompkin	lbw b Young	21	—	not out	87
C. H. Palmer	b Young	71	—	b Bennett	18
V. E. Jackson	c Compton b Robertson	21	—	b Moss	4
G. A. Smithson	b Robertson	0	—	not out	15
V. S. Munden	b Robertson	0			
J. E. Walsh	lbw b Young	3			
J. Firth	c Edrich b Robertson	4			
C. T. Spencer	b Young	1			
R. L. Pratt	not out	1			
	B 9, l-b 8	18		B 6, l-b 5, n-b 1	12

1/53 2/100 3/112 4/168 5/170　　　216
6/174 7/177 8/200 9/207

1/52 2/133　　　(4 wkts.) 228
3/170 4/185

Leicestershire Bowling

	O.	M.	R.	W.		O.	M.	R.	W.
Spencer	20	5	56	3	....	14	5	23	3
Pratt	11.4	2	31	3	....	8	1	31	0
Jackson	13	4	28	1	....	31	15	43	3
Walsh	16	3	51	0					
Munden	34	19	25	1	....	17	6	46	1
Lester	18	7	48	2	....	9	1	26	3
Palmer	5	4	10	0					

Middlesex Bowling

	O.	M.	R.	W.	O.	M.	R.	W.
Moss	15	5	29	0	.... 17.5	4	66	2
Warr	12	2	43	1	 11	0	47	0
Young	35.1	16	54	4	 9	2	38	1
Bick	10	2	35	1				
Robertson	22	9	37	4	 9	0	41	0
Bennett					 6	2	24	1

Umpires: E. Cooke and K. McCanlis.

At Bath, June 25, 27, 28. LEICESTERSHIRE drew with SOMERSET.

LEICESTERSHIRE v. GLAMORGAN

At Loughborough, July 2, 4, 5. Leicestershire won by 21 runs. After being outplayed for most of the match Glamorgan made a bold attempt to make 287 for victory and failed narrowly. Although Glamorgan were handicapped by injuries to three bowlers, Wooller, Lewis and McConnon, the Leicestershire batsmen, apart from Palmer and Jackson, showed little enterprise on the first day. Their total, however, proved useful when Goodwin, in a sustained spell of fast-medium bowling, caused Glamorgan to collapse. Shepherd and Watkins bowled equally well in Leicestershire's second innings, and remained unchanged until a declaration gave Glamorgan a seemingly heavy task. Yet so well did they bat, especially Parkhouse and Pleass, that only excellent catches enabled Leicestershire to win.

Leicestershire

G. Lester lbw b McConnon	40	— c Parkhouse b Shepherd ...	26
M. R. Hallam lbw b McConnon	27	— lbw b Watkins	5
M. Tompkin c Jones b Watkins	2	— c Jones b Watkins	80
C. H. Palmer run out	44	— b Watkins	3
V. E. Jackson c and b Pressdee	61	— b Shepherd	4
G. A. Smithson c Davies b Shepherd	45	— c Davies b Shepherd	6
L. R. Gardner not out	9	— b Watkins	14
V. S. Munden not out	35	— c Pressdee b Watkins	3
C. T. Spencer (did not bat)		— c and b Shepherd	0
J. Firth (did not bat)		— not out	0
J. Goodwin (did not bat)		— not out	0
B 5, l-b 6, n-b 1	12	B 4, l-b 6	10

1/47 2/52 3/111 4/120 (6 wkts., dec.) 275
5/204 6/231

1/14 2/54 (9 wkts., dec.) 151
3/65 4/90 5/98 6/143
7/150 8/151 9/151

Glamorgan

W. G. A. Parkhouse lbw b Spencer	5	— c Hallam b Palmer	81
B. R. Edrich b Goodwin	2	— c Firth b Spencer	0
B. Hedges b Goodwin	2	— c Smithson b Palmer	29
W. E. Jones b Goodwin	31	— c Goodwin b Spencer	16
A. J. Watkins b Spencer	12	— b Spencer	0
J. Pleass c Spencer b Goodwin	38	— c Smithson b Goodwin	62
J. Pressdee c Spencer b Jackson	17	— c Spencer b Palmer	33
J. E. McConnon c Munden b Goodwin	17	— run out	19
H. G. Davies b Jackson	2	— not out	6
K. H. Lewis c Smithson b Goodwin	12	— c Firth b Goodwin	12
D. J. Shepherd not out	0	— b Palmer	3
L-b 1, n-b 1	2	B 2, l-b 1, n-b 1	4

1/8 2/8 3/16 4/41 5/70 6/106 7/112 140
8/124 9/128

1/17 2/111 3/112 4/113 265
5/136 6/211 7/244 8/248
9/262

Glamorgan Bowling

	O.	M.	R.	W.		O.	M.	R.	W.
Lewis	5	1	10	0					
Shepherd	32	7	76	1	....	24	3	78	4
Watkins	24	2	57	1	....	23	6	63	5
McConnon	43	16	62	2					
Pressdee	21	4	58	1					

Leicestershire Bowling

	O.	M.	R.	W.		O.	M.	R.	W.
Spencer	21	5	64	2	....	20	1	82	3
Goodwin	23.4	4	59	6	....	18	3	56	2
Jackson	10	5	15	2	....	16	6	28	0
Lester						10	2	40	0
Munden						11	4	24	0
Palmer						18.3	8	31	4

Umpires: F. Chester and T. Spencer.

At The Oval, July 6, 7, 8. LEICESTERSHIRE lost to SURREY by five wickets.

LEICESTERSHIRE v. DERBYSHIRE

At Ashby-de-la-Zouch, July 9, 11, 12. Drawn. A remarkable feature of this match was that Carr, the Derbyshire captain, used all eleven players of his side as bowlers on the last day when Eato and Morgan were hurt, but he failed to prevent Leicestershire from making a draw. On the first day Leicestershire did not make full use of excellent batting conditions. Against accurate bowling, they took almost the whole day to make 248. In contrast, Derbyshire scored their 413 in under five and a half hours. Carr, vigorous and stylish, hit three 6's and eighteen 4's, and Dawkes hit so freely that he made 86 in sixty-six minutes, including three 6's and eight 4's. A sound century by Jackson (sixteen 4's) in an innings lasting just under four hours did most to save Leicestershire. Diment, in his first match for the county, helped in a sixth wicket stand of 128.

Leicestershire

G. Lester lbw b Eato	5	— lbw b Gladwin		5
M. J. K. Smith lbw b Revill	29	— c Morgan b Eato		7
M. Tompkin c Morgan b Gladwin	67	— lbw b Gladwin		36
C. H. Palmer c Morgan b Smith	47	— lbw b Gladwin		18
V. E. Jackson c Carr b Smith	10	— b Kelly		100
G. A. Smithson b Revill	50	— b Gladwin		55
R. A. Diment c and b Morgan	0	— lbw b Johnson		71
V. S. Munden b Smith	7	— not out		23
J. Firth lbw b Gladwin	1	— c and b Johnson		5
C. T. Spencer b Gladwin	11	— c Morgan b Johnson		0
J. Goodwin not out	0	— not out		11
B 6, l-b 13, n-b 2	21	B 10, l-b 4		14

1/6 2/63 3/155 4/171 5/180 6/183   248   1/7 2/39 3/61   (9 wkts.) 345
7/200 8/214 9/248   4/72 5/160 6/288 7/302
                                    8/316 9/316

Derbyshire

J. Kelly c Spencer b Goodwin	3	C. Gladwin not out	15
C. Lee c Smith b Spencer	63	E. Smith c Smithson b Munden	10
A. Hamer c Spencer b Goodwin	28		
A. C. Revill c Tompkin b Goodwin	2	B 11, l-b 4	15
D. B. Carr lbw b Jackson	146		
H. L. Johnson c Goodwin b Spencer	43	1/7 2/41 3/51 (9 wkts., dec.)	413
D. C. Morgan b Goodwin	2	4/143 5/217 6/234 7/341 8/396	
G. O. Dawkes c Smith b Munden	86	9/413	

A. Eato did not bat.

Derbyshire Bowling

	O.	M.	R.	W.	O.	M.	R.	W.
Eato	21	3	78	1	6	1	15	1
Gladwin	30	11	70	3	35	11	71	4
Morgan	15	5	35	1	4	0	18	0
Revill	6.4	2	15	2	18	7	51	0
Smith	18	11	17	3	22	9	51	0
Carr	3	0	12	0	10	3	31	0
Hamer					4	1	18	0
Lee					10	4	16	0
Kelly					11	5	21	1
Johnson					10	4	30	3
Dawkes					1	0	9	0

Leicestershire Bowling

	O.	M.	R.	W.
Spencer	23	1	118	2
Goodwin	29	5	127	4
Palmer	5	3	5	0
Jackson	19	10	53	1
Munden	17	4	76	2
Lester	4	0	19	0

Umpires: W. F. Price and E. Cooke.

At Manchester, July 16, 18, 19. LEICESTERSHIRE lost to LANCASHIRE by an innings and 59 runs.

LEICESTERSHIRE v. HAMPSHIRE

At Leicester, July 20, 21, 22. Leicestershire won by two wickets. The match provided an exciting finish, Smithson hitting the winning runs off the fourth ball of the last over. Much of the earlier play had been tedious. After losing Marshall to the second ball of the match, Hampshire struggled in their first innings, especially against the persistent off-break bowling of Jackson. Despite accurate fast-medium bowling by Shackleton, Leicestershire batted consistently, although only Smith, who hit one 6 and twelve 4's, scored rapidly. More good bowling by Jackson left Leicestershire needing 118 runs in seventy-four minutes. They made 113 for five, but lost three more batsmen in the last few minutes before snatching the victory.

Hampshire

J. R. Gray c Firth b Jackson	29	— c Firth b Goodwin 6
R. E. Marshall b Spencer	0	— c Smith b Spencer 10
H. Horton c Hallam b Jackson	43	— c Firth b Jackson 23
E. D. R. Eagar lbw b Palmer	4	— c Hallam b Jackson 15
N. H. Rogers lbw b Lester	19	— c Spencer b Jackson 37
H. M. Barnard c Hallam b Jackson	26	— c Hallam b Jackson 1
L. Harrison c Firth b Jackson	4	— c Lester b Jackson 30
P. J. Sainsbury lbw b Palmer	33	— not out 38
D. Shackleton b Spencer	34	— st Firth b Lester 11
V. H. D. Cannings not out	3	— b Lester 0
M. D. Burden c Smithson b Goodwin	4	— c Munden b Lester 0
B 7, l-b 2, n-b 3	12	B 5, l-b 4, w 1, n-b 2 .. 12

1/0 2/72 3/74 4/86 5/127 6/127   211   1/13 2/27 3/54 4/84 5/96   183
7/138 8/182 9/203   6/97 7/145 8/167 9/171

Leicestershire

G. Lester c Harrison b Cannings	2	— run out	0
M. R. Hallam b Shackleton	23	— c Gray b Shackleton	30
M. Tompkin lbw b Shackleton	11	— c Shackleton b Cannings	9
M. J. K. Smith lbw b Shackleton	70	— c Sainsbury b Cannings	14
C. H. Palmer b Shackleton	13	— c Marshall b Cannings	40
V. E. Jackson lbw b Burden	20	— st Harrison b Shackleton	5
G. A. Smithson c Cannings b Burden	50	— not out	2
V. S. Munden lbw b Shackleton	11	— b Cannings	12
J. Firth not out	39	— run out	1
C. T. Spencer b Sainsbury	14	— not out	1
J. Goodwin b Burden	10		
B 6, l-b 8	14	B 1, l-b 3	4

1/7 2/35 3/36 4/56 5/120 6/161   277   1/0 2/21 3/45   (8 wkts.) 118
7/189 8/222 9/244   4/59 5/99 6/113 7/114 8/115

Leicestershire Bowling

	O.	M.	R.	W.		O.	M.	R.	W.
Spencer	10	2	32	2	....	20	8	31	1
Goodwin	10	1	29	1	....	11	2	23	1
Jackson	44	28	57	4	....	35	19	48	5
Munden	10	5	16	0	....	4	4	0	0
Palmer	19	12	30	2	....	8	5	6	0
Lester	10	2	35	1	....	22.4	7	63	3

Hampshire Bowling

	O.	M.	R.	W.		O.	M.	R.	W.
Shackleton	48	19	78	5	....	12	1	44	2
Cannings	47	20	59	1	....	11.4	0	70	4
Burden	16.5	2	60	3					
Sainsbury	20	5	58	1					
Gray	5	3	8	0					

Umpires: D. Davies and H. Elliott (Lancashire).

At Brentwood, July 23, 25. LEICESTERSHIRE beat ESSEX by 18 runs.

At Bournemouth, July 27, 28, 29. LEICESTERSHIRE lost to HAMPSHIRE by ten wickets.

LEICESTERSHIRE v. NORTHAMPTONSHIRE

At Leicester, July 30, August 1, 2. Northamptonshire won by nine wickets. Batting first on a pitch which favoured spin bowlers, Leicestershire could make little of the left-arm slows of Tribe, apart from Hallam, who resisted skilfully for two and a half hours. Jackson, Munden and Palmer also troubled the Northamptonshire batsmen, with the exception of the patient Brookes, who batted for the entire six hours of the innings, before being last out. Tribe helped to add 97 for the fifth wicket. Palmer played excellently in the Leicestershire second innings, hitting fifteen 4's in his 102, made in just over three hours, but again Tribe held the upper hand against other batsmen, and Northamptonshire found little difficulty in scoring the 71 needed to win.

Leicestershire

G. Lester lbw b Tribe	16	— lbw b Wild	18
M. R. Hallam b Tribe	44	— b Tyson	0
M. Tompkin b Tribe	0	— lbw b Tribe	13
M. J. K. Smith b Tyson	8	— c Arnold b Tribe	15
C. H. Palmer b Tyson	0	— b Tyson	102
V. E. Jackson c Brookes b Tribe	21	— c Tribe b Wild	14
G. A. Smithson b Tribe	0	— c Tyson b Wild	8
R. A. Diment c Andrew b Tribe	9	— lbw b Tribe	0
V. S. Munden c and b Broderick	6	— b Tribe	0
J. Firth not out	0	— lbw b Tribe	18
C. T. Spencer b Tribe	0	— not out	8
B 6, l-b 1, n-b 1	8	B 13, l-b 5	18

1/45 2/45 3/63 4/63 5/87 6/87 7/104 **112**   1/9 2/27 3/43 4/89 5/123 **214**
8/110 9/112   6/141 7/160 8/174 9/202

Northamptonshire

D. Brookes c Spencer b Palmer	117	— b Munden	22
P. Arnold lbw b Jackson	7	— not out	32
L. Livingston b Jackson	7	— not out	13
D. Barrick c Spencer b Jackson	0		
R. Subba Row b Munden	8		
G. E. Tribe c Firth b Palmer	49		
V. Broderick c Lester b Munden	27		
F. H. Tyson b Palmer	22		
K. V. Andrew c Hallam b Munden	0		
J. Wild c Smithson b Munden	4		
J. Webster not out	0		
B 4, l-b 9, n-b 2	15	B 4	4

1/16 2/28 3/30 4/45 5/142 6/193 **256**   1/40   (1 wkt.) **71**
7/228 8/245 9/251

Northamptonshire Bowling

	O.	M.	R.	W.		O.	M.	R.	W.
Tyson	12	3	19	2	....	12.4	3	33	2
Webster	7	2	11	0	....	7	1	20	0
Broderick	24	11	36	1	....	9	2	37	0
Tribe	24.3	8	38	7	....	33	11	53	5
Wild						26	12	53	3

Leicestershire Bowling

	O.	M.	R.	W.		O.	M.	R.	W.
Spencer	13	4	32	0	....	3	0	16	0
Palmer	27.1	19	25	3	....	2	0	11	0
Jackson	38	12	72	3	....	3.4	0	13	0
Munden	46	17	92	4	....	3	0	27	1
Lester	5	2	20	0					

Umpires: W. F. Price and A. J. B. Fowler.

LEICESTERSHIRE v. YORKSHIRE

At Leicester, August 3, 4, 5. Yorkshire won by two wickets, in a close finish to a match which was keenly contested throughout. Although Trueman bowled with sustained pace, and Wardle varied his left-arm slows cleverly, Leicestershire batted consistently and with great spirit on the first day, Diment and Munden adding 74 in a seventh wicket stand. When Yorkshire lost seven men for 170 against skilful spin bowling by Walsh and Jackson, Leicestershire seemed sure of the lead. Then Illingworth and Trueman batted with soundness and power in an eighth wicket stand of 133 made in 90 minutes. Apart from sound batting by Tompkin and another defiant display from Diment, Leicestershire batted unconvincingly in their second innings, but more good bowling by Walsh made Yorkshire struggle before victory was gained.

Leicestershire

G. Lester c Padgett b Trueman	19	— b Platt 7
M. R. Hallam b Platt	16	— c Binks b Wardle 12
M. Tompkin c Wilson b Wardle	43	— c and b Close............. 68
M. J. K. Smith b Trueman	11	— lbw b Trueman 3
C. H. Palmer b Trueman	22	— run out 0
V. E. Jackson lbw b Trueman	44	— c Binks b Trueman 0
R. A. Diment b Wardle	48	— c Sutcliffe b Close 47
V. S. Munden c Yardley b Wardle	50	— c Watson b Close 0
J. Firth c Trueman b Wardle	0	— lbw b Close 3
J. E. Walsh c Close b Wardle	19	— c Watson b Wardle....... 24
C. T. Spencer not out	0	— not out 2
B 15, l-b 13, n-b 1	29	L-b 9, n-b 1 10

1/29 2/39 3/68 4/108 5/123 6/180   301   1/9 2/46 3/56 4/58 5/58   176
7/254 8/258 9/299   6/110 7/118 8/128 9/166

Yorkshire

W. H. H. Sutcliffe b Jackson	17	— b Jackson 7
D. B. Close b Jackson	28	— b Jackson 49
J. V. Wilson c Smith b Walsh	68	— c and b Walsh 19
D. E. V. Padgett c Spencer b Walsh	25	— c and b Walsh 19
W. Watson b Jackson	17	— st Firth b Walsh 18
N. W. D. Yardley c Hallam b Walsh	0	— b Walsh 17
R. Illingworth c and b Walsh	61	— not out 29
J. H. Wardle b Jackson	8	— lbw b Palmer 16
F. S. Trueman b Jackson	74	— lbw b Walsh............. 0
J. G. Binks not out	7	— not out 0
R. K. Platt b Jackson	2	
B 5, l-b 5	10	B 8, l-b 1 9

1/33 2/72 3/136 4/140 5/156 6/156   317   1/12 2/75 3/75   (8 wkts.) 164
7/170 8/303 9/305   4/75 5/117 6/118 7/159
                                                   8/160

Yorkshire Bowling

	O.	M.	R.	W.		O.	M.	R.	W.
Trueman	29	2	82	4	....	20	5	35	2
Platt	17	7	22	1	....	6	3	7	1
Wardle	32.3	8	72	5	....	27.2	8	61	2
Close	18	5	47	0	....	20	6	43	4
Illingworth	20	5'	49	0	....	12	3	20	0

Leicestershire Bowling

	O.	M.	R.	W.		O.	M.	R.	W.
Spencer	14	4	60	0					
Palmer	9	2	17	0	....	6.3	3	31	1
Jackson	41.4	21	75	6	....	17	3	73	2
Walsh	38	15	107	4	....	18	3	51	5
Lester	9	1	31	0					
Munden	2	0	17	0					

Umpires: F. S. Lee and T. J. Bartley.

At Birmingham, August 6, 8, 9. Leicestershire drew with Warwickshire.

At Leicester, August 10, 11, 12. LEICESTERSHIRE lost to the SOUTH AFRICANS by an innings and 117 runs. (See SOUTH AFRICAN section.)

LEICESTERSHIRE v. SUSSEX

At Leicester, August 13, 15, 16. Leicestershire won by 143 runs. The match was a triumph for Jackson, Leicestershire's Australian all-rounder, who completed the cricketer's double for the first time. His accurate off-break bowling largely accounted for the home side's good victory. Jackson completed 1,000 runs on the first day when, on a pitch responsive to spin, Leicestershire found trouble in dealing with the off-breaks of Oakman. Sussex fared even worse against Jackson, only Oakman and Cox resisting strongly, and Tompkin soon consolidated Leicestershire's lead of 30. Mixing sound defence with powerful driving, he hit one 6 and nine 4's. Apart from an excellent innings by Sheppard, Sussex again found Jackson's off-breaks on a dusty pitch too much for them, and he completed his 100 wickets.

Leicestershire

G. Lester b James	7	— c Doggart b Marlar	1
M. J. K. Smith run out	1	— c Sheppard b Oakman	2
M. Tompkin b Oakman	12	— b James	90
C. H. Palmer c Langridge b Marlar	18	— c Sheppard b Smith	19
V. E. Jackson c Sheppard b Oakman	35	— c Langridge b Smith	24
R. A. Diment lbw b Oakman	34	— lbw b Marlar	34
V. S. Munden c Langridge b Oakman	20	— c Webb b Marlar	0
J. E. Walsh c Doggart b Oakman	0	— lbw b James	2
J. Firth c Marlar b Smith	30	— st Webb b Smith	31
C. T. Spencer c Doggart b Smith	38	— b James	29
J. Goodwin not out	11	— not out	6
B 11, l-b 2	13	B 25, l-b 3	28

1/7 2/13 3/32 4/54 5/81 6/113   **219**
7/113 8/132 9/190

1/1 2/23 3/88 4/122   **266**
5/164 6/169 7/180 8/192
9/246

Sussex

J. Langridge c Firth b Jackson	12	— c Spencer b Goodwin	3
D. V. Smith c Lester b Jackson	25	— c Lester b Jackson	23
A. S. M. Oakman c Jackson b Munden	32	— lbw b Jackson	20
J. M. Parks lbw b Jackson	6	— c Spencer b Jackson	6
D. S. Sheppard c Firth b Munden	5	— b Jackson	53
G. Cox b Munden	47	— lbw b Palmer	3
G. H. G. Doggart b Jackson	15	— c Walsh b Jackson	3
K. G. Suttle c Palmer b Jackson	21	— c Lester b Jackson	14
R. T. Webb lbw b Munden	0	— lbw b Munden	13
R. G. Marlar c Smith b Jackson	1	— c Walsh b Jackson	3
A. E. James not out	0	— not out	3
B 19, l-b 6	25	B 5, l-b 3, w 1	9

1/18 2/68 3/76 4/88 5/100 6/139   **189**
7/181 8/181 9/184

1/16 2/29 3/94 4/109   **153**
5/109 6/128 7/132 8/132
9/136

Sussex Bowling

	O.	M.	R.	W.	O.	M.	R.	W.
Smith	14	4	24	2	22.4	8	72	3
James	23	10	42	1	24	10	41	3
Oakman	31	12	71	5	17	4	35	1
Marlar	28	7	65	1	29	8	90	3
Parks	1	0	4	0				

Leicestershire Bowling

	O.	M.	R.	W.		O.	M.	R.	W.
Spencer	2	0	7	0	....	2	1	3	0
Goodwin	2	0	11	0	....	4	1	14	1
Jackson	28	9	83	6	....	19	3	69	7
Palmer	4	1	8	0	....	4	0	10	1
Munden	25.1	10	48	4	....	17.4	3	48	1
Walsh	3	1	7	0					

Umpires: W. T. Jones and Harry Elliott (Derbyshire).

LEICESTERSHIRE v. ESSEX

At Leicester, August 17, 18, 19. Leicestershire won by 59 runs. Jackson punished the Essex bowlers severely, hitting one 6 and eighteen 4's in a delightful display. He and Tompkin added 103 for the fourth wicket. Despite this aggressive batting, Preston and Ralph bowled with life and accuracy for long spells. Essex made light of the Leicestershire total, two amateurs, Williams and Insole, adding 200 for the fourth wicket in just over three hours. Insole hit twelve 4's and Williams eleven, each displaying a wide range of strokes, and Essex declared with only five wickets down. Leicestershire, in turn, were able to declare, after consistent batting. They set Essex to make 201 in under two hours, a task which was attempted boldly, but without success.

Leicestershire

G. Lester c and b Preston	16	— c Insole b Ralph	32
M. J. K. Smith lbw b Preston	19	— c Greensmith b Smith	58
M. Tompkin run out	50	— run out	32
C. H. Palmer c Preston b Ralph	3	— lbw b Ralph	26
V. E. Jackson c Insole b Preston	121	— b Greensmith	30
R. A. Diment lbw b Ralph	31	— c Gibb b Preston	12
G. A. Smithson c Preston b Ralph	4	— c Gibb b Greensmith	10
V. S. Munden b Preston	12	— c Gibb b Greensmith	0
J. E. Walsh b Preston	7	— b Greensmith	6
J. Firth b Ralph	8	— not out	19
C. T. Spencer not out	2	— not out	26
B 4, l-b 5	9	B 4, l-b 4, w 1, n-b 1 ..	10

1/35 2/44 3/51 4/154 5/242 6/252   282   1/87 2/90   (9 wkts., dec.) 261
7/252 8/263 9/278   3/130 4/153 5/189 6/200
7/200 8/207 9/216

Essex

T. C. Dodds b Spencer	7	— c Palmer b Spencer	15
G. Barker c Firth b Spencer	40	— run out	13
P. A. Gibb b Spencer	18	— lbw b Walsh	0
C. C. P. Williams c Spencer b Munden	119	— b Palmer	3
D. J. Insole c Firth b Spencer	109	— c and b Walsh	40
R. Horsfall not out	21	— lbw b Palmer	3
W. T. Greensmith not out	14	— lbw b Walsh	12
R. Smith (did not bat)		— b Palmer	24
R. Ralph (did not bat)		— b Lester	14
K. C. Preston (did not bat)		— not out	15
J. A. Bailey (did not bat)		— c Smith b Lester	0
B 9, l-b 4, n-b 2	15	B 1, l-b 1	2

1/16 2/73 3/82 4/282   (5 wkts., dec.) 343   1/20 2/34 3/39 4/49 5/97   141
5/315   6/109 7/113 8/115 9/136

Essex Bowling

	O.	M.	R.	W.		O.	M.	R.	W.
Preston	25	5	79	5	....	21	1	65	1
Bailey	12	3	31	0	....	9	0	29	0
Ralph	22.5	5	58	4	....	14	2	69	2
Greensmith	12	2	58	0	....	12	3	42	4
Smith	10	1	34	0	....	14	3	46	1
Insole	2	0	13	0					

Leicestershire Bowling

	O.	M.	R.	W.		O.	M.	R.	W.
Spencer	33	5	119	4	....	10	0	54	1
Palmer	24	9	43	0	....	10	0	54	3
Munden	23	7	51	1					
Walsh	13	4	38	0	....	7	4	9	3
Jackson	25	6	68	0					
Lester	2	0	9	0	....	6.3	2	22	2

Umpires: T. Spencer and N. Oldfield.

At Cardiff, August 20, 22, 23. LEICESTERSHIRE beat GLAMORGAN by ten wickets.

At Lord's, August 24, 25, 26. LEICESTERSHIRE lost to MIDDLESEX by 40 runs.

LEICESTERSHIRE v. WORCESTERSHIRE

At Leicester, August 27, 29, 30. Leicestershire won by five wickets. After being led by 98 on first innings, Leicestershire fought back splendidly and gained their eleventh championship victory, equalling their best record, gained in 1935. Kenyon and Horton, adding 140 for the third wicket, laid the foundations for Worcestershire's good score, Kenyon scoring his fourth century in successive innings against Leicestershire, and Horton his first hundred in county cricket. Rain curtailed play on the first day, and on Monday Goodwin used drying turf so effectively that Worcestershire declared, enabling their spin bowlers, Berry and Jenkins, to give Leicestershire an uncomfortable time. In turn Worcestershire found runs hard to make, but on the last day Palmer and Jackson, with a stand of 166, gave Leicestershire victory. Jackson cover-drove splendidly and hit two 6's and fifteen 4's.

Worcestershire

D. Kenyon c Jackson b Palmer	131	— b Spencer	0
L. Outschoorn b Goodwin	19	— c Firth b Goodwin	0
R. G. Broadbent b Jackson	17	— st Firth b Walsh	38
M. J. Horton c Diment b Goodwin	103	— b Goodwin	4
G. Dews c Spencer b Goodwin	12	— c Firth b Spencer	3
J. Lister c Spencer b Goodwin	0	— not out	37
R. O. Jenkins not out	3	— c Firth b Jackson	0
H. Yarnold c Walsh b Goodwin	0	— c Tompkin b Munden	18
R. Berry not out	0	— c Spencer b Munden	0
J. Flavell (did not bat)		— lbw b Jackson	18
R. T. D. Perks (did not bat)		— c Firth b Munden	1
L-b 3, n-b 4	7	W 2, n-b 2	4

1/46 2/97 3/237 4/279   (7 wkts., dec.) 292   1/0 2/5 3/19 4/22 5/66   123
5/279 6/290 7/290   6/66 7/66 8/121 9/121

Leicestershire

G. Lester lbw b Perks	8	—	c Horton b Flavell	5
M. J. K. Smith c and b Jenkins	46	—	b Perks	4
M. Tompkin c Lister b Berry	49	—	lbw b Flavell	5
C. H. Palmer c Yarnold b Perks	9	—	c Perks b Horton	63
V. E. Jackson c Yarnold b Berry	38	—	b Horton	114
R. A. Diment c Outschoorn b Jenkins	13	—	not out	15
V. S. Munden c Yarnold b Berry	0	—	not out	4
J. E. Walsh c Dews b Jenkins	19			
J. Firth c and b Jenkins	3			
C. T. Spencer c Flavell b Jenkins	8			
J. Goodwin not out	0			
L-b 1	1		B 7, l-b 4, n-b 1	12
	194			**222**

1/18 2/100 3/104 4/115 5/162 6/162
7/164 8/181 9/194

1/5 2/9 3/34 (5 wkts.) 222
4/200 5/207

Leicestershire Bowling

	O.	M.	R.	W.		O.	M.	R.	W.
Spencer	11	1	53	0	....	9	2	26	2
Goodwin	20	4	46	5	....	10	2	28	2
Palmer	16	8	25	1	....	2	2	0	0
Walsh	11	2	51	0	....	11	3	40	1
Jackson	25	0	68	1	....	8	5	22	1
Munden	23	8	42	0	....	3.1	2	3	3

Worcestershire Bowling

	O.	M.	R.	W.		O.	M.	R.	W.
Perks	17	4	65	2	....	18.3	2	73	1
Flavell	5	2	13	0	....	12	1	36	2
Horton	8	2	37	0	....	13	1	38	2
Berry	16	5	40	3	....	13	4	41	0
Jenkins	11.3	2	38		....	4	0	22	0

Umpires: F. S. Lee and Harry Elliott (Derbyshire).

MIDDLESEX

President—R. H. TWINING

Hon. Secretary—F. G. MANN, Lord's Cricket Ground,
St. John's Wood Road, London, N.W.8

Captain—W. J. EDRICH

 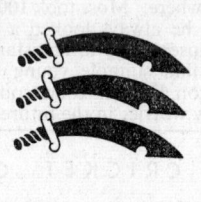 

J. D. Robertson   County Badge   F. J. Titmus

Middlesex were one of the most inconsistent sides in the Championship. At times they appeared capable of beating almost anyone, yet on other occasions they looked a poor team. They finished fifth, two places higher than in 1954, but they ought to have done better. Two defeats at the hands of struggling Kent and another by the bottom county, Somerset, showed how unreliable they were, yet they beat Yorkshire in August when the northern county were at their best.

The reason for the set-backs was not hard to find. While the side possessed one of the strongest all-round attacks in the country, the batting proved weak and collapses were frequent. Not until August 3, 4, 5, at Trent Bridge did they reach a total of 300. Undoubtedly the many absences of Denis Compton weakened the batting considerably. Through Test calls and other reasons, usually the need to rest his knee which again troubled him for most of the season, Compton missed 17 games and in 20 innings he scored no more than 590 runs; only four times did he reach 50. Edrich too, disappointed. He always appeared to be struggling to find his form and an average of 26.44 from such an accomplished batsman fell far below expectations. On the other hand Robertson recovered much of his skill and he made 1,754 runs, nearly 500 more than anyone else. Middlesex were much stronger late in the season when Dewes and Delisle became available. In his seven matches Dewes scored 644 runs and he easily headed the averages with 53.66. Delisle received his county cap following a century against Nottinghamshire.

By far the most impressive feature was the bowling of Titmus and Moss, well supported by Young and Warr. These four took 392 wickets between them in county games. Titmus became the first Middlesex player to complete the "double" since R. W. V. Robins and N. E. Haig did so in 1929. He also established a new record by taking 158 wickets in all matches for Middlesex, beating the 154 of A. E. Trott in 1900. He played in two Tests against South Africa and his selection for the tour of Pakistan completed a memorable season for him. His cleverly flighted and well-spun off-breaks worried batsmen everywhere. Moss took 100 wickets for Middlesex for the first time and he always looked a menacing fast bowler. Like Titmus he was chosen to go to Pakistan.

Unless they can find suitable young batsmen to take over eventually from Compton, Edrich, Robertson and Brown, Middlesex are likely to have many worries in the future.

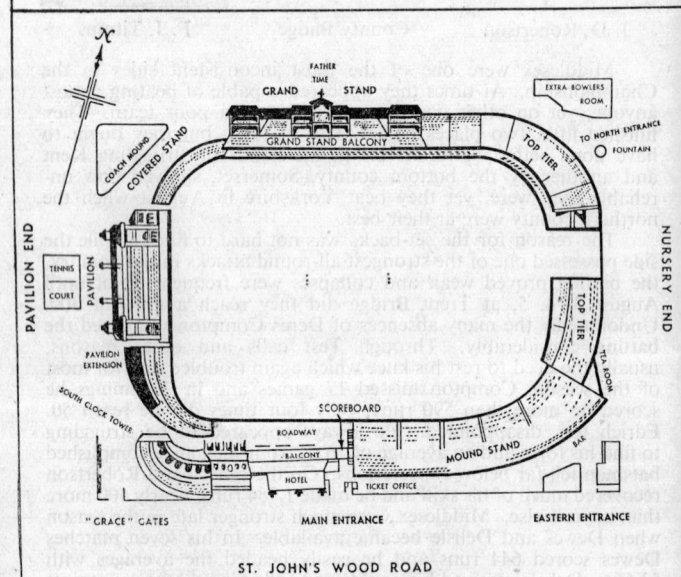

MIDDLESEX RESULTS

All First-Class Matches—Played 31, *Won* 15, *Lost* 13, *Drawn* 3

County Championship Matches—Played 28, *Won* 14, *Lost* 12, *Drawn* 2

COUNTY CHAMPIONSHIP AVERAGES

BATTING

	Birthplace	Mtchs.	Inns.	Not Outs	Runs	100's	Highest Inns.	Aver.
J. G. Dewes	*Latchford*	7	14	2	644	2	117	53.66
J. D. Robertson .	*Chiswick*	28	55	0	1754	1	137	31.89
D. C. S. Compton	*Hendon*	11	20	1	590	1	150	31.05
W. J. Edrich	*Lingwood*	28	54	2	1296	1	125*	26.44
G. P. S. Delisle..	*St. Kitts*	13	26	1	636	1	105	25.44
F. J. Titmus	*Kentish Town*	24	43	9	806	1	104	23.70
S. M. Brown ...	*Eltham*	23	45	2	929	0	83	21.60
D. Bennett......	*Wakefield*	28	52	6	981	0	99	21.32
H. P. Sharp	*Kentish Town*	6	11	3	154	0	52*	19.25
J. T. Murray	*Kensington*	2	4	0	62	0	26	15.50
D. O. Baldry ...	*Acton*	14	24	2	264	0	26	12.00
J. J. Warr	*Ealing*	27	42	4	410	0	51	10.78
A. Thompson ...	*Liverpool*	7	14	0	147	0	43	10.50
H. W. Tilley	*Edmonton*	2	3	0	31	0	20	10.33
L. H. Compton ..	*Woodford*	26	38	2	367	0	57	10.19
D. A. Bick......	*Hampstead*	5	9	0	85	0	33	9.44
J. A. Young	*Paddington*	24	36	12	171	0	18	7.12
R. J. Hurst	*Hampton Hill*	4	6	3	16	0	8	5.33
A. E. Moss	*Tottenham*	26	38	18	83	0	16	4.15
R. V. C. Robins	*Burnham*	3	6	0	10	0	7	1.66

* *Signifies not out.*

BOWLING

	Overs	Maidens	Runs	Wickets	Average
F. J. Titmus	1047	385	2075	137	15.14
A. E. Moss	684.2	141	1852	101	18.33
R. J. Hurst	101	42	223	11	20.27
J. A. Young	836.2	312	1820	88	20.68
J. J. Warr	600.1	143	1392	66	21.09
R. V. C. Robins	54.5	8	201	9	22.33
D. Bennett.............	226.4	38	596	21	28.38
D. A. Bick.............	41	10	134	4	33.50
J. D. Robertson	58	12	168	4	42.00
H. W. Tilley	75.2	15	188	4	47.00
D. C. S. Compton	127	18	488	8	61.00
W. J. Edrich	10.4	2	21	0	—

Also bowled: S. M. Brown 6—1—17—1.

Amateurs.—G. P. S. Delisle, J. G. Dewes, W. J. Edrich, R. V. C. Robins, J. J. Warr.

MIDDLESEX v. DERBYSHIRE

At Lord's, May 7, 9, 10. Drawn. A close fight ended unsatisfactorily, rain ruining the last day. The ball often rose nastily and fast and slow bowlers received plenty of help. The spin of Young and Titmus upset Derbyshire and only Hamer, who stayed two hours twenty minutes, offered much resistance. Edrich saved Middlesex from complete collapse, the others failing before Jackson and Gladwin. Useful innings came from Kelly and Revill when Derbyshire batted again 39 ahead, and an eighth wicket stand of 53 by Johnson and Gladwin put them in a good position. Middlesex needed 214 to win on the last day, but cricket was limited to two brief periods amounting to fifteen minutes.

Derbyshire

A. Hamer c Edrich b Young	56	—	c Titmus b Moss	0
J. Kelly c Compton b Warr	4	—	b Moss	52
C. Lee c Robertson b Young	0	—	c Compton b Moss	1
A. C. Revill c Titmus b Warr	27	—	b Bennett	43
D. B. Carr c Warr b Titmus	29	—	c Moss b Bennett	0
H. L. Johnson c and b Titmus	12	—	not out	31
D. C. Morgan c Titmus b Young	0	—	c Compton b Moss	0
G. O. Dawkes b Titmus	9	—	lbw b Moss	0
C. Gladwin c Bennett b Young	0	—	c Moss b Warr	21
E. Smith not out	0	—	b Moss	1
L. Jackson st Compton b Young	1			
B 10, l-b 2	12		B 10, l-b 14, n-b 1	25

1/16 2/26 3/88 4/120 5/136 6/140   150   1/0 2/10   (9 wkts., dec.) 174
7/140 8/149 9/149   3/88 4/88 5/118 6/120
                                           7/120 8/173 9/174

Middlesex

J. D. Robertson c Johnson b Gladwin	16	—	c Dawkes b Jackson	4
S. M. Brown lbw b Jackson	3	—	not out	0
W. J. Edrich c Jackson b Gladwin	44	—	not out	2
H. P. Sharp c Carr b Gladwin	10			
D. Bennett c Morgan b Gladwin	2			
D. O. Baldry st Dawkes b Smith	19			
F. J. Titmus c Carr b Jackson	1			
J. J. Warr b Jackson	1			
L. H. Compton c Revill b Jackson	4			
J. A. Young b Jackson	4			
A. E. Moss not out	5			
B 1, n-b 1	2			

1/7 2/19 3/41 4/53 5/87 6/97   111   1/4   (one wkt.)   6
7/97 8/102 9/106

Middlesex Bowling

	O.	M.	R.	W.		O.	M.	R.	W.
Moss	5	3	8	0	....	24.1	10	45	6
Warr	12	6	16	2	....	13	5	27	1
Titmus	24	5	71	3	....	6	3	7	0
Young	26.2	14	43	5	....	21	10	39	0
					Bennett	12	5	31	2

Derbyshire Bowling

	O.	M.	R.	W.		O.	M.	R.	W.
Jackson	23.2	11	27	5	....	2	0	3	1
Gladwin	27	13	48	4	....	1.2	0	3	0
Smith	8	3	16	1					
Morgan	4	0	18	0					

Umpires: H. G. Baldwin and G. S. Mobey.

MIDDLESEX v. ESSEX

At Lord's, May 11, 12, 13. Middlesex won by 70 runs. On soft drying turf which favoured spin bowlers, Middlesex were the better side. The clever off-spin bowling of Titmus proved a big factor in their success. He was freely hit in the second innings, but gained valuable wickets and finished with 11 for 157. Robertson took the batting honours with two attractive displays of stylish driving and pulling. Essex, left to make 268, lost seven men for 115 by one o'clock on the last day, but the tail-enders prolonged the game until 3.15; Smith pulled Titmus for six over the Tavern scoreboard into the road.

Middlesex

J. D. Robertson c Insole b Cousens	68	— st Gibb b Cousens 65
S. M. Brown c Gibb b J. Bailey	20	— st Gibb b Greensmith 25
W. J. Edrich c Greensmith b Cousens ...	48	— c Insole b Greensmith 0
H. P. Sharp not out..................	39	— b T. Bailey 10
D. Bennett c Taylor b Smith	5	— c Gibb b T. Bailey 6
D. O. Baldry c and b Smith	3	— b T. Bailey 0
F. J. Titmus c Gibb b Smith	9	— c Greensmith b Smith 36
J. J. Warr c sub b T. Bailey	12	— b Cousens 1
L. H. Compton (did not bat)		— c Horsfall b Greensmith ... 35
J. A. Young (did not bat)		— not out 0
A. E. Moss (did not bat)		— b Smith 1
B 2, l-b 1, n-b 2	5	B 1, l-b 6, n-b 1 8

1/35 2/139 3/139 4/154   (7 wkts., dec.) 209   1/79 2/79 3/103 4/107   187
5/162 6/190 7/209   5/107 6/122 7/123 8/184 9/186

Essex

T. C. Dodds c Edrich b Titmus........	14	— lbw b Moss 0
P. A. Gibb c Bennett b Young	24	— c Baldry b Titmus 43
G. Barker b Titmus	0	— c Moss b Titmus 0
R. Horsfall c Moss b Young	16	— c Robertson b Young...... 10
W. T. Greensmith b Titmus	1	— c Brown b Titmus 22
D. J. Insole c Moss b Titmus	25	— c Moss b Warr 19
T. E. Bailey b Titmus	8	— c Robertson b Young...... 28
B. Taylor c Warr b Titmus	10	— b Young 28
R. Smith b Titmus	22	— c Young b Titmus........ 20
J. A. Bailey c Edrich b Moss	0	— not out 14
P. Cousens not out	0	— c Edrich b Young 9
B 6, l-b 3	9	B 3, l-b 1 4

1/40 2/40 3/40 4/48 5/66 6/80   129   1/0 2/50 3/51 4/70   197
7/104 8/126 9/129   5/93 6/115 7/115 8/171 9/174

Essex Bowling

	O.	M.	R.	W.		O.	M.	R.	W.
T. Bailey	20.1	4	52	1	....	19	3	43	3
Smith	20	4	53	3	....	11	5	18	2
J. Bailey	13	3	43	1					
Cousens	22	8	38	2	....	29	8	69	2
Greensmith	5	0	18	0	....	21	8	49	3

Middlesex Bowling

	O.	M.	R.	W.		O.	M.	R.	W.
Moss	7.4	1	21	1	....	5	2	10	1
Warr..........	6	0	12	0	....	19	8	35	1
Titmus	22	10	52	7	....	24	3	105	4
Young	20	9	35	2	....	19.4	7	43	4

Umpires: F. S. Lee and J. J. Hills.

MIDDLESEX v. HAMPSHIRE

At Lord's, May 14, 16, 17. Middlesex won by 55 runs. On this occasion the faster bowlers, especially Moss, made best use of the rain-affected pitch. Eagar was rewarded for his enterprise in sending in Middlesex. The game began so sensationally that the first five wickets fell for 11, but Titmus, despite several painful blows, stood his ground and saw the total reach 100. Hampshire offset the splendid bowling of Shackleton and Cannings by their unsound batting, for only their opening pair, Marshall in the first innings, and later Gray, gave any trouble. Middlesex possessed a match-winner in Moss. Consistently fast and accurate Moss achieved his best analysis with seven wickets for 34, and when the game finished in the extra half-hour his full figures were 12 wickets for 61—a truly fine performance.

Middlesex

J. D. Robertson c Cannings b Shackleton	7	— lbw b Cannings	17
H. P. Sharp c Sainsbury b Cannings	0	— b Shackleton	9
W. J. Edrich b Cannings	1	— c Eagar b Shackleton	6
D. C. S. Compton c Marshall b Cannings	3	— c Eagar b Shackleton	32
D. Bennett b Shackleton	0	— c Eagar b Cannings	6
D. O. Baldry c Harrison b Shackleton	14	— c Sainsbury b Cannings	1
F. J. Titmus c Cannings b Shackleton	61	— lbw b Cannings	6
L. H. Compton b Shackleton	14	— run out	4
J. J. Warr c Eagar b Shackleton	0	— b Shackleton	12
J. A. Young c Rogers b Sainsbury	0	— c Gray b Cannings	0
A. E. Moss not out	0	— not out	0
		B 7, l-b 1, w 1	9

1/0 2/8 3/8 4/11 5/11 6/73 7/91   100   1/19 2/29 3/37 4/47   102
8/99 9/100   5/53 6/63 7/73 8/101 9/102

Hampshire

J. R. Gray b Moss	0	— c Young b Titmus	37
R. E. Marshall c Baldry b Moss	26	— c and b Moss	0
H. Horton c L. Compton b Warr	5	— b Moss	0
E. D. R. Eagar b Moss	5	— c Titmus b Warr	1
N. H. Rogers c L. Compton b Moss	8	— b Moss	12
A. W. H. Rayment c and b Warr	0	— b Young	17
L. Harrison b Moss	0	— b Titmus	0
P. J. Sainsbury c Bennett b Moss	5	— lbw b Titmus	0
D. Shackleton b Moss	11	— b Moss	14
V. H. D. Cannings c L. Compton b Warr	0	— b Moss	4
M. D. Burden not out	1	— not out	0
		N-b 1	1

1/0 2/29 3/31 4/42 5/43 6/44   61   1/0 2/2 3/3 4/23 5/48   86
7/47 8/54 9/57   6/49 7/59 8/82 9/86

Hampshire Bowling

	O.	M.	R.	W.		O.	M.	R.	W.
Shackleton	27.1	11	40	6	....	23.1	12	35	4
Cannings	25	13	48	3	....	17	3	44	5
Sainsbury	4	1	4	1	....	7	3	10	0
Gray	1	0	2	0					
Burden	1	0	6	0	....	1	0	4	0

Middlesex Bowling

	O.	M.	R.	W.		O.	M.	R.	W.
Moss	14	4	34	7	....	11.3	3	27	5
Warr.........	11	5	18	3	....	5	3	3	1
Young	2	0	9	0	....	14	2	45	1
				Titmus	....	11	4	10	3

Umpires: N. Oldfield and W. T. Jones.

At Oxford, May 18, 19, 20. MIDDLESEX drew with OXFORD UNIVERSITY.

At Rushden, May 21, 23, 24. MIDDLESEX beat NORTHAMPTONSHIRE by six wickets.

At Bristol, May 25, 26, 27. MIDDLESEX lost to GLOUCESTERSHIRE by 60 runs.

MIDDLESEX v. SUSSEX

(H. P. Sharp and A. Thompson—Joint Benefit)

At Lord's, May 28, 30, 31. Drawn. A superb innings by Denis Compton transcended all else in a game restricted to two days by rain. After a blank Saturday Compton held the Middlesex batting together. He reached 50 out of 64; 100 out of 135 and 150 out of 195, and a crowd of more than 20,000 on Whit Monday gave him an ovation when finally he was caught on the edge of the boundary. When Sussex, in turn, faltered against the pace bowling of Moss it looked as though Middlesex would gain first innings lead but a seventh wicket partnership of 66 between Suttle and Potter helped to give Sussex four points.

Middlesex

H. P. Sharp b Thomson	2	— not out	52
J. D. Robertson c Suttle b James	2	— c and b Marlar	15
W. J. Edrich c Smith b Thomson	7		
D. C. S. Compton c Suttle b Marlar 150		— st Webb b Cox	2
A. Thompson c Langridge b James......	1	— b Potter	25
D. Bennett c Langridge b Marlar	2	— b Cox	16
F. T. Titmus c Langridge b Oakman	8	— not out	0
J. J. Warr b Thomson	13		
L. H. Compton c Langridge b Marlar ..	12		
J. A. Young not out	4		
A. E. Moss st Webb b Marlar	4		
L-b 1	1		

1/4 2/4 3/23 4/24 5/54 6/105 206 1/20 2/61 (4 wkts.) 110
7/133 8/188 9/199   3/100 4/106

Sussex

J. Langridge b Moss............	10	G. Potter not out	48
D. V. Smith c D. Compton b Young	36	N. I. Thomson b Warr	28
A. S. M. Oakman b Moss	6	R. G. Marlar b Moss	11
R. T. Webb lbw b Moss	31	A. E. James b Moss	1
J. M. Parks b Moss	23	B 8, n-b 2	10
K. G. Suttle c and b Moss	63		
G. Cox c L. Compton b D. Comp-		1/24 2/36 3/82 4/107 5/116	281
ton	14	6/150 7/216 8/252 9/277	

Sussex Bowling

	O.	M.	R.	W.	O.	M.	R.	W.
Thomson	30	12	42	3	2	0	4	0
James	21	9	47	2	2	1	4	0
Smith	4	0	16	0				
Marlar	20.5	9	50	4	14	2	45	
Oakman	18	6	50	1				
Potter					14	5	29	1
Parks					5	0	12	0
Cox					5	1	12	2
Langridge					1	0	4	0

Middlesex Bowling

	O.	M.	R.	W.
Moss	33.5	4	124	7
Warr	20	3	62	1
Titmus	26	13	47	0
D. Compton	12	2	29	1
Young	3	1	5	1
Bennett	2	0	4	0

Umpires: E. A. Roberts and J. J. Hills.

At Cambridge, June 1, 2, 3. MIDDLESEX beat CAMBRIDGE UNIVERSITY by three wickets

MIDDLESEX v. WORCESTERSHIRE

At Lord's, June 4, 6. Middlesex won by an innings and 110 runs. Worcestershire gave dismal batting displays in losing within two days for the second successive match. Their first innings lasted two hours forty minutes and the second three-quarters of an hour less. Titmus bowled off-breaks skilfully on a good pitch, but his match analysis of nine wickets for 20 runs reflected in the main the inadequacy of the opposition. Robertson and Brown gave Middlesex their best start thus far and D. Compton batted well until losing patience when tied to defence by the accuracy of Berry's left-arm slow bowling.

Worcestershire

D. Kenyon b Moss	18	— b Warr	12
L. Outschoorn c Titmus b Warr	10	— b Moss	0
G. Dews c L. Compton b Titmus	15	— lbw b Titmus	14
L. N. Devereux c and b Titmus	18	— lbw b Moss	8
R. G. Broadbent c D. Compton b Warr	9	— b Bennett	15
J. P. Whitehead c Edrich b Warr	8	— not out	9
M. J. Horton b Titmus	0	— lbw b Bennett	0
H. Yarnold b Titmus	2	— b Bennett	4
R. T. D. Perks c Baldry b Titmus	0	— c Robertson b Titmus	1
R. Berry not out	1	— b Titmus	1
J. Flavell c Baldry b Warr	0	— b Titmus	0
B 7, n-b 1	8	B 4, n-b 2	6

1/28 2/29 3/63 4/74 5/76 6/76　　89　　　1/2 2/22 3/34 4/48　　70
7/82 8/82 9/87　　　　　　　　　　　　5/58 6/58 7/62 8/63 9/66

Middlesex

S. M. Brown c and b Horton	46	L. H. Compton lbw b Berry	3
J. D. Robertson c Yarnold b Berry	79	R. J. Hurst not out	5
W. J. Edrich b Berry	6	A. E. Moss b Berry	2
D. C. S. Compton st Yarnold b Berry	51		
D. Bennett b Flavell	23	B 7, l-b 4, n-b 3	14
D. O. Baldry c Broadbent b Berry	5		
F. J. Titmus hit wkt b Perks	13	1/87 2/106 3/185 4/198 5/222	269
J. J. Warr b Flavell	22	6/226 7/255 8/259 9/267	

Middlesex Bowling

	O.	M.	R.	W.		O.	M.	R.	W.
Moss	9	2	23	1	....	7	1	19	2
Warr	12.3	5	23	4	....	7	1	17	1
Hurst	10	5	24	0					
Titmus	14	7	11	5	....	9.1	3	9	4
D. Compton						1	0	5	0
Bennett						11	3	14	3

Worcestershire Bowling

	O.	M.	R.	W.
Perks	19	4	38	1
Flavell	19	2	69	2
Outschoorn	1	1	0	0
Berry	37.2	20	61	6
Horton	34	11	87	1

Umpires: A. E. Pothecary and H. Elliott (Lancashire).

MIDDLESEX v. KENT

At Lord's, June 8, 9, 10. Kent won by six wickets, despite much time being lost through rain. Clever bowling by Wright upset Middlesex, who were dismissed in just over three hours. A storm prevented further cricket on the first day and on Thursday only seventy-five minutes' play was possible. By lunch time on Friday only one innings apiece had been completed and a definite result seemed unlikely. Middlesex, 18 ahead, reached 109 for five, but lost their last five wickets in thirteen balls for the addition of nine runs. Page, with off-breaks, took six for 33, the best performance of his career. Kent needed 137 in 140 minutes and steady batting by Phebey helped towards victory with ten minutes to spare.

Middlesex

J. D. Robertson st Ufton b Wright	40	—	lbw b Spanswick	25
S. M. Brown lbw b Dixon	7	—	c Wilson b Page	16
W. J. Edrich c Fagg b Wright	6	—	c Disbury b Page	3
A. Thompson c Fagg b Dixon	7	—	b Dixon	43
D. Bennett c Ufton b Page	14	—	b Page	4
D. O. Baldry b Wright	20	—	c Dixon b Page	8
F. J. Titmus c Disbury b Spanswick	26	—	st Ufton b Dixon	15
J. J. Warr c Wilson b Wright	0	—	b Page	0
L. H. Compton lbw b Wright	0	—	b Page	0
R. J. Hurst not out	2	—	not out	0
A. E. Moss b Spanswick	3	—	c Fagg b Dixon	2
B 5, l-b 1, n-b 2	8		L-b 2	2

1/38 2/49 3/56 4/67 5/78 6/113   133   1/39 2/41 3/50 4/69 5/81   118
7/113 8/113 9/126   6/109 7/110 8/112 9/116

Kent

A. E. Fagg c Bennett b Warr	3	—	c Hurst b Titmus	19
A. H. Phebey lbw b Warr	31	—	run out	49
P. Hearn lbw b Warr	0	—	b Titmus	0
J. Pettiford c Hurst b Warr	11	—	not out	8
A. Dixon c Bennett b Moss	3			
R. C. Wilson b Titmus	3	—	not out	32
B. E. Disbury not out	26			
D. G. Ufton b Titmus	24	—	lbw b Titmus	20
D. V. P. Wright b Titmus	2			
J. C. T. Page b Titmus	0			
J. Spanswick lbw b Titmus	3			
B 5, l-b 1, n-b 3	9		B 1, l-b 6, n-b 2	9

1/9 2/9 3/25 4/31 5/42 6/56   115   1/37 2/37 3/95   (4 wkts.) 137
7/93 8/101 9/109   4/119

Kent Bowling

	O.	M.	R.	W.		O.	M.	R.	W.
Spanswick	8.4	1	21	2	....	10	2	34	1
Disbury	4	0	22	0	....	3	1	13	0
Dixon	12	5	29	2	....	3	0	13	3
Wright	16	6	21	5	....	3	0	23	0
Page	6	3	10	1	....	12	1	33	6
Pettiford	7	2	22	0					

Middlesex Bowling

	O.	M.	R.	W.		O.	M.	R.	W.
Moss	16	3	32	1	....	16	2	50	0
Warr	24	12	39	4	....	4	0	9	0
Titmus	23.3	9	35	5	....	20.1	6	46	3
					Hurst	8	2	23	0

Umpires: A. E. Pothecary and E. Cooke.

MIDDLESEX v. LANCASHIRE

At Lord's, June 11, 13.   Lancashire won by an innings and 13 runs.   Caught on a rain-damaged pitch, Middlesex lost twenty wickets on the second day. On Saturday the first two Lancashire wickets fell for two runs, but they recovered through a stand of 171 between Washbrook and Grieves.   Washbrook stayed four hours and Grieves also gave a stylish display.   Moss and Warr, with the new ball, caused a collapse and the last six wickets went down for 41.   Middlesex could do little against balls which frequently rose nastily.   Goodwin, on his first appearance at Lord's, caused their first collapse and when Middlesex followed on 166 behind, the spin of Hilton, Tattersall and Ikin upset them.

Lancashire

J. T. Ikin lbw b Warr	0
A. Wharton c Compton b Moss	2
G. A. Edrich, c Edrich b Bennett	22
C. Washbrook c Compton b Moss	97
K. Grieves b Moss	84
P. Marner lbw b Moss	21
R. Collins b Warr	13
A. Wilson c Robertson b Moss	0
M. J. Hilton b Warr	1
R. Tattersall b Warr	0
F. Goodwin not out	5
B 5, l-b 9, n-b 1	15

1/2 2/2 3/48 4/219 5/232   260
6/243 7/243 8/253 9/253

Middlesex

J. D. Robertson c Edrich b Goodwin	22	— c Ikin b Goodwin	5
S. M. Brown c Grieves b Tattersall	22	— c Wharton b Hilton	26
W. J. Edrich c Ikin b Goodwin	1	— c Wharton b Hilton	30
A. Thompson c Edrich b Goodwin	2	— c and b Hilton	9
D. Bennett c Wilson b Hilton	8	— c Collins b Hilton	25
D. O. Baldry c Hilton b Goodwin	1	— c Collins b Ikin	15
F. J. Titmus not out	7	— c Grieves b Ikin	24
J. J. Warr c Collins b Hilton	14	— b Tattersall	15
L. H. Compton c Washbrook b Goodwin	9	— c Wharton b Tattersall	0
J. A. Young run out	0	— st Wilson b Tattersall	0
A. E. Moss c Marner b Hilton	1	— not out	0
N-b 6	6	B 3, n-b 1	4

1/26 2/32 3/34 4/55 5/60 6/61   94
7/77 8/87 9/88

1/6 2/54 3/68 4/71   153
5/113 6/127 7/153 8/153
9/153

Middlesex Bowling

	O.	M.	R.	W.	O.	M.	R.	W.
Moss	16	3	31	5				
Warr	25.4	9	58	4				
Young	21	8	57	0				
Bennett	11	1	26	1				
Titmus	26	6	62	0				
Edrich	4	1	11	0				

Lancashire Bowling

	O.	M.	R.	W.	O.	M.	R.	W.
Goodwin	20	8	35	5	10	1	18	1
Wharton	4	2	4	0	5	3	2	0
Marner	5	3	5	0				
Tattersall	9	4	9	1	18	7	25	3
Hilton	11.3	5	35	4	36	18	65	4
Collins					4	1	15	0
Ikin					13.1	5	24	2

Umpires: A. Skelding and J. J. Hills.

MIDDLESEX v. SOMERSET

At Lord's, June 18, 20, 21. Middlesex won by nine wickets, the match being over after three-quarters of an hour on the third day. Somerset broke down before the clever off-break bowling of Titmus who, although receiving little help from the pitch, baffled the batsmen by clever variation of flight and spin. Robertson took complete command when Middlesex went in and reached his century in two hours. Altogether he batted just under three hours for 137, hitting a six and fifteen 4's. Compton gave him good support and Middlesex declared 142 ahead. Somerset looked like being beaten by an innings, but Tremlett stayed two and three-quarter hours and McMahon helped him add 50 for the ninth wicket. Even so, Middlesex needed only 48 to win.

Somerset

H. W. Stephenson c Bennett b Warr	27	— c Titmus b Warr	0
Yawar Saeed c L. Compton b Moss	1	— run out	22
J. Lawrence b Titmus	27	— b Moss	8
G. G. Tordoff b Titmus	24	— c D. Compton b Titmus	18
P. B. Wight lbw b Titmus	0	— c Moss b Young	12
M. F. Tremlett run out	7	— c Warr b Titmus	92
J. G. Lomax c L. Compton b Titmus	3	— c Baldry b Titmus	12
G. M. Tripp c Edrich b Titmus	8	— c Moss b Young	2
J. Hilton c D. Compton b Titmus	11	— c Edrich b Young	8
J. W. McMahon not out	5	— c Titmus b Warr	7
B. Lobb c Edrich b Titmus	14	— not out	0
B 7, l-b 4, w 1, n-b 7	19	B 4, l-b 4	8

1/16 2/64 3/80 4/80 5/89 6/104   146   1/0 2/17 3/43 4/55 5/61   189
7/109 8/126 9/127   6/88 7/119 8/139 9/189

Middlesex

J. D. Robertson c sub b McMahon	137	— st Stephenson b Lawrence	28
S. M. Brown c Lawrence b Lobb	13	— not out	16
W. J. Edrich c Lomax b Hilton	19	— not out	3
D. C. S. Compton c Tordoff b Hilton	48		
D. Bennett run out	24		
D. O. Baldry not out	23		
F. J. Titmus not out	18		
B 1, l-b 4, w 1	6	N-b 1	1

1/60 2/143 3/198 4/224 (5 wkts., dec.) 288   1/36   (1 wkt.) 48
5/257

J. J. Warr, L. H. Compton, J. A. Young and A. E. Moss did not bat.

Middlesex Bowling

	O.	M.	R.	W.	O.	M.	R.	W.
Moss	18	2	46	1	9	4	17	1
Warr	19	4	37	1	10.4	1	32	2
Bennett	4	0	13	0				
Titmus	24.3	11	31	7	35	6	64	3
Young					33	9	68	3

Somerset Bowling

	O.	M.	R.	W.	O.	M.	R.	W.
Lobb	22	5	84	1	4	0	10	0
Yawar Saed	4	0	19	0				
Lomax	12	1	59	0				
McMahon	14	3	43	1				
Hilton	23	6	54	2				
Tordoff	10	1	23	0	8	2	21	0
Tremlett					1	0	7	0
Lawrence					3.2	1	9	1

Umpires: F. Chester and K. McCanlis.

At Leicester, June 22, 23, 24. MIDDLESEX lost to LEICESTERSHIRE by six wickets.

At Bath, June 29, 30. MIDDLESEX lost to SOMERSET by 63 runs.

At Worcester, July 2, 4, 5. MIDDLESEX beat WORCESTERSHIRE by eight wickets.

At Birmingham, July 9, 11, 12. MIDDLESEX lost to WARWICKSHIRE by one wicket.

At Liverpool, July 13, 14, 15. MIDDLESEX beat LANCASHIRE by two wickets.

MIDDLESEX v. YORKSHIRE

At Lord's, July 16, 18, 19. Yorkshire won by eight wickets, holding the initiative for most of the match, which was played on a fast and lively pitch. Trueman's pace soon troubled Middlesex, but Denis Compton, in his most dashing form, hit 84 in ninety minutes, including thirteen 4's, and the fourth wicket stand of 107 with Delisle lasted little over an hour. After Compton's dismissal, fifth out, Middlesex collapsed, and Trueman finished the innings by taking four wickets in nine balls. Lowson, batting nearly five hours for his first century of the season and hitting a 5 and fourteen 4's, earned chief credit for Yorkshire gaining a lead of 56. Sound in defence, he drove well. Wilson helped him in a stand of 102 for the second wicket. Apart from good hooking by Edrich, Middlesex could do little in the second innings against the fiery pace of Trueman and Appleyard, who made his off-breaks turn and lift, and Yorkshire were set to make only 79, finishing the match just before lunch on the third day.

Middlesex

J. D. Robertson b Trueman	6	— c Lowson b Appleyard..... 15
S. M. Brown b Illingworth	44	— c and b Yardley 14
W. J. Edrich b Trueman	18	— b Appleyard 37
D. C. S. Compton c Wardle b Appleyard	84	— b Trueman 0
G. P. S. Delisle c Yardley b Appleyard	31	— c Wilson b Appleyard 1
D. Bennett c Binks b Trueman	12	— b Trueman 11
F. J. Titmus c Wilson b Yardley	1	— c Binks b Appleyard..... 7
J. J. Warr c Binks b Trueman	11	— c Wilson b Appleyard 17
L. H. Compton c Illingworth b Trueman	1	— c Binks b Appleyard..... 12
J. A. Young not out	0	— b Trueman 0
A. E. Moss lbw b Trueman	0	— not out 0
B 7, 1-b 8	15	B 10, 1-b 6, n-b 4 20

1/23 2/68 3/79 4/186 5/198 6/201   223
7/221 8/222 9/223

1/15 2/52 3/53 4/60   134
5/79 6/108 7/111 8/125
9/126

Yorkshire

F. A. Lowson c L. Compton b Titmus	116	— c L. Compton b Moss 12
D. E. V. Padgett c L. Compton b Moss	4	— b Titmus 14
J. V. Wilson b Titmus	55	— not out 30
W. H. H. Sutcliffe c Bennett b Titmus	1	— not out 18
W. Watson retired hurt	16	
N. W. D. Yardley b Warr	18	
R. Illingworth c Moss b Warr	30	
J. H. Wardle b Titmus	5	
F. S. Trueman lbw b Moss	18	
J. G. Binks c Brown b Titmus	2	
R. Appleyard not out	1	
B 6, 1-b 4, n-b 3	13	B 5.................. 5

1/8 2/110 3/112 4/177 5/246 6/256   279
7/257 8/277

1/26 2/28   (2 wkts.) 79

Yorkshire Bowling

	O.	M.	R.	W.		O.	M.	R.	W.
Trueman	20.5	3	49	6	....	19	5	48	3
Appleyard	14	3	51	2	....	17.5	2	51	6
Wardle	11	1	48	0	....	4	2	6	0
Illingworth	15	4	46	1					
Yardley	6	0	14	1	....	5	3	9	1

Middlesex Bowling

	O.	M.	R.	W.		O.	M.	R.	W.
Moss	23	2	80	2	....	13	2	28	1
Warr.........	20	9	41	2	....	1	0	3	0
Titmus	25.2	10	65	5	....	12	4	37	1
Bennett	1	0	1	0					
Young	21	9	37	0	....	1	0	6	0
D. Compton ...	7	1	42	0					
					Edrich	0.3	0	0	0

Umpires: F. S. Lee and G. S. Mobey.

MIDDLESEX v. NORTHAMPTONSHIRE

At Lord's, July 20, 21, 22. Middlesex won by 13 runs, after an exciting
finish with only five minutes to spare. It was a well-fought match in which both
sides collapsed on a pitch bare of grass in places, yet both did better at the second
attempt. Thanks to Robertson, who shaped splendidly in each innings, Middlesex
reached 152 for four on the first day and then broke down before Tribe, the last

wickets falling for 38. Tribe turned the ball from a good length and took six for 49. Brookes and Arnold overcame some short pitched fast bowling by Moss and Warr but the later batsmen broke down against the spin of Titmus and Robins, the last six wickets falling on the second morning for 52 more runs. Middlesex exercised more care in their second innings and Edrich declared setting Northamptonshire to make 323 in five and a quarter hours. In a fine display of driving against the fast bowlers Barrick hit sixteen 4's, scoring his 139 in four hours ten minutes. Broderick and Tribe also batted skilfully but, with fifteen minutes left and two wickets to fall, 30 were still needed and although Clarke made a gallant effort Middlesex just got home.

Middlesex

J. D. Robertson c Andrew b Tribe	67	— c Barrick b Subba Row	77
S. M. Brown c Clarke b Webster	5	— c and b Webster	28
W. J. Edrich lbw b Webster	0	— c Greasley b Clarke	55
G. P. S. Delisle lbw b Tribe	38	— lbw b Tribe	0
D. Bennett b Tribe	34	— not out	60
F. J. Titmus st Andrew b Tribe	20	— c Brookes b Broderick	42
R. V. C. Robins lbw b Tribe	2	— c Arnold b Broderick	7
J. J. Warr c Clarke b Greasley	8	— not out	8
L. H. Compton b Tribe	4		
J. A. Young run out	2		
A. E. Moss not out	0		
B 4, 1-b 6	10	B 7, 1-b 3	10

1/7 2/7 3/70 4/152 5/153 6/165 7/184   **190**   1/68 2/120   (6 wkts., dec.) **287**
8/188 9/190   3/122 4/192 5/267 6/275

Northamptonshire

D. Brookes c Young b Titmus	40	— b Warr	7
P. Arnold c Compton b Titmus	42	— b Warr	0
L. Livingston b Titmus	18	— lbw b Robins	30
K. V. Andrew b Titmus	0	— c Robertson b Titmus	1
D. Barrick b Titmus	2	— b Young	139
J. Webster b Moss	3	— not out	1
R. Subba Row b Robins	27	— lbw b Titmus	25
D. G. Greasley b Moss	0	— b Titmus	0
G. E. Tribe not out	14	— c Young b Warr	33
V. Broderick c Titmus b Robins	0	— c Compton b Warr	48
R. W. Clarke lbw b Robins	1	— st Compton b Robins	15
B 2, 1-b 4, n-b 2	8	B 2, 1-b 8	10

1/73 2/98 3/98 4/102 5/107 6/122   **155**   1/0 2/19 3/51 4/134   **309**
7/123 8/141 9/149   5/142 6/220 7/264 8/293
                                                    9/299

Northamptonshire Bowling

	O.	M.	R.	W.		O.	M.	R.	W.
Clarke	11	1	45	0	....	21	3	54	1
Webster	12	3	25	2	....	20	6	65	1
Barrick	8	1	22	0	....	6	2	13	0
Tribe	28	9	49	6	....	22	6	51	1
Subba Row	1	1	0	0	....	13	1	44	1
Broderick	19	7	37	0	....	16	5	37	2
Greasley	2	1	2	1	....	4	0	13	0

Middlesex Bowling

	O.	M.	R.	W.	O.	M.	R.	W.
Moss	18	5	42	2	12	3	50	0
Warr..........	8	2	13	0	15	3	33	4
Titmus	27	8	56	5	38	4	88	3
Robins	13.5	3	36	3	17	1	74	2
Young					19	8	39	1
Bennett					4	0	15	0

Umpires: H. G. Baldwin and E. A. Roberts.

At Bournemouth, July 23, 25, 26. MIDDLESEX lost to HAMPSHIRE by an innings and six runs.

At Cardiff, July 27, 28, 29. MIDDLESEX beat GLAMORGAN by one wicket.

At Hove, July 30, August 1, 2. MIDDLESEX beat SUSSEX by six wickets.

At Nottingham, August 3, 4, 5. MIDDLESEX lost to NOTTINGHAMSHIRE by seven wickets.

At The Oval, August 6, 8, 9. MIDDLESEX lost to SURREY by 39 runs.

MIDDLESEX v. WARWICKSHIRE

At Lord's, August 10, 11. Middlesex won by 24 runs, a fitting result to a close struggle on a pitch which showed many bare patches. Bannister, fast-medium, troubled Middlesex in the first innings, and but for brisk hitting by L. Compton, once missed, they would have fared disastrously. Moss, taking five of the first six wickets for 34 runs, caused a Warwickshire collapse and though Townsend batted pluckily, he could find nobody to stay with him. Leading by 36, Middlesex found the spin bowling of Hollies and Townsend awkward, but Robertson batted skilfully for an hour and three-quarters and he and D. Compton, who punished Thompson for a 6 and three 4's in an over, put on 62. So Warwickshire needed 193 to win. Wolton, let off three times, shared with Horner in a stand of 63, but the last eight wickets fell to the spin bowling of Titmus and Young for 100 runs.

Middlesex

J. D. Robertson c Bannister b Carter....	17	— c Gardner b Hollies	54
S. M. Brown b Bannister	12	— c Townsend b Bannister ...	8
W. J. Edrich c Thompson b Bannister	11	— c Dollery b Carter	13
D. C. S. Compton c Dollery b Bannister.	1	— c Dollery b Hollies	34
G. P. S. Delisle c Townsend b Bannister..	5	— b Townsend	23
D. Bennett c Wolton b Carter	14	— c Spooner b Townsend	11
F. J. Titmus lbw b Bannister	10	— c Spooner b Townsend ...	1
L. H. Compton b Hollies	57	— b Townsend	7
J. J. Warr b Bannister	2	— not out	1
J. A. Young c Wolton b Thompson	18	— lbw b Hollies	1
A. E. Moss not out	4	— run out	2
B 1, l-b 1, n-b 2	4	L-b 1	1

1/25 2/35 3/36 4/45 5/50 6/71 7/73   155   1/17 2/42 3/104 4/109   156
8/101 9/126   5/134 6/140 7/149 8/152
                                                         9/153

Warwickshire

F. C. Gardner lbw b Moss	2	— lbw b Warr	3
N. F. Horner b Moss	16	— c D. Compton b Titmus	29
A. V. Wolton b Moss	2	— b Titmus	45
R. T. Spooner c L. Compton b Warr	4	— c Warr b Titmus	5
H. E. Dollery b Moss	1	— lbw b Young	17
R. E. Hitchcock c D. Compton b Moss	16	— c Edrich b Titmus	24
A. Townsend not out	47	— b Titmus	21
J. D. Bannister c Warr b Bennett	14	— c D. Compton b Young	2
R. G. Carter b Bennett	1	— not out	0
R. G. Thompson b Titmus	0	— c Bennett b Young	1
W. E. Hollies run out	0	— b Young	2
B 9, l-b 6, n-b 1	16	B 11, l-b 8	19
	119		**168**

1/12 2/16 3/25 4/30 5/30 6/67   119   1/5 2/68 3/78 4/89 5/129   168
7/89 8/99 9/102   6/133 7/136 8/162 9/162

Warwickshire Bowling

	O.	M.	R.	W.		O.	M.	R.	W.
Thompson	16	3	38	1		7	0	40	0
Bannister	26	6	79	6		10	2	31	1
Carter	10	0	34	2		4	0	29	1
Hollies	0.3	0	0	1		16	5	31	3
Townsend						9.2	1	24	4

Middlesex Bowling

	O.	M.	R.	W.		O.	M.	R.	W.
Moss	15	1	49	5		4	0	18	0
Warr	13	4	24	1		5	1	15	1
Titmus	6	0	21	1		20	7	47	5
Bennett	4	1	9	2					
Young						21.4	4	69	4

Umpires: A. E. Pothecary and W. T. Jones.

At Leeds, August 13, 15, 16. MIDDLESEX beat YORKSHIRE by five wickets.

MIDDLESEX v. GLAMORGAN

At Lord's, August 17, 18, 19. Middlesex won by 164 runs. Apart from a stand of 101 between Dewes and Brown, Middlesex fared none too well in the first innings, and the last eight wickets fell for 84. Glamorgan experienced disaster against the fast bowling of Moss and Warr following rain on the second morning. Five wickets were down for 18 and Watkins, struck on the right elbow by Warr, retired from the match. Wooller and Pressdee then added 82, Wooller batting courageously for just over two and a half hours. An opening partnership of 110 by Robertson and Dewes led to a Middlesex declaration in the second innings. Set 306 to get, Glamorgan lost five men for 72. Again Wooller and Pressdee stemmed the tide, putting on 63, but Moss virtually ended the game by dismissing Wooller, H. G. Davies and H. D. Davies with the first, fourth and last balls of an over for two runs.

Middlesex

J. D. Robertson lbw b H. D. Davies	20	— c H. G. Davies b Wooller	58
J. G. Dewes b H. D. Davies	46	— not out	85
S. M. Brown hit wkt b H. D. Davies	60	— c and b Wooller	16
W. J. Edrich b Pressdee	22	— lbw b Wooller	4
G. P. S. Delisle b Pressdee	3	— b Wooller	6
D. Bennett b Pressdee	0	— b H. D. Davies	22
F. J. Titmus c H. G. Davies b Watkins	24	— not out	8
L. H. Compton b Watkins	9		
J. J. Warr c and b Pressdee	5		
J. A. Young b Watkins	17		
A. E. Moss not out	3		
B 12, l-b 1	13	L-b 5, n-b 4	9

1/37 2/138 3/141 4/144 5/144 6/175   222   1/110 2/132 (5 wkts., dec.) 208
7/193 8/198 9/212   3/136 4/152 5/200

Glamorgan

P. B. Clift b Moss	0	— c Bennett b Moss	0
W. G. A. Parkhouse c Compton b Warr	6	— b Titmus	12
D. Ward c Compton b Moss	0	— c Robertson b Warr	1
W. E. Jones b Moss	8	— c Titmus b Moss	37
A. J. Watkins retired hurt	0	— absent hurt	0
J. Pleass c Moss b Warr	0	— lbw b Young	13
W. Wooller c and b Titmus	73	— lbw b Moss	17
J. Pressdee lbw b Young	33	— c Compton b Brown	35
H. G. Davies lbw b Young	0	— lbw b Moss	1
H. D. Davies b Young	1	— b Moss	0
D. J. Shepherd not out	0	— not out	3
L-b 2, n-b 2	4	B 18, l-b 4	22

1/6 2/6 3/6 4/8 5/18 6/100 7/106   125   1/0 2/1 3/31 4/68 5/72   141
8/125 9/125   6/135 7/137 8/137 9/141

Glamorgan Bowling

	O.	M.	R.	W.	O.	M.	R.	W.
H. D. Davies	24	5	67	3	18	3	78	1
Watkins	27	10	58	3				
Shepherd	9	1	22	0	27	7	72	0
Wooller	9	2	21	0	18	2	49	4
Pressdee	27	12	41	4				

Middlesex Bowling

	O.	M.	R.	W.	O.	M.	R.	W.
Moss	22	7	60	3	11	1	26	5
Warr	17	4	27	2	6	4	6	1
Bennett	7	1	24	0				
Young	10	3	10	3	19	7	42	1
Titmus	2.5	2	0	1	20	11	28	1
Brown					6	1	17	1

Umpires: F. Chester and A. J. B. Fowler.

Q

MIDDLESEX v. SURREY
(H. P. Sharp and A. Thompson—Joint Benefit)

At Lord's, August 20, 22, 23. Surrey won by nine wickets. They were much stronger all round and once more Lock proved a match-winning bowler. He decided to play only at the last minute because a sore finger had been troublesome. A crowd of 20,000 saw him take five for 62 on Saturday when after a good innings from Delisle, Middlesex collapsed. Their last five wickets fell for 18. Barrington and E. Bedser shared a stand of 114 and with Stewart also showing fine form, Surrey led by 84. On a dusty pitch Middlesex broke down again and Lock made his match record nine for 108. Surrey needed only 32 to win.

Middlesex

J. D. Robertson c Stewart b Surridge ...	16	— c McIntyre b Lock 16
J. G. Dewes run out	37	— lbw b A. Bedser 15
S. M. Brown c McIntyre b A. Bedser...	21	— c Stewart b A. Bedser 2
W. J. Edrich c McIntyre b Lock	20	— c Stewart b Lock.......... 10
G. P. S. Delisle c Loader b Lock	51	— b A. Bedser 0
J. T. Murray b E. Bedser	26	— b E. Bedser 22
D. Bennett c Clark b Lock............	0	— c Barrington b E. Bedser .. 9
F. J. Titmus c Stewart b E. Bedser	0	— lbw b E. Bedser 25
J. J. Warr c Surridge b Lock	0	— c Stewart b Lock.......... 8
J. A. Young not out	0	— not out 5
A. E. Moss c Barrington b Lock.......	4	— st McIntyre b Lock 2
B 12, l-b 8, n-b 3	23	B 1................. 1

1/33 2/75 3/84 4/122 5/180 6/194   198
7/194 8/194 9/194

1/28 2/34 3/34 4/34 5/52   115
6/67 7/80 8/107 9/109

Surrey

T. H. Clark c and b Young	11	— b Moss 0
M. J. Stewart c and b Young	73	— not out 10
P. B. H. May lbw b Warr	16	— not out 16
E. A. Bedser c Moss b Warr	79	
B. Constable b Moss	1	
K. Barrington b Moss	51	
A. J. McIntyre c Titmus b Warr	11	
G. A. R. Lock b Moss	0	
W. S. Surridge b Warr	1	
P. J. Loader b Warr	18	
A. V. Bedser not out	5	
B 6, l-b 8, n-b 2	16	B 4, l-b 2 6

1/45 2/79 3/129 4/130 5/244 6/246   282
7/246 8/259 9/260

1/1   (1 wkt.)   32

Surrey Bowling

	O.	M.	R.	W.		O.	M.	R.	W.
A. Bedser......	18	6	26	1	....	18	6	28	3
Loader	8	3	14	0					
Surridge	15	5	41	1	....	2	0	5	0
Lock	25.5	10	62	5	....	28.1	10	46	4
E. Bedser	9	4	16	2	....	16	4	31	3
Clark	4	0	16	0	....	4	1	4	0

Middlesex Bowling

	O.	M.	R.	W.		O.	M.	R.	W.
Moss	29	6	74	3	....	5	0	17	1
Warr	20.1	5	41	5					
Titmus	45	21	69	0	....	5.3	4	8	0
Young	31	13	66	2					
Bennett	6	1	16	0					
Edrich						1	0	1	0

Umpires: D. Davies and T. Spencer.

MIDDLESEX v. LEICESTERSHIRE

At Lord's, August 24, 25, 26. Middlesex won by 40 runs after a keen, even fight. Robertson and Dewes opened with 114 for Middlesex, who batted consistently. Edrich, Delisle and Bennett also played good innings. Tompkin dominated the Leicestershire batting. Driving powerfully, he hit two 6's and eleven 4's in 121. Palmer made 38 towards the third wicket stand of 102. Walsh and Firth put Leicestershire ahead in a partnership of 66 for the eighth wicket and they declared one run in front. Middlesex scored at over 70 an hour in their second innings and set Leicestershire to get 219 in 165 minutes. In poor light Leicestershire failed in their chase for the runs.

Middlesex

J. D. Robertson c and b Walsh	75	— lbw b Jackson	34
J. G. Dewes c Firth b Munden	53	— c Tompkin b Munden	29
W. J. Edrich c Spencer b Goodwin	59	— c Tompkin b Jackson	14
D. C. S. Compton b Munden	19	— st Firth b Munden	10
G. P. S. Delisle c Firth b Spencer	55	— c Walsh b Munden	39
D. Bennett not out	48	— b Munden	36
F. J. Titmus not out	11	— c Jackson b Palmer	30
L. H. Compton (did not bat)		— b Walsh	8
J. J. Warr (did not bat)		— not out	8
J. A. Young (did not bat)		— c Lester b Walsh	2
A. E. Moss (did not bat)		— b Walsh	0
L-b 3, n-b 2	5	B 4, l-b 3, n-b 2	9

1/114 2/145 3/175 4/219 (5 wkts., dec.) 325
5/295

1/60 2/74 3/84 4/94   219
5/149 6/197 7/197 8/209
9/211

Leicestershire

G. Lester b Titmus	24	— c L. Compton b Moss	13
M. J. K. Smith b Moss	1	— c and b Young	33
M. Tompkin b Titmus	121	— c Dewes b Young	19
C. H. Palmer c Edrich b Titmus	38	— b Titmus	5
V. E. Jackson b Titmus	12	— c Robertson b Young	36
R. A. Diment run out	4	— run out	14
V. S. Munden c L. Compton b Moss	29	— c Bennett b Young	9
J. E. Walsh not out	57	— b Titmus	1
J. Firth not out	19	— not out	24
C. T. Spencer (did not bat)		— b Titmus	14
J. Goodwin (did not bat)		— c Moss b Young	2
B 12, l-b 5, w 2, n-b 2	21	B 4, l-b 4	8

1/8 2/55 3/157 4/191   (7 wkts., dec.) 326
5/197 6/211 7/260

1/14 2/60 3/70 4/70 5/107   178
6/133 7/134 8/136 9/162

Leicestershire Bowling

	O.	M.	R.	W.		O.	M.	R.	W.
Spencer	21	1	78	1	....	6	1	30	0
Goodwin	22	5	78	1	....	4	0	18	0
Jackson	19	6	54	0	....	9	1	47	2
Palmer	8	3	16	0	....	7	3	17	1
Munden	15	4	45	2	....	26	7	64	4
Walsh	18	2	49	1	....	11.2	3	34	3

Middlesex Bowling

	O.	M.	R.	W.		O.	M.	R.	W.
Moss	21	2	76	2	....	6	2	17	1
Warr	8	0	20	0	....	1	0	8	0
Titmus	49.5	23	74	4	....	23	4	61	3
D. Compton	19	2	71	0					
Young	30	10	64	0	....	19	1	84	5

Umpires: F. S. Lee and G. Morton.

At Lord's, August 27, 29, 30. MIDDLESEX lost to SOUTH AFRICANS by 235 runs. (See SOUTH AFRICAN section.)

At Folkestone, August 31, September 1, 2. MIDDLESEX lost to KENT by nine wickets.

NORTHAMPTONSHIRE

President—T. E. MANNING

Secretary—LIEUT.-COL. A. ST. G. COLDWELL, County Cricket
Ground, Wantage Road, Northampton

Captain—DENNIS BROOKES

D. Brookes   County Badge   G. E. Tribe

As Northamptonshire won only one of their first fourteen
matches they stood within a few places of the bottom of the table
midway through the summer. Then came a splendid recovery
and they went unbeaten from July 22 till the end of the season.
They began their revival with six successive victories, finishing with
a memorable victory over Surrey. Eventually the team equalled
their nine wins of 1954 which was the most successful season since
1949.

Almost certainly they would have fared even better but for
an injury which deprived them of the help of Tyson for half the
season. After his wonderful performances in Australia the previous
winter much was expected from Tyson and, indeed, when he did
play his value as the spearhead of the attack was indispensable.

When Tyson was away the seam bowlers rarely seemed
capable of achieving a break-through, but fortunately Tribe, with
his varied left-handed spin, enjoyed his best season since entering
county cricket. He took 98 more wickets than the next most
successful bowler, Broderick, and completed the double of 1,000
runs and 100 wickets for the fourth successive year.

Two left-handers, Subba Row and Livingston, were among
the five batsmen who exceeded 1,000 runs in Championship games.
Subba Row, who joined the county from Surrey by special registration, marked his association with his new club by hitting the
highest individual score in the history of Northamptonshire cricket;
260 not out against Lancashire at Northampton, and it was also
the highest of the season in first-class cricket.

Livingston remained the most successful run-getter, again passing 2,000 in all matches, though much responsibility was removed from his shoulders by the excellent form of both opening batsmen. Arnold enjoyed his best season. He scored his first first-class century against Glamorgan, and followed with another next time he batted. Brookes again led the side in splendid fashion and batted most confidently. With Arnold, he formed one of the very few reliable first wicket partnerships in the country. Early in July they put on 100 three times in consecutive innings. Barrick interspersed good scores with periods when little would go right for him.

Broderick regained form with the bat and Andrew maintained his reputation behind the stumps. In Lightfoot there emerged a young pace-bowler of promise. The main weakness was the lack of a high-class off-spinner, for Starkie took only 13 wickets in the Championship games and these were expensive.

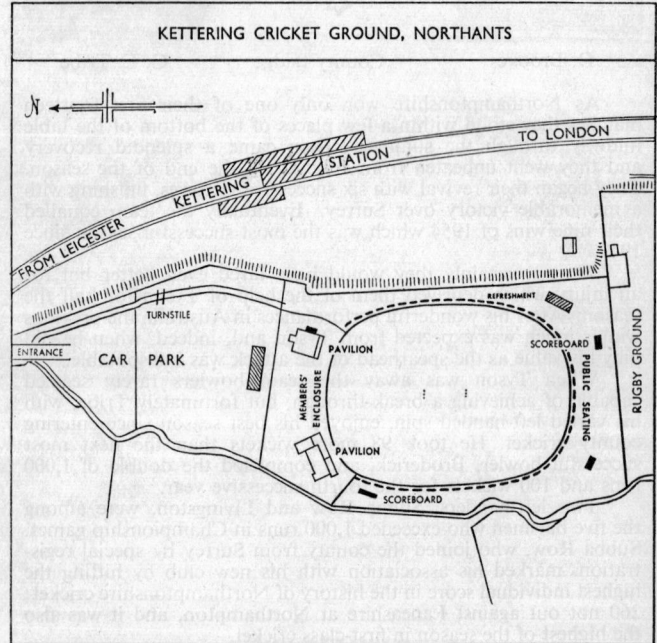

KETTERING CRICKET GROUND, NORTHANTS

NORTHAMPTONSHIRE RESULTS

All First-Class Matches—Played 30*, Won* 9*, Lost* 10*, Drawn* 11

County Championship Matches—Played 28*, Won* 9*, Lost* 10,
Drawn 9

COUNTY CHAMPIONSHIP AVERAGES
BATTING

	Birthplace	Mtchs.	Inns.	Not Outs	Runs	100's	Highest Inns.	Aver.
L. Livingston .	*Sydney*	28	51	5	1957	5	172*	42.54
R. Subba Row .	*Croydon*	24	36	5	1230	4	260*	39.67
D. W. Barrick .	*Fitzwilliam*	23	39	7	1188	2	139	37.12
D. Brookes .	*Kippax*	28	51	4	1629	3	177	34.65
P. Arnold	*Wellington, N.Z.*	28	52	2	1523	3	122	30.46
B. Reynolds ..	*Kettering*	11	18	3	383	0	64*	25.53
G. E. Tribe ...	*Melbourne*	28	44	5	958	0	80*	24.56
V. Broderick .	*Bacup*	28	41	6	760	0	68	21.71
D. G. Greasley .	*Hull*	7	12	1	210	0	63	19.09
F. H. Tyson .	*Bolton*	15	18	2	228	0	72	14.25
R. W. Clarke .	*Finedon*	21	29	13	182	0	27*	11.37
K. W. Andrew .	*Oldham*	24	31	10	235	0	32	11.19
S. Starkie.....	*Burnley*	11	16	1	107	0	60	7.13
J. Wild	*Northampton*	12	14	1	92	0	25	7.07
A. Lightfoot .	*Woore, Crewe*	3	5	0	35	0	17	7.00
R. Hogan	*Tamorra, N.S.W.*	2	4	0	18	0	8	4.50
J. Webster ...	*Bradford*	10	10	4	11	0	3	1.83

Also batted: A. G. Liddell (*Northampton*) 0, 29; A. L. Wells (*Leeds*) 9, 1;
E. Davis (*Brackley*) 25.

* *Signifies not out.*

BOWLING

	Overs	Maidens	Runs	Wickets	Average
F. H. Tyson	437.5	97	1074	58	18.51
G. E. Tribe	1220.1	328	3155	169	18.66
A. G. Liddell	55	13	134	6	22.33
A. Lightfoot	78	19	182	8	22.75
R. Subba Row	121.4	26	376	14	26.85
V. Broderick	871.5	312	2061	71	29.02
J. Webster	233.2	64	617	15	41.13
S. Starkie	223.1	69	548	13	42.15
R. W. Clarke	565	101	1576	33	47.75
J. Wild	223.3	48	748	14	53.42
D. G. Greasley	35	5	129	2	64.50
D. W. Barrick..........	143	29	415	5	83.00
R. Hogan	34	5	155	1	155.00

Also bowled: P. Arnold 1—1—0—0; A. L. Wells 48—15—121—0.

Amateurs.—A. G. Liddell, R. Subba Row, J. Webster, A. L. Wells, J. Wild.

NORTHAMPTONSHIRE v. LEICESTERSHIRE

At Northampton, May 4, 5. Drawn. Northamptonshire 251 (P. Arnold
89; G. Lester five for 49) and 178 for six wickets (L. Livingston 91; V. S. Munden
four for 32); Leicestershire 320 (M. Tompkin 67, G. A. Smithson 55, J. E. Walsh 50).
(Friendly match.)

At Bradford, May 7, 9. NORTHAMPTONSHIRE lost to YORKSHIRE by 78 runs.

At Manchester, May 11, 12, 13. NORTHAMPTONSHIRE drew with LANCASHIRE. (Friendly match.)

NORTHAMPTONSHIRE v. WORCESTERSHIRE

At Northampton, May 14, 16, 17. Drawn. Tyson, playing before his home crowd for the first time since the M.C.C. Australasian tour, bowled splendidly. When Worcestershire reached 112 for one wicket by lunch they seemed set for a big score; afterwards no batsman looked impressive against Tyson. Subba Row batted well on his first home appearance for Northamptonshire, and his 80 was top score of the match. With Broderick he shared a sixth wicket stand of 107. When Worcestershire batted again 55 behind Kenyon hit freely, but rain prevented play on the third day.

Worcestershire

D. Kenyon c and b Tribe	15	— not out 33
L. Outschoorn c Broderick b Tyson	55	— not out 3
G. Dews c Clarke b Tyson	63	
L. N. Devereux c Starkie b Tyson	2	
R. G. Broadbent c Arnold b Tyson	16	
J. P. Whitehead b Tyson	16	
M. J. Horton c Andrew b Tyson	2	
H. Yarnold b Tyson	2	
R. T. D. Perks st Andrew b Tribe	10	
J. Flavell st Andrew b Tribe	8	
R. Berry not out	3	
B 4, l-b 2, n-b 2	8	

1/30 2/123 3/125 4/154 5/157   200   (No wkt.) 36
6/159 7/167 8/182 9/196

Northamptonshire

D. Brookes lbw b Horton	37
P. Arnold c Broadbent b Flavell	24
L. Livingston c Flavell b Perks	0
D. Barrick c Dews b Berry	31
R. Subba Row c Yarnold b Whitehead	80
G. E. Tribe c Broadbent b Horton	5
V. Broderick b Whitehead	56
F. H. Tyson c Outschoorn b Whitehead	4
S. Starkie run out	11
R. W. Clarke not out	1
B 2, n-b 4	6

1/36 2/38 3/90   (9 wkts., dec.) 255
4/98 5/119 6/226 7/236 8/253 9/255

K. V. Andrew did not bat.

Northamptonshire Bowling

	O.	M.	R.	W.	O.	M.	R.	W.
Tyson	30.2	14	44	7	4	2	8	0
Clarke	12	2	38	0	2	0	8	0
Tribe	26	6	77	3	2	0	20	0
Starkie	5	0	23	0				
Broderick	7	2	10	0				

Worcestershire Bowling

	O.	M.	R.	W.
Perks	15	3	47	1
Flavell	19	6	60	1
Berry	26	6	60	1
Horton	21	4	60	2
Whitehead	5.5	0	22	3

Umpires: T. Spencer and W. F. Price.

NORTHAMPTONSHIRE v. MIDDLESEX

At Rushden, May 21, 23, 24. Middlesex won by six wickets. Fine batting by Brookes, who went in lower in the order, Reynolds and Broderick, helped Northamptonshire to a respectable total after six wickets had fallen cheaply. Northamptonshire gained a narrow lead on first innings thanks mainly to Tyson and Tribe. Livingston who narrowly missed a century averted a second innings collapse, and Middlesex were set to get 207 to win. Their first three wickets went cheaply, but Edrich was missed at the start of his innings, and Bennett added 158 and only one run was needed when they were separated.

Northamptonshire

R. Subba Row b Warr	7	— run out	10
P. Arnold c Edrich b Moss	5	— lbw b Moss	25
L. Livingston b Warr	7	— c Compton b Moss	93
D. Barrick c Edrich b Warr	9	— c and b Moss	19
D. Brookes c and b Hurst	56	— b Hurst	4
B. L. Reynolds b Moss	38	— b Hurst	0
G. E. Tribe c Compton b Moss	1	— lbw b Moss	20
V. Broderick not out	57	— c Compton b Moss	7
F. H. Tyson b Hurst	2	— b Moss	11
S. Starkie b Bennett	0	— b Moss	1
R. W. Clarke b Warr	12	— not out	9
B 3, l-b 9, w 1, n-b 3	16	B 1, l-b 2	3

1/8 2/20 3/22 4/34 5/107 6/111   210
7/143 8/149 9/150

1/36 2/36 3/80 4/99   202
5/105 6/162 7/174 8/185 9/191

Middlesex

J. D. Robertson c and b Tribe	68	— b Tyson	30
H. P. Sharp b Tyson	2	— b Tyson	8
W. J. Edrich b Tyson	0	— not out	87
A. Thompson c Tyson b Broderick	31	— b Clarke	2
D. Bennett c Clarke b Tribe	32	— st Livingston b Subba Row	68
D. O. Baldry lbw b Tribe	2	— not out	1
D. A. Bick lbw b Tribe	2		
J. J. Warr c Brookes b Broderick	40		
L. H. Compton lbw b Tyson	13		
R. J. Hurst b Tyson	8		
A. E. Moss not out	0		
B 4, l-b 2, w 1, n-b 1	8	B 8, l-b 2, w 1	11

1/31 2/31 3/99 4/111 5/114 6/116   206
7/185 8/185 9/205

1/36 2/45 3/48   (4 wkts.) 207
4/206

Middlesex Bowling

	O.	M.	R.	W.		O.	M.	R.	W.
Moss	31	3	80	3	....	22.2	4	61	7
Warr	26.2	8	46	4		20	1	72	0
Bennett	15	2	19	1		8	1	14	0
Hurst	15	4	30	2		9	3	32	2
Bick	4	1	19	0					
Robertson						7	0	20	0

Northamptonshire Bowling

	O.	M.	R.	W.		O.	M.	R.	W.
Tyson	22.3	6	77	4		20	0	62	2
Clarke	7	1	29	0		16	3	36	1
Broderick	15	5	31	2		16	3	32	0
Tribe	22	6	52	4		18	7	38	0
Starkie	4	1	9	0		9	3	15	0
Subba Row						3	0	13	1

Umpires: P. Corrall and Harry Elliott (Derbyshire).

NORTHAMPTONSHIRE v. LEICESTERSHIRE

At Northampton, May 28, 30, 31. Drawn. After rain had restricted the first day to 55 minutes Livingston completed his third century in successive innings against Leicestershire, and with Arnold shared 175 for the second wicket. When Leicestershire seemed likely to gain first innings points, Tribe took three wickets for 15 runs in 17 balls, and with the departure of Tompkin Leicestershire's chances of the lead vanished. Subba Row batted confidently in the Northamptonshire second innings.

Northamptonshire

R. Subba Row c Jackson b Spencer	....	0	— not out	60
P. Arnold c Tompkin b Jackson	....	82	— b Lester	23
L. Livingston b Jackson	....	105	— not out	17
D. Barrick c Tompkin b Jackson	....	30		
D. Brookes run out	....	0		
G. E. Tribe c Hallam b Munden	....	10		
V. Broderick b Spencer	....	29		
F. H. Tyson b Boshier	....	19		
K. V. Andrew b Boshier	....	3		
S. Starkie c Hallam b Boshier	....	0		
R. W. Clarke not out	....	0		
B 11, l-b 3, w 2	....	16	B 4, l-b 4, w 1	9
		294	(1 wkt.)	109

1/1 2/176 3/207 4/216 5/230   1/81
6/236 7/290 8/294 9/294

Leicestershire

G. Lester c Tribe b Tyson	....	32	J. E. Walsh b Tribe	2
M. R. Hallam c Subba Row b Clarke	....	43	C. T. Spencer run out	4
			B. Boshier not out	0
M. Tompkin b Tribe	....	89	J. Firth absent hurt	0
C. H. Palmer b Tyson	....	1	B 3, l-b 7, n-b 2	12
V. E. Jackson lbw b Tribe	....	29		
G. A. Smithson b Tyson	....	10	1/69 2/87 3/91 4/150 5/165	242
V. S. Munden b Tribe	....	20	6/219 7/223 8/242 9/242	

Leicestershire Bowling

	O.	M.	R.	W.		O.	M.	R.	W.
Spencer	20.1	5	56	2	....	5	0	22	0
Boshier	16	3	58	3	....	5	1	12	0
Palmer	4	2	10	0					
Jackson	31	15	53	3					
Munden	32	15	76	1	....	6	4	9	0
Lester	3	1	15	0	....	9	1	33	1
Walsh	2	0	10	0	....	4	0	24	0

Northamptonshire Bowling

	O.	M.	R.	W.
Tyson	23	2	71	3
Clarke	15	3	37	1
Tribe	14.3	2	61	4
Barrick	3	0	9	0
Broderick	9	2	24	0
Starkie	15	6	28	0

Umpires: F. Chester and H. G. Baldwin.

NORTHAMPTONSHIRE v. HAMPSHIRE

At Peterborough, June 1, 2, 3. Hampshire won by seven wickets. The vastly improved Hampshire team proved stronger in every department. Arnold and Broderick in the first Northamptonshire innings were the only batsmen to last long against a well-balanced attack, and an innings defeat seemed likely until Tyson hit a brisk 72. Marshall dominated the Hampshire first innings, hitting 91 out of an opening stand of 131 in less than an hour and three-quarters. Northamptonshire's bowling appeared as ineffective as that of Hampshire was dangerous.

Northamptonshire

B. L. Reynolds b Cannings	9	— lbw b Shackleton	38
P. Arnold c Harrison b Shackleton	30	— lbw b Cannings	0
L. Livingston b Shackleton	1	— lbw b Burden	11
D. Barrick b Barnard	13	— b Shackleton	4
D. Brookes b Burden	6	— b Marshall	15
R. Subba Row b Burden	6	— c Eagar b Shackleton	6
G. E. Tribe b Burden	10	— lbw b Sainsbury	26
V. Broderick lbw b Sainsbury	42	— b Sainsbury	23
F. H. Tyson run out	5	— b Sainsbury	72
K. V. Andrew b Sainsbury	6	— not out	7
R. W. Clarke not out	1	— b Sainsbury	0
B 8, l-b 9	17	B 14, l-b 12	26

1/10 2/11 3/47 4/58 5/60 6/80   142   1/0 2/32 3/37 4/75   228
7/83 8/94 9/141   5/83 6/85 7/134 8/147 9/228

Hampshire

J. R. Gray c Clarke b Tyson	44	— not out	15
R. E. Marshall c Tyson b Clarke	91	— b Broderick	3
N. H. Rogers c Tyson b Tribe	28	— lbw b Broderick	1
A. W. H. Rayment lbw b Tribe	23	— b Subba Row	4
H. M. Barnard c Arnold b Broderick	27	— not out	2
E. D. R. Eagar c Andrew b Tribe	53		
L. Harrison c Clarke b Barrick	8		
P. J. Sainsbury lbw b Barrick	0		
D. Shackleton c Brookes b Tyson	47		
V. H. D. Cannings not out	2		
M. D. Burden b Tyson	0		
B 15, l-b 4	19	B 4	4

1/131 2/152 3/183 4/214 5/228 6/249   342   1/4 2/18 3/27   (3 wkts.)   29
7/251 8/340 9/342

Hampshire Bowling

	O.	M.	R.	W.		O.	M.	R.	W.
Shackleton	20	13	11	2		25	7	46	3
Cannings	16	6	23	1		6	2	13	1
Sainsbury	16	5	24	2		19.4	4	51	4
Gray	2	1	6	0		2	0	3	0
Burden	22	6	59	3		13	1	41	1
Barnard	1	0	2	1		1	0	6	0
Marshall						18	9	42	1

Northamptonshire Bowling

	O.	M.	R.	W.	O.	M.	R.	W.
Tyson	23	6	50	3				
Clarke	15	3	50	1				
Tribe	31	4	108	3				
Broderick	19	3	88	1	9.1	5	12	2
Barrick	8	1	27	2				
Subba Row					9	2	13	1

Umpires: H. G. Baldwin and A. Skelding.

At Coventry, June 4, 6, 7. NORTHAMPTONSHIRE drew with WARWICKSHIRE.

At Horsham, June 8, 9, 10. NORTHAMPTONSHIRE lost to SUSSEX by 73 runs.

NORTHAMPTONSHIRE v. NOTTINGHAMSHIRE

At Northampton, June 11, 13, 14. Northamptonshire won by ten wickets, their first win of the season. Partnerships between Livingston and Barrick and the left-handers, Subba Row and Tribe, enabled them to reach 300 for five wickets, but the remaining batsmen fell cheaply in trying to force the pace. With three leading Nottinghamshire batsmen failing to score in the first innings, and only Dooland showing confidence against spin bowling in the second, Northamptonshire needed only six to win.

Northamptonshire

D. Brookes b Harvey	32	— not out	2
P. Arnold c Rowe b Smales	4	— not out	4
L. Livingston b Smales	84		
D. Barrick c Dooland b Smales	65		
R. Subba Row b Smales	48		
G. E. Tribe b Smales	50		
V. Broderick c Clay b Smales	16		
A. Lightfoot c and b Dooland	1		
S. Starkie c Giles b Smales	10		
R. W. Clarke c Rowe b Dooland	0		
K. V. Andrew not out	9		
L-b 7	7		

1/14 2/52 3/175 4/188 5/273 326　　　　(No wkt.) 6
6/303 7/307 8/310 9/310

Nottinghamshire

R. T. Simpson c Tribe b Lightfoot	25	— lbw b Tribe	32
J. D. Clay c Subba Row b Lightfoot	0	— lbw b Lightfoot	10
C. J. Poole c Clarke b Lightfoot	0	— c Andrew b Clarke	2
J. Hardstaff c Livingston b Clarke	0	— c Andrew b Broderick	23
E. J. Martin c and b Lightfoot	9	— b Broderick	15
R. Giles b Tribe	18	— c Tribe b Starkie	9
P. F. Harvey c and b Tribe	26	— c Andrew b Broderick	0
B. Dooland b Starkie	12	— b Starkie	54
K. Smales c Clarke b Tribe	22	— c Clarke b Tribe	7
A. Jepson c Barrick b Starkie	20	— c Arnold b Tribe	20
E. J. Rowe not out	7	— not out	5
B 3, l-b 5, w 1	9	B 6	6

1/2 2/2 3/7 4/27 5/38 6/77 7/80　　148　　　1/16 2/21 3/55 4/71　　183
8/96 9/126　　　　　　　　　　　　　　　　5/89 6/91 7/91 8/121 9/148

Nottinghamshire Bowling

	O.	M.	R.	W.	O.	M.	R.	W.
Jepson	23	4	54	0				
Smales	36	8	104	7				
Dooland	37	13	95	2				
Harvey	21	6	66	1				
Hardstaff					1	0	1	0
Clay					0.3	0	5	0

Northamptonshire Bowling

	O.	M.	R.	W.	O.	M.	R.	W.
Clarke	8	2	8	1	10	1	31	1
Lightfoot	24	9	37	4	10	2	25	1
Tribe	23	8	48	3	18	5	52	3
Starkie	19	5	34	2	13	5	24	2
Broderick	5	2	12	0	32	17	45	3

Umpires: K. McCanlis and W. T. Jones.

NORTHAMPTONSHIRE v. GLAMORGAN

At Northampton, June 15, 16, 17. Drawn. For the greater part of the three days the cricket was dreary and unenterprising, neither side setting their sights any higher than the winning of first innings points. On an easy pitch, the responsibility for producing worthwhile cricket rested with the batsmen, but except for Brookes, Arnold and Livingston before lunch on the third day they failed lamentably. Bowlers, aided by defensive fields, were allowed to dictate terms to batsmen unwilling to take any risk. Glamorgan, set to score 246 in 200 minutes to win, made no attempt to force a result, even though they had won first innings points. An hour before the end, with the Glamorgan total 100, Brookes gave up hope of inducing the visitors to go for runs.

Northamptonshire

D. Brookes c Wooller b Lewis	23	— not out	102
P. Arnold c Watkins b McConnon	22	— c McConnon b Pressdee	113
L. Livingston b Watkins	11	— not out	37
D. Barrick c and b Pressdee	50		
R. Subba Row lbw b Watkins	0		
G. E. Tribe c Davies b McConnon	4		
V. Broderick c and b Pressdee	68		
F. H. Tyson c Watkins b Pressdee	5		
S. Starkie c Wooller b Pressdee	2		
R. W. Clarke c Watkins b Pressdee	5		
K. V. Andrew not out	5		
B 4, 1-b 6, n-b 1	11	B 3	3

1/37 2/59 3/63 4/63 5/74 6/143   206   1/197   (1 wkt., dec.) 255
7/175 8/193 9/199

Glamorgan

W. G. A. Parkhouse b Tyson	24 — retired hurt	3
W. Wooller lbw b Tribe	13 — c Andrew b Tyson	0
B. Hedges c Subba Row b Tribe	87 — not out	54
W. E. Jones c Starkie b Broderick	35 — lbw b Starkie	35
A. J. Watkins c Tribe b Broderick	5 — not out	42
J. Pressdee lbw b Tribe	8	
B. R. Edrich b Tribe	5	
J. Pleass b Tyson	1	
J. E. McConnon lbw b Tribe	12	
H. G. Davies not out	5	
K. H. Lewis st Andrew b Tribe	6	
B 15	15	

1/24 2/42 3/125 4/143 5/181 6/188   216   1/0 2/63   (2 wkts.) 134
7/192 8/194 9/208

Glamorgan Bowling

	O.	M.	R.	W.	O.	M.	R.	W.
Wooller	16	4	36	0	12	0	59	0
Lewis	17	1	40	1	22	5	57	0
Watkins	15	5	21	2	9	4	26	0
McConnon	28	13	37	2	8	0	30	0
Pressdee	21.4	8	35	5	21	1	80	1
Jones	10	2	26	0				

Northamptonshire Bowling

	O.	M.	R.	W.	O.	M.	R.	W.
Tyson	26	6	44	2	7	3	7	1
Clarke	10	3	16	0	7	0	22	0
Tribe	30.2	9	72	6	8	2	21	0
Starkie	12	6	20	0	15	5	27	1
Broderick	16	4	49	2	9	4	22	0
Subba Row					7	3	9	0
Barrick					4	0	26	0
Arnold					1	1	0	0

Umpires: L. H. Gray and A. J. B. Fowler.

At Tunbridge Wells, June 18, 20, 21. NORTHAMPTONSHIRE lost to KENT by 142 runs.

NORTHAMPTONSHIRE v. YORKSHIRE

At Northampton, June 22, 23, 24. Yorkshire won by six wickets. Even without Trueman, Appleyard, Wardle and Cowan, the Yorkshire bowling was too strong for Northamptonshire. Close seized the opportunity to return his best figures for some time, and in the second innings Illingworth enjoyed a good spell. Nevertheless, Northamptonshire gained first innings lead, but their meagre second innings total set Yorkshire a moderate task. With Hutton showing greater confidence than in previous matches and Sutcliffe playing another good innings, victory was assured.

Northamptonshire

D. Brookes run out	9	— c Close b Leadbeater	53
P. Arnold c Watson b Van Geloven	12	— run out	26
L. Livingston c Illingworth b Close	44	— lbw b Illingworth	24
D. Barrick b Close	41	— c Hutton b Leadbeater	6
R. Subba Row lbw b Close	28	— c Wilson b Illingworth	5
G. E. Tribe c Close b Leadbeater	9	— c Van Geloven b Illingworth	5
V. Broderick b Close	23	— lbw b Illingworth	5
R. Hogan c Hutton b Close	6	— b Close	8
K. V. Andrew not out	24	— c Wilson b Close	2
S. Starkie b Leadbeater	4	— b Close	0
R. W. Clarke b Illingworth	17	— not out	2
B 11, l-b 3	14	B 4, l-b 5	9

1/17 2/23 3/108 4/108 5/123 6/158   231
7/164 8/184 9/189

1/70 2/103 3/109   145
4/110 5/117 6/126 7/126
8/139 9/139

Yorkshire

L. Hutton c Andrew b Clarke	13	— c Hogan b Starkie	62
W. H. H. Sutcliffe c Brookes b Tribe	86	— c Andrew b Broderick	68
J. V. Wilson c Subba Row b Clarke	27	— b Starkie	5
E. Lester lbw b Tribe	24	— b Starkie	9
W. Watson c Andrew b Tribe	2	— not out	5
D. B. Close c Brookes b Starkie	10	— not out	5
N. W. D. Yardley c Barrick b Broderick	23		
R. Illingworth b Tribe	0		
J. Van Geloven lbw b Tribe	16		
R. Booth b Tribe	7		
E. Leadbeater not out	3		
B 7, l-b 2	9	B 5, l-b 1	6

1/28 2/80 3/124 4/134 5/149 6/172   220
7/172 8/198 9/210

1/107 2/123   (4 wkts.) 160
3/147 4/151

Yorkshire Bowling

	O.	M.	R.	W.		O.	M.	R.	W.
Van Geloven	15	4	41	1	....	4	1	22	0
Close	43	14	88	5	....	24.1	9	47	3
Wilson	3	0	16	0					
Illingworth	14.3	10	12	1	....	28	11	48	4
Leadbeater	24	7	60	2	....	6	1	17	2
Yardley						3	1	2	0

Northamptonshire Bowling

	O.	M.	R.	W.		O.	M.	R.	W.
Clarke	20	4	45	2	....	11	1	33	0
Hogan	5	1	15	0	....	4	1	11	0
Tribe	40.2	16	73	6	....	16	3	30	0
Starkie	18	8	31	1	....	10.1	2	39	3
Broderick	19	6	47	1	....	14	4	41	1

Umpires: E. A. Roberts and E. Davies.

At Guildford, June 25, 27, 28. NORTHAMPTONSHIRE lost to SURREY by 69 runs.

At Northampton, June 29, 30, July 1. NORTHAMPTONSHIRE drew with SOUTH
AFRICANS. (See SOUTH AFRICAN section.)

NORTHAMPTONSHIRE v. GLOUCESTERSHIRE

At Kettering, July 2, 4, 5. Gloucestershire won by 154 runs. Fine batting by Young and Graveney for Gloucestershire, and Brookes, the home captain, was the feature of a keen match. Young scored a century in each innings, and Graveney narrowly failed to join the ranks of those who have scored a hundred before lunch. The Gloucestershire score passed 250 for two in under three hours, but the later batsmen failed against Tribe. Brookes, despite bruised ribs which gave him considerable pain, shared a stand of 106 with Arnold, this being Northamptonshire's third century opening partnership in successive innings, but after Arnold left only Broderick gave the captain useful assistance. Gloucestershire's declaration did not give Graveney the chance of following Young's example of scoring two hundreds in the match, but the England batsman was rewarded by the best bowling figures when Northamptonshire batted again. Northamptonshire were handicapped by Tyson's absence, and an injury to Subba Row, who cut his hand over the week-end and took no further part in the match.

Gloucestershire

D. M. Young b Tribe	121	—	not out	117
C. C. Milton lbw b Hogan	10	—	b Clarke	29
T. W. Graveney c Arnold b Wild	101	—	not out	75
J. F. Crapp c and b Tribe	32			
G. M. Emmett c Clarke b Tribe	12			
G. E. Lambert not out	45			
J. Mortimore c Andrew b Clarke	5			
P. Rochford lbw b Tribe	2			
C. Cook c Reynolds b Tribe	7			
B. D. Wells run out	1			
F. P. McHugh st Andrew b Tribe	8			
B 9, l-b 9, n-b 1	19		B 5, l-b 2	7

1/17 2/198 3/272 4/286 5/287 6/310   363   1/67   (1 wkt., dec.) 228
7/321 8/341 9/350

Northamptonshire

D. Brookes c Graveney b McHugh	95	—	c Milton b Wells	20
P. Arnold b McHugh	56	—	c Milton b Lambert	0
L. Livingston c Milton b Lambert	22	—	c Wells b Lambert	0
B. Reynolds b Lambert	0	—	b Graveney	50
G. E. Tribe b Mortimore	9	—	c Wells b Mortimore	51
V. Broderick c Young b Lambert	36	—	lbw b Wells	1
K. V. Andrew b McHugh	32	—	c Milton b Graveney	14
J. Wild b Lambert	4	—	c Emmett b Graveney	0
R. Hogan c Rochford b Lambert	4	—	lbw b Wells	0
R. W. Clarke not out	18	—	not out	0
R. Subba Row absent hurt	0	—	absent hurt	0
B 2, l-b 5, w 1	8		B 3, l-b 14	17

1/106 2/138 3/146 4/163 5/219 6/228   284   1/7 2/9 3/59 4/61 5/97   153
7/241 8/251 9/284   6/142 7/142 8/145 9/153

Northamptonshire Bowling

	O.	M.	R.	W.		O.	M.	R.	W.
Clarke	27	9	56	1	....	15	1	57	1
Hogan	14	1	67	1	....	11	2	62	0
Tribe	25	3	116	6	....	13	0	37	0
Broderick	22	7	67	0	....	8	1	34	0
Wild	12	3	38	1	....	6	0	31	0

Gloucestershire Bowling

	O.	M.	R.	W.		O.	M.	R.	W.
Lambert	34	9	81	5	....	12	4	23	2
McHugh	32	6	87	3	....	11	7	14	0
Wells	13	3	20	0	....	19	5	66	3
Graveney	6	1	20	0	....	5.5	2	18	3
Cook	18	6	35	0	....	2	0	5	0
Mortimore	19	7	33	1	....	7	2	10	1

Umpires: E. A. Roberts and K. McCanlis.

NORTHAMPTONSHIRE v. WARWICKSHIRE

At Northampton, July 6, 7, 8. Drawn. Despite three declarations a definite result was not achieved mainly because of the cautious batting of both teams which delayed the decision for the first innings points until the third morning. Tribe bowled skilfully on a docile pitch in taking five wickets for 81, but the two left-handers, Spooner and Hitchcock, hit well. Another left-hander, Livingston, stood out for Northamptonshire and showed a welcome return to form, getting his century in three hours. Greasley, on his first appearance of the season, spent an hour over his first 10 runs, but afterwards scored so freely that he hit eleven 4's. Warwickshire made a commendable bid to achieve a result by scoring 232 in a little over three hours and they left Northamptonshire to make the same number of runs in two hours twenty-five minutes, but the home county soon fell behind the clock. For Warwickshire, Hitchcock was always venturesome and he scored 141 runs in the match without being dismissed.

Warwickshire

F. C. Gardner c and b Clarke	44	— b Tribe	43
N. F. Horner c Clarke b Broderick	34	— lbw b Clarke	35
A. V. Wolton c Andrew b Tribe	31	— c Greasley b Tribe	28
R. T. Spooner c Reynolds b Tribe	77	— c Reynolds b Clarke	34
H. E. Dollery lbw b Tribe	3	— b Wild	6
R. E. Hitchcock not out	82	— not out	59
A. Townsend st Andrew b Tribe	7	— not out	18
J. D. Bannister b Tribe	0		
R. T. Weeks not out	23		
B 3	3	B 5, w 4	9

1/72 2/84 3/170 4/180   (7 wkts., dec.) 304   1/53 2/94   (5 wkts., dec.) 232
5/207 6/219 7/219   3/111 4/122 5/180
R. G. Thompson and W. E. Hollies did not bat.

Northamptonshire

D. Brookes c Horner b Thompson	5	— c Thompson b Townsend	24
P. Arnold c Townsend b Bannister	0	— c Spooner b Thompson	10
L. Livingston st Spooner b Hitchcock	101	— c Horner b Townsend	21
D. Barrick c Spooner b Bannister	14	— not out	51
B. Reynolds b Hitchcock	19	— not out	8
D. G. Greasley c Spooner b Bannister	63		
G. E. Tribe run out	44		
V. Broderick not out	33		
K. V. Andrew not out	19		
B 2, l-b 3, w 1, n-b 1	7		

1/5 2/5 3/30 4/75 5/174   (7 wkts., dec.) 305   1/20 2/54 3/55   (3 wkts.) 114
6/225 7/265

J. Wild and R. W. Clarke did not bat.

Northamptonshire Bowling

	O.	M.	R.	W.		O.	M.	R.	W.
Clarke	31	4	75	1	....	14	1	68	2
Barrick	15	2	58	0	....	6	3	12	0
Wild	17	3	37	0	....	10	0	47	1
Tribe	32	14	81	5	....	17	6	43	2
Greasley	1	0	2	0	....	8	3	39	0
Broderick	26	10	48	1	....	7	3	14	0

Warwickshire Bowling

	O.	M.	R.	W.		O.	M.	R.	W.
Bannister	32.5	6	74	3	....	7	1	14	0
Thompson	22	3	60	1	....	7	1	19	1
Townsend	11	1	27	0	....	7	2	32	2
Hollies	33	15	52	0	....	5	0	20	0
Hitchcock	12	0	56	2	....	2	0	5	0
Weeks	5	1	29	0	....	5	1	14	0
			Gardner		....	1	0	10	0

Umpires: F. Chester and L. H. Gray.

At Romford, July 9, 11, 12. NORTHAMPTONSHIRE beat ESSEX by 124 runs.

At Gloucester, July 13, 14, 15. NORTHAMPTONSHIRE lost to GLOUCESTERSHIRE by 40 runs.

At Cardiff, July 16, 18, 19. NORTHAMPTONSHIRE beat GLAMORGAN by four wickets.

At Lord's, July 20, 21, 22. NORTHAMPTONSHIRE lost to MIDDLESEX by 13 runs.

NORTHAMPTONSHIRE v. LANCASHIRE

At Northampton, July 23, 25, 26. Match drawn. Subba Row's excellent performance overshadowed all else. His score of 260 was a record for the county, and the highest for the season to date. He batted seven and three-quarter hours and hit twenty-eight boundaries. With Tribe he put on 161 for the fifth wicket, but when Starkie joined him Northamptonshire still needed 46 for first innings points. The ninth wicket pair swiftly put paid to Lancashire's hopes with a record ninth wicket partnership for the county of 156. Hilton scored a maiden championship century for Lancashire, and Ikin and Dyson were in good form.

Lancashire

J. T. Ikin lbw b Tribe	92	—	not out	17
J. Dyson c Andrew b Liddell	84	—	lbw b Tribe	2
G. A. Edrich lbw b Tribe	0			
C. Washbrook lbw b Tribe	1			
A. Wharton c Starkie b Tribe	2			
K. Grieves c Subba Row b Broderick	61			
K. B. Standring c Andrew b Liddell	0	—	not out	6
J. Jordan b Liddell	3			
M. J. Hilton not out	100			
F. W. Moore lbw b Clarke	14			
R. Tattersall not out	0			
B 6, l-b 9	15			

1/153 2/159 3/161 4/177 (9 wkts., dec.) 372   1/7   (1 wkt.) 25
5/204 6/214 7/218 8/267 9/363

Northamptonshire

D. Brookes c Wharton b Moore ..	3	K. V. Andrew b Tattersall 3
P. Arnold c Jordan b Ikin	50	S. Starkie b Wharton 60
L. Livingston c Hilton b Tattersall	43	R. W. Clarke not out 5
R. Subba Row not out 260		B 8, l-b 8 16
E. Davis c Tattersall b Ikin......	25	
G. E. Tribe b Hilton	52	1/8 2/90 3/117 (9 wkts., dec.) 517
V. Broderick c Grieves b Tattersall	0	4/151 5/312 6/313 7/317 8/337
A. G. Liddell c Grieves b Tattersall	0	9/493

Northamptonshire Bowling

	O.	M.	R.	W.		O.	M.	R.	W.
Clarke	32	5	72	1	....	2	0	4	0
Liddell	24	9	62	3	....	3	0	4	0
Starkie	18	3	52	0	....	2	0	9	0
Tribe	39	8	117	4	....	3	1	8	1
Broderick......	16	6	47	1					
Subba Row ...	3	1	7	0					

Lancashire Bowling

	O.	M.	R.	W.
Moore	29	5	107	1
Standring	17	1	46	0
Hilton	61	22	137	1
Tattersall	57	21	115	4
Ikin...........	19	2	56	2
Wharton ..?...	10	2	26	1
Dyson	9	4	14	0

Umpires: H. Elliott (Lancashire) and K. McCanlis.

At Chesterfield, July 27, 28, 29. NORTHAMPTONSHIRE beat DERBYSHIRE by six wickets.

At Leicester, July 30, August 1, 2. NORTHAMPTONSHIRE beat LEICESTERSHIRE by nine wickets.

NORTHAMPTONSHIRE v. SOMERSET

At Northampton, August 3, 4, 5. Northamptonshire won by eight wickets. Their attack, with Tyson in his best form, was too strong for Somerset. In the first innings only a rally by the later batsmen enabled the visitors to reach 156. Northamptonshire gained a lead of 165, due mainly to enterprising batting by Livingston, Barrick and Tribe. The Somerset batting failed for a second time, but Stephenson played an attacking innings when things were going badly. Northamptonshire easily obtained the 52 needed for victory.

Somerset

G. G. Tordoff lbw b Webster	1	— b Tyson	13
F. L. Angell b Tyson.................	14	— st Andrew b Subba Row ..	35
J. Lawrence c Subba Row b Webster ..	8	— b Tyson	0
M. F. Tremlett c Subba Row b Tribe ...	7	— c Tyson b Broderick	35
P. B. Wight c Wild b Tyson............	5	— c Webster b Subba Row ...	4
J. G. Lomax b Tyson	0	— st Andrew b Tribe	38
Yawar Saeed c Tribe b Tyson.........	14	— b Tyson	15
H. W. Stephenson lbw b Tribe	31	— b Tyson	53
J. Hilton run out	31	— b Tribe	2
J. W. McMahon not out	23	— not out	15
B. Lobb st Andrew b Tribe	12	— c Tribe b Broderick	4
B 4, l-b 5, n-b 1	10	B 1, l-b 1	2

1/1 2/19 3/23 4/28 5/28 6/42 7/79   156   1/20 2/20 3/73 4/87   216
8/82 9/132   5/97 6/118 7/187 8/196 9/197

Northamptonshire

D. Brookes b Lobb	18	—	b Lobb		2
P. Arnold c Stephenson b Lobb	23	—	b Lawrence		17
L. Livingston c McMahon b Tordoff	55	—	not out		27
D. Barrick c Lomax b Hilton	87	—	not out		1
R. Subba Row c Lomax b Lawrence	20				
G. E. Tribe c Wight b Hilton	58				
V. Broderick lbw b Hilton	39				
F. H. Tyson c Tremlett b Lawrence	8				
J. Wild c Tremlett b Lawrence	0				
K. V. Andrew not out	7				
J. Webster st Stephenson b Lawrence	1				
B 2, l-b 2, n-b 1	5		B 4, n-b 1		5

1/27 2/72 3/121 4/169 5/258 6/289   321   1/2 2/47   (2 wkts.)   52
7/310 8/310 9/314

Northamptonshire Bowling

	O.	M.	R.	W.		O.	M.	R.	W.
Tyson	15	6	38	4	....	15	1	48	4
Webster	10	2	38	2	....	5	0	23	0
Tribe	14.1	2	43	3	....	21	6	50	2
Wild	7	3	19	0	....	2	0	17	0
Broderick	4	1	5	0	....	16.3	8	37	2
Subba Row	2	0	3	0	....	12	4	39	2

Somerset Bowling

	O.	M.	R.	W.		O.	M.	R.	W.
Lobb	22	3	65	2	....	6	2	21	1
Yawar Saeed	13	1	48	0	....	5	0	20	0
Lomax	8	3	21	0					
McMahon	8	1	43	0					
Tordoff	5	0	9	1	....	1	1	0	0
Hilton	27	8	55	3					
Lawrence	20.3	2	75	4	....	1.3	0	6	1

Umpires: L. H. Gray and E. Cooke.

NORTHAMPTONSHIRE v. ESSEX

At Wellingborough, August 6, 8, 9. Northamptonshire won by seven wickets. They gained a spectacular victory, scoring the 332 needed in 202 minutes, with fifteen minutes of extra time to spare. The first day was notable for fine batting by Williams, Bailey and Insole, and despite a gallant innings by Subba Row Northamptonshire finished 86 behind. When Essex batted again Smith enhanced his considerable reputation as a hitter by reaching the fastest century of the season in 73 minutes. His record was immediately in danger, for Livingston, of Northamptonshire, reached 82 in 59 minutes, but later batted with more restraint. He lost Arnold at 183, but partnerships with Barrick and Subba Row took the score to 288 before Tribe joined his fellow Australian in the winning stand. Livingston's 172 took only two hours forty minutes, and included two 6's and twenty-three 4's.

Essex

T. C. Dodds lbw b Tyson	1	— b Tribe	29
G. Barker b Tribe	30	— lbw b Tribe	51
T. E. Bailey c Subba Row b Wild	72		
C. C. P. Williams b Wild	93	— b Tribe	0
D. J. Insole lbw b Wild	57	— lbw b Broderick	45
P. A. Gibb b Wild	28	— not out	0
R. Smith c Tribe b Broderick	7	— not out	101
R. Horsfall not out	44	— st Andrew b Broderick	17
W. T. Greensmith not out	5		
B 4, l-b 8, n-b 2	14	L-b 2	2

1/2 2/45 3/193 4/202   (7 wkts., dec.) 351
5/261 6/272 7/328
R. Ralph and K. C. Preston did not bat.

1/62 2/97   (5 wkts., dec.) 245
3/97 4/101 5/241

Northamptonshire

D. Brookes b Bailey	9	— retired hurt	14
P. Arnold lbw b Preston	18	— c Preston b Insole	80
L. Livingston c Horsfall b Ralph	41	— not out	172
D. Barrick c Insole b Ralph	17	— b Bailey	22
R. Subba Row not out	90	— c and b Insole	14
G. E. Tribe st Gibb b Greensmith	31	— not out	28
V. Broderick c Williams b Greensmith	10		
K. V. Andrew b Greensmith	1		
J. Wild st Gibb b Smith	25		
J. Webster c Insole b Bailey	3		
F. H. Tyson b Preston	5		
B 4, l-b 9, n-b 2	15	L-b 2, w 1, n-b 1	4

1/22 2/30 3/82 4/99 5/161 6/179   265
7/187 8/216 9/252

1/183 2/251 3/288 (3 wkts.) 334

Northamptonshire Bowling

	O.	M.	R.	W.		O.	M.	R.	W.
Tyson	18	3	57	1					
Webster	20	7	37	0	....	9	0	38	0
Barrick	6	2	17	0	....	4	0	10	0
Tribe	23	6	67	1	....	27.2	8	80	3
Broderick	23	11	46	1	....	20	7	57	2
Subba Row	4	0	15	0	....	2	0	19	0
Wild	23	4	98	4	....	10	3	39	0

Essex Bowling

	O.	M.	R.	W.		O.	M.	R.	W.
Bailey	17	3	50	2	....	21	3	58	1
Preston	12.5	1	44	2	....	6	0	35	0
Ralph	15	3	46	2	....	4	0	34	0
Smith	26	10	36	1	....	8	0	63	0
Greensmith	21	3	74	3	....	8	0	65	0
Insole					....	12	0	65	2
Barker					....	1	0	6	0
Williams					....	0.1	0	4	0

Umpires: D. Davies and T. J. Bartley.

At Stourbridge, August 10, 11.   NORTHAMPTONSHIRE beat WORCESTERSHIRE by an
innings and 51 runs.

NORTHAMPTONSHIRE v. SURREY

At Northampton, August 17, 18, 19. Northamptonshire won by six wickets. Two fine innings by Arnold, and a splendid all-round performance by Tribe, were mainly responsible for Northamptonshire's victory over the champions. Surrey's chances of first innings lead seemed slender when Brookes and Arnold took Northamptonshire's first wicket stand to 122. Devastating bowling by Loader and Cox brought such a collapse that Surrey led by 29. Tribe took six for 66 in their second innings. Then, with Northamptonshire needing 202 to win, he shared stands of 105 with Arnold and 60 with Broderick. Owing to the final Test Surrey were without May, Laker and Lock.

Surrey

T. H. Clark c Andrew b Tyson	16	— c Subba Row b Tribe	11
M. J. Stewart b Tyson	29	— c sub b Tribe	27
B. Constable c Wild b Webster	11	— b Tyson	5
K. Barrington c Subba Row b Tribe	1	— b Broderick	15
R. C. E. Pratt c Subba Row b Tribe	30	— c Subba Row b Tyson	16
E. A. Bedser lbw b Tyson	7	— c Subba Row b Tribe	23
A. J. McIntyre c Arnold b Webster	21	— b Tyson	22
D. F. Cox b Tribe	36	— b Tribe	15
W. S. Surridge lbw b Tyson	0	— c sub b Tribe	12
P. J. Loader st Andrew b Webster	57	— c Subba Row b Tribe	17
A. V. Bedser not out	0	— not out	1
B 1, l-b 6	7	B 6, l-b 3	9

1/20 2/56 3/61 4/61 5/70 6/102   215   1/34 2/45 3/45 4/81 5/81   173
7/130 8/131 9/197   6/119 7/142 8/142 9/165

Northamptonshire

D. Brookes c McIntyre b A. Bedser	29	— c McIntyre b Loader	7
P. Arnold b Cox	86	— lbw b Loader	80
L. Livingston c Surridge b Cox	22	— lbw b A. Bedser	9
D. Barrick c and b Cox	25		
R. Subba Row b Loader	1	— c Cox b Loader	4
G. E. Tribe c Stewart b Cox	1	— not out	80
V. Broderick c McIntyre b Cox	2	— not out	20
F. H. Tyson b Loader	0		
J. Wild c McIntyre b Cox	1		
J. Webster b Loader	2		
K. V. Andrew not out	6		
B 3, l-b 7, n-b 1	11	B 2, l-b 3	5

1/122 2/123 3/158 4/161 5/164 6/171   186   1/18 2/31 3/40   (4 wkts.) 205
7/172 8/176 9/178   4/145

Northamptonshire Bowling

	O.	M.	R.	W.		O.	M.	R.	W.
Tyson	19	5	53	4	....	22	8	47	3
Webster	19.2	8	45	3	....	17	6	31	0
Barrick	4	0	11	0					
Tribe	20	7	62	3	....	26.3	5	66	6
Broderick	5	1	11	0	....	9	3	20	1
Wild	3	0	26	0					

Surrey Bowling

	O.	M.	R.	W.		O.	M.	R.	W.
A. Bedser	19	5	62	1	....	21	6	45	1
Loader	26.5	5	53	3	....	22	3	65	3
E. Bedser	7	0	33	0	....	13	4	35	0
Cox	15	3	27	6	....	5	1	20	0
Clark						10	4	15	0
Barrington						2.5	0	20	0

Umpires: E. A. Roberts and W. F. Price.

NORTHAMPTONSHIRE v. KENT

At Northampton, August 20, 22, 23. Drawn. After a run of six successive victories, Northamptonshire were lucky to escape defeat. At the close they were 79 behind, with only one wicket left. Allan, the Oxford Blue, was in excellent batting form for the visitors. He hit a century in each innings, and in the second shared a stand of 173 with Phebey, whose 122 was his highest score in first class cricket. Extras, contributed no fewer than 73—more than any single batsman— to Northamptonshire's first innings total. Sunburn seriously impeded Catt's movements, and he found difficulty in taking Wright, who spun the ball sharply. In the Northamptonshire second innings the Kent captain made a determined attempt to bowl his side to victory, with six for 32, but Webster survived the final over.

Kent

A. E. Fagg c Tribe b Webster	3	— b Webster	15
A. H. Phebey b Tribe	16	— c Reynolds b Tribe	122
J. M. Allan not out	121	— c Broderick b Greasley	105
R. C. Wilson c Livingston b Tribe	24	— st Livingston b Subba Row	26
J. Pettiford c Brookes b Tribe	4	— not out	40
P. Hearn c Webster b Subba Row	27	— not out	37
B. E. Disbury lbw b Tribe	0		
A. Dixon c Greasley b Tribe	11		
A. W. Catt b Tribe	4		
J. Spanswick st Livingston b Subba Row	0		
D. V. P. Wright st Livingston b Subba Row	0		
B 5, l-b 3	8	B 8, l-b 4	12

1/5 2/23 3/104 4/116 5/172 6/177   218   1/23 2/62   (4 wkts., dec.) 357
7/205 8/217 9/218   3/235 4/293

Northamptonshire

D. Brookes c Phebey b Dixon	26	— lbw b Wright	15
P. Arnold c and b Disbury	1	— c Fagg b Spanswick	3
L. Livingston b Dixon	62	— b Disbury	19
R. Subba Row c Phebey b Allan	33	— c Allan b Wright	6
B. Reynolds run out	47	— c Fagg b Wright	30
D. G. Greasley lbw b Wright	23	— lbw b Wright	0
G. E. Tribe c Allan b Pettiford	0	— c Disbury b Wright	28
V. Broderick c Fagg b Allan	55	— not out	8
F. H. Tyson c Dixon b Allan	36	— b Wright	0
J. Wild c Disbury b Allan	17	— b Pettiford	2
J. Webster not out	1	— not out	0
B 48, l-b 23, w 2	73	B 1, l-b 9, w 1	11

1/3 2/76 3/103 4/212 5/212 6/239   374   1/20 2/38 3/80   (9 wkts.) 122
7/263 8/322 9/366   4/80 5/89 6/94 7/105
                                             8/105 9/116

Northamptonshire Bowling

	O.	M.	R.	W.		O.	M.	R.	W.
Tyson	16	3	37	0	....	17	4	39	0
Webster	13	5	25	1	....	9	0	38	1
Tribe	27	5	76	6	....	26	6	84	1
Broderick	15	8	23	0	....	22	3	59	0
Subba Row	10.5	3	22	3	....	10	3	35	1
Wild	8	0	27	0	....	17	4	53	0
Greasley						7	0	37	1

Kent Bowling

	O.	M.	R.	W.		O.	M.	R.	W.
Spanswick	13	3	43	0	....	6	0	26	1
Disbury	4	2	16	1	....	7	1	33	1
Allan	22	7	81	4					
Dixon	23	4	61	2					
Wright	22	8	58	1	....	12	6	32	6
Pettiford	16	6	42	1	....	10	4	20	1

Umpires: G. S. Mobey and J. J. Hills.

At Nottingham, August 24, 25, 26. NORTHAMPTONSHIRE drew with NOTTINGHAM-SHIRE.

At Taunton, August 27, 29, 30. NORTHAMPTONSHIRE drew with SOMERSET.

NOTTINGHAMSHIRE

President—J. ASHLEY PLAYER
Secretary—H. A. BROWN, County Cricket Ground, Nottingham
Captain—R. T. SIMPSON

R. J. Giles   County Badge   G. Goonesena

Nottinghamshire, having climbed steadily to fifth place in the Championship table during the two previous seasons, fell to eleventh in 1955. Their fall was not so drastic as might appear as the team again won ten matches and their total of 132 points was only slightly fewer than the year before. The number of defeats, however, rose from six to eleven.

The chief factor in Nottinghamshire's decline was the reduced effectiveness of Dooland who, like many players from the Commonwealth, seemed to be feeling the strain of continuous cricket. Troubled for much of the summer by a split spinning finger, Dooland did not meet with the success anticipated on the prevailing hard, fast pitches which should have favoured his leg-breaks and googlies. By normal standards, the Australian had a good season, taking 142 wickets in Championship matches at an average cost of 22.15 each, but he was not so often the devastating force of the previous two seasons.

By way of consolation, Smales surpassed all hopes by taking over 100 wickets for the first time in his career. His feat was all the more remarkable for the fact that in the four years since his special registration from Yorkshire he had taken a total of only 79 wickets for Nottinghamshire. In the absence of an experienced bowler to open the attack with Jepson, Smales shared the new ball in many matches, but it was in his customary role as an off-spinner that he became an established and valuable member of the team. Twice he claimed seven wickets in an innings and on four occasions six, so leaving his previous best performance of five for 33 far behind.

The county's spin attack was completed after the Cambridge

term by the return of Goonesena, who also enjoyed his best season so far. The little Singhalese, whose zest for the game is a delight to watch, had never before obtained 100 wickets or 1,000 runs. Yet he not only accomplished both, but was the first player to complete the "double." He also hit his maiden first-class century. The inclusion of the Australian left-arm bowler, A. K. Walker, was expected to strengthen the new ball attack considerably in 1956.

Although five players scored over 1,000 runs in Championship matches compared with only two in 1954, the batting again was not wholly satisfactory. The captain, Simpson, still fell short of his best form and the left-handed Stocks, though consistency itself at Trent Bridge, could hardly score a run elsewhere. Poole overcame a barren spell in June in admirable style but the most heartening feature of the batting was the performance of Giles. After several lean seasons, Giles did not find a place in the side for the first seven matches, but having done so he became most dependable.

TRENT BRIDGE GROUND, NOTTINGHAM

NOTTINGHAMSHIRE RESULTS

All First-Class Matches—Played 29, Won 10, Lost 11, Drawn 8

County Championship Matches—Played 28, Won 10, Lost 11, Drawn 7

COUNTY CHAMPIONSHIP AVERAGES

BATTING

	Birthplace	Mtchs.	Inns.	Not Outs	Runs	100's	Highest Inns.	Aver.
R. J. Giles	*Chilwell*	20	40	3	1293	3	142	34.94
R. T. Simpson .	*Sherwood*	21	40	0	1350	2	105	33.75
C. J. Poole	*Forest Town*	26	49	3	1547	2	122	33.63
F. W. Stocks ..	*Carcroft*	19	36	3	1099	0	99	33.30
J. Hardstaff ..	*Nuncargate*	13	22	0	732	1	134	33.27
J. D. Clay	*W. Bridgford*	27	52	2	1308	2	127	26.16
G. Goonesena..	*Colombo*	13	25	4	544	1	107*	25.90
J. Kelly	*Conisborough*	6	10	3	172	0	41	24.57
B. Dooland ...	*Adelaide*	25	40	3	887	0	91	23.97
E. J. Martin ..	*Lambley*	19	34	4	672	0	76	22.40
K. J. Poole	*Thurgarton*	11	21	2	362	0	58	19.05
P. F. Harvey ..	*Linby*	17	29	4	443	0	54*	17.72
K. Smales	*Horsforth*	28	43	16	433	0	41	16.03
A. Jepson	*Selsdon*	25	40	6	496	0	52*	14.58
E. J. Rowe	*Netherfield*	27	35	14	124	0	16	5.90
C. S. Matthews	*Worksop*	4	5	1	12	0	8	3.00
M. Wood......	*Nottingham*	4	5	2	5	0	4	1.66

Also batted: A. Clevely (*Chaddesden*) 4*, 0; J. P. Springall (*London*) 3, 2; M. Winfield (*Gainsborough*) 4, 38.

* Signifies not out.

BOWLING

	Overs	Maidens	Runs	Wickets	Average
C. S. Matthews.........	79.1	29	166	9	18.44
G. Goonesena..........	444.3	108	1214	57	21.29
B. Dooland	1156.1	314	3146	142	22.15
K. Smales	1112.1	365	2757	114	24.18
A. Jepson	766.5	203	1861	62	30.01
J. Kelly	61	28	123	4	30.75
F. W. Stocks	37	6	132	4	33.00
P. F. Harvey	307.1	89	808	18	44.88
M. Wood	66.5	9	231	4	57.75
K. J. Poole	183.4	31	612	7	87.42

Also bowled: J. D. Clay 0.3—0—5—0; A. Clevely 38—9—107—3; J. Hardstaff 1—0—1—0; C. J. Poole 0.1—0—4—0; R. T. Simpson 0.2—0—4—0.

Amateurs.—G. Goonesena, R. T. Simpson.

NOTTINGHAMSHIRE v. DERBYSHIRE

At Nottingham, May 2, 3. Drawn. Derbyshire 195 for four wickets, declared (C. Lee 54, A. C. Revill 53 not out); Nottinghamshire 30 for one wicket. (Friendly match.)

NOTTINGHAMSHIRE v. SUSSEX

At Nottingham, May 7, 9, 10. Drawn. Rain ruined the prospect of an exciting finish by restricting the final day's play to less than an hour and a half. Oakman deserved chief credit for giving Sussex first innings points. With his long reach, he alone mastered the spin of Dooland and Smales and his economical bowling was invaluable. A thrilling struggle took place for the lead, Smales and Rowe defying the Sussex attack for sixty-five minutes before Rowe was run out.

Sussex

J. Langridge c Rowe b Smales	0	— b Dooland	28
D. V. Smith b Jepson	13	— lbw b Dooland	1
A. S. M. Oakman c Martin b Smales	80	— c Poole b Dooland	16
J. M. Parks c Rowe b Dooland	18	— c Stocks b Smales	14
K. G. Suttle b Dooland	1	— lbw b Dooland	5
G. Cox c Stocks b Dooland	7	— c Stocks b Smales	10
G. Potter lbw b Smales	5	— b Dooland	2
N. I. Thomson b Dooland	3	— not out	35
A. E. James b Dooland	17	— c Rowe b Smales	22
R. T. Webb b Jepson	18	— not out	6
R. G. Marlar not out	22		
L-b 4	4	B 3, l-b 1	4

1/1 2/23 3/50 4/58 5/78 6/105   188   1/10 2/29 3/44   (8 wkts.) 143
7/114 8/134 9/154   4/49 5/53 6/78 7/78 8/129

Nottinghamshire

R. T. Simpson b James	4	K. Smales not out	15
J. D. Clay c Parks b Marlar	46	A. Jepson run out	0
C. J. Poole lbw b Oakman	17	E. J. Rowe run out	11
J. Hardstaff c Oakman b James	51		
E. J. Martin b Oakman	9	B 2, l-b 2	4
F. W. Stocks c Parks b Thomson	7		
P. F. Harvey c Webb b James	18	1/9 2/68 3/68 4/87 5/102	185
B. Dooland b Marlar	3	6/146 7/153 8/159 9/161	

Nottinghamshire Bowling

	O.	M.	R.	W.		O.	M.	R.	W.
Jepson	16.4	8	29	2	....	20	5	32	0
Smales	29	11	59	3	....	22.3	8	53	3
Dooland	31	8	85	5	....	29	14	46	5
Harvey	6	3	11	0	....	5	3	8	0

Sussex Bowling

	O.	M.	R.	W.
Thomson	21	6	39	1
James	27	4	48	3
Oakman	40	20	37	2
Potter	5	1	18	0
Marlar	31	15	39	2

Umpires: J. S. Buller and A. Skelding.

At Portsmouth, May 11, 12, 13. NOTTINGHAMSHIRE beat HAMPSHIRE by nine wickets.

At Nottingham, May 14, 16, 17. NOTTINGHAMSHIRE drew with the SOUTH AFRICANS. (See SOUTH AFRICAN section.)

At Taunton, May 21, 23, 24. NOTTINGHAMSHIRE beat SOMERSET by eight runs.

NOTTINGHAMSHIRE v. SURREY

At Nottingham, May 28, 30, 31. Surrey won by eight wickets, finishing the match with a hurricane display when set to get 188 in two hours. The Surrey attack met with its first check of the season on the first day when Simpson stayed for four hours thirty-five minutes for 100. Poole helped him add 93 and Hardstaff shared a stand of 139. Surrey began shakily before a 25,000 crowd on Whit Monday, but Barrington and McIntyre added 177. McIntyre took only 108 minutes over his century and Barrington obtained his second hundred in succession. He was awarded his county cap during the innings. After consistent Nottinghamshire batting and a declaration, Surrey went for runs and McIntyre again showed grand form. He and May added 149 in fifty-seven minutes and Surrey won with 33 minutes to spare. McIntyre's 79 included four 6's and nine 4's. In the match he made 189 for once out.

Nottinghamshire

R. T. Simpson b Loader	100	— c Lock b Surridge	21
J. D. Clay lbw b Bedser	10	— c Clark b Lock	20
C. J. Poole b Loader	55	— c Loader b Laker	24
J. Hardstaff lbw b Loader	70	— c McIntyre b Lock	14
F. W. Stocks c Loader b Laker	18	— not out	3
P. F. Harvey c Surridge b Lock	5	— c McIntyre b Lock	32
B. Dooland c Fletcher b Lock	56	— b Laker	27
A. Jepson c Fletcher b Lock	4	— c Constable b Lock	19
K. Smales b Loader	5	— not out	34
E. J. Rowe c and b Lock	13		
M. Wood not out	1		
B 8, l-b 7, w 1	16	B 5, l-b 1, w 2	8

1/13 2/106 3/245 4/260 5/269 6/279   353   1/37 2/51   (7 wkts., dec.) 202
7/293 8/319 9/351   3/73 4/81 5/143 6/143 7/182

Surrey

T. H. Clark c Simpson b Wood	4	— b Jepson	23
D. G. W. Fletcher b Rowe b Dooland	40	— b Jepson	6
P. B. H. May b Wood	4	— not out	74
B. Constable c Harvey b Dooland	34		
K. Barrington c Hardstaff b Harvey	126		
A. J. McIntyre c Harvey b Dooland	110	— not out	79
J. C. Laker not out	42		
W. S. Surridge not out	4		
B 1, l-b 3	4	B 4, l-b 2	6

1/7 2/11 3/64 4/112   (6 wkts., dec.) 368   1/28 2/39   (2 wkts.) 188
5/289 6/353

P. J. Loader, A. V. Bedser and G. A. R. Lock did not bat.

Surrey Bowling

	O.	M.	R.	W.	O.	M.	R.	W.
Bedser	33	6	81	1	8	2	26	0
Loader	34	11	57	4	8	1	9	0
Lock	36.1	11	86	4	31	11	81	4
Laker	29	9	82	1	23	11	32	2
Surridge	6	0	19	0	9	2	24	1
Clark	4	0	12	0				
Barrington					4	0	22	0

Nottinghamshire Bowling

	O.	M.	R.	W.	O.	M.	R.	W.
Jepson	25	7	64	0	10	0	50	2
Wood	21	3	68	2	5	0	28	0
Smales	16	4	53	0	2	0	24	0
Dooland	32	6	123	3	7	0	55	0
Harvey	15	2	56	1	4	0	21	0
Simpson					0.2	0	4	0

Umpires: A. Skelding and N. Oldfield.

At Leicester, June 1, 2, 3. NOTTINGHAMSHIRE lost to LEICESTERSHIRE by three wickets.

At Blackheath, June 4, 6, 7. NOTTINGHAMSHIRE drew with KENT.

At Llanelly, June 8, 9, 10. NOTTINGHAMSHIRE drew with GLAMORGAN.

At Nottingham, June 9, 10, 11, 13. ENGLAND beat SOUTH AFRICA by an innings and five runs. (First Test Match.) (See SOUTH AFRICAN section.)

At Northampton, June 11, 13, 14. NOTTINGHAMSHIRE lost to NORTHAMPTONSHIRE by ten wickets.

NOTTINGHAMSHIRE v. LEICESTERSHIRE

At Nottingham, June 18, 20, 21. Nottinghamshire won by two wickets with eight minutes to spare largely through a gallant innings by their captain, Simpson. Set to score 276 in three hours, they appeared to be heading for defeat when Simpson, batting number eight because of a leg injury, reached the crease. Although forced to use a runner, Simpson hit so boldly that in fifty minutes he and Harvey added 97 and made victory possible. Earlier Leicestershire had been on top, Palmer batting specially well in each innings. Dooland ended the first by taking five wickets in three overs for nine runs.

Leicestershire

G. Lester c Smales b Jepson	7	— c Dooland b Smales 14
M. R. Hallam c Rowe b Jepson	86	— c Jepson b Smales 21
M. Tompkin lbw b Dooland	31	— c Poole b Dooland 63
C. H. Palmer c Martin b Smales	128	— not out 87
V. E. Jackson c Martin b Harvey	12	— not out 14
G. A. Smithson c Martin b Dooland	27	
V. S. Munden c Clay b Dooland	43	
J. E. Walsh c Hardstaff b Dooland	3	
C. T. Spencer c and b Dooland	0	
R. L. Pratt not out	8	
J. Firth c Smales b Dooland	1	
B 2, l-b 17	19	B 1, l-b 6 7

1/8 2/56 3/219 4/281 5/281 6/342   365
7/352 8/353 9/359

1/33 2/50   (3 wkts., dec.) 206
3/149

Nottinghamshire

R. T. Simpson c Palmer b Lester	82	—	c Smithson b Spencer	67
J. D. Clay b Lester	20	—	b Munden	68
C. J. Poole b Spencer	9	—	c Palmer b Spencer	7
J. Hardstaff c Pratt b Spencer	61	—	b Spencer	8
E. J. Martin c Smithson b Pratt	48	—	lbw b Spencer	4
R. J. Giles c Hallam b Pratt	0	—	b Palmer	18
P. F. Harvey b Palmer	19	—	not out	54
K. Smales not out	28	—	not out	3
A. Jepson not out	17	—	c Lester b Munden	18
B Dooland (did not bat)		—	c Tompkin b Munden	26
B 5, l-b 7	12		B 2, l-b 1	3

1/37 2/88 3/148   (7 wkts., dec.) 296   1/14 2/32 3/38   (8 wkts.) 276
4/209 5/209 6/242 7/264   4/103 5/115 6/135 7/155
                                                     8/252

E. J. Rowe (did not bat)

Nottinghamshire Bowling

	O.	M.	R.	W.		O.	M.	R.	W.
Jepson	33	3	92	2	....	17	3	70	0
Smales	43	15	90	1	....	14	5	32	2
Dooland	34.3	9	105	6	....	13	1	60	1
Harvey	22	6	59	1	....	10	1	37	0

Leicestershire Bowling

	O.	M.	R.	W.		O.	M.	R.	W.
Spencer	27	8	47	2	....	13	0	58	4
Pratt	12	2	48	2	....	6	0	32	0
Jackson	12	5	20	0	....	5.2	0	46	0
Lester	20	1	74	2					
Walsh	20	1	69	0					
Palmer	9	5	9	1	....	14	1	60	1
Munden	11	4	17	0	....	13	0	77	3

Umpires: L. H. Gray and E. Davies.

At Manchester, June 22, 23, 24. NOTTINGHAMSHIRE beat LANCASHIRE by ten
wickets.

NOTTINGHAMSHIRE v. YORKSHIRE

At Nottingham, June 25, 27, 28. Drawn. Batsmen dominated the game on
an easy-paced pitch and there was never much prospect of a definite result. The
game was specially notable for the return to form of Hutton who, after a run of
low scores, batted just under five hours for the highest individual innings of the
summer to that point. He hit three 6's and twenty-four 4's, his last 94 runs taking
only sixty-five minutes. Giles, deputising as opening batsman for the injured
Simpson, also distinguished himself by following his century in the previous game
with the highest score of his career. Hardstaff and Martin also batted excellently
against a Yorkshire attack weakened by the absence of Wardle, Appleyard and
Trueman.

Nottinghamshire

J. D. Clay c Wilson b Van Geloven.....	3	— c Binks b Yardley	1
R. J. Giles b Illingworth..	142	— c Binks b Van Geloven	46
C. J. Poole run out	1	— c Binks b Close	6
J. Hardstaff b Close..................	75	— c Hutton b Wilson	134
E. J. Martin c Lowson b Illingworth ...	76	— not out	64
P. F. Harvey c Wilson b Close	21	— c Illingworth b Lester	9
B. Dooland c Van Geloven b Close	4		
J. Kelly c and b Close	30	— not out	10
K. Smales c and b Close..............	13		
A. Jepson run out	6		
E. J. Rowe not out	0		
B 1, l-b 9, n-b 3	13	B 9, w 1	10

1/4 2/21 3/148 4/298 5/308 6/321   384   1/5 2/22 3/87   (5 wkts.) 280
7/339 8/375 9/384   4/248 5/269

Yorkshire

L. Hutton c Jepson b Harvey 194		J. Van Geloven b Dooland	0
F. A. Lowson c Dooland b Jepson. 16		E. Leadbeater not out	17
J. V. Wilson c and b Kelly 35		J. G. Binks not out.............	1
W. H. H. Sutcliffe lbw b Jepson .. 44			
E. Lester c Rowe b Dooland 16		B 2, l-b 7	9
D. B. Close b Dooland 24			
N. W. D. Yardley c Martin b Smales 11		1/33 2/125 3/271 (9 wkts., dec.) 389	
R. Illingworth lbw b Jepson 22		4/306 5/306 6/334 7/360 8/360 9/382	

Yorkshire Bowling

	O.	M.	R.	W.	O.	M.	R.	W.
Van Geloven...	15	3	47	1	16	3	55	1
Close	41.1	11	95	5	18	2	45	1
Leadbeater	19	2	71	0	12	2	44	0
Illingworth	40	11	107	2	27	7	70	0
Yardley	9	4	15	0	6	3	11	1
Wilson	10	1	36	0	7	0	35	1
				Lester	3	1	10	1

Nottinghamshire Bowling

Jepson	32	8	55	3
Smales	33	14	77	1
Dooland	50	13	155	3
Harvey	21	2	68	1
Kelly	10	4	25	1

Umpires: K. McCanlis and E. A. Roberts.

At Birmingham, June 29, 30, July 1. NOTTINGHAMSHIRE lost to WARWICKSHIRE by 150 runs.

NOTTINGHAMSHIRE v. ESSEX

At Nottingham, July 2, 4, 5. Essex won by 95 runs after setting Nottinghamshire to score 215 for victory in just over two hours. Nottinghamshire began their task discouragingly but continued to go all out for runs until the last wicket fell with forty minutes to spare. Essex were indebted to Barker, whose first Championship century occupied three and a quarter hours, for their first innings recovery, but Nottinghamshire went ahead with only six wickets down. K. Poole batted well on his first appearance. Forceful batting by Barker and Insole enabled Essex to declare

Essex

T. C. Dodds c Rowe b K. Poole	21	—	c Martin b Dooland		48
G. Barker lbw b Smales	104	—	c Martin b Harvey		62
P. A. Gibb c C. Poole b Dooland	15	—	c Harvey b Cleveley		6
R. Horsfall run out	2	—	c Martin b Dooland		38
D. J. Insole lbw b Dooland	0	—	b Harvey		62
T. E. Bailey c Clay b Dooland	37	—	b Cleveley		17
R. Smith c K. Poole b Smales	16	—	lbw b Cleveley		21
W. T. Greensmith not out	23	—	not out		5
G. S. Smith c Martin b Dooland	2				
R. Ralph b Dooland	40	—	st Rowe b Harvey		4
K. C. Preston c Harvey b Dooland	0				
B 1, l-b 3	4		B 1, l-b 6		7

1/31 2/57 3/63 4/63 5/176 6/199   264   1/75 2/93   (8 wkts., dec.) 270
7/199 8/208 9/264   3/119 4/177 5/223 6/261
7/261 8/270

Nottinghamshire

R. T. Simpson c Gibb b Bailey	41	—	c Barker b Bailey		8
J. D. Clay c Gibb b Bailey	102	—	c G. Smith b Preston		12
R. J. Giles c Preston b Greensmith	34	—	lbw b Bailey		13
C. J. Poole c R. Smith b Greensmith	0	—	c and b Preston		11
E. J. Martin c and b Preston	21	—	c Bailey b Greensmith		36
K. J. Poole c Insole b Bailey	34	—	c Barker b Greensmith		8
P. F. Harvey c Bailey b R. Smith	14	—	c and b Dodds		5
B. Dooland c Preston b Bailey	41	—	c Insole b Greensmith		21
K. Smales b Bailey	15	—	b Greensmith		4
A. Cleveley not out	4	—	st Gibb b Dodds		0
E. J. Rowe c Ralph b Preston	1	—	not out		0
B 4, l-b 6, w 1, n-b 2	13		L-b 1		1

1/86 2/161 3/161 4/187 5/236 6/242   320   1/17 2/22 3/45 4/47   119
7/268 8/310 9/317   5/64 6/86 7/100 8/119 9/119

Nottinghamshire Bowling

	O.	M.	R.	W.		O.	M.	R.	W.
Cleveley	17	3	44	0	....	21	6	63	3
Smales	27	13	64	2	....	18	3	50	0
K. Poole	13	4	47	1	....	4	0	18	0
Dooland	42.4	21	82	6	....	32	3	116	2
Harvey	14	5	23	0	....	8.1	2	16	3

Essex Bowling

	O.	M.	R.	W.		O.	M.	R.	W.
Preston	30.3	7	66	2	....	5	0	28	2
R. Smith	23	6	56	1					
Greensmith	34	10	90	2	....	6.1	1	27	4
Ralph	4	0	16	0					
Bailey	28	10	63	5	....	6	1	32	2
G. Smith	8	3	16	0					
Dodds						6	1	31	2

Umpires: P. Corrall and W. F. Price.

NOTTINGHAMSHIRE v. LANCASHIRE

At Nottingham, July 9, 11, 12. Nottinghamshire won by 32 runs, Smales ending the match by performing the first hat-trick of his career. Rowe helped him to dismiss Hilton and Moore and with the first ball of his next over Smales bowled Smith. Nottinghamshire scored freely on the opening day, Giles hitting one 6 and seventeen 4's in his second century of the season against Lancashire and, despite a stubborn innings by Ikin, they gained a big lead. After more bright batting, Simpson set Lancashire the reasonable task of scoring 265 at a run a minute. Ikin and Washbrook began with a partnership of 95 in an hour and a quarter but once they were parted Smales and Goonesena held the upper hand.

Nottinghamshire

R. T. Simpson c Ikin b Tattersall	44	— c Grieves b Tattersall	13
J. D. Clay c and b Dyson	87	— c and b Hilton	26
R. J. Giles st Grieves b Hilton	115	— c Edrich b Tattersall	1
F. W. Stocks c Washbrook b Hilton	56	— not out	53
K. J. Poole c and b Ikin	13	— c Edrich b Tattersall	6
G. Goonesena c Hilton b Tattersall	28	— b Hilton	14
B. Dooland b Tattersall	16	— c Edrich b Hilton	23
E. J. Martin not out	3	— b Tattersall	1
M. Wood b Tattersall	4		
K. Smales not out	3	— not out	5
E. J. Rowe (did not bat)		— c sub b Tattersall	9
B 4	4	B 6, l-b 1	7

1/79 2/181 3/288 4/311 (8 wkts., dec.) 373
5/331 6/357 7/364 8/370

1/29 2/33 (8 wkts., dec.) 158
3/45 4/56 5/89 6/91 7/114
8/144

Lancashire

J. T. Ikin b Dooland	114	— c and b Dooland	57
J. Dyson c and b Dooland	31	— c Stocks b Goonesena	13
G. A. Edrich c Rowe b Smales	1	— c Rowe b Goonesena	21
C. Washbrook c Stocks b Dooland	12	— lbw b Smales	53
A. Wharton hit wkt b Goonesena	11	— c and b Goonesena	5
K. Grieves b Goonesena	31	— c Simpson b Goonesena	14
C. S. Smith c Wood b Dooland	28	— b Smales	36
J. Jordan c and b Dooland	13	— c Stocks b Smales	0
M. J. Hilton b Smales	0	— st Rowe b Smales	11
F. W. Moore not out	1	— c Rowe b Smales	0
R. Tattersall c Simpson b Smales	2	— not out	0
B 16, l-b 6, n-b 1	23	B 8, l-b 13, n-b 1	22

1/44 2/59 3/80 4/101 5/146 6/220 267
7/255 8/256 9/262

1/95 2/124 3/130 4/166 232
5/166 6/197 7/198 8/227
9/227

Lancashire Bowling

	O.	M.	R.	W.	O.	M.	R.	W.
Smith	15	2	53	0	4	1	15	0
Moore	15	1	54	0	2	0	8	0
Tattersall	29	6	78	4	25	10	59	5
Hilton	39	9	107	2	19	6	61	3
Dyson	21	8	42	1	4	0	8	0
Ikin	7	1	35	1				

Nottinghamshire Bowling

	O.	M.	R.	W.	O.	M.	R.	W.
Wood	12	3	38	0	2	0	7	0
Poole	8	1	19	0	2	0	7	0
Dooland	31	11	60	5	28	5	71	1
Smales	33.5	13	61	3	23.1	10	37	5
Goonesena	20	7	46	2	27	4	88	4
Stocks	8	1	20	0				

Umpires: F. Chester and E. A. Roberts.

NOTTINGHAMSHIRE v. DERBYSHIRE

At Nottingham, July 13, 14, 15. Derbyshire won by 111 runs, largely through a remarkable innings by Hamer. Seven wickets had fallen to Dooland and Smales for 133 before Hamer found a reliable partner in Smith. In an hour and a half these two added 157 and after Smith's dismissal for 57—his highest first-class score—Hamer continued to punish the bowling until he was last out. Hamer spent nearly five hours over the first double-century innings of the season, and the first of his career. He hit five 6's and twenty-seven 4's. Nottinghamshire fought back well on a wearing pitch, restricting Derbyshire's lead to 107, and then Smales produced his best bowling performance. An overnight storm flooded the ground, however, and the next morning Gladwin in particular made the ball lift sharply. Giles, going in at number five, batted excellently in the conditions, hitting 70 out of 103, but received little support.

Derbyshire

A. Hamer lbw b Jepson	227	—	c Jepson b Smales		25
J. Kelly lbw b Dooland	8	—	c Stocks b Smales		7
C. Lee lbw b Smales	17	—	c Rowe b Dooland		0
A. C. Revill c Clay b Smales	0	—	c Giles b Dooland		11
D. B. Carr c Stocks b Smales	5	—	c Poole b Smales		10
H. L. Johnson c Stocks b Dooland	8	—	c Stocks b Smales		29
G. O. Dawkes c Clay b Dooland	0	—	c Stocks b Smales		15
C. Gladwin c Rowe b Dooland	0	—	c and b Dooland		3
E. Smith c Rowe b Jepson	57	—	b Smales		6
R. Carter lbw b Dooland	9	—	c Poole b Smales		5
D. Hall not out	6	—	not out		1
B 5, l-b 11, w 1	17		B 7, l-b 2, w 1		10
	354				122

1/45 2/94 3/94 4/120 5/133 6/133
7/133 8/290 9/328

1/32 2/32 3/33 4/50 5/55
6/82 7/89 8/104 9/113

Nottinghamshire

R. T. Simpson c Carr b Gladwin	83	—	c Revill b Gladwin		1
J. D. Clay b Gladwin	16	—	lbw b Hall		0
R. J. Giles run out	15	—	b Carr		70
F. W. Stocks c Kelly b Gladwin	25	—	c Carr b Gladwin		0
K. J. Poole c Revill b Gladwin	5	—	b Smith		0
E. J. Martin c Revill b Smith	8	—	run out		14
P. F. Harvey c Gladwin b Smith	34	—	c Carter b Gladwin		20
B. Dooland b Smith	12	—	c Carr b Hall		2
K. Smales not out	11	—	not out		4
A. Jepson c and b Carr	5	—	c Revill b Carr		1
E. J. Rowe c Revill b Carr	0	—	b Hall		5
B 14, l-b 11, n-b 8	33		L-b 1		1
	247				118

1/45 2/102 3/142 4/148 5/157 6/182
7/200 8/234 9/240

1/1 2/5 3/8 4/50 5/50
6/55 7/111 8/112 9/117

Nottinghamshire Bowling

	O.	M.	R.	W.		O.	M.	R.	W.
Jepson	15.1	4	50	2	....	2	0	13	0
Poole	13	3	47	0					
Dooland	30	6	95	5	....	22	5	42	3
Smales	34	8	103	3	....	24.2	9	44	7
Harvey	13	2	42	0					
Stocks						2	0	13	0

Derbyshire Bowling

	O.	M.	R.	W.	O.	M.	R.	W.
Hall	5	2	14	0	12	5	16	3
Gladwin	33	11	57	4	15	6	38	3
Smith	35	9	80	3	11	3	39	1
Carter	5	0	25	0				
Carr	12.1	1	38	2	7.3	2	24	2

Umpires: H. Elliott (Lancashire) and L. H. Gray.

At Kidderminster, July 16, 18, 19. NOTTINGHAMSHIRE lost to WORCESTERSHIRE by 117 runs.

NOTTINGHAMSHIRE v. GLOUCESTERSHIRE

At Nottingham, July 20, 21, 22. Gloucestershire won by 146 runs. A fast-scoring partnership between Emmett and Crapp assured them of a useful first innings total and when Stocks and Poole looked like retrieving Nottinghamshire's poor start Wells improved Gloucestershire's position with a fine spell of off-spin bowling. After dismissing both the left-handers, he took four more wickets in succession. Young, Crapp and Emmett all scored briskly when Gloucestershire batted again and Emmett set his opponents to make 301 in four hours five minutes. After a spirited innings by Hardstaff, who hit six 4's, Wells and Cook took command.

Gloucestershire

D. M. Young c Rowe b Smales	19	— c Harvey b Goonesena	63
C. A. Milton b Goonesena	23	— lbw b Goonesena	18
J. F. Crapp lbw b Jepson	70	— c Goonesena b Harvey	44
G. M. Emmett b Goonesena	95	— b Smales	77
W. Knightley-Smith c Goonesena b Stocks	17	— c Martin b Smales	11
A. E. Wilson c Clay b Goonesena	21	— not out	2
G. E. Lambert c Clay b Smales	13	— not out	12
J. Mortimore not out	12	— c Rowe b Jepson	0
B. D. Wells c Martin b Smales	0	— c Giles b Smales	3
C. Cook c Clay b Goonesena	0		
F. P. McHugh lbw b Goonesena	5		
B 9, l-b 10, w 3	22	B 4, l-b 7	11

1/42 2/62 3/183 4/235 5/252 6/273	297	1/35 2/120 (7 wkts., dec.) 241
7/285 8/285 9/285		3/147 4/209 5/210 6/226
		7/234

Nottinghamshire

J. D. Clay c Crapp b Lambert	18	— b Wells	11
J. Hardstaff c Young b McHugh	3	— c Wells b McHugh	32
R. J. Giles b McHugh	3	— b McHugh	14
F. W. Stocks c Milton b Wells	64	— c Milton b Wells	18
C. J. Poole lbw b Wells	63	— c Cook b Lambert	28
E. J. Martin c Crapp b Wells	28	— lbw b Wells	17
G. Goonesena b Wells	28	— c Emmett b Cook	17
P. F. Harvey lbw b Wells	4	— c Mortimore b Cook	2
K. Smales st Wilson b Cook	13	— c Milton b Wells	2
A. Jepson c Wilson b Wells	7	— c Lambert b Cook	2
E. J. Rowe not out	0	— not out	4
B 2, l-b 3, n-b 2	7	B 2, l-b 5	7

1/5 2/17 3/43 4/136 5/171 6/198	238	1/45 2/47 3/69 4/89 154
7/215 8/218 9/238		5/111 6/144 7/144 8/148
		9/148

Nottinghamshire Bowling

	O.	M.	R.	W.	O.	M.	R.	W.
Jepson	22	8	38	1	18	4	55	1
Smales	29	4	92	3	23	4	81	3
Goonesena	29.3	7	101	5	18	3	60	2
Harvey	8	2	23	0	8	2	20	1
Stocks	4	0	21	1	4	1	14	0

Gloucestershire Bowling

	O.	M.	R.	W.	O.	M.	R.	W.
Lambert	18	2	44	1	10	1	41	1
McHugh	20	1	47	2	16	4	36	2
Wells	40	20	66	6	24	6	64	4
Cook	27.2	8	50	1	5.4	3	6	3
Mortimore	8	2	24	0				

Umpires: T. Spencer and K. McCanlis.

At Ilkeston, July 23, 25, 26. NOTTINGHAMSHIRE drew with DERBYSHIRE.

NOTTINGHAMSHIRE v. SOMERSET

At Nottingham, July 27, 28, 29. Nottinghamshire won by 261 runs. Somerset never mastered the spin bowling of Smales and Goonesena, who shared all but one of their wickets. Lawrence bowled exceptionally well during a marathon spell on the first day despite severe punishment from the left-handers, Poole and Stocks, and it was only through his effort with the bat that Somerset avoided following on. Nottinghamshire strengthened their position by bold hitting in which Poole and Stocks again led the way and Somerset were left the immense task of scoring 405 to win. Tordoff and Angell began with an admirable opening partnership of 80 in an hour, but in another seventy minutes it was all over.

Nottinghamshire

J. D. Clay c Lomax b McMahon	61	— c Lomax b Walker	25
R. J. Giles lbw b Lawrence	24	— lbw b McMahon	45
E. J. Martin c and b Lawrence	4	— c Lawrence b McMahon	2
F. W. Stocks c McMahon b Lawrence	44	— c Tremlett b McMahon	69
C. J. Poole c Tordoff b Lawrence	70	— c and b Yawar Saeed	67
G. Goonesena st Stephenson b Lawrence	2	— c Wight b Lobb	14
P. F. Harvey c Stephenson b Lawrence	0	— not out	25
J. Kelly b Yawar Saeed	38	— not out	23
K. Smales c Lawrence b Yawar Saeed	9		
C. S. Matthews not out	2		
E. J. Rowe b Yawar Saeed	2		
B 3, l-b 11, w 5	19	B 2, l-b 3	5

1/83 2/91 3/127 4/167 5/193 6/193   275   1/70 2/70   (6 wkts., dec.) 275
7/236 8/266 9/271   3/101 4/187 5/220 6/228

Somerset

F. L. Angell c Poole b Matthews	0	—	c Poole b Smales	37
M. Walker b Smales	14	—	c Goonesena b Smales	5
J. Lawrence c Poole b Smales	61	—	c Stocks b Smales	17
J. W. McMahon lbw b Smales	0	—	not out	0
G. G. Tordoff b Goonesena	24	—	st Rowe b Smales	33
M. F. Tremlett b Goonesena	19	—	c Poole b Goonesena	0
P. B. Wight c Harvey b Goonesena	7	—	c and b Goonesena	5
J. G. Lomax b Smales	3	—	st Rowe b Goonesena	4
H. W. Stephenson c Clay b Goonesena	14	—	st Rowe b Goonesena	10
Yawar Saeed c Poole b Goonesena	1	—	st Rowe b Smales	15
B. Lobb not out	0	—	b Smales	0
B 6, l-b 4	10		B 13, l-b 3, w 1	17
	146			143

1/2 2/24 3/29 4/56 5/82 6/82 7/87
8/104 9/146

1/80 2/85 3/92 4/102
5/106 6/114 7/124 8/138
9/143

Somerset Bowling

	O.	M.	R.	W.	O.	M.	R.	W.
Lobb	12	1	32	0	6	1	40	1
Yawar Saeed	9.1	2	16	3	7	0	46	1
Lomax	4	1	7	0				
Lawrence	37	7	97	6	19	4	65	0
McMahon	18	5	44	1	21	6	55	3
Walker	17	5	60	0	10	2	36	1
Wight					5	0	28	0

Nottinghamshire Bowling

	O.	M.	R.	W.	O.	M.	R.	W.
Matthews	10	6	13	1	3	0	15	0
Smales	29	13	75	4	22	4	47	6
Goonesena	20.4	3	48	5	20	4	64	4

Umpires: D. Davies and W. F. Price.

At The Oval, July 30, August 1, 2. NOTTINGHAMSHIRE lost to SURREY by an innings and 3 runs.

NOTTINGHAMSHIRE v. MIDDLESEX

At Nottingham, August 3, 4, 5. Nottinghamshire won by seven wickets. Splendid all-round cricket by Dooland enabled them to make a remarkable recovery. With only four wickets left, Nottinghamshire needed another 47 to avoid following-on when Dooland went to the crease. He promptly launched a furious attack on the bowling and, with considerable help from Smales and Jepson, reduced the Middlesex lead to 57 before he was last out. Then Dooland upset the Middlesex second innings with his leg-breaks and googlies and left his side to make 222 at a rate of one a minute. After being given a sound start, the left-handers Stocks and Poole hit off the last 105 runs in fifty minutes, Nottinghamshire winning with forty minutes to spare. Delisle hit his maiden Championship century on the first day when Dewes and Bennett also batted excellently for Middlesex.

Middlesex

J. D. Robertson c Dooland b Goonesena	19	— c Goonesena b Jepson	2
J. G. Dewes lbw b Dooland	69	— lbw b Dooland	17
W. J. Edrich c K. Poole b Goonesena	57	— c Stocks b Dooland	47
D. C. S. Compton c Clay b Dooland	7	— c sub b Dooland	0
S. M. Brown hit wkt b Dooland	8	— lbw b Dooland	43
G. P. S. Delisle c Jepson b Smales	105	— c Clay b Dooland	0
D. Bennett not out	81	— c Stocks b Dooland	26
F. J. Titmus not out	15	— c Rowe b Goonesena	8
L. H. Compton (did not bat)		— c and b Goonesena	11
J. J. Warr (did not bat)		— c K. Poole b Dooland	0
J. A. Young (did not bat)		— not out	0
B 7, l-b 3, n-b 3	13	B 5, l-b 4, w 1	10

1/75 2/109 3/127 4/135   (6 wkts., dec.) 374   1/4 2/37 3/37 4/56 5/90   164
5/212 6/328   6/143 7/143 8/162 9/164

Nottinghamshire

J. D. Clay b Titmus	76	— b Titmus	23
R. J. Giles c and b Young	22	— c Robertson b Titmus	30
E. J. Martin lbw b D. Compton	3	— b Titmus	30
F. W. Stocks c Young b Titmus	39	— not out	82
C. J. Poole b Titmus	22	— not out	52
K. J. Poole c and b Young	22		
G. Goonesena c and b Titmus	0		
B. Dooland c Robertson b Titmus	77		
K. Smales lbw b Titmus	11		
A. Jepson b Young	21		
E. J. Rowe not out	9		
B 5, l-b 10	15	B 3, l-b 2	5

1/65 2/72 3/137 4/154 5/178 6/178   317   1/37 2/60 3/117   (3 wkts.) 222
7/206 8/233 9/303

Nottinghamshire Bowling

	O.	M.	R.	W.		O.	M.	R.	W.
Jepson	19	4	54	0	....	4	0	10	1
K. Poole	12	0	50	0	....	4	0	12	0
Goonesena	37	9	110	2	....	20	3	58	2
Dooland	40	6	99	3	....	24.4	3	67	7
Smales	14	5	48	1	....	4	1	7	0

Middlesex Bowling

	O.	M.	R.	W.		O.	M.	R.	W.
Warr	16	3	45	0	....	1	0	2	0
Bennett	16	3	34	0	....	1	0	8	0
Young	40	11	92	3	....	27	11	67	0
D. Compton	13	0	57	1	....	6	0	45	0
Titmus	32.5	13	74	6	....	37	11	78	3
Robertson						3	0	13	0
Edrich						1	0	4	0

Umpires: F. Chester and K. McCanlis.

NOTTINGHAMSHIRE v. KENT

At Nottingham, August 6, 8, 9. Nottinghamshire won by 278 runs. After struggling in their first innings against the spin of Wright and Allan, Nottinghamshire established complete superiority. The match was specially notable for the achievement of Goonesena, who secured the runs and wickets he needed to record the first "double" of the season, and the first of his career. Afterwards he was awarded his county cap. Simpson, after three weeks' absence through sinus trouble, batted attractively for his second century of the summer and was helped in fast-scoring stands by Giles and Stocks. With the exception of Pretlove and Pettiford, the Kent batsmen gave a poor exhibition.

Nottinghamshire

R. T. Simpson c Wilson b Allan	39	— c Fagg b Pettiford.........105
J. D. Clay lbw b Spanswick	11	— b Wright 28
R. J. Giles b Allan...................	31	— c and b Allan 41
F. W. Stocks c Cowdrey b Phillips	5	— c Fagg b Phillips 75
C. J. Poole b Phillips................	2	— c and b Phillips 4
G. Goonesena c Allan b Wright	22	— not out 39
B. Dooland c Cowdrey b Wright	32	— c Fagg b Allan 19
K. Smales not out	16	
A. Jepson c Wilson b Wright..........	13	— not out 12
C. S. Matthews run out	1	
E. J. Rowe lbw b Wright	0	
B 2, l-b 5, w 1, n-b 3	11	B 8, l-b 7, n-b 1....... 16

1/16 2/82 3/90 4/92 5/104 6/141   183   1/51 2/136 (6 wkts., dec.) 339
7/158 8/178 9/179   3/232 4/239 5/280 6/320

Kent

A. E. Fagg b Dooland	24	— lbw b Goonesena 9
M. C. Cowdrey b Matthews............	11	— c Dooland b Goonesena ... 2
R. C. Wilson c Clay b Goonesena	8	— lbw b Dooland 4
J. F. Pretlove c Clay b Dooland	35	— c Rowe b Jepson 22
A. W. Catt c Stocks b Dooland	1	— c Stocks b Smales........ 1
J. Pettiford c and b Goonesena	17	— lbw b Jepson 42
J. M. Allan b Dooland	1	— lbw b Goonesena 13
A. F. Brazier b Goonesena	5	— c Stocks b Smales 0
J. Spanswick b Goonesena	13	— c Rowe b Dooland 5
D. V. P. Wright not out	6	— not out 5
J. B. Phillips b Dooland	0	— c Matthews b Smales 8
B 9, l-b 3	12	L-b 8 8

1/30 2/49 3/57 4/61 5/83 6/88   133   1/22 2/23 3/27 4/32 5/36   111
7/101 8/121 9/133   6/104 7/105 8/105 9/111

Kent Bowling

	O.	M.	R.	W.	O.	M.	R.	W.
Spanswick	16	2	35	1	13	1	74	0
Phillips	18	5	42	2	11	1	49	2
Wright	16.2	4	49	4	10	0	70	1
Allan	34	15	46	2	19	3	64	2
Pettiford					18	5	66	1

Nottinghamshire Bowling

	O.	M.	R.	W.	O.	M.	R.	W.
Jepson	6	3	15	0	9	3	19	2
Matthews......	8	2	14	1	2	0	2	0
Dooland	30	13	47	5	14	3	37	2
Goonesena	26	9	45	4	17	5	39	3
Smales........					10.5	7	6	3

Umpires: T. Spencer and A. E. Pothecary.

At Scarborough, August 10, 11, 12. NOTTINGHAMSHIRE lost to YORKSHIRE by nine wickets.

NOTTINGHAMSHIRE v. HAMPSHIRE

At Nottingham, August 13, 15, 16. Drawn. Excellent bowling by Jepson, who in intense heat maintained a lively pace for nearly two hours, brought Hampshire near to defeat after they had been set to make 140 in two hours five minutes. A brilliant catch by Dooland that sent back Marshall turned events in Nottinghamshire's favour, for no other batsman could force matters effectively. Marshall's brilliant batting and a spirited last-wicket stand between Burden and Harrison, who limped badly, enabled Hampshire to win a keen tussle for first innings lead. Sainsbury bowled well in causing Nottinghamshire's cheap dismissal in the second innings.

Nottinghamshire

R. T. Simpson run out	82	— b Shackleton	5
J. D. Clay c Barnard b Burden	21	— b Sainsbury	39
C. J. Poole c Barnard b Gray	60	— b Shackleton	1
F. W. Stocks c Marshall b Burden	56	— b Burden	15
K. J. Poole lbw b Burden	3	— lbw b Sainsbury	14
E. J. Martin b Sainsbury	7	— lbw b Burden	1
G. Goonesena lbw b Shackleton	39	— hit wkt b Sainsbury	43
B. Dooland c Marshall b Shackleton	47	— c Barnard b Sainsbury	20
A. Jepson b Shackleton	7	— b Burden	0
K. Smales lbw b Gray	0	— not out	1
E. J. Rowe not out	0	— lbw b Sainsbury	0
B 1, l-b 5, n-b 1	7	B 6, l-b 2	8

1/73 2/146 3/178 4/202 5/227 6/239   329   1/8 2/12 3/44 4/68 5/87   147
7/287 8/307 9/312   6/94 7/136 8/137 9/147

Hampshire

J. R. Gray c Clay b Dooland	21	— b Jepson	15
R. E. Marshall c Smales b Dooland	105	— c Dooland b Jepson	31
H. Horton c Rowe b K. Poole	43	— b Jepson	10
A. W. H. Rayment c and b Goonesena	0	— b Dooland	6
N. H. Rogers c Simpson b Smales	85	— st Rowe b Dooland	0
H. M. Barnard b Jepson	0	— c K. Poole b Goonesena	11
P. J. Sainsbury lbw b Dooland	3	— b Smales	2
L. Harrison not out	24	— not out	2
D. Shackleton lbw b Dooland	10	— lbw b Jepson	4
V. H. D. Cannings b Dooland	0	— not out	8
M. D. Burden c Martin b Smales	30		
B 9, l-b 6, n-b 1	16	B 4, l-b 8, w 1	13

1/57 2/166 3/172 4/234 5/245 6/262   337   1/52 2/59 3/74   (8 wkts.)   102
7/276 8/288 9/288   4/74 5/75 6/86 7/92 8/94

Hampshire Bowling

	O.	M.	R.	W.		O.	M.	R.	W.
Shackleton	27.2	4	60	3	....	10	4	8	2
Cannings	29	5	80	0	....	7	1	23	0
Gray	25	7	68	2	....	4	0	12	0
Sainsbury	25	4	58	1	....	28.5	13	47	5
Burden	23	9	56	3	....	30	8	49	3

Nottinghamshire Bowling

	O.	M.	R.	W.		O.	M.	R.	W.
Jepson	24	8	40	1	....	17	3	33	4
K. Poole	9	3	28	1	....	2	0	10	0
Dooland	42	11	87	5	....	15	5	36	2
Goonesena	24	3	79	1	....	4	2	8	1
Smales	25.1	5	87	2	....	4	3	2	1

Umpires: N. Oldfield and P. Corrall.

NOTTINGHAMSHIRE v. WARWICKSHIRE

At Nottingham, August 17, 18, 19. Nottinghamshire won by six wickets. They gained a firm grip on the game on the opening day when, H. E. Dollery apart, Warwickshire batted disappointingly against the leg-spin of Goonesena. By the close Nottinghamshire were only 54 runs behind with eight wickets standing and the left-handers C. J. Poole and Stocks made sure of a substantial lead next morning by taking their third-wicket stand to 124. Poole batted brightly but Stocks spent nearly five hours over 99. The Warwickshire attack was handicapped by the loss of Hollies through a bruised finger, but Bannister deserved better reward for his whole-hearted bowling on a dead pitch. Smales caused most trouble in Warwickshire's second innings, Horner alone facing his off-breaks confidently, and Nottinghamshire were left with a light task.

Warwickshire

F. C. Gardner b K. Poole	6	— c Dooland b Smales 23
N. F. Horner lbw b Jepson	5	— c Kelly b Goonesena 82
A. V. Wolton c C. Poole b Goonesena	21	— b Smales 0
A. Townsend run out	4	— lbw b Dooland 7
H. E. Dollery c Clay b Goonesena	61	— b Smales 5
R. E. Hitchcock c Stocks b Smales	10	— c Clay b Smales............ 20
T. W. Cartwright b Goonesena	14	— b Smales 17
E. B. Lewis lbw b Goonesena	0	— c Goonesena b Smales 14
J. D. Bannister c Dooland b Smales	2	— not out 15
R. G. Thompson st Rowe b Goonesena	6	— b Goonesena 0
W. E. Hollies not out	2	— c Rowe b Goonesena 10
B 1, l-b 6	7	B 12, l-b 6, w 1 19
	138	**212**

1/9 2/17 3/23 4/53 5/84 6/123
7/123 8/128 9/130

1/73 2/73 3/93 4/97 5/133 6/159 7/179 8/188
9/188

Nottinghamshire

R. T. Simpson c Hollies b Bannister	17	— c Gardner b Bannister 12
J. D. Clay c Bannister b Hollies	13	— b Hitchcock 10
C. J. Poole c and b Bannister	96	— c Gardner b Hitchcock 11
F. W. Stocks c Bannister b Thompson	99	— c Bannister b Hitchcock ... 18
K. J. Poole b Hitchcock	7	— not out 0
G. Goonesena c Cartwright b Townsend	4	— not out 4
J. Kelly c Lewis b Hitchcock	3	
B. Dooland c Hitchcock b Bannister	10	
K. Smales not out	18	
A. Jepson c and b Bannister	18	
B 1, l-b 6, n-b 2	9	B 4 4
	294	**59**

1/27 2/33 3/157 4/182   (9 wkts., dec.) 294
5/189 6/214 7/243 8/263 9/294

1/22 2/24 3/51   (4 wkts.) 59
4/55

E. J. Rowe did not bat.

Nottinghamshire Bowling

	O.	M.	R.	W.	O.	M.	R.	W.
Jepson	14	3	29	1	7	5	7	0
K. Poole	8	1	20	1	5	4	2	0
Goonesena	23	8	51	5	19	6	38	3
Dooland	8	2	18	0	26	8	53	1
Smales	9	3	13	2	35	15	84	6
Kelly					4	1	9	0

Warwickshire Bowling

	O.	M.	R.	W.		O.	M.	R.	W.
Thompson	30	9	95	1	....	5	1	12	0
Bannister	38.2	12	82	4	....	7	2	24	1
Hollies	7	2	30	1					
Townsend	18	2	41	1	....	2	0	3	0
Hitchcock	17	7	37	2	....	4	1	16	3

Umpires: Harry Elliott (Derbyshire) and P. Corrall.

At Hove, August 20, 22, 23. NOTTINGHAMSHIRE lost to SUSSEX by ten wickets.

NOTTINGHAMSHIRE v. NORTHAMPTONSHIRE

At Nottingham, August 24, 25, 26. Drawn. After outplaying Nottinghamshire on the first two days Northamptonshire were baulked of victory because the home team batted resolutely on a pitch still in excellent condition. They did badly in their first innings and lost half the side for 64 before Stocks and Goonesena doubled the score. A splendid partnership of 281—the highest all season against Nottinghamshire—between the left-handers Livingston and Subba Row placed Northamptonshire in a commanding position. Each hit powerfully after giving an early chance, Livingston getting three 6's and twenty-three 4's and Subba Row sixteen 4's. Nottinghamshire began the last day 203 behind with eight wickets left, but again Stocks led a recovery. This time he received better support, specially from Goonesena and K. Poole who shared an unfinished stand of 155. Goonesena completed his first century for the county in the final over and Poole also made his highest score.

Nottinghamshire

R. T. Simpson st Livingston b Tribe	26	— c Arnold b Tribe	10
R. J. Giles hit wkt b Broderick	20	— b Tyson	21
C. J. Poole c Reynold b Tribe	1	— c Greasley b Tribe	34
F. W. Stocks c Broderick b Wild	63	— lbw b Tribe	62
M. Winfield lbw b Tyson	4	— b Tribe	38
K. J. Poole b Tyson	0	— not out	57
G. Goonesena b Tyson	14	— not out 107
B. Dooland run out	40		
J. P. Springall c Livingston b Tyson....	3	— lbw b Tyson	2
K. Smales not out	20		
A. Jepson c Reynolds b Wild	0		
L-b 5, n-b 1...................	6	B 8, l-b 7	15

1/47 2/47 3/51 4/62 5/64 6/128   197   1/22 2/29 3/42   (6 wkts.) 346
7/138 8/149 9/196   4/81 5/176 6/191

Northamptonshire

D. Brookes c K. Poole b Dooland	25	V. Broderick not out	1
P. Arnold c Goonesena b Smales	28	F. H. Tyson c Springall b Jepson .	0
L. Livingston c Goonesena b Smales	170		
R. Subba Row b Stocks 132		B 28, l-b 7, w 1	36
B. Reynolds lbw b Goonesena	16		
G. E. Tribe c Goonesena b Stocks.	5	1/54 2/78 3/359 (9 wkts., dec.) 438
J. Wild c C. Poole b Goonesena...	4	4/401 5/405 6/410 7/425 8/438
D. G. Greasley b Jepson	21	9/438

J. Webster did not bat.

Northamptonshire Bowling

	O.	M.	R.	W.		O.	M.	R.	W.
Tyson	21	4	52	4	....	23	3	55	2
Webster	8	4	13	0	....	15	3	52	0
Tribe	28	10	50	2	....	33	9	92	4
Broderick	22	12	40	1	....	16	4	29	0
Subba Row	8	3	8	0	....	8	1	34	0
Wild	10.3	4	28	2	....	19	4	57	0
					Greasley	5	0	12	0

Nottinghamshire Bowling

	O.	M.	R.	W.
Jepson	16.5	2	74	2
K. Poole	10	1	45	0
Goonesena	29	6	87	2
Dooland	35	12	82	1
Smales	33	11	73	2
Stocks	11	2	41	2

Umpires: H. Elliott (Lancashire) and G. S. Mobey.

At Southend, August 27, 29, 30. NOTTINGHAMSHIRE beat ESSEX by two wickets.

PLAYING NO LONGER

Nottinghamshire

HARDSTAFF, J. (Nottinghamshire). Debut 1930. Delightful batsman with free, flowing strokes. Played in 23 Tests for England, opposing Australia, South Africa, West Indies, New Zealand and India. Scored 31,841 runs (average 44.34) with highest innings of 266 against Leicestershire at Leicester in 1937. Hit 83 centuries in career.

Somerset

LAWRENCE, J. (Somerset). Debut 1946. Yorkshire born. Clever leg-break bowler, sound batsman and smart field. Total runs 9,183; total wickets 798. Highest score 111 against Essex in 1952 and best bowling eight for 63 against Hampshire in 1949.

SOMERSET

President—The Bishop of Bath and Wells

Hon. Secretary—Air Vice-Marshal M. L. Taylor, County Cricket Ground, St. James's Street, Taunton

Captain—G. G. Tordoff

M. F. Tremlett County Badge B. Lobb

Once more the Somerset team consisted mostly of players lacking the skill required to form a good match-winning combination and the county finished at the bottom for the fourth consecutive year. Two most depressing experiences occurred during the Weston-super-Mare festival where they were dismissed for 36 by Surrey and 37 by Hampshire, the two lowest totals of the season.

Tordoff, the newly-elected captain and left-handed batsman who was on special leave from the Royal Navy, stood little chance of bringing a transformation in the fortunes of the club, but he marked his first full season of county cricket by scoring 1196 runs. From the beginning Tordoff found his batting order a jig-saw puzzle without the right men to fit the holes, but strangely five completed 1,000 runs in a summer when Surrey, the Champions, produced only two able to achieve the same feat in Championship games.

Tremlett, whose superb driving some equalled but few surpassed, topped the averages, and scoring 1850 runs he enjoyed his best season since 1951 when his aggregate was 2101. Wight, a polished stroke-player, maintained his form and would probably have fared much better in a stronger side. Lawrence retained the distinction of being the best all-rounder, but this little Yorkshireman was released from his contract at his own request and ended a career which lasted nine seasons. Walker, another Yorkshireman, raised hopes of developing into an attractive opening batsman when he hit 100 against Essex at Romford. Angell, handicapped by injury early in the season, scarcely faced the new ball with that degree of confidence required of a Number One batsman and Lomax, from Lancashire, disappointed in his second season.

Lobb, a tall loose-limbed fast bowler, previously with Warwickshire, appeared to be the best discovery made by Somerset for some years and he headed his county's bowling with 86 wickets at 25.59 each. Deceptive inswingers and deliveries which moved off the pitch at great speed brought him much success. McMahon, Lawrence and Hilton were useful spin bowlers of varying types, but on the whole the attack never attained the standard needed to lift Somerset up the table.

Whatever their shortcomings Somerset, always rich in wicket-keepers, again found Stephenson a stalwart behind the stumps. More than once on the short list for Test honours, he received official recognition of his skill when chosen for the M.C.C. tour of Pakistan.

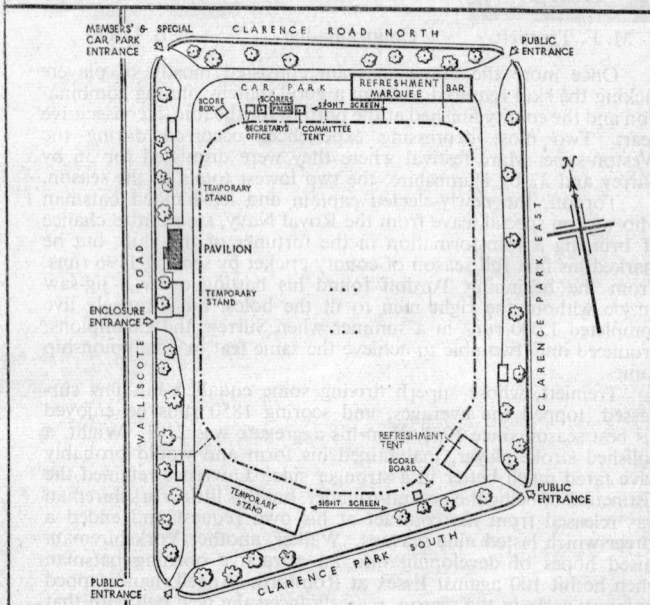

COUNTY CRICKET GROUND, WESTON-SUPER-MARE

SOMERSET RESULTS

All First-Class Matches—Played 29, Won 4, Lost 18, Drawn 7

County Championship Matches—Played 28, Won 4, Lost 17, Drawn 7

COUNTY CHAMPIONSHIP AVERAGES

BATTING

	Birthplace	Mtchs.	Inns.	Not Outs	Runs	100's	Highest Inns.	Aver.
M. F. Tremlett .	Stockport	28	55	1	1830	2	153	33.88
P. B. Wight	Georgetown	28	54	3	1323	1	106	25.94
J. Lawrence	Leeds	26	50	1	1101	1	122	22.46
G. G. Tordoff ..	Whitwood	27	53	3	1091	1	145*	21.82
J. G. Lomax	Rochdale	24	46	6	868	0	71	21.70
H. W. Stephenson	Stockton-on-Tees	27	51	4	1016	0	85*	21.61
F. L. Angell	Norton St. Philip	16	32	0	578	0	90	18.06
M. Walker......	Mexborough	8	15	0	239	1	100	15.93
Yawar Saeed ...	Pakistan	23	44	2	664	0	64	15.80
C. F. Davey	Petherton	5	10	1	132	0	46	14.66
J. Hilton	Chadderton	20	37	8	388	0	61*	13.37
B. Langford	Birmingham	2	4	0	48	0	41	12.00
J. W. McMahon.	S. Australia	28	48	21	247	0	24	9.14
R. Smith	Taunton	5	9	0	72	0	21	8.00
K. E. Palmer....	Winchester	3	6	1	35	0	12*	7.00
G. M. Tripp	Clevedon	2	4	0	20	0	8	5.00
G. L. Williams ..	Kidwelly	3	6	0	30	0	24	5.00
B. Lobb........	Birmingham	27	46	13	110	0	14	3.33
L. Pickles.......	Wakefield	2	4	0	4	0	2	1.00

Also batted: G. Atkinson (*Lofthouse*) 8, 2; K. D. Biddulph (*Chingford*) 1, 1; D. G. Hughes (*Taunton*) 2.

* Signifies not out.

BOWLING

	Overs	Maidens	Runs	Wickets	Average
B. Lobb	754	152	2201	86	25.59
J. Lawrence	594.5	113	1855	71	26.12
M. Walker.............	85	15	329	12	27.41
K. E. Palmer...........	24	5	56	2	28.00
J. Hilton	368.1	88	1019	36	28.30
J. W. McMahon........	800.3	223	2129	75	28.38
Yawar Saeed	385.3	50	1403	38	36.92
K. D. Biddulph	43.2	5	148	4	37.00
G. G. Tordoff	108.1	24	344	9	38.22
J. G. Lomax	362	77	1031	19	54.26
M. F. Tremlett	38	6	122	1	122.00
P. B. Wight	12	0	58	0	—

Also bowled: B. Langford 1—0—8—0.

Amateurs.—G. G. Tordoff, G. L. Williams, Yawar Saeed.

At Taunton, April 28, 29. SOMERSET drew with GLAMORGAN. (Friendly match.) Somerset 288 for four wickets, declared (J. Lawrence 95, G. G. Tordoff 67, R. Smith 56); Glamorgan 71 for three wickets.

At Southampton, May 4, 5. SOMERSET drew with HAMPSHIRE. (Friendly match.)

At Birmingham, May 7, 9, 10. SOMERSET drew with WARWICKSHIRE.

At Taunton, May 11, 12, 13. SOMERSET beat ROYAL AIR FORCE by 131 runs. (Not first-class.) Somerset 278 (P. B. Wight 148; A/C M. J. Cowan six for 65) and 209 for nine wickets, declared (R. Smith 65, H. W. Stephenson 62); Royal Air Force 149 (J. Lawrence five for 44) and 207 (A/C S. Leary 62).

At The Oval, May 14, 16. SOMERSET lost to SURREY by an innings and four runs.

At Leeds, May 18, 19, 20. SOMERSET lost to YORKSHIRE by 163 runs.

SOMERSET v. NOTTINGHAMSHIRE

At Taunton, May 21, 23, 24. Nottinghamshire won by eight runs with two minutes to spare. They began moderately, but Clay and Stocks effected a recovery in a fifth wicket partnership of 185. Against the slow bowling of Dooland, Somerset lost six men for 93 and stood in danger of following on. Then Tremlett played a faultless and judicious innings of three and a half hours which included one 6 and fifteen 4's. He and Hilton put on 149 and on the last day Tordoff declared 83 behind. Nottinghamshire accepted the challenge. Poole (two 6's, seven 4's), missed before scoring, hit 71 in sixty-five minutes and Simpson in turn declared, leaving Somerset to get 286 in three hours twenty minutes. Brisk work by the earlier batsmen was followed by strong hitting from Yawar Saeed, but Dooland and Harvey brought about a collapse during the extra half-hour, the last four wickets falling for 22 runs.

Nottinghamshire

R. T. Simpson c Hughes b Lomax	14	— c Smith b Yawar Saeed 54
J. D. Clay lbw b Lobb	127	— lbw b Lobb 1
C. J. Poole c Yawar Saeed b Lomax	0	— c Tordoff b McMahon 71
J. Hardstaff c Hilton b Lobb	6	— b Yawar Saeed 30
E. J. Martin b McMahon	13	— not out 8
F. W. Stocks c Lomax b Lawrence......	92	— c Yawar Saeed b Lobb ... 1
P. F. Harvey st Hughes b McMahon ...	29	
B. Dooland b Lobb	0	— c Lomax b Lobb 12
K. Smales b Lawrence	1	
A. Jepson c Tordoff b Lawrence	21	— c Lawrence b Lobb........ 6
E. J. Rowe not out	2	
B 12, l-b 8	20	B 13, l-b 5, n-b 1...... 19

1/43 2/43 3/52 4/84 5/269 6/277   325
7/277 8/278 9/300

1/2 2/103 (7 wkts., dec.) 202
3/171 4/171 5/184
6/192 7/202

Somerset

G. G. Tordoff b Dooland..............	31	— b Dooland 42
J. G. Lomax b Jepson	15	— b Jepson 25
J. Lawrence c Clay b Dooland	5	— c Clay b Dooland 22
P. B. Wight c Poole b Dooland........	0	— c Rowe b Dooland 39
R. Smith c Rowe b Dooland	1	— c Clay b Dooland 21
M. F. Tremlett lbw b Dooland	120	— c Simpson b Dooland 39
Yawar Saeed b Jepson	8	— c Hardstaff b Harvey 61
J. Hilton not out ...,.............	61	— b Harvey 2
D. G. Hughes (did not bat)		— c Smales b Dooland 2
J. W. McMahon (did not bat)		— not out 10
B. Lobb (did not bat)		— b Dooland 8
W 1	1	B 1, l-b 4, n-b 1...... 6

1/41 2/51 3/51 4/51   (7 wkts., dec.) 242
5/56 6/93 7/242

1/39 2/75 3/94 4/152   277
5/188 6/255 7/257 8/257 9/268

Somerset Bowling

	O.	M.	R.	W.	O.	M.	R.	W.
Lobb	31	3	89	3	 12	1	47	4
Tremlett	16	2	51	0	 1	0	15	0
Lomax	12	4	16	2	 11	2	39	0
Lawrence	22	1	71	3	 2	0	18	0
McMahon	26.3	5	58	2	 9	2	54	1
Hilton	9	2	20	0				
Yawar Saeed					.. 5	1	10	2

Nottinghamshire Bowling

	O.	M.	R.	W.	O.	M.	R.	W.
Jepson	29	9	54	2	 12	2	55	1
Smales	24	8	52	0	 14	2	59	0
Dooland	36	10	111	5	.... 20.5	1	110	7
Harvey	15	8	24	0	 18	4	47	2

Umpires: D. Davies and A. E. Pothecary.

SOMERSET v. GLOUCESTERSHIRE

At Taunton, May 28, 30, 31. Drawn. Batsmen were in complete command and only 21 wickets fell in the match for 1,022 runs. Somerset batted carefully at the start. Wight and Lawrence added 105 for the third wicket and Lomax also showed sound form. Gloucestershire quickly took command and declared shortly after taking the lead. Milton and Young began with 91 and then Graveney helped Milton put on 191 in 170 minutes. Tordoff soon removed any possibility of a Somerset defeat, racing to his century in ninety-nine minutes. He batted just under three hours for the highest score of his career. Gloucestershire did not attempt to go for the 261 needed for victory at two a minute.

Somerset

G. G. Tordoff b Lambert	20	— not out	145
F. L. Angell b McHugh	16	— lbw b Wells	22
J. Lawrence lbw b Mortimore	60		
P. B. Wight run out	60	— c Rochford b McHugh	0
M. F. Tremlett c Young b Lambert	30	— b Mortimore	47
J. G. Lomax b McHugh	53		
Yawar Saeed c Wells b Lambert	26	— not out	43
H. W. Stephenson b Lambert	16	— c Graveney b Mortimore	6
J. Hilton b McHugh	7		
J. W. McMahon not out	7		
B. Lobb b Graveney	11		
L-b 6, n-b 2	8	B 5, l-b 2	7

1/28 2/51 3/156 4/161 5/224 6/259   314   1/68 2/195 (4 wkts., dec.) 270
7/284 8/293 9/301   3/203 4/203

Gloucestershire

C. A. Milton b Yawar Saeed	138	— not out	44
D. M. Young c Stephenson b Lawrence	37	— c Tremlett b Tordoff	43
T. W. Graveney c Tordoff b Yawar Saeed	104		
J. F. Crapp c Stephenson b Lobb	10		
G. M. Emmett b Lobb	22		
R. B. Nicholls not out	6	— st Stephenson b Lawrence	5
J. Mortimore not out	1	— not out	5
B 2, l-b 3, n-b 1	6	B 10, l-b 6, n-b 1	17

1/91 2/282 3/296   (5 wkts., dec.) 324   1/76 2/88   (2 wkts.) 114
4/310 5/323

G. E. Lambert, P. Rochford, B. D. Wells and F. P. McHugh did not bat.

Gloucestershire Bowling

	O.	M.	R.	W.	O.	M.	R.	W.
Lambert	28	5	84	4	10	1	41	0
McHugh	38	8	84	3	18	1	87	1
Wells	29	12	72	0	8	0	44	1
Mortimore.....	29	9	52	1	17	1	83	2
Graveney	5	1	14	1				
Emmett					1	0	4	0
Milton........					0.4	0	4	0

Somerset Bowling

	O.	M.	R.	W.	O.	M.	R.	W.
Lobb	25	3	63	2	5	1	10	0
Lomax	11	0	49	0	4	0	11	0
Yawar Saeed ..	18	2	63	2	3	1	4	0
Lawrence	19	3	49	1	7	4	21	1
McMahon	17	2	56	0	10	5	19	0
Hilton	17	3	38	0				
Tordoff					6	1	32	1

Umpires: G. S. Mobey and A. J. B. Fowler.

SOMERSET v. SUSSEX

At Frome, June 4, 6, 7. Somerset won by 50 runs, their first victory of the season. Excitement rose when the teams tied on the first innings. In the end Somerset owed most to the deceptive slow left-arm bowling of McMahon, who when Sussex went in a second time, troubled everybody. Before McMahon triumphed, Lobb, a promising young pace bowler, served Somerset well. On a green pitch runs were generally difficult to get and 59 by Lomax for Somerset was the highest score. Parks made a great effort to save the game for Sussex staying an hour and three-quarters, being stumped six minutes from time.

Somerset

G. G. Tordoff c and b James...........	5	—	b James...................	0
F. L. Angell c Langridge b James	21	—	c Langridge b Thomson....	8
J. Lawrence c Langridge b Marlar	2	—	c Smith b Thomson	4
P. B. Wight lbw b James	25	—	c Oakman b James	58
M. F. Tremlett b James	16	—	b James...................	38
J. G. Lomax st Webb b Oakman	1	—	c Cox b James	59
Yawar Saeed c Potter b Marlar........	9	—	st Webb b James	31
H. W. Stephenson run out	41	—	c Langridge b Thomson....	7
J. Hilton not out	31	—	run out	0
J. W. McMahon run out	24	—	not out	1
B. Lobb b Marlar	9	—	st Webb b Thomson	9
B 4, l-b 1	5		B 4, l-b 1	5

1/9 2/21 3/37 4/67 5/74 6/74   189   1/1 2/8 3/23 4/97   220
7/91 8/131 9/168   5/114 6/178 7/201 8/207 9/210

Sussex

J. Langridge b Lobb	13	—	lbw b McMahon	18
D. V. Smith lbw b Lobb	4	—	c Angell b McMahon	23
A. S. M. Oakman c Tordoff b Lobb	26	—	c Stephenson b McMahon.	0
R. T. Webb c Lomax b McMahon	8	—	not out	12
J. M. Parks lbw b Yawar Saeed	48	—	st Stephenson b McMahon	46
K. G. Suttle c Lawrence b Yawar Saeed	52	—	b Hilton	12
G. Cox b Lobb	9	—	run out	0
G. Potter c Stephenson b Lobb	2	—	c Lomax b McMahon	9
N. I. Thomson b Lawrence	10	—	b McMahon	21
A. E. James not out	4	—	st Stephenson b Lawrence	12
R. G. Marlar b Lawrence	9	—	b Hilton	2
L-b 4	4		B 10, l-b 5	15

1/8 2/17 3/54 4/58 5/141 6/154   189   1/36 2/36 3/53 4/67   170
7/164 8/176 9/176   5/69 6/70 7/74 8/103 9/132

Sussex Bowling

	O.	M.	R.	W.		O.	M.	R.	W.
Thomson	22	2	51	0	....	19	3	74	4
James	31	13	54	4	....	24	3	65	5
Marlar	20.4	3	56	3	....	10	0	48	0
Oakman	10	3	23	1	....	8	1	28	0

Somerset Bowling

	O.	M.	R.	W.		O.	M.	R.	W.
Lobb	30	12	50	5	....	12	2	23	0
Lomax	13	4	36	0	....	5	2	13	0
McMahon	11	4	29	1	....	23.2	6	66	6
Lawrence	12.3	1	33	2	....	12	2	35	1
Hilton	6	2	12	0	....	16	8	18	2
Yawar Saeed	12	2	25	2					

Umpires: E. A. Roberts and J. S. Buller.

SOMERSET v. KENT

At Yeovil, June 11, 13, 14. Somerset won by three wickets. Besides profiting from Kent mistakes in the field, they were much indebted to McMahon. The Australian left-arm slow bowler, by clever variation of flight and spin, nearly routed Kent in the first innings, equalling his previous best analysis. Fagg offered strong resistance, but like all his colleagues experienced difficulty in getting the ball away. A spirited sixth wicket stand of 103 by Lawrence and Lomax put Somerset on the way to a lead of 55. When Kent went in again Witherden and Pettiford batted doggedly, but Hilton, exploiting off-spinners skilfully, eased the final task for Somerset.

Kent

A. E. Fagg b McMahon	62	—	c Lomax b McMahon	19
E. G. Witherden b Lobb	6	—	c Hilton b Lawrence	69
A. H. Phebey c Yawar Saeed b McMahon	34	—	lbw b Lobb	14
P. Hearn c Lawrence b McMahon	0	—	c Stephenson b Hilton	21
J. Pettiford c Lawrence b Lawrence	37	—	not out	32
R. C. Wilson b McMahon	4	—	c Lawrence b Hilton	3
B. E. Disbury c Hilton b McMahon	2	—	st Stephenson b Lawrence	10
D. G. Ufton b McMahon	1	—	b Hilton	0
D. V. P. Wright b McMahon	13	—	c Lomax b Hilton	5
J. Spanswick c and b McMahon	0	—	c Tordoff b Lawrence	6
J. C. T. Page not out	0	—	b Hilton	0
B 8, l-b 1, w 4	13		L-b 5	5

1/19 2/93 3/93 4/120 5/126 6/134   172   1/37 2/37 3/90 4/139   184
7/136 8/172 9/172   5/151 6/168 7/169 8/177 9/184

Somerset

G. G. Tordoff c Disbury b Spanswick	.. 1	— c Pettiford b Spanswick	... 5
F. L. Angell c Spanswick b Page	 14	— c Pettiford b Spanswick	... 9
J. Lawrence b Spanswick	 80	— c Spanswick b Page	... 37
P. B. Wight b Page	 13	— c Fagg b Spanswick	 31
M. F. Tremlett b Wright	 9	— b Wright	 0
J. Hilton c Phebey b Wright	 0	— b Wright	 4
J. G. Lomax b Page	 71	— not out	 26
Yawar Saeed c Spanswick b Page	 5	— run out	 2
H. W. Stephenson b Page	 8	— not out	 4
J. W. McMahon not out	 5		
B. Lobb c Ufton b Wright	 2		
B 14, l-b 5	 19	B 11, l-b 1, n-b 2	 14
	—		—
	227	(7 wkts.)	132

1/2 2/34 3/64 4/83 5/83 6/186   227
7/206 8/219 9/220

1/14 2/19 3/25   (7 wkts.) 132
4/63 5/66 6/114 7/120

Somerset Bowling

	O.	M.	R.	W.		O.	M.	R.	W.
Lobb	24	8	39	1	....	8	2	25	1
Lomax	25	10	35	0	....	4	2	11	0
Yawar Saeed	4	0	13	0					
Lawrence	10.1	1	23	1	....	31	9	71	3
McMahon	32	14	46	8	....	19	8	46	1
Hilton	3	1	3	0	....	31.2	20	26	5

Kent Bowling

	O.	M.	R.	W.		O.	M.	R.	W.
Spanswick	16	4	52	2	....	13	3	38	3
Wright	21.1	5	63	3	....	23	5	50	2
Page	21	4	64	5	....	10	2	30	1
Pettiford	6	0	19	0					
Hearn	4	1	10	0					

Umpires: E. A. Roberts and W. F. Price.

At Taunton, June 15, 16, 17. SOMERSET lost to SOUTH AFRICANS by an innings and 32 runs. (See SOUTH AFRICAN section.)

At Lord's, June 18, 20, 21. SOMERSET lost to MIDDLESEX by nine wickets.

At Newport, June 22, 23, 24. SOMERSET lost to GLAMORGAN by eight wickets.

SOMERSET v. LEICESTERSHIRE

At Bath, June 25, 27, 28. Drawn. Splendid forcing cricket by both sides featured a struggle which ended with honours almost even. Set 319 for victory, Leicestershire were 113 short of their target with seven wickets standing when rain terminated the game. After losing five batsmen for 117 in the second innings, Somerset adopted bold methods. Tremlett and Stephenson attacked the bowling so fiercely that 100 came for the sixth wicket in forty-eight minutes. Stephenson twice drove the new ball for six. Tompkin and Jackson were also full of aggression for Leicestershire, joining in an unbroken fourth wicket stand of 110.

Somerset

G. G. Tordoff c Hallam b Spencer	4	— c Smithson b Jackson	29
Yawar Saeed b Lester	13	— c Walsh b Spencer	44
P. B. Wight c Firth b Jackson	34	— b Jackson	7
M. F. Tremlett c Palmer b Jackson	47	— b Pratt	92
J. G. Lomax b Walsh	8	— not out	10
C. F. Davey c Lester b Munden	46	— b Spencer	2
B. Langford lbw b Spencer	41	— lbw b Spencer	0
H. W. Stephenson b Pratt	41	— not out	85
J. Hilton not out	18		
J. W. McMahon b Walsh	5		
B. Lobb lbw b Walsh	0		
B 1, w 4	5	L-b 3	3

1/10 2/32 3/83 4/108 5/114 6/178   262   1/67 2/75   (6 wkts., dec.) 272
7/234 8/244 9/262   3/101 4/103 5/117 6/229

Leicestershire

G. Lester c Yawar Saeed b Lobb	13	— c Yawar Saeed b Lobb	10
M. Hallam c Stephenson b Yawar Saeed	6	— c Stephenson b Lobb	14
M. Tompkin lbw b Yawar Saeed	42	— not out	89
C. H. Palmer c Lomax b Lobb	74	— st Stephenson b McMahon	32
V. E. Jackson c Stephenson b Lomax	45	— not out	56
G. A. Smithson c Yawar Saeed b Lomax	6		
V. S. Munden b McMahon	14		
J. E. Walsh b Lomax	0		
J. Firth not out	4		
C. T. Spencer run out	2		
R. L. Pratt c Yawar Saeed b Lomax	2		
B 1, l-b 6, w 1	8	L-b 5	5

1/9 2/35 3/85 4/151 5/169 6/200   216   1/22 2/33 3/96   (3 wkts.) 206
7/205 8/209 9/211

Leicestershire Bowling

	O.	M.	R.	W.	O.	M.	R.	W.
Spencer	22	2	53	2	18	2	105	3
Pratt	17	5	28	1	13	0	70	1
Lester	12	3	53	1	2	0	15	0
Walsh	22	5	45	3				
Jackson	18	5	43	2	20	11	64	2
Munden	12	6	27	1				
Palmer	4	0	8	0	13	9	15	0

Somerset Bowling

	O.	M.	R.	W.	O.	M.	R.	W.
Lobb	19	4	50	2	15	5	54	2
Yawar Saeed	18	3	67	2	7.2	0	30	0
McMahon	18	7	46	1	17	3	63	1
Hilton	4	1	10	0				
Langford	1	0	8	0				
Lomax	14	2	27	4	9	0	41	0
Tordoff					3	0	13	0

Umpires: Harry Elliott (Derbyshire) and D. Davies.

SOMERSET v. MIDDLESEX

At Bath, June 29, 30. Somerset won by 63 runs. This was not the fault of Titmus, whose skilful off-break bowling brought him an analysis of fifteen wickets for 95 runs, but the Middlesex batting twice failed against a varied attack. Somerset looked like building up a huge total when Tordoff and Saeed began with a stand of 108, but thanks to Titmus the last nine wickets fell for 66. After the first Middlesex collapse, only Tordoff and Wight achieved much for Somerset on wearing turf, and the Metropolitan county never appeared likely to get the 161 required for victory.

Somerset

G. G. Tordoff b Titmus		53	— b Titmus		28
Yawar Saeed c Edrich b Titmus		64	— b Warr		5
M. F. Tremlett c Young b Titmus		16	— b Titmus		7
P. B. Wight c Edrich b Titmus		6	— lbw b Young		48
C. F. Davey b Titmus		4	— c Bennett b Titmus		4
B. Langford st Compton b Young		3	— c Robertson b Titmus		4
H. W. Stephenson c and b Titmus		0	— c Baldry b Titmus		1
J. Hilton b Young		6	— c Bennett b Titmus		8
K. Palmer b Titmus		10	— c L. Compton b Titmus		3
J. W. McMahon not out		7	— not out		4
B. Lobb b Titmus		0	— b Young		2
B 3, l-b 2		5	B 6, l-b 2		8

1/108 2/136 3/136 4/146 5/149 6/149   174   1/8 2/27 3/60 4/64   122
7/151 8/162 9/174   5/68 6/76 7/96 8/110 9/120

Middlesex

J. D. Robertson c Stephenson b Lobb		23	— c Tremlett b Yawar Saeed		8
S. M. Brown c Stephenson b Yawar Saeed		8	— c Stephenson b Lobb		7
W. J. Edrich c Tremlett b McMahon		8	— b Hilton		15
D. Bennett c McMahon b Palmer		7	— not out		9
D. O. Baldry c Hilton b McMahon		12	— run out		26
F. J. Titmus lbw b Palmer		1	— c Yawar Saeed b Hilton		2
D. A. Bick lbw b Yawar Saeed		33	— b Hilton		3
J. J. Warr b Lobb		13	— c Stephenson b Lobb		20
L. H. Compton c Wight b Lobb		11	— c Yawar Saeed b Lobb		0
J. A. Young not out		12	— c Tremlett b McMahon		2
A. E. Moss lbw b Lobb		0	— st Stephenson b McMahon		0
B 1, l-b 6, n-b 1		8	B 2 l-b 2, w 1		5

1/32 2/32 3/47 4/47 5/52 6/80 7/100   136   1/14 2/24 3/35 4/41   97
8/124 9/136   5/65 6/66 7/88 8/88 9/95

Middlesex Bowling

	O.	M.	R.	W.		O.	M.	R.	W.
Moss	15	4	51	0	....	3	0	10	0
Warr	9	1	30	0	....	5	1	8	1
Bennett	3	0	15	0					
Titmus	25.2	11	44	8	....	31	13	51	7
Young	17	8	29	2	....	28.3	16	45	2

Somerset Bowling

	O.	M.	R.	W.		O.	M.	R.	W.
Lobb	17.2	5	46	4	....	15	6	24	3
Yawar Saeed	17	5	46	2	....	6	0	13	1
McMahon	14	7	20	2	....	18.4	8	21	2
Palmer	10	4	16	2					
Hilton						10	1	34	3

Umpires: Harry Elliott (Derbyshire) and D. Davies.

SOMERSET v. WARWICKSHIRE

At Bath, July 2, 4, 5. Warwickshire won by six wickets. A stubborn innings by Gardner, who batted almost through the first day for 167, placed them in a comfortable position. Yet Lawrence, the Somerset leg-break and googly bowler, was never really mastered, and three of his six wickets for 67 runs came in four balls at the end of the innings. Facing a total of 326, Somerset crumbled before Thompson's pace, and followed on 189 behind. Then Tremlett, Wight, Stephenson and Tordoff all batted attractively, but Warwickshire were left the easy task of scoring 70 to win. Before they gained success, however, Lobb dismissed Gardner, Wolton and Hitchcock in ten deliveries for five runs.

Warwickshire

F. C. Gardner c Hilton b Lawrence	 167	—	c Stephenson b Lobb	9
N. F. Horner c Stephenson b Lawrence	. 39	—	b McMahon	28
A. V. Wolton c Hilton b Lobb	 18	—	c Tremlett b Lobb	1
R. E. Hitchcock c Stephenson b Lawrence	1	—	lbw b Lobb	2
H. E. Dollery b Hilton	13	—	not out	23
R. T. Spooner lbw b Hilton	 22	—	not out	3
A. Townsend run out	 46			
K. R. Dollery not out	13			
R. T. Weeks lbw b Lawrence	 0			
R. G. Thompson lbw b Lawrence	 0			
W. E. Hollies c Stephenson b Lawrence	. 0			
B 7	 7		B 4	4

1/77 2/111 3/112 4/147 5/189 6/286   326   1/14 2/16 3/22   (4 wkts.)   70
7/324 8/324 9/324   4/62

Somerset

G. G. Tordoff lbw b Thompson	 3	—	b Hitchcock	33
Yawar Saeed b Thompson	 19	—	b K. Dollery	0
J. Lawrence b Thompson	 4	—	c Spooner b K. Dollery	0
M. F. Tremlett c Spooner b Weeks	 29	—	b Hollies	89
P. B. Wight c Spooner b K. Dollery	 1	—	lbw b Hollies	39
C. F. Davey c Townsend b Thompson	.. 1	—	lbw b Hollies	12
H. W. Stephenson c Gardner b Hollies	.. 58	—	c Townsend b Hollies	34
J. Hilton not out	 10	—	c Weeks b Thompson	20
K. Palmer c Townsend b Hitchcock	.. 2	—	not out	12
J. W. McMahon c Gardner b Hitchcock	. 4	—	c Spooner b Thompson	0
B. Lobb b Hitchcock	 0	—	b Townsend	1
B 4, n-b 2	 6		B 8, l-b 8, n-b 2	18

1/4 2/22 3/30 4/31 5/42 6/73 7/121   137   1/4 2/4 3/85 4/175 5/180   258
8/129 9/137   6/187 7/229 8/255 9/257

Somerset Bowling

	O.	M.	R.	W.		O.	M.	R.	W.
Lobb	21	3	44	1	....	10	1	35	3
Yawar Saeed	12	1	40	0	....	6	1	21	0
Palmer	12	1	33	0					
Lawrence	38	12	67	6					
McMahon	13	2	41	0	....	4	1	10	1
Hilton	24	6	70	2					
Tordoff	4	0	24	0					

Warwickshire Bowling

	O.	M.	R.	W.		O.	M.	R.	W.
Thompson	12	2	28	4	....	9	1	22	2
K. Dollery	15	3	44	1	....	8	1	38	2
Hollies	21	10	33	1	....	32	11	71	4
Weeks	6	1	21	1	....	17	7	36	0
Hitchcock	9.1	7	5	3	....	19	7	52	1
					Townsend	8.5	0	21	1

Umpires: H. G. Baldwin and J. J. Hills.

At Romford, July 6, 7, 8. SOMERSET lost to ESSEX by five wickets.

At Portsmouth, July 9, 11, 12. SOMERSET lost to HAMPSHIRE by eight wickets.

SOMERSET v. WORCESTERSHIRE

At Taunton, July 13, 14, 15. Somerset won by nine wickets. For the first victory at their headquarters since June 1954, they were chiefly indebted to Wight, a West Indian, whose maiden Championship century occupied three and three-quarter hours. Lomax helped him add 150 for the fifth wicket in quick time, and lively methods by Stephenson put Somerset in the lead. Worcestershire were soon disturbed in their second innings by the determined seam bowling of Lobb, Biddulph, and Saeed. Losing their first three wickets for 24 they never recovered, but Jenkins stayed nearly an hour without being beaten. Stephenson, Somerset wicket-keeper, made eight catches in the match.

Worcestershire

L. Outschoorn lbw b Yawar Saeed	33	— c Stephenson b Lobb	0
J. Lister c Stephenson b Lobb	74	— c Stephenson b Lobb	6
D. W. Richardson c Stephenson b Lawrence	35	— c Wight b Biddulph	9
M. J. Horton c and b Lawrence	53	— b Yawar Saeed	56
G. Dews c Walker b Lobb	16	— c Wight b Yawar Saeed	11
R. G. Broadbent c Stephenson b Lobb	5	— c Stephenson b Yawar Saeed	0
T. Davies c Tremlett b Lawrence	8	— c and b Lawrence	5
R. O. Jenkins c Stephenson b Lobb	8	— not out	21
H. Yarnold c Stephenson b Biddulph	33	— b Lawrence	0
R. T. D. Perks b Biddulph	3	— lbw b Lawrence	14
R. Berry not out	23	— c sub b Lawrence	0
B 7, l-b 7	14	W 2	2
	305		**124**

1/57 2/136 3/145 4/162 5/169 6/193 7/242 8/245 9/262

1/0 2/11 3/24 4/70 5/71 6/88 7/98 8/98 9/124

Somerset

M. Walker run out	26		
J. Lawrence c Broadbent b Berry	32	— not out	24
M. F. Tremlett st Yarnold b Berry	29	— not out	20
P. B. Wight c Dews b Berry	106		
R. Smith c Davies b Horton	1	— c Broadbent b Perks	6
J. G. Lomax c Outschoorn b Horton	64		
H. W. Stephenson st Yarnold b Jenkins	68		
Yawar Saeed c Berry b Jenkins	19		
K. Biddulph run out	1		
J. W. McMahon not out	7		
B. Lobb c Dews b Jenkins	5		
B 6, l-b 12, n-b 4	22	L-b 2, w 1	3
	380	(1 wkt.)	**53**

1/58 2/69 3/113 4/118 5/268 6/292 7/361 8/367 9/368

1/18

Somerset Bowling

	O.	M.	R.	W.		O.	M.	R.	W.
Lobb	26	6	65	4	....	7	1	34	2
Biddulph	20.2	3	74	2	....	7	0	19	1
Yawar Saeed ..	10	4	25	1	....	11	2	46	3
Lomax	12	1	44	0	....	2	0	9	0
Lawrence	24	5	65	3	....	8.5	4	14	4
McMahon	9	4	18	0					

Worcestershire Bowling

	O.	M.	R.	W.		O.	M.	R.	W.
Perks	18	3	61	0	....	4	1	6	1
Outschoorn ...	10	2	36	0					
Jenkins	23.3	4	114	3					
Berry	39	14	71	3	....	2.5	0	25	0
Davies	2	0	11	0					
Horton	24	4	65	2	....	1	0	4	0
Richardson....						2	0	15	0

Umpires: P. Corrall and A. Skelding.

SOMERSET v. ESSEX

At Taunton, July 16, 18, 19. Drawn. After less than two hours' play on the second day through rain, first innings points became the main issue, and a keen struggle ended in favour of Somerset by nine runs. Wight gave another impressive demonstration of polished stroke-play, and was unfortunate to miss a second century in consecutive innings by only three runs. For Essex, Dodds drove and hooked in a delightful manner, and when Smith and Greensmith added 98 for the eighth wicket their hopes of getting in front were bright. Biddulph, an Essex-born pace bowler, turned the scales for Somerset by disposing of Smith. When Somerset batted again Tremlett completed 1,000 runs for the seventh time.

Somerset

G. G. Tordoff c Taylor b Smith	4		
F. L. Angell c Taylor b Ralph..........	31	— c Taylor b Preston	3
J. Lawrence c Taylor b Insole..........	77	— b Preston	4
M. F. Tremlett c Preston b Greensmith..	1	— c and b Insole	22
P. B. Wight c Preston b Ralph	97	— not out	35
C. F. Davey c Williams b Greensmith ..	16	— not out	33
H. W. Stephenson c Williams b Green-			
smith	5		
Yawar Saeed c Ralph b Preston	28		
K. Biddulph c Taylor b Ralph	1		
J. W. McMahon not out	10		
B. Lobb c Barker b Preston	1		
B 15, l-b 14	29	B 1, l-b 3	4
	300	(3 wkts.)	101

1/13 2/91 3/96 4/168 5/207 6/215   1/8 2/18 3/51
7/267 8/288 9/289

Essex

T. C. Dodds c Lawrence b Yawar Saeed....	94	W. T. Greensmith st Stephenson b Lawrence 52
G. Barker lbw b Lawrence	5	R. Ralph c Angell b McMahon .. 22
P. A. Gibb c Stephenson b Lobb .	0	K. C. Preston not out 0
C. C. P. Williams b Yawar Saeed .	21	
D. J. Insole c Tremlett b McMahon	29	B 5, l-b 11 16
R. Horsfall c Wight b Yawar Saeed	0	
B. Taylor b Yawar Saeed	2	1/22 2/29 3/99 4/148 5/154 291
R. Smith b Biddulph	50	6/156 7/160 8/258 9/291

Essex Bowling

	O.	M.	R.	W.	O.	M.	R.	W.
Preston	20.5	5	51	2	9	1	21	2
Smith	19	2	71	1	7	1	16	0
Ralph	23	3	51	3				
Insole	16	5	28	1	6	1	19	1
Greensmith	30	10	70	3				
Dodds					7	0	28	0
Barker					3	0	13	0

Somerset Bowling

	O.	M.	R.	W.
Lobb	17	0	57	1
Biddulph	16	2	55	1
Yawar Saeed	18	4	72	4
Lawrence	22	4	60	2
McMahon	28	13	28	2
Tremlett	1	0	3	0

Umpires: P. Corrall and A. Skelding.

SOMERSET v. YORKSHIRE

At Taunton, July 20, 21, 22. Yorkshire won by eight wickets. After conceding first innings points, Yorkshire fought back in exhilarating fashion and hit off the 285 runs required for victory in three and a half hours. Promoted to opening batsman, Close showed his aptitude for the task by scoring 143 out of 212 in 160 minutes. Wilson, who remained unbeaten for 109, never equalled Close in aggression, but the two left-handers mostly thwarted Somerset by their second wicket stand of 191. Splendid fast bowling by Trueman and Cowan were also important factors in Yorkshire's success. For Somerset, Angell figured in century stands for the first and second wicket, and Lawrence, whose leg-breaks earned him six wickets for 39, gained the best analysis in the match.

Somerset

G. G. Tordoff b Cowan	57	— b Trueman	28
F. L. Angell lbw b Trueman	90	— c Wilson b Cowan	8
J. Lawrence b Trueman	58	— run out	5
M. F. Tremlett b Cowan	6	— b Illingworth	42
P. B. Wight not out	33	— b Illingworth	25
J. G. Lomax b Illingworth	8	— c sub b Trueman	18
C. F. Davey b Cowan	0	— c Wilson b Illingworth	14
H. W. Stephenson c Binks b Trueman	10	— c Illingworth b Close	6
Yawar Saeed b Trueman	0	— lbw b Trueman	0
J. W. McMahon b Cowan	0	— b Cowan	2
B. Lobb b Cowan	0	— not out	1
B 5, l-b 12, w 8, n-b 1	26	N-b 3	3

1/109 2/211 3/228 4/242 5/259 6/260   288
7/275 8/275 9/288

1/33 2/38 3/42 4/87 5/94   152
6/116 7/141 8/141 9/144

Yorkshire

W. H. H. Sutcliffe b Lobb	4			
D. E. V. Padgett b Lobb	6	— not out	12	
J. V. Wilson c Tremlett b Lawrence	31	— not out	109	
E. Lester c Tordoff b Lobb	39			
D. B. Close st Stephenson b Lawrence	32	— c Davey b Lobb	143	
N. W. D. Yardley b Lawrence	17	— c Davey b Lobb	11	
R. Illingworth c and b Lawrence	10			
F. S. Trueman b Lawrence	5			
J. G. Binks c Lomax b Lawrence	1			
R. Appleyard b Lobb	4			
M. J. Cowan not out	1			
L-b 6, w 1	7	B 10	10	

1/11 2/16 3/78 4/83 5/136 6/137   157   1/21 2/212   (2 wkts.) 285
7/143 8/145 9/149

Yorkshire Bowling

	O.	M.	R.	W.		O.	M.	R.	W.
Trueman	30	11	39	4	....	15	1	49	3
Cowan	39	8	75	5	....	18	4	53	2
Appleyard	18	2	75	0					
Illingworth	25	9	51	1	....	10	1	31	3
Close	7	2	22	0	....	6	2	16	1

Somerset Bowling

	O.	M.	R.	W.		O.	M.	R.	W.
Lobb	16	3	60	4	....	11	3	38	2
Yawar Saeed	9	1	33	0	....	7	0	37	0
Lawrence	16	4	39	6	....	22	5	68	0
McMahon	9	2	18	0	....	22.4	5	102	0
					Wight	7	0	30	0

Umpires: Harry Elliott (Derbyshire) and W. T. Jones.

At Nottingham, July 27, 28, 29. SOMERSET lost to NOTTINGHAMSHIRE by 61 runs.

At Bristol, July 30, August 1, 2. SOMERSET drew with GLOUCESTERSHIRE.

At Northampton, August 3, 4, 5. SOMERSET lost to NORTHAMPTONSHIRE by eight wickets.

At Worcester, August 6, 8, 9. SOMERSET drew with WORCESTERSHIRE.

SOMERSET v. SURREY

At Weston-super-Mare, August 10, 11. Surrey won by an innings and 100 runs. The Somerset batsmen were no match for Surrey's bowlers on a spiteful pitch. Surrey did well to score 227, but they owed most to May who gave a delightful display against the lifting and turning ball. Then came a dramatic breakdown, Somerset being dismissed for the lowest total of the season. They found Lock and A. Bedser almost unplayable. Lock did the hat-trick for the first time in his career when he dismissed McMahon and Lobb at the end of the first innings and Angell with his first ball when Somerset followed on 191 behind. Only an hour and a quarter was needed on the second day, Lock and A. Bedser again routing the home county. Lock took ten for 54 in the match and A. Bedser nine for 46.

Surrey

T. H. Clark c Tremlett b Lomax ..	6	G. A. R. Lock lbw b Lobb	......	36
M. J. Stewart c Angell b Tordoff...	14	W. S. Surridge c Tordoff b Lobb	.	22
P. B. H. May c Angell b McMahon	93	P. J. Loader c Tordoff b McMahon		17
B. Constable c Lomax b McMahon	1	A. V. Bedser not out	....	1
K. Barrington c Tremlett b McMahon	1	L-b 1	....	1
E. A. Bedser c Angell b McMahon	31			—
A. J. McIntyre c Angell b McMahon	4	1/6 2/42 3/47 4/61 5/135 6/139		227
		7/170 8/190 9/226		

Somerset

F. L. Angell c Surridge b A. Bedser	....	1	— c May b Lock	0
G. G. Tordoff c Lock b A. Bedser	......	13	— c Loader b A. Bedser	19
J. Lawrence b Loader	....	1	— c McIntyre b Lock	9
M. F. Tremlett c Lock b A. Bedser	.....	11	— c Clark b Lock	26
G. L. Williams c May b A. Bedser	.....	0	— c Surridge b Lock	1
P. B. Wight c McIntyre b Lock	....	5	— c Lock b A. Bedser	7
M. Walker c May b Lock	....	0	— b A. Bedser	0
J. G. Lomax not out	....	1	— c Clark b Lock	13
H. W. Stephenson c McIntyre b A. Bedser		0	— c Constable b A. Bedser ...	0
J. W. McMahon b Lock	....	0	— c Clark b Lock	5
B. Lobb st McIntyre b Lock	....	0	— not out	0
B 4	....	4	B 9, l-b 1	10
		—		—
1/10 2/15 3/21 4/21 5/31 6/35 7/35		36	1/0 2/32 3/32 4/38 5/45	91
8/35 9/36			6/49 7/64 8/74 9/91	

Somerset Bowling

	O.	M.	R.	W.		O.	M.	R.	W.
Lobb	20.3	3	64	2					
Lomax	9	3	16	1					
McMahon	29	11	79	6					
Tordoff	7	3	14	1					
Lawrence	2	1	10	0					
Walker	9	0	43	0					

Surrey Bowling

	O.	M.	R.	W.		O.	M.	R.	W.
A. Bedser......	9	3	14	5	....	14	5	32	4
Loader	6	1	13	1					
Lock	3.5	2	5	4	....	13.4	3	49	6

Umpires: E. Davies and J. J. Hills.

SOMERSET v. GLAMORGAN

At Weston-super-Mare, August 13, 15, 16. Glamorgan won by an innings and 15 runs. The fast-medium bowling of Shepherd, who claimed six wickets in each innings on a lively pitch, proved too much for Somerset. Glamorgan took advantage of loose bowling on the first day, bright stands coming from Pressdee and Ward, and Watkins and Clift. Watkins hit McMahon for three 6's in one over. Somerset broke down and followed on 163 behind. Glamorgan tried hard to end the match in two days, but after they claimed the extra half-hour rain intervened. The match was over inside an hour on the third day. The victory took Glamorgan from the bottom of the Championship table.

Glamorgan

W. E. Jones c Lawrence b Lobb ..	7		H. G. Davies b McMahon	....	5
J. Pressdee b McMahon	 43		D. Shepherd c Tordoff b Walker ..		17
D. Ward c Lawrence b Walker	... 34		H. D. Davies b McMahon	....	4
P. B. Clift b Walker	 45				
J. Pleass b Lobb	 28		B 3, l-b 2	....	5
A. J. Watkins c Williams b Walker	48				
B. R. Edrich not out	 23		1/9 2/85 3/85 4/115 5/197		271
A. Rees b Walker	 12		6/217 7/241 8/246 9/263		

Somerset

G. G. Tordoff b Shepherd	....	5	— b Watkins	....	1
F. L. Angell b Shepherd	....	4	— lbw b Shepherd	....	6
J. Lawrence c Ward b Shepherd	......	6	— c Clift b Shepherd	....	65
M. F. Tremlett c Pressdee b Shepherd	...	17	— b Shepherd	....	10
P. B. Wight c H. G. Davies b Watkins	..	1	— c Clift b Shepherd	....	16
G. L. Williams b Shepherd	....	24	— c Edrich b H. D. Davies	..	1
M. Walker b Shepherd	....	4	— b Shepherd	....	0
J. G. Lomax b Watkins	....	17	— b Shepherd	....	19
H. W. Stephenson st H. G. Davies b Pressdee	....	13	— c H. G. Davies b Watkins	..	18
J. W. McMahon not out	....	2	— c Edrich b Watkins	....	8
B. Lobb c H. G. Davies b Pressdee	.....	0	— not out	....	0
B 9, l-b 3, n-b 3	....	15	W 2, n-b 2	....	4
1/9 2/18 3/27 4/42 5/42 6/51 7/81		108	1/6 2/15 3/31 4/69 5/80		148
8/106 9/106			6/81 7/111 8/134 9/146		

Somerset Bowling

	O.	M.	R.	W.	O.	M.	R.	W.
Lobb	15	4	52	2				
Lomax	6	2	14	0				
McMahon	33.1	12	103	3				
Lawrence	2	0	11	0				
Walker	25	7	76	5				
Tordoff	2	0	10	0				

Glamorgan Bowling

	O.	M.	R.	W.		O.	M.	R.	W.
Shepherd	28	11	42	6	.....	33.3	15	49	6
H. D. Davies ..	2	0	3	0	....	3	0	14	1
Watkins	24	9	47	2	....	33	11	73	3
Pressdee	3	2	1	2	....	11	6	8	0

Umpires: J. S. Buller and A. Skelding.

SOMERSET v. HAMPSHIRE

At Weston-super-Mare, August 17, 18. Hampshire won by 264 runs. Remarkable bowling by Shackleton gave them their decisive victory. He accomplished one of the best performances in the history of the game in taking eight wickets for four runs in 11.1 overs in the first innings and he followed with six for 25 when Somerset batted again. Rain before the start and during lunch restricted the first day's play when Hampshire did fairly well until the spin took effect. Then Hilton did the hat-trick for the first time, dismissing Harrison, Shackleton and Burden. The pitch was extremely awkward and the Somerset batsmen were helpless. They were all out in 74 minutes and Hampshire, leading by 117, scored readily. Rayment made his only hundred of the season and Horton and Harrison helped in good stands. Somerset, needing 363, again failed dismally, only Stephenson offering resistance with a hard-hit 52.

Hampshire

J. R. Gray c Lawrence b Hilton	43	— b McMahon	4
R. E. Marshall c Stephenson b Yawar Saeed	5	— c Lobb b Yawar Saeed	12
H. Horton c Lawrence b Hilton	43	— b Tordoff	59
A. W. H. Rayment c Lawrence b McMahon	12	— c Tordoff b McMahon	104
N. H. Rogers c Williams b Hilton	2	— c Williams b Tordoff	10
H. M. Barnard b McMahon	19	— b McMahon	5
L. Harrison c Williams b Hilton	9	— not out	35
P. J. Sainsbury not out	13		
D. Shackleton st Stephenson b Hilton	0		
M. D. Burden b Hilton	0	— b Hilton	4
V. H. D. Cannings c Hilton b McMahon	0		
B	8	B 7, l-b 5	12

1/11 2/78 3/91 4/94 5/126 6/136   154
7/149 8/149 9/149

1/12 2/16   (7 wkts., dec.) 245
3/107 4/127 5/136 6/239
7/245

Somerset

G. G. Tordoff b Shackleton	0	— c Marshall b Shackleton	0
G. L. Williams c Rogers b Shackleton	2	— c Burden b Shackleton	2
J. Lawrence lbw b Shackleton	0	— c Gray b Sainsbury	4
M. F. Tremlett c Gray b Shackleton	8	— b Shackleton	0
P. B. Wight c Marshall b Shackleton	2	— c and b Burden	10
J. G. Lomax c Rogers b Sainsbury	0	— c Rayment b Shackleton	20
H. W. Stephenson not out	18	— c Horton b Sainsbury	52
Yawar Saeed c Barnard b Shackleton	0	— c Barnard b Shackleton	0
J. Hilton b Shackleton	0	— b Shackleton	0
J. W. McMahon run out	1	— not out	9
B. Lobb c Rayment b Shackleton	0	— c Burden b Sainsbury	0
L-b	6	L-b 1	1

1/0 2/0 3/3 4/10 5/10 6/20 7/20   37
8/26 9/27

1/0 2/3 3/4 4/16 5/16   98
6/81 7/81 8/81 9/89

Somerset Bowling

	O.	M.	R.	W.		O.	M.	R.	W.
Lobb	11	4	23	0	....	6	1	12	0
Yawar Saeed	7	2	16	1	....	5	0	14	1
Hilton	24	7	49	6	....	12.2	0	50	1
McMahon	27.3	10	58	3	....	32	2	122	3
Lomax						2	1	2	0
Tordoff						11	1	33	2

Hampshire Bowling

	O.	M.	R.	W.		O.	M.	R.	W.
Shackleton	11.1	7	4	8	....	16	7	25	6
Cannings	4	2	5	0	....	4	2	3	0
Sainsbury	7	2	22	1	....	13.4	0	63	3
Burden						2	0	6	1

Umpires: A. Skelding and J. S. Buller.

At Manchester, August 20, 22, 23. SOMERSET lost to LANCASHIRE by an innings and 79 runs.

At Chesterfield, August 24, 25, 26. SOMERSET lost to Derbyshire by 115 runs.

SOMERSET v. NORTHAMPTONSHIRE

At Taunton, August 27, 29, 30. Drawn. Somerset nearly pulled off an unexpected victory after Northamptonshire had lost only five wickets in the match. The pitch gave bowlers no help and batsmen were in complete command.

Northamptonshire scored briskly, Brookes and Arnold leading the way with an opening stand of 230. Brookes, missed first ball, stayed four and three-quarter hours for 177 and Arnold's 122 in three and a quarter hours was the highest of his career. After losing three wickets cheaply to Tyson, Somerset recovered, Tremlett and Wight adding 130. Tremlett, missed twice, batted just over five and a half hours for 153. Brookes and Livingston put on 156 when Northamptonshire batted again 91 ahead. Set to get 282 in 205 minutes, Somerset made a fine effort but failed by four runs. Twelve were needed in the final over. Stephenson and Wight, adding 112 in an hour, gave Somerset their chance.

Northamptonshire

D. Brookes b Lawrence	177	—	not out	80
P. Arnold c Wight b Lawrence	122	—	c Stephenson b Lobb	4
L. Livingston b Lobb	36	—	c Wight b McMahon	79
G. E. Tribe not out	47			
D. Barrick not out	29	—	not out	18
B 4, l-b 4	8		B 7, l-b 2	9

1/230 2/299 3/361   (3 wkts., dec.) 419   1/9 2/165   (2 wkts., dec.) 190

R. Subba Row, B. Reynolds, V. Broderick, F. H. Tyson, R. W. Clarke and J. Webster did not bat.

Somerset

F. L. Angell b Tribe	28	—	c Tribe b Subba Row	54
M. Walker b Tyson	4	—	b Webster	8
J. Lawrence b Tyson	4	—	c Clarke b Tribe	6
M. F. Tremlett c Brookes b Broderick	153	—	c and b Clarke	49
P. B. Wight b Tribe	67	—	c Subba Row b Tribe	68
G. G. Tordoff b Tyson	12	—	not out	7
J. G. Lomax b Tyson	3	—	not out	3
H. W. Stephenson c Barrick b Tribe	27	—	c Brookes b Tribe	65
Yawar Saeed run out	8	—	st Reynolds b Tribe	4
J. W. McMahon c Webster b Tribe	3			
B. Lobb not out	1			
B 4, l-b 14	18		B 9, l-b 4, w 1	14

1/7 2/15 3/53 4/183 5/223 6/235   328   1/9 2/96 3/139   (7 wkts.) 278
7/307 8/322 9/325   4/251 5/262 6/264 7/267

Somerset Bowling

	O.	M.	R.	W.	O.	M.	R.	W.
Lobb	21	2	88	1	12	0	40	1
Yawar Saeed	15	0	78	0	9	1	30	0
Lomax	11	0	36	0	8	0	47	0
Lawrence	20	2	100	2	5.3	0	24	0
McMahon	15	2	48	0	11	0	40	1
Tordoff	4	0	27	0				
Walker	6	1	34	0				

Northamptonshire Bowling

	O.	M.	R.	W.	O.	M.	R.	W.
Tyson	26	1	76	4	11	0	45	0
Webster	15	1	53	0	8	1	27	1
Tribe	31	7	86	4	15	1	64	4
Clarke	14	2	40	0	12	2	50	1
Subba Row	1	0	8	0	7	1	29	1
Broderick	17.3	6	47	1	3	0	27	0
Barrick					4	0	22	0

Umpires: E. Davies and A. E. Pothecary.

At Hove, August 31, September 1. SOMERSET lost to SUSSEX by nine wickets.

SURREY

PATRON—HER MAJESTY THE QUEEN

President—MARSHAL OF THE ROYAL AIR FORCE LORD TEDDER

Secretary—B. K. CASTOR, Kennington Oval, London, S.E.11

Captain—W. STUART SURRIDGE

P. B. H. May   County badge   A. J. McIntyre

Surrey, desperately pursued by Yorkshire, won the Championship for the fourth consecutive season with Stuart Surridge as their captain, a feat only twice previously accomplished under the same leader—Yorkshire (A. B. Sellers) 1937–46 and Nottinghamshire (Alfred Shaw) 1883–86. Moreover, Surrey set up new records for 28 matches with their total number of points reaching 284 and their number of victories 23.

Yorkshire, too, surpassed the previous best in both instances, but they simply could not hold Surrey whose objective throughout the season was decisive results. In these days when so many sides make first innings points and immunity from defeat their first consideration it was most refreshing to find Surrey going through the summer without once being engaged in a drawn match. They played 34 matches, won 27 and lost seven. If winning the toss was a secret to success Surrey would have failed miserably, as between them Surridge and May lost it 23 times in the 34 matches.

Surrey began by winning their first 12 engagements. These included two victories against Cambridge University and one against M.C.C. Their first defeat came in the middle of June in the return match with Yorkshire at Leeds. The second setback provided the sensation of the season when on July 12th the lowly Kent team overthrew Surrey at The Oval, but all the time Surrey stood at the top of the table. Indeed only for four days during the four months did Surrey yield the first position to Yorkshire (at times they were bracketed together) and that was at the end of July following defeat by Warwickshire at Coventry.

Later, in the absence of May, Laker and Lock who were

engaged in the final Test, Surrey failed against Northamptonshire at Northampton and after they had clinched the Championship against Sussex at The Oval on August 26, they suffered an anticlimax losing two of their last three matches to Hampshire at Bournemouth and The Rest at The Oval. Their other defeat was at the hands of the South Africans when to the delight of everyone associated with Surrey, their Patron, the Queen, attended a match at The Oval for the first time.

Again Surrey owed their success mainly to their brilliant work in the field, where Surridge once more set a wonderful example by his enthusiastic and enterprising leadership as well as his splendid catching. As many as seven Surrey players appeared for England (Yorkshire provided six), but thanks to their capable understudies, Surrey were usually able to fill the gaps adequately, though for the most part the batting was thin in the absence of May.

The bowling averages clearly revealed Surrey's strength. Between them the four England players, Alec Bedser, Lock, Laker and Loader took 422 wickets in the Championship compared with 375 in 1954. Although Alec Bedser no longer claimed a regular place in the Test XI—he played only at Manchester—his value to Surrey remained undiminished for he was consistently good. Lock enjoyed his best season, taking altogether 216 wickets.

After his success in Australia, May returned in his best form, but his appearances for Surrey were restricted as he had the honour of leading England in all five Tests against South Africa. He headed both the first-class and the Surrey batting averages. Two young batsmen, Barrington and Stewart, scored many more runs than hitherto and firmly established themselves in the county side. A solidly built cricketer with a deadly aim in the field, Barrington hit the ball really hard. He began the summer so well that he was chosen for the first two Tests, but although he made top score in England's disappointing first innings at Lord's he did not retain his place. Still, Barrington was always a potential run-getter and at the end of the season the Cricket Writers awarded him their trophy for the most promising young player of the year.

Stewart had to wait his opportunity, but he soon became a regular member of the team. He hit his two centuries, 118 against Kent at Blackheath and 104 against Leicestershire at The Oval, in successive matches in the first week in July. Like Barrington, Stewart showed himself to be a forceful and enterprising batsman, and both stood out in this most excellent set of fielders. In fact, in all matches, Stewart (52 catches), shared with Surridge (56) and Lock (48) the honours for snapping up close-to-the-wicket chances.

McIntyre not only enjoyed a highly successful benefit year financially, but he celebrated it with many fine performances with the bat as well as behind the stumps. His aggressiveness in the middle of the order often helped to turn the issue of a match and he gained the distinction of being the season's leading wicket-keeper with 85 victims. When Evans was injured, McIntyre proved a worthy deputy at Leeds as the England wicket-keeper, but, in turn, McIntyre was hurt and consequently the selectors would not risk playing him in the final Test.

Constable alone took part in all the Championship matches, scoring 1029 runs which compared favourably with his work of the previous summer. At first, Surrey depended on Clark and Fletcher as their opening batsmen, but neither flourished on the lively Oval pitches. Partly because of hip trouble, Clark played in six fewer matches and his aggregate fell by nearly 800 runs, a factor which was offset by the advance of Barrington and Stewart, but there were important occasions when Clark took wickets with his off-breaks. Similarly, Eric Bedser did useful work as an all-rounder when he returned to the side midway through the season.

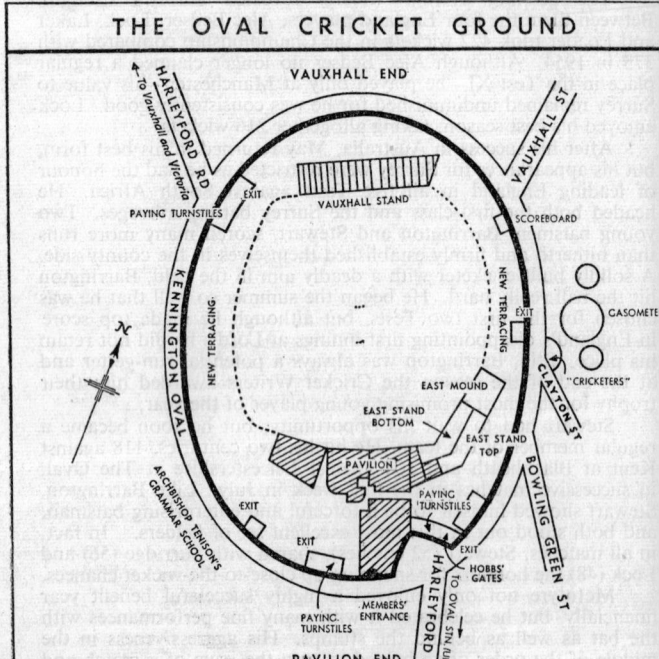

SURREY RESULTS

All First-Class Matches—Played 34, Won 27, Lost 7
County Championship Matches—Played 28, Won 23, Lost 5

COUNTY CHAMPIONSHIP AVERAGES
BATTING

	Birthplace	Mtchs.	Inns.	Not Outs	Runs	100's	Highest Inns.	Aver
P. B. H. May ...	*Reading*	16	26	4	921	2	122*	41.86
K. F. Barrington.	*Reading*	25	38	6	1262	2	135*	39.43
M. J. Stewart ...	*Herne Hill*	20	36	5	923	2	118	29.77
A. J. McIntyre ..	*Kennington*	23	34	6	807	1	110	28.82
J. C. Laker	*Bradford*	24	28	5	613	0	78*	26.65
B. Constable ...	*Molesey*	28	45	6	1029	2	132	26.38
D. W. G. Fletcher	*Sutton*	17	31	3	726	0	84	25.92
E. A. Bedser	*Reading*	18	28	3	637	0	79	25.48
D. F. Cox	*Bermondsey*	6	8	1	147	0	57	21.00
R. Swetman	*Croydon*	5	7	1	116	0	36	19.33
P. J. Loader ...	*Wallington*	17	20	4	307	0	81	19.18
G. A. R. Lock ..	*Limpsfield*	22	24	5	351	0	55	18.47
R. C. E. Pratt ..	*Balham*	12	19	0	333	0	43	17.52
T. H. Clark ...	*Luton*	20	35	0	596	0	87	17.02
W. S. Surridge ..	*Herne Hill*	25	32	5	291	0	26*	10.77
A. V. Bedser ...	*Reading*	26	26	17	92	0	19*	10.22

Also batted: M. D. Willett (*Norwood*) 25, H. R. A. Kelleher (*Bermondsey*)
played in three matches but did not bat.

* Signifies not out.

BOWLING

	Overs	Maidens	Runs	Wickets	Average
D. F. Cox	70.5	19	163	14	11.64
G. A. R. Lock	905	336	1840	149	12.34
H. R. A. Kelleher	74	15	179	12	14.91
P. J. Loader	408.1	95	893	54	16.53
A. V. Bedser	882	247	1980	117	16.92
J. C. Laker	846.4	274	1850	102	18.13
E. A. Bedser	288.3	84	672	36	18.66
T. H. Clark	145.2	36	341	18	18.94
W. S. Surridge	280.4	67	683	26	26.26

Also bowled: K. F. Barrington 6.5—0—42—0; B. Constable 8—0—47—0;
R. C. E. Pratt 6—4—8—0.

Amateurs.—P. B. H. May and W. S. Surridge.

At Cambridge, April 30, May 2, 3. SURREY beat CAMBRIDGE UNIVERSITY by an
innings and 70 runs.

At Lord's, May 4, 5, 6. SURREY beat M.C.C. by seven wickets.

SURREY v. GLOUCESTERSHIRE

At The Oval, May 7, 9, 10. Surrey won by eight wickets. In a match
dominated by bowlers, Lock and Loader served Surrey admirably. Rain the day
before the game began and a well-grassed pitch provided ideal conditions for
them especially against batsmen who apart from Mortimore—he hit five of his
six 4's from Bedser—showed little initiative. For Surrey, Barrington, Surridge

and Loader revealed welcome enterprise. A blow on the head while fielding caused Graveney to bat at number five in Gloucestershire's second innings and he and Crapp, in a bold stand of 71, averted an innings defeat. On the last day Surrey, after taking the last five wickets for the addition of 21, began the task of scoring 32 with a heavy thunderstorm approaching. In the quest for runs they lost their opening pair in the first over and they still wanted three when the rain came, but Constable promptly hooked Cook to the boundary to settle the issue.

Gloucestershire

D. M. Young c May b Bedser	20	— c McIntyre b Loader	4
T. W. Graveney c Lock b Loader	1	— c and b Lock	42
G. M. Emmett lbw b Lock	16	— run out	12
C. A. Milton c Surridge b Bedser	22	— b Lock	14
J. F. Crapp c McIntyre b Loader	7	— c Surridge b Laker	32
G. E. Lambert c Clark b Lock	18	— run out	19
J. Mortimore c Clark b Lock	30	— b Loader	3
P. Rochford c Constable b Lock	4	— b Lock	5
C. Cook b Loader	1	— st McIntyre b Lock	2
B. D. Wells b Loader	5	— c Loader b Lock	0
F. P. McHugh not out	0	— not out	1
B 1, w 1	2	L-b 3	3

1/4 2/33 3/37 4/47 5/78 6/86   126   1/6 2/28 3/35 4/106   137
7/115 8/122 9/122   5/106 6/121 7/132 8/134
                                     9/134

Surrey

T. H. Clark c Rochford b Lambert	8	— c Rochford b Lambert	0
D. G. W. Fletcher c Rochford b McHugh	18	— b Lambert	11
P. B. H. May c Crapp b Wells	8	— not out	11
B. Constable c Rochford b Lambert	19	— not out	11
K. Barrington c Emmett b Mortimore	46		
A. J. McIntyre b McHugh	19		
J. C. Laker c Graveney b Lambert	36		
W. S. Surridge c Graveney b Wells	25		
G. A. R. Lock c Rochford b Cook	0		
A. V. Bedser not out	5		
P. J. Loader b Cook	39		
B 6, l-b 1, n-b 2	9		

1/8 2/36 3/42 4/107 5/107 6/153   232   1/11 2/14   (2 wkts.)   33
7/171 8/184 9/188

Surrey Bowling

	O.	M.	R.	W.		O.	M.	R.	W.
Bedser	19	3	52	2	....	16	6	22	0
Loader	15.1	6	27	4	....	23	5	42	2
Lock	23	7	45	4	....	27.1	17	21	5
Laker						24	10	43	1
Surridge						1	0	6	0

Gloucestershire Bowling

	O.	M.	R.	W.		O.	M.	R.	W.
Lambert	30	7	65	3	....	3	0	16	2
McHugh	27	5	63	2	....	1	0	7	0
Wells	17	3	53	2					
Cook	18.4	8	25	2	....	2.1	1	10	0
Mortimore	5	0	17	1					

Umpires: F. Chester and A. E. Pothecary.

SURREY v. SOMERSET

At The Oval, May 14, 16. Surrey won by an innings and four runs. Not unexpectedly, the Champions outplayed the bottom county. The match was a triumph for Lock, who took eleven wickets for 78 runs. The pitch was damp enough to help bowlers and Lock acquired lift as well as spin. Wight resisted the rising ball for two hours, but none of the Somerset batsmen attempted venture-some methods. At first Lomax and Lobb bowled well for Somerset, but when tiring they were punished by Fletcher, who excelled with the hook and cut. Consequently Surrey led by 12 runs with seven wickets standing at the end of the first day and strong hitting by Barrington, McIntyre and Surridge put them in an almost invincible position. Somerset collapsed so badly when batting again that seven men were out for 47 before Tremlett and Hilton, by bold methods, added 56 in the visitors' best stand of a one-sided match.

Somerset

G. G. Tordoff c Clark b Laker	18	—	c McIntyre b Bedser	0
J. G. Lomax c Surridge b Lock	12	—	c Laker b Lock	10
J. Lawrence b May b Lock	4	—	b Lock	11
P. B. Wight not out	32	—	c and b Lock	17
R. Smith c Laker b Lock	14	—	c Laker b Lock	1
M. F. Tremlett b Bedser	3	—	b Laker	37
L. Pickles lbw b Lock	1	—	c Barrington b Lock	0
H. W. Stephenson c Laker b Bedser	9	—	c Clark b Laker	4
J. Hilton c Clark b Bedser	3	—	c McIntyre b Bedser	29
J. W. McMahon b Lock	0	—	c and b Laker	7
B. Lobb c Bedser b Lock	0	—	not out	1
B 1, l-b 2	3		L-b 4	4
	99			121

1/31 2/37 3/37 4/72 5/81 6/82
7/95 8/98 9/99

1/0 2/16 3/33 4/37
5/42 6/42 7/47 8/103 9/119

Surrey

T. H. Clark c Tremlett b Lomax	3	W. S. Surridge c Hilton b Lobb	25
D. G. W. Fletcher run out	62	G. A. R. Lock c Tordoff b Lobb	0
P. B. H. May c Tremlett b Lobb	11	P. J. Loader b McMahon	4
B. Constable lbw b Lobb	8	A. V. Bedser not out	3
K. Barrington b McMahon	64	B 6, l-b 2	8
A. J. McIntyre c Stephenson b McMahon	30		224
J. C. Laker c Lomax b McMahon	6	1/6 2/25 3/47 4/112 5/161	
		6/173 7/204 8/204 9/219	

Surrey Bowling

	O.	M.	R.	W.	O.	M.	R.	W.
Bedser	17	6	33	3	12	4	20	2
Loader	4	0	15	0				
Laker	16	8	20	1	23.3	9	44	3
Lock	21.4	11	25	6	24	8	53	5
Clark	2	0	3	0				

Somerset Bowling

	O.	M.	R.	W.
Lomax	15	4	30	1
Lobb	16	2	48	4
McMahon	25	8	59	4
Hilton	18	4	61	0
Lawrence	3	0	11	0
Tremlett	3	1	7	0

Umpires: H. G. Baldwin and A. Skelding.

At Ilford, May 18, 19, 20. SURREY beat ESSEX by five wickets.

At Leicester, May 21, 23, 24. SURREY beat LEICESTERSHIRE by seven wickets.

SURREY v. LANCASHIRE

At The Oval, May 25, 26, 27. Surrey won by an innings and 143 runs. They gave a vastly superior all-round display against a disappointing Lancashire side. On a pitch which helped him to move the ball sharply, Bedser caused a collapse at the start, taking four wickets for seven runs in one spell. Apart from Statham, Lancashire also bowled below form and Surrey quickly established a mastery. Barrington overshadowed May in an unbroken fourth wicket stand of 218 and his 135 was then the best of his career. He completed his hundred in two hours twenty-five minutes and altogether hit nineteen 4's. May spent five hours thirty-five minutes over 122. Lancashire again failed in their second innings, but Jordan, a young wicket-keeper, made a promising Championship debut.

Lancashire

J. T. Ikin, b Bedser	19	— b Loader	2
S. Smith c May b Loader	2	— c May b Bedser	2
G. A. Edrich lbw b Bedser	4	— c Surridge b Lock	23
C. Washbrook b Bedser	1	— c Lock b Bedser	18
A. Wharton b Surridge	0	— c Surridge b Lock	31
K. Grieves st McIntyre b Bedser	13	— lbw b Lock	6
M. J. Hilton c May b Bedser	1	— c Surridge b Lock	0
J. B. Statham b Surridge	13	— c McIntyre b Laker	1
J. Jordan c Lock b Surridge	9	— c Surridge b Laker	11
R. Tattersall not out	2	— not out	1
T. Greenough st McIntyre b Bedser	14	— c Surridge b Laker	0
B 11, l-b 5	16	B 11, l-b 1, w 1	13
	—		—
	94		108

1/14 2/23 3/26 4/27 5/27 6/28
7/63 8/63 9/79

1/3 2/5 3/34 4/76
5/84 6/105 7/105 8/106
9/106

Surrey

T. H. Clark b Statham	33	K. Barrington not out	135	
D. G. W. Fletcher b Statham	14	B 1, l-b 3, n-b 1	5	
P. B. H. May not out	122			
B. Constable lbw b Tattersall	36	1/43 2/54 3/127	(3 wkts., dec.)	345

A. J. McIntyre, J. C. Laker, W. S. Surridge, G. A. R. Lock, P. J. Loader and A. V. Bedser did not bat.

Surrey Bowling

	O.	M.	R.	W.	O.	M.	R.	W.
Bedser	24.1	13	36	6	 13	2	23	2
Loader	11	4	20	1	 11	3	20	1
Surridge	15	5	22	3	 5	1	9	0
Lock					18	9	17	4
Laker					20	10	26	3

Lancashire Bowling

	O.	M.	R.	W.
Statham	36	10	92	2
Wharton	12	4	32	0
Tattersall	44	16	84	1
Hilton	35	11	93	0
Greenough	12	3	34	0
Ikin	3	1	5	0

Umpires: F. S. Lee and F. Chester.

At Nottingham, May 28, 30, 31. SURREY beat NOTTINGHAMSHIRE by eight wickets.

SURREY v. GLAMORGAN

At The Oval, June 1, 2, 3. Surrey won by eight wickets. After two days of tediously slow cricket, bold hitting by Fletcher and McIntyre carried them to their seventh successive victory with fifty minutes to spare. Excellent fielding and defensive bowling so tied down Surrey on the first day that even May found few opportunities to display his strokes. After a bright start by Parkhouse, Glamorgan failed completely against controlled swing-bowling on the second morning and were all out in under two hours. Led by Parkhouse, they gave a more resolute exhibition after following-on 183 behind and until McConnon and Davies came together concentrated on defence. Surrey, left two hours twenty minutes in which to score 105, also had to contend with the rain, which fell heavily while Fletcher and McIntyre hit off the last 55 runs in twenty minutes.

Surrey

T. H. Clark b Watkins	14	— b Watkins	30
D. G. W. Fletcher c Davies b Lewis	1	— not out	46
P. B. H. May b Watkins	79	— c Parkhouse b Wooller	1
B. Constable lbw b Wooller	1		
K. Barrington b Wooller	31		
A. J. McIntyre c Davies b Wooller	6	— not out	23
R. C. E. Pratt b Watkins	26		
J. C. Laker c Davies b Watkins	19		
W. S. Surridge lbw b Watkins	17		
G. A. R. Lock c Ward b Lewis	18		
A. V. Bedser not out	16		
B 7, l-b 4	11	B 5	5

1/2 2/29 3/44 4/122 5/130 6/134   239   1/45 2/50   (2 wkts.) 105
7/180 8/189 9/200

Glamorgan

W. G. A. Parkhouse c Lock b Bedser	23	— lbw b Surridge	81
W. E. Jones c Laker b Bedser	2	— c and b Bedser	5
B. Hedges c Lock b Bedser	10	— b Surridge	16
J. Pressdee c McIntyre b Surridge	3	— c May b Surridge	38
A. J. Watkins b Surridge	1	— lbw b Clark	22
W. Wooller c Lock b Bedser	13	— lbw b Lock	11
D. Ward lbw b Bedser	2	— lbw b Surridge	15
J. E. McConnon lbw b Surridge	0	— b Lock	29
H. G. Davies lbw b Surridge	0	— c McIntyre b Clark	32
D. J. Shepherd c Lock b Surridge	0	— c Constable b Surridge	8
K. H. Lewis not out	0	— not out	8
L-b 2	2	B 8, l-b 13, n-b 1	22

1/25 2/26 3/37 4/39 5/41 6/52   56   1/17 2/65 3/150 4/151   287
7/53 8/53 9/53   5/183 6/197 7/223 8/266
                            9/266

Glamorgan Bowling

	O.	M.	R.	W.		O.	M.	R.	W.
Lewis	21.3	2	58	2	....	7	0	16	0
Shepherd	19	5	36	0	....	6	2	22	0
Wooller	24	9	61	3	....	6	0	30	1
Watkins	28	7	63	5	....	5	0	32	1
McConnon	6	2	10	0					

Surrey Bowling

	O.	M.	R.	W.		O.	M.	R.	W.
Bedser	18.5	7	30	5	...	40	14	62	1
Surridge	18	8	24	5	...	43.4	14	93	5
Laker						25	11	35	0
Lock						38	22	45	2
Pratt						5	4	3	0
Clark						14	3	27	2

Umpires: H. Elliott (Lancashire) and W. F. Price.

SURREY v. YORKSHIRE
(A. J. McIntyre's Benefit)

At The Oval, June 4, 6, 7. Surrey won by 41 runs. The meeting of these two great rivals for the Championship drew crowds of Test match proportions on the first two days and altogether 45,000 paid, a collection for McIntyre on the Saturday yielding £535. With the ground saturated, Yardley sent in Surrey and they were all out in two and a half hours, the batsmen being helpless against Appleyard, whose rising off-spinners made his leg-trap a persistent danger. With Hutton bowled for a "duck" in his second consecutive innings, Yorkshire, for whom Watson batted admirably, took three hours to gain the lead. Every ball mattered and no one complained that six hours' cricket on the first day yielded only 193 runs. Lock bowled magnificently for Surrey and in dismissing Lowson made a marvellous right-handed return catch while lying across the pitch. Batting a second time, Surrey exercised great care, Fletcher taking four and a half hours over 84. May alone showed enterprise. More rain changed the conditions on the last day and when play was resumed after an hour's delay, Yorkshire themselves were trapped on a difficult pitch. Bedser always troubled them, but Sutcliffe showed great defensive skill for two hours twenty minutes until Bedser brought off a grand left-handed return catch. The match provided something unique in the appearance of the two current England captains, May and Hutton, serving under their two official County captains, Surridge and Yardley.

Surrey

T. H. Clark c Lowson b Trueman	7	— c Booth b Trueman 33
D. G. W. Fletcher c Sutcliffe b Appleyard	12	— c Wardle b Close 84
P. B. H. May c Trueman b Appleyard	6	— c and b Trueman 56
B. Constable c Watson b Appleyard	5	— not out 32
K. Barrington c Close b Appleyard	1	— b Wardle 11
A. J. McIntyre c Watson b Appleyard	10	— b Wardle 9
J. C. Laker c Wilson b Appleyard	0	— c sub b Close 5
W. S. Surridge b Trueman	10	— c Appleyard b Close 15
G. A. R. Lock not out	21	— not out 0
P. J. Loader b Wardle	5	
A. V. Bedser c and b Appleyard	0	
B 5, l-b 3	8	B 9, l-b 5, n-b 2 16

1/20 2/22 3/28 4/33 5/39 6/41 7/52   85   1/67 2/167   (7 wkts., dec.) 261
8/62 9/74   3/205 4/225 5/235 6/242 7/261

Yorkshire

L. Hutton c McIntyre b Loader	0	— b Loader	1
F. A. Lowson c and b Lock	16	— c Lock b Bedser	0
J. V. Wilson c Surridge b Laker	10	— c Barrington b Lock	9
W. H. H. Sutcliffe b Lock	7	— c and b Bedser	40
W. Watson b Loader	32	— c Surridge b Lock	30
D. B. Close b Lock	1	— c Barrington b Laker	3
N. W. D. Yardley c McIntyre b Lock	24	— lbw b Bedser	15
J. H. Wardle c Lock b Bedser	2	— b Bedser	41
R. Booth b Loader	22	— c May b Bedser	3
F. S. Trueman b Loader	4	— not out	14
R. Appleyard not out	1	— c Laker b Lock	9
B 4, l-b 7, w 1	12	L-b 6, w 1, n-b 2	9

1/0 2/28 3/30 4/64 5/66 6/95   131   1/2 2/4 3/32 4/82 5/85   174
7/99 8/111 9/126   6/100 7/133 8/141 9/150

Yorkshire Bowling

	O.	M.	R.	W.	O.	M.	R.	W.
Trueman	15	2	32	2	22	7	37	2
Appleyard	18	6	29	7	30	9	66	0
Wardle	6	2	16	1	27	9	47	2
Close					29	7	87	3
Yardley					4	1	8	0

Surrey Bowling

	O.	M.	R.	W.	O.	M.	R.	W.
Loader	20.3	5	38	4	12	2	38	1
Bedser	9	3	18	1	25	11	38	5
Lock	27	12	36	4	25.2	8	63	3
Laker	12	7	23	1	15	6	26	1
Surridge	2	1	4	0				

Umpires: T. Spencer and E. Davies.

SURREY v. ESSEX

At The Oval, June 11, 13, 14. Surrey won by 62 runs after being sent in to bat. On the first day they found run-getting difficult on turf affected by mid-week rain and, despite an opening stand of 55, lost half their wickets for 130. Fletcher stayed nearly three hours. Thanks to hard hitting by Laker and Lock and steady play by Constable, the last five wickets realised 113. Though Insole batted skilfully, Essex were 100 behind on the first innings and Surrey in turn fared badly against the fast-medium bowling of Preston. Left 210 to get, Essex began disastrously, but Barker batted skilfully and Taylor stayed with Insole while 57 were added before unluckily playing on. Then came another collapse and, though Smith punished Laker for 18 in an over, the last five wickets fell for 35.

Surrey

D. G. W. Fletcher b Bailey	55	— c Gibb b Smith	1
T. H. Clark c and b Smith	35	— c Dodds b Preston	38
M. J. Stewart c Gibb b Preston	15	— run out	4
B. Constable c Taylor b Preston	56	— c Gibb b Preston	28
R. C. E. Pratt lbw b Insole	8	— lbw b Preston	7
A. J. McIntyre run out	3	— c Greensmith b Preston	12
J. C. Laker c and b Insole	21	— b Preston	1
G. A. R. Lock b Bailey	34	— c Horsfall b Greensmith	0
P. J. Loader b Preston	1	— not out	9
A. V. Bedser b Preston	1	— c Bedser b Greensmith	2
W. S. Surridge not out	6	— c Bear b Greensmith	6
B 3, l-b 5	8	L-b 1	1

1/55 2/104 3/106 4/127 5/130 6/160   243   1/2 2/13 3/61 4/78   109
7/219 8/224 9/226   5/85 6/92 7/92 8/96 9/103

Essex

T. C. Dodds c Fletcher b Bedser	20	— c Clark b Loader	3
P. A. Gibb b Loader	1	— c Constable b Bedser	0
G. Barker b Bedser	23	— lbw b Bedser	31
R. Horsfall c McIntyre b Bedser	13	— c Stewart b Laker	4
D. J. Insole c Stewart b Clark	34	— lbw b Laker	41
B. Taylor c McIntyre b Bedser	16	— b Clark	27
M. Bear c Fletcher b Clark	6	— c Lock b Laker	0
R. Smith c Pratt b Clark	19	— c Loader b Clark	27
W. T. Greensmith c Surridge b Laker	0	— not out	1
K. C. Preston not out	3	— lbw b Laker	0
J. A. Bailey b Laker	0	— run out	1
B 6, l-b 2	8	B 8, l-b 3, n-b 1	12

1/12 2/52 3/52 4/75 5/101 6/118   **143**
7/125 8/140 9/143

1/3 2/3 3/30 4/55 5/112   **147**
6/118 7/121 8/145 9/146

Essex Bowling

	O.	M.	R.	W.		O.	M.	R.	W.
Preston	24.1	5	68	4	....	16	5	37	5
Bailey	24	6	48	2	....	6	0	13	0
Smith	21	2	44	1	....	6	1	21	1
Insole	12	1	50	2	....	3	0	5	0
Greensmith	9	1	25	0	....	11.4	2	32	3

Surrey Bowling

	O.	M.	R.	W.		O.	M.	R.	W.
Bedser	23	8	36	4	....	12	4	25	2
Loader	6	2	9	1	....	7	1	20	1
Laker	18.4	2	51	2	....	19	2	46	4
Lock	8	0	28	0	....	11	6	23	0
Clark	7	1	11	3	....	12	5	21	2

Umpires: H. G. Baldwin and G. S. Mobey.

SURREY v. CAMBRIDGE UNIVERSITY

At The Oval, June 15, 16, 17. Surrey won by an innings and 23 runs. The fast bowling of Loader, who took 11 wickets for 69 runs, proved the deciding factor on lively turf. He was almost unplayable in the first innings when Cambridge were out in three and a half hours, but O'Brien defied him nearly all that time and won a place in the team for Lord's. Surrey, captained by Ransom of the Second XI in the absence of Surridge, were indebted to Stewart, E. Bedser and McIntyre for excellent driving against steady bowling. With a lead of 225, the county saw Loader break the back of the Cambridge batting in the second innings by taking the first three wickets for six runs, and although the left-handed Pretlove and Singh hit gallantly—Singh pulled Clark out of the ground—the match was over before lunch on the third day.

Cambridge University

D. R. W. Silk b Loader	0	— b Loader	4
R. O'Brien c Stewart b Lock	44	— c Stewart b Loader	2
G. Goonesena b Loader	0	— c and b Bedser	19
V. R. Lumsden c Barrington b Loader	12	— lbw b Lock	27
J. F. Pretlove b Ransom	0	— c Barrington b Lock	56
S. Singh lbw b Loader	4	— c Stewart b Loader	52
A. B. D. Parsons c Stewart b Lock	21	— b Loader	6
P. D. Croft run out	4	— lbw b Lock	13
C. S. Smith not out	22	— lbw b Lock	1
M. E. L. Melluish c Pratt b Loader	0	— b Loader	5
D. J. Smith b Loader	0	— not out	0
L-b 5	5	B 12, l-b 5	17

1/0 2/0 3/14 4/15 5/20 6/71 7/79   112   1/3 2/11 3/14 4/56   202
8/108 9/112   5/154 6/167 7/192 8/197 9/200

Surrey

D. G. W. Fletcher st Melluish b Pretlove	31	V. J. Ransom c Melluish b Goonesena	2
T. H. Clark c Pretlove b C. Smith	0	G. A. R. Lock c Parsons b Goonesena	14
M. J. Stewart c Melluish b D. Smith	93	P. J. Loader not out	5
B. Constable lbw b D. Smith	28		
K. Barrington b D. Smith	9	B 7, l-b 6, w 1, n-b 1	15
R. C. E. Pratt c Goonesena b Singh	17		
E. A. Bedser c Croft b Goonesena	71	1/4 2/75 3/142 4/167 5/168	337
A. J. McIntyre c Melluish b Goonesena	52	6/207 7/296 8/298 9/326	

Surrey Bowling

	O.	M.	R.	W.	O.	M.	R.	W.
Loader	16.5	6	17	6	24	8	52	5
Ransom	14	5	21	1				
Lock	26	14	41	2	35	13	57	4
Bedser	13	4	28	0	19	6	44	1
Clark					5	1	12	0
Constable					7	2	20	0

Cambridge University Bowling

	O.	M.	R.	W.
C. Smith	28	9	49	1
D. Smith	33	11	86	3
Goonesena	30	5	85	4
Pretlove	16	5	39	1
Singh	18	4	54	1
Lumsden	1	0	9	0

Umpires: F. Chester and A. Skelding.

At Leeds, June 18, 20, 21. SURREY lost to YORKSHIRE by six wickets.

SURREY v. OXFORD UNIVERSITY

At Guildford, June 22, 23, 24. Surrey won by an innings and 12 runs. A weakened Surrey side, led by the 49-year-old Holmes, proved too strong for the University. The Surrey bowling was not at its best on the first day, but on the second, after a slow start, the batsmen hit freely, and between lunch and tea a scoring rate of nearly 100 an hour was maintained. Clark, Cox, Holmes and Loader punished the University bowling severely. In the Oxford second innings only Fellows-Smith batted with assurance. He hit five 6's during the match.

Oxford University

M. J. K. Smith b Loader	3	— b Loader	9
J. M. Allan c and b Loader	4	— lbw b Loader	2
A. C. Walton st Swetman b Lock	27	c E. Bedser b Lock	11
C. C. P. Williams c A. Bedser b E. Bedser	34	c A. Bedser b E. Bedser	13
G. P. S. Delisle lbw b Lock	63	b A. Bedser	19
I. Gibson b Lock	21	run out	14
J. P. Fellows-Smith c Lock b A. Bedser	58	b Lock	48
A. P. Walshe b Loader	6	b Loader	21
D. C. P. R. Jowett c Swetman b Loader	2	not out	0
D. K. Fasken c Clark b A. Bedser	6	c Swetman b Constable	8
J. A. Arenhold not out	3	b Constable	0
B 2, l-b 6, n-b 3	11	B 1, l-b 3	4
	—		—
	238		149

1/3 2/12 3/62 4/83 5/135 6/176
7/225 8/227 9/235

1/2 2/21 3/43 4/51 5/63
6/79 7/114 8/117 9/143

Surrey

D. G. W. Fletcher c Walton b Allan	31	E. R. T. Holmes b Jowett	49
M. J. Stewart c Walshe b Fasken	1	G. A. R. Lock not out	14
B. Constable b Fasken	55	A. V. Bedser c Williams b Jowett	2
E. A. Bedser c Smith b Gibson	7		
R. Swetman hit wkt b Jowett	36	B 5, l-b 5, w 2, n-b 4	16
D. F. Cox c Arenhold b Gibson	54		—
T. H. Clark b Jowett	113		399
P. J. Loader c Walton b Arenhold	21	1/8 2/91 3/97 4/126 5/154	
		6/216 7/272 8/374 9/375	

Surrey Bowling

	O.	M.	R.	W.	O.	M.	R.	W.
A. Bedser	19	4	39	2	14	3	36	1
Loader	18.2	4	44	4	14	5	25	3
Cox	6	2	6	0				
Lock	21	6	48	3	15.4	4	37	2
E. Bedser	13	4	30	1	3	1	15	1
Clark	4	0	23	0				
Constable	6	0	37	0	6	0	32	2

Oxford University Bowling

Arenhold	17	4	48	1
Fasken	26	2	122	2
Fellows-Smith	13	2	32	0
Gibson	14	1	71	2
Allan	26	7	60	1
Jowett	23.5	7	50	4

Umpires: A. J. B. Fowler and A. E. Pothecary.

SURREY v. NORTHAMPTONSHIRE

At Guildford, June 25, 27, 28. Surrey won by 69 runs. Under A. Bedser, in the continued absence of Surridge through injury, they forced victory with seven minutes of extra time to spare although first innings lead was not decided until noon on the last day. Loader, who bowled excellently in the first innings, retired early in the second with a pulled side muscle. Northamptonshire, set to make 225 in two and a half hours, were given a chance when Barrick, who drove a ball from E. Bedser through the asbestos top of the sightscreen, reached fifty in 38 minutes, but the guile of Lock and Laker turned the fortunes of the game. McIntyre, Fletcher, Clark, E. Bedser and Laker played attractive innings for Surrey. Brookes and Subba Row, who drove finely in hitting a century against his old colleagues on his first appearance against them, played the major part in making the issue on the first innings so close. Starkie broke a finger on the first day, but batted in both innings.

Surrey

D. G. W. Fletcher c Andrew b Clarke ..	34	— not out	81
T. H. Clark c Andrew b Broderick	87	— b Clarke	5
M. J. Stewart lbw b Tribe	14	— b Clarke	3
B. Constable st Andrew b Tribe	4	— c Brookes b Tribe	22
R. C. E. Pratt c Arnold b Tribe	6		
E. A. Bedser c Reynolds b Clarke	45	— not out	14
A. J. McIntyre c Broderick b Subba Row	91	— c Brookes b Tribe	64
J. C. Laker not out	54		
G. A. R. Lock not out	0		
B 4, l-b 6, w 1	11	B 1, l-b 1	2

1/84 2/131 3/145   (7 wkts., dec.) 346   1/10 2/20   (4 wkts., dec.) 191
4/145 5/162 6/232 7/345   3/63 4/169
P. J. Loader and A. V. Bedser did not bat.

Northamptonshire

D. Brookes c Stewart b Laker	72	— b Loader................	7
P. Arnold c Lock b Loader	14	— b Laker	14
L. Livingston lbw b Loader	0	— c Stewart b E. Bedser	41
D. Barrick c McIntyre b Loader	8	— st McIntyre b Lock	58
R. Subba Row c Clark b Loader	112	— lbw b Lock..............	14
B. Reynolds lbw b A. Bedser	25	— c Pratt b Laker	4
G. E. Tribe b Loader	26	— c Pratt b E. Bedser	0
V. Broderick c Laker b A. Bedser......	5	— c Stewart b Laker	4
K. V. Andrew b A. Bedser	24	— not out	12
R. W. Clarke not out	6	— c McIntyre b Laker	0
S. Starkie st McIntyre b A. Bedser	0	— b Lock	0
B 16, l-b 2, n-b 3	21	L-b 1	1

1/18 2/36 3/54 4/172 5/245 6/254   313   1/15 2/37 3/104 4/104   155
7/276 8/299 9/313   5/130 6/139 7/139 8/148
9/154

Northamptonshire Bowling

	O.	M.	R.	W.		O.	M.	R.	W.
Clarke	32	3	103	2	....	15	1	53	2
Barrick	19	3	58	0	....	9	2	17	0
Starkie	14	2	46	0					
Tribe	33	17	65	3	....	19	1	57	2
Broderick	24	13	50	1	....	7	0	48	0
Subba Row	4	1	13	1	....	3	0	14	0

Surrey Bowling

	O.	M.	R.	W.		O.	M.	R.	W.
A. Bedser......	33.5	6	109	4	....	7	2	19	0
Loader	35	4	89	5	....	3	0	8	1
Laker	25	11	41	1	....	13	8	19	4
Lock	23	6	45	0	....	10.3	3	18	3
E. Bedser	5	1	8	0	....	10	0	43	2
					Constable	8	0	47	0

Umpires: A. J. B. Fowler and A. E. Pothecary.

SURREY v. WORCESTERSHIRE

At The Oval, June 29, 30. Surrey won by ten wickets. For the second year in succession this fixture ended well inside two days. Kelleher, in his first Championship game, made fast-medium deliveries lift on drying turf and Worcestershire, sent in to bat, were dismissed in two hours twenty minutes. Surrey, forcing the pace, declared thirty-five minutes before the close on the first day and though, largely through a determined display by Broadbent, Worcestershire almost doubled their first innings total, they left Surrey to get only 83. These Fletcher and Stewart hit off in fifty minutes. Kelleher finished with ten wickets for 73.

Worcestershire

D. Kenyon c Lock b A. Bedser	6	— c Fletcher b A. Bedser	....	31
L. N. Devereux c Constable b Kelleher .	0	— c Fletcher b A. Bedser	....	5
M. J. Horton c McIntyre b Kelleher	10	— c Stewart b Kelleher	....	21
R. G. Broadbent c McIntyre b Lock	7	— c McIntyre b Kelleher	....	52
G. Dews c McIntyre b Kelleher	25	— c McIntyre b Kelleher	.....	0
D. W. Richardson c Lock b Laker	9	— b Kelleher	......	0
R. O. Jenkins not out	4	— c Cox b Lock.............		11
H. Yarnold c McIntyre b Kelleher	1	— run out	.....	14
R. T. D. Perks c McIntyre b Kelleher....	7	— c Lock b Kelleher	.....	10
R. Berry c Stewart b Laker	1	— run out	.....	2
L. Coldwell c Stewart b Laker.........	0	— not out	......	0
B 3, l-b 1, n-b 3	7	B 5, l-b 2		7

1/7 2/7 3/25 4/38 5/62 6/62 7/63　　　　77　　　　1/23 2/45 3/64 4/72　　　　153
8/73 9/77　　　　　　　　　　　　　　　　　　　5/78 6/103 7/125 8/150 9/153

Surrey

D. G. W. Fletcher c Yarnold b Coldwell	10	— not out	....	48
M. J. Stewart c Yarnold b Coldwell	39	— not out	....	35
B. Constable c Broadbent b Perks	9			
K. Barrington c Richardson b Perks	32			
E. A. Bedser not out	39			
A. J. McIntyre c Berry b Coldwell	3			
D. F. Cox not out	12			
B 1, l-b 1, n-b 2	4			

1/18 2/29 3/92 4/102　　(5 wkts., dec.) 148　　　　　　(No wkt.) 83
5/105

J. C. Laker, G. A. R. Lock, A. V. Bedser and H. R. A. Kelleher did not bat.

Surrey Bowling

	O.	M.	R.	W.		O.	M.	R.	W.
A Bedser	11	4	22	1	....	18	5	40	2
Kelleher	14	5	23	5	....	20	3	50	5
Lock	10	4	16	1	....	14.1	7	27	1
Laker	8	3	9	3	....	7	1	29	0

Worcestershire Bowling

	O.	M.	R.	W.		O.	M.	R.	W.
Perks	17	1	72	2	....	4	0	14	0
Coldwell	14	3	62	3	....	5	0	27	0
Berry	2	0	10	0					
Horton						5	1	21	0
Jenkins						3	0	21	0

Umpires: T. Spencer and E. A. Roberts.

At Blackheath, July 2, 4. Surrey beat Kent by an innings and 28 runs.

SURREY v. LEICESTERSHIRE

At The Oval, July 6, 7, 8. Surrey won by five wickets. For the second time during the season Leicestershire worried the Champions. Hitting two 6's and fourteen 4's, Lester, who batted for five hours and forty minutes, made his highest score and he and Smithson by adding 123 took part in the first three-figure stand of the summer against Surrey at Kennington. Palmer declared first thing on Thursday morning, Leicestershire's 314 being then the highest by any visiting side, and then Surrey, thanks to centuries by Stewart—very strong in hitting to leg— and Constable gave Surrey the mastery. The pitch, which at first proved fast, became dusty on the third day when Eric Bedser seized the chance to accomplish the best bowling performance of his career. Surridge distinguished himself by making seven catches, most of them brilliant. Surrey wanted 161 in two hours thirty-five minutes. The batsmen hurried to the crease and by consistent forcing cricket Surrey gained their thirteenth Championship victory by a comfortable margin of wickets but with only ten minutes left of the extra half-hour.

Leicestershire

G. Lester c Stewart b Cox 143	— c Laker b Cox	7
M. R. Hallam c Surridge b Kelleher	1 — c Surridge b Bedser	43
M. Tompkin c McIntyre b Surridge	1 — c Surridge b Bedser	44
M. J. K. Smith c Surridge b Laker	63 — lbw b Cox	3
C. H. Palmer c Stewart b Bedser	11 — c Cox b Bedser	15
V. E. Jackson c Cox b Bedser	8 — st McIntyre b Bedser	6
G. A. Smithson b Surridge.............	34 — c Surridge b Bedser	0
V. S. Munden c Surridge b Laker	24 — c Constable b Clark	28
J. Firth not out	2 — c Surridge b Bedser......	8
C. T. Spencer c Barrington b Cox	13 — b Bedser	0
J. Goodwin (did not bat)	— not out	0
B 4, l-b 8, n-b 2	14 B 4, l-b 4, n-b 3	11

1/4 2/9 3/138 4/161   (9 wkts., dec.) 314   1/39 2/72 3/81 4/100   165
5/177 6/293 7/293 8/299 9/314   5/113 6/113 7/138 8/155
                                      9/159

Surrey

D. G. W. Fletcher lbw b Jackson	40 — b Spencer	4
T. H. Clark b Goodwin	2 — b Jackson	31
M. J. Stewart b Goodwin 105	— c Palmer b Spencer	37
B. Constable b Hallam b Goodwin 104	— c Smith b Jackson.........	10
K. Barrington not out	27 — not out	28
E. A. Bedser run out	19 — c Palmer b Jackson	24
A. J. McIntyre not out	4 — not out	21
L-b 14, n-b 4...................	18 B 1, l-b 5	6

1/5 2/81 3/259 4/266   (5 wkts., dec.) 319   1/5 2/52 3/72   (5 wkts.) 161
5/311   4/85 5/125

J. C. Laker, W. S. Surridge, D. F. Cox and H. R. A. Kelleher did not bat.

Surrey Bowling

	O.	M.	R.	W.		O.	M.	R.	W.
Surridge	29	5	69	2	....	4	2	4	0
Kelleher	19	3	58	1	....	10	0	36	0
Cox...........	15.5	6	32	2	....	14	1	48	2
Laker	41	15	91	2	....	14	6	13	0
Bedser	23	7	50	2	....	29	15	33	7
			Clark			7.2	3	20	1

Leicestershire Bowling

	O.	M.	R.	W.		O.	M.	R.	W.
Spencer	26	6	82	0	....	16	2	49	2
Goodwin	26	3	102	3	....	9	2	37	0
Jackson	26	10	50	1	....	12.4	1	52	3
Palmer	7	2	17	0					
Munden	13.2	5	35	0					
Lester	5	1	15	0					
			Palmer			3	1	17	0

Umpires: W. F. Price and P. Corrall.

SURREY v. KENT

At The Oval, July 9, 11, 12. Kent won by 13 runs in one of the most dramatic finishes of the season and so avenged their crushing defeat by the Champions the previous week. Surrey seemed certain of victory when, with Barrington and Pratt batting comfortably and six wickets to fall, they needed only 29 more runs. Then Allan, who had bowled his left-arm slows with persistent accuracy on a pitch giving no help, dismissed Pratt and for the second time in the match Surrey collapsed in astonishing fashion. Reckless strokes accounted for McIntyre, Laker and Surridge; Cox was out first ball and then Barrington, having batted excellently for two and a quarter hours, fell in trying to score the single needed to keep the bowling. The last six wickets went down in twenty minutes, Allan claiming four of them in fifteen deliveries. Kent batted poorly on the first day when, in ideal conditions, Pettiford alone offered much resistance to Surrey's weakened attack. Surrey appeared to be heading for a useful lead when Wright and Allan caused the first breakdown, the score moving from 123 for three to 132 for nine in half an hour. Kent reached 91 for five before a cloudburst ended play on the second evening and the following morning Laker and Bedser made full use of the rain-affected turf. When this dried out Surrey appeared to have a simple task.

Kent

A. E. Fagg b Cox	28	— lbw b Laker		49
A. H. Phebey c Pratt b Loader	5	— lbw b Loader		5
J. M. Allan c Stewart b Surridge	0	— lbw b Laker		10
R. C. Wilson b Cox	24	— c Surridge b Laker		13
J. Pettiford lbw b Cox	50	— c Pratt b Bedser		12
J. F. Pretlove c Laker b Loader	5	— c Surridge b Laker		8
P. Hearn c McIntyre b Surridge	14	— c Stewart b Cox		0
D. G. Ufton b Laker	14	— c Surridge b Bedser		0
D. V. P. Wright not out	17	— c Clark b Bedser		3
J. C. T. Page c Constable b Laker	3	— not out		3
J. B. Phillips c Stewart b Laker	0	— b Laker		4
B 14, l-b 4, w 1, n-b 2	21	B 4, l-b 5		9

1/14 2/15 3/43 4/74 5/92 6/119   181   1/19 2/52 3/65 4/71   116
7/148 8/178 9/181   5/91 6/95 7/96 8/104 9/108

Surrey

T. H. Clark c Wilson b Wright	32	— c Ufton b Phillips		0
M. J. Stewart c Allan b Wright	20	— c and b Allan		11
B. Constable run out	30	— c Phebey b Wright		14
K. Barrington c Wilson b Allan	27	— lbw b Allan		72
E. A. Bedser lbw b Wright	12	— lbw b Wright		6
R. C. E. Pratt st Ufton b Allan	1	— c Fagg b Allan		23
A. J. McIntyre b Allan	2	— c and b Allan		4
J. C. Laker c Phillips b Wright	1	— c Wilson b Allan		1
D. F. Cox b Wright	0	— c Phebey b Wright		0
W. S. Surridge b Allan	15	— b Wright		0
P. J. Loader not out	2	— not out		0
L-b 3, n-b 1	4	L-b 4, n-b 3		7

1/49 2/56 3/108 4/123 5/126 6/126   146   1/0 2/15 3/30 4/46 5/123   138
7/129 8/129 9/132   6/127 7/133 8/134 9/134

Surrey Bowling

	O.	M.	R.	W.		O.	M.	R.	W.
Loader	17	4	35	2	....	9	3	25	1
Surridge	19	3	45	2	....	4	1	7	0
Laker	20.5	8	34	3	....	23.5	9	48	5
Cox	14	5	23	3	....	6	3	10	1
Bedser	10	2	23	0	....	13	6	16	3

Kent Bowling

	O.	M.	R.	W.	O.	M.	R.	W.
Phillips	19	2	39	0	 3	1	3	1
Allan	31.3	12	49	4	.... 22.4	4	60	5
Wright	17	3	45	5	 14	1	45	4
Page	4	1	9	0	 6	1	23	0

Umpires: H. Elliott (Lancashire) and K. McCanlis.

At The Oval, July 16, 18, 19. SURREY lost to SOUTH AFRICANS by 82 runs. (See SOUTH AFRICAN section.)

At Swansea, July 20, 21. SURREY beat GLAMORGAN by nine wickets.

At Worcester, July 23, 25, 26. SURREY beat WORCESTERSHIRE by eight wickets.

At Coventry, July 27, 28, 29. SURREY lost to WARWICKSHIRE by 131 runs.

SURREY v. NOTTINGHAMSHIRE

At The Oval, July 30, August 1, 2. Surrey won by an innings and three runs. The match took a sensational turn late on the second day when Nottinghamshire batted a second time 43 runs behind. They went in at 5.25 p.m.; one hour later six wickets were down for 25 and Laker's analysis read: 6—5—1—4. No one anticipated the breakdown, and as well as Laker bowled on a dusty pitch he owed much to some magnificent fielding. In fact a wonderful left-handed catch by Stewart at silly mid-on, only eight yards from the bat, began the trouble for Notts when he held a powerful drive by Giles. Lock and Surridge also made brilliant catches. Surridge claimed the extra half-hour but Kelly, despite an injured left arm, stayed forty minutes. Close of play found Notts with only one wicket left, their score being 30 for nine. Next morning seven minutes sufficed, Lock and Laker each bowling one more maiden before Surridge caught his rival captain, Jepson, splendidly with the right hand at slip.

Nottinghamshire

J. D. Clay st McIntyre b A Bedser	4	— c Surridge b Laker	7
R. J. Giles b A. Bedser	10	— c Stewart b A. Bedser	2
C. J. Poole c Laker b A. Bedser	63	— run out	11
F. W. Stocks c Stewart b Lock	56	— lbw b Laker	3
J. Kelly run out	41	— lbw b Lock..............	2
G. Goonesena b Loader	36	— c Lock b Laker	0
B. Dooland c May b Loader	6	— c A. Bedser b Laker	0
K. Smales c May b Loader	17	— c Lock b Laker	2
A. Jepson lbw b Loader	0	— c Surridge b Lock	4
C. S. Matthews b Loader	8	— b Laker	1
E. J. Rowe not out	7	— not out	2
B 3, n-b 1	4	B 6..................	6

1/4 2/33 3/107 4/159 5/187 6/210   252
7/227 8/227 9/239

1/5 2/21 3/22 4/25 5/25   40
6/25 7/29 8/29 9/30

Surrey

M. J. Stewart b Jepson	15	W. S. Surridge c Giles b Goonesena	0
E. A. Bedser c Goonesena b Dooland	52	G. A. R. Lock lbw b Goonesena...	5
		P. J. Loader c Goonesena b Dooland	6
P. B. H. May c sub b Dooland ...	23	A. V. Bedser not out	0
B. Constable run out	98	B 5, l-b 3	8
K. Barrington b Stocks	43		
A. J. McIntyre c Poole b Smales..	27	1/36 2/82 3/101 4/176 5/214	
J. C. Laker c Rowe b Goonesena .	18	6/265 7/271 8/286 9/291	295

Surrey Bowling

	O.	M.	R.	W.		O.	M.	R.	W.
A. Bedser	30	7	78	3	....	5	0	13	1
Loader	27.3	8	59	5	....	4	2	5	0
Laker	13	3	30	0	....	16	11	5	6
Surridge	7	0	25	0					
Lock	18	5	36	1	....	11.4	8	9	2
E. Bedser	8	1	20	0	....	3	2	2	0

Nottinghamshire Bowling

	O.	M.	R.	W.
Jepson	14	6	20	1
Matthews	14	8	24	0
Dooland	34.2	9	101	3
Smales	28	8	79	1
Goonesena	27	9	55	3
Stocks	3	1	8	1

Umpires: L. H. Gray and A. Skelding.

At Manchester, August 3, 4, 5. SURREY beat LANCASHIRE by seven wickets.

SURREY v. MIDDLESEX

At The Oval, August 6, 8, 9. Surrey won by 39 runs. After they had won the toss for only the fourth time in 21 Championship matches, they lost four wickets for six runs against some admirable bowling by Warr and Moss who exploited a green pitch and heavy atmosphere. Surrey fought back and a sixth wicket stand of 92 by Barrington (he batted splendidly for three and a quarter hours) and Swetman gave them a sporting chance on a pitch that turned in favour of the spin bowlers on the second day. Lock revelled in the conditions taking 13 wickets for the second successive match, but Dewes proved to be in his best form and he carried his bat for 101 in an innings lasting four hours. His leg hitting and strong driving brought him most of his nine 4's. Then Stewart showed the same determination for Surrey who left Middlesex to make 166. Whereas Laker, troubled through his spinning finger becoming sore, accomplished little, Lock, supported by excellent fielding, again thwarted Middlesex, the turning-point coming when he held a fierce return from Dewes, who was third out at 64.

Surrey

M. J. Stewart c Edrich b Warr	0	—	c Robertson b Young	60
D. G. W. Fletcher b Warr	2	—	b Moss	4
P. B. H. May b Moss	3	—	run out	3
B. Constable c Moss b Warr	0	—	lbw b Young	13
K. Barrington c Compton b Titmus	73	—	c Delisle b Young	2
E. A. Bedser run out	16	—	c Robertson b Titmus	11
R. Swetman b Young	36	—	b Moss	19
J. C. Laker b Moss	17	—	c Moss b Young	30
W. S. Surridge b Titmus	1	—	c Compton b Moss	10
G. A. R. Lock lbw b Moss	14	—	lbw b Young	12
A. V. Bedser not out	0	—	not out	0
L-b 7, n-b 2	9		B 13, l-b 11, n-b 5	29

1/1 2/4 3/4 4/6 5/41 6/133 7/145　171　　1/13 2/29 3/56 4/56 5/93　193
8/146 9/166　　　　　　　　　　　　　6/120 7/156 8/180 9/184

Middlesex

J. D. Robertson c Lock b A. Bedser	5	— c E. Bedser b A. Bedser	0
J. G. Dewes not out	101	— c and b Lock	35
S. M. Brown c Stewart b A. Bedser	1	— c Swetman b Lock	18
W. J. Edrich b Lock	23	— c Fletcher b Laker	13
J. J. Warr b Laker	7	— c Swetman b A. Bedser	2
G. P. S. Delisle c Surridge b Lock	13	— c Surridge b Lock	16
D. Bennett c Surridge b Lock	3	— c Stewart b Lock	8
F. J. Titmus c Lock b Laker	24	— c Swetman b Lock	7
L. H. Compton c May b Lock	12	— not out	6
J. A. Young b Lock	0	— c Laker b Lock	7
A. E. Moss lbw b Lock	0	— c E. Bedser b Lock	3
B 12, l-b 2	14	B 7	7

1/10 2/12 3/42 4/68 5/85 6/99   203   1/4 2/49 3/64 4/74 5/96   122
7/171 8/189 9/189   6/97 7/104 8/107 9/116

Middlesex Bowling

	O.	M.	R.	W.		O.	M.	R.	W.
Moss	20.1	6	42	3	....	9.5	0	18	3
Warr	18	2	32	3	....	4	0	8	0
Bennett	13	2	30	0					
Titmus	25	15	35	2	....	34	16	55	1
Young	10	2	23	1	....	41	18	68	5
Robertson						4	2	15	0

Surrey Bowling

	O.	M.	R.	W.		O.	M.	R.	W.
A. Bedser	13	3	24	2	....	15	4	40	2
Surridge	5	2	8	0	....	6	2	10	0
Laker	31	6	76	2	....	9	1	41	1
Lock	25.5	5	58	6	....	17.2	8	24	7
E. Bedser	9	1	23	0					

Umpires: F. S. Lee and W. T. Jones.

At Weston-super-Mare, August 10, 11. SURREY beat SOMERSET by an innings and 100 runs.

At The Oval, August 13, 15, 16, 17. ENGLAND beat SOUTH AFRICA in Fifth Test by 92 runs. (See SOUTH AFRICAN section.)

At Cheltenham, August 13, 15. SURREY beat GLOUCESTERSHIRE by 43 runs.

At Northampton, August 17, 18, 19. SURREY lost to NORTHAMPTONSHIRE by six wickets.

At Lord's, August 20, 22, 23. SURREY beat MIDDLESEX by nine wickets.

SURREY v. SUSSEX

At The Oval, August 24, 25, 26. Surrey won by an innings and eight runs. In serious danger at the end of the first day they swung the game in emphatic style and by their victory they made certain of winning the Championship. Sussex lost four wickets for 75 at the start, but recovered through resolute batting by Parks, Suttle, Cox and Thompson. Before the close four Surrey wickets fell for 32, but next day Surrey took command. Constable, batting four hours, played a vital part in the recovery and Barrington, McIntyre and Laker supported him well. McIntyre hit tremendously hard and his 81 included fourteen 4's. Against a tiring attack Laker and Surridge added 68 in fifty minutes. Two spectacular slip catches by May off A. Bedser started the Sussex breakdown when they went in 98 behind. On a worn pitch A. Bedser and Lcck bowled so effectively that on the last morning Sussex lost their last eight wickets in ninety-five minutes for 78.

Sussex

J. Langridge c Stewart b A. Bedser	5	— c May b A. Bedser	0
D. V. Smith c Surridge b Lock	21	— lbw b A. Bedser	13
A. S. M. Oakman c Stewart b Surridge	3	— c May b A. Bedser	7
J. M. Parks lbw b Lock	68	— lbw b Lock	7
G. H. G. Doggart b Laker	10	— b A. Bedser	1
K. G. Suttle c Stewart b Lock	32	— c sub b Lock	27
G. Cox c Stewart b Laker	48	— b Laker	14
R. T. Webb c Surridge b E. Bedser	9	— c Stewart b A. Bedser	7
N. I. Thomson b Lock	35	— c and b Lock	3
R. G. Marlar st McIntyre b Lock	11	— not out	6
A. E. James not out	1	— lbw b Lock	0
L-b 2	2	L-b 4, n-b 1	5
	245		90

1/18 2/23 3/52 4/75 5/121 6/155
7/180 8/221 9/242

1/0 2/12 3/27 4/27 5/53
6/60 7/73 8/84 9/90

Surrey

R. C. E. Pratt st Webb b James	2	J. C. Laker not out	78
M. J. Stewart c Langridge b Thomson	2	G. A. R. Lock lbw b Parks	19
P. B. H. May c Webb b Smith	13	W. S. Surridge b Marlar	21
E. A. Bedser b Thomson	1		
B. Constable c Langridge b Parks	77	B 8, l-b 2	10
K. Barrington c Smith b Parks	39		
A. J. McIntyre c Thomson b Smith	81	(9 wkts., dec.)	343

A. V. Bedser did not bat.

1/4 2/4 3/15 4/26
5/99 6/194 7/242 8/275 9/343

Surrey Bowling

	O.	M.	R.	W.	O.	M.	R.	W.
A. Bedser	14	3	35	1	17	3	41	5
Surridge	10	4	23	1	1	0	1	0
Laker	28	7	77	2	1	0	7	1
Lock	24	7	70	5	17	8	36	4
E. Bedser	15	4	38	1				

Sussex Bowling

Thomson	31	9	67	2
James	33	11	77	1
Smith	28	8	66	2
Marlar	18.4	2	57	1
Oakman	6	1	13	0
Parks	13	2	53	3

Umpires: L. H. Gray and A. Skelding.

At Bournemouth, August 27, 29, 30. SURREY lost to HAMPSHIRE by 129 runs.

SURREY v. DERBYSHIRE

At The Oval, August 31, September 1. Surrey won by eight wickets and completed their Championship programme appropriately with three of their younger members, Pratt, Stewart and Barrington, batting well to bring about victory within two days. Previously, the game ran very much to form, with each side stronger in bowling and fielding than in batting. Smith, the young off-spinner, helped Derbyshire to pass 100 by hitting 22 of the last wicket stand of 32, the best partnership of the innings. Only Willett, who in his first game showed great promise, and Laker reached double figures for Surrey. They hit 63 out of a total of 101. Derbyshire collapsed in their second innings against the fast bowling of Surridge. The Surrey captain took six wickets for 56 runs, his best figures of the summer. During the match Stewart held his fiftieth catch of the season.

Derbyshire

A. Hamer c Laker b A. Bedser		11	— c Pratt b Surridge		31
J. Kelly c Constable b Lock		8	— lbw b A. Bedser		20
D. J. Green lbw b A. Bedser		0	— st McIntyre b Surridge		0
A. C. Revill b Lock		22	— c McIntyre b Surridge		33
D. B. Carr c McIntyre b A. Bedser		4	— lbw b Surridge		1
H. L. Johnson b Laker		10	— b Surridge		0
D. C. Morgan c Stewart b Lock		3	— b Surridge		13
G. O. Dawkes c Surridge b Lock		0	— c Stewart b A. Bedser		18
C. Gladwin st McIntyre b Laker		3	— not out		4
E. Smith not out		22	— c McIntyre b Laker		5
D. Hall b Lock		6	— c Barrington b Laker		0
B 9, l-b 3, n-b 2		14	B 4, n-b 1		5

1/16 2/23 3/25 4/35 5/56 6/62   103   1/54 2/54 3/58 4/63   130
7/65 8/71 9/71   5/67 6/92 7/114 8/123 9/128

Surrey

R. C. E. Pratt lbw b Morgan		8	— c Revill b Hall		22
M. J. Stewart b Gladwin		9	— not out		53
K. Barrington c Dawkes b Gladwin		1	— c Carr b Hall		50
E. A. Bedser c Carr b Gladwin		4	— not out		8
B. Constable c and b Morgan		0			
M. D. Willett c Hamer b Smith		25			
A. J. McIntyre b Morgan		2			
J. C. Laker c Carr b Hall		38			
G. A. R. Lock c Morgan b Hall		4			
W. S. Surridge b Smith		5			
A. V. Bedser not out		0			
B 4, n-b 1		5			

1/14 2/16 3/22 4/22 5/23 6/25   101   1/41 2/108   (2 wkts.) 133
7/87 8/92 9/101

Surrey Bowling

	O.	M.	R.	W.		O.	M.	R.	W.
A. Bedser	16	6	31	3	....	20	5	56	2
Surridge	1	0	8	0	....	23	5	56	6
Lock	20	7	37	5	....	8	3	7	0
Laker	5	2	13	2	....	3.3	1	6	2

Derbyshire Bowling

	O.	M.	R.	W.		O.	M.	R.	W.
Hall	11.5	1	26	2	....	12	0	53	2
Gladwin	17	10	27	3	....	10	4	18	0
Morgan	11	6	12	3	....	9	1	27	0
Smith	10	4	15	2	....	12	3	32	0
Carr	5	1	16	0	....	3	1	3	0

Umpires: F. S. Lee and L. H. Gray.

CHAMPION COUNTY (SURREY) v. THE REST

At The Oval, September 10, 12, 13, 14. The Rest won by two wickets,
Spooner providing a dramatic finish to the season by making the winning hit off
the last possible ball from Lock. Four runs were needed and Spooner got them
with a towering on drive that cleared the boundary fence first bounce. So Surrey
failed to emulate Yorkshire and Middlesex, the only two counties to have triumphed
as Champions against The Rest. An important factor in their defeat was the
decision to cover the pitch completely during the game. The turf was unprotected,

however, when heavy rain fell the day before, which meant that Surrey, who were put in by Insole, batted first on a wet pitch. Stewart and the left-handed Pratt batted soundly before lunch, but afterwards the innings broke down against the speed and spin of the Yorkshire pair, Trueman and Wardle. The Rest lost three wickets, including that of the potential "night watchman," Marlar, before the close, but in easier conditions Parks and Hamer placed them in a powerful position on the second day. Parks batted beautifully and Hamer's innings, though far less spectacular, was no less valuable. Just over two and a half hours' play was possible on the third day when, after cheerful hitting by Lock, a similar stand developed for Surrey. Pratt showed remarkable patience for four hours and helped May, in his best form, to add 175. Trueman again caused a breakdown, however, and The Rest were left to score 164 in two hours twenty minutes. Sound stroke play by Hamer, Wilson and Insole led to the exciting climax. The match drew over 11,000 spectators on the first day, but cold, dismal weather on the subsequent days kept down the attendances.

Champion County (Surrey)

R. C. E. Pratt c Parks b Marlar	20	— lbw b Shackleton	59
M. J. Stewart lbw b Wardle	45	— c Wardle b Trueman	2
P. B. H. May b Wardle	25	— hit wkt b Trueman	125
K. Barrington c Wilson b Bailey	13	— b Trueman	0
B. Constable c Spooner b Trueman	16	— c Bailey b Trueman	7
E. A. Bedser b Trueman	16	— not out	30
A. J. McIntyre b Trueman	1	— b Shackleton	8
J. C. Laker c Shackleton b Wardle	10	— c Spooner b Wardle	10
G. A. R. Lock b Wardle	1	— c Wilson b Wardle	38
P. J. Loader c Hamer b Wardle	2	— b Marlar	4
A. V. Bedser not out	0	— b Marlar	0
B 4, l-b 12	16	B 6, l-b 8	14

1/62 2/87 3/115 4/121 5/142 6/150   165
7/151 8/154 9/163

1/8 2/51 3/226 4/227   297
5/240 6/241 7/256 8/284
9/297

The Rest

D. Kenyon c E. Bedser b Loader	1	— c Barrington b A. Bedser	9
A. Hamer b Loader	81	— run out	35
J. V. Wilson c Stewart b Lock	23	— c Lock b Loader	44
R. G. Marlar st McIntyre b Lock	6	— st McIntyre b Lock	3
J. M. Parks lbw b Lock	96	— c May b Lock	10
D. J. Insole c Barrington b A. Bedser	33	— b Lock	29
T. E. Bailey c McIntyre b A. Bedser	11	— not out	7
R. T. Spooner not out	20	— not out	7
D. Shackleton b A. Bedser	0		
J. H. Wardle c Lock b Laker	17	— c E. Bedser b Loader	11
F. S. Trueman c McIntyre b Lock	1	— b Loader	1
B 5, l-b 4, w 1	10	B 1, l-b 7	8

1/1 2/42 3/48 4/191 5/229 6/250   299
7/263 8/271 9/298

1/12 2/79 3/101   (8 wkts.) 164
4/105 5/134 6/147 7/147
8/156

The Rest Bowling

	O.	M.	R.	W.		O.	M.	R.	W.
Trueman	15	5	21	3	....	26	7	71	4
Shackleton	12	2	19	0	....	24	5	58	2
Wardle	20.4	9	32	5	....	33	11	89	2
Bailey	13	5	21	1	....	8	0	31	0
Marlar	15	4	56	1	....	15.4	5	34	2

Champion County (Surrey) Bowling

	O.	M.	R.	W.	O.	M.	R.	W.
A. Bedser	28	5	71	3	 10	1	41	1
Loader	22	4	64	2	 14	1	50	3
Lock	28.3	6	67	4	 10	1	42	3
Laker	23	5	63	1	 5	1	23	0
E. A. Bedser	5	0	24	0				

Umpires: K. McCanlis and E. A. Roberts.

PLAYING NO LONGER
Glamorgan
McCONNON, J. E. (Glamorgan). Debut 1950. Durham born. Fine off-break bowler who toured Australia with the 1954-55 M.C.C. team but returned home early because of a hand injury. Knee trouble also caused him to miss part of the Commonwealth tour of India in 1953-54. Total wickets 446. Total runs 1,772. Best bowling eight for 36 against Nottinghamshire in 1953. Two Tests v. Pakistan in 1954. Retired for business reasons.

Hampshire
ROGERS, N. H. (Hampshire). Debut 1946. Reliable opening batsman on the verge of Test honours for several years. Total runs 16,056, nine times over 1,000 runs in a season. Highest score 186 against Gloucestershire in 1951. Has been twelfth man for England.

Middlesex
SHARP, H. P. (Middlesex). Debut 1946. Steady batsman and useful off-break bowler. Total runs 6,416; wickets 52. Highest score 165 against Northamptonshire in 1951. Best bowling five for 52 against Oxford University in 1949. Frequently opened the innings but usually regarded as a middle-order batsman.

THOMPSON, A. (Middlesex). Debut 1939. Liverpool born. Attacking batsman. Total runs 7,915. Highest score 158 against Worcestershire in 1952. He and Sharp shared a joint benefit in 1955.

Sussex
WOOD, D. J. (Sussex). Debut 1936. Left arm fast-medium bowler. Total wickets 589. Best bowling seven for 24 against Middlesex in 1949. Aggressive tail-end batsman and good outfield.

Yorkshire
N. W. D. YARDLEY (Yorkshire). Debut 1935. Fine all-rounder; attractive batsman, particularly strong on the leg-side, useful medium-pace bowler and splendid field. Total runs 18,173, wickets 279. Highest score 183 not out against Hampshire in 1951; best bowling six for 29 for M.C.C. against Cambridge University in 1946. Played in 20 Tests, 14 as captain. Cambridge Blue four years, captain in 1938. Toured India, South Africa, Australia and New Zealand. Yorkshire captain from 1948. Has been on Test selection committee, Chairman in 1951 and 1952.

SUSSEX

President—THE DUKE OF NORFOLK

Secretary—LIEUT.-COL. G. D. GRIMSTON, County Ground,
Eaton Road, Hove 3, Sussex

Captain—R. G. MARLAR

| R. G. Marlar | County Badge | D. V. Smith |

Though never serious challengers for the title, Sussex under Marlar, their fourth captain in as many years, enjoyed increased success and in winning five more games than in 1954 rose from ninth to fourth position in the Championship. They finished the season in fine style, winning four of their last five engagements.

The fact that, for the first time since 1947, six men exceeded 1,000 runs in Championship fixtures illustrated the strength of the batting. Parks, than whom no player hit harder in front of the wicket, easily headed the averages. In making 205 not out in three and a half hours against Somerset in his county's last match, he obtained the highest score of his career and for the first time completed 2,000 runs. Oakman, less used as an off-break bowler, flourished as a batsman, his runs increasing by 662 and his average by nearly 10; against Derbyshire he enjoyed the satisfaction of reaching his first century. John Langridge, who earned the award for holding more catches—69—than any other fieldsman in the country, and Cox wound up their first-class careers in highly satisfactory form, and the left-handers, Suttle and Smith, completed an impressive run-getting combination which Sheppard periodically augmented.

To Marlar, James, Thomson and Smith went practically all the bowling honours, for between them they dismissed no fewer than 406 batsmen in Championship games. Each of the first-named three took over 100 wickets. Thomson and James formed a most effective opening pair, as Yorkshire, for one, could testify. In the match with the northern county at Hove, James, with nine wickets for 60 in the first innings, and Thomson, with six for 55 in the second, paved the way to victory by 21 runs. The skilfully-controlled off-breaks of Marlar brought him more victims than in any other season, 121 as against 59 in 1954, his best analysis being nine for 46 against Lancashire at Hove. The most remarkable feature of the bowling, however, was the performance of Donald Smith. Rarely tried with the ball in previous years, he had taken no more than nine wickets, and those at a cost of 57 runs each. Yet he bowled left-arm medium-pace over the wicket to such purpose that he disposed of 72 men for less than 18 runs apiece. He did specially well against Kent, taking five wickets for 13 runs at Hastings and five for 36 at Tunbridge Wells.

Another Sussex player whose county career ended in 1955 was Wood, the left-arm fast-medium bowler, who took the match with Kent at Hastings as his benefit.

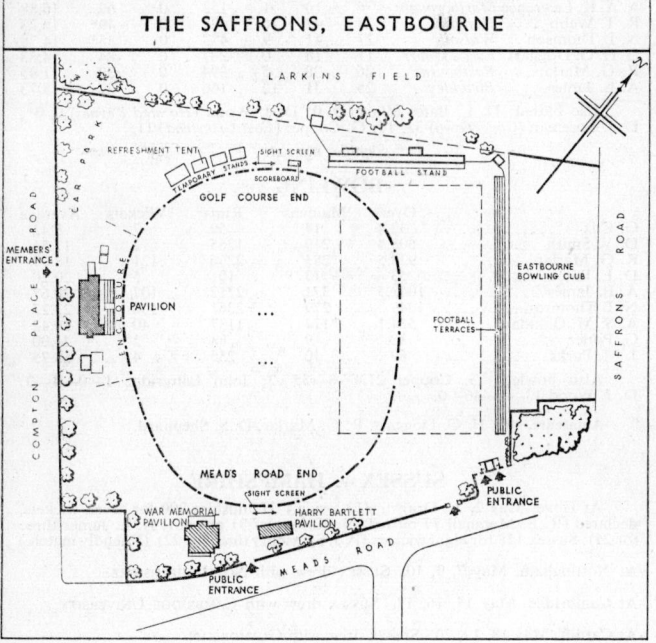

SUSSEX RESULTS

All First-Class Matches—Played 32, Won 13, Lost 10, Drawn 8, Tied 1

County Championship Matches—Played 28, Won 13, Lost 8, Drawn 6, Tied 1

COUNTY CHAMPIONSHIP AVERAGES
BATTING

	Birthplace	Mtchs.	Inns.	Not Outs	Runs	100's	Highest Inns.	Aver.
J. M. Parks ...	*Haywards Hth.*	27	47	7	1686	3	205*	42.15
D. S. Sheppard	*Reigate*	7	12	0	401	0	65	33.41
A. S. M. Oakman	*Hastings*	27	49	3	1335	1	102	29.02
K. G. Suttle ...	*Kensington*	28	48	2	1216	1	104	26.43
G. Cox	*Horsham*	26	45	3	1001	0	79	23.83
D. V. Smith ...	*Broadwater*	28	50	2	1106	0	90	23.04
John Langridge	*Chailey*	.28	49	1	1050	1	101	21.87
G. Potter	*Dormansland*	9	15	3	208	0	48*	17.33
A. A. K. Lawrence	*Marlborough*	6	10	1	152	0	63	16.88
R. T. Webb ...	*Harrow*	28	42	16	422	0	49*	16.23
N. I. Thomson .	*Walsall*	27	41	9	473	0	35*	14.78
G. H. G. Doggart	*Earl's Court*	11	18	0	267	0	84	14.83
R. G. Marlar ..	*Eastbourne*	26	38	5	394	0	39	11.93
A. E. James....	*Bletchley*	25	31	12	166	0	22	8.73

Also batted: D. L. Bates (*Hove*) 8, 0; D. J. Wood (*Horsted Keynes*) 0, 0*; D. J. Foreman (*Cape Town*) 33, 15; G. Cooper (*East Grinstead*) 11.

* Signifies not out.

BOWLING

	Overs	Maidens	Runs	Wickets	Average
G. Cox	32.4	14	59	7	8.42
D. V. Smith	608.4	219	1265	72	17.56
R. G. Marlar	928.5	283	2296	121	18.97
D. L. Bates	53	13	101	5	20.20
A. E. James...........	1042.5	371	2212	107	20.67
N. I. Thomson	1049	279	2361	106	22.27
A. S. M. Oakman	524.1	174	1137	40	28.42
G. Potter	32	9	88	2	44.00
J. M. Parks	69	10	235	4	58.75

Also bowled: G. Cooper 21.4—8—55—3; John Langridge 1—0—4—0; D. J. Wood 13—1—46—0.

Amateurs.—G. H. G. Doggart, R. G. Marlar, D. S. Sheppard.

SUSSEX v. HAMPSHIRE

At Hove, May 2, 3. Drawn. (12-a-side.) Hampshire 200 for seven wickets, declared (R. E. Marshall 77 retired, N. H. Rogers 81 not out; A. E. James three for 21); Sussex 158 for eight wickets (P. J. Sainsbury three for 22). (Friendly match.)

At Nottingham, May 7, 9, 10. SUSSEX drew with NOTTINGHAMSHIRE.

At Cambridge, May 14, 16, 17. SUSSEX drew with CAMBRIDGE UNIVERSITY.

At Cardiff, May 18, 19, 20. SUSSEX drew with GLAMORGAN.

SUSSEX v. ESSEX

At Worthing, May 21, 23, 24. Sussex won by six wickets, thanks in large measure to a stand of 72 by Langridge and Oakman. Essex began in a manner which suggested better things. Dodds shared with Gibb and Barker in partnerships of 86 and 82, but the pitch turned difficult and the last eight wickets fell to Thomson and James for 44 runs. Sussex lost five men for 96 and though Suttle and Cox added 53, Essex gained a lead of 29. The offbreaks of Oakman and Marlar troubled them, and despite a stand of 48 by Barker and Insole, Sussex needed only 137 to win.

Essex

T. C. Dodds run out	89	—	lbw b James		7
P. A. Gibb c Lawrence b Oakman	31	—	c Marlar b James		4
G. Barker c Lawrence b Thomson	48	—	c Marlar b Potter		35
R. Horsfall c Suttle b Thomson	0	—	b Marlar		5
D. J. Insole c Lawrence b Thomson	11	—	c Webb b Oakman		18
W. T. Greensmith c Potter b Thomson	0	—	c Langridge b Oakman		6
B. Taylor c Lawrence b James	0	—	b Oakman		4
R. Smith c and b James	21	—	c Langridge b Oakman		9
K. C. Preston c Langridge b James	1	—	b Marlar		3
J. A. Bailey not out	5	—	b Marlar		1
P. Cousens c Webb b James	0	—	not out		0
B 3, l-b 3	6		B 15		15

1/86 2/168 3/168 4/175 5/178 6/183   212
7/183 8/185 9/212

1/11 2/16 3/29 4/77   107
5/83 6/93 7/100 8/103 9/106

Sussex

J. Langridge lbw b Greensmith	31	—	c Dodds b Smith		43
D. V. Smith c Bailey b Smith	18	—	lbw b Preston		0
R. T. Webb c Greensmith b Bailey	0				
R. G. Marlar b Greensmith	22				
A. S. M. Oakman c and b Smith	20	—	c Preston b Smith		37
K. G. Suttle lbw b Preston	30	—	c Preston b Smith		15
G. Cox c Gibb b Greensmith	25	—	not out		11
G. Potter b Preston	7	—	not out		27
A. A. K. Lawrence b Preston	9				
N. I. Thomson not out	9				
A. E. James b Greensmith	9				
B 2, l-b 1	3		B 3, l-b 1		4

1/30 2/35 3/71 4/72 5/96 6/149   183
7/149 8/163 9/172

1/0 2/72 3/83   (4 wkts.) 137
4/109

Sussex Bowling

	O.	M.	R.	W.		O.	M.	R.	W.
Thomson	18	4	51	4	....	9	4	20	0
James	24.5	7	56	4	....	13	5	26	2
Oakman	21	5	55	1	....	10	4	17	4
Marlar	15	2	44	0	....	15.4	8	22	3
Potter						4	1	7	1

Essex Bowling

	O.	M.	R.	W.		O.	M.	R.	W.
Preston	18	7	36	3	....	12	2	26	1
Bailey	14	2	41	1	....	17	8	24	0
Smith	21	8	45	2	....	18	7	32	3
Greensmith	21.5	8	40	4	....	13	3	28	0
Cousens	3	1	13	0	....	10	6	18	0
Insole	3	1	5	0					
Dodds						1.1	0	5	0

Umpires: H. G. Baldwin and W. F. Price.

SUSSEX v. GLAMORGAN

At Worthing, May 25, 26, 27. Drawn, heavy rain ending cricket before lunch on the last day. Glamorgan batted without enterprise in the first innings. Watkins, their leading scorer, stayed nearly three hours for 51. Thanks to a stand of 70 between Parks and Suttle and good work by the stubborn Langridge and Cox, Sussex were able to declare two runs ahead. Against the off-breaks of Oakman and Marlar, Glamorgan fared none too well in the second innings until the weather broke.

Glamorgan

W. G. A. Parkhouse lbw b Thomson	49	— c Parks b Oakman	11
W. E. Jones run out	9	— b Oakman	41
B. Hedges lbw b Smith	28	— run out	15
J. Pressdee c Smith b Oakman	27	— c Smith b Oakman	25
A. J. Watkins c Potter b Thomson	51	— c Thomson by Marlar	20
W. Wooller st Webb b Oakman	35	— not out	5
P. B. Clift c Oakman b James	9	— c Suttle b Marlar	6
D. Ward st Webb b James	19	— not out	6
J. E. McConnon b Smith	5		
H. G. Davies c Langridge b Smith	0		
D. Shepherd not out	4		
B 13, l-b 5, n-b 2	20	B 2, l-b 1	3
	256	(6 wkts.)	132

1/31 2/87 3/103 4/138 5/193 6/221
7/227 8/248 9/252

1/46 2/56 3/82   (6 wkts.)   132
4/113 5/116 6/126

Sussex

J. Langridge c Davies b Shepherd	46	A. E. James not out	9
D. V. Smith c Davies b Watkins	13	R. G. Marlar c Davies b Wooller	8
A. S. M. Oakman c Ward b Wooller	1	R. T. Webb not out	5
J. M. Parks c Watkins b Pressdee	67	B 4, l-b 4, n-b 1	9
K. G. Suttle c Pressdee b Watkins	34		
G. Cox c Parkhouse b Wooller	44	(9 wkts., dec.)	258
G. Potter c Wooller b Watkins	13		
N. I. Thomson c and b Watkins	9		

1/45 2/46 3/91   (9 wkts., dec.)   258
4/161 5/176 6/216 7/228 8/242
9/253

Sussex Bowling

	O.	M.	R.	W.	O.	M.	R.	W.
Thomson	29	11	59	2	12	2	39	0
James	19	6	53	2	5	5	0	0
Smith	13	3	30	3				
Oakman	32	14	42	2	14	3	52	3
Marlar	26	14	33	0	9.5	0	38	2
Potter	4	0	19	0	1	1	0	0

Glamorgan Bowling

	O.	M.	R.	W.
Wooller	40	19	79	3
Shepherd	16	4	47	1
Watkins	33.4	12	68	4
McConnon	13	1	29	0
Pressdee	9	2	26	1

Umpires: H. G. Baldwin and W. F. Price.

At Lord's, May 28, 30, 31. SUSSEX drew with MIDDLESEX.

SUSSEX v. YORKSHIRE

At Hove, June 1, 2, 3, Sussex won by 21 runs with forty-five minutes to spare. In the absence of Yardley, injured, Hutton led Yorkshire and his decision to put in Sussex may have cost his side the match as rain left them a damp pitch for the final task. In a low-scoring game runs generally came slowly. Sussex were indebted to Langridge for two stubborn innings and five slip catches, including two superb low ones with the right hand which accounted for Lester and Sutcliffe at the crisis. Yorkshire seemed well-placed at the end of the first day, but James, fast-medium, moving the ball slightly from leg, took the remaining seven wickets for 30 runs, his nine for 60 being his best performance in first-class cricket. Left to make 157, Yorkshire finished the second day 26 for two; then came a delay until 3.40 p.m. Soon four wickets were down for 45, but dazzling hitting by the left-handers, Close and Watson, gave Yorkshire a splendid chance as their stand produced 59. Finally, Thomson turned the scales for Sussex by taking the last four wickets in 17 balls while conceding four runs and so Yorkshire, who won their previous six Championship matches, lost the game and their 100 per cent record.

Sussex

J. Langridge c Wilson b Wardle	81	— b Wardle	24
D. V. Smith lbw b Trueman	5	— c and b Wardle	16
A. S. M. Oakman c Close b Appleyard	25	— c Hutton b Wardle	28
J. M. Parks lbw b Appleyard	10	— b Close	0
K. G. Suttle b Appleyard	10	— lbw b Wardle	28
G. Cox b Trueman	1	— c Wilson b Trueman	9
G. Potter b Wardle	13	— not out	9
R. T. Webb not out	4	— c Lowson b Wardle	0
N. I. Thomson run out	0	— b Close	5
A. E. James b Appleyard	0	— b Close	0
R. G. Marlar b Appleyard	6	— c Appleyard b Wardle	6
B 7, l-b 11, w 1, n-b 1	20	B 9, l-b 2, n-b 2	13

1/11 2/48 3/70 4/108 5/111 6/150   175
7/165 8/165 9/165

1/25 2/56 3/57 4/99   138
5/110 6/116 7/116 8/125
9/129

Yorkshire

L. Hutton c Oakman b James	54	— lbw b Thomson	0
F. A. Lowson st Webb b James	24	— c Potter b James	3
J. V. Wilson c Langridge b James	0	— b James	20
D. B. Close b Marlar	3	— c Langridge b Marlar	37
W. Watson lbw b James	18	— not out	42
E. Lester b James	11	— c Langridge b Thomson	1
W. H. H. Sutcliffe b James	23	— c Langridge b Thomson	0
J. H. Wardle c Langridge b James	6	— b Marlar	12
R. Booth b James	8	— c Suttle b Thomson	7
F. S. Trueman c Smith b James	0	— c and b Thomson	3
R. Appleyard not out	0	— b Thomson	0
B 4, l-b 5, w 1	10	B 4, l-b 6	10

1/40 2/40 3/43 4/106 5/113 6/120   157
7/128 8/152 9/157

1/4 2/20 3/29 4/45   135
5/104 6/120 7/123 8/131
9/135

Yorkshire Bowling

	O.	M.	R.	W.		O.	M.	R.	W.
Trueman	12	0	43	2	....	10	2	30	1
Close	14	5	25	0	....	18	6	38	3
Appleyard	22.2	9	45	5	....	13	7	18	0
Wardle	28	16	42	2	....	28.3	15	39	6

Sussex Bowling

	O.	M.	R.	W.	O.	M.	R.	W.
Thomson	12	2	30	0	18.4	2	55	6
James	33.5	13	60	9	15	5	41	2
Marlar	19	11	27	1	8	2	16	2
Oakman	13	4	30	0	2	0	13	0

Umpires: A. E. Pothecary and K. McCanlis.

At Frome, June 4, 6, 7. SUSSEX lost to SOMERSET by 50 runs.

SUSSEX v. NORTHAMPTONSHIRE

At Horsham, June 8, 9, 10. Sussex won by 73 runs. Two men saved them from a first innings failure on rain-affected turf. Oakman, very enterprising, hit twelve 4's in two hours and a quarter, and Suttle, batting a quarter of an hour less, obtained thirteen boundaries. They alone dealt confidently with the slow left-arm bowling of Tribe. Thomson, fast-medium, began a Northamptonshire breakdown, and though Tribe batted patiently for nearly four hours, Sussex gained a lead of 48. Well served by Smith, Sussex declared on the last day. Left to get 228, Northamptonshire faltered against the off-breaks of Marlar, who gained a match record of 11 wickets for 101. The one exception was Barrick (one 6, ten 4's), who hit freely for an hour and forty minutes.

Sussex

J. Langridge c Lightfoot b Starkie	17	— b Clarke	17
D. V. Smith lbw b Tribe	31	— c Tribe b Broderick	56
A. S. M. Oakman b Tribe	90	— c Clarke b Tribe	10
G. Potter b Starkie	2	— c Broderick b Starkie	35
J. M. Parks st Andrew b Tribe	4	— not out	23
R. T. Webb lbw b Tribe	2		
K. G. Suttle b Tribe	80	— c Barrick b Tribe	17
N. I. Thomson c Brookes b Broderick	2	— not out	10
D. L. Bates st Andrew b Tribe	8		
A. E. James not out	4		
R. G. Marlar c Brookes b Tribe	0		
B 6, l-b 5	11	B 7, l-b 4	11

1/39 2/89 3/92 4/109 5/119 6/186   251   1/23 2/46   (5 wkts., dec.) 179
7/201 8/220 9/251   3/109 4/135 5/169

Northamptonshire

D. Brookes b Thomson	18	— b Marlar	21
P. Arnold b Thomson	10	— c Suttle b Marlar	24
L. Livingston c Langridge b Thomson	16	— c Suttle b Marlar	3
D. Barrick b Thomson	5	— c Bates b Thomson	64
R. Subba Row hit wkt b Oakman	26	— b Marlar	3
G. E. Tribe c Webb b Marlar	64	— c Potter b Oakman	10
V. Broderick b Oakman	9	— c Suttle b Marlar	0
A. Lightfoot st Webb b Marlar	6	— c and b Marlar	10
S. Starkie not out	11	— run out	4
K. V. Andrew lbw b Marlar	0	— c and b Marlar	5
R. W. Clarke c Webb b Marlar	9	— not out	2
B 19, l-b 8, w 1, n-b 1	29	B 6, l-b 2	8

1/28 2/33 3/50 4/53 5/117 6/147   203   1/39 2/45 3/60 4/74   154
7/164 8/191 9/191   5/87 6/87 7/143 8/147 9/147

Northamptonshire Bowling

	O.	M.	R.	W.		O.	M.	R.	W.
Clarke	9	3	13	0	....	16	3	37	1
Lightfoot	7	1	16	0	....	12	4	27	0
Starkie	24	6	76	2	....	11	3	32	1
Broderick......	21	4	66	1	....	9	2	43	1
Tribe	26.2	6	69	7	....	19	10	29	2

Sussex Bowling

	O.	M.	R.	W.		O.	M.	R.	W.
Thomson	34	9	55	4	....	11	2	47	1
Bates	6	1	14	0	....	5	0	12	0
James	17	9	24	0	....	4	1	18	0
Smith	5	3	4	0					
Marlar	27	9	48	4	....	24.2	8	53	7
Oakman	28	17	29	2	....	12	3	16	1

Umpires: F. Chester and T. Spencer.

SUSSEX v. CAMBRIDGE UNIVERSITY

At Horsham, June 11, 13, 14. Cambridge University won by four wickets. Set to get 265 in just over four hours, they succeeded eight minutes from time, thanks largely to a stand of 94 by Goonesena and Lumsden. Parks overshadowed everybody else in the Sussex first innings. For four and a half hours he pulled and drove freely, hitting one 6 and twenty-three 4's. Foreman and Cox helped him in stands of 130 and 115. Against a depleted Sussex attack Cambridge batted unevenly and they found defensive tactics unprofitable. Parsons, who stayed three and a half hours for 46, shared with Lumsden in a partnership of 101, but the University narrowly avoided following on.

Sussex

G. Potter c Melluish b C. Smith	2	— b Lumsden	32
D. V. Smith c Goonesena b C. Smith ...	10	— b D. Smith	11
K. G. Suttle b Goonesena	45	— not out	20
J. M. Parks not out	175		
D. S. Sheppard b D. Smith	12	— c Melluish b Lumsden	24
D. J. Foreman b Lumsden	38	— st Melluish b Goonesena ..	1
G. Cox b Goonesena...................	48	— b D. Smith	17
D. N. Mantell c Melluish b Goonesena .	2		
R. G. Marlar (did not bat).............		— not out	5
D. L. Bates (did not bat)			
D. J. Wood (did not bat)			
B 21, l-b 6, n-b 2	29	B 15, l-b 10..........	25

1/2 2/35 3/87 4/114	(7 wkts., dec.) 361	1/23 2/67 (5 wkts., dec.) 135
5/244 6/359 7/361		3/68 4/90 5/124

Cambridge University

R. O'Brien c Sheppard b Wood	1	— b Wood	1
A. B. D. Parsons c Foreman b Marlar	46	— not out	14
G. Goonesena b Bates	14	— c Marlar b Bates	61
V. R. Lumsden b Marlar	47	— c Cox b Wood	90
D. R. W. Silk b Parks	26	— b Parks	25
S. Singh c and b Parks	39	— lbw b Bates	26
P. D. Croft b Marlar	6	— c Parks b Wood	26
W. Knightley-Smith not out	13		
C. S. Smith b Marlar	4	— not out	7
M. E. L. Melluish lbw b Marlar	16		
D. J. Smith lbw b Parks	0		
B 8, l-b 11, w 1	20	B 6, l-b 10, n-b 1	17
	—		—
	232	(6 wkts.)	267

1/2 2/14 3/115 4/122 5/184 6/195
7/195 8/201 9/227

1/4 2/55 3/149   4/210 5/233 6/249

Cambridge University Bowling

	O.	M.	R.	W.		O.	M.	R.	W.
C. Smith	29	3	106	2	....	10	4	20	0
D. Smith	27	6	84	1	....	17	0	32	2
Singh	14	5	37	0					
Goonesena	21	4	68	3	....	19	5	41	1
Lumsden	8	0	37	1	....	11	6	17	2

Sussex Bowling

	O.	M.	R.	W.		O.	M.	R.	W.
Wood	16	8	13	1	....	16	4	33	3
Bates	15	3	32	1	....	22	7	58	2
Marlar	48	20	89	5	....	26.1	5	98	0
Smith	15	4	27	0	....	6	1	25	0
Potter	16	5	28	0					
Parks	16.5	6	23	3	....	11	4	36	1

Umpires: F. Chester and T. Spencer.

At Dudley, June 15, 16, 17. SUSSEX beat WORCESTERSHIRE by 108 runs.

At Hove, June 18, 20, 21. SUSSEX lost to SOUTH AFRICANS by nine wickets. (See SOUTH AFRICAN section.)

At Tunbridge Wells, June 22, 23, 24. SUSSEX lost to KENT by 104 runs.

SUSSEX v. OXFORD UNIVERSITY

At Hove, June 25, 27, 28. Drawn. On a pitch which gave bowlers little help, Oxford began with a stand of 133 between Allan (thirteen 4's) and Smith (fourteen 4's), and Walton and Williams, who hit one 6 and fourteen 4's in a stay of two and a half hours, also scored readily. For Sussex, who declared 15 runs ahead, Langridge was the most prominent batsman. Always master of the bowling, he made the 75th century of his career in nearly four hours, with three 6's and eighteen 4's among his figures. Lawrence helped him add 144 and Sheppard and Foreman punished the Oxford attack. Smith took the honours in the University second innings, hitting two 6's and eleven 4's, but Thomson and Bates dismissed the last seven batsmen for 90. Sussex needed 264 to win and though losing two men cheaply, were never in danger.

Oxford University

J. M. Allan c Sheppard b Bates		69	— c Langridge b Bates		25
M. J. K. Smith b Oakman		89	— lbw b Thomson		100
A. C. Walton c Lawrence b Bates		68	— c Potter b Willson		29
C. C. P. Williams c Foreman b Thomson		95	— c Willson b Lawrence		37
G. P. S. Delisle b Bates		10	— run out		14
J. P. Fellows-Smith not out		25	— c Langridge b Bates		15
I Gibson (did not bat)			— b Bates		14
A. P. Walshe (did not bat)			— b Thomson		18
D. K. Fasken (did not bat)			— c Marlar b Bates		11
D. C. P. R. Jowett (did not bat)			— b Thomson		0
J. B. Phillips (did not bat)			— not out		0
B 4, l-b 2, w 1		7	B 8, l-b 7		15

1/133 2/175 3/279   (5 wkts., dec.) 363
4/309 5/363

1/43 2/114 3/188 4/207   278
5/221 6/242 7/259 8/276
9/278

Sussex

J. Langridge b Fasken		153	— c Walton b Phillips		15
G. Potter b Fasken		27	— c Gibson b Phillips		4
A. S. M. Oakman c Phillips b Fasken		3			
A. A. K. Lawrence c Williams b Phillips		62	— not out		63
D. S. Sheppard not out		58	— c Fellows-Smith b Allan		38
R. H. Willson c Walshe b Fasken		25	— c Delisle b Jowett		5
D. J. Foreman not out		40	— not out		15
B 7, l-b 3		10	B 4, l-b 1, w 1		6

1/94 2/102 3/246 4/256   (5 wkts., dec.) 378
5/289

1/17 2/21 3/110   (4 wkts.) 146
4/124

N. I. Thomson, R. T. Webb, R. G. Marlar and D. L. Bates did not bat.

Sussex Bowling

	O.	M.	R.	W.		O.	M.	R.	W.
Thomson	20.2	1	84	1	....	16	7	46	3
Bates	26	3	78	3	....	23.1	5	79	4
Oakman	21	4	46	1	....	7	2	26	0
Willson	7	0	35	0	....	7	0	42	1
Potter	13	3	42	0	....	8	2	40	0
Marlar	17	3	71	0	....	3	0	16	0
					Lawrence	2	0	14	1

Oxford University Bowling

	O.	M.	R.	W.		O.	M.	R.	W.
Phillips	25	2	99	1	....	14	3	36	2
Fasken	35	5	102	4	....	17	1	61	0
Fellows-Smith	12	2	41	0					
Jowett	15	2	51	0	....	4	0	13	1
Allan	22	5	70	0	....	8	1	25	1
Gibson	1	0	5	0					
					Williams	2	0	5	0

Umpires: F. S. Lee and J. J. Hills.

At Liverpool, June 29, 30, July 1. SUSSEX drew with LANCASHIRE.

SUSSEX v. HAMPSHIRE

At Eastbourne, July 2, 4, 5. A tie. Set 140 to get to win, Hampshire fared so badly against the medium-pace bowling of James that eight men were out for 84. Sainsbury and Cannings joined in a stubborn partnership of 55 which brought the scores level, but in trying to turn Thomson to leg for the winning run, Cannings was bowled and each side took six Championship points. The pitch always favoured bowlers. When Sussex were sent in to bat, Langridge stayed three and

T

a half hours and prevented a bad batting breakdown against the fast-medium bowling of Shackleton and Cannings. The same pair of bowlers were responsible for the collapse of Sussex when they batted a second time 19 runs ahead.

Sussex

J. Langridge c Harrison b Cannings	48	— b Cannings	6
D. V. Smith b Cannings	0	— lbw b Shackleton	1
A. S. M. Oakman c Marshall b Shackleton	3	— b Shackleton	8
J. M. Parks lbw b Sainsbury	29	— lbw b Cannings	12
K. G. Suttle b Cannings	20	— c Sainsbury b Cannings	13
G. Cox run out	28	— lbw b Shackleton	6
A. A. K. Lawrence c Harrison b Shackleton	5	— c Harrison b Shackleton	13
R. T. Webb c Barnard b Shackleton	12	— lbw b Sainsbury	8
N. I. Thomson c Burden b Shackleton	7	— c Shackleton b Gray	12
A. E. James not out	8	— not out	11
R. G. Marlar c Barnard b Cannings	6	— c Gray b Shackleton	23
B 2, l-b 4	6	B 2, l-b 5	7

1/0 2/5 3/64 4/88 5/123 6/138 7/151   172   1/7 2/7 3/24 4/34 5/43   120
8/151 9/164   6/50 7/69 8/71 9/89

Hampshire

J. R. Gray c Marlar b Thomson	12	— c Oakman b James	4
R. E. Marshall c Smith b Thomson	14	— c Webb b James	2
H. Horton b James	40	— lbw b Marlar	19
A. W. H. Rayment c Langridge b Marlar	31	— lbw b Smith	30
H. M. Barnard c Webb b Oakman	7	— c Langridge b James	0
E. D. R. Eagar b Langridge b Oakman	2	— b James	14
L. Harrison b Thomson	13	— b Thomson	2
P. J. Sainsbury c Lawrence b James	3	— b James	22
D. Shackleton c Oakman b James	13	— c Webb b Thomson	13
V. H. D. Cannings not out	3	— b Thomson	25
M. D. Burden b James	6	— not out	0
B 7, l-b 2	9	B 4, l-b 3, n-b 1	8

1/24 2/33 3/80 4/95 5/101 6/125   153   1/5 2/10 3/55 4/55 5/59   139
7/131 8/133 9/147   6/74 7/84 8/84 9/139

Hampshire Bowling

	O.	M.	R.	W.		O.	M.	R.	W.
Shackleton	26	9	45	4	....	26.2	13	42	5
Cannings	27.5	9	53	4	....	22	5	55	3
Gray	19	5	35	0	....	5	3	6	1
Sainsbury	20	11	28	1	....	9	5	10	1
Burden	3	2	5	0					

Sussex Bowling

	O.	M.	R.	W.		O.	M.	R.	W.
Thomson	27	11	43	3	....	29.4	11	42	3
James	32.3	14	60	4	....	33	14	49	5
Smith	3	3	0	0	....	10	2	20	1
Oakman	17	4	29	2	....	2	0	10	0
Marlar	4	0	12	1	....	8	4	10	1

Umpires: H. Elliott (Lancashire) and E. Cooke.

SUSSEX v. GLOUCESTERSHIRE

At Eastbourne, July 6, 7. Sussex won by an innings and 173 runs. They batted consistently. Smith made many good strokes in front of the wicket; Suttle (fourteen 4's) drove and cut well for two and three-quarter hours, he and Parks adding 108, and Lawrence (ten 4's) and Cox (eight 4's) punished the bowling so severely that they put on 86 in twenty-eight minutes. A gallant innings of three hours forty minutes by the left-handed Crapp, who hit one 6 and thirteen 4's, chiefly drives, could not prevent Gloucestershire following on 274 behind, and in the second innings they collapsed against the fast-medium bowling of Thomson.

Sussex

J. Langridge c Rochford b Lambert	14	G. Cox b Cook 49
D. V. Smith lbw b Wells	69	N. I. Thomson not out 12
A. S. M. Oakman c Rochford b Cook	31	R. G. Marlar not out 19
J. M. Parks run out	54	B 19, l-b 7, w 1, n-b 1 28
K. G. Suttle b Milton	104	
A. A. K. Lawrence c Crapp b Cook	63	1/38 2/116 3/124 (7 wkts., dec.) 443
		4/232 5/322 6/408 7/415

A. E. James and R. T. Webb did not bat.

Gloucestershire

D. M. Young b Smith	6	— c Webb b Thomson	2
C. A. Milton lbw b James	37	— c Langridge b Thomson....	34
J. F. Crapp st Webb b Cox	101	— c Webb b James	10
G. M. Emmett c Webb b James	0	— c Webb b Thomson	9
W. Knightley-Smith b James	0	— not out	23
G. E. Lambert c Cox b James	3	— b Thomson...............	3
J. Mortimore c Lawrence b Cox	5	— c Cox b James	8
P. Rochford lbw b Smith	1	— lbw b Smith	1
C. Cook b Smith	0	— st Webb b Smith	2
B. D. Wells not out	0	— c Suttle b Thomson	2
F. P. McHugh c Lawrence b Cox........	0	— b Smith	2
B 9, l-b 7	16	B 5..................	5
1/21 2/85 3/89 4/95 5/127 6/162	169	1/10 2/45 3/58 4/59 5/63	101
7/165 8/165 9/169		6/74 7/83 8/95 9/98	

Gloucestershire Bowling

	O.	M.	R.	W.		O.	M.	R.	W.
Lambert	28	4	98	1					
McHugh	28	4	97	0					
Milton	19	6	50	1					
Wells	32	6	99	1					
Cook	17	3	63	3					
Mortimore.....	2	1	8	0					

Sussex Bowling

	O.	M.	R.	W.		O.	M.	R.	W.
Thomson	20	4	50	0	....	20	5	41	5
James	26	11	34	4	....	16	4	39	2
Smith	21	10	19	3	....	7	1	12	3
Marlar	5	0	23	0					
Cox...........	4.4	2	7	3	....	3	2	4	0
Oakman	3	0	20	0					

Umpires: H. Elliott (Lancashire) and E. Cooke.

At Sheffield, July 9, 11, 12. SUSSEX lost to YORKSHIRE by eight wickets.

SUSSEX v. ROYAL NAVY

At Hove, July 14, 15. Sussex won by an innings and 89 runs. Royal Navy 90 (D. V. Smith four for seven) and 102 (W. H. Bagust four for 40); Sussex 281 for six wickets, declared (A. S. M. Oakman 69, D. J. Foreman 60 not out, G. Potter 56).

SUSSEX v. KENT

(D. J. Wood's Benefit)

At Hastings, July 16, 18, 19. Sussex won by nine wickets. This match was virtually decided half an hour after lunch on the first day when Kent, who won the toss, were all out on a green-looking pitch for 66. As at Tunbridge Wells a few weeks earlier they were baffled by the seam bowlers, and Donald Smith, left-arm over the wicket attacking the right-hander's leg stump, took five of the last six wickets. Sussex soon lost Langridge, but Smith showed his all-round quality by driving well and he and Oakman put Sussex completely on top in a stand of 118. With Parks, Sheppard and Suttle all enjoying themselves, Sussex declared 233 ahead. Then Oakman brought off two smart catches and Kent again looked like breaking down, but Pettiford and Shirreff defied the bowling for one and three-quarter hours, their stand yielding 102. Altogether Pettiford stayed three hours twenty minutes. Thomson and Smith, however, were too good for the tail and Sussex were left with a very easy task in the fourth innings.

Kent

A. E. Fagg lbw b Thomson	1	— c Oakman b James 20
A. H. Phebey c Oakman b Thomson ...	0	— c Oakman b Thomson 2
J. M. Allan lbw b James	0	— c Webb b Oakman 20
R. C. Wilson c Webb b Thomson	17	— not out 2
J. Pettiford c Webb b Smith	20	— c Sheppard b Smith 90
J. F. Pretlove not out	9	— c Langridge b Oakman ... 8
A. C. Shirreff lbw b Smith	0	— c Webb b Thomson 55
D. G. Ufton c James b Smith	8	— c Parks b Thomson 18
G. Smith c Langridge b Smith	0	— c Parks b Thomson 4
D. V. P. Wright b Smith	0	— c Parks b Thomson 13
J. C. T. Page b Thomson	1	— b Smith 6
B 4, l-b 5, n-b 1	10	B 8, l-b 12, n-b 1 21

1/5 2/5 3/5 4/41 5/45 6/45 7/59   66   1/18 2/24 3/46 4/73   259
8/59 9/59   5/175 6/225 7/229 8/243
     9/253

Sussex

J. Langridge c Smith b Shirreff	0	
D. V. Smith lbw b Shirreff	65	— not out 15
A. S. M. Oakman lbw b Allan	65	— not out 8
J. M. Parks c Fagg b Shirreff	59	
D. S. Sheppard lbw b Wright	52	
K. G. Suttle not out	43	
G. Cox lbw b Wright	9	— c Shirreff b Smith 4
N. I. Thomson c Fagg b Smith	0	
R. T. Webb c Pretlove b Wright	0	
R. G. Marlar c Shirreff b Wright	0	
B 6	6	

1/0 2/118 3/155 4/232   (9 wkts., dec.) 299   1/6   (1 wkt.) 27
5/267 6/295 7/296 8/299 9/299

A. E. James did not bat.

Sussex Bowling

	O.	M.	R.	W.		O.	M.	R.	W.
Thomson	19.1	8	18	4	....	40.4	9	94	5
James	11	4	25	1	....	31	14	56	1
Smith	13	8	13	5	....	13	4	29	2
Oakman						13	5	24	2
Marlar						10	3	35	0

Kent Bowling

	O.	M.	R.	W.		O.	M.	R.	W.
Shirreff	28	5	92	3	....	4.2	1	13	0
Smith	27	6	83	1	....	5	0	14	1
Wright	15	3	59	4					
Allan	14	8	24	1					
Pretlove	3	1	10	0					
Page	3	0	25	0					

Umpires: W. F. Price and A. J. B. Fowler.

SUSSEX v. WARWICKSHIRE

At Hastings, July 20, 21, 22. Sussex won by 56 runs. Two seam bowlers were in their element on a green pitch. Roland Thompson, of Warwickshire, took eleven wickets for 108 runs and Ian Thomson, of Sussex, ten for 95. Naturally Warwickshire, having sent in Sussex, considered they had done well in dismissing them for 178. The match went against the visitors when they lost half their wickets for 39. Sussex gained a lead of 69 and thanks to strong confident strokes by the left-handed Smith they left Warwickshire to make 203. This time James disposed of Horner, Wolton and Hitchcock while conceding only a single, but H. E. Dollery rallied his side in a brilliant display. In two and a half hours the Warwickshire captain scored 82, hitting ten 4's, and his stand with Gardner realised 111 before he was smartly stumped just before the close of the second day. That was the final turning-point, for next day Thomson, acquiring much lift, was mainly responsible for the last six wickets falling for the addition of only 29 runs.

Sussex

D. V. Smith c Gardner b Thompson	6	— b Thompson	38
J. Langridge c Bannister b Thompson ..	0	— lbw b Thompson	3
A. S. M. Oakman b Thompson	40	— c Spooner b Thompson	6
J. M. Parks c Spooner b K. Dollery	19	— b Thompson	5
K. G. Suttle c H. Dollery b Thompson..	44	— lbw b Hollies	14
A. A. K. Lawrence not out	33	— lbw b Thompson	9
G. Cox c Bannister b Thompson	4	— b Bannister	7
R. T. Webb c Townsend b Thompson	0	— not out	20
N. I. Thomson run out	10	— c Horner b Bannister	11
A. E. James b Hollies	2	— c Spooner b Bannister	1
R. G. Marlar c and b Thompson	0	— st Spooner b Bannister	3
B 10, l-b 5, n-b 5	20	B 4, l-b 7, w 4, n-b 1 ..	16

1/1 2/10 3/63 4/103 5/137 6/149   178   1/5 2/31 3/43 4/63 5/87   133
7/149 8/171 9/177   6/98 7/107 8/124 9/125

Warwickshire

F. C. Gardner c Lawrence b Thomson ..	6	— c Langridge b Thomson	30
N. F. Horner st Webb b James	3	— c Langridge b James	1
A. V. Wolton b Smith	12	— b James	0
R. E. Hitchcock run out	5	— c Langridge b James	2
H. E. Dollery c Langridge b Marlar	31	— st Webb b James	82
R. T. Spooner c Webb b Thomson	0	— c Smith b Thomson	0
A. Townsend lbw b Thomson	21	— run out	1
K. R. Dollery lbw b Thomson	0	— lbw b Smith	19
J. D. Bannister c Webb b Thomson	4	— c Marlar b Thomson	4
R. G. Thompson c Langridge b Thomson	9	— not out	1
W. E. Hollies not out	1	— c Marlar b Thomson	0
B 8, l-b 8, n-b 1	17	B 6	6

1/4 2/29 3/29 4/37 5/39 6/83 7/87   109   1/4 2/4 3/6 4/117 5/118   146
8/93 9/100   6/122 7/123 8/13 3 9/145

Warwickshire Bowling

	O.	M.	R.	W.		O.	M.	R.	W.
Thompson	23	2	61	6	....	21	6	47	5
Bannister	16	4	41	1	....	17.1	5	48	4
K. Dollery	14	1	48	1	....	6	1	13	0
Townsend	2	1	3	0					
Hollies	4	1	5	1	....	5	1	9	1

Sussex Bowling

	O.	M.	R.	W.		O.	M.	R.	W.
Thomson	20.2	8	36	6	....	28.1	7	59	4
James	9	3	23	1	....	25	7	54	4
Smith	13	2	33	1	....	12	8	7	1
Marlar	1	1	0	1	....	5	2	11	0
Cox						4	2	3	0
Oakman						2	0	6	0

Umpires: W. F. Price and A. J. B. Fowler.

At Bristol, July 23, 25, 26. SUSSEX lost to GLOUCESTERSHIRE by 16 runs.

SUSSEX v. WORCESTERSHIRE

At Hove, July 27, 28, 29. Sussex won by six wickets. Again Thomson put Sussex on top, for Worcestershire, winning the toss, decided to bat; but first thing the pitch was green and they were powerless against capable swing bowlers. Taking the lead for the loss of only three men, Sussex pursued an enterprising policy. The left-handed Suttle pulled and drove freely, hitting nine 4's, and Cox who batted an hour less, made his 69 (two 6's and nine 4's) in eighty minutes. Worcestershire also revelled in the easier conditions when they batted a second time and Kenyon, one 6 and thirteen 4's, gave a delightful display until Parks caught him brilliantly close to the ground at cover. A bruised heel kept Thomson off the field and Broadbent, after exercising much patience, hit four 6's, two from Marlar clearing the ground. The younger Richardson excelled with the off-drive but, thanks to the untiring efforts of James and the persistent off-spin of Marlar, Sussex needed only 100 for victory.

Worcestershire

D. Kenyon c Oakman b James	6	— c Parks b James	94
J. Lister lbw b Thomson	0	— lbw b James	2
L. Outschoorn b Thomson	2	— c sub b Marlar	14
R. G. Broadbent c Suttle b Thomson ..	37	— c Webb b Smith	71
M. J. Horton b Thomson	9	— lbw b Smith	1
D. W. Richardson c Langridge b Smith .	11	— c Oakman b Marlar	61
R. O. Jenkins c Webb b Smith	0	— c Langridge b Marlar	15
H. Yarnold b Smith	0	— lbw b Marlar	18
R. T. D. Perks b Thomson	3	— c sub b Marlar	12
G. H. Chesterton not out	22	— c Webb b Smith	17
J. Flavell b Smith	4	— not out	0
B 10, n-b 1	11	B 23, l-b 1, n-b 1	25

1/1 2/5 3/13 4/34 5/53 6/53 7/57   105
8/65 9/85

1/46 2/140 3/155 4/196   330
5/199 6/266 7/289 8/306
9/324

Sussex

J. Langridge c sub b Chesterton	47	— c Yarnold b Jenkins 26
D. V. Smith c Outschoorn b Flavell	11	— c Yarnold b Perks......... 10
A. S. M. Oakman b Chesterton	40	— not out 41
J. M. Parks lbw b Chesterton	13	— not out 7
K. G. Suttle c Outschoorn b Chesterton	75	— b Jenkins 2
G. H. G. Doggart c Outschoorn b Chesterton	28	— c Yarnold b Jenkins 7
G. Cox c Chesterton b Perks	69	
R. T. Webb run out	1	
N. I. Thomson not out	20	
A. E. James st Yarnold b Chesterton	15	
B 4, l-b 6, w 1, n-b 6	17	L-b 5, w 1, n-b 1 7

1/19 2/102 3/102 4/129   (9 wkts., dec.) 336   1/18 2/74 3/82   (4 wkts.) 100
5/202 6/269 7/280 8/299 9/336   4/84

R. G. Marlar did not bat.

Sussex Bowling

	O.	M.	R.	W.		O.	M.	R.	W.
Thomson	16	6	24	5	....	3	1	4	0
James	19	5	49	1	....	55	24	88	2
Smith	9.2	5	21	4	....	36	15	67	3
Marlar						35.4	12	101	5
Oakman						11	2	45	0
Cox						1	1	0	0

Worcestershire Bowling

	O.	M.	R.	W.		O.	M.	R.	W.
Perks	26	2	•109	1	....	15.3	3	40	1
Flavell	22	3	71	1	....	11	5	23	0
Chesterton	30	6	139	6	....	5	1	17	0
Jenkins						7	1	13	3

Umpires: L. H. Gray and E. Cooke.

SUSSEX v. MIDDLESEX

At Hove, July 30, August 1, 2. Middlesex won by six wickets, an excellent performance after being 105 behind on the first innings. Chief credit belonged to the left-hander, Dewes, playing in his first county game of the season. He batted without mistake for four hours fifty minutes, hitting one 6 and fifteen 4's. Another left-hander, Smith, gave Sussex a capital start on the opening day, strong drives bringing him ten 4's. Oakman helped him add 102 and Parks pulled freely, but Bennett and Warr, fast-medium, got down the last six wickets for 40 runs. Apart from Brown and Edrich, who put on 71, the Middlesex batsmen failed against the medium-pace cutters of James in the first innings, and though the pitch gave bowlers little help, Sussex would have been cheaply dismissed at the second attempt but for a hard-hitting last wicket partnership of 55 between Marlar and Webb.

Sussex

J. Langridge lbw b Bennett	13	—	c Titmus b Warr		7
D. V. Smith c Titmus b Young	90	—	c Titmus b Bennett		35
A. S. M. Oakman c Dewes b Young	50	—	c Titmus b Warr		4
J. M. Parks c Edrich b Bennett	53	—	b Bennett		18
K. G. Suttle lbw b Warr	15	—	b Titmus		12
G. H. G. Doggart b Bennett	12	—	b Titmus		4
G. Cox lbw b Bennett	5	—	b Titmus		10
R. G. Marlar c Bennett b Warr	3	—	b Bennett		39
R. T. Webb b Warr	8	—	not out		34
A. E. James b Bennett	4	—	run out		6
N. I. Thomson not out	0	—	c Delisle b Warr		1
B 5, l-b 7	12		B 2, l-b 12, w 4		18

1/40 2/142 3/165 4/225 5/241 6/246   265
7/251 8/253 9/263

1/16 2/20 3/62 4/71 5/76   188
6/95 7/106 8/117 9/130

Middlesex

J. D. Robertson lbw b Thomson	4	—	c Langridge b Thomson		27
J. G. Dewes c Langridge b James	9	—	b Thomson		117
S. M. Brown c Webb b Smith	55	—	b Marlar		41
G. P. S. Delisle c Parks b Thomson	6	—	not out		45
W. J. Edrich c Langridge b James	28	—	b James		49
D. Bennett c Langridge b James	10	—	not out		6
F. J. Titmus b James	0				
J. J. Warr b Smith	3				
H. W. Tilly b Smith	3				
L. H. Compton not out	28				
J. A. Young b James	1				
B 13	13		B 4, l-b 5		9

1/4 2/18 3/35 4/106 5/118 6/125   160
7/128 8/128 9/155

1/55 2/136 3/231 (4 wkts.) 294
4/245

Middlesex Bowling

	O.	M.	R.	W.		O.	M.	R.	W.
Warr	24.4	4	48	3	....	18	1	66	3
Tilly	15	0	53	0	....	4	1	16	0
Bennett	21	2	75	5	....	15.4	2	56	3
Titmus	16	4	32	0	....	18	8	32	3
Young	22	8	45	2					

Sussex Bowling

	O.	M.	R.	W.		O.	M.	R.	W.
Thomson	25	10	33	2	....	32	12	75	2
James	33.2	12	67	5	....	26	5	73	1
Smith	17	3	39	3	....	22	7	61	0
Marlar	2	0	8	0	....	25.3	9	76	1

Umpires: E. Cooke and N. Oldfield.

At Chelmsford, August 3, 4, 5. SUSSEX drew with ESSEX.

At Portsmouth, August 6, 8, 9. SUSSEX lost to HAMPSHIRE by 151 runs.

At Derby, August 10, 11, 12. SUSSEX beat DERBYSHIRE by 49 runs.

At Leicester, August 13, 15, 16. SUSSEX lost to LEICESTERSHIRE by 143 runs.

SUSSEX v. LANCASHIRE

At Hove, August 17, 18, 19. Sussex won by 87 runs. To the batting of Sheppard and the off-break bowling of Marlar who, in taking nine wickets for 46 runs in the Lancashire second innings achieved the best performance of his career, went most honours. In the match Marlar dismissed fifteen batsmen for 119 runs. Sheppard played admirably on the opening day, his stand of 110 with Doggart and one of 57 by Webb and Thomson retrieving a bad start. Apart from Washbrook, who displayed marked skill for two and three-quarter hours, none of the Lancashire batsmen dealt effectively with Marlar. Leading by 71, Sussex would have collapsed against the off-spin of Tattersall but for Sheppard who, because of a leg injury, employed a runner. Marlar dispelled any Lancashire hopes of scoring 193 to win by disposing of three men in his second over.

Sussex

J. Langridge c Barber b Wharton	13	— b Wharton	1
D. V. Smith c Wilson b Moore	11	— c Wilson b Wharton	4
A. S. M. Oakman st Wilson b Wharton	12	— b Wharton	0
J. M. Parks c Wilson b Moore	2	— lbw b Tattersall	15
D. S. Sheppard lbw b Standring	65	— c Collins b Tattersall	61
G. H. G. Doggart b Tattersall	51	— c Edrich b Tattersall	9
K. G. Suttle c Wilson b Tattersall	11	— lbw b Standring	2
R. T. Webb not out	49	— c Moore b Tattersall	18
N. I. Thomson c Wilson b Standring	32	— not out	10
R. G. Marlar c Barber b Moore	25	— c Washbrook b Moore	0
A. E. James run out	2	— b Tattersall	0
B 1, l-b 1	2	B 1	1

1/18 2/35 3/38 4/40 5/150 6/156   275
7/166 8/223 9/258

1/5 2/6 3/9 4/41 5/59   121
6/62 7/91 8/91 9/120

Lancashire

A. Wharton c Webb b Smith	26	— c Smith b Marlar	16
S. Smith b Marlar	9	— c Suttle b Marlar	19
G. A. Edrich c Langridge b Marlar	23	— c Langridge b Marlar	17
G. Pullar c Smith b Marlar	11	— c Smith b Marlar	5
C. Washbrook c Doggart b James	94	— c Suttle b Marlar	0
R. W. Barber c Doggart b Marlar	0	— b Marlar	6
R. Collins lbw b James	23	— c Suttle b Marlar	24
K. B. Standring c Webb b Marlar	0	— c Langridge b Marlar	2
F. W. Barber run out	7	— b James	16
A. Wilson b Marlar	2	— c Oakman b Marlar	0
R. Tattersall not out	0	— not out	0
B 2, l-b 7	9		

1/31 2/55 3/64 4/87 5/113 6/150   204
7/161 8/181 9/204

1/35 2/38 3/38 4/69   105
5/80 6/83 7/91 8/105 9/105

Lancashire Bowling

	O.	M.	R.	W.	O.	M.	R.	W.
Wharton	21	4	52	2	13	3	40	3
Moore	28	6	74	3	18.2	8	34	1
Standring	15	2	42	2	8	5	7	1
Tattersall	27	7	79	2	20	11	30	5
Collins	8.3	3	18	0	7	4	9	0
Barber	1	0	8	0				

Sussex Bowling

	O.	M.	R.	W.	O.	M.	R.	W.
Thomson	19	7	31	0	 4	0	12	0
James	28.3	5	56	2	 28	13	45	1
Smith	16	5	35	1	 2	1	2	0
Marlar	33	10	73	6	.... 23.2	8	46	9

Umpires: G. S. Mobey and J. J. Hills.

SUSSEX v. NOTTINGHAMSHIRE

At Hove, August 20, 22, 23. Sussex won by ten wickets. After losing their first two wickets cheaply they took complete control and gained an easy success. Oakman and Parks led the recovery with a stand of 78 and Parks and Suttle put on 158 in just over two hours for the fifth wicket. Parks hit two 6's and fourteen 4's in a delightful innings, and ten of Suttle's sixteen 4's came in his first 50. C. J. Poole alone offered resistance for Nottinghamshire who disappointed on a good pitch, and followed on 230 behind. They showed better form in the second innings, when conditions became more difficult, but Sussex needed only three to win.

Sussex

J. Langridge c K. Poole b Jepson	4		
D. V. Smith lbw b Jepson	18		
A. S. M. Oakman lbw b Goonesena	44		
J. M. Parks c and b Smales	117		
G. H. G. Doggart b Goonesena	0		
K. G. Suttle lbw b Dooland	93	— not out	4
G. Cox run out	26		
R. G. Marlar b Dooland	39		
R. T. Webb not out	8	— not out	0
N. I. Thomson b Jepson	1		
B 6, l-b 4	10		

1/20 2/33 3/111 4/111   (9 wkts., dec.) 360   (No wkt.) 4
5/269 6/299 7/316 8/357 9/360
A. E. James did not bat.

Nottinghamshire

R. T. Simpson st Webb b Marlar	5	— c Webb b Marlar	59
J. D. Clay b Smith	19	— c Langridge b Smith	6
E. J. Rowe c Oakman b Thomson	6	— st Webb b Smith	3
R. J. Giles lbw b Thomson	4	— b James	28
F. W. Stocks c and b Thomson	1	— c Doggart b James	0
C. J. Poole not out	59	— c Webb b Marlar	39
K. J. Poole b James	11	— b Marlar	40
G. Goonesena c Oakman b Marlar	5	— st Webb b Parks	8
B. Dooland b James	1	— c Webb b Marlar	6
K. Smales lbw b James	2	— not out	23
A. Jepson c Parks b Marlar	12	— st Webb b Thomson	12
B 4, l-b 1	5	B 5, l-b 2, w 1	8

1/11 2/30 3/30 4/35 5/40 6/53 7/90   130   1/28 2/78 3/82 4/93   232
8/91 9/99
5/161 6/182 7/188 8/188
9/229

Nottinghamshire Bowling

	O.	M.	R.	W.	O.	M.	R.	W.
Jepson	20.5	7	44	3				
K. Poole	13	2	53	0				
Smales	32	9	96	1				
Dooland	25	3	109	2				
Goonesena	16	3	48	2				
C. Poole					0.1	0	4	0

Sussex Bowling

	O.	M.	R.	W.	O.	M.	R.	W.
Thomson	18	6	35	3	19	5	49	1
James	21	7	45	3	15	7	28	2
Marlar	12.2	4	21	3	32	9	88	4
Smith	9	2	24	1	12.1	5	28	2
Cox					4	2	12	0
Parks					13	4	19	1

Umpires: L. H. Gray and H. G. Baldwin.

At The Oval, August 24, 25, 26. SUSSEX lost to SURREY by an innings and eight runs.

SUSSEX v. DERBYSHIRE

At Hove, August 27, 29, 30. Sussex won by 94 runs. The batting of Oakman and Parks and the bowling of Marlar were the outstanding features of their triumph. On the first day Oakman made the first hundred of his career, batting faultlessly for two hours fifty minutes and hitting fifteen 4's. Parks helped him add 85 for the fourth wicket. Smith, who worried most of the other batsmen, took his 100th wicket in his first full season. Derbyshire lost three wickets for 37, but Willatt and Carr proved stubborn. Leading by 92, Sussex consolidated their position with another fine innings by Parks, whose unbeaten 101 took two and three-quarter hours. Set to get 323 Derbyshire were upset for the second time by Marlar, who in the match took twelve wickets for 156 runs.

Sussex

J. Langridge b Smith	30	— c Carr b Morgan	35
D. V. Smith c Hall b Gladwin	18	— lbw b Hall	2
G. H. G. Doggart c Morgan b Hall	6		
J. M. Parks c Willatt b Smith	63	— not out	101
A. S. M. Oakman b Smith	102	— c Smith b Gladwin	12
K. G. Suttle c Green b Smith	17		
G. Cox b Smith	9	— st Dawkes b Carr	79
R. G. Marlar c Hall b Smith	18		
N. I. Thomson not out	25		
R. T. Webb st Dawkes b Gladwin	8		
B 3, l-b 3	6	B 1	1

1/27 2/43 3/77 4/162   (9 wkts., dec.) 302   1/2 2/15   (4 wkts., dec.) 230
5/217 6/243 7/269 8/269 9/302   3/72 4/230

A. E. James did not bat.

Derbyshire

A. Hamer b Thomson	2	— b Thomson	0
J. Kelly b Marlar	5	— c Doggart b Thomson	6
E. Smith b Smith	5	— not out	24
G. L. Willatt c Doggart b Oakman	68	— c Langridge b Marlar	32
A. C. Revill c Langridge b Smith	25	— c Smith b Marlar	32
D. B. Carr c James b Marlar	51	— c Oakman b Marlar	66
D. J. Green c Suttle b Marlar	19	— c Langridge b Marlar	25
D. C. Morgan not out	24	— b Marlar	8
G. O. Dawkes c Suttle b Marlar	0	— b Marlar	0
C. Gladwin c Langridge b Smith	0	— c Langridge b Marlar	16
D. Hall c Suttle b Marlar	0	— b Oakman	6
B 4, l-b 6, w 1	11	B 13	13
	210		228

1/2 2/9 3/37 4/98 5/114 6/182
7/187 8/187 9/187

1/0 2/21 3/58 4/118
5/157 6/180 7/180 8/185
9/207

Derbyshire Bowling

	O.	M.	R.	W.	O.	M.	R.	W.
Hall	21	6	58	1	14	2	55	1
Gladwin	19.4	4	58	2	17	4	54	1
Morgan	12	2	33	0	11	3	46	1
Smith	32	12	80	6	16	3	61	0
Revill	8	3	35	0				
Carr	6	0	32	0	1.2	0	8	1
Hamer					2	0	5	0

Sussex Bowling

	O.	M.	R.	W.	O.	M.	R.	W.
Thomson	20	7	33	1	11	3	24	2
Smith	20	8	44	3	9	5	12	0
Marlar	23.2	5	58	5	24	8	98	7
James	6	2	17	0				
Parks	3	0	11	0	8	0	46	0
Oakman	15	5	36	1	14.1	4	35	1

Umpires: F. Chester and J. S. Buller.

SUSSEX v. SOMERSET

At Hove, August 31, September 1. Sussex won by nine wickets. The batting of Parks dominated the match. He scored 205 not out in only three and a half hours and for the first time completed 2,000 runs in a season. His innings was also the best of his career. In a glorious display he hit five 6's and twenty-five 4's. Smith, Oakman, Cox and Marlar supported him strongly. In six and a half hours on the first day 530 runs were scored. Somerset fought reasonably well, but could not avoid defeat in two days. Wight, Saeed and Lomax offered resistance in the first innings, but only Tremlett held up the attack when they followed on 171 behind. In the final phase Langridge and Cox, making their last appearances in county cricket, walked out to open the Sussex second innings with the crowd standing and cheering them to the wicket. Nor did they forget Lawrence, the Somerset all-rounder, who was also retiring.

Sussex

J. Langridge b Lobb	12	— not out	9
D. V. Smith c Stephenson b Lawrence	52		
A. S. M. Oakman c Tordoff b Lomax	47		
J. M. Parks not out	205		
G. Cox c Stephenson b Yawar Saeed	38	— c Walker b Tordoff	
K. G. Suttle c sub b Yawar Saeed	11		
G. H. G. Doggart c Lomax b Lawrence	18		
R. T. Webb c Wight b Lawrence	26		
N. I. Thomson run out	1		
R. G. Marlar c Tordoff b Walker	38	— not out	1
B 5, l-b 9, w 1, n-b 1	16		

1/24 2/112 3/112 4/214 (9 wkts., dec.) 464 1/17 (1 wkt.) 18
5/283 6/321 7/392 8/402 9/464

A. E. James did not bat.

Somerset

F. L. Angell c Langridge b James	16	— b Marlar	22
M. Walker c Langridge b James	38	— b James	22
J. Lawrence c Smith b Marlar	9	— b Smith	19
M. F. Tremlett b Thomson	17	— c Oakman b Marlar	68
P. B. Wight run out	61	— c Oakman b Smith	4
G. G. Tordoff b James	12	— c James b Marlar	7
H. W. Stephenson c Langridge b Marlar	4	— c Langridge b Smith	8
J. G. Lomax not out	47	— c Langridge b Smith	0
Yawar Saeed c Suttle b Smith	62	— b Marlar	3
J. W. McMahon c Parks b Thomson	5	— c Doggart b Marlar	10
B. Lobb c Oakman b Thomson	4	— not out	2
B 12, l-b 5, n-b 1	18	B 11, l-b 12	23

1/41 2/66 3/81 4/99 5/129 6/142   293 1/40 2/73 3/95 4/102   188
7/180 8/263 9/277   5/106 6/125 7/139 8/152
                                   9/185

Somerset Bowling

	O.	M.	R.	W.	O.	M.	R.	W.
Lobb	14	1	90	1				
Yawar Saeed	15	1	72	2				
Lomax	9	0	48	1				
Lawrence	27	0	159	3	2.2	0	12	0
McMahon	9	1	46	0				
Walker	8	0	33	1				
Tordoff					3	1	6	1

Sussex Bowling

	O.	M.	R.	W.	O.	M.	R.	W.
Thomson	25.2	6	80	3	9	0	34	0
James	36	9	105	3	7	1	28	1
Smith	10	4	25	1	17	5	40	4
Marlar	11	3	44	2	18.2	2	63	5
Oakman	6	1	21	0				

Umpires: F. Chester and J. S. Buller.

PLAYING NO LONGER

Cox, G. (Sussex). Debut 1931. Hard-hitting batsman and cheerful personality, splendid cover point and useful medium-paced bowler. Scored 22,639 runs in his career. Highest score 234 not out against the Indians at Hove in 1946. Exceeded 1,000 runs in a season 13 times. Appointed coach at Winchester College.

Langridge, John (Sussex). Debut 1928. Splendidly consistent opening batsman and brilliant slip fieldsman who scored 34,380 runs in career (average 37.45). Highest score 250 not out against Glamorgan at Hove in 1933. Exceeded 1,000 runs in a season 17 times. Held 69 catches in 1955, which had only twice been bettered.

WARWICKSHIRE

President—Dr. STANLEY BARNES
Secretary—L. T. DEAKINS, County Ground, Birmingham 3
Captain—H. E. DOLLERY

R. E. Hitchcock   County Badge   J. D. Bannister

The performances of Warwickshire during 1955 fell below what had been expected from them in a predominately dry season. Although obtaining 140 points, the same total as in the previous summer, they dropped four places to tenth in the County Championship table. The decline could not be attributed to any single cause. The attack clearly lacked balance. Seam was adequately covered by Bannister, Thompson and K. R. Dollery but the spin bowling relied too much upon the leg-breaks of Hollies and Hitchcock.

Another disappointing aspect of the team's playing record concerned the batting. True, six players reached 1,000 runs, but this was a modest aggregate for any batsman in such a summer. Equally true, and certainly of greater significance, were the failures on good pitches. Gardner and Horner were seldom able to give the side a sound start and once things began to go badly no one, except H. E. Dollery, seemed capable of exerting a steadying influence on the course of the innings.

Towards the end of the summer Dollery announced his impending retirement from the first-class game. Warwickshire, and indeed the English county scene, will not seem the same without this genial and intelligent player. As the county committee so rightly recorded at the time Dollery made his decision: "He has given a new status and dignity to the professional player, both as a cricketer and as a leader."

Fortunately for Warwickshire another distinguished member of their pre-war playing staff, Hollies, is likely to continue in the game for a while yet. He again took 100 wickets and, on his day, made the best batsmen look ill at ease. Hitchcock not only advanced as a bowler but also as a left-handed batsman whose punishing stroke-play brought to life many a leisurely day's cricket. Bannister, maintaining his improvement, took nine wickets for thirty-five in an innings against Yorkshire at Sheffield in May. Thompson illustrated the importance of accuracy when pitches were not helping him, and K. R. Dollery, a useful batsman, deserved more opportunities, though it was difficult to fit him in without omitting one of the other fast bowlers.

Among the batsmen H. E. Dollery played some notable innings, not least his 156 at Westcliff. Wolton, without quite living up to the high promise of the previous summer, impressed most when making use of his attacking strokes. Spooner, a dependable wicket-keeper-batsman, who appeared for England in the fifth Test, also seemed better suited to a more aggressive batting role.

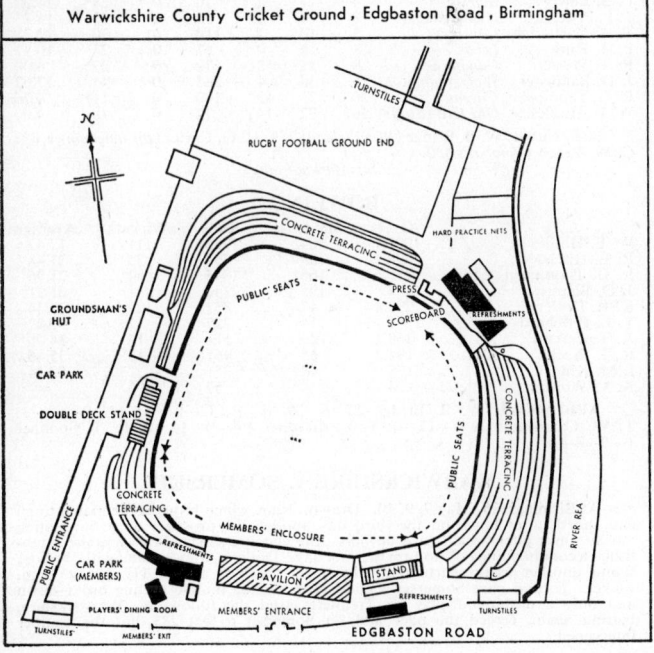

Warwickshire County Cricket Ground, Edgbaston Road, Birmingham

WARWICKSHIRE RESULTS

All First-Class Matches—Played 32, *Won* 10, *Lost* 11, *Drawn* 11

County Championship Matches—Played 28, *Won* 10, *Lost* 9,
Drawn 9

BATTING

	Birthplace	Mtchs.	Inns.	Not Outs	Runs	100's	Highest Inns.	Aver.
R. E. Hitchcock	New Zealand	28	49	6	1507	4	128	35.04
H. E. Dollery .	Reading	27	47	2	1558	4	156	34.62
A. V. Wolton .	Maidenhead	27	51	4	1470	1	107	31.27
R. T. Spooner.	Stockton-on-Tees	25	48	5	1307	1	125	30.39
F. C. Gardner .	Covertry	25	48	3	1287	1	167	28.60
N. F. Horner .	Queensbury	21	41	0	1110	1	119	27.07
K. R. Dollery .	Australia	13	22	8	289	0	37	20.64
A. Townsend .	Stockton-on-Tees	28	48	6	800	0	84	19.04
W. J. Stewart .	Carmarthenshire	6	7	2	95	0	28*	19.00
E. B. Lewis ...	Shirley	4	7	2	70	0	28*	14.00
T. L. Pritchard	New Zealand	3	4	0	55	0	23	13.75
T. W. Cartwright	Coventry	5	10	1	110	0	30	12.22
I. M. King....	Leeds	8	8	0	87	0	23	10.87
R. T. Weeks ..	Camborne	8	11	2	72	0	23*	8.00
J. D. Bannister	Wolverhampton	26	39	4	267	0	45	7.62
R. G. Thompson	Coventry	25	33	12	100	0	11*	4.76
W. E. Hollies .	Old Hill (Staffs)	26	32	14	72	0	18	4.00

Also batted: W. B. Bridge (*Birmingham*) 2, 3; R. G. Carter (*Birmingham*) 1, 0*;
C. W. Leach (*Bombay*) 0, 0.

* Signifies not out.

BOWLING

	Overs	Maidens	Runs	Wickets	Average
W. E. Hollies	1002.1	384	1935	111	17.43
R. E. Hitchcock	298.1	89	752	35	21.48
R. G. Thompson	736.5	166	1845	84	21.96
J. D. Bannister	857	195	2140	91	23.51
K. R. Dollery	293.4	47	851	29	29.34
T. L. Pritchard	91	14	227	7	32.42
A. Townsend	168.1	26	511	15	34.06
R. T. Weeks	194.2	65	461	13	35.46
I. M. King.............	178	68	351	7	50.14
A. V. Wolton	24	4	57	0	

Also bowled: W. B. Bridge 22—6—39—1; R. G. Carter 14—0—63—3;
T. W. Cartwright 2—0—15—0; F. C. Gardner 1.4—0—14—0; R. T. Spooner
1—0—4—0.

WARWICKSHIRE v. SOMERSET

At Birmingham, May 7, 9, 10. Drawn. Rain, which brought the match to an end shortly after lunch on the third day, spoiled the prospect of an interesting finish. On a pitch which gave bowlers little encouragement Warwickshire established a commanding position on the first day. Dollery, after a stand with Wolton, found another useful partner in Hitchcock, the pair adding 117 for the sixth wicket. Tordoff gave Somerset a good start but the middle batting broke down and only a dashing display by Tremlett saved the follow-on. Warwickshire, batting again, forced the pace and set Somerset to get 288, but the weather intervened.

Warwickshire

F. C. Gardner c Wight b McMahon	28	— b Lobb	14
N. F. Horner c Tremlett b Lawrence	42	— c Lomax b McMahon	36
A. V. Wolton b McMahon	74	— not out	65
R. T. Spooner c Stephenson b Lawrence	24	— not out	37
H. E. Dollery b Lawrence	105		
A. Townsend c Stephenson b McMahon	1		
R. E. Hitchcock run out	51		
R. T. Weeks c Lobb b Lawrence	5	— c Stephenson b Lawrence	0
T. L. Pritchard st Stephenson b Lawrence	16		
J. D. Bannister run out	8		
W. E. Hollies not out	1		
L-b 4	4	B 4, l-b 3	7

1/69 2/75 3/128 4/193 5/205   359   1/30 2/82   (3 wkts., dec.) 159
6/322 7/331 8/341 9/358   3/83

Somerset

G. G. Tordoff c Townsend b Bannister	67	— not out	45
F. L. Angell b Pritchard	9	— c Weeks b Bannister	11
J. Lawrence c Gardner b Pritchard	35		
P. Wight c and b Weeks	31		
R. Smith c Gardner b Pritchard	3		
M. F. Tremlett c Bannister b Weeks	55		
J. G. Lomax c Townsend b Hollies	3	— not out	9
H. W. Stephenson c Gardner b Hollies	0		
J. Hilton b Bannister	18		
J. W. McMahon b Hollies	4		
B. Lobb not out	1		
B 4, l-b 1	5	B 1	1

1/36 2/113 3/117 4/128 5/164   231   1/37   (one wkt.) 66
6/177 7/177 8/215 9/225

Somerset Bowling

	O.	M.	R.	W.	O.	M.	R.	W.
Lobb	17	2	55	0	13	1	46	1
Tremlett	6	1	22	0				
McMahon	53	18	101	3	23	5	62	1
Lawrence	34.5	7	98	5	2	1	1	1
Hilton	18	2	60	0	10.2	1	40	0
Lomax	4	0	19	0	2	1	3	0

Warwickshire Bowling

Bannister	15.3	4	53	2	10	3	24	1
Pritchard	21	4	55	3	8	0	28	0
Hollies	32	8	72	3	4	0	12	0
Weeks	29	12	46	2	1	0	1	0

Umpires: E. Davies and W. F. Price.

WARWICKSHIRE v. WORCESTERSHIRE

At Birmingham, May 11, 12, 13. Drawn. Rain again ruined the match, no play being possible on the final day. When Gardner and Horner began with a stand of 92 Warwickshire looked set for a big score, but the nine remaining wickets fell for 50. Perks, making an occasional ball lift, and Berry, genuine left-arm spin, caused the breakdown. Kenyon and Outschoorn were even more successful in their opening partnership but, like their opponents, most of the other Worcestershire batsmen were dismissed cheaply. Hollies, whose leg-breaks and googlies accounted for seven wickets, became the first Warwickshire bowler to pass 2,000 wickets in his career. A fighting stand of 93 between Dollery and Spooner helped Warwickshire to recover.

Warwickshire

F. C. Gardner c Kenyon b Berry	40	— lbw b Perks	9
N. F. Horner c Broadbent b Perks	51	— b Perks	7
A. V. Wolton c Outschoorn b Perks	0	— b Berry	35
R. T. Spooner b Perks	6	— not out	62
H. E. Dollery c Broadbent b Berry	4	— c Yarnold b Horton	47
A. Townsend b Berry	5	— not out	2
R. E. Hitchcock c Devereux b Berry	20		
R. T. Weeks b Horton	0		
J. D. Bannister c Berry b Horton	0		
T. L. Pritchard c Jenkins b Perks	12		
W. E. Hollies not out	0		
N-b 4	4	B 5, l-b 4	9
	142	**(4 wkts.)**	**171**

1/92 2/92 3/98 4/102 5/105 6/110 7/113 8/117 9/142

1/15 2/24 3/68 4/161

Worcestershire

D. Kenyon c Townsend b Hollies	74	R. O. Jenkins lbw b Weeks	1
L. Outschoorn c Gardner b Hollies	31	H. Yarnold b Hollies	14
G. Dews b Hollies	17	R. T. D. Perks b Hollies	17
L. N. Devereux c Horner b Pritchard	33	R. Berry not out	1
R. G. Broadbent c Gardner b Hollies	1	B 8, l-b 1, n-b 1	10
J. P. Whitehead c Gardner b Weeks	19		**223**
M. J. Horton b Hollies	5		

1/104 2/127 3/132 4/134 5/179 6/181 7/182 8/188 9/222

Worcestershire Bowling

	O.	M.	R.	W.	O.	M.	R.	W.
Perks	23.1	9	55	4	17	2	47	2
Whitehead	4	2	6	0	7	0	32	0
Berry	30	16	49	4	28	17	23	1
Horton	16	7	28	2	19	4	47	1
Jenkins					3	0	13	0

Warwickshire Bowling

	O.	M.	R.	W.
Bannister	20	5	49	0
Pritchard	18	5	43	1
Hollies	49	20	69	7
Weeks	30	13	52	2

Umpires: N. Oldfield and W. T. Jones.

At Oxford, May 14, 16, 17. WARWICKSHIRE drew with OXFORD UNIVERSITY.

At Manchester, May 18, 19, 20. WARWICKSHIRE lost to LANCASHIRE by 72 runs.

WARWICKSHIRE v. GLAMORGAN

At Birmingham, May 21, 23, 24. Warwickshire won by six wickets. They recovered splendidly after Glamorgan began the final day 113 runs ahead with seven wickets intact. Thompson wrested the initiative from Glamorgan by dismissing Watkins and Pressdee in his first two overs and Hollies hastened the second innings collapse. This left Warwickshire to score 183 and a sound display by Spooner, deputising for Gardner, injured, as opening batsman, helped them to succeed with thirty-five minutes to spare.

Glamorgan

W. Wooller c Hitchcock b Bannister	9	— lbw b Hollies	40
W. G. A. Parkhouse c Townsend b Thompson	67	— c Dollery b Bannister	8
B. Hedges b Thompson	3	— b Hollies	4
W. E. Jones b Hollies	18	— b Hollies	41
J. Pressdee c Spooner b Thompson	27	— c Horner b Thompson	7
P. B. Clift c Spooner b Bannister	17	— hit wkt b Hollies	20
D. Ward b Weeks	11	— b Bannister	7
J. E. McConnon c Bannister b Hollies	18	— not out	4
A. J. Watkins not out	7	— c Stewart b Thompson	34
D. Shepherd not out	23	— lbw b Hollies	4
H. G. Davies (did not bat)		— b Bannister	3
B 2, l-b 2, n-b 1	5	B 2, l-b 2	4

1/16 2/23 3/65 4/111   (8 wkts., dec.) 205
5/127 6/150 7/173 8/173

1/14 2/35 3/60 4/113   176
5/123 6/148 7/165 8/167
9/173

Warwickshire

R. T. Spooner b Jones	25	— c Pressdee b McConnon	57
N. F. Horner lbw b Wooller	10	— st Davies b Wooller	2
A. V. Wolton c Davies b Watkins	22	— c and b McConnon	44
R. E. Hitchcock c Davies b Watkins	0	— b Pressdee	38
H. E. Dollery b Pressdee	47	— not out	30
A. Townsend c Davies b Pressdee	44	— not out	3
W. J. Stewart b Pressdee	27		
R. T. Weeks b McConnon	3		
J. D. Bannister c Ward b McConnon	0		
W. E. Hollies lbw b Watkins	3		
R. G. Thompson not out	0		
B 9, l-b 9	18	B 4, l-b 5	9

1/17 2/69 3/69 4/69 5/158 6/167   199
7/178 8/182 9/199

1/5 2/68 3/138   (4 wkts.) 183
4/168

Warwickshire Bowling

	O.	M.	R.	W.		O.	M.	R.	W.
Bannister	29	10	62	2	....	18.2	4	44	3
Thompson	22	8	30	3	....	23	7	47	2
Hollies	32	17	49	2	....	27	15	33	5
Weeks	17	5	45	1	....	11	0	44	0
Wolton	3	0	14	0					
Townsend					....	2	0	4	0

Glamorgan Bowling

	O.	M.	R.	W.		O.	M.	R.	W.
Shepherd	6	1	14	0	....	9	1	41	0
Wooller	7	2	26	1	....	11	0	40	1
Watkins	21	4	46	3	....	10	1	31	0
McConnon	19	6	38	2	....	9.1	1	36	2
Jones	14	3	35	1					
Pressdee	14.1	3	22	3	....	10	3	26	1

Umpires: E. A. Roberts and T. J. Bartley.

At Sheffield, May 25, 26 27. WARWICKSHIRE lost to YORKSHIRE by five wickets.

WARWICKSHIRE v. DERBYSHIRE

At Birmingham, May 28, 30, 31. Drawn. Derbyshire enjoyed the better of a game restricted to two days by rain. Only Spooner, eighth out, batted with any assurance for Warwickshire on a pitch helpful to bowlers. Derbyshire showed more consistency and largely through Morgan and Dawkes, who hit 91 in forty-five minutes, Warwickshire went in again needing 139 to avoid an innings defeat. They lost three wickets cheaply but a splendid display by the left-hander, Hitchcock, thwarted Derbyshire's bid for victory.

Warwickshire

R. T. Spooner c Morgan b Smith	57	—	b Smith	14
T. W. Cartwright b Gladwin	1	—	c Revill b Gladwin	8
A. V. Wolton c and b Gladwin	11	—	b Gladwin	0
R. E. Hitchcock st Dawkes b Smith	15	—	not out	72
H. E. Dollery c Gladwin b Carr	8	—	lbw b Jackson	30
A. Townsend b Smith	12	—	run out	0
W. J. Stewart b Carr	3	—	not out	18
J. D. Bannister b Carr	0			
I. M. King c Morgan b Carr	6			
R. G. Thompson c Carr b Smith	0			
W. E. Hollies not out	0			
N-b 1	1		L-b 2, n-b 1	3

1/8 2/30 3/46 4/69 5/93 6/103   114   1/23 2/23   (5 wkts.) 145
7/103 8/109 9/114   3/23 4/101 5/102

Derbyshire

A. Hamer b Hollies	42	D. C. Morgan b Hollies	47
J. Kelly c Spooner b Bannister	3	G. O. Dawkes not out	52
C. Lee b Thompson	0	B 1, l-b 3	4
A. C. Revill b King	58		
D. B. Carr c Hollies b Bannister	30	1/9 2/10 3/64 (7 wkts., dec.) 253
H. L. Johnson b Hollies	17	4/123 5/142 6/162 7/253

C. Gladwin, E. Smith and L. Jackson did not bat.

Derbyshire Bowling

	O.	M.	R.	W.	O.	M.	R.	W.
Jackson	10	3	22	0	8	1	22	1
Gladwin	16	6	29	2	18	6	43	2
Morgan	7	1	19	0	6	4	5	0
Smith	22	11	31	4	16	7	32	1
Carr	9.4	2	12	4	9	0	38	0
Hamer					3	2	1	0
Revill					1	0	1	0

Warwickshire Bowling

	O.	M.	R.	W.
Bannister	23	6	66	2
Thompson	14	2	43	1
Hollies	32.2	11	77	3
King	24	9	48	1
Cartwright	2	0	15	0

Umpires: W. T. Jones and T. Spencer.

WARWICKSHIRE v. COMBINED SERVICES

At Birmingham, June 1, 2, 3, Drawn. Rain prevented play on the last day. Apart from the left-handers Richardson and Leary, few of the Services' batsmen looked at ease against the right-arm leg-break bowling of Hitchcock, who took four wickets in five overs without cost. Warwickshire built up a commanding lead through consistent batting. Wolton, strong in cover driving, hit a 6 and eighteen 4's. Gardner retired because of a strained thigh.

Combined Services

Cpl. P. E. Richardson c Gardner b Hitchcock	73	— c Lewis b Dollery 78
S/Ldr. A. C. Shirreff b Dollery	0	— not out 59
A/C W. B. Stott c Lewis b Latham	17	
Lt. Comdr. M. L. Y. Ainsworth b Latham	0	
Comdr. A. L. Thackara c Stewart b Hitchcock	34	
A/C J. T. Murray b Hitchcock	14	
A/C S. E. Leary not out	59	
A/C D. A. Allen lbw b Hitchcock	0	
F/O G. H. McKinna lbw b Hitchcock ..	1	
L/Bdr. C. S. Matthews st Lewis b Hitchcock	19	
A/C M. J. Cowan b Paul	22	
B 6, l-b 5, n-b 1	12	

1/0 2/34 3/38 4/109 5/140 6/145   251   1/137   (1 wkt.) 137
7/145 8/149 9/183

Warwickshire

F. C. Gardner retired hurt	36	E. B. Lewis b Allen	29
R. T. Spooner b Cowan	10	K. R. Dollery lbw b Allen	8
A. V. Wolton c Cowan b McKinna	136	H. J. Latham b Shirreff	2
A. Townsend lbw b Allen	22	I. M. King not out	0
R. E. Hitchcock c Ainsworth b Allen	45	B 4, l-b 9, n-b 1	14
W. J. Stewart b Cowan	3	1/11 2/173 3/226 4/229 5/296	345
N. A. Paul c Murray b Allen	40	6/315 7/338 8/345 9/345	

Warwickshire Bowling

	O.	M.	R.	W.		O.	M.	R.	W.
Latham	22	4	73	2	....	7	0	22	0
Dollery........	22	2	83	1	....	6.5	1	18	1
Paul	9.2	2	13	1	....	6	1	19	0
King	7	3	16	0	....	5	1	15	0
Hitchcock	22	9	54	6	....	14	6	25	0
Townsend						6	0	29	0
Wolton						3	1	9	0

Combined Services Bowling

	O.	M.	R.	W.
Cowan	21	3	65	2
McKinna	16	1	63	1
Shirreff	22	5	78	1
Matthews......	11	2	36	0
Allen	19.1	2	58	5
Leary	4	0	31	0

Umpires: F. Chester and D. Davies.

WARWICKSHIRE v. NORTHAMPTONSHIRE

At Coventry, June 4, 6, 7. Drawn. Again the last day's play was lost through rain which probably cost Warwickshire victory. By the end of the second day Northamptonshire, with six wickets left, required 65 runs to avoid defeat by an innings. Northamptonshire, deciding to bat first on lively turf, were quickly in difficulties against the fast-medium bowling of Bannister, who made the ball swing in the heavy atmosphere. Gardner, batting nearly three hours and a half, Hitchcock (a 6 and ten 4's) and Townsend, were chiefly responsible for Warwickshire establishing a lead of 142.

Northamptonshire

B. L. Reynolds b Bannister	6	— c Spooner b Thompson	4
P. Arnold b Bannister	11	— b Bannister	7
L. Livingston c Townsend b Bannister	37	— c Townsend b Thompson	25
D. Barrick c Spooner b Bannister	0	— not out	31
D. Brookes lbw b Hollies	9	— lbw b Thompson	8
R. Subba Row b Thompson	31	— not out	1
G. E. Tribe c Spooner b Hollies	10		
V. Broderick b Hollies	3		
F. H. Tyson not out	23		
K. V. Andrew b Thompson	0		
A. L. Wells b Thompson	9		
L-b 9, n-b 1	10	N-b 1	1
	149	(4 wkts.)	77

1/17 2/36 3/38 4/69 5/69 6/101 7/113 8/115 9/115

1/8 2/14 3/66 4/76

Warwickshire

F. C. Gardner b Tyson	50	W. J. Stewart not out	28
R. T. Spooner b Tyson	25		
A. V. Wolton c Reynold b Tribe	10		
I. M. King run out	22	B 8, l-b 7, w 4, n-b 1	20
H. E. Dollery lbw b Tyson	7		
R. E. Hitchcock c Tyson b Tribe	69	(7 wkts., dec.)	291
A. Townsend b Tyson	60		

1/35 2/52 3/103 4/132 5/152 6/215 7/291

J. D. Bannister, R. G. Thompson and W. E. Hollies did not bat.

Warwickshire Bowling

	O.	M.	R.	W.		O.	M.	R.	W.
Bannister	19	2	44	4	....	8	0	33	1
Thompson	19.3	6	47	3	....	13	0	40	3
Hollies	17	4	48	3	....	5	4	3	0

Northamptonshire Bowling

	O.	M.	R.	W.
Tyson	32.2	8	71	4
Wells	23	6	62	0
Tribe	27	6	68	2
Broderick	21	10	37	0
Subba Row	3	0	12	0
Barrick	4	0	21	0

Umpires: F. S. Lee and T. J. Bartley.

WARWICKSHIRE v. LANCASHIRE

At Birmingham, June 8, 9, 10. Drawn. After a blank first day Ikin, the Lancashire left-hander, showed both concentration and technical skill while batting for three hours 40 minutes on a rain-affected pitch. After he and Wharton hit 83 in just over an hour for the fourth wicket, Collins enjoyed the satisfaction of scoring his first fifty in county cricket. Warwickshire, 119 for three at lunch on the third day, collapsed against Goodwin and Hilton, the last seven wickets falling for 28. They followed on 144 runs behind under the two-day rule, but there was never any prospect of a second batting breakdown.

Lancashire

J. T. Ikin b Hollies	78	M. J. Hilton b Hollies	0
S. Smith c Gardner b Hollies	9	A. Wilson b Thompson	8
G. A. Edrich c Wolton b King	15	F. Goodwin not out	3
C. Washbrook c King b Hollies	21		
A. Wharton c Spooner b Thomson	63	L-b 3, n-b 1	4
K. Grieves b Hollies	26		
J. Dyson c and b Hollies	12	1/18 2/41 3/76 (9 wkts., dec.) 291
R. Collins not out	52	4/159 5/199 6/223 7/226 8/226 9/264

Warwickshire

F. C. Gardner lbw b Goodwin	41	— not out	32
R. E. Hitchcock b Wharton	5		
I. M. King b Collins	23		
A. V. Wolton c Wharton b Collins	5		
R. T. Spooner c Wharton b Hilton	48	— not out	31
H. E. Dollery lbw b Goodwin	0		
A. Townsend c Grieves b Hilton	0		
W. J. Stewart c and b Hilton	11		
J. D. Banister lbw b Goodwin	0		
R. G. Thompson c Wilson b Goodwin	3		
W. E. Hollies not out	3		
L-b 2	2	W 1	1

1/6 2/51 3/69 4/122 5/122 6/123   147   (No wkt.) 64
7/130 8/131 9/143

Warwickshire Bowling

	O.	M.	R.	W.	O.	M.	R.	W
Bannister	19	3	69	0				
Thompson	21	5	53	2				
Hollies	41	12	85	6				
King	27	14	45	1				
Hitchcock	4	0	19	0				
Wolton	6	0	16	0				

Lancashire Bowling

	O.	M.	R.	W.	O.	M.	R.	W
Goodwin	17	4	32	4	2	0	12	0
Wharton	7	1	19	1	3	0	12	0
Hilton	31	14	37	3				
Collins	23	10	43	2				
Dyson	6	2	11	0	9	3	11	0
Ikin	3	1	3	0				
Grieves					9	2	28	0

Umpires: H. Elliott (Lancashire) and H. G. Baldwin.

At Hinckley, June 11, 13, 14. WARWICKSHIRE beat LEICESTERSHIRE by nine wickets.

WARWICKSHIRE v. GLOUCESTERSHIRE

At Birmingham, June 15, 16, 17. Gloucestershire won by seven wickets. After two tedious days the character of the match was transformed. Warwickshire set the pattern by scoring 206 runs in two hours five minutes and Gloucestershire, emulating this example, responded to Dollery's declaration challenge by obtaining the 206 runs needed for victory in two hours. Emmett, displaying a wide variety of strokes, reached 100 in ninety-two minutes, seventeen 4's testifying to the power of his hits. Earlier both sides adopted such painstaking batting methods that first innings lead was not determined until the last morning.

Warwickshire

F. C. Gardner b Graveney	35	— b Lambert	16
R. T. Spooner lbw b McHugh	16	— c McHugh b Mortimore	70
A. V. Wolton c Nicholls b Cook	26	— not out	78
R. E. Hitchcock b McHugh	44	— not out	39
H. E. Dollery b Lambert	85		
A. Townsend b Mortimore	12		
W. J. Stewart c Emmett b Cook	8		
J. D. Bannister st Rochford b Cook	45		
I. M. King b Cook	14		
R. G. Thompson c Graveney b Cook	5		
W. E. Hollies not out	4		
B 13, l-b 2, n-b 1	16	B 2, n-b 1	3

1/37 2/78 3/97 4/162 5/198 6/221   **310**   1/42 2/114   (2 wkts., dec.) **206**
7/252 8/294 9/305

Gloucestershire

D. M. Young lbw b Hollies	74		
C. A. Milton c and b Hollies	65	— lbw b Hollies	20
T. W. Graveney c Dollery b Bannister	27	— st Spooner b Bannister	33
J. F. Crapp not out	100	— not out	9
G. M. Emmett b Thompson	1	— b Bannister	113
R. B. Nicholls b Thompson	1		
G. E. Lambert not out	31		
J. Mortimore (did not bat)		— not out	22
B 7, l-b 4, n-b 1	12	B 1, l-b 8	9

1/139 2/142 3/210   (5 wkts., dec.) **311**   1/58 2/168 3/175   (3 wkts.) **206**
4/213 5/215

P. Rochford, C. Cook and F. P. McHugh did not bat.

Gloucestershire Bowling

	O.	M.	R.	W.	O.	M.	R.	W.
Lambert	15	1	60	1	9	0	45	1
McHugh	25	3	72	2	9.3	0	33	0
Cook	47.2	18	55	5	12	5	42	0
Mortimore	24	5	57	1	4	0	26	1
Graveney	17	2	50	1	6	0	46	0
Emmett					2	0	11	0

Warwickshire Bowling

	O.	M.	R.	W.	O.	M.	R.	W.
Bannister	35	6	83	1	13	0	75	2
Thompson	25	6	60	2	10	0	55	0
Hollies	40	19	69	2	11	0	50	1
King	24	6	58	0	2	0	17	0
Townsend	9	3	13	0				
Hitchcock	1	0	6	0				
Wolton	5	0	10	0				

Umpires: Harry Elliott (Derbyshire) and P. Corrall.

WARWICKSHIRE v. CAMBRIDGE UNIVERSITY

At Birmingham, June 18, 20, 21. Cambridge University won by 53 runs. The match provided a personal triumph for Goonesena, the all-rounder from Ceylon, who obtained his maiden hundred in first-class cricket and took 10 wickets in the match for 137. Goonesena, adept at cutting and driving, shared a third wicket partnership of 142 in two hours with Lumsden. Warwickshire passed 100 for the loss of two wickets, but Goonesena's leg-breaks caused a collapse. After good bowling by Hitchcock and Carter, the county were left to get 282 to win. The task always appeared too much for them, although Ibadulla and K. Dollery provided unexpected resistance in a last wicket stand of 85.

Cambridge University

D. R. W. Silk	b Carter	2	— c Lewis b Hitchcock		10
R. O'Brien	b Dollery	2	— b Carter		5
G. Goonesena	c Townsend b Carter	118	— b Townsend		26
V. R. Lumsden	c Lewis b Dollery	69	— b Hitchcock		4
W. Knightley-Smith	c Lewis b Dollery	2	— b Hitchcock		0
S. Singh	b Dollery	36	— c Leach b Carter		56
A. B. D. Parsons	lbw b Dollery	13	— lbw b Carter		27
P. D. Croft	c Lewis b Dollery	8	— b Carter		19
J. F. Pretlove	c Lewis b Dollery	15	— c Lewis b Paul		12
C. S. Smith	c Carter b King	39	— c Dollery b Hitchcock		7
M. E. L. Melluish	not out	11	— not out		0
	B 4, l-b 4, n-b 2	10	B 3, l-b 3		6

1/3 2/11 3/153 4/157 5/217 6/238   325   1/14 2/18 3/26 4/28   172
7/255 8/260 9/297   5/58 6/117 7/152 8/153 9/172

Warwickshire

T. W. Cartwright	b Smith	58	— lbw b Smith		2
C. W. Leach	c and b Goonesena	23	— b Goonesena		25
A. V. Wolton	c Melluish b Goonesena	30	— b Parsons b Smith		16
R. E. Hitchcock	c Smith b Singh	22	— c Silk b Singh		17
K. Ibadulla	b Goonesena	35	— not out		66
A. Townsend	c O'Brien b Singh	4	— st Melluish b Goonesena		24
N. A. Paul	c Knightley-Smith b Singh	25	— b Goonesena		5
E. B. Lewis	b Goonesena	4	— b Singh		2
I. M. King	c Silk b Goonesena	0	— b Goonesena		3
K. R. Dollery	not out	0	— lbw b Singh		38
R. G. Carter	(did not bat)		— b Goonesena		18
	B 7, l-b 8	15	B 4, l-b 6, w 2		12

1/55 2/99 3/140 4/140   (9 wkts., dec.) 216   1/2 2/20 3/59 4/83   228
5/148 6/201 7/207 8/207 9/216   5/89 6/94 7/126 8/130 9/143

Warwickshire Bowling

	O.	M.	R.	W.		O.	M.	R.	W.
Dollery	37	3	121	7	....	10	3	24	0
Carter	14	1	44	2	....	21	8	39	4
Paul	17	6	28	0	....	3.3	2	5	1
King	20.1	3	57	1	....	9	6	6	0
Hitchcock	11	0	49	0	....	30	6	68	4
Townsend	7	2	16	0	....	6	1	24	1

Cambridge University Bowling

	O.	M.	R.	W.		O.	M.	R.	W.
Smith	22	6	30	1	....	16	1	58	2
Silk	2	0	2	0					
Goonesena	22.2	6	58	5	....	29	5	79	5
Singh	33	8	90	3	....	29	4	74	3
Pretlove	6	2	21	0	....	3	1	5	0
Lumsden	1	1	0	0					

Umpires: D. Davies and Harry Elliott (Derbyshire).

At Westcliff, June 22, 23, 24. WARWICKSHIRE beat ESSEX by 142 runs.

At Dudley, June 25, 27, 28. WARWICKSHIRE beat WORCESTERSHIRE by 151 runs.

WARWICKSHIRE v. NOTTINGHAMSHIRE

At Birmingham, June 29, 30, July 1. Warwickshire won by 150 runs. Splendid batting in each innings by their captain, H. E. Dollery, played a leading part in the victory. Warwickshire would have been in serious trouble but for his seventh wicket stand of 76 with K. R. Dollery. Nottinghamshire never recovered from the shock of losing the first three wickets in nine balls to Thompson and Warwickshire built up a commanding position. H. E. Dollery shared partnerships of 86 for the fourth wicket with Horner, and 183 in two hours for the sixth with Townsend, during which he completed the 50th hundred of his career. Nottinghamshire, losing seven wickets for 125, were rallied by Dooland and Smales who added 105, but once they were parted the innings soon closed.

Warwickshire

F. C. Gardner b Jepson	2	— c Poole b Jepson	1
N. F. Horner b Jepson	16	— c and b Dooland	49
A. V. Wolton c Jepson b Dooland	37	— b Dooland	4
R. E. Hitchcock b Smales	13	— lbw b Dooland	8
H. E. Dollery c Clay b Dooland	65	— c Simpson b Harvey 151	
R. T. Spooner c Dooland b Smales	0	— b Dooland	0
A. Townsend c Dooland b Jepson	6	— lbw b Harvey	84
K. R. Dollery st Rowe b Dooland	37	— not out	5
R. T. Weeks b Dooland	8	— b Dooland	3
J. D. Bannister st Rowe b Smales	1	— c Harvey b Dooland	1
R. G. Thompson not out	4		
B 5, l-b 1	6	B 1, w 2	3

1/18 2/19 3/68 4/68 5/68 6/84   195
7/160 8/170 9/175

1/4 2/19   (9 wkts., dec.) 309
3/31 4/117 5/117 6/300
7/300 8/307 9/309

Nottinghamshire

R. T. Simpson c Townsend b Thompson	1	— b Weeks	14
J. D. Clay b Bannister	10	— lbw b Thompson	30
R. Giles c Bannister b Thompson	0	— c Gardner b Weeks	14
J. Hardstaff b Thompson	0	— b Thompson	8
C. J. Poole b K. Dollery	31	— c Townsend b Hitchcock ..	48
E. J. Martin lbw b K. Dollery	20	— lbw b Hitchcock	9
P. F. Harvey not out	28	— b K. Dollery	1
B. Dooland st Spooner b Weeks	12	— c H. Dollery b K. Dollery..	68
K. Smales lbw b Hitchcock	1	— b K. Dollery	41
A. Jepson b Weeks	4	— not out	7
E. J. Rowe lbw b Weeks..............	0	— c Townsend b K. Dollery ..	2
B 2, w 1, n-b 1	4	N-b 1	1

1/4 2/4 3/4 4/18 5/65 6/66 7/97   111
8/104 9/111

1/36 2/50 3/62 4/74   243
5/119 6/125 7/125 8/230
9/241

Nottinghamshire Bowling

	O.	M.	R.	W.		O.	M.	R.	W.
Jepson	22	7	42	3	....	23	4	73	1
Smales	32	11	67	3	....	27	7	84	0
Dooland	27.5	8	76	4	....	28.4	3	93	6
Harvey	3	1	4	0	....	13	3	56	2

Warwickshire Bowling

	O.	M.	R.	W.		O.	M.	R.	W.
Bannister	20	6	27	1	....	19	2	42	0
Thompson	19	4	41	3	....	20	3	68	2
K. Dollery	8	2	23	2	....	15	0	41	4
Weeks	10	4	16	3	....	18	7	35	2
Hitchcock	4	4	0	1	....	23	10	36	2
					Townsend	5	1	30	0

Umpires: T. J. Bartley and W. T. Jones.

At Bath, July 2, 4, 5. WARWICKSHIRE beat SOMERSET by six wickets.

At Northampton, July 6, 7, 8. WARWICKSHIRE drew with NORTHAMPTONSHIRE.

WARWICKSHIRE v. MIDDLESEX

At Birmingham, July 9, 11, 12. Warwickshire won by one wicket, Hollies making the winning hit off the fifth ball of the last over. In each innings Middlesex were saved from a batting breakdown by a fine individual performance. On the opening day Bennett, going in when three wickets had fallen for ten runs, defied the bowlers for four hours twenty minutes, being dismissed when one short of three figures. Middlesex owed most in their second innings to the captain, Edrich, who was quick to punish anything short of a length during a chanceless display. Warwickshire, whose first innings failure was largely due to indeterminate stroke play, displayed more resolution when set to score 283 in four hours. Wolton and Gardner hit 117 for the second wicket in an hour and thirty-five minutes and though half the side were out for 147, Spooner swung the game in Warwickshire's favour.

Middlesex

J. D. Robertson c Gardner b Bannister .	5	— b Thompson 21
S. M. Brown b Thompson	0	— lbw b K. Dollery.......... 22
W. J. Edrich c Townsend b K. Dollery .	18	— not out 125
A. Thompson c H. Dollery b Thompson .	3	— c Spooner b Hollies 2
D. Bennett c Spooner b Hollies.........	99	— b Bannister............... 12
D. O. Baldry c H. Dollery b K. Dollery .	20	— b Thompson 14
D. A. Bick c Spooner b K. Dollery	7	— st Spooner b Hollies 6
J. J. Warr b Hollies	1	— run out 0
L. H. Compton run out	21	— c Wolton b Hollies 0
J. A. Young b Hollies	14	— not out 7
A. E. Moss not out	1	
B 7, l-b 9, n-b 1	17	B 1, l-b 1, n-b 1....... 3

1/7 2/7 3/10 4/51 5/110 6/132 7/141   206   1/36 2/48   (8 wkts., dec.) 212
8/187 9/203   3/57 4/101 5/153 6/180
                                               7/180 8/183

Warwickshire

F. C. Gardner c Compton b Warr	14	— c Compton b Moss	1
N. F. Horner c Compton b Warr	1	— b Moss	0
A. V. Wolton b Moss	6	— lbw b Young	7
R. E. Hitchcock b Bick	47	— b Moss	0
H. E. Dollery c Compton b Young	25	— c Brown b Young	1
R. T. Spooner c Compton b Bick	18	— c and b Young	82
A. Townsend c Brown b Bick	12	— c Young b Moss	20
K. R. Dollery not out	9	— run out	16
J. D. Bannister b Moss	0	— b Young	1
R. G. Thompson b Moss	0	— not out	0
W. E. Hollies run out	3	— not out	6
W 1	1	B 5, l-b 15	20
	—		—
	136	(9 wkts.)	284

1/7 2/18 3/32 4/89 5/103 6/124
7/127 8/127 9/128

1/23 2/140 3/140 (9 wkts.) 284
4/142 5/147 6/207 7/267
8/271 9/278

Warwickshire Bowling

	O.	M.	R.	W.	O.	M.	R.	W.
Bannister	19	6	27	1	18	3	52	1
Thompson	11	3	21	2	18	5	43	2
K. Dollery	27	6	73	3	20	3	44	1
Hollies	29.5	11	53	3	34	12	60	3
Hitchcock	7	2	15	0	5	2	10	0

Middlesex Bowling

	O.	M.	R.	W.	O.	M.	R.	W.
Moss	17	2	43	3	27	7	70	4
Warr	19	4	36	2	8	0	33	0
Bennett	2	0	9	0	4	1	6	0
Young	15	6	26	1	33.5	7	106	4
Bick	11	5	21	3	7	1	24	0
Robertson					4	0	25	0

Umpires: A. J. B. Fowler and J. S. Buller.

WARWICKSHIRE v. HAMPSHIRE

At Birmingham, July 13, 14. 15. Drawn. The curious reluctance of Hampshire to accept the task set them in the fourth innings spoiled the prospect of an interesting finish. H. E. Dollery's declaration left Hampshire to score 172 to win in two hours, but Marshall, normally an enterprising stroke player, and his opening partner, Gray, made only 72 in an hour and a half. Stumps were drawn without the extra half-hour being claimed. A first wicket stand of 99 between Gardner and Horner, and 111 for the third wicket between Wolton and Hitchcock enabled Warwickshire to build a sound total in their first innings. Hampshire, for whom Marshall and Ingleby-Mackenzie showed the best batting, failed by 16 to gain the lead

Warwickshire

F. C. Gardner b Barnard	41	—	b Cannings		0
N. F. Horner b Barnard	60	—	c Ingleby-Mackenzie b Shackleton		7
A. V. Wolton c Shackleton b Gray	67	—	c Eagar b Shackleton		14
R. E. Hitchcock c Marshall b Cannings	65	—	b Burden		38
R. T. Spooner c Rogers b Shackleton	19	—	c Marshall b Burden		26
A. Townsend c Ingleby-Mackenzie b Shackleton	2	—	c Sainsbury b Burden		5
K. R. Dollery run out	12	—	lbw b Shackleton		14
J. D. Bannister not out	5	—	c Eagar b Burden		0
E. B. Lewis not out	2	—	not out		28
R. G. Thompson (did not bat)		—	not out		11
B 4, l-b 1, n-b 1	6		B 4, l-b 9		13

1/99 2/112 3/223 4/254 (7 wkts., dec.) 279
5/257 6/272 7/272

1/3 2/9 3/34 (8 wkts., dec.) 156
4/37 5/101 6/114 7/114
8/117

W. E. Hollies did not bat.

Hampshire

J. R. Gray b Thompson	14	—	not out		28
R. E. Marshall b Thompson	51	—	not out		37
H. Horton st Lewis b Hollies	56				
E. D. R. Eagar b Hollies	19				
N. H. Rogers hit wkt b Townsend	18				
H. M. Barnard b K. Dollery	2				
A. C. D. Ingleby-Mackenzie c Horner b Bannister	34				
P. J. Sainsbury c Lewis b K. Dollery	4				
D. Shackleton b Thompson	12				
V. H. D. Cannings not out	15				
M. D. Burden b Thompson	17				
B 8, l-b 13, n-b 1	22		L-b 7		7

1/50 2/85 3/122 4/164 5/167 6/184 264
7/210 8/226 9/236

(No wkt.) 72

Hampshire Bowling

	O.	M.	R.	W.		O.	M.	R.	W.
Shackleton	23	2	61	2	....	19	5	27	3
Cannings	21	2	62	1	....	19	3	43	1
Gray	14	4	24	1	....	12	0	33	0
Sainsbury	17	6	55	0					
Burden	20	7	43	0	....	11	2	40	4
Barnard	13	5	28	2					

Warwickshire Bowling

	O.	M.	R.	W.		O.	M.	R.	W.
Bannister	17	3	56	1	....	5	1	11	0
Thompson	19.5	4	46	4	....	6	0	18	0
Hollies	29	8	62	2	..	6	1	15	0
K. Dollery	17	5	42	2	....	5	0	9	0
Hitchcock	3	0	10	0	....	2	0	8	0
Townsend	8	1	26	1					
Wolton						1	1	0	0
Spooner						1	0	4	0

Umpires: F. Chester and F. S. Lee.

At Bristol, July 16, 18, 19. WARWICKSHIRE beat GLOUCESTERSHIRE by an innings and 39 runs.

At Hastings, July 20, 21, 22. WARWICKSHIRE lost to SUSSEX by 56 runs.

WARWICKSHIRE v. YORKSHIRE

At Birmingham, July 23, 25, 26. Yorkshire won by ten wickets. They were stronger in all phases of the game. A third wicket partnership of 228 between the left-hander, Wilson, and Padgett provided the feature of their innings. Padgett, making many runs off the back foot during a display rich in promise, completed a maiden hundred in first-class cricket in five minutes under three hours. Wilson, whose hundred took half an hour longer, was given "run out" when 54 but as he returned to the pavilion spectators protested that the ball struck a boundary flag and was therefore "dead" when Horner threw in. After consulting the fieldsman and Pothecary, his fellow-umpire, Spencer signalled a boundary hit and Wilson was recalled to resume his innings. Warwickshire's batting broke down on a good pitch against the fast bowling of Trueman. They followed on 256 runs behind and this time displayed more determination, Wolton setting the example. He dominated the innings and completed a hundred out of 117 in two hours ten minutes. Yet Yorkshire were left only the formal task of scoring 43 for victory.

Yorkshire

D. B. Close c Wolton b K. Dollery	.....	42	— not out	34
K. Taylor lbw b Hollies	....	17	— not out	12
J. V. Wilson not out	....	132		
D. E. V. Padgett b K. Dollery	....	115		
W. Watson not out	....	26		
B 10, l-b 10, n-b 2	....	22		

1/62 2/62 3/290   (3 wkts., dec.) 354   (No wkt.) 46

E. Lester, N. W. D. Yardley, R. Illingworth, F. S. Trueman, J. G. Binks and M. J. Cowan did not bat.

Warwickshire

F. C. Gardner c Wilson b Trueman	....	1	— c Lester b Trueman	 21
N. F. Horner hit wkt b Trueman	....	9	— c Wilson b Trueman	 13
A. V. Wolton b Trueman	....	26	— b Taylor	 107
J. D. Bannister lbw b Trueman	....	13	— c Lester b Cowan	 7
R. E. Hitchcock c and b Close	....	1	— b Cowan	 12
H. E. Dollery b Trueman	....	3	— c and b Trueman	 24
R. T. Spooner lbw b Cowan	....	13	— c Padgett b Illingworth	... 61
A. Townsend b Cowan	....	1	— c Binks b Cowan	 27
K. R. Dollery c Binks b Cowan	....	16	— c Binks b Trueman	 4
R. G. Thompson not out	....	10	— c and b Close	 1
W. E. Hollies c Taylor b Close	....	0	— not out	 0
N-b 5	....	5	B 6, l-b 12, n-b 3	 21

1/11 2/14 3/49 4/51 5/56 6/63 7/67   98   1/25 2/121 3/175 4/213   298
8/72 9/97   5/239 6/267 7/277 8/295
                                                        9/296

Warwickshire Bowling

	O.	M.	R.	W.	O.	M.	R.	W.
Thompson	18	4	46	0	3	0	16	0
Bannister	22	4	60	0	1	0	5	0
K. Dollery	18	1	80	2				
Hollies	29	5	90	0	4	0	7	0
Hitchcock	7	0	36	0	3	0	14	0
Townsend	3	0	20	0				
Gardner					0.4	0	4	0

Yorkshire Bowling

	O.	M.	R.	W.	O.	M.	R.	W.
Trueman	12	2	31	5	24	1	68	4
Cowan	11	0	26	3	20.5	2	80	3
Close	14	2	36	2	21	8	42	1
Illingworth					31	14	60	1
Taylor					14	4	27	1

Umpires: T. Spencer and A. E. Pothecary.

WARWICKSHIRE v. SURREY

At Coventry, July 27, 28, 29. Warwickshire won by 131 runs, in a game notable for a fine hundred by their left-hander Hitchcock. Warwickshire, with a total of 134 for three, were well placed at lunch on the first day, but Surrey wrested the initiative afterwards when Laker, switching ends, took five of the last seven wickets for 32. Earlier he had been struck for three 6's by Wolton. Surrey lost half their side for 58 to the fast bowling of Thompson and Bannister before Barrington and Swetman staged a partial recovery. Warwickshire, leading by 56, might not have established such a strong position but for a glorious exhibition of strokes by Hitchcock whose hundred in as many minutes contained seven 6's, five off Laker, and twelve 4's. Surrey possessed a chance of obtaining the 307 needed for victory so long as Barrington remained but when he was sixth out at 145, after a stay of two hours, all hope disappeared.

Warwickshire

F. C. Gardner b Laker	23	— c E. Bedser b Laker	27
N. F. Horner c Swetman b Loader	10	— c A. Bedser b Lock	38
A. V. Wolton b Laker	76	— lbw b Lock	1
A. Townsend c Fletcher b Laker	17	— c Swetman b Lock	5
H. E. Dollery c Swetman b Laker	24	— c Laker b Lock	5
R. E. Hitchcock b Lock	1	— not out	123
K. R. Dollery lbw b Laker	2	— c Surridge b E. Bedser	4
E. B. Lewis c Constable b Lock	9	— lbw b Laker	0
J. D. Bannister b Laker	12	— lbw b Laker	2
R. G. Thompson not out	7	— b E. Bedser	3
W. E. Hollies c Fletcher b Laker	11	— st Swetman b Lock	18
B 17, l-b 1	18	B 18, l-b 6	24

1/28 2/67 3/123 4/138 5/139 6/160   210
7/171 8/175 9/188

1/49 2/50 3/60 4/70   250
5/112 6/155 7/162 8/180
9/207

Surrey

D. G. W. Fletcher b Thompson	1	— b Bannister	10
M. J. Stewart b Bannister	3	— c Gardner b Hitchcock	26
B. Constable c Hollies b Thompson	0	— lbw b Hollies	23
K. Barrington run out	49	— b Bannister	34
E. A. Bedser b Bannister	9	— c Townsend b Bannister	13
J. C. Laker c Hitchcock b Hollies	16	— c Wolton b Bannister	16
R. Swetman c Thompson b K. Dollery	14	— not out	10
G. A. R. Lock run out	8	— b Hollies	17
W. S. Surridge not out	26	— c Wolton b Hollies	2
P. J. Loader b Thompson	12	— c Bannister b Hollies	4
A. V. Bedser c H. Dollery b Hollies	2	— c and b Bannister	0
B 7, l-b 6, n-b 1	14	B 16, l-b 4	20
	—		—
	154		175

1/7 2/7 3/9 4/29 5/58 6/97 7/108   154
8/111 9/135

1/26 2/53 3/93 4/115   175
5/134 6/145 7/160 8/162
9/166

Surrey Bowling

	O.	M.	R.	W.		O.	M.	R.	W.
A. Bedser	8	1	18	0	....	4	0	18	0
Loader	9	1	31	1	....	4	1	8	0
Lock	26	11	48	2	....	19.5	3	68	5
Laker	24	3	95	7	....	27	3	90	3
					E. Bedser	16	4	42	2

Warwickshire Bowling

	O.	M.	R.	W.		O.	M.	R.	W.
Thompson	16	4	37	3	....	6	0	17	0
Bannister	21	2	51	2	....	24.1	3	57	5
Hollies	17	5	31	2	....	29	6	57	4
Hitchcock	7	0	16	0	....	6	1	18	1
K. Dollery	5	3	5	1	....	3	1	6	0
					Townsend	1	1	0	0

Umpires: N. Oldfield and P. Corrall.

At Derby, July 30, August 1, 2. WARWICKSHIRE beat DERBYSHIRE by 164 runs.

At Birmingham, August 3, 4, 5. WARWICKSHIRE lost to the SOUTH AFRICANS by
ten wickets. (See SOUTH AFRICAN section.)

WARWICKSHIRE v. LEICESTERSHIRE

At Birmingham, August 6, 8, 9. Drawn. Bolder methods by both teams
would probably have brought a definite result on an easy-paced pitch. As it was,
too much time was lost through negative stroke play. Spooner, who batted three
and a quarter hours, and Wolton, shared a third wicket stand of 146 for Warwickshire, but Leicestershire gained the lead with only three wickets down. Lester,
though tedious to watch, made no errors during a stay of nearly five hours.
Palmer, more fluent in his strokes, helped put on 130 for the third wicket. Hallam
was unable to continue his innings on the second morning because of a chill.
Facing arrears of 100 Warwickshire lost Gardner and Townsend for three runs,
but Hitchcock and Horner, displaying welcome aggression, increased the total
by 104 in just over an hour. Soon after Hitchcock's departure rain brought the
game to a premature end when everything pointed to an interesting finish.

Warwickshire

F. C. Gardner c Hallam b Boshier	.....	3	— c Diment b Palmer	2
N. F. Horner b Palmer	....	9	— c Tompkin b Walsh	35
A. V. Wolton c Jackson b Munden	.....	56	— not out	0
R. T. Spooner run out	....	125	— not out	20
H. E. Dollery c Firth b Munden	.....	3	— b Munden	18
R. E. Hitchcock c Firth b Palmer	......	31	— lbw b Munden	86
A. Townsend c Hallam b Palmer	....	22	— lbw b Palmer	0
K. R. Dollery not out	....	1		
J. D. Bannister b Walsh	....	17		
R. G. Thompson lbw b Walsh	....	0		
W. E. Hollies c Tompkin b Walsh	......	0		
B 8, l-b 16, n-b 1	....	25	B 2, l-b 2	4

1/10 2/14 3/160 4/173 5/218 6/261   292   1/3 2/3 3/107   (5 wkts.) 165
7/266 8/286 9/286   4/134 5/161

Leicestershire

G. Lester b Townsend	....	109	J. E. Walsh c K. Dollery b Ban-	
M. R. Hallam retired ill	....	57	nister	13
M. Tompkin lbw b Thompson	...	17	J. Firth c and b Bannister	2
M. J. K. Smith lbw b Hitchcock	....	35	B. Boshier not out	0
C. H. Palmer c Horner b Bannister		126	B 6, l-b 6, n-b 1	13
V. E. Jackson b Hollies	....	5		
R. A. Diment lbw b Hollies	......	1	1/109 2/162 3/292 4/306 5/311	392
V. S. Munden b Bannister	....	14	6/371 7/371 8/387 9/392	

Leicestershire Bowling

	O.	M.	R.	W.	O.	M.	R.	W.
Boshier	29	4	88	1	9	1	35	0
Palmer	26	3	58	3	10	3	34	2
Jackson	20	11	48	0	4	1	14	0
Walsh	6.5	0	32	3	10	1	49	1
Munden	15	5	41	2	14	5	29	2

Warwickshire Bowling

	O.	M.	R.	W.
Thompson	26	3	90	1
Bannister	31.3	6	84	4
K. Dollery	14	3	63	0
Hollies	32	8	79	2
Hitchcock	19	6	29	1
Townsend	9	1	34	1

Umpires: H. G. Baldwin and L. H. Gray.

At Lord's, August 10, 11. WARWICKSHIRE lost to MIDDLESEX by 24 runs.

At Dover, August 13, 15, 16. WARWICKSHIRE drew with KENT.

At Nottingham, August 17, 18, 19. WARWICKSHIRE lost to NOTTINGHAMSHIRE by six wickets.

U

WARWICKSHIRE v. ESSEX

At Birmingham, August 20, 22, 23. Essex won by 36 runs with six minutes to spare after a closely contested game. Although without Hollies and Thompson, injured, Warwickshire dismissed half the Essex side for 104. Bannister bowled especially well, but when he tired the later order batsmen took command, Smith scoring 69 in under an hour. Warwickshire also lost five wickets cheaply before a dashing display by the left-hander, Hitchcock, set them on the way to a fine recovery. He scored all but 58 of the 191 runs added with Townsend in two hours 25 minutes for the fifth wicket. Largely through an attractive opening partnership of 132 between Dodds and Barker, Essex were able to declare a second time and set their opponents to score 202 to win in just under two hours. Warwickshire, altering their batting order, went boldly for the runs, and they appeared to hold a chance while Gardner and Wolton were together in a sixth wicket stand which added 63 in half an hour. Once they were parted, however, Essex gained control.

Essex

T. C. Dodds c Townsend b Bannister ...	17	— c Spooner b King	57
G. Barker b Bannister	5	— c Townsend b Pritchard....	106
P. A. Gibb b Bannister	32	— not out	22
D. J. Insole lbw b Hitchcock	29	— run out	13
T. E. Bailey c Townsend b King	32	— run out	1
R. Horsfall c Townsend b Bannister	7	— c Spooner b Bannister	1
M. Bear b Bannister	53	— not out	13
W. T. Greensmith c Bannister b K. Dollery	40	— lbw b Pritchard	2
R. Smith not out	69	— c sub b Pritchard	3
R. Ralph c Leach b K. Dollery	2	— lbw b King	0
K. C. Preston not out	13		
B 7, l-b 6, n-b 2	15	B 1, l-b 3, n-b 1.......	5

1/5 2/36 3/83 4/83 (9 wkts., dec.) 314
5/104 6/160 7/219 8/243 9/284

1/132 2/135 (8 wkts., dec.) 223
3/162 4/171 5/176 6/191
7/192 8/198

Warwickshire

F. C. Gardner c Preston b Greensmith ..	24	— lbw b Insole	31
C. W. Leach lbw b Bailey	0	— run out	0
A. V. Wolton c Gibb b Bailey	58	— b Greensmith	59
R. T. Spooner c Preston b Greensmith ..	17	— c Gibb b Bailey	0
H. E. Dollery c Ralph b Bailey	1	— lbw b Preston	2
R. E. Hitchcock c Ralph b Greensmith..	128	— b Preston	22
A. Townsend c Gibb b Bailey	58	— lbw b Preston	5
K. R. Dollery not out	9	— lbw b Dodds	18
T. L. Pritchard c Bear b Greensmith	23	— run out	4
J. D. Bannister b Bailey	0	— not out	8
I. M. King (did not bat)		— c Preston b Dodds	7
B 14, l-b 1, w 2, n-b 1	18	B 3, l-b 3, w 3	9

1/9 2/75 3/103 4/106 (9 wkts., dec.) 336
5/110 6/301 7/303 8/332 9/336

1/1 2/5 3/45 4/53 5/61 165
6/124 7/124 8/127 9/151

Warwickshire Bowling

	O.	M.	R.	W.		O.	M.	R.	W.
Bannister	34	5	114	5	....	19	5	43	1
Pritchard	23	4	48	0	....	21	1	53	3
K. Dollery	20	5	59	2	....	11	0	44	0
King	29	13	40	1	....	20	6	40	2
Hitchcock	21	7	34	1	....	10	2	38	0
Townsend	3	1	4	0					

Essex Bowling

	O.	M.	R.	W.		O.	M.	R.	W.
Bailey	24.1	1	74	5	....	9	0	40	1
Preston	18	0	51	0	....	7	0	46	3
Smith	9	0	35	0					
Ralph	14	2	62	0					
Greensmith	24	7	93	4	....	9	0	49	1
Insole	1	0	3	0	....	4	0	9	1
Dodds						3.5	1	12	2

Umpires: E. Davies and A. J. B. Fowler.

At Neath, August 24, 25. WARWICKSHIRE lost to GLAMORGAN by an innings and 80 runs.

PLAYING NO LONGER

Warwickshire

DOLLERY, H. E. (Warwickshire). Debut 1934, but previously with Berkshire. Attractive all-round batsman and good slip. Played four times for England, twice against Australia and once each against South Africa and West Indies. Captained Warwickshire from 1948 and led them to the Championship in 1951. Scored 24,413 runs in career with highest innings of 212 against Leicestershire in 1952.

Worcestershire

PERKS, R. T. D. (Worcestershire). Debut 1930. A leading fast bowler for many years and hard-hitting left-handed batsman. Has taken 100 wickets or more in a season 16 times. Only W. Rhodes and A. P. Freeman have done better. Total wickets in career 2,233; total runs 8,956. Best bowling nine for 42 against Gloucestershire in 1946. Captained Worcestershire in 1955, first professional to do so. Two Tests—one each against South Africa and West Indies.

WORCESTERSHIRE

President—MAJOR M. F. S. JEWELL
Secretary—MAJOR BRYAN BAYLY, County Ground, Worcester
Captain—R. T. D. PERKS   1956—P. E. RICHARDSON

M. J. Horton

County Badge

J. Flavell

There was a genuine desire in Worcestershire for the county to do well under the captaincy of one of its most faithful servants, R. T. D. Perks, the first professional to lead the side. An auspicious start brought victory over the South Africans, which subsequently proved to be the only defeat of the touring team outside of the Tests, but afterwards there was little of note in the county's performances. Not until the beginning of July did they gain their first victory in the Championship, and with only five wins in all they finished third from bottom in the table.

Towards the end of this disappointing season, Perks announced that after 27 years with the club he would retire at the end of the summer. Even at the age of 43 he remained the most successful and hardworking bowler, and in all matches he took over 100 wickets for the sixteenth consecutive time. Only A. P. Freeman, of Kent (17 times), exceeded that figure in successive years, and as a slow bowler he was not subjected to the same physical strain. Appropriately Perks completed this wonderful feat in his last match; and at Bournemouth, where when 16 he embarked on his county career as twelfth man and scorer.

Much of the weakness of Worcestershire could be traced to a lack of determination in batting. With P. E. Richardson still on Army service a lot of responsibility again rested on the shoulders of Kenyon. Apart from a lean period midway through the summer he responded magnificently, exceeding 2,000 runs for the sixth successive season. Outschoorn supported him reasonably well as opening batsman, although it was not his normal position, and Broadbent occasionally showed the form of which he is capable.

There was little scoring power lower in the order and until D. W. Richardson, the younger brother of P. E. Richardson, and J. Lister, the assistant secretary, came into the side during June it was no exaggeration to say that the tail sometimes commenced on the fall of the third wicket. D. W. Richardson also helped to improve the catching and ground fielding.

Perks received limited support in the attack. Horton started well by taking nine for 56 with off-breaks in the South African second innings and Flavell, fast-medium, surpassed that analysis with nine for 30 against Kent at Dover, but generally the bowling lacked "bite" and consistency. Jenkins, recovering from illness, did something to rectify these shortcomings during the later months.

Undoubtedly the most heartening feature was the progress made by 21-year-old Horton as an all-rounder. He completed the double of 100 wickets and 1,000 runs in his first full season.

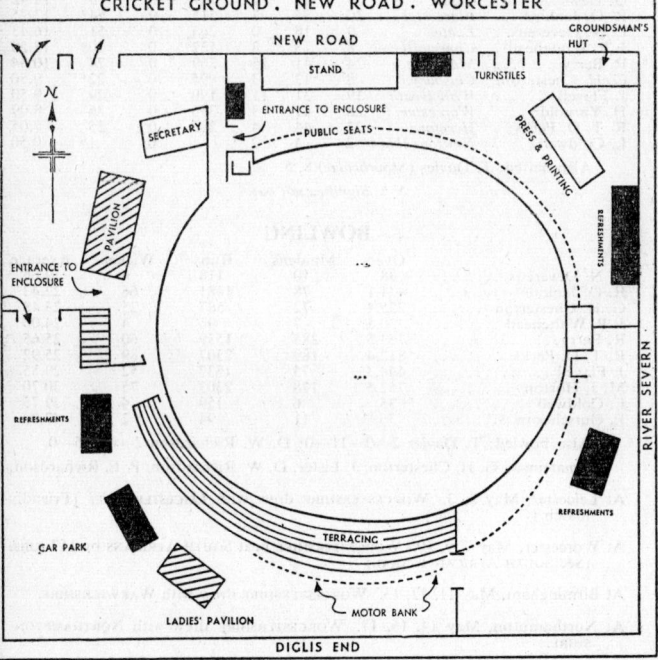

WORCESTERSHIRE RESULTS

All First-Class Matches—Played 32, Won 8, Lost 18, Drawn 6

County Championship Matches—Played 28, Won 5, Lost 17, Drawn 6

COUNTY CHAMPIONSHIP AVERAGES

BATTING

	Birthplace	Mtchs.	Inns.	Not Outs	Runs	100's	Highest Inns.	Aver.
P. E. Richardson	Hereford	6	12	3	508	0	91*	56.44
D. Kenyon	Wordsley	24	45	3	1637	4	131	38.97
L. Outschoorn ..	Ceylon	24	44	2	1247	2	150*	29.69
R. G. Broadbent	Beckenham	28	51	1	1312	2	146	26.24
D. W. Richardson	Hereford	17	32	2	742	1	126	24.73
J. Lister	Thirsk	12	24	1	549	0	99	23.86
M. J. Horton ...	Worcester	28	53	4	1131	1	103*	23.08
G. Dews	Ossett	23	41	1	737	0	73	18.42
R. O. Jenkins ...	Worcester	20	36	7	515	0	54*	17.75
L. N. Devereux .	Exeter	9	16	0	263	0	51	16.43
J. P. Whitehead .	Uppermill	8	13	3	132	0	20*	13.20
R. Berry........	Manchester	24	41	15	269	0	24	10.34
G. H. Chesterton	Chisbury	8	13	3	95	0	22*	9.50
J. Flavell	Wall Heath	19	31	11	190	0	29	9.50
H. Yarnold	Worcester	28	47	3	356	0	36	8.09
R. T. D. Perks ..	Hereford	27	44	4	282	0	25	7.05
L. Coldwell	Newton Abbot	2	4	2	1	0	1*	0.50

Also batted: T. Davies (*Stourbridge*) 8, 5.

* *Signifies not out.*

BOWLING

	Overs	Maidens	Runs	Wickets	Average
L. N. Devereux	38	10	118	6	19.66
R. O. Jenkins	434.1	78	1481	66	22.43
G. H. Chesterton	225.4	72	587	25	23.48
J. P. Whitehead	30.5	7	96	4	24.00
R. Berry..............	753.5	285	1539	60	25.65
R. T. D. Perks	812.4	189	2307	89	25.92
J. Flavell	448.3	73	1537	52	29.55
M. J. Horton	752.5	178	2303	75	30.70
L. Coldwell	35	6	159	4	39.75
L. Outschoorn	36	11	94	2	47.00

Also bowled: T. Davies 2—0—11—0; D. W. Richardson 2—0—15—0.

Amateurs.—G. H. Chesterton, J. Lister, D. W. Richardson, P. E. Richardson.

At Leicester, May 2, 3. WORCESTERSHIRE drew with LEICESTERSHIRE. (Friendly match.)

At Worcester, May 7, 9, 10. WORCESTERSHIRE beat SOUTH AFRICANS by 117 runs. (See SOUTH AFRICAN section.)

At Birmingham, May 11, 12, 13. WORCESTERSHIRE drew with WARWICKSHIRE.

At Northampton, May 14, 16, 17. WORCESTERSHIRE drew with NORTHAMPTON-SHIRE.

WORCESTERSHIRE v. HAMPSHIRE

At Worcester, May 18, 19, 20. Drawn. The game was at an interesting stage when rain ended the match one hour after the start on Friday. Worcestershire were then 126 runs on with three wickets to fall. The faster bowlers held command throughout. Shackleton and Cannings each took four wickets on the first day and Perks, who took three wickets at a personal cost of 11 runs in one spell, followed with a splendid performance on a pitch giving little sign of life. Richardson, the only batsman to show complete confidence, looked set for a century when he batted throughout the innings but ran out of partners on the first day.

Worcestershire

D. Kenyon lbw b Cannings	11	— c Gray b Sainsbury	47
P. E. Richardson not out	91	— c Harrison b Cannings	0
L. Outschoorn b Cannings	6	— lbw b Shackleton	4
G. Dews c Harrison b Shackleton	2	— b Cannings	0
R. G. Broadbent lbw b Shackleton	0	— c Harrison b Shackleton	1
J. P. Whitehead b Gray	17	— not out	20
M. J. Horton b Shackleton	0	— b Sainsbury	1
R. O. Jenkins lbw b Cannings	1	— not out	0
H. Yarnold b Cannings	0		
R. T. D. Perks c Eagar b Shackleton	5		
R. Berry c Gray b Sainsbury	2	— b Gray	1
B 13, l-b 7	20	B 3, l-b 6	9
	155	**(7 wkts.)**	**83**

1/23 2/43 3/54 4/56 5/94 6/95 7/101 8/101 9/108

1/0 2/13 3/22 4/35 5/36 6/75 7/79

Hampshire

R. E. Marshall b Perks	8	D. Shackleton c Broadbent b Perks	8
J. R. Gray lbw b Whitehead	8	V. H. D. Cannings not out	0
H. Horton c Yarnold b Perks	2	M. D. Burden b Perks	0
A. W. H. Rayment lbw b Perks	17		
N. H. Rogers lbw b Berry	23		
E. D. R. Eagar c Jenkins b Perks	23	L-b 5, w 1, n-b 1	7
L. Harrison b Berry	7		**112**
P. J. Sainsbury c Outschoorn b Berry	9		

1/16 2/18 3/18 4/61 5/61 6/86 7/96 8/112 9/112

Hampshire Bowling

	O.	M.	R.	W.		O.	M.	R.	W
Shackleton	33	17	42	4	....	16	6	30	2
Cannings	37	13	68	4	....	16	5	28	2
Gray	9	3	15	1	....	8	3	15	1
Burden	5	0	9	0					
Sainsbury	1.5	1	1	1	....	5	4	1	2

Worcestershire Bowling

	O.	M.	R.	W.
Perks	24.4	10	44	6
Whitehead	11	4	25	1
Berry	16	11	10	3
Horton	7	0	26	0

Umpires: E. Cooke and T. J. Bartley.

At Glasgow, May 21, 23, 24. WORCESTERSHIRE beat SCOTLAND by 197 runs.

WORCESTERSHIRE v. LEICESTERSHIRE

At Dudley, May 25, 26, 27. Drawn. A fine, forcing century by Kenyon, his first of the season, helped Worcestershire to make a good start. He hit seventeen 4's during a stay of three and a half hours and always looked for runs. Broadbent also drove well. Tompkin replied with an equally good hundred for Leicestershire. Without his innings and that of Hallam, who batted attractively for 90 minutes, they would have been in serious trouble. Worcestershire led on the first innings by 126, but with rain reducing play on the second day a definite result never looked likely once Leicestershire saved the follow-on.

Worcestershire

D. Kenyon b Lester	129	
P. E. Richardson c Hallam b Munden	39	— not out 9
L. Outschoorn c Jackson b Lester	28	
G. Dews c Palmer b Munden	4	
R. G. Broadbent c Firth b Boshier	69	
J. P. Whitehead c Firth b Boshier	10	— not out 0
M. J. Horton b Jackson	42	
H. Yarnold c Smithson b Boshier	36	
R. T. D. Perks b Spencer	1	
R. Berry not out	23	
J. Flavell b Spencer	2	
B 2, l-b 2	4	L-b 1 1

1/99 2/189 3/198 4/211 5/242   387   (No wkt.) 10
6/305 7/345 8/352 9/372

Leicestershire

G. Lester c Dews b Berry	16		J. Firth lbw b Horton	6
M. R. Hallam c and b Horton	65		C. T. Spencer not out	0
M. Tompkin c Richardson b Berry	131		B. Boshier c Perks b Berry	0
C. H. Palmer b Flavell	36			
G. A. Smithson b Flavell	4		B 2	2
V. E. Jackson c Broadbent b Berry	1			
V. S. Munden c Yarnold b Flavell	0		1/44 2/99 3/184 4/192 5/203	261
J. E. Walsh b Flavell	0		6/204 7/204 8/261 9/261	

Leicestershire Bowling

	O.	M.	R.	W.		O.	M.	R.	W.
Spencer	29.3	7	87	2	....	2	0	4	0
Boshier	32	4	113	3	....	2	1	1	0
Walsh	9	2	38	0					
Jackson	25	13	56	1					
Munden	30	9	70	2					
Lester	10	4	19	2					
Tompkin						1	0	4	0

Worcestershire Bowling

	O.	M.	R.	W.
Perks	15	4	38	0
Flavell	22	2	75	4
Berry	35	10	70	4
Horton	26	5	76	2

Umpires: N. Oldfield and E. A. Roberts.

WORCESTERSHIRE v. ESSEX

At Worcester, May 28, 30, 31. Drawn. A blank day on Saturday brought the total number of playing hours lost so far by Worcestershire to 33. When play started, Richardson, driving delightfully, and Broadbent alone batted with freedom, but Essex were later just as unenterprising. Gibb, first in, defied the bowlers until Insole declared with a lead of one run. Afterwards Kenyon gave a polished display, but because of the time lost there was little chance of a definite result.

Worcestershire

D. Kenyon c Taylor b Greensmith	20	— not out	90
P. E. Richardson lbw b Greensmith	53	— run out	51
L. Outschoorn c Bailey b Insole	32		
G. Dews c Gibb b Preston	5		
R. G. Broadbent c Gibb b Smith	47		
J. P. Whitehead c Gibb b Insole	6		
M. J. Horton lbw b Greensmith	1	— not out	0
H. Yarnold b Smith	15		
R. T. D. Perks b Smith	2		
R. Berry not out	8		
J. Flavell c Taylor b Smith	6		
B 1, l-b 2	3	B 1, l-b 1	2

1/45 2/88 3/99 4/136 5/142 6/143   198   1/142   (1 wkt., dec.) 143
7/179 8/181 9/188

Essex

T. C. Dodds b Berry	27		
P. A. Gibb not out	72		
G. Barker lbw b Berry	1	— not out	6
R. Horsfall b Horton	36		
D. J. Insole b Horton	15		
T. E. Bailey b Berry	4		
B. Taylor c Richardson b Berry	6		
B. Knight c Kenyon b Berry	22		
R. Smith not out	4		
W. T. Greensmith (did not bat)		— not out	18
B 2, l-b 10	12	L-b 1	1

1/48 2/62 3/124 4/148   (7 wkts., dec.) 199   (No wkt.) 25
5/159 6/165 7/193

K. C. Preston did not bat.

Essex Bowling

	O.	M.	R.	W.		O.	M.	R.	W.
Bailey	23	9	34	0	....	13	2	31	0
Preston	14	4	30	1	....	11	2	25	0
Smith	10	2	37	4	....	10	2	34	0
Greensmith	32	7	72	3	....	5	0	26	0
Insole	11	5	22	2	....	4	0	25	0

Worcestershire Bowling

	O.	M.	R.	W.		O.	M.	R.	W.
Perks	14	4	35	0	....	2	1	3	0
Flavell	8	1	23	0	....	3	1	5	0
Horton	33	10	66	2	....	3	1	5	0
Berry	34	11	63	5	....	4	1	11	0

Umpires: E. Davies and P. Corrall.

WORCESTERSHIRE v. DERBYSHIRE

At Worcester, June 1, 2. Derbyshire won by 144 runs. Their third wicket pair, Johnson and Revill, were criticised for slow scoring, but in adding 92 they laid the foundations of the total before Dawkes hit nine 4's during an enterprising stand with Gladwin. Worcestershire never recovered from the loss of Kenyon to a slip catch without a run scored. Their batsmen, apart from Broadbent in the first innings, faltered first against the off-breaks of Smith and later the spin and pace of Carr and Gladwin. Derbyshire did little better on the second day when 26 wickets fell in six and a half hours.

Derbyshire

A. Hamer b Horton	34	— c Whitehead b Perks		8
J. Kelly lbw b Chesterton	11	— b Perks		15
H. L. Johnson st Yarnold b Berry	50	— c Perks b Chesterton		0
A. C. Revill c Chesterton b Horton	53	— c Broadbent b Horton		33
D. B. Carr st Yarnold b Berry	19	— c Broadbent b Horton		19
C. Lee b Horton	0	— c Yarnold b Berry		7
D. C. Morgan run out	6	— c Perks b Berry		1
G. O. Dawkes b Berry	51	— c Perks b Horton		22
C. Gladwin c Broadbent b Horton	29	— not out		29
E. Smith b Horton	12	— c Dews b Horton		8
L. Jackson not out	4	— st Yarnold b Berry		16
L-b 7, n-b 1	8	B 4, l-b 6		10

1/35 2/51 3/143 4/159 5/159   277
6/175 7/176 8/261 9/269

1/12 2/15 3/25 4/63   160
5/76 6/80 7/102 8/133 9/133

Worcestershire

D. Kenyon c Smith b Jackson	0	— b Smith		19
L. Outschoorn c Morgan b Carr	22	— c Jackson b Gladwin		6
G. Dews b Smith	16	— c Morgan b Gladwin		0
R. G. Broadbent b Smith	54	— b Carr		32
J. P. Whitehead c Hamer b Smith	8	— b Carr		15
J. Flavell b Carr	23	— not out		7
R. T. D. Perks run out	0	— c Johnson b Carr		25
M. J. Horton b Smith	4	— run out		0
H. Yarnold b Smith	0	— b Gladwin		4
G. H. Chesterton b Smith	9	— b Gladwin		8
R. Berry not out	16	— c Gladwin b Carr		8
B 7, l-b 4	11	B 5, l-b 1		6

1/0 2/38 3/38 4/47 5/110 6/123   163
7/133 8/133 9/134

1/12 2/12 3/48 4/61   130
5/67 6/72 7/82 8/109 9/120

Worcestershire Bowling

	O.	M.	R.	W.		O.	M.	R.	W.
Perks	13	6	34	0		6	1	25	2
Flavell	8	2	29	0		1	0	3	0
Chesterton	19	5	40	1		4	1	4	1
Horton	34.4	10	123	5		25	6	66	4
Berry	31	14	43	3		25.2	11	52	3

Derbyshire Bowling

	O.	M.	R.	W.		O.	M.	R.	W.
Jackson	6	1	12	1		5	0	15	0
Gladwin	12	3	38	0		18.2	5	65	4
Morgan	2	1	1	0					
Smith	22.1	5	45	6		5	1	18	1
Carr	18	3	56	2		7	2	21	4
Hamer						2	0	5	0

Umpires: E. Davies and P. Corrall.

At Lord's, June 4, 6. WORCESTERSHIRE lost to MIDDLESEX by an innings and 110 runs.

WORCESTERSHIRE v. R.A.F.

At Worcester, June 8, 9, 10. Abandoned without a ball being bowled.

Worcestershire

J. Lister, D. W. Richardson, L. Outschoorn, R. G. Broadbent, J. P. Whitehead, M. J. Horton, L. N. Devereux, A. Tipton, L. Coldwell, D. Pearson, T. Davies.

R.A.F.

S/Ldr. A. C. Shirreff, F/Lt. R. Leggett, F/Lt. R. Gebbels, F/O G. H. McKinna, A/C J. T. Murray, A/C M. J. Cowan, A/C W. B. Stott, A/C S. E. Leary, A/C R. A. Tindall, A/C P. McKelvey, A/C D. A. Allen.

Umpires: D. Davies and L. H. Gray.

At Oxford, June 11, 13, 14. WORCESTERSHIRE beat OXFORD UNIVERSITY by five wickets.

WORCESTERSHIRE v. SUSSEX

At Dudley, June 15, 16, 17. Sussex won by 108 runs and owed a lot to Sheppard in his first championship match of the season. He helped Smith to add 78 runs on the first day and again played attractively, particularly in off-driving, when Sussex batted brightly in the second innings. Cox, 43 years old, hit three 6's and two 4's off one over from Perks, of the same age. Set to score 361 in four and three-quarter hours, Worcestershire never looked like saving the game. Broadbent and Horton were associated in a lively stand before Thomson hastened the end by taking four of the last five wickets at a personal cost of 12 runs.

Sussex

J. Langridge c Dews b Perks	7	— c Perks b Horton	42
D. V. Smith c Yarnold b Horton	71	— b Berry	19
A. S. M. Oakman c Kenyon b Perks	5	— c Broadbent b Devereux	57
J. M. Parks b Flavell	3	— c Dews b Perks	61
D. S. Sheppard b Horton	43	— c Richardson b Horton	57
K. G. Suttle lbw b Berry	15	— c Lister b Berry	28
G. Cox lbw b Horton	1	— not out	63
N. I. Thomson c Dews b Perks	35	— c Devereux b Perks	6
A. E. James c and b Berry	3		
R. T. Webb not out	28		
R. G. Marlar lbw b Horton	19	— not out	3
		B 1, l-b 6, w 1, n-b 1	9

1/17 2/23 3/28 4/106 5/139 6/140   230   1/44 2/107   (7 wkts., dec.) 345
7/147 8/172 9/203   3/153 4/221 5/267 6/284
                                                 7/299

Worcestershire

D. Kenyon c Parks b Marlar	60	— c Suttle b James	2
J. Lister lbw b Marlar	19	— c Smith b Marlar	18
L. N. Devereux b Thomson	4	— lbw b Oakman	51
D. W. Richardson c and b Marlar	6	— run out	15
M. J. Horton run out	24	— c Webb b Thomson	59
R. G. Broadbent c and b Oakman	48	— b Thomson	56
G. Dews st Webb b Thomson	20	— lbw b Marlar	24
H. Yarnold c Suttle b Oakman	3	— b Thomson	0
R. T. D. Perks c Oakman b James	21	— lbw b Thomson	12
R. Berry b James	6	— b Thomson	6
J. Flavell not out	1	— not out	3
B 2, l-b 3	5	B 3, l-b 3	6

1/67 2/82 3/92 4/92 5/164 6/164   215
7/172 8/210 9/210

1/5 2/44 3/87 4/89   252
5/186 6/229 7/229 8/235
9/247

Worcestershire Bowling

	O.	M.	R.	W.		O.	M.	R.	W.
Flavell	17	3	47	1	....	15	3	56	0
Perks	23	4	64	3	....	17	4	80	2
Berry	24	6	47	2	....	25	13	49	2
Horton	31	15	72	4	....	23	2	105	2
Devereux						6	0	46	1

Sussex Bowling

	O.	M.	R.	W.		O.	M.	R.	W.
Thomson	21	4	61	2	....	18	1	57	5
James	20.4	10	38	2	....	7	1	21	1
Marlar	18	7	67	3	....	25	6	82	2
Oakman	15	3	40	2	....	22	4	60	1
Parks	1	1	0	0	....	4	0	20	0
Smith	1	0	4	0	....	3	2	6	0

Umpires: D. Davies and T. J. Bartley.

At Manchester, June 18, 20, 21. WORCESTERSHIRE lost to LANCASHIRE by eight wickets.

WORCESTERSHIRE v. CAMBRIDGE UNIVERSITY

At Worcester, June 22, 23. Cambridge University won by an innings and 76 runs with a day and a half to spare, mainly through the good all-round form of Singh and Goonesena and the splendid batting of Lumsden, who contributed 225 to the University total of 262. Before the close of the first day Singh, bowling at medium pace, took three wickets for ten runs. He repeated this performance at the start of the second day, when Worcestershire were out for 47, and with four wickets for 43 runs in the second innings he gained match figures of ten for 63. Towards the end, Goonesena, leg-breaks, exploited a worn patch.

Cambridge University

W. Knightley-Smith b Perks	5	D. R. W. Silk run out	6
A. B. D. Parsons b Coldwell	2	M. E. L. Melluish b Coldwell	5
G. Goonesena b Coldwell	47	D. J. Smith c Yarnold b Perks	0
V. R. Lumsden b Davies	99		
J. F. Pretlove b Jenkins	0	B 1, w 1, n-b 3	5
S. Singh not out	79		
P. D. Croft c Richardson b Davies	0	1/8 2/8 3/117 4/118 5/188 262
R. O'Brien b Perks	16	6/188 7/224 8/248 9/261

Worcestershire

M. J. Horton c Singh	1	— c Melluish b Singh 5
L. N. Devereux c Lumsden b Singh	4	— c Silk b Goonesena....... 21
L. Outschoorn c Melluish b Smith	5	— b Singh 0
R. G. Broadbent c Melluish b Smith	0	— b Goonesena 9
D. W. Richardson c Melluish b Singh	24	— b Goonesena 7
R. Jones b Singh	2	— c and b Goonesena 23
T. Davies b Goonesena	0	— lbw b Goonesena 15
H. Yarnold b Smith	1	— c Knightley-Smith b Singh.. 10
R. O. Jenkins not out	0	— c Parsons b Singh........ 8
R. T. D. Perks c and b Singh	5	— c O'Brien b Goonesena .. 18
L. Coldwell b Singh	4	— not out 0
L-b 1	1	B 17, l-b 6 23

1/3 2/10 3/10 4/13 5/18 6/30   47   1/9 2/13 3/30 4/51   139
7/35 8/37 9/43   5/54 6/78 7/105 8/105 9/139

Worcestershire Bowling

	O.	M.	R.	W.	O.	M.	R.	W
Perks	17.4	4	39	3				
Coldwell	25	7	69	3				
Horton	11	1	42	0				
Jenkins	21	5	51	1				
Devereux	11	2	34	0				
Davies	5	1	22	2				

Cambridge University Bowling

	O.	M.	R.	W.		O.	M.	R.	W
Smith	16	8	21	3	....	10	5	24	0
Singh	13	4	20	6	....	25.1	11	43	4
Goonesena	3	1	5	1	....	22	7	49	6

Umpires: W. F. Price and N. Oldfield.

WORCESTERSHIRE v. WARWICKSHIRE

At Dudley, June 25, 27, 28. Warwickshire won by 151 runs. They always looked the more polished side on a pitch taking spin. Horner in particular batted well against the turning ball and, with scores of 71 and 90, made an auspicious return to the side after injuring a finger at the beginning of the month. Apart from Dews and D. W. Richardson in the first innings and later P. E. Richardson, the Worcestershire batsmen failed against the leg-breaks of Hollies and Hitchcock.

Warwickshire

F. C. Gardner c Yarnold b Jenkins	31	— lbw b Horton............ 28
N. F. Horner c Yarnold b Berry	71	— st Yarnold b Berry........ 90
A. V. Wolton c Broadbent b Coldwell	99	— c D. Richardson b Horton. 15
R. E. Hitchcock c D. Richardson b Jenkins	4	— c Yarnold b Horton 0
H. E. Dollery c Broadbent b Devereux	53	— lbw b Berry 40
R. T. Spooner c Broadbent b Perks	26	— c D. Richardson b Horton 14
A. Townsend lbw b Jenkins	27	— lbw b Horton............ 0
K. R. Dollery c Yarnold b Jenkins	5	— not out 17
J. D. Bannister st Yarnold b Berry	8	— c Broadbent b Horton 4
R. G. Thompson c Broadbent b Jenkins	4	— b Horton 1
W. E. Hollies not out	0	— c and b Berry........... 0
B 8, l-b 3, w 1	12	B 7, l-b 8 n-b 2 17

1/99 2/105 3/109 4/223 5/281   340   1/69 2/97 3/97 4/170   226
6/291 7/323 8/330 9/336   5/189 6/189 7/209 8/214
                                      9/225

Worcestershire

P. E. Richardson c Hitchcock b Thompson	5	— c Gardner b Hollies	52
L. N. Devereux b Bannister	14	— lbw b Hollies	34
M. J. Horton c and b Hollies	28	— c Gardner b Hitchcock	31
R. G. Broadbent b Hitchcock	3	— c Bannister b Hollies	12
G. Dews c Gardner b Townsend	69	— b Hollies	26
D. W. Richardson b Townsend b Hollies	47	— c Gardner b Hitchcock	1
R. O. Jenkins b Hitchcock	33	— not out	5
H. Yarnold c and b Hollies	1	— c Spooner b Hitchcock	21
R. T. D. Perks c Bannister b Hollies	4	— b Hitchcock	0
R. Berry b Hollies	11	— c Bannister b Hitchcock	4
L. Coldwell not out	1	— c and b Hitchcock	0
B 3, l-b 9	12	L-b 1	1

1/5 2/38 3/50 4/60 5/149 6/191   228
7/192 8/200 9/216

1/81 2/96 3/130 4/134   187
5/148 6/158 7/159 8/165
9/187

Worcestershire Bowling

	O.	M.	R.	W.		O.	M.	R.	W.
Perks	16	2	49	1	....	4	2	10	0
Coldwell	13	3	63	1	....	3	0	7	0
Berry	43	15	70	2	....	29.2	8	62	3
Jenkins	37.2	10	106	5	....	5	0	17	0
Horton	8	1	36	0	....	24	2	111	7
Devereux	5	3	4	1	....	1	0	2	0

Warwickshire Bowling

	O.	M.	R.	W.		O.	M.	R.	W.
Bannister	13	2	38	1	....	1	0	5	0
Thompson	16	4	32	1	....	6	1	10	0
Hollies	36	15	65	5	....	35	13	67	4
Hitchcock	8	3	24	2	....	25.5	4	67	6
Townsend	10	1	37	1	....	0	0	18	0
K. Dollery	6	1	20	0	....	2	1	5	0
					Wolton	4	0	14	0

Umpires: H. Elliott (Lancashire) and N. Oldfield.

At The Oval, June 29, 30. WORCESTERSHIRE lost to SURREY by ten wickets.

WORCESTERSHIRE v. MIDDLESEX

At Worcester, July 2, 4, 5. Middlesex won by eight wickets and on a dusty pitch owed most to Titmus, their off-spinner, who took ten wickets for 147 runs in the match. He captured his hundredth wicket on the first day a few hours after Lock (Surrey) became the first bowler to reach that target. Batsmen generally found runs hard to score after Kenyon and Outschoorn put on 123 for the first wicket. Middlesex, helped by a last wicket stand of 61 by Warr and Moss, led by eight runs and they won comfortably after causing Worcestershire much trouble in their second innings. D. Compton reached 50 in thirty-four minutes and the winning hit came before lunch on the third day.

Worcestershire

D. Kenyon c L. Compton b Titmus	65	— c Moss b Titmus	31
L. Outschoorn lbw b Moss	53	— c Baldry b Young	15
L. N. Devereux c L. Compton b Titmus .	23	— c L. Compton b Titmus ...	1
M. J. Horton c Titmus b D. Compton .	34	— b Titmus	18
R. G. Broadbent c Warr b Titmus	4	— c Robertson b D. Compton	34
G. Dews lbw b D. Compton	5	— c L. Compton b Moss	36
J. Lister c Edrich b Titmus	25	— c Titmus b D. Compton ...	4
H. Yarnold b Titmus	1	— c Edrich b Young	4
R. T. D. Perks c L. Compton b Moss ...	12	— b Moss	7
R. Berry c Brown b Titmus	16	— c L. Compton b Titmus ...	1
J. Flavell not out	10	— not out	0
B 5, l-b 9, n-b 1	15	B 5, l-b 4	9

1/123 2/128 3/178 4/186 5/191 6/222   263
7/222 8/237 9/239

1/26 2/46 3/64 4/67   160
5/121 6/126 7/135 8/159
9/160

Middlesex

J. D. Robertson c Kenyon b Flavell.....	55	— c Dews b Horton	45
S. M. Brown lbw b Perks	19	— c Dews b Perks	0
W. J. Edrich c Kenyon b Horton.......	44	— not out	56
D. Bennett c Broadbent b Perks	20		
D. C. S. Compton lbw b Perks	23	— not out	50
D. O. Baldry c Flavell b Horton	17		
F. J. Titmus c Dews b Horton	6		
J. J. Warr c Broadbent b Berry	51		
L. H. Compton lbw b Perks	0		
J. A. Young b Perks	10		
A. E. Moss not out	14		
B 6, l-b 3, n-b 3	12	L-b 4, w 1	5

1/54 2/98 3/131 4/159 5/166 6/185   271
7/192 8/192 9/210

1/1 2/85   (2 wkts.) 156

Middlesex Bowling

	O.	M.	R.	W.		O.	M.	R.	W.
Moss	16	5	45	2	....	5	1	5	2
Warr..........	6	0	24	0	....	4	0	13	0
Young	17	7	30	0	....	27	15	37	2
Titmus	39.4	20	81	6	....	34.2	10	66	4
D. Compton ...	16	3	61	2	....	6	1	30	2
Bennett	3	1	7	0					

Worcestershire Bowling

	O.	M.	R.	W.		O.	M.	R.	W.
Flavell	16	1	70	1	....	2	0	14	0
Perks	34	6	93	5	....	12	1	34	1
Horton	20	5	70	3	....	19	9	49	1
Berry	19.1	13	19	1	....	24	8	54	0
Devereux	1	0	7	0					

Umpires: Harry Elliott (Derbyshire) and J. S. Buller.

WORCESTERSHIRE v. KENT

At Worcester, July 6, 7, 8. Worcestershire won by 188 runs, their first championship success of the season. The pitch took spin from the start and only bold methods brought runs. Lister, promoted to open the innings in the absence of Kenyon, hit twelve 4's before losing his leg stump to a full toss when one short of a maiden century. Kent failed to follow Lister's example and, batting timidly, were all out 152 runs behind. Their second effort was little better and they never appeared likely to score the 369 runs required for victory. Only Allan and Ufton attacked Jenkins, whose leg-breaks and googlies always held danger for batsmen tied to their crease. Jenkins' match analysis was nine wickets for 105 runs.

Worcestershire

L. Outschoorn c Ufton b Page	33	— b Page	32
J. Lister b Page	99	— lbw b Spanswick	10
D. W. Richardson b Wright	42	— c Fagg b Allan	10
L. N. Devereux lbw b Wright	6	— b Page	8
M. J. Horton b Wright	0	— lbw b Wright	53
R. G. Broadbent c Phebey b Wright	4	— c Phebey b Dixon	10
G. Dews lbw b Allan	5	— c and b Allan	26
R. O. Jenkins lbw b Pettiford	40	— b Page	17
H. Yarnold lbw b Wright	5	— not out	30
R. T. D. Perks c Hearn b Page	10	— b Wright	16
R. Berry not out	0	— c Pettiford b Wright	0
B 16, l-b 1, n-b 3	20	L-b 4	4

1/61 2/137 3/153 4/157 5/172 6/182   264
7/238 8/254 9/264

1/25 2/36 3/60 4/61 5/90   216
6/153 7/153 8/193 9/216

Kent

A. E. Fagg lbw b Berry	26	— c Outschoorn b Perks	15
A. H. Phebey lbw b Outschoorn	4	— b Outschoorn	4
J. M. Allan b Perks	24	— c Outschoorn b Devereux	53
R. C. Wilson c Richardson b Jenkins	13	— c Devereux b Perks	5
J. Pettiford c Outschoorn b Jenkins	7	— not out	40
P. Hearn c Outschoorn b Jenkins	4	— lbw b Jenkins	6
D. G. Ufton c Richardson b Jenkins	0	— b Jenkins	35
A. L. Dixon c Dews b Perks	1	— b Jenkins	1
J. Spanswick lbw b Horton	24	— c Lister b Horton	0
D. V. P. Wright not out	8	— b Horton	2
J. C. T. Page c Lister b Jenkins	1	— st Yarnold b Jenkins	12
		B 2, l-b 4, n-b 1	7

1/14 2/36 3/52 4/66 5/70 6/70 7/71   112
8/82 9/111

1/17 2/25 3/45 4/92   180
5/103 6/147 7/149 8/150
9/159

Kent Bowling

	O.	M.	R.	W.	O.	M.	R.	W.
Spanswick	4	0	18	0	7	2	20	1
Wright	24	4	94	5	12.5	1	45	3
Page	14.4	2	51	3	18	5	74	3
Allan	23	3	59	1	24	10	46	2
Pettiford	6	0	22	1				
Dixon					5	0	27	

Worcestershire Bowling

	O.	M.	R.	W.	O.	M.	R.	W.
Perks	17	10	18	2	12	3	35	2
Outschoorn	9	3	15	1	5	1	18	1
Horton	9	2	24	1	17	5	30	2
Berry	6	3	8	1	3	1	11	0
Jenkins	14.1	4	39	5	20.5	4	66	4
Devereux	5	1	8	0	8	3	13	1

Umpires: Harry Elliott (Derbyshire) and A. J. B. Fowler.

At Gloucester, July 9, 11, 12. WORCESTERSHIRE lost to GLOUCESTERSHIRE by 138 runs.

At Taunton, July 13, 14, 15. WORCESTERSHIRE lost to SOMERSET by nine wickets.

WORCESTERSHIRE v. NOTTINGHAMSHIRE

At Kidderminster, July 16, 18, 19. Worcestershire won by 117 runs. They held the initiative thanks to Kenyon and Lister making 100 for the opening partnership. Perks, helped by rain on the second day, caused a lot of concern with the occasional ball which kept low. He hit the stumps four times during Nottinghamshire's first innings and took seven wickets for 71 runs—an excellent performance. C. J. Poole, hitting twelve 4's in the highest individual score of the game, batted well for Nottinghamshire, who were unsuccessful in their attempt to score 293 at just over a run a minute.

Worcestershire

D. Kenyon c K. Poole b Goonesena	58	— lbw b Jepson 29
J. Lister lbw b Jepson	46	— c Stocks b Jepson 50
L. Outschoorn c and b Dooland	53	— lbw b K. Poole 16
D. W. Richardson c Jepson b Smales ..	36	— c Simpson b Jepson 11
M. J. Horton c Rowe b Smales	0	— run out 21
R. G. Broadbent c Rowe b Jepson	28	— c C. Poole b Smales 9
R. O. Jenkins lbw b Dooland	8	— c Rowe b Jepson 13
H. Yarnold b Jepson	14	— b Smales 1
R. T. D. Perks b Jepson	4	— not out 3
R. Berry b Dooland	9	— absent ill 0
J. Flavell not out	2	— c Giles b Jepson 0
B 11, l-b 8, n-b 1	20	B 1, l-b 5, w 1, n-b 1 .. 8

1/100 2/120 3/200 4/201 5/204   278   1/44 2/66 3/97 4/117   161
6/219 7/261 8/265 9/272   5/136 6/145 7/160 8/160

Nottinghamshire

R. T. Simpson c Yarnold b Perks	3	— c Richardson b Flavell .. 37
J. D. Clay c Broadbent b Perks	0	— lbw b Flavell 11
R. J. Giles b Perks................	47	— c Jenkins b Flavell 4
F. W. Stocks b Perks	28	— lbw b Horton.......... 3
C. J. Poole c sub b Flavell	8	— c Richardson b Horton .. 70
K. J. Poole b Perks	2	— b Perks 24
G. Goonesena b Flavell	20	— c Yarnold b Horton .. 3
K. Smales c sub b Perks	14	— lbw b Perks 6
A. Jepson b Perks	13	— b Horton................ 0
B. Dooland not out	7	— not out 12
E. J. Rowe b Flavell	1	— c sub b Perks 0
N-b 4	4	L-b 4, n-b 1 5

1/1 2/8 3/74 4/83 5/88 6/93 7/125   147   1/41 2/53 3/54 4/68   175
8/125 9/140   5/149 6/153 7/161 8/161
   9/167

Nottinghamshire Bowling

	O.	M.	R.	W.		O.	M.	R.	W.
Jepson	20	4	60	4	....	22	6	49	5
K. Poole	16	2	51	0	....	14	3	24	1
Goonesena	18	4	50	1					
Smales	19	6	53	2	....	11.4	2	61	2
Dooland	18.2	4	44	3	....	8	2	19	0

Worcestershire Bowling

	O.	M.	R.	W.		O.	M.	R.	W.
Perks	28	7	71	7	....	14.4	2	52	3
Flavell	24.4	6	59	3	....	14	1	61	3
Outschoorn ...	2	0	8	0					
Horton	3	1	5	0	....	18	5	47	4
					Jenkins	2	0	10	0

Umpires: J. J. Hills and E. Davies.

WORCESTERSHIRE v. ROYAL NAVY

At Worcester, July 20, 21. Worcestershire won by an innings and 66 runs. Royal Navy 129 (R. O. Jenkins seven for 53) and 147 (R. O. Jenkins eight for 46); Worcestershire 342 (R. G. Broadbent 98, R. O. Jenkins 69, L. Outschoorn 64; C/P/O G. D. Steer four for 98).

WORCESTERSHIRE v. SURREY

At Worcester, July 23, 25, 26. Surrey won by eight wickets. They were put on the right road by Stewart and Constable, whose second wicket stand realised 104 in eighty minutes. Constable completed the first century of the season on the Worcester ground, hitting one 5 and sixteen 4's in three hours forty minutes before his first mistake, a mistimed hook, cost him his wicket. The Surrey bowlers, and A. Bedser and Laker in particular, built on the solid foundations laid by the batsmen. On the second day they took seventeen wickets and when stumps were drawn Worcestershire still needed two runs to avoid an innings defeat. Richardson and Outschoorn, and Jenkins on the final day, were the only batsmen who caused Surrey much trouble.

Surrey

M. J. Stewart b Flavell	83	—	st Yarnold b Jenkins		19
D. G. W. Fletcher b Perks	20	—	b Berry		1
B. Constable c Yarnold b Flavell	132	—	not out		7
K. Barrington lbw b Horton	18	—	not out		8
T. H. Clark c and b Flavell	28				
E. A. Bedser c and b Jenkins	41				
R. C. E. Pratt b Jenkins	38				
R. Swetman b Jenkins	17				
J. C. Laker not out	6				
W. S. Surridge not out	0				
L-b 9, n-b 2	11				

1/48 2/152 3/193 4/269 (8 wkts., dec.) 394
5/292 6/366 7/373 8/394
1/20 2/24 (2 wkts.) 35

A. V. Bedser did not bat.

Worcestershire

D. Kenyon b A. Bedser	0	—	b Laker		39
P. E. Richardson lbw b Clark	38	—	lbw b Clark		44
L. Outschoorn c Stewart b Laker	49	—	b A. Bedser		46
J. Lister b Laker	13	—	b Clark		2
M. J. Horton lbw b Laker	11	—	c and b Laker		19
R. G. Broadbent c and b E. Bedser	0	—	lbw b Clark		36
R. O. Jenkins c E. Bedser b Laker	29	—	not out		54
H. Yarnold b E. Bedser	0	—	b Laker		7
R. T. D. Perks b A. Bedser	2	—	c A. Bedser b E. Bedser		3
R. Berry c Laker b A. Bedser	11	—	c Fletcher b Laker		9
J. Flavell not out	0	—	b A. Bedser		5
B 4, l-b 1	5		B 2, l-b 4		6

1/4 2/91 3/95 4/115 5/116 6/116 158
7/116 8/122 9/152
1/59 2/105 3/113 4/151 270
5/151 6/208 7/215 8/237
9/263

Worcestershire Bowling

	O.	M.	R.	W.	O.	M.	R.	W.
Perks	26	4	72	1	 1	0	3	0
Flavell	24	3	77	3				
Berry	26	6	86	0	 4	3	3	1
Jenkins	15.3	1	69	3	.... 5.1	0	17	1
Horton	18	1	79	1	 2	0	12	0

Surrey Bowling

	O.	M.	R.	W.	O.	M.	R.	W.
A. Bedser......	18	4	33	3	.... 17.5	3	50	2
Surridge	7	0	23	0	 3	0	19	0
Laker	24.3	6	63	4	 25	5	49	4
E. Bedser	11	1	28	2	 21	6	65	1
Clark	3	1	6	1	 21	0	76	3
					Pratt 1	0	5	0

Umpires: W. T. Jones and P. Corrall.

At Hove, July 27, 28, 29. WORCESTERSHIRE lost to SUSSEX by six wickets.

At Chelmsford, July 30, August 1, 2. WORCESTERSHIRE beat ESSEX by 115 runs.

At Swansea, August 3, 4. WORCESTERSHIRE lost to GLAMORGAN by an innings and 23 runs.

WORCESTERSHIRE v. SOMERSET

At Worcester, August 6, 8, 9. Drawn. Worcestershire held a commanding position after a slow start. Broadbent, forty-five minutes over his first four runs, reached a century in two and three-quarter hours, and altogether hit one 6 and sixteen 4's. Somerset failed to master the leg-breaks and googlies of Jenkins, who bowled skilfully on an unresponsive pitch, and on losing four wickets for 39 runs after following-on 174 behind, they appeared to be heading for defeat inside two days. Then Tremlett and Lawrence, the 41-year-old all-rounder, whose highest innings in first-class cricket, 122, included thirteen 4's, put on 156 for the fifth wicket. Even so, Worcestershire would probably have won but for rain, which reduced the final day's play to two and three-quarter hours.

Worcestershire

D. Kenyon b Lobb	35		
L. Outschoorn c Angell b Lomax	60		
R. G. Broadbent c Tordoff b Hilton	146		
G. Dews c Yawar Saeed b McMahon ..	16		
M. J. Horton c and b Hilton	37	— not out	13
D. W. Richardson not out	62	— not out	7
R. O. Jenkins c Hilton b Tordoff	16		
G. H. Chesterton b Tordoff	0		
R. T. D. Perks b Hilton	0		
R. Berry c Stephenson b Tordoff	24		
H. Yarnold not out	1		
B 8, l-b 8	16		

1/56 2/149 3/200 4/282 (9 wkts., dec.) 413   (No wkt.) 20
5/307 6/361 7/361 8/362 9/403

Somerset

F. L. Angell lbw b Chesterton	6	— lbw b Perks	1
G. G. Tordoff c Broadbent b Jenkins	53	— b Perks	20
J. Lawrence c and b Berry	24	— c Outschoorn b Perks	122
M. F. Tremlett b Jenkins	1	— c Broadbent b Jenkins	96
P. B. Wight c Yarnold b Jenkins	36	— b Chesterton	2
J. G. Lomax c and b Jenkins	21	— lbw b Perks	0
Yawar Saeed c Richardson b Jenkins	12	— lbw b Jenkins	26
H. W. Stephenson lbw b Chesterton	46	— c Chesterton b Perks	15
J. Hilton b Perks	4	— c Yarnold b Perks	17
J. W. McMahon not out	9	— not out	5
B. Lobb c Richardson b Perks	13	— c Outschoorn b Perks	0
B 6, l-b 5, w 1, n-b 2	14	B 5, l-b 4, n-b 3	12
	239		**316**

1/41 2/65 3/67 4/106 5/142 6/162
7/183 8/217 9/221

1/13 2/31 3/38 4/39
5/195 6/224 7/275 8/299
9/312

Somerset Bowling

	O.	M.	R.	W.		O.	M.	R.	W.
Lobb	25	3	82	1	....	2	0	8	0
Yawar Saeed	17	1	75	0					
Lomax	18	1	59	1					
Lawrence	9	2	44	0					
McMahon	13	3	34	1					
Hilton	12	0	78	3					
Tordoff	6	2	25	3	....	1	0	12	0

Worcestershire Bowling

	O.	M.	R.	W.		O.	M.	R.	W.
Perks	17	5	49	2	....	28.3	6	105	7
Chesterton	23	10	29	2	....	27	8	68	1
Jenkins	31	7	105	5	....	20	2	74	2
Berry	9	4	12	1	....	17	6	31	0
Horton	11	3	30	0	....	8	2	26	0

Umpires: E. Davies and H. Elliott (Lancashire).

WORCESTERSHIRE v. NORTHAMPTONSHIRE

At Stourbridge, August 10, 11. Northamptonshire won by an innings and 51 runs and eighteen of Worcestershire's twenty wickets fell to the left-arm slow bowling of Broderick (eleven for 79) and Tribe (seven for 121). Both were able to turn the ball on a helpful pitch at Stourbridge, where no county cricket had taken place for three years. The only resistance came from Outschoorn and Broadbent during the second wicket partnership of 127 runs on the first day. Worcestershire were dismissed in two and a quarter hours in their second innings. Northamptonshire batted with much more assurance, although Livingston, who scored his second century in successive innings, was dropped twice off sharp chances before reaching fifty. Subba Row gave a polished display for two and a half hours. This was Worcestershire's sixth two-day defeat of the season.

Worcestershire

D. Kenyon c Andrew b Webster	7	—	b Broderick		19
L. Outschoorn st Andrew b Broderick	106	—	b Broderick		4
R. G. Broadbent st Andrew b Broderick	54	—	run out		0
M. J. Horton hit wkt b Broderick	1	—	lbw b Tribe		2
G. Dews c Wild b Broderick	3	—	c Tribe b Broderick		18
D. W. Richardson b Broderick	14	—	lbw b Broderick		33
R. O. Jenkins lbw b Tribe	3	—	b Tribe		1
H. Yarnold lbw b Broderick	5	—	c Tribe b Broderick		0
G. H. Chesterton b Tribe	0	—	b Tribe		0
R. T. D. Perks c and b Tribe	6	—	b Tribe		16
R. Berry not out	7	—	not out		3
B 2, l-b 1, n-b 1	4		B 1, l-b 2, w 1		4

1/14 2/141 3/153 4/163 5/182 6/191   210   1/22 2/23 3/25 4/27 5/75   100
7/193 8/197 9/197   6/80 7/80 8/80 9/81

Northamptonshire

D. Brookes c Richardson b Berry	41	J. Wild c Perks b Chesterton		1
P. Arnold lbw b Horton	24	R. W. Clarke not out		27
K. V. Andrew lbw b Horton	0	J. Webster c Dews b Jenkins		0
L. Livingstone c and b Chesterton	107			
D. Barrick c and b Chesterton	43	B 4, l-b 8		12
R. Subba Row c Yarnold b Jenkins	102			
G. E. Tribe c Broadbent b Perks	4	1/63 2/63 3/73 4/170 5/270		361
V. Broderick lbw b Chesterton	0	6/275 7/276 8/278 9/357		

Northamptonshire Bowling

	O.	M.	R.	W.		O.	M.	R.	W.
Webster	13	6	17	1	....	4	1	18	0
Clarke	6	1	14	0	....	4	1	4	0
Tribe	27.1	4	81	3	....	18.2	7	40	4
Broderick	33	17	54	6	....	22	10	25	5
Wild	12	0	40	0	....	3	1	9	0

Worcestershire Bowling

Perks	19	5	62	1
Chesterton	25	7	79	4
Berry	31	9	62	1
Horton	39	10	129	2
Jenkins	6	0	17	2

Umpires: T. J. Bartley and H. G. Baldwin.

At Buxton, August 13, 15, 16. WORCESTERSHIRE lost to DERBYSHIRE by seven wickets.

At Dover, August 17, 18, 19. WORCESTERSHIRE beat KENT by 52 runs.

WORCESTERSHIRE v. YORKSHIRE

At Worcester, August 20, 22, 23. Yorkshire won by nine wickets and after recovering from the loss of their first four wickets for sixteen runs never conceded the advantage. Watson led the revival with a splendid innings particularly notable for the off-drive and cut. He batted nearly five hours for 214, his highest score for Yorkshire, and hit one 6 and thirty 4's. Yardley helped Watson to add 214 runs in two and a half hours. Worcestershire had no real answer to the turning ball and eleven of their wickets fell to the left-arm slow bowling of Wardle at a personal cost of 136 runs. Close, the off-spinner, took four wickets for 59 runs in the first innings and he completed a successful all-round performance by hitting 59 runs (ten 4's) out of 63 in thirty-eight minutes to end the match.

Yorkshire

D. B. Close b Flavell	3	— not out	59
W. H. H. Sutcliffe c Yarnold b Flavell	4		
J. V. Wilson c Yarnold b Perks	1		
D. E. V. Padgett c Yarnold b Perks	7	— lbw b Horton	1
W Watson not out	214	— not out	1
R. Illingworth b Jenkins	35		
N. W. D. Yardley c Perks b Jenkins	76		
J. H. Wardle b Horton	11		
F. S. Trueman not out	12		
B 7, l-b 6, w 1, n-b 1	15	N-b 2	2

1/7 2/8 3/10 4/16 5/110 (7 wkts., dec.) 378
6/324 7/364

1/28 (1 wkt.) 63

J. G. Binks and M. J. Cowan did not bat.

Worcestershire

D. Kenyon b Trueman	20	— b Wardle	10
L. Outschoorn c Wilson b Wardle	53	— c Close b Cowan	6
R. G. Broadbent c Wilson b Illingworth	24	— c Cowan b Wardle	52
M. J. Horton b Close	38	— c Wilson b Wardle	48
G. Dews c Close b Wardle	9	— c Watson b Wardle	23
D. W. Richardson c Wilson b Close	6	— run out	31
R. O. Jenkins lbw b Wardle	10	— b Wardle	47
H. Yarnold hit wkt b Wardle	4	— b Wardle	1
R. Berry not out	14	— c Padgett b Close	1
J. Flavell c Watson b Close	12	— st Binks b Wardle	4
R. T. D. Perks c Sutcliffe b Close	3	— not out	0
B 6, l-b 4	10	B 9, l-b 4	13

1/44 2/90 3/106 4/148 5/148 6/164   203
7/164 8/173 9/194

1/12 2/44 3/75 4/112   236
5/150 6/214 7/228 8/231
9/235

Worcestershire Bowling

	O.	M.	R.	W.		O.	M.	R.	W.
Flavell	14	0	77	2	....	2	0	5	0
Perks	21	6	68	2	....	3	0	21	0
Berry	9	3	32	0	....	2	0	15	0
Jenkins	28	8	98	2	....	1	0	7	0
Horton	34	7	88	1	....	4	1	13	1

Yorkshire Bowling

	O.	M.	R.	W.		O.	M.	R.	W.
Trueman	9	0	30	1	....	10	1	19	0
Cowan	7	3	13	0	....	7	1	21	1
Close	21	6	59	4	....	35	9	92	1
Wardle	31	12	64	4	....	39.1	13	72	7
Illingworth	9	2	27	1	....	11	4	19	0

Umpires: J. S. Buller and P. Corrall.

WORCESTERSHIRE v. GLOUCESTERSHIRE

At Worcester, August 24, 25, 26. Worcestershire won by seven wickets in an exciting finish to their home programme. Set to score 219 runs in two and a half hours, they were given an excellent start by Kenyon and Outschoorn, who scored 182 runs in two hours. Both were out at that total and Broadbent was bowled two runs later, but victory came with five minutes to spare. Maiden centuries were hit by D. W. Richardson, the 20-year-old Worcestershire left-hander, and Lambert, who was capped by Gloucestershire before the war, but the match will be remembered mostly for the splendid batting of Graveney. He hit 61 of his side's 108 during their first innings, when six batsmen failed to score, and reached his third century of the summer after Gloucestershire followed on 226 runs behind. Young completed 2,000 runs for the season.

Worcestershire

D. Kenyon c Rochford b Wells	27	—	c McHugh b Cook	108
L. Outschoorn c Milton b Graveney	78	—	b Cook	73
R. G. Broadbent c Graveney b Wells	4	—	b Lambert	1
M. J. Horton c Graveney b McHugh	3	—	not out	15
G. Dews c Milton b Wells	1	—	not out	20
D. W. Richardson b McHugh	126			
R. O. Jenkins lbw b McHugh	10			
H. Yarnold c Milton b Mortimore	36			
R. Berry c Lambert b Mortimore	21			
J. Flavell run out	2			
R. T. D. Perks not out	11			
B 8, l-b 5, w 1, n-b 1	15		B 1, n-b 1	2

1/44 2/52 3/65 4/69 5/185 6/241   **334**   1/182 2/182   (3 wkts.) **219**
7/260 8/314 9/321   3/184

Gloucestershire

D. M. Young c Horton b Flavell	0	—	run out	28
C. A. Milton c Broadbent b Flavell	9	—	c Yarnold b Jenkins	10
T. W. Graveney lbw b Horton	61	—	b Jenkins	128
G. M. Emmett c Outschoorn b Flavell	0	—	c Dews b Jenkins	3
W. Knightley-Smith c Broadbent b Perks	0	—	lbw b Jenkins	64
J. Mortimore b Jenkins	28	—	c Broadbent b Horton	73
G. E. Lambert c Yarnold b Horton	7	—	not out	100
P. Rochford c Dews b Jenkins	0	—	lbw b Horton	1
C. Cook lbw b Horton	1	—	c Kenyon b Jenkins	15
B. D. Wells c sub b Jenkins	0	—	lbw b Horton	2
F. P. McHugh not out	0	—	not out	0
B 1, n-b 1	2		B 4, l-b 9, w 1, n-b 6	20

1/2 2/19 3/20 4/21 5/91 6/105   **108**   1/51 2/166   (9 wkts., dec.) **444**
7/108 8/108 9/108   3/190 4/204 5/285 6/372
    7/390 8/432 9/440

Gloucestershire Bowling

	O.	M.	R.	W.		O.	M.	R.	W.
Lambert	18.4	0	77	0	....	8	0	48	1
McHugh	26	5	66	3	....	10	0	46	0
Wells	34	11	79	3	....	3	0	18	0
Cook	12	2	32	0	....	16	2	64	2
Mortimore	16	6	33	2	....	12	2	41	0
Graveney	7	1	32	1					

Worcestershire Bowling

	O.	M.	R.	W.		O.	M.	R.	W.
Flavell	10	5	20	3	....	18	3	70	0
Perks	12	6	31	1	....	20	7	39	0
Jenkins	15.2	4	29	3	....	46.2	10	160	5
Horton	12	4	26	3	....	41	6	129	3
Berry						18	7	26	0

Umpires: P. Corrall and A. J. B. Fowler.

At Leicester, August 27, 29, 30. WORCESTERSHIRE lost to LEICESTERSHIRE by five wickets.
At Bournemouth, August 31, September 1, 2. WORCESTERSHIRE lost to HAMPSHIRE by 79 runs.
Career of R. T. D. Perks, playing no longer for Worcestershire, see p. 611.

YORKSHIRE

President—T. L. TAYLOR

Secretary—J. H. NASH, Old Bank Chambers, Park Row, Leeds, 1

Captain in 1955—N. W. D. YARDLEY
Captain in 1956—W. H. H. SUTCLIFFE

| W. H. H. Sutcliffe | County Badge | J. H. Wardle |

Again Yorkshire provided the only real challenge to Surrey for the Championship, but for the second year running they had to be satisfied with the position of runners-up. The extent of Yorkshire's effort could be judged from the fact that their total points of 268 broke the record since the present scoring system came into force in 1938. Yorkshire, themselves, had previously obtained most points in a season, 260 in 1939, but even though getting eight more than last season they could do little more than give Surrey a mild fright.

Yorkshire and Surrey started the season neck-and-neck, but after six successive victories, Yorkshire fell back. Three defeats in a row at the hands of Sussex, Surrey and Hampshire early in June cost them their chance. Later, they gained revenge over Surrey and in July they momentarily went into first place with a lead of eight points, but Surrey then had two games in hand and were never really in danger of losing the title. In the end Yorkshire were 16 points behind, but the great fight between these two counties brought intense keenness to the county season.

Those who judge by the highest standards must have seen some weaknesses in all departments of the side, but even they will admit that only a little stiffening was needed to the batting, bowling and fielding for Yorkshire to become once more the power they were in the pre-war years.

To enjoy such a successful season lacking the full assistance of Hutton, their leading batsman, and Appleyard, one of, if not the best of their bowlers, reflected great credit on the side as a whole. Hutton's ill health proved a severe blow to England as well as to Yorkshire and he played in only ten county matches. Even then he was rarely able to find his true form. Appleyard began the season in great style, but because of shoulder trouble he could play in only three matches after June. Nevertheless he took 73 wickets and his low average of 11.54 gave him first place in the averages.

Wardle, making more use of the left-hander's off-break than previously, bowled extremely well, as did Trueman, whose deadly fast bowling often swung the course of a game. The consistent batting of the left-handers, Watson and Wilson, served Yorkshire well but perhaps more satisfaction as far as the future was concerned came from the form shown by Sutcliffe, Illingworth and Padgett, who all made considerable advancement. Sutcliffe's success was specially welcomed and he was appointed captain of the county on the retirement of Yardley because of business reasons.

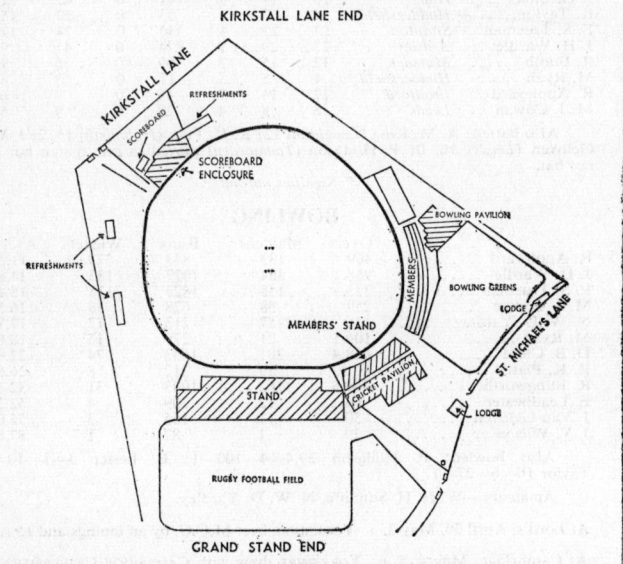

HEADINGLEY GROUND

KIRKSTALL LANE END

KIRKSTALL LANE

REFRESHMENTS

SCOREBOARD

SCOREBOARD ENCLOSURE

BOWLING PAVILION

REFRESHMENTS

BOWLING GREENS

LODGE

MEMBERS' STAND

MEMBERS

STAND

CRICKET PAVILION

ST. MICHAEL'S LANE

LODGE

RUGBY FOOTBALL FIELD

GRAND STAND END

YORKSHIRE RESULTS

All First-Class Matches—Played 33, Won 23, Lost 6, Drawn 4

County Championship Matches—Played 28, Won 21, Lost 5, Drawn 2

COUNTY CHAMPIONSHIP AVERAGES

BATTING

	Birthplace	Mtchs.	Inns.	Not Outs	Runs	100's	Highest Inns.	Aver.
W. Watson	Bolton-on-Dearne	22	38	13	1424	4	214*	56.96
W. H. H. Sutcliffe	Armley	21	35	3	1124	3	161*	35.12
R. Illingworth .	Pudsey	22	28	6	772	1	116	35.09
J. V. Wilson ...	Scampton	28	47	4	1480	3	132*	34.41
E. Leadbeater .	Huddersfield	3	4	3	30	0	17*	30.00
L. Hutton	Pudsey	10	18	0	535	1	194	29.72
D. E. V. Padgett	Bradford	13	21	1	560	1	115	28.00
D. B. Close ..	Rawdon	23	39	5	941	0	143	27.67
F, Lowson	Bradford	20	36	2	835	1	116	24.55
N. W. D. Yardley	Barnsley	26	36	5	722	1	100*	23.29
E. Lester	Scarborough	11	16	0	323	0	54	20.18
J. G. Binks	Hull	16	17	9	141	0	42*	17.62
K. Taylor	Huddersfield	4	7	1	93	0	27	15.50
F. S. Trueman .	Stainton	23	27	4	330	0	74	14.34
J. H. Wardle ..	Ardsley	23	29	1	274	0	41	9.78
R. Booth	Marsden	12	15	3	109	0	36	9.08
M. Ryan	Huddersfield	4	5	3	17	0	10	8.50
R. Appleyard ..	Bradford	12	14	7	46	0	9	6.57
M. J. Cowan ..	Leeds	8	8	4	20	0	9	5.00

Also batted: A. M. King (*Laughton*) 12; R. K. Platt (*Holmfirth*) 1*, 2; J. Van Geloven (*Leeds*) 16, 0; P. Hodgson (*Todmorden*) played in one match but did not bat.

* *Signifies not out.*

BOWLING

	Overs	Maidens	Runs	Wickets	Average
R. Appleyard	409	133	843	73	11.54
J. H. Wardle	988.1	384	1977	133	14.86
F. S. Trueman	753.3	158	1823	118	15.44
M. J. Cowan	259	58	628	38	16.52
N. W. D. Yardley	136	57	213	12	17.75
M. Ryan	106.5	21	279	15	18.60
D. B. Close	668.4	201	1692	74	22.86
R. K. Platt	101.3	29	212	8	26.50
R. Illingworth	465.5	162	1003	31	32.35
E. Leadbeater	64	12	209	4	52.25
J. Van Geloven.........	50	11	165	3	55.00
J. V. Wilson	20	1	87	1	87.00

Also bowled: P. Hodgson 29.4—4—100—1; E. Lester 3—1—10—1; Taylor 16—6—27—1.

Amateurs.—W. H. H. Sutcliffe, N. W. D. Yardley.

At Lord's, April 30, May 2, 3. YORKSHIRE beat M.C.C. by an innings and 15 runs.

At Cambridge, May 4, 5, 6. YORKSHIRE drew with CAMBRIDGE UNIVERSITY.

YORKSHIRE v. NORTHAMPTONSHIRE

At Bradford, May 7, 9. Yorkshire won by 78 runs. A rain-damaged pitch, ideally suited to spin bowlers, produced astonishing cricket, the game being over in seven and a half hours of actual playing time. Tribe, the Northamptonshire slow left-arm bowler, had the mixed experience of accomplishing the best match performance of his career, but being on the losing side. His full figures were 15 wickets for 75 runs, including nine for 45 in the second innings. After leading by 33, Yorkshire lost eight batsmen in their second innings for 60 before play ended on Saturday. Much depended on the conditions on Monday. Fortunately for Yorkshire the pitch remained almost unplayable and Northamptonshire never looked like scoring the 138 they needed to win.

Yorkshire

F. A. Lowson st Andrew b Broderick ...	22 — c Brookes b Tribe	7
W. H. H. Sutcliffe b Tribe	13 — c Barrick b Tribe	8
J. V. Wilson c Subba Row b Tribe	20 — b Tribe	0
D. B. Close b Tribe	15 — lbw b Tribe	0
W. Watson c Andrew b Broderick	2 — c and b Tribe	32
E. Lester st Andrew b Broderick........	3 — c Clarke b Broderick	11
N. W. D. Yardley lbw b Broderick	5 — c Clarke b Tribe	10
J. H. Wardle lbw b Tribe	8 — c Clarke b Tribe	7
R. Booth c Tyson b Tribe	3 — lbw b Tribe	0
F. S. Trueman c Tyson b Tribe	0 — c Tyson b Tribe	21
R. Appleyard not out	0 — not out	2
B 3	3 L-b 6	6

1/27 2/57 3/73 4/73 5/76 6/82   94   1/8 2/8 3/8 4/17 5/36   104
7/91 8/91 9/94   6/47 7/55 8/59 9/85

Northamptonshire

D. Brookes b Appleyard...............	8 — b Wardle	7
P. Arnold c Close b Trueman	0 — lbw b Appleyard	5
L. Livingston c Lester b Appleyard	19 — b Appleyard	1
D. Barrick b Wardle	7 — c Watson b Wardle.......	4
R. Subba Row c Lowson b Appleyard ..	0 — c Booth b Wardle	15
G. E. Tribe lbw b Appleyard	12 — c Appleyard b Wardle	6
V. Broderick c Lowson b Wardle	0 — run out	3
F. H. Tyson not out	8 — c Lowson b Appleyard.....	1
S. Starkie c Wilson b Wardle...........	1 — b Appleyard	3
K. V. Andrew b Appleyard	0 — not out	2
R. W. Clarke c Lowson b Appleyard ...	0 — b Appleyard	2
L-b 6	6 B 2, l-b 6, n-b 2......	10

1/5 2/26 3/37 4/37 5/41 6/41   61   1/10 2/11 3/18 4/34   59
7/51 8/52 9/61   5/43 6/48 7/50 8/50 9/55

Northamptonshire Bowling

	O.	M.	R.	W.		O.	M.	R.	W.
Tyson	5	3	2	0	....	2	0	2	0
Clarke	3	0	13	0					
Broderick......	15	5	46	4	....	21	8	51	1
Tribe	13.1	0	30	6	....	19.2	5	45	9

Yorkshire Bowling

	O.	M.	R.	W.		O.	M.	R.	W.
Trueman	2	0	12	1	....	3	0	6	0
Appleyard	11.5	4	25	6	....	13.1	4	23	5
Wardle	11	6	18	3	....	12	2	20	4

Umpires: E. Cooke and Harry Elliott (Derbyshire).

At Oxford, May 11, 12. YORKSHIRE beat OXFORD UNIVERSITY by an innings and 23 runs.

At Bristol, May 14, 16. YORKSHIRE beat GLOUCESTERSHIRE by an innings and 54 runs.

YORKSHIRE v. SOMERSET

At Leeds, May 18, 19, 20. Yorkshire won by 163 runs. The Somerset batsmen never offered a serious challenge. Rain delayed the start and on a difficult pitch Yorkshire fought hard for runs. Hutton, playing his first game following his return from Australasia, stayed an hour for 11 and in the cold, miserable weather none of the batsmen was at his best. Somerset scored 31 for one before the close but next day they collapsed, the remaining nine wickets falling for 53. Yorkshire, 77 ahead, consolidated their position with an opening stand of 90 by Hutton and Lowson, and Wilson followed with a hard-hitting innings. After a declaration, Somerset needed 291 to win, but Tremlett and Stephenson, who added 54 for the seventh wicket, alone showed fight.

Yorkshire

L. Hutton c Lomax b Lobb	11	— c Smith b McMahon	66
F. A. Lowson c and b Lobb	11	— c Lomax b McMahon	60
J. V. Wilson c Stephenson b Lomax	14	— c Stephenson b Lobb	68
D. B. Close c Tremlett b Hilton	34	— c Tordoff b Hilton	1
W. Watson c Hilton b Lomax	10	— not out	14
W. H. H. Sutcliffe c Tremlett b McMahon	37	— not out	1
N. W. D. Yardley b Hilton	23		
J. H. Wardle b McMahon	5		
R. Booth not out	7		
F. S. Trueman c Tordoff b McMahon	0		
R. Appleyard b Hilton	8		
L-b 1	1	L-b 1, w 2	3

1/19 2/32 3/44 4/80 5/80 6/140   161   1/90 2/161   (4 wkts., dec.) 213
7/140 8/153 9/153   3/162 4/204

Somerset

G. G. Tordoff b Wardle	3	— b Trueman	7
J. G. Lomax st Booth b Wardle	33	— b Trueman	4
J. Lawrence b Appleyard	21	— b Appleyard	7
P. B. Wight c Wilson b Appleyard	0	— b Trueman	13
R. Smith c Wilson b Appleyard	19	— b Trueman	6
M. F. Tremlett b Wardle	3	— c Watson b Appleyard	53
L. Pickles lbw b Wardle	1	— lbw b Wardle	2
H. W. Stephenson b Appleyard	0	— c Lowson b Wardle	25
J. Hilton b Wardle	0	— b Appleyard	0
J. W. McMahon b Appleyard	0	— c Sutcliffe b Appleyard	1
B. Lobb not out	0	— not out	0
B 1, l-b 2, n-b 1	4	B 8, l-b 1	9

1/10 2/48 3/48 4/65 5/78 6/82   84   1/5 2/16 3/18 4/22   127
7/82 8/82 9/84   5/36 6/47 7/101 8/115 9/122

Somerset Bowling

	O.	M.	R.	W.		O.	M.	R.	W.
Lobb	16	5	29	2	....	13	1	55	1
Tremlett	7	1	13	0					
Lomax	16	5	32	2	....	13	2	35	0
Hilton	18	2	55	3	....	15	1	71	1
McMahon	8	1	25	3	....	24.2	4	47	2
Lawrence	1	0	6	0	....	1	0	2	0

Yorkshire Bowling

	O.	M.	R.	W.		O.	M.	R.	W.
Trueman	5	2	13	0	....	15	1	42	4
Appleyard	22.2	13	21	5	....	16.5	9	26	4
Wardle	21	9	42	5	....	13	6	18	2
Close	1	0	4	0	....	11	1	32	0

Umpires: E. A. Roberts and J. S. Buller.

At Chesterfield, May 21, 23, 24. YORKSHIRE beat DERBYSHIRE by 139 runs.

YORKSHIRE v. WARWICKSHIRE

At Sheffield, May 25, 26, 27. Yorkshire won by five wickets despite a remarkable bowling performance by Bannister for Warwickshire. After sharing a partnership of 60 with Townsend, Bannister caused a complete collapse. His nine wickets for 35 runs, the best achievement of his career, included the hat-trick when he dismissed Wilson, Yardley and Lester. Bannister's previous best, eight for 54, was also against Yorkshire in 1954. Leading by 75, Warwickshire again struggled, but they set Yorkshire to get 217 to win. A fine third wicket stand of 118 between Watson and Close decided the match. Close played many excellent forcing strokes and Watson's patience proved invaluable. He stayed five hours twenty minutes.

Warwickshire

R. T. Spooner lbw b Close	14	— c Lowson b Wardle	27
N. F. Horner b Trueman	4	— b Wardle	12
A. V. Wolton c Booth b Trueman	13	— b Trueman	12
T. W. Cartwright b Trueman	27	— b Trueman	4
H. E. Dollery b Close	5	— c Booth b Appleyard	32
A. Townsend lbw b Wardle	40	— b Appleyard	14
R. E. Hitchcock b Trueman	9	— lbw b Trueman	3
J. D. Bannister c Booth b Appleyard	23	— c Lowson b Appleyard	16
I. M. King c and b Wardle	1	— lbw b Wardle	3
R. G. Thompson b Trueman	7	— not out	3
W. E. Hollies not out	0	— b Wardle	0
L-b 1, w 2, n-b 2	5	B 4, l-b 8, n-b 3	15

1/4 2/23 3/44 4/64 5/66 6/80   **148**
7/140 8/140 9/142

1/18 2/46 3/68 4/99   **141**
5/110 6/111 7/126 8/130
9/134

Yorkshire

F. A. Lowson lbw b Bannister	8	— b Thompson	26
W. Watson b Bannister	24	— not out	64
J. V. Wilson b Bannister	17	— c Spooner b Bannister	3
D. B. Close lbw b Thompson	1	— b Hollies	85
E. Lester c and b Bannister	1	— c Cartwright b Hollies	12
N. W. D. Yardley c Townsend b Bannister	0	— lbw b Hollies	7
R. Illingworth b Bannister	7	— not out	15
J. H. Wardle b Bannister	1		
R. Booth c Cartwright b Bannister	8		
F. S. Trueman b Bannister	4		
R. Appleyard not out	0		
L-b 2	2	B 2, l-b 3, n-b 1	6

1/28 2/41 3/50 4/52 5/52 6/53   **73**
7/61 8/62 9/70

1/44 2/47 3/165   (5 wkts.) **218**
4/179 5/192

Yorkshire Bowling

	O.	M.	R.	W.		O.	M.	R.	W.
Trueman	18.4	4	35	5	....	20	6	57	3
Appleyard	17	6	35	1	....	23	7	38	3
Close	17	1	59	2	....	4	2	15	0
Wardle	8	4	14	2	....	7.5	3	16	4

Warwickshire Bowling

	O.	M.	R.	W.		O.	M.	R.	W.
Thompson	16	3	36	1	....	32	4	90	1
Bannister	15.2	5	35	9	....	31	5	58	1
Hollies						24	13	26	3
Townsend						3	0	15	0
King						8	1	23	0

Umpires: A. Skelding and H. Elliott (Lancashire).

At Manchester, May 28, 30, 31. YORKSHIRE beat LANCASHIRE by five wickets.

At Hove, June 1, 2, 3. YORKSHIRE lost to SUSSEX by 21 runs.

At The Oval, June 4, 6, 7. YORKSHIRE lost to SURREY by 41 runs.

YORKSHIRE v. HAMPSHIRE

At Bradford, June 11, 13. Hampshire won by an innings and 43 runs, their first victory in Yorkshire since 1932. Caught on drying turf on Monday, Yorkshire collapsed twice and suffered their third successive defeat. When Hampshire batted first the pitch was easy and Marshall scored freely for eighty minutes. Stands of 51 by Barnard and Harrison and 56 by Sainsbury and Cannings enabled Hampshire to recover when Yorkshire looked to be getting on top. Yorkshire lost two wickets for 23 before rain ended play eighty-five minutes early on Saturday. Following week-end downpours they were dismissed for 62 and followed on 162 behind. Sainsbury, the slow left-arm bowler, celebrated his 21st birthday by dismissing Hutton twice and clever bowling brought him nine wickets for 62 in the match. Marshall, with off-breaks, also took nine wickets cheaply.

Hampshire

J. R. Gray c Wilson b Trueman...	29
R. E. Marshall c Lowson b Illingworth	52
N. H. Rogers b Illingworth......	1
A. W. H. Rayment lbw b Illingworth	0
H. M. Barnard c Watson b Cowan	33
E. D. R. Eagar c Trueman b Illingworth	3
L. Harrison b Cowan	12
P. J. Sainsbury b Trueman	25
D. Shackleton c Watson b Trueman	14
V. H. D. Cannings not out	36
M. D. Burden b Cowan	0
B 8, l-b 9, n-b 2	19

1/85 2/86 3/86 4/86 5/93 6/144   224
7/145 8/167 9/223

Yorkshire

W. H. H. Sutcliffe lbw b Shackleton	4	— c Rayment b Marshall	37
F. A. Lowson b Cannings	4	— c Rogers b Sainsbury	5
J. V. Wilson c Rogers b Marshall	26	— lbw b Sainsbury	4
L. Hutton b Sainsbury	17	— lbw b Sainsbury	4
W. Watson b Sainsbury	0	— b Marshall	19
D. B. Close c Harrison b Marshall	3	— c Gray b Marshall	2
R. Illingworth c Harrison b Sainsbury..	0	— lbw b Marshall	13
R. Booth b Marshall	0	— b Marshall	5
F. S. Trueman c Cannings b Sainsbury ..	1	— b Marshall	9
E. Leadbeater b Shackleton b Sainsbury .	2	— not out	8
M. J. Cowan not out..................	0	— c Barnard b Sainsbury	5
B 4, l-b 1	5	B 4, l-b 4	8

1/7 2/9 3/45 4/45 5/54 6/55 7/59   62   1/15 2/23 3/43 4/68   119
8/60 9/60   5/70 6/75 7/81 8/100 9/110

Yorkshire Bowling

	O.	M.	R.	W.	O.	M.	R.	W.
Trueman	20	5	59	3				
Cowan	19.4	6	41	3				
Close	18	6	54	0				
Illingworth ...	19	7	34	4				
Leadbeater	3	0	17	0				

Hampshire Bowling

	O.	M.	R.	W.	O.	M.	R.	W.
Shackleton.....	12	5	14	1	4	3	1	0
Cannings	6	1	14	1	3	3	0	0
Burden	2	1	4	0	16	9	23	0
Sainsbury......	18.3	8	19	5	23.5	13	43	4
Marshall	11	8	6	3	21	8	44	6

Umpires: H. Elliott (Lancashire) and N. Oldfield.

YORKSHIRE v. KENT

At Hull, June 15, 16, 17. Yorkshire won by ten wickets, this victory coinciding with a return to form of Hutton. At first it looked as if they were to have another hard match, for on an easy pitch Fagg and Phebey opened for Kent with a stand of 126. Subsequently only Pettiford and Wilson, who added 69, did much. Hutton, going in first again after batting number four against Hampshire, helped Lowson in a partnership of 120 and he batted three hours twenty minutes. Wilson and Sutcliffe added 114 for the third wicket, Sutcliffe, who hit eighteen 4's, taking only two and a quarter hours over 107. Kent, 126 behind, collapsed before the spin of Close and Wardle.

Kent

A. E. Fagg c Close b Wardle	82	— b Close	15
A. H. Phebey run out	45	— lbw b Trueman	28
A. C. Shirreff b Illingworth	0	— c and b Close..............	5
P. Hearn st Booth b Wardle	2	— b Close	0
J. Pettiford lbw b Close	48	— c Trueman b Close	21
R. C. Wilson b Trueman	31	— b Close	9
B. E. Disbury c Booth b Close	13	— not out	25
D. G. Ufton c Wilson b Wardle	0	— b Wardle	15
D. V. P. Wright not out	6	— b Wardle	2
J. Spanswick c Sutcliffe b Close	4	— b Wardle	8
J. C. T. Page b Wardle	3	— run out	2
B 14, l-b 1	15	L-b 2	2

1/126 2/126 3/131 4/136 5/206   249   1/43 2/45 3/48 4/51   132
6/226 7/227 8/234 9/238   5/65 6/86 7/113 8/115
9/125

Yorkshire

L. Hutton c Ufton b Page	85		
F. A. Lowson b Spanswick	62		
J. V. Wilson c Hearn b Spanswick	77		
W. H. H. Sutcliffe b Page..............	107		
W. Watson not out	19		
D. B. Close b Ufton b Wright	1		
N. W. D. Yardley not out	5		
R. Booth (did not bat)		— not out	0
R. Illingworth (did not bat)		— not out	7
B 8, l-b 11	19		

1/120 2/190 3/304   (5 wkts., dec.) 375   (No wkt.) 7
4/360 5/361

J. H. Wardle and F. S. Trueman did not bat.

Yorkshire Bowling

	O.	M.	R.	W.	O.	M.	R.	W.
Trueman	28	5	65	1	 20	3	40	1
Close	10	2	38	3	.... 30.5	14	55	5
Wardle	42.5	20	75	4	 17	4	35	3
Illingworth	32	16	44	1				
Yardley	11	5	12	0				

Kent Bowling

	O.	M.	R.	W.				
Spanswick	25	3	87	2				
Shirreff	27	3	91	0				
Wright	18	2	55	1				
Page	23	4	79	2				
Pettiford	18	9	37	0				
Disbury	2	0	7	0				
Phebey					1	1	0	0
Wilson					0.5	0	7	0

Umpires: N. Oldfield and J. S. Buller.

YORKSHIRE v. SURREY

At Leeds, June 18, 20, 21. Yorkshire won by six wickets. This thrilling struggle between the two leading sides in the country drew over 60,000 people and the atmosphere resembled that of a Test Match. Surrey struggled hard to preserve their record, but were beaten for the first time in 16 consecutive games, their previous defeat being in July 1954. The gates were closed on Saturday when 35,000 saw Surrey fight back after losing their first eight wickets for 119. Lock and Loader, who added 96, each made his highest score. Loader and Bedser completed the recovery with a last wicket stand of 53. Yorkshire found runs hard to get against accurate bowling, but Wilson defended well for nearly three hours and helped to save the follow-on. Then Surrey, leading by 102, broke down completely in the last 100 minutes on Monday, losing seven men for 27 in poor light against the fast bowling of Trueman and Cowan. Next day the last three wickets added 48 and Yorkshire needed 178 to win in three hours ten minutes. Until the last half-hour they were behind the clock, but they obtained the runs with eleven minutes to spare. Wilson and Lowson put on 91 for the second wicket and Watson and Sutcliffe 71 for the fourth.

Surrey

T. H. Clark hit wkt b Trueman.........	12	— b Trueman	7
D. G. W. Fletcher c Hutton b Wardle ..	31	— c Lowson b Cowan........	0
P. B. H. May c Wilson b Wardle	15	— c Booth b Trueman	9
B. Constable lbw b Appleyard..........	24	— b Cowan	1
K. Barrington c Wilson b Appleyard	5	— b Trueman	0
A. J. McIntyre c Booth b Appleyard	4	— c Booth b Trueman	7
J. C. Laker b Wardle	10	— b Wardle	20
W. S. Surridge lbw b Trueman	7	— b Cowan	1
G. A. R. Lock c Cowan b Trueman.....	55	— not out	20
P. J. Loader c Booth b Wardle	81	— b Cowan	3
A. V. Bedser not out	14	— c Trueman b Cowan.......	0
L-b 7, n-b 3....................	10	L-b 5, n-b 2	7

1/24 2/53 3/76 4/87 5/93 6/96	268	1/7 2/17 3/20 4/21	75
7/108 8/119 9/215		5/21 6/26 7/27 8/35 9/64	

Yorkshire

L. Hutton lbw b Bedser	6	— b Bedser	1
F. A. Lowson c Fletcher b Bedser	27	— c McIntyre b Bedser	52
J. V. Wilson b Loader	48	— b Lock	43
W. H. H. Sutcliffe c McIntyre b Lock	1	— b Loader	21
W. Watson c Fletcher b Lock	0	— not out	51
N. W. D. Yardley c McIntyre b Laker	23	— not out	2
J. H. Wardle c May b Lock	20		
R. Booth c Clark b Lock	1		
F. S. Trueman not out	26		
R. Appleyard c Surridge b Loader	1		
M. J. Cowan b Loader	2		
B 9, l-b 2	11	L-b 7, w. 1	8

1/19 2/46 3/47 4/49 5/80 6/125   166   1/8 2/99 3/99   (4 wkts.) 178
7/126 8/146 9/150   4/170

Yorkshire Bowling

	O.	M.	R.	W.		O.	M.	R.	W.
Trueman	30	9	81	3	....	19	6	31	4
Cowan	18	1	62	0	....	15	7	15	5
Appleyard	19	7	36	3					
Wardle	31.3	9	79	4	....	9	4	22	1

Surrey Bowling

	O.	M.	R.	W.		O.	M.	R.	W.
Loader	17.3	3	29	3	....	14.4	2	43	1
Bedser	27	13	37	2	....	20	4	57	2
Surridge	1	0	1	0					
Laker	5	2	17	1					
Lock	27	8	71	4	....	21	4	70	1

Umpires: J. S. Buller and W. T. Jones.

At Northampton, June 22, 23, 24. YORKSHIRE beat NORTHAMPTONSHIRE by six wickets.

At Nottingham, June 25, 27, 28. YORKSHIRE drew with NOTTINGHAMSHIRE.

At Bournemouth, June 29, 30. YORKSHIRE beat HAMPSHIRE by 96 runs.

At Sheffield, July 2, 4, 5. YORKSHIRE lost to SOUTH AFRICANS by 193 runs. (See SOUTH AFRICAN section.)

YORKSHIRE v. GLAMORGAN

At Harrogate, July 6, 7, 8. Glamorgan won by four wickets, a remarkable triumph after narrowly saving the follow-on. Several splendid individual feats were accomplished, with that of Pleass on the last day the best. Padgett batted splendidly on his first appearance of the season for Yorkshire. Sutcliffe, who hit three 6's and twenty-two 4's in 161 not out, helped Padgett add 138 and with Illingworth put on 84 in thirty-five minutes. Vigorous hitting by Shepherd in a last wicket stand of 56 enabled Glamorgan to save the follow-on. Padgett again showed good form when Yorkshire went in again 136 ahead. Glamorgan, needing 334 to win, lost five wickets for 166 but Pleass, missed before scoring, made his first century after nine years in first-class cricket. Glamorgan won with twenty minutes to spare and so gained the second victory in their history over Yorkshire.

Yorkshire

F. A. Lowson st H. G. Davies b McConnon	15	— b H. D. Davies	23
D. E. V. Padgett c and b Pressdee	96	— c Shepherd b Jones	64
J. V. Wilson b Watkins	4	— b Watkins	81
W. H. H. Sutcliffe not out	161	— b McConnon	7
W. Watson b Pressdee	0	— not out	15
D. B. Close b Shepherd	31		
N. W. D. Yardley c H. D. Davies b Watkins	25		
R. Illingworth not out	33		
B 2, l-b 11, n-b 3	16	B 1, l-b 4, n-b 2	7

1/37 2/48 3/186 4/188   (6 wkts., dec.) 381
5/257 6/297

1/73 2/117   (4 wkts., dec.) 197
3/128 4/197

J. H. Wardle, J. G. Binks and P. Hodgson did not bat.

Glamorgan

W. G. A. Parkhouse c Watson b Wardle	20	— c Wilson b Wardle	80
B. R. Edrich c Wilson b Close	5	— c Close b Wardle	21
B. Hedges c Padgett b Yardley	3	— c Watson b Wardle	7
W. E. Jones c Illingworth b Close	79	— c Binks b Wardle	37
J. Pleass c Watson b Wardle	4	— not out	102
A. J. Watkins c Yardley b Illingworth	18	— lbw b Close	4
J. Pressdee c Watson b Illingworth	20	— not out	33
J. E. McConnon c Sutcliffe b Wardle	37	— lbw b Illingworth	28
H. G. Davies c Binks b Wardle	0		
H. D. Davies not out	6		
D. J. Shepherd c Binks b Hodgson	48		
B 1, l-b 4	5	B 10, l-b 12	22

1/10 2/24 3/28 4/40 5/144 6/176   245
7/189 8/189 9/189

1/53 2/75 3/145   (6 wkts.) 334
4/154 5/166 6/263

Glamorgan Bowling

	O.	M.	R.	W.		O.	M.	R.	W.
Shepherd	29	6	77	1	....	10	1	42	0
H. D. Davies	23	1	82	0	....	10	0	78	1
McConnon	20	4	43	1	....	6	0	37	1
Watkins	24	3	108	2	....	0.4	0	3	1
Pressdee	13	2	55	2					
Jones						7	0	30	1

Yorkshire Bowling

	O.	M.	R.	W.		O.	M.	R.	W.
Hodgson	17.4	4	49	1	....	12	0	51	0
Close	23	6	66	2	....	30	13	75	1
Wardle	35	12	102	4	....	38	9	110	4
Yardley	6	4	7	1	....	2	0	10	0
Illingworth	19	11	16	2	....	25.3	6	66	1

Umpires: T. Spencer and A. Skelding.

YORKSHIRE v. SUSSEX

At Sheffield, July 9, 11, 12. Yorkshire won by eight wickets and celebrated the centenary match at Bramall Lane in splendid style.   Sussex, on an easy pitch, started well, but a good spell with the new ball by Platt, a 22-year-old medium paced bowler making his debut, caused a collapse. Sussex lost their last six wickets for 36. Yorkshire began badly, but Watson hit his first century of the

season and batted five and three-quarter hours for 163 which included two 6's
and fifteen 4's. Sutcliffe retired during his innings with a pulled leg muscle, but in
his two spells with Watson 145 were added. Sussex lost six wickets before clearing
their arrears of 90 and only Parks resisted the attack. Yorkshire needed 69 to win.

Sussex

J. Langridge b Illingworth	38	— c Close b Yardley	4
D. V. Smith c Wilson b Wardle	54	— lbw b Yardley	26
A. S. M. Oakman c Wardle b Close	32	— b Yardley	3
J. M. Parks run out	69	— not out	86
K. G. Suttle c Close b Platt	18	— lbw b Platt	2
G. Cox lbw b Platt	0	— c Close b Wardle	2
A. A. K. Lawrence lbw b Platt	0	— c Wilson b Wardle	10
R. T. Webb not out	8	— c Lowson b Wardle	6
N. I. Thomson b Yardley	0	— c Wilson b Wardle	5
A. E. James b Yardley	8	— c Wilson b Wardle	2
R. G. Marlar b Platt	10	— c and b Close	4
B 10, l-b 2, n-b 1	13	B 6, l-b 2	8

1/84 2/100 3/164 4/214 5/214 6/222   250   1/9 2/33 3/42 4/47 5/75   158
7/225 8/225 9/235   6/81 7/127 8/137 9/153

Yorkshire

F. A. Lowson run out	1	— not out	32
D. E. V. Padgett lbw b Thomson	0	— b Oakman	14
W. H. H. Sutcliffe c Cox b James	89		
W. Watson c Marlar b Thomson	163	— not out	1
J. V. Wilson c Langridge b Marlar	16	— c Webb b Oakman	22
D. B. Close b Oakman	14		
N. W. D. Yardley c Lawrence b James	5		
R. Illingworth run out	23		
J. H. Wardle c Oakman b Marlar	4		
J. G. Binks b James	18		
R. K. Platt not out	1		
L-b 6	6		

1/1 2/1 3/155 4/192 5/209 6/258   340   1/29 2/61   (2 wkts.) 69
7/270 8/286 9/332

Yorkshire Bowling

	O.	M.	R.	W.		O.	M.	R.	W.
Platt	28.3	7	70	4	....	27	7	43	1
Close	17	4	54	1	....	11	4	18	1
Yardley	17	6	28	2	....	18	9	34	3
Illingworth	25	10	43	1	....	9	2	24	0
Wardle	29	17	42	1	....	21	10	31	5

Sussex Bowling

	O.	M.	R.	W.		O.	M.	R.	W.
Thomson	41	9	111	2	....	2	1	5	0
James	36.3	16	52	3	....	3	0	16	0
Smith	10	4	32	0	....				
Marlar	30	7	92	2	....	9	2	24	0
Oakman	16	3	47	1	....	10	3	24	2

Umpires: T. J. Bartley and L. H. Gray.

At Lord's, July 16, 18, 19. YORKSHIRE beat MIDDLESEX by eight wickets.

At Taunton, July 20, 21, 22. YORKSHIRE beat SOMERSET by eight wickets.

At Leeds, July 21, 22, 23, 25, 26. SOUTH AFRICA beat ENGLAND in the fourth Test by 224 runs. (See SOUTH AFRICAN section.)

At Birmingham, July 23, 25, 26. YORKSHIRE beat WARWICKSHIRE by ten wickets.

YORKSHIRE v. ESSEX

At Bradford, July 27, 28, 29. Yorkshire won by ten wickets. Things did not go well for them on the first day when Essex, after losing their first three wickets for 56, reached 286 for five. They owed everything to Insole and Trevor Bailey who, staying together three and a quarter hours, never made a poor stroke in a stand of 163. Insole hit eighteen 4's in his splendid 142 which occupied four and a half hours before Wardle turned the scales. In the course of his last 27 deliveries Wardle took five of the last six wickets for four runs. The three left-handers, Close, Wilson and Watson led Yorkshire in a revel of run-making. In two and three-quarter hours Wilson (one 6 and twenty 4's) and Watson (fourteen 4's) put on 192, neither offering a real chance. Essex were handicapped through Trevor Bailey being unable to bowl and when they faced a deficit of 144 they broke down against some steady off-spin bowling by Close who was admirably supported at the other end by Wardle. Only an enterprising eighth wicket stand of 52 by Trevor Bailey and Ralph saved Essex from an innings defeat.

Essex

T. C. Dodds lbw b Platt	21	—	c Trueman b Close	23
G. Barker lbw b Yardley	10	—	c Binks b Close	12
P. A. Gibb c Wardle b Trueman	19	—	c sub b Close	20
D. J. Insole c Watson b Wardle	142	—	st Binks b Wardle	5
T. E. Bailey b Trueman	65	—	not out	38
W. T. Greensmith c Close b Wardle	28	—	b Close	0
B. Taylor st Binks b Wardle	0	—	c Yardley b Close	8
R. Smith c Binks b Wardle	1	—	c Lester b Wardle	14
R. Ralph c Illingworth b Close	0	—	run out	37
K. C. Preston c Close b Wardle	5	—	b Close	4
J. A. Bailey not out	0	—	b Close	0
B 4, l-b 6, n-b 1	11		B 4, l-b 9	13

1/29 2/33 3/56 4/219 5/286 6/286   302   1/43 2/44 3/53 4/89 5/90   174
7/297 8/297 9/297   6/98 7/117 8/169 9/174

Yorkshire

F. A. Lowson c J. Bailey b Greensmith	25			
D. B. Close c Dodds b Ralph	60	—	not out	25
J. V. Wilson b Insole	132			
E. Lester c Barker b Greensmith	29			
W. Watson st Taylor b Greensmith	105	—	not out	9
N. W. D. Yardley c Taylor b J. Bailey	17			
R. Illingworth not out	16			
J. H. Wardle b Insole	17			
F. S. Trueman not out	20			
B 11, l-b 8, n-b 6	25			

1/87 2/95 3/138 4/330   (7 wkts., dec.) 446   (No wkt.) 34
5/393 6/393 7/413

J. G. Binks and R. K. Platt did not bat.

Yorkshire Bowling

	O.	M.	R.	W.		O.	M.	R.	W.
Trueman	18	2	59	2	....	8	2	19	0
Platt	20	4	64	1	....	3	1	6	0
Yardley	6	2	12	1					
Wardle	34.3	12	74	5	....	31	15	59	2
Illingworth	12	5	25	0	....	3	0	15	0
Close	24	8	57	1	....	24.4	9	62	7

Essex Bowling

	O.	M.	R.	W.		O.	M.	R.	W.
Preston	19	4	73	0	....	3	2	16	0
Smith	9	3	37	0					
J. Bailey	23	3	80	1					
Ralph	13	2	39	1	....	2	0	5	0
Greensmith	29	7	118	3					
Insole	10	0	48	2					
Dodds	7	1	26	0	....	5	0	13	0

Umpires: F. Chester and F. S. Lee.

YORKSHIRE v. LANCASHIRE

At Sheffield, July 30, August 1, 2. Drawn. Rain, which held up cricket following lunch on the last day till after half-past four, robbed Yorkshire of deserved victory. They began so badly against the fast bowling of Statham, who took three of the first four wickets for 20 runs, that five men were out for 60, but a masterly innings by the left-hander, Watson, restored the balance. Great help came from Illingworth, who batted stubbornly for three and a half hours while 188 were added. Watson, driving spendidly, made 174, including two 6's and twenty 4's, in four and three-quarter hours without a chance. Lancashire, despite a stand of 51 for the eighth wicket between Grieves and Hilton, broke down against the left-arm bowling of Cowan, fast-medium, and Wardle, slow, and followed on 173 behind. Thanks chiefly to Washbrook, they cleared the arrears for the loss of five wickets, and stern defence by Edrich latterly enabled Lancashire to save the game.

Yorkshire

D. B. Close b Statham	20
K. Taylor run out	0
J. V. Wilson b Statham	16
D. E. V. Padgett c Wharton b Statham	2
W. Watson run out	174
N. W. D. Yardley c Jordan b Wharton	6
R. Illingworth c Edrich b Statham	53
J. H. Wardle b Hilton	10
F. S. Trueman b Tattersall	0
J. G. Binks not out	8
M. J. Cowan c Statham b Tattersall	9
B 7, l-b 5, n-b 2	14

1/8 2/24 3/37 4/40 5/60 6/248 312
7/294 8/295 9/295

Lancashire

J. T. Ikin b Yardley	8	— c Trueman b Cowan 37
J. Dyson c Wilson b Cowan	1	— c Close b Cowan 17
J. Jordan c Wilson b Cowan	17	— not out 4
G. A. Edrich c Illingworth b Wardle	6	— not out 37
C. Washbrook c Wardle b Cowan	20	— c and b Close 66
A. Wharton c Binks b Wardle	5	— b Wardle 9
K. Grieves not out	49	— b Wardle 12
P. Marner st Binks b Wardle	0	— c and b Close 8
M. J. Hilton b Cowan	23	— c Wilson b Wardle 1
J. B. Statham c Cowan b Close	7	
R. Tattersall run out	0	
N-b 3	3	B 2, l-b 10 12

1/3 2/19 3/27 4/54 5/60 6/60 7/60 139
8/111 9/135

1/29 2/50 3/116 (7 wkts.) 203
4/119 5/149 6/176 7/185

Lancashire Bowling

	O.	M.	R.	W.	O.	M.	R.	W.
Statham	26	6	72	4				
Wharton	11	2	29	1				
Marner........	15	2	50	0				
Tattersall	26.5	8	78	2				
Hilton	20	5	53	1				
Ikin..........	8	3	16	0				

Yorkshire Bowling

	O.	M.	R.	W.		O.	M.	R.	W.
Trueman	16	4	32	0	....	16	3	24	0
Cowan	21	8	44	4	....	20	4	39	2
Yardley	11	5	10	1	....	2	2	0	0
Wardle	21	6	47	3	....	49	21	67	3
Taylor	1	1	0	0					
Close	2.4	0	3	1	....	36	17	49	2
					Illingworth ...	7	2	12	0

Umpires: F. S. Lee and T. J. Bartley.

At Leicester, August 3, 4, 5. YORKSHIRE beat LEICESTERSHIRE by two wickets.

YORKSHIRE v. DERBYSHIRE

At Bradford, August 6, 8. Yorkshire won by an innings and 94 runs. They thoroughly overplayed Derbyshire, who never looked like making a fight on a pitch favouring run-getting. In the first Derbyshire innings only Revill, who played doggedly for two and a quarter hours, offered much resistance to the fast-medium bowling of Trueman and Melville Ryan, a twenty-two-year-old colt playing in his first Championship match. When facing arrears of 266 they broke down against the spin of Close, following an opening partnership of 56 between Hamer and Carr. The Yorkshire batting provided a strong contrast. Sutcliffe took chief honours, reaching by sound methods his third century of the season. Padgett played attractively, as did Illingworth who hit eleven 4's in a stay of an hour and three-quarters. He was awarded his county cap.

Derbyshire

A. Hamer b Trueman	21	— c Padgett b Close	21
J. Kelly retired hurt	4	— c Ryan b Close	24
G. L. Willatt c Close b Ryan.........	0	— c Trueman b Close	1
A. C. Revill not out	35	— c Trueman b Close	24
D. B. Carr c Wilson b Trueman	1	— c Illingworth b Close	42
H. L. Johnson c and b Ryan	1	— c Trueman b Wardle	0
D. C. Morgan b Ryan	2	— lbw b Wardle	0
G. O. Dawkes c Close b Trueman	3	— c Ryan b Illingworth	38
R. Carter b Trueman	0	— b Wardle	10
E. Smith c Binks b Ryan	9	— not out	4
D. Hall b Wardle	6	— b Close	1
B 1, l-b 6	7	L-b 7	7
	94		**172**

1/29 2/35 3/39 4/44 5/58 6/61 7/61 8/76

1/56 2/64 3/66 4/68 5/73 6/92 7/140 8/162 9/167

Yorkshire

W. H. H. Sutcliffe st Dawkes b Carr 133		J. H. Wardle c sub b Hall	14
D. B. Close c Johnson b Morgan .	16	F. S. Trueman b Hall...........	24
J. V. Wilson c sub b Morgan	21	J. G. Binks b Morgan	0
D. E. V. Padgett c Dawkes b Carter	41	M. Ryan not out..............	4
R. Illingworth c Dawkes b Hall....	63		
A. M. King c Morgan b Hall	12	1/24 2/49 3/144 4/248 5/280	**360**
N. W. D. Yardley c and b Morgan	32	6/293 7/323 8/332 9/350	

Yorkshire Bowling

	O.	M.	R.	W.		O.	M.	R.	W.
Trueman	17	3	31	4	....	6	3	12	0
Ryan	20	5	44	4	....	4	0	16	0
Yardley	1	0	1	0					
Illingworth	2	0	2	0	....	4	0	23	1
Wardle	5.2	4	4	1	....	23	9	51	3
Close	1	0	5	0	....	17.1	3	63	6

Derbyshire Bowling

	O.	M.	R.	W.
Hall	26.3	7	83	4
Morgan	34	11	110	4
Smith	16	5	70	0
Revill	11	2	36	0
Carter	8	3	30	1
Carr	7	1	31	1

Umpires: P. Corrall and K. McCanlis.

YORKSHIRE v. NOTTINGHAMSHIRE

At Scarborough, August 10, 11, 12. Yorkshire won by nine wickets. The fast bowling of Trueman played a leading part in the success. In the first innings he did the hat-trick for the second time against Nottinghamshire, sending back Giles, Stocks and C. Poole. His other hat-trick was at Trent Bridge in 1951. A useful innings by K. Poole and hard hitting by Jepson enabled Nottinghamshire to recover slightly. Yorkshire also found run-getting difficult, but Illingworth batted three and a quarter hours in fine style and Binks helped him add 92 for the ninth wicket stand, which put Yorkshire ahead. At the close of the second day Nottinghamshire led by one run with eight wickets left, but they were out in another forty-five minutes. Trueman accomplished his best performance of the season in taking seven for 23. Yorkshire needed only 18 to win.

Nottinghamshire

R. T. Simpson c Illingworth b Wardle ..	28	— c Wardle b Trueman	44
J. D. Clay c Sutcliffe b Ryan	1	— c Wilson b Ryan	11
R. J. Giles c Binks b Trueman	17	— b Trueman	30
F. W. Stocks c Wilson b Trueman	0	— c Illingworth b Trueman ...	0
C. J. Poole c Lowson b Trueman	0	— b Wardle	2
K. J. Poole c Wardle b Close..........	43	— c Wardle b Trueman	2
G. Goonesena b Wardle	23	— b Wardle	3
B. Dooland c Yardley b Wardle	0	— not out	1
K. Smales c Binks b Ryan	23	— c Binks b Trueman	1
A. Jepson not out	52	— b Trueman	6
E. J. Rowe b Ryan	2	— b Trueman	0
B 1, l-b 11, w 1, n-b 1	14	L-b 1, n-b 4	5

1/7 2/34 3/34 4/34 5/61 6/117		203	1/34 2/89 3/89 4/92
7/119 8/135 9/201			5/92 6/97 7/97 8/99 9/105

105

Yorkshire

W. H. H. Sutcliffe b K. Poole	30	— b Smales	3
D. B. Close c Clay b Smales	36	— not out	7
J. V. Wilson c K. Poole b Goonesena	13		
D. E. V. Padgett b Jepson	16		
F. A. Lowson c Dooland b Jepson	11		
R. Illingworth c K. Poole b Smales	94		
N. W. D. Yardley b K. Poole	19		
J. H. Wardle c C. Poole b Smales	5		
F. S. Trueman c Clay b Goonesena	11		
J. G. Binks not out	42	— not out	8
M. Ryan b Goonesena	0		
L-b 13, n-b 1	14		

1/54 2/74 3/92 4/102 5/111 6/156　　291　　1/5　　　(1 wkt.)　18
7/163 8/198 9/290

Yorkshire Bowling

	O.	M.	R.	W.		O.	M.	R.	W.
Trueman	27	7	71	3	....	18.2	7	23	7
Ryan	9.3	0	22	3	....	10	2	15	1
Yardley	8	1	16	0					
Wardle	21	7	55	3	....	13	3	37	2
Close	4	0	25	1	....	4	1	13	0
Illingworth						9	6	12	0

Nottinghamshire Bowling

	O.	M.	R.	W.		O.	M.	R.	W.
Jepson	29	15	47	2					
K. Poole	21	4	59	2	....	3.4	0	14	0
Dooland	33	7	86	0					
Smales	18	10	33	3	....	3	1	4	1
Goonesena	17.2	5	52	3					

Umpires: P. Corrall and T. Spencer.

YORKSHIRE v. MIDDLESEX

At Leeds, August 13, 15, 16. Middlesex won by five wickets, and in repeating their victory of last season on the same ground they again ruined Yorkshire's chances of winning the Championship. Put in to bat on a lively rain-damaged pitch, Yorkshire were always struggling, but they fought back when Middlesex batted. Trueman caused the early collapse, and Cowan upset the later batsmen, but Middlesex led by eight. Sutcliffe showed good form in Yorkshire's second innings and when the third wicket fell they led by 101, but the last seven went to 66. Middlesex needed 168 to win and Robertson and Brown played a big part towards the success by adding 67. Robertson batted faultlessly for nearly three hours.

Yorkshire

W. H. H. Sutcliffe b Moss	0	— b Titmus	59
F. A. Lowson c Compton b Bennett	24	— lbw b Warr	4
J. V. Wilson c Compton b Moss	14	— b Moss	32
D. E. V. Padgett c Young b Bennett	8	— c Compton b Young	29
R. Illingworth c Bennett b Titmus	11	— lbw b Young	6
N. W. D. Yardley b Titmus	21	— c and b Titmus	21
K. Taylor lbw b Moss	16	— lbw b Titmus	0
J. H. Wardle c Bennett b Warr	9	— c Warr b Young	0
F. S. Trueman b Warr	23	— c Dewes b Titmus	9
J. G. Binks b Titmus	9	— c and b Titmus	4
M. J. Cowan not out	0	— not out	3
B 8, l-b 6, n-b 2	16	B 5, l-b 2, n-b 1	8

1/0 2/22 3/41 4/62 5/64 6/97 7/115   151
8/115 9/149

1/11 2/77 3/109 4/126   175
5/143 6/144 7/147 8/156
9/168

Middlesex

J. G. Dewes c Wardle b Trueman	29	c Binks b Trueman	2
J. D. Robertson c Illingworth b Trueman	8	b Trueman	82
S. M. Brown c Binks b Trueman	2	b Wardle	28
W. J. Edrich c Wilson b Cowan	38	lbw b Wardle	7
G. P. S. Delisle c Illingworth b Cowan	26	c Yardley b Trueman	4
D. Bennett c Binks b Cowan	4	not out	24
F. J. Titmus not out	14	not out	11
L. H. Compton c Yardley b Trueman	9		
J. J. Warr b Cowan	4		
J. A. Young b Cowan	8		
A. E. Moss b Cowan	0		
B 4, l-b 8, n-b 5	17	L-b 7, w 1, n-b 4	12

1/8 2/22 3/55 4/111 5/123 6/124   159
7/137 8/149 9/159

1/9 2/76 3/86   (5 wkts.) 170
4/99 5/142

Middlesex Bowling

	O.	M.	R.	W.		O.	M.	R.	W.
Moss	17	6	40	3	....	13	1	56	1
Warr	12.2	3	39	2	....	8	2	11	1
Bennett	9	3	12	2	....	7	2	9	0
Titmus	22	5	44	3	....	33.3	16	58	5
Young	2	2	0	0	....	22	10	33	3

Yorkshire Bowling

	O.	M.	R.	W.		O.	M.	R.	W.
Trueman	22	4	52	4	....	18	7	48	3
Cowan	20.5	4	52	6	....	10	1	32	0
Wardle	11	3	30	0	....	25	14	41	2
Illingworth	2	0	8	0	....	10.1	3	37	0
					Taylor	1	1	0	0

Umpires: H. Elliott (Lancashire) and E. Cooke.

YORKSHIRE v. GLOUCESTERSHIRE

At Huddersfield, August 17, 18, 19. Yorkshire won by 67 runs after being in serious trouble. They broke down completely before the fast bowling of their former player, McHugh, who accomplished the best performance of his career, and were dismissed in a little over two hours. Gloucestershire went ahead for the loss of only three wickets, but failed to press home their advantage. They led on first innings by 68 and sent back the opening pair, Sutcliffe and Lowson, for seven.

Then the Yorkshire recovery started with Wilson and Padgett adding 116. Gloucestershire, needing 152, were helpless against the pace of Trueman, only three players reaching double figures. The pitch could not be blamed, the batsmen being beaten by speed.

Yorkshire

W. H. H. Sutcliffe b Lambert	1	— c Lambert b McHugh 0
F. A. Lowson c Rochford b McHugh ...	5	— c Young b Lambert 2
J. V. Wilson c Rochford b McHugh ...	1	— c Rochford b Wells 79
D. E. V. Padgett c Young b McHugh ...	36	— c Rochford b Wells 44
R. Illingworth c Rochford b McHugh	13	— st Rochford b Wells 23
N. W. D. Yardley c Rochford b McHugh	2	— lbw b Wells 0
K. Taylor lbw b Wells	27	— c Rochford b Mortimore ... 21
J. H. Wardle b Wells............	4	— c Wells b Mortimore 9
F. S. Trueman c and b McHugh	1	— b Wells 12
J. G. Binks c Crapp b McHugh	0	— not out 2
M. Ryan not out	0	— c Mortimore b Wells 10
B 9, l-b 1	10	B 8, l-b 6, n-b 3 17

1/11 2/12 3/19 4/55 5/57 6/95 7/99   100   1/2 2/7 3/123 4/142   219
8/100 9/100   5/142 6/177 7/190 8/205
                          9/205

Gloucestershire

D. M. Young c Sutcliffe b Trueman.....	12	— c Lowson b Trueman 4
C. A. Milton c Trueman b Wardle ...	21	— c and b Trueman 7
J. F. Crapp c Wilson b Ryan..........	28	— c and b Ryan 10
G. M. Emmett c Ryan b Wardle	42	— c Binks b Trueman 30
J. V. C. Griffths lbw b Wardle	6	— c Wilson b Ryan........ 19
G. E. Lambert c Wilson b Trueman.....	16	— lbw b Trueman 1
J. Mortimore c Binks b Trueman	12	— not out 5
G. G. M. Wiltshire c Binks b Wardle ...	13	— c Yardley b Trueman 0
P. Rochford b Wardle................	10	— b Wardle 5
B. D. Wells b Trueman................	1	— b Trueman 0
F. P. McHugh not out	0	— b Trueman 0
B 5, l-b 2	7	B 1, l-b 2 3

1/31 2/41 3/95 4/105 5/120 6/135   168   1/10 2/19 3/50 4/66 5/67   84
7/156 8/167 9/168   6/74 7/78 8/83 9/84

Gloucestershire Bowling

	O.	M.	R.	W.		O.	M.	R.	W.
Lambert	13	3	53	1	....	23	5	56	1
McHugh	16	6	32	7	....	22	4	52	1
Wells	4.1	1	5	2	....	32.4	9	69	6
Mortimore						17	9	25	2

Yorkshire Bowling

	O.	M.	R.	W.		O.	M.	R.	W.
Trueman	28.1	6	71	4	....	12	5	30	7
Ryan	24	7	49	1	....	9	2	32	2
Wardle	10	2	41	5	....	10	3	19	1

Umpires: H. Elliott (Lancashire) and E. Cooke.

At Worcester, August 20, 22, 23. Yorkshire beat Worcestershire by nine wickets.

At Southend, August 24, 25, 26. Yorkshire beat Essex by nine wickets.

At Jesmond, August 29, 30. Yorkshire beat Northumberland by 83 runs. Two-day match.)

YORKSHIRE v. M.C.C.

At Scarborough, August 31, September 1, 2. Drawn. Yorkshire were the superior all-round side, but they could not force victory. They began by losing four wickets cheaply to Hall, the Somerset fast-medium bowler, but once the pitch eased their batsmen gained control. Illingworth scored his second century in successive innings and also the 1000th recorded in all Yorkshire matches. He once more showed his value in a crisis, batting four and a quarter hours and hitting seventeen 4's. Wilson helped him add 128. Rain caused long delays on the second day when M.C.C. struggled for runs, particularly against Trueman. Following on 152 behind, M.C.C. were indebted to Graveney, also their most successful batsman in the first innings. He scored 101 (a 6 and thirteen 4's) out of 130 in two hours. A defiant Insole helped him to save the match.

Yorkshire

D. B. Close b Hall	0	F. S. Trueman c Gibb b Hall	2
F. A. Lowson c Insole b Hall	11	J. G. Binks not out	25
J. V. Wilson c Gibb b Shepherd	78	M. Ryan not out	9
D. E. V. Padgett c Gibb b Hall	11	B 3, l-b 5, n-b 6	14
E. Lester b Hall	4		
R. Illingworth b Munden	138	1/0 2/16 3/36 (9 wkts., dec.)	304
N. W. D. Yardley b Shepherd	1	4/42 5/170 6/174 7/201 8/220	
J. H. Wardle c Gibb b Wells	11	9/290	

M.C.C.

R. T. Simpson lbw b Trueman	31	— b Ryan	8
P. E. Richardson b Trueman	23	— c Trueman b Close	3
T. W. Graveney not out	40	— c Padgett b Close	101
W. H. H. Sutcliffe lbw b Trueman	4	— c Yardley b Wardle	7
D. J. Insole c Trueman b Close	8	— c Wilson b Close	26
T. E. Bailey c Close b Wardle	24	— not out	14
P. A. Gibb c Close b Wardle	0	— run out	4
V. S. Munden b Close	3		
D. J. Shepherd b Trueman	5		
T. A. Hall b Trueman	11		
B. D. Wells b Trueman	0		
B 1, l-b 2	3	L-b 2	2
1/51 2/54 3/58 4/80 5/111 6/125	152	1/11 2/15 3/58 (6 wkts.)	165
7/130 8/136 9/152		4/141 5/161 6/165	

M.C.C. Bowling

	O.	M.	R.	W.	O.	M.	R.	W.
Hall	22	6	50	5				
Shepherd	18	1	75	2				
Bailey	20	3	70	0				
Munden	21	5	46	1				
Wells	16	2	49	1				

Yorkshire Bowling

	O.	M.	R.	W.	O.	M.	R.	W.
Trueman	18	3	45	6	8	1	20	0
Ryan	13	2	35	0	5	2	16	1
Yardley	1	1	0	0	0.3	0	0	0
Wardle	15	6	38	2	13	3	50	1
Close	10	2	31	2	21	7	45	3
				Illingworth	9	1	32	0

Umpires: H. Elliott (Lancashire) and A. Skelding.

THE UNIVERSITIES IN 1955

CAMBRIDGE

Captain—D. R. W. SILK (Christ's Hospital and
Corpus Christi)

Hon. Secretary—M. E. L. MELLUISH (Rossall and Caius)

Captain for 1956—M. E. L. MELLUISH

Hon. Secretary—G. GOONESENA (Royal College, Colombo, and
Queen's)

Cambridge were a most unpredictable side; they had no English
player of really outstanding merit and for most of the season they
relied to a considerable extent upon the three overseas players,
G. Goonesena, S. Singh and V. R. Lumsden. This was particularly
noticeable during the four weeks' tour, although strangely enough
these three failed to rise to their previous heights in the all-important
match against Oxford when the Light Blues had to fight hard
against the clock to stave off defeat.

Once again the team left Fenner's without a victory, having
been beaten by Surrey, Leicestershire and Middlesex, and drawn
with Yorkshire, Essex, Sussex, South Africans and Free Foresters;
but during the eight matches on tour they jumped into form with a
win against Colonel Stevens's XI in a two days' game at Eastbourne,
and followed by defeating Sussex, Warwickshire and Worcestershire, but lost to Surrey and Gloucestershire. The two final matches
at Lord's against the M.C.C. and Oxford were drawn.

For the captain, D. R. W. Silk, it was a most unsettling time.
Unable to find a reliable opening partner, he experimented with
five or six, and this, added to indisposition early in June, had a
considerable effect on his own play. When at Bristol he and
O'Brien began with a stand of 100 he decided to retain O'Brien,
but again his own form deserted him, so that finally he resigned
himself to the middle of the batting order. Easily the best all-
rounder was Gamini Goonesena who not only achieved several
capital performances with his varied leg spin bowling, but vastly
improved his batting; he hit 118 against Warwickshire at Edgbaston.

Swaranjit Singh, the turbaned and bearded Sikh, twelfth man
in 1954, steadily forced his way into the side by his vigorous left-
handed batting, besides distinguishing himself as a slow bowler
in support of Goonesena, his best effort being six wickets for 20
against Worcestershire. At The Oval he drove a ball from Lock
over the stand into the road near the gas-holders. Vincent Lumsden,

the West Indian, in the side for the third time, again found a particular liking for the Worcester ground. He followed his 93 and 107 there in 1954 with another exhilarating innings in which he missed a century by only a single.

During the season at Fenner's the team greatly missed the services of J. F. Pretlove, whose stern attention to scholastic studies allowed him to play in only four matches, but after scoring a fine 110 against Middlesex his real reward came in the Inter-Varsity match when by dogged determination he hit an invaluable 114.

Colin Smith, the fast bowler, experienced a less successful season, his six for 35 against the Free Foresters at Fenner's being his best performance. Later, in the middle of the tour, an attack of neuritis in his right shoulder necessitated medical attention and kept him out of two matches. Donald Smith, a Freshman from Southport, despite his modest stature, was successful in maintaining speed and accuracy. Knightley-Smith, after making 95 against Essex early in May, lost his form completely, and for the second year in succession he failed to gain a place. Melluish, who leads the side this year, kept wicket efficiently. Goonesena and Pretlove played for the Gentlemen at Lord's.

P. PIGGOTT.

CAMBRIDGE UNIVERSITY RESULTS

First-Class Matches—Played 15, Won 3, Lost 5, Drawn 7

AVERAGES
First-Class Matches
BATTING

	Matches	Inns.	Not Outs	Runs	100's	Highest Innings	Average
G. Goonesena.........	15	26	2	809	1	118	33.70
J. F. Pretlove	10	19	1	537	2	114	29.83
S. Singh	14	25	1	707	0	94	29.45
V. R. Lumsden	12	22	0	627	0	99	28.50
A. D. Buckingham.....	4	8	1	155	0	52*	22.14
R. O'Brien............	13	24	2	429	0	49	19.50
W. Knightley-Smith....	10	16	2	264	0	95	18.85
A. B. D. Parsons	13	24	2	391	0	46	17.77
C. S. Smith	12	21	5	273	0	40*	17.06
D. R. W. Silk	14	26	0	425	0	63	16.34
R. W. Barber	5	9	3	93	0	36*	15.50
M. E. L. Melluish	12	20	6	197	0	36	14.07
P. D. Croft	11	20	0	246	0	47*	12.30
D. J. Smith	14	19	12	64	0	18*	9.14

Also batted: R. H. M. Arkell 1, 3; R. B. Blatcher 15, 1; R. G. Newcombe 0, 4; J. C. W. Riley 0*, 0; P. G. Whiteside 0, 1

* *Signifies not out.*

BOWLING

	Overs	Maidens	Runs	Wickets	Average
G. Goonesena	520.2	140	1290	60	21.50
J. F. Pretlove	96.2	24	262	12	21.83
S. Singh	416.3	107	1032	43	24.00
C. S. Smith	358.3	81	921	36	25.58
D. J. Smith	439	90	1220	42	29.04
V. R. Lumsden	36	10	122	3	40.66
R. W. Barber	23	3	124	0	—

Also bowled: R. H. M. Arkell 8—1—23—0; R. B. Blatcher 16—2—59—2; D. R. W. Silk 2.3—0—7—0.

CAMBRIDGE UNIVERSITY v. SURREY

At Cambridge, April 30, May 2, 3. Surrey won by an innings and 70 runs. The considerable task confronting the University players in their opening first-class match of playing the Champions proved insurmountable, though Cambridge fought back creditably in the follow-on through Singh, Goonesena and D. J. Smith. After capturing the first three Surrey wickets for 17 the University bowlers toiled without effect against May and Barrington, who added 128, and the later batsmen scored briskly. A rain-soaked pitch brought disaster when Cambridge began their reply. Lock, the Surrey left-arm slow bowler, turned the ball to such an extent that no one faced him confidently and he finished with ten wickets for only 66 runs.

Surrey

T. H. Clark b D. Smith	4
D. G. W. Fletcher b C. Smith	3
P. B. H. May c Parsons b C. Smith	72
B. Constable c Parsons b D. Smith	7
K. Barrington c D. Smith b Singh	66
R. C. E. Pratt c Pretlove b Singh	18
A. J. McIntyre c Whiteside b C. Smith	29
J. C. Laker c Buckingham b D. Smith	44
W. S. Surridge c Silk b Goonesena	33
G. A. R. Lock c Pretlove b Goonesena	36
P. J. Loader not out	0
B 9, l-b 6, n-b 1	16
	328

1/9 2/9 3/17 4/145 5/169
6/188 7/252 8/261 9/312

Cambridge University

D. R. W. Silk c Lock b Loader	6	— c McIntyre b Lock	12
A. D. Buckingham c McIntyre b Loader	14	— st McIntyre b Lock	13
A. B. D. Parsons b Laker	11	— lbw b Lock	4
V. R. Lumsden c Pratt b Lock	4	— run out	8
J. F. Pretlove c Surridge b Lock	0	— c McIntyre b Laker	6
S. Singh c and b Lock	10	— c Fletcher b Loader	41
R. W. Barber b Laker b Lock	5	— st McIntyre b Laker	3
C. S. Smith c and b Lock	15	— b Loader	12
G. Goonesena not out	12	— b Lock	47
D. J. Smith c Laker b Lock	0	— not out	18
P. G. Whiteside lbw b Laker	0	— c Surridge b Constable	1
L-b 3, n-b 2	5	B 2, l-b 8, n-b 1	11
	82		176

1/16 2/29 3/36 4/37 5/44 6/51
7/54 8/81 9/81

1/19 2/29 3/38 4/39
5/45 6/64 7/95 8/116 9/171

Cambridge Bowling

	O.	M.	R.	W.	O.	M.	R.	W.
C. Smith	21	7	59	3				
D. Smith	28	5	103	3				
Goonesena	20.1	1	93	2				
Singh	17	1	40	2				
Barber	4	2	17	0				

Surrey Bowling

	O.	M.	R.	W.	O.	M.	R.	W.
Loader	13	9	10	2	18	8	24	2
Surridge	10	3	16	0	3	1	3	0
Lock	27	16	29	6	27	11	37	4
Laker	24.4	16	22	2	30	15	35	2
Clark					7	4	8	0
Constable					9.1	2	27	1
Barrington					7	0	31	0

Umpires: F. S. Lee and H. Palmer.

CAMBRIDGE UNIVERSITY v. YORKSHIRE

At Cambridge, May 4, 5, 6. Drawn. Three left-handed batsmen dominated a match in which the easy nature of the pitch always made a draw probable. After Yorkshire had lost two wickets for 21, Wilson and Close added 224 in two and a half hours, both driving particularly well. Close in that time hit one 6 and eleven 4's; Wilson, batting three hours, hit eleven 4's. After early successes for Van Geloven, a Colt in his first county game, Singh batted splendidly for Cambridge. Despite accurate bowling, he drove and pulled strongly, and hit thirteen 4's. Lowson and Watson made 114 for the first wicket before Yorkshire declared their second innings and, with rain causing a delay, Cambridge did not really attempt their final task.

Yorkshire

F. A. Lowson c Parsons b C. Smith	7	— c Whiteside b Singh	54
W. Watson b C. Smith	10	— not out	52
J. V. Wilson b D. Smith	110		
D. B. Close lbw b C. Smith	114		
E. Lester c Whiteside b D. Smith	6		
N. W. D. Yardley not out	74		
R. Illingworth b Singh	28		
J. van Geloven not out	1		
B 13, l-b 11	24	B 6, l-b 2	8

1/16 2/21 3/245 4/260   (6 wkts., dec.) 374   1/114   (1 wkt., dec.) 114
5/271 6/373

R. Booth, F. S. Trueman and R. Appleyard did not bat.

Cambridge University

D. R. W. Silk b van Geloven	15	— c Appleyard b Close	28
A. D. Buckingham b van Geloven	10	— b Close	43
A. B. D. Parsons lbw b Trueman	36		
V. R. Lumsden c and b Trueman	25	— c Illingworth b Close	0
R. O'Brien c Booth b Close	6	— not out	16
S. Singh c Illingworth b van Geloven	94	— c Watson b Illingworth	38
R. W. Barber b Illingworth	0	— not out	3
C. S. Smith c Lowson b Appleyard	37		
G. Goonesena c and b Trueman	4		
D. J. Smith not out	0		
B 3, l-b 6, n-b 4	13	B 4, l-b 5, n-b 1	10

1/24 2/29 3/68 4/84   (9 wkts., dec.) 240   1/60 2/60 3/80   (4 wkts.) 138
5/144 6/149 7/224 8/229 9/240   4/131

P. G. Whiteside did not bat.

Cambridge Bowling

	O.	M.	R.	W.	O.	M.	R.	W.
C. Smith	20	2	73	3	7	1	16	0
D. Smith	27	2	84	2	11	2	32	0
Singh	17	0	86	1	6.4	0	27	1
Goonesena	25	5	76	0	11	1	31	0
Barber	5	1	31	0				

Yorkshire Bowling

	O.	M.	R.	W.	O.	M.	R.	W.
Trueman	25	6	74	3	12	3	19	0
van Geloven	17	4	46	3	7	1	13	0
Close	17	5	40	1	12	4	35	3
Appleyard	23.4	12	35	1	12	3	26	0
Illingworth	17	5	32	1	5	0	35	1

Umpires: F. S. Lee and H. Palmer.

CAMBRIDGE UNIVERSITY v. ESSEX

At Cambridge, May 7, 9, 10. Drawn. Chief interest centred on the struggle for first innings lead which Cambridge gained by two runs. Essex recovered after a disappointing start through the efforts of two former Light Blues, Insole and T. E. Bailey, who shared a fifth wicket partnership of 92, but a long stay by the left-hander Knightley-Smith who surpassed his previous best helped Cambridge into the lead. Rain restricted play on the final day when the University were set to make 193 in one hour forty minutes.

Essex

T. C. Dodds c Melluish b C. Smith	2	— c Singh b Goonesena	50
P. A. Gibb c Silk b Goonesena	16	— lbw b C. Smith	17
G. Barker run out	24	— not out	67
R. Horsfall c Melluish b Goonesena	5	— not out	40
D. J. Insole c Silk b Goonesena	84		
T. E. Bailey b Singh	28		
B. Taylor c Melluish b Goonesena	0		
R. Smith c Silk b Goonesena	6		
W. T. Greensmith not out	30		
J. A. Bailey b Singh	1		
P. Cousens run out	3		
B 10, l-b 9, n-b 2	21	B 17, l-b 3	20

1/2 2/30 3/55 4/55 5/147 6/151   220   1/53 2/98   (2 wkts., dec.) 194
7/162 8/191 9/192

Cambridge University

D. R. W. Silk b Smith	1	— c T. Bailey b Greensmith	20
A. D. Buckingham c Gibb b T. Bailey	0	— not out	52
R. O'Brien c sub b Greensmith	27		
V. R. Lumsden b T. Bailey	18		
W. Knightly-Smith c Dodds b Smith	95		
S. Singh c Insole b Greensmith	0		
R. W. Barber st Gibb b Greensmith	10	— not out	36
C. S. Smith b J. Bailey	0		
G. Goonesena b Greensmith	20		
M. E. L. Melluish b T. Bailey	36		
D. J. Smith not out	5		
B 6, l-b 1, w 1, n-b 2	10	L-b 2	2

1/1 2/1 3/34 4/71 5/71 6/88   222   1/29   (1 wkt.) 110
7/101 8/137 9/203

Cambridge Bowling

	O.	M.	R.	W.		O.	M.	R.	W.
C. Smith	10	4	18	1	....	13	4	31	1
D. Smith	11	2	28	0	....	12	0	39	0
Goonesena	44.4	17	70	5	....	18	5	35	1
Singh	33	12	61	2	....	7	2	14	0
Barber	4	0	22	0	....	4	0	26	0
					Lumsden	8	2	29	0

Essex Bowling

	O.	M.	R.	W.		O.	M.	R.	W.
T. Bailey	24.1	7	43	3					
Smith	22	7	43	2	....	7	1	13	0
J. Bailey	15	3	33	1	....	10	2	23	0
Greensmith	27	5	72	4	....	6	1	23	1
Cousens	17	7	21	0	....	8	1	39	0
					Insole	2	0	10	0

Umpires: F. S. Lee and H. Palmer.

CAMBRIDGE UNIVERSITY v. LEICESTERSHIRE

At Cambridge, May 11, 12, 13. Leicestershire won by three wickets. An exciting race against the clock ended in victory for Leicestershire with only three minutes left. Set to make 151 in two and a quarter hours, the county looked assured of victory when Palmer and Smithson added 61 for the fourth wicket, but as soon as they were dismissed in quick succession an interesting struggle developed. Singh and Goonesena took the batting honours for the University and Goonesena also bowled his leg-breaks successfully.

Cambridge University

D. R. W. Silk c Firth b Boshier	0	— st Firth b Munden	28
R. O'Brien lbw b Munden	34	— c Hallam b Munden	46
V. R. Lumsden c Firth b Walsh	23	— b Munden	13
S. Singh run out	53	— c Hallam b Boshier	49
W. Knightley-Smith b Munden	14	— b Boshier	15
C. S. Smith lbw b Walsh	11	— c Hallam b Spencer	4
P. D. Croft b Lester	8	— c Spencer b Boshier	13
G. Goonesena not out	56	— b Spencer	14
M. E. L. Melluish c Smithson b Lester	13	— c Tompkin b Boshier	1
D. J. Smith c Smithson b Walsh	5	— not out	3
R. H. M. Arkell b Walsh	1	— c and b Boshier	8
B 3, l-b 1, w 1	5	B 1, l-b 7	2

1/15 2/57 3/59 4/79 5/136 6/136   223   1/65 2/84 3/89 4/139   196
7/164 8/202 9/217   5/158 6/176 7/182 8/185 9/192

Leicestershire

G. Lester lbw b Goonesena	62	—	c Knightley-Smith b D. Smith		7
M. R. Hallam b Goonesena	35	—	c Silk b C. Smith		13
M. Tompkin c Melluish b Goonesena	15	—	b D. Smith		30
C. H. Palmer lbw b C. Smith	87	—	c Melluish b D. Smith		43
G. A. Smithson lbw b D. Smith	14	—	b C. Smith		22
V. E. Jackson b D. Smith	0	—	not out		12
V. S. Munden b C. Smith	17	—	run out		3
J. E. Walsh lbw b C. Smith	0	—	c Melluish b D. Smith		6
J. Firth not out	18	—	not out		2
C. T. Spencer c and b Goonesena	12				
B. Boshier c Melluish b Goonesena	0				
B 2, 1-b 7	9		B 8, 1-b 6, n-b 1		15

1/68 2/88 3/167 4/214 5/214 6/220   269   1/11 2/49 3/59   (7 wkts.) 153
7/220 8/249 9/269   4/120 5/124 6/128 7/135

Leicestershire Bowling

	O.	M.	R.	W.		O.	M.	R.	W.
Spencer	13	5	33	0	....	24	3	62	2
Boshier	9	3	25	1	....	21.5	9	49	5
Walsh	25	3	75	4	....	8	0	34	0
Munden	21	11	38	2	....	18	12	16	3
Jackson	9	6	7	0					
Lester	12	2	40	2	....	8	1	27	0

Cambridge Bowling

	O.	M.	R.	W.		O.	M.	R.	W.
C. Smith	22	2	69	3	....	14.3	2	49	2
D. Smith	20	1	65	2	....	18	3	58	4
Singh	19	4	54	0	....	6	0	18	0
Goonesena	26	8	49	5	....	10	4	13	0
Arkell	8	1	23	0					

Umpires: E. Davies and H. Palmer.

CAMBRIDGE UNIVERSITY v. SUSSEX

At Cambridge, May 14, 16, 17. Drawn. Rain ruined the game, no play being possible on the last day. The Cambridge batsmen, through lack of concentration, gave an indifferent display on a pitch that was never really difficult. Thomson, with steady pace and accurate length, always troubled them. Sussex began well enough but the middle batsmen were hesitant against Singh's annoying spin and only after a keen struggle did the county gain the lead. Then they struck two vital blows by removing the Cambridge opening batsmen, but the opportunity of exploiting this promising position was lost because of the weather.

Cambridge University

D. R. W. Silk lbw b Thomson	9	—	lbw b Smith		3
R. O'Brien run out	49	—	c Oakman b James		0
A. B. D. Parsons c Mantell b Marlar	21	—	not out		0
S. Singh c Oakman b Thomson	9				
W. Knightley-Smith c James b Marlar	39				
P. D. Croft c Parks b Thomson	24				
G. Gonnesena c Smith b Thomson	0				
C. S. Smith c and b Thomson	11				
R. W. Barber lbw b Thomson	11				
M. E. L. Melluish not out	6				
D. J. Smith not out	2	—	not out		0
B 16, 1-b 1	17				

1/16 2/67 3/93 4/100   (9 wkts., dec.) 198   1/3 2/3   (2 wkts.) 3
5/157 6/161 7/166 8/184 9/187

Sussex

J. Langridge lbw b Goonesena ... 28	D. N. Mantell c Croft b Goonesena 11
D. V. Smith c Parsons b D. Smith . 18	R. G. Marlar not out 14
A. S. M. Oakman c Melluish b Singh 17	N. I. Thomson not out 0
J. M. Parks b Singh 30	B 5, w 1, n-b 1 7
K. G. Suttle lbw b Singh 21	
G. Cox b Singh 44	1/50 2/54 3/86 (8 wkts., dec.) 199
G. Potter c Melluish b Singh...... 9	4/111 5/132 6/158 7/177 8/193

A. E. James did not bat.

Sussex Bowling

	O.	M.	R.	W.	O.	M.	R.	W.
Thomson	39	5	81	6				
James	27	9	48	0	6	5	3	1
Marlar	32	17	42	2				
Oakman	10	5	10	0				
Smith					6	6	0	1

Cambridge Bowling

	O.	M.	R.	W.
C. Smith	13	3	26	0
D. Smith	10	0	39	1
Goonesena ...	23.3	6	65	2
Singh	26	7	62	5

Umpires: F. S. Lee and H. Palmer.

At Cambridge, May 18, 19, 20. CAMBRIDGE UNIVERSITY drew with the SOUTH AFRICANS. (See SOUTH AFRICAN section.)

CAMBRIDGE UNIVERSITY v. MIDDLESEX

At Cambridge, June 1, 2, 3. Middlesex won by three wickets. Considering that examinations forced the University to field their weakest side of the season, they did extremely well to hold Middlesex to such a narrow margin. After the county had established a lead of 120 Cambridge were indebted to an excellent all-round display by Pretlove. He hit their first century of the summer and, in partnership with Goonesena, added 111 for the fifth wicket. Middlesex, needing 157, made a good start through Brown, but steady left-arm slow bowling by Pretlove caused them anxious moments before they achieved their objective.

Cambridge University

A. D. Buckingham c Edrich b Robins ..	18	— lbw b Bennett	5
R. W. Barber c Compton b Bennett	4	— retired hurt...............	21
R. O'Brien c Brown b Warr............	4	— not out	11
G. Goonesena b Robins	16	— c Compton b Bick	45
A. B. D. Parsons b Robins	13	— b Warr	24
W. Knightley-Smith c Titmus b Robins..	29	— b Bennett	20
J. F. Pretlove c Compton b Bennett	44	— st Compton b Titmus	110
P. D. Croft b Titmus.................	9	— b Titmus	14
D. J. Smith c Bick b Titmus	11	— c Robins b Hurst	17
R. B. Blatcher b Bennett	15	— c and b Hurst	1
J. C. W. Riley not out	0	— b Hurst	0
L-b 1	1	B 4, l-b 4	8

1/10 2/17 3/36 4/53 5/64 6/94   164   1/15 2/57 3/89 4/89   276
7/103 8/125 9/157   5/200 6/257 7/271 8/276
                                         9/276

Middlesex

J. D. Robertson c and b Pretlove	49	— c Parsons b Smith	25
S. M. Brown c Parsons b Goonesena	17	— c Parsons b Pretlove	70
W. J. Edrich b Blatcher	88	— c Pretlove b Smith	10
D. Bennett c Riley b Smith	37	— b Pretlove	0
D. O. Baldry b Pretlove	24	— st Riley b Pretlove	6
D. A. Bick b Smith	1		
R. V. C. Robins c Croft b Blatcher	17	— b Pretlove	3
F. J. Titmus not out	27	— not out	35
J. J. Warr b Pretlove	1	— b Pretlove	8
L. H. Compton b Goonesena	1	— not out	1
R. J. Hurst b Pretlove	7		
B 12, l-b 3	15	B 1	1

1/63 2/81 3/194 4/204 5/205 6/226   284   1/45 2/64 3/64   (7 wkts.) 159
7/250 8/252 9/253   4/92 5/107 6/137 7/146

Middlesex Bowling

	O.	M.	R.	W.		O.	M.	R.	W.
Warr	12	3	33	1	....	26	6	60	2
Bennett	7.1	0	21	3	....	21	3	41	2
Robins	20	8	39	4	....	6	3	13	0
Hurst	14	7	30	0	....	40.5	21	56	3
Bick	7	2	21	0	....	4	0	13	1
Titmus	19	11	19	2	....	32	13	66	2
Edrich						2	0	9	0
Baldry						5	2	10	0

Cambridge Bowling

	O.	M.	R.	W.		O.	M.	R.	W.
Blatcher	13	2	51	2	....	3	0	8	0
Smith	34	9	79	2	....	21	3	65	2
Pretlove	33.1	8	66	4	....	11.1	0	55	5
Goonesena	39	18	45	2	....	6	0	30	0
Barber	6	0	28	0					

Umpires: F. S. Lee and H. Palmer.

CAMBRIDGE UNIVERSITY v. FREE FORESTERS

At Cambridge, June 4, 6, 7. Drawn. Again rain prevented play on the last day and this time it ruined the University's hopes of success. The weather played an important part in shaping the pattern of the cricket. Mann was influenced by the effect of prolonged rain on the pitch before the start and put Cambridge into bat, but useful stands between Parsons and Goonesena and C. S. Smith and Melluish and a delightful innings by Silk upset his calculations and the University were able to declare. The Foresters offered little resistance against the hostile pace bowling of C. S. Smith and Cambridge with a lead of 103 proceeded to establish a strong position.

Cambridge University

A. B. D. Parsons c Shaddick b Hall	 34	— b Hall 11
P. D. Croft lbw b Hall	 8	— b Kenny 0
G. Goonesena c Blake b Kenny	 48	— c Willenkin b Kenny 78
S. Singh c Dowding b Hall	 1	— c Shaddick b Robins 48
D. R. W. Silk c Burger b Robins	 41	
W. Knightley-Smith st Blake b Shaddick.	9	— run out 1
J. F. Pretlove c Blake b Shaddick	 0	— b Robins 3
R. G. Newman lbw b Robins	 0	— c and b Kenny 4
C. S. Smith not out	 40	— not out 14
M. E. L. Melluish c Hall b Dickenson..	36	— not out 18
B 10, l-b 6, w 1, n-b 1	 18	B 4 ....,.. 4

1/19 2/88 3/91   (9 wkts., dec.) 235   1/8 2/20 3/101   (7 wkts.) 181
4/104 5/131 6/131 7/132 8/167 9/235   4/119 5/127 6/148 7/151

D. J. Smith did not bat.

Free Foresters

D. E. Blake c Croft b Goonesena..	42	T. A. Hall not out 8
B. C. G. Willenkin c Silk b C. Smith	 5	D. C. Dickenson b C. Smith...... 5
		C. J. M. Kenny b C. Smith....... 0
A. L. Dowding c Parsons b D. Smith	0	R. A. Shaddick b Goonesena 1
A. E. R. Rutter b C. Smith.......	45	
F. G. Mann c Melluish b Goonesena	 2	B 12, l-b 6 18
C. G. Burger b C. Smith	4	1/10 2/13 3/93 4/103 5/108 132
R. V. C. Robins lbw b C. Smith ..	2	6/112 7/115 8/125 9/125

Free Foresters Bowling

	O.	M.	R.	W.		O.	M.	R.	W.
Hall	18	6	50	3	....	8	1	22	1
Kenny	30	5	68	1	....	26	11	61	3
Shaddick	13	2	40	2	....	10	3	20	0
Dickenson	3.1	0	9	1	....	7	1	22	0
Robins	17	2	50	2	....	13	1	52	2

Cambridge Bowling

	O.	M.	R.	W.
C. Smith.......	21	5	35	6
D. Smith	11	4	25	1
Goonesena	22.4	8	35	3
Singh	10	4	19	0

Umpires: H. Palmer and E. Wye.

At Eastbourne, June 9, 10. (Two-day Match.) CAMBRIDGE beat L. C. STEVENS'S XI by three wickets.

At Horsham, June 11, 13, 14. CAMBRIDGE beat SUSSEX by four wickets.

At The Oval, June 15, 16, 17. CAMBRIDGE lost to SURREY by an innings and 23 runs.

At Birmingham, June 18, 20, 21. CAMBRIDGE beat WARWICKSHIRE by 53 runs.

At Worcester, June 22, 23. CAMBRIDGE beat WORCESTERSHIRE by an innings and 76 runs.

At Bristol, June 25, 27, 28. CAMBRIDGE lost to GLOUCESTERSHIRE by seven wickets.

At Lord's, June 29, 30, July 1. CAMBRIDGE drew with M.C.C.

At Lord's, July 2, 4, 5. CAMBRIDGE drew with OXFORD. (See OTHER MATCHES AT LORD'S.)

OXFORD

Captain—C. C. P. WILLIAMS (Westminster and Christ Church)
Hon. Secretary—M. J. K. SMITH (Stamford and St. Edmund Hall)
Captain for 1956—M. J. K. SMITH
Hon. Secretary—A. C. WALTON (Radley and Lincoln)

Oxford were a disappointing side and many of the individual players with reputations already established did little to enhance them. Throughout the season they did not win one match, which was sufficiently lamentable, but it became even more so when one realized that the last victory was against Cambridge in 1951.

The weather was certainly against them and in all their ten home games none was played through without some interference from rain and, altogether, nine and a half days of playing time were lost. That in itself may have undermined the determination of the side, though a more likely handicap to the individual players was the length of time C. C. P. Williams took to decide who would be in the XI to meet Cambridge. The freshmen were particularly affected and when the weeks passed and they were still playing for their places none of them was able to relax and play a natural game.

As a side the University were lacking in two essentials. Match after match showed an inability to face fast bowling; Statham and Trueman, for instance, had the batsmen in all sorts of difficulties though many of those could have been resolved if greater confidence had been shown. The other great need was a fast bowler. J. B. Phillips of King's School, Canterbury, went nearest to solving the problem. He played in nearly every match, bowling with great consistency, and at times brilliantly, but he was never more than medium fast. J. H. Bowman, the Fettes freshman, was given an ample trial but he was never quite able to find a length and the wickets which he took cost many runs. J. M. Allan, with his slow left arm deliveries, was the most successful of the Oxford bowlers but at times he was roughly treated by top class batsmen. Some sixes over the sight screen off his bowling did something to break the monotony of dreary matches. A. P. Walshe who kept wicket in 1953, but lost his place to A. Kamm in 1954, came back into his best form.

On paper the batting looked strong and down to number seven there were men who were capable of making a lot of runs. The fickle weather certainly militated against steady batting but, time after time, there were surprising failures. M. J. K. Smith, for instance, hit a double century against Cambridge in 1954, and looked a most accomplished stroke player, but in nearly all the home matches he failed to find anything like his best form and it was only when he got to Lord's that he played the sort of innings expected of him. He and Allan, unfortunately, were not a success as an opening pair and too often left a formidable task to those who followed them.

Williams began well, but the cares of captaincy and of examinations seemed to affect his batting. A. C. Walton, G. P. S. Delisle and I. Gibson played with delicacy, but many times had to show undue restraint when the earlier batsmen had failed.

The omission of J. Baker from the side to play Cambridge was puzzling. He had his limitations in the field but he was a useful stock bowler and the most consistent batsman. He was the only one who, in every circumstance, played a natural game and many times, going in far later than his batting warranted, he rescued the side from threatened disaster.

In the field Oxford were patchy. Williams generally set a good example and was well backed up by Smith, Delisle, Walton and Gibson and, of course, by Walshe, but others in the side were guilty of errors through laziness.

To sum up, Oxford were a poor side, comparing ill with some of the great University teams of the past.

C. VENABLES.

OXFORD UNIVERSITY RESULTS
First-Class Matches—Played 15, *Drawn* 9, *Lost* 6

AVERAGES
First-Class Matches
BATTING

	Matches	Inns.	Not Outs	Runs	100's	Highest Inns.	Average
J. Baker	5	8	2	221	0	91*	36.83
M. J. K. Smith	15	27	1	943	3	118	36.26
C. C. P. Williams	13	24	2	765	1	120	34.77
J. P. Fellows-Smith	8	16	2	385	0	58	27.50
J. M. Allan	15	28	2	653	0	69	25.11
G. P. S. Delisle	15	27	2	549	1	113	21.96
A. C. Walton	15	28	0	612	0	68	21.85
I. Gibson	15	25	3	464	0	52*	21.09
A. P. Walshe	14	24	3	361	0	77	17.19
S. G. Metcalfe	4	7	0	106	0	73	15.14
D. K. Fasken	4	6	0	66	0	29	11.00
D. C. P. R. Jowett	13	19	5	135	0	30*	9.64
J. A. Arenhold	6	10	3	57	0	32*	8.14
R. Bowman	3	4	1	17	0	9	5.66
J. D. Anderson	2	3	2	4	0	4*	4.00
J. B. Phillips	14	17	6	41	0	20	3.72

Also batted: J. J. McInerny 2, 1; F. Slaven 13, 0; A. Kamm 9*.

* Signifies not out.

BOWLING

	Overs	Maidens	Runs	Wickets	Average
J. M. Allan	431.4	130	1173	46	25.50
J. B. Phillips	364.5	90	1016	38	26.73
J. Baker	64	14	199	7	28.42
D. C. P. R. Jowett	286.3	71	774	27	28.66
J. D. Anderson	36	9	118	4	29.50
J. P. Fellows-Smith	153.4	37	430	14	30.71
D. K. Fasken	121	21	367	11	33.36
J. A. Arenhold	109	20	329	8	41.12
C. C. P. Williams	11.2	0	56	1	56.00
R. Bowman	42	8	150	2	75.00
I. Gibson	89	12	364	4	91.00

Also bowled: S. G. Metcalfe 4—0—15—1.

OXFORD UNIVERSITY v. GLOUCESTERSHIRE

At Oxford, April 30, May 2, 3. Drawn. Batsmen generally dominated the first big match of the season in The Parks and there were four centuries, those of Delisle and Mortimore being their first in first-class cricket. Careful play by Allan and Walton was followed by some beautiful stroke play by Williams and Delisle whose stand yielded 190 in two hours twenty minutes. Each hit one 6 and Williams also claimed fourteen 4's compared with ten 4's by Delisle. The death of his father-in-law caused Graveney to leave the match, but Gloucestershire held their own thanks to a grand innings of 170 by Young (one 6, fourteen 4's), who with Mortimore (one 6 and fifteen 4's) put on 215 for the fifth wicket. At no time did the pitch give any encouragement to the bowlers.

Oxford University

M. J. K. Smith c Milton b Lambert	8	
J. M. Allan c Wells b Cook	54	— not out 36
A. C. Walton b Mortimore	52	— b Lambert 5
C. C. P. Williams c McHugh b Cook	120	— not out 64
G. P. S. Delisle c Emmett b Mortimore	113	
F. Slaven c Mortimore b Wells	13	
A. P. Walshe c Rochford b Wells	1	
D. C. P. R. Jowett b Mortimore	5	
J. A. Arenhold not out	1	
I. Gibson (did not bat)		— c Milton b Cook 3
B 12, l-b 4	16	B 1, l-b 2 3

1/13 2/107 3/132 4/322   (8 wkts., dec.) 383   1/15 2/24   (2 wkts.) 111
5/369 6/375 7/377 8/383

J. B. Phillips did not bat.

Gloucestershire

D. M. Young c Williams b Allan	.170	P. Rochford b Jowett 0
C. A. Milton c and b Jowett	30	B. D. Wells st Walshe b Allan 12
G. M. Emmett run out	14	F. P. McHugh not out............ 1
J. F. Crapp c Williams b Jowett	17	B 3, l-b 1 4
G. E. Lambert c Walton b Arenhold	0	1/66 2/90 3/124 (8 wkts., dec.) 368
J. Mortimore c Williams b Jowett	120	4/125 5/340 6/341 7/360 8/368

T. W. Graveney and C. Cook did not bat.

Gloucestershire Bowling

	O.	M.	R.	W.		O.	M.	R.	W.
Lambert	22	5	54	1	....	7	1	17	1
McHugh	31	10	71	0	....	5	1	8	0
Wells	35	11	73	2	....	9	5	13	0
Mortimore.....	23.2	2	83	3	....	5	4	1	0
Cook	28	15	38	2	....	9	4	15	1
Graveney	8	3	30	0					
Milton	3	0	18	0		6	0	23	0
Emmett						3	0	31	0
Crapp						2	2	0	0

Oxford Bowling

	O.	M.	R.	W.
Arenhold	20	2	58	1
Phillips	28	13	65	0
Allan	38.4	18	91	2
Gibson	17	1	47	0
Jowett	22	1	97	4
Williams	1	0	6	0

Umpires: D. Hendren and F. Chester.

OXFORD UNIVERSITY v. LANCASHIRE

At Oxford, May 4, 5, 6. Rain wiped out half of the first day and brought the match to an end after an hour of the third day. The University batsmen were obviously nervous against Statham, Tattersall and Hilton, and some of them left to unworthy strokes. Despite the presence of five freshmen in the Oxford team, Lancashire were also unhappy, and only a tenacious innings by Place enabled them to exceed Oxford's 111. Allan, Phillips and Jowett bowled splendidly for Oxford and later Allan and Williams shaped well with the bat.

Oxford University

M. J. K. Smith b Statham	0	— b Statham................	0
J. M. Allan b Hilton	10	— not out	44
A. C. Walton b Statham................	19	— b Statham................	10
C. C. P. Williams b Tattersall	12	— run out	44
G. P. S. Delisle c Ikin b Hilton	0	— not out	23
F. Slaven c Wharton b Hilton	0		
I. Gibson c Wharton b Hilton	11		
A. P. Walshe c Statham b Tattersall	14		
R. Bowman c Hilton b Tattersall	0		
D. C. P. R. Jowett not out.............	30		
J. B. Phillips c Hilton b Tattersall	5		
B 7, l-b 2, n-b 1	10	B 2, l-b 3	5

1/0 2/31 3/44 4/48 5/48 6/50 7/70 111   1/0 2/10 3/82   (3 wkts.) 126
8/71 9/80

Lancashire

J. T. Ikin c Slaven b Allan	18	A. Wilson c Slaven b Phillips	21
S. Smith c Walton b Phillips......	7	R. Tattersall c Williams b Allan ..	4
A. Wharton c and b Allan	7	T. Greenhough not out	0
C. Washbrook c Bowman b Jowett	14		
W. Place lbw b Phillips	52	B 6....................	6
K. Grieves lbw b Allan	9		
M. J. Hilton c Delisle b Allan	5	1/14 2/27 3/46 4/46 5/57	159
J. B. Statham lbw b Jowett	16	6/62 7/91 8/150 9/159	

Lancashire Bowling

	O.	M.	R.	W.		O.	M.	R.	W.
Statham	10	4	17	2	....	14	1	31	2
Wharton	6	1	11	0	....	3	2	1	0
Tattersall	22	11	42	4	....	4	1	14	0
Hilton	23	16	26	4	....	15.2	7	33	0
Greenhough	5	3	5	0	....	19	6	39	0
			Ikin			3	1	3	0

Oxford Bowling

	O.	M.	R.	W.
Bowman	5	1	19	0
Phillips	11	3	21	3
Allan	23.3	8	60	5
Jowett	14	1	34	2
Gibson	3	1	19	0

Umpires: D. Hendren and H. G. Baldwin.

OXFORD UNIVERSITY v. YORKSHIRE

At Oxford, May 11, 12. Yorkshire won by an innings and 23 runs. All round superiority enabled the county to win with a day to spare. A dour innings by Lowson and enterprising batting by Lester, Yardley and Booth helped Yorkshire gain a substantial total. Oxford found Trueman's pace too much and they did little better after following-on 179 runs behind, for Trueman finished the match with ten wickets for 32.

Yorkshire

F. A. Lowson c Baker b Allan	...	72
W. H. H. Sutcliffe c Delisle b Anderson		25
W. Watson c Bowman b Anderson		7
E. Lester b Allan		53
R. Illingworth b Allan		14
D. B. Close c Allan b Anderson	..	11
N. W. D. Yardley c Allan b Bowman		72
J. H. Wardle c Baker b Anderson	..	0
R. Booth c Williams b Phillips	...	48
F. S. Trueman c Anderson b Phillips		0
R. Appleyard not out		4
B 8, l-b 3		11
		317

1/61 2/93 3/125 4/166 5/185
6/185 7/185 8/304 9/304

Oxford University

M. J. K. Smith c Illingworth b Appleyard	23	—	c Booth b Appleyard	10
J. M. Allan b Trueman	0	—	c sub b Trueman	1
A. C. Walton b Trueman	10	—	c sub b Illingworth	25
A. P. Walshe c Watson b Wardle	27	—	b Appleyard	24
C. C. P. Williams c Booth b Trueman	25	—	b Trueman	3
G. P. S. Delisle c sub b Trueman	14	—	b Wardle	26
I. Gibson lbw b Wardle	7	—	c Appleyard b Close	43
J. Baker b Wardle	7	—	c Booth b Close	11
R. Bowman b Trueman	1	—	not out	7
J. D. Anderson not out	0	—	b Trueman	0
J. B. Phillips b Trueman	0	—	b Trueman	0
B 9, l-b 10, n-b 5	24		B 2, l-b 2, n-b 2	6
	138			156

1/1 2/21 3/65 4/68 5/113 6/119
7/132 8/137 9/138

1/8 2/16 3/28 4/55 5/75
6/96 7/149 8/151 9/152

Oxford Bowling

	O.	M.	R.	W.	O.	M.	R.	W.
Bowman	19	5	50	1				
Phillips	21.1	4	66	2				
Anderson	25	6	68	4				
Allan	34	8	87	3				
Baker	4	1	20	0				
Gibson	4	1	15	0				

Yorkshire Bowling

	O.	M.	R.	W.	O.	M.	R.	W.
Trueman	18	10	23	6	11.3	5	9	4
Appleyard	15	7	30	1	11	2	34	2
Close	10	3	24	0	10	5	19	2
Wardle	21	10	37	3	21	7	59	1
Illingworth ...					11	4	29	1

Umpires: D. Hendren and H. G. Baldwin.

OXFORD UNIVERSITY v. WARWICKSHIRE

At Oxford, May 14, 16, 17. Drawn. Fine bowling by Allan, Phillips and Jowett justified Williams's decision to send in Warwickshire. Though Warwickshire were dismissed for a modest total, Oxford were in turn caught on a tricky pitch early on the second day, and after the first three wickets had fallen for 61, Thompson and Weekes baffled the remaining batsmen. The pitch played easier after tea when Warwickshire flayed the Oxford attack. Wolton was most aggressive being particularly severe on Allan. Rain prevented any play on the third day.

Warwickshire

F. G. Gardner c Allan b Jowett	28	— lbw b Allan	8
N. F. Horner c Kamm b Phillips	21	— c Walton b Allan	9
A. V. Wolton c Jowett b Phillips	17	— not out	105
W. J. Stewart b Jowett	0	— not out	33
R. E. Hitchcock c Anderson b Allan	53		
N. A. Paul lbw b Phillips	5		
R. T. Weekes c Anderson b Phillips	0		
E. B. Lewis c Delisle b Allan	16		
R. G. Carter c and b Allan	0		
I. King not out	5		
R. G. Thompson c Jowett b Allan	0		
B 3, l-b 1	4	B 8, l-b 1	9

1/34 2/51 3/51 4/77 5/82 6/86   149   1/14 2/33   (2 wkts.) 164
7/143 8/145 9/145

Oxford University

M. J. K. Smith c Wolton b Carter	17	J. Baker st Lewis b Weeks	18
J. M. Allan b Thompson	26	D. C. P. R. Jowett b Thompson ..	9
A. C. Walton c Paul b Thompson	13	J. B. Phillips c Paul b Weeks	2
C. C. P. Williams c Lewis b Weeks	16	J. D. Anderson not out	4
I. Gibson c Stewart b Thompson..	11	N-b 5	5
G. P. S. Delisle c Hitchcock b			
Thompson	4	1/36 2/55 3/61 4/80 5/88	134
A. Kamm retired hurt	9	6/95 7/116 8/132 9/134	

Oxford Bowling

	O.	M.	R.	W.	O.	M.	R.	W.
Phillips	16	7	34	4	 18	6	33	0
Baker	5	1	18	0	 5	0	17	0
Jowett	18	5	38	2	 13	3	27	0
Allan	14.3	8	24	4	 21	6	51	2
Anderson	8	3	31	0	 3	0	19	0
					Gibson 3	0	8	0

Warwickshire Bowling

	O.	M.	R.	W.
Carter.........	17	3	45	1
Thompson	29	12	55	5
Weeks	12.5	4	29	3

Umpires: D. Hendren and F. Chester.

OXFORD UNIVERSITY v. MIDDLESEX

At Oxford, May 18, 19, 20. Drawn. Oxford had established a favourable position when a storm ended this much interrupted game. On the first day play did not begin until 4.45 and on a pitch suited for bowling only Allan and Delisle reached double figures. Nevertheless, Middlesex broke down against some excellent bowling by Phillips and Jowett, but at the critical moment Jowett lost his length and fearless batting by Warr who hit two 6's sent the county ahead. On the last day Oxford made a great recovery after four wickets had gone for 35. Williams and Walshe, with seventeen 4's between them, hit in such carefree style that they put on 154. Finally Oxford left Middlesex to make 211 in two hours twenty minutes, but within one minute of the declaration the storm broke and the pitch was flooded.

Oxford University

M. J. K. Smith b Warr	0	— b Warr	17
J. M. Allan b Titmus	54	— c Warr b Titmus...........	0
A. C. Walton b Moss	3	— c and b Titmus	10
C. C. P. Williams b Bick	5	— c Baldry b Bick	80
G. P. S. Delisle b Titmus	30	— not out	8
I. Gibson c Titmus b Warr	0	— b Titmus	0
J. P. Fellows-Smith b Titmus.........	8	— c Moss b Hurst	20
A. P. Walshe st L. Compton b Hurst ..	4	— hit wkt b Bick	77
J. A. Arenhold run out	2	— c Titmus b Bick...........	0
D. C. P. R. Jowett not out............	1	— c D. Compton b Bick......	4
J. B. Phillips c Moss b Hurst	2		
B 14, l-b 1	15	B 9, l-b 3, w 1, n-b 2 ..	15

1/0 2/9 3/31 4/107 5/112 6/113   124   1/2 2/2 3/20 (9 wkts., dec.) 231
7/115 8/122 9/122   4/35 5/189 6/214 7/221
8/225 9/231

Middlesex

J. D. Robertson lbw b Arenhold..	22	J. J. Warr c Gibson b Jowett	36
A. Thompson b Phillips..........	14	R. J. Hurst c Phillips b Jowett ...	7
D. O. Baldry b Phillips	1	A. E. Moss not out	1
D. C. S. Compton b Phillips	0		
F. J. Titmus c Gibson b Jowett....	24	B 4, l-b 2	6
D. A. Bick lbw b Fellows-Smith ..	14		
W. J. Edrich b Jowett	14	1/19 2/25 3/25 4/37 5/75	145
L. H. Compton c Smith b Phillips..	6	6/76 7/85 8/106 9/139	

Middlesex Bowling

	O.	M.	R.	W.		O.	M.	R.	W.
Warr..........	11	5	9	2	....	16	2	50	1
Moss	4	1	11	1	....	14	1	38	0
Bick	12	3	32	1	....	9.3	1	40	4
Hurst	18	9	38	2	....	13	3	40	1
Titmus	12	6	19	3	....	7	2	14	3
D. Compton ..						2	0	13	0
Baldry						5	1	21	0

Oxford Bowling

	O.	M.	R.	W.
Arenhold	13	4	39	1
Phillips	17	9	24	4
Fellows-Smith .	13	3	26	1
Jowett	14.4	4	45	4
Allan	6	4	5	0

Umpires: D. Hendren and F. Chester.

At Oxford, May 25, 26, 27. OXFORD lost to SOUTH AFRICANS by an innings and
137 runs. (See SOUTH AFRICAN section.)

OXFORD UNIVERSITY v. FREE FORESTERS

At Oxford, May 28, 30, 31. Free Foresters won by five wickets. Although
rain washed out the first day enterprising cricket led to a definite result. Oxford
had lost six men for 73 when Baker, a Taunton Freshman, arrived at the crease.
He hit three 6's off Brown, the former England captain, and also one 5 and seven
4's. Blake batted splendidly for Foresters in both innings, hitting eleven 4's in
his 81 and Brown played his usual forcing game. Despite falling 55 behind, Oxford
fought back, but Foresters set to make 187 in one and three-quarter hours were
indebted to Blake and Ingleby-Mackenzie for a sparkling stand before Kimmins
made the winning hit eight minutes from time.

Oxford University

M. J. K. Smith c Kimmins b Brown	35	— c and b Brown............	24
J. M. Allan c Kimmins b Bransdon	19	— c Barton b Kimmins.......	19
S. G. Metcalfe run out	1	— run out	73
A. C. Walton b Whitcombe	9	— c Wyatt b Brown	21
J. J. McInerny run out	2	— b Brown	1
G. P. S. Delisle c Ingleby-Mackenzie b Whitcombe	1	— c Kimmins b Bransdon	22
I. Gibson b Brown....................	23	— not out	51
J. Baker not out	91	— retired hurt..............	8
A. P. Walshe b Bransdon	5	— not out	17
R. Bowman c Dowding b Whitcombe ..	9		
J. B. Phillips b Kimmins	20		
B 1, l-b 10, n-b 2	13	L-b 5	5

1/48 2/50 3/61 4/70 5/71 6/73 7/131   228
8/146 9/165

1/31 2/55   (6 wkts., dec.) 241
3/87 4/95 5/140 6/171

Free Foresters

D. E. Blake c and b Allan	81	—	c Gibson b Baker		60
M. D. Corke c Gibson b Phillips	3	—	c Walshe b Phillips		4
A. C. D. Ingleby-Mackenzie c Allan b Bowman	9	—	b Metcalfe		68
R. E. S. Wyatt c Baker b Allan	18				
A. L. Dowding c Phillips b Allan	34	—	c Smith b Allan		15
M. R. Barton b Phillips	13				
F. R. Brown c McInerny b Baker	70	—	lbw b Allan		23
P. A. Whitcombe c and b Allan	21				
S. E. A. Kimmins b Baker	9	—	not out		15
A. G. Powell c Bowman b Allan	8	—	not out		0
J. Bransdon not out	2				
B 11, l-b 3, n-b 1	15		L-b 2		2

1/7 2/16 3/65 4/152 5/156 6/196   283   1/13 2/101 3/134 (5 wkts.) 187
7/262 8/263 9/277   4/155 5/181

Free Foresters Bowling

	O.	M.	R.	W.		O.	M.	R.	W.
Whitcombe	23	8	39	3	....	15	1	68	0
Kimmins	25.1	8	52	1	....	17	6	64	1
Brown	24	7	77	2	....	16	2	43	3
Bransdon	18	3	41	2	....	12	0	29	1
Dowding	6	3	6	0	....	6	0	32	0

Oxford Bowling

	O.	M.	R.	W.		O.	M.	R.	W.
Phillips	21	2	86	2	....	9	0	53	1
Bowman	14	2	50	1	....	4	0	31	0
Baker	10	2	26	2	....	5	0	52	1
Allan	18.3	4	74	5	....	8	1	34	2
Gibson	7	0	32	0					
					Metcalfe	4	0	15	1

Umpires: D. Hendren and K. McCanlis.

OXFORD UNIVERSITY v. THE ARMY

At Oxford, June 1, 2, 3. Drawn. The Army 172 (J. M. Allan six for 67) and 220 for eight wickets (Capt. G. S. Seaton 60); Oxford University 233 (I. Gibson 61; Pte D. Gibson five for 45). (Not first-class.)

OXFORD UNIVERSITY v. LEICESTERSHIRE

At Oxford, June 8, 9, 10. Drawn. With only fifteen minutes' play possible on the first day and none on the second, cricket on the final day was of the light-hearted variety. The Oxford innings was notable for some big hitting by Allan, who took 27 off an over from Jackson—4—6—6—4—4—3.

Oxford University

M. J. K. Smith c Spencer b Jackson	30	J. Baker b Walsh		37
J. M. Allan c Jackson b Munden	56	A. P. Walshe st Smith b Walsh		9
S. G. Metcalfe b Jackson	1	D. C. P. R. Jowett not out		0
C. C. P. Williams c Hallam b Munden	1	J. B. Phillips lbw b Walsh		0
A. C. Walton c Smithson b Munden	1	L-b 2		2
G. P. S. Delisle lbw b Walsh	17	1/87 2/88 3/89 4/91 5/96		154
I. Gibson b Munden	0	6/96 7/133 8/153 9/154		

Leicestershire

G. Lester not out 45	V. S. Munden not out 24
M. R. Hallam lbw b Baker 6	
M. Tompkin c Allan b Phillips ... 6	L-b 1 1
C. H. Palmer c Smith b Phillips... 0	
V. E. Jackson c Walshe b Phillips . 5	1/10 2/19 3/31 4/43 (5 wkts.) 87
G. A. Smithson b Phillips 0	5/45

J. E. Walsh, C. T. Spencer, J. W. R. Smith and J. Goodwin did not bat.

Leicestershire Bowling

	O.	M.	R.	W.
Spencer	6	0	20	0
Goodwin	8	5	8	0
Palmer	2	1	2	0
Munden	17	9	38	4
Jackson	21	7	75	2
Walsh	5	1	9	4

Oxford Bowling

	O.	M.	R.	W.
Phillips	12	3	30	4
Baker	6	0	13	1
Jowett	8	3	17	0
Gibson	5	1	17	0
Williams	2	0	9	0

Umpires: D. Hendren and G. S. Mobey.

OXFORD UNIVERSITY v. WORCESTERSHIRE

At Oxford, June 11, 13, 14. Worcestershire won by five wickets with four minutes to spare. They took the honours after gaining a mastery on the opening day when, thanks to a fine stand by Horton and Devereux, they finished only 55 behind with nine wickets left. Gibson was awarded his Blue after his chanceless 50. When Oxford batted a second time, Smith alone of the early batsmen showed confidence. Worcestershire wanted 194 in two and a quarter hours, but for some time they fell well behind the clock. In an effort to persuade them to hit, Williams, never regarded as a bowler, put on himself and he and Allan were treated mercilessly by Dews and Broadbent. Williams made no attempt to restrict the flow of runs until Worcestershire were in sight of their target. Broadbent hit four 6's and six 4's, getting his 83 in the last sixty-four minutes.

Oxford University

M. J. K. Smith b Flavell	0	— b Flavell	73
J. M. Allan c Yarnold b Coldwell	1	— lbw b Coldwell	2
S. G. Metcalfe lbw b Coldwell	12	— c Lister b Davies	19
C. C. P. Williams b Flavell	42	— b Flavell	3
G. P. S. Delisle c and b Horton	24	— b Flavell	11
A. C. Walton c Devereux b Horton	2	— c and b Devereux	30
I. Gibson c Yarnold b Coldwell	50	— c Flavell b Devereux	40
J. Baker b Davies	29	— b Coldwell	20
A. P. Walshe lbw b Flavell	12	— b Devereux.............	10
D. C. P. R. Jowett c Devereux b Horton	6	— not out	22
J. B. Phillips not out	2	— b Coldwell	5
N-b 1	1	B 1, l-b 4, n-b 2........	7

1/0 2/6 3/15 4/77 5/81 6/85 7/138   181
8/163 9/179

1/23 2/40 3/106 4/108   242
5/122 6/127 7/192 8/193
9/230

Worcestershire

L. Outschoorn b Baker	6	— lbw b Allen	28	
M. J. Horton c Gibson b Baker	74	— c Gibson b Phillips	2	
L. N. Devereux run out	59	— c Williams b Allan	25	
G. Dews c Phillips b Allan	57	— st Walshe b Williams	25	
R. G. Broadbent c Metcalfe b Jowett	2	— not out	83	
J. Lister c Gibson b Allan	13	— not out	5	
D. W. Richardson c Walshe b Jowett	7	— c Walshe b Baker	26	
T. Davies not out	11			
B 1	1			

1/20 2/129 3/148   (7 wkts., dec.) 230   1/11 2/48 3/61   (5 wkts.) 194
4/152 5/167 6/182 7/230   4/87 5/179

L. Coldwell, J. Flavell and H. Yarnold did not bat.

Worcestershire Bowling

	O.	M.	R.	W.		O.	M.	R.	W.
Flavell	21	6	47	3	....	25	7	64	3
Coldwell	13	2	37	3	....	22.4	6	43	3
Horton	23.2	6	61	3	....	21	5	51	0
Outschoorn	8	3	19	0					
Davies	3	0	16	1	....	9	1	34	1
Devereux						18	7	43	3

Oxford Bowling

	O.	M.	R.	W.		O.	M.	R.	W.
Phillips	16	3	31	0	....	14.4	2	55	1
Baker	19	9	30	2	....	10	1	23	1
Allan	27.1	9	80	2	....	9	2	60	2
Jowett	31	10	67	2	....	6	0	23	0
Gibson	4	0	21	0					
Williams						6	0	33	1

Umpires: D. Hendren and D. Davies.

At Lord's, June 15, 16, 17. OXFORD drew with M.C.C.

At Bournemouth, June 18, 20, 21. OXFORD lost to HAMPSHIRE by six wickets.

At Guildford, June 22, 23, 24. OXFORD lost to SURREY by an innings and 12 runs.

At Hove, June 25, 27, 28. OXFORD drew with SUSSEX.

At Eastbourne, June 29, 30, July 1. OXFORD drew with D. R. JARDINE'S XI.

At Lord's July 2, 4, 5. OXFORD drew with CAMBRIDGE. (See OTHER MATCHES AT LORD'S.)

LIST OF BLUES

From 1880–1955

To save space, Blues prior to 1880 are omitted, except some of special interest for personal or family reasons.

OXFORD

Abell, G. E. B. (Marlborough), 1924, 1926–27
Allan, J. M. (Edinburgh Academy), 1953–55
Altham, H. S. (Repton), 1911–12
Arenhold, J. A. (Diocesan Coll., S.A.), 1954
Arkwright, H. A. (Eton), 1895
Arnall-Thompson, H. T. (Rugby), 1886
Asher, A. G. G. (Loretto), 1883
Awdry, R. W. (Winchester), 1904

Ballance, T. G. L. (Uppingham), 1935–37
Bannon, B. D. (Tonbridge), 1898
Barber, A. T. (Shrewsbury) (Capt. in 1929), 1927–29
Bardsley, R. V. (Shrewsbury), 1911–13
Bardsley, G. R. (Uppingham) (Capt. in 1897), 1894, 1896–97
Barlow, E. A. (Shrewsbury), 1932–34
Barnard, F. H. (Charterhouse), 1922, 1924
Barnes, R. G. (Harrow), 1906–07
Bartlett, J. N. (Chichester), 1946, 1951
Barton, M. R. (Winchester), 1936–37
Bassett, H. (Bedford House, Oxford), 1889–91
Bastard, E. W. (Sherborne), 1883–85
Bathurst, F. (Winchester), 1848
Bathurst, L. C. V. (Radley), 1893–94
Bathurst, R. A. (Winchester), 1838–39
Bathurst, S. E. (Winchester), 1836
Bell, G. F. (Repton), 1919
Belle, B. H. (Forest School), 1936
Benn, A. (Harrow), 1935
Benson, E. T. (Blundell's), 1928–29
Berkeley, G. F. H. (Wellington), 1890–93
Bettington, R. H. B. (The King's School, Parramatta) (Capt. in 1923), 1920–23
Bickmore, A. F. (Clifton), 1920–21
Bird, W. S. (Malvern) (Capt. in 1906), 1904–06
Birrell, H. B. (St. Andrews, South Africa), 1953–54
Blagg, P. H. (Shrewsbury), 1939
Blaikie, K. G. (Maritzburg), 1924

Blake, P. D. S. (Eton) (Capt. in 1952), 1950–52
Bloy, N. C. F. (Dover), 1946–47
Boger, A. J. (Winchester), 1891
Bolitho, W. E. T. (Harrow), 1883, 1885
Bonham-Carter, M. (Winchester), 1902
Boobbyer, B. (Uppingham), 1949–52
Bosanquet, B. J. T. (Eton), 1898–1900
Boswell, W. G. K. (Eton), 1913–14
Bowring, T. (Rugby), 1907–08
Bradby, H. C. (Rugby), 1890
Braddell, R. L. (Charterhouse), 1910–11
Bradshaw, W. H. (Malvern), 1930–31
Brain, J. H. (Clifton) (Capt. in 1887), 1884–87
Brain, W. H. (Clifton), 1891–93
Brandt, D. R. (Harrow), 1907
Branston, G. T. (Charterhouse), 1904–06
Brett, P. J. (Winchester), 1929
Bristowe, O. C. (Eton), 1914
Bromley-Martin, G. E. (Eton), 1897–98
Brooke, R. H. J. (St. Edward's, Oxford), 1932
Brougham, H. (Wellington), 1911
Brownlee, L. D. (Clifton), 1904
Bruce, C. N. (now Lord Aberdare) (Winchester), 1907–08
Buckland, E. H. (Marlborough), 1884–87
Burn, R. C. W. (Winchester), 1902–05
Bush, J. E. (Magdalen Coll. Sch.), 1952
Butterworth, R. E. C. (Harrow), 1927
Buxton, R. V. (Eton), 1906

Campbell, I. P. (Canford), 1949–50
Campbell, I. P. F. (Repton) (Capt. in 1913), 1911–13
Carlisle, K. M. (Harrow) (Capt. in 1905), 1903–05
Carr, D. B. (Repton) (Capt. in 1950), 1949–51
*Case, T. B. (Winchester), 1891–92
Cazalet, P. V. F. (Eton), 1927
Chalk, F. G. H. (Uppingham) (Capt. in 1934), 1931–34
Champain, F. H. B. (Cheltenham) (Capt. in 1899), 1897–1900
Chesterton, G. H. (Malvern), 1949
Cobb, A. R. (Winchester), 1886

* Case came into the game of 1891, by permission of the Cambridge captain, through the Hon. F. J. N. Thesiger being injured soon after play began.

Y

Cochrane, A. H. J. (Repton), 1885–86, 1888

Colebrooke, E. L. (Charterhouse), 1880

Collins, L. P. (Marlborough), 1899

Colman, G. R. R. (Eton), 1913–14

Coutts, I. D. F. (Dulwich), 1952

Cowdrey, M. C. (Tonbridge) (Capt. in 1954), 1952–54

Coxon, A. J. (Harrow C.S.), 1952

Crawford, J. W. F. (Merchant Taylors), 1900–01

Crawley, A. M. (Harrow), 1927–30

Croome, A. C. M. (Wellington), 1888–89

Crutchley, G. E. V. (Harrow), 1912

Cunliffe, F. H. E. (Eton) (Capt. in 1898) 1895–98

Curwen, W. J. H. (Charterhouse), 1906

Darwall-Smith, R. F. H. (Charterhouse), 1935–38

Dauglish, M. J. (Harrow), 1889–90

Davidson, W. W. (Brighton), 1947–48

Davies, P. H. (Brighton), 1913–14

Delisle, G. P. S. (Stoneyhurst), 1955

De Montmorency, R. H. (Cheltenham and St. Paul's), 1899

de Saram, F. C. (Royal College, Colombo), 1934–35

Dillon, E. W. (Rugby), 1901–02

Divecha, R. V. (Bombay University), 1950–51

Dixon, E. J. H. (St. Edward's, Oxford) (Capt. in 1939), 1937–39

Donnelly, M. P. (Canterbury University, New Zealand) (Capt. in 1947), 1946–47

Dowding, A. L. (St. Peter's, Adelaide) (Capt. in 1953), 1952–53

Dyson, J. H. (Charterhouse), 1936

Eagar, E. D. R. (Cheltenham), 1939

Eccles, A. (Repton), 1897–99

Eggar, J. D. (Winchester), 1938

Evans, A. H. (Rossall and Clifton) (Capt. in 1881), 1878–81

Evans, A. J. (Winchester) (Capt. in 1911), 1909–12

Evans, E. N. (Haileybury), 1932

Evans, G. (St. Asaph), 1939

Evans, W. H. B. (Malvern) (Capt. in 1904), 1902–05

Evelyn, F. L. (Rugby), 1880

Fane, F. L. (Charterhouse) 1897–98

Fasken, D. K. (Wellington), 1953–55

Fellows-Smith, J. P. (Durban High School, South Africa), 1953–55

Findlay, W. (Eton) (Capt. in 1903), 1901–03

Fisher, C. D. (Westminster), 1900

Forbes, D. H. (Eton), 1894

Ford, G. J. (King's College, London), 1839–40

Ford, N. M. (Harrow), 1928–30

Forster, H. W. (Eton), 1887–89

Foster, G. N. (Malvern), 1905–08

Foster, H. K. (Malvern), 1894–96

Foster, R. E. (Malvern) (Capt. in 1900), 1897–1900

Fowler, G. (Clifton), 1888

Fox, R. W. (Wellington), 1897–98

Franklin, H. W. F. (Christ's Hospital), 1924

Fraser, J. N. (Church of England Grammar School, Melbourne, and Melbourne University), 1912–13

Frazer, J. E. (Winchester), 1924

Fry, C. B. (Repton) (Capt. in 1894), 1892–95

Garland-Wells, H. M. (St. Paul's), 1928–30

Garthwaite, P. F. (Wellington), 1929

Gibson, I (Manchester G.S.), 1955

Gilbert, H. (Charterhouse), 1907–09

Gilliat, I. A. W. (Charterhouse), 1925

Gilligan, F. W. (Dulwich) (Capt. in 1920), 1919–20

Gordon, J. H. (Winchester), 1906–07

Greenstock, J. W. (Malvern), 1925–27

Greeson, F. H. (Winchester), 1887–89

Grover, J. N. (Winchester) (Capt. in 1938), 1936–38

Guise, J. L. (Winchester) (Capt. in 1925), 1924–25

Halliday, J. G. (City of Oxford High School), 1935

Hamilton, W. D. (Haileybury), 1882

Harris (Lord), G. R. C. (Eton), 1871–72, 1874

Harrison, G. C. (Malvern and Clifton), 1880–81

Hart, T. M. (Strathallar), 1931–32

Hartley, J. C. (Marlborough and Tonbridge), 1896–97

Hatfeild, C. E. (Eton), 1908

Hedges, L. P. (Tonbridge), 1920–22

Henderson, D. (St. Edwards, Oxford), 1950

Henley, D. F. (Harrow), 1947

Henley, F. A. H. (Forest School), 1905

Hewetson, E. P. (Shrewsbury), 1923–25

Hewett, H. T. (Harrow), 1886

Hildyard, L. D'Arcy (Private), 1884–86

Hill, V. T. (Winchester), 1892

Hill-Wood, C. K. (Eton), 1928–30

Hill-Wood, D. J. (Eton), 1928

Hine-Haycock, T. R. (Wellington), 1883–84

Hirst, E. T. (Rugby), 1878–80

Hofmeyr, M. B. (Pretoria, South Africa) (Capt. in 1951), 1949–51

Holdsworth, R. L. (Repton), 1919–22

Hollins, A. M. (Eton), 1899

Hollins, F. H. (Eton), 1901

Holmes, E. R. T. (Malvern) (Capt. in 1927), 1925–27

Hone, B. W. (Adelaide University) (Capt. in 1933), 1931–33

Hooman, C. V. L. (Charterhouse), 1909–10

Hopkins, H. O. (St. Peter's College, Adelaide), 1923

Howell, M. (Repton) (Capt. in 1919), 1914, 1919

Hurst, C. S. (Uppingham) (Capt. in 1909), 1907–09

Jackson, K. L. T. (Rugby), 1934

Jardine, D. R. (Winchester), 1920–21, 1923

Jardine, M. R. (Fettes) (Capt. in 1891), 1889–92

Jenkins, V. G. J. (Llandovery), 1933

Jones, R. T. (Eton), 1892

Jose, A. D. (Adelaide University), 1950–51

Jowett, D. C. P. R. (Sherborne), 1952–55

Kamm, A. (Charterhouse), 1954

Kardar, A. H. (Punjab University), 1947–49

Keighley, W. G. (Eton), 1947–48

Kelly, G. W. F. (Stonyhurst), 1901–02

Kemp, M. C. (Harrow) (Capt. in 1883–84), 1881–84

Key, K. J. (Clifton), 1884–87

Kimpton, R. C. M. (Melbourne University), 1935, 1937–38

Kingsley, P. G. T. (Winchester) (Capt. in 1930), 1928–30

Knight, D. J. (Malvern), 1914, 1919

Knight, N. S. (Uppingham), 1934

Knott, C. H. (Tonbridge) (Capt. in 1924), 1922–24

Knott, F. H. (Tonbridge) (Capt. in 1914), 1912–14

Knox, F. P. (Dulwich) (Capt. in 1901), 1899–1901

Lagden, R. O. (Marlborough), 1909–12

Le Couteur, P. R. (Warrnambool Academy and Melbourne University), 1909–11

Lee, E. C. (Winchester), 1898

Legard, A. R. (Winchester), 1932, 1935

Legge, G. B. (Malvern) (Capt. in 1926), 1925–26

Leslie, C. F. H. (Rugby), 1881–83

Leveson Gower, H. D. G. (Winchester) (Capt. in 1896), 1893–96

Lewis, D. J. (Cape Town University), 1951

Lewis, R. P. (Winchester), 1894–96

Lindsay, W. O'B. (Harrow), 1931

Llewellyn, W. D. (Eton), 1890–91

Lomas, J. M. (Charterhouse), 1938–39

Lowe, J. C. M. (Uppingham), 1907–09

Lowndes, W. G. L. F. (Eton), 1921

Lyon, B. H. (Rugby), 1922–23

Lyon, G. W. F. (Brighton), 1925

McBride, W. N. (Westminster), 1926

McCanlis, M. A. (Cranleigh) (Capt. in 1928), 1926–28

Macindoe, D. H. (Eton) (Capt. in 1946), 1937–39, 1946

McIntosh, R. I. F. (Uppingham), 1927–28

M'Iver, C. D. (Forest School), 1903–04

McKinna, G. H. (Manchester Grammar School), 1953

M'Lachlan, N. (Loretto) (Capt. in 1882), 1879–82

Mallett, A. W. H. (Dulwich), 1947–48

Marshall, J. C. (Rugby), 1953

Marsham, A. J. B. (Eton), 1939

Marsham, C. D. B. (Private) (Capt. in 1857–58), 1854–58

Marsham, C. H. B. (Eton) (Capt. in 1902), 1900–02

Marsham, C. J. B. (Private), 1851

Marsham, R. H. B. (Private), 1856

Marsland, G. P. (Rossall), 1954

Martin, E. G. (Eton), 1903–06

Martyn, H. (Exeter Grammar School), 1899–1900

Matthews, M. H. (Westminster), 1936–37

Maudsley, R. H. (Malvern), 1946–47

Mayhew, J. F. N. (Eton), 1930

Medlicott, W. S. (Harrow), 1902

Melle, B. G. von B. (South African College School and South African College, Cape Town), 1913–14

Melville, A. (Michaelhouse, South Africa) (Capt. in 1931–32), 1930–33

Mitchell, R. A. H. (Eton) (Capt. in 1863–65), 1862–65

Mitchell, W. M. (Dulwich), 1951–52

Mitchell-Innes, N. S. (Sedbergh) (Capt. in 1936), 1934–37

Monro, R. W. (Harrow), 1860

Moore, D. N. (Shrewsbury) (Capt. in 1931, when he did not play v. Cambridge, owing to illness), 1930

Mordaunt, G. J. (Wellington) (Capt. in 1895), 1893–96

More, R. E. (Westminster), 1900–01

Moss, R. H. (Radley), 1889

Munn, J. S. (Forest School), 1901

Murray-Wood, W. (Mill Hill), 1936

Naumann, F. C. G. (Malvern), 1914, 1919

Nepean, E. A. (Sherborne), 1887–88

Neser, V. H. (South African College, Cape Town), 1921

Newman, G. C. (Eton), 1926–27

Newton, A. E. (Eton), 1885

Newton-Thompson, J. O. (Diocesan College, Rondebosch, South Africa), 1946

Nicholls, B. E. (Winchester), 1884

Nunn, J. A. (Sherborne), 1926–27

O'Brien, T. C. (St. Charles' College, Notting Hill), 1884–85

Oldfield, P. C. (Repton), 1932–33

Ottaway, C. J. (Eton) (Capt. in 1873), 1870–73

Owen-Smith, H. G. (Diocesan College, South Africa), 1931–33

Page, H. V. (Cheltenham) (Capt. in 1885–86), 1883–86

Palairet, L. C. H. (Repton) (Capt. in 1892–93), 1890–93

Palairet, R. C. N. (Repton), 1893–94

Pataudi, Nawab of (Chief's College, Lahore), 1929–31

Patten, M. (Winchester), 1922–23

Patterson, J. I. (Chatham House, Ramsgate), 1882

Patterson, W. H. (Chatham House, Ramsgate, and Harrow), 1880–81

Pawson, A. C. (Winchester), 1903

Pawson, A. G. (Winchester) (Capt. in 1910), 1908–11

Pawson, H. A. (Winchester) (Capt. in 1948), 1947–48

Payne, A. (Private) (Capt. in 1856), 1852, 1854–56

Payne, A. F. (Private), 1855

Payne, C. A. L. (Charterhouse), 1906–07

Peake, E. (Marlborough), 1881–83

Pearse, G. V. (Maritzburg College, Natal), 1919

Peat, C. U. (Sedbergh), 1913

Peebles, I. A. R. (Glasgow Academy), 1930

Pershke, W. J. (Uppingham), 1938

Pether, S. (Magdalen College School), 1939

Philipson, H. (Eton) (Capt. in 1889), 1887–89

Phillips, F. A. (Rossall), 1892, 1894–95

Phillips, J. B. (King's, Canterbury), 1955

Pilkington, C. C. (Eton), 1896

Pilkington, H. C. (Eton), 1899–1900

Pilkington, W. (Midhurst), 1827

Potts, H. J. (Stand G. S.), 1950

Price, V. R. (Bishop's Stortford) (Capt. in 1921), 1919–22

Proud, R. B. (Winchester), 1939

Pycroft, J. (Bath), 1836

Raikes, D. G. (Shrewsbury), 1931

Raikes, G. B. (Shrewsbury), 1894–95

Raikes, T. B. (Winchester), 1922–24

Randolph, B. M. (Charterhouse), 1855–56

Randolph, C. (Eton), 1844–45

Randolph, J. (Westminster), 1843

Randolph, L. C. (Westminster), 1845

Raphael, J. E. (Merchant Taylors), 1903–05

Rashleigh, W. (Tonbridge) (Capt. in 1888), 1886–89

Rice, R. W. (Cardiff), 1893

Richardson, J. V. (Uppingham), 1925

Ricketts, G. W. (Winchester), 1887

Ridding A. (Winchester), 1846–50

Ridding, C. H. (Winchester), 1845–49

Ridding, W. (Winchester) (Capt. in 1849 and 1852, also in 1851 but did not play v. Cambridge, owing to illness), 1849–50, 1852–53

Robertson-Glasgow, R. C. (Charterhouse), 1920–23

Robinson, G. E. (Burton), 1881–83

Robinson, H. B. (North Shore College, Vancouver), 1947–48

Robinson, R. L. (St. Peter's College, Adelaide, and Adelaide University), 1908–09

Royle, Vernon (Rossall), 1875–76

Rucker, C. E. S. (Charterhouse), 1914

Rucker, P. W. (Charterhouse), 1919

Rudd, C. R. D. (Eton), 1949

Ruggles-Brise, H. G. (Winchester), 1883

Rumbold, J. S. (St. Andrew's College, New Zealand), 1946

Sale, R. (Repton), 1910

Sale, R. (*junior*) (Repton), 1939, 1946

Salter, M. G. (Cheltenham), 1909–10

Samson, O. M. (Cheltenham), 1903

Schwann, H. S. (Clifton), 1890

Scott, Lord Geo. (Eton), 1887–89

Scott, K. B. (Winchester), 1937

Scott, R. S. G. (Winchester), 1931

Seamer, J. W. (Marlborough), 1934–36

Seitz, J. A. (Scotch College and Melbourne University), 1909

Shaw, E. A. (Marlborough), 1912, 1914

Shaw, E. D. (Forest School), 1882

Simpson, E. T. B. (Harrow), 1888

Sinclair, E. H. (Winchester), 1924

Singleton, A. P. (Shrewsbury) (Capt. in 1937), 1934–37

Skeet, C. H. L. (St. Paul's), 1920

Skene, R. W. (Sedbergh), 1928

Smith, E. (Clifton), 1890–91

Smith, G. O. (Charterhouse), 1895–96

Smith, M. J. K. (Stamford), 1954–55

Stainton, R. G. (Malvern), 1933

Stanning, J. (Winchester), 1939

Stephenson, J. S. (Shrewsbury). 1925–26

Stevens, G. T. S. (University College School), (Capt. in 1922), 1920–23
Stewart-Brown, P. H. (Harrow), 1925–26
Stocks, F. W. (Lancing and Denstone), 1898–99
Sutton, M. A. (Ampleforth), 1946

Taylor, C. H. (Westminster), 1923–26
Teesdale, H. (Winchester), 1908
*Thesiger, F. J. N., 1st Visct. Chelmsford (Winchester) (Capt. in 1890), 1888, 1890
Thornton, W. A. (Winchester), 1879–82
Tindall, R. G. (Winchester), 1933–34
Townsend, D. C. H. (Winchester), 1933–34
Travers, B. H. (Sydney University), 1946, 1948
Trevor, A. H. (Winchester), 1880–81
Tuff, F. N. (Malvern), 1910
Twining, R. H. (Eton) (Capt. in 1912), 1910–13
Tylecote, E. F. S. (Clifton) (Capt. in 1871–72), 1869–72
Tylecote, H. G. (Clifton), 1874–77

Udal, N. R. (Winchester), 1905–06

Van der Bijl, P. G. (Diocesan College, South Africa), 1932
Van Ryneveld, C. B. (Diocesan College, South Africa) (Capt. in 1949), 1948–50
Vidler, J. L. S. (Repton), 1910–12
Von Ernsthausen, A. C. (Uppingham), 1902–04

Waddy, P. S. (The King's School, Parramatta), 1896–97
Waldock, F. A. (Uppingham), 1919–20
Walford, M. M. (Rugby), 1936, 1938
Walker, D. F. (Uppingham) (Capt. in 1935), 1933–35
Walker, J. G. (Loretto), 1882–83
Walker, R. D. (Harrow), 1861–65
Walton, A. C. (Radley), 1955

Walshe, A. P. (Milton, Rhodesia), 1953, 55
Ward, H. P. (Shrewsbury), 1919, 1921
Warner, P. F. (Rugby), 1895–96
Watson, A. K. (Harrow), 1889
Watson, H. D. (Harrow), 1891
Webb, H. E. (Winchester), 1948
Webbe, A. J. (Harrow) (Capt. in 1877–78), 1875–78
Webbe, H. R. (Winchester) (Capt. in 1879), 1877–79
Wellings, E. M. (Cheltenham), 1929, 1931
Wheatley, G. A. (Uppingham), 1946
Whitby, H. O. (Leamington), 1884–87
Whitcombe, P. A. (Winchester), 1947–49
Whitcombe, P. J. (Worcester G.S.), 1951–52
White, H. (Denstone), 1900
Whitehouse, P. M. (Marlborough), 1938
Whiting, A. O. (Sherborne), 1881–82
Wickham, A. P. (Marlborough), 1878
Wiley, W. G. E. (Diocesan Coll., Rondebosch, S.A.), 1952
Wilkinson, W. A. C. (Eton), 1913
Williams, C. C. P. (Westminster), (Capt. in 1955), 1953–55
Williams, R. A. (Winchester), 1901–02
Wilson, G. L. (Brighton), 1890–91
Wilson, T. S. B. (Bath College), 1892–93
Winn, C. E. (King's College School, Wimbledon), 1948–51
Wood, J. B. (Marlborough), 1892–93
Wordsworth, Chas. (Harrow) (Capt. both years, First Oxford Capt.), 1827, 1829
Wright, E. C. (Clergy Orphan School), 1897
Wright, E. L. (Winchester) (Capt. in 1907–08), 1905–08
Wrigley, M. H. (Harrow), 1949
Wyld, H. J. (Harrow), 1901–03

Young, D. E. (King's College School, Wimbledon), 1938

* Thesiger began to play in the game of 1891, but retired injured soon after the start. The Cambridge captain allowed his place to be taken by T. B. Case.

CAMBRIDGE

Aird, R. (Eton), 1923
Alexander, F. C. M. (Wolmer's Coll., Jamaica), 1952–53
Allen, A. W. (Eton), 1933–34
Allen, B. O. (Clifton), 1933
Allen, G. O. (Eton), 1922–23
Allom, M. J. C. (Wellington), 1927–28
Arnold, A. C. P. (Malvern), 1914
Ashton, C. T. (Winchester) (Capt. in 1923), 1921–23

Ashton, G. (Winchester) (Capt. in 1921), 1919–21
Ashton, H. (Winchester) (Capt. in 1922), 1920–22
Austin, H. M. (Melbourne), 1924

Baggallay, M. E. C. (Eton), 1911
Bagnall, H. F. (Harrow), 1923
Bailey, T. E. (Dulwich), 1947–48
Baily, E. P. (Harrow), 1872, 1874

Baily, R. E. H. (Harrow), 1908
Bainbridge, H. W. (Eton) (Capt. in 1886), 1884–86
Baker, E. C. (Brighton), 1912. 1914
Bartlett, H. T. (Dulwich) (Capt. in 1936), 1934–36
Bennett, C. T. (Harrow) (Capt. in 1925, 1923, 1925
Blake, J. P. (Aldenham), 1939
Blaker, R. N. (Elizabeth College, Guernsey), 1842–43
Blaker, R. N. R. (Westminster), 1900–02
Bligh, Ivo F. W. (Lord Darnley) (Eton) (Capt. in 1881), 1878–81
Block, S. A. (Marlborough), 1929
Blundell, E. D. (Waitaki, New Zealand), 1928–29
Bodkin, P. E. (Bradfield) (Capt. in 1946), 1946
Bray, E. (Westminster), 1871–72
Bray, E. H. (Charterhouse), 1896–97
Bridgeman, W. C. (Eton), 1887
Brocklebank, J. M. (Eton), 1936
Brodhurst, A. H. (Malvern), 1939
Bromley-Davenport, H. R. (Eton), 1892–93
Brooke-Taylor, G. P. (Cheltenham), 1919–20
Brown, F. R. (Leys), 1930–31
Browne, F. B. R. (Aldro School and Eastbourne College), 1922
Brunton, J. du V. (Lancaster Grammar School), 1894
Bryan, J. L. (Rugby), 1921
Buchanan, J. N. (Charterhouse) (Capt. in 1909), 1906–09
Buckston, G. M. (Eton), 1903
Burnett, A. C. (Lancing), 1949
Burnup, C. J. (Malvern), 1896–98
Burrough, J. (King's School, Bruton, and Shrewsbury), 1895
Bushby, M. H. (Dulwich) (Capt. in 1954), 1952–54
Butler, E. M. (Harrow), 1888–89
Butterworth, H. R. W. (Rydal Mount), 1929
Buxton, C. D. (Harrow) (Capt. in 1888), 1885–88

Calthorpe, F. S. G. (Repton), 1912–14, 1919
Cameron, J. H. (Taunton), 1935–37
Cangley, B. G. (Felsted), 1947
Carris, B. D. (Harrow), 1938–39
Carris, H. E. (Mill Hill), 1930
Cawston, E. (Lancing), 1932
Chapman, A. P. F. (Oakham and Uppingham), 1920–22
Christopherson, J. C. (Uppingham), 1931
Cobbold, P. W. (Eton), 1896
Cobbold, R. H. (Eton), 1927
Cobden, F. C. (Harrow), 1870–72

Cockett, J. A. (Aldenham), 1951
Colbeck, L. G. (Marlborough), 1905–06
Collins, D. C. (Wellington College, Wellington, N.Z.), 1910–11
Comber, J. T. H. (Marlborough), 1931–33
Conradi, E. R. (Oundle), 1946
Coode, A. T. (Fauconberge School, Beccles), 1898
Cowie, A. G. (Charterhouse), 1910
Crawley, E. (Harrow), 1887–89
Crawley, L. G. (Harrow), 1923–25
Croft, P. D. (Gresham's, Holt), 1955
Crookes, D. V. (Michaelhouse, South Africa), 1953
Cumberlege, B. S. (Durham), 1913

Daniell, J. (Clifton), 1899–1901
Datta, P. B. (Asutosh College, Calcutta), 1947
Davies, G. B. (Rossall), 1913–14
Davies, J. G. W. (Tonbridge), 1933–34
Dawson, E. W. (Eton) (Capt. in 1927), 1924–27
Day, S. H. (Malvern) (Capt. in 1901), 1899–1902
De Little, E. R. (Geelong Grammar School), 1889
De Paravicini, P. J. (Eton), 1882–85
De Zoete, H. W. (Eton), 1897–98
Dewes, J. G. (Aldenham), 1948–50
Dickinson, D. C. (Clifton), 1953
Dickinson, P. J. (K.C.S., Wimbledon), 1939
Doggart, A. G. (Bishop's Stortford), 1921–22
Doggart, G. H. G. (Winchester) (Capt. in 1950), 1948–50
Dorman, A. W. (Dulwich), 1886
Douglas, J. (Dulwich), 1892–94
Douglas, R. N. (Dulwich), 1890–92
Downes, K. D. (Rydal), 1939
Dowson, E. M. (Harrow) (Capt. in 1903), 1900–03
Driffield, L. T. (Leatherhead), 1902
Druce, N. F. (Marlborough) (Capt. in 1897), 1894–97
Druce, W. G. (Marlborough) (Capt. in 1895), 1894–95
Duleepsinhji, K. S. (Cheltenham), 1925–26, 1928

Ebden, C. H. M. (Eton), 1902–03
Elgood, B. C. (Bradfield), 1948
Enthoven, H. J. (Harrow) (Capt. in 1926), 1923–26
Estcourt, N. S. D. (Plumtree, Southern Rhodesia), 1954
Evans, R. G. (King Edward, Bury St. Edmunds), 1921
Eyre, C. H. (Harrow) (Capt. in 1906), 1904–06

Fabian, A. H. (Highgate), 1929–31

Fairbairn, G. A. (Church of England Grammar School, Geelong), 1913–14, 1919

Falcon, M. (Harrow) (Capt. in 1910), 1908–11

Fargus, A. H. C. (Clifton and Haileybury), 1900–01

Farnes, K. (Royal Liberty School, Romford), 1931–33

Fernie, A. E. (Wellingborough), 1897, 1900

Fiddian-Green, C. A. (Leys), 1921–22

Field, E. (Clifton), 1894

Foley, C. P. (Eton), 1889–91

Foley, C. W. (Eton), 1880

Ford, A. F. J. (Repton), 1878–81

Ford, F. G. J. (Repton) (Capt. in 1889) 1887–90

Ford, W. J. (Repton), 1873

Francis, T. E. S. (Tonbridge), 1925

Franklin, W. B. (Repton), 1912

Fraser, T. W. (Jeppe, S. Africa), 1937

Freeman-Thomas F. (Lord Willingdon) (Eton), 1886–89

Frere, J. (Eton), 1827

Fry, K. R. B. (Cheltenham), 1904

Gaddum, F. D. (Uppingham and Rugby), 1882

Gay, L. H. (Marlborough and Brighton), 1892–93

Gibb, P. A. (St. Edward's, Oxford), 1935–38

Gibson, C. H. (Eton), 1920–21

Gillespie, D. W. (Uppingham), 1939

Gilligan, A. E. R. (Dulwich), 1919–20

Gilman, J. (St. Paul's), 1902

Godsell, R. T. (Clifton), 1903

Goodwin, H.J. (Marlborough), 1907–08

Goonesena, G. (Royal Coll., Colombo), 1954–55

Gosling, R. C. (Eton), 1888–90

Grace, W. G., junr. (Clifton), 1895–96

Grant, G. C. (Trinidad), 1929–30

Grant, R. S. (Trinidad), 1933

Gray, H. (Perse), 1894–95

Green, C. E. (Uppingham) (Capt. in 1868), 1865–68

Grierson, H. (Bedford Grammar), 1911

Griffith, S. C. (Dulwich), 1935

Griffiths, W. H. (Charterhouse), 1946–48

Grimshaw, J. W. T. (King William's College, Isle of Man), 1934–35

Hadingham, A. W. G. (St. Paul's), 1932

Hale, H. (Hutchins School, Hobart), 1887, 1889–90

Hall, P. J. (Geelong), 1949

Harbinson, W. K. (Marlborough), 1929

Harper, L. V. (Rossall), 1901–03

Harrison, W. P. (Rugby), 1907

Hawke, M. B. (Lord) (Eton) (Capt. in 1885), 1882–83, 1885

Hawkins, H. H. B. (Whitgift), 1898–99

Hayward, W. I. D. (St. Peter's College, Adelaide), 1950–51, 1953

Hazlerigg, A. G. (Eton) (Capt. in 1932), 1930–32

Hemingway, W. McG. (Uppingham), 1895–96

Henery, P. J. T. (Harrow), 1882–83

Hewan, G. E. (Marlborough), 1938

Hill, A. J. L. (Marlborough), 1890–93

Hill-Wood, W. W. (Eton), 1922

Hind, A. E. (Uppingham), 1898–1901

Hobson, R. S. (Taunton), 1946

Holloway, N. J. (Leys), 1910–12

Hone, N. T. (Rugby), 1881

Hopley, F. J. V. (Harrow), 1904

Hopley, G. W. V. (Harrow), 1912

Hotchkin, N. S. (Eton), 1935

Howard-Smith, G. (Eton), 1903

Hughes, O. (Malvern), 1910

Hunt, R. G. (Aldenham) 1937

Human, J. H. (Repton) (Capt. in 1934), 1932–34

Human, R. H. C. (Repton), 1930–31

Imlay, A. D. (Clifton), 1907

Insole, D. J. (Monoux, Walthamstow) (Capt. in 1949), 1947–49

Ireland, J. F. (Marlborough) (Capt. in 1911), 1908–11

Irvine, L. G. (Taunton), 1926–27

Jackson, F. S. (Harrow) (Capt. in 1892–93), 1890–93

Jagger, S. T. (Malvern), 1925–26

Jahangir Khan, M. (Lahore), 1933–36

Jenner, C. H. (Eton), 1829

Jenner, Herbert (Eton) (Capt. in 1827, First Cambridge Capt.), 1827

Jenner, H. L. (Harrow), 1841

Jephson, D. L. A. (Manor House, Clapham), 1890–92

Jessop, G. L. (Cheltenham Grammar) (Capt. in 1899), 1896–99

Johnson, P. R. (Eton), 1901

Johnstone, C. P. (Rugby), 1919-20

Jones, A. O. (Bedford Modern), 1893

Jones, R. S. (Chatham House, Ramsgate), 1879–80

Judd, A. K. (St. Paul's), 1927

Kaye, M. A. C. P. (Harrow), 1938

Keigwin, R. P. (Clifton), 1903–06

Kelland, P. A. (Repton), 1950

Kemp, G. M. (Mill Hill and Shrewsbury), 1885–86, 1888

Kemp-Welch, G. D. (Charterhouse) (Capt. in 1931), 1929–31

Kenny, C. J. M. (Ampleforth), 1952

Khanna, B. C. (Lahore), 1937

Kidd, E. L. (Wellington) (Capt. in 1912), 1910–13
Killick, E. T. (St. Paul's), 1928–30
King, F. (Dulwich), 1934
Knatchbull-Hugessen, C. M. (Eton), 1886
Knightley-Smith, W. (Highgate), 1953

Lacey, F. E. (Sherborne), 1882
Lacy-Scott, D. G. (Marlborough), 1946
Lagden, R. B. (Marlborough), 1912–14
Lancashire, O. P. (Lancing), 1880
Lang, A. H. (Harrow), 1913
Langley, J. D. A. (Stowe), 1938
Latham, P. H. (Malvern) (Capt. in 1894), 1892–94
Lawrence, A. S. (Harrow), 1933
Lewis, L. K. (Taunton), 1953
Lockhart, J. H. B. (Sedbergh), 1909–10
Longfield, T. C. (Aldenham), 1927–28
Longman, G. H. (Eton) (Capt. in 1874–75), 1872–75
Longman, H. K. (Eton), 1901
Longrigg, E. F. (Rugby), 1927–28
Lowe, R. G. H. (Westminster), 1925–27
Lowe, W. W. (Malvern), 1895
Lowry, T. C. (Christ's College, N.Z.) (Capt. in 1924), 1923–24
Lucas, A. P. (Uppingham), 1875–78
Lumsden, V. R. (Munro College, Jamaica), 1953–55
Lyon, M. D. (Rugby), 1921–22
Lyttelton, 4th Lord (Eton), 1838
Lyttelton, Alfred (Eton) (Capt. in 1879), 1876–79
Lyttelton, C. F. (Eton), 1908–09
Lyttelton, C. G. (Lord Cobham) (Eton), 1861–64
Lyttelton, Edward (Eton) (Capt. in 1878), 1875–78
Lyttelton, G. W. S. (Eton), 1866–67

MacBryan, J. C. W. (Exeter), 1920
McCarthy, C. N. (Pietermaritzburg Coll., S.A.), 1952
McDonell, H. C. (Winchester), 1903–05
MacGregor, G. (Uppingham) (Capt. in 1891), 1888–91
Machin, R. S. (Lancing), 1927
Mackinnon, F. A. (Harrow), 1870
MacLeod, K. G. (Fettes), 1908–09
Mainprice, H. (Blundell's), 1906
Mann, E. W. (Harrow) (Capt. in 1905), 1903–05
Mann, F. G. (Eton), 1938–39
Mann, F. T. (Malvern), 1909–11
Mann, J. E. F. (Geelong), 1924
Mansfield, J. W. (Winchester), 1883–84
Marchant, F. (Rugby and Eton) (Capt. in 1887), 1884–87
Marlar, R. G. (Harrow) (Capt. in 1953), 1951–53

Marriott, C. S. (St. Columba's), 1920–21
Marriott, H. H. (Malvern), 1895–98
Marsh, J. F. (Amersham Hall), 1904
Martineau, L. (Uppingham), 1887
Mathews, K. P. A. (Felsted), 1951
May, P. B. H. (Charterhouse), 1950–52
May, P. R. (Private), 1905–06
Melluish, M. E. L. (Rossall), 1954–55
Meyer, R. J. O. (Haileybury), 1924–26
Meyrick-Jones, F. (Marlborough), 1888
Mills, J. M. (Oundle) (Capt. in 1948), 1946–48
Mischler, N. M. (St. Paul's), 1946–47
Mitchell, F. (St. Peter's, York) (Capt. in 1896), 1894–97
Money, W. B. (Harrow) (Capt. in 1870), 1868–71
Moon, L. J. (Westminster), 1899–1900
Morcom, A. F. (Repton), 1905–07
Mordaunt, H. J. (Eton), 1888–89
Morgan, J. T. (Charterhouse) (Capt. in 1930), 1928–30
Morgan, M. N. (Marlborough), 1954
Morris, R. J. (Blundell's), 1949
Morrison, J. S. F. (Charterhouse) (Capt. in 1919), 1912, 1914, 1919
Morton, P. H. (Rossall), 1878–80
Mugliston, F. H. (Rossall), 1907–08
Mulholland, H. G. H. (Eton) (Capt. in 1913), 1911–13

Napier, G. G. (Marlborough), 1904–07
Nason, J. W. W. (University School, Hastings), 1909–10
Naumann, J. H. (Malvern), 1913, 1919
Nelson, R. P. (St. George's, Harpenden), 1936
Norman, C. L. (Eton), 1852–53
Norman, F. H. (Eton) (Capt. in 1860), 1858–60

O'Brien, R. (Wellington), 1955
Olivier, E. (Repton), 1908–09
Orford, L. A. (Uppingham), 1886–87

Page, C. C. (Malvern), 1905–06
Palmer, C. (Uppingham), 1907
Parker, G. W. (Crypt Gloucester) (Capt. in 1935), 1934–35
Parry, D. M. (Merchant Taylors), 1931
Parsons, A. B. D. (Brighton), 1954–55
Partridge, N. E. (Malvern), 1920
Patterson, W. S. (Uppingham) (Capt. in 1877), 1875–77
Pawle, J. H. (Harrow), 1936–37
Payne, A. U. (St. Edmund's, Canterbury), 1925
Payne, M. W. (Wellington) (Capt. in 1907), 1904–07
Payton, W. E. G. (Nottingham High School), 1937
Pelham, A. G. (Eton), 1934

Pelham, F. G. (Eton) (Capt. in 1866–67), 1864–67
Penn, E. F. (Eton), 1899, 1902
Pepper, J. (The Leys), 1946–48
Perkins, H. (Bury St. Edmunds), 1854
Perkins, T. T. N. (Leatherhead), 1893–94
Phillips, E. S. (Marlborough), 1904
Pickering, E. H. (Eton) (Capt. in 1829), 1827, 1829
Pickering, W. P. (Eton), 1840, 1842
Ponsonby, F. G. B. (Lord Bessborough) (Harrow), 1836
Pope, C. G. (Harrow), 1894
Popplewell, O. B. (Charterhouse), 1949–51
Powell, A. G. (Charterhouse), 1934
Prest, E. B. (Eton), 1850
Prest, H. E. W. (Malvern), 1909, 1911
Pretlove, J. F. (Alleyn's), 1954–55
Pryer, B. J. K. (City of London), 1948

Ramsay, R. C. (Harrow), 1882
Ranjitsinhji, K. S. (Rajkumar College, India), 1893
Ratcliffe, A. (Rydal School), 1930–32
Rees-Davies, W. R. (Eton), 1938
Riddell, V. H. (Clifton), 1926
Riley, W. N. (Worcester Grammar School), 1912
Rimell, A. G. J. (Charterhouse), 1949–50
Roberts, F. B. (Rossall), 1903
Robertson, W. P. (Harrow), 1901
Robins, R. W. V. (Highgate), 1926–28
Robinson, J. J. (Appleby), 1894
Rock, C. W. (Launceston Grammar School, Tasmania), 1884–86
Roe, W. N. (Clergy Orphan School, Canterbury), 1883
Rotherham, G. A. (Rugby), 1919
Rought-Rought, D. C. (Private), 1937
Rought-Rought, R. C. (Private), 1930, 1932
Rowe, F. C. C. (Harrow), 1881
Rowell, W. I. (Marlborough), 1891

Savile, A. (Eton), 1840
Savile, G. (Eton and Rossall), 1868
Saville, S. H. (Marlborough) (Capt. in 1914), 1911–14
Seabrook, F. J. (Haileybury) (Capt. in 1928), 1926–28
Seddon, R. (Bridgnorth Grammar School), 1846–47
Shelmerdine, G. O. (Cheltenham), 1922
Sheppard, D. S. (Sherborne) (Capt. in 1952), 1950–52
Sherwell, N. B. (Tonbridge), 1923–25
Shine, E. B. (King Edward VI School, Saffron Walden), 1896–97
Shirley, W. R. (Eton), 1924
Shirreff, A. C. (Dulwich), 1939

Shuttleworth, G. M. (Queen Elizabeth Grammar School), 1946–48
Silk, D. R. W. (Christ's Hospital), (Capt. in 1955), 1953–55
Singh, S. (Khalsa and Punjab U.), 1955
Slack, J. K. E. (U.C.S.), 1954
Smith, C. A. (Charterhouse), 1882–85
Smith, C. S. (William Hulme's G.S.), 1954–55
Smith, D. J. (Stockport G.S.), 1955
Spencer, R. (Harrow), 1881
Spiro, D. G. (Harrow), 1884
Stanning, J. (Rugby), 1900
Steel, A. G. (Marlborough) (Capt. in 1880), 1878–81
Steel, D. Q. (Uppingham), 1876–79
Stevenson, M. H. (Rydal), 1949–52
Stogdon, J. H. (Harrow), 1897–99
Streatfeild, E. C. (Charterhouse), 1890–93
Studd, C. T. (Eton) (Capt. in 1883), 1880–83
Studd, G. B. (Eton) (Capt. in 1882), 1879–82
Studd, J. E. K. (Eton) (Capt. in 1884), 1881–84
Studd, P. M. (Harrow) (Capt. in 1939), 1937–39
Studd, R. A. (Eton), 1895
Subba Row, R. (Whitgift), 1951–53
Suttery, A. M. (Uppingham and Oundle), 1887

Taylor, T. L. (Uppingham) (Capt. in 1900), 1898–1900
Thompson, J. R. (Tonbridge), 1938–39
Thornton, C. I. (Eton) (Capt. in 1872), 1869–72
Tindall, M. (Harrow) (Capt. in 1937), 1935–37
Tomlinson, W. J. V. (Felsted), 1923
Topham, H. G. (Repton), 1883–84
Toppin, C. (Sedbergh), 1885–87
Tordoff, G. G. (Normanton G.S.), 1952
Trapnell, B. M. W. (U.C.S.), 1946
Tufnell, N. C. (Eton), 1909–10
Turnbull, M. J. (Downside) Capt. in 1929), 1926, 1928–29
Turner, J. A. (Uppingham), 1883–86

Urquhart, J. R. (King Edward VI School, Chelmsford), 1948

Valentine, B. H. (Repton), 1929
Vincent, H. G. (Haileybury), 1914

Wait, O. J. (Dulwich), 1949, 1951
Ward, E. E., Rev. (Bury St. Edmunds), 1870–71
Warr, J. J. (Ealing County Grammar School) (Capt. in 1951), 1949–52
Watts, H. E. (Downside), 1947

Webster, J. (Bradford G.S.), 1939
Webster, W. H. (Highgate), 1932
Weigall, G. J. V. (Wellington), 1891–92
Wells, C. M. (Dulwich), 1891–93
Wells, T. U. (King's College, Auckland, N.Z.), 1950
White, A. F. T. (Uppingham), 1936
White, A. H. (Geelong), 1924
Whitfeld, H. (Eton), 1878–81
Wilcox, D. R. (Dulwich) (Capt. in 1933), 1931–33
Wild, J. V. (Taunton), 1938
Willatt. G. L. (Repton) (Capt. in 1947), 1946–47
Wilson, C. E. M. (Uppingham) (Capt. in 1898), 1895–98
Wilson, C. P. (Uppingham and Marlborough), 1880–81
Wilson, E. R. (Rugby) (Capt. in 1902), 1899–02
Wilson, F. B. (Harrow) (Capt. in 1904), 1902–04
Wilson, G. (Harrow), 1919

Winlaw, R. de W. K. (Winchester), 1932–34
Winter, A. H. (Westminster), 1865–67
Winter, C. E. (Uppingham), 1902
Winter, G. E. (Winchester), 1898–99
Wood, G. E. C. (Cheltenham) (Capt. in 1920), 1914, 1919–20
Woodroffe, K. H. C. (Marlborough), 1913–14
Woods, S. M. J. (Brighton) (Capt. in 1890), 1888–91
Wooller, W. (Rydal), 1935–36
Wright, C. C. G. (Tonbridge), 1907–08
Wright, C. W. (Charterhouse), 1882–85
Wright, P. A. (Wellingborough), 1922–24
Wykes, N. G. (Oundle), 1928

Yardley, N. W. D. (St. Peter's, York) (Capt. in 1938), 1935–38
Yardley, W. (Rugby) (Capt. in 1871), 1869–72
Young, R. A. (Repton) (Capt. in 1908), 1905–08

BENEFITS IN 1956

J. C. Laker—Surrey v. Yorkshire at The Oval, June 16, 18, 19.

F. W. Stocks—Notts v. Yorkshire at Trent Bridge, July 7, 9, 10.

W. Watson—Yorkshire v. Surrey at Sheffield, July 21, 23, 24.

K. Grieves—Lancashire v. Northants at Blackpool, August 1, 2, 3.

V. E. Jackson—Leicestershire v. Hampshire at Leicester, August 11, 13, 14.

M. F. Tremlett—Somerset v. Middlesex at Glastonbury, July 7, 9, 10.

TESTIMONIALS: G. O. Dawkes (Derbyshire), C. J. Scott (Gloucestershire), N. H. Rogers (Hampshire), G. E. Tribe (Northamptonshire), James Langridge (Sussex), and Dennis Hendren (Middlesex and Durham), sponsored by Oxford University.

OTHER MATCHES IN 1955

SCOTLAND v. WORCESTERSHIRE

At Glasgow, May 21, 23, 24. Worcestershire won by 197 runs. Fielding errors proved costly for Scotland and a third wicket partnership of 128 between Dews and Broadbent put Worcestershire on top. Dews batted faultlessly in scoring a century but Broadbent, who also reached three figures, was dropped at 42. In addition, Kenyon and Outschoorn, who shared in an opening stand of 90, each gave two chances. The Rev. J. Aitchison, who established a new record for Scottish cricket by reaching 2,173 runs in 65 innings, took the batting honours for his country although no one countered the clever swing bowling of Perks in the second innings.

Worcestershire

D. Kenyon c Cosh b Chisholm	63	— c Brown b Youngson 94
L. Outschoorn c Brown b Nichol	54	— c and b Youngson 56
G. Dews b Youngson	105	— c Brown b Nichol 6
R. G. Broadbent c and b Drummond	106	— not out 5
D. W. Richardson not out	36	— not out 6
M. J. Horton not out	0	
B 5, l-b 9, n-b 4	18	B 5, l-b 1, w 1 7

1/90 2/153 3/281 4/378   (4 wkts., dec.) 382   1/154 2/159 (3 wkts., dec.) 174
3/165

J. P. Whitehead, R. O. Jenkins, H. Yarnold, R. T. D. Perks and J. E. Chadd did not bat.

Scotland

R. H. Chisholm b Horton	26	— c Yarnold b Perks......... 2
J. F. Mendl b Jenkins	59	— c Broadbent b Perks...... 12
J. Aitchison c Dews b Horton	81	— c Yarnold b Perks......... 11
J. D. Matthews c Broadbent b Horton ..	8	— c Dews b Outschoorn...... 5
S. H. Cosh c Jenkins b Horton	31	— c Yarnold b Horton 11
W. Nichol c Outschoorn b Horton	1	— b Perks 8
W. A. Edward c Broadbent b Perks	16	— c Yarnold b Jenkins 6
J. Brown c Yarnold b Perks	6	— b Perks 14
D. W. Drummond b Whitehead	7	— c Dews b Perks 32
J. W. Souness c Broadbent b Jenkins ...	7	— c Dews b Perks 0
G. W. Youngson not out	0	— not out 0
B 6, l-b 5, n-b 3	14	B 1, n-b 1 2

1/73 2/97 3/126 4/166 5/174 6/208   256   1/2 2/19 3/26 4/32 5/46   103
7/227 8/236 9/256   6/57 7/61 8/90 9/90

Scotland Bowling

	O.	M.	R.	W.	O.	M.	R.	W.
Souness	23	3	81	0	 10	1	31	0
Youngson	35	11	81	1	.... 22.2	3	68	2
Edward	30	5	87	0	 7	0	21	0
Nichol	20	2	72	1	 18	2	44	1
Chisholm	6	0	24	1				
Drummond ...	10	3	19	1	 1	0	3	0

Worcestershire Bowling

	O.	M.	R.	W.	O.	M.	R.	W.
Perks	16	7	40	2	.... 14.4	5	32	7
Whitehead	15	2	56	1	 3	1	14	0
Outschoorn ...	2	1	4	0	 4	1	9	1
Horton	27.1	9	52	5	 8	0	22	1
Jenkins	29	6	85	2	 6	2	15	1
Chadd	1	0	5	0	 5	2	9	0

Umpires: G. C. Black and A. Reid.

At Eastbourne, June 9, 10. Cambridge University won by three wickets. Cambridge University 246 for eight wickets, declared (A. B. D. Parsons 82; Major J. H. G. Deighton four for 44) and 163 for seven (S. Singh 61; Lt. T. E. Dickenson four for 74); Colonel L. C. Stevens' XI 78 (D. J. Smith six for 27) and 327 for five wickets, declared (Lt.-Cmd. M. L. Y. Ainsworth 112 not out, J. G. Rogers 81).

D. R. JARDINE'S XI v. OXFORD UNIVERSITY

At Eastbourne, June 29, 30, July 1. Drawn. Oxford's chances of forcing a win were dashed by rain which prevented play on the third day. The University batted attractively in both innings with Smith and Walton setting splendid examples. Jardine's XI failed against the medium paced deliveries of Fellows-Smith, who caused a collapse among the middle batsmen, and they looked to be in an almost impossible position at the close on the second day when they were left to get 354 to win. Then rain came to their rescue.

Oxford University

J. M. Allan c Thoy b Robertson	21	— c Lewis b Robertson	3
M. J. K. Smith c Holmes b Wyatt	64	— run out	36
A. C. Walton c Thackara b Wyatt......	49	— st Lewis b Cowdrey	56
C. C. P. Williams c Robertson b Arenhold	1	— b Arenhold...............	37
G. P. S. Delisle b Arenhold	4	— b Cowdrey	9
I. Gibson b Arenhold	11	— not out	45
J. P. Fellows-Smith c Sommerville b Arenhold	5	— c Arenhold b Cowdrey.....	4
A. P. Walshe c Thackara b Arenhold ..	12	— st Lewis b Robertson	19
D. K. Fasken c Thackara b Arenhold ..	29	— c Robertson b King	8
D. C. P. R. Jowett c Thoy b Arenhold ..	16	— c Holmes b Robertson	6
J. B. Phillips not out	1	— lbw b Robertson	0
L-b 1, n-b 1....................	2	B 5, l-b 3, w 2	10

1/23 2/127 3/129 4/135 5/141 6/156   215   1/7 2/55 3/130 4/142   233
7/156 8/172 9/214.   5/148 6/156 7/207 8/217
                                            9/232

D. R. Jardine's XI

R. E. S. Wyatt lbw b Fellows-Smith	18	E. B. Lewis b Fellows-Smith......	0
R. E. Thoy c Allan b Phillips	6	J. A. Arenhold b Fellows-Smith...	0
M. C. Cowdrey c and b Allan	7	K. King b Fellows-Smith	27
C. M. A. Thackara lbw b Fellows-Smith	8	L. G. Robertson not out	2
R. J. Sommerville b Allan	3	B 2.....................	2
K. Walker b Fellows-Smith	13	1/11 2/22 3/39 4/42 5/42 6/51	95
E. R. T. Holmes b Fellows-Smith .	9	7/51 8/53 9/68	

Jardine's XI Bowling

	O.	M.	R.	W.	O.	M.	R.	W.
Arenhold	27	5	97	7	11	1	26	1
Robertson	6	2	16	1	18	4	44	4
Walker	9	2	43	0	8	1	39	0
King	8	2	26	0	10	0	27	1
Cowdrey	1	0	7	0	12	1	64	3
Wyatt	12	5	24	2	6	2	23	0

Oxford Bowling

	O.	M.	R.	W.
Phillips	8	2	17	1
Fasken	3	1	5	0
Allan	14	4	34	2
Fellows-Smith	11.2	4	26	7
Jowett	2	1	11	0

Umpires: F. C. Quaife and F. Collins.

At Aldershot, July 5, 6. Drawn. The Army 202 (C. Pickett five for 51) and 187 for six wickets, declared (R. A. Gale 82 not out); Club Cricket Conference 259 for six wickets, declared (R. E. Evans 103) and 118 for six wickets.

At Camberley, July 16, 17. Drawn. The Army 202 for seven wickets, declared (T. W. Cartwright 87; S. T. G. Morgan four for 58) and 219 for eight wickets, declared (N. Hill 80); R.M.A. (Sandhurst) 157 (R. A. Gale five for 25) and 153 for six.

At Aldershot, July 21, 22. Drawn. Civil Service 296 for five wickets, declared (R. Fox 137, E. C. Jenkins 63) and 219 for three wickets, declared (L. Singsworth 73 not out); The Army 299 for three wickets, declared (P. E. Richardson 127) and 120 for four.

IRELAND v. SCOTLAND

At Dublin, July 23, 25. Scotland won by an innings and 24 runs, racing to victory with twenty minutes to spare on the second day. Accurate left-arm slow bowling by Allan, the Oxford University and Kent cricketer, brought about the downfall of Ireland after Scotland established a first innings advantage of 119. Scotland were helped by a last wicket stand of 55 between Brown and Kerrigan. Of the Irish batsmen O'Brien alone met Allan confidently.

Ireland

R. O'Brien c Brown b Edward	8	— c Kemsley b Allan	49
S. F. Bergin b Edward	25	— b Edward	5
L. Warke b Drummond	2	— lbw b Allan	16
J. D. Caprani c and b Kerrigan	44	— hit wkt b Allan	1
J. S. Pollock c Brown b Drummond	19	— absent hurt	0
H. Martin c Dudman b Allan	19	— c Allan b Kerrigan	5
A. E. Marks c Cosh b Edward	13	— c Wilson b Allan	0
J. Bowden c and b Edward	1	— c Chisholm b Kerrigan	9
S. S. Huey c Brown b Kerrigan	4	— c Wilson b Allan	6
C. M. J. Kenny run out	1	— not out	0
E. H. Bodell not out	11	— c Dudman b Allan	2
B 2, l-b 3, n-b 1	6	L-b 1, n-b 1	2

1/9 2/16 3/45 4/100 5/104 6/123	153	1/28 2/55 3/57 4/76 5/78	95
7/125 8/134 9/136		6/78 7/85 8/93 9/95	

Scotland

R. H. E. Chisholm b Kenny	3	N. Kemsley c Marks b Kenny	20
R. Wilson c Warke b Bodell	3	J. Brown b Warke	55
J. Aitchison c Warke b Kenny	34	M. Kerrigan not out	18
L. C. Dudman c Marks b Huey	7		
J. M. Allan c Bergin b Bowden	34	B 15, l-b 8, n-b 5	28
S. M. Cosh c Warke b Kenny	39		
W. A. Edward st Marks b Huey	28	1/6 2/6 3/48 4/78 5/129 6/154	272
D. W. Drummond b Kenny	3	7/158 8/188 9/217	

Scotland Bowling

	O.	M.	R.	W.	O.	M.	R.	W.
Drummond	21	9	33	2	3	0	17	0
Allan	16.3	6	41	1	18.1	10	17	6
Edward	29	10	51	4	6	2	14	1
Kerrigan	12	8	17	2	16	4	45	2
Chisholm	3	1	5	0				

Ireland Bowling

	O.	M.	R.	W.
Kenny	39	11	111	5
Huey	26	14	34	2
Bowden	22	5	59	1
Bodell	16	5	40	1
Warke	0.2	0	0	1

Umpires: C. Fox and J. Connerton.

At Stoke-on-Trent, July 27, 28. Minor Counties drew with South Africans. (See SOUTH AFRICANS section.)

SCOTLAND v. DERBYSHIRE

At Edinburgh, August 3, 4, 5. Derbyshire won by eight wickets. Splendid off-spin bowling by Smith and a century by Willatt, a former Scotland captain, helped the county to their easy success. The Scottish batsmen shaped soundly enough in the first innings, particularly Aitchison and Courtenay, who added 110 for the third wicket, but Derbyshire gained a narrow lead of a single, mainly through the efforts of Willatt. He batted four hours forty minutes without giving a chance and hit eleven 4's. Smith followed up his triumph in the later stages of the first innings by taking nine wickets in succession, but was denied all ten by Hamer, who claimed the last wicket. Left to get 104, Derbyshire hit off the runs for the loss of Hamer and Kelly.

Scotland

R. H. E. Chisholm c Dawkes b Carr	33	— c Carr b Smith	31
R. Wilson lbw b Revill	16	— b Smith	29
J. A. Aitchison c Revill b Carr	74	— c Carr b Smith	18
G. W. L. Courtenay c Hall b Smith	69	— c Morgan b Smith	0
L. C. Dudman lbw b Smith	8	— c Carr b Smith	0
S. H. Cosh b Smith	0	— lbw b Smith	10
W. A. Edward c Hall b Smith	45	— c Morgan b Smith	2
J. Brown lbw b Hall	8	— lbw b Smith	3
M. Kerrigan lbw b Smith	11	— c Morgan b Smith	0
G. Miller not out	6	— c Furniss b Hamer	2
R. J. Nichol c Willatt b Carr	1	— not out	8
B 13, l-b 2, n-b 3	18	B 1	1

1/44 2/75 3/185 4/209 5/209 6/217   289   1/45 2/47 3/61 4/61   104
7/233 8/278 9/283   5/67 6/90 7/91 8/91 9/94

Derbyshire

A. Hamer c and b Kerrigan	43	— c Dudman b Kerrigan	16
J. Kelly lbw b Edward	57	— c sub b Edward	20
G. L. Willatt c and b Edward	133	— not out	40
A. C. Revill c Brown b Kerrigan	0	— not out	24
D. B. Carr c Wilson b Kerrigan	5		
H. L. Johnson b Nichol	16		
D. C. Morgan c and b Kerrigan	23		
G. O. Dawkes b Kerrigan	8		
E. Smith c Chisholm b Nichol	0		
D. Hall c Brown b Kerrigan	1		
J. B. Furniss not out	0		
B 1, l-b 3	4	B 4, l-b 1	5

1/58 2/135 3/136 4/156 5/209 6/262   290   1/28 2/57   (2 wkts.) 105
7/270 8/271 9/290

Derbyshire Bowling

	O.	M.	R.	W.		O.	M.	R.	W.
Hall	17	2	47	1	....	3	1	7	0
Furniss	14	5	31	0	....	3..	0	10	0
Revill	7	0	23	1					
Smith	39	12	66	5	....	26	14	46	9
Carr	29.1	7	91	3	....	7	1	21	0
Hamer	4	1	13	0	....	13.2	8	12	1
Morgan						6	3	7	0

Scotland Bowling

	O.	M.	R.	W.		O.	M.	R.	W.
Nichol	24	4	79	2	....	2	0	12	0
Miller	16	1	50	0					
Kerrigan	42.2	9	87	6	....	18	6	39	1
Edward	36	13	59	2	....	19.5	3	49	1
Chisholm	2	0	11	0					

Umpires: J. Boyd and F. Walkinshaw.

At Woolwich, August 11, 12. R.A.F. won by six wickets. Army 254 (P. Marner 72, P. E. Richardson 58; S. E. Leary four for 44) and 176 for two, declared (T. W. Cartwright 82 not out); R.A.F. 191 (S. E. Leary 75, W. B. Stott 60; A. Lightfoot six for 44) and 243 for four (R. Leggett 144 not out).

At Manchester, August 24, 25, 26. Lancashire beat Combined Services by 107 runs. (See LANCASHIRE section.)

At Jesmond, August 29, 30. Yorkshire won by 83 runs. Yorkshire 122 (D. E. V. Padgett 50 not out, K. J. Earl four for 41, L. McGibbon four for 33) and 321 for seven, declared (R. Illingworth 111 not out, F. A. Lowson 74); Northumberland 167 (F. S. Trueman six for 62) and 193 (R. W. Smithson 52, D. B. Close six for 86).

At Sunderland, September 3, 5. Durham lost to South Africans by an innings and 324 runs. (See SOUTH AFRICANS section.)

At Carlisle, September 10. Cumberland and Westmorland drew with South Africans. (See SOUTH AFRICANS section.)

SCARBOROUGH FESTIVAL

At Scarborough, August 31, September 1, 2. Yorkshire drew with M.C.C. (See
  YORKSHIRE section.)

GENTLEMEN v. PLAYERS

At Scarborough, September 3, 5, 6. Players won by two wickets in a thrilling
finish. Set to get 215 in two hours ten minutes the professionals achieved their
task with five minutes to spare, A. V. Bedser, the captain, and Trueman, the ninth
pair, scoring 47 runs in twenty-five minutes.   Edrich dominated the Gentlemen's
innings with a forceful display which brought him two 6's and seventeen 4's in his
133. Graveney, who batted superbly, and Munden took the honours for the Players.
Goonesena again showed admirable control with his leg-breaks, claiming five
wickets in each of the Players' innings.

Gentlemen

R. T. Simpson c Graveney b A. Bedser .	3 —	b Illingworth 33
P. E. Richardson b Munden	46 —	b Shepherd 23
W. J. Edrich c Trueman b A. Bedser	...133 —	c Munden b Wardle 18
W. H. H. Sutcliffe b Wardle	55 —	c A. Bedser b Wardle 2
D. J. Insole c Close b Wardle	3 —	run out 48
T. E. Bailey c Trueman b Illingworth ...	54 —	not out 25
N. W. D. Yardley c Wilson b Trueman..	7 —	c Illingworth b E. Bedser .. 6
G. Goonesena c Wilson b Wardle	13	
J. J. Warr not out...................	6	
W. S. Surridge lbw b Wardle	1	
E. B. Lewis b Illingworth	3	
B 5, l-b 2	7	L-b 3, n-b 1 4

1/5 2/92 3/198 4/212 5/273 6/287   331   1/41 2/65   (6 wkts., dec.) 159
7/315 8/323 9/324   3/75 4/85 5/152 6/159

Players

D. B. Close b Warr	8 —	c Richardson b Bailey 53
T. W. Graveney c Bailey b Goonesena .	96 —	c Lewis b Goonesena 27
J. V. Wilson c Goonesena b Bailey......	31 —	c Lewis b Bailey 13
R. Illingworth c Yardley b Goonesena	1 —	run out 20
E. A. Bedser c Edrich b Goonesena	2 —	st Lewis b Goonesena 12
V. S. Munden b Bailey.................	61 —	b Goonesena 3
J. H. Wardle b Goonesena	20 —	lbw b Goonesena 24
G. O. Dawkes lbw b Bailey	1 —	c sub b Goonesena 3
F. S. Trueman c Surridge b Bailey	7 —	not out 29
A. V. Bedser not out	43 —	not out 19
D. J. Shepherd c Simpson b Goonesena .	1	
L-b 5	5	L-b 9, w 4, n-b 1 14

1/23 2/85 3/88 4/94 5/177 6/201   276   1/71 2/95 3/108   (8 wkts.) 217
7/204 8/216 9/265   4/144 5/150 6/156 7/168
                                                    8/168

Players Bowling

	O.	M.	R.	W.		O.	M.	R.	W.
Trueman	17	1	60	1	....	4	0	13	0
A. Bedser......	16	4	39	2	....	6	1	17	0
Shepherd	14	3	34	0	....	5	1	24	1
Wardle	24	5	81	4	....	13	6	43	2
Close	11	3	48	0					
Munden	12	3	32	1					
Illingworth	10.5	3	30	2	....	10	1	39	1
					E. Bedser	2.5	0	19	1

Gentlemen Bowling

	O.	M.	R.	W.		O.	M.	R.	W.
Warr..........	20	1	83	1	....	8.5	1	53	0
Surridge	7	0	22	0	....	4	0	28	0
Goonesena	24	3	100	5	....	15	1	77	5
Bailey	21	5	66	4	....	9	0	45	2

Umpires: H. G. Baldwin and A. Skelding.

At Scarborough, September 7, 8, 9. T. N. Pearce's XI lost to the South Africans by four wickets. (See SOUTH AFRICANS section.)

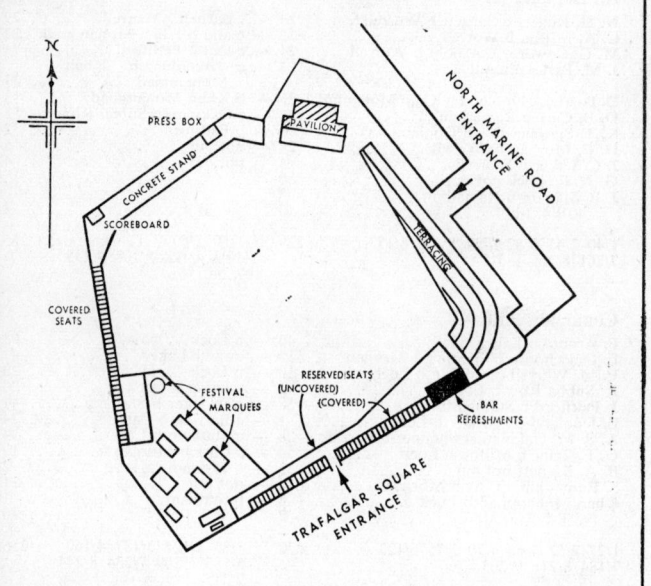

SCARBOROUGH CRICKET GROUND

HASTINGS FESTIVAL

At Hastings, August 31, September 1, 2. An England XI drew with South Africans.
(See SOUTH AFRICANS section.)

AN ENGLAND XI v. THE COMMONWEALTH

At Hastings, September 3, 5, 6. An England XI won by 56 runs. Fine driving, cutting and pulling by Carr enabled them to recover from a moderate start. In two hours ten minutes Carr scored 131 out of 218, hitting one 6 and nineteen 4's without fault. Barrick, Morgan and Lock gave excellent help. The Commonwealth lost half their wickets for 75, but Pettiford scored readily and Tribe hit four 6's and five 4's in forty-eight minutes, so that first innings arrears were no more than 57. Cowdrey, mainly by cuts and drives, hit ten 4's and Carr (one 6, eight 4's) hit 52 at one a minute before declaring and leaving the Commonwealth 313 to get. Arnold (three 6's, six 4's) and Outschoorn began with a stand of 85, but despite more good batting by Pettiford, the remaining wickets fell for 171. In dismissing Worrell, Lock took his 200th wicket of the season.

An England XI

N. H. Rogers c Barnett b Worrell	23	— c Barnett b Worrell	29
C. A. Milton b Worrell	12	— c and b Khan Mohammad	22
M. C. Cowdrey c Arnold b Worrell	24	— c and b Pettiford	71
J. M. Parks run out	24	— c Arnold b Khan Mohammad	23
D. Barrick c Dooland b Khan Mohammad	35	— b Khan Mohammad	13
D. B. Carr b Ramadhin	131	— c Oakman b Subba Row	52
R. T. Spooner lbw b Dooland	6	— b Pettiford	32
D. C. Morgan b Worrell	24	— not out	5
J. C. Laker b Worrell	4	— not out	4
G. A. R. Lock not out	30		
J. B. Statham b Ramadhin	3		
B 4, l-b 9	13	B 4	4

1/40 2/41 3/82 4/99 5/150 6/173   329   1/50 2/60   (7 wkts., dec.) 255
7/261 8/265 9/317   3/95 4/128 5/168 6/235
                                           7/246

Commonwealth XI

P. Arnold b Laker	40	— b Lock	63
L. Outschoorn c Spooner b Morgan	15	— c and b Laker	41
F. M. Worrell c Morgan b Lock	10	— b Lock	20
R. Subba Row b Lock	5	— c Laker b Lock	20
J. Pettiford c Statham b Lock	58	— c Spooner b Statham	41
B. Dooland c Spooner b Lock	1	— c Barrick b Carr	24
A. S. M. Oakman st Spooner b Barrick	28	— c Statham b Carr	4
G. E. Tribe c Milton b Lock	54	— c Carr b Morgan	19
B. A. Barnett not out	35	— b Morgan	2
S. Ramadhin c Carr b Morgan	16	— not out	11
Khan Mohammad b Lock	8	— b Statham	1
L-b 2	2	B 8, l-b 2	10

1/27 2/52 3/66 4/70 5/75 6/123   272   1/85 2/125 3/137 4/160   256
7/184 8/216 9/263   5/185 6/209 7/234 8/244
                                         9/245

Commonwealth Bowling

Worrell	27	5	77	5	....	16	2	60	1
Outschoorn	10	4	20	0				
Ramadhin	14	1	59	2				
Dooland	14	1	68	1				
Khan Moh'd	11	2	64	1	....	18	1	58	3
Tribe	5	0	28	0				
Oakman			4	0				21	0
Pettiford			9	0				61	2
Subba Row			6	0				51	1

An England XI Bowling

Statham	9	1	33	0	....	10.4	1	30	2
Morgan	15	1	46	2	....	9	2	40	2
Lock	17.4	2	49	6	....	20	1	90	3
Laker	11	1	52	1	....	13	0	59	1
Parks	4	1	23	0				
Barrick	9	1	41	1				
Cowdrey	4	0	26	0				
Carr						5	0	27	2

Umpires: F. Chester and A. E. Pothecary.

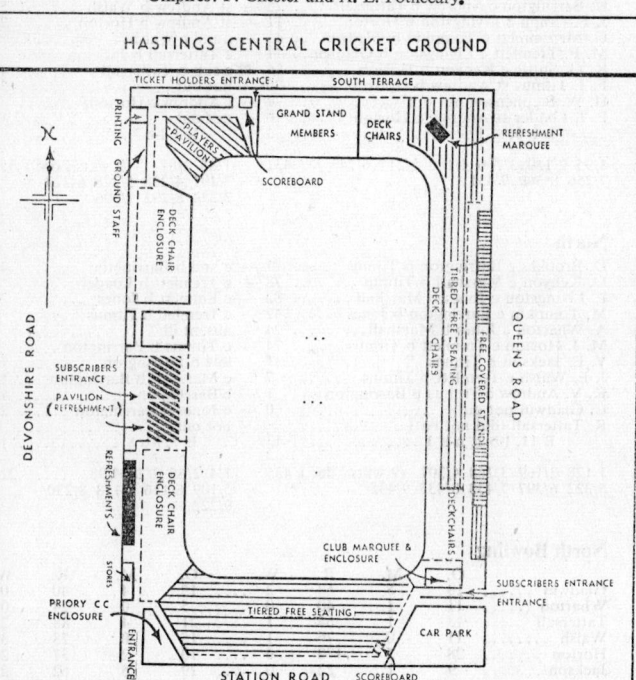

HASTINGS CENTRAL CRICKET GROUND

TORQUAY FESTIVAL

NORTH v. SOUTH

At Torquay, September 3, 5, 6. South won by 109 runs. A batsman's pitch and sunny weather encouraged free scoring, and the players, with Marshall and Livingston in dashing form, gave the crowd fine entertainment. Marshall's 72 came out of 95 in the opening hour. Both Horton and Titmus demonstrated their value as forcing batsmen and skilful off-spin bowlers. North, left to score 332 in two hours fifty minutes, were handicapped by the absence of Wharton, and against some unexpectedly clever leg-spin bowling by Barrington they never looked likely to succeed.

South

J. D. Robertson c Tattersall b Horton	..	54	— c Livingston b Jackson	 52
R. E. Marshall c Livingston b Walsh	...	72	— b Tattersall	34
W. E. Jones c and b Horton	....	32	— c Brookes b Walsh	 71
K. Barrington c Andrew b Tattersall	.....	25	— st Andrew b Walsh	 52
J. F. Crapp c Livingston b Horton	.....	11	— st Andrew b Horton	 21
G. M. Emmett c Tompkin b Gladwin	..	45	— c and b Walsh	 0
M. F. Tremlett c Livingston b Gladwin	.	11	— c Tattersall b Jackson	 1
K. G. Suttle c Kenyon b Horton	....	66	— c sub b Tattersall	 40
F. J. Titmus st Andrew b Horton	......	70	— not out	 37
H. W. Stephenson not out	....	39	— c Andrew b Horton	 2
P. J. Loader st Andrew b Horton	......	0	— not out	 19
L-b 5, w 1	....	6	B 3, l-b 3	 6

1/95 2/159 3/166 4/182 5/217 6/243   431   1/85 2/87   (9 wkts., dec.) 335
7/256 8/369 9/431   3/191 4/228 5/228 6/229
                                                        7/254 8/292 9/306

North

D. Brookes c Barrington b Titmus	.....	77	— c and b Barrington	 49
D. Kenyon c Marshall b Titmus	......	78	— c Tremlett b Loader	 4
L. Livingston c Jones b Marshall	....	82	— c Emmett b Jones	 29
M. Tompkin c Barrington b Jones	......	42	— c Tremlett b Titmus	 1
A. Wharton c Jones b Marshall	....	24	— absent ill	 0
M. J. Horton c Tremlett b Titmus	.....	74	— c Titmus b Barrington	 5
V. E. Jackson b Titmus	....	37	— lbw b Barrington	 13
J. E. Walsh c Tremlett b Titmus	...	7	— c Marshall b Barrington	 59
K. V. Andrew c Titmus b Barrington	...	1	— b Barrington	 19
C. Gladwin not out	....	0	— c Jones b Barrington	 28
R. Tattersall (did not bat)	....		— not out	 0
B 11, l-b 1, n-b 1	....	13	B 7, l-b 8	 15

1/128 2/169 3/268 4/307 (9 wkts., dec.) 435   1/4 2/65 3/78 4/98   222
5/322 6/397 7/433 8/435 9/435   5/109 6/116 7/158 8/220
                                                     9/222

North Bowling

	O.	M.	R.	W.		O.	M.	R.	W.
Gladwin	18	5	53	2	....	15	4	40	0
Wharton	11	1	40	0	....	5	0	24	0
Tattersall	13	1	64	1	....	21	4	88	2
Walsh	11	0	76	1	....	15	0	78	3
Horton	28	5	170	6	....	10	2	37	2
Jackson	9	1	22	0	....	19	5	62	2

South Bowling

	O.	M.	R.	W.		O.	M.	R.	W.
Loader	20	0	86	0	....	5	0	14	1
Marshall	15	0	59	2	....	5	1	10	0
Titmus	27	6	100	5	....	14	2	52	1
Jones	9	0	62	1	...,	10	0	39	1
Tremlett	15	0	73	0					
Barrington	5	0	42	1	....	15.4	0	70	6
Robertson						6	0	22	0

Umpires: W. F. Price and J. S. Buller.

AN ENGLAND XI v. COMMONWEALTH XI

At Torquay, September 7, 8, 9. Commonwealth won by three runs. Again batting and bowling of high standard gave the crowd enjoyment. Marshall and Worrell were brilliant in their powerful stroke-play, and Marshall hit seven 4's and three 6's in 72 of which the last 40 came in ten minutes. Worrell excelled off the back foot. Kenyon and Brookes were other successful batsmen of pleasing style, and Lock and Mankad took the eye for first-rate spin bowling. The England XI, needing 308 runs in three hours, made a bold bid despite the absence through a wrenched knee of Emmett. Titmus played a gallant innings, but, in an exciting finish, he fell off the fifth ball of the last over and Commonwealth snatched the honours.

Commonwealth XI

R. E. Marshall c Kenyon b Tattersall ...	72	—	c and b Lock	47
V. Mankad c Titmus b Lock	37	—	not out	6
L. Livingston lbw b Tattersall	1	—	c Loader b Titmus	56
F. M. Worrell b Titmus	100	—	c Kenyon b Lock	48
C. L. McCool c Titmus b Loader ...	15	—	c Kenyon b Lock	52
B. Dooland c Andrew b Lock	5	—	c Lock b Titmus	19
D. G. Phadkar c Emmett b Lock	63	—	c Loader b Tattersall	16
V. E. Jackson c Andrew b Gladwin	1	—	not out	51
G. E. Tribe c Robertson b Lock	50	—	c sub b Tattersall	2
B. A. Barnett not out	9	—	c Andrew b Gladwin.......	5
S. Ramadhin c Emmett b Lock	5	—	c Tattersall b Gladwin	16
B 1, l-b 2	3	—	B 5, l-b 5	10

1/96 2/102 3/126 4/154 5/159 6/269   361
7/270 8/330 9/349

1/85 2/123   (9 wkts., dec.) 328
3/172 4/226 5/229 6/266
7/280 8/287 9/305

An England XI

D. Brookes st Barnett b Mankad	55	—	c Marshall b Dooland	77
J. D. Robertson lbw b Jackson	7	—	c Dooland b Mankad......	54
D. Kenyon c Worrell b Mankad 117		—	c Barnett b Mankad	1
G. M. Emmett st Barnett b Mankad	36	—	absent hurt	0
M. Tompkin b Ramadhin	68	—	c Livingston b Ramadhin ..	25
F. J. Titmus c Worrell b Mankad	1	—	b McCool	80
G. A. R. Lock st Barnett b Tribe	38	—	c McCool b Dooland	30
C. Gladwin not out	31	—	c Barnett b Ramadhin	14
P. J. Loader st Barnett b Ramadhin....	1	—	c Tribe b Mankad........	1
K. V. Andrew not out	16	—	b McCool	6
R. Tattersall (did not bat)		—	not out	0
B 5, l-b 7	12	—	B 5, l-b 10, w 1	16

1/27 2/123 3/195 4/238   (8 wkts., dec.) 382
5/247 6/314 7/350 8/352

1/93 2/98 3/149 4/152   304
5/188 6/206 7/262 8/289
9/304

An England XI Bowling

	O.	M.	R.	W.		O.	M.	R.	W.
Loader	18	1	73	1	....	5	0	24	0
Gladwin	14	3	45	1	....	15.1	3	64	2
Lock	22.5	2	127	5	....	18	0	113	3
Tattersall	18	5	68	2	....	13	1	68	2
Titmus	12	2	45	1	....	12	1	49	2

Commonwealth XI Bowling

	O.	M.	R.	W.		O.	M.	R.	W.
Phadkar	5	1	10	0	....	6	0	24	0
Worrell	4	0	13	0	....	5	0	35	0
Jackson	11	3	32	1					
Ramadhin	32	6	92	2	....	13	1	43	2
McCool	10	1	22	0	....	13.5	1	59	2
Mankad	19	4	62	4	....	15	1	80	3
Dooland	18	1	74	0	....	15	0	47	2
Tribe	12	1	65	1					

Umpires: W. F. Price and J. S. Buller.

At The Oval, September 10, 12, 13, 14. Champions (Surrey) los to The Rest by two wickets. (See SURREY section.)

At Carlisle. September 16. Cumberland and Westmorland drew with South Africans. (See SOUTH AFRICANS section.)

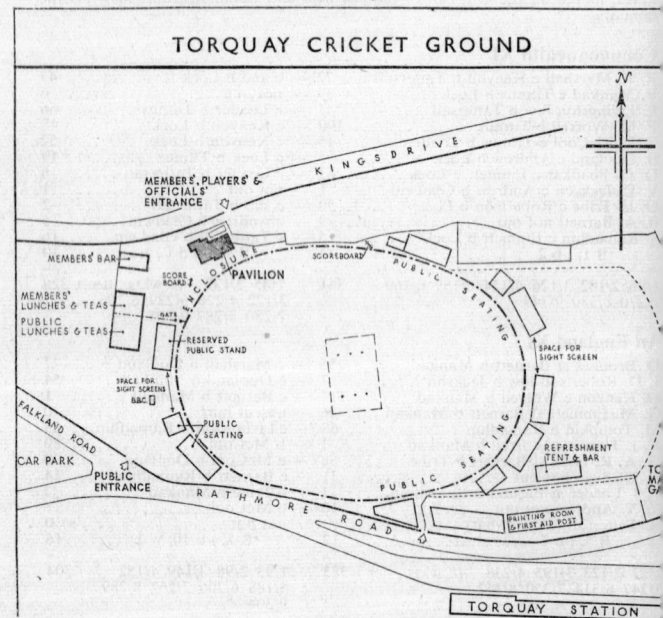

TORQUAY CRICKET GROUND

THE MINOR COUNTIES IN 1955

The second elevens of the major cricket organisations continued to dominate the Minor Counties Competition. They maintained their superiority in 1955 through the splendid efforts of **Surrey**, who won the Championship for the third time in five years and for the second successive season. As can be seen on page 207, second elevens have finished top seven times out of ten since the competition was resumed in 1946. Only Suffolk (1946), Buckinghamshire (1952) and Berkshire (1953) of the genuine Minor Counties have won the title since 1938.

Surrey deserved their success because of their bowling strength. The phenomenal summer conditions and the docility of many pitches taxed the ingenuity of most captains to reach decisions, but V. J. Ransom was helped in his task by a well-balanced attack. Three of the bowlers, E. A. Bedser, who headed the Second-Class averages, H. R. A. Kelleher, now with Northamptonshire, and Ransom, himself, finished among the top six. J. H. Edrich, formerly with Norfolk, proved a useful acquisition to the batting and the side quickly established a reputation of being able to press home the slightest advantage.

Northumberland found this to their cost in the Challenge match at Kennington Oval where the dismissal of G. Walton, their leading batsman, without a run on the board, brought about a second innings collapse. The Challengers enjoyed their most successful season since 1925 thanks to consistent all-round cricket. For the first time in Northumberland's history a player scored a century in each innings of a match, Walton hitting 119 and 102 not out against Cheshire at Newcastle.

Durham finished third, thus maintaining the improvement shown last year. Every opportunity was given to the younger players who proved a great asset to the side which was capably led by D. W. Hardy in his first season as captain. The bowling did not impress as much as in the previous seasons, but this was mainly because R. Aspinall could not open the attack as an injury compelled him to reduce his pace.

On the other hand, pace bowling, allied to sound batting, helped **Somerset Second Eleven** into fourth position in their first venture into the competition. Enthusiasm in the field and a welcome desire to achieve results were other factors which played important parts in the success of this young combination, so expertly handled by E. Hill. A possible weakness was the lack of a recognised leg-break bowler.

Bedfordshire must have given great pleasure to Mr. Frank Crompton in his thirtieth year as honorary secretary, for they enjoyed their best season since 1950. In spite of the absence through injury of R. Davies, the South African fast bowler, and B. Martin, a good opening batsman, the eleven was well balanced. Two youngsters, I. Davison, a bowler from Berkhamsted School, and G. Millman, a wicket-keeper from Bedford Modern School, gave rich promise for the future.

Hertfordshire fell away after an excellent start, but even so they were well satisfied with their performance which was a marked improvement on 1954. R. C. V. L. Marques and T. G. Morley took full advantage of the dry pitches and between them shared nearly half the wickets.

The second elevens of **Kent, Middlesex, Northamptonshire** and **Lancashire** occupied the next four places. All used the competition as a testing ground for young players with satisfactory results. T. A. Crawford, the Kent captain, was able to play in only two games because of a leg injury, but C. Lewis, the county coach, stepped into the breach, proving an admirable deputy. Playing 20 matches, more than any other team in the competition, Lancashire were well pleased with the younger batsmen but the bowling still left much to be desired, though C. Hilton, a young fast bowler from Atherton Colliery, looked extremely promising.

An 18-year-old all-rounder, P. H. Parfitt, headed both batting and bowling averages for **Norfolk,** who experienced mixed success, as did **Warwickshire Second Eleven** and **Yorkshire Second Eleven.** Warwickshire were particularly pleased with the batting ability of D. R. Cook, who hit 149 not out against Northamptonshire Second Eleven. A product of Warwick School, he opened the bowling for the Public Schools at Lord's.

Two cricketers were outstanding for **Devon** in both batting and bowling—D. H. Cole and H. D. Fairclough. Cole scored 106 and 235 not out in the two matches against Dorset; 91 and 83 not out against Berkshire at Newbury and 100, 82 and 92 against Somerset Second Eleven. Not surprisingly Cole headed the Second-Class batting with an average of 89.10 and thus became the first player to win the "Wilfred Rhodes" trophy, which is being presented to the Minor Counties batsman with the best average for the season from a minimum of eight innings.

After an absence of twenty-three years, **Leicestershire Second Eleven** re-entered the competition without achieving much success, and **Cumberland,** another newcomer, ended the summer in bottom place. Cumberland's relative failure was anticipated by the County after the change-over from Saturday afternoon club cricket, but their officials are hopeful of building a reasonable team during the next few years.

MINOR COUNTIES' CHAMPIONSHIP

FINAL RESULTS, 1955

	Played	Won	Lost	Won 1st Inns.	Lost 1st Inns.	No Result	Points	Average
Surrey 2nd XI	14	10	0	1	1	2	108	7.71
Northumberland	12	6	0	4	1	1	75	6.25
Durham	10	5	2	1	1	1	56	5.60
Somerset 2nd XI ...	8	3	0	4	0	1	44	5.50
Bedfordshire	8	3	2	2	0	1	38	4.75
Hertfordshire	10	4	3	2	1	0	47	4.70
Kent 2nd XI	10	4	1	0	4	1	46	4.60
Middlesex 2nd XI ...	10	3	1	4	1	0	45	4.50
Northants 2nd XI ...	12	4	*3	1	4	0	50	4.16
Lancashire 2nd XI ..	20	6	*3	4	6	1	83	4.15
Norfolk	10	3	†4	1	2	0	41	4.10
Buckinghamshire	10	3	4	2	1	0	37	3.70
Staffordshire	10	3	3	1	3	0	36	3.60
Warwickshire 2nd XI	14	3	†5	4	2	0	50	3.57
Yorkshire 2nd XI....	18	4	5	7	1	1	64	3.55
Cambridgeshire	8	2	2	2	2	0	28	3.50
Dorset	12	2	1	5	4	0	39	3.25
Essex 2nd XI	10	2	*6	2	0	0	29	2.90
Oxfordshire	10	1	1	4	4	0	26	2.60
Notts 2nd XI	14	1	1	6	4	2	36	2.57
Cornwall	10	1	1	3	5	0	24	2.40
Suffolk	8	1	*3	1	3	0	19	2.37
Devon	10	1	*3	2	4	0	23	2.30
Berkshire	10	1	2	2	5	0	21	2.10
Derbyshire 2nd XI ..	8	0	1	3	3	1	14	1.75
Leicestershire 2nd XI.	8	0	2	3	2	1	13	1.62
Lincolnshire	8	0	1	1	5	1	10	1.25
Wiltshire	8	0	*6	1	0	1	8	1.00
Cheshire............	8	0	4	1	3	0	6	0.75
Cumberland	8	0	6	0	2	0	2	0.25

    * 1st innings points in one match lost.
    † 1st innings points in two matches lost.

System of Scoring:—

  Ten points for a win in a completed Two-Day Match, and for a lead on the
   first innings in a One-Day Match, provided the match cannot be played
   out.

  Three points to the winner and one to the loser in a Two-Day Match decided
   on the first innings.

  Two points to each County in a Match in which there is no result on the
   first innings.

  When the Match is a tie, the ten points shall be equally divided.

  For a tie on 1st innings in an unfinished Match, two points to each side.

  First innings qualifying points (3) gained shall be retained irrespective of
   final result of a Match provided that a County shall receive not more
   than 10 points in such Match.

  **In the challenge match between Surrey 2nd XI and Northumberland at The
Oval on September 3, 5, 6, Surrey won by 14 runs and became Champion County.**

CHALLENGE MATCH

SURREY II v. NORTHUMBERLAND

At The Oval, September 3, 5, 6. Surrey Second Eleven won by 14 runs. After an exciting struggle they retained the Championship by dismissing Northumberland with five minutes of extra time remaining. Thanks to the efforts of the opening bowlers, Earl and McGibbon, the Challengers established a first innings supremacy, but they threw away this advantage by uncertain catching. Brown, the Beddington amateur and top scorer, profited from five escapes before falling to Watson, who captured eight wickets with his medium-paced bowling. Left to score 123, Northumberland suffered a blow when Walton, their leading batsman, fell without a run scored and, though Smithson offered stubborn resistance, they never recovered from that early disaster.

Surrey II

A. H. Brown c Henderson b Earl	2	— b Watson	59
R. C. E. Pratt b Watson	19	— c Liddell b Earl	1
J. Edrich b Earl	2	— c Walton b Watson	9
A. B. Parsons c Smithson b McGibbon	26	— c Smithson b Watson	0
M. D. Willett lbw b Watson	6	— lbw b Watson	14
R. A. E. Tindall st Henderson b McGibbon	5	— b Earl	0
D. E. Pratt c Henderson b Earl	1	— c Walton b Watson	35
R. Swetman b Earl	0	— c Earl b Watson	28
V. J. Ransom b McGibbon	18	— b Watson	7
H. R. A. Kelleher not out	7	— not out	2
D. Halfyard c Liddell b McGibbon	5	— c and b Watson	0
L-b 5, n-b 1	6	B 7, l-b 3, w 1, n-b 1	12
	97		167

1/6 2/12 3/33 4/40 5/57 6/62 7/62 8/82 9/83

1/17 2/36 3/46 4/78 5/81 6/101 7/146 8/158 9/165

Northumberland

G. Walton c Tindall b D. Pratt	53	— b Halfyard	0
K. G. Davidson c R. Pratt b Halfyard	5	— c Brown b Ransom	30
K. D. Smith c Swetman b Kelleher	1	— c Swetman b Halfyard	5
R. Jowsey b R. Pratt	9	— c Swetman b Kelleher	3
R. W. Smithson b Halfyard	35	— run out	45
L. E. Liddell not out	24	— b Halfyard	1
J. M. Watson c Parsons b Halfyard	0	— c Swetman b Halfyard	7
H. B. Henderson c Swetman b Halfyard	0	— b Ransom	7
K. J. Earl not out	1	— c Parsons b Ransom	6
L. McGibbon (did not bat)		— c Swetman b Halfyard	1
K. Norton (did not bat)		— not out	0
B 8, l-b 2, n-b 4	14	L-b 1, n-b 2	3
	(7 wkts., dec.) 142		108

1/16 2/28 3/54 4/92 5/137 6/139 7/139

1/0 2/10 3/21 4/44 5/45 6/53 7/64 8/79 9/104

Northumberland Bowling

	O.	M.	R.	W.		O.	M.	R.	W.
Earl	21	7	41	4		19	5	50	2
McGibbon	27.3	12	37	4		9	3	26	0
Watson	7	3	13	2		26.3	6	65	8
Norton						8	3	14	0

Surrey II Bowling

	O.	M.	R.	W.	O.	M.	R.	W.
Kelleher	11	2	24	1	6	0	17	1
Halfyard	21	6	46	4	17	2	54	5
R. Pratt	14	4	29	1				
D. Pratt	8	3	21	1				
Ransom	9	6	8	0	11	0	34	3

Umpires: L. D'Arcy and W. E. Brown.

BEDFORDSHIRE

Secretary—FRANK CROMPTON, Shire Hall, Bedford

Matches 8—Won 3, Lost 2, Won on first innings 2, No result 1

		1st Innings	2nd Innings	Result
June 6, 7	Lincolnshire	292	—	No result
Grantham	Bedfordshire	85 for 2		
June 22, 23	Cambridgeshire	226	182* for 3	Won by three
Ely	Bedfordshire	230* for 5	182 for 7	wickets
July 6, 7	Bedfordshire	121	266* for 6	Lost by three
Hertford	Hertfordshire	244	146 for 7	wickets
July 26, 27	Lincolnshire	280	103* for 5	Won on first
Luton	Bedfordshire	281* for 3	89 for 6	innings
August 1, 2	Bedfordshire	333* for 5	108* for 5	Won on first
Bedford School	Cambridgeshire	222	152 for 7	innings
August 3, 4	Bedfordshire	304* for 7	122* for 3	Won by 101
Bedford School	Buckinghamshire	205* for 5	120	runs
August 5, 6	Bedfordshire	136	264* for 6	Won by 68 runs
Bedford School	Hertfordshire	128	204	
August 17, 18	Buckinghamshire	173	142	Lost by 34 runs
Slough	Bedfordshire	87	194	

* Innings declared closed.

Batting Averages

	Innings	Not Outs	Runs	Highest Innings	Average
N. S. Gunn	12	2	543	146	54.30
J. A. R. Oliver†	10	4	295	74	49.16
J. G. Owen	13	3	371	98	37.10
G. Millman	13	0	445	80	34.23
P. D. Watts	7	4	92	53*	30.66
G. L. B. August	14	1	370	116	28.46
S. T. Morris	10	0	249	86	24.90
I. Davison	7	2	93	26	18.60

Also batted: V. Grimshaw 1, 82, 0; P. McEwan 12, 30, 2; A. G. Coomb 7*, 3, 0, 0, 3; M. W. Crouch 4*, 7; D. G. Jenkins 1, 0, 0*; M. L. Kilby 0, 0, 0, 14, 15; R. W. Street 0, 13, 1; V. J. Harris 3, 2*; M. S. Meeson 3, 4.

R. D. Gardiner played but did not bat.

* *Signifies not out.* † Captain.

Bowling Averages

	Overs	Maidens	Runs	Wickets	Average
A. G. Coomb	213.1	52	593	35	16.94
I. Davison	146	29	441	23	19.17
D. G. Jenkins	75	9	220	10	22.00
R. D. Gardiner	157.2	33	429	19	22.57

	Overs	Maidens	Runs	Wickets	Average
J. G. Owen	170	29	542	19	28.52
J. A. R. Oliver	57	9	177	6	29.50

Also bowled: G. Brice 28—6—65—3; H. Hayhurst 13—2—44—2; P. D. Watt 39.4—6—147—3; T. D. Matthews 20.2—2—53—1.

Professionals.—None.

BERKSHIRE

Secretary—H. L. LEWIS, c/o Huntley & Palmers Ltd., Reading

Matches 10—Won 1, Lost 2, Won on first innings 2, Lost on first innings 5

		1st Innings	2nd Innings	Result
July 27, 28	Cornwall	111	226	Won by innings
Camborne	Berkshire	385* for 6	—	and 48 runs
July 29, 30	Berkshire	294	215 for 7	Lost on first
Exeter	Devon	296* for 7	—	innings
August 1, 2	Berkshire	237	183* for 8	Won on first
Reading	Buckinghamshire	226	142 for 8	innings
August 3, 4	Oxfordshire	269	—	Lost by innings
Reading	Berkshire	107	90	and 72 runs
August 5, 6	Buckinghamshire	327	—	Lost on first
High Wycombe	Berkshire	209	278	innings
August 10, 11	Berkshire	229	—	Won on first
Reading	Cornwall	194	—	innings
August 12, 13	Berkshire	123	275	Lost by eight
Newbury	Devon	241* for 8	158 for 2	wickets
August 17, 18	Dorset	312* for 2	149* for 8	Lost on first
Reading	Berkshire	214* for 8	212 for 8	innings
August 22, 23	Dorset	284* for 6	184* for 3	Lost on first
Weymouth	Berkshire	255* for 9	185 for 7	innings
August 26, 27	Oxfordshire	206	212* for 5	Lost on first
Oxford	Berkshire	187	207 for 8	innings

* Innings declared closed.

Batting Averages

	Innings	Not Outs	Runs	Highest Innings	Average
G. R. Langdale	6	0	275	91	45.83
R. M. James	7	0	240	69	34.28
A. A. Hillary	18	0	557	142	30.94
A. C. Walton	11	0	338	134	30.72
J. G. C. Surridge	13	1	343	103	28.58
J. A. Mence†	18	0	501	91	27.83
M. N. Morgan	11	3	178	35	22.25
J. R. Ford	8	4	78	23	19.50
J. R. Tovey	6	0	102	28	17.00
C. E. W. Brooks	13	2	161	36	14.63
D. H. Wagham	8	2	73	35	12.16
T. Ingram	6	3	35	11	11.66
M. A. Salmon...............	6	0	67	30	11.16
D. E. Young	6	0	40	30	6.66
A. J. Sly..................	10	4	34	21*	5.66
A. G. Robinson	6	2	7	5	1.75

Also batted: F. C. Pickett 75*, 53, 1, 0, 2; B. G. Brockenhurst 4, 10, 1, 90; A. T. Davis 0, 31, 51, 0, 20; P. D. R. Smith 11, 1, 28, 50; A. D. Brow 19*, 6, 24, 19; C. M. S. Crombie 1, 13; E. Palmer 9, 4; A. W. Flatman 0*, 0, 12, 0*, 0; J. R. Digby 9, 0.

* *Signifies not out.* † Captain.

Bowling Averages

	Overs	Maidens	Runs	Wickets	Average
M. N. Morgan	182	40	454	21	21.61
C. E. W. Brooks	193.4	29	647	28	23.10
A. G. Robinson	96.5	16	328	13	25.23
A. J. Sly	199.1	57	544	19	28.63
J. R. Ford	127	27	357	8	44.62
A. W. Flatman	94	17	271	6	45.16

Also bowled: F. C. Pickett 67—27—138—5; R. M. James 65.2—9—210—5; G. R. Langdale 29—8—93—2; A. A. Hillary 61—11—187—4; J. R. Digby 12—0—40—0; J. G. C. Surridge 19—2—64—1; A. C. Walton 1—0—6—0; J. A. Mence 2.1—1—10—0; M. A. Salmon 2—0—14—0; D. E. Young 9—0—40—0.

Professionals.—None.

BUCKINGHAMSHIRE

Secretary—C. ANTHONY PRINCE, 10, Ashbourne Road, London, W.5

Matches 10—Won 3, Lost 4, Won on first innings 2, Lost on first innings 1

		1st Innings	2nd Innings	Result
July 27, 28	Buckinghamshire	257	137	Lost by six wickets
Lakenham	Norfolk	307* for 5	88 for 4	
July 29, 30	Buckinghamshire	284	9 for 0	Won by ten wickets
Cowley	Oxfordshire	182	108	
August 1, 2	Berkshire	237	183* for 8	Lost on first innings
Reading	Buckinghamshire	226	142 for 8	
August 3, 4	Bedfordshire	304* for 7	122* for 3	Lost by 101 runs
Bedford School	Buckinghamshire	205* for 5	120	
August 5, 6	Buckinghamshire	327	—	Won on first innings
High Wycombe	Berkshire	209	278	
August 10, 11	Buckinghamshire	200	83	Lost by ten wickets
Bishops Stortford	Hertfordshire	264	20 for 0	
August 12, 13	Buckinghamshire	304	—	Won on first innings
Wing	Oxfordshire	174	212 for 8	
August 15, 16	Buckinghamshire	310* for 6	—	Won by innings and 57 runs
Slough	Hertfordshire	132	121	
August 17, 18	Buckinghamshire	173	142	Won by 35 runs
Aspros, Slough	Bedfordshire	87	194	
August 24, 25	Buckinghamshire	157	233	Lost by six wickets
Chesham	Norfolk	228	163 for 4	

* Innings declared closed.

Batting Averages

	Innings	Not Outs	Runs	Highest Innings	Average
K. Butler	6	0	254	96	42.33
P. L. Stoddart	15	1	505	90	36.07
G. Reynolds†	14	1	414	119	31.84
C. Pickett	13	1	330	80	27.50
J. A. Cockett	13	0	317	74	24.38
D. R. Peppiatt	8	2	114	41*	19.00
R. Plested	5	2	50	24*	16.66
C. G. Hawkins	5	0	81	30	16.20

* *Signifies not out.* † **Captain.**

	Innings	Not Outs	Runs	Highest Innings	Average
H. Taylor	15	1	215	52	15.37
M. Tilbury	15	1	213	37	15.21
B. Lucas	7	0	103	26	14.71
P. Jackson	5	0	68	28	13.60
S. G. Healey	11	2	83	24	9.22
C. W. Smith	13	6	50	16*	7.14
A. J. Hughes	7	2	24	10	4.80

Also batted: B. A. Barnett 146, 8; P. Isherwood 56, 23; D. Rickard 32*, 1; A. Hawes 47, 3; N. V. Butler 26, 0; R. Nickless 10, 5; R. Avery 1, 1.

* Signifies not out.

Bowling Averages

	Overs	Maidens	Runs	Wickets	Average
A. J. Hughes	197	45	375	27	13.88
R. Plested	93	17	128	6	21.33
C. Pickett	450.5	104	854	38	22.47
D. R. Peppiatt	60	10	160	7	22.85
C. W. Smith	460.5	96	1046	44	23.77
G. Reynolds	72.5	14	181	7	25.85
K. Butler	152.3	30	363	11	33.00

Also bowled: N. V. Butler 27.4—3—66—6; P. Isherwood 25—2—96—2; D. Rickard 19—1—57—1; P. R. B. Stoddart 1—0—6—1.

Professionals.—None.

CAMBRIDGESHIRE

Secretary—F. W. WILKINSON, "Charnwood," 43, Cambridge Road, Ely

Matches 8—*Won* 2, *Lost* 2, *Won on first innings* 2, *Lost on first innings* 2

		1st Innings	2nd Innings	Result
May 31, June 1	Lincolnshire	191	230* for 4	Won on first innings
March	Cambridgeshire	196* for 5	152 for 4	
June 15, 16	Cambridgeshire	213	196* for 5	Lost by six wickets
Witham	Essex II	215* for 8	197 for 4	
June 22, 23	Cambridgeshire	226	182* for 3	Lost by three wickets
Ely	Bedfordshire	230* for 5	182 for 7	
July 6, 7	Lincolnshire	92	96	Won by innings and 139 runs
Bourne	Cambridgeshire	327* for 8	—	
July 19, 20	Essex II	146* for 2	169	Won by three wickets
Cambridge	Cambridgeshire	146* for 1	173 for 7	
August 1, 2	Bedfordshire	333* for 5	108* for 5	Lost on first innings
Bedford	Cambridgeshire	222	152 for 7	
August 17, 18	Hertfordshire	178	267 for 6	Won on first innings
Sawston	Cambridgeshire	235* for 9	—	
August 22, 23	Hertfordshire	383* for 8	16* for 1	Lost on first innings
Watford	Cambridgeshire	219	165 for 8	

* Innings declared closed.

Batting Averages

	Innings	Not Outs	Runs	Highest Innings	Average
M. A. Crouch†	12	3	496	141	55.11
R. Gautrey	9	3	259	65	43.16
M. Kassipillai	5	1	151	117	37.75
F. C. M. Alexander	13	2	388	78	35.27
W. B. Morris	13	1	390	91	32.50
R. A. Taylor	6	2	127	54*	31.75
R. Hawes	10	0	284	90	28.40
B. A. Thomas	11	3	178	65*	22.25
C. J. Harrisson	9	0	173	52	19.22
J. Hoyles	4	1	57	29*	19.00
H. A. Godfrey	5	0	47	26	9.40
V. Lumsden	6	0	52	28	8.66

Also batted: L. C. S. Jerman 0*, 0; R. Nunn 0; A. H. South 11*, 1; I. Craig 6; T. R. Morton 7*.

     * Signifies not out.   *† Captain.*

Bowling Averages

	Overs	Maidens	Runs	Wickets	Average
I. Craig	62.3	22	109	7	15.57
H. A. Godfrey	77	18	199	9	22.11
L. C. S. Jerman	163.1	34	399	16	24.93
J. Hoyles	143	28	413	16	25.81
W. B. Morris	209	46	570	22	25.90
G. Thomas	134	12	408	13	31.38
R. A. Taylor	136.4	26	376	11	34.18

Also bowled: A. H. South 20—1—103—3; V. Lumsden 44—2—104—3; T. R. Morton 16—5—42—1; M. Kassipillai 18—1—99—1.

Professional.—W. B. Morris.

CHESHIRE

Secretary—LEWIS WILSON, 50, Oxford Road, Bootle, Liverpool, 20

Matches 8—Lost 4, Won on first innings 1, Lost on first innings 3

		1st Innings	2nd Innings	Result
May 18, 19	Staffordshire	141	124	Won on first innings
Neston	Cheshire	200* for 6	59 for 1	
June 1, 2	Cheshire	195	128	Lost by ten wickets
Oxton	Lancashire II	301* for 9	23 for 0	
June 15, 16	Yorkshire II	245* for 5	—	Lost on first innings
Macclesfield	Cheshire	91	166 for 8	
June 27, 28	Lancashire II	200	133* for 9	Lost on first innings
Old Trafford	Cheshire	166	70 for 4	
July 11, 12	Northumberland	272	189* for 2	Lost by 132 runs
Nantwich	Cheshire	195	134	
July 18, 19	Yorkshire II	385* for 5	0 for 0	Lost on first innings
Bridlington	Cheshire	314	—	
July 20, 21	Cheshire	298	148* for 6	Lost by eight wickets
Jesmond	Northumberland	303* for 8	146 for 2	
August 3, 4	Staffordshire	291* for 5	—	Lost by innings and 60 runs
Porthill Park	Cheshire	135	76	

     * Innings declared closed.

Batting Averages

	Innings	Not Outs	Runs	Highest Innings	Average
F. W. Millett	14	1	386	158*	29.69
B. H. Williams	4	0	116	70	29.00
G. H. Wigglesworth	5	0	136	94	27.20
A. Vickery	7	1	160	57	26.66
B. M. Lowe†	14	1	337	75	25.92
J. R. Cook	7	1	150	43	25.00
B. E. Jones	5	1	97	57	24.25
J. R. L. Davies	7	1	135	45*	22.50
D. J. Smith	7	2	92	40	18.40
C. Cannon.................	6	0	100	37	16.66
K. E. Young	11	0	150	65	13.63
E. L. Hartley	3	0	39	24	13.00
S. G. Shepherd	9	5	47	15*	11.75
W. Bardsley	3	0	33	19	11.00
P. J. Wilkinson	3	2	7	7	7.00
W. G. Allen	4	0	25	22	6.25
E. C. Nicholls	5	1	24	8	6.00
E. Ford	4	0	24	16	6.00

Also batted: A. Gilbert 25*, 13; L. B. P. Adams 31*, 7; A. J. Grindrod 42, 2; W. L. Edgar 16, 12; F. A. Jones 21, 0; M. Yeadon 5, 1*; W. L. Goodwin 9, 2; F. R. Allen 4*, 1; J. Selby 2, 2; R. J. Dignam 2, 1; K. Holding 2, 0; J. A. Hardman 2, 0; H. Simpson 1, 0; A. B. Storer 0.

Signifies not out. † Captain.

Bowling Averages

	Overs	Maidens	Runs	Wickets	Average
E. C. Nicholls	129.3	60	265	14	18.92
K. E. Young	85	16	296	10	29.60
S. G. Shepherd	222	68	651	20	32.55
D. J. Smith	124	29	444	13	34.15

Also bowled: A. J. Grindrod 7—1—25—2; W. L. Edgar 20—4—71—4; M. Yeadon 3—0—18—1; F. R. Allen 44.2—15—92—4; R. J. Dignam 64.2—17—220—7; P. J. Wilkinson 37—9—105—3; A. Vickery 54.4—21—117—3; C. Cannon 16—6—57—1; B. E. Jones 48.2—8—196—2; W. L. Goodwin 7—1—16—0; W. Bardsley 6—3—10—0; A. B. Storer 5—1—10—0; J. R. L. Davies 3.2—1—10—0; F. W. Millett 3—1—13—0.

Professionals.—None.

CORNWALL

Secretary—A. Lugg, "Wendron," 18, Trevean Road, Truro

Matches 10—Won 1, Lost 1, Won on first innings 3, Lost on first innings 5

		1st Innings	2nd Innings	Result
June 10, 11	Cornwall	85	223	Lost on first
Falmouth	Somerset II	126	157 for 7	innings
July 1, 2	Devon	139	271 for 9	Won on first
Liskeard	Cornwall	250	—	innings
July 13, 14	Cornwall	135	273	Won by 50 runs
Torquay	Devon	230	128	
July 27, 28	Cornwall	111	226	Lost by innings
Camborne	Berkshire	385* for 6	—	and 48 runs
July 29, 30	Cornwall	392* for 3	143 for 5	Won on first
Penzance	Dorset	295* for 9	—	innings

* Innings declared closed.

		1st Innings	2nd Innings	Result		
August 3, 4	Somerset II	346	205 for 7	Lost	on	first
Taunton	Cornwall	306	—	innings		
August 5, 6	Cornwall	284	221* for 8	Lost	on	first
Poole	Dorset	287* for 5	133 for 7	innings		
August 8, 9	Oxfordshire	277* for 9	126 for 5	Won	on	first
Oxford	.Cornwall	285	—	innings		
August 10, 11	Berkshire	229	—	Lost	on	first
Reading	Cornwall	194	—	innings		
August 19, 20	Oxfordshire	281* for 9	176 for 6	Lost	on	first
Camborne	Cornwall	248	—	innings		

* Innings declared closed.

Batting Averages

	Innings	Not Outs	Runs	Highest Innings	Average
J. Vincent	10	2	336	122	42.00
R. Harris	11	2	344	106*	38.22
C. Callaway	10	1	321	101*	35.66
J. W. Murphy	14	1	459	175	35.30
R. F. Hosking	11	0	379	73	34.45
A. Opie	3	1	53	24	26.50
W. N. Dorning†	13	1	260	45*	21.66
C. Casley	4	0	86	52	21.50
R. D. I. Charlesworth	10	0	211	71	21.10
H. Watts	8	1	144	42	20.57
R. W. Hosen...............	9	0	182	76	20.22
A. W. Smith	3	0	50	28	16.66
G. J. Dunstan	6	1	70	35*	14.00
M. J. Tobin...............	4	1	33	14	11.00
J. P. O'Brien	3	0	32	16	10.66
T. W. Cory	7	0	57	24	8.14
I. F. M. Hine	3	0	24	21	8.00
O. Trenwith	7	3	28	11*	7.00
O. Gregor	5	2	15	12	5.00
T. B. Bax	9	1	27	13	3.37

Also batted: G. Hocking 21, 17; D. Opie 5.

* *Signifies not out.*   † Captain.

Bowling Averages

	Overs	Maidens	Runs	Wickets	Average
A. W. Smith	74	17	174	14	12.42
O. Trenwith	145.2	38	391	18	21.72
A. Opie	61.4	17	181	8	22.62
G. J. Dunstan	103.4	20	283	12	23.58
J. W. Murphy	124.3	27	351	13	27.00
T. W. Cory	86.4	21	200	7	28.57
H. Watts	124.5	30	408	14	29.14
O. Gregor	86	14	263	9	29.22
C. Callaway	100	25	268	8	33.50
R. W. Hosen...............	190.5	33	610	17	35.88
R. F. Hosking	68	5	296	7	42.28

Also bowled: J. Vincent 4—0—18—1; W. N. Dorning 2—0—29—1; C. Casley 36—6—94—3; D. Opie 2—0—2—0; R. Harris 4—1—13—0.

Professionals.—None.

Z

CUMBERLAND

Secretary—N. WISE, 18, Banklands, Workington

Matches 8—Lost 6, Lost on first innings 2

		1st Innings	2nd Innings	Result
May 25, 26	Yorkshire II	187	—	Lost by innings
Carlisle	Cumberland	76	76	and 35 runs
June 6, 7	Northumberland	403* for 9	6 for 0	Lost on first
Newcastle	Cumberland	260	326* for 9	innings
June 8, 9	Durham	219	—	†Lost by 99 runs
West Hartlepool	Cumberland	120	—	
June 27, 28	Yorkshire II	213	182* for 3	Lost on first
Redcar	Cumberland	160	42 for 2	innings
July 27, 28	Cumberland	94	138	Lost by innings
Carlisle	Northumberland	258	—	and 26 runs
August 3, 4	Cumberland	139	110	Lost by innings
Keswick	Lancashire II	264 for 8*	—	and 15 runs
August 15, 16	Lancashire II	202	6 for 0	Lost by ten
Manchester	Cumberland	92	115	wickets
August 24, 25	Cumberland	70	181	Lost by nine
Whitehaven	Durham	215	37 for 1	wickets

* Innings declared closed.

† Reduced to one day because of rain.

Batting Averages

	Innings	Not Outs	Runs	Highest Innings	Average
W. Lawton	12	0	342	120	28.50
R. S. Ellwood†	10	1	252	68*	28.00
J. M. S. Burrow	9	1	181	57	22.62
R. Shepherd	4	2	42	20	21.00
N. Baxter	3	2	17	14	17.00
D. W. Wardle	3	0	48	28	16.00
J. F. Dennis	12	0	181	67	15.08
A. Clulow	4	0	59	30	14.75
R. Bowman	4	0	54	28	13.50
R. Stewart	6	0	76	38	12.66
R. Talbot	11	1	126	30	12.60
J. H. Millican	13	1	142	50*	11.83
E. Walmsley	4	1	33	27*	11.00
T. Atkinson	8	0	74	20	9.25
E. Fallows	4	3	9	4	9.00
R. K. Arnold	8	0	66	36	8.25
C. Dalzell	9	2	46	13	6.57
R. English	4	0	25	23	6.25
T. Thompson	3	1	12	10*	6.00
N. Emery	6	0	21	6	3.50
P. Sergeant	3	1	4	4	2.00
J. Denvir	6	0	10	7	1.66

Also batted: A. J. Dickinson 6, 5; P. R. Smith 9, 1; I. Forsyth 5, 4; J. C. Johnstone 6, 1; J. F. Raw 4, 0.

* *Signifies not out.*　　　　　　　† Captain.

Bowling Averages

	Overs	Maidens	Runs	Wickets	Average
J. F. Raw	13	1	43	3	14.33
W. Lawton	229.2	79	466	23	20.26
J. H. Millican	91.2	15	274	12	22.83
T. Atkinson	62	15	177	7	25.28
C. Dalzell	76	11	220	8	27.50
R. S. Ellwood	32	2	123	4	30.75
R. Stewart	23	2	93	3	31.00
J. F. Dennis	167.4	18	516	15	34.40

Also bowled: T. Thompson 11—2—32—1; N. Baxter 22—1—78—1; J. M. S. Burrow 1.5—0—2—0; P. Sergeant 9—1—31—2; A. Clulow 11—0—51—2.

Professionals.—J. F. Dennis, W. Lawton.

DEVON

Secretary—H. G. CATH, Kenilworth, Southfield Avenue, Paignton

Matches 10—Won 1, Lost 3, Won on first innings 2, Lost on first innings 4

		1st Innings	2nd Innings	Result
July 1, 2	Devon	139	271 for 9	Lost on first
Liskeard	Cornwall	250	—	innings
July 13, 14	Cornwall	135	273	Lost by 50 runs
Torquay	Devon	230	128	
July 29, 30	Berkshire	294	215 for 7	Won on first
Exeter	Devon	296* for 7	—	innings
August 1, 2	Devon	247	194	Lost by seven
Exeter	Dorset	249* for 4	193 for 3	wickets
August 8, 9	Devon	391* for 5	—	Lost on first
Blandford	Dorset	392 for 5		innings
August 10, 11	Oxfordshire	138	315* for 9	Won on first
Oxford	Devon	208	101 for 5	innings
August 12, 13	Berkshire	123	275	Won by eight
Newbury	Devon	241* for 8	158 for 2	wickets
August 22, 23	Devon	304* for 7	91 for 2	Lost on first
Torquay	Oxfordshire	426* for 7	—	innings
August 24, 25	Somerset II	356* for 7	175* for 6	Lost on first
Sidmouth	Devon	281	23 for 0	innings
September 1, 2	Somerset II	304* for 8	172* for 4	Lost by 24 runs
Taunton	Devon	228	224	

* Innings declared closed.

Batting Averages

	Innings	Not Outs	Runs	Highest Innings	Average
D. H. Cole	12	2	891	235*	89.10
H. D. Fairclough	16	1	600	118	40.00
G. W. Parker†	5	1	117	58	29.25
A. N. S. Burnett	11	3	215	43	26.87
T. J. Wood	9	1	199	51*	24.87
C. T. Reichwald	5	0	123	74	24.60
S. G. Mountford	7	0	166	64	23.71
M. E. C. Comer	7	2	114	48	22.80
P. Atkinson	12	3	204	47	22.66
N. C. F. Bloy	10	1	199	51	22.11

* Signifies not out. † Captain.

	Innings	Not Outs	Runs	Highest Innings	Average
R. D. Healey	9	4	79	33*	15.80
N. H. Humphries	5	0	78	39	15.60
C. E. Wensley	9	0	93	46	10.33
F. R. Bulley	11	3	65	16*	8.12

Also batted: R. Pamplin 0, 0; R. V. Turner 22, 25, 0, 0; J. G. Turner 0, 30; E. D. Forward 0, 6*, 0, 6; R. S. Mitchell 9, 19; D. L. Haines 5, 4*; J. Evans 0; K. C. Kinnersley 55, 28, 0; C. B. R. Fetherstonhaugh 13; H. B. C. Gardner 67, 26, 27, 31; E. R. Crowe 0, 0, 9; G. R. Byfield 8*; A. Brett 0*, 11*; D. J. Rippon 0, 0.

* Signifies not out.

Bowling Averages

	Overs	Maidens	Runs	Wickets	Average
D. H. Cole	196.5	36	549	25	21.96
H. D. Fairclough	210	41	596	24	24.83
R. D. Healey	226.4	30	781	29	26.93
G. W. Parker	100	29	263	9	29.22
F. R. Bulley	125	20	434	12	36.16
P. Atkinson	227	38	716	13	55.07

Also bowled: E. D. Forward 13—0—52—1; D. L. Haines 39.3—21—69—4; K. C. Kinnersley 19—2—68—0; N. H. Humphries 3—0—21—0; H. B. C. Gardner 14—0—50—0; C. T. Reichwald 47—7—170—3; N. C. F. Bloy 30—0—157—2; D. J. Rippon 23—0—73—1.

Professionals.—None.

DERBYSHIRE SECOND ELEVEN

Secretary—W. T. TAYLOR, County Cricket Ground, Nottingham Road, Derby

Matches 8—Lost 1, Won on first innings 3, Lost on first innings 3, No result 1

		1st Innings	2nd Innings	Result
May 30, 31	Warwickshire II	265* for 9	—	Lost on first innings
Derby	Derbyshire II	163	204 for 7	
June 1, 2	Derbyshire II	223	106* for 8	Won on first innings
Ilkeston	Notts II	128* for 4	148 for 7	
June 13, 14	Lancashire II	271* for 6	—	No result
Old Trafford	Derbyshire II	95 for 7		
June 15, 16	Derbyshire II	208	166* for 5	Lost by three wickets
Carrington	Notts II	209* for 9	168 for 7	
July 13, 14	Derbyshire II	312	—	Won on first innings
Derby	Leicestershire II	191	141 for 5	
August 1, 2	Warwickshire II	311* for 5	103* for 4	Lost on first innings
Birmingham	Derbyshire II	192	152 for 8	
August 8, 9	Lancashire II	306* for 7	93* for 7	Lost on first innings
Chesterfield	Derbyshire II	208	82 for 0	
August 22, 23	Derbyshire II	304* for 7	74 for 4	Won on first innings
Leicester	Leicestershire II	266	—	

* Innings declared closed.

Batting Averages

	Innings	Not Outs	Runs	Highest Innings	Average
C. Lee	8	1	394	113	56.28
G. Wyatt	11	2	355	109*	39.44
J. A. Holmes............	5	0	156	52	31.20
H. J. Rhodes.............	6	0	153	57	25.50
K. Mohan	11	1	248	63	24.80
I. Buxton	6	0	128	63	21.33
A. H. Collard†	8	0	162	59	20.25
G. Beet	10	3	137	43*	19.57
R. DeVille	9	3	87	29	14.50
R. Carter	10	1	126	35	14.00
D. Milner	12	1	122	34	11.09

Also batted: J. D. Short 15, 9, 17, 0; A. Eato 14*, 48, 9, 6; D. Hall 0, 2*, 3, 7,* J. B. Furniss 0, 11*, 15; R. Gillard 2, 0, 30; J. Warner 19, 15; B. Vickers 7, 0; D. J. Green 51; H. L. Johnson 19; D. Kerry 2*; L. R. Flint 0; G. Clark 0*.

* *Signifies not out.* † Captain.

Bowling Averages

	Overs	Maidens	Runs	Wickets	Average
K. Mohan	23	8	46	5	9.20
H. J. Rhodes.............	109.2	27	245	14	17.50
D. Hall	131	21	363	17	21.35
A. Eato	52	17	131	6	21.83
R. Carter	103.4	27	305	9	33.88
R. DeVille	126	19	514	14	36.71
J. B. Furniss	69	4	272	6	45.33

Also bowled: G. Beet 47—12—166—3; A. Bonsall 15—4—39—0; I. Buxton 4—0—5—0; G. Clark 26—14—23—3; J. A. Holmes 3—0—21—0; H. L. Johnson 13—2—26—2; D. Kerry 60—9—113—4; C. Lee 13.3—2—47—1; D. Milner 38—7—115—1; J. D. Short 4—2—3—0; B. Vickers 4—0—16—0.

Amateurs.—I. Buxton, A. H. Collard, R. DeVille, R. Gillard, J. A. Holmes, J. D. Short.

DORSET

R. G. RAYMOND, 30, West Street, Wimborne

Matches 12—Won 2, Lost 1, Won on first innings 5, Lost on first innings 4

		1st Innings	2nd Innings	Result
July 29, 30	Cornwall	392* for 3	143 for 5	Lost on first
Penzance	Dorset	295* for 9	—	innings
August 1, 2	Devon	247	194	Won by seven
Exeter	Dorset	249* for 4	193 for 3	wickets
August 5, 6	Cornwall	284	221* for 8	Won on first
Poole	Dorset	287* for 5	133 for 7	innings
August 8, 9	Devon	391* for 5	—	Won on first
Blandford	Dorset	392 for 5		innings
August 10, 11	Dorset	206	156 for 6	Lost on first
Dorchester	Wiltshire	254		innings
August 12, 13	Wiltshire	139	262	Won by five
Chippenham	Dorset	192	211 for 5	wickets
August 15, 16	Oxfordshire	293	152 for 3	Won on first
Banbury	Dorset	380	—	innings

* Innings declared closed.

		1st Innings	2nd Innings	Result
August 17, 18	Dorset	312* for 2	149* for 8	Won on first
Reading	Berkshire	214* for 8	212 for 8	innings
August 19, 20	Dorset	92	157	Lost by ten
Sherborne	Somerset II	244* for 7	8 for 0	wickets
August 22, 23	Dorset	284* for 6	184* for 3	Won on first
Weymouth	Berkshire	255* for 9	185 for 7	innings
August 24, 25	Dorset	299* for 6	174* for 8	Lost on first
Weymouth	Oxfordshire	308	68 for 2	innings
August 26, 27	Somerset II	293* for 3	171* for 6	Lost on first
Glastonbury	Dorset	214* for 8	239 for 6	innings

* Innings declared closed.

Batting Averages

	Innings	Not Outs	Runs	Highest Innings	Average
M. M. Walford	21	0	1025	126	48.80
D. E. Lawes	8	1	307	120	43.85
G. W. L. Courtenay	14	1	506	142*	38.92
D. J. W. Bridge†	18	6	448	106	37.33
G. W. Thompson	19	3	518	94	32.37
G. E. S. Woodhouse	16	0	517	91	32.31
H. W. Joynt	10	3	206	53	29.42
H. G. Hunt	9	1	205	63	25.62
C. F. Deacon	8	1	168	71*	24.00
R. R. Dovey	10	4	85	20*	14.16

Also batted: D. C. P. R. Jowett 4, 6*, 1, 4*, 3*; W. H. Ives 9*; D. R. Foyle 2, 10, 14*; L. A. Stiles 0, 22; J. J. M. Barron 15, 17, 5, 20; A. T. W. Oxford 1*; S. P. Tindall 2, 0*, 0*, 1; J. S. W. Lush 23, 6, 0, 0; D. F. J. Hardwicke 10, 29, 5*; 6*, 20, 26*; C. White 1, 0; P. A. Deane 55*, 10; G. G. L. Hebden 40, 54*; D. W. Foot 15, 13, 40*, 0; M. E. Doggrell 0, 1; M. Hardwicke 7*, 15*.

* *Signifies not out.* † *Captain.*

Bowling Averages

	Overs	Maidens	Runs	Wickets	Average
D. J. W. Bridge	170.1	36	544	22	24.72
D. C. P. R. Jowett	375.2	81	906	35	25.88
R. R. Dovey	555	168	1293	49	26.38
H. W. Joynt	186.2	28	598	15	39.86
M. E. Doggrell	67.1	11	226	5	45.20
P. A. Deane	60.5	17	179	3	59.66
S. P. Tindall	66	4	347	5	69.40

Also bowled: J. J. M. Barron 42—5—159—3; W. H. Ives 25—1—103—1; M. M. Walford 7—1—32—0; L. A. Stiles 14—3—58—0; G. E. S. Woodhouse 2—0—18—1; J. S. W. Lush 23—7—75—4; G. G. L. Hebden 10—1—46—0; H. Hall 4—0—19—0; M. Hardwicke 3—0—15—0.

Professionals.—None.

DURHAM

Secretary—J. ILEY, "Farndale," Fieldhouse Lane, Durham City

Matches 10—Won 5, Lost 2, Won on first innings 1, Lost on first innings 1, No result 1

		1st Innings	2nd Innings	Result
May 30, 31	Durham	230	150	Lost by nine
Jesmond	Northumberland	323* for 8	61 for 1	wickets
June 8, 9	Durham	219	—	Won by 99 runs
West Hartlepool	Cumberland	120	—	
June 22, 23	Durham	198	—	Lost on first
South Shields	Staffordshire	205 for 7	—	innings
July 13, 14	Durham	265	41 for 0	Won by ten
Blackhill	Lancashire II	145	160	wickets
July 18, 19	Durham	334* for 8	—	Won on first
Stafford	Staffordshire	138	308 for 6	innings
July 20, 21	Durham	197	207* for 8	Lost by two
Manchester	Lancashire II	238	167 for 8	wickets
August 1, 2,	Durham	305	—	No result
Sunderland	Northumberland	218 for 4		
August 3, 4	Durham	176	214* for 1	Won by 31 runs
Scarborough	Yorkshire II	143	216	
August 17, 18	Yorkshire II	181	164	Won by two
Bishop Auckland	Durham	263	86 for 8	wickets
August 24, 25	Cumberland	70	181	Won by nine
Whitehaven	Durham	215	31 for 1	wickets

* Innings declared closed.

Batting Averages

	Innings	Not Outs	Runs	Highest Innings	Average
H. D. Bell	16	2	547	101	39.07
K. Williamson	4	0	127	111	31.75
D. W. Hardy†	12	0	380	132	31.66
G. M. Crawford	6	0	174	44	29.00
G. C. Lamb	12	1	316	107	28.72
R. Aspinall	9	1	210	56	26.25
N. W. Owen	7	2	131	30*	26.20
J. G. Keeler	16	1	372	76	24.80
M. E. Scott	13	2	265	50	24.09
J. G. Williamson	12	1	180	81	16.36
J. Brown	3	1	30	26	15.00
K. Longstaff	8	2	82	29*	13.66
J. G. Fox	12	6	79	11	13.16
K. Land	4	0	52	24	13.00
E. T. Waller	4	2	8	3*	4.00

Also batted: R. B. Proud 15, 13; F. Robson 13, 6; J. M. Camburn 6, 5; G. F. Fairley 3; W. Wake 0; T. Birtle 0; G. F. Perks 0.

* *Signifies not out.*   † Captain.

Bowling Averages

	Overs	Maidens	Runs	Wickets	Average
K. Williamson	76	29	158	14	11.28
M. E. Scott	252.3	69	609	36	16.91
R. Aspinall	170.1	57	389	20	19.45
J. G. Williamson	246.1	71	675	32	21.09

	Overs	Maidens	Runs	Wickets	Average
D. W. Hardy	129.1	44	252	11	22.90
J. Brown	99.5	16	309	10	30.90
E. T. Waller	49	4	169	5	33.80
N. W. Owen	123.5	35	288	7	41.14

Also bowled: T. Birtle 11—6—6—1; G. M. Crawford 7—2—19—1; W. Wake 10—2—19—1; H. D. Bell 1.2—0—10—0.

Professionals.—R. Aspinall, H. D. Bell, J. G. Keeler, N. W. Owen.

ESSEX SECOND ELEVEN

Secretary—T. E. BAILEY, 60, London Road, Chelmsford

Matches 10—Won 2, Lost 6, Won on first innings 2

		1st Innings	2nd Innings	Result
June 1, 2	Kent II	143	248* for 8	Won on first innings
Dartford	Essex II	145* for 9	169 for 8	
June 15, 16	Cambridgeshire	213	196* for 5	Won by six wickets
Witham	Essex II	215* for 8	197 for 4	
June 27, 28	Essex II	171	117	Lost by four wickets
Chingford	Surrey II	163	126 for 6	
July 1, 2	Suffolk	147	195	Won by eight wickets
Mistley	Essex II	292* for 9	51 for 2	
July 6, 7	Essex II	200	139	Lost by nine wickets
Enfield	Middlesex II	241	101 for 1	
July 13, 14	Essex II	139	161	Lost by nine wickets
Harlow	Kent II	248	53 for 1	
July 16, 18	Essex II	245	125	Lost by seven wickets
Frinton-on-Sea	Middlesex II	271* for 7	100 for 3	
July 19, 20	Essex II	146* for 2	169	Lost by three wickets
Cambridge	Cambridgeshire	146* for 1	173 for 7	
August 1, 2	Essex II	224	183* for 8	Won on first innings
Felixstowe	Suffolk	138	252 for 6	
August 20, 22	Essex II	163	175	Lost by seven wickets
The Oval	Surrey II	263	80 for 3	

* Innings declared closed.

Batting Averages

	Innings	Not Outs	Runs	Highest Innings	Average
F. Rist	6	0	230	98	38.33
R. Trimby	4	0	134	63	33.50
A. B. Quick†	17	2	460	74	30.66
P. Gunary	13	1	360	102*	30.00
R. E. Evans	4	0	104	37	26.00
G. West	6	0	136	54	22.66
A. Stanyard	17	3	314	57	22.42
R. Ralph	4	0	84	46	21.00
P. Shott	4	0	78	31	19.50
B. Taylor	7	0	118	55	16.85
B. Knight	16	0	256	99	16.00
P. Palmer	5	1	62	32*	15.50
D. Mills	4	0	58	28	14.50
L. Saville	4	0	58	28	14.50
E. Palmer	12	4	111	17	13.87
G. Smith	10	0	129	42	12.90
M. Bear	10	0	128	32	12.80

* *Signifies not out.*   † *Captain.*

	Innings	Not Outs	Runs	Highest Innings	Average
B. Flinders	4	1	31	16*	10.33
D. Bryant	6	0	52	30	8.66
R. Vickers	4	0	30	19	7.50
J. Dray	3	1	8	7	4.00
P. Cousens	13	7	7	4*	1.16

Also batted: J. V. Wright 75, 21*; J. Taylor 13*, 9; B. Spurgeon 8, 5*; G. Horrex 5*, 3; R. Horsfall 11, 1; J. Cadman 2, 0; T. Lester 0, 0; R. Vowels 39; A. Durley 33; A. Pallett 3; I. Garwood 13*; D. Watkins 21*.

* Signifies not out.

Bowling Averages

	Overs	Maidens	Runs	Wickets	Average
I. Garwood	34	16	56	7	8.00
P. Shott	22.5	10	45	5	9.00
R. Ralph	68	19	177	10	17.70
E. Palmer	259.4	58	821	42	19.54
B. Knight	226	50	746	31	24.06
P. Cousens	160.1	41	406	12	33.83
G. Smith	92.3	15	301	7	43.00

Also bowled: D. Bryant 8—1—16—1; D. Mills 21.4—2—85—3; J. Cadman 9—0—35—1; H. Debnam 26—4—111—3; B. Flinders 20—7—54—1; R. Vickers 48—6—173—3; P. Gunary 18—5—61—1; A. B. Quick 24—3—134—1; A. Durley 6—0—20—0; R. Vowels 4—0—19—0; M. Bear 1—0—5—0; F. Rist 0.3—0—4—0.

Professionals.—M. Bear, P. Cousens, R. Horsfall, B. Knight, F. Rist, L. Saville, G. Smith, A. Stanyard, B. Taylor.

HERTFORDSHIRE

Secretary—MAJOR H. G. LAY, High Croft, Springfields, Broxbourne

Matches 10—Won 4, Lost 3, Won on first innings 2, Lost on first innings 1

		1st Innings	2nd Innings	Result
July 6, 7	Bedfordshire	121	266* for 6	Won by three wickets
Hertford	Hertfordshire	244	146 for 7	
August 1, 2	Norfolk	344* for 3	143 for 2	Won on first innings
Norwich	Hertfordshire	345* for 4	—	
August 5, 6	Bedfordshire	136	264* for 6	Lost by 68 runs
Bedford	Hertfordshire	128	204	
August 8, 9	Suffolk	237* for 8	123* for 9	Won by seven wickets
Felixstowe	Hertfordshire	192	171 for 3	
August 10, 11	Buckinghamshire	200	83	Won by ten wickets
Bishops Stortford	Hertfordshire	264	20 for 0	
August 15, 16	Buckinghamshire	310* for 6	—	Lost by innings and 57 runs
Slough	Hertfordshire	132	121	
August 17, 18	Hertfordshire	178	267 for 6	Lost on first innings
Sawston	Cambridgeshire	235	—	
August 22, 23	Hertfordshire	383* for 8	16* for 1	Won on first innings
Watford	Cambridgeshire	219	165 for 8	
August 24, 25	Hertfordshire	263	140	Lost by seven wickets
Letchworth	Suffolk	265* for 6	141 for 3	
August 26, 27	Hertfordshire	163	191	Won by 42 runs
St. Albans	Norfolk	170	142	

* Innings declared closed.

Batting Averages

	Innings	Not Outs	Runs	Highest Innings	Average
D. J. Carnill	15	4	463	105*	42.09
T. W. Tyrwhitt-Drake†	12	0	479	96	39.91
R. Marriott	5	1	147	73	36.75
G. F. Webb................	11	1	365	165	36.50
A. N. Bradbeer............	12	3	267	48	29.66
D. B. Parkin	10	1	255	68	28.33
R. G. Simons	10	0	281	88	28.10
D. V. Cooper	8	1	153	44	21.85
R. C. V. L. Marques	13	3	213	43	21.30
G. A. Harrington	4	1	60	23	20.00
R. N. Smith	4	0	78	41	19.50
A. O'Neill	5	0	97	43	19.40
C. M. Clapham	10	1	143	34	15.88
T. G. Morley	12	1	159	58	14.45
G. M. Ellis	9	0	94	27	10.44
R. C. Hughes	10	1	69	16	7.66
G. Meadowcroft............	7	2	14	13	2.80
R. Vine	8	3	7	2	1.40
C. J. Higby	4	0	4	4	1.00

Also batted: D. J. Atkins 11, 5: A. A. Grimsdell 1, 1.

Signifies not out.　　　　　† *Captain.*

Bowling Averages

	Overs	Maidens	Runs	Wickets	Average
G Meadowcroft..........	103	23	305	15	20.33
R. C. V. L. Marques	194	35	575	27	21.29
R. Vine	131	28	349	16	21.81
T. G. Morley	280	67	778	34	22.88
C. J. Higby	125	26	312	12	26.00
R. C. Hughes	147	25	523	19	27.52

Also bowled: A. N. Bradbeer 2 wickets for 169 runs; D. J. Carnhill 2—104; T. W. Tyrwhitt-Drake 1—134; D. B. Parkin 0—16; D. V. Cooper 0—27; G. F. Webb 1—7.

Professionals—None.

KENT SECOND ELEVEN

Secretary—N. CHRISTOPHERSON, St. Lawrence Ground, Canterbury

Matches 10—*Won* 4, *Lost* 1, *Lost on first innings* 4, *No result* 1

		1st Innings	2nd Innings	Result
May 25, 26	Middlesex II	230	142* for 9	Lost on first
Crouch End	Kent II	137	175 for 8	innings
The Oval	Kent II	175* for 9	—	No result
May 28, 30	Surrey II	172 for 9	—	
June 1, 2	Kent II	143	248* for 8	Lost on first
Dartford	Essex II	145* for 9	169 for 8	innings
June 22, 23	Kent II	177* for 6	189 for 3	Won by seven
Tonbridge	Wiltshire	146	216	wickets
June 29, 30	Kent II	200	221* for 4	Lost on first
Gravesend	Middlesex II	205	177 for 9	innings

* Innings declared closed.

		1st Innings	2nd Innings	Result
July 13, 14	Essex II	139	161	Won by nine wickets
Harlow	Kent II	248	53 for 1	
July 18, 19	Kent II	166	178 for 9	Lost on first innings
Sevenoaks	Norfolk	172	235* for 5	
July 28, 29	Kent II	177	164	Lost by nine wickets
Beckenham	Surrey II	281* for 7	61 for 1	
August 10, 11	Norfolk	265	121	Won by eight wickets
Lakenham	Kent II	210	177 for 2	
August 15, 16	Wiltshire	223	203	Won by 6 runs
Marlborough	Kent II	105	327	

* Innings declared closed.

Batting Averages

	Innings	Not Outs	Runs	Highest Innings	Average
B. E. Disbury	16	1	561	135*	37.40
E. G. Witherden	11	1	368	76	36.80
S. E. Leary	9	2	255	93*	36.42
A. W. Catt	11	3	278	94	34.75
P. Hearn	9	3	202	89	33.66
A. F. Brazier	10	2	255	85*	31.87
P. H. Jones	7	1	144	51	24.00
D. M. Sayer	4	3	24	15*	24.00
D. G. Ufton	7	0	133	58	19.00
A. J. Woodhouse	4	0	76	30	19.00
A. L. Dixon	8	0	145	69	18.12
L. Hellmuth	13	2	196	38	17.81
J. G. Spanswick	8	3	84	39*	16.80
S. Knight	4	2	16	6*	8.00
J. C. T. Page	5	1	23	10	5.75
J. Spalding	6	1	27	24*	5.40
D. Moor	4	0	21	13	5.25
C. Lewis	7	2	20	12*	4.00

Also batted: C. B. Howland 72, 0, 0; G. W. Cook 5, 9, 27; T. A. Crawford† 28, 0, 0; C. Dring 23, 0, 17; J. B. Phillips 2, 2*, 10; R. O'Brien 3, 0, 0; A. H. Phebey 25, 44; G. V. Lukehurst 39, 14; J. M. Broadley 8, 23; A. R. B. Neame 9, 11; J. G. Prodger 6, 5; J. Davey 19; W. L. Bircumshaw 15; B. W. Luckhurst 0; S. Capon 0.

* *Signifies not out.*   † Captain.

Bowling Averages

	Overs	Maidens	Runs	Wickets	Average
C. Lewis	61	19	113	10	11.30
E. G. Witherden	86.1	31	161	11	14.63
J. B. Phillips	50	9	138	9	15.33
J. C. T. Page	73	18	185	12	15.41
A. L. Dixon	97.4	32	242	14	17.28
S. E. Leary	77.2	16	275	15	18.33
S. Knight	106	35	262	14	18.71
D. Sayer	87.5	21	236	12	19.66
J. G. Spanswick	123	34	345	14	24.64
L. Hellmuth	192.3	59	523	21	24.90
A. W. Catt	46.5	7	136	4	34.00
A. F. Brazier	55	14	115	3	38.33
B. E. Disbury	81	21	254	5	50.80

Also bowled: J. Davey 15—1—52—2; G. W. Cook 16—7—38—2; S. Capon 22—5—54—0; J. M. Broadley 7—1—41—0; P. Hearn 14.4—6—22—1; P. H. Jones 2—0—9—0; B. W. Luckhurst 14—7—20—2; J. G. Prodger 2—0—5—1; J. Spalding 6—4—8—0; G. V. Lukehurst 2—1—4—1.

Amateurs.—W. L. Bircumshaw, J. M. Broadley, S. Capon, G. W. Cook T. A. Crawford, J. Davey, C. B. Howland, G. V. Lukehurst, D. Moor, A. R. B Neame, R. O'Brien, J. B. Phillips, D. M. Sayer, A. J. Woodhouse.

LANCASHIRE SECOND ELEVEN

Secretary—C. G. HOWARD, Old Trafford, Manchester, 16

Matches 20—*Won* 6, *Lost* 3, *Won on first innings* 4, *Lost on first innings* 6, *No result* 1

		1st Innings	2nd Innings	Result
May 18, 19	Lancashire II	206* for 7	53* for 5	Lost by six
Coventry	Warwickshire II	141	119 for 4	wickets
May 25, 26	Lancashire II	155	77	Lost by ten
Old Trafford	Surrey II	226* for 8	7 for 0	wickets
May 30, 31	Lancashire II	318* for 8	102	Won on firs
Harrogate	Yorkshire II	252	5 for 1	innings
June 1, 2	Cheshire	195	128	Won by ten
Oxton, Birkenhead	Lancashire II	301* for 9	23 for 0	wickets
June 6, 7	Lancashire II	112	4 for 0	Lost on firs
Rothwell	Northants II	155	—	innings
June 8, 9	Warwickshire II	136	52	Won by nine
Lancaster	Lancashire II	97	93 for 1	wickets
June 13, 14	Lancashire II	271* for 6	—	No result
Old Trafford	Derbyshire II	96 for 6		
June 15, 16	Northants II	144	60	Won by one
Old Trafford	Lancashire II	98	107 for 9	wicket
June 27, 28	Lancashire II	200	133* for 9	Won on firs
Old Trafford	Cheshire	166	70 for 4	innings
June 29, 30	Lancashire II	259* for 7	211 for 2	Lost on firs
Worksop	Notts II	284* for 8		innings
July 6, 7	Lancashire II	227	224* for 6	Lost on firs
Newcastle	Northumberland	250* for 3	130 for 6	innings
July 13, 14	Durham	265	41 for 0	Lost by ten
Blackhill, Consett	Lancashire II	145	160	wickets
July 20, 21	Durham	197	207* for 8	Won by twe
Old Trafford	Lancashire II	238	167 for 8	wickets
July 25, 26	Surrey II	271	175 for 4	Won on firs
Beddington	Lancashire II	274* for 8	—	innings
August 1, 2	Yorkshire II	250	133* for 5	Lost on firs
Old Trafford	Lancashire II	203	54 for 2	innings
August 3, 4	Cumberland	139	110	Won by inning
Keswick	Lancashire II	264* for 8	—	and 15 runs
August 8, 9	Lancashire II	306* for 7	93* for 7	Won on firs
Chesterfield	Derbyshire II	208	82 for 0	innings
August 10, 11	Northumberland	236	174* for 6	Lost on firs
Old Trafford	Lancashire II	234	81 for 5	innings
August 15, 16	Lancashire II	202	6 for 0	Won by ten
Old Trafford	Cumberland	92	115	wickets
August 17, 18	Notts II	228* for 9	133 for 4	Lost on firs
Great Crosby	Lancashire II	184	—	innings

* *Innings declared closed.*

Batting Averages

	Innings	Not Outs	Runs	Highest Innings	Average
R. W. Barber	6	1	224	93	44.80
J. Dyson	8	2	267	127*	44.50
K. B. Standring	11	4	273	62	39.00

* *Signifies not out.*

	Innings	Not Outs	Runs	Highest Innings	Average
W. Place	16	4	412	65	34.33
J. D. Bond	29	4	73	107*	29.40
I. Gibson	10	1	263	86	29.22
S. Smith	25	2	624	115*	27.13
F. W. Moore	8	3	109	59	21.80
D. Johnson	9	2	147	44	21.00
R. Collins	12	1	228	52	20.72
P. Barcroft.............	30	2	568	61	20.28
K. Bowling	22	2	403	58	20.15
G. Pullar	18	0	296	80	16.44
J. Wood	17	4	195	44	15.00
E. Thomas..............	6	4	30	14*	15.00
M. G. Rhodes†	27	1	301	73	11.57
F. D. Parr	9	0	96	27	10.66
A. Wilson	8	0	45	15	5.62
T. Greenhough	16	5	61	20	5.54

Also batted: G. Edrich 111; P. Marner 47*, 15; C. S. Smith 23, 4; R. Tattersall 1, 26; W. Heys 25*, 6, 0; W. Holt 5*, 4, 1; W. Horsfield 5; J. Jordan 7, 2, 0; M. Hilton 1; H. Farrar 0*, 0*, 9*, 2*; G. H. Elson 0*; C. Hilton 2*, 0*; G. Blight 2, 0; F. Goodwin 6, 0, 3*, 10*.

Signifies not out.   † *Captain.*

Bowling Averages

	Overs	Maidens	Runs	Wickets	Average
M. Hilton	55.5	30	62	11	5.63
R. Tattersall	80.5	30	150	16	9.37
C. S. Smith	47	9	146	13	11.23
J. Dyson	115.3	46	262	18	14.55
T. Greenhough	409.1	130	977	62	15.75
H. Farrar...............	86	30	170	10	17.00
F. Moore	280.5	85	633	37	17.10
C. Hilton	46.4	3	159	6	26.50
K. B. Standring	195	64	506	19	26.63
R. Collins	138.5	9	327	12	27.25
F. Goodwin	86.4	11	194	7	27.71
J. Wood	237	87	580	18	32.22
E. Thomas..............	96.1	27	295	9	32.77
I. Gibson	64	9	268	8	33.50

Also bowled: M. G. Rhodes 1—0—1—1; W. Horsfield 30.4—7—75—6; R. W. Barber 15—3—56—3; W. B. Holt 34—11—91—3; D. Johnson 105—13—374—4; S. Smith 1—0—9—0; P. Marner 4—0—22—0; G. H. Elson 4—2—8—0.

Amateurs.—R. W. Barber, G. A. Elson, H. Farrar, I. Gibson, C. Hilton, W. Holt, W. Horsfield, G. Pullar, M. G. Rhodes. C. S. Smith, K. B. Standring.

LEICESTERSHIRE SECOND ELEVEN

Secretary—C. H. PALMER, Spencer Chambers, Market Place, Leicester

Matches 8—Lost 2, Won on first innings 3, Lost on first innings 2, No result 1

		1st Innings	2nd Innings	Result
May 18, 19	Leicestershire II	155	87	Lost by eight wickets
Northampton	Northants II	185* for 9	58 for 2	
June 6, 7	Notts II	317* for 7	—	No result
Leicester	Leicestershire II	52 for 4		

* *Innings declared closed.*

		1st Innings	2nd Innings	Result
June 20, 21	Leicestershire II	204* for 6	115* for 4	Won on firs
Leicester	Northants II	131	101 for 1	innings
July 12, 13	Derbyshire II	312	—	Lost on first
Derby	Leicestershire II	191	141 for 5	innings
July 25, 26	Leicestershire II	147	170* for 5	Lost by two
Leicester	Warwickshire II	169	149 for 8	wickets
August 22, 23	Derbyshire II	304* for 7	74 for 4	Lost on first
Leicester	Leicestershire II	266	—	innings
August 24, 25	Warwickshire II	402* for 7	—	Won on first
Birmingham	Leicestershire II	403 for 6	—	innings
August 29, 30	Notts II	153	271 for 4	Won on first
Nottingham	Leicestershire II	310	—	innings

* Innings declared closed.

Batting Averages

	Innings	Not Outs	Runs	Highest Innings	Average
G. A. Smithson	3	0	233	138	77.66
P. T. Smith	12	1	432	188*	39.27
L. R. Gardner	12	0	418	69	34.83
E. F. Phillips..............	7	2	158	69*	31.60
R. A. Diment†	9	1	237	101*	29.62
P. H. Jaques	7	1	82	51	13.66
B. S. Boshier	3	0	39	22	13.00
F. M. Turner...............	4	1	38	19*	12.66
F. W. Parker...............	9	1	99	46	12.37
J. S. Savage	8	1	59	20	8.42
F. Foulds.................	7	0	42	17	6.00
J. W. R. Smith	3	0	18	14	6.00

Also batted: B. R. Wright 0, 8; T. J. Goodwin 6, 6; M. F. Hickman 24*, 0;
R. A. Day 46*, 2*; B. A. F. Smith 18; O. Vann 64, 1*; G. A. Hickinbottom 0;
R. Smith 11*; R. Julian 9; J. E. Walsh 17, 4; E. Lowe 0; R. L. Pratt 9*, 5*, 16*,
20*, 8, 16*, 3.

* *Signifies not out.* † *Captain.*

Bowling Averages

	Overs	Maidens	Runs	Wickets	Average
R. Smith	41.5	17	77	9	8.55
J. E. Walsh	28	7	74	7	10.57
J. T. Goodwin	69	17	211	9	23.44
J. S. Savage	245	60	727	28	25.96
F. M. Turner	99	22	358	12	29.83
R. L. Pratt	128.3	17	467	11	42.45
B. S. Boshier	121.5	13	450	10	45.00

Also bowled: F. Parker 27—11—61—2; L. R. Gardner 1—0—7—0; E. Lowe
9—1—32—0; R. A. Day 6—3—6—0; R. A. Diment 3—0—29—0.

Amateurs.—R. A. Day, R. A. Diment, G. A. Hickinbottom, P. H. Jaques,
E. Lowe, B. A. F. Smith, J. W. R. Smith, O. Vann.

LINCOLNSHIRE

Secretary—R. J. CHARLTON, Welbourn Hall, Nr. Lincoln

*Matches 8—Lost 1, Won on first innings 1, Lost on first innings 5,
No result 1*

		1st Innings	2nd Innings	Result
May 25, 26	Notts II	295* for 6	—	Lost on first
Grimsby	Lincolnshire	171	180 for 9	innings

* Innings declared closed.

		1st Innings	2nd Innings	Result
May 31, June 1	Lincolnshire	191	230* for 4	Lost on first
March	Cambridgeshire	196* for 5	152 for 4	innings
June 6, 7	Lincolnshire	292	—	No result
Grantham	Bedfordshire	85 for 2	—	
June 29, 30	Lincolnshire	291	40 for 1	Lost on first
Hull	Yorkshire II	357	—	innings
July 6, 7	Lincolnshire	92	96	Lost by innings
Bourne	Cambridgeshire	327* for 8		and 139 runs
July 26, 27	Lincolnshire	280	103* for 5	Lost on first
Luton	Bedfordshire	281* for 3	89 for 6	innings
August 1, 2	Lincolnshire	338* for 9	131* for 4	Won on first
Trent Bridge	Notts II	240* for 8	88 for 0	innings
August 8, 9	Yorkshire II	337		Lost on first
Scunthorpe	Lincolnshire	215	191 for 8	innings

Innings declared closed.

Batting Averages

	Innings	Not Outs	Runs	Highest Innings	Average
D. Taylor	11	1	442	125	44.20
G. A. Marlow	10	3	269	58	38.42
R. Tunstall	10	2	307	83	38.37
J. R. C. Todd	10	1	276	85*	30.66
J. H. Taylor	11	0	331	96	30.09
R. P. Lascelles	6	0	174	48	29.00
N. A. Maddison	4	0	103	55	25.75
D. Merryweather	7	0	140	44	20.00
M. H. Parker	6	0	107	36	17.83
B. C. Ehrenfried†	14	2	204	51	17.00
J. L. Thompson	4	0	49	27	12.25
G. Berry	4	2	20	9*	10.00
J. G. Watson	4	0	38	15	9.50
D. G. Pearce	10	1	57	18	6.33

Also batted: A. Whitworth 26; S. Beckett 23, 2*; N. Chatterton 8, 21*, 4; R. F. J. Godby 12; J. W. H. Travers 1, 21; B. Humpage 10; R. Smith 2, 0, 5; A. Longmate 2, 8; R. Creasey 7, 2; P. H. M. Clark 0, 7, 3; D. Jenkinson 5, 0, 1; B. K. Dexter 0, 0; S. E. Stroud 0, 0; J. Stone 2*, 0, 5*.

Signifies not out.   † Captain.

Bowling Averages

	Overs	Maidens	Runs	Wickets	Average
N. A. Maddison	35	5	107	4	26.75
N. Chatterton	60	21	141	5	28.20
D. G. Pearce	76.3	11	237	6	39.50
P. H. M. Clark	59	7	216	5	43.20
G. A. Marlow	180.2	21	521	12	43.41
J. G. Watson	90	16	318	7	45.42
G. Berry	101	6	339	4	84.75

Also bowled: D. Jenkinson 3—0—15—1; J. Stone 20—5—46—2; R. F. J. Godby 30—5—94—3; B. C. Ehrenfried 8—0—31—1; D. Merryweather 41—7—135—3; A. Whitworth 12—1—51—1; B. Humpage 2—0—11—0; S. E. Stroud 3—0—23—0; R. P. Lascelles 3—0—15—0; R. Tunstall 2—0—15—0; J. H. Taylor 3—0—17—0; J. R. C. Todd 4—0—27—0.

Professionals.—None.

MIDDLESEX SECOND ELEVEN

Secretary—F. G. MANN, Lord's Cricket Ground,
London, N.W.8

*Matches 10—Won 3, Lost 1, Won on first innings 4, Lost on
first innings 1, No result 1*

		1st Innings	2nd Innings	Result
May 11, 12	Middlesex II	131	120	Lost by ten
Winchmore Hill	Northants II	224	29 for 0	wickets
May 25, 26	Middlesex II	230	142* for 9	Won on first
Hornsey	Kent II	137	175 for 8	innings
June 8, 9	Surrey II	—	—	No result
Mitcham	Middlesex II	—	—	
June 29, 30	Kent II	200	221* for 4	Won on firs
Gravesend	Middlesex II	205	177 for 9	innings
July 6, 7	Essex II	200	139	Won by nine
Enfield	Middlesex II	241	101 for 1	wickets
July 16, 18	Essex II	245	125	Won by seven
Frinton-on-Sea	Middlesex II	271* for 7	100 for 3	wickets
July 27, 28	Middlesex II	297	158* for 9	Won by 93 runs
Brackley	Northants II	181	181	
August 5, 6	Middlesex II	254	144* for 4	Won on first
Felixstowe	Suffolk	155* for 9	116 for 4	innings
August 13, 15	Middlesex II	172	78 for 4	Lost on first
Lord's	Surrey II	190	—	innings
August 22, 23	Middlesex II	119	258* for 6	Won on first
Finchley	Suffolk	105	153 for 5	innings

* Innings declared closed.

Batting Averages

	Innings	Not Outs	Runs	Highest Innings	Average
J. L. Swann	5	0	205	81	41.00
J. T. Murray	6	0	234	74	39.00
D. L. Newman†	15	5	379	99*	37.90
A. Thompson	12	1	327	69	29.72
D. A. Bick	16	3	372	128*	28.61
D. O. Baldry	8	1	194	43	27.71
H. J. Felton	4	0	104	43	26.00
A. J. Drew	5	1	101	59*	25.25
H. W. Tilly	14	2	234	66	19.50
H. P. Sharp	10	0	194	49	19.40
A. Biggs	6	1	94	54*	18.80
T. Angus	8	6	30	16	15.00
R. J. Hurst	11	2	132	21*	14.66
W. E. Russell	8	0	104	31	13.00
D. Widows	5	0	63	24	12.60
M. D. Scott	5	0	46	40	9.20
R. V. Bell	4	0	22	16	5.50
B. C. Hall	5	0	13	9	2.60

Also batted G. Nolan 12, 1, 21; G. C. J. Winchester 0, 0*, 2; S. M. Brown
27, 17; K. Day 0, 0; S. J. Ilsley 1, 2; A. Lowe 3*, 0*; M. P. Murray 62, 14; D.
Nute 15, 1; J. A. Young 0, 7.

* *Signifies not out.* 　　　　　† Captain.

Bowling Averages

	Overs	Maidens	Runs	Wickets	Average
H. W. Tilly	266.4	73	661	43	15.37
R. J. Hurst	227.3	70	609	39	15.61
A. Biggs	69	22	141	8	17.62
T. Angus	144.4	23	455	20	22.75
R. V. Bell	43	14	105	4	26.25
D. A. Bick	91.1	16	328	9	36.44
J. L. Swann	23	4	79	2	39.50
B. C. Hall	27	5	92	2	46.00

Also bowled: D. O. Baldry 7—0—16—0; W. E. Russell 14—4—41—1; H. P. Sharp 7—2—14—0; J. A. Young 22—10—31—3; S. J. Ilsley 5—0—21—1; D. L. Newman 2—0—2—0.

Amateurs.—A. J. Drew, H. J. Felton, M. P. Murray, D. L. Newman, G. Nolan, D. Nute, M. D. Scott, J. L. Swann, G. C. J. Winchester.

NORFOLK

Secretary—G. A. STEVENS, 37, St. Peter's Street, Norwich

Matches 10—*Won* 3, *Lost* 4, *Won on first innings* 1, *Lost on first innings* 2

		1st Innings	2nd Innings	Result
July 18, 19	Norfolk	172	235* for 5	Won on first
Sevenoaks	Kent II	166	178 for 9	innings
July 20, 21	Norfolk	132	218	Lost by eight
The Oval	Surrey II	193* for 7	158 for 2	wickets
July 27, 28	Buckinghamshire	257	137	Won by six
Lakenham	Norfolk	307* for 5	88 for 4	wickets
August 1, 2	Norfolk	344* for 3	143 for 2	Lost on first
Lakenham	Hertfordshire	345* for 4	—	innings
August 3, 4	Norfolk	316* for 5	176* for 7	Won by 65 runs
Lakenham	Suffolk	245* for 2	182	
August 5, 6	Norfolk	203	235* for 8	Lost by four
Lakenham	Surrey II	238* for 3	201 for 6	wickets
August 10, 11	Norfolk	265	121	Lost by eight
Lakenham	Kent II	210	177 for 2	wickets
August 12, 13	Norfolk	256* for 7	—	Lost on first
Lowestoft	Suffolk	257* for 5	—	innings
August 24, 25	Buckinghamshire	157	233	Won by six
Chesham	Norfolk	228	163 for 4	wickets
August 26, 27	Hertfordshire	163	191	Lost by 42 runs
St. Albans	Norfolk	170* for 8	142	

* *Innings declared closed.*

Batting Averages

	Innings	Not Outs	Runs	Highest Innings	Average
P. H. Parfitt	10	3	401	131	57.28
N. H. Moore	11	3	431	103*	53.87
J. C. Bate	11	0	401	86	36.45
R. H. G. Hoff	7	1	215	118	35.83
W. O. Thomas	16	0	560	105	35.00
M. E. Thorne	8	2	181	65	30.16
P. G. Powell†	18	0	496	83	27.55
C. S. R. Boswell	15	3	329	94	27.41
A. J. Corran	6	1	127	52*	25.40
D. D. Carter	4	0	99	63	24.75
J. Reynolds	7	0	98	30	14.00

* *Signifies not out.*　　　　　† *Captain.*

	Innings	Not Outs	Runs	Highest Innings	Average
N. J. Tilney	6	1	66	26*	13.20
J. H. Parfitt	4	1	37	27*	12.33
P. G. Walmsley	8	5	27	13*	9.00
C. B. Grant	12	3	74	29	8.22
B. G. Stevens	12	1	81	21*	7.36
M. A. Gorrod	4	2	14	12	7.00

Also batted: W. L. Drinkwater 7, 10*; D. C. Thorne 3, 0, 2*; D. Drake 0; R. Schofield played in one match and did not bat.

* Signifies not out.

Bowling Averages

	Overs	Maidens	Runs	Wickets	Average
P. H. Parfitt	61.5	13	175	10	17.50
P. G. Walmsley	297.1	83	848	38	22.31
C. S. R. Boswell	296.1	76	820	31	26.45
N. J. Tilney	102	26	266	10	26.60
M. A. Gorrod	55	7	213	7	30.42
D. C. Thorne	101.1	27	281	9	31.22
N. H. Moore	57	12	222	7	31.71
C. B. Grant	131.3	23	429	11	39.00
A. J. Corran	39	10	110	2	55.00

Also bowled: W. L. Drinkwater 7—0—19—0; P. G. Powell 2—0—12—0; J. Reynolds 2—1—6—0; R. Schofield 23—2—112—0; W. O. Thomas 4—1—10—0.

Professionals.—C. S. R. Boswell, J. Reynolds.

NORTHAMPTONSHIRE SECOND ELEVEN

Secretary—Lt.-Col. A. St. G. Coldwell, County Ground, Northampton

Matches 12—Won 4, Lost 3, Won on first innings 1, Lost on first innings 4

		1st Innings	2nd Innings	Result
May 11, 12	Middlesex II	131	120	Won by ten
Winchmore Hill	Northants II	224	29 for 0	wickets
May 18, 19	Leicestershire II	155	87	Won by eight
Northampton	Northants II	185* for 9	58 for 2	wickets
June 1, 2	Yorkshire II	313	73 for 7	Lost by three
Saltaire	Northants II	158	227	wickets
June 6, 7	Lancashire II	112	4 for 0	Won on first
Rothwell	Northants II	155	—	innings
June 15, 16	Northants II	144	60	Lost by one
Old Trafford	Lancashire II	98	107 for 9	wicket
June 20, 21	Leicestershire II	204* for 6	115* for 4	Lost on first
Leicester	Northants II	131	101 for 1	innings
July 11, 12	Northants II	161	255 for 5	Lost on first
Northampton	Notts II	304* for 7	—	innings
July 18, 19	Warwickshire II	348* for 6	185* for 6	Won by six
Northampton	Northants II	277* for 7	257 for 4	wickets
July 25, 26	Northants II	195	291 for 8	Lost on first
Newark	Notts II	286	—	innings
July 27, 28	Middlesex II	297	158* for 9	Lost by 93 runs
Brackley	Northants II	181	181	
August 15, 16	Northants II	293* for 9	224* for 1	Won by 126
Northampton	Yorkshire II	217* for 7	174	runs
August 17, 18	Warwick II	234	62	Lost on first
Rugby	Northants II	180	91 for 3	innings

* Innings declared closed.

Batting Averages

	Innings	Not Outs	Runs	Highest Innings	Average
P. Pickering	6	3	215	116*	71.66
B. Reynolds	11	4	345	102*	49.28
P. Davis	17	6	388	62	35.27
M. Tate	7	3	136	54*	34.00
M. Norman	10	0	315	67	31.50
E. Davis	16	1	451	112	30.06
D. Greasley	15	2	357	101*	27.46
S. Leadbetter	17	1	425	68	26.56
R. Hogan	19	1	441	75	24.50
M. Allen	14	2	289	71*	24.08
S. Starkie	8	0	127	30	15.87
J. Dale	6	2	38	28	9.50
J. Wild	7	0	57	20	8.14
A. L. Wells†	9	1	59	21*	7.37
M. White	14	4	34	16	3.40

Also batted: R, Subba Row 47, 29; R. W. Clarke 9; A. Lightfoot 2, 40, 7; L. Rowe 16, 5; W. Aylen 3; T. Freeman 5, 2; J. Care 3*, 0; A. Liddell 14.

Signifies not out.   † Captain.

Bowling Averages

	Overs	Maidens	Runs	Wickets	Average
A. Lightfoot	26.5	5	74	8	9.25
M. Tate	35	12	84	7	12.00
A. L. Wells	138.1	42	320	23	13.91
J. Dale	86	19	236	16	14.75
D. Greasley	89.5	31	216	12	18.00
S. Starkie	150.3	37	449	23	19.52
M. Allen	147.5	37	376	18	20.88
J. Wild	122.4	31	279	12	23.25
R. Hogan	244	51	794	32	24.81
M. White	92.4	25	249	10	24.90

Also bowled: M. Warrington 9—2—31—1; T. Freeman 16—4—62—2; R. W. Clarke 16.4—4—41—1; J. Care 30—5—122—5; R. Subba Row 1—0—17—0; G. Harris 13—1—54—0.

Amateurs.—W. Aylen, J. Care, T. Freeman, G. Harris, A. Liddell, P. Pickering, R. Subba Row, L. Rowe, A. L. Wells, M. Warrington, J. Wild.

Correction: In 1955 averages, initials of Arkell should be R. H. M. and not H. J. D.

NORTHUMBERLAND

Secretary—G. H. MALLEN, 94, St. George's Terrace,
Newcastle upon Tyne, 2

Matches 13—Won 6, Lost 1, Won on first innings 4, Lost on first innings 1, No result 1

		1st Innings	2nd Innings	Result
May 30, 31	Durham	230	150	Won by nine
Newcastle	Northumberland	323* for 8	61 for 1	wickets
June 6, 7	Northumberland	403* for 9	6 for 0	Won on first
Newcastle	Cumberland	260	326* for 9	innings
June 20, 21	Staffordshire	221	—	†Won by seven
Newcastle	Northumberland	222 for 3	—	wickets
June 22, 23	Yorkshire II	100	209	Won by five
Newcastle	Northumberland	254* for 9	59 for 5	wickets

* Innings declared closed.   † Reduced to one day because of rain.

		1st Innings	2nd Innings	Result
July 6, 7	Lancashire II	227	224* for 6	Won on first
Newcastle	Northumberland	250* for 3	130 for 6	innings
July 11, 12	Northumberland	272	189* for 2	Won by 132
Nantwich	Cheshire	195	134	runs
July 13, 14	Yorkshire II	399* for 8	—	Lost on first
Middlesbrough	Northumberland	364		innings
July 20, 21	Cheshire	298	148* for 6	Won by eight
Newcastle	Northumberland	303* for 8	146 for 2	wickets
July 27, 28	Cumberland	94	138	Won by innings
Carlisle	Northumberland	258	—	and 26 runs
August 1, 2	Durham	305	—	No result
Sunderland	Northumberland	218 for 4	—	
August 8, 9	Staffordshire	104	5 for 0	Won on first
Uttoxeter	Northumberland	181* for 7		innings
August 10, 11	Northumberland	236	174* for 6	Won on first
Old Trafford	Lancashire II	234	81 for 5	innings
Challenge Match				
September 3, 5, 6	Surrey II	97	167	Lost by 14 runs
The Oval	Northumberland	142* for 7	108	

* Innings declared closed.

Batting Averages

	Innings	Not Outs	Runs	Highest Innings	Average
P. Shaw	5	1	240	156	60.00
R. W. Smithson	11	2	460	86	51.11
G. Walton	13	1	583	119	48.58
K. D. Smith	13	2	513	115	46.63
R. Jowsey	16	2	605	86	43.21
K. G. Davidson	13	1	468	126	39.00
L. E. Liddell†	14	3	283	48	25.72
R. G. Clough	7	1	143	52	23.83
J. Oakes	13	2	225	66	20.45
J. M. Watson	11	2	171	75	19.00
K. J. Earl	5	2	41	19	13.66
H. B. Henderson	10	1	105	22	11.66
L. McGibbon	3	1	20	19	10.00
M. McKendrick	9	2	31	14	4.42
C. Pearson	4	1	13	12	4.33
K. Norton	6	6	4	3*	—

Also batted: C. L. Routledge 118, 1*; P. Forster 15, 6; N. G. Loraine 1, 1; A. Bartle 9; D. Hall 7; J. T. Hounsome 10*; D. Rutherford 12*.

Signifies not out. † Captain.

Bowling Averages

	Overs	Maidens	Runs	Wickets	Average
L. McGibbon	174.5	53	412	26	15.84
K. Norton	136	50	306	18	17.00
K. J. Earl	277.5	66	700	39	17.94
M. McKendrick	240.3	60	633	31	20.41
J. T. Hounsome	26	7	62	3	20.66
J. M. Watson	300.4	71	851	41	20.75
K. D. Smith	29.4	10	97	4	24.25
P. Forster	47	11	148	6	24.66
N. G. Loraine	68	17	175	7	25.00
D. Hall	41.1	16	136	5	27.20
J. Oakes	189	42	587	16	36.68

Professional.—J. Oakes.

NOTTINGHAMSHIRE SECOND ELEVEN

Secretary—H. A. BROWN, County Ground, Trent Bridge, Nottingham

Matches 14—Won 1, Lost 1, Won on first innings 6, Lost on first innings 4, No result 2

		1st Innings	2nd innings	Result
May 16, 17	Notts II	183	—	No result
Barnsley	Yorkshire II	58 for 6	—	
May 25, 26	Lincolnshire	171	180 for 9	Won on first
Grimsby	Notts II	295* for 6	—	innings
June 1, 2	Derbyshire II	223	106* for 8	Lost on first
Ilkeston	Notts II	128* for 4	148 for 7	innings
June 6, 7	Notts II	317* for 7	—	No result
Leicester	Leicestershire II	52 for 4	—	
June 15, 16	Derbyshire II	208	166* for 5	Won by three
Nottingham	Notts II	209* for 9	168 for 7	wickets
(Police Ground)				
June 22, 23	Notts II	130	217	Lost on first
Trent Bridge	Warwickshire II	178	143 for 6	innings
June 29, 30	Lancashire II	259* for 7	211 for 2	Won on first
Worksop	Notts II	284* for 8	—	innings
July 6, 7	Yorkshire II	198	180* for 1	Lost by seven
Shireoaks	Notts II	114	257	runs
July 11, 12	Northants II	161	255* for 4	Won on first
Northampton	Notts II	304* for 7	—	innings
July 25, 26	Northants II	195	291* for 7	Won on first
Newark	Notts II	286	—	innings
August 1, 2	Lincolnshire	338	131* for 4	Lost on first
Trent Bridge	Notts II	240	88 for 0	innings
August 10, 11	Notts II	275	224* for 7	Won on first
Nuneaton	Warwickshire II	160	—	innings
August 17, 18	Notts II	228	133 for 5	Won on first
Great Crosby	Lancashire II	184	—	innings
August 29, 30	Notts II	153	271 for 4	Lost on first
Nottingham	Leicestershire II	310	—	innings
(Police Ground)				

* Innings declared closed.

Batting Averages

	Innings	Not Outs	Runs	Highest Innings	Average
E. J. Martin	4	1	259	138*	86.33
K. Poole	9	1	292	101	36.50
R. C. Vowles	18	4	509	145*	36.35
P. F. Harvey	6	1	174	78	34.80
M. Winfield	21	2	609	82	32.05
R. Giles	4	0	116	55	29.00
N. F. Hill	6	0	174	71	29.00
A. P. Potter	9	1	210	78	26.25
H. R. Cox†	5	2	77	34*	25.66
M. Wood	9	4	115	50*	23.00
J. B. Riley	13	3	222	42*	22.20
J. Kelly	13	2	240	77*	21.81
J. D. Springall	18	2	292	70*	18.25
M. J. Hall	15	0	270	46	18.00

* *Signifies not out.* † Captain.

	Innings	Not Outs	Runs	Highest Innings	Average
A. Cleveley	7	2	71	38*	14.20
B. Notley	8	3	63	29*	12.60

Also batted: K. Brealey 3; J. Rutherford 11, 7; J. S. Hodgkins 23, 15; P. Blatherwick 0, 4; P. Forman 2, 4, 6*; M. Palfreyman 1, 1; F. W. Stocks 0, 114, 124; A. J. Underwood 26, 22; A. Crookes 0, 2*, 0; C. J. Poole 66; J. Hardstaff 23; P. Cullen 20; J. H. Newsome 0; G. Yates 45, 24.

Signifies not out.

Bowling Averages

	Overs	Maidens	Runs	Wickets	Average
P. Forman	83	26	197	15	13.13
P. F. Harvey	127	43	308	17	18.11
H. R. Cox	57	29	88	5	17.60
B. Notley	91	22	235	12	19.58
K. Jackson	22	2	80	4	20.00
A. P. Potter..............	189.3	49	559	27	20.70
J. Kelly	253	99	506	24	21.08
A. Cleveley	153	30	422	18	23.44
F. W. Stocks	47	14	123	5	24.60
R. C. Vowles	125	27	373	14	26.64
M. Wood...............	205	36	596	19	31.36

Also bowled: K. Poole 62—7—210—3; J. Rutherford 40—7—103—4; N. F. Hill 7—2—33—0; M. Palfreyman 39—5—134—4; M. Winfield 8—2—23—1; A. J. Underwood 31—10—83—2; A. Crookes 49—8—192—4; C. J. Poole 11—2—40—1; G. Yates 35—9—92—4; J. H. Newsome 20—11—29—1; P. Cullen 5—2—18—2; J. B. Riley 5—1—6—2; M. Hall 1—0—8—0.

Amateurs.—P. Blatherwick, K. Brealey, H. R. Cox, P. Cullen, P. Forman, J. S. Hodgkins, J. H. Newsome, B. Notley, M. Palfreyman, J. B. Riley, J. Rutherford, A. J. Underwood, G. Yates.

OXFORDSHIRE

Secretary—L. B. Frewer, "Tal-y-Fan," Highfield Avenue, Oxford

Matches 10—Won 1, Lost 1, Won on first innings 4, Lost on first innings 4

		1st Innings	2nd Innings	Result
July 29, 30	Buckinghamshire	284	9 for 0	Lost by ten
Cowley	Oxfordshire	182	108	wickets
August 1, 2	Oxfordshire	269	—	Won by innings
Reading	Berkshire	107	90	and 72 runs
August 8, 9	Oxfordshire	277* for 9	126 for 5	Lost on first
Oxford (Sports Club)	Cornwall	285	—	innings
August 10, 11	Oxfordshire	138	315* for 9	Lost on first
Oxford (Sports Club)	Devon	208	101 for 5	innings
August 12, 13	Oxfordshire	174	212* for 7	Lost on first
Ascott Park, Wing	Buckinghamshire	304	—	innings
August 15, 16	Oxfordshire	293	152 for 3	Lost on first
Banbury	Dorset	380	—	innings
August 19, 20	Oxfordshire	281* for 9	176 for 6	Won on first
Camborne	Cornwall	248	—	innings
August 22, 23	Devon	304* for 7	91 for 2	Won on first
Torquay	Oxfordshire	426* for 7	—	innings

Innings declared closed.

		1st Innings	2nd Innings	Result	
August 24, 25	Dorset	299* for 6	174* for 8	Won on	first
Weymouth	Oxfordshire	308	—	innings	
August 26, 27	Oxfordshire	206	212* for 5	Won on	first
Oxford	Berkshire	187	207 for 8	innings	
(Sports Club)					

* Innings declared closed.

Batting Averages

	Innings	Not Outs	Runs	Highest Innings	Average
K. Talboys	9	2	321	183	45.85
J. W. Carter	8	0	280	125	35.00
E. J. Gardner	11	2	304	56	33.77
J. F. Mendl	8	0	265	71	33.12
H. J. Locke	10	1	287	61	31.88
D. Banton	16	3	401	62*	30.84
D. J. Laitt	12	1	322	71	29.27
B. C. G. Wilenkin	18	0	525	96	29.16
W. H. Miller	10	0	289	98	28.90
W. W. Inge†	15	4	243	37*	22.09

Also batted: G. F. Betts 3 innings—3 not outs—18 runs; J. E. Bush 3—0—89; D. Cummings 3—0—9; D. K. Fasken 3—0—1; T. Gibson 8—0—57; H. Goldie 1—1—7; C. M. Lowe 3—1—37; D. MacDonald 4—4—9; R. H. Pitkin 4—1—7; A. H. Reynolds 2—0—31; J. E. Smith 7—1—54; T. V. Strange 4—2—77; R. D. J. Surman 4—0—79.

* Signifies not out.   † Captain.

Bowling Averages

	Overs	Maidens	Runs	Wickets	Average
D. J. Laitt	170	58	575	46	12.50
T. Gibson	61	16	172	9	19.11
D. Banton	242	53	700	25	28.00
H. J. Locke	118	31	369	13	28.38
R. H. Pitkin	90	6	311	9	34.55
G. F. Betts	106	26	299	7	42.71

Also bowled: J. E. Bush 1—0—4—0; D. Cummings 13—0—54—1; D. K. Fasken 63—17—159—2; E. J. Gardner 1—0—4—0; C. M. Lowe 3—0—11—0; J. F. Mendl 1—0—1—0; D. MacDonald 34—7—89—2; W. H. Miller 1—0—4—0; A. H. Reynolds 5—1—19—0; T. V. Strange 47—14—135—5; R. D. J. Surman 7—0—38—0; K. Talboys 1—0—1—0; B. C. G. Wilenkin 10—1—51—2.

Professionals.—None.

SOMERSET SECOND ELEVEN

Secretary—Air Vice-Marshal M. L. Taylor, County Ground, Taunton

Matches 8—Won 3, Won on first innings 4, No result 1

		1st Innings	2nd Innings	Result	
June 10, 11	Cornwall	85	223	Won on	first
Falmouth	Somerset II	126	157 for 7	innings	
July 29, 30	Wiltshire	244	203* for 7	Won by	two
Trowbridge	Somerset II	279* for 6	169 for 8	wickets	
August 3, 4	Somerset II	346	205 for 7	Won on	first
Taunton	Cornwall	306	—	innings	

* Innings declared closed.

		1st Innings	2nd Innings	Result
August 8, 9	Somerset II	373* for 5	—	No result
Bath	Wiltshire	256 for 6	—	
August 19, 20	Dorset	92	157	Won by ten
Sherborne	Somerset II	244* for 7	8 for 0	wickets
August 24, 25	Somerset II	256* for 7	175* for 6	Won on first
Sidmouth	Devon	281	23 for 0	innings
August 26, 27	Somerset II	293* for 3	171* for 6	Won on first
Glastonbury	Dorset	214* for 8	239 for 6	innings
September 1, 2	Somerset II	304	172* for 4	Won by 24 runs
Taunton	Devon	228	224	

* Innings declared closed.

Batting Averages

	Innings	Not Outs	Runs	Highest Innings	Average
J. Baker	11	4	355	84	50.71
G. L. Williams	7	1	294	139	49.00
M. Walker................	6	0	279	99	46.50
P. Eele	6	0	276	112	46.00
G. Atkinson	15	1	590	88	42.14
L. Pickles................	7	3	161	50*	40.25
J. Currie	12	2	400	102*	40.00
E. Hill†	10	2	232	40*	29.00
P. Fussell	6	3	86	23*	28.66
B. Langford	5	0	142	64	28.40
K. Palmer	6	2	94	45*	23.50
R. Smith	12	4	171	38	21.37
G. Tripp	3	1	23	13	11.50
C. Davey	7	0	43	20	6.14
K. Biddulph	3	0	14	6	4.66

Also batted: T. Clements 1*, 0*; J. Hilton 15.

Signifies not out.　　　　† Captain.

Bowling Averages

	Overs	Maidens	Runs	Wickets	Average
J. Hilton	53.3	17	119	12	9.91
K. Palmer	41	11	93	6	15.50
J. Baker	118.5	35	308	19	16.21
M. Walker................	25.1	7	66	4	16.50
P. Fussell	165.3	38	411	21	19.57
B. Langford	59.5	25	137	6	22.83
K. Biddulph	253	50	795	32	24.84
E. Hill	52	15	175	7	25.00
G. Atkinson	86	13	320	5	64.00
L. Pickles	34	5	130	2	65.00

Also bowled: R. Smith 10—4—17—0; C. Davey 2—1—2—0; J. Currie 2—1—2—0; G. L. Williams 2—0—4—0.

Amateurs.—J. Baker, K. Biddulph, T. Clements, J. Currie, P. Eele, P. Fussell, E. Hill.

STAFFORDSHIRE

Secretary—L. W. HANCOCK, 4, Kingsland Avenue,
Oakhill, Stoke-on-Trent

Matches 10—Won 3, Lost 3, Won on first innings 1, Lost on first innings 3

		1st Innings	2nd Innings	Result
May 18, 19	Staffordshire	141	124	Lost on first
Neston	Cheshire	200* for 6	59 for 1	innings
May 25, 26	Staffordshire	153	169* for 7	Lost by eight
Birmingham	Warwickshire II	177	146 for 2	wickets
June 8, 9	Staffordshire	110	123	Lost by nine
Bradford	Yorkshire II	217* for 0	17 for 1	wickets
June 20, 21	Staffordshire	221* for 9	—	†Lost by seven
Newcastle	Northumberland	222 for 3	—	wickets
June 22, 23	Durham	198	—	Won on first
South Shields	Staffordshire	205 for 7	—	innings
July 13, 14	Warwickshire II	142	156* for 7	Won by one
Knypersley	Staffordshire	164	140 for 9	wicket
July 18, 19	Durham	334	—	Lost on first
Stafford	Staffordshire	138	308* for 6	innings
August 3, 4	Staffordshire	291* for 5	—	Won by innings
Porthill	Cheshire	155	76	and 60 runs
August 8, 9	Staffordshire	104	5 for 0	Lost on first
Uttoxeter	Northumberland	181* for 7	—	innings
August 10, 11	Staffordshire	144	266* for 5	Won by 108
Longton	Yorkshire II	76	226	runs

* Innings declared closed.

† Reduced to one day because of rain.

Batting Averages

	Innings	Not Outs	Runs	Highest Innings	Average
D. Russell	5	0	176	107	35.20
H. Boon..................	12	1	357	102*	32.45
B. Shardlow	14	3	337	91*	30.63
C. Pollard	3	0	88	57	29.33
F. Apperley	9	0	262	74	29.11
F. Butler	10	0	282	91	28.20
D. M. Haynes†	10	1	221	81	24.55
S. Crump	7	0	139	60	19.85
N. G. W. Banks	8	3	97	26*	19.40
B. Crump	11	2	146	44	16.22
A. Leake	6	0	94	39	15.66
S. B. Boon	3	0	43	33	14.33
B Hayward	4	0	55	31	13.75
A. J. Gott	4	0	54	37	13.50
G. J. Gregory	5	2	34	19*	11.33
E. G. Smith.............	3	1	21	14	10.50
F. R. Bailey	6	1	42	18	8.40
J. S. Hall	6	0	50	36	8.33
W. T. Jolley	6	2	27	10	6.75
J. Bailey	6	2	12	5	3.00
G. M. Lawton	3	1	6	5*	3.00
J. C. Norcup	3	1	1	1	0.50

Also batted: R. Curwen 34*; J. S. Rider 1, 23; W. Boon 11, 2*; H. Shardlow 0, 12; G. Pedley 8, 3*; B. J. Mayers 2, 8; D. S. G. Swift 10; H. H. Wood 4, 6; S. Norcup 1; E. Shaw 0; D. Turner 0.

* *Signifies not out.*   † *Captain.*

Bowling Averages

	Overs	Maidens	Runs	Wickets	Average
S. B. Boon...............	59.3	15	139	14	9.92
B. Crump	74.2	12	230	14	16.42
S. Crump	101	44	166	9	18.44
B. Shardlow	222	65	552	28	19.71
E. G. Smith.............	42.4	6	150	7	21.42

	Overs	Maidens	Runs	Wickets	Average
B. Hayward	40	7	132	5	26.40
G. J. Gregory	63.4	13	186	6	31.00
D. Russell	28	5	119	3	39.66
W. Boon	32.3	4	80	2	40.00
W. T. Jolley	103.2	26	275	6	45.83
J. C. Norcup	80.3	12	284	6	47.33

Also bowled: N. G. W. Banks 16—1—49—1; F. Butler 15—6—37—1; S. Norcup 8—0—31—0; H. Boon 5.3—4—6—0.

Professionals.—None.

SUFFOLK

Secretary—G. T. BARNARD, 24 and 26, Museum Street, Ipswich

Matches 8—Won 1, Lost 3, Won on first innings 1, Lost on first innings 3

		1st Innings	2nd Innings	Result
July 1, 2	Suffolk	147	195	Lost by eight
Mistley	Essex II	292* for 9	51 for 2	wickets
August 1, 2	Essex II	224	183* for 5	Lost on first
Felixstowe	Suffolk	138	252 for 6	innings
August 3, 4	Norfolk	216* for 5	176* for 7	Lost by 66 runs
Norwich	Suffolk	245* for 2	182	
August 5, 6	Middlesex II	254	144* for 4	Lost on first
Felixstowe	Suffolk	155* for 9	116 for 4	innings
August 8, 9	Suffolk	237* for 8	123* for 9	Lost by seven
Felixstowe	Hertfordshire	192	171 for 3	wickets
August 12, 13	Norfolk	256* for 7	—	Won on first
Lowestoft	Suffolk	257 for 5		innings
August 22, 23	Middlesex II	119	258* for 6	Lost on first
Finchley	Suffolk	105	153 for 5	innings
August 24, 25	Hertfordshire	263	140	Won by seven
Letchworth	Suffolk	265* for 6	141 for 3	wickets

* Innings declared closed.

Batting Averages

	Innings	Not Outs	Runs	Highest Innings	Average
C. B. T. Gibbons	13	3	481	116*	48.10
B. H. Belle	8	1	215	128*	30.71
D. F. Henley-Welch	10	1	272	90	30.22
M. D. Corke†	15	3	350	85	29.16
B. A. Wilson	12	3	252	57	28.00
K. C. Girkin	15	0	372	71	24.80
P. R. Downing	13	1	215	36	17.91
E. J. Unwin	3	0	50	25	16.66
R. F. Clark	5	2	44	12	14.66
E. A. Goodwyn	3	0	41	16	13.66
G. C. Perkins	9	2	76	27	10.85
J. N. Stevens	5	2	29	12	9.66
H. S. Hargreaves	6	2	22	10	5.50

Also batted: E. R. Baker 4, 8; L. F. Roper 7*, 4; A. F. Skinner 41; A. H. Finch 0; E. J. Branton 14, 4*; I. F. Hammond 0; C. H. C. Piper 10*, 0*; R. A. Collinge 7, 24; A. Waldous 1.

* *Signifies not out.*   † Captain.

Bowling Averages

	Overs	Maidens	Runs	Wickets	Average
G. C. Perkins	254.1	88	557	35	15.91
R. A. Collinge	50.3	10	196	10	19.60
H. S. Hargreaves	183	38	588	23	25.56
B. A. Wilson	58.4	10	226	8	28.25
K. C. Girkin	65.2	8	223	7	31.85
D. F. Henley-Welch	72	12	249	7	35.57
P. R. Downing	43	3	153	4	38.25
J. N. Stevens	158	43	457	8	57.12

Also bowled: I. F. Hammond 3—0—9—1; E. J. Unwin 9—0—34—0; E. J. Branton 35—7—120—1; M. D. Corke 1—0—12—0; L. F. Roper 10—0—43—0.

Professionals.—H. S. Hargreaves, G. C. Perkins, B. A. Wilson.

SURREY SECOND ELEVEN

Secretary—B. K. Castor, Kennington Oval, S.E.11

Matches 15—Won 11, Won on first innings 1, Lost on first innings 1, No result 2

		1st Innings	2nd Innings	Result
May 25, 26	Lancashire II	155	77	Won by ten
Old Trafford	Surrey II	226* for 8	7 for 0	wickets
May 28, 30	Kent II	175* for 9	—	No result
The Oval	Surrey II	172 for 9		
June 8, 9	Surrey II	—	—	No result
Mitcham	Middlesex II	—	—	
June 13, 14	Surrey II	93	110	Won by four
Sutton	Warwickshire II	90	109	runs
June 20, 21	Wiltshire	132	229	Won by six
The Oval	Surrey II	254* for 3	108 for 4	wickets
June 27, 28	Essex II	171	117	Won by four
Chingford	Surrey II	163	126 for 6	wickets
July 6, 7	Warwickshire II	196	151	Won by eight
Birmingham	Surrey II	232* for 6	116 for 2	wickets
July 20, 21	Norfolk	132	218	Won by eight
The Oval	Surrey II	193* for 7	158 for 2	wickets
July 25, 26	Surrey II	271	175 for 4	Lost on first
Beddington	Lancashire II	274* for 8	—	innings
July 28, 29	Surrey II	281* for 7	61 for 1	Won by nine
Beckenham	Kent II	177	164	wickets
August 1, 2	Wiltshire	113	238	Won by nine
Swindon	Surrey II	246* for 5	106 for 1	wickets
August 5, 6	Norfolk	203	235* for 8	Won by four
Lakenham	Surrey II	238* for 3	201 for 6	wickets
August 13, 15	Middlesex II	172	78 for 4	Won on first
Lord's	Surrey II	190	—	innings
August 20, 22	Essex II	163	175	Won by seven
The Oval	Surrey II	263	80 for 3	wickets
Challenge Match				
September 3, 5, 6	Surrey II	97	167	Won by 14 runs
The Oval	Northumberland	142* for 7	108	

* Innings declared closed.

Batting Averages

	Innings	Not Outs	Runs	Highest Innings	Average
J. Edrich	23	6	762	100	44.82
R. Swetman	12	4	286	52	35.75
D. F. Cox	7	2	175	49*	35.00
R. C. E. Pratt	11	3	276	54	34.50
M. D. Willett	22	5	571	84	33.58
G. J. Chidgey	7	1	195	71	32.50
A. H. Brown	19	1	553	121*	30.72
D. E. Pratt	20	3	423	59	24.88
A. B. D. Parsons	8	0	188	60	23.50
R. A. E. Tindall	8	1	122	32	17.42
E. A. Bedser	6	0	89	32	14.83
V. J. Ransom†	12	3	117	34*	13.00
H. R. A. Kelleher	11	5	48	10	8.00
D. Halfyard	10	2	31	9	3.87

Also batted: R. J. Attawell 28; R. A. Bowles 51, 0, 5, 3; P. D. Croft 3; D Gibson 19, 1; L. A. Johnson 0, 1*; P. G. McKelvey 2*, 2*, 0*, 4; A. Morley Brown 30, 0; N. D. Parks 4, 6, 65, 10; M. J. Stewart 7, 4*, 61. N. Armstrong, H. K Christian, J. K. Hall and D. Sydenham played but did not bat.

* Signifies not out. † *Captain.*

Bowling Averages

	Overs	Maidens	Runs	Wickets	Average
E. A. Bedser	144.3	73	201	24	8.37
H. R. A. Kelleher	357.4	105	791	59	13.40
V. J. Ransom	164.3	45	353	25	14.12
D. Halfyard	333	111	880	54	16.29
D. F. Cox	94.3	18	242	13	18.61
R. C. E. Pratt	134	48	266	12	22.17
D. E. Pratt	233	68	645	29	22.24

Also bowled: A. H. Brown 2—1—4—0; H. K. Christian 24—4—51—3 D. Gibson 25—8—73—2; J. K. Hall 28—5—118—2; P. G. McKelvey 40.4—6—140—3; A. Morley Brown 3—1—12—0; A. B. D. Parsons 4—1—18—1; D Sydenham 13—1—45—1; R. A. E. Tindall 23—4—75—3; M. D. Willett 14—4—36—2.

Amateurs.—N. Armstrong, R. J. Attawell, R. A. Bowles, A. H. Brown G. J. Chidgey, H. K. Christian, P. D. Croft, J. K. Hall, A. Morley Brown, N. D Parks, A. B. D. Parsons, V. J. Ransom.

WARWICKSHIRE SECOND ELEVEN

Secretary—L. T. DEAKINS, County Ground, Edgbaston, Birmingham, 5

Matches 14—Won 3, Lost 5, Won on first innings 4, Lost on first innings 2

		1st Innings	2nd Innings	Result
May 18, 19	Lancashire II	206* for 7	53* for 5	Won by six
Coventry	Warwickshire II	141	119 for 4	wickets
May 25, 26	Staffordshire	153	169* for 7	Won by eigh
Edgbaston	Warwickshire II	177	146 for 2	wickets
May 30, 31	Warwickshire II	265* for 9	—	Won on firs
Derby	Derbyshire II	163	204 for 7	innings
June 8, 9	Warwickshire II	136	52	Lost by nine
Lancaster	Lancashire II	97	93 for 1	wickets

* Innings declared closed.

		1st Innings	2nd Innings	Result
June 13, 14	Surrey II	93	110	Lost by four runs
Sutton	Warwickshire II	90	109	
June 22, 23	Notts II	130	217	Won on first innings
Nottingham	Warwickshire II	178	143 for 6	
July 6, 7	Warwickshire II	196	151	Lost by eight wickets
M. & B. Ground, Birmingham	Surrey II	232* for 6	116 for 2	
July 13, 14	Warwickshire II	142	156* for 7	Lost by one wicket
Knypersley	Staffordshire	164	140 for 9	
July 18, 19	Warwickshire II	348* for 6	185* for 6	Lost by six wickets
Northampton	Northants II	277* for 7	257 for 4	
July 25, 26	Leicestershire II	147	170* for 5	Won by two wickets
Leicester	Warwickshire II	169	149 for 8	
August 1, 2	Warwickshire II	311* for 5	103* for 4	Won on first innings
Edgbaston	Derbyshire II	192	152 for 8	
August 10, 11	Warwickshire II	160	224* for 7	Lost on first innings
Nuneaton	Notts II	275* for 9	—	
August 17, 18	Warwickshire II	234	62	Won on first innings
Rugby	Northants II	180	91 for 3	
August 24, 25	Warwickshire II	402* for 7	—	Lost on first innings
Edgbaston	Leicestershire II	403* for 6	—	

* Innings declared closed.

Batting Averages

	Innings	Not Outs	Runs	Highest Innings	Average
D. R. Cook	5	1	188	149*	47.00
B. E. Fletcher	9	1	292	164*	36.50
W. J. Stewart	17	1	525	99	32.81
R. E. G. Steward	7	1	181	57*	30.16
R. T. Weeks	17	4	355	77*	27.30
C. W. Leach	22	0	590	68	26.81
P. H. Bromley	11	0	253	72	23.00
J. S. Ord†	23	4	389	105*	20.47
I. M. King	11	5	98	27*	16.33
T. L. Pritchard	12	1	179	58	14.91
N. A. Paul	12	1	162	40*	14.72
W. B. Bridge	19	5	182	38	13.00
G. Hill	8	1	91	27*	13.00
J. R. M. Branston	4	0	47	29	11.75
R. G. Carter	10	3	81	31*	11.57
W. J. Slater	3	0	32	31	10.66
K. R. Dollery	9	3	56	23	9.33
W. G. R. Couldrick	8	0	70	25	8.75
T. P. Barnes	15	3	75	22	6.25

Also batted: N. F. Horner 80, 10; A. C. Smith 71, 6; M. M. Burton 44, 16; T. S. Cox 35, 14; R. Sewell 37, 13; M. L. Simms 38, 1; A. R. Collicutt 14, 3; V. G. Gabriel 8, 0*; R. Whitton 6, 1; O. S. Wheatley 4*, 1; D. White 4, 0.

* *Signifies not out.*   † Captain.

Bowling Averages

	Overs	Maidens	Runs	Wickets	Average
J. R. M. Branston	33	10	82	6	13.66
R. G. Carter	206	53	453	29	15.62
K. R. Dollery	195	55	405	25	16.20
I. M. King	240.3	109	446	27	16.51
N. A. Paul	96.5	27	233	12	19.41
G. H. Hill	112	37	259	13	19.92
W. J. Slater	45	10	116	5	23.20

	Overs	Maidens	Runs	Wickets	Average
R. T. Weeks	302.2	123	627	24	26.12
P. H. Bromley	58.4	12	143	5	28.60
T. L. Pritchard	241.3	52	691	19	36.36
W. B. Bridge	242.1	68	651	17	38.29

Also bowled: O. S. Wheatley 12.4—3—24—3; C. W. Leach 31.5—6—140—3
J. Billingham 2—0—14—0; D. R. Cook 25—5—90—0.

Professionals.—T. B. Barnes, W. B. Bridge, R. G. Carter, K. R. Dollery
N. F. Horner, I. M. King, C. W. Leach, J. S. Ord, T. L. Pritchard, W. J. Stewart
R. T. Weeks, R. Whitton.

WILTSHIRE

Secretary—R. A. C. FORRESTER, 11–12, High Street,
Chippenham

Matches 8—Lost 6, Won on first innings 1, No result 1

June 20, 21	Surrey II	254* for 3	108 for 4	Lost by six
The Oval	Wiltshire	132	229	wickets
June 22, 23	Wiltshire	146	216	Lost by seven
Tonbridge School	Kent II	177* for 6	189 for 3	wickets
July 29, 30	Wiltshire	244	203* for 7	Lost by two
Trowbridge	Somerset II	279* for 6	169 for 8	wickets
August 1, 2	Wiltshire	113	238	Lost by nine
Swindon	Surrey II	246* for 5	106 for 1	wickets
(B.R. ground)				
August 8, 9	Somerset II	373* for 5	—	No result
Bath	Wiltshire	256 for 6		
August 10, 11	Dorset	206	156 for 6	Won on first
Dorchester	Wiltshire	254	—	innings
August 12, 13	Wiltshire	139	262	Lost by five
Chippenham	Dorset	192	211 for 5	wickets
August 15, 16	Wiltshire	223	203	Lost by six runs
Marlborough Coll.	Kent II	105	327	

* Innings declared closed.

Batting Averages

	Innings	Not Outs	Runs	Highest Innings	Average
J. R. Thompson	10	0	442	140	44.20
L. R. Lomax	12	1	312	84*	28.36
A. H. Mills	12	0	331	55	27.58
R. J. Knight	12	0	326	96	27.16
J. Hurn†	14	0	358	100	25.57
G. P. Gent	8	0	121	70	15.12
A. E. H. Rutter	10	0	140	43	14.00
J. H. Merryweather	14	6	103	19*	12.87
A. G. Marshall	12	3	91	54	10.11
D. S. Milford	7	1	52	20	8.66
M. H. Martin	8	2	36	28*	6.00

Also batted: D. M. Richards 20, 15, 14, 1; G. C. Emery 1, 0, 15, 9; A. J.
Wheeler 13, 27, 0, 0; G. Pratt 20, 15, 14, 1; R. C. Robinson 0, 8, 0, 1; A. M.
Smith 0, 28; N. C. B. Creek 8, 60*; P. A. Naylor 10*, 41, 3, 17; J. B. Russell 17, 45*.

* *Signifies not out.*   † Captain.

Bowling Averages

	Overs	Maidens	Runs	Wickets	Average
J. R. Thompson	55	10	168	8	21.00
I. R. Lomax	51	6	212	10	21.20
P. A. Naylor	48	13	149	6	24.83
A. G. Marshall	193.1	39	649	22	29.50
D. S. Milford	91	22	315	9	35.00
R. J. Knight	41.4	6	147	4	36.75
J. H. Merryweather	221.5	31	928	25	37.12
M. H. Martin	96	21	316	5	63.20

Also bowled: A. J. Wheeler 4—0—12—1; J. Hurn 1—0—11—0.

Professional.—A. G. Marshall.

YORKSHIRE SECOND ELEVEN

Secretary—J. H. Nash, Old Bank Chambers, Leeds, 1

Matches 18—Won 4, Lost 5, Won on first innings 7, Lost on first innings 1, No result 1

		1st Innings	2nd Innings	Result
May 16, 17	Notts II	183	—	No result
Barnsley	Yorkshire II	59 for 6	—	
May 25, 26	Cumberland	76	76	Won by innings
Carlisle	Yorkshire II	187	—	and 35 runs
May 30, 31	Lancashire II	318	102	Lost on first
Harrogate	Yorkshire II	252	5 for 1	innings
June 1, 2	Northants II	158	227	Won by three
Salts	Yorkshire II	313	73 for 7	wickets
June 8, 9	Staffordshire	110	123	Won by nine
Bradford	Yorkshire II	217* for 0	17 for 1	wickets
June 15, 16	Yorkshire II	245* for 5	—	Won on first
Macclesfield	Cheshire	91	166 for 8	innings
June 22, 23	Yorkshire II	100	209	Lost by five
Jesmond	Northumberland	254* for 9	59 for 5	wickets
June 27, 28	Yorkshire II	213	182* for 3	Won on first
Redcar	Cumberland	160	42 for 2	innings
June 29, 30	Lincolnshire	291	40 for 1	Won on first
Hull	Yorkshire II	357	—	innings
July 6, 7	Yorkshire II	198	180* for 1	Won by seven
Shireoaks	Notts II	114	257	runs
July 13, 14	Yorkshire II	399	—	Won on first
Middlesbrough	Northumberland	364	—	innings
July 18, 19	Yorkshire II	385* for 5	0 for 0	Won on first
Bridlington	Cheshire	314	—	innings
August 1, 2	Yorkshire II	260	133* for 5	Won on first
Old Trafford	Lancashire II	203	54 for 2	innings
August 3, 4	Durham	176	214* for 1	Lost by 31 runs
Scarborough	Yorkshire II	143	216	
August 8, 9	Yorkshire II	337	—	Won on first
Scunthorpe	Lincolnshire	215	191 for 8	innings
August 10, 11	Staffordshire	144	266* for 6	Lost by 108
Longton	Yorkshire II	76	226	runs
August 15, 16	Northants II	293* for 9	224* for 1	Lost by 126
Northampton	Yorkshire II	217* for 7	174	runs
August 17, 18	Yorkshire II	181	164	Lost by two
Bishop Auckland	Durham	263	86 for 8	wickets

* Innings declared closed.

Batting Averages

	Innings	Not Outs	Runs	Highest Innings	Average
D. E. V. Padgett	13	2	747	183	67.90
K. Taylor	14	2	619	177*	51.58
E. I. Lester	15	0	700	129	46.66
A. M. King	12	3	381	89	42.33
R. Booth	16	3	450	77	34.61
J. van Geloven	15	1	480	100*	34.28
J. R. Burnet†	22	1	623	101	29.66
E. Leadbeater	8	3	110	40	22.00
A. Kettleborough	9	0	178	60	19.77
F. W. Goddard	5	0	82	62	16.40
B. Cromack	7	2	76	24	15.20
H. D. Bird	10	1	129	41*	14.33
G. W. Moore	7	1	80	45	13.33
A. B. Bainbridge	12	4	96	26*	12.00
J. G. Binks	7	2	49	24*	9.80
W. F. Oates	5	0	45	24	9.00
B. C. Moor	5	1	34	12*	8.50
R. Wood	5	2	22	9	7.33
M. Ryan	8	2	42	8	7.00
G. Booth	9	0	45	13	5.00
B. Jackson	8	2	27	7*	4.50
P. Hodgson	5	1	10	6	2.50

Also batted: P. Broughton 0, 1, 0; J. C. Brown 9, 15, 0; D. B. Close 80; K. M. Goddard 21, 18, 1; B. Handley 8, 3, 13; G. A. Hare 1, 8; C. Helliwell 0, 1, 8*, 18; R. Illingworth 23; S. G. Metcalfe 15, 16, 3, 16; B. Milner 27*, 15, 4; J. A. Pitt 4; R. H. Platt 2*, 1, 8*, 1*; P. J. Sharpe 33, 23, 5, 18; W. B. Stott 27; F. S. Trueman 8; T. G. Webster 3, 1, 0*. R. Appleyard played in one match and did not bat.

* Signifies not out. † Captain.

Bowling Averages

	Overs	Maidens	Runs	Wickets	Average
G. A. Hare	17	6	32	5	6.40
R. Appleyard	30	11	66	5	13.20
E. Leadbeater	201	45	564	41	13.75
J. van Geloven	223	53	591	36	16.41
R. K. Platt	126	36	313	19	16.47
J. R. Burnet	19.5	0	102	6	17.00
H. D. Bird	11	0	51	3	17.00
R. Illingworth	49	11	156	9	17.33
P. Hodgson	128.3	32	322	18	17.88
T. G. Webster	71.5	19	191	10	19.10
G. Booth	169.1	35	508	26	19.53
M. Ryan	139.5	24	425	19	22.36
J. C. Brown	48	12	113	5	22.60
B. Jackson	127	36	322	12	26.83
C. Helliwell	70.4	25	162	6	27.00
A. B. Bainbridge	121.1	38	264	9	29.33
R. Wood	85.3	24	221	7	31.57
B. Milner	58	18	182	5	36.40
B. Cromack	67	7	245	5	49.00
K. Taylor	56	15	161	3	53.66

Also bowled: P. Broughton 43—5—170—2; D. B. Close 28.4—13—69—2; F. W. Goddard 2—1—4—0; K. M. Goddard 19—3—59—1; A. M. King 7—4—16—1; E. I. Lester 16—7—36—1; B. C. Moor 15—1—50—1; G. W. Moore 5—2—23—0; W. F. Oates 1—0—4—0; D. E. V. Padgett 7.4—1—19—1; J. A. Pitt 6—1—20—1; F. S. Trueman 28—5—101—2.

Amateurs.—J. R. Burnet, S. G. Metcalfe, G. W. Moore, P. J. Sharpe.

MINOR COUNTIES' AVERAGES, 1955

BATTING

(Qualification: 8 innings, average 25.00)

	County	Innings	Not Outs	Runs	Highest Innings	Average
D. H. Cole	Devon	12	2	891	235*	89.10
D. E. V. Padgett ..	Yorkshire II	13	2	747	183	67.90
P. H. Parfitt	Norfolk	10	3	401	131	57.28
C. Lee	Derbyshire II	8	1	394	113	56.28
M. A. Crouch	Cambridgeshire	12	3	496	141	55.11
N. S. Gunn	Bedfordshire	12	2	543	146	54.30
N. H. Moore	Norfolk	11	3	431	103	53.87
K. Taylor	Yorkshire II	14	2	619	177*	51.58
R. W. Smithson ...	Northumberland	11	2	460	86	51.11
J. Baker	Somerset II	11	4	355	84	50.71
B. Reynolds	Northants II	11	4	345	102*	49.28
J. A. R. Oliver	Bedfordshire	10	4	295	74	49.16
M. M. Walford ...	Dorset	21	0	1025	126	48.80
G. Walton	Northumberland	13	1	583	119	48.58
C. B. T. Gibbons .	Suffolk	13	3	481	116*	48.10
E. I. Lester	Yorkshire II	15	0	700	129	46.66
K. D. Smith	Northumberland	13	2	513	115*	46.63
K. Tallboys	Oxfordshire	9	2	321	183	45.85
J. Edrich	Surrey II	23	6	762	100	44.82
J. Dyson	Lancashire II	8	2	267	127*	44.50
J. R. Thompson ...	Wiltshire	10	0	442	140	44.20
D. W. Taylor	Lincolnshire	11	1	442	125	44.20
D. E. Lawes	Dorset	8	1	307	120	43.85
R. Jowsey	Northumberland	16	2	605	86*	43.21
R. Gautrey	Cambridgeshire	9	3	259	65	43.16
A. M. King	Yorkshire II	12	3	381	89	42.33
G. Atkinson	Somerset II	15	1	590	88	42.14
D. J. Carnill	Hertfordshire	15	4	463	105*	42.09
J. Vincent	Cornwall	10	2	336	122	42.00
H. D. Fairclough .	Devon	16	1	600	118	40.00
J. Currie	Somerset II	12	2	400	102*	40.00
T. W. Tyrwhitt-Drake	Hertfordshire	12	0	479	96	39.91
G. Wyatt	Derbyshire II	11	2	355	109*	39.44
P. T. Smith	Leicestershire II	12	1	432	188*	39.27
H. D. Bell	Durham	16	2	547	101*	39.07
K. B. Standring ...	Lancashire II	11	4	273	62	39.00
K. G. Davidson ...	Northumberland	13	1	468	126	39.00
G. W. L. Courtenay	Dorset	14	1	506	142*	38.92
G. A. Marlow.....	Lincolnshire	10	3	269	58	38.42
R. Tunstall	Lincolnshire	10	2	307	83	38.37
R. Harris	Cornwall	11	2	344	108*	38.22
D. L. Newman ...	Middlesex II	15	5	379	99*	37.90
B. E. Disbury	Kent II	16	1	561	135*	37.40
D. J. W. Bridge ...	Dorset	18	6	448	106	37.33
J. G. Owen	Bedfordshire	13	3	371	98	37.10
E. G. Witherden...	Kent II	11	1	368	76	36.80
B. E. Fletcher	Warwickshire II	9	1	292	164*	36.50
K. Poole	Notts II	9	1	292	101	36.50
G. F. Webb.......	Hertfordshire	11	1	365	165	36.50
J. C. Bate	Norfolk	11	0	401	86	36.45
S. E. Leary	Kent II	9	2	255	93*	36.42
R. C. Vowles	Notts II	18	4	509	145*	36.35
P. L. Stoddart.....	Buckinghamshire	15	1	505	90	36.07

* Signifies not out.

AA

	County	Innings	Not Outs	Runs	Highest Innings	Average
R. Swetman	*Surrey II*	12	4	286	52	35.75
C. Callaway	*Cornwall*	10	1	321	101*	35.66
J. W. Murphy	*Cornwall*	14	1	459	175	35.30
F. C. M. Alexander	*Cambridgeshire*	13	2	388	78	35.27
P. Davis	*Northants II*	17	6	388	62	35.27
J. W. Carter	*Oxfordshire*	8	0	280	125	35.00
W. O. Thomas	*Norfolk*	16	0	560	105	35.00
L. R. Gardner ...	*Leicestershire II*	12	0	418	69	34.83
A. W. Catt	*Kent II*	11	3	278	94	34.75
R. Booth	*Yorkshire II*	16	3	450	77	34.61
R. C. E. Pratt	*Surrey II*	11	3	276	54	34.50
R. F. Hosking ...	*Cornwall*	11	0	379	73	34.45
W. Place	*Lancashire II*	16	4	412	65	34.33
J. van Geloven	*Yorkshire II*	15	1	480	100*	34.28
G. Millman	*Bedfordshire*	13	0	445	80	34.23
E. J. Gardner	*Oxfordshire*	11	2	304	56	33.77
P. Hearn	*Kent II*	9	3	202	89	33.66
M. D. Willett	*Surrey II*	22	5	571	84	33.58
J. F. Mendl	*Oxfordshire*	8	0	265	71	33.12
W. J. Stewart	*Warwickshire II*	17	1	525	99	32.81
W. B. Morris	*Cambridgeshire*	13	1	390	91	32.50
H. Boon..........	*Staffordshire*	12	1	357	102*	32.45
G. W. Thomson ..	*Dorset*	19	3	518	94*	32.37
G. E. S. Woodhouse	*Dorset*	16	0	517	91	32.31
M. Winfield.......	*Notts II*	21	2	609	82	32.05
H. J. Locke	*Oxfordshire*	10	1	287	61	31.88
A. F. Brazier......	*Kent II*	10	2	255	85*	31.87
G. Reynolds	*Buckinghamshire*	14	1	414	119	31.84
D. W. Hardy	*Durham*	12	0	380	132	31.66
M. Norman.......	*Northants II*	10	0	315	67	31.50
A. A. Hillary	*Berkshire*	18	0	557	142	30.94
D. Banton	*Oxfordshire*	16	3	401	62*	30.84
A. C. Walton	*Berkshire*	11	0	338	134	30.72
A. H. Brown	*Surrey II*	19	1	553	121*	30.72
B. H. Belle	*Suffolk*	8	1	215	128*	30.71
J. R. C. Todd	*Lincolnshire*	10	1	276	85*	30.66
A. B. Quick.......	*Essex II*	17	2	460	74	30.66
B. Shardlow	*Staffordshire*	14	3	337	91*	30.63
D. F. Henley-Welch	*Suffolk*	10	1	272	90	30.22
J. H. Taylor	*Lincolnshire*	11	0	331	96	30.09
E. Davis..........	*Northants II*	16	1	451	112	30.06
P. Gunary	*Essex II*	13	1	360	102*	30.00
A. Thompson	*Middlesex II*	12	1	327	69	29.72
F. W. Millett	*Cheshire*	14	1	386	158*	29.69
A. N. Bradbeer....	*Hertfordshire*	12	3	267	48	29.66
J. R. Burnet	*Yorkshire II*	22	1	623	101	29.66
R. A. Diment	*Leicestershire II*	9	1	237	101*	29.62
H. W. Joynt	*Dorset*	10	3	206	53	29.42
J. D. Bond	*Lancashire II*	29	4	735	107*	29.40
D. J. Laitt	*Oxfordshire*	12	1	322	71	29.27
I. Gibson	*Lancashire II*	10	1	263	86	29.22
M. D. Corke	*Suffolk*	15	3	350	85	29.16
B. C. G. Wilenkin..	*Oxfordshire*	18	0	525	96	29.16
F. Apperley	*Staffordshire*	9	0	262	74	29.11
E. Hill	*Somerset II*	10	2	232	40*	29.00
W. H. Miller	*Oxfordshire*	10	0	289	98	28.90
G. C. Lamb	*Durham*	12	1	316	107	28.72
D. A. Bick........	*Middlesex II*	16	3	372	128*	28.61
J. G. C. Surridge ..	*Berkshire*	13	1	343	103	28.58

* *Signifies not out.*

	County	Innings	Not Outs	Runs	Highest Innings	Average
W. Lawton	*Cumberland*	12	0	342	120	28.50
G. L. B. August ..	*Bedfordshire*	14	1	370	116	28.46
R. Hawes.........	*Cambridgeshire*	10	0	284	90	28.40
I. R. Lomax	*Wiltshire*	12	1	312	84*	28.36
D. B. Parkin	*Hertfordshire*	10	1	255	68	28.33
F. Butler	*Staffordshire*	10	0	282	91	28.20
R. G. Simons	*Hertfordshire*	10	0	281	88	28.10
R. S. Ellwood	*Cumberland*	10	1	252	68*	28.00
B. A. Wilson	*Suffolk*	12	3	252	57	28.00
J. A. Mence	*Berkshire*	18	0	501	91	27.83
D. O. Baldry	*Middlesex II*	8	1	194	43	27.71
A. H. Mills	*Wiltshire*	12	0	331	55	27.58
P. G. Powell	*Norfolk*	18	0	496	83	27.55
C. Pickett	*Buckinghamshire*	13	1	330	80	27.50
D. Greasley	*Northants II*	15	2	357	101*	27.46
C. S. R. Boswell ..	*Norfolk*	15	3	329	94	27.41
R. T. Weeks	*Warwickshire II*	17	4	355	77*	27.30
R. J. Knight	*Wiltshire*	12	0	326	96	27.16
S. Smith	*Lancashire II*	25	2	624	115*	27.13
A. N. S. Burnett...	*Devon*	11	3	215	43	26.87
C. W. Leach	*Warwickshire II*	22	0	590	68	26.81
S. Leadbetter ...	*Northants II*	17	1	425	68	26.56
A. P. Potter.......	*Notts II*	9	1	210	78	26.25
R. Aspinall	*Durham*	9	1	210	56	26.25
B. M. Lowe.......	*Cheshire*	14	1	337	75	25.92
L. E. Liddell	*Northumberland*	14	3	283	48	25.72
H. G. Hunt	*Dorset*	9	1	205	63	25.62
J. Hurn	*Wiltshire*	14	0	358	100	25.57

* *Signifies not out.*

BOWLING

(Qualification: 20 wickets, average 24.00)

	County	Overs	Maidens	Runs	Wickets	Average
E. A. Bedser	*Surrey II*	144.3	73	201	24	8.37
D. J. Laitt	*Oxfordshire*	170	58	575	46	12.50
H. R. A. Kelleher	*Surrey II*	357.4	105	791	59	13.40
E. Leadbeater ..	*Yorkshire II*	201	45	564	41	13.75
A. J. Hughes	*Buckinghamshire*	197	45	375	27	13.88
A. L. Wells	*Northants II*	138.1	42	320	23	13.91
V. J. Ransom	*Surrey II*	164.3	45	353	25	14.12
H. W. Tilly	*Middlesex II*	266.4	73	661	43	15.37
R. J. Hurst	*Middlesex II*	227.3	70	609	39	15.61
R. G. Carter ...	*Warwickshire II*	206	53	453	29	15.62
T. Greenhough ...	*Lancashire II*	409.1	130	977	62	15.75
L. McGibbon ...	*Northumberland*	174.5	53	412	26	15.84
G. C. Perkins ...	*Suffolk*	254.1	88	557	35	15.91
K. R. Dollery ...	*Warwickshire II*	195	55	405	25	16.20
D. Halfyard	*Surrey II*	333	111	880	54	16.29
J. Van Geloven ...	*Yorkshire II*	223	53	591	36	16.41
I. M. King......	*Warwickshire II*	240.3	109	446	27	16.51
M. E. Scott	*Durham*	252.3	69	609	36	16.91
A. G. Coomb ...	*Bedfordshire*	213.1	52	593	35	16.94
F. Moore	*Lancashire II*	280.5	85	633	37	17.10
K. J. Earl	*Northumberland*	277.5	66	700	39	17.94
I. Davidson	*Bedfordshire*	146	29	441	23	19.17
R. Aspinall	*Durham*	170.1	57	389	20	19.45
S. Starkie	*Northants II*	150.3	37	449	23	19.52
G. Booth	*Yorkshire II*	169.1	35	508	26	19.53

County		Overs	Maidens	Runs	Wickets	Average
P. Palmer.......	*Essex II*	259.4	58	821	42	19.54
P. Fussell	*Somerset II*	165.3	38	411	21	19.57
B. Shardlow	*Staffordshire*	222	65	552	28	19.71
W. Lawton	*Cumberland*	229.2	79	466	23	20.26
M. McKendrick .	*Northumberland*	240.3	60	633	31	20.41
A. P. Potter.....	*Notts II*	189.3	49	559	27	20.70
J. M. Watson ...	*Northumberland*	300.4	71	851	41	20.75
J. Kelly	*Notts II*	253	99	506	24	21.08
J. G. Williamson	*Durham*	246.1	71	675	32	21.09
R. C. Marques ..	*Hertfordshire*	194	35	575	27	21.29
M. N. Morgan ..	*Berkshire*	182	40	454	21	21.61
D. H. Cole	*Devon*	196.5	36	549	25	21.96
D. E. Pratt	*Surrey II*	233	68	645	29	22.24
P. G. Walmsley .	*Norfolk*	297.1	83	848	38	22.31
C. Pickett	*Buckinghamshire*	450.5	104	854	38	22·47
T. Angus	*Middlesex II*	144.4	23	455	20	22.75
T. G. Morley ...	*Hertfordshire*	280	67	778	34	22.88
C. E. W. Brooks .	*Berkshire*	193.4	29	647	28	23.10
C. W. Smith	*Buckinghamshire*	460.5	96	1046	44	23.77

THE CRICKET SOCIETIES

Cricket Societies continue to flourish, and they are holding a joint meeting at Lilleshall, Shropshire, in June, 1956. The Cricket Society, originally formed in 1945 as "The Society of Cricket Statisticians," has over 750 members and aims to provide contacts between cricket lovers all over the world. It organises matches, social functions and discussion meetings, publishes news letters and bulletins and has a free circulating library. The Hon. Secretary is C. V. P. Airey, 71 Lincoln's Inn Fields, London, W.C.2.

The Northern Cricket Society has over 600 members and a full programme of talks, film shows, lunches, dinners and matches. Hon. Secretary, C. R. Yeomans, 88 Church Lane, Cross Gates, Leeds.

Also over 600 in membership is the Cricket Society of Scotland, who have extended their activities from Edinburgh and Glasgow to many other parts, with many well-known cricketers as speakers. Private premises have been obtained in Edinburgh for regular meetings and a library is available. Hon. Secretary: J. M. Fleming, 31 Murrayfield Gardens, Edinburgh 12.

The youngest society is the Wombwell Cricket Lovers Society, formed in late 1952. In addition to social functions they provide winter and summer coaching for local youngsters and sponsor a cricket league for young players. Annually, they present a trophy to their Cricketer of the Year, the 1955 choice being P. B. H. May. Secretary: Mr. J. Sokell, 20 Orchard Street, Wombwell, Barnsley, Yorks.

THE PUBLIC SCHOOLS IN 1955

By E. M. WELLINGS

Public School cricketers of 1955 improved on acquaintance. When they first arrived at Lord's for their four days of representative cricket they looked a decidedly moderate crowd. By the end of the fourth day they had created a much better impression, and in the last innings of all there was even a welcome improvement in the fielding standard. On the whole, however, that was again much below what we have every right to expect from youngsters enjoying continuous opportunities for practice. Nothing will induce me to become really enthusiastic about Public School cricket until this fielding weakness has been put right.

At one time during the first day of the match between the chosen XI and Combined Services I made note that in succession G. W. Cook (Dulwich), B. L. Reed (Winchester) and M. D. Duck (Wellingborough) allowed the ball to go between their legs. There will doubtless be some who will ask why these three offenders should be named. My answer is that general criticism of the fielding standard seems to get us nowhere. Let us therefore proceed from the general to the particular. Then the young cricketers who offer themselves for our approval annually at Lord's may take more pains to fit themselves as fielders for that experience. There can be no excuse for such players to allow the ball through their legs now that the fielding quality of the playing area at Lord's has been improved. If they fail to that extent they deserve to be noted and named.

Young English cricketers have need to pay more attention to their fielding than boys of most other cricketing countries. The reason is that the majority of those who prosper as batsmen or bowlers are astonishingly awkward movers. There seems to be no grace of movement about most of them, and they contrast greatly with the easy movers from other parts of the Commonwealth. It might be that athletic and gymnastic instruction would benefit our young cricketers.

No amount of help, however, will avail them if they will not devote much more time to fielding practice. G. W. Cook, for instance, is a large fellow who moves ponderously. If he wishes to get anywhere in the game, he therefore needs to do everything to overcome his natural handicap. He has not allowed it to hold him back as batsman and bowler. Why then should he let it so hamper his fielding? He and the many other young players whose state is similar, should reflect that it is much easier to make oneself into a good fielder while young than at any other period during a playing career.

If I have given the impression that the fielding was unusually bad this year, that is not what was intended. It has indeed been worse, but it is still so far below a good standard that it seems wise to state the case strongly. There was happily an improvement before the end of the four days, and generally the catching was superior to the ground fielding. A. R. B. Neame of Harrow, who was a highly accomplished all-rounder, took a most brilliant catch in the big match against the Services. Moreover, from first to last the wicket-keeping was so good that it seemed a pity that both the stumpers on trial, C. B. Howland (Dulwich) and A. C. Smith (King Edward's, Birmingham), could not advance into the representative side.

There are fortunately signs that some of the schools are mindful of the importance of fielding. Bradfield, for instance, claim that their success—nine wins against two defeats—was largely due to their catching and throwing. Charterhouse, who won seven times and lost only once, report somewhat similarly. So do Marlborough, who won more often than they lost in spite of having weak batting. Moreover, those reporting on the success of the three schools with claims to be considered the year's leaders, Wellington, Winchester and Dulwich, also mentioned their standard in the field. Of the three, Wellington perhaps have the strongest claims to be placed first. They were unbeaten and they won seven times. Moreover, they were outstanding against other schools, among whom Eton, Harrow and Haileybury were heavily beaten. All three of the leaders were deservedly represented by two players each at Lord's. They helped the South to beat the Rest by a wide margin, and all six then went forward to the representative match.

That trial game was played on a pitch which might charitably have been described as sporting. It played well enough on the first day, but before the end it was rough, though not perhaps quite rough enough to account for the collapse of both batting sides. In a well-beaten side from northern parts P. J. Sharpe justified the batting reputation which had preceded him from Worksop. There he had made 1,251 runs for the school team, with an average of 113.7. Among his seven centuries were two exceeding 200 and two others which were scored in the same match. In his spare time Sharpe had also taken 23 wickets. It may be that he had made too many runs and some of those rather too easily. That would account for the one obvious weakness he showed at Lord's. It was a weakness of outlook, for he was inclined to be careless and to take liberties which cost him his wicket needlessly.

Sharpe did not, for that reason, score as freely in these representative matches as outstanding batsmen of the past, most notably P. B. H. May. But I have not the slightest hesitation in describing him as an outstanding schoolboy batsman. He was a stockily built young cricketer with a maturity of technique beyond his age. He

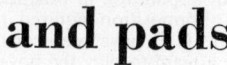

had a wide range of solid and well-managed strokes, and he looked equally good off front and back foot. To a bowler his bat must have looked not only illegally wide but uncompromisingly straight. His bat indeed appeared as broad as his person, and between the two he allowed no gap. The one technical flaw was a tendency to try to play the ball pitched on the leg stump too square on the leg side—a flaw which has often cost leading Test batsmen their wickets while touring on the faster Australian pitches.

In common with several others, Sharpe was also an indifferent runner between wickets. He squandered several runs by that failing, and, like fielding, this is one of the arts which suffers from neglect in the schools. One who was worse in this respect was also one of the faulty fielders, and may here be allowed anonymity. He never seemed prepared for an over-throw, nor for a second run when the ball was misfielded. Lazy running is common in all ranks of the game today, but there is less excuse for it among boys than among any other group of players.

As a team the Public Schools played with considerable spirit against an apparently superior Combined Services side, which proved disappointing in practice. The Services have not provided the type of opposition required in this match, and it is not surprising that the M.C.C. have been considering making themselves responsible for a team to play the boys.

On this occasion the Schools were not far from victory at the close, after having fought back from a position of almost certain disaster. In their second innings they had three men, including Sharpe, out for 30 and were still three runs behind. They were saved by D. J. Mordaunt (Wellington) and G. W. Cook, who put on 71 for the fourth wicket. In previous innings Cook had appeared to some to be unnecessarily cautious, but now his powers of concentration and his solid defence came in extremely handy. He provided the stubbornness while Mordaunt boldly challenged the Service bowlers and deprived them of the initiative. It was a notable piece of cricket.

Cook, who had made 734 runs at an average of 66.7 for Dulwich, based his soundness on a brief back lift. Mordaunt was a free batsman with an obvious love of driving, and, if his bat was not always quite straight while driving, the fault was not vital. He did, too, appear to sacrifice control by holding the bat close to the top of the handle, in spite of which he was clearly a most excellent schoolboy batsman. He and the other Wellington representative, I. A. Addison, had splendid seasons for their school side. Not otherwise perhaps would Mordaunt have won through to the representative side. In the trial game he was stumped for a small score in the first innings, and in the second he was monstrously unlucky. He received a ball which kicked so sharply from a good length that he was struck on the right shoulder, and on appeal he was given out caught in the gully. In the end all came right for him, since in the representative match he was top scorer in each innings.

Addison was the highly successful captain of Wellington, the leading batsman and also the wicket-keeper. He could not keep wicket at Lord's, but he turned his talents to slip fielding with conspicuous success. His batting was sound and sensible, and his cover driving most attractive. He resembled Sharpe in not making all the runs at Lord's that he appeared worth.

The main batting of the schools was completed by a couple of diminutive cricketers, B. L. Reed of Winchester and Neame. Though he began with an innings of 33, Reed had a disappointing run. He appeared to be passing through a temporary spell of staleness, during which he got out in some rather elementary ways. His Winchester record against good opposition places him in a high class, but just how high we were not allowed to judge. Neame, who had also been one of the leading players of the previous year, batted particularly well in the trial match. On the second day of that game, when the pitch was unreliable, his 45 not out while his side could total only 118 was an excellent innings. He watches the ball closely, has a good defence and bases his play on nimble footwork. He was also the team's off-break bowler, and a good one with a springy action.

As though being the leading all-rounder was not enough, Neame had a busy summer captaining his school and then his two teams at Lord's. His own play seemed rather better than his captaincy. It is a difficult job captaining a scratch team of school-boys insufficiently grounded in the cricketing arts. Both Neame and M. D. Duck, who led the Rest, suffered from the ignorance of the fielding positions shown by several of their followers. Some very peculiar positions were taken for the slow left-arm bowling of D. M. Alty (Merchant Taylors, Crosby) and the fast left-hander, D. R. Cook (Warwick). The latter suffered not a little from the habit of his short-leg fielders to stand too deep and also on occasions from the absence of a short fine leg.

D. R. Cook was one of a trio of good seam bowlers chosen against the Services. He was the fastest of them and one who looked likely to develop into a really good bowler. He had a good, powerful action, and in addition to his natural in-swing he could move the ball away from the batsman off the pitch. He was successful in both matches and deservedly so. He was also an uninhibited clouter of the ball with the bat, and that he batted at number ten indicated the absence of a tail in the representative side.

The other two opening type bowlers were C. A. A. Black, who had taken 54 wickets at 12.8 for Winchester, and Duck, who was an all-rounder with particular emphasis at Lord's on his bowling. All three were able to bowl accurately, and it was pleasing to see that each could move the ball towards the slips. It was as much due to the persistence of their attack as to lack of enterprise on the part of the batsmen that the Combined Services could manage only 131 for 7, when set to hit 184 in 145 minutes on the last afternoon.

In spite of Neame, the spin was not so impressive as the faster bowling. The attack was completed in its main form by Alty, a slow left-hander who made little use of spin. He did not take many wickets, but he played his part usefully in the big match as a batsmen with a free style. G. W. Cook and Mordaunt were also bowlers of some ability.

There was some curious captaincy in the trial game which kept A. Hurd, of Chigwell, out of the Rest attack until seven Southern wickets were down in the second innings. Having batted at number eleven, he must have been wondering about his exact role, when a belated message from the pavilion reminded his captain that he was selected as an off-break bowler. Hurd then took two of the remaining three wickets and actually looked the most promising spin bowler in the game. He had a good, lively action and spun the ball more than anyone else, which, incidentally, brought out the best of Smith's wicket-keeping. Happily Hurd was due to remain at school for another year and could expect another chance of playing in the big match.

So many of the leading boy players both bat and bowl—even if they sometimes neglect their fielding—that it is not easy to give all a full chance in a trial game lasting two days. Several of those who remained reserves figured only briefly and inconclusively in the proceedings. As the game went the reserve strength appeared slight, so that only Smith, Hurd and R. C. Coke-Wallis, another useful seam bowler from Marlborough, challenged the chosen XI at all closely.

It is not so long ago that the trial game was between Lord's Schools and the Rest. In 1955 only three members of school teams who play at Lord's were selected for the Southern Schools and the Rest game. They were Neame, Coke-Wallis and E. McQ. Rose of Rugby. The change has obviously benefited schools cricket by widening the field of choice, though the strength of the Southern Schools is habitually such that even in its present form the game is not entirely satisfactory.

Among the Lord's schools without a representative was Eton. In recent seasons they have contributed comparatively little to these games, which is a source of weakness, for they were formerly a school who provided the representative team with a solid foundation. In 1955 they had an unusually young side, some of whom may now develop into representative class players. There were others in the schools of obvious promise for 1956, including J. R. Bernard, who topped both the batting and bowling averages at

Clifton. H. J. Conlin, who took 50 wickets for Downside, was another scheduled for another year at school, while G. J. Sharman (Lancing) and R. M. Prideaux (Tonbridge), though still younger, were among the successful cricketers of the year of whom we should soon hear more.

The signs for 1956 were good, but obviously the fulfilment of the considerable promise shown by these younger players will depend in part on their willingness to tackle the fielding question. Even the best batsman or bowler may find himself disregarded by the selectors at Lord's unless he can field well. It happened to P. B. H. May during his last but one year at Charterhouse. He had played for the representative side in the previous year, and after the gap he did so again two years later, since when there can have been few complaints about his fielding. If the selectors at Lord's could drop May, then no lazy fielder among the leading school cricketers has reason to consider himself safe.

Following are destinations of some of the members of last years' school elevens:

	OXFORD	CAMBRIDGE
Aldenham	D. J. Mundy	
Bloxham	R. E. Towner	
Bradfield	J. B. Brow	N. E. R. Robson
Brentwood...........	G. P. Harrison	N. A. Maryan Green
Christ's Hospital		R. H. Stevens
Cranleigh		C. D. White
Dean Close		F. C. Welles
Dulwich		G. W. Cook
		C. B. Howland
		M. A. Shirley
		N. C. Tinworth
Eastbourne		T. C. Wilson
Edinburgh Academy ..		F. H. D. Walker
Felsted		R. M. Moody
Highgate	A. J. Murray	
Ipswich		J. R. S. Mash
King's, Canterbury ...	C. J. Lainé	
King William's, I.o.M.		B. K. Colvin
		S. G. S. Scott
Lancing		G. G. B. Wilkes
Marlborough	R. C. Coke-Wallis	

	OXFORD	CAMBRIDGE
Monkton Combe	R. C. Holt	
	S. H. Maslen	
Nottingham..........		R. Foster
		N. Warren
Oakham		P. I. D. James
Oundle		A. J. T. Crabbe
St. Bees		F. Booth
St. Edward's, Oxford..	J. R. Friend	
St. Paul's		P. Wheeler
Sutton Valence		B. G. Keeble
Worcester	J. G. Wilkinson	
	D. L. Williams	

THE SCHOOLS

† Indicates captain.   ** Signifies not out.*

ALDENHAM SCHOOL

The Aldenham side proved one of the best of recent years and were concerned in a number of exciting finishes. The all-round ability of D. J. Mundy stood out for the third successive year and a young leg-spin bowler, A. R. Day, showed considerable promise. The batting was well balanced and the fielding alert.

Played 15, Won 5, Lost 2, Drawn 8

Batting

	Innings	Not outs	Runs	Highest inns.	Average
†R. S. G. Heslop	16	5	315	68*	28.63
S. A. Hussain	15	0	312	71	20.80
D. J. Mundy	16	0	299	65	18.68
P. A. Boitel-Gill	16	0	279	61	17.43
A. R. Day	15	0	238	54	15.86

Bowling

	Overs	Maidens	Runs	Wickets	Average
R. T. Rainey	123	24	278	26	10.69
D. J. Mundy	179	50	409	30	13 63
A. R. Day	146	17	447	32	13.96
J. H. Riley	170	36	369	22	16.77

ALLEYN'S SCHOOL

Played 15, Won 7, Lost 4, Drawn 4

Batting

	Innings	Not outs	Runs	Highest inns.	Average
†P. A. Badmin	14	4	402	65	40.20
D. Jacobs	8	2	128	48	21.33
I. N. Trafford	14	2	253	68	21.08

Bowling

	Overs	Maidens	Runs	Wickets	Average
R. F. Dorey	62	19	172	26	6.61
J. A. Saunders	146	52	290	24	12.08
G. F. Pye	67	9	315	21	15.00
P. A. Badmin	123	39	308	19	16.21
M. J. Edwards	116	25	379	23	16.47

ALLHALLOWS SCHOOL

Played 14, Won 3, Lost 3, Drawn 8

Batting

	Innings	Not outs	Runs	Highest inns.	Average
†M. J. Farwell	14	2	400	86*	33.33
D. W. Palmer	13	2	291	68	26.45
P. J. Colson	14	1	282	68*	21.69
P. G. Rowe	10	4	126	42	21.00
K. G. Cliff	10	2	144	38*	18.00
R. Connett	13	1	209	63	17.41

Bowling

	Overs		Maidens		Runs		Wickets		Average
D. W. Palmer	91	..	14	..	256	..	14	..	18.28
P. R. Ward	90	..	16	..	240	..	13	..	18.46
P. G. Rowe	140	..	10	..	557	..	26	..	21.42
A. J. Stutter	227	..	37	..	570	..	26	..	21.92
J. M. McFadyean	81	..	12	..	242	..	10	..	24.20

AMPLEFORTH COLLEGE

Bad weather during May gave Ampleforth no chance to practise and results did not do full justice to their potential strength. J. H. Sullivan was the best cricketer both with bat and ball but too much responsibility fell on his shoulders.

Played 10, Won 0, Lost 5, Drawn 5

Batting

	Innings		Not outs		Runs		Highest inns.		Average
J. H. Sullivan	11	..	4	..	435	..	69*	..	62.14
D. M. Thompson	8	..	0	..	260	..	80	..	32.50
T. J. Perry	11	..	3	..	254	..	77*	..	31.75
M. Dougal	9	..	1	..	147	..	38	..	18.37
B. J. Morris	11	..	0	..	173	..	66	..	15.72

Bowling

	Overs		Maidens		Runs		Wickets		Average
Master of Lovat	51.5	..	12	..	158	..	13	..	12.15
R. Lorimer	110.4	..	22	..	325	..	22	..	14.77
J. H. Sullivan	200	..	57	..	511	..	28	..	18.25
J. M. Morton	95.5	..	10	..	411	..	17	..	24.18

ARDINGLY COLLEGE

Played 12, Won 5, Lost 1, Drawn 6

Batting

	Innings		Not outs		Runs		Highest inns.		Average
†B. L. Morris	12	..	1	..	328	..	74*	..	29.81
T. F. Baiden	12	..	3	..	254	..	68*	..	28.22
E. P. Kirk	9	..	4	..	125	..	38*	..	25.00
D. E. Wilmshurst	12	..	0	..	232	..	49	..	19.33
R. W. Joyce	9	..	2	..	134	..	38*	..	19.14
A. P. H. Whyte	12	..	1	..	209	..	52*	..	19.00

Bowling

	Overs		Maidens		Runs		Wickets		Average
M. J. Mance	40.5	..	9	..	96	..	16	..	6.00
S. C. Mounsey	219.2	..	73	..	444	..	33	..	13.45
B. L. Morris	152	..	48	..	341	..	24	..	14.20
M. B. Allingham	93.5	..	18	..	373	..	26	..	14.34

BANCROFT'S SCHOOL

Played 13, Won 4, Lost 4, Drawn 5

Batting

	Innings		Not outs		Runs		Highest inns.		Average
†D. N. Macfarlane	11	..	1	..	248	..	83	..	24.80
M. C. Meredith	13	..	1	..	269	..	63	..	22.41
G. L. Rice	13	..	1	..	167	..	35*	..	13.91
A. G. Meredith	13	..	3	..	136	..	38	..	13.60

Bowling

	Overs		Maidens		Runs		Wickets		Average
A. G. Johnson	159	..	44	..	361	..	35	..	10.31
D. N. Macfarlane	187.2	..	39	..	464	..	38	..	12.21
T. J. Whittingdale	58	..	12	..	182	..	11	..	16.54
P. W. Green	72.3	..	9	..	255	..	14	..	18.21

BEAUMONT COLLEGE

Played 12, Won 3, Lost 3, Drawn 6

Batting

	Innings		Not outs		Runs		Highest inns.		Average
R. J. Mills-Owen	13	..	2	..	432	..	114	..	39.27
†D. A. Bulfield	12	..	1	..	383	..	104*	..	34.81
J. P. Bedford............	11	..	2	..	301	..	101*	..	33.44
P. D. Bird	12	..	2	..	231	..	59	..	23.10
M. H. Barnes	12	..	1	..	185	..	87	..	16.81
G. M. Hoghton	13	..	1	..	200	..	71	..	16.66

Bowling

	Overs		Maidens		Runs		Wickets		Average
R. MacQueen	128	..	32	..	363	..	27	..	13.44
M. H. Barnes	262	..	69	..	623	..	44	..	14.15
D. A. Bulfield	194	..	35	..	510	..	26	..	19.61
R. Quinn	87	..	19	..	233	..	11	..	21.18

BEDFORD MODERN SCHOOL

Results were disappointing, mainly through the inability of leading batsmen to speed the scoring when they were well established. The captain, D. J. Wilson, and P. D. Watts, enjoyed successes with both bat and ball and W. Chamberlain proved a sound opening batsman. The fielding was generally good.

Played 11, Won 3, Lost 2, Drawn 6

Batting

	Innings		Not outs		Runs		Highest inns.		Average
W. Chamberlain	12	..	1	..	472	..	111*	..	42.90
P. D. Watts	11	..	1	..	315	..	88	..	31.50
†D. J. Wilson	12	..	2	..	217	..	73*	..	21.70
P. J. Stretton...........	9	..	3	..	129	..	41	..	21.50
P. E. G. White	7	..	2	..	107	..	35*	..	21.40
K. H. Richardson	12	..	4	..	118	..	28*	..	14.75

Bowling

	Overs		Maidens		Runs		Wickets		Average
D. J. Wilson	178.2	..	41	..	416	..	32	..	13.00
P. E. G. White	119.4	..	25	..	281	..	21	..	13.38
P. D. Watts	106	..	21	..	270	..	20	..	13.50
K. H. Richardson	122	..	34	..	227	..	16	..	14.18

BEDFORD SCHOOL

A young team gained in experience as the season progressed and, with ten remaining for 1956, prospects are bright. In school games, Bedford were beaten only by the strong Dulwich XI. They defeated Stowe and The Leys and drew with Tonbridge, Haileybury and Aldenham. The Oundle match was rained off for the fourth consecutive year. K. Rischmiller, who hit centuries against the XL Club and Old Bedfordians, was the best batsman and J. N. Ferro, captain next year, formed a hostile opening attack with R. G. Bass.

Played 13, *Won* 3, *Lost* 4, *Drawn* 6

Batting

	Innings	Not outs	Runs	Highest inns.	Average
K. Rischmiller	13	2	380	121	34.54
C. Kapur	15	3	273	50	22.75
P. M. Howlett	12	1	219	49	19.90
R. L. J. Kilby	10	3	114	33	16.28
†R. H. Meadows	12	1	160	50	14.54

Bowling

	Overs	Maidens	Runs	Wickets	Average
J. N. Ferro	125.3	15	540	32	16.87
D. C. Eldridge	182	31	495	28	17.67
R. G. Bass..............	232	30	513	27	19.00
D. G. Conniff	73	10	377	12	31.41

BISHOP'S STORTFORD COLLEGE

Played 11, *Won* 3, *Lost* 2, *Drawn* 6

Batting

	Innings	Not outs	Runs	Highest inns.	Average
R. Bailey	10	1	216	51	24.00
H. W. Lambert.........	11	2	177	42*	19.66
A. R. Mason...........	9	0	119	42	13.22
P. C. Chapman.........	11	1	108	35*	10.80

Bowling

	Overs	Maidens	Runs	Wickets	Average
R. Bailey	74.3	11	232	17	13.64
T. S. Herring	62	9	205	14	14.64
P. C. Chapman.........	68.4	8	187	12	15.58
M. J. Covill...........	99	21	246	13	18.92

BLOXHAM SCHOOL

Played 13, *Won* 5, *Lost* 4, *Drawn* 4

Batting

	Innings	Not outs	Runs	Highest inns.	Average
*R. E. Towner	13	2	292	55	26.54
J. D. Lilwall	13	0	263	75	20.23
M. F. Elkington	13	1	233	86	19.41
D. L. Pearson	13	0	212	46	16.30
C. R. Jones	12	1	145	52	13.18
J. S. Morgan	10	1	116	44	12.88

Bowling

	Overs	Maidens	Runs	Wickets	Average
D. L. Pearson	57.5	12	155	15	10.33
J. W. Carter	113.1	22	286	26	11.00
A. J. Kaye	94.3	27	264	18	14.66
C. R. Jones	128	27	366	22	16.63
M. F. Elkington	110.3	26	373	20	18.65

BLUNDELL'S SCHOOL

With J. J. M. Street, the only old colour, the team proved more successful than was expected. Street deserved credit for his firm, confident leadership and R. J. Firth, a sound opening batsman, showed consistently good form. A. J. N. Edwards repeatedly gave the side an encouraging start in the field by dismissing opposing opening batsmen cheaply with in-swingers.

Played 16, Won 6, Lost 4, Drawn 6

Batting

	Innings	Not outs	Runs	Highest inns.	Average
R. J. Firth	15	0	605	103	40.33
A. R. Tinniswood	16	4	373	105*	31.08
†J. J. M. Street	13	2	262	62	23.81
R. A. W. Sharp	16	0	288	78	18.00
F. J. Davis	16	1	228	41	15.20
C. J. A. Clarke	12	1	166	43*	15.09

Bowling

	Overs	Maidens	Runs	Wickets	Average
A. J. N. Edwards	155.1	36	411	30	13.70
C. J. A. Clarke	173.3	42	449	32	14.03
A. R. Tinniswood	122.3	23	361	23	15.69
F. J. Davis	161	32	486	21	23.14

BRADFIELD COLLEGE

In terms of matches won, Bradfield enjoyed their best season and the only defeats were by margins of one wicket and two wickets respectively. N. E. R. Robson inspired an excellent team-spirit, specially in the field where the catching and throwing were first-rate. The batting was strong and P. J. Workman far exceeded expectations as an opener in his first year. R. S. H. Brewer's total of 53 wickets has only once been surpassed at Bradfield.

Played 13, Won 9, Lost 2, Drawn 2

Batting

	Innings	Not outs	Runs	Highest inns.	Average
J. B. Brow	12	2	345	84	34.50
M. C. F. Cox	11	4	234	67*	33.42
P. J. Workman	13	2	347	80*	31.54
†N. E. R. Robson	12	4	221	52*	27.62
A. W. Fuller	10	1	229	55*	25.44
A. J. Duvivier	13	1	225	38	18.75

Bowling

	Overs	Maidens	Runs	Wickets	Average
R. S. H. Brewer	270.4	84	680	53	12.83
E. J. W. Lewis	235.3	83	514	36	14.26
E. N. Thomas	83	13	238	15	15.86
A. J. Duvivier	68	13	197	10	19.70

BRADFORD GRAMMAR SCHOOL

Played 10, Won 7, Lost 3

Batting

	Innings		Not outs		Runs		Highest inns.		Average
†R. L. Jowett	10	..	0	..	233	..	50	..	23.30
I. M. Hewitt	10	..	1	..	158	..	90*	..	17.55
M. S. Throup	9	..	1	..	119	..	39*	..	14.87
A. J. C. Gray	9	..	0	..	128	..	36	..	14.22

Bowling

	Overs		Maidens		Runs		Wickets		Average
J. P. Bailey	85.5	..	16	..	200	..	31	..	6.45
R. L. Jowett	68	..	14	..	173	..	19	..	9.10
I. M. Hewitt	74.2	..	23	..	144	..	13	..	11.07

BRENTWOOD SCHOOL

The batting suffered from timidity but the team's cricket reached a high standard in the field, where G. P. Harrison, the captain, excelled. J. Barber, a quickish right-arm in-swing bowler, kept the ball well up to the batsman and was rarely off the stumps.

Played 13, Won 6, Lost 5, Drawn 2

Batting

	Innings		Not outs		Runs		Highest inns.		Average
M. J. Davey	12	..	1	..	209	..	56	..	19.00
†G. P. Harrison	13	..	1	..	215	..	46	..	17.91
N. R. Amery	8	..	0	..	124	..	44	..	15.50
N. A. Maryan Green....	13	..	2	..	169	..	59*	..	15.36
J. I. Bowden	12	..	0	..	136	..	41	..	11.33

Bowling

	Overs		Maidens		Runs		Wickets		Average
J. Barber	226.1	..	90	..	399	..	50	..	7.98
J. R. Collyer	174.5	..	49	..	385	..	25	..	15.40
P. A. Hayes............	49.4	..	3	..	227	..	12	..	18.91

BRIGHTON COLLEGE

At their best Brighton played good cricket, J. A. Lush being a capable captain and right-hand batsman who hit hard and deserved his selection for the Southern Schools. He was well supported by D. J. Pickering, a Colt who is a most promising right-hand bat and off-spinner. Another Colt, P. G. Mayle, was the leading member of the attack and has considerable possibilities as a slow left-arm bowler.

Played 13, Won 7, Lost 4, Drawn 2

Batting

	Innings		Not outs		Runs		Highest inns.		Average
†J. A. Lush	13	..	1	..	565	..	101	..	47.08
D. J. Pickering	13	..	1	..	413	..	126	..	34.41
R. C. Usherwood	9	..	3	..	156	..	32	..	26.00
R. W. Lewis	11	..	3	..	191	..	43*	..	23.87
N. V. Abraham	13	..	0	..	267	..	87	..	20.53
M. A. Lansdall	12	..	2	..	200	..	34	..	20.00
P. G. Dalzell	10	..	1	..	114	..	31	..	12.66

Bowling

	Overs		Maidens		Runs		Wickets		Average
P. G. Mayle	167	..	41	..	419	..	28	..	14.96
M. A. Lansdall	85	..	24	..	206	..	13	..	15.84
D. J. Pickering	132	..	29	..	397	..	25	..	15.88
W. N. Wren	96	..	20	..	296	..	16	..	18.50
M. Keith	103	..	25	..	309	..	14	..	22.07

BRISTOL GRAMMAR SCHOOL

Played 11, *Won* 4, *Lost* 2, *Drawn* 5

Batting

	Innings		Not outs		Runs		Highest inns.		Average
R. C. Spiller	11	..	1	..	349	..	66*	..	34.90
†Q. G. Stevens	10	..	2	..	230	..	105	..	28.75
M. F. Barnes	10	..	2	..	116	..	29	..	14.50

Bowling

	Overs		Maidens		Runs		Wickets		Average
B. J. Roberts	72.4	..	25	..	151	..	12	..	12.58
Q. G. Stevens	112.5	..	26	..	337	..	26	..	12.96
A. C. D. Mann	71	..	16	..	193	..	13	..	14.84
M. F. Barnes	173.1	..	43	..	375	..	22	..	17.04

BROMSGROVE SCHOOL

Played 11, *Won* 5, *Lost* 4, *Drawn* 2

Batting

	Innings		Not outs		Runs		Highest inns.		Average
C. W. Kleiser	11	..	3	..	459	..	72*	..	57.37
J. M. M. Huins	11	..	1	..	214	..	48	..	21.40
R. G. Black	10	..	0	..	164	..	72	..	16.40

Bowling

	Overs		Maidens		Runs		Wickets		Average
M. D. Baker	144	..	39	..	349	..	30	..	11.63
K. Garbett	99	..	25	..	256	..	18	..	14.22
R. C. Mackenzie	123.4	..	26	..	343	..	22	..	15.59

BRYANSTON SCHOOL

R. V. Jeffreys, a right-handed opening bat, scored 181 against Canford, but in general the batting was undependable and the bowling undistinguished. In spite of this, the team retained an unbeaten record against other schools dating from May 1953.

Played 12, *Won* 4, *Lost* 3, *Drawn* 5

Batting

	Innings		Not outs		Runs		Highest inns.		Average
R. V. Jeffreys	12	..	0	..	379	..	181	..	31.58
†R. A. M. Purver	13	..	1	..	211	..	73	..	17.58
J. R. C. Lecomber	13	..	2	..	193	..	51	..	17.54
D. S. Anderson	13	..	2	..	178	..	65*	..	16.18
M. F. J. Checksfield	12	..	2	..	143	..	23	..	14.30

Bowling

	Overs		Maidens		Runs		Wickets		Average
R. N. M. Warde	159.5	..	53	..	330	..	27	..	12.22
R. A. M. Purver	206.4	..	61	..	454	..	33	..	13.75
R. S. Kilburn	64.1	..	12	..	169	..	11	..	15.36
P. G. Rhoades	83	..	15	..	256	..	16	..	16.00

CANFORD SCHOOL

Played 11, Won 4, Lost 2, Drawn 5

Batting

	Innings		Not outs		Runs		Highest inns.		Average
M. L. A. Cowan	13	..	1	..	429	..	94	..	35.75
R. H. Palin	13	..	2	..	255	..	102	..	23.18
P. A. T. Traill	13	..	0	..	252	..	54	..	19.38
N. N. Bown	12	..	1	..	174	..	48	..	15.81
R. S. Morton	8	..	0	..	120	..	30	..	15.00
C. M. Campbell	10	..	2	..	117	..	27	..	14.65

Bowling

	Overs		Maidens		Runs		Wickets		Average
H. P. Garon	102.7	..	30	..	236	..	19	..	12.42
H. S. Davenport	67.5	..	15	..	206	..	15	..	13.73
N. N. Bown	154	..	35	..	335	..	18	..	18.61
J. S. Scrivener	80.5	..	9	..	274	..	12	..	22.83

CATERHAM SCHOOL

Played 12, Won 2, Lost 7, Drawn 3

Batting

	Innings		Not outs		Runs		Highest inns.		Average
N. J. Harper	10	..	1	..	203	..	78*	..	22.55
S. D. Mayes	11	..	1	..	178	..	38	..	17.80

Bowling

	Overs		Maidens		Runs		Wickets		Average
J. R. Mathias	86.2	..	34	..	152	..	17	..	8.94
M. Naysmith	43.5	..	9	..	132	..	13	..	10.15
†J. H. Darley	107.5	..	18	..	309	..	21	..	14.71

CHARTERHOUSE SCHOOL

Charterhouse had a most successful season, yet all the inter-school matches were drawn. Ably led by T. R. Jakobson, the team proved to be fairly strong all round, and they owed much of their success to outstanding ability in the field. J. J. Carless, a fine stroke player, was the most consistent batsman, and he received good support from at least half the side. One of the best innings was 100 by P. J. de Q. Adams in ninety minutes on a wet pitch against the Grasshoppers. The bowling, backed up by fine catching, was useful, but rather lacking in penetration. A. T. C. Allom did well with accurate medium pace and G. E. F. Gross bowled steadily. Seven of the XI remain for 1956.

Played 14, Won 7, Lost 1, Drawn 6

Batting

	Innings		Not outs		Runs		Highest inns.		Average
J. J. Carless	15	..	0	..	537	..	104	..	35.80
D. C. Burrows	15	..	0	..	400	..	60	..	26.66
P. J. de Q. Adams ...	16	..	2	..	325	..	100*	..	23.21
A. T. C. Allom	14	..	2	..	270	..	51	..	22.50
†T. R. Jakobson........	15	..	2	..	290	..	71*	..	22.30
A. J. South	12	..	6	..	125	..	37	..	20.83
D. B. Lees	14	..	0	..	275	..	61	..	19.64

Bowling

	Overs		Maidens		Runs		Wickets		Average
A. T. C. Allom	224.4	..	70	..	551	..	34	..	16.20
A. J. South	238	..	57	..	626	..	37	..	16.91
G. E. F. Gross	228.1	..	51	..	599	..	28	..	21.39
J. C. W. Murray	115.1	..	17	..	361	..	16	..	22.56

CHELTENHAM COLLEGE

Though weak in batting, Cheltenham were a better team than their record suggests and nearly all their defeats were by narrow margins. D. J. G. James, the captain, was called upon to build a new side and two fine young spin bowlers, J. A. Wichers (left arm) and A. F. Benke (off-breaks), came to the fore. A good fast bowler would have made the bowling formidable. Besides keeping wicket well, C. D. Marsden showed high promise with the bat, as did P. W. F. Stutchbury, a Colt.

Played 11, Won 2, Lost 7, Drawn 2

Batting

	Innings		Not outs		Runs		Highest inns.		Average
C. D. Marsden	16	..	2	..	381	..	69	..	27.21
P. W. F. Stutchbury	16	..	1	..	324	..	70	..	21.60
J. A. Hancock	12	..	2	..	187	..	87*	..	18.70
G. J. Cleland	14	..	1	..	221	..	67	..	17.08
J. A. S. Donald	16	..	0	..	264	..	41	..	16.50
†D. J. G. James	16	..	0	..	211	..	67	..	13.18
T. H. Coke	16	..	0	..	201	..	36	..	12.56
P. F. Ross	10	..	1	..	106	..	39	..	11.77

Bowling

	Overs		Maidens		Runs		Wickets		Average
J. A. Wichers	242.3	..	43	..	663	..	47	..	14.10
A. F. Benke	218	..	41	..	657	..	42	..	15.64
D. J. G. James	149.5	..	33	..	432	..	22	..	19.63
S. E. Khazzam	65	..	6	..	260	..	10	..	26.00

CHIGWELL SCHOOL

Although not a well-balanced side, Chigwell enjoyed a most successful season, chiefly because of the excellent bowling of A. Hurd (off-breaks), who was outstanding for the third successive year, and D. L. Reeves (slow-medium).

Played 10, Won 8, Lost 1, Drawn 1

Batting

	Innings		Not outs		Runs		Highest inns.		Average
J. P. Josling	14	..	2	..	415	..	90	..	34.58
D. L. Reeves	14	..	5	..	304	..	46	..	33.77
B. J. Styles	14	..	2	..	315	..	102*	..	26.25
†G. E. Hurd	13	..	4	..	221	..	56*	..	24.55

Bowling

	Overs		Maidens		Runs		Wickets		Average
A. Hurd	291.5	..	107	..	509	..	64	..	7.95
D. L. Reeves	218.4	..	70	..	399	..	40	..	9.97

CHRIST'S HOSPITAL

R. H. Stevens, a good batsman, led a cheerful side extremely well and made the most of limited bowling resources. P. J. Hill, who will be captain in 1956, scored an admirable century against the Sussex Martlets and the batting generally was sound.

Played 14, *Won* 4, *Lost* 8, *Drawn* 2

Batting

	Innings		Not outs		Runs		Highest inns.		Average
†R. H. Stevens	13	..	0	..	419	..	67	..	32.23
P. J. Hill	14	..	1	..	330	..	102*	..	25.38
N. P. Thompson	14	..	2	..	293	..	72*	..	24.41
E. J. Crutchley	12	..	0	..	233	..	63	..	19.41
J. M. Brougham	14	..	4	..	186	..	50*	..	18.60
J. G. B. Martin	13	..	1	..	210	..	55*	..	17.50
P. G. Crook	8	..	0	..	138	..	42	..	17.25
S. G. Hoare	14	..	0	..	194	..	68	..	13.85

Bowling

	Overs		Maidens		Runs		Wickets		Average
P. G. Crook	95.2	..	15	..	344	..	19	..	18.10
J. M. Brougham	173.2	..	43	..	487	..	20	..	24.35
N. P. Thompson	187.3	..	36	..	619	..	22	..	28.13
C. W. Grace	84.5	..	12	..	321	..	10	..	32.10

CITY OF LONDON SCHOOL

Under D. A. Bignell, a useful left-arm bowler, the team enjoyed fair success. I. F. C. Brown, a particularly strong driver and sound in defence, and G. Duckworth, an all-rounder, showed special promise.

Played 14, *Won* 6, *Lost* 3, *Drawn* 5

Batting

	Innings		Not outs		Runs		Highest inns.		Average
I. F. C Brown	13	..	3	..	314	..	76	..	31.40
G. Duckworth	11	..	2	..	265	..	92*	..	29.44
A. McPherson	11	..	1	..	155	..	37	..	15.50
J. R. Petzold	13	..	1	..	133	..	58	..	11.08

Bowling

	Overs		Maidens		Runs		Wickets		Average
†D. A. Bignell	163.2	..	41	..	378	..	32	..	11.81
L. Levy	104.5	..	35	..	189	..	16	..	11.81
G. Duckworth	119.5	..	22	..	301	..	25	..	12.04
G. Call	97	..	23	..	254	..	19	..	13.36
M. A. Frankel	110.3	..	19	..	325	..	24	..	13.54

CLIFTON COLLEGE

Clifton perhaps were not more than average in batting and bowling, but excelled in fielding throughout the season. D. C. Mills was a most able captain, and, it is expected, will again lead the team in 1956. J. R. Bernard, a young all-rounder, showed himself to be the most promising cricketer Clifton have had for some years. C. A. H. White kept wicket well for the third year in succession, and R. W. Mathias, a 15-year-old left-hander, showed distinct ability. All the other players had their moments of success, specially R. H. Whitty, a creditable fast-bowler and very safe slip catcher.

Played 15, Won 4, Lost 3, Drawn 8

Batting

	Innings		Not outs		Runs		Highest inns.		Average
J. R. Bernard	14	..	0	..	378	..	93	..	27.00
C. A. H. White	14	..	1	..	337	..	53	..	25.92
R. W. Mathias	10	..	4	..	138	..	55*	..	23.00
†D. C. Mills	17	..	0	..	387	..	50	..	22.75
W. S. Linnell	14	..	2	..	213	..	54*	..	17.75
M. R. Williams	18	..	4	..	237	..	40*	..	16.92
P. A. Brain	13	..	2	..	161	..	36*	..	14.63

Bowling

	Overs		Maidens		Runs		Wickets		Average
J. R. Bernard	239.5	..	48	..	607	..	43	..	14.11
R. H. Whitty	200.4	..	27	..	670	..	35	..	19.14
D. C. Mills	167.2	..	25	..	623	..	30	..	20.76
J. C. M. Whittaker	163.2	..	33	..	453	..	16	..	28.31

CRANBROOK SCHOOL

J. A. H. Townsend, the captain, established a school record by taking fifty-eight wickets with his right-arm leg-breaks and the wicket-keeper, A. E. S. Bond, who gave him excellent support, also beat the previous best for Cranbrook. He claimed twenty-nine victims, nineteen of them stumped. They shared the honours of a successful season with A. J. S. Todman, a fine all-rounder.

Played 15, Won 7, Lost 3, Drawn 5

Batting

	Innings		Not outs		Runs		Highest inns.		Average
A. J. S. Todman	14	..	2	..	397	..	80	..	33.08
J. C. Watts	14	..	4	..	243	..	46*	..	24.30
B. R. Watts	12	..	2	..	182	..	41*	..	18.20
K. G. D. Bachelor	14	..	1	..	218	..	58*	..	16.76
A. E. S. Bond	14	..	1	..	186	..	50	..	14.30
B. L. Hartley	11	..	2	..	119	..	38*	..	13.22
†J. A. H. Townsend	14	..	0	..	172	..	68	..	12.28

Bowling

	Overs		Maidens		Runs		Wickets		Average
A. J. S. Todman	148.5	..	50	..	320	..	33	..	9.69
J. A. H. Townsend	242.5	..	72	..	642	..	58	..	11.06
B. L. Hartley	178	..	62	..	318	..	25	..	12.72
I. Weltman	138.1	..	48	..	295	..	16	..	18.43

CRANLEIGH SCHOOL

All the batsmen were willing to hit the ball hard but only C. D. White, the captain, showed much consistency. More than one collapse in the middle of the order was retrieved by the "tail-enders," notably R. J. Farrar at No. 9. The bowling was weakened by the lack of both off- and leg-spin but there was always willing support in the field. Every player threw well.

Played 12, Won 4, Lost 4, Drawn 4

Batting

	Innings		Not outs		Runs		Highest inns.		Average
†C. D. White	13	..	2	..	426	..	71	..	38.72
R. J. Farrar	9	..	3	..	147	..	41*	..	24.50
J. W. McDermott	13	..	2	..	249	..	89*	..	22.63
A. Wright	12	..	2	..	176	..	44	..	17.60
B. D. Hickman	12	..	0	..	179	..	30	..	14.91
B. L. George	13	..	0	..	169	..	52	..	13.00

Bowling

	Overs		Maidens		Runs		Wickets		Average
A. M. Forth	157.3	..	32	..	392	..	29	..	13.51
J. W. McDermott	87	..	25	..	207	..	11	..	18.81
R. J. Farrar	125.4	..	22	..	404	..	18	..	22.44
D. R. Bond	112	..	28	..	321	..	14	..	22.92

CULFORD SCHOOL

One of the features of a satisfactory season was the wicket-keeping of D. W. Simms, who stumped seventeen batsmen and caught fifteen.

Played 14, Won 5, Lost 5, Drawn 4

Batting

	Innings		Not outs		Runs		Highest inns.		Average
P. J. Revill	13	..	2	..	325	..	88	..	29.54
J. M. Fisher	13	..	4	..	243	..	53*	..	27.00
J. M. Kirkup	12	..	2	..	264	..	58*	..	26.40

Bowling

	Overs		Maidens		Runs		Wickets		Average
C. E. Wright	99	..	6	..	441	..	33	..	13.36
D. O. Punchard	150	..	19	..	474	..	35	..	13.54
J. L. Davidson	105	..	27	..	268	..	16	..	16.75
O. F. Howes	137	..	34	..	322	..	18	..	17.88

DEAN CLOSE SCHOOL

Played 11, Won 2, Lost 3, Drawn 6

Batting

	Innings		Not outs		Runs		Highest inns.		Average
†F. C. Welles	11	..	1	..	401	..	91	..	40.10
J. H. Robinson	10	..	2	..	140	..	49*	..	17.50
W. J. Benton-Evans	11	..	1	..	165	..	40*	..	16.50
R. I. Ireland	11	..	1	..	164	..	36	..	16.40
E. A. L. Bird	10	..	3	..	106	..	29*	..	15.14
M. T. Robinson	11	..	1	..	148	..	56	..	14.80
P. A. C. Blackmore	11	..	0	..	131	..	33	..	11.90
D. B. Grigg	11	..	2	..	107	..	23*	..	11.88

Bowling

	Overs		Maidens		Runs		Wickets		Average
P. H. Knight	90.2	..	12	..	312	..	23	..	13.56
C. E. N. Blake	75.4	..	20	..	226	..	12	..	18.83
D. B. Grigg	110.2	..	20	..	361	..	13	..	27.76

DENSTONE COLLEGE

The batting depended heavily on E. J. Everall, a fine left-hander, who overshadowed his colleagues. He also gained marked success as a right-arm fast-medium bowler, though in this department he received better support, notably from J. Y. Kelly (leg-breaks).

Played 10, Won 3, Lost 3, Drawn 4

Batting

	Innings		Not out		Runs		Highest inns.		Average
E. J. Everall	12	..	2	..	463	..	107*	..	46.30
†A. H. Marshall	11	..	0	..	178	..	57	..	16.18
G. D. Blenkinsop	12	..	1	..	174	..	57	..	15.81
R. S. D. Jones	10	..	1	..	120	..	47	..	13.33
D. A. E. Bloor	10	..	0	..	133	..	72	..	13.30

Bowling

	Overs		Maidens		Runs		Wickets		Average
J. Y. Kelly	96	..	16	..	243	..	25	..	9.72
E. J. Everall	128.5	..	22	..	313	..	24	..	13.04
T. J. Burke	123.5	..	21	..	305	..	15	..	20.33

DOUAI SCHOOL
Played 13, *Won* 5, *Lost* 5, *Drawn* 3

Batting

	Innings		Not outs		Runs		Highest inns.		Average
C. E. Allanson	5	..	2	..	150	..	54*	..	50.00
C. R. Segal	13	..	0	..	251	..	72	..	19.30
J. B. Moriarty	12	..	5	..	115	..	30	..	16.42
D. W. Hopkin	11	..	0	..	163	..	34	..	14.81
J. A. Stodart	11	..	1	..	133	..	36	..	13.30
J. C. McNally	13	..	0	..	151	..	38	..	11.61

Bowling

	Overs		Maidens		Runs		Wickets		Average
C. R. Segal	154	..	51	..	360	..	38	..	9.47
D. W. Hopkin	173	..	36	..	485	..	42	..	11.54

DOVER COLLEGE

The general standard of cricket at Dover continued to show improvement, though the season would have been more successful if some of the technically competent batsmen had not frequently thrown away their wickets by lack of concentration. The bowling was above average, with P. J. P. Grilli and G. V. Sherren maintaining an accurate opening attack and being well supported by the slow bowlers, E. M. S. Woodman, left hand, and J. R. A. Widgery, right hand. The fielding was generally keen.

Played 14, *Won* 6, *Lost* 5, *Drawn* 3

Batting

	Innings		Not outs		Runs		Highest inns.		Average
E. M. S. Woodman	14	..	1	..	350	..	67*	..	26.92
D. J. P. Biggs	14	..	2	..	269	..	78*	..	22.41
R. P. Heaton	14	..	2	..	211	..	38	..	17.58
J. R. A. Widgery	12	..	2	..	142	..	64	..	14.20
M. C. S. Weston	13	..	1	..	146	..	36	..	12.16

Bowling

	Overs		Maidens		Runs		Wickets		Average
P. J. P. Grilli	151.1	..	47	..	365	..	31	..	11.77
G. V. Sherren	155	..	42	..	322	..	24	..	13.41
E. M. S. Woodman	166	..	49	..	423	..	29	..	14.58
J. R. A. Widgery	117	..	20	..	312	..	20	..	15.60

DOWNSIDE SCHOOL

As the only experienced batsman left from the previous year, the captain, A. W. Gooda, held a responsible position and when he failed there was often no one to take over. Nevertheless two talented young batsmen were found in P. A. Kavanagh, still of Colts age, and E. F. Maynard. H. J. Conlin bowled consistently well with a fine action and promised to be really fast by the time he leaves as he still has another year in the XI. Gooda, the other opening bowler, was also above medium-pace. The fielding was steady but lacked aggression.

Played 13, *Won* 5, *Lost* 4, *Drawn* 4

Batting

	Innings		Not outs		Runs		Highest inns.		Average
†A. W. Gooda	15	..	1	..	322	..	68	..	23.00
E. F. Maynard	12	..	2	..	229	..	51	..	22.90
P. M. Murphy	15	..	3	..	258	..	79	..	21.50
J. G. Wells	10	..	1	..	192	..	58	..	21.33
J. F. Bone	12	..	3	..	163	..	38	..	18.11
P. A. Kavanagh	14	..	1	..	229	..	56	..	17.61
H. J. Conlin	10	..	1	..	143	..	40	..	15.88

Bowling

	Overs		Maidens		Runs		Wickets		Average
H. J. Conlin	236.2	..	53	..	639	..	50	..	12.78
A. W. Gooda	120	..	28	..	320	..	23	..	13.91
E. F. Maynard	87	..	26	..	199	..	13	..	15.30
M. H. Radcliffe	178.2	..	25	..	631	..	28	..	22.53
R. E. Davenhill	145.3	..	38	..	311	..	10	..	31.10

DULWICH COLLEGE

C. B. Howland, captain and wicket-keeper, and G. W. Cook, an exceptionally gifted right-handed batsman, were the leading members of the most successful team in the school's history. Both represented the Schools at Lord's for the second time and played for Kent II. These two received excellent support. M. A. Shirley played many fine innings and the advance of E. W. Anderson as a right-arm medium-pace bowler contributed much to the side's record. P. L. Hulston, a young left-hander, proved a valuable all-rounder. The fielding was good with Howland, and P. J. Holliday, a fine slip catcher, outstanding.

Played 16, *Won* 10, *Lost* 1, *Drawn* 5

Batting

	Innings		Not outs		Runs		Highest inns.		Average
G. W. Cook	15	..	4	..	734	..	131	..	66.72
B. G. Rogers	6	..	3	..	118	..	41*	..	39.33
P. L. Hulston	11	..	4	..	274	..	57	..	39.14
M. A. Shirley	15	..	3	..	391	..	103*	..	32.58
†C. B. Howland	14	..	1	..	331	..	100*	..	25.46
P. J. Holliday	15	..	0	..	363	..	66	..	24.20
N. C. Tinworth	13	..	1	..	224	..	50	..	18.66

Bowling

	Overs		Maidens		Runs		Wickets		Average
E. W. Anderson	264.5	..	74	..	635	..	44	..	14.43
P. L. Hulston	169.3	..	28	..	490	..	32	..	15.31
D. G. Read	170.3	..	63	..	341	..	21	..	16.23
G. W. Cook	188.1	..	53	..	441	..	23	..	19.17

DURHAM SCHOOL

Apart from the fielding, which was at times slow and untidy, Durham played good cricket. They possessed a strong, well-varied attack and the batting was solid.

Played 13, *Won* 8, *Lost* 3, *Drawn* 2

Batting

	Innings		Not outs		Runs		Highest inns.		Average
M. P. Weston	12	..	2	..	301	..	54	..	30.10
J. R. Donald	13	..	0	..	292	..	82	..	22.46
F. H. Curry...........	13	..	1	..	249	..	43	..	20.75
W. L. Taylor...........	12	..	2	..	199	..	64	..	19.90
†M. R. Neesham	10	..	4	..	118	..	39*	..	19.66
J. B. H. Fenwick	12	..	1	..	127	..	27*	..	11.54

Bowling

	Overs		Maidens		Runs		Wickets		Average
J. B. H. Fenwick	171.2	..	39	..	404	..	36	..	11.22
M. R. Neesham	118.1	..	25	..	341	..	29	..	11.75
M. P. Weston	106.4	..	13	..	366	..	24	..	15.25

EASTBOURNE COLLEGE

J. Watt, captain for 1956, was the outstanding cricketer and he ended a most successful season with a not-out innings of 128 against Radley and 84 against Free Foresters. The strength of the batting lay in the absence of a tail: against the Old Eastbournians there was an unbroken last-wicket stand of 102 between P. G. Parsons and R. D. B. Howell.

Played 14, Won 5, Lost 3, Drawn 6

Batting

	Innings		Not outs		Runs		Highest inns.		Average
J. Watt	15	..	5	..	535	..	129*	..	53.50
P. C. de S. Botcherby ...	11	..	2	..	227	..	49*	..	25.22
I. R. B. Fraser	14	..	3	..	231	..	103*	..	21.00
R. D. B. Howell	8	..	3	..	104	..	36*	..	20.80
M. W. E. Hind	15	..	0	..	307	..	69	..	20.46
P. H. Madath	12	..	4	..	143	..	36	..	17.87
T. C. Wilson	12	..	2	..	161	..	36	..	16.10
A. K. Hutchison	14	..	1	..	194	..	37	..	14.92

Bowling

	Overs		Maidens		Runs		Wickets		Average
C. J. Peake	145.2	..	41	..	396	..	25	..	15.84
T. C. Wilson	203.4	..	55	..	574	..	28	..	20.50
P. C. de S. Botcherby ...	166	..	48	..	436	..	21	..	20.76
J. Watt	100	..	25	..	318	..	13	..	24.46
I. R. B. Fraser	123.3	..	29	..	400	..	16	..	25.00

THE EDINBURGH ACADEMY

Edinburgh Academy had a moderately successful season with victories over Glenalmond and Watson's, defeats by Fettes and Loretto, and draws with Merchiston and Royal High School. The improvement on the previous season's record was due to the captaincy and batting of F. H. D. Walker, the ability of more than half the team to make a reasonable score, R. Stirling's wicket-keeping, and the bowling of D. B. Gillan (slow left-arm) and K. L. G. Sinclair (leg-breaks and googlies).

Played 14, Won 6, Lost 4, Drawn 4

Batting

	Innings	Not outs	Runs	Highest inns.	Average
†F. H. D. Walker	13	1	426	111	35.50
M. H. Bond	16	1	358	56*	23.86
A. J Cook	16	1	357	54	23.80
D. M. Henderson	14	3	254	65	23.09
R. W. G. Ross	16	1	300	79*	20.00
P. J. Burnet	14	3	219	53	19.90
G. Pryde	9	1	145	49	18.12

Bowling

	Overs	Maidens	Runs	Wickets	Average
D. M. Henderson	143	28	349	22	15.86
D. B. Gillan	187	18	631	37	17.05
K. L. G. Sinclair	123	18	470	25	18.80
A. J. Cook	164	32	414	19	21.78

ELTHAM COLLEGE

Played 14, Won 3, Lost 4, Drawn 7

Batting

	Innings	Not outs	Runs	Highest inns.	Average
†J. A. Napier	13	0	382	65	29.38
J. N. Levick	14	1	256	49	19.69
J. H. Bradnock	12	3	145	44	16.11
I. B. Waller	12	3	140	37*	15.55
H. I. Fordyce	14	0	190	35	13.57
I. R. Gillham	14	1	131	41	10.07

Bowling

	Overs	Maidens	Runs	Wickets	Average
J. A. Napier	44	14	126	11	11.45
I. B. Waller	129.2	31	324	25	12.96
A. J. Glock	101.4	18	317	22	14.40
D. R. Chesterton	86.2	16	255	16	15.93
G. Avery	82.4	16	243	12	20.25

EPSOM COLLEGE

Played 13, Won 4, Lost 6, Drawn 3

Batting

	Innings	Not outs	Runs	Highest inns.	Average
A. G. Johnson	14	2	464	69	38.66
J. J. J. Bell	14	0	390	70	27.85
W. D. J. Crawford	14	1	295	71	22.69
G. W. Patterson	12	0	188	81	15.66
P. M. Whelan	13	0	202	57	15.53
R. J. Farrow	11	1	123	27	12.30

Bowling

	Overs	Maidens	Runs	Wickets	Average
J. J. J. Bell	183.1	31	516	25	20.64
G. A. Wood-Wilson	102	12	404	19	21.26
N. P. de Morgan	150.3	37	382	15	25.46
†D. P. M. Howells	110	23	368	11	33.45

ETON COLLEGE

Fielding their youngest side for many years—including three fifteen-year-olds—Eton experienced a season of mixed fortunes. Harrow, the old enemy, were beaten at Lord's, but defeats were suffered from both Winchester and Wellington. The batting, led by a sound opening pair in C. T. M. Pugh and D. R. Stoddart, was quite strong. A. R. B. Burrows, a newcomer to the XI, showed special promise and there was no pronounced "tail." C. H. Gibson, an admirable captain on and off the field, would have welcomed a bowler of genuine pace to add penetration to the attack, which was accurate rather than hostile. Two medium-paced bowlers, S. Douglas Pennant, a left-hander, and I. A. C. Sinclair, did most work and E. J. Lane Fox gave valuable support with left-arm spin. The fielding was good. Sinclair will have six old colours, including all the bowlers, under him next season.

Played 12, Won 5, Lost 3, Drawn 4

Batting

	Innings		Not outs		Runs		Highest inns.		Average
C. T. M. Pugh	15	..	2	..	536	..	113*	..	41.23
A. R. B. Burrows	14	..	2	..	404	..	102*	..	33.66
D. R. Stoddart	15	..	0	..	378	..	92	..	25.20
E. J. Lane Fox	12	..	3	..	225	..	71	..	25.00
I. A. C. Sinclair	14	..	2	..	262	..	74	..	21.83
A. M. Wolfe-Murray....	12	..	2	..	207	..	46*	..	20.70
†C. H. Gibson	14	..	0	..	274	..	71	..	19.57
A. P. M. Marsham	8	..	2	..	101	..	34	..	16.83
H. C. Blofeld	12	..	1	..	152	..	37	..	13.81

Bowling

	Overs		Maidens		Runs		Wickets		Average
S. Douglas Pennant	231	..	84	..	597	..	33	..	18.09
I. A. C. Sinclair	243	..	71	..	646	..	31	..	20.83
E. J. Lane Fox	190	..	54	..	510	..	24	..	21.25

EXETER SCHOOL

Played 12, Won 7, Lost 2, Drawn 3

Batting

	Innings		Not outs		Runs		Highest inns.		Average
†D. Mullins.............	13	..	1	..	267	..	70	..	22.25
D. B. Ellis	11	..	2	..	197	..	51	..	21.88
F. L. B. Vigers	10	..	4	..	106	..	24	..	17.66
R. R. Cockroft	13	..	2	..	169	..	36*	..	15.36
P. G. Farrell	13	..	2	..	161	..	34	..	14.63

Bowling

	Overs		Maidens		Runs		Wickets		Average
F. L. B. Vigers	168.3	..	55	..	307	..	46	..	6.67
M. J. C. Tozer	73.2	..	21	..	191	..	19	..	10.05
D. E. Mettam	52.4	..	10	..	181	..	14	..	12.92
J. A. Jago	140	..	41	..	340	..	25	..	13.60

FELSTED SCHOOL
Played 10, *Won* 4, *Lost* 0, *Drawn* 6

Batting

	Innings		Not outs		Runs		Highest inns.		Average
†R. M. Moody	11	..	3	..	319	..	81*	..	39.87
R. A. G. Luckin	12	..	1	..	315	..	82	..	28.63
G. C. Willsher	12	..	1	..	268	..	84	..	24.36
R. A. Jowit	11	..	2	..	218	..	60	..	24.22

Bowling

	Overs		Maidens		Runs		Wickets		Average
R. J. Stapleton	210	..	69	..	425	..	28	..	15.17
R. L. Tyrrell	114	..	31	..	288	..	14	..	20.57
G. C. Willsher	78	..	21	..	245	..	11	..	22.27
C. P. Boyle	111	..	21	..	296	..	12	..	24.66
R. A. G. Luckin	108	..	13	..	392	..	15	..	26.13

FETTES COLLEGE

D. W. Horne was the best of a powerful set of batsmen who showed plenty of fight and determination under the leadership of D. M. A. Steel. Apart from Horne, Steel will have all his leading players available again in 1956.

Played 18, *Won* 7, *Lost* 2, *Drawn* 9

Batting

	Innings		Not outs		Runs		Highest inns.		Average
D. W. Horne	19	..	5	..	636	..	107	..	45.42
D. C. Ferguson	16	..	3	..	391	..	128	..	30.71
†D. M. A. Steel	18	..	0	..	479	..	107	..	26.61
R. J. B. Hoare	19	..	1	..	460	..	66*	..	25.55
T. C. Garner	14	..	4	..	214	..	50	..	21.40
P. A. L. Williamson	18	..	3	..	219	..	34*	..	14.60
D. C. Cameron	19	..	0	..	271	..	46	..	14.26

Bowling

	Overs		Maidens		Runs		Wickets		Average
A. W. M. Bain	275.3	..	90	..	594	..	58	..	10.24
D. R. Miller	75	..	16	..	240	..	20	..	12.00
D. M. A. Steel	98.5	..	25	..	239	..	19	..	12.57
D. M. Lumsden	193.2	..	56	..	444	..	26	..	17.07
J. D. D. MacBean	109.2	..	19	..	435	..	17	..	25.58

FOREST SCHOOL
Played 15, *Won* 3, *Lost* 11, *Drawn* 1

Batting

	Innings		Not outs		Runs		Highest inns.		Average
C. J. Foster	12	..	0	..	140	..	33	..	11.66
E. R. Fox	11	..	1	..	113	..	27	..	11.30

Bowling

	Overs		Maidens		Runs		Wickets		Average
A. V. Martin	59.3	..	5	..	236	..	14	..	16.85

GEORGE HERIOT'S SCHOOL

E. McKeating, captain for the third year, led Heriot's to their best season since the war. The batting was good, with K. J. F. Scotland outstanding; the bowling keen and hostile and the fielding excellent. In only three games did the entire XI need to bat.

Played 19, Won 16, Lost 0, Drawn 3

Batting

	Innings	Not outs	Runs	Highest inns.	Average
K. J. F. Scotland	17	3	524	91	37.42
E. H. Tainsh	19	3	492	102	30.75

Bowling

	Overs	Maidens	Runs	Wickets	Average
G. R. Wright	49.4	16	95	22	4.31
G. F. Goddard	222.5	87	335	63	5.31
†E. McKeating	126.2	40	269	37	7.27
C. J. Horton	147	62	229	28	8.17

GEORGE WATSON'S BOYS' COLLEGE

Played 15, Won 3, Lost 6, Drawn 6

Batting

	Innings	Not outs	Runs	Highest inns.	Average
†J. C. Burton	14	2	255	59	21.25
J. P. Cruickshank.......	11	2	175	62	19.44
J. S. Hogg	13	0	237	50	18.23
I. A. N. Wilson	15	2	202	70	15.53
D. G. Leitch	14	1	197	41	15.15
A. M. Kemsley	13	1	165	35	13.75
W. A. Marshall	12	2	122	48*	12.20

Bowling

	Overs	Maidens	Runs	Wickets	Average
J. S. Hogg	176.5	43	432	36	12.00
D. G. Leitch	85	20	233	13	17.92
W. A. Marshall	160.5	45	429	21	20.42
I. R. Sutherland	97.1	22	267	13	20.53

GIGGLESWICK SCHOOL

Played 10, Won 3, Lost 6, Drawn 1

Batting

	Innings	Not outs	Runs	Highest inns.	Average
J. P. B. Golding	9	0	142	28	15.77
J. R. Linley	9	0	133	29	14.77

Bowling

	Overs	Maidens	Runs	Wickets	Average
I. W. M. Smith.........	130.2	65	235	28	8.39
D. Garforth	95.1	20	235	23	10.21

GORDONSTOUN SCHOOL
Played 9, Won 5, Lost 1, Tied 1, Drawn 2

Batting

	Innings	Not outs	Runs	Highest inns.	Average
R. A. P. George	10	1	203	65*	22.55
†P. St. J. Whitworth	11	1	181	31	18.10
C. M. Flesch	11	2	135	46	15.00
J. A. Innes	9	0	117	50	13.00

Bowling

	Overs	Maidens	Runs	Wickets	Average
J. A. Innes	44	20	98	17	5.76
W. L. Fuller	93	23	257	28	9.17
J. Vallance	35	4	157	14	11.21

GRESHAM'S SCHOOL, HOLT

A. J. Corran, who played for The Rest at Lord's and for Norfolk in the Minor Counties Championship, built a side that, on top form, showed few weaknesses. It was notable that a year which brought P. D. Croft, the 1952 captain, the school's first Blue, also marked a return to the aggressive cricket lacking in the school team for some time. The batsmen attacked even in a crisis and the bowlers were keenly supported in the field.

Played 11, Won 5, Lost 2, Drawn 4

Batting

	Innings	Not outs	Runs	Highest inns.	Average
†A. J. Corran	11	1	377	146*	37.70
R. J. Simpson	11	3	288	57	36.00
K. G. D. Croft	11	1	316	95	31.60
K. D. Henderson	10	1	200	56*	22.22
R. G. Blyth	10	1	130	40	14.44

Bowling

	Overs	Maidens	Runs	Wickets	Average
A. J. Corran	199.4	64	428	45	9.51
R. D. A. Galbraith	123	25	328	30	10.93
D. J. B. Arnold	98.4	25	265	20	13.25

HABERDASHERS' ASKE'S SCHOOL
Played 15, Won 4, Lost 7, Drawn 4

Batting

	Innings	Not outs	Runs	Highest inns.	Average
I. D. Scofield	15	1	196	57*	14.00
†N. A. Fuller	14	1	136	25*	10.46
D. W. Curtis	15	1	140	56*	10.00

Bowling

	Overs	Maidens	Runs	Wickets	Average
N. A. Fuller	89.4	30	173	20	8.65
I. D. Scofield	130.1	30	375	36	10.41
G. T. Wheal	140	46	284	25	11.36
G. A. Butler	112	31	272	21	12.95

HAILEYBURY AND I.S.C.

Because of bad weather at the beginning of the season, most of the batsmen did not run into form until late in June. D. J. Newsom was easily the most consistent and held the side together several times. M. G. P. Foster, the captain, showed his best form when he promoted himself to open the innings with Newsom and D. L. Stretton Cox played attractively against Cheltenham at Lord's. A. D. N. Smith, left-arm medium-pace, bowled consistently well but C. R. Leighton did not maintain his early successes with medium-paced off-breaks. The captain kept wicket well but the fielding generally fell short of the excellent standard set the previous year.

Played 12, Won 3, Lost 4, Drawn 5

Batting

	Innings	Not outs	Runs	Highest inns.	Average
D. J. Newsom	16	0	502	70	31.38
D. L. Stretton Cox	15	2	312	52	24.00
†M. G. P. Foster	14	3	216	66	19.63
J. R. Thompson	12	0	159	32	13.25
D. J. E. Foster	15	0	186	48	12.40
C. R. Leighton	16	3	149	29	11.46

Bowling

	Overs	Maidens	Runs	Wickets	Average
A. D. N. Smith	215.4	50	627	44	14.25
R. A. B. Hall	95	13	302	17	17.76
A. J. Claxton	86	15	284	14	20.28
C. R. Leighton	216	44	628	29	21.65

HARROW SCHOOL

Harrow possessed several players of above average ability, notably the captain, A. R. B. Neame, and two left-handed batsmen, R. S. Miller and J. M. Parker, but never as a team did they do themselves full justice. Haileybury provided the only victory over a school side, though Winchester and Charterhouse both had cause for relief when stumps were drawn. The matches against Eton and Wellington were lost. Neame, who again bowled off-spin effectively, was not the prolific scorer of the previous year and more runs were expected from G. D. Massy, whose natural talent suffered through recklessness. L. J. Champniss, steadier than most leg-break bowlers, deserved better reward; a promising opening bowler was found in 15-year-old M. L. Maydon.

Played 12, Won 2, Lost 4, Drawn 6

Batting

	Innings		Not outs		Runs		Highest inns.		Average
R. S. Miller	14	..	2	..	526	..	109	..	43.83
J. M. Parker	15	..	0	..	622	..	97	..	41.46
†A. R. B. Neame	13	..	0	..	330	..	61	..	25.38
G. D. Massy	15	..	3	..	250	..	50	..	20.83
A. S. R. Winlaw	6	..	0	..	100	..	31	..	16.66
J. C. T. Harvey	11	..	1	..	160	..	44	..	16.00
L. J. Champniss	10	..	2	..	123	..	49	..	15.37

Bowling

	Overs		Maidens		Runs		Wickets		Average
A. R. B. Neame	163.5	..	36	..	418	..	30	..	13.93
M. L. Maydon	83	..	15	..	236	..	12	..	19.66
R. S. Miller	119	..	32	..	306	..	15	..	20.40
N. Davies-Barker	103.2	..	15	..	349	..	14	..	24.92
L. J. Champniss	149.4	..	53	..	402	..	15	..	26.80

HEREFORD CATHEDRAL SCHOOL
Played 12, Won 3, Lost 5, Drawn 4

Batting

	Innings		Not outs		Runs		Highest inns.		Average
R. B. Brown	11	..	1	..	208	..	52*	..	20.80
†G. V. Miller	11	..	1	..	163	..	66*	..	16.30
J. B. Brown	10	..	1	..	134	..	37	..	14.88
J. S. Daybell	10	..	0	..	111	..	19	..	11.10
A. M. Pyke	11	..	0	..	117	..	34	..	10.63

Bowling

	Overs		Maidens		Runs		Wickets		Average
A. Howgate	57	..	10	..	162	..	19	..	8.52
J. G. Underwood	113	..	32	..	218	..	22	..	9.90
P. T. V. Grimshaw	103.3	..	22	..	276	..	20	..	13.80
J. B. Brown	79.1	..	12	..	278	..	19	..	14.63

HIGHGATE SCHOOL

The batting became very steady with the arrival of hard pitches but the bowling proved a great disappointment. Most of the bowlers who had done well the previous season appeared to have lost some of their control and the most reliable was D. B. Sowter from the Colts.

Played 15, Won 3, Lost 5, Drawn 7

Batting

	Innings		Not outs		Runs		Highest inns.		Average
D. M. Bland	12	..	4	..	249	..	61*	..	31.12
C. D. Drybrough	14	..	0	..	422	..	73	..	30.14
A. J. Murray	13	..	3	..	240	..	41*	..	24.00
†J. K. Fawcett	15	..	0	..	251	..	58	..	16.73
R. P. Juniper	15	..	0	..	231	..	45	..	15.40
C. J. S. Garner	13	..	2	..	131	..	24	..	11.90
M. D. Field	13	..	1	..	141	..	35*	..	11.75

Bowling

	Overs		Maidens		Runs		Wickets		Average
D. B. Sowter	133	..	31	..	365	..	23	..	15.86
J. K. Fawcett	149	..	35	..	309	..	18	..	17.16
C. D. Drybrough	149	..	31	..	367	..	21	..	17.47
I. G. Jenkins	125	..	35	..	247	..	12	..	20.58

HURSTPIERPOINT COLLEGE

Played 12, Won 2, Lost 8, Drawn 2

Batting

	Innings		Not outs		Runs		Highest inns.		Average
T. S. Grove	11	..	0	..	192	..	55	..	17.45
H. N. B. Morgan	12	..	0	..	186	..	46	..	15.50
†A. M. Syson	11	..	0	..	166	..	53	..	15.09
C. Davies..............	11	..	0	..	135	..	38	..	12.27

Bowling

	Overs		Maidens		Runs		Wickets		Average
W. E. Cobbett	165	..	43	..	309	..	27	..	11.44
C. Davies..............	84	..	15	..	252	..	18	..	14.00
W. G. Pollock	76	..	17	..	224	..	12	..	18.66
A. M. Syson	117	..	25	..	340	..	18	..	18.88

IPSWICH SCHOOL

Played 13, Won 3, Lost 6, Drawn 4

Batting

	Innings		Not outs		Runs		Highest inns.		Average
C. H. C. Piper	13	..	1	..	445	..	100*	..	37.08
W. D. Buxton	11	..	2	..	172	..	36	..	19.11
J. J. Greenwood	13	..	1	..	198	..	65	..	16.50
T. M. Cracknell	10	..	2	..	122	..	65	..	15.25
J. R. S. Mash	12	..	1	..	136	..	31	..	12.36
N. R. Jarrold	11	..	0	..	122	..	50	..	11.09

Bowling

	Overs		Maidens		Runs		Wickets		Average
W. A. D. Whitfield	57.1	..	11	..	147	..	12	..	12.25
J. R. S. Mash	163.3	..	39	..	418	..	29	..	14.41
C. T. Catton	76	..	18	..	231	..	12	..	19.25

KELLY COLLEGE

Played 12, Won 7, Lost 2, Drawn 3

Batting

	Innings		Not outs		Runs		Highest inns.		Average
D. J. Powell	12	..	2	..	238	..	66*	..	23.80
J. E. Perkins	9	..	3	..	133	..	42	..	22.16
R. G. James	11	..	1	..	216	..	88	..	21.60
A. S. Heazell...........	10	..	2	..	162	..	42*	..	20.25
S. D. F. Molineux	9	..	2	..	116	..	36*	..	16.57
D. A. Cotton	12	..	0	..	198	..	45	..	16.50
A. P. B. Lissett	12	..	0	..	175	..	34	..	14.58

Bowling

	Overs	Maidens	Runs	Wickets	Average
R. G. James	139	.. 29	.. 385	.. 39	.. 9.84
S. A. Menne	86.1	.. 21	.. 283	.. 28	.. 10.10
A. P. B. Lissett	104	.. 30	.. 278	.. 18	.. 15.44
S. D. F. Molineux	72	.. 18	.. 222	.. 10	.. 22.20

KING EDWARD'S SCHOOL, BIRMINGHAM
Played 18, Won 3, Lost 1, Drawn 14

Batting

	Innings	Not outs	Runs	Highest inns.	Average
†A. C. Smith...........	16	.. 2	.. 805	.. 134*	.. 57.50
P. F. Williams	17	.. 3	.. 338	.. 56	.. 24.14
M. Wilkins	17	.. 0	.. 299	.. 50	.. 17.58
J. Mulford	17	.. 2	.. 224	.. 45	.. 14.93

Bowling

	Overs	Maidens	Runs	Wickets	Average
R. G. Dauncey	147.3	.. 53	.. 339	.. 20	.. 16.95
J. Mulford	250	.. 51	.. 635	.. 31	.. 20.48
E. L. B. Saxon	161.4	.. 38	.. 457	.. 16	.. 28.56

KING EDWARD'S SCHOOL, STOURBRIDGE

J. M. Cockin led his young team with distinction and against schoolboy batsmen often proved devastating with leg-breaks and googlies. He and R. J. Clements represented Worcestershire Schools.

Played 9, Won 5, Lost 0, Drawn 4

Batting

	Innings	Not outs	Runs	Highest inns.	Average
D. Sturman	9	.. 2	.. 225	.. 69*	.. 32.14
†J. M. Cockin..........	9	.. 1	.. 217	.. 100*	.. 27.12
R. J. Clements	9	.. 0	.. 131	.. 46	.. 14.55
J. Mees	9	.. 0	.. 102	.. 33	.. 11.33

Bowling

	Overs	Maidens	Runs	Wickets	Average
J. M. Cockin..........	97.5	.. 30	.. 133	.. 36	.. 3.69
R. J. Clements	52.4	.. 19	.. 109	.. 13	.. 8.38
R. F. Snow	92	.. 30	.. 179	.. 19	.. 9.42

KING WILLIAM'S COLLEGE, ISLE OF MAN
Played 16, Won 7, Lost 5, Drawn 4

Batting

	Innings	Not outs	Runs	Highest inns.	Average
S. Quirk	12	.. 5	.. 251	.. 66	.. 35.85
†B. K. Colvin	17	.. 3	.. 323	.. 57*	.. 23.07
S. R. Donaldson	17	.. 3	.. 317	.. 61	.. 22.64
S. G. S. Scott	16	.. 0	.. 316	.. 68	.. 19.75
E. Q. Bashforth	13	.. 3	.. 140	.. 34*	.. 14.00
T. A. J. E. Connor	12	.. 4	.. 104	.. 43*	.. 13.00

Bowling

	Overs		Maidens		Runs		Wickets		Average
A. H. Johnson	49	..	18	..	126	..	14	..	9.00
B. K. Colvin	150	..	37	..	363	..	34	..	10.67
W. R. Kneen	100	..	3	..	355	..	30	..	11.83
W. N. Ward	112	..	20	..	280	..	20	..	14.00
S. Quirk	102	..	16	..	299	..	14	..	21.35

KING'S COLLEGE, TAUNTON

King's, Taunton, possessed their best team for some years and with more penetration in attack many of the drawn matches could have been won.

Played 12, Won 4, Lost 1, Drawn 7

Batting

	Innings		Not outs		Runs		Highest inns.		Average
†N. E. Giles	17	..	0	..	460	..	73	..	27.05
J. Watson	11	..	5	..	150	..	36	..	25.00
A. Elliot	17	..	0	..	420	..	72	..	24.70
M. Gower	14	..	2	..	233	..	63*	..	19.41
R. Wadland	16	..	2	..	231	..	49	..	16.50

Bowling

	Overs		Maidens		Runs		Wickets		Average
D. Hillier	104	..	17	..	288	..	26	..	11.08
J. Watson	169	..	46	..	423	..	26	..	16.26
R. Blake	224	..	40	..	656	..	38	..	17.26
N. E. Giles	97	..	10	..	358	..	16	..	22.37

KING'S COLLEGE SCHOOL, WIMBLEDON

Played 13, Won 3, Lost 4, Drawn 6

Batting

	Innings		Not outs		Runs		Highest inns.		Average
†P. D. Kelly	13	..	4	..	263	..	56*	..	29.22
J. F. Dowden	13	..	0	..	359	..	93	..	27.61
K. M. Arnott	13	..	0	..	339	..	93	..	26.08
B. Z. Myers	13	..	2	..	165	..	41	..	15.00
P. H. Elkington	12	..	1	..	118	..	28	..	10.72

Bowling

	Overs		Maidens		Runs		Wickets		Average
P. D. Kelly	75.3	..	16	..	236	..	22	..	10.72
I. P. McLeish	110.2	..	27	..	333	..	21	..	15.85
P. H. Elkington	161	..	36	..	495	..	16	..	30.93
D. Cox	164	..	40	..	560	..	14	..	40.00

KING'S SCHOOL, BRUTON

Played 11, Won 2, Lost 6, Drawn 3

Batting

	Innings		Not outs		Runs		Highest inns.		Average
J. J. M. Hewlett	11	..	0	..	361	..	100	..	32.81
J. R. Evans	10	..	4	..	135	..	22	..	22.50
C. G. Holt	11	..	2	..	198	..	84*	..	22.00
†J. R. W. Bolton	11	..	0	..	130	..	34	..	11.81

Bowling

	Overs	Maidens	Runs	Wickets	Average
D. M. Murray	125.2 ..	35	.. 255	.. 19	.. 13.42
M. J. Gould	59.2 ..	11	.. 175	.. 10	.. 17.50
M. G. Moore	86 ..	12	.. 272	.. 14	.. 19.42
N. A. Charles	107.1 ..	33	.. 240	.. 11	.. 21.81

KING'S SCHOOL, CANTERBURY
Played 16, *Won* 7, *Lost* 4, *Drawn* 5

Batting

	Innings	Not outs	Runs	Highest inns.	Average
†C. N. Lainé	16 ..	4	.. 534	.. 125* ..	44.50
R. J. C. Collins	16 ..	1	.. 368	.. 115* ..	24.53
R. M. Sutton	13 ..	1	.. 293	.. 81 ..	24.41
M. E. W. Vincent	15 ..	1	.. 340	.. 72 ..	24.28

Bowling

	Overs	Maidens	Runs	Wickets	Average
P. B. Harding	154.3 ..	54	.. 336	.. 30	.. 11.20
C. M. J. Whittington....	78.4 ..	16	.. 229	.. 20	.. 11.45
I. C. Potter	228.5 ..	57	.. 620	.. 38	.. 16.31
M. E. W. Vincent	81.3 ..	17	.. 242	.. 14	.. 17.28
R. J. C. Collins	60 ..	10	.. 253	.. 13	.. 19.46

KINGS' SCHOOL, ELY

R. S. Wood, the captain, played a conspicuous part in a successful season, heading both the batting and bowling figures.

Played 17, *Won* 9, *Lost* 2, *Drawn* 6

Batting

	Innings	Not outs	Runs	Highest inns.	Average
†R. S. Wood	17 ..	7	.. 365	.. 68 ..	36.50
M. B. Glenister	17 ..	2	.. 354	.. 54* ..	23.60
R. E. Hix..............	16 ..	3	.. 271	.. 52* ..	20.84
R. W. Clarke	14 ..	2	.. 219	.. 55 ..	18.25

Bowling

	Overs	Maidens	Runs	Wickets	Average
R. S. Wood	230.3 ..	67	.. 544	.. 62	.. 8.77
N. J. Entwistle	191.1 ..	61	.. 366	.. 39	.. 9.38
R. W. Clarke	142.1 ..	50	.. 353	.. 30	.. 11.76
J. P. Cuthbert	104.1 ..	38	.. 238	.. 19	.. 12.52

KING'S SCHOOL, MACCLESFIELD
Played 15, *Won* 6, *Lost* 5, *Tied* 1, *Drawn* 3

Batting

	Innings	Not outs	Runs	Highest inns.	Average
M. P. Holland	15 ..	5	.. 255	.. 96 ..	25.50
C. D. R. Barker	15 ..	2	.. 331	.. 60* ..	25.46
D. R. A. Ridyard.......	12 ..	1	.. 116	.. 33 ..	10.54

Bowling

	Overs		Maidens		Runs		Wickets		Average
S. Foley	90	..	21	..	200	..	20	..	10.00
C. D. R. Barker	146.1	..	46	..	284	..	28	..	10.14
†G. Bickerton	138.4	..	37	..	318	..	29	..	10.96
D. R. A. Ridyard.......	110.1	..	27	..	313	..	21	..	14.90

KINGSWOOD SCHOOL

Played 14, *Won* 7, *Lost* 3, *Drawn* 4

Batting

	Innings		Not outs		Runs		Highest inns.		Average
H. R. Kedward	14	..	2	..	361	..	95	..	30.83
P. W. Thomson	14	..	0	..	302	..	51	..	21.57
J. Badcock	13	..	3	..	198	..	55*	..	19.80
M. E. Dodds...........	12	..	1	..	203	..	54	..	18.45
A. W. Sutcliffe	13	..	0	..	186	..	64	..	14.30

Bowling

	Overs		Maidens		Runs		Wickets		Average
H. R. Kedward	78.1	..	15	..	191	..	26	..	7.34
A. W. Fearn	116.4	..	31	..	281	..	24	..	11.70
†J. J. L. Crosby	186.1	..	39	..	451	..	31	..	14.63

LANCING COLLEGE

Through an epidemic of glandular fever, the young Lancing side were often below full strength. But for this, their record would have been even better. G. J. Sharman, who has two more years in the team before going to Oxford, showed particular promise and ended the season with innings of 116, 23, 0, 69, 94 and 67 not out. A fine leg-break and googly bowler also, he achieved the hat-trick against Westminster. G. G. B. Wilkes, who raised his total wickets for four years in the XI to 100, led the side astutely and B. A. Rodgers also enjoyed a good season.

Played 14, *Won* 6, *Lost* 5, *Drawn* 3

Batting

	Innings		Not outs		Runs		Highest inns.		Average
G. J. Sharman	13	..	2	..	425	..	116	..	38.63
B. A. Rodgers..........	13	..	2	..	342	..	103*	..	31.09
D. V. Bedford..........	13	..	1	..	231	..	69*	..	19.25
J. W. Bridge	12	..	1	..	184	..	48*	..	16.72
†G. G. B. Wilkes	12	..	0	..	193	..	69	..	16.08
T. J. Goodwin	14	..	2	..	183	..	40*	..	15.25
R. J. V. Steward........	12	..	2	..	131	..	29	..	13.10

Bowling

	Overs		Maidens		Runs		Wickets		Average
G. G. B. Wilkes	156	..	31	..	400	..	35	..	11.42
B. A. Rodgers..........	101.3	..	26	..	270	..	23	..	11.73
R. J. V. Steward........	132.5	..	32	..	350	..	27	..	12.96
G. J. Sharman	70	..	12	..	249	..	16	..	15.56
N. G. Anderson	74	..	11	..	195	..	11	..	17.72

LEEDS GRAMMAR SCHOOL
Played 13, *Won* 4, *Lost* 4, *Drawn* 5

Batting

	Innings	Not outs	Runs	Highest inns.	Average
J. G. Wooldridge	8	2	184	47	30.66
P. G. Whitworth	13	1	349	102	29.08
D. A. Hill	12	2	269	63*	26.90
†J. D. Fretwell	11	1	213	40	21.30
J. D. Brooke	9	2	149	39	21.28
R. J. Williams	11	1	210	58	21.00
D. H. Lupton	7	2	103	29*	20.60

Bowling

	Overs	Maidens	Runs	Wickets	Average
D. Senior	71.3	11	275	24	11.45
D. A. Hill	157	26	482	29	16.62
R. Grant	54	8	172	10	17.20

LEIGHTON PARK SCHOOL
Played 9, *Won* 4, *Lost* 3, *Drawn* 2

Batting

	Innings	Not outs	Runs	Highest inns.	Average
A. G. Barker	14	1	482	94	37.07
P. B. Cotton	14	1	429	91	33.00
A. J. Richmond	13	2	191	44	17.36
†D. J. H. Richmond	11	1	150	47	15.00
J. G. Morris	9	2	101	25	14.42
D. Doncaster	9	2	99	45	14.14

Bowling

	Overs	Maidens	Runs	Wickets	Average
D. J. H. Richmond	100	27	242	19	12.73
A. G. Barker	145.2	18	451	34	13.26
W. J. Hopkins	69	3	272	19	14.31

THE LEYS SCHOOL

Apart from N. H. Payne, none of the batsmen could be relied upon for runs and this was to blame for the team's poor record. The outcricket was more satisfactory and most opponents were dismissed for modest totals. Payne will have five other colours under him in 1956.

Played 12, *Won* 1, *Lost* 7, *Drawn* 4

Batting

	Innings	Not outs	Runs	Highest inns.	Average
N. H. Payne	13	2	367	84*	33.36
R. A. W. Walker	12	3	209	53*	23.22
J. J. Firth	11	1	184	55	18.40
J. S. Holmes	13	1	162	55	13.50
C. R. Fairey	12	0	127	43	10.58

Bowling

	Overs	Maidens	Runs	Wickets	Average
D. H. M. Christie	98 ..	28 ..	218 ..	20 ..	10.90
N. H. Payne	57.4 ..	15 ..	150 ..	10 ..	15.00
P. W. Barker	116.4 ..	14 ..	480 ..	22 ..	21.81
A. H. B. Turner	138.1 ..	36 ..	347 ..	14 ..	24.78
†B. J. Wilkins	139 ..	35 ..	347 ..	12 ..	28.91

LIVERPOOL COLLEGE

Played 9, Won 5, Lost 2, Drawn 2

Batting

	Innings	Not outs	Runs	Highest inns.	Average
J. E. L. Prendiville	7 ..	4 ..	95 ..	24* ..	31.66
J. A. Cogan	8 ..	3 ..	132 ..	59* ..	26.40
†D. C. Hughes	8 ..	0 ..	163 ..	50 ..	20.37

Bowling

	Overs	Maidens	Runs	Wickets	Average
J. A. Cogan	127.1 ..	27 ..	289 ..	29 ..	9.96
A. J. Windsor	127.4 ..	24 ..	344 ..	27 ..	12.74

LLANDOVERY COLLEGE

Under the captaincy of T. B. Williams, what was expected to prove a weak team improved out of recognition. Their record suffered through the lack of reliable spin-bowling. M. G. Pearn kept wicket splendidly.

Played 12, Won 3, Lost 2, Tied 1, Drawn 6

Batting

	Innings	Not outs	Runs	Highest inns.	Average
M. Charles	12 ..	4 ..	204 ..	52* ..	25.50
†T. B. Williams	10 ..	2 ..	191 ..	51 ..	23.87
D. I. Gealy	12 ..	0 ..	267 ..	53 ..	22.25
R. Williams	12 ..	0 ..	222 ..	37 ..	18.50
J. D. P. Evans	11 ..	2 ..	140 ..	30 ..	15.55

Bowling

	Overs	Maidens	Runs	Wickets	Average
J. B. Rowlands	149.1 ..	41 ..	320 ..	26 ..	12.30
H. E. D. Bevan	52.4 ..	3 ..	177 ..	14 ..	12.64
T. B. Williams	165 ..	32 ..	407 ..	30 ..	13.56

LORETTO SCHOOL

Although their captain, H. B. Langlands, won a place in the Schools trial at Lord's as an off-spin bowler, Loretto owed their impressive record chiefly to the solidity of their batting. A. K. Thomson, the best batsman, received most support from D. B. McMurray and Langlands.

Played 16, Won 8, Lost 2, Drawn 6

Batting

	Innings		Not outs		Runs		Highest inns.		Average
A. K. Thomson	18	..	4	..	605	..	100*	..	43.21
D. B. McMurray	17	..	3	..	483	..	81*	..	34.50
†H. B. Langlands	17	..	4	..	280	..	46*	..	21.53
I. R. Brooks	17	..	1	..	308	..	57	..	19.25
P. D. C. Crisp	18	..	0	..	321	..	56	..	17.83
P. B. Dowson	17	..	1	..	269	..	50	..	16.81
P. R. Prenter	17	..	1	..	265	..	33	..	16.56
G. R. A. Milligan	14	..	4	..	135	..	42	..	13.50

Bowling

	Overs		Maidens		Runs		Wickets		Average
I. Macaulay	50	..	11	..	110	..	11	..	10.00
H. B. Langlands	217.3	..	36	..	742	..	61	..	12.16
D. B. McMurray	123	..	25	..	313	..	22	..	14.22
J. C. G. Barr	107	..	24	..	282	..	19	..	14.84
R. J. Williamson	170	..	32	..	446	..	23	..	19.39

MALVERN COLLEGE

Malvern discovered a fine young batsman in P. G. Hatch but the bowling again proved weak. Hatch, a latecomer to the side, hit two centuries and three fifties in his eight innings. He and I. C. MacLaurin, the most successful captain since the war, added 192 for the second wicket against Clifton. Another successful experiment was the introduction of J. M. Costeloe, an opening bowler, who gave C. M. G. Hunter fine support in the last few matches. Their efforts, however, could not disguise the absence of a match-winning spin bowler.

Played 11, Won 5, Lost 2, Drawn 4

Batting

	Innings		Not outs		Runs		Highest inns.		Average
P. G. Hatch	8	..	0	..	377	..	125	..	47.12
†I. C. MacLaurin	15	..	2	..	349	..	105	..	26.84
C. M. G. Hunter	11	..	2	..	230	..	54	..	25.55
R. J. Devereux	11	..	1	..	238	..	61	..	23.80
M. J. D. Newbury	12	..	0	..	258	..	81	..	21.50
J. L. Smith	13	..	0	..	196	..	52	..	15.07
N. B. Potter	11	..	2	..	131	..	23	..	14.55

Bowling

	Overs		Maidens		Runs		Wickets		Average
C. M. G. Hunter	195.5	..	59	..	490	..	31	..	15.80
J. M. Costeloe	148.5	..	39	..	370	..	23	..	16.08
I. C. MacLaurin	103.4	..	19	..	417	..	24	..	17.37
N. B. Potter	96	..	16	..	358	..	15	..	23.86

MANCHESTER GRAMMAR SCHOOL

Although without their four main bowlers from 1954, Manchester had another good season. S. M. Jackson stood out as a batsman and wicket-keeper of high promise and two young players, G. Hambleton and D. M. Green, did well.

Played 18, Won 10, Lost 3, Drawn 5

Batting

	Innings		Not outs		Runs		Highest inns.		Average
S. M. Jackson	18	..	4	..	542	..	129*	..	38.71
†P. N. Hutson	18	..	3	..	447	..	84*	..	29.80
T. M. Richardson	15	..	3	..	347	..	53	..	28.91
C. E. Druce	12	..	1	..	187	..	43	..	17.00
G. Hambleton	13	..	3	..	155	..	30	..	15.50
D. M. Green	17	..	1	..	218	..	44	..	13.62

Bowling

	Overs		Maidens		Runs		Wickets		Average
D. H. Wrigley	212.2	..	64	..	381	..	41	..	9.29
T. M. Richardson	150	..	34	..	344	..	31	..	11.09
C. E. Druce	206.4	..	51	..	461	..	38	..	12.13
B. D. Jones	120	..	32	..	298	..	20	..	14.90

MAGDALEN COLLEGE SCHOOL
Played 13, *Won* 7, *Lost* 3, *Drawn* 3

Batting

	Innings		Not outs		Runs		Highest inns.		Average
R. A. Winstone	12	..	4	..	384	..	93*	..	48.00
D. Tinbergen	7	..	2	..	221	..	65*	..	44.20
†B. J. T. Britton	9	..	1	..	163	..	60	..	20.37
D. R. H. Jones	12	..	1	..	136	..	36	..	12.36
J. S. Baxter	12	..	3	..	103	..	26*	..	11.44

Bowling

	Overs		Maidens		Runs		Wickets		Average
D. R. L. Serjeant	125.5	..	25	..	343	..	31	..	11.06
M. R. Bowley	82	..	15	..	200	..	15	..	13.33
S. G. Salway	128.3	..	24	..	326	..	23	..	14.17
R. A. Winstone	133	..	16	..	429	..	30	..	14.30

MARLBOROUGH COLLEGE

Powerful bowling and often brilliant fielding compensated Marlborough's young side for their batting deficiencies, and after a moderate start, they finished the season in grand style with victories over Sherborne, Cheltenham and Rugby. R. C. Coke-Wallis, the captain, set a fine example with bat and ball and A. J. B. Sabine showed much promise as a fast bowler. Ten of the team remained for 1956.

Played 13, *Won* 5, *Lost* 4, *Drawn* 4

Batting

	Innings		Not outs		Runs		Highest inns.		Average
†R. C. Coke-Wallis	16	..	1	..	399	..	80	..	26.60
B. A. C. Marr	14	..	2	..	296	..	53	..	24.66
N. M. Stratford	16	..	1	..	302	..	64	..	20.13
R. E. Coote	16	..	0	..	285	..	59	..	17.81
V. Roberts	8	..	2	..	103	..	43	..	17.16
D. M. Slatter	8	..	2	..	102	..	26	..	17.00
G. A. Morris	16	..	0	..	248	..	62	..	15.50
P. R. Chamberlain	12	..	2	..	131	..	53	..	13.10
J. A. C. Gardiner	14	..	2	..	150	..	32*	..	12.50

Bowling

	Overs	Maidens	Runs	Wickets	Average
A. J. B. Sabine	125.4 ..	30 ..	297 ..	21 ..	14.14
R. C. Coke-Wallis	233 ..	50 ..	704 ..	42 ..	16.76
V. Roberts.............	81 ..	17 ..	243 ..	13 ..	18.69
A. J. H. Gardiner	133.1 ..	32 ..	417 ..	21 ..	19.38
D. M. Slatter	134 ..	25 ..	407 ..	15 ..	27.13

MERCERS' SCHOOL

Played 14, Won 5, Lost 6, Drawn 3

The bowling was more suited to the softer pitches prevailing at the start of the season than the later hard wickets. The batting was unreliable but the fielding came well up to standard. G. R. Pearce was a good captain and M. J. Cooper did very well as wicket-keeper.

Batting

	Innings	Not outs	Runs	Highest inns.	Average
M. J. Horne	13 ..	0 ..	238 ..	47 ..	18.30
D. H. Talks............	11 ..	1 ..	149 ..	40* ..	14.90
†G. R. Pearce	11 ..	3 ..	106 ..	39* ..	13.25
J. E. K. Tabert	12 ..	1 ..	140 ..	35 ..	12.72
R. H. C. McKenzie	10 ..	1 ..	109 ..	43 ..	12.11
B. F. Taylor	14 ..	2 ..	126 ..	37* ..	10.50
D. L. Moxey	11 ..	0 ..	110 ..	28 ..	10.00

Bowling

	Overs	Maidens	Runs	Wickets	Average
G. R. Pearce	102.5 ..	28 ..	248 ..	25 ..	9.92
J. Seez	122.3 ..	27 ..	238 ..	23 ..	10.34
M. J. Horne	139.2 ..	35 ..	335 ..	32 ..	10.46
B. Moore	109 ..	24 ..	297 ..	20 ..	14.85

MERCHANT TAYLORS' SCHOOL

With only three old colours, the side did well to lose only to a strong M.C.C. XI. R. D. Montgomerie, the captain, had a fine season as No. 4 batsman and leg-spin bowler, but W. D. S. Kay-Smith, a lively opening bowler, missed the latter part of the season through back trouble.

Played 14, Won 7, Lost 1, Drawn 6

Batting

	Innings	Not outs	Runs	Highest inns.	Average
†R. D. Montgomerie ...	12 ..	6 ..	355 ..	65* ..	59.16
M. E. Whitehead	14 ..	1 ..	245 ..	60 ..	18.84
R. W. Wiles	14 ..	3 ..	205 ..	46* ..	18.63
J. D. Collins	11 ..	1 ..	136 ..	37 ..	13.60

Bowling

	Overs	Maidens	Runs	Wickets	Average
W. D. S. Kay-Smith ...	110 ..	27 ..	239 ..	20 ..	11.95
R. D. Montgomerie	181.4 ..	34 ..	491 ..	38 ..	12.92
J. D. Collins	103.5 ..	23 ..	219 ..	13 ..	16.84
M. J. Christie	232.3 ..	63 ..	507 ..	28 ..	18.10
M. E. Whitehead	89 ..	33 ..	209 ..	11 ..	19.00

MERCHANT TAYLORS' SCHOOL, CROSBY

Although a great deal depended on the all-round ability of left-hander D. M. Alty, who played in the Schools games at Lord's, the success of the young opening batsmen, I. A. Corless and R. W. Myall, augured well for the future. The main bowling honours went to L. N. Treeby, medium in-swing, and under the captaincy of J. Hollowood the school maintained their reputation for first-class fielding.

Played 15, *Won* 9, *Lost* 2, *Drawn* 4

Batting

	Innings		Not outs		Runs		Highest inns.		Average
D. M. Alty	14	..	5	..	351	..	80*	..	39.00
I. A. Corless	15	..	3	..	354	..	70*	..	29.50
†J. Hollowood	15	..	4	..	267	..	73*	..	24.27
R. W. Myall	15	..	0	..	242	..	51	..	16.13

Bowling

	Overs		Maidens		Runs		Wickets		Average
L. N. Treeby	225	..	55	..	558	..	49	..	11.38
D. M. Alty	221	..	67	..	425	..	35	..	12.14
J. Bryson	70	..	19	..	201	..	15	..	13.40

MERCHISTON CASTLE SCHOOL

Particularly strong in bowling, Merchiston were unbeaten in school matches, gaining victories against Loretto and Watson's and drawing with Fettes, Glenalmond and Edinburgh Academy.

Played 18, *Won* 8, *Lost* 1, *Drawn* 9

Batting

	Innings		Not outs		Runs		Highest inns.		Average
†A. M. Zuill	19	..	2	..	536	..	66	..	31.52
A. M. B. Sym	16	..	2	..	415	..	79	..	29.78
J. M. Boyle	21	..	3	..	438	..	59	..	24.33
N. O. Kilpatrick	18	..	6	..	261	..	47	..	21.75
A. B. Gourlay	19	..	2	..	256	..	33	..	15.05
J. E. Jackson	13	..	5	..	107	..	19	..	13.37
I. McLauchlan	18	..	4	..	182	..	24	..	13.00

Bowling

	Overs		Maidens		Runs		Wickets		Average
I. Leddie	231.2	..	77	..	512	..	49	..	10.44
J. M. Boyle	178.1	..	32	..	606	..	56	..	10.82
I. H. Morris	252.1	..	78	..	552	..	46	..	12.00
A. C. W. Boyle	56.4	..	8	..	203	..	10	..	20.30
I. McLauchlan	121	..	30	..	280	..	10	..	28.00

MILL HILL SCHOOL
Played 13, Won 0, Lost 3, Drawn 10

Batting

	Innings		Not outs		Runs		Highest inns.		Average
J. M. Bunyard	11	..	3	..	229	..	53	..	28.62
M. R. Zilka............	11	..	0	..	254	..	72	..	23.09
D. H. Wickenden	10	..	0	..	153	..	47	..	15.30
†K. L. W. Armistead ...	11	..	1	..	150	..	32	..	15.00
R. J. Auld	11	..	0	..	161	..	50	..	14.63
A. Scobie	9	..	2	..	102	..	37	..	14.57
A. R. Bramley-Harker ..	11	..	0	..	122	..	30	..	11.09

Bowling

	Overs		Maidens		Runs		Wickets		Average
M. A. Roberts	92	..	21	..	247	..	15	..	16.46
K. L. W. Armistead ..	148	..	54	..	317	..	18	..	17.61
R. G. Freeman	84	..	28	..	238	..	12	..	19.83

MONKTON COMBE SCHOOL
Played 11, Won 2, Lost 2, Drawn 7

Batting

	Innings		Not outs		Runs		Highest inns.		Average
J. S. Davies	7	..	2	..	149	..	30*	..	29.80
†S. H. Maslen...........	11	..	1	..	141	..	45	..	14.10

Bowling

	Overs		Maidens		Runs		Wickets		Average
I. H. Glasgow	121.5	..	18	..	371	..	28	..	13.25
C. G. Reeves...........	63.3	..	5	..	168	..	11	..	15.27
J. S. Davies	103.5	..	19	..	301	..	14	..	21.50

MOUNT ST. MARY'S COLLEGE
Played 10, Won 3, Lost 2, Drawn 5

Batting

	Innings		Not outs		Runs		Highest inns.		Average
E. D'Andrade	12	..	0	..	285	..	63	..	23.75
H. D'Andrade	12	..	2	..	225	..	58	..	22.50
†P. Davison	12	..	0	..	233	..	41	..	19.41
J. Hall	10	..	2	..	106	..	42	..	13.25
R. Place	12	..	1	..	117	..	28	..	10.63

Bowling

	Overs		Maidens		Runs		Wickets		Average
P. Davison	89	..	22	..	233	..	23	..	10.13
E. D'Andrade	141.1	..	35	..	283	..	27	..	10.48
P. Cullen	75	..	17	..	182	..	16	..	11.37
J. Hall	100	..	12	..	271	..	19	..	14.26

NEWCASTLE ROYAL GRAMMAR SCHOOL
Played 19, Won 12, Lost 2, Drawn 5

Batting

	Innings	Not outs	Runs	Highest inns.	Average
G. K. Knox	17	2	576	103*	38.40
†A. R. Taylor	20	5	486	72*	32.40
B. M. Darling	16	1	320	63	21.33
W. J. Martin	16	4	194	55	16.16
R. Napper	13	4	145	27	16.11
P. D. Brodrick	19	1	284	121	15.77

Bowling

	Overs	Maidens	Runs	Wickets	Average
R. W. Willey	96.4	23	218	21	10.38
G. K. Knox	165.2	37	476	43	11.06
J. G. Duncan	174	37	480	40	12.00
P. D. Brodrick	209.4	39	553	45	12.28

NOTTINGHAM HIGH SCHOOL
Played 18, Won 11, Lost 3, Drawn 4

Batting

	Innings	Not outs	Runs	Highest inns.	Average
S. P. Unwin	8	3	220	67	44.00
J. E. Hotchin	18	3	635	92	42.33
B. Calvert	18	3	424	100*	28.26
J. T. Bexon	17	3	319	58	22.78
J. D. Morris	7	2	104	25	20.80
†D. J. Lipman	14	4	178	44*	17.80

Bowling

	Overs	Maidens	Runs	Wickets	Average
D. J. Palfreman	145.3	39	338	27	12.51
R. Foster	137.2	29	364	29	12.55
S. P. Unwin	220.1	58	576	43	13.39
J. D. Morris	153	29	480	29	16.55

OAKHAM SCHOOL
Played 14, Won 3, Lost 4, Drawn 7

Batting

	Innings	Not outs	Runs	Highest inns.	Average
A. P. Marrion	14	0	553	130	39.50
A. R. Boffey	14	1	453	123	34.84
W. N. Houghton	12	2	337	74	33.70
R. J. Peberdy	14	0	337	86	24.07
P. I. D. James	14	1	309	79	23.76

Bowling

	Overs	Maidens	Runs	Wickets	Average
E. M. E. Garner	175.4	44	423	28	15.10
R. J. Peberdy	173.4	51	387	22	17.59
D. W. Foode	190	41	553	31	17.83

ORATORY SCHOOL

Played 16, Won 5, Lost 5, Drawn 6

Batting

	Innings	Not outs	Runs	Highest inns.	Average
J. Moore	17	3	384	76	27.42
†T. Hinds	17	5	286	61*	23.83
R. Nicol	12	3	188	50*	20.88
J. Latham	15	2	196	47	15.07

Bowling

	Overs	Maidens	Runs	Wickets	Average
J. Latham	131	30	420	31	13.54
R. Nicol	189.1	48	478	23	14.05
T. Hinds	163.1	24	529	37	14.29
A. Duch	110	15	386	17	22.70

OUNDLE SCHOOL

T. W. O. Herbert, wicket-keeper for the fourth year, managed a young side well, and the batting was generally reliable, though it failed against the M.C.C. and Rugby. R. V. Lawry batted with distinction on many occasions and J. D. Appleyard, son of the former Essex bowler, developed into a skilful left-arm spin bowler.

Played 11, Won 2, Lost 2, Drawn 7

Batting

	Innings	Not outs	Runs	Highest inns.	Average
R. V. Lawry	12	4	454	104*	56.75
J. F. Doubleday	12	0	375	133	31.25
A. J. T. Crabbe	11	1	230	69	23.00
†T. W. O. Herbert	11	1	183	73*	18.30
J. M. Foulds	11	2	161	35*	17.88
G. M. Boyce	12	0	191	59	15.91

Bowling

	Overs	Maidens	Runs	Wickets	Average
J. D. Appleyard	182.4	54	396	28	14.14
G. H. Saul	122.5	33	423	20	21.15
P. H. Mitchell	138.2	34	383	16	23.93

PERSE SCHOOL

D. E. Nightingale, the captain, enjoyed an exceptional season. He dominated the batting and on favourable pitches proved an effective off-spin bowler. J. H. Lidstone (left-arm slow) also bowled well, but the attack was less penetrative on hard pitches.

Played 16, Won 10, Lost 2, Drawn 4

Batting

	Innings	Not outs	Runs	Highest inns.	Average
†D. E. Nightingale	16	7	649	93*	72.11
D. H. Perkins	16	2	276	49*	19.71
C. W. Seamons	12	2	164	39*	16.40
I. R. W. Stone	9	2	106	36*	15.14

Bowling

	Overs		Maidens		Runs		Wickets		Average
J. H. Lidstone	155	..	34	..	404	..	50	..	8.08
D. E. Nightingale	185.4	..	63	..	366	..	37	..	9.89
B. L. Hunt	130	..	34	..	271	..	20	..	13.55

QUEEN ELIZABETH GRAMMAR SCHOOL, WAKEFIELD

C. J. Littlewood, one of four aggressive left-handers, and his team did well to overcome in such convincing manner the loss through injury of C. C. Nichols, the leading bowler in 1954. Their best performance was the dismissal of Bradford for 28 when J. A. Holt took five for six.

Played 16, *Won* 7, *Lost* 1, *Tied* 1, *Drawn* 7

Batting

	Innings		Not outs		Runs		Highest inns.		Average
†C. J. Littlewood	15	..	2	..	355	..	69	..	27.30
I. Plimmer	13	..	2	..	288	..	55*	..	26.18
T. Cass	15	..	1	..	228	..	77*	..	16.28
D. A. Harrison	14	..	1	..	161	..	31	..	12.38
J. M. Bromley	14	..	0	..	142	..	36	..	10.14

Bowling

	Overs		Maidens		Runs		Wickets		Average
B. T. Lomas	100.2	..	24	..	256	..	33	..	7.75
J. A. Holt	82.2	..	25	..	176	..	18	..	9.77
P. N. Lees	145.5	..	35	..	350	..	32	..	10.93
R. G. Smith	125.1	..	38	..	282	..	22	..	12.81

RADLEY COLLEGE

Particularly strong in batting, Radley enjoyed a successful season with victories over Westminster, St. Edwards and Eastbourne to set against their defeats by Bradfield and Stowe. Although kept out of five games by injury, G. B. C. Hopton batted attractively on the hard pitches in July and led the way in several feats of fast-scoring. The bowlers lacked penetration and even A. R. Duff, the most successful, did not improve as expected.

Played 13, *Won* 6, *Lost* 2, *Drawn* 5

Batting

	Innings		Not outs		Runs		Highest inns.		Average
G. B. C. Hopton	8	..	2	..	269	..	79	..	44.83
D. W. M. Berkley	15	..	3	..	418	..	100*	..	34.83
D. W. H. McCowen	15	..	2	..	389	..	73	..	29.92
†W. D. G. Lewis	15	..	0	..	440	..	107	..	29.33
J. C. Lewis	12	..	3	..	249	..	56*	..	27.66
F. T. A. Hole	15	..	0	..	360	..	87	..	24.00
T. W. Morkill	11	..	2	..	164	..	50*	..	18.22
A. R. V. McGarrigle	7	..	0	..	105	..	27	..	15.00

Bowling

	Overs		Maidens		Runs		Wickets		Average
A. R. Duff	226	..	48	..	604	..	35	..	17.25
T. W. Morkill	189	..	46	..	589	..	28	..	21.07
W. D. G. Lewis	140.5	..	31	..	461	..	21	..	21.95
J. C. Lewis	113.3	..	23	..	272	..	11	..	24.72
D. W. H. McCowen	150	..	27	..	482	..	13	..	37.07

READING SCHOOL

Played 15, Won 4, Lost 1, Drawn 10

Batting

	Innings		Not outs		Runs		Highest inns.		Average
J. R. Digby	15	..	4	..	420	..	72*	..	38.18
P. A. Merrett	14	..	4	..	312	..	70*	..	31.20
B. G. F. Shepheard	14	..	0	..	375	..	72	..	26.78
J. Sansom	10	..	4	..	137	..	31*	..	22.83
R. W. Briggs	10	..	4	..	135	..	27	..	22.50
A. P. Sadler	14	..	1	..	277	..	60	..	21.30
†D. N. Dominy	10	..	1	..	166	..	52	..	18.44

Bowling

	Overs		Maidens		Runs		Wickets		Average
R. A. Alexander	79	..	4	..	309	..	19	..	16.26
D. N. Dominy	136.1	..	15	..	386	..	23	..	16.78
J. R. Digby	180	..	47	..	423	..	24	..	17.62
A. P. Sadler	80	..	11	..	299	..	15	..	19.93

REPTON SCHOOL

Repton, though difficult to beat, were not up to the standard of recent years. There were three formidable fast bowlers in J. R. Fletcher and B. M. Betts, both left-handed, and J. R. H. Sale, and two steady leg-spinners in P. J. Barber and A. Jollie. The batting depended too much on P. H. Vaughan, a natural hitter, and P. R. Starkey, an attacking opening batsman. The fielding was good and A. W. S. Robinson improved as a wicket-keeper. Six old colours, led by P. J. Barber, remain for 1956.

Played 14, Won 6, Lost 1, Drawn 7

Batting

	Innings		Not outs		Runs		Highest inns.		Average
P. H. Vaughan	16	..	3	..	550	..	110	..	42.30
P. R. Starkey	14	..	1	..	396	..	71	..	30.46
†R. G. Gillard	16	..	1	..	309	..	61	..	20.60
J. R. H. Sale	8	..	3	..	101	..	23*	..	20.20
P. J. Barber	15	..	3	..	235	..	49*	..	19.58
A. Jollie	12	..	3	..	148	..	30*	..	16.44
J. B. Hall	15	..	2	..	184	..	49	..	14.15
A. W. S. Robinson	12	..	3	..	103	..	24*	..	11.44
R. J. Pilkington	11	..	1	..	101	..	34	..	10.10

Bowling

	Overs	Maidens	Runs	Wickets	Average
J. R. Fletcher	248	.. 86	.. 516	.. 47	.. 10.97
B. M. Betts	136.1	.. 40	.. 331	.. 29	.. 11.41
J. R. H. Sale	143	.. 50	.. 294	.. 23	.. 12.78
P. J. Barber	148.1	.. 37	.. 365	.. 21	.. 17.38
A. Jollie	99.3	.. 22	.. 295	.. 15	.. 19.66

ROSSALL SCHOOL

Despite the overwhelming proportion of drawn games, Rossall always played attractive cricket. The batting never really failed, and the catching and ground-fielding were the best for many years. The side's weakness lay in the absence of bowlers capable of running through the opposition. J. G. Wildman, the captain, set a fine example and others who distinguished themselves particularly were I. T. C. Glen, a superb close-field, and C. J. Fryer, whose peculiarity of style did not prevent his being a most consistent batsman.

Played 12, Won 2, Lost 1, Drawn 9

Batting

	Innings	Not outs	Runs	Highest inns.	Average
†J. G. Wildman	13	.. 1	.. 341	.. 61	.. 28.41
C. J. Fryer	14	.. 1	.. 365	.. 85	.. 28.07
D. R. M. Collinge	10	.. 3	.. 195	.. 39*	.. 27.85
I. T. C. Glen	13	.. 2	.. 261	.. 91	.. 23.72
M. J. Reece	14	.. 3	.. 208	.. 52*	.. 18.90
I. S. Foster	10	.. 1	.. 161	.. 56	.. 17.88
G. M. Attenborough	13	.. 0	.. 213	.. 35	.. 16.38

Bowling

	Overs	Maidens	Runs	Wickets	Average
J. S. Bowns	136.2	.. 25	.. 398	.. 25	.. 15.92
D. R. M. Collinge	149	.. 38	.. 394	.. 23	.. 17.13
M. J. Reece	197.5	.. 61	.. 467	.. 26	.. 17.96
I. T. C. Glen	176.5	.. 53	.. 407	.. 17	.. 23.94

RUGBY SCHOOL

Brittle batting prevented Rugby from having a strong side. There were several attractive stroke-players but too few with correct technique. In attack, the faster men performed creditably but did not receive the support expected from the spin bowlers. E. McQ. Rose led the side well and ensured a steady improvement in the fielding.

Played 14, Won 4, Lost 7, Drawn 3

Batting

	Innings	Not outs	Runs	Highest inns.	Average
C. R. B. Neame	13	.. 1	.. 392	.. 74	.. 32.66
†E. McQ. Rose	16	.. 1	.. 471	.. 83	.. 31.40
P. R. Colville	13	.. 1	.. 223	.. 49	.. 18.58
M. A. Oddy	13	.. 0	.. 223	.. 65	.. 17.15
G. D. G. Shaw	9	.. 0	.. 141	.. 30	.. 15.66
H. M. Fox	14	.. 1	.. 153	.. 43	.. 11.76

Bowling

	Overs		Maidens		Runs		Wickets		Average
G. S. Harcourt	151.3	..	37	..	344	..	29	..	11.86
R. Lancaster	100.4	..	25	..	291	..	21	..	13.85
T. B. L. Coghlan	207.5	..	45	..	506	..	33	..	15.33

RUTHIN SCHOOL

Ruthin were strong in bowling and the fielding generally reached a high standard. J. F. Foster, R. G. Reynolds and P. B. Schofield all bowled most efficiently, Reynolds and Schofield, both aged 15 and both seam bowlers, were new to the side and showed much promise.

Played 17, *Won* 10, *Lost* 3, *Drawn* 4

Batting

	Innings		Not outs		Runs		Highest inns.		Average
†G. Neil-Dwyer	17	..	3	..	424	..	73*	..	30.28
N. S. Casson	13	..	4	..	127	..	33	..	14.11
L. W. Houghton	14	..	0	..	159	..	45	..	11.35
J. Wynne-Williams......	18	..	3	..	168	..	48	..	11.20
S. Kerruish	17	..	2	..	165	..	30	..	11.00

Bowling

	Overs		Maidens		Runs		Wickets		Average
P. B. Legg	32.3	..	11	..	53	..	12	..	4.41
P. B. Schofield	75.4	..	22	..	163	..	27	..	6.03
J. F. Foster	200.1	..	93	..	316	..	50	..	6.32
R. G. Reynolds	168.1	..	60	..	308	..	41	..	7.51

RYDAL SCHOOL

Rydal were not beaten until they met M.C.C. in the last match, a specially satisfying record considering that C. D. Pighills, the appointed captain, was unable to play at all. It is hoped he will be fit to lead the side in 1956. K. R. F. Bearne, who took over the captaincy, showed fine all-round form.

Played 10, *Won* 3, *Lost* 1, *Tied* 1, *Drawn* 5

Batting

	Innings		Not outs		Runs		Highest inns.		Average
R. M. Hillman	10	..	1	..	237	..	67*	..	26.33
J. A. T. Burton.........	8	..	1	..	162	..	67*	..	23.14
†K. R. F. Bearne	10	..	0	..	217	..	58	..	21.70
D. R. Bott	9	..	0	..	162	..	38	..	18.00
C. H. Thompson	9	..	2	..	118	..	33	..	16.85
J. N. Sefton............	10	..	1	..	142	..	57	..	15.77

Bowling

	Overs		Maidens		Runs		Wickets		Average
K. R. F. Bearne	125.3	..	25	..	346	..	30	..	11.53
M. W. Corry...........	108.1	..	12	..	343	..	25	..	13.72
A. G. Greenwood	123.4	..	19	..	375	..	19	..	19.73

ST. ALBANS SCHOOL
Played 11, Won 2, Lost 7, Drawn 2

Batting

	Innings	Not outs	Runs	Highest inns.	Average
D. H. Levy	12	1	184	95	16.72
G. A. Luffman	10	0	148	71	14.80
A. G. Buchanan	11	0	160	48	14.54
D. Thorpe	11	2	122	40	13.55
†S. S. Lazarus	11	3	101	29	12.62

Bowling

	Overs	Maidens	Runs	Wickets	Average
G. A. Luffman	87	16	256	17	15.05
S. S. Lazarus	130	26	398	24	16.58

ST. BEES SCHOOL

Victories over both Rossall and Giggleswick made the season specially satisfying. F. Booth inspired a cheerfully aggressive spirit, and this was reflected in the batting and fielding.

Played 14, Won 5, Lost 5, Drawn 4

Batting

	Innings	Not outs	Runs	Highest inns.	Average
J. W. Parker	14	3	434	67*	39.45
A. E. Townsend	12	2	257	67	25.70
H. J. Corrie	14	2	283	55*	23.58
J. F. Laxton	13	0	168	39	12.92

Bowling

	Overs	Maidens	Runs	Wickets	Average
D. R. Dowzer	48	7	146	15	9.73
†F. Booth	113.4	23	275	22	12.50
A. E. Townsend	143	32	350	26	13.46
R. L. Newton	72	22	174	10	17.40
H. J. Corrie	151	30	361	18	20.05

ST. EDMUND'S, CANTERBURY
Played 13, Won 5, Lost 5, Drawn 3

Batting

	Innings	Not outs	Runs	Highest inns.	Average
I. Taylor	13	2	444	138*	43.63
D. Pettit	12	2	261	58*	26.10
M. Baxter	12	1	228	123*	20.72
F. Wood	12	1	215	44*	19.54
A. Courtauld	9	2	101	28*	14.42
P. Cook	10	1	127	31	14.11

Bowling

	Overs	Maidens	Runs	Wickets	Average
D. Pettit	148.3	48	346	34	10.17
A. Courtauld	118.4	33	363	29	12.51
J. Martin	39	5	141	11	12.81
F. Howells	42	6	198	10	19.80

ST. EDWARD'S SCHOOL, OXFORD

Although St. Edward's possessed no player of outstanding ability, they were well balanced and achieved a creditable record, including the school's first victory over Free Foresters.

Played 15, Won 7, Lost 2, Drawn 6

Batting

	Innings	Not outs	Runs	Highest inns.	Average
H. J. E. Emson	10	5	220	55	44.00
D. L. Hosie	15	0	464	88	30.93
†J. R. Friend	16	3	375	57	28.84
J. D. B. Gardiner	16	0	398	62	24.87
B. G. Powell-Harper	13	2	246	44	22.36
C. F. Dobson	16	0	304	82	19.00
M. Oldaker	11	3	110	31*	13.75
R. J. C. Sprague	11	1	111	29	11.10

Bowling

	Overs	Maidens	Runs	Wickets	Average
M. Oldaker	207.5	55	622	36	17.27
M. H. Spence	209	42	712	35	20.34
C. E. L. Balmer	60	13	204	10	20.40
J. R. Friend	101	17	428	15	28.53

ST. GEORGE'S SCHOOL, HARPENDEN

Played 18, Won 6, Lost 8, Drawn 4

Batting

	Innings	Not outs	Runs	Highest inns.	Average
†H. C. Bang	18	4	523	100*	37.35
R. Noyes	16	1	150	23	10.00

Bowling

	Overs	Maidens	Runs	Wickets	Average
E. S. Mallett	184.3	50	462	50	9.24
C. G. Gilbert	185.3	54	480	40	12.00
H. C. Bang	100.3	21	271	18	15.05
R. F. Gilbert	75.5	18	260	11	23.63

ST. LAWRENCE COLLEGE, RAMSGATE

Played 15, Won 1, Lost 6, Drawn 8

Batting

	Innings	Not outs	Runs	Highest inns.	Average
D. J. Minshall	14	1	332	115*	25.53
R. L. Thomas	15	1	337	74	24.07
†P. Cherry	15	3	214	48	17.83
E. A. Baxter	10	1	146	73	16.22
D. G. Austin-Jones	12	2	142	46*	14.20
J. L. Williams	14	1	134	68	10.30

Bowling

	Overs	Maidens	Runs	Wickets	Average
E. J. Coomes	171	22	615	35	17.57
E. A. Baxter	123	22	343	17	20.17
M. O. Ormerod	128	11	477	19	25.10
D. T. Bowesman	163	19	569	14	40.64

ST. PAUL'S SCHOOL
Played 13, *Won* 2, *Lost* 7, *Drawn* 4

Batting

	Innings	Not outs	Runs	Highest inns.	Average
†P. Wheeler	12	2	325	62*	32.50
A. N. Sperryn	10	2	193	78*	24.12
J. D. Davies	6	0	108	35	18.00
R. A. Godfrey	13	2	186	48	16.90
P. N. Sperryn	11	1	138	50	13.80
G. R. Gosheron	11	0	117	37	10.63

Bowling

	Overs	Maidens	Runs	Wickets	Average
R. E. M. Freeman	131.2	27	295	24	12.29
R. A. Godfrey	121.5	32	322	23	14.00
W. G. S. Haddow	95.1	15	287	17	16.88
I. K. R. Brown	75	8	280	11	25.54

ST. PETER'S SCHOOL, YORK

After a depressing start to the season St. Peter's made a splendid recovery and finished with a reasonable record. Mediocre bowling was made effective by first-class fielding. From mid-June onwards, the team scored heavily and four centuries were made—two by M. Willstrop, one by D. A. MacPherson and one by D. Kirby. R. G. Bough (captain) had a disappointing season with the bat, but he was an astute tactician and set an excellent example in the field.

Played 11, *Won* 6, *Lost* 3, *Drawn* 2

Batting

	Innings	Not outs	Runs	Highest inns.	Average
D. Kirby	12	2	519	111*	51.90
M. Willstrop	12	2	405	136*	40.50
D. A. MacPherson	12	1	219	111*	19.90
P. B. Clayton	12	0	190	54	15.83
†R. G. Bough	11	0	115	33	10.45

Bowling

	Overs	Maidens	Runs	Wickets	Average
A. Burrows	176.3	67	283	24	11.79
M. Willstrop	171.5	46	369	28	13.17
D. Kirby	112.3	29	235	16	14.68
P. M. Hewson	90.1	14	277	18	15.38

SEDBERGH SCHOOL

Lack of net-practice in the first three weeks of the season made team-building a difficult process for the captain, W. H. R. Meageen, and prevented players of high promise from showing their full potential. The outstanding individual was D. Smith, a fine left-handed batsman and fast-medium bowler, who scored centuries against two adult teams, Catterick Garrison and Durham Pilgrims. G. R. James bowled off-breaks well but the attack was weakened through an injury to J. R. Miller, who missed the later games.

Played 11, *Won* 5, *Lost* 3, *Drawn* 3

Batting

	Innings	Not outs	Runs	Highest inns.	Average
D. Smith	10	.. 3	.. 515	.. 41*	.. 73.57
†W. H. R. Meageen	11	.. 1	.. 237	.. 39*	.. 23.70
P. T. Dransfield	10	.. 2	.. 176	.. 43	.. 22.00
R. D. Sangwin	10	.. 1	.. 183	.. 49	.. 20.33
B. W. J. G. Wilson	6	.. 0	.. 121	.. 36	.. 20.16
P. L. Hogarth	10	.. 0	.. 102	.. 30	.. 10.20

Bowling

	Overs	Maidens	Runs	Wickets	Average
D. H. Charlton..........	69.1	.. 14	.. 168	.. 12	.. 14.00
G. R. James	160.4	.. 33	.. 488	.. 31	.. 15.74
D. Smith	159.1	.. 41	.. 391	.. 24	.. 16.29
J. R. Miller	82.4	.. 17	.. 223	.. 11	.. 20.27

SEVENOAKS SCHOOL
Played 12, *Won* 5, *Lost* 2, *Drawn* 5

Batting

	Innings	Not outs	Runs	Highest inns.	Average
L. J. Humble	9	.. 2	.. 304	.. 107	.. 43.42
J. R. F. Martin.........	12	.. 1	.. 224	.. 62	.. 20.36
C. C. Richardson	11	.. 0	.. 195	.. 45	.. 17.72
C. A. C. Cooper........	12	.. 2	.. 145	.. 43	.. 14.50
R. F. Stewart	8	.. 0	.. 114	.. 45	.. 14.25

Bowling

	Overs	Maidens	Runs	Wickets	Average
D. J. Russell	82.1	.. 18	.. 193	.. 14	.. 13.78
C. C. Richardson	121.3	.. 39	.. 319	.. 23	.. 13.86
M. J. Burden	80.1	.. 18	.. 230	.. 16	.. 14.37
R. C. Clifford	69.2	.. 14	.. 204	.. 10	.. 20.40

SHERBORNE SCHOOL

The absence of a hostile new-ball attack prevented Sherborne from developing into a really good side. The batting was attractive and consistent; the fielding thoroughly sound and there were two fine spin bowlers in S. P. Tindall (leg-breaks) and J. Lawrence (off-breaks). G. P. Gent handled the team well and M. B. Wilson distinguished himself behind the wicket.

Played 12, *Won* 3, *Lost* 3, *Drawn* 6

Batting

	Innings	Not outs	Runs	Highest inns.	Average
C. C. T. Henfrey	11	.. 2	.. 308	.. 105	.. 34.22
M. B. Wilson	12	.. 2	.. 321	.. 85	.. 32.10
P. D. Cowell	14	.. 1	.. 355	.. 118*	.. 27.30
†G. P. Gent	15	.. 1	.. 380	.. 74	.. 27.14
C. R. J. Eglinton	14	.. 1	.. 320	.. 64*	.. 24.61
J. Lawrence	10	.. 1	.. 162	.. 33	.. 18.00
P. C. Eglinton..........	15	.. 1	.. 251	.. 53	.. 17.92
J. P. Devitt	11	.. 3	.. 125	.. 28	.. 15.62

Bowling

	Overs		Maidens		Runs		Wickets		Average
S. P. Tindall	216.1	..	53	..	632	..	48	..	13.16
J. Lawrence	172	..	59	..	365	..	20	..	18.25
J. J. Barber	151	..	37	..	347	..	12	..	28.91

SHREWSBURY SCHOOL

Although the team contained several able batsmen, the middle of the order proved unreliable. This factor contributed much to the defeats by Repton and Malvern, and nearly cost the match with Rossall. J. L. Ward, left-arm slow, did not keep such an accurate length as the previous season but he and R. N. Carter, right-arm medium-pace, were again the most successful bowlers. T. J. Lewis led the side admirably.

Played 10, Won 3, Lost 5, Drawn 2

Batting

	Innings		Not outs		Runs		Highest inns.		Average
J. M. Nicolson	12	..	0	..	317	..	55	..	26.41
J. L. Ward	13	..	2	..	270	..	56	..	24.54
T. H. E. Moore	13	..	0	..	253	..	51	..	19.46
A. N. Duerr	12	..	2	..	193	..	44	..	19.30

Bowling

	Overs		Maidens		Runs		Wickets		Average
J. L. Ward	149.1	..	39	..	454	..	30	..	15.13
R. N. Carter	127.2	..	37	..	295	..	19	..	15.52
A. G. P. Lewis	136	..	33	..	368	..	19	..	19.36
J. A. Harvey	119	..	27	..	352	..	10	..	35.20

SOLIHULL SCHOOL

Played 14, Won 6, Lost 1, Drawn 7

Batting

	Innings		Not outs		Runs		Highest inns.		Average
D. Stratford	13	..	2	..	337	..	103*	..	30.63
G. Vaughan	11	..	1	..	297	..	86*	..	29.70
P. Taylor	10	..	2	..	183	..	59	..	22.87
†J. Stratford	9	..	1	..	109	..	30	..	13.62

Bowling

	Overs		Maidens		Runs		Wickets		Average
D. Smith	132	..	33	..	398	..	32	..	12.43
A. Hames	124	..	18	..	439	..	28	..	15.67
P. Bailey	171	..	56	..	452	..	24	..	18.83

STAMFORD SCHOOL

Played 12, Won 4, Lost 2, Drawn 6

Batting

	Innings		Not outs		Runs		Highest inns.		Average
J. B. Bayley	12	..	2	..	271	..	88	..	27.10
A. Nickerson	11	..	3	..	216	..	73*	..	27.00
I. D. Norton	12	..	1	..	279	..	71	..	25.36
P. C. Compton	11	..	1	..	241	..	101*	..	24.10

Bowling

	Overs	Maidens	Runs	Wickets	Average
M. J. Barwell	151	56	333	31	10.74
P. C. Compton	44	14	134	12	11.16
I. D. Norton	160	40	448	22	20.36

STONYHURST COLLEGE

Though the season was inevitably one of rebuilding, the batting was exceptionally weak and caused defeat in all save one of the school matches. The bowling was steady without being particularly dangerous. I. P. Fisher, a fast-medium in-swinger, and M. T. Corbett, left-arm medium, were the most successful members of an attack that lacked variety.

Played 12, *Won* 0, *Lost* 8, *Drawn* 4

Batting

	Innings	Not outs	Runs	Highest inns.	Average
R. G. Mackenzie	14	0	231	48	16.50
J. St. F. Dare	14	3	162	29*	14.72
J. G. Parker	14	0	206	39	14.71
P. L. Recordon	14	0	204	73	14.57
K. J. Garry	13	0	162	45	12.46

Bowling

	Overs	Maidens	Runs	Wickets	Average
I. P. Fisher	159	33	420	24	17.50
M. T. Corbett	129	26	378	19	19.89
K. J. Garry	124	17	420	19	22.10

STOWE SCHOOL

Stowe had a young and inexperienced side, the batting in particular being inadequate, though J. P. Kerr was consistent and played one outstanding innings and J. A. Boyd-Smith showed promise. D. Cameron was a hostile and persistent opening bowler and was well supported by J. B. Hamer, also right-handed. F. N. Rushton was a most competent wicket-keeper, and R. W. Slater (slow medium right-hand) bowled steadily and captained the side with quiet efficiency.

Played 12, *Won* 4, *Lost* 7, *Drawn* 1

Batting

	Innings	Not outs	Runs	Highest inns.	Average
J. P. Kerr	13	0	465	175	35.76
R. A. Opperman	9	1	266	95*	33.25
J. A. Boyd-Smith	13	1	219	38	18.25
R. A. B. Day	10	0	162	59	16.20
J. H. Harris	13	2	174	53*	15.81
J. B. Hamer	12	1	170	34	15.54
D. Cameron	11	1	145	45	14.50

Bowling

	Overs	Maidens	Runs	Wickets	Average
†R. W. Slater	85.3	15	261	14	18.64
J. B. Hamer	146	28	373	18	20.72
D. Cameron	188.3	27	589	28	21.03
M. D. Miall	126.2	11	482	15	32.13
C. J. G. Shillington	105.3	9	398	11	36.18

SUTTON VALENCE SCHOOL

Fast scoring was the feature of the school's best season for many years, the rate more than once exceeding 100 runs an hour. Under the fine captaincy of B. G. Keeble the out-cricket was equally aggressive.

Played 13, Won 9, Lost 3, Drawn 1

Batting

	Innings	Not outs	Runs	Highest inns.	Average
C. D. Gerty	10	4	276	83*	46.00
R. E. B. Craven	13	2	440	95	40.00
P. N. Goddard	11	3	258	101*	32.25
†B. G. Keeble	13	2	322	50	29.27
W. E. Ellis	11	5	162	46*	27.00
E. M. Hollingsworth	12	0	150	50	12.50

Bowling

	Overs	Maidens	Runs	Wickets	Average
P. N. Goddard	135	46	349	35	9.97
A. C. Nash	117	48	258	20	12.90
D. F. Fenton	123	25	352	26	13.54
R. E. B. Craven	180	51	541	22	24.59

TAUNTON SCHOOL

Played 14, Won 4, Lost 6, Drawn 4

Batting

	Innings	Not outs	Runs	Highest inns.	Average
D. R. Dale	7	2	137	69*	27.40
D. F. Miller	8	2	140	86	23.33
M. D. Steyn	9	2	159	42	22.71
†G. Gill	14	1	285	72*	21.92
W. D. L. Erasmus	12	1	162	74*	14.72

Bowling

	Overs	Maidens	Runs	Wickets	Average
G. Gill	186.3	41	504	35	14.40
C. Webb	144.5	43	313	16	19.56
D. R. Williams	96	22	226	11	20.54
M. D. Steyn	85	16	259	12	21.58

TONBRIDGE SCHOOL

Tonbridge varied between extremes. At their best, as in beating M.C.C., they were most impressive; at other times, as against Westminster, equally bad. R. M. K. Gracey, the captain, reserved his best bowling for Lord's, where he shattered Clifton's second innings, and it was unfortunate that P. Meredith, the steadiest

bowler, should have been hampered by back trouble for most of
the season. The brightest feature was the batting of the youngest
player, R. M. Prideaux, an enterprising stroke-player of high
promise. He and his hard-hitting colleagues in the middle of the
order owed much to the soundness of G. E. Godfrey and C. M.
Smith, who usually saw the shine off the ball.

Played 13, *Won* 6, *Lost* 3, *Drawn* 4

Batting

	Innings		Not outs		Runs		Highest inns.		Average
R. M. Prideaux	13	..	6	..	405	..	104*	..	57.85
G. E. Godfrey	16	..	2	..	441	..	118*	..	31.50
N. Héroys	15	..	4	..	288	..	63	..	26.18
A. B. E. Hudson	8	..	2	..	148	..	36	..	24.66
C. J. Crang	15	..	1	..	313	..	84*	..	22.35
†R. M. K. Gracey	16	..	3	..	256	..	81	..	19.69
C. M. Smith	16	..	0	..	290	..	44	..	18.12
R. Ward	15	..	2	..	176	..	36*	..	13.53

Bowling

	Overs		Maidens		Runs		Wickets		Average
P. Meredith	105.4	..	25	..	256	..	19	..	13.47
N. R. B. Prowse	139.5	..	29	..	371	..	26	..	14.26
M. H. Foster	152.3	..	36	..	422	..	27	..	15.62
A. B. E. Hudson	126	..	16	..	366	..	23	..	15.91
R. M. K. Gracey	126.2	..	24	..	330	..	19	..	17.36

TRENT COLLEGE

Played 14, *Won* 3, *Lost* 8, *Drawn* 3

Batting

	Innings		Not outs		Runs		Highest inns.		Average
P. J. H. Neal..........	13	..	1	..	277	..	79	..	23.08
D. L. Bullard	12	..	0	..	231	..	61	..	19.25
R. M. Jolly	14	..	0	..	183	..	32	..	13.07
J. B. Bell	14	..	3	..	126	..	40	..	11.45
A. K. Blakeley	13	..	1	..	135	..	34	..	11.25

Bowling

	Overs		Maidens		Runs		Wickets		Average
†D. E. C. Spalding	155.3	..	40	..	443	..	34	..	13.02
J. H. G. Turner	79	..	11	..	256	..	18	..	14.22
G. R. Atkinson	98	..	17	..	328	..	16	..	20.50
A. K. Blakeley	71.5	..	8	..	274	..	11	..	24.90

TRINITY COLLEGE, GLENALMOND

After a poor start, the team improved considerably and
deserved credit for their fighting cricket in a remarkable series of
close finishes. These included victory by three runs over Fettes.

Played 19, *Won* 7, *Lost* 4, *Drawn* 8

Batting

	Innings		Not outs		Runs		Highest inns.		Average
D. E. Denholm	18	..	3	..	468	..	76*	..	31.20
D. H. Macpherson	16	..	2	..	319	..	50	..	22.78
H. S. U. Steven	19	..	1	..	295	..	63	..	17.17
A. T. Macdonald	15	..	1	..	162	..	51	..	11.57
B. H. Stowell	16	..	2	..	146	..	35	..	10.42

Bowling

	Overs		Maidens		Runs		Wickets		Average
W. E. Crawford	185.3	..	66	..	337	..	33	..	10.21
A. T. Macdonald	166	..	30	..	458	..	40	..	11.45
†J. A. G. Murray	244.2	..	61	..	583	..	38	..	15.34
D. H. Macpherson	78.3	..	10	..	320	..	18	..	17.77

UNIVERSITY COLLEGE SCHOOL

Played 12, Won 5, Lost 6, Drawn 1

Batting

	Innings		Not outs		Runs		Highest inns.		Average
A. Landsberg	12	..	1	..	155	..	41	..	14.09
A. G. Smith	12	..	1	..	139	..	27	..	12.63
A. P. A. Trayling	12	..	0	..	150	..	39	..	12.50
†P. T. Leney	12	..	1	..	123	..	44	..	11.18

Bowling

	Overs		Maidens		Runs		Wickets		Average
C. D. Smith	133	..	42	..	289	..	50	..	5.78
H. D. Wilsdon	46	..	10	..	131	..	14	..	9.35
M. L. Hawken	106	..	34	..	232	..	24	..	9.66

UPPINGHAM SCHOOL

Uppingham, with their strongest side for some years, enjoyed a fairly successful season, only the first two matches being lost. The number of drawn games was unsatisfactory but the school held the upper hand in most of them, and in no case were they in serious danger of defeat. J. H. Purves was the outstanding batsman and most of the side could make runs if necessary. C. Traub and M. J. K. Robson (fast) and C. R. Terras (leg breaks) were the principal bowlers and the left-handed J. B. R. Vartan completed a well-varied attack. The ground fielding, catching and throwing were extremely good.

Played 11, Won 3, Lost 2, Drawn 6

Batting

	Innings		Not out		Runs		Highest inns.		Average
J. H. Purves	14	..	2	..	489	..	110	..	40.75
J. B. R. Vartan	12	..	2	..	255	..	64	..	25.50
W. D. Leppington	14	..	2	..	298	..	68	..	24.83
J. H. Chatterton	11	..	2	..	214	..	52	..	23.77
W. N. Greig	11	..	1	..	229	..	54	..	22.90
M. J. K. Robson	11	..	2	..	191	..	72*	..	21.22

Bowling

	Overs		Maidens		Runs		Wickets		Average
J. B. R. Vartan	67	..	15	..	186	..	12	..	15.50
C. R. Terras	150.5	..	32	..	383	..	23	..	16.65
C. Traub	184	..	42	..	471	..	28	..	16.82
M. J. K. Robson	178.3	..	48	..	468	..	27	..	17.33

VICTORIA COLLEGE, JERSEY

Played 14, Won 8, Lost 3, Drawn 3

Batting

	Innings		Not outs		Runs		Highest inns.		Average
P. J. B. Le Brocq	12	..	4	..	305	..	90	..	38.12
†A. B. Carter	13	..	0	..	337	..	76	..	25.92
B. R. Le Marquand	11	..	3	..	166	..	50*	..	20.75
R. A. Furness	14	..	2	..	243	..	74	..	20.25
I. N. S. Ross-Roberts ...	14	..	0	..	214	..	58	..	15.28
B. P. Le Geyt	11	..	1	..	133	..	40	..	13.20
R. B. Hooper	14	..	1	..	161	..	26	..	12.38

Bowling

	Overs		Maidens		Runs		Wickets		Average
R. A. Furness	22	..	3	..	72	..	10	..	7.20
F. P. Le Quesne	47	..	8	..	259	..	23	..	11.26
A. B. Carter	163	..	46	..	460	..	39	..	11.79
F. R. Falle	109	..	31	..	334	..	24	..	13.91

WALLASEY GRAMMAR SCHOOL

Played 16, Won 10, Lost 4, Drawn 2

Batting

	Innings		Not outs		Runs		Highest inns.		Average
†J. C. Tomkins	16	..	3	..	518	..	106	..	39.84
G. J. Brown	15	..	4	..	378	..	107*	..	34.36
J. B. McGlashan	15	..	2	..	315	..	100*	..	24.23
R. D. Watkins	15	..	0	..	192	..	55	..	12.80
P. M. Townsend........	14	..	0	..	173	..	54	..	12.35

Bowling

	Overs		Maidens		Runs		Wickets		Average
J. B. McGlashan	337.5	..	85	..	760	..	68	..	11.17
J. M. Atkinson	213.2	..	42	..	607	..	53	..	11.45
R. W. Kent	148.1	..	37	..	416	..	26	..	16.00

WELLINGBOROUGH SCHOOL

Wellingborough were fortunate in possessing two such experienced players as the captain, M. D. Duck, and wicket-keeper, R. J. Mayes, both of whom set a fine all-round example to their younger colleagues. Of these, M. Iqbal, from Pakistan, enjoyed considerable success as a leg-break bowler, and R. L. Peck did good work with bat and ball.

Played 14, Won 5, Lost 3, Drawn 6

Batting

	Innings		Not outs		Runs		Highest inns.		Average
R. J. Mayes............	14	..	4	..	504	..	139*	..	50.40
†M. D. Duck	12	..	2	..	425	..	67*	..	42.50
R. L. Peck	12	..	3	..	222	..	34*	..	24.66
M. J. R. Barker	13	..	1	..	212	..	42*	..	17.66

Bowling

	Overs		Maidens		Runs		Wickets		Average
M. D. Duck	158.3	..	54	..	257	..	30	..	8.57
M. Iqbal	131.3	..	15	..	398	..	33	..	12.06
R. L. Peck	73.2	..	11	..	269	..	19	..	14.15
J. C. Branson	87	..	26	..	172	..	12	..	14.33

WELLINGTON COLLEGE

Wellington had their best season in living memory. Eton and Harrow were both beaten by large margins; Haileybury were overwhelmed by an innings before lunch on the second day and the matches with Charterhouse and Bradfield were favourably drawn. Not a ball was bowled in the Marlborough game. Splendidly led by I. A. Addison, whose 791 runs established a school record, the team were happy and well balanced. D. J. Mordaunt's powerful hitting earned him a place alongside Addison in the Schools XI at Lord's. The bowling was hostile and varied, S. J. S. Clarke showing special promise with leg-breaks and googlies. In an excellent fielding combination the captain set an inspiring example behind the stumps.

Played 13, Won 7, Lost 0, Drawn 6

Batting

	Innings		Not outs		Runs		Highest inns.		Average
†I. A. Addison	14	..	0	..	791	..	111	..	56.50
D. J. Mordaunt	14	..	2	..	524	..	100*	..	43.66
R. J. de M. Gainher	11	..	7	..	131	..	33*	..	32.75
R. J. B. Yeldham	11	..	3	..	246	..	75	..	30.75
S. J. S. Clarke..........	14	..	0	..	309	..	82	..	22.07
C. J. R. Goode	13	..	2	..	192	..	27	..	17.45
D. M. Lee	13	..	0	..	199	..	47	..	15.30
D. K. T. Vaughan-Arbuckle	9	..	1	..	112	..	25	..	14.00

Bowling

	Overs		Maidens		Runs		Wickets		Average
P. A. Langston	177.2	..	53	..	356	..	27	..	13.18
R. J. de M. Gainher	83	..	23	..	245	..	18	..	13.61
S. J. S. Clarke	127	..	32	..	438	..	32	..	13.68
G. M. W. Williams	189.2	..	48	..	396	..	24	..	16.50
D. J. Mordaunt	151	..	34	..	364	..	19	..	19.15

WELLINGTON SCHOOL

Played 16, Won 7, Lost 4, Drawn 5

Batting

	Innings		Not outs		Runs		Highest inns.		Average
†P. Benson	16	..	5	..	481	..	104	..	43.72
P. Ball	16	..	2	..	275	..	60	..	19.64
F. Mawji	16	..	0	..	268	..	52	..	16.75
P. Hopley	12	..	3	..	148	..	42	..	16.44
P. Brice	16	..	0	..	234	..	39	..	14.62

Bowling

	Overs		Maidens		Runs		Wickets		Average
J. James	79.5	..	20	..	222	..	18	..	12.33
T. Lane	185.4	..	29	..	482	..	37	..	13.02
F. Mawji	54	..	9	..	242	..	17	..	14.23
P. Benson	141	..	30	..	399	..	28	..	14.25
M. Colman	61	..	6	..	209	..	13	..	16.07

WESTMINSTER SCHOOL

Weak batting accounted largely for Westminster's disappointing record. Though he handled the side well, D. J. A. Delmotte never produced his best form with the bat and only J. W. Myring scored with any consistency. The bowling was more praiseworthy, specially that of M. J. Hyam, medium-pace, who played a vital part in the sole victory over Tonbridge. J. F. Mortimer, leg-breaks, also bowled well.

Played 11, Won 1, Lost 7, Drawn 3

Batting

	Innings		Not outs		Runs		Highest inns.		Average
J. W. Myring	12	..	0	..	442	..	104	..	36.83
W. D. J. Turner	11	..	3	..	139	..	43	..	17.37
J. A. Lauder	11	..	0	..	182	..	70	..	16.54
P. G. K. Saunders	12	..	0	..	184	..	50	..	15.33
†D. J. A. Delmotte	12	..	1	..	136	..	35	..	12.36
J. F. Mortimer	11	..	0	..	122	..	44	..	11.09

Bowling

	Overs		Maidens		Runs		Wickets		Average
J. F. Mortimer	174	..	28	..	564	..	31	..	18.19
M. J. Hyam	254	..	59	..	738	..	33	..	22.36

WHITGIFT SCHOOL

Played 13, Won 2, Lost 6, Drawn 5

Batting

	Innings		Not outs		Runs		Highest inns.		Average
J. A. D. Webb	8	..	1	..	267	..	99*	..	38.14
D. Evans	11	..	2	..	194	..	44*	..	21.55
†P. R. Grant	11	..	1	..	195	..	39*	..	19.50
J. F. H. Trott	11	..	1	..	176	..	38*	..	17.60

Bowling

	Overs		Maidens		Runs		Wickets		Average
T. R. King	116.4	..	17	..	386	..	25	..	15.44
P. L. James	61	..	15	..	180	..	10	..	18.00
J. D. Ewart	144.2	..	36	..	374	..	15	..	24.93

WINCHESTER COLLEGE

The strong Winchester side contained two players of outstanding ability in B. L. Reed and C. A. A. Black, both of whom were chosen for the Public Schools XI at Lord's. Reed, a right-handed batsman with a wide range of fluent attacking strokes, scored a century against Eton and later made runs freely for Hampshire II. Black, right-arm medium-pace, formed the spearhead of the attack with his controlled away-swingers and deserved his 54 wickets. D. R. McCarthy's example behind the wicket inspired an excellent standard of fielding, Reed being brilliant, and there were three valuable all-rounders in P. R. Stevens, D. E. D. Campbell and A. E. Seager.

Played 14, Won 7, Lost 2, Drawn 5

Batting

	Innings		Not outs		Runs		Highest inns.		Average
B. L. Reed..............	16	..	3	..	559	..	129*	..	43.00
D. E. D. Campbell	15	..	4	..	332	..	74*	..	30.18
A. E. Seager	16	..	4	..	346	..	60*	..	28.83
P. R. Stevens	16	..	1	..	341	..	60	..	22.73
M. D. Barton	16	..	0	..	341	..	87	..	21.31
T. C. Travers	13	..	0	..	228	..	58	..	17.53
W. S. Aylen	10	..	3	..	109	..	28*	..	15.57

Bowling

	Overs		Maidens		Runs		Wickets		Average
C. A. A. Black	267.2	..	71	..	691	..	54	..	12.79
P. R. Stevens	175.2	..	38	..	464	..	24	..	19.33
D. C. le F. Edwards	118.5	..	19	..	443	..	21	..	21.09
A. E. Seager	112.2	..	18	..	367	..	15	..	24.46
D. E. D. Cambell.......	164.2	..	33	..	448	..	14	..	32.00

WORCESTER ROYAL GRAMMAR SCHOOL

The much improved record was due to a great extent to the batting of F. B. Wheeler and his fine form behind the stumps; he earned his place in the English School's XI.

Played 21, Won 12, Lost 6, Drawn 3

Batting

	Innings		Not outs		Runs		Highest inns.		Average
F. B. Wheeler	22	..	3	..	564	..	112*	..	29.68
C. G. Clarke	22	..	2	..	361	..	41	..	18.05
D. L. Williams	18	..	6	..	201	..	44*	..	16.75
J. G. Wilkinson	23	..	2	..	255	..	50*	..	12.14
†A. E. Stubbs	21	..	2	..	218	..	32*	..	11.47

Bowling

	Overs		Maidens		Runs		Wickets		Average
G. W. Meredith	57.5	..	14	..	157	..	26	..	6.04
A. E. Stubbs	160.1	..	29	..	487	..	40	..	12.17
E. P. Ellison	156.2	..	26	..	442	..	34	..	13.00
D. E. Rodway	93	..	22	..	247	..	18	..	13.72
J. G. Wilkinson	202.2	..	62	..	460	..	31	..	14.83
P. J. Payne	219.2	..	63	..	495	..	25	..	19.80

WORKSOP COLLEGE

For a very good season, in which four of the five inter-school matches were conclusively won, Worksop owed much to their captain, P. J. Sharpe, who scored two double-centuries and five centuries and averaged over a hundred, a fine record which earned him selection for both the Schools matches at Lord's. The other batsmen were overshadowed, but W. G. D. Sykes and R. M. Wilcockson were useful all-rounders. The attack was well balanced, with P. G. Patchett (fast-medium right-hand) again a most successful opening bowler with Wilcockson (fast-medium left-hand). D. H. McNaught (slow right-hand) and Sykes (slow left-hand) proved a formidable pair of young spin bowlers, of whom much is expected. Excellent catching was a decisive factor in several matches. T. C. Jones will be captain in 1956 and will be able to call on five other old colours.

Played 15, Won 10, Lost 2, Drawn 3

Batting

	Innings		Not outs		Runs		Highest inns.		Average
†P. J. Sharpe	16	..	5	..	1251	..	240	..	113.72
W. G. D. Sykes	13	..	3	..	218	..	57*	..	21.80
R. M. Wilcockson	12	..	3	..	162	..	52*	..	18.00
T. C. Jones	15	..	3	..	185	..	50*	..	15.41
N. J. Emmens	12	..	2	..	145	..	44	..	14.50

Bowling

	Overs		Maidens		Runs		Wickets		Average
D. H. McNaught	121.3	..	21	..	401	..	27	..	14.85
W. G. D. Sykes	98.2	..	22	..	337	..	22	..	15.31
P. G. Patchett	214.5	..	49	..	658	..	42	..	15.66
R. M. Wilcockson	131.1	..	29	..	350	..	22	..	15.90
P. J. Sharpe	133.2	..	32	..	400	..	23	..	17.39

WREKIN COLLEGE

Wrekin enjoyed a better season. W. P. Krinks captained them admirably and always set a splendid example in the field. He also had a fair season as a batsman. K. A. Radin and C. J. Richardson batted consistently and the most successful bowlers were J. H. E. Baldwin, N. E. Lingard (right-hand) and T. W. Bullivant (left-hand). The ground fielding was good but the catching, with the exception of C. J. Richardson, was uncertain.

Played 13, Won 5, Lost 6, Drawn 2

Batting

	Innings		Not outs		Runs		Highest inns.		Average
K. A. Radin	9	..	1	..	257	..	72	..	32.12
C. J. Richardson	15	..	5	..	313	..	56	..	31.30
†W. P. Krinks	15	..	1	..	359	..	55	..	25.64
J. J. White	13	..	2	..	169	..	40	..	15.36
N. H. Grenfell	15	..	0	..	174	..	28	..	11.60

Bowling

	Overs		Maidens		Runs		Wickets		Average
N. E. Lingard	93	..	25	..	251	..	14	..	17.78
T. W. Bullivant	127	..	11	..	486	..	24	..	20.25
J. H. E. Baldwin	160	..	34	..	480	..	23	..	20.86
J. H. Thornburn	80	..	18	..	247	..	11	..	22.45

WYCLIFFE COLLEGE

The satisfactory record was due to the determined efforts of the team as a whole rather than individual achievements. The batting was generally mediocre but exceptional promise was shown by a 14-year-old, L. R. Drury.

Played 12, Won 5, Lost 3, Drawn 4

Batting

	Innings		Not outs		Runs		Highest inns.		Average
P. W. Bateman	11	..	1	..	165	..	64	..	16.50
K. F. Thompson	11	..	1	..	145	..	43	..	14.50
W. B. Gauntlett	12	..	0	..	161	..	33	..	13.41
†J. R. Lewis	12	..	1	..	143	..	39	..	13.00
M. J. Graydon	10	..	0	..	109	..	21	..	10.90

Bowling

	Overs		Maidens		Runs		Wickets		Average
M. J. Graydon	152	..	47	..	269	..	29	..	9.27
R. A. Bazley	108	..	37	..	229	..	21	..	10.90
P. J. Skinner	129	..	21	..	389	..	34	..	11.44
H. P. Williams	55	..	10	..	173	..	11	..	15.72

WYGGESTON GRAMMAR SCHOOL

Played 13, Won 3, Lost 4, Drawn 6

Batting

	Innings		Not outs		Runs		Highest inns.		Average
R. Oakley	13	..	2	..	319	..	50*	..	29.00
†W. H. Mann	11	..	4	..	166	..	37*	..	23.71
D. E. Holland	13	..	0	..	246	..	45	..	18.92
D. L. Sellicks	13	..	2	..	178	..	49	..	16.18

Bowling

	Overs		Maidens		Runs		Wickets		Average
W. H. Bassett	155.1	..	29	..	433	..	34	..	12.73
F. N. Tarratt	98	..	30	..	261	..	15	..	17.40
P. G. Addison	123.1	..	26	..	302	..	17	..	17.76

PUBLIC SCHOOL MATCHES IN 1955

For Eton v. Harrow, Beaumont v. Oratory, Clifton v. Tonbridge, Rugby v. Marlborough, Cheltenham v. Haileybury, Southern Schools v. The Rest, Combined Services v. Public Schools, see Other Matches at Lord's.

ROSSALL v. SHREWSBURY

At Rossall, May 31, June 1. Drawn. After an even first innings, Shrewsbury's batting broke down unexpectedly on a good pitch, but they escaped thanks to the stubborn defence of Harvey and Duerr. Rossall just failed to score 55 in twenty minutes.

Shrewsbury

R. H. C. Waters c Reece b Collinge	....	14	— b Glen	3
J. M. Nicolson c Foster b Reece	....	28	— lbw b Collinge	14
T. H. E. Moore c Fielden b Collinge	.....	24	— c Glen b Collinge	2
J. L. Ward c Reece b Collinge	....	56	— c A. Fryer b Bowns	8
A. G. P. Lewis lbw b Collinge	....	2	— b Glen	7
A. G. Cordle c Gillott b Bowns	....	12	— c Collinge b Bowns	0
J. A. Harvey not out	....	19	— not out	14
A. N. Duerr c Collinge b Bowns	......	23	— b Reece	19
R. N. Carter b Reece	....	1	— c Glen b Reece	0
T. V. Hutchinson lbw b Reece	......	0	— lbw b Collinge	0
T. J. Lewis b Collinge	....	9	— lbw b Reece	1
Extras	....	8	Extras	1
		196		**69**

Rossall

J. G. Wildman run out	....	24	— c and b Carter	11
G. M. Attenborough b Harvey	.....	18		
C. J. Fryer c Hutchinson b Harvey	....	1	— not out	10
I. T. C. Glen c Moore b Carter	....	91		
M. J. Reece b A. Lewis	....	2	— c T. Lewis b Carter	0
I. S. Foster b Carter	....	56		
D. R. M. Collinge lbw b Carter	....	2	— not out	16
J. A. H. Fielden b A. Lewis	....	4		
D. W. M. Gillott not out	....	1		
A. G. Fryer b A. Lewis	....	1		
J. S. Bowns c Waters b A. Lewis	......	0		
Extras	....	11	Extras	3
		211	**(2 wkts.)**	**40**

BRADFIELD v. RADLEY

At Bradfield, June 17, 18. Bradfield won by an innings and 33 runs. The strength of their middle batting proved the conclusive factor, for Radley broke down twice against the bowling of Lewis (nine for 48) and Brewer.

Bradfield

J. B. Brow lbw b Morkill	....	39	E. J. W. Lewis not out	6
P. J. Workman lbw b W. Lewis	..	0	C. J. Davis c W. Lewis b Morkill	5
A. J. Duvivier c Hole b W. Lewis	..	17	J. Hilliard not out	8
A. W. Fuller c Morkill b McCowen		44	B 11, l-b 3	14
M. C. F. Cox c Slocock b W. Lewis		64		
N. E. R. Robson b W. Lewis	....	35	**(7 wkts., dec.)**	**232**

R. S. H. Brewer and E. N. Thomas did not bat.

Radley

D. W. H. McCowen c Davis b Duvivier .	15	— lbw b Brewer	10
F. T. A. Hole lbw b Brewer	16	— b Brewer	0
P. F. Dale b Duvivier	0	— b Lewis	0
D. W. M. Berkley b Brewer	2	— b Lewis	8
W. D. G. Lewis b Lewis	6	— b Lewis	9
J. C. Lewis b Workman	12	— b Brewer	5
N. A. Slocock c Thomas b Lewis	2	— c Cox b Lewis	7
T. W. Morkill c Cox b Duvivier	15	— c Robson b Lewis	19
A. R. V. McGarrigle b Lewis	20	— b Brewer	27
J. J. Wilson not out	2	— b Lewis	3
A. R. Duff b Brewer	1	— not out	7
L-b 3, n-b 1	4	B 4, l-b 5	9
	95		**104**

HARROW v. CHARTERHOUSE

At Harrow, June 17, 18. Drawn. Harrow gained a grip on the game through a fine sustained spell of bowling by Champniss and an excellent innings by Parker. Allom and Lees batted stubbornly in the Charterhouse second innings and Harrow were unable to force victory.

Charterhouse

D. B. Lees c Cable b Champniss	13	— lbw b Neame	42
D. C. Burrows st Cable b Champniss	11	— b Maydon	6
J. J. Carless c Cable b Miller	1	— b Miller	8
P. J. de Q. Adams lbw b Champniss	2	— lbw b Champniss	9
A. T. C. Allom b Neame	49	— lbw b Maydon	30
T. R. Jakobson b Champniss	33	— c Cable b Maydon	0
J. C. W. Murray b Champniss	6	— lbw b Neame	0
A. J. South c Cable b Maydon	37	— run out	7
A. V. Sutton c Champniss b Neame	0	— c Cable b Harvey	9
F. M. Aston b Champniss	0	— c Stewart-Brown b Harvey .	12
G. E. F. Gross not out	15	— not out	0
B 14, l-b 5, n-b 3	22	B 8, l-b 1, n-b 2	11
	189		**134**

Harrow

J. M. Parker c Burrows b Gross	97	— c Carless b South	2
A. R. B. Neame b South	40	— c Burrows b Allom	0
R. S. Miller run out	27	— not out	1
G. D. Massy c Aston b South	8	— c Allom b South	11
I. H. Stewart-Brown c Lees b South	14	— not out	6
A. S. R. Winlaw c Jakobson b Gross	19		
J. C. T. Harvey run out	15	— c and b Allom	5
L. J. Champniss not out	35		
C. A. Atha b Murray	3		
M. L. Maydon not out	0		
B 9, l-b 2, w 4	15	L-b 2, w 4, n-b 2	8
	(8 wkts., dec.) 273		**(4 wkts.) 33**

A. B. Cable did not bat.

WORKSOP v. WREKIN

At Worksop, June 17, 18. Worksop won by an innings and 30 runs. Steady batting by Wrekin on a good pitch in their first innings seemed to ensure them at least safety from defeat. Then followed a remarkable attacking innings by Sharpe, who scored 240 in 206 minutes, hitting thirty 4's and two 6's, and Worksop's excellent bowling on the second afternoon turned an apparent stalemate into victory with a quarter of an hour to spare.

Wrekin

W. P. Krinks c Scott b King	55	—	c Sharpe b Patchett	2
N. H. Grenfell b Sharpe	13	—	c Scott b Patchett	1
K. A. Radin c Sykes b McNaught	72	—	b McNaught	33
D. J. Edwards, c Patchett b McNaught	2	—	b Wilcockson	3
C. J. Richardson c Jones b Sharpe	56	—	c Scott b Patchett	5
J. J. White, c Sharpe b King	8	—	lbw b Sykes	1
J. H. Thornburn lbw b Sharpe	10	—	b Sykes	0
J. H. E. Baldwin b Wilcockson	3	—	st Scott b McNaught	0
T. W. Bullivant b McNaught	23	—	lbw b McNaught	15
N. E. Lingard c Patchett b Sharpe	0	—	b Sykes	2
B. K. Douglas not out	11	—	not out	10
Extras	13		Extras	10
	266			**82**

Worksop

P. J. Sharpe b Bullivant	240	R. A. Bradwell lbw b Thornburn	17
T. C. Jones b Thornburn	11	R. M. King b Lingard	14
J. B. R. Walker, lbw b Thornburn	13	P. G. Patchett c Baldwin b Krinks	9
N. J. Emmens c Krinks b Thornburn	0	Extras	6
W. G. D. Sykes b White	16		
R. M. Wilcockson not out	52	(8 wkts., dec.)	378

J. B. Scott and D. H. McNaught did not bat.

SHERBORNE v. DOWNSIDE

At Sherborne, June 18. Sherborne won by 49 runs, due mainly to the accurate slow bowling of Lawrence and Tindall, who gave the Downside batsmen no opportunity to score quickly.

Sherborne

G. P. Gent b Radcliffe	42	M. B. Wilson c Murphy b Davenhill	39
P. C. Eglington b Conlin	2	J. Lawrence c Bone b Conlin	15
C. R. J. Eglington c Gooda b Radcliffe	31	M. Maley b Conlin	8
P. D. Cowell b Davenhill	9	J. J. Barber b Conlin	0
C. C. T. Henfrey c Radcliffe b Davenhill	4	S. P. Tindall not out	0
		B 8, l-b 1	9
J. P. Devitt c and b Radcliffe	6		
			165

Downside

A. W. Gooda b Barber	2	J. G. Wells c Maley b Tindall	9
P. M. Murphy c Wilson b Lawrence	9	J. de Aguirre not out	13
P. A. Kavanagh b Lawrence	24	M. H. Radcliffe c P. Eglington b Barber	0
J. F. Bone b Lawrence	5	B 2, l-b 1	3
E. F. Maynard st Wilson b Tindall	25		
H. J. Conlin lbw b Tindall	14		
M. T. Gwynne c Wilson b Barber	1		
R. E. Davenhill b Tindall	11		**116**

WESTMINSTER v. LANCING

At Westminster, June 18. Lancing won by 105 runs, the match providing a personal triumph for Sharman. After hitting a splendid century, he routed the Westminster batsmen with leg-breaks, taking seven for 42, including the hat-trick.

Lancing

T. J. Goodwin c Turner b Hyam .	34
G. J. Sharman run out	116
N. H. S. Evans c Hyam b Delmotte	9
B. A. Rodgers b Hyam	2
G. G. B. Wilkes c Hyam b Mortimer	0
D. V. Bedford b Hyam	1
J. W. Bridge b Mortimer	9
J. L. Newbury not out	18
R. J. V. Steward not out	3
B 4, l-b 1, w 1	6
(7 wkts., dec.)	198

R. Naylor and C. J. Saunders did not bat.

Westminster

J. W. Myring lbw b Steward	2
J. F. Mortimer b Sharman	20
P. G. K. Saunders c and b Wilkes	20
M. J. Hyam lbw b Sharman	0
C. B. M. Hunt b Sharman	1
A. D. C. Stout c and b Sharman	0
D. J. A. Delmotte c Goodwin b Sharman	14
W. D. J. Turner b Sharman	0
J. A. Lauder b Sharman	3
P. C. Bonavia b Steward	14
N. C. Roope not out	14
B 4, l-b 1	5
	93

WINCHESTER v. ETON

At Winchester, June 24, 25. Winchester won by seven wickets after one of the finest games in the long series of meetings between the two schools. Winchester's thoroughly deserved success was specially gratifying as their first over Eton at New Field since 1920, and was founded chiefly on the performances of Reed and Black. After steady batting by Eton, Reed retrieved Winchester's poor start with a brilliant innings lasting just over two hours. McCarthy's declaration three runs ahead seemed to some over-generous but Black again bowled well and despite stout resistance by the Eton "tail," Winchester were left to make 137 in two hours twenty-five minutes. Confident strokes brought them victory with half an hour to spare.

Eton

C. T. M. Pugh lbw b Edwards	25	— b Stevens	11
D. R. Stoddart c Seager b Edwards	17	— b Black	13
I. A. C. Sinclair b Black	45	— c McCarthy b Edwards	7
C. H. Gibson c and b Black	8	— c Barton b Black	2
A. R. B. Burrows c Seager b Black	32	— lbw b Black	0
E. J. Lane Fox, c McCarthy b Stevens	0	— c Travers b Stevens	1
A. M. Wolfe-Murray c McCarthy b Black	20	— b Stevens	30
H. C. Blofeld, c and b Black	18	— c Reed b Edwards	23
A. P. M. Marsham b Seager	34	— c Stevens b Black	15
S. Douglas Pennant not out	5	— c McCarthy b Seager	12
G. E. D. Pearson not out	9	— not out	22
B 1, l-b 1, w 2	4	B 1, l-b 1, n-b 1	3
(9 wkts. dec.)	217		139

Winchester

M. D. Barton c Burrows b Douglas Pennant	0	— b Douglas Pennant 21
T. C. Travers c Pugh b Pearson	5	
B. L. Reed not out....................	129	— c Pugh b Sinclair.......... 34
D. E. D. Campbell c Douglas Pennant b Lane Fox	25	— not out 10
P. R. Stevens b Sinclair	5	— not out 18
A. E. Seager c Stoddart b Lane Fox	20	— st Blofeld b Pearson 44
W. S. Aylen not out	21	
B 10 l-b 5	15	B 8, l-b 5 13
(5 wkts., dec.)	220	(3 wkts.) 140

J. J. B. Rowe, D. C. le F. Edwards, D. R. McCarthy and C. A. A. Black did not bat.

Winchester Bowling

	O.	M.	R.	W.		O.	M.	R.	W.
Black	28	7	68	5	....	18	4	40	4
Stevens	17	5	45	1	....	18	2	56	3
Seager	11	4	24	1	....	2.2	0	11	1
Edwards.......	12	1	40	2	....	11	2	16	2
Campbell	18	4	36	0	....	8	3	13	0

Eton Bowling

Douglas Pennant	17	7	37	1	....	16	1	40	1
Sinclair	21	8	77	1	....	13	2	40	1
Pearson	19	2	52	1	....	4.5	1	22	1
Lane Fox	13	2	39	2	....	7	0	25	0

From 1826 to 1854 inclusive the match was played at Lord's, but since 1855 (when the sides met at Eton), the games have taken place alternately on the Eton and Winchester grounds. Excluding the one-day war-time matches, the sides have met 114 times. Eton have won 55 and Winchester 28, one match ended in a tie and 30 have been drawn.

RESULTS SINCE THE WAR

1947	No match (illness)	1952	Drawn
1948	Winchester won by nine wickets	1953	Eton won by four wickets
1949	Drawn	1954	Drawn
1950	Drawn	1955	Winchester won by seven wickets
1951	Eton won by 62 runs		

REPTON v. MALVERN

At Repton, July 5, 6. Drawn. After gaining the better of a close first-innings tussle, Malvern came near to defeat in their attempt to make 164 to win, Betts taking four for 26. Vaughan played two fine innings for Repton and Hatch also batted attractively for Malvern.

Repton

R. G. Gillard c Newbury b Costeloe	....	23	— c Newbury b Potter	1
P. R. Starkey c Newbury b Costeloe	....	6	— c and b Costeloe	10
J. B. Hall c Smith b Costeloe	....	0	— b Potter	8
P. H. Vaughan b Costeloe	....	74	— lbw b Costeloe............	66
P. J. Barber b Costeloe	....	0	— b Costeloe	2
A. Jollie c Hatch b Potter	....	2	— c Newbury b Hunter	16
A. W. S. Robinson b Potter	....	6	— c Hunter b Kemp	10
R. J. Pilkington b Costeloe	....	4	— c MacLaurin b Hunter......	34
J. R. H. Sale lbw b Kemp	....	23	— c Straker b Hunter	10
J. R. Fletcher not out	....	7	— not out	5
B. M. Betts lbw b Kemp	....	0	— c Newbury b Costeloe	3
Extras	....	5	Extras	4
		150		169

Malvern

J. L. Smith b Fletcher	....	1	— c Pilkington b Fletcher ...	13
P. G. Hatch run out	....	70	— c Robinson b Betts	5
P. V. Straker b Betts	....	2	— b Sale	17
R. J. Devereux c Vaughan b Fletcher	....	34	— b Betts	0
I. C. MacLaurin c Robinson b Betts	....	1	— b Fletcher	2
C. M. G. Hunter c Robinson b Fletcher	.	1	— b Betts	20
M. J. D. Newbury b Sale	....	10	— b Barber	8
J. M. Davies c Jollie b Fletcher	....	6	— not out	18
N. B. Potter c Pilkington b Betts	....	14	— c Robinson b Betts	18
J. M. Costeloe c Betts b Barber	....	9	— not out	0
J. N. Kemp not out	....	0		
Extras	....	9	Extras	12
		156	(8 wkts.)	113

WELLINGTON v. HAILEYBURY

At Crowthorne, July 8, 9. Wellington won by an innings and 71 runs, a victory that clearly demonstrated the power of their formidable XI. Whereas Haileybury could do little against the leg-spin of Clarke (ten for 41) on a good pitch, Wellington batted confidently and well. Mordaunt and Yeldham both gave dashing displays despite the wholehearted bowling of Smith.

Haileybury

D. J. Newsom b Clarke	....	15	— c Lee b Gainher	46
M. G. P. Foster c Robertson b Williams	..	2	— st Addison b Clarke	1
D. L. Stretton-Cox c and b Clarke	....	13	— b Mordaunt	0
D. J. E. Foster c Langston b Clarke	....	16	— c Addison b Williams	1
J. R. Thompson c Clarke b Langston	....	6	— st Addison b Clarke	11
R. A. B. Hall hit wkt b Clarke	....	4	— lbw b Clarke	4
H. J. K. Bagnall-Oakeley c and b Clarke	.	2	— c Mordaunt b Clarke	0
C. R. Leighton c Langston b Clarke	....	0	— c Langston b Gainher	2
B. E. Simmons b Langston	....	0	— c Vaughan-Arbuckle b Mordaunt	16
A. D. N. Smith not out	....	4	— not out	10
A. J. Claxton b Langston	....	4	— c Yeldham b Gainher......	1
L-b 2, n-b 2	....	4	B 7, l-b 4, n-b 1	12
		71		104

Wellington

I. A. Addison c Smith b Leighton..	22
D. M. Lee c M. Foster b Smith....	4
S. J. S. Clarke c M. Foster b Smith	13
D. J. Mordaunt b Claxton	65
R. J. B. Yeldham b Smith	75
C. J. R. Goode b Hall	25
W. D. Robertson lbw b Hall	5
D. K. T. Vaughan-Arbuckle c M. Foster b Smith	24
R. J. de M. Gainher c M. Foster b Smith	3
P. A. Langston not out..........	4
G. M. W. Williams b Smith	1
B 2, l-b 1, n-b 2.............	5
	246

STONYHURST v. DENSTONE

At Stonyhurst, July 20, 21. Denstone won by ten wickets. Everall played a prominent part in their success and Burke brought about Stonyhurst's first innings' collapse by taking six for 27.

Stonyhurst

J. G. Parker lbw b Everall	0	— lbw b Everall	31
R. Unsworth b Burke	10	— b Everall	1
P. L. Recordon b Burke	10	— c Marshall b Burke........	10
R. G. Mackenzie b Burke	5	— st Bloor b Kelly	17
D. Black b Kelly	3	— c Bloor b Kelly	0
K. J. Garry c Everall b Burke	2	— c Bloor b Kelly	13
P. O'Callaghan b Burke	1	— c Bloor b Kelly	11
J. St. F. Dare not out	29	— b Everall	14
I. P. Fisher b Shilton...............	16	— c Bloor b Everall........	2
M. T. Corbett b Burke	1	— run out	0
C. P. Cheetham c Bloor b Shilton	5	— not out	0
Extras........................	9	Extras	13
	91		112

Denstone

E. J. Everall c Fisher b Cheetham	39	— not out	29
E. D. Blenkinsop lbw b Garry..........	1	— not out	29
A. H. Marshall b Fisher	1		
R. S. D. Jones b Cheetham	11		
N. H. Wood hit wkt b Cheetham	43		
D. V. King b Corbett	28		
D. A. E. Bloor b Corbett	0		
P. W. Shilton b Corbett	0		
D. W. W. Burnside not out	5		
J. Y. Kelly c Black b Cheetham	0		
C. J. Burke b Corbett	4		
Extras........................	13	Extras	2
	145	(no wkts)	60

M.C.C. TEAM IN AUSTRALIA AND NEW ZEALAND, 1954–55

By Norman Preston

Under the zealous and skilful captaincy of Len Hutton, England won the rubber in Australia for the first time for twenty-two years and so retained the Ashes they took from A. L. Hassett's side at Kennington Oval in 1953. On paper the success gained by the players who sailed from Tilbury in September appears most convincing and rather suggests a comfortable tour against indifferent opposition. That was far from the case. It was a hard tour with its days of triumph and days of regret, but in the end superb fast bowling by Tyson and Statham turned the scales so that finally the Australian batsmen were completely humbled.

Some people in England never expected the side would return home conquerors by three victories to one—the final match, ruined by rain, was drawn heavily in their favour. In fact not only was the choice of Hutton as captain in the balance until mid-July, but the omission of the three bowlers, F. S. Trueman, G. A. R. Lock and J. C. Laker, who took 15 of the 19 wickets in that victory at The Oval in 1953, occasioned much surprise. In addition, M. C. Cowdrey was given a place although he had not approached his splendid form of the previous year.

At first only seventeen were selected, but Compton became doubtful owing to a recurrence of his knee trouble. He stayed behind for treatment, travelled by air and joined the team at Adelaide. Consequently, Wilson, the Yorkshire left-hander, was a late addition to the party which comprised:

L. Hutton (captain), Yorkshire (38);
P. B. H. May (vice-captain), Surrey (24);
R. T. Simpson, Nottinghamshire (34);
W. J. Edrich, Middlesex (38);
T. E. Bailey, Essex (30);
M. C. Cowdrey, Kent (21);
D. C. S. Compton, Middlesex (36);
A. V. Bedser, Surrey (36);
T. G. Evans, Kent (33);
J. H. Wardle, Yorkshire (31);
J. B. Statham, Lancashire (24);
T. W. Graveney, Gloucestershire (27);
R. Appleyard, Yorkshire (30);
J. E. McConnon, Glamorgan (31);
P. J. Loader, Surrey (24);
F. H. Tyson, Lancashire (24);
K. V. Andrew, Northamptonshire (24); and

J. V. Wilson, Yorkshire (33).

C. G. Howard, Lancashire (*manager*);

G. Duckworth, Lancashire (*scorer and baggage master*); and

H. W. Dalton, Essex (*masseur*).

Thus the complete party numbered 21 and at once I desire to emphasise the important parts played by the three officials. Geoffrey Howard carried out his duties as manager in a pleasant and efficient manner and was very well received by the Australian officials; George Duckworth, with his vast experience of numerous tours, was a cheering and inspiring influence, especially when things were going badly, and Harold Dalton, if only by keeping Tyson and Statham at the peak of condition for seven Tests, proved the wisdom of M.C.C. in sending out from England for the first time their own masseur.

The tour took three courses. There was early evidence that given fast pitches Statham would be a thorn in the side of the Australians. M.C.C. won their first two matches in Perth with some ease, but going to Adelaide they encountered a slow pitch and could only scramble home by 21 runs against South Australia. Rain spoiled what was virtually an Australian Test Trial at Melbourne and then New South Wales, under the dynamic captaincy of Keith Miller, severely shook M.C.C. in a drawn match which was saved only by the splendid batting of Hutton and Cowdrey—three centuries between them.

So M.C.C. flew to Brisbane in mid-November for the first Test not completely satisfied with their performances but nevertheless still unbeaten and knowing they were developing into a real team. Little did they realise they were entering the second phase and would soon be touching rock bottom. Against Queensland they found the fast pitch they desired, but although Simpson and Compton hit centuries against an attack which included Lindwall, the batting was still inconsistent. No one anticipated the devastating blow the team were about to receive from the pick of Australia, and indeed it might not have occurred if the fielding had approached even a reasonable level.

On the eve of the match, Evans was stricken ill and could not play. His absence was a severe loss and may well have been the turning-point, but that was only one of three factors which told so much against England. The second was Hutton's decision on winning the toss to send in Australia. I do not blame Hutton for taking the course he did. In four of the six first-class matches the team had played, the captain who won the toss preferred to take the field: Hutton and May at Perth; Miller at Sydney and Archer at Brisbane. In the previous match against Queensland, the pitch was ideally suited to fast bowlers and Hutton anticipated the same conditions, but this did not turn out to be the case as the

Test pitch could not be watered immediately before the match because of the Queensland game. Yet if the England fielders had held their catches Hutton might have been hailed as a wise man; but when twelve chances go unaccepted, how can a side expect to win?

The third factor was a mishap to Compton on the very first morning when, trying to save a boundary, he ran into the wooden fence palings and fractured a bone in his left hand. Small wonder Australia won by an innings and 154 runs. So M.C.C. approached Christmas and the second Test at Sydney with none of their batsmen at all sure of themselves and knowing that Australia, somewhat doubtful about their ability before Brisbane, were now brimful of confidence as to the destiny of the Ashes.

Just as England suffered through ill luck, so did Australia in their turn. Neither Ian Johnson, their captain, nor Keith Miller were fit for the second Test. The Englishmen thought this would be the vital match. Even a draw would be useful. Meanwhile Hutton having entered the Brisbane Test with an attack of four seam bowlers, Bedser, Statham, Tyson and Bailey, decided variety was essential. He felt the need to include Appleyard as an off spinner and Wardle, left-arm slow, and so he sacrificed Bedser.

This time Morris, the Australian captain, put in England and no one in that country condemned him when Hutton's men were dismissed for 154, but it proved a very low scoring match. Only three men made 50—May 104, Cowdrey 54 and Neil Harvey 92 not out, but Tyson and Statham began their deadly combination and England won by 38 runs. All was square, the second phase was over and what turned out to be the long triumphant third phase had begun. M.C.C. were on the crest of the wave.

That Sydney victory restored confidence and, with May and Cowdrey developing high-class and reliable batsmanship, Evans keeping wicket at his very best, Bailey always doing something useful, and the tail, notably Wardle, making important little scores, England assumed the mastery; but above everything else counted the pace of Tyson and Statham.

The New Year brought a thrilling win in the Third Test at Melbourne by 128 runs, Tyson taking seven for 27 in the final innings. Then after a holiday in the lovely temperate climate of Tasmania M.C.C. went back to Adelaide for the fourth Test, which provided another hard tussle before England, thanks to 80 by Hutton, 79 by Cowdrey and some excellent bowling by Tyson, Statham, Appleyard and Bailey, won by five wickets and clinched the rubber. The last two months, February and March, provided an anti-climax. The tension was over but there were still three more Tests awaiting decision. Owing to rain, nothing could be done in the fifth Test at Sydney until the fourth day and then England outplayed Australia, though time prevented them gaining the victory they deserved.

Finally, a brief tour of New Zealand where both Tests were won, the team setting the seal on their great work in the last innings of all when they routed New Zealand for 26, the lowest total in the history of Test cricket. Hutton made his farewell to International cricket in that match. Certainly he could not have wished for a more triumphant finale to a wonderful career.

Only twice in the Tests did a team exceed 300. Australia reached 601 at Brisbane and England 371 in the fifth match at Sydney. While credit must be given to the bowlers the fact remains that no longer did the batsmen find themselves on shirt-front or even easy-paced pitches. As in England, the modern Australian groundsmen leave some grass and the pitches do not undergo so much rolling as in the days when Sir Jack Hobbs and Sir Donald Bradman were in their prime.

Most surprising was the deterioration in Australian batting. During the tour only four hundreds were hit against M.C.C. and none after the first Test, whereas nineteen were hit by Hutton's men including two in New Zealand. England never found a satisfactory opening pair. Here are the figures for the first wicket in the five Tests: Brisbane 4, 22 by Hutton and Simpson; Sydney 14 and 18 by Hutton and Bailey; Melbourne 14 and 40 by Hutton and Edrich; Adelaide 60 and 3 by Hutton and Edrich; Sydney 6 by Hutton and Graveney. Hutton had four different partners and the burden he carried in this respect, added to all the care and attention he gave to the captaincy both on and off the field, severely taxed him both mentally and physically.

At first there was no indication of any decline in Hutton as a batsman; his first three first-class matches yielded him scores of 145 not out, 37, 98, 102 and 87. Then came the Test matches and for the remainder of the tour he reached 50 only four times, his best being 80, a most valuable innings in the fourth Test at Adelaide. Indeed it was the highest of that match and went a long way towards winning the rubber.

For May, the vice-captain, the tour brought enhanced reputation, for not only did it reveal his qualities of leadership on the few occasions when Hutton rested, but it put beyond shadow of doubt his ability as a batsman. Compton, after his wretched experiences of the previous tour when eight Test innings brought him an aggregate of no more than 53, average 7.57, quickly found his form against South Australia and Queensland, but his fielding mishap at Brisbane accounted for his low scores in the first Test and not until late in the tour did he look his real self again although his aggregate of 78 for once out at Adelaide was an important factor in England's success.

Edrich, nearing the end of his career, never revealed his

former powers and Wilson, the Yorkshire left-hander, always a magnificent fielder, could not settle down on the fast Australian pitches. Both Simpson and Graveney were unreliable although Graveney, when the tension had gone, finished in a blaze of glory.

Against all these batting disappointments was the success of Cowdrey, the Oxford captain of the previous English season. From the moment the ship stopped for a day at Colombo he rarely knew failure. Any hesitation which may have existed in Hutton's mind about including Cowdrey in the Tests disappeared when, on the team's first appearance in Sydney, Cowdrey hit 110 and 103 against New South Wales. In the second innings of that match, Hutton switched places with Cowdrey and when this brilliant young batsman of only 21 years of age made his second hundred Hutton had serious thoughts about opening with him in the Tests. As it was Cowdrey proved his worth lower in the order, notably when he made 102 out of a total of 191 in the first innings at Melbourne.

Before the party was chosen in England the decision was reached to assail Australia with a battery of fast bowlers. The attack was well endowed numerically and in variety. There were five seamers, Bedser, Statham, Bailey, Tyson and Loader, and three spinners, Appleyard, Wardle and McConnon. The accent on speed turned out far more successful than anyone dared to hope.

Moreover it was accomplished without much assistance from Bedser. That was the big surprise. Bedser fell ill with shingles soon after the team landed in Perth. He was scarcely fit for the first Test at Brisbane and let down by fielders who missed seven catches he finished with one wicket for 131. Hutton included Bedser among the twelve for Sydney, but on the morning of the match he made the dramatic announcement that Bedser would be omitted. This must have been a very hard decision for Hutton, but there were many factors including the difficulty of "hiding" him in the field. Events alone justified Hutton, but above everything else the transformation of Tyson between the first and second Tests saved the captain from adverse criticism long before the last ball of the tour was bowled.

After taking only one wicket for 160 runs at Brisbane, Tyson shortened his run and gained complete control over length and direction without losing any of his fire. In the next three Tests he took 26 wickets and, with 15 falling to Statham, a devastating alliance was formed between these two young Lancashire-born players. Thanks to their efforts all the other bowlers had a very light tour.

Neither Loader nor McConnon could gain a place in any of the Tests, but Loader who took 41 wickets in first-class matches, bowled extremely well. McConnon suffered from injuries and after receiving a broken finger while fielding at Hobart he returned home before the fourth Test. By this time the presence of eighteen players in the party was an encumbrance, for with lack of match practice it was difficult to keep the understudies in form. Simpson, Graveney and to some extent Wilson were handicapped in this respect.

Mention has already been made of the wonderful work of Evans behind the stumps. Always brimful of energy no matter how exhausting the heat of the day, he was an inspiration to the whole team and especially the bowlers. Andrews, the deputy wicket-keeper, lacked Evans's effervescence, but he was neat and efficient in an ordinary way.

For Australia, three defeats in successive Tests came as a severe blow to their cricketing pride. The three selectors, Sir Donald Bradman, Jack Ryder and D. Seddon were the target of harsh criticism from some quarters but they were unshaken in their belief that they chose the best players available and later events in the West Indies upheld their opinion. The same men who went down before England showed there was little wrong with Australian cricket that concentration and determination could not put right. A word of praise must be given to the Australian umpires who achieved miracles by satisfying almost everyone.

Clearly England won on their merit and to Hutton, particularly, must be given the credit for the way he conducted himself and his men. For me it was a privilege and pleasure to accompany M.C.C. on this eventful tour as the representative of *Reuters* and the *Press Association*. I should add that the team were showered with hospitality wherever they went and although rivalry was as keen as it should be, the true spirit of cricket and good-fellowship always existed between the two teams.

SUMMARY OF THE TOUR—RESULTS OF ALL MATCHES

All Matches—Played 28, Won 17, Lost 2, Drawn 9

First-Class Matches—Played 21, Won 12, Lost 2, Drawn 7

Test Matches—Played 7, Won 5, Lost 1, Drawn 1

SUMMARY OF ALL MATCHES

		1st Innings	2nd Innings	Result
†Sept. 30 Colombo	M.C.C. Ceylon	178* for 8 101 for 4	— —	Drawn
†Oct. 11, 12 Bunbury	M.C.C. Western Country	344* for 5 116	— 128 for 6	Drawn
Oct 15, 16, 18, 19 Perth	Western Australia M.C.C.	103 321	255 40 for 3	Won by seven wickets
Oct. 22, 23, 25 Perth	Combined XI M.C.C.	86 311	163 —	Won by inns. and 62 runs

* Signifies innings declared closed.   † Signifies not a first-class fixture.

Oct. 29, 30, Nov. 1, 2 Adelaide	M.C.C. South Australia	246 254	181 152	Won by 21 runs
Nov. 5, 6, 8, 9, 10 Melbourne	M.C.C. Australian XI	205 167 for seven	— —	Drawn
Nov. 12, 13, 15, 16 Sydney	M.C.C. New South Wales	252 382	327 78 for 2	Drawn
Nov. 19, 20, 22, 23 Brisbane	M.C.C. Queensland	304 288	288 25 for 2	Drawn
Nov. 26, 27, 29, 30 and Dec. 1	Australia England	601* for 8 190	— 257	Lost by inns. and 154 runs
		(First Test Match)		
† Dec. 4, 6 Rockhampton	M.C.C. Country XI	317 95	— 210	Won by inns. and 12 runs
†Dec. 8 Canberra	M.C.C. Prime Minister's XI	278* for 7 247	— —	Won by 31 runs
Dec. 10, 11, 13, 14 Melbourne	M.C.C. Victoria	312 277	236* for 5 88 for 3	Drawn
Dec. 17, 18, 20, 21, 22 Sydney	England Australia	154 228	296 184	Won by 38 runs
		(Second Test Match)		
†Dec. 27, 28, 29 Newcastle	Northern N.S.W. M.C.C.	211 438	246 20 for 1	Won by nine wickets
Dec. 31, Jan. 1, 3, 4, 5 Melbourne	England Australia	191 231	279 111	Won by 128 runs
		(Third Test Match)		
Jan. 8, 10, 11 Hobart	Combined XI M.C.C.	221 242	184* for 6 99 for 2	Drawn
Jan. 13, 14, 15 Launceston	M.C.C. Tasmania	427* for 7 117	133* for 6 200	Won by 243 runs
†Jan. 18, 19 Mount Gambier	M.C.C. S.A. Country XI	328 106	— 45	Won by inns. and 177 runs
Jan. 21, 22, 24 Adelaide	South Australia M.C.C.	185 451	123 —	Won by inns. and 143 runs
Jan. 28, 29, 31, Feb. 1, 2 Adelaide	Australia England	323 341	111 97 for 5	Won by five wickets
		(Fourth Test Match)		
†Feb. 5, 7 Yallourn	Vic. Country XI M.C.C.	182 307* for 8	99 —	Won by inns. and 26 runs
Feb. 11, 12, 14, 15 Melbourne	Victoria M.C.C.	113 90 for 1	— —	Drawn

* Signifies innings declared closed.
† Signifies not a first-class fixture.

Feb. 18, 19, 21, 22 Sydney	New South Wales M.C.C.	172 172	314* for 8 269	Lost by 45 runs
Feb. 25, 26, 28, Mar. 1, 2, 3 Sydney	England Australia	371* for 7 221	— 118 for 6	Drawn
	(Fifth Test Match)			
Mar. 5, 7, 8 Christchurch	Canterbury M.C.C.	140 302	206 45 for 3	Won by seven wickets
Mar. 11, 12, 14, 15, 16 Dunedin	New Zealand England	125 209* for 8	132 49 for 2	Won by eight wickets
	(First Test Match)			
Mar. 19, 21, 22 Wellington	M.C.C. Wellington	207 127	201 94	Won by 187 runs
Mar, 25, 26, 28 Auckland	New Zealand England	200 246	26 —	Won by inns. and 20 runs
	(Second Test Match)			

* Signifies innings declared closed.

ENGLAND BATTING AVERAGES IN THE TESTS AGAINST AUSTRALIA

	Matches	Inns.	Not Outs	Runs	Highest Inns.	Average
T. W. Graveney	2	3	0	132	111	44.00
P. B. H. May	5	9	0	351	104	39.00
D. C. S. Compton	4	7	2	191	84	38.20
T. E. Bailey	5	9	1	296	88	37.00
M. C. Cowdrey	5	9	0	319	102	35.44
L. Hutton	5	9	0	220	80	24.44
W. J. Edrich	4	8	0	180	88	22.50
R. Appleyard	4	5	3	44	19*	22.00
J. H. Wardle	4	6	1	109	38	21.80
T. G. Evans	4	7	1	102	37	17.00
J. B. Statham	5	7	1	67	25	11.16
F. H. Tyson	5	7	1	66	37*	11.00
R. T. Simpson	1	2	0	11	9	5.50
K. V. Andrew	1	2	0	11	6	5.50
A. V. Bedser	1	2	0	10	5	5.00

* Signifies not out.

ENGLAND BOWLING AVERAGES IN THE TESTS AGAINST AUSTRALIA

	Overs	Maidens	Runs	Wickets	Average
R. Appleyard	79	22	224	11	20.36
F. H. Tyson	151	16	583	28	20.82
J. H. Wardle	70.6	15	229	10	22.90
J. B. Statham	143.3	16	499	18	27.72
T. E. Bailey	73.4	8	306	10	30.60

Also Bowled: A. V. Bedser 37—4—131—1; W. J. Edrich 3—0—28—0; T. W. Graveney 6—0—34—1; L. Hutton 0.6—0—2—1.

AUSTRALIAN BATTING AVERAGES IN THE TESTS

	Matches	Inns.	Not Outs	Runs	Highest Inns.	Average
I. W. Johnson	4	6	4	116	41	58.00
C. C. McDonald	2	4	0	186	72	46.50
R. N. Harvey	5	9	1	354	162	44.25
P. Burge	1	2	1	35	18*	35.00
A. R. Morris	4	7	0	223	153	31.85
L. Maddocks	3	5	0	150	69	30.00
R. R. Lindwall	4	6	2	106	64*	26.50
K. R. Miller	4	7	0	167	49	23.85
J. Burke	2	4	0	81	44	20.25
L. Favell	4	7	0	130	30	18.57
G. B. Hole	3	5	0	85	57	17.00
R. G. Archer	4	7	0	117	49	16.71
R. Benaud	5	9	0	148	34	16.44
A. K. Davidson	3	5	0	71	23	14.20
W. Watson	1	2	0	21	18	10.50
G. R. Langley	2	3	0	21	16	7.00
W. A. Johnston	4	6	2	25	11	6.25

* Signifies not out.

AUSTRALIAN BOWLING AVERAGES IN THE TESTS

	Overs	Maidens	Runs	Wickets	Average
R. G. Archer	97.6	32	215	13	16.53
I. W. Johnson	111	37	243	12	20.25
W. A. Johnston	141.4	37	423	19	22.26
K. R. Miller	88.4	28	243	10	24.30
R. R. Lindwall	130.6	28	381	14	27.21
R. Benaud	116.7	23	377	10	37.70
A. K. Davidson	71	16	220	3	73.33

Also bowled: J. Burke 2—0—7—0.

M.C.C. TEAM BATTING AVERAGES—FIRST-CLASS MATCHES IN AUSTRALIA AND NEW ZEALAND

	Matches	Inns.	Not Outs	Runs	Highest Inns.	Average
D. C. S. Compton	11	16	2	799	182	57.07
L. Hutton	15	25	2	1059	145*	46.04
T. W. Graveney	15	22	3	855	134	45.00
P. B. H. May	18	29	3	1096	129	42.15
M. C. Cowdrey	17	31	1	1019	110	33.96
T. E. Bailey	15	21	2	551	88	29.00
R. T. Simpson	16	27	3	644	136	26.83
F. H. Tyson	14	20	4	286	62*	17.87
J. V. Wilson	11	19	2	301	72	17.70
J. H. Wardle	18	23	3	341	63	17.05
W. J. Edrich	11	18	0	293	88	16.27
J. E. McConnon	5	7	1	85	22	14.16
T. G. Evans	14	20	2	244	40	13.55
J. B. Statham	13	14	4	132	25	13.20
R. Appleyard	13	17	9	82	19*	10.25
A. V. Bedser	7	11	2	85	30	9.44
P. J. Loader	11	13	2	90	22	8.18
K. V. Andrew	8	11	2	71	28*	7.88

* Signifies not out.

M.C.C. TEAM BOWLING AVERAGES—FIRST-CLASS MATCHES IN AUSTRALIA AND NEW ZEALAND

	Balls	Maidens	Runs	Wickets	Average
R. Appleyard	1962	82	656	44	14.90
J. B. Statham	2445	69	916	54	16.96
F. H. Tyson	2764	65	1140	64	17.81
P. J. Loader	1902	42	817	41	19.92
J. V. Wilson	183	0	100	5	20.00
J. H. Wardle	3153	135	1166	57	20.45
T. E. Bailey	1898	49	769	36	21.36
A. V. Bedser	1655	33	659	24	27.45
J. E. McConnon.......	601	18	267	8	33.37
T. W. Graveney	102	3	47	1	47.00
D. C. S. Compton	128	1	101	2	50.50
M. C. Cowdrey	68	1	71	1	71.00

Also bowled; W. J. Edrich 64—2—53—0; L. Hutton 6—0—2—1; R. T. Simpson 28—1—5—2.

Note. In Australia eight balls were bowled to the over; in New Zealand six balls to the over.

The following nineteen three-figure innings were played for M.C.C. during the tour:—

P. B. H. May (6):
157   v. Northern N.S.W. at Newcastle.†
129   v. Combined XI at Perth.
114   v. South Australia at Adelaide.
105*   v. Victoria at Melbourne.
104   v. Australia at Sydney (Second Test).
101   v. Prime Minister's XI at Canberra.†

T. W. Graveney (4):
134   v. Tasmania at Launceston.
111   v. Australia at Sydney (Fifth Test).
102   v. Wellington at Wellington.
101   v. Canterbury at Christchurch.

D. C. S. Compton (3):
182   v. South Australia at Adelaide.
113   v. South Australia at Adelaide.
110   v. Queensland at Brisbane.

M. C. Cowdrey (3):
101 }
103 } v. New South Wales at Sydney.
102   v. Australia at Melbourne (Third Test).

L. Hutton (2):
145*   v. Western Australia at Perth.
102   v. New South Wales at Sydney.

R. T. Simpson (1):
136   v. Queensland at Brisbane.

The following four three-figure innings were played against M.C.C.:—

R. N. Harvey (1):
162   v. England at Brisbane (First Test).

K. Meuleman (1):
109   for Western Australia at Perth.

A. R. Morris (1):
153   v. England at Brisbane (First Test).

W. Watson (1):
155   for New South Wales at Sydney.

* *Signifies not out.*   † Not a first-class fixture.

M.C.C. FIELDING IN 21 FIRST-CLASS MATCHES

T. G. Evans 41 wickets (34 caught, 7 stumped), T. W. Graveney 20, K. V. Andrew 18 wickets (16 caught, 2 stumped), P. B. H. May 16, M. C. Cowdrey 13, J. V. Wilson 10, J. H. Wardle 9, R. Appleyard 8, T. E. Bailey 7, L. Hutton 7, P. J. Loader 6, J. B. Statham 6, W. J. Edrich 5, R. T. Simpson 5, A. V. Bedser 3, D. C. S. Compton 3, F. H. Tyson 3, J. E. McConnon 2, Substitute 2 (Wilson 2).

M.C.C. v. CEYLON

At Colombo, September 30. Drawn. Cowdrey gave early evidence of his ability to settle down to tropical heat and a fast pitch. Excelling with drives and cuts he hit eleven 4's in a most attractive display which lasted eighty minutes. Simpson, Edrich, Graveney and May were dismissed before lunch for 59 but M.C.C. made their runs in two and half hours before May declared. Although Statham soon took two wickets Ceylon were never in any danger. F. C. de Saram, their captain, hit cheerfully in the last hour of this very pleasant match which attracted a large and jubilant crowd.

M.C.C. 178 for eight wickets declared (M. C. Cowdrey 66 not out); Ceylon 101 for four wickets (F. C. de Saram 43).

M.C.C. v. WESTERN AUSTRALIAN COUNTRY XI

At Bunbury, October 11, 12. Drawn. In bright sunshine and before enthusiastic crowds M.C.C. gained valuable match practice. They scored at a good rate when put in. Edrich struggling at first but later driving and pulling strongly for four 6's and nine 4's, hit the first hundred of the tour. Graveney was most fluent and Hutton and Cowdrey also impressed. After an opening stand of 51, the Country XI collapsed before the varied attack of McConnon and Loader, and followed on 228 behind with 160 minutes left. As in the first innings the opening batsman, Stephen, proved very dogged and in the match he batted 280 minutes for 53 runs, doing much to help his side avert defeat.

M.C.C.

L. Hutton b Outridge	59	T. E. Bailey b Herbert 12
W. J. Edrich c McCormack b Snell	129	J. E. McConnon not out 18
J. V. Wilson c Snell b Herbert	17	B 2, w 1 3
T. W. Graveney c Slattery b Sheppard	58	1/79 2/134 3/249 (5 wkts., dec.) 344
M. C. Cowdrey not out	48	4/267 5/300

J. H. Wardle, K. V. Andrew, P. J. Loader and F. H. Tyson did not bat.

Western Australian Country XI

J. Hutchinson b Tyson	37	.. c and b Wardle	9
E. Stephen c Hutton b Loader	13	— b Cowdrey	40
A. Sampson b Loader	2	— not out	10
T. Outridge c Loader b McConnon	5	— c Bailey b Cowdrey	21
M. Herbert c Tyson b McConnon	14	— c Graveney b Cowdrey	29
B. Sheppard c Tyson b McConnon	27	— c and b McConnon	14
G. McCormack c Bailey b McConnon	0	— st Andrew b Cowdrey	4
H. Slattery st Andrew b McConnon	7		
J. Morris b Loader	10		
E. James b Loader	0		
H. Snell not out	0		
W 1	1	N-b 1	1

1/51 2/53 3/58 4/60 5/87 6/87 7/95	116	1/24 2/45 3/83 (6 wkts.)	128
8/112 9/112		4/110 5/116 6/128	

Western Australian Country XI Bowling

	O.	M.	R.	W.	O.	M.	R.	W.
Snell	12	0	28	1				
Slattery	6	1	33	0				
James	11	0	75	0				
Outridge	21	0	110	1				
Herbert	15	0	64	2				
Sheppard	4	1	31	1				

M.C.C. Bowling

	O.	M.	R.	W.	O.	M.	R.	W.
Tyson	11	3	32	1	4	1	12	0
Loader	14	3	35	4	6	1	11	0
Bailey	3	0	9	0	2	0	11	0
Wardle	2	0	9	0	17	8	31	1
McConnon	12	3	30	5	6	1	27	1
Cowdrey					5.5	0	35	4

Umpires: Robins and Foley.

M.C.C. v. WESTERN AUSTRALIA

At Perth, October 15, 16, 18, 19. M.C.C. won by seven wickets, McConnon making the winning hit just before lunch on the fourth day. Statham paved the way for victory by bowling in devastating fashion on a fast true pitch aided by a strong cool wind after Hutton sent in the State team to bat. When the score was seven for three wickets rain caused a slight delay. On resuming, the first ball from Statham struck Carmody, the oposing captain, on the right temple and he did not resume until the fall of the sixth wicket, being last out. In batting M.C.C. were carried by Hutton who, not always faultless, spent four hours reaching his hundred. After lunch he hit brilliantly getting nine boundaries in his last 45 runs. A slightly injured leg muscle caused him to retire from the match, May taking over the captaincy. Western Australia wanted 218 to save an innings defeat. Meuleman, who batted two hours on Friday, went in again for the final half-hour on Saturday and then defied M.C.C. the whole of Monday, his chanceless 109 occupying six and a half hours. A fine right-handed catch by Statham at square leg ended a stubborn stand between Meuleman and Carmody who were together three hours fifty minutes. M.C.C. thus gained their first wicket on Monday from the last ball bowled before tea.

Western Australia

J. Rutherford b Statham	0	— b Loader	9
R. Sarre c Evans b Bailey	0	— b Statham	5
P. McCarthy b Statham	3	— c May b Wardle	13
K. Meuleman c Evans b Loader	23	— c Evans b Statham	109
D. K. Carmody b Loader	25	— c Statham b McConnon	75
L. Pavy c May b Statham	20	— c Evans b Loader	0
M. Herbert b Statham	0	— run out	0
R. Strauss c Loader b Bailey	10	— lbw b McConnon	4
J. Munro b Statham	15	— c Evans b Bailey	6
H. R. Gorringe b Statham	0	— c May b Statham	4
R. H. Price not out	0	— not out	21
L-b 5, n-b 2	7	L-b 6, n-b 3	9

1/0 2/0 3/7 4/38 5/38 6/57 7/57   103
8/101 9/101

1/7 2/25 3/32 4/160 5/163   255
6/171 7/178 8/197 9/236

M.C.C.

L. Hutton retired hurt	145				
R. T. Simpson c Munro b Gorringe	7	— b Price			4
J. V. Wilson c Munro b Gorringe	38	— c Rutherford b Sarre			9
P. B. H. May c Rutherford b Herbert	8	— not out			3
M. C. Cowdrey c Gorringe b Strauss	41	— c Pavy b Sarre			6
T. E. Bailey c Munro b Gorringe	0				
J. E. McConnon run out	12	— not out			13
J. H. Wardle c Munro b Strauss	5				
P. J. Loader c Strauss b Herbert	22				
T. G. Evans b Gorringe	18				
J. B. Statham not out	5				
B 9, l-b 5, w 3, n-b 3	20	B 4, w 1			5

1/23 2/94 3/125 4/252 5/252 6/266   321   1/11 2/24 3/25   (3 wkts.) 40
7/297 8/297 9/321

M.C.C. Bowling

	O.	M.	R.	W.		O.	M.	R.	W.
Statham	10	4	23	6	....	23.3	6	68	3
Bailey	11	2	36	2	....	21	6	51	1
Loader	9.2	4	26	2	....	22	5	56	2
Wardle	5	2	11	0	....	10	1	29	1
McConnon						19	7	42	0

Western Australia Bowling

	O.	M.	R.	W.		O.	M.	R.	W.
Price	20	0	72	0	....	4	0	9	1
Gorringe	27.5	4	102	4	....	1	0	6	0
Meuleman	7	0	23	0					
Strauss	12	1	57	2					
Herbert	16	4	47	2	....	5	2	9	0
Sarre						2.5	0	11	2

Umpires: O. Cooley and R. Lethbridge.

M.C.C. v. COMBINED XI

At Perth, October 22, 23, 25. M.C.C. won by an innings and 62 runs. This was not only the first time in four matches that the Englishmen had beaten the Combined side on this ground, but also the first time M.C.C. had opened a tour by winning both first-class matches in Perth. As in the previous match the captain, this time May, put in the opposition on a very fast pitch and after taking eighty minutes to break the opening stand M.C.C. never looked back. In both innings the Eastern State players, Harvey, Hole and Johnson, made no more than 60. The bowling and fielding were always extremely good, Wilson bringing off three dazzling catches on the last day. When the first three M.C.C. wickets fell for 42 late on the opening day, the Australians had a slight chance of recovery, but May and Wilson remained together until just before tea, their steady stand producing 179 in four hours. Wilson was content to play the minor part, giving splendid support to May who, batting five hours twenty minutes, never took the slightest risk but on occasion drove, pulled and hooked superbly, hitting fourteen 4's. Owing to knee trouble, Meuleman could not assist the losers, whose opening batsmen, Rutherford, an 18-year-old left hander, and Sawle, both of West Australia University, offered stubborn opposition. Throughout the batting of both sides was singularly unenterprising.

Combined XI

J. Rutherford c and b Wardle	39	— c Wilson b Tyson	0
L. Sawle c Evans b Bailey	7	— c Bailey b Wardle	25
R. N. Harvey c Evans b Bailey	3	— c Evans b Bailey	8
G. B. Hole c Evans b Tyson	4	— c Graveney b Appleyard	33
D. K. Carmody c Statham b Tyson	8	— c Wilson b Bailey	38
L. Pavy st Evans b Wardle	9	— not out	36
I. W. Johnson lbw b Statham	2	— c Tyson b Appleyard	10
J. Munro not out	5	— c and b Appleyard	5
R. H. Price c Evans b Statham	4	— c Appleyard b Wardle	0
E. James b Statham	0	— b Wardle	0
H. R. Gorringe run out	0	— c Wilson b Wardle	4
L-b 4, n-b 1	5	B 1, l-b 3	4

1/19 2/25 3/35 4/48 5/74 6/77   86   1/4 2/22 3/61 4/76 5/117   163
7/77 8/86 9/86   6/144 7/154 8/159 9/163

M.C.C.

W. J. Edrich b Price	0	J. H. Wardle st Munro b James	6
R. T. Simpson c Rutherford b Johnson	28	F. H. Tyson c Sawle b Gorringe	21
P. B. H. May c Rutherford b Price	129	R. Appleyard c Harvey b James	0
T. W. Graveney c Munro b Johnson	0	J. B. Statham not out	12
J. V. Wilson c Hole b Gorringe	72	B 3, w 3, n-b 2	8
T. E. Bailey c Sawle b Johnson	35		
T. G. Evans c Pavy b Price	0	1/1 2/42 3/42 4/221 5/236 6/243	311
		7/252 8/289 9/294	

M.C.C. Bowling

	O.	M.	R.	W.	O.	M.	R.	W.
Statham	8.5	3	21	3	12	3	41	0
Tyson	9	3	14	2	11	6	13	1
Bailey	11	4	16	2	13	3	35	2
Appleyard	10	5	19	2	17	4	36	3
Wardle	4	0	11	2	11.6	2	34	4

Combined XI Bowling

	O.	M.	R.	W.
Price	25	7	73	3
Gorringe	19	4	61	2
James	32	6	92	2
Johnson	22.6	7	44	3
Harvey	1	0	8	0
Hole	6	0	25	0

Umpires: O. Cooley and J. Mackley.

M.C.C. v. SOUTH AUSTRALIA

At Adelaide, October 29, 30, November 1, 2. M.C.C. won by 21 runs. After the fast pitches of Perth, most of the M.C.C. batsmen cut a sorry figure on the slower one they found here, but this was no excuse for their poor display. Compton, who joined the side only two days before the match following a tiring and adventurous flight from London, was in his most enterprising mood; Favell hit splendidly in both innings for South Australia, who seemed to have established a winning position at lunch time on the last day when with seven wickets standing they needed only 74 more runs. Immediately after the interval Tyson bowled Favell by sheer speed and then Appleyard, coming on at 140, took the next four wickets in three overs for only five runs before Loader, who earlier had made a brilliant right-hand return catch from Harris, put an end to M.C.C.'s troubles by disposing of Wilson. Hutton held his men together for two days, first by staying four and a quarter hours and finally maintaining a keen attack by shrewd bowling changes and careful field placing.

M.C.C.

L. Hutton c Roxby b Wilson	37	— c Hole b Roxby	98
W. J. Edrich c and b Horsnell	0	— c Langley b Drennan	2
R. T. Simpson c sub b Wilson	26	— b Drennan	16
D. C. S. Compton st Langley b Wilson	.113	— b Drennan	2
T. W. Graveney b Drennan	20	— c Langley b Hole	34
M. C. Cowdrey st Langley b Roxby	20	— c Hole b Wilson	7
J. E. McConnon st Langley b Roxby	4	— lbw b Wilson	12
F. H. Tyson c Hole b Roxby	8	— not out	4
P. J. Loader c Ridings b Wilson	6	— c Pinch b Wilson	4
K. V. Andrew c Favell b Wilson	2	— c Hole b Wilson	0
R. Appleyard not out	5	— b Roxby	0
B 4, l-b 1	5	B 1, l-b 1	2

1/4 2/45 3/93 4/162 5/211 6/225   246   1/5 2/29 3/31 4/96 5/111   181
7/227 8/234 9/236   6/173 7/173 8/173 9/181

South Australia

L. Favell c Hutton b Tyson	84	— b Tyson	47
D. Harris b Tyson	43	— c and b Loader	0
G. B. Hole c Simpson b Loader	12	— c McConnon b Appleyard..	10
C. Pinch b McConnon	12	— c Andrew b Appleyard	9
P. L. Ridings c Andrew b Loader	19	— c Graveney b McConnon	27
N. Dansie c Hutton b Tyson	11	— lbw b Appleyard	18
G. R. Langley not out	36	— b McConnon	23
R. Roxby lbw b McConnon	4	— not out	6
J. Drennan b Tyson	2	— c Simpson b Appleyard	1
K. Horsnell b Tyson	0	— b Appleyard	2
J. Wilson run out	0	— b Loader	2
B 3, l-b 3, n-b 1	7	B 5, l-b 1, n-b 1	7

1/119 2/136 3/146 4/167 5/182 6/186   254   1/2 2/42 3/95 4/102   152
7/246 8/249 9/253   5/127 6/142 7/142 8/144
                                              9/147

South Australia Bowling

	O.	M.	R.	W.		O.	M.	R.	W.
Drennan	7	1	16	1	....	16	3	32	3
Horsnell	13	2	38	1	....	8	0	34	0
Roxby	23.6	4	82	3	....	16.5	3	59	2
Wilson	24	4	81	5	....	16	5	32	4
Hole	1	0	1	0	....	10	3	14	1
Dansie	5	0	23	0	....	5	1	8	0

M.C.C. Bowling

	O.	M.	R.	W.		O.	M.	R.	W.
Tyson	19	3	62	5	....	12	3	37	1
Loader	17	0	73	2	....	8.6	2	25	2
Edrich	5	2	25	0					
Appleyard	9	2	31	0	....	11	1	46	5
McConnon	11.1	1	56	2	....	8	0	37	2

Umpires: M. J. McInnes and K. C. Butler.

M.C.C. v. AN AUSTRALIAN XI

At Melbourne, November 5, 6, 8, 9, 10. Drawn. After an even struggle for two days, continuous rain put an end to the proceedings although on the third evening an extra day was added not so much for the purpose of obtaining a result as to help the players of both sides to get into form for the Brisbane Test. A dry true pitch gave no encouragement to the bowlers, yet they were generally on top, uninspiring displays by most batsmen being extremely disappointing. Only

Simpson, May and Benaud showed any initiative, the others being leaden-footed and strokeless. The two Australian spinners, Johnson (off-breaks) and Benaud (leg-breaks) seldom turned the ball and they had to rely mainly on variation of flight and length. In contrast, M.C.C. pace bowlers, Bailey, Statham and Bedser, commanded the utmost respect, Bedser on his first appearance of the tour being content to tune himself up carefully.

M.C.C.

R. T. Simpson c and b Benaud ...	74	T. G. Evans b Johnson..........	1
W. J. Edrich c R. N. Harvey b Johnson	11	J. H. Wardle b Johnson..........	8
		A. V. Bedser b Johnson.........	3
P. B. H. May c Drennan b Archer .	45	J. B. Statham c R. N. Harvey b Johnson	13
D. C. S. Compton c Maddocks b Benaud	16	W 1, n-b 1	2
J. V. Wilson c Archer b Benaud..	6		
T. W. Graveney not out	22	1/48 2/111 3/135 4/153 5/159	205
T. E. Bailey c McDonald b Johnson	4	6/166 7/168 8/181 9/185	

Australian XI

C. C. McDonald lbw b Statham ..	4	L. Maddocks not out	24
R. Briggs b Bailey..............	48	I. W. Johnson not out	5
R. N. Harvey c Evans b Statham..	4		
R. Harvey c Edrich b Bailey	7	B 4, n-b 1	5
J. H. de Courcy lbw b Bailey	0		—
R. Benaud c Evans b Bedser......	47	1/12 2/18 3/44 4/44 (7 wkts.)	167
R. G. Archer b Bailey	23	5/110 6/115 7/156	

J. Drennan and W. A. Johnston did not bat.

Australian XI Bowling

	O.	M.	R.	W.
Drennan	8	1	27	0
Archer........	12	4	22	1
Johnston	11	2	30	0
Johnson	17.6	2	66	6
Benaud	19	4	58	3

M.C.C. Bowling

	O.	M.	R.	W.
Statham	14	3	29	2
Bedser	16	2	39	1
Bailey	17.1	3	53	4
Wardle	21	9	41	0

Umpires: R. Wright and R. Hele.

M.C.C. v. NEW SOUTH WALES

At Sydney, November 12, 13, 15, 16. Drawn. To Cowdrey fell the distinction of hitting two centuries in the same match before he had even hit one in the County Championship. Watson, of N.S.W., also accomplished an unusual performance, for in only his second first-class innings he hit his maiden century in any type of cricket. Miller, winning the toss, requested M.C.C. to bat and Crawford, a tall young fast bowler, began so well that four men left for 38 before Cowdrey and Hutton, by excellent batting, put on 163. Throughout the Australians fielded magnificently, Watson and Simpson making some grand slip catches. With Watson and Miller adding 161 together, New South Wales came within 40 of the M.C.C.'s 252 before their third wicket fell. Watson, sixth out, stayed six and quarter hours, hitting eighteen 4's. On M.C.C. batting again Cowdrey opened for the first time in his life, being accompanied by Wilson, Hutton going in sixth. Finally, New South Wales faced an impossible task, needing 198 in seventy-five minutes. They threw away their chance of victory when on Saturday with forty-five minutes left, De Courcy suggested to Hutton that the light was too bad to continue. It was not in Hutton's interest that his tired bowlers should be punished and he agreed to the game being stopped. After a delay of twenty-four minutes the cricket continued but soon the umpires upheld an appeal against the light.

M.C.C.

L. Hutton c Davidson b Treanor	102	— c Simpson b Treanor 87
W. J. Edrich c Watson b Crawford	7	— c Burke b Davidson 37
R. T. Simpson c Simpson b Crawford	0	— b Crawford 21
P. B. H. May c Lambert b Treanor	1	— c de Courcy b Treanor..... 16
J. V. Wilson c Simpson b Miller	9	— b Crawford 0
M. C. Cowdrey c and b Davidson	110	— lbw b Crawford 103
T. G. Evans c Watson b Crawford	11	— c Simpson b Davidson 7
F. H. Tyson c Simpson b Treanor	7	— b Crawford 15
A. V. Bedser c Lambert b Davidson	0	— c Simpson b Treanor 5
P. J. Loader c and b Davidson	0	— c Burke b Treanor 16
R. Appleyard not out	0	— not out 9
L-b 2, w 1, n-b 2	5	L-b 5, w 1, n-b 5 11
	252	**327**

1/24 2/24 3/25 4/38 5/201 6/245   252
7/249 8/252 9/252

1/0 2/39 3/69 4/158   327
5/226 6/253 7/292 8/298 9/312

New South Wales

A. R. Morris c Simpson b Bedser	26	
W. Watson lbw b Tyson	155	— c May b Loader 8
R. Benaud c May b Tyson	2	
K. R. Miller c Wilson b Bedser	86	
J. Burke lbw b Bedser	6	— not out 34
J. H. de Courcy b Appleyard	20	
R. L. Simpson c Evans b Tyson	22	— b Loader................ 4
A. K. Davidson c Loader b Bedser	30	— not out 27
O. Lambert c Wilson b Loader	6	
J. Treanor c Wilson b Tyson	12	
P. Crawford not out	0	
B 8, l-b 4, n-b 5	17	L-b 2, n-b 3 5
	382	**(2 wkts.) 78**

1/48 2/51 3/212 4/253 5/294 6/328   382
7/335 8/343 9/374

1/16 2/29   (2 wkts.) 78

New South Wales Bowling

	O.	M.	R.	W.	O.	M.	R.	W
Crawford	17	6	51	3	19	1	86	4
Davidson	19.2	3	41	3	27	10	63	2
Treanor	16	3	64	3	25.5	6	96	4
Miller	8	0	31	1	6	1	8	0
Benaud	15	2	50	0	29	11	52	0
Burke	3	0	6	0	1	1	0	0
Simpson	2	0	4	0	3	1	11	0

M.C.C. Bowling

Bedser	24.5	3	117	4	4	0	13	0
Tyson	25	2	98	4	2	1	1	0
Loader	18	2	92	1	4	0	14	2
Appleyard	21	3	58	1	3	1	7	0
Cowdrey					3	0	38	0

Umpires: H. Elphinstone and H. MacKinnon.

M.C.C. v. QUEENSLAND

At Brisbane, November, 19, 20, 22, 23. Drawn In a match of batting contrasts M.C.C. faced Lindwall for the first time during the tour. Cowdrey again opened the innings but the experiment failed and Hutton did not try it again. Again the captain winning the toss, K. Archer sent in his opponents, and Cowdrey, May and Bailey were out for 18. Then came a magnificent stand of 234—the best of the tour by any side—by Simpson and Compton. Before completing his century Simpson made only one rash stroke and he hit one 6 and eighteen 4's; yet never again did he reveal the same power of concentration. Compton, with seventeen 4's, excelled with the late cut, the square drive past point and the leg sweep. Queensland batted for ten minutes before the close of the first day and McConnon at silly mid-on was severely injured in the groin from a hard drive by Harvey. He spent a week in hospital. With rain reducing play to two and a quarter hours on the second day and Queensland not showing any initiative until the last pair added 54 quickly, their innings occupied seven and a half hours. The new ball did not become available until 78 eight-ball overs were delivered—the equivalent of 104 overs in England. Throughout the M.C.C.'s long stay in the field Bedser bowled splendidly. M.C.C. used the last day mainly for batting practice. Simpson, possibly because of the heat, was completely out of touch but May and, once again, Compton shaped splendidly.

M.C.C.

R. T. Simpson c Grout b Walmsley	136	—	c Bratchford b Raymer	....	38
M. C. Cowdrey c Grout b Lindwall	..	4	—	b R. Archer	0
T. E. Bailey b Lindwall.............		0	—	not out	51
P. B. H. May c Bratchford b R. Archer	.	0	—	lbw b Mackay	77
D. C. S. Compton c Grout b Mackay	110	—	c Bratchford b Flynn	...	69
J. V. Wilson c and b Lindwall	....	4	—	b Flynn	0
J. E. McConnon b Lindwall	....	1	—	absent hurt	0
J. H. Wardle c Harvey b R. Archer	.....	1	—	lbw b R. Archer	27
A. V. Bedser c Burge b Mackay	....	30	—	c K. Archer b Walmsley	..	16
K. V. Andrew b Bratchford	....	15	—	b Bratchford	0
J. B. Statham not out	....	1	—	b Walmsley	0
L-b 1, n-b 1....................		2		B 9, l-b 1	10
		304			**288**

1/17 2/17 3/18 4/252 5/252 6/253   304
7/258 8/258 9/302

1/1 2/8 3/60 4/72 5/156   288
6/205 7/245 8/288 9/288

Queensland

K. Archer c Andrew b Bedser	....	23	— c Bedser b Simpson	9
C. Harvey c Andrew b Bedser	....	49	— b Simpson	9
K. Mackay b Bailey	....	33	— not out	3
P. Burge b Wilson	....	26		
R. G. Archer c Andrew b Bailey	....	22		
J. Bratchford c Andrew b Statham	....	21		
W. Walmsley c Cowdrey b Statham	....	34		
N. V. Raymer c Cowdrey b Statham	....	11		
W. Grout not out	....	32		
B. Flynn b Bailey	....	26		
R. R. Lindwall absent ill	....	0		
B 7, l-b 3, n-b 1	....	11	B 4..................	4
		288	**(2 wkts.)**	**25**

1/41 2/111 3/115 4/150 5/177 6/209   288
7/225 8/234 9/288

1/20 2/25   (2 wkts.) 25

Queensland Bowling

	O.	M.	R.	W.		O.	M.	R.	W.
Lindwall	15	0	66	4					
R. Archer	15	4	37	2	....	15	1	34	2
Bratchford	10	1	27	1	....	8	2	22	1
Flynn	11	1	73	0	....	15	1	80	2
Walmsley	10	1	54	1	....	20	1	90	2
Raymer	8	1	40	0	....	13	1	39	1
Mackay	3.2	1	5	2	....	9	3	13	1

M.C.C. Bowling

	O.	M.	R.	W.		O.	M.	R.	W.
Statham	23	4	74	3					
Bedser	31	9	56	2					
Bailey	20.3	2	74	3					
Wardle	19	7	57	0					
Compton	1	0	5	0					
Wilson	4	0	11	1	....	4	0	16	0
Simpson						3.4	1	5	2

Umpires: L. Townsend and C. Hoy.

ENGLAND v. AUSTRALIA

First Test Match

At Brisbane, November 26, 27, 29, 30, December 1. Australia won by an innings and 154 runs at ten minutes past four on the fifth day with a day to spare. Nothing went right for the Englishmen. Before the match Evans fell ill with sunstroke and on the first morning Compton, when fielding, ran into the wooden palings, breaking a bone in the back of his left hand, but above everything else the whole course of the game probably turned on the decision of Hutton, after winning the toss, to give Australia first innings. Never before had an England captain taken such a gamble in Australia and certainly never before in a Test match had a side replied with a total of 601 after being sent in to bat.

Hutton may have made up his mind some time earlier that he would take this course if the decision rested with him. Four times already on the tour the procedure had been adopted always with satisfactory results for the fielding side and for this game England had banked on an all-speed attack of four bowlers. Hutton inspected the pitch most carefully with several of his colleagues. It looked a beauty, but he carried out his plan and although on subsequent events he could be condemned, the fact remains that besides the loss of Compton England allowed about twelve possible chances to go astray, including one from Morris to Andrew off Bedser in the third over of the match before he scored. If the England fielding had approached any decent standard Hutton might well have achieved his objective.

Australia, who omitted Davidson from the chosen twelve and were captained for the first time by Ian Johnson, averaged just over 40 runs an hour on the first day when they scored 208 for the loss of Favell and Miller. A splendid catch near his boots by Cowdrey at square-leg removed Favell and then Miller charmed the crowd of 20,000 for eighty-five minutes before he chopped a harmless-looking ball into his stumps. So at three o'clock the two left-handers, Morris and Harvey, entered on a long partnership. Both flicked at balls outside the off stump and never during the two hours and ten minutes they were together on the first day did they establish a complete mastery over the bowling. Immediately after tea Bailey at deep long-leg gave Morris a life when he was 55 and the total 145. That mistake alone cost England dearly.

With the new ball available first thing on Saturday there was still hope, but now Morris and Harvey took absolute control and thanks to their example and enterprise Australia added 295 that day for the loss of four more wickets. Taking into consideration the length of time the fast bowlers occupied completing an over this was extremely fast scoring in present-day Test matches. Hutton realised it would be futile to persist with an attacking field. He placed his men with the idea of saving runs and Tyson cut yards off his run in order to gain accuracy: but not until mid-afternoon did England meet with their first success of the day when Cowdrey, the only slip, held a waist-high catch from a chop by Morris who, with two 6's and seven 4's, batted seven hours for his 153. The stand produced 202 in four hours ten minutes.

England had to wait another two hours for their next wicket, Harvey and Hole putting on 131 before a fine throw by Tyson from long-leg ran out Hole. Then with seven more runs added Harvey fell to a brilliant catch at backward square-leg, Bailey rolling over as he held a hard pull. Harvey's 162, made in six hours twenty minutes, was easily his highest against England and also his first hundred against them in Australia. He hit one 5 and seventeen 4's.

Archer soon gave an easy catch to gully, but more trouble came from Lindwall and Benaud for both hit with great power. Australia, 503 for six at the week-end, kept England in the field until lunch time on Monday, Lindwall continuing his sparkling hitting which brought him eleven 4's. Altogether the Australian innings lasted eleven and a half hours.

After his spell of ninety minutes with the bat on the third morning, Lindwall came out fresh and bowled superbly for an hour during which time the first four England wickets crashed for 25 runs. Not until Bailey arrived was there any sign of stability and then in two hours forty minutes he and Cowdrey added 82, Cowdrey in his first Test match hit seven splendid 4's and gave a foretaste of the great innings he was to play later in the series. The end of the third day found England 107 for five wickets and defeat was obviously only a matter of time unless rain came to the rescue.

Having made 38 in two hours forty minutes, Bailey continued the fight. He soon lost Tyson, Bedser and Andrew but Statham kept up his end for thirty-five minutes and when he left Bailey had reached 81. Against medical advice Compton decided to bat, but he was almost helpless and so Bailey, who had batted without error, hit out and was bowled. He stayed four hours twenty minutes for his highest score against Australia and besides eleven 4's he hit one 6 and one 5. When he drove Johnson for his six, Bailey won the prize of £A100 offered by a local businessman for the first English 6.

By two o'clock England followed on 411 behind and in the first hour they lost Simpson and Hutton. Simpson foolishly tried a single when Hutton was dropped by Favell in the slips off Lindwall, but Edrich and May checked the opposition in a defiant stand. They took the total to 130 at the close but next day Australia were on top again. May, playing at a short ball, was lbw when the partnership had added 124 in just under two and a half hours, and next Edrich, having shaped splendidly, especially against Lindwall, also fell to a short ball which took his middle stump when he was too soon with his hook. Edrich batted three hours ten minutes and hit one 6 and thirteen 4's. Subsequently only Bailey and Tyson gave the Australian bowlers any trouble. Scoring 111 runs in the match Bailey defended resolutely for just under six hours. In less than half an hour after tea the last four wickets fell to the spin of Benaud and Johnson, the match ending with a glorious running catch in the deep by Harvey when Statham tried to lift Benaud for 6.

The full attendance of 77,008 was below Brisbane's best of 93,143 in the 1932–33 series, but the receipts of £21,000 were easily a record for the capital city of Queensland.

Australia

. Favell c Cowdrey b Statham	23	R. R. Lindwall not out		64
. R. Morris c Cowdrey b Bailey	153	G. R. Langley b Bailey		16
. R. Miller b Bailey	49	I. W. Johnson not out		24
. N. Harvey c Bailey b Bedser	162	B 11, l-b 7, n-b 1		19
. B. Hole run out	57			
. Benaud c May b Tyson	34	1/51 2/123 3/325 (8 wkts., dec.)		601
. G. Archer c Bedser b Statham	0	4/456 5/463 6/464 7/545 8/572		

. A. Johnston did not bat.

England

L. Hutton c Langley b Lindwall	4	— lbw b Miller	13
R. T. Simpson b Miller	2	— run out	9
W. J. Edrich c Langley b Archer	15	— b Johnston	88
P. B. H. May b Lindwall	1	— lbw b Lindwall	44
M. C. Cowdrey c Hole b Johnston	40	— b Benaud	10
T. E. Bailey c Johnston	88	— c Langley b Lindwall	23
F. H. Tyson b Johnson	7	— not out	37
A. V. Bedser b Johnson	5	— c Archer b Johnson	
K. V. Andrew b Lindwall	6	— b Johnson	
J. B. Statham b Johnson	11	— c Harvey b Benaud	14
D. C. S. Compton not out	2	— c Langley b Benaud	
B 3, l-b 6	9	B 7, l-b 2	9

1/4 2/10 3/11 4/25 5/107 6/132   **190**
7/141 8/156 9/181

1/22 2/23 3/147 4/163   **257**
5/181 6/220 7/231 8/242
9/243

England Bowling

	O.	M.	R.	W.	O.	M.	R.	W
Bedser	37	4	131	1				
Statham	34	2	123	2				
Tyson	29	1	160	1				
Bailey	26	1	140	3				
Edrich	3	0	28	0				

Australia Bowling

	O.	M.	R.	W.	O.	M.	R.	W
Lindwall	14	4	27	3	17	3	50	2
Miller	11	5	19	1	12	2	30	1
Archer	4	1	14	1	15	4	28	0
Johnson	19	5	46	3	17	5	38	2
Benaud	12	5	28	0	8.1	1	43	3
Johnston	16.1	5	47	2	21	8	59	1

Umpires: M. J. McInnes (Adelaide) and C. Hoy (Brisbane).

M.C.C. v. QUEENSLAND COUNTRY XI

At Rockhampton, December 4, 6.   M.C.C. won by an innings and 12 runs. Hutton came in for some severe and apparently unjust criticism because he per suaded the local captain, Johnson, to extend the playing time in order to brin about a definite result. The fact that Hutton had given permission for the pitc to be more or less re-made on the Sunday by watering and rolling to ensure som reasonable cricket on the second day was ignored by the protesters. Afte batting in light-hearted fashion M.C.C. were held up only by Brown, a soun left-hander who batted well for three hours.

M.C.C.

L. Hutton c Duckham b Watt	40	R. Appleyard not out	
W. J. Edrich c Brown b Greenough	74	P. J. Loader c Duckham b Watt	
P. B. H. May c Johnson b Watt	69	K. V. Andrew b Jenkins	
T. W. Graveney st Thorpe b Watt	29	A. V. Bedser c Sippel b Watt	
J. V. Wilson c Johnson b Jenkins	61	B 2, l-b 4	
M. C. Cowdrey c Bichel b Greenough	19		
J. H. Wardle c Greenough b Jenkins	7	1/112 2/117 3/191 4/242 5/291	31
		6/305 7/305 8/308 9/312	

Queensland Country XI

W. Brown run out		22	—	b Graveney	78
L. Westaway c Graveney b Loader		0	—	b Bedser	1
R. Sippel b Wardle		17	—	b Appleyard	45
D. Watt c Graveney b Appleyard		4	—	c Wilson b Appleyard	29
L. Thorpe b Appleyard		0	—	c Andrew b Graveney	22
F. Greenough b Wardle		10	—	st Andrew b Appleyard	0
K. Jenkins c and b Loader		4	—	b Appleyard	8
L. Johnson b Loader		4	—	b Appleyard	2
D. Bichel not out		15	—	b Appleyard	1
D. Duckham st Andrew b Graveney		9	—	not out	4
J. Sneddon c Wilson b Graveney		0	—	b Appleyard	0
B 5, n-b 5		10		B 10, l-b 5, n-b 5	20
		—			—
		95			210

1/10 2/48 3/49 4/49 5/60 6/67   1/9 2/117 3/153 4/183
7/71 8/71 9/95   5/183 6/203 7/203 8/208
                                 9/208

Country XI Bowling

	O.	M.	R.	W.	O.	M.	R.	W.
Johnson	11	0	39	0				
Greenough	12	0	75	2				
Sneddon	5	1	11	0				
Bichel	12	0	70	0				
Watt	18.2	0	56	5				
Jenkins	8	0	44	3				
Duckham	2	0	16	0				

M.C.C. Bowling

	O.	M.	R.	W.	O.	M.	R.	W.
Bedser	4	0	15	0	14	1	38	1
Loader	6	1	22	3	4	1	19	0
Wardle	19	9	22	2	11	1	33	0
Appleyard	11	4	18	2	14.7	4	51	7
Graveney	2.1	0	8	2	12	0	49	2

Umpires: A. C. Barnes and A. Scott.

M.C.C. v. PRIME MINISTER'S XI

At Canberra, December 8. M.C.C. won by 31 runs. Free hitting was the order of this gay charity match in which local businessmen offered thirty shillings for each 6 and ten shillings for each 4. They paid out £35 10s., the Englishmen costing them £20 with three 6's and thirty-one 4's and the Australians £15 10s., five 6's, all by Benaud, and sixteen 4's. Yorkshire figured prominently in an exciting finish. Wilson caught Benaud, Miller and Harvey just in front of the sightscreen off Wardle, and Hutton, taking three of the last four wickets in eleven balls, helped his side to win in the final over. Sir William Slim, Governor-General of Australia, graced the match with his presence and pleased everyone by "fielding" one of Benaud's 6's in the enclosure.

M.C.C.

L. Hutton c Miller b Backen		15	J. H. Wardle not out	37
W. J. Edrich b Robin		0	J. E. McConnon not out	14
P. B. H. May c Harvey b O'Reilly		101		
J. V. Wilson c Gibb b Johnson		29	L-b 4	4
T. W. Graveney st Gibb b Benaud		56		
M. C. Cowdrey lbw b Hassett		8	1/3 2/25 3/123 (7 wkts., dec.)	278
T. G. Evans b Hassett		14	4/199 5/207 6/219 7/236	

A. V. Bedser and F. H. Tyson did not bat.

Prime Minister's XI

I. W. Johnson lbw b Edrich	4	J. Backen c Edrich b Hutton	11
R. Benaud c Wilson b Wardle	113	K. Gibb st Evans b Hutton	0
S. J. Loxton st Evans b McConnon	47	B. Robin not out	0
K. R. Miller c Wilson b Wardle	38		
R. Bellchambers b Edrich	4		
R. N. Harvey c Wilson b Wardle	8	B 4, l-b 1, n-b 2	7
A. L. Hassett c Tyson b Hutton	11		
J. O'Reilly b Wardle	4	1/23 2/107 3/195 4/200 5/214	247
		6/228 7/234 8/241 9/247	

Prime Minister's XI Bowling

	O.	M.	R.	W.
Robin	5	0	29	1
Backen	6	0	35	1
O'Reilly	8	0	41	1
Hassett	5	0	34	2
Benaud	6	0	55	1
Johnson	5	0	20	1
Miller	2	0	15	0
Bellchambers	1	0	11	0
Loxton	2	0	34	0

M.C.C. Bowling

	O.	M.	R.	W.
Bedser	2	0	17	0
Edrich	5	0	41	2
Tyson	3	0	16	0
Graveney	3	0	26	0
McConnon	7	0	52	1
Wardle	9	0	73	4
Hutton	1.3	0	15	3

Umpires: J. Fingleton and C. Morrison.

M.C.C. v. VICTORIA

At Melbourne, December 10, 11, 13, 14. Drawn. Rain which reduced play by nearly four hours on the Saturday accounted mainly for the stalemate, but the match itself brought M.C.C. satisfaction, for here they began the long climb up the ladder which led to three consecutive Test wins. Of the batsmen Simpson alone failed. Hutton and Bailey began with the best stand so far for the first wicket, but neither made any attempt to take the initiative, yet there was some fine hitting by Graveney and Cowdrey. McConnon defended stubbornly in a valuable ninth wicket parternship of 53 with Cowdrey. When Victoria batted Tyson continued the experiment he began in the Brisbane Test of reducing his run to fifteen yards, beginning with six shuffling steps and finishing with ten deliberate raking strides. His six wickets for 68 was at that stage his best analysis in first class cricket. Although Neil Harvey made 93 for once out and batted splendidly against the other bowlers he was not convincing or certain when opposed to Tyson. Hutton prolonged the M.C.C. second innings for May to complete a fine hundred (ten 4's) and consequently Victoria, wanting 272 in only two hours, were content to play out time. Ian Johnson pulled a leg muscle while fielding—an injury which kept him out of the second Test.

M.C.C.

L. Hutton lbw b Loxton	41	— c Maddocks b Loxton	25
T. E. Bailey c Maddocks b Loxton	60	— b Power	9
P. B. H. May c Maddocks b Johnston	4	— not out	105
T. W. Graveney c Power b Johnston	48	— c Maddocks b Loxton	12
M. C. Cowdrey run out	79	— c McDonald b Johnson	54
R. T. Simpson c and b Hill	3	— c Chambers b Hill	4
T. G. Evans c Maddocks b Hill	14	— not out	11
J. H. Wardle b Power	16		
F. H. Tyson c Hill b Power	15		
J. E. McConnon c Loxton b Johnson	21		
P. J. Loader not out	3		
B 5, l-b 1, w 1, n-b 1	8	B 12, l-b 1, w 1, n-b 2	16
1/97 2/104 3/126 4/192 5/195 6/213	312	1/26 2/52 (5 wkts., dec.)	236
7/233 8/253 9/306		3/69 4/189 5/199	

Victoria

C. C. McDonald c Evans b Tyson	24	— retired hurt	0
J. Hallebone b Tyson	17	— lbw b Loader	7
R. Harvey b Tyson	11	— c Hutton b McConnon	38
R. N. Harvey b Tyson	59	— not out	34
J. Chambers run out	42	— lbw b Wardle	1
S. J. Loxton b Bailey	26	— not out	6
L. Maddocks c Cowdrey b Loader	35		
I. W. Johnson b Tyson	5		
J. C. Hill not out	34		
J. Power b Tyson	5		
W. A. Johnston c Loader b Wardle	4		
B 8, l-b 5, n-b 2	15	B 1, l-b 1	2

1/37 2/54 3/59 4/159 5/160 6/225   277   1/29 2/53 3/68   (3 wkts.)   88
7/225 8/248 9/258

Victoria Bowling

	O.	M.	R.	W.		O.	M.	R.	W.
Power	14	1	67	2	....	10	0	63	1
Loxton	15	2	54	2	....	14	2	67	2
Johnston	23	6	60	2	....	10	4	37	0
Hill	22	1	71	2	....	12	3	30	1
Johnson	15.6	1	52	1	....	7	2	23	1

M.C.C. Bowling

	O.	M.	R.	W.		O.	M.	R.	W.
Tyson	21	3	68	6	....	6	0	33	0
Bailey	10	0	48	1					
Loader	15	2	60	1	....	5	0	16	1
Wardle	12.5	2	41	1	....	4	0	14	1
McConnon	11	2	45	0	....	11	5	23	1

Umpires: R. Hele and R. Wright.

ENGLAND v. AUSTRALIA
Second Test Match

At Sydney, December 17, 18, 20, 21, 22. England won by 38 runs at twelve minutes past three on the fifth day with one day in hand. Such a victory seemed beyond any possibility when England—this time they were put in by the Australian captain, Morris—lost eight wickets for 88, but among a crop of batting failures in both teams the tail-enders made their presence felt. In addition May hit his first Test century against Australia and Neil Harvey made a supreme effort of 92 not out for his side.

The match was a triumph for pace bowlers and in particular for Tyson and Statham. Many people feared that Tyson had been seriously hurt when, batting just before lunch on the fourth day, he turned his back on a bouncer from Lindwall and it struck him on the back of the head. Temporarily, Tyson was knocked out but not only did he resume his innings but the next day he knocked out Australia, taking six wickets for 85 runs.

Tyson won the match for England because he kept his head. After his painful experience he might well have been tempted to hurl down bouncers, particularly at Lindwall, but he never did so. Possibly Lindwall expected retaliation, for Tyson yorked him as he did Burke and Hole in the same innings. The cricket at this vital stage emphasised that, above everything else in bowling, perfect length and direction win matches.

Both teams made changes compared with the first Test at Brisbane. England brought in Evans, Graveney, Wardle and Appleyard for Andrew, Compton, Simpson and Bedser, while Australia had Burke and Davidson for Ian Johnson and Miller, both injured. The omission of Bedser from the twelve on the morning of the match created a controversy, but subsequent events justified the introduction of both Appleyard and Wardle who brought variety to the attack.

Yet in this match the seam bowlers of both teams controlled the play; in fact Morris achieved what Hutton, the England captain, hoped but failed to accomplish at Brisbane, England being dismissed in four and a quarter hours. Hutton stayed two hours but the promotion of Bailey was a failure and it was not repeated in subsequent Tests.

Lindwall, rarely bowling short and swinging the ball either way while aiming persistently at the stumps, kept the hesitant opposition on tenterhooks, and Archer, Johnston and Davidson were equally menacing. The fielding, as usual, reached the best Australian traditions with Davidson outstanding. The loss of Bailey and May for 19 put Hutton completely on the defensive and in ninety minutes before lunch England mustered only 34 runs. Between lunch and tea came a dreadful collapse, five wickets falling for 60, and as Cowdrey and Appleyard soon went on resuming, nine men were out for 111. Then two left-handers, Wardle and Statham, struck heartily at almost every ball and their partnership of 43 was the best of the innings.

The only enjoyable moment that day for England came with the last ball when Hutton at leg-slip caught his rival captain, Morris, leaving Australia 18 for one wicket. Next day the bowlers recovered much of the ground lost by the batsmen. At first Favell and Burke made speedy progress, paying little respect to Bailey and Statham, but on Bailey changing ends and sharing the attack with Tyson the tempo changed. Graveney held Favell at second slip, so that at lunch Australia were 88 for two wickets—and quite comfortable.

Bailey continued to bowl splendidly and with Tyson causing much trouble Australia were not only put on the defensive but in one hour fifty minutes between lunch and tea they lost four more men for the addition of 70. A daring and lucky effort by Archer saved Australia. Although constantly missing when trying to cut Tyson and more than once fortunate not to be bowled, Archer pulled Appleyard for 6 and hit six 4's, his stand of 52 in an hour with Davidson being the best of the match for Australia whose first innings occupied just over five hours.

England, having restricted their deficit to 74, went in again first thing on Monday, but at the lunch interval with Hutton, Bailey and Graveney gone for 58, it seemed that Australia might win without any serious challenge. Happily, May, who began his innings just after midday, found a worthy partner in Cowdrey and their fourth wicket stand of 116 in three and a quarter hours altered the structure of the match.

It was most heartening to see these two young amateurs, one from Oxford and the other from Cambridge, master the Australian bowling by their sureness in defence and their willingness to hit the half-volley or any loose ball. Seldom were they beaten and never did they offer the semblance of a chance until Cowdrey, trying to hit himself out of a quiet spell, attempted to drive Benaud for 6 when there were two men waiting in the deep. Powerful cover drives and hard hits to leg brought Cowdrey most of his runs. May used a wide range of strokes and compelled Morris to remove his array of leg fielders behind the wicket. His punishing strokes were beautifully timed.

With twenty-five minutes remaining before the close Edrich and May took the total to 204 for five, and May needed only two for his hundred, but Australia had the right to the new ball first thing in the morning.

Because of the wet state of the outfield Morris delayed claiming the second new ball, but May having completed his century from the second ball of the day added only three more runs in the next fifty minutes. Then at 222 Lindwall and Archer went into action with the new ball and immediately the bowlers took charge so that the position changed to 250 for nine.

May, who hit ten 4's in a stay of five hours, was bowled when playing forward to a late inswinger and in twelve overs on this fourth day Lindwall claimed three wickets for 20 runs. Wardle could not repeat his first innings performance, but the last pair, Appleyard and Statham, faced the situation calmly and, unafraid to play forward to the well-pitched up ball, they added 46 runs in fifty minutes—another invaluable late stand.

Australia wanted 223 for victory, not an unreasonable task, but at once Statham and Tyson, with more pace than Lindwall, made the ball fly nastily.

In Statham's first over Edrich could not hold a hot chance from Favell. Statham gave Morris a terrible time, beating him four times in the last over before tea and removing him leg before with the seventh ball.

The interval came within twenty-five minutes of the start of the innings, giving the two England bowlers time to rest. On resuming Tyson, with his sixth ball, beat Favell by sheer pace, Edrich taking a nice catch in front of his chest, and both the opening batsmen were out for 34. That was a great start, but Harvey, after a shaky beginning, settled down. Burke did not score for nearly an hour and the pair played through the last seventy-eight minutes, seeing the total to 72 for two at nightfall.

Australia now needed 151 more runs and first thing the odds were in their favour. Though much rain fell during the night, the ground was perfect and the protected pitch played with less fire than at any stage of the match, but it was never slow. Tyson struck in the second over of the day when he yorked both Burke and Hole. Hutton did not overtax either Tyson or Statham at this stage and Bailey and Appleyard entered the attack. In the Yorkshireman's second over, Benaud hooked a skier which Tyson held and half the wickets were down for 106.

At lunch the total stood at 118 for five; Harvey 51, Archer 5, and no one cared to hazard a guess as to the ultimate result. The match was resumed at twenty minutes to two and Statham and Tyson virtually clinched the issue in the next fifty minutes when they removed Archer, Davidson, Lindwall and Langley for only 27, making Australia 145 for nine.

For some time Harvey had played a lone hand and as his partners disappeared the more brilliant he became. When Johnston arrived he and Harvey held a mid-wicket conference and obviously they agreed that Harvey should have most of the strike. Harvey hit boldly, but never chanced anything when a defensive stroke was imperative.

Johnston made some queer strokes but he lasted thirty-seven minutes, playing only 16 of 80 balls sent down during a stand which added 39. He hit runs to long leg off the back-hand until at length he flicked a catch to Evans standing back. Harvey remained unbeaten, having played one of his finest innings for Australia. For four hours twenty minutes he faced England unflinchingly, hitting nine 4's.

While justice must be done to Tyson who bowled without relief for over ninety minutes down wind in that vital spell in which his figures were 7.4 overs, 1 maiden, 41 runs, 3 wickets, England could not have won without the valuable work Statham accomplished bowling into the wind for eighty-five minutes. With ten wickets for 130 runs in the match, Tyson was England's hero, and the whole of Hutton's party faced Christmas and the New Year in a new frame of mind—optimistic that their luck had changed and that the rubber could be won. Attendance 135,350. Receipts £19,485.

England

L. Hutton c Davidson b Johnston	30	— c Benaud b Johnston	28
T. E. Bailey b Lindwall	0	— c Langley b Archer	6
P. B. H. May c Johnston b Archer	5	— b Lindwall	104
T. W. Graveney c Favell b Johnston	21	— c Langley b Johnston	0
M. C. Cowdrey c Langley b Davidson	23	— c Archer b Benaud	54
W. J. Edrich c Benaud b Archer	10	— b Archer	29
F. H. Tyson b Lindwall	0	— b Lindwall	9
T. G. Evans c Langley b Archer	3	— c Lindwall b Archer	4
J. H. Wardle c Burke b Johnston	35	— lbw b Lindwall	8
R. Appleyard c Hole b Davidson	8	— not out	19
J. B. Statham not out	14	— c Langley b Johnston	25
L-b 5	5	L-b 6, n-b 4	10

1/14 2/19 3/58 4/63 5/84 6/85   154   1/18 2/55 3/55 4/171   296
7/88 8/99 9/111   5/222 6/232 7/239 8/249
                                                     9/250

Australia

A. R. Morris c Hutton b Bailey	12	—	lbw b Statham	10
L. Favell c Graveney b Bailey	26	—	c Edrich b Tyson	16
J. Burke c Graveney b Bailey	44	—	b Tyson	14
R. N. Harvey c Cowdrey b Tyson	12	—	not out	92
G. B. Hole b Tyson	12	—	b Tyson	0
R. Benaud lbw b Statham	20	—	c Tyson b Appleyard	15
R. G. Archer c Hutton b Tyson	49	—	b Tyson	8
A. K. Davidson b Statham	20	—	c Evans b Statham	0
R. R. Lindwall c Evans b Tyson	19	—	b Tyson	1
G. R. Langley b Bailey	5	—	b Statham	6
W. A. Johnston not out	0	—	c Evans b Tyson	12
B 5, l-b 2, n-b 2	9		L-b 7, n-b 3	10

1/18 2/65 3/100 4/104 5/122 6/141　　228
7/193 8/213 9/224

1/27 2/34 3/77 4/77　　184
5/106 6/122 7/127 8/136
9/145

Australia Bowling

	O.	M.	R.	W.		O.	M.	R.	W.
Lindwall	17	3	47	2	....	31	10	69	3
Archer	12	7	12	3	....	22	9	53	3
Davidson	12	3	34	2	....	13	2	52	0
Johnston	13	3	56	3	....	19.3	2	70	3
Benaud						19	3	42	1

England Bowling

	O.	M.	R.	W.		O.	M.	R.	W.
Statham	18	1	83	2	....	19	6	45	3
Bailey	17.4	3	59	4	....	6	0	21	0
Tyson	13	2	45	4	....	18.4	1	85	6
Appleyard	7	1	32	0	....	6	1	12	1
Wardle						4	2	11	0

Umpires: M. J. McInnes and R. Wright.

M.C.C. v. N.S.W. NORTHERN DISTRICTS XI

At Newcastle, December 27, 28, 29. M.C.C. won by nine wickets. Although three days were given to this match it did not rank as first-class, but the ability of the home side was far superior to some met in Tasmania and New Zealand. At one time the District side threatened to make a big total; they reached 171 for four. Then Wardle broke an enterprising stand of 86 between McDonald and Stephenson and he took the last six wickets for 11 runs. M.C.C. gave a joyous display against much capable bowling and keen fielding. Compton, in his first match since his Brisbane injury, confirmed that he was completely fit again and May in a dazzling exhibition hit his fourth century in consecutive matches. Superb driving was the feature of his 157 which included twenty-six 4's. The Districts batted more consistently the second time and a grand second day's cricket yielded 465 runs in five hours twenty minutes. Thanks to good bowling by Bedser and Appleyard M.C.C. completed a comfortable win soon after lunch the next day.

N.S.W. Northern Districts XI

A. Dews c Bedser b Loader	21	— run out	27
K. Hill c Evans b Loader	6	— b Appleyard	28
R. Harvey c McConnon b Bedser	41	— b Bedser	36
R. Wotton b Appleyard	13	— b Bedser	52
R. McDonald c Evans b Wardle	63	— lbw b Appleyard	10
C. Stephenson c Evans b Wardle	30	— b Appleyard	3
J. Bull b Wardle	22	— c Graveney b Bedser	4
D. O'Connor b Wardle	0	— b Wardle	24
W. Wellham c Evans b Wardle	6	— c Loader b Appleyard	33
L. Fowler b Wardle	0	— b Appleyard	0
B. O'Sullivan not out	0	— not out	4
B 1, l-b 2, n-b 6	9	B 10, l-b 11, n-b 4	25

1/7 2/51 3/85 4/85 5/171 6/192   211
7/192 8/200 9/200

1/57 2/73 3/145 4/161   246
5/166 6/171 7/177 8/228
9/237

M.C.C.

W. J. Edrich c O'Connor b Bull	3		
J. E. McConnon c Fowler b O'Sullivan	43	— not out	4
T. W. Graveney b Bull	2		
D. C. S. Compton st O'Connor b O'Sullivan	60		
J. V. Wilson c and b O'Sullivan	3	— not out	14
P. B. H. May c Bull b McDonald	157		
T. G. Evans b Bull	69	— b Fowler	2
J. H. Wardle b Bull	29		
A. V. Bedser c Stephenson b Bull	33		
R. Appleyard not out	9		
P. J. Loader c Harvey b O'Sullivan	21		
B 5, l-b 2, n-b 2	9		

1/4 2/16 3/101 4/104 5/125 6/243   438   1/4   (1 wkt.) 20
7/290 8/392 9/409

M.C.C. Bowling

	O.	M.	R.	W.		O.	M.	R.	W.
Bedser	10	0	37	1	....	13	1	49	3
Loader	12	0	56	2	....	5	0	18	0
Appleyard	12	2	44	1	....	19.2	2	59	5
Wardle	10.2	1	36	6	....	14	1	73	1
McConnon	5	0	29	0	....	3	0	22	0

N.S.W. Northern Districts XI Bowling

	O.	M.	R.	W.		O.	M.	R.	W.
Bull	21	5	80	5					
Wellham	15	1	90	0					
O'Sullivan	20.4	4	107	4					
Hill	5	0	44	0					
Fowler	13	0	81	0	....	2.5	0	16	1
McDonald	3	0	27	1					
Dews						2	0	4	0

Umpires: T. Locker and J. Sandeman.

ENGLAND v. AUSTRALIA
Third Test Match

At Melbourne, December 31, January 1, 3, 4, 5.   England won by 128 runs at nineteen minutes past one on the fifth day with a day to spare.   As in the previous Test, the combined speed of Tyson and Statham proved too much for Australia and again the two young amateur batsmen, Cowdrey (102) and May (91), carried the England batting on a sporting pitch which was said to have been "doctored" on the Sunday.   Certainly large cracks were evident on Saturday yet on Monday these had closed and for a time the surface behaved more kindly to batsmen.   The Victorian Cricket Association and the Melbourne Cricket Club held an inquiry into a report published in *The Age* alleging watering and issued the following statement:

"After a searching inquiry it is emphatically denied that the pitch or any part of the cricket ground has been watered since the commencement of the third Test match on Friday, December 31."

With Compton fit England had their strongest side (Bedser again being omitted) and Australia welcomed back Ian Johnson, their captain, and Miller, but Langley, the wicket-keeper, stood down through injury which gave Maddocks his opportunity to make his debut in Test cricket.

This time Hutton, winning the toss, decided to bat, but apart from Cowdrey, Evans and Bailey England made a sorry show.   Cowdrey went in when Edrich and May had fallen for 21 and soon he saw Hutton and Compton follow, these four wickets going down in less than an hour for 41.

Then another defiant amateur, Bailey, joined Cowdrey and they checked the Australian bowlers for two hours, adding 74, following which there came a Kent partnership by Cowdrey and Evans that produced 54, before the last four wickets fell for 22.   For four hours Cowdrey batted without mistake, getting his body and bat behind short rising balls which Lindwall and Miller were able to bowl off this pitch almost at will.   Cowdrey specialised in perfectly-timed drives, both straight and to cover, and he forced the ball skilfully off his legs.

Miller bowled magnificently throughout the ninety minutes before lunch when his figures were 9 overs, 8 maidens, 5 runs, 3 wickets.   There were only two scoring strokes against him, a cover drive for 3 by Compton and one for 2 by Cowdrey.   As Miller's knee was still suspect Johnson later preferred to conserve his energy for batting.   Hutton, troubled by a heavy cold, decided only at the last minute to play.

So England faced the second day knowing that yet again the bowlers must rescue them from a crisis, and thanks to Tyson and Statham ably assisted by Bailey and Appleyard the first eight Australian wickets fell for 151.   Hutton used his bowlers in short spells, for the heat was stifling.   As Compton could not field, having bruised his thumb when he fell to a bouncer, Wilson acted as substitute, excelling in the leg trap.

Maddocks, who had kept wicket neatly and efficiently, rallied Australia.   Arriving when six men had gone for 115 he saw the total to 188 for eight at the close, having made 36 in two and a quarter hours.   Maddocks batted another half-hour making top score, 47.   He and Johnson added 54 and with Johnson lasting altogether two hours Australia gained a lead of 40, their last four wickets adding 116 against England's 22.

It was essential that the early England batsmen did not let down their side a second time and the arrears were cleared before a turning ball across the wicket took Edrich's off stump.   So at eight minutes to three May joined Hutton and proceeded to play masterly cricket in which the straight drive predominated.   There was always the possibility that he might be trapped by a "creeper," but May watched the ball intently.   At 96 he saw Hutton fall to one which moved fast and low from outside the off stump.   The captain had served his side well by remaining nearly two and a half hours and giving a fine example of watchfulness and concentration.   With May in such form, Cowdrey preferred to take the defensive, but soon he played on, England being 159 for three at the close; May 83, Compton 10.

On the fourth day May soon left having batted three hours twenty minutes and hit eight 4's.   Bailey defended for two and three-quarter hours but Evans and Wardle hit gaily, Wardle taking 16 in one over from Johnston and 14 from the next by Johnson.   Actually Wardle hit 38 out of 46 in forty minutes, but this time the rest of the tail failed so that Australia were left to make 240 to win.

A superb right-hand catch by Cowdrey at forward short-leg when he disposed of Morris brought England their first success at 23, but in order to keep Miller fresh, Benaud came next and both he and Favell exercised great care until Appleyard yorked Favell. Nearly half an hour remained that day and Benaud (19) and Harvey (9) raised the total to 79 for two.

This meant that Australia still required 165, a task that seemed far from impossible. The pitch was worn and the experts predicted that England must look to Appleyard, pointing out that the conditions were made for his off spin, and probably they were right, but Tyson and Statham saw England home without Hutton having to look elsewhere for any bowling.

Sheer speed through the air coupled with the chance of a shooter at any moment left the Australian batsmen nonplussed. Tyson blazed through them like a bush fire. In seventy-nine minutes the match was all over, the eight remaining wickets crashing for 36 runs. Here are the bowling figures:

Tyson   6.3 overs, 0 maidens, 16 runs, 6 wickets.
Statham   6 overs, 1 maiden, 19 runs, 2 wickets.

A wonderful leg-side catch by Evans when Harvey glanced the seventh ball of the day heralded the collapse. The loss of Harvey was a terrible blow to Australia and with Benaud hooking too soon and Edrich catching Miller at slip from a ball which lifted, Tyson claimed three wickets in 21 balls in the first half-hour.

Then Statham accounted for Hole, who flashed; Maddocks played on to Tyson and in the same over Lindwall went to drive a half-volley which shot under his bat. Next Statham bowled Archer with a fast full toss and finally Evans took his third catch, this time from Johnston high with the left hand, Australia being all out in three hours and five minutes.

The full attendance for the match was 300,270. The receipts, £A47,933, were a record for any Australian match.

England

L. Hutton c Hole b Miller	12	—	lbw b Archer	42
W. J. Edrich c Lindwall b Miller	4	—	b Johnston	13
P. B. H. May c Benaud b Lindwall	0	—	b Johnston	91
M. C. Cowdrey b Johnson	102	—	b Benaud	7
D. C. S. Compton c Harvey b Miller	4	—	c Maddocks b Archer	23
T. E. Bailey c Maddocks b Johnston	30	—	not out	24
T. G. Evans lbw b Archer	20	—	c Maddocks b Miller	22
J. H. Wardle b Archer	0	—	b Johnson	38
F. H. Tyson b Archer	6	—	c Harvey b Johnston	6
J. B. Statham b Archer	3	—	c Favell b Johnston	0
R. Appleyard not out	1	—	b Johnston	6
B 9	9		B 2, l-b 4, w 1	7
	191			**279**

1/14 2/21 3/29 4/41 5/115 6/169   191
7/181 8/181 9/190

1/40 2/96 3/128 4/173   279
5/185 6/211 7/257 8/273
9/273

Australia

L. Favell lbw b Statham	25	—	b Appleyard	30
A. R. Morris lbw b Tyson	3	—	c Cowdrey b Tyson	4
K. R. Miller c Evans b Statham	7	—	c Edrich b Tyson	6
R. N. Harvey b Appleyard	31	—	c Evans b Tyson	11
G. B. Hole b Tyson	11	—	c Evans b Statham	5
R. Benaud c sub b Appleyard	15	—	b Tyson	22
R. G. Archer b Wardle	23	—	b Statham	15
L. Maddocks c Evans b Statham	47	—	b Tyson	0
R. R. Lindwall b Statham	13	—	lbw b Tyson	0
I. W. Johnson not out	33	—	not out	4
W. A. Johnston b Statham	11	—	c Evans b Tyson	0
B 7, l-b 3, n-b 2	12		B 1, l-b 13	14
	231			**111**

1/15 2/38 3/43 4/65 5/92 6/115   231
7/134 8/151 9/205

1/23 2/57 3/77 4/86 5/87   111
6/97 7/98 8/98 9/110

Australia Bowling

	O.	M.	R.	W.		O.	M.	R.	W.
Lindwall	13	0	59	1	....	18	3	52	0
Miller	11	8	14	3	....	18	6	35	1
Archer	13.6	4	33	4	....	24	7	50	2
Benaud	7	0	30	0	....	8	2	25	1
Johnston	12	6	26	1	....	24.5	2	85	5
Johnson	11	3	20	1	....	8	2	25	1

England Bowling

	O.	M.	R.	W.		O.	M.	R.	W.
Tyson	21	2	68	2	....	12.3	1	27	7
Statham	16.3	0	60	5	....	11	1	38	2
Bailey	9	1	33	0	....	3	0	14	0
Appleyard	11	3	38	2	....	4	1	17	1
Wardle	6	0	20	1	....	1	0	1	0

Umpires: M. J. McInnes and C. Hoy.

M.C.C. v. COMBINED XI

At Hobart, January 8, 10, 11. Drawn. The game attracted 20,783 people, the best attendance for any first-class game in Tasmania, and although they saw some excellent bowling and catching the batting of both teams was mostly colourless. Four Test players, Favell, Neil Harvey, Benaud and Davidson, helped the locals who had six left-handed batsmen: Smith, Thomas, Harvey, Davidson, Brownlow and Cowley. Harvey provided one exception, for he always sought runs and made his 82 in two hours, but Rodwell, the local captain, spent seventy minutes reaching double figures before finding freedom against Bedser, Loader and Bailey who swung the ball awkwardly. M.C.C. needed five and a half hours to equal their opponents 221 and only a late stand of 40 between Andrew and Bedser saw them in front. Again Harvey hit well and Benaud showed better form than in the Tests, but by the time Rodwell declared a stalemate seemed certain. M.C.C. wanted 164 in an hour and forty minutes and when Andrew opened the innings with Simpson everyone knew the task would not be attempted. On the last day, McConnon, fielding a hard drive from Harvey, received a fracture of the little finger of the right hand. As medical opinion considered he would not be fit until the last two weeks in New Zealand he was advised to return home.

Combined XI

L. Favell c McConnon b Bedser	0	— b Loader	9
L. Smith c Andrew b Loader	21	— c Bedser b McConnon	17
M. Thomas c Graveney b Loader	6	— b Loader	6
R. N. Harvey b Bailey	82	— b Bedser	47
R. Benaud b Bailey	13	— not out	68
E. Rodwell c Bailey b Bedser	70	— b Bailey	17
A. K. Davidson c Graveney b Bedser	5	— c Simpson b Bailey	7
B. Brownlow c Andrew b Bailey	0	— not out	0
T. Cowley c Wardle b Loader	12		
W. Hird not out	4		
B. Considine c Wilson b Loader	5		
B 2, l-b 1	3	B 10, l-b 2, n-b 1	13

1/0 2/15 3/46 4/72 5/132 6/140   221   1/21 2/30   (6 wkts., dec.) 184
7/146 8/200 9/216   3/64 4/100 5/159 6/182

M.C.C.

L. Hutton c Hird b Cowley	15				
R. T. Simpson c Smith b Cowley	28	— not out			37
T. W. Graveney c Brownlow b Davidson	7	— lbw b Hird			26
D. C. S. Compton c Favell b Davidson	46				
J. V. Wilson c Favell b Considine	3	— not out			33
T. E. Bailey c Benaud b Davidson	53				
J. E. McConnon c Davidson b Benaud	22				
J. H. Wardle lbw b Hird	9				
K. V. Andrew not out	28	— b Cowley			1
A. V. Bedser b Benaud	19				
P. J. Loader b Davidson	1				
B 5, l-b 1, n-b 5	11	L-b 2			2

1/46 2/46 3/63 4/77 5/114 6/147   242   1/2 2/53   (2 wkts.)   99
7/167 8/199 9/239

M.C.C. Bowling

	O.	M.	R.	W.		O.	M.	R.	W.
Bedser	15	3	56	3	....	13	0	42	1
Loader	16.2	1	81	4	....	8	2	21	2
Wardle	9	3	26	0	....	11	3	38	0
Bailey	8	0	29	3	....	6	0	19	2
McConnon	7	2	26	0	....	8	1	38	1
Wilson						2	0	13	0

Combined XI Bowling

	O.	M.	R.	W.		O.	M.	R.	W.
Considine	19	1	54	1	....	4	1	12	0
Cowley	17	5	36	2	....	5	0	25	1
Davidson	18.5	2	45	4	....	5	0	10	0
Benaud	19	0	79	2					
Hird	8	2	17	1	....	7	1	31	1
Favell						2	0	14	0
Rodwell						1	0	5	0

Umpires: H. Uhr-Henry and R. Miller

M.C.C. v. TASMANIA

At Launceston, January 13, 14, 15. M.C.C. won by 243 runs. Hutton timed everything so well in this one-sided match that he provided an exciting finish for the spectators who saw Wardle take the final wicket with fifteen minutes to spare. Graveney thrived on fielding errors in hitting his first hundred of the tour. He shared three-figure stands with Hutton and Compton; for sheer mastery and execution of strokes Compton stood alone. Loader's inswing and pace were too much for the opposition, but in order to ensure plenty of cricket on the last day (Saturday) M.C.C., although leading by 310, did not enforce the follow-on. They declared at lunch time and Tasmania did reasonably well while Hutton did not call on his front-line bowlers. Hyland and Maddox put on 60 in half an hour, mainly at the expense of Compton and Cowdrey, but as soon as pressure was exerted the last seven wickets went for 98.

M.C.C.

L. Hutton lbw b Considine	61	— not out	21
R. T. Simpson c Cowley b Considine	4	— c and b Cowley	18
T. W. Graveney c Smith b Diprose	134		
D. C. S. Compton c Rodwell b Considine	50	— b Diprose	20
M. C. Cowdrey b Diprose	27	— c Richarson b Cowley	11
J. V. Wilson not out	62	— b Cowley	9
J. H. Wardle c Brownlow b Diprose	63	— not out	12
F. H. Tyson c Brownlow b Diprose	15	— c Hyland b Cowley	27
R. Appleyard not out	1	— c Richardson b Diprose	14
B 5, l-b 3, n-b 2	10	B 1	1

1/11 2/138 3/242 4/276   (7 wkts., dec.) 427
5/281 6/393 7/413

1/21 2/57   (6 wkts., dec.) 133
3/69 4/70 5/93 6/114

K. V. Andrew and P. J. Loader did not bat.

Tasmania

M. Thomas c Andrew b Loader	17	— st Andrew b Wilson	10
L. Smith lbw b Loader	6	— c Andrew b Cowdrey	18
M. Hyland lbw b Appleyard	18	— c Wilson b Loader	49
J. Maddox b Wardle	19	— not out	62
E. Rodwell b Wardle	11	— b Tyson	13
B. Richardson b Wardle	22	— c Appleyard b Tyson	0
B. Brownlow b Compton	3	— c Compton b Wardle	11
T. Cowley c Simpson b Loader	12	— c and b Wardle	10
W. Hird not out	6	— b Wardle	19
N. Diprose b Loader	0	— b Compton	5
B. Considine c and b Loader	1	— b Wardle	1
B 1, l-b 1	2	L-b 2	2

1/19 2/24 3/52 4/71 5/78 6/100   117
7/106 8/111 9/115

1/13 2/42 3/102 4/126   200
5/126 6/147 7/161 8/192
9/199

Tasmania Bowling

	O.	M.	R.	W.	O.	M.	R.	W.
Considine	20	0	93	3				
Cowley	19	1	84	0	15	2	53	4
Hird	22	1	94	0	9	0	34	0
Diprose	27	2	107	4	13	1	45	2
Richardson	6	0	39	0				

M.C.C. Bowling

	O.	M.	R.	W.	O.	M.	R.	W.
Tyson	9	0	22	0	6	1	20	2
Loader	12	3	22	6	10	1	34	1
Wardle	9	2	29	2	13.1	2	37	4
Wilson	3	0	6	0	1	0	1	1
Appleyard	6	0	15	1	4	2	6	0
Compton	4	0	21	1	11	1	75	1
					Cowdrey	4	0	25	1

Umpires: M. Blakeney and R. Harrison.

M.C.C. v. SOUTH AUSTRALIAN COUNTRY XI

At Mount Gambier, January 18, 19. M.C.C. won by an innings and 177 runs. This was a fine performance which delighted the local inhabitants who were celebrating their town achieving city status. The early M.C.C. batsmen scored so freely on an easy-paced pitch that the side needed only four hours to make 328. Statham took a wicket in his first over, but Bennett and Hanna played through the last seventy minutes, both shaping soundly. On the second and last day nineteen wickets fell for 111 runs, seventeen of them shared by Statham, Bedser and Appleyard in just over four hours. Bennett carried his bat in the follow-on, but perhaps he was fortunate to keep away from Statham who, in a devastating spell beginning at 27 for three wickets, took six wickets all clean bowled without conceding a run. So despite the loss of forty minutes first thing in the morning M.C.C. completed the match with twenty minutes to spare.

M.C.C.

W. J. Edrich c Eaton b Gwynne....	22	A. V. Bedser not out	18
R. T. Simpson c Gross b Pengilley	68	J. B. Statham b Darling..........	23
P. B. H. May c Gwynne b Beare...	62	R. Appleyard b Darling..........	5
T. W. Graveney c Darling b Beare.	44		
D. C. S. Compton b Darling......	53	B 12, l-b 6	18
T. E. Bailey lbw b Gross	0		—
T. G. Evans b Gross	15	1/60 2/119 3/197 4/214 5/215	328
F. H. Tyson b Gross	0	6/234 7/234 8/280 9/322	

South Australian Country XI

G. Fuller b Statham	5	— b Bedser	0
H. Bennett b Bailey	25	— not out	14
K. Hanna lbw b Bedser	34	— lbw b Bedser	2
J. Milnes b Statham	1	— b Bedser	0
P. Eaton c Evans b Appleyard	2	— b Statham..................	15
J. Gwynne b Appleyard	1	— b Statham..................	0
L. Curtis not out	20	— b Statham..................	0
M. Darling lbw b Appleyard	0	— b Statham..................	0
L. Beare c Statham b Appleyard	4	— b Statham..................	0
W. Pengilley c Evans b Appleyard	0	— b Statham..................	0
G. Gross c Graveney b Appleyard	6	— lbw b Bailey	14
B 7, l-b 1	8		—

1/8 2/52 3/59 4/70 5/75 6/78 7/80	106	1/0 2/2 3/2 4/27 5/27	45
8/88 9/88		6/26 7/27 8/31 9/31	

South Australian Country XI Bowling

	O.	M.	R.	W.	O.	M.	R.	W.
Beare	9	0	64	2				
Gross	8	0	31	3				
Curtis	7	1	44	0				
Gwynne	10	0	47	1				
Darling	13.4	0	55	3				
Pengilley	11	0	69	1				

M.C.C. Bowling

	O.	M.	R.	W.		O.	M.	R.	W.
Tyson	3	0	10	0	....	6	1	16	0
Statham	8	3	16	2	..	4	3	3	6
Bedser	11	1	22	1	....	6	1	11	3
Appleyard	12.2	4	26	6	....	7	4	8	0
Compton	1	0	9	0					
Bailey	8	2	15	1	....	1.3	0	7	1

Umpires: A. Tye and R. Marks.

M.C.C. v. SOUTH AUSTRALIA

At Adelaide, January 21, 22, 24. M.C.C. won by an innings and 143 runs with a day to spare. It was the heaviest defeat M.C.C. had inflicted on this State for 43 years, the 1911–12 team having won there by an innings and 194. The only blemish in the display was the shoddy fielding which came as a disappointment after many recent improved displays. Only Ridings, the State captain, and Langley, left out of the Test side, gave M.C.C. much trouble and when in turn the Englishmen lost four wickets for 91 a close fight appeared possible, but the three Test players, Cowdrey, Compton and May, completely changed the outlook, all making their strokes with the utmost confidence. Compton, with eighteen 4's, played the highest individual innings of the tour in four and three-quarter hours and the total of 451 was the M.C.C.'s best of the whole tour. The stand of 234 in three hours by Compton and May equalled the highest of the tour between Compton and Simpson against Queensland. The Surrey seam bowlers, Bedser and Loader, were responsible for half the South Australian wickets falling for 29, and although Wardle came in for punishment while Ridings and Trowse added 67, Loader returned and broke the stand before finishing the match with Wardle.

South Australia

L. Favell c Andrew b Bedser	1	— c Cowdrey b Bedser	11
N. Dansie b Appleyard	29	— c Appleyard b Bedser	2
C. Pinch c Edrich b Bedser	1	— run out	4
G. B. Hole c Wilson b Loader	2	— c Graveney b Loader	40
P. L. Ridings c May b Loader	40	— not out	40
D. Trowse lbw b Appleyard	21	— lbw b Loader	32
G. R. Langley b Wardle	53	— c Andrew b Bedser	5
J. Osborn c Compton b Loader	1	— b Loader	0
K. Horsnell b Wardle	23	— b Wardle	1
J. Wilson b Wardle	6	— lbw b Wardle	2
J. Gregg not out	2	— b Loader	4
B 1, l-b 2, n-b 3	6	B 5, l-b 7, w 1, n-b 8	21
	185		123

1/4 2/13 3/18 4/38 5/80 6/117   1/13 2/17 3/18 4/22 5/29
7/120 8/160 9/172   6/96 7/96 8/108 9/118

M.C.C.

W. J. Edrich b Gregg	14	K. V. Andrew not out	6
T. W. Graveney c Favell b Gregg	21	R. Appleyard c Langley b Horsnell	1
J. V. Wilson lbw b Wilson	22	P. J. Loader c Pinch b Gregg	10
J. H. Wardle c Langley b Gregg	7		
M. C. Cowdrey b Wilson	64	B 1, l-b 4, w 3, n-b 2	10
D. C. S. Compton c Favell b Wilson	182		
P. B. H. May b Horsnell	114	1/35 2/40 3/55 4/91 5/183	451
A. V. Bedser c Langley b Harsnell	0	6/417 7/419 8/436 9/440	

M.C.C. Bowling

	O.	M.	R.	W.	O.	M.	R.	W.
Bedser	14	2	41	2	11	3	20	3
Loader	14	1	52	3	13	2	32	4
Appleyard	17	6	50	2	4	2	13	0
Wardle	16.5	5	36	3	17	6	37	2

South Australia Bowling

	O.	M.	R.	W.
Gregg	26.3	0	117	4
Horsnell	23	2	88	3
Wilson	30	7	78	3
Osborn	15	0	87	0
Dansie	7	0	35	0
Hole	7	1	36	0

Umpires: K. C. Butler and J. M. Kierse.

ENGLAND v. AUSTRALIA
Fourth Test Match

At Adelaide, January 28, 29, 31, February 1, 2. England won by five wickets at twenty minutes past five on the fifth day, the first four Tests all being concluded with one day to spare. This victory gave England the rubber for the first time in Australia since 1932–33, and again the fast bowlers, Tyson and Statham, who were well supported by Bailey and Appleyard, played a major part. It was the only match of the series won by the side batting last.

While England were at full strength—they relied on the side which succeeded at Melbourne—Australia left out Hole and Favell and a leg injury in a State game caused Lindwall to withdraw. Originally Morris was also omitted but he replaced Lindwall in the chosen eleven to which Davidson was added. Favell, at first named to play, was dropped and McDonald and Burke completed the side. As Langley, the local wicket-keeper, was fit there was much indignation about Maddocks being retained, but the crowd gave him a great reception and he responded by making the top score for Australia.

With the temperature hovering near 100 degrees both sides wanted to win the toss; Ian Johnson was the lucky man and when the lunch interval arrived with Australia 51 for nought trouble seemed likely for England.

In each session Hutton used Tyson and Statham in short spells. When 12 Morris offered a low chance off Statham to Hutton's left hand, otherwise there was no encouragement for the bowlers on this placid pitch until after the interval. Then Tyson made one ball rise and it touched Morris's glove in transit to Evans; so Australia's first wicket fell after one hour and fifty minutes.

McDonald (43) received a life off Statham from Compton at mid-on and next over, trying to hit himself out of a negative spell, he was taken by May. Back came Tyson and he trapped Burke at short-leg, England going to tea satisfied with Australia 119 for three.

On resuming, Bailey put in a very fine effort from the Cathedral end while Tyson and Statham attacked in turn from the Torrens river end. Harvey edged Bailey to slip, but Benaud and Miller avoiding all risks remained together for the last seventy-five minutes taking the score to 161 for four—a very fine first day for England.

With the new ball coming later Hutton gave Tyson and Statham only two overs each the next morning and switching to Appleyard he made an unsuspected and wise change. The Yorkshire off-spinner took the wickets of Benaud and Miller in the course of only three overs. Archer greeted Wardle by pulling him for 6 first ball, and on taking the new ball England soon accounted for both Archer and Davidson, making Australia 229 for eight on a perfect pitch. Here Ian Johnson joined Maddocks and by sensible batsmanship they added 92 in as many minutes, though the stand should have ended at 270 when with both batsmen at the same end Appleyard at square-leg shied the ball high over Evans.

England wilted in the heat, Evans notably missing chances, and Statham was handicapped with a sore foot caused by the removal of a toe nail a few days before the match. Hutton and Edrich relieved the tension by making the best opening stand of the series. England waged a hard fight on the third day and thanks to Hutton, Cowdrey and Compton they reached 230 for three wickets at the close.

First thing, Australia struck two swift blows, dismissing Edrich and May. Johnson put down Edrich's off stump and Archer at first slip made a wonderful low right-hand catch. Already the pitch was favouring spin, but by cultured batting Hutton and Cowdrey added 99 before Hutton also fell to an amazing catch after batting four and a half hours for 80, the best score of the match. Hutton unerringly hooked a long hop and Davidson, only a few yards from the bat at forward short-leg, turned his back, shot out his hands to protect himself and the ball stayed. Although the new ball became due forty minutes before the end of the day Johnson preferred to rely on his spinners.

On the fourth day England continued with Cowdrey 77 and Compton 44 and at once Miller and Davidson struck with the new ball, both men falling for the addition of only two runs. Cowdrey batted five hours and Compton two, but happily for England Evans hit cleanly and impudently and some steady efforts by Wardle and as usual Bailey led to a first innings advantage of 18 by mid-afternoon, the innings altogether lasting nine hours.

Some Australians felt that England were playing for a draw which would have sufficed to ensure the retention of the Ashes. In any case the initiative rested with Australia, but England's objective was outright victory.

On Australia batting a second time, Hutton gave only two overs to Statham before introducing Appleyard at 24 and this move, hailed as a touch of genius, gave England the upper hand. Exploiting worn patches caused by bowlers' footmarks, Appleyard removed Morris, Burke and Harvey in his first six overs at a personal cost of six runs and he finished the day with these figures: 10 overs, 5 maidens, 13 runs, 3 wickets, Australia's score standing at 69 for three wickets.

On this evidence alone, most people reckoned Appleyard would be unplayable next day, yet again those two demon fast bowlers, Tyson and Statham, denied him his chance. Statham, freed from pain by having a hole cut in his left boot which allowed the injured toe to move freely, staggered Australia by removing McDonald, Miller and Maddocks in his first three overs of the day between which Tyson yorked Benaud. Subsequently, Tyson accounted for Archer and Johnston so that at lunch Australia were 103 for nine. Bowling unchanged for ninety minutes, Tyson and Statham had caused six wickets to fall for 34 runs and their analyses during this breath-taking period read: Statham 7—0—12—3; Tyson 7—1—17—3.

Appleyard did not get his opportunity until after the interval and then Wardle dismissed Davidson leg before. Davidson, who alone offered any resistance, batted for seventy-five minutes. One would emphasise that Tyson and Statham broke down the opposition without delivering one bouncer and as in the other successful Tests they were forced to rely on an orthodox field as England could not afford to give away runs.

England wanted only 94 and though no one sensed any real danger Miller provided shocks when in the course of bowling 20 balls he disposed of Edrich, Hutton and Cowdrey. Next he caught May brilliantly at cover, but Compton and Bailey were equal to the situation and saw England within four runs of their objective before Bailey was lbw. So those two old campaigners, Compton and Evans, were there at the finish, Evans making the winning hit.

After the match Hutton, reviewing the series, paid tribute to Statham, Tyson, Cowdrey, May and Evans and thanked the Australian crowds for their patience when the number of overs had been restricted during the day. "Fast bowlers must take time over their overs," he said, "and I feel that as youngsters they need my help in placing the field." Commenting on the success of the fast bowlers during the later stages of the Tests, Hutton said that whereas one would have expected the spinners to succeed the habit of the ball to come through on this tour at varying heights made the fast bowlers trickier to face.

The total attendance was 165,038; receipts £25,816.

Australia

C. C. McDonald c May b Appleyard....	48 — b Statham..........................	29
A. R. Morris c Evans b Tyson	25 — c and b Appleyard	16
J. Burke c May b Tyson	18 — b Appleyard	5
R. N. Harvey c Edrich b Bailey	25 — b Appleyard	7
K. R. Miller c Bailey b Appleyard	44 — b Statham.................	14
R. Benaud c May b Appleyard	15 — lbw b Tyson	1
L. Maddocks run out	69 — lbw b Statham	2
R. G. Archer c May b Tyson	21 — c Evans b Tyson..........	3
A. K. Davidson c Evans b Bailey	5 — lbw b Wardle	23
I. W. Johnson c Statham b Bailey	41 — not out	3
W. A. Johnston not out	0 — c Appleyard b Tyson	3
B 3, l-b 7, n-b 2	12 — B 4, l-b 1	5

1/59 2/86 3/115 4/129 5/175 6/182   323   1/24 2/40 3/54 4/69 5/76   111
7/212 8/229 9/321   6/77 7/79 8/83 9/101

England

L. Hutton c Davidson b Johnston	80	— c Davidson b Miller 5
W. J. Edrich b Johnson	21	— b Miller 0
P. B. H. May c Archer b Benaud	1	— c Miller b Johnston 26
M. C. Cowdrey c Maddocks b Davidson	79	— c Archer b Miller 4
D. C. S. Compton lbw b Miller	44	— not out 34
T. E. Bailey c Davidson b Johnston	38	— lbw b Johnston 15
T. G. Evans c Maddocks b Benaud	37	— not out 6
J. H. Wardle c and b Johnson	23	
F. H. Tyson c Burke b Benaud	1	
R. Appleyard not out	10	
J. B. Statham c Maddocks b Benaud	0	
B 1, l-b 2, n-b 4	7	B 3, l-b 4 7

1/60 2/63 3/162 4/232 5/232 6/283   341   1/3 2/10 3/18   (5 wkts.)   97
7/321 8/323 9/336   4/49 5/90

England Bowling

	O.	M.	R.	W.		O.	M.	R.	W.
Tyson	26.1	4	85	3	....	15	2	47	3
Statham	19	4	70	0	....	12	1	38	3
Bailey	12	3	39	3					
Appleyard	23	7	58	3	....	12	7	13	3
Wardle	19	5	59	0	....	4.2	1	8	1

Australia Bowling

	O.	M.	R.	W.		O.	M.	R.	W.
Miller	11	4	34	1	....	10.4	2	40	3
Archer	3	0	12	0	....	4	0	13	0
Johnson	36	17	46	2					
Davidson	25	8	55	1	....	2	0	7	0
Johnston	27	11	60	2	....	8	2	20	2
Benaud........	36.6	6	120	4	....	6	2	10	0
Burke	2	0	7	0					

Umpires: M. J. McInnes and R. Wright.

M.C.C. v. VICTORIA COUNTRY XI

At Yallourn, February 5, 7. M.C.C. won by an innings and 26 runs. For this match they included Geoffrey Howard, the manager, and though there were only three recognised bowlers they carried all before them. Neither in batting nor bowling could the opposition rise to the occasion. Hutton and Simpson, who made the best opening stand of the tour, and Graveney all enjoyed some batting practice and Wardle took twelve wickets for 91 runs.

Victoria Country XI

N. F. Chapman c Compton b Loader....	1	— c and b Wardle 18
R. R. Walker c Wilson b Loader	14	— absent hurt 0
W. Young b Loader	56	— b Wardle 4
C. H. Miles c Evans b Wilson	13	— st Evans b Wardle 1
R. Milne c Edrich b Wardle	26	— not out 25
J. G. Bath not out	29	— b Bedser 10
G. B. Tozer c Evans b Loader........	9	— b Wardle 0
R. T. Sagar lbw b Wardle	2	— st Evans b Wardle 3
R. H. Hollioake c Wilson b Wardle	1	— c and b Wardle 18
L. Baker st Evans b Wardle	15	— c Wardle b Compton 3
K. H. Grant b Wardle	0	— b Wardle 6
B 8, l-b 4, w 2, n-b 2	16	B 8, l-b 3 11

1/1 2/24 3/56 4/109 5/127 6/145   182   1/21 2/34 3/38 4/41   99
7/148 8/158 9/182   5/43 6/51 7/81 8/92 9/99

M.C.C.

L. Hutton c Miles b Tozer	75	J. H. Wardle run out 17
R. T. Simpson c and b Tozer	59	C. G. Howard not out 0
T. W. Graveney c Miles b Hollioake	50	A. V. Bedser not out 2
J. V. Wilson b Hollioake..........	17	B 5, l-b 3, w 2 10
D. C. S. Compton c Tozer b Bath..	24	
W. J. Edrich c Walker b Bath	36	1/137 2/144 3/178 (8 wkts., dec.) 307
T. G. Evans c Grant b Tozer	17	4/215 5/249 6/280 7/303 8/303

P. J. Loader did not bat.

M.C.C. Bowling

	O.	M.	R.	W.		O.	M.	R.	W.
Bedser	13	1	63	0	....	6	0	20	1
Loader	11	1	29	4	....	6	2	13	0
Wardle	16	5	46	5	....	8.5	3	45	7
Wilson	2	0	18	1					
Graveney	1	0	10	0					
Compton						3	0	10	1

Victoria Country XI Bowling

	O.	M.	R.	W.
Grant	12	0	78	0
Hollioake......	11	0	69	2
Tozer	15	0	75	3
Baker	8	1	48	0
Bath	5	0	27	2

Umpires: R. Oswald and G. Morgan.

M.C.C. v. VICTORIA

At Melbourne, February 11, 12, 14, 15. Drawn. M.C.C. ran into bad weather for the remainder of their stay in Australia. No play was possible on three of the four days in this match, making seven days lost in four engagements at Melbourne where only the Test was uninterrupted. After a blank first day, Loxton, in the absence of Ian Johnson, injured, led Victoria and he chose to bat, but grand bowling by Statham, Bailey and Appleyard who exploited the humidity brought about a collapse. Six wickets fell for 39 before Dick, wearing glasses, made the only stand with Loxton. Bailey fractured a finger of his right hand. Confident batting by Edrich, Simpson and May placed M.C.C. in a strong position by the close on Saturday and then severe downpours over the week-end which caused at least one death and dislocated the city's telephones left the ground under water.

Victoria

C. C. McDonald b Statham	10	A. Dick c Compton b Appleyard.. 41
R. Harvey c Graveney b Statham..	0	J. C. Hill c Wardle b Appleyard .. 0
R. N. Harvey b Bailey b Statham..	17	W. A. Johnston c Loader b Wardle 1
J. Shaw lbw b Bailey	9	J. Power not out 4
K. Kendall c Andrew b Bailey ...	1	B 1, l-b 2 3
S. J. Loxton c Statham b Apple-		
yard	27	1/3 2/26 3/33 4/34 5/39 6/39 113
L. Maddocks lbw b Bailey	0	7/92 8/92 9/109

M.C.C.

W. J. Edrich lbw b Johnston	23	N-b 1 1
R. T. Simpson not out	33	
P. B. H. May not out............	33	1/37 (1 wkt.) 90

J. B. Statham, P. J. Loader, T. E. Bailey, R. Appleyard, J. H. Wardle, T. W. Graveney, D. C. S. Compton, K. V. Andrew did not bat.

M.C.C. Bowling

	O.	M.	R.	W.
Statham	10	1	23	3
Loader	10	1	33	0
Bailey	10	4	22	3
Appleyard	6.1	2	14	3
Wardle	3	0	18	1

Victoria Bowling

	O.	M.	R.	W.
Power	5	0	22	0
Loxton	6	2	16	0
Johnston	5	1	9	1
Dick	6	0	22	0
Hill	3	0	20	0

Umpires: R. Hele and J. Ward.

M.C.C. v. NEW SOUTH WALES

At Sydney, February 18, 19, 21, 22. New South Wales won by 45 runs. The result provided a big surprise for several reasons. In the first place, owing to the effects of vacination for the West Indies tour, N.S.W. lost both their regular opening batsmen, Morris and Watson. When Miller, on winning the toss, decided to bat—he sent in M.C.C. in the first match—Bedser, Tyson and Loader used the new ball to such purpose that half their wickets fell for 26 before two young school-teachers, Philpott (20) and Booth (19), pressed into service at the last minute, played excellently. Four fine slip catches did much to earn Graveney a place in the final Test. M.C.C. also broke down, but Hutton, going in late, enabled them to tie on first innings. The third day went against M.C.C. They lost the help of Tyson, whose left leg was injured, and the depleted attack was mastered by Burke and Simpson whose stand realised 159. M.C.C. bowled and fielded in rain for some time before Hutton led his men off the field after receiving permission from the umpires, but the batsmen were not consulted. This caused trouble and on resuming Simpson, who wanted only two for his hundred at the break, made a wild stroke and was stumped. Possibly his concentration was disturbed and the crowd angrily barracked Hutton. Later Miller, who captained his side splendidly, hit freely with Benaud before declaring. On the last day, M.C.C. appeared to be making a close challenge, but Miller bowled May when his fourth-wicket stand with Hutton had yielded 77 and, several bowling changes meeting with early success, New South Wales gained a well-deserved win.

New South Wales

R. Briggs c Evans b Bedser	0	— b Tyson	0
J. Burke c Cowdrey b Bedser	0	— c Graveney b Wardle	62
R. Simpson c Graveney b Tyson	6	— st Evans b Wardle	98
R. Benaud c Wardle b Bedser	1	— st Evans b Wardle	57
K. R. Miller c Graveney b Loader	11	— c May b Bedser	71
P. Philpott st Evans b Bedser	46	— b Wardle	11
B. Booth not out	74	— c Evans b Bedser	0
A. K. Davidson c Graveney b Bedser	9	— c Cowdrey b Wardle	0
P. Crawford c Evans b Wilson	19	— not out	0
O. Lambert c Cowdrey b Wardle	1		
J. Treanor c Graveney b Wilson	0		
B 1, l-b 3, n-b 1	5	L-b 10, w 2, n-b 3	15

1/0 2/1 3/3 4/16 5/26 6/109 7/127   172

8/167 9/168

1/2 2/161   (8 wkts., dec.) 314

3/161 4/196 5/260 6/263

7/314 8/314

M.C.C.

R. T. Simpson c Briggs b Davidson	6	— c Davidson b Benaud	24
J. V. Wilson b Miller	0	— b Davidson	4
P. B. H. May c Lambert b Crawford	3	— b Miller	42
P. J. Loader b Davidson................	0	— c Benaud b Treanor	8
T. W. Graveney c Lambert b Davidson..	35	— lbw b Benaud	28
M. C. Cowdrey c Lambert b Davidson ..	12	— c Simpson b Booth	33
L. Hutton c Simpson b Treanor	48	— c Simpson b Burke	59
T. G. Evans b Crawford	40	— c Miller b Davidson	39
J. H. Wardle c Crawford b Treanor	16	— c Philpott b Treanor......	12
F. H. Tyson run out	3	— c Benaud b Treanor	0
A. V. Bedser not out	2	— not out	0
B 1, l-b 1, n-b 5	7	B 13, l-b 3, w 1, n-b 3 ..	20

1/1 2/4 3/10 4/13 5/35 6/94   172....1/36 2/63 3/68 4/145   269
7/135 8/153 9/157   5/189 6/222 7/250 8/261
                                          9/261

M.C.C. Bowling

	O.	M.	R.	W.		O.	M.	R.	W.
Bedser	19	3	57	5	....	22.2	4	87	2
Tyson	16	4	27	1	....	9	2	24	1
Loader	11	2	56	1	....	10	2	28	0
Wardle	8	2	26	1	....	25	0	118	5
Wilson	1.1	0	1	2	....	4	0	42	0

New South Wales Bowling

	O.	M.	R.	W.		O.	M.	R.	W.
Crawford	15	3	47	2	....	8	0	37	0
Miller	10	0	31	1	....	5	0	15	1
Davidson	12	3	25	4	....	13	1	43	2
Treanor	11	4	44	2	....	13.7	1	54	3
Benaud........	3	0	10	0	....	21	7	62	2
Philpott	1	0	8	0	....	6	2	22	0
					Burke	3	1	6	1
					Booth	2	0	10	1

Umpires: C. Wigzell and J. Bowden.

ENGLAND v. AUSTRALIA

Fifth Test Match

At Sydney, February 25, 26, 28, March 1, 2, 3. Drawn. Abnormal downpours, the worst experienced in New South Wales for fifty years, caused loss of life and millions of pounds of damage in the Hunter River valley and also held up play in this final Test until two o'clock on the fourth day. M.C.C.'s tour profits suffered to the extent of nearly £8,000. The delay gave time for Bailey (fractured finger), Cowdrey (tonsilitis following a broken nose while fielding in the Adelaide Test), Tyson (strained leg muscles) and Maddocks (bruised finger) to recover. Australia included Watson and Burge for the first time besides having Lindwall and Favell in the side again, and Graveney replaced Edrich in the England eleven.

Instead of thirty hours, playing time was reduced to thirteen hours ten minutes, Ian Johnson won the toss and preferred not to risk first innings on a rain-affected pitch, for the covers had been of little use in the deluge. As it happened the pitch gave not the slightest help to the bowlers. The ball came through at an easy pace and at a nice height. Hutton left to the fourth ball of the match, Burge catching him at the second attempt at leg-slip, but Graveney and May played glorious cricket, their stand realising 182 in two hours forty minutes before Graveney fell to a grand return catch. Magnificent drives were the feature of his superb innings. His first Test hundred against Australia contained fourteen 4's.

Cowdrey went first ball and in the last over May, taken at slip, was out after batting just over three hours so that England's total was 196 for four. Next day, Compton, already having spent twenty minutes without scoring, exercised much care with Bailey, but after lunch he treated the bowling with less respect, his last 62 runs coming in eighty minutes. The partnership yielded 134 and finally Evans and Bailey both fell to Lindwall who thus reached 100 wickets in Australia–England Tests, a unique feat for a fast bowler. Bailey actually allowed himself to be bowled and then he went down the pitch, being the first to congratulate Lindwall. Very slow and tedious early in the day, Bailey hit only four 4's and occupied three and a quarter hours for his 72.

The pitch was livelier than on the previous day and Australia were pleased to see their opening pair, McDonald and Watson, survive the first onslaught of Statham and Tyson, but Watson played on in Wardle's fourth over and Favell soon went in Tyson's second spell.

McDonald (45) and Harvey (12) saw the total to 82 for two at nightfall but on the last day only McDonald and Maddocks played with much confidence against the varied spin of Wardle. When Compton ran out Ian Johnson from cover, Australia failed by one run to avoid the follow-on. As less than two hours remained, a definite result was unlikely, but Hutton offered no respite, and although Tyson, to save time, cut down his run to six yards he employed five slips and two short legs and still looked very fast.

As in the first innings, Hutton used Wardle for long periods and again Australia broke down, leaving no doubt that besides being vulnerable to pace they were just as unsafe against the turning ball. England, so often criticised for loose fielding, gave almost nothing away on this their final appearance in Australia. Cowdrey ran out Miller smartly and Tyson, Appleyard, Graveney and Wardle brought off excellent catches.

It was the first time since Hutton's 364 at The Oval in 1938 that England had made Australia follow on. Watson, Favell and Harvey were out for 29, but McDonald again showed determination, so the outside chance of bringing off an unexpected victory vanished. Towards the end Hutton relaxed and called on Graveney to bowl. He dismissed McDonald in his second over and appropriately Hutton finished the tour of Australia by sending down the final over and getting the last wicket when he bowled Benaud.

During the day 14 Australian wickets fell for 257 runs and Wardle claimed seven of them in 29 overs for 115 runs. One could excuse him amusing the crowd by bowling his final over almost on his knees! The full attendance for the three days was 29,844; receipts £4,285.

England

L. Hutton c Burge b Lindwall	....	6
T. W. Graveney c and b Johnson	.	111
P. B. H. May c Davidson b Benaud		79
M. C. Cowdrey c Maddocks b Johnson		0
D. C. S. Compton c and b Johnson		84
T. E. Bailey b Lindwall	....	72

T. G. Evans c McDonald b Lindwall		10
J. H. Wardle not out	....	5
B 1, l-b 3	....	4
		—
	(7 wkts., dec.)	371

1/6 2/188 3/188 4/196 5/330 6/359 7/371

F. H. Tyson, R. Appleyard and J. B. Statham did not bat.

Australia

W. Watson b Wardle	18	— c Graveney b Statham	3
C. C. McDonald c May b Appleyard	72	— c Evans b Graveney	37
L. Favell b Tyson	1	— c Graveney b Wardle	9
R. N. Harvey c and b Tyson	13	— c and b Wardle	1
K. R. Miller run out	19	— b Wardle	28
P. Burge c Appleyard b Wardle	17	— not out	18
R. Benaud b Wardle	7	— b Hutton	22
L. Maddocks c Appleyard b Wardle	32		
A. K. Davidson c Evans b Wardle	18		
I. W. Johnson run out	11		
R. R. Lindwall not out	2		
B 10, l-b 1	11		

1/52 2/53 3/85 4/129 5/138 6/147   221   1/14 2/27 3/29   (6 wkts.) 118
7/157 8/202 9/217   4/67 5/87 6/118

Australia Bowling

	O.	M.	R.	W.	O.	M.	R.	W.
Lindwall	20.6	5	77	3				
Miller	15	1	71	0				
Davidson	19	3	72	0				
Johnson	20	5	68	3				
Benaud	20	4	79	1				

England Bowling

	O.	M.	R.	W.	O.	M.	R.	W.
Tyson	11	1	46	2	5	2	20	0
Statham	9	1	31	0	5	0	11	1
Appleyard	16	2	54	1				
Wardle	24.4	6	79	5	12	1	51	3
Graveney					6	0	34	1
Hutton					0.6	0	2	1

Umpires: M. J. McInnes and R. Wright.

M.C.C. v. CANTERBURY

At Christchurch, March 5, 7, 8. M.C.C. won by seven wickets. Another dazzling century by Graveney overshadowed everything else in this match after M.C.C. had dismissed Canterbury in just over three hours. Excelling with the drive, Graveney made his 101 out of 148 in ninety-five minutes, hitting one 6 and seventeen 4's. His first wicket stand with Hutton realised 97 in fifty-seven minutes, but later the Test bowlers, Hayes and Burtt, met with success before Tyson, who twice hooked Burtt for 6 and also hit nine 4's, helped himself to 62 in an hour, he and Statham adding 75 for the last wicket. Then Leggat defied M.C.C. for four and a half hours. When 98 he gave a simple chance to Wardle at short-leg but for all his luck and patience he missed a century through calling Guillen for an impossible single. Burtt, the left-arm slow bowler, finished his first-class career by hitting Wardle for 24 in one over, two 6's and three 4's. M.C.C. needed only 45 and play was extended for twenty-five minutes in order to finish the match before lunch.

Canterbury

J. G. Leggat b Wilson	22	—	run out	99
M. B. Poore c Andrew b Wardle	35	—	c May b Loader	21
M. E. Chapple b Tyson	6	—	c Wardle b Loader	4
P. G. Harris c Andrew b Statham	20	—	c and b Wardle	16
P. W. O'Malley lbw b Loader	12	—	lbw b Wardle	0
R. T. Dowker c May b Loader	12	—	c Andrew b Loader	8
S. C. Guillen st Andrew b Wardle	9	—	b Tyson	9
A. R. MacGibbon c and b Wardle	6	—	b Statham	1
T. B. Burtt b Wardle	6	—	not out	30
J. A. Hayes b Loader	0	—	b Statham	0
K. J. McNicholl not out	0	—	lbw b Statham	0
B 6, l-b 5, w 1	12		B 11, l-b 4, n-b 3	18
	140			206

1/60 2/70 3/71 4/102 5/116 6/127
7/127 8/138 9/140

1/67 2/73 3/114 4/114
5/127 6/169 7/173 8/178
9/182

M.C.C.

L. Hutton b Hayes	33			
T. W. Graveney b MacGibbon	101	—	not out	12
R. T. Simpson c Chapple b Hayes	22	—	not out	13
J. V. Wilson b MacGibbon	0	—	b Hayes	0
P. B. H. May b Burtt	31			
M. C. Cowdrey c Chapple b Hayes	0	—	lbw b MacGibbon	17
J. H. Wardle c McNicholl b Burtt	12			
K. V. Andrew st Guillen b Burtt	6	—	c Leggat b Hayes	2
P. J. Loader b Burtt	4			
F. H. Tyson not out	62			
J. B. Statham c Poore b McNicholl	21			
B 2, l-b 3, n-b 5	10		N-b 1	1
	302			45

1/97 2/148 3/156 4/182 5/184 6/205
7/205 8/210 9/227

1/0 2/17 3/19   (3 wkts.)   45

M.C.C. Bowling

	O.	M.	R.	W.		O.	M.	R.	W.
Statham	9	2	15	1	....	14.4	4	32	3
Tyson	8	2	26	1	....	9	1	22	1
Loader	11	1	34	3	....	23	8	26	3
Wardle	21.3	7	46	4	....	31	11	84	2
Graveney	3	1	3	0	....	6	2	10	0
Wilson	1	0	4	1	....	4	0	6	0
Cowdrey					....	2	0	8	0

Canterbury Bowling

	O.	M.	R.	W.		O.	M.	R.	W.
MacGibbon	12	4	36	2	....	4	0	31	1
McNicholl	13	0	90	1	....				
Hayes	18	2	55	3	....	5	1	12	2
Burtt	14	2	74	4	....	0.1	0	1	0
Poore	4	0	37	0					

Umpires: L. C. Johnston and B. Vine.

ENGLAND v. NEW ZEALAND
First Test Match

At Dunedin, March 11, 12, 14, 15, 16. England won by eight wickets, despite the loss of the third and fourth days through rain. In all respects excepting some sound left-handed batting by Sutcliffe, England were clearly superior. Although the conditions were not particularly favourable to bowlers, Hutton, winning the toss, sent in New Zealand who adopted a negative policy. Rabone, their captain, set the example by occupying three hours over 18. He persuaded Sutcliffe to copy him, but when the supply of partners was running short Sutcliffe adopted a more natural game. Playing through the innings of four and a half hours, Sutcliffe was last out having hit Bailey, Appleyard and Wardle each for 6.

England began their reply next day and with Graveney again in sparkling form they passed 50 in thirty-five minutes, whereupon Reid, MacGibbon and Cave bowled short of a length to a defensive field. England went ahead in two and a half hours. When bad light stopped play they held an advantage of 84 but rain set in and nothing more could be done before Wednesday.

Hutton declared first thing and this time Sutcliffe opened with Rabone, the score at lunch being 67 for one. Immediately after the interval a brilliant return by May from long-leg ran out Sutcliffe and between them Tyson, Appleyard and Wardle soon accounted for the remainder. There was a break of half an hour before England began their task of scoring 49 as Rabone claimed ten minutes between innings as well as twenty minutes for tea, but the quibble made no difference, England never being pressed for time.

New Zealand

G. O. Rabone st Evans b Wardle	18	— lbw b Wardle		7
M. E. Chapple b Statham	0	— b Statham		20
B. Sutcliffe c Statham b Bailey	74	— run out		35
J. R. Reid b Statham	4	— b Tyson		28
S. N. McGregor b Tyson	2	— c Cowdrey b Appleyard		8
L. A. Watt b Tyson	0	— b Appleyard		2
H. B. Cave b Tyson	1	— b Tyson		1
A. N. Moir b Statham	7	— lbw b Tyson		10
R. W. Blair b Statham	0	— b Wardle		3
A. R. MacGibbon c Evans b Bailey	7	— b Tyson		0
I. A. Colquhoun not out	0	— not out		1
B 5, l-b 4, n-b 3	12	B 7, l-b 10		17

1/3 2/63 3/68 4/72 5/76 6/86 7/103   125   1/24 2/68 3/75 4/96 5/98   132
8/113 9/122   6/103 7/103 8/123 9/126

England

L. Hutton c Colquhoun b Reid	11	— c Colquhoun b Blair		3
T. W. Graveney b Cave	41	— not out		32
P. B. H. May b MacGibbon	10	— b MacGibbon		13
M. C. Cowdrey lbw b Reid	42	— not out		0
R. T. Simpson b Cave	21			
T. E. Bailey lbw b Reid	0			
T. G. Evans b Reid	0			
J. H. Wardle not out	32			
F. H. Tyson c McGregor b MacGibbon	16			
R. Appleyard not out	0			
B 12, l-b 18, n-b 6	36	L-b 1		1

1/60 2/77 3/101 4/150   (8 wkts., dec.) 209   1/22 2/47   (2 wkts.) 49
5/152 6/152 7/156 8/208

J. B. Statham did not bat.

England Bowling

	O.	M.	R.	W.	O.	M.	R.	W.
Tyson	19	8	23	3	 12	6	16	4
Statham	17	9	24	4	 15	5	30	1
Bailey	12.2	6	19	2	 8	4	9	0
Wardle	26	15	31	1	.... 14.3	4	41	2
Appleyard	7	3	16	0	 7	2	19	2

New Zealand Bowling

	O.	M.	R.	W.	O.	M.	R.	W.
Blair	8	1	29	0	 4	0	20	1
MacGibbon....	24.5	11	39	2	.... 7.2	2	16	1
Reid	27	11	36	4	 4	2	12	0
Cave	24	15	27	2				
Moir	9	1	42	0				

Umpires: R. G. Currie and S. G. Tonkinson.

M.C.C. v. WELLINGTON

At Wellington, March 19, 21, 22. M.C.C. won by 187 runs. Another grand hundred by Graveney—his third in four consecutive matches—and accurate spin bowling by the two Yorkshiremen, Appleyard and Wardle, who took 18 of the Wellington wickets, gave the Englishmen another comfortable win. Again exquisite driving between cover and mid-on marked Graveney's stylish display, and with twelve 4's he made his 102 out of 152 in two and a half hours. Next highest scorer was May who occupied fifty minutes over 22. Wellington, winners of the Plunket Shield, looked a better team in the field than New Zealand. They were well led by Reid and the fielding approached almost the best Australian standard. Blair, dropped from the Test team, maintained a fast aggressive attack and Dempster showed himself a skilful left-arm slow bowler, but owing to business he was not available for either Test.

M.C.C.

R. T. Simpson b Blair	10	— b Reid	37
T. W. Graveney c Smith b Blair 102		— b Reid	35
W. J. Edrich c McMahon b Blair	2	— c McMahon b Morrison ...	17
M. C. Cowdrey c and b Dempster	19	— c McMahon b Morrison ...	29
J. V. Wilson lbw b Blair	13	— c Blair b Reid	17
P. B. H. May c Reid b Dempster	22	— lbw b Reid	41
T. E. Bailey b Morrison	15	— c McMahon b Smith	10
J. H. Wardle lbw b Morrison	4	— c Beck b Smith	2
T. G. Evans c and b Dempster	1	— b Reid	0
R. Appleyard not out	2	— run out	0
P. J. Loader c and b Miller b Reid	10	— not out	6
B 5, l-b 2	7	B 3, l-b 4	7

1/16 2/22 3/98 4/135 5/152 6/180   207   1/54 2/89 3/93 4/135   201
7/185 8/194 9/194   5/160 6/190 7/194 8/194
                                      9/194

Wellington

D. S. St. John c Evans b Loader	6	— lbw b Appleyard	18
K. F. H. Smith lbw b Wardle	9	— c Graveney b Appleyard	26
L. S. M. Miller b Appleyard	13	— b Wardle	6
P. T. Barton b Wardle	0	— st Evans b Wardle	0
J. R. Reid c Wilson b Appleyard	31	— b Appleyard	5
J. E. F. Beck c Graveney b Bailey	29	— b Appleyard	0
R. T. Barber b Wardle	20	— c Graveney b Appleyard	14
E. W. Dempster b Wardle	9	— st Evans b Wardle	3
T. G. McMahon b Appleyard	2	— b Wardle	4
R. W. Blair not out	0	— c Cowdrey b Appleyard	4
D. B. Morrison b Wardle	0	— not out	0
B 6, l-b 1, n-b 1	8	B 10, l-b 4	14

1/12 2/22 3/22 4/46 5/83 6/93   127
7/110 8/123 9/127

1/25 2/38 3/42 4/49 5/49   94
6/79 7/84 8/88 9/88

Wellington Bowling

	O.	M.	R.	W.		O.	M.	R.	W.
Blair	16	2	50	4	....	6	1	25	0
Morrison	16	4	67	2	....	16	2	63	2
Reid	23	7	51	1	....	20	4	65	5
Dempster	16	5	32	3	....	14	9	29	0
Smith					....	4.5	0	12	2

M.C.C. Bowling

	O.	M.	R.	W.		O.	M.	R.	W.
Loader	10	3	24	1	....	2	0	12	0
Bailey	14	5	17	1	....	1	0	1	0
Appleyard	20	7	36	3	....	21.4	13	21	6
Wardle	15.4	5	42	5	....	21	8	46	4

Umpires: J. McLellan and J. C. Clarke.

ENGLAND v. NEW ZEALAND
Second Test Match

At Auckland, March 25, 26, 28. England won by an innings and 20 runs with two days to spare. Hutton's team finished their triumphant tour by setting up a world record. They dismissed New Zealand in the second innings for 26, the lowest total in the history of Test cricket. The previous lowest score was 30, made twice by South Africa against England. The first was at Port Elizabeth in 1895–96 when George Lohmann took eight wickets for seven runs including the hat-trick. The second was at Edgbaston in 1924 when Tate and Gilligan routed South Africa, and Arthur Gilligan was in Auckland on this occasion when Appleyard for the second time in the match took two wickets with successive balls only to be denied the hat-trick.

After winning the toss, New Zealand were soon in trouble against Tyson, losing Leggat and Poore for 13, but Sutcliffe and Reid batted well in a stand of 63 before Sutcliffe, hooking a bouncer, was caught at mid-on. As at Dunedin, Rabone offered a dead bat for two and a half hours and his partnership of 78 in two and a quarter hours with Reid was the best of the match. Dismissing MacGibbon and Colquhoun with the last two balls of the day, Appleyard failed to trap Moir the next morning, but four balls from Statham sufficed to dispose of Moir and Hayes.

Instead of the ideal conditions of the first day, England were confronted with the task of batting on a pitch affected by heavy rain and in light that was dull for most of the day.   In addition, more rain which caused two breaks of half an hour left the outfield so heavy that rarely did the batsmen gain full value for their strokes. This was specially true in the case of May whose 48 in two hours included seven 3's.

England owed much to Hutton who, going in at number five, saw the total reach 148 for four at the end of the second day. Bailey stayed over two hours with his captain who proceeded to make the highest score of the match before being ninth out soon after lunch when MacGibbon took the new ball. Hutton batted three and a quarter hours. In a final stand Tyson and Statham added 28, two more than New Zealand were about to total.

Actually the issue appeared to be evenly balanced, but in one hour and forty-four minutes the game and the tour were completed. As in Australia, Tyson and Statham were mainly responsible for the collapse by getting rid of the early batsmen. In the seven Tests during the tour, Tyson took 39 wickets and Statham 30.

It was exactly three o'clock on a glorious summer's day when New Zealand began their task. The pitch was dry and not particularly fast, but the ball went through at varying heights and took spin. In forty minutes before tea New Zealand lost Leggat, Poore and Reid for 13 runs.

By clever strategy Hutton brought on Wardle, left arm slow, to tackle Sutcliffe, New Zealand's talented left-handed batsman. That move made the record lowest score possible as Wardle tempted Sutcliffe into a big hit against his "chinaman" and he was completely deceived and bowled.

With four men out for 14, Appleyard entered the attack, relieving Tyson, and he removed McGregor, Cave, MacGibbon and Colquhoun, who went first ball in each innings. In fact Appleyard claimed three wickets in four balls but Moir again prevented a hat-trick, the ball falling only just short of Graveney who was in great form in the leg trap.

Hutton decided to give Statham and Tyson the chance of making the kill, but one over from Statham sufficed. First he got Rabone leg before with his fourth delivery and finally established the new world record by sending Hayes' middle stump flying. New Zealand's previous lowest scores were 42 and 54 against Australia at Wellington in March 1946.

So M.C.C. won all four matches in New Zealand and finished with the best record of any visiting team to the Antipodes. Large crowds flocked to the New Zealand grounds, the receipts amounting to £26,000, leaving approximately a profit of £16,000 for the benefit of cricket in the two islands.

New Zealand

B. Sutcliffe c Bailey b Statham	49	— b Wardle	11
J. G. Leggat lbw b Tyson	4	— c Hutton b Tyson	1
M. B. Poore c Evans b Tyson	0	— b Tyson	0
J. R. Reid c Statham b Wardle	73	— b Statham	1
G. O. Rabone c Evans b Statham	29	— lbw b Statham	7
S. M. McGregor not out	15	— c May b Appleyard	1
H. B. Cave c Bailey b Appleyard	6	— c Graveney b Appleyard	5
A. R. MacGibbon b Appleyard	9	— lbw b Appleyard	0
A. R. Colquhoun c sub b Appleyard	0	— c Graveney b Appleyard	0
A. N. Moir lbw b Statham	0	— not out	0
E. A. Hayes b Statham	0	— b Statham	0
B 3, l-b 6, w 4, n-b 2	15		
	200		**26**

1/13 2/13 3/76 4/154 5/171 6/189   200   1/6 2/8 3/9 4/14 5/14   26
7/199 8/199 9/200   6/22 7/22 8/22 9/26

England

R. T. Simpson c and b Moir	23	F. H. Tyson not out	27
T. W. Graveney c Rabone b Hayes	13	R. Appleyard c Colquhoun b Hayes	6
P. B. H. May b Hayes	48	J. B. Statham c Reid b Moir	13
M. C. Cowdrey b Moir	22		
L. Hutton b MacGibbon	53	B 12, l-b 3, n-b 8	23
T. E. Bailey c Colquhoun b Cave	18		
T. G. Evans c Reid b Moir	0	1/21 2/56 3/112 4/112 5/163 246
J. H. Wardle c Reid b Moir	0	6/164 7/164 8/201 9/218

England Bowling

	O.	M.	R.	W.		O.	M.	R.	W
Tyson	11	2	41	2	....	7	2	10	2
Statham	17.4	7	28	4	....	9	2	9	3
Bailey	13	2	34	0					
Appleyard .	16	4	38	3	....	6	3	7	4
Wardle	31	19	44	1	....	5	5	0	1

New Zealand Bowling

	O.	M.	R.	W.
Hayes	23	7	71	3
MacGibbon....	20	7	33	1
Reid	25	10	28	0
Cave	24	10	25	1
Moir	25.1	3	62	5
Rabone	2	0	4	0

Umpires: J. McLennan and J. C. Harris.

AUSTRALIANS IN WEST INDIES, 1955

Following their defeat at home by England, Australia fully rehabilitated themselves in the eyes of the cricket world when visiting the West Indies in 1955. Not only did they complete the tour without a reverse, but, in winning three of the Test matches and drawing two, they became the first overseas team to triumph in a series in the Caribbean. Furthermore they proved immensely popular wherever they played, so that their programme was carried through without any of the rancour and ugly incidents which marred the visit to the Islands of Hutton's M.C.C. Team a year earlier. For this, much credit belonged to the tact displayed by Ian Johnson, who proved a most able captain both on and off the field.

The batting failures against England naturally gave rise to misgivings before the start of the tour as to how the Australians would fare when facing the side with whom their conquerors could do no better than share the rubber in 1953–54. In the event, the run-getting formed the main strength of the side, as was amply demonstrated by the scoring of twelve centuries for Australia in the five Test matches. Admittedly the pitches were easy-paced and never did they face anyone of the calibre of Tyson or Statham, but against King and Dewdney, the best fast bowlers available, the batsmen successfully set to work to show themselves complete masters.

This was accomplished by purely orthodox means. Gone were the somewhat apprehensive cross-bat methods which so frequently led to disaster against England. In their place the batsmen demonstrated to their own satisfaction and for the benefit of cricketers in general the undoubted value of the straight bat. The left-handed Harvey hit three splendid hundreds, with 204 in the closing game the highest, and Miller also reached three figures on three occasions. McDonald, a reliable Number One, scored two centuries, shared in three opening partnerships exceeding 100 and, in helping Harvey to add 295 in the final match, set up a new third-wicket record for Australia.

Once again Lindwall and Miller, who between them took 40 wickets, formed the spearhead of the attack. Both bowled at a fine pace, using the occasional short-pitched ball judiciously, and in the fifth Test Miller enjoyed the dual distinction of taking eight wickets and hitting a century. Johnson, with off-breaks, at times was ineffective, but his seven wickets for 44 runs in the second innings paved the way to victory in the Third Test and put Australia thus early beyond all fear of defeat in the rubber. Benaud and Archer, both of whom scored maiden Test centuries, accomplished much valuable work as all-rounders.

The efficiency of Langley behind the wicket in the last four representative matches is worthy of special mention. He helped in the dismissal of twenty batsmen and in the eight innings in which he kept wicket conceded no more than 22 byes while 2,464 runs were scored. In the third and fifth games he equalled a world's Test record by getting rid of five men in an innings, and he equalled another when disposing of eight in a match when the last sweeping success at Kingston set the seal on the Australian supremacy.

Not all the Test match honours went to the Australians. Indeed, the most prominent batsman on either side was undoubtedly Walcott. By fearless but discriminating batting, he performed feats achieved by no other player in history for both at Port o Spain and Kingston he hit a century in each innings of a match and altogether five in the series. Moreover his aggregate of 827 runs was the highest recorded in a rubber for West Indies. Too often Walcott bore the chief burden of an innings, for though Weekes improved from a moderate start, Worrell never reached the form expected of him. In the fourth Test at Bridgetown Atkinson and Depeiza enabled their side to effect a remarkable recovery by adding 348, a world's record for the seventh wicket in first-class cricket. Each scored his first Test match century.

Injuries to Stollmeyer could not have helped the West Indies. Stollmeyer, who captained the side against England in the previous season, hurt a finger while practising before the first Test and inexperienced Atkinson took over the leadership. Stollmeyer returned to the captaincy for the next two Tests, but damaged a collar-bone while fielding in the third, so that Atkinson was again appointed for the fourth and final representative games.

SUMMARY OF THE TOUR—RESULTS OF FIRST-CLASS MATCHES
Played 9, Won 5, Drawn 4

TEST MATCHES AGAINST WEST INDIES
Played 5, Won 3, Drawn 2

AUSTRALIA BATTING AVERAGES IN THE TESTS

	Matches	Inns.	Not Outs	Runs	100's	Highest Inns.	Average
R. N. Harvey	5	7	1	650	3	204	108.33
K. R. Miller	5	6	0	439	3	147	73.16
C. C. McDonald	5	8	1	449	2	127	64.14
R. G. Archer	5	6	0	364	1	128	60.66
I. W. Johnson	5	6	2	191	0	66	47.75
G. R. Langley..........	4	4	2	91	0	53	45.50
A. R. Morris...........	4	6	0	266	1	111	44.33
L. Favell	2	3	0	125	0	72	41.66
R. Benaud	5	6	0	246	1	121	41.00
R. R. Lindwall	5	6	1	187	1	118	37.40
W. Watson	3	5	1	85	0	30	21.15

Also batted: P. Burge 14; J. C. Hill 8* and 1; W. A. Johnston 0* and 1*; L. Maddocks 1 and 12*.

* Signifies not out.

AUSTRALIA BOWLING AVERAGES IN THE TESTS

	Overs	Maidens	Runs	Wickets	Average
R. Benaud	185	49	486	18	27.00
I. W. Johnson	151.2	51	406	14	29.00
K. R. Miller	189.2	37	640	20	32.00
R. R. Lindwall	176	25	643	20	32.15
R. G. Archer	129	27	413	11	37.54
W. A. Johnston	53	7	188	2	94.00

Also bowled: R. N. Harvey 5—0—18—0; J. C. Hill 35—11—115—1; W. Watson 1—0—5—0.

WEST INDIES BATTING AVERAGES IN THE TESTS

	Matches	Inns.	Not Outs	Runs	100's	Highest Inns.	Average
C. L. Walcott	5	10	0	827	5	155	82.70
E. D. Weekes	5	10	0	469	1	139	58.62
D. Atkinson	4	8	1	311	1	219	44.42
C. Depeiza	3	6	2	169	1	122	42.25
G. Sobers	4	8	2	231	0	64	38.50
O. G. Smith	4	8	0	206	1	104	25.75
F. M. Worrell	4	8	0	206	0	61	25.75
J. K. Holt	5	10	0	251	0	60	25.10
J. B. Stollmeyer	2	4	0	89	0	42	22.25
A. L. Valentine	3	4	3	8	0	4*	8.00
F. King	4	7	1	46	0	21	7.66
S. Ramadhin	4	6	1	27	0	12*	5.40
T. Dewdney	2	3	0	2	0	2	0.66

Signifies not out.

Also batted: A. P. Binns 0 and 0; L. Butler 16; H. Furlonge 4 and 28; G. Gibbs 12 and 0; N. Marshall 0 and 8; C. McWatt 4.

WEST INDIES BOWLING AVERAGES IN THE TESTS

	Overs	Maidens	Runs	Wickets	Average
D. Atkinson	215.1	78	459	13	35.30
G. Sobers	93.5	36	213	6	35.50
C. L. Walcott	71	24	152	4	38.00
T. Dewdney	67	15	263	5	52.60
O. G. Smith	134.4	38	340	5	68.00
A. L. Valentine	140	42	349	5	69.80
S. Ramadhin	139	33	379	5	75.80
F. M. Worrell	115	23	311	3	103.66
F. King	113	16	403	3	134.33

Also bowled: L. Butler 40—7—151—2; G. Gibbs 4—1—7—0; J. K. Holt 4—1—20—1; N. Marshall 46.3—21—63—2; J. B. Stollmeyer 6—0—12—0; E. D. Weekes 2.2—0—8—1.

AUSTRALIANS BATTING AVERAGES IN ALL FIRST-CLASS MATCHES

	Matches	Inns.	Not Outs	Runs	100's	Highest Inns.	Average
R. N. Harvey	8	12	2	789	3	204	78.90
C. C. McDonald	7	12	1	583	2	127	53.00
A. R. Morris	7	11	0	577	2	157	52.45
K. R. Miller	8	11	0	577	3	147	52.45
R. G. Archer	8	11	1	478	1	128	47.80
L. Maddocks	4	7	3	181	0	83	45.25
R. Benaud	8	11	1	446	1	121	44.60
W. Watson	6	10	1	393	1	122	43.66

	Matches	Inns.	Not Outs	Runs	100's	Highest Inns.	Average
G. R. Langley	5	5	2	118	0	53	39.33
P. Burge	5	8	0	310	1	177	38.75
L. Favell	5	8	0	287	0	72	35.87
A. K. Davidson	3	4	2	70	0	34*	35.00
R. R. Lindwall	7	9	2	227	1	118	32.42
I. W. Johnson	8	9	2	200	0	66	28.57
J. C. Hill	4	4	2	32	0	22*	16.00
W. A. Johnston	6	5	3	14	0	6	7.00

* *Signifies not out.*

AUSTRALIAN BOWLING AVERAGES IN ALL FIRST-CLASS MATCHES

	Overs	Maidens	Runs	Wickets	Average
J. C. Hill	146.4	53	380	18	21.11
R. R. Lindwall	237.4	36	808	28	28.85
I. W. Johnson	243.2	74	672	23	29.21
K. R. Miller	245.2	51	791	26	30.42
R. Benaud	240.5	59	671	21	31.95
R. G. Archer	220	47	682	18	37.88
A. K. Davidson	63.2	9	202	4	50.50
W. A. Johnston	119	18	405	8	50.62

Also bowled: R. N. Harvey 12—0—67—0; A. R. Morris 4—0—12—0
W. Watson 5—0—22—0.

The following fifteen three-figure innings were played for the Australians in first-class matches:

R. N. Harvey (3):
    204 v. West Indies, at Kingston (Fifth Test).
    133 v. West Indies, at Kingston (First Test).
    133 v. West Indies, at Port of Spain (Second Test).

K. R. Miller (3):
    147 v. West Indies, at Kingston (First Test).
    137 v. West Indies, at Bridgetown (Fourth Test).
    109 v. West Indies, at Kingston (Fifth Test).

C. C. McDonald (2):
    127 v West Indies, at Kingston (Fifth Test).
    110 v. West Indies, at Port of Spain (Second Test).

A. R. Morris (2):
    157 v. Jamaica, at Kingston.
    111 v. West Indies, at Port of Spain (Second Test).

R. G. Archer (1):
    128 v. West Indies, at Kingston (Fifth Test).

R. Benaud (1):
    121 v. West Indies, at Kingston (Fifth Test).

P. Burge (1):
    177 v. British Guiana, at Georgetown.

R. R. Lindwall (1):
    118 v. West Indies, at Bridgetown (Fourth Test).

W. Watson (1):
    122 v. Barbados, at Bridgetown.

The following thirteen three-figure innings were played against the Australians in first-class matches:

C. L. Walcott (5):
155
110 } for West Indies, at Kingston (Fifth Test).
126
110 } for West Indies, at Port of Spain (Second Test).
108 for West Indies, at Kingston (First Test).

O. G. Smith (2):
169 for Jamaica, at Kingston.
104 for West Indies, at Kingston (First Test).

E. D. Weekes (2):
139 for West Indies, at Port of Spain (Second Test).
132 for Barbados, at Bridgetown.

D. Atkinson (1):
219 for West Indies, at Bridgetown (Fourth Test).

A. P. Binns (1):
151 for Jamaica, at Kingston.

C. Depeiza (1):
122 for West Indies, at Bridgetown (Fourth Test).

H. Furlonge (1):
150* for Trinidad, at Port of Spain.

* Signifies not out.

JAMAICA v. AUSTRALIANS

At Kingston, March 19, 21, 22, 23. Drawn. In their opening match the Australians found the batting conditions to their liking. Following a chance when 21, the left-handed Morris scored readily all round, his 157 including two 6's and twenty-three 4's. McDonald also played well and Benaud and Maddocks hit so freely that they put on 84 in less than half an hour. Jamaica badly felt the absence of Valentine through injury. The fall of five wickets for 81 placed them in an unhappy position, but Smith (two 6's, twenty-three 4's) and Binns (twenty-one 4's) mastered the bowling in a fine stand of 277 in three hours fifty minutes. Facing arrears of 21, the Australians, despite good bowling by Worrell, again made runs briskly, but no chance of a definite result existed.

Australians

A. R. Morris c Rae b Smith	157	— c Binns b Holt	22
C. C. McDonald lbw b Minott	73	— c Barclay b Worrell	27
P. Burge b Dewdney	29	— c Smith b Worrell	69
R. N. Harvey b Smith	21	— b Minott	37
K. R. Miller lbw b Mullings	13	— c Mullings b Worrell	39
R. Benaud b Scarlett	55	— b Worrell	20
L. Maddocks c and b Scarlett	62	— c Dewdney b Mullings	83
A. K. Davidson b Smith	27	— absent hurt	0
I. W. Johnson c Worrell b Scarlett	2	— c Binns b Minott	7
R. R. Lindwall not out	4	— c Bonitto b Worrell	10
W. A. Johnston c Rae b Smith	5	— not out	2
L-b 3, w 2	5	L-b 2, n-b 1	3

1/150 2/232 3/283 4/286 5/305 6/389   453
7/438 8/442 9/444

1/7 2/51 3/142 4/164   319
5/213 6/253 7/271 8/308

EE

Jamaica

J. K. Holt c Morris b Johnson	25	— not out 6
A. Rae c Burge b Lindwall	1	— not out 21
N. L. Bonitto c Benaud b Davidson	10	
F. M. Worrell c Maddocks b Johnston	24	
K. Barclay lbw b Johnston	14	
O. G. Smith c and b Johnston	169	
A. P. Binns c Burge b Benaud	151	
R. Scarlett lbw b Johnson	25	
C. Minott b Lindwall	14	
T. Dewdney not out	13	
L. Mullings c Archer b Benaud	5	
B 11, l-b 7, w 2, n-b 3	23	L-b 1 1
	474	(No wkt.) 28

1/5 2/29 3/43 4/69 5/81 6/358 7/408
8/446 9/458

Jamaica Bowling

	O.	M.	R.	W.		O.	M.	R.	W.
Dewdney	20	1	93	1	....	5	0	26	0
Minott	12	1	53	1	....	13	2	49	2
Worrell	5	1	20	0	....	22.5	4	87	5
Smith	44.4	10	103	4	....	6	0	25	0
Scarlett	33	5	97	3	....	13	1	40	0
Mullings	16	1	82	1	....	15	0	69	1
Holt						6	1	16	1
Bonitto						1	0	4	0

Australia Bowling

	O.	M.	R.	W.		O.	M.	R.	W.
Lindwall	25	3	81	2	....	3	1	5	0
Miller	21	4	65	0	....	2	0	4	0
Johnston	28	2	97	3	....	2	0	7	0
Davidson	13	0	52	1					
Johnson	31	6	77	2	....	2	1	5	0
Benaud	20.5	3	79	2	....	1	0	6	0

WEST INDIES v. AUSTRALIA
First Test Match

At Kingston, March 26, 28, 29, 30, 31. Australia won by nine wickets with a day in hand. They took command from the start. McDonald and Morris began with a partnership of 102 and Harvey, scoring his thirteenth Test match century, and Miller shared in a third wicket stand of 224. Each hit fifteen 4's. Profiting from missed chances, Walcott made a brave effort for the West Indies, but they could not recover from the loss of five wickets for 101. Walcott drove with fine power, especially off the back foot, and he hit twelve 4's. Apart from Smith, who stayed while the fifth wicket realised 138, he received poor support, and when the big stand ended Lindwall, whose accurate fast bowling deserved better reward, soon finished the innings.

So the West Indies followed on 256 behind and for a time they fared better, thanks largely to admirable batting by Smith and Holt. Smith hooked and drove splendidly and well deserved the distinction of hitting a century on his first appearance in a Test match. His 104 occupied three hours forty minutes and contained fourteen 4's. Then the bowlers regained the mastery, the last six wickets going down for 66, and Australia needed only 20 runs to win.

In the absence of Johnson, who hurt a foot while batting, Miller captained Australia for much of the game.

Australia

C. C. McDonald st Binns b Valentine ...	50	— not out 7
A. R. Morris lbw b Valentine	65	— c Gibbs b Weekes 1
R. N. Harvey b Valentine	133	
K. R. Miller lbw b Walcott	147	
R. R. Lindwall lbw b Ramadhin........	10	
P. Burge c and b Atkinson	14	
L. Maddocks b Valentine	1	— not out 12
R. Benaud b Walcott	46	
R. G. Archer c Walcott b Holt	24	
I. W. Johnson not out.................	18	
W. A. Johnston not out	0	
B 3, l-b 3, w 1	7	

1/102 2/137 3/361 4/391 (9 wkts., dec.) 515   (1 wkt.) 20
5/417 6/430 7/435 8/475 9/506   1/6

West Indies

J. K. Holt c Benaud b Lindwall	31	— c Maddocks b Benaud 60
G. Gibbs lbw b Archer	12	— b Johnston 0
A. P. Binns c Burge b Archer	0	— lbw b Miller 0
E. D. Weekes run out	19	— c and b Benaud 1
C. L. Walcott c Benaud b Miller	108	— c Archer b Lindwall 39
F. M. Worrell b Johnston	9	— b Archer 9
O. G. Smith b Lindwall	44	— c Harvey b Miller 104
D. Atkinson c Harvey b Miller	1	— c Benaud b Miller 30
F. King c Maddocks b Lindwall	4	— b Lindwall 21
S. Ramadhin not out.................	12	— c Lindwall b Archer 3
A. L. Valentine b Lindwall	0	— not out 2
B 14, l-b 2, n-b 3	19	B 5, n-b 1 6

1/27 2/27 3/56 4/75 5/101 6/239   259   1/20 2/122 3/132 4/209   275
7/240 8/243 9/253   5/213 6/213 7/239 8/253
                                         9/270

West Indies Bowling

	O.	M.	R.	W.	O.	M.	R.	W.
King	28	7	122	0	2	0	10	0
Worrell	7	2	13	0				
Atkinson	23	9	46	1				
Ramadhin	46	12	112	1				
Valentine	54	20	113	3				
Smith	11	0	27	0				
Walcott	26	9	50	3				
Gibbs	3	1	5	0	1	0	2	0
Holt	3	0	20	1				
Weekes					2.2	0	8	1

Australia Bowling

	O.	M.	R.	W.	O.	M.	R.	W.
Lindwall	24	6	61	4	16.1	3	63	2
Archer	19	8	39	2	12	3	44	2
Johnston	23	4	75	1	16	2	54	1
Benaud........	19	7	29	0	23	9	44	2
Miller	16	5	36	2	28	9	62	3
Harvey					1	0	2	0

Umpires: P. Burke and T. Ewart.

TRINIDAD v. AUSTRALIANS

At Port of Spain, April 4, 5, 6, 7. Drawn. Apart from H. Furlonge and
Gomez, the Trinidad batsmen fared moderately in the first innings against the
pace and swing of Lindwall. In turn Butler caused trouble to the Australians
and, in taking five wickets, earned himself a place in the second Test match; but
Watson batted beautifully for an hour and a quarter and Favell helped substantially towards a lead of 82. Stollmeyer and H. Furlonge soon staved off all
ideas of defeat for Trinidad. They scored 204 together, setting up a first wicket
record for Trinidad against a team from abroad. H. Furlonge made his maiden
century in first-class cricket in four and a half hours with twenty-four 4's among
his figures. Watson again showed good form in the Australian second innings.

Trinidad

H. Furlonge b Lindwall	57	— not out	150
J. B. Stollmeyer b Lindwall	9	— lbw b Archer	95
R. Legall c Burge b Archer	0	— lbw b Johnston	3
R. Tangchoon lbw b Johnston	12		
G. Gomez b Hill	45		
W. Rodriquez b Lindwall	26	— c Lindwall b Archer	7
C. Furlonge lbw b Archer	9	— c Langley b Johnston	7
S. Oliver not out	25	— not out	10
W. Ferguson b Lindwall	18		
K. Babb b Lindwall	0		
L. Butler lbw b Lindwall	0		
B 9, l-b 7	16	B 2, l-b 10, w 6	18

1/23 2/24 3/51 4/95 5/135 6/160   217   1/204 2/213 (4 wkts., dec.) 290
7/167 8/213 9/213   3/240 4/265

Australians

L. Favell c Oliver b Butler	71	— c Tangchoon b Gomez	2
A. R. Morris run out	21		
R. N. Harvey c Stolmeyer b Butler	2	— not out	21
W. Watson c C. Furlonge b Butler	70	— b Rodriguez	50
P. Burge st Legall b Ferguson	0	— c C. Furlonge b Babb	2
R. Benaud c C. Furlonge b Babb	42	— c Gomez b Ferguson	20
R. G. Archer c C. Furlonge b Butler	7	— not out	10
R. A. Lindwall c C. Furlonge b Butler	26		
G. R. Langley c Oliver b Ferguson	27		
J. C. Hill not out	22		
W. A. Johnston c Butler b Ferguson	6		
B 2, l-b 2, n-b 1	5	B 4, l-b 1, n-b 4	9

1/44 2/47 3/115 4/115 5/209 6/209   299   1/10 2/31 3/58 (4 wkts.) 114
7/229 8/248 9/291   4/87

Australians Bowling

	O.	M.	R.	W.		O.	M.	R.	W.
Lindwall	19.4	6	41	6	....	14	1	38	0
Archer	20	4	46	2	....	23	4	63	2
Johnston	20	8	49	1	....	16	1	64	2
Benaud	12	5	29	0					
Hill	19	7	32	1	....	13	6	33	0
Harvey	1	0	4	0	....	6	0	45	0
Watson						4	0	17	0
Morris						4	0	12	0

Trinidad Bowling

	O.	M.	R.	W.		O.	M.	R.	W.
Butler	26	5	93	5					
Gomez	18	8	41	0	....	6	1	16	1
Babb	18	4	57	1	....	5	0	19	1
Oliver	16	2	42	0	....	4	0	20	0
Ferguson	18.5	4	59	3	....	5	0	14	1
Rodriguez	1	0	2	0	....	3	0	20	1
Tangchoon ...					....	3	0	11	0
C. Furlonge ...					....	1	0	5	0

WEST INDIES v. AUSTRALIA
Second Test Match

At Port of Spain, April 11, 12, 13, 14, 15, 16. Drawn. A century in each innings by Walcott, who became the third West Indies cricketer to achieve this feat in a Test match, and the return to his best form of Weekes enabled West Indies to share the honours in a game of heavy scoring. So great was public interest that on the opening day the gates were closed before the start, and a crowd estimated at 28,000 comprised the biggest ever to watch a match in the West Indies.

Rain limited the first day's cricket to eighty-five minutes in which time West Indies lost two wickets for 73. Next day Weekes and Walcott, scoring 242 together, established a new record for any West Indies wicket in a Test with Australia. Both employed powerful strokes all round. Weekes gave a masterly display for three and a half hours, hitting one 6 and twenty-four 4's, and Walcott obtained seventeen 4's. On the third morning the last five wickets fell, four of them to Lindwall, for 27 runs, and McDonald and Morris followed with sound batting. Nine bowlers tried without success to part them before the close when the total stood at 147, and despite the handicap of injuries they stayed till their stand reached 191, a record for an Australian first wicket against West Indies.

Harvey completed his second century of the series and fierce hitting came from Archer (one 6, twelve 4's) and Johnson. So Australia gained a first innings advantage of 218.

West Indies went ahead for the loss of two wickets, Walcott and Weekes adding 127 together. Walcott, whose forcing tactics took him to three figures in just over an hour and fifty minutes, hit thirteen boundaries.

The game, the first Test match to be played in Trinidad on a turf pitch, yielded 1,255 runs for the loss of twenty-three wickets.

West Indies

J. K. Holt c Johnston b Lindwall	25	— lbw b Archer	21
J. B. Stollmeyer b Lindwall	14	— b Johnson.............	42
C. L. Walcott st Langley b Benaud	126	— c Watson b Archer	110
E. D. Weekes c Johnson b Benaud	139	— not out	87
O. G. Smith b Benaud	0	— c Langley b Archer	0
G. Sobers c Langley b Lindwall	47	— not out	8
C. McWatt c Benaud b Miller	4		
F. King b Lindwall	2		
S. Ramadhin b Lindwall...............	0		
L. Butler c Johnson b Lindwall	16		
A. L. Valentine not out	4		
B 1, l-b 3, n-b 1	5	L-b 3, w 2	5

1/39 2/40 3/282 4/282 5/323 6/355   382   1/40 2/103 3/230 (4 wkts.) **273**
7/360 8/360 9/361   4/236

Australia

C. C. McDonald c Walcott b Valentine 110	R. R. Lindwall not out 37
A. R. Morris c King b Butler 111	G. R. Langley c King b Walcott .. 9
R. N. Harvey lbw b King 133	W. A. Johnston not out.......... 1
W. Watson lbw b Ramadhin 27	B 5, l-b 6, w 1, n-b 2 14
R. Benaud c Walcott b Ramadhin. 5	
K. R. Miller run out 3	1/191 2/259 3/328 (9 wkts., dec.) 600
R. G. Archer c McWatt b Valentine 84	4/336 5/345 6/439
I. W. Johnson c McWatt b Butler. 66	7/529 8/570 9/594

Australia Bowling

	O.	M.	R.	W.		O.	M.	R.	W.
Lindwall	24.5	3	95	6	....	16	1	70	0
Miller	28	9	96	1	....	12	0	52	0
Archer	9	0	42	0	....	8	1	37	3
Johnston	7	1	28	0	....	7	0	31	0
Johnson	19	5	72	0	....	7	2	26	1
Benaud	17	3	44	3	....	12	2	52	0

West Indies Bowling

Butler	40	7	151	2
King	37	7	98	1
Holt	1	1	0	0
Ramadhin	32	8	90	2
Valentine	49	12	133	2
Walcott	19	5	45	1
Sobers	3	1	10	0
Smith	15	1	48	0
Stollmeyer	5	0	11	0

Umpires: E. Lee Kow and C. Jordan.

BRITISH GUIANA v. AUSTRALIANS

At Georgetown, April 20, 21, 22. Australians won by an innings and 134 runs. The absence of Walcott from their second innings ruined whatever chance British Guiana might have possessed of saving the match. Only he and Kanhai on the opening day and Butcher on the last achieved much against the leg-breaks of Hill, who came out with an analysis of ten wickets for 65 runs. Burge (two 6's, twenty-two 4's) stayed four hours twenty minutes, he and Archer putting on 155 for the fifth Australian wicket, and as Harvey and Benaud scored freely, the touring team gained a first innings advantage of 299.

British Guiana

B. Pairaudeau c Maddocks b Miller	4	— lbw b Johnson	17
G. Gibbs c Maddocks b Archer	0	— c Archer b Miller	2
R. Kanhai lbw b Hill	51	— st Maddocks b Hill	27
C. L. Walcott run out	51	— absent hurt	0
B. Butcher c Maddocks b Benaud	8	— b Johnson..................	46
C. McWatt c Harvey b Davidson	14	— b Hill	28
C. Paul lbw b Hill	19	— st Maddocks b Johnson	11
N. Wight c Maddocks b Hill	8	— not out	15
W. Edun not out	17	— b Hill	6
L. Madray b Hill....................	1	— b Hill	0
P. Legall b Hill....................	1	— b Hill	5
B 1, n-b 2	3	B 2, l-b 2, n-b 4	8

1/5 2/19 3/91 4/116 5/116 6/141	177	1/11 2/43 3/47 4/94 5/138	165
7/154 8/159 9/161		6/139 7/155 8/155 9/165	

Australians

L. Favell c McWatt b Wight	18	L. Maddocks lbw b Wight	0
W. Watson c McWatt b Edun	31	A. K. Davidson not out	34
R. N. Harvey c Wight b Madray	58	L-b 3, w 1, n-b 2	6
P. Burge c Pairaudeau b Madray	177		
K. R. Miller c Kanhai b Wight	33	1/48 2/50 3/137 (7 wkts., dec.)	476
R. G. Archer c Edun b Madray	56	4/216 5/371 6/388	
R. Benaud not out	63	7/389	

J. C. Hill and I. W. Johnson did not bat.

Australian Bowling

	O.	M.	R.	W.		O.	M.	R.	W.
Miller	6	3	9	1	....	5	1	15	1
Archer	11	3	30	1	....	7	2	34	0
Johnson	7	1	31	0	....	17	5	39	3
Hill	21.3	8	50	5	....	16	9	15	5
Benaud	11	2	36	1	....	11	0	35	0
Davidson	10	3	18	1	....	7	2	19	0

British Guiana Bowling

	O.	M.	R.	W.
Legall	11	0	46	0
Edun	22	0	78	1
Walcott	1	0	4	0
Wight	35	6	112	3
Madray	23	0	122	3
Butcher	14	2	43	0
Gibbs	16	0	65	0

WEST INDIES v. AUSTRALIA
Third Test Match

At Georgetown, April 26, 27, 28, 29. Australia won by eight wickets, thus making themselves safe from defeat in the rubber. Four West Indies alterations, involving the inclusion for the first time of Marshall, behind the wicket, and Depeiza, did not strengthen the side in the manner expected, and an unchanged Australian team, despite the absence from the attack of the left-handed Johnston injured, triumphed with well over two days to spare.

Miller began the West Indies troubles on the first day and by lunch-time five men were out for 86. Weekes did his best to stem the tide, but when he left Benaud, with leg-breaks, caused another collapse, taking four wickets in the course of 23 deliveries for 15 runs. Though McDonald and Morris began with a partnership of 71, Australia lost half their wickets in gaining a lead, and for their first innings advantage of 75 owed much to brisk hitting by Benaud.

The fall of three wickets for 25 in the second innings virtually sealed the fate of West Indies. Walcott and Worrell effected a recovery by adding 125, but, splendidly supported by Langley behind the wicket, Johnson brought about such a breakdown that the last five wickets realised only 57. Langley, in sharing in the dismissal of five batsmen in an innings, equalled the record of Oldfield.

Set 133 to get, Australia won in the first over after lunch on the fourth day.

West Indies

J. K. Holt c and b Miller	12	— c Langley b Miller 6
J. B. Stollmeyer c Archer b Miller	16	— c and b Johnson 17
C. L. Walcott c and b Archer	8	— hit wkt b Lindwall 73
E. D. Weekes c Archer b Benaud	81	— c Langley b Johnson 0
F. M. Worrell c Johnson b Archer	9	— b Benaud 56
G. Somers c Watson b Johnson	12	— b Johnson 11
D. Atkinson b Lindwall	13	— st Langley b Johnson 16
C. Depeiza not out	16	— st Langley b Johnson 13
N. Marshall b Benaud	0	— c sub b Johnson 8
S. Ramadhin c Archer b Benaud	0	— st Langley b Johnson 2
F. King c Langley b Benaud	13	— not out 0
B 1, l-b 1	2	B 1, l-b 2, n-b 2 5

1/23 2/30 3/42 4/52 5/83 6/124   182   1/25 2/25 3/25 4/150   207
7/156 8/156 9/160   5/162 6/175 7/186 8/204
                                               9/204

Australia

C. C. McDonald b Atkinson	61	— b Atkinson 31
A. R. Morris c Sobers b Atkinson	44	— c Walcott b Marshall 38
R. N. Harvey c Holt b Ramadhon	38	— not out 41
W. Watson c and b Ramadhin	6	— not out 22
K. R. Miller c Depeiza b Sobers	33	
R. Benaud c sub b Marshall	68	
R. G. Archer st Depeiza b Sobers	2	
I. W. Johnson c Stollmeyer b Sobers	0	
R. R. Lindwall b Atkinson	2	
G. R. Langley not out	1	
W. A. Johnston absent hurt	0	
L-b 2	2	N-b 1 1

1/71 2/135 3/147 4/161 5/215 6/231   257   1/70 2/70   (2 wkts.) 133
7/231 8/238

Australia Bowling

	O.	M.	R.	W.	O.	M.	R.	W.
Lindwall	12	0	44	1	18	1	54	1
Miller	9	1	33	2	9	3	18	1
Archer	10	0	46	2	12	3	43	0
Johnson	9	1	42	1	22.2	10	44	7
Benaud	3.5	1	15	4	14	3	43	1

West Indies Bowling

	O.	M.	R.	W.	O.	M.	R.	W.
King	12	1	37	0	3	0	10	0
Worrell	9	2	17	0	7	2	20	0
Ramadhin	26	9	54	2	9	1	29	0
Atkinson	37	13	85	3	15.5	5	32	1
Marshall	33.3	15	41	1	13	6	22	1
Stollmeyer	1	0	1	0				
Sobers	16	10	20	3	11	4	19	0

Umpires: E. Lee Kow and Wing Gillette.

BARBADOS v. AUSTRALIANS

At Bridgetown, May 7, 9, 10, 11. Australians won by three wickets, their closest struggle of the tour. Though handicapped for most of his innings by a damaged right hand, Weekes made his second century from the Australian bowling, hitting twenty 4's without offering a chance. He and D. Atkinson put on 112 in just over an hour and a quarter for the fifth Barbados wicket. Watson took batting honours for the Australians who gained a lead of 28. Quiet for a long time, Watson later showed freedom and he hit one 6 and seventeen 4's. Barbados seemed doomed to defeat when losing six wickets for 75. Then Sobers (ten 4's) and Goddard added 63 and in the end the Australians needed 203. The pitch played none too easily, but the steadiness of Morris ensured success.

Barbados

C. Hunte c Archer b Miller	0	— lbw b Johnson	3
C. Depeiza run out	27	— b Archer	0
C. Smith c Hill b Miller	4	— c Archer b Johnson	24
E. D. Weekes c Davidson b Miller	132	— c and b Hill	10
G. Sobers b Miller	0	— st Maddocks b Hill	62
D. Atkinson c Davidson b Archer	78	— st Maddocks b Johnson	2
C. B. Williams c Favell b Hill	24	— b Johnson	5
E. Atkinson b Hill	1	— c Archer b Hill	23
N. Marshall run out	19	— b Davidson	7
J. D. Goddard not out	11	— not out	77
A. E. Mayers b Hill	4	— b Davidson	3
L-b 3, n-b 2	5	B 5, l-b 6, w 1, n-b 2	14

1/0 2/8 3/101 4/102 5/214 6/265   305   1/3 2/31 3/32 4/48 5/61   230
7/269 8/276 9/297   6/75 7/138 8/190 9/213

Australians

C. C. McDonald b Mayers	29	— c Goddard b D. Atkinson	5
L. Favell c Goddard b Marshall	49	— b D. Atkinson	22
A. R. Morris lbw b D. Atkinson	33	— lbw b Goddard	78
W. Watson c Depeiza b Marshall	122	— lbw b Marshall	35
P. Burge run out	17	— b Goddard	2
K. R. Miller lbw b D. Atkinson	36	— lbw b Williams	17
R. G. Archer c Depeiza b Marshall	22	— lbw b D. Atkinson	19
A. K. Davidson c Smith b D. Atkinson	4	— not out	5
L. D. Maddocks not out	13	— not out	10
I. W. Johnson c Depeiza b Marshall	0		
J. C. Hill c Weekes b D. Atkinson	1		
B 1, l-b 4, w 1, n-b 1	7	B 10, l-b 1	11

1/44 2/113 3/113 4/162 5/212 6/293   333   1/28 2/29 3/102   (7 wkts.) 204
7/308 8/322 9/322   4/128 5/137 6/189 7/189

Australians Bowling

	O.	M.	R.	W.		O.	M.	R.	W.
Miller	17	3	51	4	....	5	3	7	0
Archer	15	2	67	1	....	15	5	29	1
Johnson	8	1	39	0	....	27	9	75	4
Davidson	24	3	89	0	....	9.2	1	24	2
Hill	17.1	5	54	3	....	25	7	81	3

Barbados Bowling

	O.	M.	R.	W.		O.	M.	R.	W.
Mayers	14	3	90	1	....	1	0	7	0
E. Atkinson	10	0	40	0					
D. Atkinson	26.4	10	58	4	....	31	13	55	3
Sobers	11	6	23	0	....	9	4	19	0
Marshall	32	8	59	4	....	30	14	51	1
Goddard	9	1	35	0	....	22.2	10	32	2
Williams	7	1	21	0	....	9	1	29	1

WEST INDIES v. AUSTRALIA
Fourth Test Match

At Bridgetown, May 14, 16, 17, 18, 19, 20. Drawn, a result which sufficed to give Australia the rubber. The match was rendered memorable by a huge partnership by Atkinson and Depeiza during the first West Indies innings. In putting on 348 they established a world's record for the seventh wicket, beating the 344 by K. S. Ranjitsinhji and W. Newham for Sussex against Essex at Leyton in 1902.

The Australian batsmen lost no time in mastering the bowling. For the third time in the series they began with a three-figure stand, Favell (thirteen 4's) and McDonald scoring 108 together. The Australian innings lasted till the third day. Miller, batting in aggressive style, hit twenty-two 4's and Archer helped him to add 206 for the sixth wicket. Lindwall (two 6's, fifteen 4's) also punished wilting bowlers, reaching his second century in Test cricket, and Langley scored readily.

Another Australian victory appeared in prospect after six West Indies batsmen were dismissed for 146, but Atkinson and Depeiza came to the rescue, defying the attack for more than a day. Atkinson, the leading personality in the stand, hit one 6 and twenty-six 4's. In the end Australia's lead was restricted to 158, and as the pitch showed signs of wear Johnson did not enforce the follow-on. Favell batted skilfully and a good innings came from Johnson, so that in the end West Indies were left to make 408 in less than three hours and fifty minutes. This was clearly beyond them, but another good innings by Walcott made them safe from defeat.

Australia

C. C. McDonald run out	46	—	b Smith	17
L. Favell c Weekes b Atkinson	72	—	run out	53
R. N. Harvey c Smith b Worrell	74	—	c Valentine b Smith	27
W. Watson c Depeiza b Dewdney	30	—	b Atkinson	0
K. R. Miller c Depeiza b Dewdney	137	—	lbw b Atkinson	10
R. Benaud c Walcott b Dewdney	1	—	b Sobers	5
R. G. Archer b Worrell	98	—	lbw b Atkinson	28
R. R. Lindwall c Valentine b Atkinson	118	—	b Atkinson	10
I. W. Johnson b Dewdney	23	—	c Holt b Smith	57
G. R. Langley b Sobers	53	—	not out	28
J. C. Hill not out	8	—	c Weekes b Atkinson	1
B 1, l-b 2, w 4, n-b 1	8		B 9, l-b 4	13

1/108 2/126 3/226 4/226 5/233 6/439   668
7/483 8/562 9/623

1/71 2/72 3/73 4/87   249
5/107 6/119 7/151 8/177
9/241

West Indies

J. K. Holt b Lindwall	22	—	lbw b Hill	49
G. Sobers c Hill b Johnson	43	—	lbw b Archer	11
C. L. Walcott c Langley b Benaud	15	—	b Benaud	83
E. D. Weekes c Langley b Miller	44	—	run out	6
F. M. Worrell run out	16	—	c Archer b Miller	34
O. G. Smith c Langley b Miller	2	—	b Lindwall	11
D. Atkinson c Archer b Johnson	219	—	not out	20
C. Depeiza b Benaud	122	—	not out	11
S. Ramadhin c and b Benaud	10			
T. Dewdney b Johnson	0			
A. L. Valentine not out	2			
B 5, l-b 4, w 2, n-b 4	15		B 6, l-b 2, w 1	—

1/52 2/69 3/105 4/142 5/143 6/146   510
7/494 8/504 9/504

1/38 2/67 3/81   (6 wkts.) 234
4/154 5/193 6/207

West Indies Bowling

	O.	M.	R.	W.		O.	M.	R.	W.
Worrell	40	7	120	2	....	7	0	25	0
Dewdney	33	7	125	4	....	10	4	23	0
Walcott	26	10	57	0					
Valentine	31	9	87	0	....	6	1	16	0
Ramadhin	24	3	84	0	....	2	0	10	0
Atkinson	48	14	108	2	....	36.2	16	56	5
Smith	22	8	49	0	....	34	12	71	3
Sobers	11.5	6	30	1	....	14	3	35	1

Australia Bowling

	O.	M.	R.	W.		O.	M.	R.	W.
Lindwall	25	3	97	1	....	8	1	39	1
Miller	22	2	112	2	....	21	3	66	1
Archer	15	4	44	0	....	7	1	11	1
Johnson	35	12	77	3	....	14	4	30	0
Harvey	4	0	16	0					
Watson	1	0	5	0					
Benaud	31.1	6	73	3	....	11	3	35	1
Hill	24	9	71	0	....	11	2	44	1

Umpires: E. Lee Kow and C. Jordan.

WINDWARD ISLANDS v. AUSTRALIANS

At St. George's, Grenada, May 26, 27, 28. Drawn.
Windward Islands 265 (A. Roberts 37, V. Felix 56; W. A. Johnston four for 56) and 114 for two wickets, declared (I. Neverson 62 not out); Australians 219 (R. R. Lindwall 68, I. W. Johnson 67; C. Charles seven for 45) and 49 for two wickets.

LEEWARD ISLANDS v. AUSTRALIANS

At St. John's, June 1, 2, 3. Australians won by an innings and 219 runs.
Australians 499 (R. Benaud 104, L. Maddocks 91, L. Favell 74, A. K. Davidson 50); Leeward Islands 99 (R. Benaud four for 35) and 181 (J. C. Hill five for 42).

G. HEADLEY'S XI v. AUSTRALIANS

At Montego Bay, Jamaica, June 6, 7. Abandoned without a ball being bowled.

WEST INDIES v. AUSTRALIA
Fifth Test Match

At Kingston, June 11, 13, 14, 15, 16, 17. Australia won by an innings and 82 runs a game in which more records were established. First and foremost was the performance of Walcott in hitting for the second time during the series two separate centuries in a match, a feat never before accomplished. Furthermore he became the first player to reach three figures on five occasions in a Test rubber. The Australian total, besides being the biggest ever recorded in a Test match by a team from the Commonwealth, yielded two other records—the scoring of five centuries in an innings and the highest third wicket stand in history for Australia.

By the end of the opening day West Indies appeared likely to make a better fight, for with six wickets down they had 327 runs on the board. They began badly on a pitch "full of runs," losing two wickets, including that of the new opening batsman, Furlonge, for 13. Then Walcott led a recovery in which Weekes and Worrell rendered able support. Let off when 21 by Johnston, who twisted a knee in attempting the catch and did not bowl in the match, Walcott offered only one more chance, at 105, during a stay of nearly five hours. While always strong in defence, he drove, cut and pulled with great power. Weekes, who injured a thigh muscle early in his innings, hit so fiercely all round that in scoring 56 of the 82 added for the third wicket, he registered no fewer than ten boundaries. Worrell, with a discriminating display, helped Walcott to put on 110 before falling to a splendid left-handed catch on the leg side behind the wicket by Langley, who gave a capital exhibition and in the two innings allowed only eight byes. Next day Miller bowled so effectively that the remaining four wickets went down for 30 runs. Three of them fell to Miller at a cost of 15 runs, and he finished with six for 107.

Australia in turn made a poor start, losing two men for seven runs, but from that point they were the masters. McDonald and Harvey, proceeding unhurriedly, put on 295 in a little over five hours. Harvey, staying till his side stood 16 ahead, batted for seven hours five minutes and hit one 6 and twenty-four 4's. Very slow at first, Miller shared with Archer in a stand which realised 220, and there followed a dazzling display of forcing batsmanship by Benaud. So mercilessly did Benaud flog a tiring attack that, with two 6's and fifteen 4's among his figures, he reached 100 in seventy-eight minutes. Upon his dismissal Johnson declared with Australia 401 ahead.

Three West Indies wickets went down for 65, but again Walcott checked the success of bowlers. He found a steady partner in Sobers, who stayed three hours while 179 runs were added, but when they were parted such a breakdown occurred that the innings and the match were all over for another 75 runs early on the sixth day.

West Indies

J. K. Holt c Langley b Miller	4	— c Langley b Benaud	21
H. Furlonge c Benaud b Lindwall	4	— c sub b Miller	28
C. L. Walcott c Langley b Miller	155	— c Langley b Lindwall	110
E. D. Weekes b Benaud	56	— not out	36
F. M. Worrell c Langley b Lindwall	61	— b Johnson	12
O. G. Smith c Langley b Miller	29	— c and b Benaud	10
G. Sobers not out	35	— c Favell b Lindwall	64
D. Atkinson run out	8	— c Langley b Archer	4
C. Depeiza c Langley b Miller	0	— b Miller	6
F. King b Miller	0	— c Archer b Johnson	6
T. Dewdney b Miller	2	— lbw b Benaud	0
L-b 2, w 1	3	B 8, l-b 6, w 1	15

1/4 2/13 3/95 4/205 5/268 6/327   357   1/47 2/60 3/65 4/244   319
7/341 8/347 9/347   5/244 6/268 7/273 8/283
                                   9/289

Australia

C. C. McDonald b Worrell	127	R. Benaud c Worrell b Smith 121
L. Favell c Weekes b King	0	I. W. Johnson not out	2
A. R. Morris lbw b Dewdney	7	
R. N. Harvey c Atkinson b Smith	204	B 8, l-b 7, w 9, n-b 1	25
K. R. Miller c Worrell b Atkinson	109	
R. G. Archer c Depeiza b Sobers	128	1/0 2/7 3/302 (8 wkts., dec.) 758
R. R. Lindwall c Depeiza b King	10	4/373 5/593 6/597 7/621 8/758

G. R. Langley and W. A. Johnston did not bat.

Australia Bowling

	O.	M.	R.	W.		O.	M.	R.	W.
Lindwall	12	2	64	2	....	20	5	56	2
Miller	25.2	2	107	6	....	19	3	58	2
Archer	11	1	39	0	....	26	6	68	1
Benaud........	24	5	75	1	....	30	10	76	3
Johnson	22	7	69	0	....	23	10	46	2

West Indies Bowling

	O.	M.	R.	W.
Dewdney	24	4	115	1
King	31	1	126	2
Atkinson	55	21	132	1
Smith	52.4	17	145	2
Worrell	45	10	116	1
Sobers	38	12	99	1

Umpires: P. Burke and T. Ewart.

INDIA IN PAKISTAN, 1954–55

The first official Test series to be played in Pakistan did little credit to cricket generally. Pakistan and India faced each other like two boxers tentatively sparring for an opening, but being afraid to strike the first blow in case some unexpected counter might be forthcoming. With neither side prepared to take the initiative the series ended in stalemate, all five Tests being drawn for the first time in history. Fear of defeat remained uppermost in the minds of the two teams and it does appear that until the two countries realise that the loss of a Test Match is not the shattering tragedy they seem to imagine, games between them are likely to remain dull and practically devoid of interest.

Perhaps the years will bring greater understanding on the cricket field, but it is to be hoped that in the meantime the public will not lose interest in the game. Certainly on this tour the crowds were large and enthusiastic, but the many who must have been watching international cricket for the first time saw little to make them want to go again. Both sides adopted the same defensive batting tactics and negative bowling to deep-set fields. As a result the average rate of scoring in the Tests was barely 30 runs an hour.

If there were any honours to be gained these went to the bowlers, who toiled hard for their wickets on pitches generally in favour of batsmen. Pakistan relied almost exclusively on the fast-medium attack of Khan Mohammad, Fazal Mahmood and Mahmood Hussain; between them they took 51 of the 58 wickets which fell to bowlers.

For India the spinners did best, Gupte taking 21 wickets with leg-breaks and the slow left-hander, Mankad, who captained the side, coming next with 12. Few batsmen distinguished themselves. The most successful were Alim-ud-Din, the Pakistan opening batsman, and Umrigar, the hard-hitting Indian. Hanif Mohammad, the young Pakistani, regarded as one of the leading opening batsmen in the world, played an innings of 142 in the second Test, but otherwise scarcely lived up to his reputation. Manjrekar again showed himself to be probably the most stylish stroke-player in India.

Kardar, who captained Pakistan, won the toss in four matches and four times his side led on first innings. In no case was the lead substantial, and the teams could be considered evenly matched in nearly every respect. India went through the tour unbeaten, winning five and drawing nine matches. In the games outside the Tests, Patel, an off-break bowler, as well as Gupte, achieved considerable success and Umrigar and Manjrekar remained the leading batsmen.

SUMMARY OF THE TOUR—RESULTS OF ALL MATCHES
Matches—Played 14, Won 5, Drawn 9

TEST MATCHES
Matches—Played 5, Drawn 5

INDIA BATTING AVERAGES IN THE TESTS

	Matches	Inns.	Not Outs	Runs	Highest Inns.	Average
P. R. Umrigar	5	7	2	271	108	54.20
V. L. Manjrekar	5	8	2	270	74*	45.00
P. Roy	5	10	2	272	77	34.00
G. S. Ramchand	5	6	1	147	53	29.40
C. V. Gadkari	3	5	2	64	26*	21.33
N. S. Tamhane	5	6	2	77	54*	19.25
P. L. Punjabi	5	10	0	164	33	16.40
C. D. Gopinath	2	3	0	49	41	16.33
D. G. Phadkar	3	3	1	30	13	15.00
V. Mankad	5	6	1	51	33	10.20
S. P. Gupte	5	5	2	19	15	6.33
Ghulam Ahmed	4	4	0	18	8	4.50

Also batted: P. Bhandari 19, M. K. Mantri 0 and 2, J. S. Patel O.

INDIA BOWLING AVERAGES IN TESTS

	Overs	Maidens	Runs	Wickets	Average
G. S. Ramchand	111	44	200	10	20.00
S. P. Gupte	276.5	107	475	21	22.61
P. R. Umrigar	121	43	184	8	23.00
D. G. Phadkar	129.1	40	243	8	30.37
V. Mankad	263.3	130	399	12	33.25
Ghulam Ahmed	167	41	335	9	37.22

Also bowled: J. S. Patel 40—13—71—3.

PAKISTAN BATTING AVERAGES IN TESTS

	Matches	Inns.	Not Outs	Runs	Highest Inns.	Average
Alim-ud-Din	5	9	1	332	103	41.50
Hanif Mohammad	5	9	1	273	142	34.12
Waqar Hassan	5	9	1	244	52	30.50
Maqsood Ahmed	5	9	0	250	99	27.77
Imtiaz Ahmed	5	9	0	233	69	25.88
A. H. Kardar	5	8	0	207	93	25.87
Wazir Mohammad	5	7	1	139	55	23.16
Shuja-ud-Din	5	9	0	132	40	14.66
Fazal Mahmood	4	5	1	39	15*	9.75
Khan Mohammad	4	6	3	27	15*	9.00
Mahmood Hussain	5	7	1	30	14	5.00
Miran Bux	2	3	2	1	1*	1.00

* Signifies not out.

PAKISTAN BOWLING AVERAGES IN TESTS

	Overs	Maidens	Runs	Wickets	Average
Khan Mohammad	170.5	54	349	22	15.86
Fazal Mahmood..........	223.2	93	331	15	22.06
Mahmood Hussain	153.1	37	372	14	26.57
Hanif Mohammad	18	5	41	1	41.00
A. H. Kardar	51	14	90	2	45.00
Maqsood Ahmed	32	13	48	1	48.00
Miran Bux...............	58	22	115	2	57.50
Shuja-ud-Din	49	20	77	1	77.00

Also bowled: Alim-ud-Din 8—0—25—0; Imtiaz Ahmed 1—1—0—0; Wazir Mohammad 2—0—5—0.

INDIA BATTING AVERAGES IN FIRST-CLASS MATCHES

	Matches	Inns.	Not Outs	Runs	Highest Inns.	Average
P. R. Umrigar	11	13	3	650	151	65.00
V. L. Manjrekar	11	15	4	687	129*	62.45
C. D. Gopinath	9	10	4	350	130*	58.33
C. G. Borde	6	7	3	200	99	50.00
G. S. Ramchand	13	14	3	427	85*	38.81
P. Roy	11	17	2	576	105	38.40
V. Mankad	11	14	2	366	130	30.50
H. T. Dani	7	7	3	116	42*	29.00
C. V. Gadkari..........	8	10	3	190	36	27.14
P. L. Punjabi	11	17	0	393	111	23.11
N. S. Tamhane	9	7	3	90	54*	22.50
P. Bhandari	8	7	2	108	30*	21.60
M. K. Mantri	8	8	0	134	51	16.75
D. G. Phadkar	7	5	2	47	14	15.66
S. P. Gupte	9	5	2	19	15	6.33
Ghulam Ahmed	6	4	0	18	8	4.50
J. S. Patel	8	3	1	2	1*	1.00

Also batted: L. Amarnath 54*.

INDIA BOWLING AVERAGES IN FIRST-CLASS MATCHES

	Overs	Maidens	Runs	Wickets	Average
J. S. Patel	221	95	374	35	10.68
H. T. Dani .'.............	78	27	152	10	15.20
S. P. Gupte	479.3	165	892	55	16.21
P. R. Umrigar	169	61	252	14	18.00
V. Mankad	385.3	190	583	29	20.10
G. S. Ramchand	215	94	365	18	20.27
D. G. Phadkar	216.1	81	393	19	20.68
C. V. Gadkari..........	12	4	21	1	21.00
P. Bhandari	72	44	103	4	25.75
Ghulam Ahmed	243	61	502	16	31.37
C. G. Borde	121	45	270	3	90.00

Also bowled: L. Amarnath 20—8—39—2; C. D. Gopinath 4—1—19—0; V. L. Manjrekar 1—0—6—0.

Signifies not out.

The following nine three-figure innings were played by the Indians on the tour:—

V. L. Manjrekar (3):
    129*   v. Punjab C.A. at Sialkot.
    103*   v. Karachi C.A. at Karachi.
    100   v. Central Zone at Montgomery.

P. R. Umrigar (2):
    151   v. Services at Rawalpindi.
    108   v. Pakistan at Peshawar (Fourth Test).

C. D. Gopinath (1):
    130*   v. Combined Schools at Karachi.

V. Mankad (1):
    130   v. Karachi C.A. at Karachi.

P. L. Punjabi (1):
    111   v. Karachi C.A. at Karachi.

P. Roy (1):
    105   v. Punjab C.A. at Sialkot.

The following five three-figure innings were played against the Indians on the tour:—

Hanif Mohammad (2):
    163   for Combined Schools at Karachi.
    142   for Pakistan at Bahawalpur (Second Test).

Alim-ud-Din (1):
    103*   for Pakistan at Karachi (Fifth Test).

Imtiaz Ahmed (1):
    105   for Services, at Rawalpindi.

Shakoor Ahmed (1):
    104   for Central Zone at Montgomery.

* Signifies not out.*

At Chittagong, December 28, 29, 30. India won by an innings and 15 runs. East Pakistan S.A. 98 (S. P. Gupte four for 19, D. G. Phadkar four for 40) and 87 (Gupte six for 37); India 200 for seven, declared (M. K. Mantri 51).

PAKISTAN v. INDIA
(First Test)

At Dacca, January 1, 2, 3, 4. Drawn. The first official Test Match to be played in Pakistan set the pattern for the series, both sides playing grim, defensive cricket. At no time did a definite result look likely. Pakistan, who won the toss, batted steadily. Hanif and Waqar Hassan put on 53 for the second wicket and Imtiaz Ahmed also showed good form. At the close of the first day Pakistan were 207 for five, but they were out for the addition of 50. Ghulam Ahmed bowled unchanged for 40 overs. India collapsed before the fast-medium attack of Mahmood Hussain and Khan Mohammad and Pakistan led by 109. They strengthened their position with a second wicket stand of 92 by Alim-ud-Din and Waqar Hassan and although Gupte's leg-breaks caused a collapse India were set to get 268 to win. After losing two wickets for 17 they did not attempt the task. Only 710 runs were scored in the four days.

Pakistan

Hanif Mohammad c Tamhane b Ghulam	41	— c Umrigar b Phadkar	14
Alim-ud-Din c Phadkar b Ghulam	7	— c sub b Gupte	51
Waqar Hassan c and b Ghulam	52	— st Tamhane b Gupte	51
Maqsood Ahmed c Tamhane b Ghulam	11	— c Mantri b Gupte	16
Wazir Mohammad c Phadkar b Gupte	23	— run out	0
Imtiaz Ahmed b Phadkar	54	— c Umrigar b Gupte	5
A. H. Kardar b Ramchand	29	— c Mantri b Phadkar	3
Shuja-ud-Din st Tamhane b Mankad	25	— run out	1
Fazal Mahmood c Tamhane b Ramchand	0	— not out	15
Mahmood Hussain b Ghulam	9	— c Punjabi b Gupte	0
Khan Mohammad not out	4	— run out	0
Extras	2	Extras	2

1/21 2/74 3/88 4/125 5/157 6/207   257
7/227 8/227 9/240

1/24 2/116 3/122 4/137   158
5/139 6/140 7/140 8/156
9/158

India

P. Roy b Hussain	0	— not out	67
P. L. Punjabi b Khan	26	— lbw b Khan	3
M. K. Mantri b Hussain	0	— c Imtiaz b Khan	2
V. L. Manjrekar b Khan	18	— not out	74
P. R. Umrigar c Kardar b Hussain	32		
G. S. Ramchand c Imtiaz b Hussain	37		
D. G. Phadkar c Imtiaz b Hussain	11		
V. Mankad c Imtiaz b Hussain	2		
N. S. Tamhane b Khan	5		
Ghulam Ahmed b Khan	2		
S. P. Gupte not out	1		
Extras	14	Extras	1

1/17 2/19 3/45 4/56 5/115 6/129   148
7/131 8/143 9/145

1/15 2/17   (2 wkts.) 147

India Bowling

	O.	M.	R.	W.	O.	M.	R.	W.
Phadkar	18	11	24	1	28.1	11	57	2
Ramchand	15	7	19	2	19	10	31	0
Gupte	46	14	79	1	6	0	17	5
Mankad	12.2	3	24	1	18	6	34	0
Ghulam	45	8	109	5				
Umrigar					15	8	17	0

Pakistan Bowling

	O.	M.	R.	W.	O.	M.	R.	W.
Fazal	25	19	18	0	23	11	34	0
Hussain	27	6	67	6	7	2	21	0
Khan	26.5	12	42	4	12	5	18	2
Shuja-ud-Din	4	2	7	0	14	6	25	0
Maqsood					3	1	4	0
Kardar					12	4	17	0
Hanif					5	1	14	0
Alim-ud-Din					5	0	13	0
Imtiaz					1	1	0	0

At Karachi, January 7, 8, 9. Drawn. India 404 for four, declared (V. Mankad 130, P. Punjabi 111, V. L. Manjrekar 103 not out) and 31 for no wicket. Karachi C.A. 268 for eight, declared (Wazir Mohammad 96, Alim-ud-Din 55).

At Hyderabad, January 11, 12, 13. India won by an innings and 70 runs. Sind C.A. 97 (W. Mathias 50 not out) and 116 (S. P. Gupte four for 39); India 283 for five, declared (P. R. Umrigar 95).

PAKISTAN v. INDIA

(Second Test)

At Bahawalpur, January 15, 16, 17, 18. Drawn. Again slow scoring prevented a decision and not even three innings were completed in the match. India fared badly after winning the toss and despite a good innings by Manjrekar, seven men were out for 107. Improvement came from the later batsmen, particularly Ramchand and Tamhane who added 82. Hanif and Alim-ud-Din began with a stand of 127 for Pakistan, who took the lead with six wickets in hand. Hanif gave a fine display and scored his first century in Test cricket. Umrigar, not normally recognised as a leading Test bowler, sent down 59 overs and took six wickets. Going in again 77 behind, India were never in danger of defeat. Roy and Manjrekar put on 123 for the third wicket.

India

P. Roy b Fazal	0	— c Kardar b Khan	77
P. L. Punjabi b Khan	18	— c Maqsood b Hussain	33
V. Mankad c Imtiaz b Fazal	6	— c Imtiaz b Fazal	1
V. L. Manjrekar c Hussain b Khan	50	— c Imtiaz b Fazal	59
P. R. Umrigar b Khan	20		
G. S. Ramchand b Hussain	53		
C. V. Gadkari lbw b Khan	2	— not out	8
C. D. Gopinath c Waqar b Fazal	0	— c Maqsood b Khan	8
N. S. Tamhane not out	54	— not out	9
S. P. Gupte b Khan	15		
Ghulam Ahmed b Fazal	8		
Extras	9	Extras	14

1/0 2/12 3/61 4/93 5/98 6/100 7/107 235
8/189 9/205

1/58 2/62 3/185 (5 wkts.) 209
4/189 5/193

Pakistan

Hanif Mohammad c Gadkari b Umrigar	142
Alim-ud-Din b Ghulam	64
Waqar Hassan c Gupte b Umrigar	48
Maqsood Ahmed c Gadkari b Umrigar	10
Imtiaz Ahmed st Tamhane b Gupte	3
A. H. Kardar c Punjabi b Umrigar	13
Fazal Mahmood b Umrigar	9
Mahmood Hussain c Gadkari b Umrigar	0

Shuja-ud-Din run out 7
Wazir Mohammad not out 4
Khan Mohammad not out 1

Extras 11

1/127 2/220 (9 wkts., dec.) 312
3/226 4/229 5/258 6/286 7/286
8/301 9/307

Pakistan Bowling

	O.	M.	R.	W.		O.	M.	R.	W.
Fazal	62.5	23	86	4	....	28	6	58	2
Hussain	25	8	56	1	....	17	3	47	1
Khan	33	7	74	5	....	22	6	50	2
Shuja-ud-Din	9	4	10	0	....	8	6	2	0
					Maqsood	7	3	19	0
					Kardar	7	0	19	0

India Bowling

	O.	M.	R.	W.
Ramchand	13	5	26	0
Umrigar	59	25	74	6
Gupte	17	8	49	1
Ghulam	36	4	63	1
Mankad	40	19	89	0

At Montgomery, January 21, 22, 23. Drawn. Central Zone 123 (Nayyar Hussain 60 not out, S. P. Gupte six for 51) and 304 (Shakoor Ahmed 104, Shuja-ud-Din 62, V. Mankad four for 56, S. P. Gupte four for 110); India 307 for seven, declared (V. L. Manjrekar 100, V. Mankad 61, C. D. Gopinath 60) and 110 for four.

At Lahore, January 25, 26, 27. India won by an innings and 10 runs. Universities XI 69 (J. Patel four for 22) and 85 (Patel eight for 25); India 164 (P. R. Umrigar 58, Aziz four for 62).

PAKISTAN v. INDIA
(Third Test)

At Lahore, January 29, 30, 31, February 1. Drawn. For the third Test running Pakistan enjoyed slight superiority without being able to force victory. Pakistan, who won the toss, began shakily but the middle batsmen brought recovery. Maqsood Ahmed was unfortunate to miss a century by one run and with Kardar added 136 for the fourth wicket. Good innings also came from Wazir Mohammad and Imtiaz Ahmed. Gupte accomplished a remarkable performance in sending down 73.5 overs in the innings, 33 being maidens. India again owed most to their later batsmen. Half the side fell for 117, but Umrigar, well supported by Gopinath and Mankad, restricted the Pakistan lead to 77. Pakistan failed to score at the necessary pace in their second innings and when they declared insufficient time remained for them to dismiss India again.

Pakistan

Hanif Mohammad c Tamhane b Gupte..	12	— not out	0
Alim-ud-Din run out	38	— b Mankad	58
Waqar Hassan c Mankad b Gupte	9	— c Tamhane b Mankad	12
Maqsood Ahmed st Tamhane b Gupte ..	99	— c Punjabi b Mankad	15
A. H. Kardar c Ramchand b Mankad ..	44		
Wazir Mohammad lbw b Mankad	55		
Imtiaz Ahmed run out	55	— c Tamhane b Gupte	9
Shuja-ud-Din c Mankad b Ghulam	3	— c sub b Gupte	40
Fazal Mahmood st Tamhane b Gupte ..	12		
Mahmood Hussain b Gupte	0		
Miran Bux not out	1		
Extras........................	0	Extras	2

1/32 2/55 3/62 4/198 5/202 6/286   328   1/83 2/109   (5 wkts., dec.)136
7/302 8/327 9/327   3/112 4/136 5/136

India

P. Roy b Hussain.....................	23	— c Imtiaz b Kardar	23
P. L. Punjabi b Miran................	27	— c Maqsood b Kardar	1
C. V. Gadhari b Fazal	13	— not out	26
V. L. Manjrekar b Miran	0	— not out	23
P. R. Umrigar c Hanif b Hussain	78		
G. S. Ramchand c Maqsood b Fazal.....	12		
C. D. Gopinath c Fazal b Shuja	41		
V. Mankad c Imtiaz b Hussain	33		
N. S. Tamhane c Imtiaz b Hussain......	0		
Ghulam Ahmed c Imtiaz b Fazal	0		
S. P. Gupte not out	0		
Extras........................	24	Extra	1

1/52 2/56 3/58 4/91 5/117 6/179   251   1/3 2/40   (2 wkts.) 74
7/228 8/243 9/244

India Bowling

	O.	M.	R.	W.		O.	M.	R.	W.
Umrigar	14	4	23	0					
Ramchand	10	5	12	0	....	6	1	20	0
Gupte	73.5	33	133	5	....	36.3	11	34	2
Ghulam	46	11	95	1	....	14	2	47	0
Mankad	44	25	65	2	....	28	17	33	3

Pakistan Bowling

	O.	M.	R.	W.		O.	M.	R.	W.
Hussain	26.1	6	70	4	....	1	0	1	0
Fazal	47	24	62	3	....	1	0	2	0
Miran	48	20	82	2					
Shuja	7	2	13	1	....	7	0	20	0
Maqsood						4	2	4	0
Kardar						12	3	20	2
Alim						3	0	12	0
Hanif						3	0	9	0
Wazir						2	0	5	0

At Sialkot, February 3, 5, 6. India won by an innings and 162 runs. India 422 for six, declared (V. L. Manjrekar 129 not out, P. Roy 105, G. S. Ramchand 56, M. K. Mantri 50, S. F. Rehman four for 103); Punjab C.A. 153 (J. S. Patel four for 34, Ghulam Ahmed four for 81) and 107.

At Rawalpindi, February 8, 9, 10. India won by an innings and 20 runs. Services XI 101 (Imtiaz Ahmed 59) and 183 (Imtiaz Ahmed 105, V. Mankad five for 68, S. P. Gupte four for 87); India 304 for five, declared (P. R. Umrigar 151, V. Mankad 64, L. Amarnath 54 not out).

PAKISTAN v. INDIA
(Fourth Test)

At Peshawar, February 12, 13, 14, 15. Drawn. The scoring was slower than ever, only 638 runs being obtained in four days. For the first time India finished on top, but once more there was little to choose between the sides. Pakistan made only 129 for the loss of six wickets on the first day, the batsmen again finding the leg-breaks of Gupte troublesome. India owed nearly everything to Umrigar, who obtained his country's only century of the series and alone showed any enterprise in the match. Although going ahead for the loss of only four wickets, India could not force home their position, and Pakistan went in again no more than 57 behind. As many as four batsmen were run out in the India innings. Pakistan looked to be in trouble when they lost their fourth wicket at 70, but Maqsood Ahmed and Imtiaz Ahmed saved them with a stand of 83. India needed 126 to win, but only an hour remained.

Pakistan

Hanif Mohammad c Phadkar b Gupte	13	—	c and b Mankad	21
Alim-ud-Din b Ramchand	0	—	lbw b Ghulam	4
Waqar Hassan c and b Gupte	43	—	lbw b Gupte	16
Maqsood Ahmed c Punjabi b Phadkar	31	—	c and b Mankad	44
Imtiaz Ahmed b Phadkar	0	—	c Punjabi b Mankad	69
Wazir Mohammad b Mankad	34	—	b Mankad	0
A. H. Kardar b Gupte	11	—	b Phadkar	0
Shuja-ud-Din c Tamhane b Gupte	37	—	run out	11
Khan Mohammad c Mankad b Ghulam	4	—	c sub b Mankad	3
Mahmood Hussain not out	5	—	st Tamhane b Phadkar	2
Miran Bux lbw b Gupte	0	—	not out	0
Extras	10		Extras	12

1/2 2/32 3/81 4/81 5/96 6/111 7/171   **188**   1/10 2/50 3/68 4/70   **182**
8/176 9/188   5/153 6/156 7/177 8/178 9/182

India

P. Roy run out	16	—	not out	13
P. I. Punjabi b Khan	16	—	b Hanif	6
P. R. Umrigar run out	108	—	not out	3
V. L. Manjrekar run out	32			
C. V. Gadkari c Maqsood b Hussain	15			
G. S. Ramchand c Shuja b Khan	18			
V. Mankad not out	3			
N. S. Tamhane run out	0			
D. G. Phadkar b Khan	13			
S. P. Gupte c Waqar b Hussain	2			
Ghulam Ahmed b Khan	8			
Extras	14		Extra	1
	—			—
	245		(1 wkt.)	23

1/30 2/44 3/135 4/182 5/210 6/218   245   1/19   (1 wkt.) 23
7/219 8/232 9/235

India Bowling

	O.	M.	R.	W.		O.	M.	R.	W.
Phadkar	21	14	19	2	....	18	2	42	2
Ramchand	7	2	13	1	....	2	1	3	0
Gupte	41.3	22	63	5	....	35	16	52	1
Mankad	61	34	71	1	....	54.1	26	64	5
Ghulam	13	7	12	1	....	13	9	9	1

Pakistan Bowling

	O.	M.	R.	W.		O.	M.	R.	W.
Khan	36	14	79	4	....	4	0	10	0
Hussain	38	11	78	2	....	2	1	2	0
Miran	8	2	30	0	....	2	0	3	0
Kardar	19	6	34	0	....	1	1	0	0
Maqsood	7	3	10	0	....	6	2	6	0
					Hanif	4	3	1	1

At Lyallpur, February 18, 19, 20. Drawn. India 300 for eight, declared (P. Roy 73, C. D. Gopinath 55 not out, Israr Ali four for 134) and 191 for two (G. S. Ramchand 85 not out, P. Roy 70); North Zone 153 (Nissar 50, J. Patel seven for 69).

At Karachi, February 22, 23, 24. Drawn. India 352 for five, declared (C. D. Gopinath 130 not out, C. G. Borde 99, G. S. Ramchand 56) and 36 for two; Combined Schools 267 for nine, declared (Hanif Mohammad 163).

PAKISTAN v. INDIA
(Fifth Test)

At Karachi, February 26, 27, 28, March 1. Drawn. When it seemed that a result might be possible at last, a heavy thunderstorm interfered on the third day, and so the series ended with all five matches drawn. The fast-medium bowling of Ramchand worried Pakistan when they won the toss for the fourth time. India fared just as badly against Khan Mohammad and Fazal Mahmood, and they finished 17 behind on first innings. These two innings were over by the second day but Pakistan were held up by the rain which limited play to an hour and forty minutes on the third day. Alim-ud-Din checked a collapse and made his first Test century for Pakistan. Kardar helped him add 155 at almost a run a minute, some of the fastest scoring of the series, but too much time had been lost for a result when India went in to get 259 to win.

Pakistan

Hanif Mohammad c Tamhane b Phadkar	2	— c Tamhane b Umrigar	28
Alim-ud-Din c Tamhane b Ramchand	7	— not out	103
Waqar Hassan c Umrigar b Ramchand	12	— not out	1
Maqsood Ahmed c Tamhane b Ramchand	22	— c Bhandari b Umrigar	2
Imtiaz Ahmed c Ramchand b Patel	37	— run out	1
Wazir Mohammad c Phadkar b Patel	23		
A. H. Kardar c Tamhane b Ramchand	14	— st Tamhane b Gupte	93
Shuja-ud-Din c Mankad b Ramchand	0	— b Ramchand	8
Fazal Mahmood lbw b Patel	3		
Khan Mohammad not out	15		
Mahmood Hussain c Phadkar b Ramchand	14		
Extras	13	Extras	5

1/2 2/19 3/37 4/66 5/88 6/119   162   1/25 2/69 (5 wkts., dec.) 241
7/119 8/122 9/135   3/77 4/81 5/236

India

P. Roy c Kardar b Khan	37	— lbw b Maqsood	16
P. L. Punjabi lbw b Khan	12	— c Imtiaz b Fazal	22
P. R. Umrigar b Fazal	16	— not out	14
V. L. Manjrekar c Kardar b Khan	14		
V. Mankad c Maqsood b Fazal	6		
G. S. Ramchand c Hanif b Fazal	15	— not out	12
N. S. Tamhane b Fazal	9		
P. Bhandari b Khan	19		
D. G. Phadkar not out	6		
J. Patel lbw b Khan	0		
S. P. Gupte c Shuja b Fazal	1		
Extras	10	Extras	5

1/22 2/45 3/68 4/89 5/95 6/110   145   1/34 2/49   (2 wkts.) 69
7/131 8/144 9/145

India Bowling

	O.	M.	R.	W.	O.	M.	R.	W.
Ramchand	28	9	49	6	11	4	27	1
Phadkar	10	6	7	1	34	6	94	0
Patel	33	12	49	3	7	1	22	0
Gupte	15	3	24	0	6	0	24	1
Mankad	5	0	16	0	1	0	3	0
Umrigar	5	3	4	0	28	3	66	2

Pakistan Bowling

	O.	M.	R.	W.	O.	M.	R.	W.
Khan	30	5	72	5	7	5	4	0
Hussain	7	0	14	0	3	0	16	0
Fazal	27.3	6	49	5	9	4	22	1
Hanif					6	1	17	0
Maqsood					5	2	5	1

OVERSEAS CRICKET, 1954–55

AUSTRALIAN INTER-STATE MATCHES

By T. L. GOODMAN

SHEFFIELD SHIELD RESULTS

	Played	Won	Won on 1st Inns.	Lost on 1st Inns.	Lost	Drawn	Points	Per cent
Points awarded ...	—	5	3	1	—	2	—	
New South Wales..	4	2	1	0	1	0	13	65.00
Victoria	4	1	2	0	1	0	11	55.00
Western Australia .	2	0	1	0	0	1	5	50.00
Queensland	4	1	0	2	1	0	7	35.00
South Australia ...	4	0	0	2	1	1	4	20.00

New South Wales won the Sheffield Shield for the fifth time in nine post-war inter-State competitions. The Shield series took second place to the M.C.C. tour. Moreover, the programme had been cut from sixteen to nine matches by the "Inter-State Conference." Western Australia, who had been allowed to continue experimentally in the competition on a modified programme of four matches, were limited to two fixtures, both against South Australia. The other four States played four instead of seven games.

This drastic curtailment was designed to limit financial losses, but it proved to be false economy. Promising players on the fringe of Test selection had their opportunities severely restricted, and, as a result, the work of Australian and State selection committees was hampered. Before the season was over representatives of the Shield States decided to discontinue the experiment and they drew up a normal programme for 1955–56.

K. R. Miller, again appointed captain of New South Wales, had to miss two of the four matches, but some excellent reserves were available when key players were required for the Tests. New South Wales and Victoria each lost one match—to each other. Victoria won in Melbourne by 36 runs but after being sent in to bat on a fast Sydney pitch they lost the return game by nine wickets in two days. The teams took advantage of a new rule which allowed extra time on the second day if a definite result was in sight. Test men played in these two games. New South Wales also defeated Queensland in Sydney with one day to spare, having claimed extra time on the third day. In this match the pace bowlers took 35 of the 39 wickets that fell.

It seemed ludicrous that, under the restricted programme, Western Australia after beating South Australia in Adelaide on the first innings could have won the Shield with an outright victory in their only other fixture—against South Australia in Perth— but rain prevented even a first innings result being recorded there.

J. Rutherford, the Western Australia opening batsman, scored a century in each of the two matches against South Australia, and he headed the Sheffield Shield batting averages, with 303 runs in three innings, average 101. Neil Harvey (Victoria) despite the calls of Test cricket, scored most runs, 401, at 57.28. Rutherford also had the best average among Australian batsmen for all first-class cricket, 68.40 (5 innings, 342 runs), and Neil Harvey hit most runs, 1,009, at 45.8.

A number of young batsmen fared well in inter-State and international games and L. Favell (South Australia), P. Burge (Queensland) and W. Watson (New South Wales) were chosen for the Australian team to tour West Indies at the end of the season. Burge against New South Wales in Brisbane repeated his century of the previous season. Of the others to impress, R. Simpson (New South Wales) at least, might also have been chosen for the tour. Simpson, a tall right-handed batsman, aged 18, scored a valuable maiden century in first-class cricket against Victoria in Sydney. He is a brilliant slip fieldsman, as he showed when playing against M.C.C.

P. Philpott made an impressive debut in Shield cricket by scoring 71 and 39 for New South Wales when runs were needed against Queensland in Sydney, and later he did well against M.C.C. J. Chambers (Victoria) and L. Pavy (Western Australia), both left-handers, played some good innings. D. Harris showed much promise in a big opening partnership with Favell for South Australia against M.C.C., but he did not maintain his form in the inter-State series.

Whereas spin bowlers took the chief honours the previous summer, pace bowlers triumphed in Shield cricket at the same time as Tyson and Statham of England were upsetting Australia's batsmen in the Tests. Well-grassed pitches, particularly at Sydney, contributed to this factor.

An outstanding feature was the discovery of Pat Crawford, the 21-year-old New South Wales right-arm fast bowler, who met with astonishing successes after graduating through the inter-State Colts match against Queensland. He headed the Shield bowling averages with 12.96 and took most wickets, 25. Having taken nine wickets for New South Wales against M.C.C., he shared with his State colleague, A. K. Davidson, left-arm fast-medium, the distinction of taking most wickets, 34, in first-class cricket. Crawford led the averages with 16.02.

Crawford captured 12 wickets against Queensland in Sydney, after taking eight against Victoria in Melbourne. He is over 6 ft. tall, has good command of length and pace, and can move the ball into, or away from a batsman. Crawford was favoured by the fast Sydney pitches, but nevertheless his success in his initial season in "big" cricket was very encouraging. Crawford, and also

Philpott, later went to England for a season in Lancashire League
cricket.

    A. Dick (Victoria), an exponent of top-spin, who deputised
for I. W. Johnson in some of the matches, followed Crawford in
the Shield averages, with 10 wickets at 13.40. J. Treanor the New
South Wales right-arm leg-spin bowler, performed the "hat-
trick" in Queensland's second innings in Brisbane. In the same
match, the first of the competition, R. R. Lindwall made his first
appearance for Queensland, against his native New South Wales,
and although receiving no help from the pitch he took the first
four wickets.

    J. Drennan, right-arm fast-medium, who is tall and has a
good action, showed promise, but his State, South Australia,
missed G. Noblet, who retired from first-class cricket after being
the mainstay of the attack for many years.

    The New South Wales Cricket Association, anxious to make
up leeway in recognising the services of former internationals,
decided to stage two joint testimonial matches in Sydney: one
for A. A. Mailey and J. M. Taylor in 1955–6 and the other for
S. J. McCabe and W. J. O'Reilly in 1956–7.

    For the 1955–56 season Western Australia, on trial since they
first entered the Sheffield Shield competition in 1947–48, were
elevated to permanent status, but they will still play fewer matches
than the four other members in the Eastern States.

QUEENSLAND v. NEW SOUTH WALES

    At Brisbane, October 29, 30, November 1, 2. New South Wales won on
first innings. For Queensland, Burge did a lot of hard driving and, like Benaud
for New South Wales, repeated his feat of the previous season in reaching three-
figures in this fixture. K. Archer figured in an opening stand of 132 with Harvey,
who was missed in the slips before scoring. Lindwall, the Test fast bowler,
playing for the first time against his native State, gained no help from the pitch,
but took the first four wickets. Benaud and Burke were chiefly responsible for
their team's substantial total. Though facing Lindwall with the new ball, Burke
batted all the third day for 124. In Queensland second innings the brothers
Archer scored well and MacKay, by solid left-hand batting, played a chanceless
innings. Treanor, leg-breaks, performed the hat-trick when dismissing K. Archer,
Sanders and Burge.

Queensland

K. Archer b Treanor	51	— lbw b Treanor	52
C. Harvey b O'Reilly	90	— c Simpson b Benaud	9
K. Mackay, c Simpson b Treanor	32	— not out	106
L. Sanders b Treanor	0	— b Treanor	0
R. G. Archer lbw b Treanor	9	— not out	75
P. Burge c Cotton b Miller	122	— lbw b Treanor	0
J. Bratchford c Miller b Simpson	58		
R. R. Lindwall b Treanor	5		
V. N. Raymer b O'Reilly	11		
W. Grout b O'Reilly	1		
B. Flynn not out	25		
Extras	1	Extras	19
	405	**(4 wkts.) 26**	

New South Wales

R. Briggs b Lindwall	30	J. Burke c Grout b R. Archer	137
A. R. Morris c Grout b Lindwall	27	E. Cotton retired hurt	41
R. Benaud lbw b Lindwall	125	O. Lambert c R. Archer b Raymer	1
K. R. Miller c Lindwall b Flynn	46	J. Treanor not out	7
H. de Courcy lbw b Lindwall	3	Extras	9
R. Simpson c and b Flynn	24		
O'Reilly c Grout b Raymer	19		469

New South Wales Bowling

	O.	M.	R.	W.		O.	M.	R.	W.
Miller	16	1	39	1	....	15	0	58	0
Cotton	8	0	33	0					
Benaud	27	4	87	0	....	11	3	21	1
Treanor	37	10	146	5	....	13	0	59	3
Burke	7	2	17	0	....	12	5	26	0
Simpson	1	0	4	1	....	11	2	39	0
O'Reilly	22	3	78	3	....	15	4	24	0
Briggs						1	0	7	0
de Courcy						2	1	8	0

Queensland Bowling

	O.	M.	R.	W.
Lindwall	35	8	90	4
K. Archer	28	2	57	1
Flynn	41	4	161	2
Raymer	38.4	6	96	2
Mackay	15	3	25	0
Cratchford	6	0	31	0
R. Archer	1	1	0	0

SOUTH AUSTRALIA v. WESTERN AUSTRALIA

At Adelaide, November 12, 13, 15, 16. Western Australia won on first innings. Hole and Pinch achieved most in the South Australia first innings when the pace bowler, Gorringe, took five wickets and the wicket-keeper, Buggins, aged 19, playing in his first inter-State game, held four catches. Western Australia went ahead for the loss of three batsmen, all run out. Rutherford stayed five and a half hours and hit twenty-one 4's, giving no chance till passing 100. Pinch and Langley were conspicuous in the South Australia second innings and paved the way to a declaration. The left-hander, Edwards, prevented a Western Australia batting collapse against the left-arm slows of Wilson and the speed of Drennan.

South Australia

Favell c Buggins b Price	34	— b Gorringe	48
Harris c Buggins b Gorringe	8	— b Rutherford	43
B. Hole c Pavy b James	64	— c Meuleman b Rutherford	40
Dansie c Edwards b Gorringe	5	— c Rutherford b Price	21
Pinch b Rutherford	46	— not out	108
Ridings b Herbert	41	— c Rutherford b Price	6
R. Langley b Price	31	— b Gorringe	52
Roxby c Buggins b Gorringe	34	— lbw b Price	4
Drennan lbw b Gorringe	0	— lbw b Gorringe	0
Horsnell not out	10	— c Pavy b Price	29
Wilson c Buggins b Gorringe	9	— not out	1
Extras	14	Extras	14
	296	(9 wkts., dec.)	366

Western Australia

L. Sawle run out	35	— c Langley b Drennan			8
J. Rutherford b Hole	167	— c Dansie b Roxby			2
D. K. Carmody run out	59	— c Favell b Drennan			
K. Meuleman run out	44	— c Pinch b Drennan			
M. Herbert c Dansie b Hole	9	— not out			3
A. Edwards c Hole b Wilson	57	— c Favell b Wilson			7.
L. Pavy run out	7	— c Ridings b Wilson			2
R. Buggins c Hole b Horsnell	8	— b Dansie			
H. Price not out	3	— not out			1
E. James c Langley b Wilson	1				
H. Gorringe, c Horsnell b Wilson	0				
Extras	7	Extras			
	397	(7 wkts.)			**18**

Western Australia Bowling

	O.	M.	R.	W.		O.	M.	R.	W
Price	15	4	56	2	....	31	2	90	4
Gorringe	18.2	1	92	5	....	22	1	97	3
Herbert	13	3	48	1	....	8	0	39	0
James	10	0	70	1	....	9	2	47	0
Rutherford	4	2	8	1	....	19	1	59	2
Meuleman	1	0	8	0					
Edwards						4	0	20	0

South Australia Bowling

	O.	M.	R.	W.		O.	M.	R.	W
Drennan	31	2	108	0	....	12	1	52	3
Horsnell	19	4	64	1	....	7	1	19	0
Roxby	12	0	63	0	....	9	2	31	1
Wilson	32.3	10	104	3	....	19	4	45	2
Dansie	5	2	19	0	....	9	2	27	1
Hole	12	0	32	2	....	4	0	10	0

VICTORIA v. SOUTH AUSTRALIA

At Melbourne, November 19, 22, 23. Victoria won on first innings. Rai
prevented play on the second day and until mid-afternoon on the third. Rai
averted a rout in the first South Australia innings and by staying four and a quarte
hours in the second staved off any possibility of defeat. For Victoria, the lef
handers, Neil Harvey and Chambers, batted brightly and a good effort by th
wicketkeeper, Maddocks, helped to establish a lead of 158.

South Australia

L. Favell b Johnston	56	— b Power			16
D. Harris b Power	3	— b Hill			4
G. B. Hole c Power b Loxton	1	— c Maddocks b Johnson			
C. Pinch lbw b Loxton	0	— c sub b Johnston			
N. Danzie, lbw b Johnston	15	— b Johnston			3
P. Ridings lbw b Johnston	21	— b Power			
G. R. Langley st Maddocks b Johnson	5	— c R. N. Harvey b Johnston.			
R. Roxby not out	26	— not out			2
J. Drennan lbw b Johnson	0	— not out			
K. Horsnell b Johnston	9	— c R. N. Harvey b Johnson.			
J. Wilson st Maddocks b Hill	9				
Extras	8	Extras			
	153	(8 wkts., dec.)			**35**

Victoria

M. Hallebone lbw b Wilson 12	L. Maddocks not out 65
C. C. McDonald run out......... 18	I. W. Johnson c Wilson b Hole ... 4
Ray Harvey b Drennan 16	J. C. Hill not out 12
R. N. Harvey b Horsnell 69	Extras 10
J. Chambers st Langley b Wilson 102	
S. J. Loxton b Horsnell 3	(7 wkts., dec.) 311

W. A. Johnston and W. Power did not bat.

Victoria Bowling

	O.	M.	R.	W.		O.	M.	R.	W.
Power	4	0	18	1	....	12	0	67	2
Loxton	6	0	37	2	....	17	1	76	0
Johnston	11	1	44	4	....	19	1	79	3
Johnson	11	2	36	2	....	21	0	87	2
Hill	4.6	2	10	1	....	10	0	35	1

South Australia Bowling

	O.	M.	R.	W.
Drennan	22	1	77	1
Horsnell	16	3	64	2
Wilson	19	1	81	2
Dansie	3	0	21	0
Roxby	3	0	26	0
Hole	7	0	32	1

SOUTH AUSTRALIA v. QUEENSLAND

At Adelaide, December 25, 27, 28, 29. Queensland won by 34 runs. The match was marked by promising work by the young South Australia fast-medium right-arm bowler, John Drennan, who took nine wickets for 100 runs. Queensland batted determinedly. The left-hander, Mackay, spent three and a quarter hours over 55 and K. Archer and R. Archer also played slow but valuable innings. Hole, fighting to retain his Test place, batted stubbornly, but South Australia were 76 behind on the first innings. Queensland broke down when batting a second time, and South Australia needed 253 to win. While Ridings, their experienced captain, stayed they possessed a chance of success, but when he was bowled the end soon came. Walmsley, with spin bowling, brought his match record to eight wickets for 174 runs. When keeping wicket, Langley received a cut eyebrow which forced his withdrawal from Australia's team for the third Test.

Queensland

K. Archer c Trowse b Drennan.........	40 —	not out 1
C. Harvey c Harris b Gregg............	31 —	lbw b Horsnell........... 35
K. Mackay, c and b Horsnell	55 —	b Gregg 9
P. Burge lbw b Drennan	1 —	c Harris b Gregg 11
E. Toovey lbw b Wilson	16 —	c Harris b Drennan 10
R. G. Archer c Langley b Drennan	66 —	b Wilson 44
J. Bratchford b Drennan	39 —	c Hole b Wilson 14
W. Walmsley c Hole b Wilson	10 —	c Horsnell b Drennan 7
V. N. Raymer, c Langley b Drennan ...	24 —	b Gregg 30
W. Grout c Drennan b Hole	17 —	c Pinch b Drennan 0
B. Flynn not out	22 —	c Wilson b Drennan 7
Extras......................	17	Extras 8
	——	——
	338	176

South Australia

L. Favell c and b R. Archer	21	— lbw b R. Archer	4
D. Harris c R. Archer b Bratchford	9	— lbw b Bratchford	
C. Pinch st Grout b Walmsley	43	— lbw b R. Archer	
G. B. Hole c Walmsley b R. Archer	140	— b Bratchford	
P. Ridings c R. Archer b Walmsley	17	— b Walmsley	9
D. Trowse c R. Archer b Walmsley	0	— c R. Archer b Walmsley	
G. R. Langley c Toovey b Walmsley	13	— absent injured	
J. Drennan lbw b R. Archer	0	— c Bratchford b Mackay	3?
K. Horsnell b Bratchford	4	— c Raymer b Walmsley	
J. Wilson c Harvey b Walmsley	1	— not out	
J. Gregg not out	5	— b R. Archer	2?
Extras	9	Extras	
	262		**21**

South Australia Bowling

	O.	M.	R.	W.	O.	M.	R.	W
Drennan	28	6	58	5	13.2	1	42	4
Horsnell	17	2	57	1	6	0	25	1
Gregg	23	4	72	1	11	2	28	3
Wilson	33	9	103	2	16	4	53	2
Hole	15.3	3	31	1	4	1	20	0

Queensland Bowling

	O.	M.	R.	W.	O.	M.	R.	W
R. Archer	18.6	4	67	3	16.3	3	47	3
Bratchford	7	0	37	2	6	0	29	2
Flynn	5	0	24	0	1	0	8	0
Mackay	9	2	22	0	13	2	27	1
Walmsley	24	2	84	5	20	2	90	3
Raymer	9	4	19	0	4	2	10	0

VICTORIA v. NEW SOUTH WALES

At Melbourne, December 25, 27, 28, 29. Victoria won by 36 runs. Despite capital bowling by Pat Crawford, twenty-one-year-old fast right-arm, playing in his first Shield game, and Treanor, leg-breaks, each of whom took eight wickets, and a fine second innings recovery, New South Wales could not atone for a first innings breakdown. After offering a sharp chance when seven, McDonald drove and pulled strongly for nearly three hours. He and R. N. Harvey (one 6, nine 4's) bore leading parts in Victoria's first innings, and this pair and Maddocks took the batting honours in the second. Benaud, fielding close in, held three smart catches in each innings. New South Wales in the first innings struggled against good spin bowling by Johnston, Hill and Dick. When they faced the task of scoring 400 to win, Morris gave them a fine start. On the last day they needed 261 with eight wickets in hand, but despite a fighting stand of 142 by de Courcy (fourteen 4's) and Benaud, they failed mainly because of the persistency of those three slow bowlers.

Victoria

C. C. McDonald c Benaud b Treanor ...	94	— c Benaud b Crawford	54
J. Hallebone c Cotton b Crawford	13	— c Lambert b Crawford	3
Ray Harvey b Benaud...............	25	— b Crawford	3
R. N. Harvey c Davidson b Benaud.....	62	— c Benaud b Davidson	62
J. Chambers c and b Treanor	32	— lbw b Treanor	23
S. J. Loxton c Lambert b Crawford	29	— c Lambert b Crawford	8
L. Maddocks c Benaud b Treanor	10	— not out	69
A. Dick st Lambert b Treanor	13	— c and b Benaud	9
J. C. Hill c Benaud b Crawford........	18	— c Morris b Crawford	3
W. A. Johnston not out	19	— c Crawford b Treanor	6
J. Power b Treanor	19	— b Treanor	2
Extras................	12	Extras	11
	352		253

New South Wales

R. Simpson lbw b Johnston	33	— lbw b Dick	14
R. Briggs b Loxton	19	— lbw b Hill	24
A. R. Morris lbw b Hill	28	— c Hill b Loxton	78
J. Burke c McDonald b Dick	26	— b Dick	36
J. H. de Courcy c Johnston b Dick	26	— b Hill	95
R. Benaud b Dick	3	— lbw b Hill	64
E. Cotton c Loxton b Dick	35	— lbw b Hill	9
A. K. Davidson c Power b Hill	18	— c Chambers b Hill ...	15
O. Lambert c Hallebone b Dick	8	— st Maddocks b Johnston ...	2
J. Treanor c Hill b Johnston	0	— c Loxton b Dick	2
P. Crawford not out	7	— not out	4
Extras................	3	Extras	20
	206		363

New South Wales Bowling

	O.	M.	R.	W.	O.	M.	R.	W.
Crawford	13	1	79	3	19	0	76	5
Davidson	9	0	48	0	17	4	66	1
Benaud........	16	0	101	2	12	1	45	1
Treanor	15.6	0	97	5	10	1	41	3
Cotton	3	0	15	0	4	0	14	0

Victoria Bowling

	O.	M.	R.	W.	O.	M.	R.	W.
Power	6	2	29	0	14	2	28	0
Loxton	9	0	38	1	11	2	52	1
Johnston	15	2	51	2	22	5	85	1
Dick	14.4	5	31	5	25	5	66	3
Hill	15	3	54	2	35.1	6	112	5

NEW SOUTH WALES v. QUEENSLAND

At Sydney, January 1, 3, 4. New South Wales won by 48 runs with a day to spare. They were without Miller, Morris, Benaud and Burke. Two young batsmen, Philpott and Booth, were promoted to fill vacancies. A grassy pitch suited pace bowlers and they took thirty-five of the thirty-nine wickets that fell. Crawford enjoyed another triumph, for he followed his Melbourne success by dismissing six men in each Queensland innings. For Queensland, Fisher took eight wickets in the match. New South Wales began by losing four men for 44, but Briggs batted solidly for a good century and Philpott showed poise in a difficult situation. He batted splendidly for nearly two and a half hours while making 71. It was a most impressive debut. With Watson injuring a finger, New South Wales fared badly in their second innings, but Philpott again played well and Crawford hit strongly. Queensland were always challenging their opponents and Burge,

especially, shaped attractively in a good stand with the solid left-handed Mackay
Set 216 to win, Queensland reached 119 for two wickets at tea, but they crumple
before the lively pace of Crawford and the left-handed Davidson. Under a new
rule, the umpires allowed play to be extended for seven minutes in order to finish
the match on the third day.

New South Wales

W. Watson b Fisher	1	— absent injured
R. Briggs lbw b Walmsley	100	— c Searle b Bratchford
R. Simpson c Grout b Searle	22	— c Harvey b Fisher
J. H. de Courcy c Raymer b Bratchford	1	— b Fisher
B. Booth c Fisher b Searle	0	— c Harvey b Fisher
C. Johnston c Harvey b Bratchford	3	— b Bratchford
A. K. Davidson b Fisher	18	— b Bratchford
P. Philpott c Raymer b Searle	71	— b Fisher
J. Treanor b Fisher	21	— c Searle b Fisher
O. Lambert c Mackay b Searle	15	— b Walmsley
P. Crawford not out	16	— not out
Extras	10	Extras
	278	

Queensland

C. Harvey c Philpott b Crawford	0	— not out
W. Grout c Lambert b Crawford	0	— c Lambert b Crawford
K. Mackay lbw b Crawford	59	— b Davidson
P. Burge c Lambert b Philpott	90	— c Lambert b Davidson
E. Toovey b Crawford	6	— lbw b Crawford
J. Bratchford b Crawford	6	— b Crawford
W. Walmsley c Lambert b Philpott	16	— c Crawford b Davidson
V. N. Rayner c Lambert b Davidson	37	— lbw b Crawford
B. Flynn c Simpson b Crawford	6	— c Philpott b Davidson
B. Fisher not out	0	— c Lambert b Crawford
R. Seale b Davidson	0	— c Philpott b Crawford
Extras	10	Extras
	230	

Queensland Bowling

	O.	M.	R.	W.	O.	M.	R.	W
Fisher	21	3	78	3	17	1	50	5
Searle	19.5	3	83	4	9	0	48	0
Bratchford	14	1	61	2	13	2	31	3
Mackay	4	0	16	0				
Raymer	5	2	11	0	6	1	14	0
Walmsley	3	0	11	1	3.6	0	12	1
Flynn	1	0	8	0				

New South Wales Bowling

	O.	M.	R.	W.	O.	M.	R.	W
Crawford	14	3	59	6	14.4	0	55	6
Davidson	12.6	0	70	2	16	3	71	4
Treanor	6	0	54	0	4	0	26	0
Philpott	7	1	37	2	2	0	12	0

NEW SOUTH WALES v. VICTORIA

At Sydney, January 14, 15. New South Wales won by nine wickets. O
another fast Sydney pitch, this vital match was over in two days, extra time bein
allowed so that New South Wales could score the 11 runs needed in the secon
innings. Victoria, sent in by Miller, were bundled out by Crawford and Davidso

or their lowest post-war total, 86. When New South Wales batted, Morris was ut to a mistimed hook off the first ball he received; but the team, assisted by ome dropped catches, reached 234. Briggs scored 47, and Simpson aged 18, at he crisis of the innings, batted with pluck and resource, making his first century n first-class cricket in two and a half hours. Loxton took four wickets cheaply. Miller and Davidson were the destructive bowlers when Victoria batted again, nd only a challenging 43 by Neil Harvey and a similar score by Power, who hit astily, averted an innings beating.

Victoria

C. McDonald c Lambert b Crawford	10	— c Watson b Miller	5
Hallebone c Lambert b Crawford	8	— c Simpson b Miller	8
Ray Harvey lbw b Davidson	17	— b Davidson	7
N. Harvey c Watson b Davidson	4	— b Davidson	43
Chambers c Watson b Crawford	24	— b Miller	4
J. Loxton c Simpson b Davidson	6	— c Watson b Davidson	5
Maddocks not out	4	— b Benaud	17
Dick b Crawford	0	— lbw b Davidson	3
C. Hill b Davidson	1	— c Burke b Miller	12
Power b Crawford	5	— b Miller	43
Day b Davidson	4	— not out	2
Extras	3	Extras	9
	86		**158**

New South Wales

Briggs c Ray Harvey b Dick	47		
R. Morris c Dick b Power	0		
W. Watson b Loxton	32		
Simpson c Ray Harvey b Loxton	104		
Burke lbw b Day	22		
R. Miller b Day	0		
Benaud c Maddocks b Hill	2		
K. Davidson not out	10		
Crawford lbw b Loxton	0	— not out	4
Lambert c Ray Harvey b Power	4	— not out	7
Treanor b Loxton	1	— lbw b Power	0
Extras	12	Extras	0
	234	(1 wkt.)	**11**

New South Wales Bowling

	O.	M.	R.	W.	O.	M.	R.	W.
Crawford	12	4	21	5	11	0	34	0
Miller	5	0	26	0	10.1	1	38	5
Davidson	11	1	36	5	12	1	50	4
Treanor					2	1	5	0
Benaud					2	0	22	1

Victoria Bowling

	O.	M.	R.	W.	O.	M.	R.	W.
Power	17	1	88	2	1.4	0	7	1
Loxton	18.5	7	31	4	1	0	4	0
Day	11	1	43	2				
Hill	13	2	46	1				
Dick	4	0	14	1				

QUEENSLAND v. VICTORIA

At Brisbane, January 21, 22, 23, 24. Victoria won on first innings. Despite wo splendid innings by Neil Harvey, Victoria could not force a victory owing o rain preventing play on the second day. Queensland achieved a good per-ormance in dismissing Victoria for 220, Bratchford, right-arm medium pace taking altogether seven wickets in the match. As usual Burge and Mackay proved dependable batsmen for Queensland but the others accomplished little, whereas Victoria, at their second attempt, gave a consistently sound display.

Victoria

C. C. McDonald c Lindwall b Bratchford	30 — b Bratchford	13
Ray Harvey c Grout b Walmsley	38 — c R. Archer b Raymer	44
R. N. Harvey c Bratchford b Raymer	95 — c and b Raymer	66
J. Chambers c Bratchford b Walmsley	18 — b Bratchford	49
J. Shaw st Grout b Walmsley	4 — c Harvey b R. Archer	50
S. J. Loxton run out	16 — b Bratchford	0
L. Maddocks c Grout b Bratchford	8 — c Harvey b Bratchford	
A. Dick c Lindwall b Bratchford	6 — c K. Archer b Raymer	13
J. C. Hill b R. Archer	4 — b Walmsley	17
J. Power c Harvey b R. Archer	0 — c R. Archer b Raymer	0
A. Day not out	0 — not out	0
Extras	1 Extras	
	220	26

Queensland

K. Archer c Maddocks b Power	3	R. R. Lindwall not out	
C. Harvey c McDonald b Day	16	W. Grout c Hill b Dick	2
K. Mackay c Shaw b Power	48	V. N. Raymer c Maddocks b Hill	
P. Burge c Power b Hill	53	W. Walmsley c Loxton b Hill	
T. Ayres, c Power b Hill	21	Extras	
R. G. Archer c Maddocks b Power	4		
J. Bratchford b Power	0		19

Queensland Bowling

	O.	M.	R.	W.		O.	M.	R.	W
Lindwall	11	0	47	0					
R. Archer	13	1	37	2	....	12	3	26	1
Bratchford	11	0	38	3	....	16	1	54	4
Walmsley	16	1	74	3	....	18.1	0	88	1
Raymer	5	0	23	1	....	26	7	83	4
					K. Archer	3	0	11	0

Victoria Bowling

	O.	M.	R.	W.
Power	16	0	54	4
Loxton	11	4	14	0
Day	20	1	58	1
Hill	28.4	14	43	4
Dick	14	6	23	1

WESTERN AUSTRALIA v. SOUTH AUSTRALIA

At Perth, February 12, 14, 15, 16. Drawn. Rain washed out this match after the first two days. With Rutherford again defending laboriously progress was very slow, but he had the satisfaction of making his second century of the season against South Australia. Gregg, a pace bowler, served the visitors splendidly in taking five wickets. Having lost Dansie, who retired hurt, South Australia were none too well placed when the weather intervened.

Western Australia

L. Sawle run out	31	M. Herbert c Hole b Gregg	
J. Rutherford lbw b Hole	108	R. Strauss b Horsnell	
D. K. Carmody c Hole b Gregg	26	H. Price b Horsnell	
K. Meuleman c Favell b Gregg	16	H. Gorringe not out	
A. Edwards c Favell b Gregg	38	Extras	
R. Buggins c Langley b Gregg	2		
L. Pavy b Horsnell	26		27

South Australia

G. Stevens c Buggins b Price	.....	5
L. Favell c Herbert b Price	......	20
D. Trowse not out	....	32
G. B. Hole c Buggins b Gorringe	.	5
N. Dansie retired hurt	....	6
P. Ridings not out	....	5
Extras	....	2
	(for 3 wkts.)	75

South Australia Bowling

	O.	M.	R.	W.
Gregg	24	2	91	5
Bailey	19	4	54	0
Horsnell	12.1	3	32	3
Wilson	24	9	52	0
Dansie........	4	1	9	0
Hole	12	2	27	1

Western Australia Bowling

	O.	M.	R.	W.
Gorringe	7.6	0	49	1
Price	8	0	24	2

SHEFFIELD SHIELD AVERAGES
SEASON 1954–55

NEW SOUTH WALES
BATTING

	Innings	Not Outs	Runs	100's	Highest Innings	Average
P. Crawford	6	5	64	0	33*	64.00
J. Burke	4	0	221	1	137	55.25
R. Benaud	4	0	194	1	125	48.50
E. Cotton	3	1	85	0	41*	42.50
R. Briggs	6	0	243	1	100	40.50
R. Simpson	6	0	201	1	104	33.50
A. R. Morris	4	0	133	0	78	33.25
J. H. de Courcy	5	0	125	0	95	25.00
K. R. Miller	2	0	46	0	46	23.00
W. Watson	2	0	33	0	32	16.50
A. K. Davidson	5	1	64	0	18	16.00
J. Treanor	7	1	42	0	21	7.00
D. Lambert	7	1	39	0	15	6.50

Also batted: B. Booth, 0, 19; C. Johnston 3, 21; J. O'Reilly 19; P. Philpott 1, 39.

* Signifies not out.

BOWLING

	Overs	Maidens	Runs	Wickets	Average
P. Crawford.............	83.4	8	324	25	12.96
A. K. Davidson	77.6	9	341	16	21.31
J. Treanor	87.6	12	428	16	26.75
K. R. Miller	46.1	2	161	6	26.83
R. Benaud	68	8	276	5	55.20
J. Cotton	15	0	62	0	—

Also bowled: R. Briggs 1—0—7—0; J. Burke 19—7—43—0; J. H. de Courcy —1—8—0; J. O'Reilly 37—7—102—3; P. Philpott 9—1—49—2; R. Simpson 2—2—43—1.

VICTORIA

BATTING

	Innings	Not Outs	Runs	100's	Highest Innings	Average
R. N. Harvey	7	0	401	0	95	57.28
L. Maddocks	7	3	180	0	69*	45.00
J. Chambers	7	0	252	1	102	36.00
C. C. McDonald	7	0	224	0	94	32.00
Ray Harvey	7	0	150	0	44	21.42
J. Power	6	0	72	0	43	12.00
J. C. Hill	7	1	67	0	18	11.16
S. J. Loxton	7	0	67	0	29	9.57
J. Hallebone	5	0	44	0	13	8.80
A. Dick	6	0	44	0	13	7.33
A. Day	4	3	6	0	4	6.00

Also batted: I. W. Johnson 4; W. A. Johnston 25*, 6; J. Shaw 4, 50.

* Signifies not out.

BOWLING

	Overs	Maidens	Runs	Wickets	Average
A. Dick	57.4	16	134	10	13.40
J. C. Hill	106.3	27	300	14	21.42
W. A. Johnston	67	9	259	10	25.90
J. Power	70.4	5	291	10	29.10
S. J. Loxton	73.5	14	252	8	31.50
A. Day	31	2	101	3	33.66

Also bowled: I. W. Johnson 32—2—123—4.

WESTERN AUSTRALIA

BATTING

	Innings	Not Outs	Runs	100's	Highest Innings	Average
J. Rutherford	3	0	303	2	167	101.00
A. Edwards	3	0	170	0	75	56.66
D. K. Carmody	3	0	85	0	59	28.33
L. Pavy	3	0	54	0	26	28.00
L. Sawle	3	0	74	0	35	24.66
M. Herbert	3	1	47	0	38*	23.50
H. Price	3	2	22	0	14*	22.00
K. Meuleman	3	0	60	0	44	20.00
H. Gorringe	2	1	5	0	5*	5.00
R. Buggins	3	0	10	0	8	3.33

Also batted: E. James 1; R. Strauss 8.

* Signifies not out.

BOWLING

	Overs	Maidens	Runs	Wickets	Average
H. Price	54	6	170	8	21.25
H. Gorringe	48	2	238	9	26.44

Also bowled: A. Edwards 4—0—20—0; M. Herbert 21—3—87—1 E. James 19—2—117—1; K. Meuleman 1—0—8—0; J. Rutherford 23—3—67—3.

QUEENSLAND

BATTING

	Innings	Not Outs	Runs	100's	Highest Innings	Average
K. Mackay	7	1	316	1	106*	52.66
R. G. Archer	5	1	198	0	75*	49.50
P. Burge	7	0	318	1	122	45.42
K. Archer	5	1	147	0	52	36.75
C. Harvey	7	1	184	0	90	30.66
B. Flynn	5	2	68	0	25*	22.66
V. N. Raymer	6	0	120	0	37	20.00
J. Bratchford	6	0	117	0	58	19.50
W. Grout	6	0	110	0	63	18.33
E. Toovey	4	0	45	0	16	11.25
W. Walmsley	5	0	53	0	16	10.60
R. R. Lindwall	2	1	10	0	5*	10.00

Also batted: T. Ayres 21; B. Fisher 0*, 4; L. Sanders 0, 0; R. Searle 0, 0.

* Signifies not out.

BOWLING

	Overs	Maidens	Runs	Wickets	Average
J. Bratchford	73	4	281	16	17.56
R. G. Archer	88.1	13	234	10	23.40
W. Walmsley	84.7	5	359	14	25.64
R. R. Lindwall	46	8	137	4	34.25
V. N. Raymer	93.4	22	256	7	36.57
K. Mackay	41	7	90	1	90.00
B. Flynn	48	4	201	2	100.50
K. Archer	4	1	11	0	—

Also bowled: B. Fisher 38—4—128—8; R. Searle 28.5—3—131—4.

SOUTH AUSTRALIA

BATTING

	Innings	Not Outs	Runs	100's	Highest Innings	Average
L. Favell	7	0	381	1	160	54.42
R. Roxby	4	2	85	0	34	42.50
C. Pinch	6	1	204	1	108*	40.80
P. Ridings	7	1	228	0	92	38.00
G. B. Hole	7	0	253	0	140	36.14
G. R. Langley	5	0	120	0	52	24.00
N. Dansie	5	1	81	0	34	20.25
D. Trowse	3	1	37	0	32*	18.50
D. Harris	6	0	108	0	43	18.00
K. Horsnell	6	1	68	0	29	13.60
J. Drennan	6	1	39	0	39	7.80
J. Wilson	5	2	22	0	9	7.33

Also batted: J. Gregg 5*, 24; G. Stevens 5; W. Bailey played in one match but did not bat.

* Signifies not out.

BOWLING

	Overs	Maidens	Runs	Wickets	Average
J. Gregg	58	8	191	9	21.22
J. Drennan	106.2	11	337	13	25.92
G. B. Hole	54.3	6	152	5	30.40
K. Horsnell	77.1	13	261	8	32.62
J. Wilson	147.3	37	438	11	39.81
N. Dansie	21	5	76	1	76.00
R. Roxby	24	2	120	1	120.00

Also bowled: W. Bailey 19—4—54—0.

HOLDERS OF THE SHEFFIELD SHIELD

1892–93	Victoria	1923–24	Victoria
1893–94	South Australia	1924–25	Victoria
1894–95	Victoria	1925–26	New South Wales
1895–96	New South Wales	1926–27	South Australia
1896–97	New South Wales	1927–28	Victoria
1897–98	Victoria	1928–29	New South Wales
1898–99	Victoria	1929–30	Victoria
1899–1900	New South Wales	1930–31	Victoria
1900–1	Victoria	1931–32	New South Wales
1901–2	New South Wales	1932–33	New South Wales
1902–3	New South Wales	1933–34	Victoria
1903–4	New South Wales	1934–35	Victoria
1904–5	New South Wales	1935–36	South Australia
1905–6	New South Wales	1936–37	Victoria
1906–7	New South Wales	1937–38	New South Wales
1907–8	Victoria	1938–39	South Australia
1908–9	New South Wales	1939–40	New South Wales
1909–10	South Australia	1940–46	No competition
1910–11	Victoria	1946–47	Victoria
1911–12	New South Wales	1947–48	Western Australia
1912–13	South Australia	1948–49	New South Wales
1913–14	New South Wales	1949–50	New South Wales
1914–15	Victoria	1950–51	Victoria
1915–19	No competition	1951–52	New South Wales
1919–20	New South Wales	1952–53	South Australia
1920–21	New South Wales	1953–54	New South Wales
1921–22	Victoria	1954–55	New South Wales
1922–23	New South Wales		

New South Wales have won the Shield 27 times, Victoria 18, South Australia 7, Western Australia 1, Queensland 0.

(Queensland participated for the first time in 1926–27, and Western Australia entered the competition in 1947–48.)

PLAYING NO LONGER

A. R. Morris (Australia). Debut 1940–41. Splendid left-hand opening batsman and a leading Test player since 1946. Missed only one match in five Test series against England, scoring 2,080 runs, including eight centuries, and averaging just over 50 an innings. In all, played in 46 Tests. Began first-class career with 148 and 111 in first match for New South Wales against Queensland.

CRICKET IN SOUTH AFRICA, 1954–55

Natal, who played attacking cricket under the inspiring captaincy of D. J. McGlew, deservedly regained the Currie Cup. The final placings were:—

SECTION A

Points awarded	Played —	Won 6	Lost —	First Innings Won 3	First Innings Lost 1	Points —
Natal	6	4	0	1	1	28
Transvaal................	6	3	1	1	1	22
Western Province	6	1	2	1	2	11
Orange Free State	6	0	5	1	0	3

SECTION B

Eastern Province	6	4	1	1	0	27
Rhodesia	6	3	2	1	0	21
Border	6	3	3	0	0	18
North-Eastern Transvaal ...	6	2	3	0	1	13
Griqualand West	6	1	4	0	1	7

A new third wicket record for the Currie Cup competition was established by O. C. Dawson and K. N. Kirton. They put on 255 runs for Border v. Rhodesia at East London. Both batsmen scored a century before lunch.

CURRIE CUP DETAILS

At Salisbury, November 20, 21. North-Eastern Transvaal 147 and 155 (P. N. F. Mansell five for 36); Rhodesia 442 for eight wickets declared (D. J. Lewis 170 not out, J. H. A. Wallace 109, P. N. F. Mansell 72). Rhodesia won by an innings and 140 runs.

At Bloemfontein, November 20, 22, 23. Orange Free State 417 (R. C. le Sueur 162, L. B. Koch 111, S. Hanson 58) and 242 for seven wickets declared (L. B. Koch 56); Western Province 315 (J. E. Cheetham 81, R. J. Westcott 51, L. Tuckett four for 70) and 158 for three wickets (K. Cummins 64). Orange Free State won on the first innings.

At Welkom, November 26, 27, 29. Orange Free State 278 (S. Hanson 112, D. E. J. Ironside four for 56) and 184 (E. Hoffman 71, C. Richardson 56); Transvaal 283 (J. H. B. Waite 155, P. S. Heine eight for 92) and 181 for one wicket (W. R. Endean 87 not out). Transvaal won by nine wickets.

At Durban, November 26, 27, 29. Natal 406 for six wickets declared (H. J. Keith 111 not out, D. J. McGlew 91, L. Upton 68 not out) and 95 for no wicket (T. L. Goddard 53 not out); Western Province 297 (A. W. Marshall 70, H. J. Tayfield five for 116). Natal won on the first innings.

At Pretoria, November 27. 29, 30. Eastern Province 468 (S. D. du Toit 116, D. L. Fernley 106); North-Eastern Transvaal 153 (A. R. A. Murray five for 33) and 352. (R. Richardson 140 not out, J. H. Richardson 72, A. R. A. Murray four for 48). Eastern Province won on the first innings.

At Kimberley, December 3, 4, 6. Griqualand West 336 (E. J. Draper 117, M. McMillan 83) and 200 (D. H. Buckley 90, M. Wild four for 38); Border 298 (K. N. Kirton 114, P. C. Cornell 80, J. E. Waddington seven for 111) and 241 for six wickets (R. I. Geach 86). Border won by four wickets.

At Johannesburg, December 3, 4. Transvaal 511 for eight wickets declared (A. I. Taylor 180, W. R. Endean 127, P. L. Winslow 78); Western Province 115 (N. A. T. Adcock four for 29) and 90 (J. C. Kerby three for 19, N. A. T. Adcock three for 23). Transvaal won by an innings and 306 runs.

At Bulawayo, December 4, 5, 6. Eastern Province 265 (I. Long 66, B. Bradfield 50, B. J. McBride six for 45) and 95 (P. N. F. Mansell five for 25); Rhodesia 347 (J. H. A. Wallace 91, A. J. Pithey 77) and 14 for one wicket. Rhodesia won by nine wickets.

At Durban, December 10, 11, 13. Natal 278 (T. L. Goddard 94) and 284 for eight wickets declared (D. J. McGlew 89, B. Armitage 72 not out, D. E. J. Ironside four for 63); Transvaal 316 (A. I. Taylor 118, K. J. Funston 90) and 99 (H. J. Tayfield seven for 24). Natal won by 147 runs.

At Pretoria, December 10. 11. North-Eastern Transvaal 128 (I. Hay four for 51, M. Wild three for 19) and 239 (B. A. Wiles 58); Border 58 (G. V. Middlewick six for 22) and 149 (B. A. Wiles six for 50). North-Eastern Transvaal won by 160 runs.

At Salisbury, December 11, 12, 13. Rhodesia 138 for two wickets declared (C. A. R. Duckworth 61) and 7 for three wickets; Griqualand West 128 (B. A. Goble 73, D. C. Napier four for 39). Rhodesia won on the first innings.

At Kimberley, December 17, 18, 20. Griqualand West 233 (R. G. Draper 60) and 261 (C. Helfrich 101, R. G. Draper 50, I. Hay five for 95); North-Eastern Transvaal 197 (R. Richardson 86, J. E. Waddington five for 61) and 184 (J. H. Richardson 58 not out, J. E. Waddington six for 68). Griqualand West won by 113 runs.

At East London, December 17, 18, 20. Border 335 (K. N. Kirton 163, D. Fenner 54) and 166 (A. McKinnon three for 30); Eastern Province 352 (H. G. Emslie 127, I. Long 108) and 151 for five wickets (G. F. Dakin 75). Eastern Province won by five wickets.

At Johannesburg, December 17, 18, 20 Transvaal 480 (W. R. Endean 235, C. Tayfield 102, I. H. Littleford five for 77); Orange Free State 146 (N. A. T. Adcock six for 41) and 208. Transvaal won by an innings and 126 runs.

At Johannesburg, December 27, 28, 29. Transvaal 166 (H. J. Tayfield five for 94) and 287 (P. L. Winslow 94, J. H. B. Waite 83, H. J. Tayfield six for 88) Natal 148 (R. A. McLean 50, N. A. T. Adcock five for 58) and 139 for eight wickets (T. L. Goddard 55). Transvaal won on the first innings.

At Port Elizabeth, December 27, 28, 29. Eastern Province 422 (A. R. A. Murray 126, G. F. Dakin 81); Rhodesia 157 (R. A. Murray four for 57) and 148 (D. O.'Connell-Jones 79, A. McKinnon four for 24). Eastern Province won by an innings and 117 runs.

At Cape Town, December 27, 28, 29. Western Province 365 (R. J. Westcott 98, J. E. Cheetham 85 not out, J. R. Liddle six for 114) and 253 (B. Pfaff 78, R. J. Westcott 68, J. R. Liddle five for 96); Orange Free State 349 (L. B. Koch 95, R. C. le Sueur 91, J. Forbes 80, A. W. Marshall five for 36) and 199 (L. B. Koch 66, C. B. van Ryneveld eight for 48). Western Province won by 70 runs.

At East London, December 27, 28, 29. Border 324 (D. Fenner 90, W. S. Farrer 77) and 182 for four wickets declared; North-Eastern Transvaal 179 (C. Kirton 64, E. F. Schreiber five for 49) and 172 (B. M. Wise 55, E. J. Pienaar 50, W. R. Chalmers six for 55). Border won by 155 runs.

At Bloemfontein, January 1, 3, 4. Natal 553 (H. J. Keith 153, D. J. McGlew 121, R. A. McLean 114, P. S. Heine five for 151); Orange Free State 273 (S. Hanson 72, P. S. Heine 67, V. I. Smith five for 78) and 244 (S. Hanson 134, P. Carlstein 54, N. E. Markham five for 52). Natal won by an innings and 36 runs.

At East London, January 1, 3, 4. Border 387 (O. C. Dawson 139, K. N. Kirton 124, J. T. Partridge eight for 124) and 269 for six wickets declared (O. C. Dawson 72, D. Fenner 57, K. N. Kirton 56 not out); Rhodesia 316 (P. N. F. Mansell 131, D. J. Lewis 69) and 332 (A. J. Pithey 112, P. N. F. Mansell 54, O. C. Dawson five for 124). Border won by 8 runs.

At Cape Town, January 1, 3, 4. Western Province 377 (R. J. Westcott 93, D. E. S. Millard 62, A. I. Taylor four for 52) and 153 for four wickets declared (C. B. van Ryneveld 73); Transvaal 280 (K. J. Funston 136 not out, C. B. van Ryneveld six for 105) and 114 for four wickets. Western Province won on the first innings.

At Port Elizabeth, January 1, 3, 4. Griqualand West 210 (E. J. Draper 86, A. R. A. Murray six for 46) and 183 (R. G. Draper 72, I. Long five for 37); Eastern Province 324 (H. B. Birrell 77, J. E. Waddington nine for 105) and 70 for one wicket. Eastern Province won by nine wickets.

At Cape Town, January 7, 8, 10. Natal 364 (D. J. McGlew 67, H. J. Keith 67, S. A. Thwaits four for 57) and 228 for eight wickets declared (R. A. McLean 85, H. J. Keith 64, S. A. Thwaits four for 67); Western Province 232 (E. R. H. Fuller 69, H. J. Tayfield eight for 129) and 253 (R. J. Westcott 80, H. J. Tayfield five for 115). Natal won by 107 runs.

At Port Elizabeth, January 7, 8. Eastern Province 434 (H. G. Emslie 81, S. D. du Toit 73, E. B. Norton 56); Border 96 (A. McKinnon six for 41, A. R. A. Murray three for 12) and 140 (A. McKinnon five for 48). Eastern Province won by an innings and 198 runs.

At Kimberley, January 7, 8. Rhodesia 471 (M. W. Davies 133, P. N. F. Mansell 111, A. J. Pithey 97, C. English four for 48); Griqualand West 95 (P. N. F. Mansell five for 35, J. T. Partridge four for 29) and 228 (R. L. Gloak 69, D. Lee 67, P. N. F. Mansell four for 64). Rhodesia won by an innings and 148 runs.

At Benoni, January 14, 15, 17. Griqualand West 184 (E. J. Draper 79) and 242 (D. de Villiers 54, R. L. Gloak 51, T. W. Bryant six for 84); North-Eastern Transvaal 380 (A. Dennis 138, B. A. Wiles 54, J. E. Waddington five for 128) and 47 for one wicket. North-Eastern Transvaal won by nine wickets.

At Pietermaritzburg, January 21, 22, 24. Natal 524 (R. A. McLean 182, L. Upton 126, F. C. Bestall 65 not out, P. S. Heine five for 168); Orange Free State 154 (R. C. le Sueur 67, V. I. Smith six for 62) and 208 (V. I. Smith five for 42). Natal won by an innings and 162 runs.

CRICKET IN NEW ZEALAND, 1954–55

PLUNKET SHIELD

(Won by Wellington)

FINAL PLACINGS

	Played	Won Outright	Won on 1st Inns.	Lost Outright	Lost on 1st Inns.	Points
Points awarded	—	8	4	—	2	—
Wellington...........	4	4	0	0	0	32
Canterbury	4	2	0	1	1	18
Otago	4	1	1	1	1	14
Central District	4	1	1	2	0	12
Auckland	4	0	0	4	0	0

Plunket Shield Holders: Auckland 14 times, Canterbury 12, Wellington 10, Otago 5, Central Districts 1.

J. R. Reid, the New Zealand Test cricketer, helped Wellington to win the Plunket Shield for the tenth time. He scored 362 runs, average 60.33, and took 20 wickets at 14.15 runs apiece, the best all-round performance of the competition. Only one other player, R. T. Dowker, of Canterbury, with 366, hit more runs. R. W. Blair, also of Wellington, took most wickets—27. B. Sutcliffe, the Otago and New Zealand opening batsman, had a comparatively poor season. In seven innings he scored 249 runs.

During the match between Canterbury and Central Districts at Christchurch, J. A. Hayes, the Canterbury batsman, was given out for obstruction. His partner, A. R. MacGibbon, hit a ball to the on. Hayes, who commenced to run, was sent back but in turning slipped and appeared to hit the ball. He also collided with a fieldsman, whose appeal on the grounds of obstruction was upheld.

PLUNKET SHIELD DETAILS

At Basin Reserve, Wellington, December 25, 27, 28. Wellington 134 (D. B. Clarke four for 45) and 292 for eight wickets declared (E. W. Dempster 75 not out, R. W. Blair 59); Auckland 115 (J. R. Reid five for 31) and 226 (T. S. Hambrook 66, R. W. Blair six for 50). Wellington won by 85 runs.

At Lancaster Park, Christchurch, December 25, 27, 28. Otago 392 for nine wickets declared (J. A. Gill 91, B. Sutcliffe 55, L. D. Smith 53) and 206 for four wickets declared (W. S. Haig 62, E. A. Watson 52); Canterbury 256 (R. T. Dowker 74, F. J. Cameron four for 65) and 227 for nine wickets (M. E. Chapple 55, F. J. Cameron four for 52). Otago won on first innings.

At Eden Park, Auckland, December 30, 31, January 1. Otago 453 for seven wickets declared (B. Sutcliffe 113, W. S. Haig 102, S. N. McGregor 72, E. A. Watson 53, L. A. Watt 51, J. A. Gill 50) and 23 for no wicket; Auckland 273 (G. O. Rabone 75, A. M. Moir five for 89) and 202 (A. M. Moir four for 104). Otago won by ten wickets.

At Lancaster Park, Christchurch, December 30, 31, January 1. Canterbury 161 and 133 (M. B. Poore 142); Central Districts 91 (A. R. MacGibbon five for 31, J. A. Hayes four for 23) and 211 (J. W. Guy 55). Canterbury won by 172 runs.

At Carisbrook, Dunedin, January 3, 4, 5. Otago 256 (L. D. Smith 95, H. B. Cave four for 52, F. E. Fisher four for 55) and 82 for two wickets; Central Districts 310 (H. B. Cave 102, J. W. Guy 87, G. W. F. Overton seven for 88). Central Districts won on first innings.

At Basin Reserve, Wellington, January 3, 4, 5. Canterbury 286 (M. E. Chapple 64, P. G. Z. Harris 62, J. R. Reid four for 62) and 134 (R. W. Blair four for 28); Wellington 265 (R. T. Barber 71, L. S. M. Miller 68) and 156 for five wickets. Wellington won by five wickets.

At Trafalgar Park, Nelson, January 7, 8, 10. Central Districts 183 (H. B. Cave 70 not out) and 250 (N. S. Harford 80 retired hurt, R. W. Blair four for 82); Wellington 228 (J. R. Reid 106, D. St. John 88, J. F. Jones four for 58) and 207 for six wickets. Wellington won by four wickets.

At Eden Park, Auckland, January 7, 8, 10. Canterbury 273 (R. T. Dowker 122, M. B. Poore 51, D. B. Clarke four for 70) and 187 (M. B. Poore 63, R. T. Dowker 50, D. B. Clarke four for 59); Auckland 202 (J. K. Everest 103, J. B. Morris 53, T. B. Burtt five for 43) and 162 (A. R. MacGibbon seven for 56). Canterbury won by 96 runs.

At Carisbrook, Dunedin, January 13, 14, 15. Otago 205 (L. A. Watt 73, J. A. McKeown four for 60) and 179; Wellington 159 (G. W. F. Overton four for 34, A. M. Moir four for 63) and 228 for eight wickets (J. R. Reid 79, L. S. M. Miller 57). Wellington won by two wickets.

At Sports Ground, Palmerston North, January 21, 22, 24. Central Districts 285 (N. S. Harford 91, D. B. Clarke four for 115) and 127 (A. F. Lissette four for 32, D. B. Clarke four for 46); Auckland 133 (D. Tarrant four for 51) and 144 (H. B. Cave four for 44). Central Districts won by 135 runs.

OTHER MATCH

A North Island v. South Island game was played to help the New Zealand selectors in choosing their side to meet England. Much of its value was lost because of rain, which prevented cricket for the greater part of the second day and for all of the third.

Summarised score: At Lancaster Park, Christchurch, February 24, 25, 26. Drawn. North Island 294 (J. W. Guy 81 not out, G. O. Rabone 67, J. A. Hayes four for 77); South Island 165 for four (M. E. Chapple 71 not out).

CRICKET IN WEST INDIES, 1954–55

The West Indies' selectors used the Quadrangular Tournament matches as trials for the visit of the Australians later in the season. F. King, who subsequently played in four of the five Tests, showed genuine pace in taking fifteen wickets for Barbados at an average of ten runs apiece. A. L. Valentine, playing for Jamaica, had an analysis of 35.5—11—78—8 in the second innings of the first match against Trinidad and in the same game L. Mullings, a leg-break bowler, also of Jamaica, took five wickets for 96 runs on his first appearance in major cricket. Centuries were scored by F. M. Worrell and N. L. Bonitto (Jamaica), N. Asgarali (Trinidad) and G. Sobers (Barbados).

QUADRANGULAR TOURNAMENT DETAILS

At Bridgetown, January 28, 29, 31, February 1. British Guiana 127 (C. L. Walcott 50, F. King four for 15) and 135 (F. King four for 39); Barbados 364 (D. Atkinson 78, C. Smith 55, C. Depeiza 52 out not, C. Hunte 51). Barbados won by an innings and 102 runs.

At Bridgetown, February 5, 7, 8, 9, 10. Barbados 326 (C. Hunte 70, C. DePeiza 64, C. B. Williams 50, G. Gibbs six for 80) and 312 for seven wickets declared (G. Sobers 104 not out, N. S. Lucas 91, C. H. Thomas four for 42); British Guiana 228 (B. Pairaudeau 85, C. B. Williams four for 87) and 266 (G. Gibbs 93, B. Butcher 62, C. A. McWatt 58, F. King four for 66). Barbados won by 144 runs.

At Kingston, February 5, 7, 8, 9, 10. Trinidad 299 (R. Legall 68, N. Marshall 56, L. Mullings five for 96) and 294 (N. Asgarali 124, A. L. Valentine eight for 78); Jamaica 295 (F. M. Worrell 100, K. Babb five for 64) and 162 (J. K. Holt, jnr. 55, N. Marshall five for 34, W. Ferguson five for 61). Trinidad won by 136 runs.

At Kingston, February 12, 14, 15, 16, 17. Trinidad 234 (R. Tangchoon 60, J. B. Stollmeyer 55) and 181 (O. G. Smith four for 84); Jamaica 163 and 253 for four wickets (N. L. Bonitto 110 not out, O. G. Smith 58 not out). Jamaica won by six wickets.

CRICKET IN INDIA, 1954–55

For the first time in their career Madras won the Ranji Trophy, their opponents in the final being Holkar, who were champions in 1946, 1948, 1951 and 1953. Madras had figured previously in the finals of 1936 and 1941, when they lost to Bombay and Maharashtra respectively.

The outstanding batsman of the season was A. G. Kripal Singh, son of A. G. Ram Singh, the former Madras all-rounder. In six innings Kripal Singh hit 636 runs, average 106.00. He played only one three-figure innings, of 208 against Travancore-Cochin, but against Bengal he twice narrowly missed his hundred, with scores of 98 and 97. In the final he made 75 and 91. M. K. Nurugesh, a left-arm slow bowler, also of Madras, took 23 wickets, average 19.65.

Altogether twenty three-figure innings were played. Kripa Singh (208) and V. S. Hazare (204 not out) were the only batsmen to exceed 200.

In a non-Trophy fixture at Bombay, S. P. Gupte, the India leg-break bowler, took all ten wickets for Bombay Cricket Association President's XI in the first innings against Services and Bahawalpur Combined XI. His analysis was 24.2—7—78—10.

RANJI TROPHY RESULTS

At New Delhi, December 3, 4, 5. Delhi 163 and 242 (Kukreja 52, Tuljaram 51, Sitaram five for 75); Services 288 (H. R. Adhikari 71, P. G. Joshi 57) and 121 for two (H. R. Adhikari 52 not out). Services won by eight wickets.

At Jorhat, December 11, 12, 13. Bihar 81 (S. K. Girdhari six for 20) and 107 (S. K. Girdhari six for 46); Assam 53 (B. Bose six for 16) and 89 (B. Bose six for 31). Bihar won by 46 runs.

At Jullundar, December 17, 18, 19. East Punjab 148 (V. N. Swamy six for 29) and 282 for seven (Satish Nanda 100 not out, Chamanlal 54, V. M. Muddiah four for 80); Services 405 (Mahipetsingh 82, V. N. Swamy 53, Sitaram 51 not out, W. Ghosh four for 88). Services won on first innings.

At Ernakulam, December 18, 19, 20. Travancore-Cochin 247 (Balan Pandit 81, P. Ravi 53, M. K. Murugesh four for 50) and 141 for six; Madras 414 for nine wickets declared (A. G. Kripal Singh 208, R. B. Alagannan 106). Madras won on first innings.

At Ahmedabad, December 18, 19, 20. Gujerat 354 (D. P. Medh 77, Salim 72); Baroda 413 for four (V. S. Hazare 204 not out, G. Kishenchand 86, J. M. Ghorpade 64 not out). Baroda won on first innings.

At Banares, December 18, 19, 20. Madhya Pradesh 251 (P. Gokhale 74, R. V. Divecha 51, L. Amarnath four for 71, Sanyal four for 51) and 123 for five wickets declared; Uttar Pradesh 211 (Daljit Singh 77, Rahim four for 48) and 70 for one. Madhya Pradesh won on first innings.

At Cuttack, December 18, 20. Bengal 329 for four wickets declared (P. B. Dutta 110, D. G. Phadkar 87 not out, S. Bose 55); Orissa 58 (N. Chowdhury four for 20, D. G. Phadkar four for 21) and 126 (A. Bhatacharjee four for 43). Bengal won by an innings and 145 runs.

At Holkar. Holkar walk over Rajaputana.

At Hyderabad, January 2, 3, 4. Hyderabad 480 for six wickets declared (Gul Mohammed 152, E. B. Aibara 104 not out, Jai Simha 90, Sriram 57); Andhra 128 (Gul Mohammed five for 30) and 245 (S. Rama Rao 119); Hyderabad won by an innings and 107 runs.

At Indore, January 15, 16, 17. Madhya Pradesh 161 (K. Kesari 68) and 100 (C. T. Sarwate four for 19); Holkar 441 (Arjun Nayudu 81, B. B. Nimbalkar 67, S. D. Dhanawade 61, N. R. Nivsarkar 58). Holkar won by an innings and 180 runs.

At Calcutta, January 16, 17, 18. Bengal 309 (P. Sen 65, A. Das Gupta 55, S. Bannerjee four for 70) and 421 for nine wickets declared (A. Bhattacharjee 125, P. B. Dutta 115, N. Chatterjee 71); Bihar 119 (P. Chatterjee five for 52, N. Chowdhury four for 34) and 169 for eight (Om Prakash 54, S. Shome four for 53). Bengal won on first innings.

At Hyderabad, January 21, 22, 23. Hyderabad 288 (Abbas Ali Baig 105, V. R. Chander four for 62) and 142 for three wickets declared; Mysore 152 (Vivek Hazare 51, Ibrahim Khan five for 58, Gul Mohammed four for 50) and 184 for two (K. L. Mahesh 60 not out, D. R. Patel 54 not out). Hyderabad won on first innings.

At Baroda, January 21, 22, 23. Bombay 258 (Y. K. Rele 68, S. W. Sohoni 57); Baroda 284 for three (D. K. Gaekwad 124, V. S. Hazare 105 not out). Baroda won on first innings.

At Rajkot, January 31, February 1, 2. Saurashtra 160 (V. Nakum 52, M. V. Mathe four for 30) and 245 for five wickets declared (Laheji 144); Maharashtra 282 (R. G. Bhadbhade 73, Bhosle 72, M. Acharya four for 93) and 37 for no wicket. Maharashtra won on first innings.

At Hyderabad, February 4, 5, 6. Madras 331 (A. G. Kripal Singh 67, D. L. Chakravarthi 61, Gul Mohammed four for 113) and 172 for six wickets declared (J. Ramakrishnan 55, M. Suryanarayan 54, Ibrahim Khan four for 54); Hyderabad 274 (M. K. Murugesh four for 64, A. K. Sarangapani four for 80) and 131 for five (D. Quereshi 59 not out). Madras won on first innings.

At New Delhi, February 11, 12, 13. Services 312 (H. R. Adhikari 137, Mahipatsinghe 91, P. Chatterjee five for 102, S. Shome five for 110); Bengal 354 (S. K. Khanna 95 not out, P. B. Dutta 72, V. M. Muddaiah four for 65). Bengal won on first innings.

At Baroda, February 19, 20, 21. Maharashtra 260 (P. G. Joshi 63, C. G. Joshi six for 75); Baroda 373 (R. D. Patel 139 retired, G. Kishenchand 90, J. M. Ghorpade 50, Sher Mohammed four for 45). Baroda won on first innings.

SEMI-FINALS

At Indore, March 5, 6, 7, 8. Holkar 492 (B. B. Nimbalkar 162, S. D. Dhanawade 82, C. T. Sarwate 67, S. R. Jadav 53, H. G. Gaekwad 51); Baroda 412 (D. K. Gaekwad 145; J. M. Ghorpade 83, J. H. Vin 61 not out, C. T. Sarwate six for 103). Holkar won on first innings.

At Madras, March 6, 7, 8, 9. Madras 347 (C. D. Gopinath 121, A. G. Kripal Singh 98, S. Shome five for 78) and 139 (A. G. Kripal Singh 97, N. Chowdhury six for 35); Bengal 174 (P. Roy 74, J. Ramakrishnan five for 64, B. C. Alva four for 59) and 155 (S. K. Khanna 50, M. K. Murugesh five for 53, A. G. Kripal Singh four for 18). Madras won by 157 runs.

FINAL

At Indore, April 2, 3, 4, 5, 6. Madras 478 (C. D. Gopinath 133, S. Balakrishnan 78, A. C. Kripal Singh 75, A. K. Sarangapani 74 not out, H. G. Gaekwad four for 137) and 311 (A. G. Kripal Singh 91, R. B. Alagannan 56 not out); Holkar 417 (N. R. Nivsarkar 85, S. R. Jadhav 77, S. Mustaq Ali 55) and 326 (C. T. Sarwate 56, R. P. Singh 54, S. Mustaq Ali 51, M. K. Murugesh five for 114, A. G. Kripal Singh four for 113). Madras won by 46 runs.

RANJI TROPHY HOLDERS

1934–35	Bombay	1945–46	Holkar
1935–36	Bombay	1946–47	Baroda
1936–37	Nawanagar	1947–48	Holkar
1937–38	Hyderabad	1948–49	Bombay
1938–39	Bengal	1949–50	Baroda
1939–40	Maharashtra	1950–51	Holkar
1940–41	Maharashtra	1951–52	Bombay
1941–42	Bombay	1952–53	Holkar
1942–43	Baroda	1953–54	Bombay
1943–44	Western India	1954–55	Madras
1944–45	Bombay		

OTHER MATCHES

At Kolhapur, November 20, 21, 22, 23. Chhatrapati's team 283 for seven wickets declared (M. K. Mantri 100, R. S. Nadkarni four for 56) and 302 for nine wickets declared (M. L. Apte 103, G. S. Ramchand 66 not out, V. Mehra 53); Board President's team 326 for eight wickets declared (P. Roy 84, P. L. Punjabi 70) and 247 for seven (H. T. Dani 69, Om Prakash 57 not out, C. G. Borde four for 71). Drawn.

At Bombay, December 3, 4, 6. Services and Bahawalpur Combined XI 152 (Shuja-ud-Din 56, S. P. Gupte ten for 78) and 145 (Shuja-ud-Din 74, V. L.

Manjrekar four for 21); Bombay Cricket Association President's XI 422 (G. S. Ramchand 101, V. L. Manjrekar 99, P. Roy 88, P. R. Umrigar 55, Shuja-ud-Din four for 127). President's XI won by an innings and 125 runs.

CRICKET IN PAKISTAN, 1954-55

Karachi, helped by several of the players who appeared for Bahawalpur, the holders, last season, won the Quaid-i-Azam Trophy. They defeated Services in the final, when Wahab, a medium pace bowler, performed the hat-trick. Hanif Mohammad, who hit 230 not out against Sind, Wazir Mohammad and Raees Mohammad were the most successful of their batsmen. Imtiaz Ahmed batted soundly for Services.

QUAID-I-AZAM TROPHY RESULTS

At Karachi, November 12, 13, 14. Pakistan Railways 183 (Mohammad Aslam 58, Ikram Elahi four for 35, Baluch four for 46) and 253 (Mohammad Aslam 80, Ehsan 68); Karachi 452 (Wazir Mohammad 120 not out, Raees Mohammad 96, Hanif Mohammad 84, Ikram Elahi 59). Karachi won by an innings and 16 runs.

At Peshawar, November 19, 20, 21. Punjab 249 (Saeed Ahmad 63, Sultan Mahmood 50, Sajjad five for 62) and 192 for five wickets declared (Shakoor Ahmed 116 not out); N.W.F.P. 102 (Aftab six for 27) and 145 (Aftab five for 52, Aziz four for 21). Punjab won by 194 runs.

At Karachi, November 19, 20, 21. Karachi 452 for three wickets declared (Hanif Mohammad 230 not out, Raees Mohammad 118 not out, Alim-ud-Din 53); Sind 134 and 244 for six wickets (Wallis 81 not out). Karachi won on first innings.

At Dacca, November 20, 21, 22. Services 210 for eight wickets declared and 148 for three wickets declared; East Pakistan 116 and 111. Services won by 131 runs.

At Bahawalpur, April 15, 16, 17. Karachi 351 (Wazir Mohammad 143, Waqar Hassan 101, F. A. Shah six for 109); Bahawalpur 173 (Iqbal 55, Baluch six for 49) and 107. Karachi won by an innings and 71 runs.

At Lahore, April 15, 16, 17. Services 335 (Imtiaz Ahmed 120, Fazal Mahmood four for 73) and 177 for seven wickets declared (Imtiaz Ahmed 75, S. F. Rehman six for 63); Punjab 147 (Fazal Mahmood 53, M. E. Z. Ghazali five for 28) and 159 for two wickets (Khawar Butt 81 not out). Services won on first innings.

FINAL

At Karachi, April 21, 22, 23, 24. Karachi 438 (Wazir Mohammad 118, Raees Mohammad 110, Hanif Mohammad 109) and 35 for one wicket; Services 221 (Imtiaz Ahmed 81, Mahmood Hussain five for 75) and 249 (M. E. Z. Ghazali 55, Wahab four for 31, Raees Mohammad four for 82). Karachi won by nine wickets.

QUAID-I-AZAM TROPHY HOLDERS

1953–54	Bahawalpur
1954–55	Karachi

OTHER MATCH

At Karachi, October 15, 17, 18. The Rest 202 (Shamsi 69, Anwar Husain 68, Fazal Mahmood four for 7) and 157 (M. E. Z. Ghazali four for 13); Pakistan 233 for eight wickets declared (Wazir Mohammad 61) and 133 for two wickets (Imtiaz Ahmed 77 not out). Pakistan won by nine wickets. (Play continued after Pakistan had won.)

CRICKET IN CANADA, 1955

Although competitions in Canada have not yet reached first-class status, more cricket was played there in 1955 than for many years. Ontario won the inter-provincial tournament for the fifth time out of six competitions staged since 1947. They were undefeated in a round robin contest with British Columbia, Alberta and Manitoba, played at Vancouver, B.C. between August 1st and 6th.

The winners, who also overwhelmed Quebec in the annual Lord Athelstan Trophy match at Toronto, possessed a splendid fielding side and were well served individually by J. W. Chappell (batsman) and B. Christen (bowler), both from Toronto.

F. J. Cameron, of London, Ontario, the West Indies Test cricketer and Canadian representative player, experienced a good all-round season. Another pleasing feature was the grand form of two young spin bowlers, M. Taylor (aged 21) of Toronto and L. A. Rowe (19) of Waterloo, Ontario. They will solve one of the country's greatest problems if they maintain this early promise.

The future of cricket in the Dominion looks bright. Apart from the provinces already mentioned, the game was played last season in Novia Scotia and it is to commence in New Brunswick in 1956. Altogether about 108 teams were in operation in 1955 and some clubs travelled 150 miles each way on a single day to fulfil fixtures. The majority of games took place in public parks on various types of pitches.

BIRTHS AND DEATHS OF CRICKETERS

Details of Cricketers who died before 1851 were omitted after the issue of 1933; of those who died before 1856 after the issue of 1936; and from the 1940 issue deaths before 1900. Those who died before 1920 were deleted from the 1947 issue and those who died between 1920 and 1925 from the 1952 issue. Members of famous cricketing families and some personalities of special interest are retained. The qualification now is ten appearances in first-class cricket during one season in England, or the award of a County Cap or University Blue. Overseas cricketers are included only if they have represented their country in a tour of England.

University Players are given in the List of Blues on page 662.

à Beckett, Mr. E. L. (Victoria), b Aug 11, 1907

Abel, R. (Surrey), b Nov 30, 1857, d Dec 10, 1936

Abel, T. E. (Surrey and Glamorgan), b Sept 10, 1890, d Jan 23, 1937

Abel, W. J. (Surrey), b Aug 29, 1887, d March 23, 1934

Abell, Sir G. E. B. (Oxford Univ. and Worcestershire), b June 22, 1904

Aberdare, 3rd Lord (*see* Bruce, Hon. C. N.)

Achong, Mr. E. (West Indies), b Feb 16, 1904

Adam, Gen. Sir Ronald, 1st Bart., President M.C.C., b Oct 30, 1885

Adams, Mr. G. C. A. (Hampshire), b May 24, 1909

Adcock, Mr. N. A. T. (South Africa), b March 8, 1931

Adhikari, Mr. H. R. (India), b Aug 12, 1919

Ahl, F. D. (Worcestershire), b Nov 24, 1908

Ainsworth, Lt.-Cdr. M. L. Y. (Worcestershire), b May 13, 1922

Aird, Mr. R. (Camb. Univ. and Hampshire, Secretary M.C.C. from 1953), b May 4, 1902

Akers-Douglas, Mr. I. S. (Kent), b Nov 16, 1909, d Dec 16, 1952

Akroyd, Mr. B. N. (Surrey), b April 27, 1850, d Nov 24, 1926

Alcock, Mr. C. W.(Sec., Surrey C.C.C. 1872-1907), b Dec 2, 1842, d Feb 26, 1907

Alderman, A. E. (Derbyshire), b Oct 30, 1907

Alexander, Mr. F. C. M. (Camb. Univ.), b Nov 2, 1928

Alexander, Mr. G. (Victoria), b April 22, 1851, d Nov 7, 1930

Alexander, Mr. H. (Victoria), b June 9, 1905

Alexander, Mr. W. C. (South Australia), b Sept 14, 1907

Alim-ud-Din (Pakistan), b April 15, 1928

Allington, Rev. H. G. (Lincolnshire and Oxford Univ.), b July 25, 1837, d Dec 2, 1928

Allcott, Mr. C. F. W. (New Zealand), b Oct 7, 1896

Allan, Mr. J. M. (Oxford Univ. and Kent), b April 2, 1932

Allen, Mr. A. W. (Camb. Univ., and Northamptonshire), b Dec 22, 1912

Allen, Mr. B. O. (Camb. Univ. and Gloucestershire), b Oct 13, 1911

Allen, D. A. (Gloucestershire), b Oct 29, 1935

Allen, Mr. G. O. (Camb. Univ. and Middlesex), b at Sydney, Australia, July 31, 1902

Allen, R. (Yorkshire), b April 1893, d Oct 14, 1950

Alletson, E. (Nottinghamshire),b March 6, 1884

Allom, Mr. M. J. C. (Camb. Univ. and Surrey), b March 23, 1906

Allsop, Mr. G. (Manager of South African Teams), b Jan 4, 1864, d Mar 27, 1927

Altham, Mr. H. S. (Oxford Univ., Surrey and Hampshire),b Nov 30,1888

Amarnath, L. (India), b Sep 11, 1911

Amar Singh (India), b Dec 4, 1910, d May 20, 1940

Ames, L. E. G. (Kent), b Dec 3, 1905

Amir Elahi (India), b Sept 1, 1908

Andrew, K. V. (Northamptonshire), b Dec 15, 1929

Andrews, Mr. T. J. E. (New South Wales), b Aug 26, 1890

Andrews, W. H. R. (Somerset), b April 14, 1909

Angell, F. L. (Somerset), b June 29, 1922

Anson, Hon. Rupert (Middlesex), b Nov 7, 1889

Appleyard, Mr. F. (Essex), b Sept 9, 1906

Appleyard, R. (Yorkshire), b June 27, 1924

Archer, Mr. R. G. (Queensland), b Oct 25, 1933

Arenhold, Mr. J. A. (Oxford Univ.), b May 9, 1931

Arkwright, Mr. H. A. (Essex and Oxford Univ.), b Nov 10, 1872, d Dec 10, 1942

Arlington, Mr. G. H. A. (Sussex), b May 28, 1872, d 1944

Armstrong, Mr. E. K. (Queensland), b Feb 5, 1881

Armstrong, N. F. (Leicestershire), b Dec 22, 1894

Armstrong, T. R. (Derbyshire), b Oct 13, 1909

Armstrong, Mr. W. W. (Victoria), b May 22, 1879, d July 13, 1947

Arnold, E. G. (Worcestershire), b Nov 7, 1877, d Oct 25, 1942

Arnold, John (Oxfordshire and Hampshire), b Nov 30, 1907

Arnold, P. (Northamptonshire), b Oct 16, 1926

Arnott, Mr. T. (Glamorgan and Monmouthshire), b Feb 16, 1902

Ashby, D.A.(Surrey and New Zealand), b June 11, 1852, d June 2, 1934

Ashcroft, Dr. E. Maynard (Derbyshire), b Sept 27, 1875, d Feb 26, 1955

Ashdown, W. H. (Kent), b Dec 27, 1898

Ashley-Cooper, Mr. F. S. (Cricket Writer) b March 2, 1877, d Jan 31, 1932

Ashman, J. R. (Yorkshire and Worcestershire), b May 20, 1926

Ashton, Sqdn.-Ldr.C.T.(Camb. Univ. and Essex), b Feb 19, 1901, d Oct 31, 1942

Ashton, Mr. G. (Camb. Univ. and Worcestershire), b Sept 27, 1896

Ashton, Mr. H. (Camb. Univ. and Essex), b Feb 13, 1898

Aspinall, R. (Yorkshire), b Nov 26, 1918

Astill, W. E. (Leicestershire), b Mar 1, 1888, d Feb 10, 1948

Astor, Major Hon. J. J. (Eton, Buckinghamshire, President M.C.C., 1937), b May 20, 1886

Atfield, A. J. (Gloucestershire and Wiltshire), b Mar 3, 1868, d Jan 1, 1949

Atkins, Mr. F. M. (Kent), b Mar 28, 1864, d Jan 13, 1941

Atkinson, Mr. B. G. W. (Northamptonshire and Middlesex), b Sept 1900

Atkinson, Mr. J. (Victoria and Tasmania), b April 4, 1896

Atkinson-Clark, Mr. J. C. (Middlesex), b July 9, 1912

Attewell, Thos. (Nottinghamshire), b Nov 7, 1869, d July 6, 1937

Attewell, W. (Nottinghamshire), b June 12, 1861, d June 11, 1927

Austin, Sir H. B. G. (Barbados), b July 15, 1877, d July 27, 1943

Austin, Mr. H. M. (Camb. Univ.), b March 8, 1903

Avery, A. V. (Essex), b Dec 19, 1914

Awdry, Mr. R. W. (Oxford Univ. and Wiltshire), b May 20, 1881, d Feb 3, 1949

Bacmeister, Mr. L. H. (Middlesex), b Nov 22, 1869

Badcock, Mr. C. L. (Tasmania and South Australia), b April 10, 1914

Badcock, Mr. F. T. (New Zealand), b Aug 9, 1898

Badcock, J. R. (Hampshire) b Oct 4, 1883

Baggallay, Mr. M. E. C. (Camb. Univ.), b Dec 7, 1887

Baggallay, Lt.-Col. R. R. C. (Derbyshire), b May 4, 1884

Baggallay, Mr. T. W., later T. W. Weeding (Surrey), b June 11, 1847, d Dec 19, 1929

Bagguley, R. (Nottinghamshire), b July 10, 1873, d 1947

Bagnall, Mr. H. F. (Camb. Univ. and Northamptonshire), b Feb 18, 1904

Bagshaw, H. (Derbyshire), b Sept 1, 1861, d Jan 31, 1927

Bailey, A. (Surrey and Somerset), b March 14, 1872

Bailey, Mr. B. T. R. (South Australia), b Dec 5, 1874

Bailey, Sir D. (Bart.) (Gloucestershire), b Aug 15, 1918

Bailey, Mr. G. H. (Tasmania), b Oct 29, 1853, d Oct 10, 1926

Bailey, J. (Hampshire), b April 6, 1908

Bailey, Mr. J. A (Essex), b June 22, 1930

Bailey, Mr. T. E. (Essex and Camb. Univ.), b Dec 3, 1923

Baily, Mr. E. P. (Camb. Univ., Somerset and Middlesex), b Jan 18, 1852, d Jan 21, 1941

Baily, Mr. R. E. H. (Camb. Univ. and Surrey), b June 6, 1885

Bainbridge, Mr. H. W. (Camb. Univ., Surrey and Warwickshire), b Assam, India, Oct 29, 1862, d Mar 3, 1940

Bairstow, A. L. (Yorkshire), b Aug 14, 1870, d Feb 21, 1948

Baiss, Mr. R. S. H. (Kent), b March 6, 1873, d May 2, 1955

Bajana, Mr. M. P. (India and Somerset), b Sept 14, 1886, d April 28, 1927

Baker, A. (Surrey), b Nov 28, 1872, d April 29, 1948

Baker, C. S. (Warwickshire and Cornwall), b Jan 5, 1883

Baker, Mr. C. V. (Middlesex), b Nov 23, 1885, d Dec 7, 1947

Baker, Mr. E. C. (Camb. Univ., Sussex and Somerset), b Jan 7, 1892

Baker, Mr. E. S. (Worcestershire), b Nov 9, 1910

Baker, G. R. (Yorkshire & Lancashire), b April 18, 1862, d Feb 6, 1938

Baker, Mr. H. Z. (Kent), b Feb 7, 1880

Baker, Mr. P. C. (Kent), b May 2, 1874, d Dec 30, 1939

Bakewell, A. H. (Northamptonshire), b Nov 2, 1908

Balaskas, Mr. X. (South Africa), b Oct 15, 1910

Baldry, D. O. (Middlesex), b Dec 26, 1931

Baldwin, C. (Surrey and Suffolk), b Dec 29, 1865, d May 2, 1947

Baldwin, H. (Hampshire), b Nov 27, 1860, d Jan 12, 1935

Baldwin, H. G. (Surrey), b March 16, 1895

Baldwin of Bewdley, 1st Earl (President, M.C.C., 1938), b Aug 3, 1867, d Dec 14, 1947

Bale, E. (Surrey and Worcestershire), b Sept 18, 1878, d July 7, 1952

Bale, F. (Leicestershire), b Jan 9, 1893

Balfour-Melville, Mr. L. M. (Scotland), b March 9, 1854, d July 16, 1937

Ballance, Major T. G. L., M.C. (Oxford Univ.), b April 21, 1916, d Dec 4, 1943

Baloo, P (India), b March 19, 1876, d July 4, 1955

Bancroft, Mr. C. K. (West Indies), b Oct 30, 1885, d 1915

Banerjee, S. (India), b Oct 3, 1913

Bannerman, Mr. A. C. (New South Wales), b March 21, 1859, d Sept 19, 1924

Bannerman, Mr. Charles (New South Wales), b in Kent, July 3, 1851, d Aug 20, 1930

Bannister, A. F. (Worcestershire), b June 15, 1875

Bannister, Mr. H. M. (Leicestershire), b June 3, 1889

Bannister, J. D. (Warwickshire), b Aug 23, 1930

Bannon, Mr. B. D. (Oxford Univ. and Kent), b Dec 7, 1874, d Dec 18, 1938

Barber, Mr. A. T. (Oxford Univ. and Yorkshire), b June 17, 1905

Barber, Mr. R. W. (Lancashire and Camb. Univ.), b Sept 26, 1935

Barber, W. (Yorkshire) b April 18, 1902

Barbour, Dr. E. P. (New South Wales), b Jan 27, 1891, d Dec 7, 1934

Bardsley, Mr. R. V. (Oxford Univ. and Lancashire), b 1890, d July 26, 1952

Bardsley, Mr. W (New South Wales), b Dec 7, 1883, d Jan 20, 1954

Baring, Mr. A. E. G. (Hampshire), b Jan 21, 1910

Barker, G. (Essex) b July 6, 1932

Barker, Mr. K. E. M. (Surrey), b Oct 27, 1877, d Aug 6, 1948

Barling, T. H. (Surrey), b Sept 1, 1906

Barlow, A. (Lancashire), b Aug 31, 1915

Barlow, Mr. E. A. (Oxford Univ., Lancashire and Denbighshire), b Feb 24, 1912

Barlow, Mr. K. (Kent), d April 5, 1930, aged 39

Barnard, Mr. F. H. (Oxford Univ.), b May 6, 1902

Barnard, H. M. (Hampshire), b July 18, 1933

Barnes, Mr. J. R. (Lancashire), b May 18, 1897, d July 22, 1945

Barnes, S. F. (Warwickshire, Lancashire and Staffordshire), b April 19, 1873

Barnes, Mr. S. G. (New South Wales), b June 5, 1916

Barnett, Mr. B. A. (Victoria and Buckinghamshire), b May 23, 1908

Barnett, C. J. (Gloucestershire), b July 3, 1910

Barnett, Mr. C. S. (Gloucestershire) b Feb 26, 1884

Barnett, Mr. E. P. (Gloucestershire), b March 22, 1885, d Jan 1, 1922

Barnwell, Mr. C. J. P. (Somerset), b June 23, 1914

Barratt, F. (Nottinghamshire), b April 12, 1894, d Jan 30, 1947

Barrett, Capt. E. I. M. (Hampshire), b June 22, 1879, d July 11, 1950

Barrick, D. (Northamptonshire), b April 28, 1926

Barrington, Mr. G. B. (Derbyshire) b April 20, 1857, d Feb 26, 1942

Barrington, K. (Surrey), b Nov 24, 1930

Barron, W. (Durham and Northamptonshire), b Oct 26, 1917

Barrow, Mr. I. (West Indies), b Jan 6, 1911

Bartholomew, Mr. A. C. (Oxford Univ.), b Feb 21, 1846, d March 29, 1940

Bartlett, Mr. E. L. (West Indies), b March 18, 1906

Bartlett, Mr. H. T. (Camb. Univ., Surrey and Sussex), b Oct 7, 1914

Bartlett, Mr. J. N. (Oxford Univ. and Sussex), b June 6, 1928

Barton, Mr. H. G. M. (Hampshire), b Oct 10, 1882

Barton, Mr. M. R. (Winchester, Oxford Univ., Norfolk and Surrey), b Oct 14, 1914

Bassett, Mr. H. (Oxford Univ., Oxfordshire and Suffolk), b Oct 5, 1868, d June 13, 1943

Bastow, John (Middlesex and Essex), b Oct 30, 1850, d June 1, 1927

Bateman-Champain, Col. C. E. (Cheltenham and Gloucestershire), b March 30, 1875

Bateman-Champain, Mr. F. H. (Gloucestershire and Oxford Univ.), b June 17, 1877, d Dec 29, 1942

Bateman-Champain, Brig.-Gen. H. F. (Cheltenham and Gloucestershire), b April 6, 1869, d Oct 7, 1933

Bates, L. A. (Warwickshire), b March 20, 1895

Bates, W. E. (Yorkshire, Glamorgan and Cheshire), b March 5, 1884

Bathurst, Mr. L. C. V. (Oxford Univ., Middlesex and Norfolk), b June 4, 1871, d Feb 22, 1939

Baumgartner, Mr. H. V. (Orange Free State and South Africa), b Nov 17, 1882, d April 8, 1938

Baxter, Mr. A. D. (Devon, Lancashire, Middlesex and Scotland), b Jan 20, 1910

Baxter, Mr. A. G. (Nottinghamshire), b Sept 21, 1931

Bayes, G. (Yorkshire), b Feb 27, 1884

Bayley, M. (Surrey), b May 7, 1843, d March 6, 1926

Bean, Mr. E. E. (Victoria), b April 17, 1866, d March 22, 1939

Beattie, Mr. F. D. (Lancashire), b Aug 18, 1909

Beaumont, H. (Yorkshire), b Oct 14, 1916

Beaumont, Mr. R. (South Africa), b Feb 4, 1884

Bedser, A. V. (Surrey), b July 4, 1918

Bedser, E. A. (Surrey), b July 4, 1918

Beet, G. (Derbyshire), b April 24, 1886, d Dec 13, 1946

Beet, G. H. (Derbyshire), b May 30, 1904, d Aug 22, 1949

Begbie, Mr. D. W. (South Africa), b Dec 12, 1914

Beldam, Mr. G. W. (Middlesex), b May 1, 1868, d Nov 23, 1937

Bell, Mr. A. J. (South Africa), b April 15, 1906

Bell, J. T. (Yorkshire an d Glamorgan, b June 16, 1898

Bell, Mr. R. M. (London County and M.C.C.), b Jan 1, 1874, d June 11, 1953

Bellamy, B. (Northamptonshire), b April 22, 1891

Belle, Mr. B. H. (Oxford Univ., Essex and Suffolk), b April 7, 1914

Beloe, Mr. G. H. (Gloucestershire), b Nov 21, 1877, d Oct 1, 1944

Benaud, Mr. R. (New South Wales), b Oct 6, 1930

Bencraft, Sir H. W. Russell (Hampshire), b March 4, 1858, d Dec 25, 1943

Benham, C. (Essex), b June 24, 1881

Benn, Mr. A. (Oxford Univ.), b Oct 7, 1912

Bennet, Col. F. W. (Kent), b Dec 13, 1850, d Oct 17, 1929

Bennett, A. (Lancashire), b May 18, 1910

Bennett, Mr. C. T. (Camb. Univ., Surrey and Middlesex), b Aug 10, 1902

Bennett, D. (Middlesex), b Dec 18, 1933

Bennett, Mr. G. M. (Somerset), b Dec 17, 1909

Bennett, J. W. (Derbyshire), b Feb 22, 1864, dead

Bennett, Mr. N. H. (Surrey), b Sep 23, 1912

Bennett, Mr. R. A. (Hampshire), b Dec 12, 1872, d July 16, 1951

Benskin, W. E. (Leicestershire and Scotland), b April 8, 1883

Benson, Mr. E. T. (Oxford Univ. and Gloucestershire), b Nov 20, 1907

Beresford, Mr. R. A. A. (Northamptonshire and Norfolk), b Aug 12, 1869, d July 12, 1941

Berkeley, Mr. G. F. H. (Oxford Univ.), b Jan 29, 1870, d Nov 14, 1955

Berkeley, Mr. M. (Essex), b Sept 6, 1872, d Aug 9, 1947

Bernard, Mr. C. A. (Somerset), b Feb 16, 1876, d 1953

Bernau, Mr. E. H. L. (New Zealand), b April 6, 1896

Berridge, Mr. W. C. M. (Leicestershire), b Dec 2, 1894

Berry, F. (Surrey), b Feb 13, 1911

Berry, L. G. (Leicestershire), b April 28, 1906

Berry, R. (Lancashire and Worcestershire), b Jan 29, 1926

Berwick, A. (Derbyshire), b July 30, 1865, dead

Bessant, J. G. (Gloucestershire), b Nov 11, 1895

Bestwick, W. (Derbyshire and Glamorgan), b Feb 24, 1876, d May 3, 1938

Betham, Mr. J. D. (Author of "Oxford and Camb. Cricket Scores and Biographies"), b Feb 13, 1874

Beton, S. (Middlesex), b Nov 22, 1895

Bettesworth, Mr. W. A. (Sussex), b Nov 24, 1856, d Feb 23, 1929

Bettington, Mr. R. H. B. (Oxford Univ., Middlesex and New South Wales), b Feb 24, 1900

Beves, Mr. G. (Nottinghamshire and Transvaal), b March 15, 1863, d March 22, 1927

Bickmore, Mr. A. F. (Oxford Univ. and Kent), b May 19, 1899

Bignell, Lt. Col. G. N. (Hampshire), b Dec 3, 1886

Binks, J. G. (Yorkshire), b Oct 5, 1935

Bird, Albert (Warwickshire and Worcestershire), b Aug. 17, 1868, d June 17, 1927

Bird, Rev. F. N. (Buckinghamshire, Gloucestershire, Northamptonshire, Devon and Suffolk), b 1876

Bird, Mr. M. C. (Lancashire and Surrey) b March 25, 1888, d Dec 9, 1933

Bird, Mr. R. C. (Hampshire), b March 17, 1874, d Oct 18, 1936

Bird, Mr. R. E. (Worcestershire), b April 4, 1915

Birkett, Mr. L. S. (West Indies), b April 14, 1905

Birrell, Mr. H. B. (Oxford Univ.), b Dec 12, 1927

Birtles, T. J. (Yorkshire), b Oct 26, 1887

Birtwell, Mr. A. J. (Buckinghamshire and Lancashire), b Dec 17, 1910

Bisgood, Mr. B. L. (Somerset) b March 11, 1881

Bishop, Mr. F. A. (Essex), b June 11, 1862

Bisset, Mr. J. J. (Natal). b Dec, 1882

Bisset, Sir M. (South Africa), b April 14, 1876, d Oct 24, 1931

Blackham, Mr. J. McC. (Victoria), b May 11, 1853, d Dec 27, 1932

Blackie, Mr. D. J (Victoria), b April 5, 1882, d April 21, 1955

Blacklock, Mr. J. P. (Wellington, N.Z.), b Feb 17, 1883, d Jan 22, 1935

Blagg, Mr. P. H. (Oxford Univ.) b Sept 11, 1918, d March 18, 1943

Blaikie, Mr. K. G. (Oxford Univ. and Somerset), b May 8, 1897

Blair, Brig.-Gen. E. M. (Kent), b July 26, 1866, d May 16, 1939

Blake, Mr. D. E. (Hampshire), b April 27, 1925

Blake, Capt. J. P. (Camb. Univ. and Hampshire), b Nov 17, 1917, d June 3, 1944

Blake, Mr. P. D. S. (Oxford Univ. and Sussex), b May 23, 1927

Blaker, Mr. R. N. R. (Camb. Univ. and Kent), b Oct 24, 1879, d Sept 11, 1950

Blanckenberg, Mr. J. M. (South Africa, b Dec 31, 1893

Bland, Cyril H. G. (Lincolnshire and Sussex), b May 23, 1872, d July 1, 1950

Bland, Mr. R. D. F. (Nottinghamshire), b May 16, 1911

Blaxland, Mr. L. B. (Derbyshire), b March 25, 1898

Bligh, Mr. A. S. (Somerset), b Oct 6, 1888, d Dec 27, 1952

Bligh, Hon. and Rev. E. V. (Oxford Univ. and Kent), b Feb 28, 1829, d April 22, 1908

Bligh, Hon. and Rev. Henry (Kent), b June 10, 1834, d March 4, 1905

Bligh, Hon. Ivo, see Darnley, 8th Earl

Bligh, Mr. L. E. (Kent), b Nov 24, 1854, d May 16, 1924

Block Mr. S. A. (Camb. Univ. and Surrey), b July 15, 1908

Blomley, B. (Lancashire), b Nov, 1885

Bloodworth, B. S. (Gloucestershire), b Dec, 1893

Bloy, Mr. N. C. F. (Oxford University), b Jan 2, 1923

Blundell, Mr. E. D. (Camb. Univ. and New Zealand), b May 29, 1907

Blunden, A. (Kent), b Sept 5, 1906

Blunt, Mr. R. C. (New Zealand), b Nov 3, 1900

Blythe, C. (Kent), b May 30, 1879, d Nov 1917

Board, J. H. (Gloucestershire), b Feb 23, 1867, d April 16, 1924

Boddington, Mr. R. A. (Lancashire), b June 30, 1892

Boden, Rev. C. A. (Leicestershire), b Dec 18, 1890

Boden, Mr. J. G. (Yorkshire), b Dec 27, 1848, d Jan 3, 1928

Bodkin, Mr. P. E. (Camb. Univ. and Hertfordshire), b Sep 15, 1924

Boger, Mr. A. J. (Oxford Univ. and Hertfordshire), b Aug 31, 1871, 1940 d June 3.

Bohlen, Mr. F. H. (Philadelphia), b July 31, 1868, d Dec 9, 1942

Bolton, Capt. R. H. D. (Dorset and Hampshire), b Jan 13, 1893

Bolus, F. (Somerset), b Nov 2, 1864

Bond, Mr. G. E. (South Africa), b April 5, 1910

Bonham-Carter, Sir M. (Oxford Univ. and Kent), b Oct 11, 1880

Bonnor, Mr. G. J. (N.S.W. and Victoria), b Feb 22, 1855, d June 27, 1912

Boobbyer, Mr. B. (Oxford Univ.), b Feb. 25, 1928

Booth, A. (Yorkshire), b Nov 3, 1902

Booth, Mr. C. (Camb. Univ., Hampshire and Lincolnshire), b May 11, 1842, d July 1, 1926

Booth, F. S. (Lancashire), b Feb 12, 1907

Booth, R. (Yorkshire), b Oct 1, 1926

Borradaile, Mr. O. R. (Essex), b May 9, 1859, d May 11, 1935

Bosanquet, Mr. B. J. T. (Middlesex and Oxford Univ.), b Oct 13, 1877, d Oct 12, 1936

Boshier, B. (Leicestershire), b March 6, 1932

Boswell, C. S. R. (Essex and Norfolk), b Jan 19, 1911

Bouch, Mr. H. E. (Kent), b April 15, 1868, dead

Boucher, Mr. J. C. (Ireland), b Dec 22, 1910

Boughton, Mr. W. A. (Gloucestershire), b Dec 23, 1854, d Nov 26, 1936

Bourne, Mr. A. A. (Camb. Univ.), b April 16, 1848, d July 17, 1931

Bowden, J. (Derbyshire), b Oct 8, 1889

Bowell, A. (Hampshire), b April 27, 1881

Bower, W. (Nottinghamshire), b Jan 2, 1895

Bowes, W. E. (Yorkshire), b July 25, 1908

Bowles, J. J. (Worcestershire), b April 3, 1891

Bowley, E. H. (Sussex), b June 7, 1890

Bowley, F. J. (Leicestershire), b Feb 20, 1909

Bowley, F. L. (Worcestershire), b Nov 9, 1875, d May 31, 1943

Bowley, T. (Northamptonshire, Surrey and Dorset), b Feb 28, 1857, d Nov 9, 1939

Bowmer, Mr. H. E. (Derbyshire), b July 14, 1891

Boxall, J. (Surrey and Hampshire), b Aug. 31, 1866, d Nov 10, 1930

Boyes, G. S. (Hampshire), b March 31, 1899

Boyington, Mr. F. (Scorer, Surrey C.C.C.), b Nov 9, 1848, d May 5, 1927

Brabourne, 4th Lord (Camb. Univ. and Kent), b Nov 27, 1863, d Feb 15, 1933

Bracey, F. (Derbyshire), b July 20, 1887

Bracher, Mr. F. C. (Gloucestershire), b Oct 25, 1868

Brackley, Visct., 4th Earl of Ellesmere (Eton), b Nov 14, 1872, d Aug 24, 1944

Bradby, Mr. H. C. (Oxford Univ.), b Dec 28, 1868, d June 28, 1947

Braddell, Mr. R. L. L. (Oxford Univ. and Suffolk), b Dec 14, 1888

Bradley, J. (Nottinghamshire), b Oct 3, 1913

Bradley, Mr. W. M. (Kent), b Jan 2, 1875, d June 19, 1944

Bradman, Sir D. G. (New South Wales and South Australia), b Aug 27, 1908

Bradshaw, J. C. (Leicestershire), b Jan 25, 1902

Brain, Mr. W. H. (Oxford Univ., Gloucestershire and Glamorgan), b July 21, 1870, d Nov 20, 1934

Brann, Mr. G. (Sussex), b April 23, 1865, d June 14, 1954

Branston, Mr. G. T. (Oxford Univ. and Nottinghamshire), b Sept 3, 1884

Braund, L. C. (Surrey and Somerset), b Oct 18, 1875, d Dec 22, 1955

Bray, Mr. C. (Essex), b April 6, 1898

Bray, Sir E. (Camb. Univ. and Surrey), b Aug 19, 1849, d June 19, 1926

Bray, Sir E. H. (Camb. Univ. and Middlesex), b April 15, 1874, d Nov 27, 1950

Braybrooke, Mr. H. M. (Kent), b Feb 11, 1869, d Oct 28, 1935

Brazier, A. F. (Surrey and Kent), b Dec 7, 1924

Brearley, Mr. W. (Lancashire and Cheshire), b March 11, 1876, d Jan 30, 1937

Brennan, Mr. D. V. (Yorkshire), b Feb 10, 1920

Brice, G. (Northamptonshire), b May 4, 1924

Brice, Mr. W. S. (New Zealand), b Nov 14, 1880

Bridgeman, 1st Visct. (Camb. Univ. and Staffordshire; President, M.C.C., 1931), b Dec 31, 1864, d Aug 14, 1935

Bridger, Rev. J. R. (Hampshire), b April 8, 1920

Bridges, Mr. J. J. (Somerset), b June 28, 1887

Bridgman, Mr. H. (South Australia), b Feb 1, 1890, d Dec 3, 1953

Brierley, T. L. (Glamorgan and Lancashire), b June 15, 1910

Briggs, John (Lancashire), b Oct 3, 1862, d Jan 11, 1902

Briggs, Canon R. (Oxford Univ.), b Dec 30, 1853, d Aug 21, 1936

Brinton, Mr. R. S. (Worcestershire), b Dec 15, 1869, d Feb 23, 1942

Briscoe, Mr. A. W. (South Africa), b Feb 6, 1911, d April 21, 1941

Bristowe, Mr. O. C. (Oxford Univ. and Essex), b April 12, 1895, d Dec 27, 1938

Broadbent, R. (Worcestershire), b June 21, 1924

Brocklebank, Mr. J. M. (Camb. Univ. and Lancashire). b Sept 3, 1915

Brocklehurst, Mr. B. G. (Somerset), b Feb 18, 1922

Brockwell, W. (Surrey), b Jan 21, 1866, d July 1, 1935

Broderick, V. (Northamptonshire), b Aug 17, 1920

Brodhurst, Mr. A. H. (Camb. Univ. and Gloucestershire), b July 21, 1916

Bromley, Mr. E. H. (Victoria). b Sept 2, 1912

Bromley, P. H. (Warwickshire), b July 30, 1930

Bromley-Davenport, Mr. H. R. (Camb. Univ., Cheshire and Middlesex), b Aug 18, 1870, d May 23, 1954

Bromley-Martin, Mr. E. G. (Worcestershire), b Oct 2, 1866, d Jan 23, 1946

Bromley-Martin, Mr. G. E. (Oxford Univ. and Worcestershire), b Oct 18, 1875, d May 31, 1941

Brook, G. W (Worcestershire), b Aug 30, 1895

Brooke, Lt.-Col. F. R. R. (Lancashire), b Oct 2, 1884

Brooke, Mr. R. H. J. (Oxford Univ. and Bucks), b June 6, 1909

Brookes, D. (Northamptonshire), b Oct 29, 1915

Brookes, Mr. W. H. (Editor of *Wisden* 1936 to 1939), b Dec 5, 1894, d May 28, 1955

Brooke-Taylor, Mr. G. P. (Camb. Univ. and Derbyshire), b Oct 25, 1895

Brooks, E. W. J. (Surrey), b July 6, 1898

Brooks, Lt.-Gen. R. A. D.(Hampshire), b Aug 22, 1896

Broughton, Mr. E. A. (Leicestershire), b April 22, 1905

Brown, E. (Warwickshire), b Nov 27, 1911

Brown, Mr. F. R. (Camb. Univ., Surrey and Northamptonshire), b Lima, Dec 16, 1910.

Brown, G. (Hampshire), b Oct 6, 1887

Brown, Mr. G. R. R. (Essex), b Dec 8, 1905

Brown, J. T. (Yorkshire), b Nov 24, 1874, d April 12, 1950

Brown, L. (Leicestershire), b March 12, 1874, d Oct 14, 1951

Brown, Mr. L. S. (South Africa), b Nov 24, 1910

Brown, S. M. (Middlesex), b Dec 8, 1917

Brown, W. (Leicestershire), b April 11, 1888

Brown, Mr. W. A. (New South Wales and Queensland), b July 31, 1912

Brown, Mr. W. C. (Northamptonshire), b Nov 13, 1900

Brown, Mr. W. S. A. (Gloucestershire), b May 23, 1877, d Sept 12, 1952

Browne, Mr. C. R. (West Indies), b Oct 8, 1890

Browne, Rev. F. B. R. (Camb Univ. and Sussex), b July 28, 1899

Browne, Mr. F. D. (Kent), b March 4, 1873, d Aug 12, 1946

Brownlee, Mr. L. D. (Oxford Univ., Gloucestershire and Somerset), b Dec 17, 1882, d Sept 22, 1955

Bruce, Hon. C. N. (3rd Lord Aberdare), (Oxford Univ. and Middlesex), b Aug 2, 1885

Bruce, Mr. W. (Victoria), b May 22, 1864, d Aug 4, 1925

Brunton, Rev. J. du V. (Camb. Univ.), b July 23, 1869

Brutton, Mr. C. P. (Hampshire and Denbighshire), b Jan 20, 1899

Bryan, Capt. G. J. (Kent), b Dec 29, 1902

Bryan, Mr J. L. (Camb. Univ. and Kent), b May 26, 1896

Bryan, Mr. R. T. (Rugby and Kent), b July 30, 1898

Bryant, Mr. H. W. (Middlesex), b June 30, 1867

Buccleuch, 7th Duke of (President, M.C.C., 1913, as Earl of Dalkeith), b May 30, 1864

Buchanan, Mr. J. N. (Camb. Univ. and Buckinghamshire), b in South Africa, May 30, 1887

Buckenham, C. P. (Essex), b Jan 16, 1876, d Feb 23, 1937

Buckingham, J. (Warwickshire), b Jan 21, 1904

Bucknill, Mr. S. P. B. (Warwickshire), b June 18, 1849, d May 8, 1930

Buckston, Mr. G. M. (Camb. Univ. and Derbyshire), b March 12, 1881, d Nov 24, 1942

Buckston, Mr. R. H. R. (Derbyshire), b Oct 10, 1908

Budd, W. L. (Hampshire), b Oct 25, 1913

Bull, Mr. A. H. (Northamptonshire), b Jan 23, 1892

Bull, C. H. (Kent and Worcestershire), b March 29, 1909, d May 28, 1939

Buller, J. S. (Worcestershire), b Aug 23, 1909

Bulsara, Mr. M. D. (India), b Sept 2, 1877

Bunce, Mr. N. (Somerset), b April 17, 1911

Burchell, T. (Sussex), b April 26, 1876, d Feb, 1950

Burden, M. D. (Hampshire), b Oct 4, 1930

Burgess, Mr. J. (Leicestershire), b Nov 22, 1880, d 1953

Burke, Mr. C. (New Zealand), b March 27, 1914

Burn, Mr. K. E. (Tasmania), b Sept 17, 1863

Burn, Mr. R. C. W. (Oxford Univ.), b Oct 29, 1882, d May 8, 1955

Burnett, Mr. A. C. (Camb. Univ.), b Oct 26, 1923

Burns, James (Lancashire and Essex), b June 20, 1865

Burnup, Mr. C. J. (Camb. Univ. and Kent), b Nov 21, 1875

Burrough, Mr. H. D. (Somerset), b Feb 6, 1909

Burrows, R. D. (Worcestershire), b June 6, 1872, d Feb 1943

Burton, Mr. D. C. F. (Yorkshire), b Sept 13, 1887

Burton, George (Middlesex), b May 1, 1851, d May 6, 1930

Burton, J. (Derbyshire), b Dec 10, 1874, d Jan 25, 1940

Burton, Mr. R. C. (Yorkshire), b April 11, 1891

Burton, T. (West Indies), b Jan 31, 1878

Burtt, Mr. T. B. (New Zealand), b Jan 22, 1915

Bury, Mr. L. (Camb. Univ.), b July 9, 1857, d Oct 30, 1935

Bury, Rev. W. (Camb. Univ. and Nottinghamshire), b Oct 14, 1839, d May 21, 1927

Buse, H. T. F. (Somerset), b Aug 5, 1910

Bush, Col. H. S. (Surrey), b Oct 7, 1871, d March 18, 1942

Bush, Mr. J. E. (Oxford Univ.), b Aug 28, 1928

Bush, Mr. R. E. (Gloucestershire), b Oct 11, 1855, d Dec 9, 1939

Bushby, Mr. M. H. (Camb. Univ.), b July 29, 1931

Buswell, J. (Northamptonshire), b July 3, 1911

Buswell, W. A. (Northamptonshire), b Jan 12, 1875, d April 24, 1950

Butler, Mr. E. H. (Tasmania & M.C.C.), b March 15, 1851, d Jan 5, 1928

Butler, Mr. E. M. (Camb. Univ. and Middlesex), b Dec 31, 1866, d Feb 11, 1948

Butler, H. J. (Nottinghamshire), b March 12, 1913

Butt, H. R. (Sussex), b Dec 27, 1865, d Dec 21, 1928

Butterworth, Mr. H. R. W. (Camb. Univ., Denbighshire and Lancashire), b Feb 4, 1909

Buxton, J. H. (Nottinghamshire), b Nov 20, 1914

Buxton, Mr. R. V. (Oxford Univ. and Middlesex), b April 29, 1883, d Oct 1, 1953

Byrne, Mr. J. F. (Warwickshire), b June 19, 1871, d May 10, 1954

Cadman, S. (Derbyshire), b Jan 29, 1880, d May 6, 1952

Cahn, Sir Julien, 1st Bart. (Nottinghamshire C.C.C.), b Oct 21, 1882, d Sept 26, 1944

Caine, Mr. C. Stewart (Editor of *Wisden* 1926 to 1933), b Oct 28, 1861, d April 15, 1933

Calthorpe, Hon. F. S. G. (Camb. Univ., Sussex and Warwickshire), b May 27, 1892, d Nov 19, 1935

Cameron, Mr. H. B. (South Africa), b July 5, 1905, d Nov 2, 1935

Cameron, Mr. J. H. (Camb. Univ., Somerset and West Indies), b April 8, 1914

Cameron, Dr. J. J. (West Indies), b May, 1882

Campbell, Mr. I. P. (Oxford Univ. and Kent), b Feb 5, 1928

Campbell, Mr. I. P. F. (Oxford Univ. and Surrey), b Nov 25, 1890

Campbell, Mr. P. (Essex), b Dec 26, 1887

Cangley, Mr. B. G. (Camb. Univ. and Cambridgeshire), b Sept 12, 1922

Cannings, V. H. D. (Warwickshire and Hampshire), b April 3, 1920

Capes, Mr. C. J. (Kent), b Jan 5, 1898, d Feb 16, 1933

Cardus, Mr. Neville (Cricket Writer), b April 2, 1890

Carey, P. A. D. (Sussex), b May 21, 1920

Carkeek, Mr. W. (Victoria), b Oct 17, 1878, d Feb 21, 1937

Carless, Mr. W. C. (Herefordshire and Manager of the Hastings Festival), b June 9, 1851, d March 17, 1929

Carlin, J. (Nottinghamshire), b Nov 3, 1861

Carlisle, Mr. K. M. (Oxford Univ.), b Aug 7, 1882

Carpenter, D. (Gloucestershire), b Sept 12, 1935

Carpenter, H. (Essex and Cambridgeshire), b July 12, 1869, d Dec 12, 1933

Carpenter-Garnier, Mr. J. (Oxford Univ.), b Feb 28, 1839, d Oct 5, 1926

Carr, Mr. A. W. (Nottinghamshire), b May 18, 1893

Carr, Mr. D. B. (Oxford Univ. and Derbyshire), b Dec 28, 1926

Carr, Mr. D. W. (Kent), b March 17, 1872, d March 23, 1950

Carrington, E. (Derbyshire), b March 25, 1914

Carris, Mr. B. D. (Camb. Univ. and Middlesex), b Oct 23, 1917

Carris, Mr. H. E. (Camb. Univ. and Middlesex), b July 7, 1909

Carrol, Mr. E. V. (Victoria), b Jan 16, 1885

Carson, Mr. W. N. (New Zealand), b July 16, 1916, d Oct 1944

Carter, Mr. C. P. (South Africa and Cornwall), b April 23, 1881, d Nov 8, 1952

Carter, Mr. H. (New South Wales), b in Yorkshire, March 14, 1878, d June 8, 1948

Carter, R. (Derbyshire), b Nov 7, 1933

Cartwright, Mr. Philip (Sussex) b at Gibraltar, Sept 26, 1880, d Nov 21, 1955

Carty, R. A. (Hampshire), b July 28, 1922

Case, Mr. C. C. (Somerset), b Sept 7, 1895

Case, Mr. T. B. (Oxford Univ. and Oxfordshire), b Feb 19, 1871, d Nov 10, 1941

Castens, Mr. H. H. (Rugby and South Africa), b Nov 23, 1864, d Oct 18, 1929

Castle, Mr. F. (Somerset), b April 9, 1909

Castledine, S. W. T. (Nottinghamshire), b April 10, 1912

Catterall, Mr. R. H. (South Africa), b July 10, 1900

Cave, Mr. H. B. (New Zealand), b Oct 10, 1922

Cave, W. (Hampshire), b Aug 4, 1867

Cawston, Mr. E. (Camb. Univ., Sussex and Berkshire), b Jan 16, 1911

Chalk, Mr. F. G. H. (Oxford Univ. and Kent), b Sept 7, 1910, d Feb 1943

Challen, Mr. J. B. (Somerset), b March 26, 1863, d June 5, 1937

Challenor, Mr. G. (West Indies), b June 28, 1888, d July 30, 1947

Chamberlain, Mr. L. W. (South Australia), b Jan 15, 1889

Chandler, Mr. A. (Surrey), b Dec 5, 1849, d Dec 25, 1926

Chaplin, Mr. H. P. (Sussex), b March 1, 1883

Chapman, Mr. A. P. F. (Camb. Univ., Berkshire and Kent), b Sept 3, 1900

Chapman, Mr. J. (Derbyshire), b March 11, 1879

Chapman, T. A. (Leicestershire), b May 14, 1919

Charlesworth, C. (Warwickshire), b Feb 12, 1877, d June 15, 1953

Charlton, Mr. P. C. (New South Wales), b April 9, 1867, d Sept 30, 1954

Cheetham, Mr. A. G. (Australia), b Dec 7, 1915

Cheetham, Mr. J. E. (South Africa), b May 26, 1920

Chester, F. (Worcestershire. Umpire), b Jan 20, 1896

Chesterfield, 10th Earl of (President, M.C.C., 1909), b March 15, 1854, d Jan 24, 1933

Chesterton, Mr. G. H. (Oxford Univ. and Worcestershire), b July 15, 1922

Chidgey, H. (Somerset), b July 25, 1879, d Nov 30, 1941

Chignell, Mr. T. A. (Hampshire), b Oct 31, 1880

Childs-Clarke, Mr. A. W. (Middlesex and Northamptonshire), b May 13, 1905

Chipperfield, Mr. A. G. (New South Wales), b Nov 17, 1905

Chowdhury, Mr. N. R. (India), b 1923

Christiani, Mr. C. M. (West Indies), b Oct 28, 1913, d April 4, 1938

Christiani, Mr. R. J. (West Indies), b July 19, 1920

Christopherson, Mr. J. C. (Camb. Univ. and Kent), b June 1, 1909

Christopherson, Mr. P. (Kent and Berkshire), b March 31, 1866, d May 4, 1921

Christopherson, Mr. Stanley (Kent, President M.C.C. 1939–46), b Nov 11, 1861, d April 6, 1949

Christy, Mr. J. A. J. (South Africa and Queensland), b Dec 12, 1904

Chubb, Mr. G. W. A. (South Africa), b April 12, 1911

Clapp, A. E. (Somerset), b May 3, 1867

Clark, Mr. D. G. (Kent), b Jan 27, 1919

Clark, E. W. (Northamptonshire), b Aug. 9, 1902

Clark, Mr. L. S. (Essex), b March 6, 1914

Clark, T. H. (Surrey), b Oct 5, 1924

Clarke Lt.-Col. B. F. (Gloucestershire and Leicestershire), b Sept 26, 1885, d May, 1940

Clarke, Dr. C. B. (West Indies and Northamptonshire), b April 7, 1918

Clarke, Mr. C. C. (Derbyshire, Staffordshire and Sussex), b Dec 22, 1910

Clarke, Mr. C. C. (Surrey and Berkshire), Writer, b April 26, 1853, d Jan 29, 1931

Clarke, R. W. (Northamptonshire), b April 22, 1924

Clarke, W. (Nottinghamshire), b March 17, 1850, d May 29, 1935

Clay, Mr. J. C. (Glamorgan), b March 18, 1898

Clay, J. D. (Nottinghamshire), b Oct 15, 1924

Clift, P. (Glamorgan), b Sept 3, 1919

Clifton, C. C. (Nottinghamshire), b Dec 8, 1885, d March 14, 1930

Clode, H. (Surrey and Durham), b Sept 7, 1878

Close, D. B. (Yorkshire), b Feb. 24, 1931

Clugston, D. L. (Warwickshire), b Feb 5, 1908

Cobb, Mr. Humphry H. (Middlesex), b July 12, 1876, d Dec 13, 1949

Cobbold, Mr. P. W. (Camb. Univ., and Suffolk), b Jan 5, 1875, d Dec 28, 1945

Cobbold, Mr. R. H. (Camb. Univ.), b May 22, 1906

Cobbold, Mr. W. N. (Kent), b Feb 4, 1863, d April 8, 1922

Cobcroft, Mr. L. T. (New South Wales and New Zealand), b Feb 12, 1869, d March 9, 1938

Cobden, Mr. F. C. (Camb. Univ.), b Oct 14, 1849, d Dec 7, 1932

Cobham, 8th Visct. (5th Baron Lyttelton) (Camb. Univ., President, M.C.C., 1886), b Oct 27, 1842, d June 9, 1922

Cobham, 9th Visct. (Hon. J. C. Lyttelton), (Worcestershire; President, M.C.C., 1935), b Oct 23, 1881, d July 31, 1949

Cobham, 10th Visct. (Hon. C. J. Lyttelton) (Worcestershire), b Aug 8, 1909

Cobley, A. (Leicestershire), b Oct 5, 1875

Cochrane, Mr. A. H. J. (Oxford Univ. and Derbyshire), b Jan 26, 1865, d Dec 14, 1948

Cochrane, Mr. R. S. T. (Sec., Derbyshire C.C.C. 1907–8), b Aug 27, 1877

Cock, Mr. D. F. (Essex), b Oct 22, 1914

Cockett, Mr. J. A. (Camb. Univ.), b Dec 23, 1927

Coe, F. (Northamptonshire), b May 26, 1867

Coe, S. (Leicestershire), b June 3, 1873, d Nov 4, 1955

Coen, Mr. S. K. (South Africa), b Oct 14, 1902

Colah, S. H. M. (India), b Sept 22, 1902, d Sept 11, 1950

Cole, C. G. (Kent), b July 7, 1916

Cole, Mr. F. L. (Gloucestershire), Oct 4, 1856, d July 1, 1941

Cole, Mr. T. G. O. (Derbyshire, Lancashire, and Denbighshire), b Nov 14, 1877, d Dec 15, 1944

Colebrooke, Rev. E. L. (Oxford Univ.), b Oct 29, 1858, d Aug 10, 1939

Coleman, C. A. (Leicestershire), b July 7, 1906

Collett, Mr. G. F. (Gloucestershire), b July 18, 1879, d Feb 26, 1945.

Collier, Mr. J. (Leicestershire), b April 18, 1851, d Oct 15, 1935

Collin, T. (Warwickshire and Durham), b April 17, 1911

Collins, Mr. A. (Sussex), b 1872, d July 1945

Collins, Mr. D. C. (Camb. Univ.), b Oct 1, 1887

Collins, G. (Kent), b Sept 21, 1889, d Jan 23, 1949

Collins, Mr. G. A. K. (Sussex), b May 16, 1909

Collins, Mr. H. L. (New South Wales), b Jan 21, 1889

Collins, Brig.-Gen. L. P. (Oxford Univ., Berkshire and India), b Nov 27, 1878

Collins, R. (Lancashire), b March 10, 1934

Collins, Mr. T. (Camb. Univ.), b Jan 31, 1841, d March 16, 1934

Collins, Mr. W. E. W. (Shropshire and M.C.C.), b 1849, d Jan 7, 1932

Collishaw, W. F. (Warwickshire), b Oct 2, 1860, d Feb 1, 1936

Colman, Mr. G. R. R. (Norfolk, and Oxford Univ.), b March 14, 1892, d March 18, 1935

Colman Sir Jeremiah, 1st Bt. (President, Surrey C.C.C., 1916 to 1923), b April 24, 1859, d Jan 15, 1942

Colman, Mr. S. (Surrey), b Jan 6, 1862, d Feb 27, 1942

Colson, G. H. (Northamptonshire), b Jan 21, 1868

Comber, G. (Surrey), b Oct 12, 1856, d Oct 18, 1929

Comber, Mr. J. T. H. (Camb. Univ.), b Feb 26, 1911

Compton, D. C. S. (Middlesex), b May 23, 1918

Compton, L. H. (Middlesex), b Sept 12, 1912

Coningham, Mr. A. (Queensland and New South Wales), b July 14, 1866, d June 13, 1939

Conradi, Mr. E. R. (Camb. Univ.), b July 25, 1920

Considine, Mr. S. G. U. (Somerset), b Aug 11, 1901, d Aug 31, 1950

Constable, B. (Surrey), b Feb 19, 1921

Constantine, L. N. (West Indies), b Sept 21, 1902

Constantine, Mr. L. S. (Trinidad), b May 25, 1874, d Jan 5, 1942

Conway, A. J. (Worcestershire), b April 1, 1886, d Nov 1, 1954

Coode, Mr. A. T. (Camb. Univ. and Middlesex), b Feb 5, 1876, d Dec 28, 1940

Cook, C. (Gloucestershire), b Aug 8, 1921

Cook, L. (Lancashire), b March 28, 1885, d Dec 2, 1933

Cook, T. E. (Sussex), b Feb 5, 1901, d Jan 15, 1950

Cook, W. (Lancashire), b Jan 16, 1882, d Dec 18, 1947

Cook, Mr. W. T. (Surrey), b Dec 6, 1891

Cooke, R. (Warwickshire), b May 25, 1900

Coope, M. (Somerset), b Nov 28, 1917

Cooper, E. (Worcestershire), b Nov 30, 1915

Cooper, F. (Worcestershire), b April 18, 1921

Cooper, H. (Derbyshire), b Dec 23, 1883

Cooper, Mr. W. H. (Victoria), b Sept 11, 1849, d April 5, 1939

Copley, S. H. (Nottinghamshire), b Nov 1, 1906

Copson, W. H. (Derbyshire), b April 27, 1909

Corbett, Mr. L. J. (Gloucestershire), b May 12, 1897

Cording, Mr. G. E. (Glamorgan), b Jan 1, 1878, d Feb 2, 1946

Cornford, J. H. (Sussex), b Dec 9, 1911

Cornford, W. (Sussex), b Dec 25, 1900

Cornwallis, Capt. Hon. W. S, 2nd Lord Cornwallis (Kent), b March 14, 1892

Corrall, P. (Leicestershire), b July 16, 1906

Cotter, Mr. A. (New South Wales), b Dec 3, 1883, d Oct 20, 1917

Coulson, S. S. (Leicestershire), b Oct 17, 1898

Coupe, E. (Derbyshire), b June 9, 1863

Court, R. C. (Hampshire), b Oct 23, 1916

Cousens, P. (Essex), b May 15, 1932

Coutts, Mr. I. D. F. (Oxford Univ.), b April 27, 1928

Coventry, 9th Earl of (Eton and President, M.C.C., 1859), b May 9, 1838, d March 13, 1930

Coventry, Col. Hon. C. J. (Worcestershire), b Feb 26, 1867, d June 2, 1929

Coventry, Hon. J. B. (Worcestershire), b Jan 9, 1903

Coverdale, W. W. (Northamptonshire), b May 30, 1912

Cowan, Capt. C. F. R. (Warwickshire), b Sept, 1883

Cowan, M. J. (Yorkshire), b June 10, 1933

Cowdrey, Mr. M. C. (Kent and Oxford Univ.), b Dec 24, 1932

Cowie, Mr. J. (New Zealand) b March 30, 1912

Cox, A. L. (Northamptonshire), b July 22, 1908

Cox, G., jun. (Sussex), b Aug 23, 1911

Cox, Mr. G. C. (Worcestershire), b July 5, 1908

Cox, G. R. (Sussex), b Nov 29, 1873, d March 24, 1949

Cox, Mr. H. R. (Nottinghamshire), b May 19, 1911

Cox, Mr. J. L. (South Africa), b June 28, 1886

Cox, M. (Northamptonshire), b May 10, 1881

Coxon, A. (Yorkshire), b Jan 18, 1917

Coxon, Mr. A. J. (Oxford Univ.), b March 18, 1930

Coxon, Mr. H. (Nottinghamshire Scorer), b Aug 8 1847, d. Nov. 5, 1929

Crabtree, Mr. H. P. (Essex), b April 30, 1906

Craig, Mr. I. D. (New South Wales), b June 12, 1935

Cranfield, L. M. (Gloucestershire), b Aug 29, 1910

Crankshaw, Major Sir E. N. S. (Gloucestershire), b July 1, 1885

Cranmer, Mr. P. (Warwickshire), b Sept 10, 1914

Cranston, Mr. K. (Lancashire), b Oct 20, 1917

Crapp, J. F. (Gloucestershire), b Oct 14, 1912

Crawford, Rev. J. C. (Kent and Surrey), b May 29, 1849, d Feb 21, 1935

Crawford, Mr. J. N. (Surrey and South Australia), b Dec 1, 1886

Crawford, Mr. R. T. (Leicestershire), b June 11, 1882, d Nov 15, 1945

Crawford, Mr. V. F. S. (Surrey and Leicestershire), b April 11, 1879, d Aug 21, 1922

Crawford, Mr. J. W. F. (Oxford Univ., Surrey and Ireland), b Nov 14, 1878, d June 22, 1939

Crawley, Mr. A. M. (Oxford Univ. and Kent), b April 10, 1908

Crawley, Mr. L. G. (Camb. Univ., Durham, Worcestershire and Essex), b July 26, 1903

Cray, S. J. (Essex), b May 29, 1921

Creber, H. (Glamorgan), b April 30, 1874, d March 27, 1939

Creese, W. L. (Hampshire), b Dec 28, 1907

Cresswell, Mr. G. F. (New Zealand), b March 22, 1915

Cresswell, J. (Warwickshire), b Dec 22, 1866, d July 19, 1932

Crisp, Mr. R. J. (South Africa and Worcestershire), b May 28, 1911

Critchley-Salmonson, Mr. H. S (Somerset), b Jan 19, 1894

Crockford, Mr. E. B. (Warwickshire) b Oct 13, 1888

Croft, Mr. P. D. (Camb. Univ.), b July 7, 1933

Cromb, Mr. I. B. (New Zealand), b June 25, 1905

Cromer, 2nd Earl of (President, M.C.C., 1934), b Nov 29, 1877

Crookes, Mr. D. V. (Camb. Univ.), b June 18, 1931

Croom, A. J. (Warwickshire), b May 23, 1897, d Aug 16, 1947

Croome, Mr. A. C. M. (Gloucestershire, Oxford Univ. and Berkshire), b Feb 21, 1866, d Sept 11, 1930

Cropper, M. (Derbyshire), b July 16, 1864

Crosse, Mr. E. M. (Northamptonshire), b Dec 11, 1882

Crossland, Mr. A. P. (Yorkshire), b Dec 10, 1863

Crow, John (Kent Scorer 1874–96), b July 19, 1847, d Jan 22, 1939

Crowe, Mr. G. L. (Worcestershire), b Jan 8, 1885

Crush, Mr. E. (Kent), b April 25, 1917

Crutchley, Mr. G. E. V. (Oxford Univ. and Middlesex), b Nov 19, 1890

Cuff, Mr. L. A. (New Zealand and Tasmania), b March 28, 1866, d Oct 9, 1954

Cuffe, J. A. (New South Wales and Worcestershire), b June 26, 1880, d May 5, 1931

Cullen, L. (Northamptonshire), b Nov 23, 1914

Cumberlege, Mr. B. S. (Camb. Univ., Northumberland and Kent), b June 5, 1891

Cumberlege, Mr. C. F. (Surrey and Northumberland), b July 29, 1851, d Feb 12, 1929

Cumming, Mr. B. L. (Sussex), b July 11, 1916

Cunningham, Mr. W. (New Zealand), b Jan 23, 1900

Curgenven, Mr. G. (Derbyshire), b Dec 1, 1882, d May 26, 1934

Curgenven, Mr. H. G. (Derbyshire), b Dec 22, 1875

Curnow, Mr. S. H. (South Africa), b Dec. 16, 1907

Currie, Mr. C. E. (Hampshire), b April 4, 1861, d Jan 2, 1937

Curtis, J. S. (Leicestershire), b Dec 21, 1887

Curzon, Viscount (Eton). See Howe, 4th Earl

Cuthbertson, Mr. G. B. (Middlesex and Northamptonshire), b March 28, 1901

Cutmore, J. A. (Essex), b Dec 28, 1900

Cuttell, Willis Robert (Yorkshire and Lancashire), b Sept 13, 1864, d Dec 9, 1929

Da Costa, Mr. O. C. (West Indies), b Sept 11, 1907, d Oct 1, 1936

Dacre, C. C. (New Zealand and Gloucestershire), b May 21, 1900

Daer, Mr. A. G. (Essex), b Nov 20, 1906

Daer, H. (Essex), b Dec 10, 1918

Daffen, Mr. A. (Kent and Berkshire), b Dec 30, 1862

Daft, H. B. (Nottinghamshire), b April 5, 1866, d Jan 12, 1945

Daily, C. (Surrey), b April 28, 1900

Dales, Mr. H. L. (Middlesex), b May 18, 1888

Daley, J. V. (Norfolk, Surrey and Suffolk), b Feb 1, 1907

Dalkeith, Earl of (President, M.C.C., 1913), see Buccleuch, 7th Duke of

Dalmeny, Lord (6th Earl of Rosebery), (Bucks, Middlesex and Surrey), b Jan 8, 1882

Dalton, Mr. E. L. (South Africa), b Dec 2, 1906

Daniell, Mr. J. (Camb. Univ. and Somerset), b Dec 12, 1878

Dare, R. (Hampshire), b Nov 26, 1921

Darling, Mr. J. (South Australia), b Nov 21, 1870, d Jan 2, 1946

Darling, Mr. L. S. (Victoria), b Aug 14, 1909

Darnley, 8th Earl of (Hon. Ivo Bligh), (Camb. Univ., Kent, and President, M.C.C., 1900), b March 13, 1859, d April 10, 1927

Dartmouth, 6th Earl of (President, M.C.C., 1893), b May 6, 1851, d March 11, 1936

Dartmouth, 7th Earl of (President, M.C.C., 1932), b Feb 22, 1881

Darwall-Smith, Mr. R. F. H. (Oxford Univ. and Sussex), b July 11, 1914

Datta, Mr. P. B. (Camb. Univ.), b 1925

David, Mr. R. F. A. (Glamorgan), b June 19, 1907

Davidson, Mr. A. K. (New South Wales), b June 14, 1929

Davidson, Mr. K. R. (Yorkshire), b Dec 24, 1905, d Dec 25, 1954

Davidson, Mr. W. W. (Oxford Univ. and Sussex), b March 20, 1920

Davies, Dai (Glamorgan), b Aug 26, 1896

Davies, D. A. (Glamorgan), b July 11, 1915

Davies, Emrys (Glamorgan), b June 27, 1904

Davies, Mr. E. Q. (South Africa), b Aug 26, 1909

Davies, Mr. G. A. (Manager Australia in England, 1953), b March 19, 1895

Davies, H. D. (Glamorgan), b July 23, 1932

Davies, H. G. (Glamorgan), b April 23, 1913

Davies, Mr. J. G. W. (Camb. Univ. and Kent), b Sept 10, 1911

Davies, Capt. P. Havelock (Oxford Univ. and Sussex), b Aug 30, 1893, d Jan 30, 1930

Davis, E. (Northamptonshire), b March 8, 1922

Davis, P. (Northamptonshire), b May 24, 1916

Davis, P. (Kent), b April 4, 1922

Davis, Mr. R. A. (Tasmania), b Oct 22, 1892

Davis, W. E. (Surrey), b Nov 26, 1880

Davy, Mr. C. V. (Kent), b Oct 24, 1869, d Sept 10, 1931

Dawkes, G. (Leicestershire and Derbyshire), b July 19, 1920

Dawson, Mr. E. W. (Camb. Univ. and Leicestershire), b Feb 13, 1904

Dawson, G. (Hampshire), b Dec 9, 1916

Dawson, Mr. O. C. (South Africa), b Sept 1, 1919

Day, Mr. A. P. (Kent), b April 10, 1885

Day, Mr. H. L. V. (Bedfordshire and Hampshire), b Aug 12, 1898

Day, J. W. (Nottinghamshire and Lincolnshire), b Sept 16, 1882

Day, Mr. S. H. (Camb. Univ. and Kent), b Dec 29, 1878, d Feb 20, 1950

Dean, H. (Lancashire and Cheshire), b Aug 13, 1885

Dean, T. A. (Hampshire), b Nov 21, 1920

Deane, Mr. H. G. (South Africa), b July 21, 1895, d Oct 21, 1939

De Caires, Mr. F. I. (West Indies), b May 12, 1909

de Courcy, Mr. J. H. (New South Wales), b April 18, 1927

Deed, Mr. J. A. (Kent), b Sept 12, 1901

Deighton, Major J. H. G. (Lancashire), b April 5, 1920

Delisle, Mr. G. P. S. (Middlesex and Oxford Univ.), b Dec 25, 1934

de Lisle, Mr. J. A. (Leicestershire), b Sept 27, 1891

De Little, Mr. E. R. (Camb. Univ.), b June 19, 1868, d Oct 1, 1926

Delme-Radcliffe, Mr. A. H. (Hampshire and Berkshire), b Nov 23, 1870, d June 30. 1950

Dempster, Mr. C. S. (New Zealand, Scotland, Leicestershire and Warwickshire), b Nov 15, 1903

Dench, C. E. (Nottinghamshire), b Sept 6, 1873

Dennett, George (Gloucestershire), b April 27, 1880, d Sept 14, 1937

Dennis, F. (Yorkshire and Cheshire), b June 11, 1907

Dennis, Mr. J. N. (Essex), b Jan 4, 1911

Denton, David (Yorkshire), b July 4, 1874, d Feb 17, 1950

Denton, J. (Yorkshire), b Feb 3, 1865, d July 19, 1946

Denton, Mr. J. S. (Northamptonshire), b Nov 2, 1890

Denton, Mr. W. H. (Northamptonshire), b Nov 2, 1890

De Robeck, Admiral Sir J. M., 1st Bart. (President, M.C.C., 1925), b June 10, 1862, d Jan 20, 1928

De Saram, Mr. F. C. (Oxford Univ. and Hertfordshire), b Sept, 1912

Desborough, 1st Lord (President M.C.C., 1911), b Oct 30, 1855, d Jan 9, 1945

de Trafford, The Hon. C. E. (Lancashire and Leicestershire), b May 21, 1864, d Nov 12, 1951

Devereux, L. N. (Worcestershire), b Oct 20, 1931

Devey, John (Warwickshire), b Dec 26, 1866, d Oct 13, 1940

Devonshire, 9th Duke of (President, M.C.C., 1912), b May 31, 1868, d May 6, 1938

Dewes, Mr. J. G. (Camb. Univ. and Middlesex), b Oct 11, 1926

De Winton, Mr. S. (Gloucestershire), b Sept 5, 1869

Dews, G. (Worcestershire), b June 5, 1921

Deyes, G. (Yorkshire and Staffordshire), b Feb 11, 1879

de Zoete, Mr. H. W. (Camb. Univ. and Essex), b Feb 14, 1871

Dickinson, Mr. D. C. (Camb. Univ.), b Dec 11, 1929

Dickinson, Mr. P. J. (Camb. Univ. and Surrey), b Aug 18, 1919

Dickson, Mr. M. R. (Scotland), b Jan 2, 1882, d Jan 10, 1940

Difford, Mr. I. D. (Transvaal, Sec., S. African Cricket Assn., 1903–14), b Jan 29, 1873, d Feb 5, 1949

Digby, Mr. R. (Oxford Univ.), b April 30, 1847, d Dec 29, 1927

Dillon, Mr. E. W. (Oxford Univ. and Kent), b Feb 15, 1881, d April 25, 1941

Diment, Mr. R. A. (Leicestershire), b Feb 9, 1927

Dines, W. J. (Essex), b Sept 14, 1916

Dipper, A. E. (Gloucestershire), b Nov 9, 1887, d Nov 9, 1945

Disney, J. (Derbyshire), b Nov 20, 1861, d June 25, 1934

Divecha, R. V. (Oxford Univ. and India), b Oct 18, 1927

Dixon, A. (Kent), b Nov 27, 1933

Dixon, Mr. A. W. (Yorkshire), b Feb 8, 1870, d May 23, 1935

Dixon, Mr. E. J. H. (Oxford Univ. and Northamptonshire), b Sept 22, 1915, d April 20, 1941

Dixon, Mr. J. A. (Nottinghamshire), b May 27, 1861, d June 8, 1931

Dixon, Mr. J. G. (Essex), b Sept 3, 1895, d Nov 19, 1954

Docker, Mr. A. R. (New South Wales), b June 3, 1848, d 1929

Docker, Mr. C. T. (Australian Imperial Forces Team), b March 3, 1884

Docker, Mr. L. C. (Derbyshire and Warwickshire, President, Warwickshire C.C.C.), b Nov 26, 1860, d Aug 1, 1940

Dodd, W. T. F. (Hampshire), b March 9, 1908

Dodds, T. C. (Essex), b May 29, 1919

Doggart, Mr. A. G. (Camb. Univ., Durham and Middlesex), b June 2, 1897

Doggart, Mr. G. H. G. (Camb. Univ. and Sussex), b July 18, 1925

Doll, Mr. M. H. C. (Hertfordshire and Middlesex), b April 5, 1888

Dollery, H. E. (Warwickshire), b Oct 14, 1914

Dollery, K. R. (Warwickshire), b Dec 9, 1924

Dolling, Mr. C. E. (South Australia), b Sept 4, 1886, d June 11, 1936

Dolphin, A. (Yorkshire), b Dec 24, 1886, d Oct 24, 1942

Donnan, Mr. H. (New South Wales), b Nov 12, 1864

Donnelly, Mr. M. P. (New Zealand, Oxford Univ., Middlesex and Warwickshire), b Oct 17, 1917

Dooland, B. (South Australia and Nottinghamshire), b Nov 1, 1923

Douglas, Col. A. P. (Surrey and Middlesex), b June 7, 1867, d Jan 24, 1953

Douglas, Mr. C. H. (Essex), b June 28, 1886, d Sept 1954

Douglas, Mr. J. (Camb. Univ. and Middlesex), b Jan 8, 1870

Douglas, Mr. J. W. H. T. (Essex), b Sept 3, 1882, d Dec 19, 1930

Douglas, Rev. R. N. (Camb. Univ., Surrey and Middlesex), b Nov 9, 1868

Douglas, S. (Yorkshire), b April 4, 1903

Douglas-Hamilton, Canon H. A. (Camb. Univ.), b May 28, 1853, d Aug 22, 1929

Dovey, R. R. (Kent), b July 18, 1920

Dowding, Mr. A. L. (Oxford Univ.), b April 4, 1929

Downes, Mr. K. D. (Camb. Univ.), b June 12, 1917

Dowson, Mr. E. M. (Camb. Univ. and Surrey), b June 21, 1880, d July 22, 1933

Drake, E. J. (Hampshire), b Aug 16, 1912

Druce, Mr. N. F. (Camb. Univ. and Surrey), b Jan 1, 1875, d Oct 27, 1954

Druce, Mr. W. G. (Camb. Univ.), b Sept 16, 1872

Ducat, A. (Surrey), b Feb 16, 1886, d July 23, 1942

Duckfield, R. (Glamorgan), b July 2, 1906

Duckworth, Mr. C. A. R. (South Africa), b March 22, 1933

Duckworth, G. (Lancashire), b May 9, 1901

Duleepsinhji, K. S. (Camb. Univ. and Sussex), b June 13, 1905

Dunell, Mr. O. R. (South Africa), b July 15, 1856, d Oct 21, 1929

Dunglass, Lord (Middlesex), b July 2, 1903

Dunkley, F. (Middlesex), b Sept 9, 1863

Dunkley, M. E. F. (Northamptonshire), b Feb 19, 1914

Dunning, Mr. J. A. (New Zealand), b Feb 6, 1903

Durnell, Mr. T. W. (Warwickshire), b June 17, 1901

Durston, T. J. (Middlesex), b July 11, 1894

Dury, Mr. T. S. (Oxford Univ. and Yorkshire), b June 12, 1854, d March 22, 1932

Dyer, Mr. D. V. (South Africa), b May 2, 1914

Dyke, Rt. Hon. Sir W. Hart, 7th Bart. (President, M.C.C., 1880), b Aug 7, 1837, d July 3, 1931

Dyson, A. H. (Glamorgan), b July 10, 1905

Dyson, J. (Lancashire), b July 8, 1934

Dyson, Mr. J. H. (Oxford Univ.), b Sept 26, 1913

Eady, Mr. C. J. (Tasmania), b Oct 29, 1870, d Dec 23, 1945

Eagar, Mr. E. D. R. (Oxford Univ., Gloucestershire and Hampshire), b Dec 8, 1917

Eaglestone, J. T. (Middlesex and Glamorgan), b July 24, 1923

Earle, Mr. G. F. (Surrey and Somerset), b Aug 24, 1891

East, W. (Northamptonshire), b Aug 29, 1876, d Dec 19, 1926

Eastman, G. (Essex), b April 7, 1903

Eastman, L. C. (Essex), b June 3, 1897, d April 17, 1941

Eaton, J. (Sussex), b June 19, 1904

Ebbisham, First Baron (George Rowland Blades) (Surrey Club, captain Lords and Commons), b April 15, 1868, d May 24, 1953

Ebden, Mr. C. H. M. (Camb. Univ., Sussex and Middlesex), b June 29, 1880, d May 24, 1949

Ebeling, Mr. H. I. (Victoria), b Jan 1, 1905

Eccles, Mr. J. (Lancashire), b April 13, 1863, d Sept 2, 1933

Eckersley, Lt. P. T., R.N.V.R., M.P. (Lancashire), b July 2, 1904, d Aug 13, 1940

Ede, Mr. E. M. C. (Hampshire), b April 24, 1881

Edrich, B. R. (Norfolk, Kent and Glamorgan), b Aug 18, 1922

Edrich, E. H. (Norfolk and Lancashire), b March 27, 1914

Edrich, G. A. (Norfolk and Lancashire), b July 13, 1918

Edrich, Mr. W. J. (Norfolk and Middlesex), b March 26, 1916

Eggar, Mr. J. D. (Oxford Univ. and Derbyshire), b Dec 1, 1916

Eglington, Mr. R. (Surrey), b April 1, 1908

Elam, Mr. F. W. (Yorkshire), b Sept 13, 1871, d March 19, 1943

Elgood, Mr. B. C. (Camb. Univ. and Berkshire), b March 10, 1922

Ellesmere, 4th Earl of (President M.C.C., 1920) (see Brackley, Lord

Elliott, C. S. (Derbyshire), b April 24, 1912

Elliott, H. (Derbyshire), b Nov 2, 1895

Ellis, H. (Northamptonshire), b March 13, 1885

Ellis, J. E. (Yorkshire), b Nov 12, 1864, d Dec 1, 1927

Ellis, Mr. J. L. (Victoria), b May 9, 1891

Ellis, W. (Derbyshire), b Aug 28, 1876

Emery, Mr. S. H. (New South Wales) b Oct 16, 1886

Emmett, G. M. (Gloucestershire) b Dec 2, 1912

Endean, Mr. W. R. (South Africa), b May 31, 1924

English, Mr. E. A. (Hampshire), b Jan 1, 1864

Enthoven, Mr. H. J. (Camb. Univ and Middlesex), b June 4, 1903

Ernle, 1st Lord (see Prothero)

Ernsthusen, Mr. A. C. von (afterwards Howeson), (Oxford Univ. and Surrey), b Oct 17, 1880, d May 29, 1928

Estcourt, Mr. N. S. D. (Camb. Univ.) b Jan 7, 1929

Etheridge, Mr. S. G. (Middlesex and Hertfordshire), b Nov 3, 1882 d Sept 3, 1945

Evans, Mr. A. H. (Somerset, Hampshire and Oxford Univ.), b in India, June 14, 1858, d March 26, 1934

Evans, Mr. A. J. (Oxford Univ., Hampshire and Kent), b May 1, 1889

Evans, Col. D. MacN. (Hampshire), b Dec 12, 1886

Evans, Mr. E. N. (Oxford Univ.), b Dec 7, 1911

Evans, Rev. F. R. (Oxford Univ.), b June 1, 1842, d March 4, 1927

Evans, Mr. G. (Oxford Univ. and Leicestershire), b Aug 13, 1915

Evans, Mr. J. (Hampshire), b July 14, 1891

Evans, Mr. R. G. (Camb. Univ.), b Aug 20, 1899

Evans, T. G. (Kent), b Aug 18, 1920

Evans, V. J. (Essex), b March 4, 1912

Evans, Mr. W. T. (Queensland), b April 9, 1876

Eve, Mr. S. C. (Essex), b Dec 8, 1925

Everett, Mr. S. C. (New South Wales), b June 17, 1901

Evers, Mr. H. A. (New South Wales and West Australia), b Feb 28, 1876

Evers, Mr. R. D. M. (Worcestershire), b Aug 11, 1913

Evershed, Sir S. H. (Derbyshire), b March 12, d March 7, 1937

Every, T. (Glamorgan), b Dec 19, 1909

Evetts, Mr. W. (Oxford Univ.), b June 30, 1847, d April 7, 1936

Fabian, Mr. A. H. (Camb. Univ.), b March 20, 1909

Fagg, A. E. (Kent), b June 18, 1915

Fairbairn, Mr. A. (Middlesex), b Jan 25, 1923

Fairbairn, Capt. G. A. (Camb. Univ. and Middlesex), b June 26, 1892

Fairbanks, Mr. W. (Gloucestershire), b April 13, 1852, d Aug 25, 1924

Fairfax, Mr. A. G. (New South Wales), b June 16, 1906, d May 17, 1955

Fairservice, C. (Kent and Middlesex), b Aug 21, 1909

Fairservice, W. J. (Kent and Northumberland), b May 16, 1881

Falcon, Mr. M. (Camb. Univ. and Norfolk), b July 21, 1888

Fallows, Mr. J. A. (Lancashire), b July 25, 1907

Fane, Mr. F. L. (Oxford Univ. and Essex), b April 27, 1875, d Dec 9, 1954

Fantham, W. E. (Warwickshire), b May 14, 1918

Farnes, P/O K. (Camb. Univ. and Essex), b July 8, 1911, d Oct 20, 1941

Farquhar, Mr. J. F. (Queensland), b Jan 1, 1887

Farrimond, W. (Lancashire), b May 23, 1903

Fasken, Mr. D. K. (Oxford Univ.), b March 23, 1932

Faulkner, Mr. G. A. (Transvaal), b Dec 17. 1881, d Sept 10, 1930

Faviell, Lt.-Col. W. F. O. (Essex and India), b June 5, 1882, d Feb 14, 1950

Fazal Mahmood (Pakistan), b Feb 18, 1927

Fellows-Smith, Mr. J. P. (Oxford Univ.), b Feb 3, 1932

Felton, Mr. R. (Middlesex), b Dec 27, 1909

Fender, Mr. P. G. H. (Sussex and Surrey), b Aug 22, 1892

Fenley, S. (Surrey and Hampshire), b Jan 4, 1896

Fereday, J. (Worcestershire and Staffordshire), b Nov 24, 1875

Ferguson, Mr. V. (Hampshire), b Jan 10, 1866

Fernandes, Mr. M. P. (West Indies), b Aug 12, 1897

Fernie, Mr. A. E. (Camb. Univ. and Staffordshire), b April 9. 1877

Fida Hussain (Manager Pakistan in England, 1954), b Dec 4, 1908

Fiddian-Green, Mr. C. A. (Camb. Univ., Warwickshire and Worcestershire), b Dec 22, 1898

Fiddling, K. (Yorkshire and Northamptonshire), b Oct 13, 1917

Field, Mr. E. (Middlesex and Camb. Univ.), b Dec 18, 1871, d Jan 9, 1947

Field, F. E. (Warwickshire), b Sept 23, 1875, d Aug 25, 1934

Fielder, Arthur (Kent), b July 19, 1878, d Aug 30, 1949

Filgate, Mr. C. R. (Gloucestershire), b Oct 16, 1849, d Sept 1, 1930

Findlay, Mr. A. P. (Tasmania), b March 17, 1892

Findlay, Mr. W. (Oxford Univ. and Lancashire; Sec. Surrey C.C.C.; Sec., M.C.C., 1926 to 1936), b June 22, 1880, d June 19, 1953

Fingleton, Mr. J. H. (New South Wales), b April 28, 1908

Firth, J. (Yorkshire and Leicestershire), b June 27, 1918

Fisher, H. (Yorkshire), b Aug 3, 1903

Fishlock, L. B. (Surrey), b Jan 2, 1907

Fishwick, Mr. T. S. (Warwickshire), b July 24, 1876, d Feb 21, 1950

Flamson, W. H. (Leicestershire), b Aug 12, 1905, d Jan 9 1945

Flavell, J. (Worcestershire), b May 15, 1929

Fleetwood-Smith, Mr. L. O'B (Victoria), b March 30, 1910

Fletcher, D. G. W. (Surrey), b July 6, 1924

Flint, B. (Nottinghamshire), b Jan 12, 1893

Flint, W. A. (Nottinghamshire), b March 21, 1890, d Feb 5, 1955

Flowers, Wilfrid (Nottinghamshire), b Dec 7, 1856, d Nov 1, 1926

Foenander, Mr. S. P. (Colombo), b April 11, 1883

Foley, Lt.-Col. C. P. (Camb. Univ., Worcestershire and Middlesex), b Nov 1, 1868, d March 9, 1936

Foley, Mr. C. W. (Camb. Univ.), b Dec. 26, 1856, d Nov 20, 1933

Foord, C. W. (Yorkshire), b June 11, 1924

Ford, Mr. A. F. J. (Camb. Univ. and Middlesex), b Sept 12, 1858, d May 20, 1931

Ford, Mr. F. G. J. (Camb. Univ. and Middlesex), b Dec 14, 1866, d Feb 7, 1940

Ford, Mr. F. W. J. (Repton), b Oct 14, 1854, d Sept 11, 1920

Ford, Mr. H. J. (Repton), b Feb 5, 1860, d Nov 19, 1941

Ford, Mr. R. (Gloucestershire), b March 3, 1907

Ford, Very Rev. L. G. B. J. (Repton), b Sept 3, 1865, d March 27, 1932

Ford, Mr. N. M. (Oxford Univ., Derbyshire and Middlesex), b Nov 18, 1906

Ford, Mr. W. A. J. (Repton), b March 20, 1861, d Aug 21, 1938

Forester, Mr. T. (Warwickshire and Derbyshire), b Sept 21, 1873, d Dec 27, 1927

Forster, 1st Lord (Oxford Univ. and Hampshire; President, M.C.C., 1919), b Jan 31, 1866, d Jan 15, 1936

Foster, Mr. B. S. (Middlesex and Worcestershire), b Feb 12, 1882

Foster, Mr. D. G. (Warwickshire), b March 19, 1907

Foster, Mr. F. R. (Warwickshire), b Jan 31, 1889

Foster, Mr. G. N. (Oxford Univ., Worcestershire and Kent), b Oct 16, 1884

Foster, Mr. H. K. (Oxford Univ. and Worcestershire), b Oct 30, 1873, d June 23, 1950

Foster, Mr. M. K. (Worcestershire), b Jan 1, 1889, d Dec 3, 1940

Foster, Mr. N. J. A. (Worcestershire), b Sept 28 1890

Foster, Mr. N. K. (Queensland), b Jan 19, 1878

Foster, Mr. P. G. (Kent), b 1916

Foster, Mr. R. E. (Oxford Univ. and Worcestershire), b April 16, 1878, d May 13, 1914

Foster, T. (Derbyshire), b Dec 15, 1848, d March 23, 1929

Foster, Major W. L. (Worcestershire), b Dec 2, 1874

Fowke, Major G. H. S. (Leicestershire), b Oct 18, 1880, d June 24, 1946

Fowler, Mr. H. (Oxford Univ. and Essex), b Oct 20, 1857, d May 6, 1934

Fowler, Mr. W. H. (Essex and Somerset), b May 28, 1856, d April 13, 1941

Fox, J. (Warwickshire and Worcestershire), b Sept 7, 1904, d April 13, 1941

Fox, Lt.-Col. R. W. (Oxford Univ. and Sussex), b July 11, 1873, d Aug 21, 1948

Fox, W. V. (Worcestershire), b Jan 8, 1898, d Feb 18, 1949

Foy, F. G. (Kent), b April 11, 1915

Foy, Mr. P. A. (Somerset and Argentine), b Oct 16, 1891

Frames, Mr. A. S. (Manager South Africa team in England 1947), b Jan 7, 1891

Francis, Mr. Guy (Gloucestershire), b Aug 16, 1860, d May 1948

Francis, G. N. (West Indies), b Dec 7, 1897, d Jan 1942

Francis, H. H. (Gloucestershire and South Africa), d Jan 7, 1936, aged 65

Francis, Mr. T. E. S. (Camb. Univ. and Somerset), b Nov 21, 1902

Frank, Mr. R. W. (Yorkshire), b May 29, 1864, d Sept 9, 1950

Franklin, Mr. H. W. F. (Oxford Univ., Surrey and Essex), b June 30, 1901

Franklin, Mr. W. B. (Camb. Univ. and Buckinghamshire), b Aug 16, 1891

Fraser, Mr. J. N. (Oxford Univ.), b Aug 6, 1890

Fraser, Mr. T. W. (Camb. Univ.), b June 26, 1912

Frazer, Mr. J. E. (Oxford Univ., Sussex and Somerset), b April 22, 1901, d Jan 2, 1927

Freeman, A. P. (Kent), b May 17, 1889

Freeman, E. C. (Essex), b Dec 7, 1860, d Oct 16, 1939

Freeman, E. J. (Essex and Dorset), b Oct 16, 1880

Freeman, G. (Nottinghamshire), b Sept 12, 1854, d Nov 22, 1931

Freeman, J. R. (Essex), b Sept 3, 1883

Freeman-Thomas, Mr. F., 1st Marquess of Willingdon (Camb. Univ. and Sussex), b Sept 12, 1866, d Aug 12, 1941

Fry, Mr. C. B. (Oxford Univ., Surrey, Sussex and Hampshire), b in Surrey, April 25, 1872

Fry, Mr. K. R. B. (Camb. Univ. and Sussex), b March 15, 1883, d June 21, 1949

Fry, Mr. Stephen (Hampshire), b May 23, 1900

Fuller, Mr. E. R. H. (South Africa), b Aug 2, 1931

Fuller, Mr. G. P. (Oxford Univ.), d Jan 8, 1833, d April 2, 1927

Fullerton, Mr. G. M. (South Africa) b Dec 8, 1922

Fynn, Mr. C. G. (Hampshire), b April 24, 1898

Gaekwad, Mr. D. K. (India), b Oct 27, 1928

Gaekwad, Mr. H. G. (India), b Aug 29, 1928

Gale, Mr. Norman (Cricket Poet), b March 4, 1862, d Oct 7, 1942

Gale, Mr. P. G. (London County), b May 22, 1865, d Sept 7, 1940

Gallichan, Mr. N. (New Zealand), b June 3, 1906

Gamble, F. C. (Surrey and Devon), b May 29, 1906

Game, Mr. W. H. (Oxford Univ. and Surrey), b Oct 2, 1853, d Aug 11, 1932

Gange, T. H. (Gloucestershire), b April 15, 1891, d March 19, 1949

Gardner, F. C. (Warwickshire), b June 4, 1922

Garland-Wells, Mr. H. M. (Oxford Univ. and Surrey), b Nov 14, 1907

Garlick, R. G. (Lancashire and Northamptonshire), b April 11, 1917

Garnier, Canon E. S. (Oxford Univ.), b April 5, 1850, d Aug 8, 1938

Garnsey, Mr. G. L. (New South Wales), b Feb 10, 1881, d April 18, 1951

Garrett, Mr. T. W. (New South Wales), b July 26, 1858, d Aug 6, 1943

Garrett, Mr. W. T. (Essex), b Jan 9, 1877, d Feb 17, 1953

Garthwaite, Mr. P. F. (Oxford Univ.), b Oct 22, 1909

Gauld, Dr. G. O. (Nottinghamshire), b June 21, 1873, d June 16, 1950

Gay, Mr. L. H. (Camb. Univ., Hampshire and Somerset), b March 24, 1871, d Nov 1, 1949

Geary, A. C. T. (Surrey), b Sept 11, 1900

Geary, G. (Leicestershire), b July 9, 1893

Gehrs, Mr. D. R. A. (South Australia), b Nov 29, 1880, d June, 1953

Gentry, Mr. J. S. B. (Hampshire, Surrey and Essex), b Oct 4, 1899

George, W. (Warwickshire), b June 29, 1874, d Dec 4, 1933

Gerrard, Major R. A. (Somerset), b Jan 18, 1912, d Jan 22, 1943

Ghazali, M. E. Z. (Pakistan), b June 15, 1924

Ghulam Ahmed (India), b July 4, 1922

Ghulam Mahomed (India), b July 12, 1898

Gibb, Mr. P. A. (Camb. Univ., Scotland, Yorkshire and Essex), b July 11, 1913

Gibbons, H. H. I. H. (Worcestershire), b Oct 10, 1904

Gibson, Mr. A. L. (Essex), b Sept 4, 1877, d July 29, 1943

Gibson, Mr. C. H. (Camb. Univ., Sussex and Argentine), b Aug 23, 1900

Gibson, Mr. I. (Oxford Univ.), b Aug 15, 1936

Gibson, Mr. K. L. (Essex), b May 1888

Giffen, Mr. George (South Australia), b March 27, 1859, d Nov 29, 1927

Giffen, Mr. Walter F. (South Australia), b Sept 10, 1863, d June 29, 1949

Gilbert, Mr. H. A. (Monmouthshire, Oxford Univ., Worcestershire and Radnorshire), b June 2, 1886

Giles, R. J. (Nottinghamshire), b Oct 17, 1919

Gill, G. C. (Somerset & Leicestershire), b April 18, 1876, d Aug 21, 1937

Giller, Mr. J. F. (Victoria), b May 1, 1870, d Jan 13, 1947

Gillespie, Mr. D. W. (Camb. Univ.), b April 26, 1917

Gilliat, Mr. I. A. W. (Oxford Univ.), b Jan 8, 1903

Gilligan, Mr. A. E. R. (Camb. Univ., Surrey and Sussex), b Dec 23, 1894

Gilligan, Mr. A. H. H. (Sussex), b June 29, 1896

Gilligan, Mr. F. W. (Oxford Univ. and Essex), b Sept 20, 1893

Gillingham, Canon F. H. (Essex), b Sept 6, 1875, d April 1, 1953

Gilman, Mr. J. (Camb. Univ., London County, Middlesex and Northumberland), b March 17, 1879

Gimblett, H. (Somerset), b Oct 19, 1914

Gladwin, C. (Derbyshire), b April 3, 1917

Glover, Mr. A. C. S. (Warwickshire), b April 19, 1872, d May 22, 1949

Glover, Mr. E. R. K. (Glamorgan), b July 19, 1911

Goatly, E. G. (Surrey), b Dec 3, 1882

Godambe, S. R. (India), b March 1, 1899

Goddard, Mr. J. D. (West Indies), b April 21, 1919

Goddard, Mr. T. L. (South Africa), b Aug 1, 1931

Goddard, T. W. (Gloucestershire), b Oct 1, 1900

Godfrey, Rev. C. J. M. (Sussex), b Nov 24, 1862, d Sept 28, 1941

Godsell, Mr. R. T. (Camb. Univ. and Gloucestershire), b Jan 9, 1880, d March, 1954

Goldie, Major K. O. (Sussex), b Sept 19, 1882, d Jan 14, 1938

Gomez, Mr. G. E. (West Indies), b Oct 10, 1919

Goodacre, Mr W. B. (Nottinghamshire), b Feb 26, 1873, d 1950

Gooder, L. (Surrey), b Feb 11, 1876

Goodman, Mr. P. A. (West Indies), b Oct 3, 1874, d April 25, 1935

Goodway, Mr. C. C. (Staffordshire and Warwickshire), b July 10, 1909

Goodwin, Mr. H. S. (Gloucestershire), b Sept 30, 1870, d Nov 13, 1955

Goodwin, J. (Leicestershire), b Jan 22, 1929

Goodwyn, Canon F. W. (Gloucestershire), b Jan 20, 1850, d April 23, 1931

Goonesena, Mr. G. (Nottinghamshire and Camb. Univ.), b Feb 16, 1931

Gopalan, M. J. (India), b June 6, 1909

Gopinath, Mr. C. D. (India), b March 1, 1930

Gordon, Mr. C. S. (Gordon-Stewart, Brig.-Gen. C. S.), (Victoria and Gloucestershire), b Sept 8, 1849, d March 24, 1930

Gordon, Sir Home, 12th Bart. (Author of "Cricket Form at a Glance," etc.), b Sept 30, 1871

Gordon, Mr. J. H. (Oxford Univ. and Surrey), b June 15, 1886, d April 23, 1933

Gordon, Mr. N. (South Africa), b Aug 6, 1911

Gorell-Barnes, Mr. R., 3rd Lord Gorell (Oxford Univ. and Suffolk), b April 16, 1884

Gothard, Mr. E. J. (Derbyshire), b Oct 1, 1904

Gouldsworthy, Mr. W. R. (Gloucestershire), b May 20, 1892

Gover, A. R. (Surrey), b Feb 29, 1908

Gowans, Lt.-Col. J. (Harrow), b April 23, 1872, d April 27, 1936

Graburn, Mr. W. T. (Surrey), b March 14, 1865, d Dec 13, 1944

Grace, Dr. Alfred, b May 17, 1840, d May 24, 1916

Grace, Dr. Alfred H. (Gloucestershire), b March 10, 1866, d Sept 16, 1929

Grace, Mr. C. B. (Clifton), b March 1882, d June 6, 1938

Grace, Dr. E. M. (Gloucestershire), b Nov 28, 1841, d May 20, 1911

Grace, Dr. Edgar M. (M.C.C.), son of E. M. Grace, b Oct 6, 1886

Grace, Mr. G. F. (Gloucestershire), b Dec 13, 1850, d Sept 22, 1880

Grace, Dr. H. M. (Father of W. G., E. M., G. F.), b Feb 21, 1808, d Dec 23, 1871

Grace, Mrs. H. M. (Mother of W. G., E. M., G. F.), b July 18, 1812, d July 25, 1884

Grace, Dr. Henry, b Jan 31, 1833, d Nov 15, 1895

Grace, Dr. W. G. (Gloucestershire), b July 18, 1848, d Oct 23, 1915

Grace, Mr. W. G., jun. (Camb. Univ. and Gloucestershire), b July 6, 1874, d March 2, 1905

Graham, H. C. (Leicestershire), b May 31, 1914

Grant, Mr. G. C. (West Indies and Camb. Univ.), b May 9, 1907

Grant, Mr. R. S. (West Indies and Camb. Univ.), b Dec 15, 1909

Grant-Asher, Sir A. G. (Oxford Univ. and Scotland), b Dec 18, 1861, d July 15, 1930

Graveney, J. K. (Gloucestershire), b Dec 16, 1924

Graveney, T. W. (Gloucestershire), b June 16, 1927

Gray, Mr. C. D. (Middlesex), b April 26, 1895

Gray, Rev. Horace (Camb. Univ. and Cambridgeshire), b Nov 29, 1874, d Jan 20, 1938

Gray, J. R. (Hampshire), b May 19, 1926

Gray, L. H. (Middlesex), b Dec 16, 1915

Greasley, D. G. (Northamptonshire), b Jan 20, 1926

Greatorex, Rev. T. (Middlesex), b Dec 14, 1864, d July 27, 1933

Green, Col. Leonard (Lancashire), b Feb 1, 1890

Green, Brig. M. A. (Gloucestershire and Essex and Manager M.C.C. Team South Africa. 1948–49, Australia, 1950–51), b Oct 3, 1891

Greene, Mr. A. D. (Oxford Univ. and Gloucestershire), b April 15, 1856, d June 18, 1928

Greenhalgh, E. (Lancashire), b May 18, 1910

Greenhough, T. (Lancashire), b Nov 9, 1931

Greensmith, W. T. (Essex), b Aug 16, 1930

Greenstock, Mr. J. W. (Oxford Univ. and Worcestershire), b May 15, 1905

Greenway, Col. C. E. (Somerset), b Oct 29, 1864, d June 17, 1934

Greenwood, Mr. F. E. (Yorkshire), b Sept 28, 1905

Greenwood, H. W. (Sussex and Northamptonshire), b Sept 4, 1909

Greenwood, P. (Lancashire), b Sept 11, 1924

Gregory, Mr. A. H. (New South Wales), b July 7, 1861, d Aug 17, 1929

Gregory, Mr. C. S. (New South Wales), b Aug 5, 1847, d April 5, 1935

Gregory, Mr. G. R. (Derbyshire), b Aug 27, 1878

Gregory, Mr. J. M. (New South Wales), b Aug 14, 1895

Gregory, Sgt.-Obsr. R. G. (Victoria), b Feb 28, 1916, d June 1942

Gregory, R. J. (Surrey), b Aug 26, 1902

Gregory, Mr. S. E. (New South Wales), b April 14, 1870, d Aug 1, 1929

Gregson, W. R. (Lancashire), b Aug 5, 1878

Greig, Rev. J. G., formerly Colonel (Hampshire), b Oct 24, 1871

Gresson, Mr. F. H. (Oxford Univ. and Sussex), b Feb 18, 1868, d Jan 31, 1949

Greswell, Mr. E. A. (Somerset), b June 6, 1885

Greswell, Mr. W. T. (Somerset), b Oct 15, 1889

Gribble, Mr. H. W. R. (Gloucestershire), b Dec 23, 1860, d June 12, 1943

Grierson, Mr. H. (Bedfordshire and Camb. Univ.), b Aug 26, 1891

Grieves, K. (New South Wales and Lancashire), b Aug 27, 1925

Grieveson, Mr. R. E. (South Africa), b Aug 24, 1909

Griffith, Mr. H. C. (West Indies), b Dec 1, 1893

Griffith, Mr. S. C. (Camb. Univ., Surrey and Sussex), b June 16, 1914

Griffiths, Mr. C. (Essex), b Dec 9, 1930

Griffiths, J. V. C. (Gloucestershire), b Jan 19, 1931

Griffiths, Mr. W. H. (Camb. Univ. and Glamorgan), b Sept 26, 1922

Grimmett, Mr. C. V. (Victoria and South Australia), b Dec 25, 1892

Grimshaw, C. H. (Yorkshire and Worcestershire), b May 12, 1880, d Sept 25, 1947

Grimshaw, V. (Worcestershire), b April 1, 1916

Grimshaw, B/S/M J. W. T. (Camb. Univ. and Kent), b Feb 17, 1912, d Sept 26, 1944

Grimshaw, N. (Northamptonshire), b May 5, 1912

Grimston, Mr. George S. (Sussex), b April 2, 1905

Grinter, Mr. T. G. (Essex), b Dec 12, 1905

Gross, Mr. F. A. (Hampshire), b Sept 17, 1902

Groube, Mr. T. U. (Victoria), b Sept 2, 1857, d Aug 5, 1927

Grove, C. W. (Warwickshire and Worcestershire), b Dec 12, 1912

Grover, Mr. J. N. (Oxford Univ. and Northumberland), b Oct 15, 1915

Groves, Mr. G. J. (Nottinghamshire), b Oct 19, 1868, d Feb 18, 1941

Guise, Mr. J. D. (India and M.C.C.), b Oct 31, 1872, d July 3, 1953

Guise, Mr. J. L. (Oxford Univ. and Middlesex), b Nov 25, 1903

Gunasekara, Dr. C. H. (Middlesex and Ceylon), b July 27, 1894

Gunn, G. (Nottinghamshire), b June 13, 1879

Gunn, G. V. (Nottinghamshire), b June 21, 1905

Gunn, J. (Nottinghamshire), b July 19, 1876

Gunn, W. (Nottinghamshire), b Dec 4, 1858, b Jan 29, 1921

Gupta, Mr. P. (India) (Manager teams in England), b Oct. 10, 1899

Hadingham, Mr. A. W. G. (Camb. Univ. and Surrey), b March 1, 1913

Hadlee, Mr. W. A. (New Zealand), b June 4, 1915

Hadow, Mr. P. F. (Middlesex), b Jan 24, 1855, d June 29, 1946

Hafeez, A. (India) (now A. H. Kardar), b Jan 17, 1925

Haggas, S. (Yorkshire and Lancashire), b April 18, 1856, d March 14, 1926

Haig, Mr. N. E. (Middlesex), b Dec 12, 1887

Haigh, Schofield (Yorkshire), b March 19, 1871, d Feb 27, 1921

Haigh Smith, Mr. H. A. (Hampshire), b Oct 21, 1884, d Oct 28, 1955

Hailsham, 1st Visct. (President, M.C.C., 1933), b Feb 28, 1872

Haines, Mr. A. H. (Gloucestershire), b Aug 27, 1877

Haines, Mr. C. V. G. (Glamorgan), b Jan 17, 1906

Hake, Mr. H. D. (Hampshire), b Nov 8, 1894

Hale, Mr. H. (Camb. Univ. and Gloucestershire), b March 27, 1867 d 1947

Hale, W. H. (Somerset and Gloucestershire), b March 6, 1870

Hall, A. E. (South Africa and Lancashire), b Jan 23, 1896

Hall, C. H. (Yorkshire), b April 5, 1906

Hall, Mr. P. J. (Camb. Univ.), b Dec 4, 1927

Hall, Mr. P. M. (Hampshire), b March 19, 1894, d Dec 11, 1945

Hall, Mr. T. A. (Derbyshire and Somerset), b Aug 19, 1930

Hallam, A. W. (Lancashire, Nottinghamshire and Leicestershire), b Nov. 12, 1872, d 1940

Hallam, H. (Derbyshire), b April 12, 1882

Hallam, M. R. (Leicestershire), b Sept 10, 1931

Halliday, H. (Yorkshire), b Feb 9, 1920

Halliday, Mr. J. G. (Oxford Univ. and Oxfordshire), b July 4, 1915, d Dec 3, 1945

Hallows, C. (Lancashire), b April 4, 1895

Hambling, Mr. M. L. (Somerset), b Dec 6, 1893

Hamence, Mr. R. A. (South Australia), b Nov 25, 1915

Hamer, A. (Derbyshire), b Dec 8, 1916

Hamilton, Rt. Hon. Lord Geo. F. (Harrow, President, M.C.C., 1881), b Dec 17, 1845, d Sept 22, 1927

Hamilton, Canon H. A. Douglas- (Camb. Univ.), b May 28, 1853, d Aug 23, 1929

Hamilton, Col. L. A. H. (Kent), b Dec 23, 1862

Hammond, H. E. (Sussex), b Nov 7, 1907

Hammond, Mr. W. R. (Gloucestershire), b in Kent, June 19, 1903

Hampden, 3rd Visct. (President, M.C.C., 1926), b Jan 29, 1869

Hampton, Mr. W. M. (Warwickshire and Worcestershire), b Jan 20, 1903

Hancock, J. W. (Derbyshire), b Nov 26, 1877, d May 23, 1939

Handford, A. (Nottinghamshire), b May 3, 1869, d Oct 15, 1935

Handford, J. (Derbyshire), b Feb 1, 1890

Handley, G. (Nottinghamshire), b Jan 10, 1876

Hands, Mr. P. A. M. (Oxford Authentics and South Africa), b March 18, 1890, d April 27, 1951

Hands, Mr. W. C. (Warwickshire), b Dec 20, 1886

Hanif Mohammad (Pakistan), b Dec 24, 1934

Harbinson, Mr. W. K. (Camb. Univ.), b July 11, 1906

Harbord, Mr. W. E. (Yorkshire), b Dec 15, 1908

Harding, N. W. (Kent), b March 19, 1916, d Sept 25, 1947

Hardinge, H. T. W. (Kent), b Feb 25, 1886

Hardisty, C. H. (Yorkshire and Northumberland), b Dec 10, 1885

Hardstaff, J. (Nottinghamshire), b Nov 9, 1882, d April 2, 1947

Hardstaff, J., jun. (Nottinghamshire), b July 3, 1911

Hardstaff, R. G. (Nottinghamshire), b Jan 12, 1863, d April 18, 1932

Hare, Mr. J. H. M. (Norfolk and Oxford Univ.), b June 1, 1857, d August 1, 1935

Harfield, L. (Hampshire), b Aug 16, 1905

Hargreave, S. (Warwickshire), b Sept 22, 1876, d Jan 2, 1929

Hargreaves, H. S. (Yorkshire), b March 22, 1913

Harkness, D. (Worcestershire), b Feb 13, 1931

Harragin, Mr. A. E. A. (Trinidad), b May 4, 1877, d May 21, 1941

Harris, 4th Lord (Oxford Univ. and Kent, President, M.C.C., 1895), b West Indies, Feb 3, 1851, d March 24, 1932

Harris, C. B. (Nottinghamshire), b Dec 6, 1908, d Aug 8, 1954

Harris, Mr. G. W. (South Australia), b Dec 11, 1898

Harris, Mr. S. S. (Gloucestershire, Surrey and Sussex), b July 19, 1881, d May 4, 1926

Harris, Mr. T. A. (South Africa), b Aug 27, 1916

Harrison, Mr. C. S. (Worcestershire), b Nov 11, 1915

Harrison, Mr. E. W. (Tasmania), b July 21, 1874

Harrison, Rear-Adml. G. C. (Hampshire), b Oct 8, 1883, d Aug 10, 1943

Harrison, G. P. (Yorkshire), b Feb 11, 1862, d Sept 14, 1940

Harrison, H. S. (Surrey), b April 12, 1883

Harrison, L. (Hampshire), b June 8, 1922

Harrison, Mr. W. P. (Kent, Camb. Univ. and Middlesex), b Nov 13, 1885

Harron, D. G. (Leicestershire), b Sep 12, 1921

Hart, G. E. (Middlesex), b Jan 13, 1902

Hart, Mr. T. M. (Oxford Univ. and Scotland), b March 1, 1909

Hartigan, Mr. G. P. D. (South Africa), b Dec 30, 1884, d Jan 7, 1955

Hartigan, Mr. R. J. (New South Wales and Queensland), b Dec 12, 1879

Hartkopf, Dr. A. E. V. (Victoria), b Dec 28, 1889

Hartley, Mr. C. R. (Lancashire), b Feb 13, 1873, d Nov 15, 1927

Hartley, Lt.-Col. J. C. (Oxford Univ. and Sussex), b Nov 15, 1874

Harvey, P. F. (Nottinghamshire), b Jan 15, 1923

Harvey, Mr. R. L. (South Africa), b Sept 14, 1911

Harvey, Mr. R. N. (Victoria), b Oct 8, 1928

Hasan, Mr. Syed (India), b 1888

Hassett, Mr. A. L. (Victoria), b Aug 28, 1913

Hathorn, Mr. M. (South Africa), b April 7, 1878, d May 17, 1920

Hawke, 7th Lord (Camb. Univ. and Yorkshire; President, M.C.C., 1914–1918), b Aug 16, 1860, d Oct 10, 1938

Hawkins, D. (Gloucestershire), b May 18, 1935

Hawkins, Major H. (Northamptonshire), b Jan 15, 1876, d Aug 12, 1930

Hawkins, Mr. H. H. B. (Camb. Univ.), b Jan 9, 1876, d Jan 1, 1933

Hawkwood, C. (Lancashire), b Nov 16, 1909

Hawson, Mr. R. J. (Tasmania), b Sept 2, 1880, d Feb 20, 1928

Hawtin, Mr. A. P. R. (Northamptonshire), b Feb 1, 1883

Hay, Mr. Douglas (New Zealand), b Aug 31, 1876

Hayes, E. G. (Surrey and Leicestershire), b Nov 6, 1876, d Dec 2, 1953

Hayes, Mr. J. A. (New Zealand), b Jan 11, 1927

Hayman, Mr. H. B. (Middlesex), b Oct 5, 1873, d July 31, 1934

Haynes, R. W. (Gloucestershire), b Aug 27, 1913

Hayter, E. (Hampshire), b Sept 8, 1913

Hayward, T. W. (Surrey), b March 29, 1871, d July 19, 1939

Hayward, Mr. W. I. D. (Cambridge Univ.), b April 15, 1930

Haywood, R. A. (Northamptonshire), b Sept 16, 1887, d June 1, 1942

Hazare, V. S. (India), b March 11, 1915

Hazell, H. L. (Somerset), b Sept 30, 1909

Hazlerigg, Lord, formerly Sir Arthur Grey, 13th Bart. (Leicestershire), b Nov 17, 1878, d May 25, 1949

Hazlerigg, Lord, 14th Bart., formerly the Hon. A. G. (Camb. Univ. and Leicestershire), b Feb 24, 1910

Headlam, Mr. C. (Middlesex), b Sept 12, 1872, d Aug 12, 1934

Headley, Mr. G. (West Indies), b May 30, 1909

Healing, Mr. J. A. (Gloucestershire), b June 14, 1873, d July 4, 1933

Heane, Mr. G. F. H. (Nottinghamshire and Lincolnshire), b Jan 2, 1904

Heap, J. S. (Lancashire), b Aug 12, 1883, d Jan 30, 1951

Hearn, P. (Kent), b Nov 18, 1925

Hearne, Alec (Kent), b July 22, 1863, d May 16, 1952

Hearne, Frank (Kent and South Africa), b Nov 23, 1858, d July 14, 1949

Hearne, G. (Buckinghamshire and Middlesex), b May 15, 1829, d Dec 9, 1904

Hearne, Mr. G. A. L. (South Africa), b March 27, 1888

Hearne, George F. (Middlesex, Pavilion Clerk, Lord's), b Oct 18, 1851, d May 29, 1931

Hearne, George G. (Kent), b July 7, 1856, d Feb 13, 1932

Hearne, Herbert (Kent), b March 15, 1862, d June 13, 1906

Hearne, J. T. (Middlesex), b May 3, 1867, d April 17, 1944

Hearne, J. W. (Middlesex), b Feb 11, 1891

Hearne, Thomas (Buckinghamshire and Middlesex), b Sept 4, 1826, d May 13, 1900

Hearne, Thomas, jun. (Middlesex and Ground Superintendent at Lord's), b Dec 29, 1849, d Jan 29, 1910

Hearne, Walter (Kent), b Jan 15, 1864, d April 2, 1925

Hearne, Wm. (Buckinghamshire), b July 15, 1828, d July 17, 1908

Heasman, Dr. W. G. (Sussex, Berkshire and Norfolk), b Dec 9, 1862, d Jan 25, 1934

Heath, Mr. A. B. (Hampshire), b Jan 19, 1865

Heath, Col. A. H. (Oxford Univ. and Gloucestershire), b May 29, 1856, d April 21, 1930

Heath, D. M. W. (Warwickshire), b Dec 4, 1931

Heath, G. E. M. (Hampshire), b Feb 20, 1913

Heather, Mr. E. D. (Secretary, Victoria Cricket Association, for 30 years), b Oct 6, 1848, d July 10, 1935

Hedges, B. (Glamorgan), b July 20, 1928

Hedges, Mr. L. P. (Oxford Univ., Kent and Gloucestershire), b July 13, 1900, d Jan 12, 1933

Hedley, Col. Sir W. C. (Kent, Somerset, Devon and Hampshire), b Dec 12, 1865, d Dec 27, 1937

Hefferan, Mr. F. W. (Queensland), b May 25, 1901

Heine, Mr. P. (South Africa), b June 28, 1929

Hemingway, Mr. W. M'G. (Camb. Univ. and Gloucestershire), b Nov 12, 1873

Henderson, Mr. D. (Oxford Univ.), b March 9, 1926

Henderson, Mr. J. T. (Editor, "South African Cricketers' Annual"), b Aug 24, 1856, d Aug 28, 1935

Henderson, Mr. M. (New Zealand), b Aug 2, 1895

Henderson, R. (Surrey), b March 30, 1865, d Jan 28, 1931

Hendren, D. (Middlesex and Durham), b Sept 25, 1882

Hendren, E. (Middlesex), b Feb 5, 1889

Hendry, Mr. H. L. (New South Wales and Victoria), b May 24, 1895

Henery, Mr. P. J. T. (Camb. Univ. and Middlesex), b June 6, 1859, d Aug 10, 1938

Henley, Mr. D. F. (Oxford Univ.), b July 21, 1923

Henley, Mr. F. A. H. (Oxford Univ., Suffolk and Middlesex), b Feb 11, 1884

Henson, W. (Nottinghamshire), b Dec 7, 1874

Herbert, Hon. M. R. H. M. (Nottinghamshire and Somerset), b Nov 27, 1882, d May 26, 1929

Herman, O. W. (Hampshire), b Sept 18, 1907

Heseltine, Lt.-Col. C., O.B.E., D.L. (Hampshire), b Nov 26, 1869, d June 13, 1944

Hever, N. (Middlesex and Glamorgan), b Dec 17, 1924

Hewan, Mr. G. E. (Camb. Univ. and Berkshire), b Dec 23, 1916

Hewetson, Mr. E. P. (Oxford Univ. and Warwickshire), b May 27, 1902

Heygate, Mr. R. B. (Sussex), b May 13, 1883

Hibbert, W. J. (Lancashire), b July 11, 1874

Hickmott, E. (Kent), b March 20, 1850, d Jan 7, 1934

Hiddleston, Mr. J. S. (New Zealand), b Dec 10, 1890, d Oct 30, 1940

Hide, Arthur (Sussex), b May 7, 1860, d Nov. 5. 1933

Higgins, Mr. H. L. (Worcestershire), b Feb 24, 1894

Higgins, Mr. J. B. (Worcestershire), b Dec 31, 1885

Higgs, Mr. K. A. (Sussex), b Oct 5, 1886

Higson, Mr. T. A. (Derbyshire, Cheshire and Lancashire), b Nov 18, 1873, d Aug 3, 1949

Higson, Mr. T. A., jun. (Derbyshire and Lancashire), b March 25, 1911

Hilder, Mr. A. L. (Kent), b Oct 8, 1901

Hildyard, Rev. L. D'Arcy (Oxford Univ., Lancashire and Somerset), b Feb 5, 1861, d April 22, 1931

Hill, Allen (Yorkshire), b Nov 14, 1845, d Aug 29, 1910

Hill, Mr. A. E. L. (Hampshire), b July 14, 1901

Hill, Mr. A. J. L. (Camb. Univ. and Hampshire), b July 26, 1871, d Sept 6, 1950

Hill, Mr. Clement (South Australia), b March 18, 1877, d Sept 5, 1945

Hill, Capt. D. V. (Worcestershire), b April 13, 1896

Hill, E. (Somerset), b July 9, 1923

Hill, G. (Hampshire), b April 15, 1913

Hill, Mr. H. (Yorkshire), b Nov 29, 1858, d Aug 14, 1935

Hill, Mr. J. C. (Victoria), b June 25, 1923

Hill, Mr. J. E. (Warwickshire), b Sept 27, 1867

Hill, Mr. M. Ll. (Somerset and Glamorgan), b June 23, 1902, d Feb 28, 1948

Hill, Mr. V. T. (Oxford Univ., Somerset and Glamorgan), b Jan 30, 1871, d Sept 29, 1932

Hill, W. A. (Warwickshire), b April 27, 1910

Hills, H. M. (Essex), b Sept 28, 1886

Hills, J. (Glamorgan), b Oct 14, 1897

Hill-Wood, Sir B. S. (Derbyshire), b Feb 5, 1900, d July 3, 1954

Hill-Wood, Mr. C. K. (Oxford Univ. and Derbyshire), b June 5, 1907

Hill-Wood, Mr. D. J. (Oxford Univ. and Derbyshire), b June 25, 1906

Hill-Wood, Sir S. H. (Derbyshire and Suffolk), b March 21, 1872, d Jan 4, 1949

Hill-Wood, Mr. W. W. (Camb. Univ. and Derbyshire), b Sept 8, 1901

Hillyard, Cmdr. G. W., R.N. (Middlesex, Hertfordshire and Leicestershire), b Feb 6, 1864, d March 24, 1943

Hilton, J. (Lancashire and Somerset), b Dec 29, 1930

Hilton, M. J. (Lancashire), b Aug 2, 1928

Hime, Mr. A. H. (Natal), b Oct 4, 1871, d Feb 16, 1931

Hind, Mr. A. E. (Camb. Univ. and Nottinghamshire), b April 7, 1878, d March 22, 1947

Hindlekar, D. D. (India), b Jan 1, 1909, d March 30, 1949

Hinds, Mr. S. A. (West Indies), b June 1, 1880

Hine-Haycock, Rev. T. R. (Oxford Univ. and Kent), b Dec 3, 1861, d Nov 2, 1953

Hipkin, A. B. (Essex), b Aug 8, 1900

Hirst, G. H. (Yorkshire), b Sept 7, 1871, d May 10, 1954

Hitch, J. W. (Surrey), b May 7, 1886

Hitchcock, R. E. (Warwickshire), b Nov 28, 1929

Hoad, Mr. E. L. G. (West Indies), b Jan 29, 1896

Hoare, Mr. C. T. (Surrey and Middlesex), b Nov 10, 1851, d Jan 22, 1935

Hobbs, Sir J. B. (Cambridgeshire and Surrey), b Dec 16, 1882

Hobson, Mr. B. S. (Camb. Univ.), b Nov 22, 1925

Hodgkinson, Mr. G. F. (Derbyshire), b Feb 19, 1914

Hodgkinson, Mr. G. W. (Somerset), b Feb 19, 1883

Hodgson, G. (Lancashire), b April 16, 1904, d June 14, 1951

Hodgson, Rev. R. G. (Kent), b March 9, 1845, d Nov 1, 1931

Hofmeyr, Mr. M. B. (Oxford Univ.), b Dec. 9, 1925

Holdsworth, Mr. R. L. (Oxford Univ., Warwickshire and Sussex), b Feb 25, 1899

Holdsworth, W. E. N. (Yorkshire), b Sept 17, 1928

Hole, Mr. G. B. (South Australia), b Jan 6, 1931

Holland, F. C. (Surrey), b Feb 10, 1876

Hollies, W. E. (Warwickshire), b June 5, 1912

Hollingdale, R. A. (Sussex), b March 6, 1906

Hollins, Sir A. M., 2nd Bart. (Oxford Univ.), b July 16, 1876, d July 30, 1938

Hollins, Sir F. H., 3rd Bart. (Oxford Univ., Cumberland and Lancashire), b Oct 31, 1877

Holloway, Mr. G. W. (Gloucestershire), b April 26, 1884

Holloway, Mr. N. J. (Camb. Univ. and Sussex), b Nov 11, 1889

Holmes, Gr. Capt. A. J. (Sussex), b June 30, 1899, d May 21, 1950

Holmes, Mr. E. R. T. (Oxford Univ. and Surrey), b Aug 21, 1905

Holmes, Percy (Yorkshire), b Nov 25, 1886

Holmes, Rev. R. S. (Cricket Writer), b March 22, 1850, d Jan 13, 1933

Holroyd, J. (Lancashire), b April 15, 1907

Holt, A. (Hampshire), b April 8, 1912

Hone, Mr. B. W. (South Australia, Oxford Univ. and Wiltshire), b July 1, 1907

Hooker, Mr. H. (New South Wales), b March 6, 1898

Hooman, Mr. C. V. L. (Oxford Univ., Devon and Kent), b Oct 3, 1887

Hopkins, Mr. A. J. (New South Wales), b May 3, 1876, d April 25, 1931

Hopkins, F. J. (Warwickshire and Hampshire), b June 30, 1875, d Jan 16, 1930

Hopkins, Mr. H. O. (Oxford Univ. and Worcestershire), b July 6, 1895

Hopkins, V. (Gloucestershire), b Jan 21, 1913

Hopley, Mr. F. J. V. (Camb. Univ. and Western Province), b Aug 27, 1883, d Aug 16, 1951

Hopwood, J. L. (Lancashire), b Oct 30, 1903

Jordern, Dr. H. V. (New South Wales and Philadelphians), b Feb 10, 1884, d June 17, 1938

Hornby, Mr. A. H. (Lancashire), b July 29, 1877, d Sept 9, 1952

Horner, N. F. (Warwickshire), b May 10, 1926

Hornibrook, Mr. P. M. (Queensland), b July 27, 1899

Horrocks, W. J. (Lancashire), b June 18, 1905

Horsfall, R. (Essex), b June 26, 1920

Horton, H. (Hampshire), b April 18, 1924

Horton, J. (Worcestershire), b Aug 12, 1916

Horton, M. J. (Worcestershire), b April 21, 1934

Horton, Mr. T. (Northamptonshire), b May 16, 1871, d June 18, 1932

Horwood, Mr. S. E. (Western Province), b July 22, 1877

Hosie, Mr. A. L. (Hampshire), b Aug 6, 1890

Hossell, Mr. J. J., junior (Warwickshire), b May 25, 1914

Hotchkin, Mr. N. S. (Camb. Univ., Lincolnshire and Middlesex), b Feb 4, 1914

Hough, Mr. G. de L. (Kent), b May 14, 1894

Houldsworth, Mr. W. H. (Lancashire), b April 6, 1873, dead

Hounsfield, Mr. T. D. (Derbyshire), b April 28, 1911

Howard, A. H. (Glamorgan), b Dec 11, 1910

Howard, Mr. B. J. (Lancashire), b May 21, 1926

Howard, J. (Leicestershire), b Nov. 24, 1917

Howard, Mr. N. D. (Lancashire), b May 18, 1925

Howard, Major R. (Lancashire and Sec. Lancashire C.C.C.), b April 17, 1890

Howe, 4th Earl (Eton, President, M.C.C., 1901), b April 28, 1861, d Jan 10, 1929

Howell, H. (Warwickshire), b Nov 29, 1890, d July 9, 1932

Howell, Mr. M. (Oxford Univ. and Surrey), b Sept 9, 1893

Howell, Mr. R. G. D. (Sussex), b Jan 23, 1877, d Sept 27, 1942

Howell, Mr. W. P. (New South Wales), b Dec 29, 1869, d July 14, 1940

Howitt, Mr. R. H. (Nottinghamshire), b July 21, 1864, d Jan 10, 1951

Howlett, Brigadier B. (Kent), b Dec 18, 1898, d Nov 1943

Howorth, R. (Worcestershire), b April 26, 1909

Hubble, J. C. (Kent), b Feb 10, 1881

Huddleston, W. (Lancashire), b Feb 27, 1875

Huggins, H. J. (Gloucestershire). b March 15, 1877, d Nov 19, 1942

Hughes, Mr. D. W. (Glamorgan), b July 12, 1910

Hughes, N. (Worcestershire), b Apr 6, 1929

Hughes, Mr. O. (Camb. Univ.), b July 7, 1889

Hughes, R. (Worcestershire), b Sept 30, 1926

Hughes-Hallett, Mr. N. M. (Derbyshire), b April 1895

Huish, F. H. (Kent). b Nov 15, 1872

Hulme, J. (Derbyshire), b June 29, 1862, dead

Hulme, J. H. A. (Middlesex), b Aug 26, 1904

Human, Mr. J. H. (Camb. Univ., Berkshire and Middlesex), b Jan 13, 1912

Human, Capt. R. H. C. (Camb. Univ., Berkshire and Worcestershire), b May 11, 1909, d Nov 1942

Humphreys, E. (Kent), b Aug 24, 1881, d Nov 6, 1949

Humphries, J. (Derbyshire), b May 18, 1876, d May 8, 1946

Hunt, F. (Kent and Worcestershire), b Sept 13, 1875

Hunt, G. (Somerset), b Sept 30, 1896

Hunt, H. (Somerset), b Nov 18, 1911

Hunt, Mr. R. G. (Camb. Univ. and Sussex), b April 13, 1915

Hunte, Mr. E. (West Indies) b Oct 3, 1905

Hunter, David (Yorkshire), b March 23, 1860, d Jan 11, 1927

Hunter, Mr. F. C. (Derbyshire and Cheshire), b Aug 23, 1886

Hurst, Mr. C. S. (Oxford Univ. and Kent), b July 20, 1886

Hurwood, Mr. A. (Queensland), b June 17, 1902

Husain, Shafqat (India), b July 17, 1885

Hussain, Dilawar (India), b March 19, 1907

Hutcheon, Mr. J. S. (Queensland), b April 5, 1882

Hutchings, Mr. F. V. (Kent), b June 3, 1880, d Aug 6, 1934

Hutchings, Mr. K. L. (Kent), b Dec 7, 1882, d Sept 3, 1916

Hutchings, Mr. W. E. C. (Kent and Worcestershire), b May 31, 1879, d March 8, 1948

Hutchinson, J. M. (Derbyshire), b Nov 29, 1897

Hutton, L. (Yorkshire), b June 23, 1916

Hylton, Mr. L. G. (West Indies), b March 29, 1905, d May 17, 1955

Hylton-Stewart, Mr. B. D. (Somerset and Hertfordshire), b Nov 27, 1891

Hyman, Mr. W. (Somerset), b March 7, 1875

Hyndson, Capt. J. G. W. (Surrey), b April 25, 1892, d Feb 23, 1935

I'Anson, J. (Lancashire), b Oct 26, 1869, d Sept 16, 1936

Iddon, J. (Lancashire), b Jan 8, 1903, d April 17, 1946

Ikin, J. T. (Lancashire), b March 7, 1918

Ikram Elahi (Pakistan), b March 3, 1934

Illingworth, R. (Yorkshire), b June 8, 1932

Imlay, Mr. A. D. (Camb. Univ. and Gloucestershire), b Feb 14, 1885

Imtiaz Ahmed (Pakistan), b Jan 5, 1928

Ineson. P. (Yorkshire), b May 5, 1867, d Oct 10, 1939

Ingle, Mr. R. A. (Somerset), b Nov 5, 1903

Ingleby-Mackenzie, Mr. A. C. D. (Hampshire), b Sept 15, 1933

Ingram, Mr. E. A. (Middlesex and Ireland), b Aug 14, 1910

Ingram, I. (Kent), b May 14, 1855

Insole, Mr. D. J. (Camb. Univ. and Essex), b April 18, 1926

Iredale, Mr. F. A. (New South Wales) b June 19, 1867, d April 15, 1926

Ireland, Mr. J. F. (Camb. Univ. and Suffolk), b Aug 12, 1888

Iremonger, A. (Nottinghamshire), b June 15, 1884

Iremonger, J. (Nottinghamshire), b March 5, 1876

Irish, A. F. (Somerset), b Nov 23, 1918

Ironmonger, H. (Queensland and Victoria), b April 7, 1887

Irvine, Mr. L. G. (Camb. Univ. and Kent), b Jan 11, 1906

Isherwood, Capt. L. C. R. (Hampshire and Sussex), b April 13, 1891

Jackson, Mr. A. A. (New South Wales) b Sept 5, 1909, d Feb 16, 1933

Jackson, Mr. A. H. M. (Derbyshire), b Nov 9, 1899

Jackson, Rt. Hon. Sir F. S. (Camb. Univ. and Yorkshire; President M.C.C., 1921), b Nov 21, 1870, d March 9, 1947

Jackson, Mr. G. R. (Derbyshire) b June 23, 1896

Jackson, Mr. K. L. T. (Oxford Univ and Berkshire), b Nov, 1913

Jackson. F. M'l. (Surrey), b May 24, 1882, dead

Jackson, L. (Derbyshire), b April 5, 1921

Jackson, P. F. (Worcestershire), b May 11, 1911

Jackson, V. E. (Leicestershire), b Oct 25, 1916

Jacques, Mr. T. A. (Yorkshire), b Feb 19, 1905

Jagger, Mr. S. T. (Camb. Univ., Worcestershire, Denbighshire and Sussex), b June 30, 1904

Jahangir Khan, M. (India and Camb. Univ.), b Feb 1, 1910

Jai, L. P. (India), b April 1, 1902

Jakeman, F. (Yorkshire and Northamptonshire), b Jan 10, 1921

James, A. E. (Sussex), b Aug 7, 1924

James, C. E. (Nottinghamshire), b Sept 14, 1885

James, K. C. (New Zealand and Northamptonshire), b March 12, 1905

Jameson, Capt. T. O. (Hampshire), b April 4, 1892

Jardine, Mr. D. R. (Oxford Univ. and Surrey), b Oct 23, 1900

Jardine, Mr. M. R. (Oxford Univ. and Middlesex), b June 8, 1869, d Jan 16, 1947

Jarrett, H. (Warwickshire), b Sept 23, 1907

Jarvis, Mr. A. H. (South Australia), b Oct 18, 1860, d Nov 15, 1933

Jarvis, Mr. L. K. (Camb. Univ. and Norfolk), b Aug 3, 1857, d May 16, 1938

Jaya Ram, Mr. B. (India and London County), b April 23, 1872

Jeacocke, Mr. A. (Surrey), b Dec 1, 1892

Jeanes, Mr. W. H. (Secretary, Australian Board of Control), b May 19, 1883

Jellicoe, Rev. F. G. G. (Oxford Univ. and Hampshire), b Feb 24, 1858, d July 29, 1927

Jenkins, R. O. (Worcestershire), b Nov 24, 1918

Jenkins, Mr. V. G. J. (Oxford Univ. and Glamorgan), b Nov 2, 1911

Jenkins, Mr. W. L. T. (Glamorgan), b Aug 26, 1898

Jenner, F. D. (Sussex), b Nov 15, 1893, d March 31, 1953

Jenner, Mr. Herbert, afterwards Herbert Jenner-Fust (Camb. Univ. and Kent; President, M.C.C., 1833), b Feb 23. 1806, d July 30, 1904

Jennings, Mr. C. B. (South Australia and Queensland), b June 5, 1884, d June 25, 1950

Jennings, T. S. (Surrey), b Nov 3, 1896

Jephson, Mr. D. I. A. (Camb. Univ. and Surrey), b Feb 23, 1871, d Jan 19, 1926

Jephson, Mr. W. V. (Hampshire), b Oct 6, 1873

Jepson, A. (Nottinghamshire), b July 12, 1915

Jessop, Mr. G. L. (Gloucestershire and Camb. Univ.), b May 19, 1874, d May 11, 1955

Jewell, Mr. M. F. S. (Sussex and Worcestershire), b Sept 15, 1885

Jilani, M. Baqa (India), b July 20, 1911, d July 2, 1941

Joginder Singh (India), b July 7, 1904

Johns, Mr. A. E. (Victoria), b Jan 22, 1868, d Feb, 1934

Johnson, Mr. G. H. (Northamptonshire), b Dec 16, 1894

Johnson, Mr. H. H. (West Indies), b July 17, 1910

Johnson, H. L. (Derbyshire), b Nov 8, 1927

Johnson, Mr. I. W. (Victoria), b Dec 8, 1918

Johnson, Mr. P. R. (New Zealand, Camb. Univ., Devon and Somerset), b Aug 5, 1880

Johnston, Col. A. C. (Hampshire), b Jan 26, 1884, d Dec 27, 1952

Johnston, Mr. A. S. (Middlesex and Essex), b March 16, 1863, d Aug 8, 1929

Johnston, Mr. W. A. (Victoria), b Feb 26, 1922

Johnstone, Mr. C. P. (Camb. Univ. and Kent), b Aug 19, 1895

Jones, Mr. A. O. (Nottinghamshire and Camb. Univ.), b Aug 16, 1872, d Dec 21, 1914

Jones, D. (Nottinghamshire), b April 9, 1914

Jones, Mr. E. (South Australia), b Sept 30, 1869, d Nov 23, 1943

Jones, E. C. (Glamorgan), b Dec 14, 1912

Jones, Mr. G. L. (Hampshire), b Feb 11, 1909

Jones, Mr. P. E. (West Indies), b June 6, 1917

Jones, Mr. R. S. (Camb. Univ. and Kent), b March 14, 1857, d May 9, 1935

Jones, Mr. R. T. (Oxford Univ. and Shropshire), b June 27, 1871, d Aug 30, 1940

Jones, Mr. S. P. (New South Wales), b Aug 1, 1861, d July 14, 1951

Jones, W. E. (Glamorgan), b Oct 31, 1916

Jordan, J. (Lancashire), b Feb 7, 1932

Jose, Mr. A. D. (Oxford Univ. and Kent), b Feb 17, 1929

Jowett, Mr. D. C. P. R. (Oxford Univ.), b Jan 24, 1931

Jowett, Mr. G. (Lancashire), b April 20, 1863, d May, 1928

Joy, Mr. F. D. H. (Somerset), b Sept 26, 1880

Joyce, Mr. F. M. (Leicestershire), b Dec 16, 1886

Joynt, Mr. H. W. (Oxford Univ.), b Jan 7, 1931

Judd, Mr. A. K. (Camb. Univ. and Hampshire), b Jan 1, 1904

Judge, P. F. (Middlesex and Glamorgan), b May 23, 1916

Jupp, Mr. V. W. C. (Sussex and Northamptonshire), b March 27, 1891

Kamm, Mr. A. (Oxford Univ.), b March 2, 1931

Kanga, Dr.H.D. (India),b April19, 1880, d Dec 29, 1945

Kapadia, B. E. (India), b April 9, 1900

Kardar, A. H. (formerly Abdul Hafeez) (India, Oxford Univ., Warwickshire and Pakistan), b Jan 17, 1925

Kaye, Lt.-Col. H. S. (Yorkshire), b Aug 9, 1882, d Nov 6, 1953

Kaye, Mr. M. A. C. P. (Camb. Univ.), b Jan 11, 1916

Keene, J. W. (Surrey, Worcestershire and Scotland), b April 25, 1874, d Jan 3, 1931

Keeton, W. W. (Nottinghamshire), b April 30, 1905

Keighley, Mr. W. G. (Oxford Univ. and Yorkshire), b Jan 10, 1925

Keigwin, Mr. R. P. (Camb. Univ. Essex and Gloucestershire), b April 8, 1883

Keith, Mr. H. J. (South Africa), b Oct 25, 1927

Kelland, Mr. P. A. (Cambridge Univ.), b Sept 20, 1926

Kelleway, Mr. C. (New South Wales), b April 25, 1889, d Nov 16, 1944

Kelly, Mr. G. W. F. (Oxford Univ. and Ireland), b April 2, 1877, d Aug 16, 1951

Kelly, J. (Derbyshire), b March 19, 1922

Kelly, J. (Nottinghamshire), b Sept 15, 1930

Kelly, Mr. J. J. (New South Wales), b May 10, 1867, d Aug 14, 1938

Kemp, Mr. C. W. M. (Oxford Univ. and Kent), b April 26, 1856, d May 15, 1933

Kemp, Lt.-Col. Sir G., 1st Lord Rochdale (Camb. Univ. and Lancashire), b June 9, 1866, d March 24, 1945

Kemp, Mr. M. C. (Oxford Univ. and Kent), b Sept 7, 1861, d June 30, 1951

Kempis, Mr. G. S. (South Africa), b Nov 25, 1871, d March 1948

Kemp-Welch, Capt. G. D. (Camb. Univ. and Warwickshire), b Aug 4, 1907, d June 18, 1944

Kennedy, A. S. (Hampshire) b Jan 24, 1891

Kenny, Mr. C. J. M. (Camb. Univ. and Essex), b May 19, 1929

Kent, Mr. K. G. (Warwickshire), b Dec 10, 1901

Kenward, Mr. R. (Derbyshire and Sussex), b May 23, 1875

Kenyon, D. (Worcestershire), b May 15, 1924

Kenyon, Mr. M. N. (Lancashire), b Dec. 25, 1886

Kermode, A. (New South Wales and Lancashire), b May 15, 1876, d July 17, 1934

Kerr, Mr. J. L. (New Zealand), b Dec 28, 1910

Kerr, Mr. J. R. (Scotland), b Dec 4, 1883

Kerr, Mr. J. (Scotland), b April 8, 1885

Key, Sir K. J., 4th Bart (Oxford Univ. and Surrey), b Oct 11, 1864, d Aug 9, 1932

Khalid Hassan (Pakistan), b July 14, 1937

Khalid Wazir (Pakistan), b April 27, 1936

Khan Mohammad (Pakistan), b Jan 1, 1928

Khanna, Mr. B. C. (Camb. Univ.), b June 22, 1914

Kidd, Mr. E. L. (Camb. Univ. and Middlesex), b Oct 18, 1889

Kidney, Mr. J. M. (Manager West Indies team in England, 1933, 1939, 1950), b Oct 29, 1888

Killick, Ernest Harry (Sussex), b Jan 17, 1875, d Sept 29, 1948

Killick, Rev. E. T. (Camb. Univ. and Middlesex), b May 9, 1907, d May 18, 1953

Kilner, N. (Yorkshire and Warwickshire), b July 21, 1896

Kilner, R. (Yorkshire), b Oct 17, 1890, d April 5, 1928

Kimmins, Mr. S. E. A. (Kent), b May 26, 1930

Kimpton, Mr. R. C. M. (Oxford Univ. and Worcestershire), b Sept 21, 1916

King, B. P. (Worcestershire and Lancashire), b April 22, 1915

King, Mr. F. (Camb. Univ.), b April 6, 1911

King, I. M. (Warwickshire), b Nov 10, 1931

King, Mr. J. B. (Philadelphia), b Oct 19, 1873

King, J. H. (Leicestershire), b April 16, 1871, d Nov 20, 1946

King, J. W. (Worcestershire and Leicestershire), b Jan 21. 1908

King, K. C. W. (Surrey), b Dec 4, 1915

Kingsley, Mr. P. G. T. (Oxford Univ. and Hertfordshire), b May 26, 1908

Kingston, Rev. F. W. (Camb. Univ. and Northamptonshire), b Dec 24, 1855, d Jan 30, 1933

Kingston, Mr. G. H. (Northamptonshire), b 1864

Kingston, Mr. H. E. (Northamptonshire), b Aug 15, 1876, d June 9, 1955

Kingston, Mr. J. P. (Northamptonshire and Warwickshire), b July 8, 1857, d March, 1929

Kingston, Mr. W. H. (Northamptonshire), b Aug 12, 1874

Kingston, Mr. W. P. (Northamptonshire), b 1867, d April 15, 1937

Kinneir, S. P. (Warwickshire), b May 13, 1873, d Oct 16, 1928

Kippax, Mr. A. F. (New South Wales), b May 25, 1897

Kirk, Mr. E. C. (Surrey), b March 21, 1884, d Dec 19, 1932

Kirk, Mr. L. (Nottinghamshire), b Nov 1, 1884, d Feb 27, 1953

Kitcat, Mr. S. A. P. (Gloucestershire), b July 20, 1868, d June 17, 1942

Kitchener, F. (Hampshire), b July 2, 1871

Kitson, D. L. (Somerset), b Sept 13, 1925

Knight, Albert E. (Leicestershire), b Oct 8, 1873, d April 1946

Knight, Mr. D. J. (Oxford Univ. and Surrey), b May 12, 1894

Knight, Mr. N. S. (Oxford Univ.), b March, 1914

Knight. Mr. R. F. (Northamptonshire), b Aug 10, 1879, d Jan 9, 1955

Knight, Mr. R. L. (Oxford Univ.), b April 21, 1858, d May 22. 1938

Knightley-Smith, Mr. W. (Middlesex, Camb. Univ. and Gloucestershire), b Aug 1, 1932

Knott, Mr. C. (Hampshire), b Nov 26, 1914

Knott, Mr. C. H. (Oxford Univ. and Kent), b March 20. 1901

Knott, Mr. F. H. (Oxford Univ., Kent and Sussex), b Oct 30, 1891

Knowles, J. (Nottinghamshire), b March 25, 1910

Knowles, Mr. W. L. (Kent and Sussex, Sec. Sussex Co. Club 1919 to 1943), b Nov 27, 1871, d Dec 1, 1943

Knox, Mr. F. P. (Oxford Univ. and Surrey), b Jan 23, 1880

Knox, Major N. A. (Surrey), b Oct 10, 1884, d March 3, 1935

Knutton, H. J. (Warwickshire), b 1867

Kortright, Mr. C. J. (M.C.C. and Essex), b Jan 9, 1871, d Dec 12, 1952

Kotze, Mr. J. J. (South Africa), b Aug 7, 1879, d July 8, 1931

Lacey, Sir F. E. (Camb. Univ. and Hampshire; Secretary, M.C.C., 1898–1926), b Oct 19, 1859, d May 26, 1946

Lacy-Scott, Mr. D. G. (Camb. Univ. and Kent), b Aug 18, 1920

Lagden, Mr. R. B. (Camb. Univ. and Surrey), b April 15, 1893, d Oct 20, 1944

Laing, Mr. J. M. (Canada), b March 3, 1874, d Nov 1, 1947

Laker, J. C. (Surrey), b Feb 9, 1922

Lall Singh (India), b Dec 16, 1909

Lamason, Mr. J. R. (New Zealand), b Oct 29, 1905

Lamb, Mr. H. J. H. (Northamptonshire), b May 3, 1912

Lambert, G. (Gloucestershire), b May 5, 1919

Lambert, W. (Middlesex), b April 19, 1843, d March 4, 1927

Lampard, Mr. A. W. (Australian Imperial Forces Team), b July 3, 1885

Lancashire, Mr. O. P. (Camb. Univ. and Lancashire), b Dec 10, 1857, d July 23, 1934

Lancashire, Mr. W. (Hampshire and Dorset). b Oct 28, 1903

Lancaster, Mr. A. J. (Sec. Kent C.C.C., 1885–1936), b April 25, 1859, d Nov 16, 1936

Lancaster, T. (Yorkshire and Lancashire), b Feb 11, 1863, d Dec 12, 1935

Lane, Mr. W. W. Claypon (Surrey), b Aug 1, 1845, d March 31, 1939

Langdale, Mr. G. R. (Norfolk, Derbyshire, Somerset and Berkshire), b March 11, 1916

Langdon, T. (Gloucestershire), b Jan 8, 1879, d Nov 30, 1944

Langford, B. (Somerset), b Dec 17, 1935

Langford, W. (Hampshire), b Oct 5, 1875

Langley, Mr. C. K. (Warwickshire), b July 11, 1888, d June 26, 1948

Langley, Mr. G. R. (South Australia), b Sept 19, 1919

Langley, Mr. J. D. A. (Camb. Univ.), b April 25, 1918

Langridge, Jas. (Sussex), b July 10, 1906

Langridge, John (Sussex), b Feb 10, 1910

Langton, Mr. A. B. C. (South Africa), b March 2, 1912, d Nov 1942

Lansdowne, 5th Marquis of (President M.C.C., 1869), b Jan 14, 1845, d June 3, 1927

Large, J. (Surrey) b March 26, 1866

Larwood, H. (Nottinghamshire), b Nov 14, 1904

Latham, Mr. T. (Camb. Univ.), b June 22, 1847, d Jan 13, 1926

Lavers, Mr. A. B. (Essex), b Sept 6, 1918

Lavis, G. (Glamorgan), b Aug 17, 1908

Lawrence, Mr. A. S. (Camb. Univ.), b March 25, 1911, d March 17, 1939

Lawrence, C. (Surrey, Middlesex, New South Wales and Australian Aboriginal Team, 1868), b Dec 16, 1828, d Jan 6, 1917

Lawrence, J. (Somerset), b March 29, 1914

Lawrence, Mr. T. P. (Essex), b April 26, 1910

Lawrie, Mr. P. E. (Hampshire), b Dec 12, 1902

Lawson, H. M. (Hampshire), b May 22, 1914

Lawton, Mr. A. E. (Derbyshire, Lancashire and Cheshire), b March 31, 1879, d Dec 25, 1955

Lawton, C. G. (Warwickshire), b April 4, 1863

Lawton, J. C. (Warwickshire), b May 9, 1862, d Jan 20, 1934

Lawton, Thomas (Warwickshire), b Jan 31, 1865

Layne, O. H. (Barbados), b July 2, 1876, d Aug, 1932

Leach, Cecil (Lancashire and Somerset), b Nov 28, 1897

Leach, G. (Sussex), b at Malta, July 18, 1881, d Jan 10, 1945

Leadbeater, E. (Yorkshire), b Aug 15, 1927

Leadbeater, Mr. H. (Yorkshire), b Dec 31, 1863, d Oct 9, 1928

Leaf, Mr. H. (Surrey), b Oct 10, 1854, d Feb 13, 1936

Leaf, Mr. H. M. (Essex), b Oct 18, 1862, d April 23, 1931

Learmond, Mr. G. C. (Trinidad), b July 4, 1875

Leatham, Mr. A. E. (Gloucestershire), b Aug 9, 1859, d July 13, 1948

Leconfield, 3rd Lord (President, M.C.C., 1927), b Feb 17, 1872

Le Couteur, Mr. P. R. (Oxford Univ.), b June 26, 1885

Lee, C. (Yorkshire and Derbyshire), b March 17, 1924

Lee, Mr. E. C. (Hampshire and Oxford Univ.), b June 18, 1877, d June 16, 1942

Lee, Mr. F. M. (Kent and Somerset), b Jan 8, 1871

Lee, F. S. (Somerset), b July 24, 1907

Lee, G. M. (Nottinghamshire and Derbyshire), b June 7, 1887

Lee, H. W. (Middlesex), b Oct 26, 1890

Lee, J. W. (Middlesex and Somerset), b Feb 1, 1904, d July 1944

Lee, Mr. P. K. (South Australia), b Sept 14, 1904

Lees, Walter S. (Surrey), b Dec 25, 1876, d Sept 10, 1924

Leese, Mr. C. P. (Lancashire and Oxford Univ.), b May 22, 1889, d Jan 19, 1947

Le Fleming, Mr. H. (Kent), b Aug 17, 1870, d Sept 5, 1949

Le Fleming, Mr. J. (Kent), b Oct 23, 1865, d Oct 9, 1942

Legard, Mr. A. R. (Oxford Univ. and Worcestershire), b Jan 17, 1912

Legge, Lt.-Cmdr. G. B., R.N.V.R., F.A.A. (Oxford Univ. and Kent), b Jan 26, 1903, d Nov 21, 1940

Le Roy, Mr. P. N. (Philadelphia), b Sept 25, 1881, d 1950

Leslie, Mr. C. F. H. (Oxford Univ., Shropshire and Middlesex), b Dec 8, 1861, d Feb 12, 1921

Lester, E. (Yorkshire), b Feb 18, 1923

Lester, G. (Leicestershire), b Dec 27, 1915

Leveson Gower, Sir H. D. G. (Oxford Univ. and Surrey), b May 8, 1873 d Feb 1, 1954

Levett, Mr. W. H. V. (Kent), b Jan 25 1909

Lewis, A. E. (Somerset), b Jan 20, 1877

Lewis, C. (Kent), b July 27, 1910

Lewis, Mr. D. J. (Oxford Univ.), b July 27, 1927

Lewis, Mr. E. B. (Warwickshire), b Jan 5, 1918

Lewis, K. H. (Glamorgan), b Nov 10 1928

Lewis, Mr. L. K. (Camb. Univ.) b Sept 25, 1929

Lewis, Mr. P. T. (Oxford Authentic and South Africa), b Oct 2, 1884

Lewisham, Viscount, *see* Dartmouth

Leyland, M. (Yorkshire), b July 20, 1900

Liddell, A. G. (Northamptonshire), b May 2, 1907

Liddicut, Mr. A. E. (Victoria), b Oct 17, 1891

Light, E. (Hampshire) b Sept, 1, 1874

Lightfoot, A. (Northamptonshire), b Jan 8, 1936

Lilford, 5th Lord (Northamptonshire) b Jan 12, 1863, d Dec 17, 1945

Lilley, A. A. (Warwickshire, b Nov 18 1867, d Nov 17, 1929

Lilley, B. (Nottinghamshire), b Feb 11, 1895, d Aug 4, 1950

Lillywhite, James (Sussex), b Feb 23, 1842, d Oct 25, 1929

Lincoln, Earl of (Nottinghamshire), b April 8, 1907

Lindley, Mr. Tinsley (Nottinghamshire), b Oct 27, 1865, d March 30, 1940

Lindsay, Mr. J. D. (South Africa), b Sept 8, 1909

Lindsay, Mr. N. V. (Transvaal), b July 30, 1887

Lindwall, Mr. R. R. (New South Wales and Queensland), b Oct 3, 1921

Ling, Mr. W. V. (Griqualand West), b Oct 3, 1891

Linney, Mr. C. K. (Somerset), b Aug 26, 1912

Lipscomb, Mr. F. (Kent), b March 13, 1864, d 1952

Lister, Mr. J. (Yorkshire and Worcestershire), b May 14, 1930

Lister, Mr. W. H. L. (Lancashire), b Oct 7, 1911

Litteljohn, Mr. E. S. (Middlesex), b Sept 24, 1878

Livesay, Brig.-Gen. R. O'H. (Kent), b June 27, 1876, d March 23, 1946

Livingston, L. (Northamptonshire), b May 3, 1920

Livsey, W. H. (Hampshire), b Sept 23, 1894

Llewellyn, G. C. B. (Natal and Hampshire), b Sept 26, 1876

Lloyd, Mr. E. W. M. (Somerset), b March 19, 1845, d Sept 27, 1928

Loader, P. J. (Surrey), b Oct 25, 1929

Lobb, B. (Warwickshire and Somerset), b Jan 11, 1931

Lock, G. A. R. (Surrey). b July 5, 1929

Lock, H. (Surrey and Devon), b May 8, 1903

Locker, W. (Derbyshire), b Feb 16, 1867, d Aug 14, 1952

Lockhart, Mr. J. H. Bruce (Berkshire and Camb. Univ.), b March 4, 1889

Lockton, Mr. J. H. (Surrey), b May 22, 1892

Lockwood, W. H. (Nottinghamshire and Surrey), b March 25, 1868, d April 26, 1932

Lohmann, G. A. (Surrey), b June 2, 1865, d Dec 1, 1901

Lomas, Mr. J. M. (Oxford Univ.), b Dec 12, 1917, d Dec 4, 1945

Lomax, J. G. (Lancashire and Somerset), b May 5, 1925

Long, Rt. Hon. W. H. (1st Visct. Long) (President, M.C.C., 1906), b July 13, 1854, d Sept 26, 1924

Longfield. Mr. T. C. (Camb. Univ. and Kent), b May 12, 1906

Longman, Mr. G. H. (Camb. Univ. and Hampshire), b Aug 3, 1852, d Aug 19, 1938

Longman, Lt.-Col. H. K. (Camb. Univ., Surrey and Middlesex), b March 8, 1881

Longrigg, Mr. E. F. (Camb. Univ. and Somerset), b April 16, 1906

Lord, A. (Leicestershire), b Aug 28, 1888

Lord, W. A. (Warwickshire), b Aug 8, 1874

Louden, Mr. G. M. (Essex), b Sept 6, 1885

Loughnan, Mr. Austin (Victoria), d Oct 1926

Love, Mr. H. S. B. (New South Wales and Victoria), b Aug 10, 1895

Loveday, F. (Essex), b Sept 14, 1894

Loveitt, Mr. F. R. (Warwickshire), b April 24, 1871, d Sept 1, 1939

Lowe, Wing-Cmdr. J. C. M. (Oxford Univ. and Warwickshire), b Feb 21, 1888

Lowe, R. F. (Surrey), b July 28, 1905

Lowe, Mr. R. G. H. (Camb. Univ. and Kent), b June 11, 1904

Lowe, Mr. W. W. (Camb. Univ. and Worcestershire), b Nov 17, 1873, d May 26, 1945

Lowndes, Mr. W. G. L. F. (Oxford Univ. and Hampshire), b Jan 24, 1898

Lowry, Mr. T. C. (Camb. Univ., Somerset and New Zealand), b Feb 17, 1898

Lowson, F.A. (Yorkshire), b July 1, 1925

Loxton, Mr. S. J. (Victoria), b March 29, 1921

Luard, Col. A. J. H. (Gloucestershire and Hampshire), b Sept 3, 1861, d May 22, 1944

Lucan Brig.-Gen., 5th Earl of (President, M.C.C., 1928), b Dec 21 1860, d April 20, 1949

Lucas, Mr. A. P. (Camb. Univ., Surrey, Middlesex and Essex), b Feb 20, 1857, d Oct 12, 1923

Lucas, Mr. E. V. (Sussex and M.C.C.), b June 12, 1868, d June 26, 1938

Lucas, Mr. M. P. (Sussex and Warwickshire), b Nov 24, 1856, d July 9, 1921

Lucas, Mr. R. S. (Middlesex), b July 17, 1867, d Jan 5, 1942

Luce, Mr. F. M. (Gloucestershire), b April 26, 1878

Luckes, W. T. (Somerset), b Jan 1, 1901

Luckin, V. V. (Hampshire), b Feb 14, 1892, d Nov 30, 1931

Lumsden, Mr. V. R. (Camb. Univ.), b July 19, 1930

Lupton, Major A. W. (Yorkshire), b Feb 23, 1879, d April 14, 1944

Luther, Major A. C. G. (Sussex and Berkshire), b Sept 17, 1880

Lynes, J. (Warwickshire), b June 6, 1872

Lyon, Mr. B. H. (Oxford Univ., Wiltshire and Gloucestershire), b Jan 19, 1902

Lyon, Mr. G. W. F. (Oxford Univ.), b May 22, 1905, d Dec 1932

Lyon, Mr. M. D. (Camb. Univ., Wiltshire and Somerset), b April 22, 1898

Lyons, Mr. J. J. (South Australia), b May 21, 1863, d July 21, 1927

Lyttelton, 4th Lord (Camb. Univ), b March 31, 1817, d April 18, 1876

Lyttelton, Rt. Hon. Alfred, M.P. (Camb. Univ., Middlesex and President, M.C.C., 1898), b Feb 7, 1857, d July 5, 1913

Lyttelton, Rt. Rev. the Hon. A. T (Eton), b Jan 7, 1852, d Feb 19, 1903

Lyttelton, Hon. and Rev. A. V. (Worcestershire), b June 29, 1844, d April 4, 1928

Lyttelton, Hon. and Rev. C. F. (Camb. Univ. and Worcestershire), b Jan 26, 1887, d Oct 3, 1931

Lyttelton, Hon. C. G. (*see* 8th Visct. Cobham)

Lyttelton, Hon. C. J. (*see* 10th Visct. Cobham)

Lyttelton, Canon the Hon. Edward (Camb. Univ. and Middlesex), b July 23, 1855, d Jan 26, 1942

Lyttelton, Hon. G. W. (Eton), b Jan 6, 1883

Lyttelton, Hon. G. W. Spencer (Camb. Univ.), b June 12, 1847, d Dec 5, 1913

Lyttelton, Hon. J. C. (*see* 9th Visct. Cobham)

Lyttelton, Gen. the Rt. Hon. Sir N. G. (Eton), b Oct 28, 1845, d July 6, 1931

Lyttelton, Hon. R. H. (Eton), b Jan 18, 1854, d Nov 7, 1939

Maartenoz, Mr. G. A. (Hampshire), b April 14, 1882

McAlister, Mr. P. A. (Victoria), b July 11, 1869, d May 10, 1938

Macan, Mr. G. (Camb. Univ.), b Sept 9, 1853, d Nov 2, 1943

Macartney, Mr. C. G. (New South Wales), b June 27, 1886

Macaulay, P/O, G. G. (Yorkshire), b Dec 7, 1897, d Dec 14, 1940

McBride, Mr. W. N. (Oxford Univ. and Hampshire), b Nov 27, 1904

MacBryan, Mr. J. C. W. (Camb. Univ. and Somerset), b July 22, 1892

McCabe, Mr. S. J. (New South Wales), b July 16, 1910

McCanlis, Mr. M. A. (Oxford Univ., Surrey and Gloucestershire), b June 17, 1906

McCarthy, Mr. C. N. (South Africa and Camb. Univ.), b March 24, 1929

McConnon, J. E. (Glamorgan), b June 21, 1923

McCool, Mr. C. L. (Queensland), b Dec 9, 1915

McCorkell, N. (Hampshire), b March 23, 1912

McCormick, Mr. E. J. (Sussex), b Nov 1, 1862, d Jan 1942

McCormick, Mr. E. L. (Victoria), b May 16, 1906

McDonald, Mr. C. C. (Victoria), b Nov 17, 1928

McDonald, E. A. (Victoria and Lancashire), b in Tasmania, Jan 6, 1892, d July 22, 1937

MacDonald, Dr. R. (Queensland and Leicestershire), b Feb 28, 1872, d May 1945

McDonell, Mr. H. C. (Camb. Univ., Surrey and Hampshire), b Sept 19, 1882

McElhone, Mr. W. P. (Australian Board of Control), b Dec 22, 1870, d April 21, 1932

McGahey, Mr. C. P. (Essex), b Feb 12, 1871, d Jan 10, 1935

McGirr, Mr. H. M. (New Zealand), b Nov 5, 1891

McGlew, Mr. D. J. (South Africa), b March 11, 1929

McGlinchy, Mr. W. W. (New South Wales and Queensland), b Jan 31, 1866, d July 1, 1946

Machin, Mr. R. S. (Camb. Univ. and Surrey), b April 16, 1904

McHugh, F. P. (Yorkshire and Glos.), b Nov 15, 1925

McIlwraith, Mr. J. (Victoria), b 1857, d July 13, 1938

Macindoe, Mr. D. H. (Oxford Univ. and Buckinghamshire), b Sept 1, 1917

McIntosh, Mr. R. I. F. (Oxford Univ.), b Aug 19, 1907

McIntyre, A. J. (Surrey), b May 14, 1918

McIntyre, A. S. (Hampshire), b May 29, 1889

McIver, Mr. C. D. (Oxford Univ. and Essex), b Jan 23, 1881, d May 13, 1954

Mackay, Mr. J. R. M. (New South Wales), b Sept 9, 1881, d June 13 1953

Mackenzie, Mr. A. C. K. (New South Wales), b Dec 10, 1870, d April 11, 1947

Mackenzie, Col. F. F. (Oxford Univ. and Kent), b 1849, d July 17, 1934

Mackenzie, P. A. (Hampshire), b Oct 5, 1918

McKibbin, Mr. T. R. (New South Wales), b Dec 10, 1870, d Dec 15, 1939

McKinna, Mr. G. H. (Oxford Univ.), b Aug 2, 1930

Mackinnon, Mr. F. A. (Camb. Univ. and Kent), b April 9, 1848, d Feb 27, 1947

McLachlan, Mr. N. (Oxford Univ.), b Oct 12, 1858, d Feb 18, 1928

MacLaren, Mr. A. C. (Lancashire), b Dec 1, 1871, d Nov 17, 1944

McLean, Mr. R. A. (South Africa), b July 9, 1930

MacLeod, Mr. K. G. (Camb. Univ. and Lancashire), b Feb 2, 1888

McLeod, Mr. A. (Hampshire), b Nov 12, 1894

McMahon, J. W. (Surrey and Somerset), b Dec 28, 1919

McMillan, Mr. Q. (South Africa), b June 23, 1904, d July 3, 1948

McMurray, T. (Surrey), b July 24, 1911

McNamee, Mr. R. J. A. (New South Wales), b Aug 26, 1899, d Sept 18, 1949

McRae, Mr. F. M. (Somerset), b Feb 12, 1916, d Feb 25, 1944

Mahmood Hussain (Pakistan), b April 2, 1932

Mahomed, Gul (India), b Oct 15, 1921

Mailey, Mr. A. A. (New South Wales), b Jan 3, 1888

Mainprice, Mr. H. (Camb. Univ. and Gloucestershire), b Nov. 27, 1882

Maitland, Mr. W. Fuller (Essex and Oxford Univ.), b May 6, 1844, d Nov 15, 1932

Makepeace, H. (Lancashire), b Aug 22 1881, d Dec 19, 1952

Makin, Mr. J. (Victoria), b Feb 11, 1904

Malden, Mr. Ernest (Kent), b Oct 10, 1870

Malden, Rev. Eustace (Kent), b Aug 19, 1863, d Dec 3, 1947

Malik, Mr. H. S. (Sussex), b Nov 30, 1894

Mallett, Mr. A. W. H. (Kent and Oxford Univ.), b Aug. 29, 1924

Mallett, Mr. R. H. (Durham), (Secretary Minor Counties), b Oct 14, 1858, d Nov 29, 1939

Manjrekar, Mr. V. L. (India), b Sept 26, 1931

Mankad, M. "Vinoo" (India), b April 12, 1917

Mann, Mr. E. W. (Camb. Univ. and Kent), b March 4, 1882, d Feb 15, 1954

Mann, Mr. F. G. (Camb. Univ. and Middlesex), b Sept 6, 1917

Mann, Mr. F. T. (Camb. Univ. and Middlesex), b March 3, 1888

Mann, Mr. J. E. F. (Camb. Univ.), b Dec 2, 1903

Mann, Mr. J. P. (Middlesex), b June 13, 1919

Mann, Mr. N. B. F. (South Africa), b Dec 28, 1921, d July 31, 1952

Manning, Mr. T. E. (Northamptonshire), b Sept 2, 1884

Mansell, Mr. P. N. F. (South Africa), b March 16, 1920

Mansfield, Hon. J. W. (Norfolk and Camb. Univ.), b Feb 12, 1862, d June 17, 1932

Mantri, Mr. M. K. (India), b Sept 1, 1921

Maqsood Ahmed (Pakistan), b March 26, 1925

March, Earl of, afterwards 6th Duke of Richmond (President, M.C.C. 1842), b Feb 27, 1818, d Sept 27, 1903

Marchant, Mr. F. (Camb. Univ. and Kent), b May 22, 1864, d April 13, 1946

Marks, Mr. A. (New South Wales), b Dec 10, 1910

Marlar, Mr. R. G. (Camb. Univ. and Sussex), b Jan 2, 1931

Marlow, F. W. (Staffordshire and Sussex), b Oct 8, 1867, d Aug 7, 1952

Marlow, W. H. (Leicestershire), b Feb 13, 1900

Marner, P. (Lancashire), b March 31, 1936

Marriott, Mr. C. (Oxford Univ. and Leicestershire), b Oct 18, 1848, d July 9, 1918

Marriott, Mr. C. S. (Camb. Univ., Lancashire and Kent), b Sept 14, 1895

Marriott, Rev. G. S. (Oxford Univ. and Leicestershire), b Oct 7, 1855, d Oct 21, 1905

Marriott, Mr. H. H. (Camb. Univ. and Leicestershire), b Jan 20, 1875, d November 15, 1949

Marriott, Mr. J. M. (Leicestershire), b March 6, 1853, d Oct 21, 1910

Marsh, E. (Derbyshire), b July 7, 1920

Marsh, Mr. E. C. (Somerset and Devon), b May 7, 1865, d Nov 27, 1926

Marsh, Mr. J. F. (Camb. Univ. and Oxfordshire), b May 11, 1875, d Oct 30, 1927

Marshal, Alan (Queensland, London County and Surrey), b June 12, 1883, d July 23, 1915

Marshall, Mr. A. G. (Somerset), b April 17, 1895

Marshall, B. (Nottinghamshire), b May 5, 1902

Marshall, Mr. Chas. (Middlesex), b Feb 20, 1843, d Feb 25, 1904

Marshall, Charles (Surrey and Leicestershire), b Oct 1, 1866, d Nov 25, 1948

Marshall, Mr. H. M. (Camb. Univ.), b Aug 1, 1841, d March 2, 1913

Marshall, Mr. J. C. (Oxford Univ), b Jan 30, 1929

Marshall, J. M. A. (Warwickshire), b Oct 26, 1916

Marshall, Canon J. W. (Camb. Univ.), b Dec 5, 1835, d Sept 10 1915

Marshall, N. D. (India), b Jan 3, 1905

Marshall, Mr. R. E. (West Indies and Hampshire), b April 25, 1930

Marsham, Mr. A. J. B. (Oxford Univ. and Kent), b Aug 14, 1919

Marsham, Rev. C. D. (Oxford Univ.), b Jan 30, 1835, d March 2, 1915

Marsham, Mr. C. H. B. (Oxford Univ. and Kent), b Feb 10, 1879, d July 18, 1928

Marsham, Mr. C. J. B. (Oxford Univ.), b Jan 18, 1829, d Aug 20, 1901

Marsham, Brig. F. W. B. (Kent), b July 13, 1883

Marsham, Mr. George (Kent), b April 10, 1849, d Dec 2, 1927

Marsham, the Hon. and Rev. John (Kent), b July 25, 1842, d Sept 16, 1926

Marsham, Mr. R. H. B. (Oxford Univ.), b Sept 3, 1833, d April 5, 1913

Marsland, Mr. G. P. (Oxford Univ.), b May 17, 1932

Martin, E. (Nottinghamshire), b Aug 17, 1925

Martin, Mr. E. G. (Oxford Univ. and Worcestershire), b March 22, 1881, d April 27, 1945

Martin, Mr. F. R. (West Indies), b Oct 12, 1893

Martin, Mr. J. W. (Kent), b Feb 16, 1917

Martin, S. H. (Worcestershire), b Jan 11, 1909

Martindale, Mr. E. A. (West Indies), b Nov 25, 1909

Martyn, Mr. H. (Oxford Univ. and Somerset), b July 16, 1877, d Aug 8, 1928

Mason, A. (Yorkshire), b May 2, 1921

Mason, Mr. J. R. (Kent), b March 26, 1874

Mason, Percy (Nottinghamshire), b Nov 19, 1874

Massie, Mr. Hugh H. (New South Wales), b April 11, 1855, d Oct 12, 1938

Matheson, Mr. A. M. (New Zealand), b Feb 27, 1906

Mathews, Mr. E. (Oxford Univ.), b May 17, 1847, d Nov 25, 1930

Mathews, Mr. J. K. (Sussex), b Feb 6, 1884

Mathews, Mr. K. P. A. (Camb. Univ.), b May 10, 1926

Matthews, A. (Gloucestershire), b May 3, 1913

Matthews, Mr. A. D. G. (Northamptonshire and Glamorgan), b May 3, 1905

Matthews, C. S. (Notts), b Oct 17, 1931

Matthews, F. C. L. (Nottinghamshire), b Aug 15, 1893

Matthews, Mr. M. H. (Oxford Univ.), b April 26, 1914, d May, 1940

Matthews, Hon. R. C. (Sponsor, Canadian Cricket Tour in England, 1936), b June 14, 1871, d Sept 20, 1952

Matthews Mr. T. J. (Victoria), b April 3, 1884, d Oct 14, 1943

Maude, Mr. J. (Oxford Univ.), b March 17, 1850, d Nov 17, 1934

Maudsley, Mr. R. H. (Oxford Univ. and Warwickshire), b April 8, 1918

Maul, Mr. H. C. (Warwickshire), b Oct 6, 1850, d Oct 10, 1940

Maxwell, Mr. C. R. (Nottinghamshire, Middlesex and Worcestershire), b May 21, 1913

Maxwell, J. (Somerset and Glamorgan), b Jan. 13, 1884

May, Mr. P. B. H. (Cambridge Univ. and Surrey), b Dec 31, 1929

May, Mr. P. R. (Camb. Univ., London County and Surrey), b March 13, 1884

Mayer, J. H. (Warwickshire), b March 2, 1902

Mayes, R. (Kent), b Oct 7, 1921

Maynard, Mr. E. A. J. (Derbyshire), b Feb 10, 1861, d Jan 10, 1931

Mayne, Mr. E. R. (South Australia and Victoria), b July 4, 1883

Mead, C. P. (Hampshire and Suffolk), b March 9, 1887

Mead, Walter (Essex), b March 25, 1869, d March 18, 1954

Meads, E. A. (Nottinghamshire), b Aug 17, 1916

Medlicott, Mr. W. S. (Oxford Univ. and Wiltshire), b Aug. 28, 1879

Mee, R. J. (Nottinghamshire and Staffordshire), b Sept 25, 1867

Meherhomji, R. P. (India), b March 4, 1877

Meherhomji, K.R. (India), b Aug 9, 1911

Mehta, A. H. (Parsees), b April 8, 1876

Mehta, D. S. (Parsees), b July 3, 1864, d June 2, 1928

Melle, Mr. B. G. von B. (South Africa, Oxford Univ. and Hampshire), b March 31, 1891

Melle, Mr. M. G. (South Africa), b June 3, 1930

Melluish, Mr. M. E. L. (Camb. Univ.), b June 13, 1932

Melsome, Capt. R. G. W. (Gloucestershire), b Jan 16, 1906

Melville, Mr. A. (Oxford Univ., Sussex and South Africa), b May 19, 1910

Mercer, J. (Sussex and Glamorgan), b April 22, 1895

Merchant, V. M. (India), b Oct 12, 1911

Merrick, Mr. H. (Gloucestershire), b Dec 21, 1887

Merritt, W. E. (New Zealand and Northamptonshire), b Aug 18,1908

Merry, Mr. C. A. (West Indies), b Jan 20, 1911

Meston, Mr. S. P. (Gloucestershire and Essex), b Nov 19, 1882

Metcalfe, Mr. E. J. (Hertfordshire and Queensland), b Sept 29, 1865, d June 14, 1951

Meyer, Mr. R. J. O. (Camb. Univ. and Somerset), b March 15, 1905

Meyer, Mr. W. E. (Gloucestershire), b Jan 12, 1883, d Oct 1, 1953

Meyrick-Jones, Rev. F. (Camb. Univ., Hampshire, Kent and Norfolk), b Jan 14, 1867, d Oct 25, 1950

Miles, Mr. P. W. H. (Nottinghamshire), b Jan 7, 1848, d Dec 4, 1933

Miles, Mr. R. F. (Oxford Univ. and Gloucestershire), b Jan 24, 1846, d Feb 26, 1930

Miller, Mr. K. R. (Victoria and N.S.W.), b Nov 28, 1919

Miller, Mr. Neville (Surrey), b Aug 27, 1874

Miller, Mr. R. A. T. (Sussex), b Nov 12, 1896, d July 1941

Miles-Lade, Hon. H. A. (Kent), b Nov 24, 1867, d July 30, 1937

Mills, Mr. J. E. (New Zealand), b Sept 3, 1905

Mills, Mr. J. M. (Camb. Univ. and Warwickshire), b July 27, 1921

Mills, John (Nottinghamshire), b Jan 28, 1855, d June 27, 1932

Mills, P. T. (Gloucestershire), b May 7, 1883, d Dec 8, 1950

Millward, A. (Cheshire and Worcestershire), b July 4, 1860, d 1932

Milton, C. A. (Gloucestershire), b March 10, 1928

Milton, Sir W. H. (Marlborough and South Africa), b Dec 3, 1854, d March 6, 1930

Minnett, Mr. L. A. (New South Wales), b May 18, 1883, d Aug 6, 1934

Minnett, Mr. R.B. (New South Wales), b June 13, 1888

Minnett, Mr. R. V. (New South Wales), b Sept 2, 1884

Mischler, Mr. N. M. (Camb. Univ.), b Oct 9, 1920

Mistri, Col. K. M. (India), b Nov 7, 1874

Mitchell, A. (Yorkshire), b Sept 13, 1902

Mitchell, Mr. B. (South Africa), b Jan 8, 1909

Mitchell, Mr. C. (Kent), b Feb 20, 1862, d Oct, 1937

Mitchell, Mr. C. G. (Somerset), b Jan 27, 1929

Mitchell, Mr. Frank (Camb. Univ., Yorkshire and South Africa), b Aug 13, 1872, d Oct 11, 1935

Mitchell, F. R. (Warwickshire), b June 3, 1922

Mitchell, T. B. (Derbyshire), b Sept 4, 1902

Mitchell, Mr. T. F. (Kent), b Oct 22, 1907

Mitchell, Mr. W. M. (Oxford Univ.), b Aug 15, 1929

Mitchell-Innes, Mr. N. S. (Oxford Univ. and Somerset), b Sept 7, 1914

Moberly, Mr. J. C. (Hampshire), b April 22, 1848, d Jan 29, 1928

Mobey, G. S. (Surrey), b March 5, 1904

Modi, R. S. (India), b Nov 11, 1924

Mohammad Aslam (Pakistan), b Jan 5, 1920

Moloney, Mr. D. A. R. (New Zealand), b Aug 11, 1910, d 1943

Monks, Mr. C. (Gloucestershire), b March 4, 1912

Montezuma, Mr. L. de (Sussex), b April 16, 1870

Montgomery, S. (Glamorgan), b July 7, 1920

Montgomery, W. (Surrey, Somerset, Wiltshire, Cheshire and Hertfordshire), b March 4, 1882

Montmorency, Mr. R. H. de (Oxford Univ., Herts and Bucks), b Oct 6, 1871, d Dec 19, 1938

Moody, Mr. C. P. (Author of *Australian Cricket and Cricketers*, etc.), b Aug 11, 1867, d Nov 29, 1937

Moon, Sir Cecil E., 2nd Bart. (London County and Wanderers, Chairman New Zealand Cricket Council. 1914–17), b Sept 2, 1867, d Feb 22 1951

Moon, Mr. W. R. (Middlesex), b June 27, 1868, d Jan 9, 1943

Mooney, Mr. F. L. H. (New Zealand), b May 26, 1921

Moore, Mr. D. N. (Oxford Univ. and Gloucestershire), b Sept 26. 1910

Moore, F. W. (Lancashire), b Jan 17, 1931

Moore, J. (Hampshire), b April 29, 1891

Moore, Mr. R. H. (Hampshire), b Nov 14, 1913

Moorhouse, F. (Warwickshire and Cheshire), b March 25, 1880, dead

Morcom, Mr. A. F. (Camb. Univ. and Bedfordshire), b Feb 16, 1885, d Feb 12, 1952

Mordaunt, Mr. E. C. (Middlesex, Kent and Hampshire), b Sept 6, 1870, d June 21, 1938

Mordaunt, Mr. G. J. (Oxford Univ. and Kent), b Jan. 20, 1873

Mordaunt, Sir H. J., 12th Bart. (Camb. Univ., Middlesex and Hampshire), b July 12, 1867, d Jan 15, 1939

Mordaunt, Lt.-Col. O. C. (Somerset), b May 26, 1876, dead

More, Mr. R. E. (Oxford Univ. and Middlesex), b Jan 3, 1879, d Nov 24, 1936

Morfee. P. E. (Kent and Scotland), b May 2, 1887, dead

Morgan, Mr. C. L. (Surrey), b May 27, 1867

Morgan, D. C. (Derbyshire), b Feb 26, 1929

Morgan, Mr. J. T. (Camb. Univ. and Glamorgan), b May 7, 1907

Morgan, Mr. M. N. (Camb. Univ.), b May 15, 1932

Morgan, Mr. W. G. (Glamorgan), b Dec 26, 1907

Morkel, Mr. D. P. B. (South Africa), b Jan 25, 1906

Morley, W. L. (Essex), b Aug 26, 1894

Morris, Mr. A. R. (New South Wales), b Jan 19, 1922

Morris, Mr. H. M. (Essex), b April 16, 1898

Morris, Mr. P. E. (Essex), b Nov 26, 1877, d July 10, 1945

Morris Mr. R. J. (Camb. Univ. and Kent), b Nov 27, 1926

Morris, W. B. (Essex), b May 28, 1917

Morrison, Mr. J. S. F. (Camb. Univ., Northumberland and Somerset), b April 17, 1892

Mortimer, Sir R G. E. (Lancashire), b July 7, 1869, d May 3, 1955

Mortimore, J. (Gloucestershire), b June 14, 1933

Morton, A. (Derbyshire), b May 7, 1884, d Dec 19, 1935

Morton, Mr. F. L. (South Australia and Victoria), b Dec 21, 1901

Morton, Mr. H. G. S. (Queensland), b Oct 14, 1881

Moses, Mr. H. (New South Wales), b Feb 13, 1858, d Dec 7, 1938

Moss, A. E. (Middlesex), b Nov 14, 1930

Moss, J. (Nottinghamshire), b Feb 7, 1864, d July 10 1950

Moss, Rev. R. H. (Oxford Univ., Lancashire, Bedfordshire and Worcestershire), b Feb 24, 1868

Moulder, J. W. H. (Surrey and Transvaal), b Sept 29, 1881, d Oct 13, 1933

Moule, Mr. W. H. (Victoria), b Jan 21, 1858, d Sept, .1939

Mounsey, Joseph T. (Yorkshire), b Aug 30, 1871, d April 6, 1949

Mounteney, A. (Leicestershire), b Feb 11, 1883, d June 1, 1933

Moyes, Mr. A. G. (South Australia and Victoria), b Jan 2, 1893

Mugliston, Mr. F. H. (Camb. Univ. and Lancashire), b June 7, 1886, d Oct 3, 1932

Muir, Mr. G. H. (Hon. Sec. Hampshire C.C.), b Sept 23, 1869, d March 29, 1939

Mulholland, Right Hon. Sir H. G. H., 1st Bart. (Camb. Univ.), b Dec 20, 1888

Mulla, H. F. (India), b May 4, 1885

Muncer, B. L. (Middlesex and Glamorgan), b Oct 23, 1913

Munden, V. (Leicestershire), b Jan 2, 1928

Murch, W. (Gloucestershire and Wiltshire), b Nov 18, 1867, d May 1, 1928

Murdin, J. V. (Northamptonshire), b Aug 16, 1891

Murdoch, Mr. W. L. (New South Wales and Sussex), b Oct 18, 1855, d Feb 18, 1911

Murray, Mr. A. L. (Warwickshire), b June 29, 1901

Murray. Mr. A. R. A. (South Africa), b April 30, 1922

Murray Willis, Mr. P. E. (Worcestershire and Northamptonshire), b July 14, 1910

Murray Wood, Mr. W. (Oxford Univ. and Kent), b June 30, 1917

Murrell, H. R. (Kent and Middlesex), b Nov 19, 1880, d Aug 15, 1952

Mushtaq Ali (India), b Dec 17, 1914

Musson, Mr. F. W. (Lancashire), b May 31, 1894

Myers, H. (Yorkshire and Tasmania), b Jan 2, 1877, d June 12, 1944

Nagel, Mr. L. E. (Victoria), b March 6, 1905

Naoomal Jeoomal (India), b April 17, 1904

Napier, Mr. G. G. (Camb. Univ. and Middlesex), b Jan 26, 1884, d Sept 25, 1915

Napier, Rev. J. R. (Marlborough and Lancashire), b Jan 5, 1859, d March 12, 1939

Nash, A. (Glamorgan), b Sept 18, 1873

Nash, Mr. L. J. (Tasmania and Victoria), b May 2, 1910

Naumann, Mr. F. C. G. (Oxford Univ. and Surrey), b April 9, 1892, d Oct 30, 1947

Naumann Mr. J. H. (Camb. Univ. and Sussex), b Sept 9, 1893

Navle, J. G. (India), b Dec 7, 1902

Nayudu, C. K. (India), b Oct 31, 1895

Nayudu, C. S. (India), b April 18, 1914

Nazir Ali, S. (India and Sussex), b June 8, 1906

Neale, W. L. (Gloucestershire), b March 3, 1904, d Oct 26, 1955

Neblett, Mr. J. M. (West Indies), b Nov 13, 1901

Needham, E. (Derbyshire), b Jan 21, 1873, d March 7, 1936

Nelson, Mr. R. P., Lieut. R.M. (Camb. Univ., Middlesex and Northamptonshire), b Aug 7, 1912, d Oct 29, 1940

Neser, Mr. V. H. (Oxford Univ. and South Africa), b June 16, 1894

Nevell, W. T. (Middlesex, Surrey and Northamptonshire), b June 13, 1916

Newham, Mr. W. (Sussex), b Dec 12, 1860, d June 26, 1944

Newman, Mr. G. C. (Oxford Univ. and Middlesex), b April 26, 1904

Newman, J. (Hampshire), b Nov 12, 1887

Newnham, Lt.-Col. A. T. H. (Gloucestershire), b Jan 17, 1861, d Dec 29, 1941

Newson, Mr. E. S. (South Africa), b Dec 2, 1910

Newstead, J T (Yorkshire), b Sept 8, 1879, d March 25, 1952

Newton, Mr. A. E. (Oxford Univ. and Somerset), b Sept 12, 1862 d, Sept 15, 1952

Newton, F. A. (Derbyshire), b Sept 16, 1887, d Aug 8, 1924

Newton-Thompson, Mr. J. O. (Oxford Univ.), b Dec 2, 1920

Nice, E. H. L. (Surrey), b Aug 1, 1875, d June 6, 1946

Nichol, M. (Worcestershire), b Sept 10, 1905, d May 21, 1934

Nicholas, Capt. F. W. H. (Essex and Bedfordshire), b July 25, 1893

Nicholls, Mr. B. E. (Oxford Univ. and Sussex), b Oct 4, 1864, d June 5, 1945

Nicholls, Mr. C. O. (New South Wales), b Dec 5, 1901

Nicholls, J. E. (Worcestershire and Staffordshire), b April 20, 1878

Nicholls, R. B. (Gloucestershire), b Dec 4, 1933

Nicholls, Mr. R. W. (Middlesex), b July 23, 1875, d Jan 22, 1948

Nichols, M. S. (Essex), b Oct 6, 1900

Nicol, Mr. D. J. (South Africa), b Dec 11, 1887

Nicolson, Mr. J. F. W. (South Africa), b July 19, 1899, d Dec 18, 1935

Nimbalkar, R. B. (India), b Dec 1, 1915

Nissar, Mahomed (India), b Aug 1, 1910

Nitschke, Mr. H. C. (South Australia), b April 14, 1906

Noble, Mr. M. A. (New South Wales), b Jan 28, 1873, d June 21, 1940

Noel, Mr. J. (South Australia), b March 28, 1858, d Jan 9, 1938

Noonon, Mr. D. J. (New South Wales), b Jan 8, 1877, d March 10, 1929

Norbury, V. (Hampshire and Lancashire), b Aug 3, 1887

Norman, Mr. N. F. (Northamptonshire), b Feb 2, 1884

North, E. J. (Middlesex), b Sept 23, 1896

Northway, Mr. R. P. (Somerset and Northamptonshire), b Aug 14, 1906, d Aug 26, 1936

Nothling, Dr. O. E. (Queensland and N.S.W.), b Aug 1, 1900

Nourse, Mr. A. D. (South Africa), b at Croydon, Jan 26, 1878, d July 8, 1948

Nourse, Mr. A. D., jun. (South Africa), b Nov 12, 1910

Nunes, Mr. R. K. (West Indies), b June 7, 1894

Nunn, Mr. J. A. (Oxford Univ. and Middlesex), b March 19, 1906

Nupen, Mr. E. P. (South Africa), b Jan 1, 1902

Nutter, A. E. (Lancashire and Northamptonshire), b June 28, 1913

Nye, J. K. (Sussex), b May 23, 1914

Oakes, C. (Sussex), b Aug 10, 1912

Oakes, J. (Sussex), b March 3, 1916

Oakley, L. (Worcestershire), b Jan 11, 1916

Oakley, William (Lancashire and Shropshire), b May 6, 1861

Oakman, A. S. M. (Sussex), b April 20, 1930

Oates, A. W. (Nottinghamshire), b Dec 9, 1908

Oates, T. W. (Nottinghamshire), b Aug 9, 1875, d June 18, 1949

O'Brien, Mr. L. P. J. (Victoria), b July 2, 1908

O'Brien, Mr. R. (Camb. Univ.), b Nov 20, 1932

O'Brien, Sir T. C., 3rd Bart. (Oxford Univ., Middlesex and Ireland), b Nov 5, 1861, d Dec 9, 1948

O'Byrne, Mr. W. F. T. (Sussex), b April 30, 1908, d Oct 23, 1951

Ochse, Mr. A. L. (South Africa), b Oct 11, 1899, d May 6, 1949

O'Connor, J. (Essex and Buckinghamshire), b Nov 5, 1899

O'Connor, Mr. J. A. (New South Wales and South Australia), b Sept 9, 1875, d Aug 23, 1941

O'Connor, Mr. L. P. D. (Queensland), b April 11, 1891

O'Halloran, J. (Victoria and Southland, N.Z.), b Jan 12, 1872

Oldfield, N. (Lancashire and Northamptonshire), b April 30, 1911

Oldfield, Mr. P. C. (Oxford Univ.), b Feb 27, 1911

Oldfield, Mr. W. A. (New South Wales), b Sept 9, 1897

Oldroyd, E. (Yorkshire), b Oct 1, 1888

O'Linn, S. (Kent), b May 5, 1927

Oliver, Mr. C. (New Zealand), b Nov 1, 1905

Oliver, Mr. L. (Derbyshire), b Oct 18, 1886, d Jan 26, 1948

Ollivierre, Mr. C. A. (West Indies and Derbyshire), b July 20, 1876, d March 25, 1949

Ollivierre, Mr. R. C. (West Indies), b 1880, d June 5, 1937

Ord, J. S. (Warwickshire), b July 12, 1912

O'Reilly, Mr. W. J. (New South Wales), b Dec 20, 1905

Orford, Mr. L. A. (Camb. Univ.), b March 12, 1865, d Jan 18, 1948

Orlebar, Rev. A. ("Arthur," of "Tom Brown's Schooldays") (Bedfordshire), b Sept 30, 1912, aged 88

Orr, Cmdr. H. J. (Hampshire), b Jan 21, 1878

Orr, Mr. J. H. (Scotland), b Oct 18, 1878

Osborn, F. (Leicestershire), b Nov 10, 1889, d Oct 12, 1954

Oscroft, Mr. P. W. (Nottinghamshire), b Nov 27, 1872, d Dec 8, 1933

Osman, J. (Surrey), b Dec 14, 1868

Outschoorn, L. (Worcestershire), b Sept 26, 1918

Ovenstone, Mr. D. M. (South Africa), b July 31, 1921

Owen, J. G. (Surrey and Bedfordshire), b Jan 23, 1909

Owen-Smith, Mr. H. G. O. (South Africa, Oxford Univ. and Middlesex), b Feb 18, 1909

Oxenham, Mr. R. K. (Queensland), b July 28, 1891, d Aug 16, 1939

Oyston, C. (Yorkshire), b May 12, 1869, d July 15, 1942

Packe, Major C. W. C. (Leicestershire), b May 2, 1909, d July 1, 1944

Packe, Mr. M. St. J. (Leicestershire), b Aug 21, 1916

Padgett, D. E. V. (Yorkshire), b July 20, 1934

Page, Mr. D. A. C. (Gloucestershire), b April 11, 1911, d Sept 2, 1936

Page, Mr. H. V. (Oxford Univ. and Gloucestershire), b Oct 30, 1862, d Aug 1, 1927

Page, J. C. T. (Kent), b May 20, 1930

Page, Mr. M. L. (New Zealand), b May 8, 1902

Pai, M. D. (India), b June 21, 1883

Paine, G. A. E. (Middlesex and Warwickshire), b June 11, 1908

Paish, A. (Gloucestershire), b April 5, 1874, d Aug 15, 1948

Palairet, Mr. L. C. H. (Oxford Univ. and Somerset), b May 27, 1870, d March 27, 1933

Palairet, Mr. R. C. N. (Oxford Univ. and Somerset), b June 25, 1871, d Feb 11, 1955

Palia, P. E. (India), b Sept 5, 1910

Palm, Mr. A. W. (South Africa), b June 8, 1901

Palmer, Mr. C. (Camb. Univ. and Middlesex), b July 14, 1885

Palmer, Mr. C. H. (Worcestershire and Leicestershire), b May 15, 1919

Palmer, Mr. G. E. (Victoria and Tasmania), b Feb 22, 1861, d Aug 22, 1910

Palmer, Mr. H. J. (Essex), b Aug 30, 1890

Papillon, Mr. G. K. (Northamptonshire), b Sept 24, 1867, d Aug 14, 1942

Pardon, Mr. Charles Frederick (five years Editor of *Wisden*), b March 28, 1850, d April 18, 1890

Pardon, Mr. Edgar S. (for twelve years associated with *Wisden*), b Sept 28, 1859, d July 16, 1898

Pardon, Mr. S. H. (Editor of *Wisden* from 1891 to 1925), b Sept 23, 1855, d Nov 20, 1925

Parfitt, Mr. J. J. (Surrey, Warwickshire and Somerset), b Dec 23, 1857, d May 17, 1926

Paris, Mr. C. G. A. (Hampshire), b Aug 20, 1911

Park, Mr. R. L. (Victoria), b July 30 1892, d Jan 24, 1947

Parker, C. W. L. (Gloucestershire), b Oct 14, 1884

Parker, Mr. G. M. (South Africa), b May 27, 1899

Parker, Mr. G. W. (Camb. Univ. and Gloucestershire), b Feb 11, 1912

Parker, J. F. (Surrey), b April 23, 1913

Parker, Mr. J. P. (Hampshire), b Nov 29, 1902

Parkhouse, W. G. A. (Glamorgan), b Oct 12, 1925

Parkin, C. H. (Durham, Yorkshire and Lancashire), b Feb 18, 1886, d June 15, 1943

Parkin, R. (Lancashire), b March 17, 1908

Parkinson, L. W. (Lancashire), b Sept 15, 1908

Parks, H. W. (Sussex), b July 18, 1906

Parks, James H. (Sussex), b May 12, 1903

Parks, J. M. (Sussex), b Oct 21, 1931

Parr, F. D. (Lancs), b June 1, 1928

Parr, Mr. H. B. (Lancashire), b June 5, 1845, d March 24, 1930

Parris, F. (Sussex), b Sept 20, 1867, d Jan 17, 1941

Parry, Mr. D. M. (Camb. Univ.), b Feb 8, 1911

Parsons, Mr. A. B. D. (Camb. Univ.), b Sept 20, 1933

Parsons, Mr. H. F. (Victoria), b May 21, 1875, d Dec 20, 1937

Parsons, Rev. J. H. (Warwickshire), b May 30, 1890

Partridge, Mr. N. E. (Camb. Univ. and Warwickshire), b Aug 10, 1900

Partridge, R. J. (Northamptonshire), b Feb 11, 1912

Pataudi, Nawab of (Oxford Univ., Worcestershire and India), b March 16, 1910, d Jan 5, 1952

Paterson, Mr. R. F. T. (Essex), b Sept 8, 1916

Patiala, H.H. the Maharaja of (India), b Oct 12, 1891, d March 23, 1938

Patten, Mr. M. (Oxford Univ. and Scotland), b July 28, 1901

Patterson, Rev. J. I. (Oxford Univ. and Kent), b March 11, 1860, d Sept 22, 1943

Patterson, Mr. W. H. (Oxford Univ. and Kent), b March 11, 1859, d May 3, 1946

Patterson, Mr. W. S. (Camb. Univ. and Lancashire), b March 19, 1854, d Oct 20, 1939

Paul, A. G. (Lancashire), b July 24, 1864, d Jan 14, 1947

Pavri, Dr. M. E. (Parsees and Middlesex), b Oct 10, 1866, d April 19, 1946

Pawle, Mr. J. H. (Camb. Univ. and Essex), b May 18, 1915

Pawson, Mr. A. C. (Oxford Univ.), b Jan 5, 1882

Pawson, Mr. A. G. (Oxford Univ. and Worcestershire), b May 30, 1888

Pawson, Mr. H. A. (Kent and Oxford Univ.), b Aug 22, 1921

Payn, Mr. L. W. (South Africa), b May 6, 1915

Payne, A. (Sussex), b April 28, 1858, d July 23, 1943

Payne, Mr. A. U. (Camb. Univ. and Buckinghamshire), b Jan 28, 1903

Payne, Mr. C. A. L. (Oxford Univ. and Middlesex), b Aug 30, 1885

Payne, Mr. J. H. (Lancashire), b March 19, 1858, d Jan 24, 1942

Payne, Mr. M. W. (Camb. Univ. and Middlesex), b May 10, 1885

Paynter, E. (Lancashire), b Nov 5, 1901

Payton, Rev. W. E. G. (Camb. Univ. Nottinghamshire and Derbyshire), b Dec. 27, 1913

Payton, W. R. D. (Nottinghamshire), b Feb 13, 1882, d May 21, 1943

Peach, C. W. (Kent), b Jan 3, 1900

Peach, H. A. (Surrey and Berkshire), b Oct 6, 1890

Peake, Rev. E. (Oxford Univ., Gloucestershire and Berkshire), b March 29, 1860, d Jan 3, 1945

Pearce, G. (Sussex), b Oct 27, 1908

Pearce, Mr. T. A. (Kent), b Dec 18, 1910

Pearce, Mr. T. N. (Essex), b Nov 3, 1905

Pearse, Mr. A. (Somerset), b April 22, 1915

Pearse, Mr. G. V. (Natal and Oxford Univ.), b Sept 7, 1891

Pearse, Mr. C. O. C. (South Africa), b Oct 10, 1884, d May 28, 1953

Pearson, Mr. A. (Oxford Univ. and Scotland), b Jan 21, 1856, d Jan 24, 1931

Pearson, F. (Worcestershire), b Sept 23, 1880

Pearson-Gregory, Mr. T. S. (Middlesex and Leicestershire), b June 20, 1851, d Nov 25, 1935

Peat, Mr. C. U. (Oxford Univ. and Middlesex), b Feb 28, 1892

Peebles, Mr. I. A. R. (Oxford Univ. and Middlesex), b Jan 20, 1908

Peel, R. (Yorkshire), b Feb 12, 1857, d Aug 12, 1941

Pegler, Mr. S. J. (South Africa and Manager South African Team in England, 1951), b July 28, 1889

Pelham, Mr. A. G. (Camb. Univ., Sussex and Somerset), b Sept 4, 1911

Pelham, Rev. Canon S. (Oxford Univ. and Norfolk), b May 16, 1849, d July 14, 1926

Pellew, Mr. C. E. (South Australia), b Sept 21, 1893

Pennington, J. (Nottinghamshire), b June 24, 1881

Pepall, G. (Gloucestershire), b Feb 29, 1876, d Jan 8, 1953

Pepper, Mr. J. (Camb. Univ.), b Oct 21, 1922

Perkins, C. (Northamptonshire and Suffolk), b June 4, 1911

Perkins, Mr. T. T. N. (Camb. Univ., Essex, Kent and Wiltshire), b Dec 19, 1870, d July 20, 1946

Perks, R. T. D. (Monmouthshire and Worcestershire), b Oct 4, 1911

Perrin, Mr. P. A. (Essex), b May 26, 1876, d Nov 20, 1945

Perry, Mr. E. H. (Worcestershire), b Jan 16, 1908

Pether, Mr. S. (Oxford Univ. and Oxfordshire), b Oct 15, 1916

Pettiford, J. (New South Wales and Kent), b Nov 29, 1919

Pewtress, Mr. A. W. (Lancashire), b Aug 27, 1891

Phadkar, Mr. D. G. (India), b Dec 12, 1925

Phebey, A. H. (Kent), b Oct 1, 1924

Philipson, Mr. H. (Oxford Univ., Northumberland and Middlesex), b June 8, 1866, d Dec 4, 1935

Phillipps, Mr. J. H. (Manager New Zealand team in England, 1949), b Jan 1, 1898

Phillips, Mr. F. A. (Essex, Somerset and Oxford Univ.), b April 11, 1873, d March 5, 1955

Phillips, James (Victoria and Middlesex), b Sept 1, 1860, d April 21, 1930

Phillips, Mr. J. B. (Oxford Univ. and Kent), b Nov 19, 1933

Phillipson, W. E. (Lancashire), b Dec 3, 1910

Pierpoint, F. G. (Surrey and Norfolk), b April 24, 1915

Pierre, Mr. L. R. (West Indies), b June 5, 1921

Pilkington, Mr. C. C. (Oxford Univ., Lancashire and Middlesex), b Dec 13, 1876, d Jan 8, 1950

Pilkington, Mr. H. C. (Oxford Univ. and Middlesex), b Oct 25, 1879, d June 17, 1942

Pinch, Mr. F. B. (Glamorgan), b Feb 24, 1891

Pitchford, L.(Glamorgan),b Dec 4,1900

Piton, Mr. J. H. (Western Province, Natal and Transvaal), b April 20, 1865, d July 20, 1942

Place, W. (Lancashire), b Dec 7, 1914

Platt, G. J. W. (Surrey), b June 9, 1882, d April 14, 1955

Pleass, J. (Glamorgan), b May 21, 1923

Plimsoll, Mr. J. B. (South Africa), b Oct 27, 1917

Plumer, Field-Marshal, 1st Visct. (President, M.C.C., 1929), b March 13, 1857, d July 16, 1932

Podmore, Mr. A. (Haileybury) (Cricket Writer), b Sept 14, 1861, d Oct 17, 1937

Poidevin, Mr. L. O. S. (New South Wales, London County and Lancashire), b Nov 5, 1876, d Nov 18, 1931

Pollard, R. (Lancashire), b June 19, 1912

Ponsford, Mr. W. H. (Victoria), b Oct 19, 1900

Pontifex, Mr. D. D. (Surrey and Somerset), b Feb 12, 1855, d Sept 27, 1914

Pool, Mr. C. J. T. (Northamptonshire), b Jan 21, 1876, d Oct 13, 1954

Poole, C. J. (Nottinghamshire), b March 13, 1921

Poole, K. J. (Nottinghamshire), b April 27, 1934

Poore, Brig.-Gen. Robert M.(Wiltshire, Hampshire and South Africa), b March 20, 1866, d July 14, 1938

Pope, A. V. (Derbyshire), b Aug 15, 1909

Pope, Mr. C. G. (Camb. Univ. and Bedfordshire), b Jan 21, 1872

Pope, D. F. (Gloucestershire and Essex), b Oct 28, 1908, d Sept 8, 1934

Pope, G. H. (Derbyshire), b Jan 27, 1911

Pope, Dr. R. J. (New South Wales and M.C.C.), b Feb 18, 1864, d July 27, 1952

Popplewell, Mr. O. B. (Camb. Univ.), b Aug 15, 1927

Porch, Mr. R. B. (Somerset), b April 3, 1875

Porter, Mr. A. (Glamorgan), b March 25, 1914

Posthuma, Mr. C. J. (Holland and London County), b Jan 11, 1868, d Dec 21, 1939

Pothecary, A. E. (Hampshire), b March 1, 1906

Pothecary, S. (Hampshire), b May 6, 1890

Potter, Mr. G. (Lancashire and Cheshire), b Oct 3, 1878

Potter, G. (Sussex), b Oct 26, 1931

Potts, Mr. H. J. (Oxford Univ.), b Jan 23, 1925

Pougher, A. D. (Leicestershire), b April 19, 1865, d May 20, 1926

Powell, Mr. A. G. (Camb. Univ., Essex and Suffolk), b Aug 17, 1912

Powell, Mr. W. A. (Kent), b May 19, 1885, d Jan 1, 1954

Poynton, Dr. F. J. (Somerset), b June 26, 1869, d Oct 29, 1943

Poyntz, Mr. E. S. M. (Somerset), b Oct 27, 1883, d Dec 26, 1934

Poyntz, Col. H. S. (Somerset), b Sept 17, 1877, d June 22, 1955

Pratt, R. C. E. (Surrey), b May 5, 1928

Preece, C. R. (Worcestershire), b Dec 15, 1888

Prentice, F. T. (Leicestershire), b April 22, 1912

Pressdee, J. (Glamorgan), b June 19, 1933

Prest, Mr. H. E. W. (Camb. Univ. and Kent), b June 9, 1890, d Jan 5, 1955

Preston, Mr. Hubert (Editor of *Wisden* 1944 to 1951), b Dec 16, 1868

Preston, H. J. (Kent), b Oct 25, 1886

Preston, K. C. (Essex), b Aug 22, 1925

Pretlove, Mr. J. F. (Camb. Univ. and Kent), b Nov, 23 1932

Pretty, Dr. Harold C. (Surrey and Northamptonshire), b Oct 23, 1875, d May 31, 1952

Price, E. (Lancashire and Essex), b Oct 27, 1918

Price, Mr. V. R. (Oxford Univ. and Surrey), b May 22, 1895

Price, W. F. (Middlesex), b April 25, 1902

Priestley, Sir A. (M.C.C.), b Nov 9, 1864, d April 10, 1933

Pritchard, T. L. (New Zealand and Warwickshire), b March 10 1917

Proffitt, S. (Essex), b Oct 8, 1911

Prothero, Mr. R. E., 1st Lord Ernle (Marlborough, Hampshire and President, M.C.C., 1924), b Sept 6, 1852, d July 1, 1937

Proud, Mr. R. B. (Oxford Univ. and Hampshire and Durham), b Sept 19, 1919

Prouton, R. (Hampshire), b March 1, 1926

Pryer, Mr. B. J. K. (Camb. Univ. and Kent), b Feb 1, 1925

Pullen, Mr. W. W. F. (Gloucestershire, Somerset and Glamorgan), b June 24, 1866, d Aug 9, 1937

Pullin, Mr. A. W. (Cricket Writer under non-de-plume of ''Old Ebor''), b July 30, 1860, d June 23, 1934

Pullinger, Mr. G. R. (Essex), b March 14, 1920

Pulman, Rev. W. W. (Oxford Univ.), b Nov. 14 1852, d Aug 22, 1936

Purdy, H. (Derbyshire), b Jan 17, 1884, dead

Purdy, T. (Derbyshire), b July 3, 1864, d 1944

Putner, F. W. (Middlesex), b Sept 26, 1912

Quaife, Mr. B. W. (Warwickshire and Worcestershire), b Nov 24, 1899

Quaife, Walter (Sussex, Warwickshire and Suffolk), b April 1, 1864, d Jan 18, 1943

Quaife, W. G. (Sussex and Warwickshire), b March 17, 1872, d Oct 13, 1951

Quentin, Rev. G. A. F. (Gloucestershire), b Nov 3, 1848, d May 6, 1928

Quick, Mr. A. B. (Essex), b Feb 10, 1915

Quinn, Mr. N. A. (South Africa), b Feb 21, 1908, d Aug 5, 1934

Quinton, Brig.-Gen. F. W. D. (Hampshire), b Dec 25, 1865, d Nov 4, 1926

Quist, Mr. K. H. (New South Wales, Western Australia and South Australia), b Aug 18, 1875

Rabone, Mr. G. O. (New Zealand), b Nov 6, 1921

Radcliffe, Mr. E. J. R. H. (Yorkshire), b Jan 27, 1884

Radcliffe, George (Lancashire), b Sept 25, 1877, d Oct 27, 1951

Radcliffe, Lees (Lancashire and Durham), b Nov 23, 1871

Radcliffe, Mr. O. G. (Somerset, Gloucestershire and Wiltshire), b Oct 20, 1859, d April 13, 1940

Rae, Mr. A. F. (West Indies), b Sept 30, 1922

Rae, Mr. E. A. (West Indies), b Nov 8, 1897

Raikes, Rev. G. B. (Oxford Univ., Hampshire and Norfolk), b March 14, 1873

Raikes, Mr. T. B. (Oxford Univ. and Norfolk), b Dec 16, 1902

Rait Kerr, Col. R. S. (Rugby and R.M.A., Woolwich, Secretary, M.C.C. 1936–52, b April 13, 1891

Ralph, Mr. R. (Essex), b May 22, 1920

Ramadhin, Mr. S. (West Indies), b May 1, 1930

Ramaswami, C. (India) b June 18, 1896

Ramchand, Mr. G. S. (India), b July 26, 1927

Ramsay, Mr. R. C. (Camb. Univ. and Somerset), b Dec 20, 1861

Ranjitsinhji, Kumar Shri, afterwards H.H. The Jam Saheb of Nawanagar (India, Camb. Univ., Cambridgeshire and Sussex), b Sept 10, 1872, d April 2, 1933

Ransford, Mr. V. S. (Victoria), b March 20, 1885

Ransom, Mr. V. J. (Hampshire), b March 17, 1918

Raphael, Mr. F. C. (Hon. Sec., New Zealand Council), b Dec 29, 1866, d June, 1940

Rashleigh, Canon W. (Oxford Univ. and Kent), b March 7, 1867, d Feb 13, 1937

Ratcliffe, Mr. A. (Camb. Univ., Denbighshire, Surrey and Buckinghamshire), b March 31, 1909

Raven, Mr. R. O. (Northamptonshire), b Nov 26, 1884, d April 4, 1936

Rawlin, E. R. (Yorkshire), b Oct 4, 1899, d Jan 11. 1943

Rayment, A. W. H. (Hampshire), b May 29, 1928

Read, Mr. A. H. (Essex), b Jan 24, 1880

Read, Mr. H. D. (Surrey and Essex), b Jan 28, 1910

Read, J. Maurice (Surrey), b Feb 9, 1859, d Feb 17, 1929

Reay, Mr. G. M. (Surrey), b Jan 24, 1887

Reddick, Mr. T. B. (Middlesex and Nottinghamshire), b Feb 17, 1912

Reddish, J. (Nottinghamshire), b Dec 22, 1906

Redgrave, Mr. S. J. (New South Wales and Queensland), b Aug 5, 1878

Redman, J. (Somerset), b March 1, 1926

Rees-Davies, Mr. W. R. (Camb. Univ.), b Nov 19, 1916

Reese, Mr. D. (New Zealand and Essex), b Jan 26, 1879, d June 12, 1953

Reeves, W. (Essex), b June 22, 1876, d March 22, 1944

Reid, Mr. J. R. (New Zealand), b June 3, 1928

Relf, A. E. (Norfolk and Sussex), b June 26, 1874, d March 26, 1937

Relf, R. R. (Berkshire and Sussex), b Sept 1, 1883

Remnant, E. R. (Hampshire), b May 1, 1884

Revill, A. (Derbyshire), b March 27, 1923

Reynolds, B. L. (Northamptonshire), b June 10, 1932

Rhodes, A. E. (Derbyshire), b Oct 10, 1916

Rhodes, A. C. (Yorkshire), b Oct 14, 1906

Rhodes, Mr. S. D. (Nottinghamshire), b March 24, 1910

Rhodes, Wilfred (Yorkshire), b Oct 29, 1877

Rice, Mr. R. W. (Gloucestershire, Oxford Univ. and Bedfordshire), b Nov 14, 1868, d Feb 11, 1938

Richards, R. (Sussex), b Sept 10, 1908

Richardson, A. (Nottinghamshire), b Oct 28, 1926

Richardson, Arthur J. (South Australia and Western Australia), b July 24, 1888

Richardson, Mr. A. G. (Bedfordshire, Somerset, Gloucestershire and Orange Free State), b July 24, 1874, d Dec 17, 1934

Richardson, Mr. A. W. (Derbyshire), b June, 1907

Richardson, B. H. (Derbyshire), b March 12, 1932

Richardson, Mr. C. A. (New South Wales and Wellington, N.Z.), b Feb 22, 1864, d Aug 17, 1949

Richardson Mr. D. W. (Worcestershire), b Nov 3, 1934

Richardson, H. (Nottinghamshire) b Oct 4, 1856, d March, 1940

Richardson, Mr. H. B. (Surrey and California), b March 10, 1873

Richardson, Mr. J. V. (Oxford Univ. and Essex), b Dec 16, 1903

Richardson, Mr. P. E. (Worcestershire), b July 4, 1931

Richardson, S. (Derbyshire), b May 22, 1844, d March 1938

Richardson, T. (Surrey and Somerset), b Aug 11, 1870, d July 2, 1912

Richardson, Mr. V. Y. (South Australia), b Sept 7, 1894

Richardson, Mr. W. A. (New South Wales), b Aug 22, 1866, d Jan 3, 1930

Riches, Mr. N. V. H. (Glamorgan), b June 9, 1883

Richmond, T. L. (Nottinghamshire), b June 23, 1892

Ricketts, Mr. G. W. (Oxford Univ. and Surrey), b June 2, 1864, d June 16, 1927

Rickman, Mr. R. B. (Derbyshire), b May 6, 1881, d 1940

Riddell, Mr. V. H. (Camb. Univ.), b July 23, 1905

Riddington, A. (Leicestershire), b Dec 22, 1911

Ridgway, F. (Kent), b Aug 10, 1923

Rigg, Mr. K. E. (Victoria), b May 21, 1906

Riley, H. (Leicestershire), b Oct 3, 1903

Riley, Mr. W N. (Camb. Univ. and Leicestershire), b Nov 24, 1892, d Nov 20, 1955

Rimell, Mr. A. G. J. (Camb. Univ. and Hampshire), b Aug 29, 1928

Ring, Mr. D. (Victoria), b Oct 14, 1918

Ringrose, W. (Yorkshire and Scotland), b Sept 2, 1871, d Sept 14, 1943

Rippon, Mr. A. D. E. (Somerset), b April 29, 1892

Rippon, Mr. A. E. S. (Somerset), b April 29, 1892

Rist, F. (Essex), b March 30, 1914

Roach, Mr. C. A. (West Indies), b March 13, 1904

Roberts, Mr. A. W. (New Zealand), b Aug. 20, 1909

Roberts, Mr. A. W. (Gloucestershire), b Sept 23, 1874

Roberts, Mr. D. (M.C.C. and Surrey), b Feb 5, 1894

Roberts, F. G. (Gloucestershire), b April 1, 1862, d April 7, 1936

Roberts, H. E. (Sussex), b Feb 8, 1890

Roberts, H. J. (Warwickshire), b May 5, 1912

Roberts, W. B. (Lancashire), b Sept 27, 1914, d Aug 24, 1951

Roberts, W. C. (Hampshire), b June 15, 1861

Robertson, J. D. (Middlesex), b Feb 22, 1917

Robertson, Mr. W. P. (Camb. Univ. and Middlesex), b Sept 5, 1879, d May 7, 1950

Robertson-Glasgow, Mr. R. C. (Oxford Univ. and Somerset), b July 15, 1901

Robertson-Walker, Mr. J. (Middlesex), b Nov 19, 1850, d March 21, 1927

Robins, Mr. R. W. V. (Camb. Univ. and Middlesex), b June 3, 1906

Robinson, A. G. (Northamptonshire), b March 22, 1917

Robinson, Canon C. D. (Natal and Buckinghamshire), b July 18, 1873, d Aug 26, 1948

Robinson, Mr. C. J. (Somerset), b May 21, 1864, d June 8, 1941

Robinson Lt.-Col. D. C. (Essex and Gloucestershire), b April 20, 1883

Robinson, E. (Yorkshire), b Nov 16, 1884

Robinson, E. P. (Yorkshire and Somerset), b Aug 10, 1911

Robinson, Mr. F. G. (Gloucestershire), b Sept 19, 1880

Robinson, Mr. G. E. (Oxford Univ.), b March 13, 1861, d Nov 30, 1944

Robinson, G. W. (Nottinghamshire), b Feb 15, 1908

Robinson, Mr. H. B. (Oxford Univ.), b March 3, 1919

Robinson, Mr. J. J. (Camb. Univ.), b June 28, 1872

Robinson, Mr. M. (Glamorgan and Warwickshire), b July 16, 1921

Robinson, Mr. P. G. (Gloucestershire), b Nov 2, 1882, d Jan 30, 1951

Robinson, Sir R. L., 1st Lord Robinson (Oxford Univ.), b May 8, 1883, d Sept 5, 1952

Robinson, Mr. Theo (Somerset), b Feb. 16, 1866

Robson, Mr. C. (Middlesex and Hampshire), b June 20, 1859, d Sept 27, 1943

Rochdale, 1st Lord, C.B. (George Kemp, Cambridge, Lancashire), b June 9, 1866, d March 24, 1945

Rochford, P. (Gloucestershire), b Aug 27, 1928

Rock, Mr. C. W. (Warwickshire, Camb. Univ. and Tasmania), b June 9, 1863, d July 27, 1950

Roe, Mr. W. N. (Camb. Univ. and Somerset), b March 21, 1861, d Oct 11, 1937

Rogers, A. (Gloucestershire), b Feb 1, 1908

Rogers, Lt.-Col. F. G. (Gloucestershire), b April 7, 1897

Rogers, H. O. (Worcestershire), b Jan 21, 1891

Rogers, N. H. (Hampshire), b March 9, 1918

Rogers, Mr. S. S. (Somerset), b March 18, 1923

Roller, Mr. W. E. (Surrey), b Feb 1, 1858, d Aug 27, 1949

Romans, Mr. G. (Gloucestershire), b Nov 30, 1876, d Jan 2, 1946

Root, C. F. (Derbyshire and Worcestershire), b April 16, 1890, d Jan 20, 1954

Rosebery, 5th Earl of (Vice-President, Surrey C.C.C.), b May 7, 1847, d May 21, 1929

Rosebery, 6th Earl of (*see* Dalmeny, Lord)

Rotherham, Mr. G. A. (Camb. Univ. and Warwickshire), b May 28, 1899

Rotherham, Mr. Hugh (Warwickshire), b March 16, 1861, d Feb 24, 1939

Rought-Rought, Mr. D. C. (Camb. Univ. and Norfolk), b May 3, 1912

Rought-Rought, Mr. R. C. (Camb. Univ. and Norfolk), b Feb 17, 1908

Routledge, R. (Middlesex), b July 7, 1920

Rowan, Mr. A. M. B. (South Africa), b Feb 7 ,1921

Rowan, Mr. E. A. B. (South Africa), b July 20, 1909

Rowe, E. J. (Nottinghamshire), b July 21, 1920

Rowe, Mr. W. (Queensland), b Jan 10, 1892

Rowlands, Mr. W. H. (Gloucestershire), b July 30, 1883, d July 30, 1948

Rowley, Mr. Ernest (Lancashire), b Jan 15, 1870

Roy, Mr. P. (India), b May 31, 1928

Royle, Rev. V. P. F. A. (Oxford Univ. and Lancashire), b Jan 29, 1854, d May 21, 1929

Rucker, Mr. C. E. S. (Oxford Univ.), b Sept 4, 1894

Rucker, Capt. P. W. (Oxford Univ.), b May 5, 1900, d May 1940

Rudd, Mr. C. R. D. (Oxford Univ.), b March 25, 1929

Rudd, Mr. G. B. F. (Leicestershire), b July 3, 1894

Rudston, H. (Yorkshire), b Nov 22, 1879

Ruffell, R. (Hampshire) b Oct 3, 1869, d, 1944

Ruggles-Brise, Major-Gen. Sir H. G. (Essex and Oxford Univ.), b March 17, 1864, d June 24, 1927

Rumbold, Mr. J. S. (Oxford Univ.), b March 5, 1920

Rundell, Mr. P. D. (South Australia), b Nov 20, 1890

Rush, Mr. T. A. (Victoria), d Oct, 1926, aged 51

Rushby, T. (Surrey), b Sept 6, 1881

Rushton, F. (Lancashire), b April 21, 1906

Russell, A. C. (Essex), b Oct 7, 1887

Russell, Mr. A. I. (Hampshire), b Feb 21, 1867

Russell, T. M. (Essex), b July 6, 1868, d Feb 28, 1927

Rutter, Mr. E. (Middlesex) b Aug 3, 1842, d Feb 4, 1926

Rutty, Mr. A. W. F. (Surrey), b Aug 22, 1872, d Jan 10, 1932

Ryan, F. (Hampshire and Glamorgan), b Nov 14, 1888, d Jan 6, 1954

Ryder, Mr. J. (Victoria), b Aug 8, 1889

Ryder, Mr. R. V. (Staffordshire and Sec., Warwickshire C.C.C.), b March 11, 1873, d Sept. 1, 1949

Rye, G. J. (Norfolk and Minor Counties Umpire), b Nov 2, 1857, d Jan 6, 1943

Rylance, H. (Sec., Lancashire C.C.C. from 1921), b Sept 15, 1884, d Jan 22, 1932

Rymill, Mr. J. W. (South Australia), b March 20, 1901

Sadler, W. C. H. (Surrey and Durham), b Sept 24, 1896

Saggers, Mr. R. A. (New South Wales), b May 15. 1917

Sainsbury, Mr. E. (Somerset and Gloucestershire), b July 5, 1851, d Oct 28, 1930

Sainsbury, P. J. (Hampshire), b June 13, 1934

St. Hill, Mr. A. B. (West Indies), d Aug. 23, 1911

St. Hill, Mr. E. (West Indies), b March 9, 1904

St. Hill, Mr. W. H. (West Indies), b July 6, 1893

Salam-ud-din, K. (India), b Oct 16, 1888

Sale, Mr. R. (Oxford Univ. and Derbyshire), b June 21, 1889

Sale, Mr. R., jun. (Oxford Univ, Warwickshire and Derbyshire), b Oct 4, 1919

Salmon, Mr. G. H. (Leicestershire), b Aug. 1, 1894

Salter, Mr. M. G. (Oxford Univ. and Gloucestershire), b May 10, 1887

Samuel, Mr. G. N. T. W. (Glamorgan), b Oct 26, 1917

Sanders, W. (Warwickshire), b April 4, 1910

Sandham, A. (Surrey), b July 6, 1890

Santall, F. R. (Warwickshire), b July 12, 1903, d Nov 3, 1950

Santall, J. F. E. (Worcestershire), b Dec 3, 1907

Santall, S. (Northamptonshire and Warwickshire), b June 10, 1873

Sarel, Major W. G. M. (Surrey, Trinidad, Northumberland, Kent and Sussex, late Sec. Sussex C.C.C.), b Dec 11, 1875, d April 5, 1950

Sargent, M. A. J. (Leicestershire), b Aug 23, 1928

Sarwate, C. T. (India). b June 22, 1920

Saunders, Mr. A. A. (Sussex), b Dec 15, 1892

Saunders, Mr. D. W. (Canada), b March 22, 1862, d June 12, 1930

Saunders, Mr. J. V. (Victoria), b Feb 3, 1876, d Dec 21, 1927

Savill, L. (Essex), b June 30, 1935

Saville, Mr. S. H. (Camb. Univ. and Middlesex), b Nov 21, 1889

Scaife, Mr. J. A. (Victoria), b Nov 14, 1909

Schneider, Mr. K. J. (South Australia and Victoria), b Aug 15, 1905, d Sept 5, 1928

Schultz (afterwards Storey), Mr. S. S. (Camb. Univ. and Lancashire), b Aug 29, 1857, d Dec 18, 1937

Schwann, Mr. H. S. (later Swann) (Oxford Univ.), b Nov 19, 1868, d May 30, 1931

Scorer, Col. R. I. (Warwickshire), b Jan 6, 1892

Scott, Canon A. T. (Camb. Univ.), b July 18, 1848, d June 18, 1925

Scott, C. J. (Gloucestershire), b May 1, 1919

Scott, Capt. Lord George W. Montagu-Douglas (Oxford Univ. and Middlesex), b Aug 21, 1866, d Feb 23, 1947

Scott, Mr. J. D. (New South Wales and South Australia), b Jan 24, 1890

Scott, Major K. B. (Oxford Univ. and Sussex), b Aug 17, 1915, d Aug 9, 1943

Scott, Mr. O. C. (West Indies), b Aug 25, 1893

Scott, Mr. R. S. G. (Oxford Univ. and Sussex), b April 26, 1909

Scott, Mr. S. W. (Middlesex), b March 24, 1854, d Oct 8, 1933

Scott, Mr. V. J. (New Zealand), b July 31, 1916

Seabrook, Mr. F. J. (Camb. Univ. and Gloucestershire), b Jan 9, 1899

Sealey, Mr. B. J. (West Indies), b Aug 12, 1899

Sealy, Mr. J. E. D. (West Indies), b Sept 11, 1912

Seamer, Mr. J. W. (Somerset and Oxford Univ.), b June 23, 1913

Searle, Mr. Jas. (New South Wales), b Aug 28, 1863, d Dec 28, 1936

Seitz, Mr. J. A. (Oxford Univ. and Victoria), b Sept 19, 1883

Sellar, Lt.-Cmdr. K. A. (Royal Navy and Sussex), b Aug 11, 1906

Sellers, Mr. A. (Yorkshire), b May 30, 1870, d Sept 25, 1941

Sellers, Mr. A. B. (Yorkshire), b March 5, 1907

Sen, Mr. P. (India), b May 31, 1926

Serjeant, Sir D. M. (Victoria), b Jan 18, 1830, d Jan 12, 1929

Sesha Chari, K. (India), b Jan. 2, 1875

Sewell, Mr. C. O. H. (Natal and Gloucestershire), b Dec 19, 1874, d Aug 19, 1951

Sewell, Mr. E. H. D. (Bedfordshire, India, Essex and Buckinghamshire), b Sept 30, 1872, d Sept 20, 1947

Seymour, James (Kent), b Oct 25, 1879, d Sept 30, 1930

Seymour, John (Sussex and Northamptonshire), b Aug 24, 1883

Shackleton, D. (Hampshire), b Aug 12, 1924

Shacklock, F. (Derbyshire, Nottinghamshire and Otago), b Sept 22, 1861, d May 3, 1937

Shakespeare, Mr. W. H. N. (Worcestershire), b Aug 24, 1893

Shakoor Ahmed (Pakistan), b Sept 15, 1928

Shardlow, W. (Derbyshire), b Sept 30, 1902

Sharp, Mr. A. T. (Leicestershire), b March 23, 1889

Sharp, H. P. (Middlesex), b Oct 6, 1917

Sharp, Mr. J. (Lancashire), b Feb 15, 1878, d Jan 27, 1938

Sharp, Capt. R. H. (Essex), b June 11, 1893

Sharpe, Rev. C. M. (Camb. Univ. and Yorkshire), b Sept 6, 1851, d June 25, 1935

Sharpe, J. W. (Surrey and Nottinghamshire), b Dec 9, 1866, d June 19, 1936

Shaw, Alfred (Nottinghamshire and Sussex), b Aug 29, 1842, d Jan 16, 1907

Shaw, Rt. Rev. E. D. (Oxford Univ., Hertfordshire, Middlesex and Buckinghamshire), b Oct 5, 1860, d Nov 5, 1937

Sheffield, E. J. (Surrey and Kent), b June 20, 1908

Sheffield, J. R. (Essex), b Nov 19, 1906

Sheldrake, Mr. E. F. T. (Hampshire), b Jan 18, 1864

Shelmerdine, Mr. G. O. (Camb. Univ. and Lancashire), b Sept 7, 1899

Shelton, Mr. A. W. (Nottinghamshire C.C.C.), b Nov 14, 1862, d Sept 10, 1938

Shepherd, D. J. (Glamorgan), b Aug 8, 1927

Shepherd, T. F. (Surrey), b Dec 5, 1890

Sheppard, Rev. D. S. (Sussex and Cambridge Univ.), b March 6, 1929

Sheppard, Mr. R. A. (Surrey), b Aug 24, 1879, d Jan 28, 1953

Sherwell, Mr. N. B. (Camb. Univ. and Middlesex), b March 16, 1904

Sherwell, Mr. P. W. (Cornwall and South Africa), b Aug 17, 1880, d April 17, 1948

Shields, Mr. J. (Leicestershire), b Feb 1, 1882

Shinde, S. G. (India), b Aug 18, 1923, d June 22, 1955

Shine, Mr. E. B. (Camb. Univ. and Kent), b July 9, 1873, d Nov 11, 1952

Shipman, A. (Leicestershire), b March 7, 1901

Shipman, W. (Leicestershire), b March 1, 1886, d Aug 26, 1943

Shipston, F. W. (Nottinghamshire), b July 29, 1906

Shirley, Mr. W. R. de la C. (Camb. Univ. and Hampshire), b Oct 13, 1900

Shirreff, Mr. A. C. (Camb. Univ., Hampshire and Kent), b Feb 12, 1919

Shivram, P. (India), b March 6, 1878

Shortland, Mr. N. A. (Warwickshire), b July 16, 1916

Shrewsbury, A. (Nottinghamshire), b April 11, 1856, d May 19, 1903

Shuja-ud-Din (Pakistan), b April 10, 1930

Shuter, Mr. L. A. (Surrey), b May 15, 1852, d July 13, 1928

Shuttleworth, Mr. G. M. (Camb. Univ.), b Nov 6, 1926

Sibbles, F. M. (Lancashire), b March 15, 1904

Sidwell, T. E. (Leicestershire), b Jan 30, 1888

Siedle, Mr. I. J. (South Africa), b Jan 11, 1903

Sievers, Mr. M. W. S. (Victoria), b April 13, 1912

Silk, Mr. D. R. W. (Camb. Univ.), b Oct 8, 1931

Sime, Mr. W. A. (Bedfordshire and Nottinghamshire), b Feb 8, 1909

Simms, Mr. H. L. (Sussex and Warwickshire), b Jan 31, 1888, d June 9, 1942

Simpson, Mr. E. T. B. (Oxford Univ. and Yorkshire), b March 5, 1867, d March 20, 1944

Simpson, Mr. R. T. (Nottinghamshire), b Feb 27, 1920

Simpson-Hayward, Mr. G. H. (Worcestershire), b June 7, 1875, d Oct 2, 1936

Sims, J. M. (Middlesex), b May 13, 1904

Sinclair, Mr. E. H. L. G. (Oxford Univ.), b Sept 10, 1904

Sinclair, Mr. J. H. (South Africa), b Oct 16, 1876, d Feb 23, 1913

Sinfield, R. A. (Gloucestershire), b Dec 24, 1901

Singh, S. (Camb. Univ.), b July 18, 1931

Singleton, Mr. A. P. (Oxford Univ. and Worcestershire), b Aug 5, 1914

Skeet, Mr. C. H. L. (Oxford Univ. and Middlesex), b Aug 17, 1895

Skelding, Alec (Leicestershire), b Sept 5, 1887

Skene, Mr. R. W. (Oxford Univ.), b May 20, 1908

Skinner, Mr. A. F. (Derbyshire and Northamptonshire), b April 22, 1913

Skinner, Mr. D. A. (Derbyshire), b March 22, 1920

Skinner, I. J. (Essex), b April 1, 1928

Slack, Mr. J. K. E. (Camb. Univ.), b Dec 23, 1930

Slater, A. G. (Derbyshire), b Nov 22, 1890, d July 22, 1949

Slight, Mr. J. (Victoria), b Nov 17, 1855, d Dec 10, 1930

Smailes, T. F. (Yorkshire), b March 27, 1910

Smales, K. (Yorkshire and Nottinghamshire), b Sept 15, 1927

Small, Mr. J. A. (West Indies), b Nov 3, 1892

Smart, C. C. (Glamorgan and Warwickshire), b July 23, 1898

Smart, Jack (Warwickshire), b April 12, 1894

Smith, Mr. A. F. (Camb. Univ. and Middlesex), b May 13, 1853, d Jan 18, 1936

Smith, Mr. B. C. (Northamptonshire and First Class Umpire), b July 10, 1859, d Nov 29, 1942

Smith, Sir C. A. (Camb. Univ., Transvaal and Sussex), b July 21, 1863, d Dec 20, 1948

Smith, C. I. J. (Wiltshire and Middlesex), b Aug 25, 1906

Smith, Mr. C. J. (Middlesex), b Jan 19, 1849, d May 8, 1930

Smith, Mr. C. L. A. (Sussex), b Jan 2, 1879, d Nov 22, 1949

Smith, Mr. C. S. (Lancashire and Camb. Univ.), b Oct 1, 1932

Smith, Denis (Derbyshire), b Jan 24, 1907

Smith, Douglas (Somerset, Glamorgan and Worcestershire), b May 29, 1874, d Aug 16, 1949

Smith, Mr. D. (Victoria), b Sept 14, 1884

Smith, Mr. D. J. (Camb. Univ.), b Oct 19, 1933

Smith, D. V. (Sussex), b June 14, 192-

Smith, Mr. Ernest (Oxford Univ. and Yorkshire), b Oct 19, 1869, d April 11, 1945

Smith, E. (Derbyshire), b Jan 2, 1934

Smith, E. J. (Warwickshire), b Feb 6, 1887

Smith, Mr. F. B. (New Zealand), b March 13, 1922

Smith, F. E. (Suffolk and Surrey), b May 13, 1872, d Dec 3, 1943

Smith, Mr. G. (Kent), b Nov 30, 192-

Smith, Mr. G. O. (Oxford Univ. and Surrey), b Nov 25, 1872, d Dec 6, 1943

Smith, H. (Gloucestershire), b May 21, 1891, d Nov 12, 1937

Smith, H. A. (Leicestershire), b March 29, 1901, d Aug 7, 1948

Smith, Mr. H. E. (Transvaal), b April 21, 1884

Smith, Mr. H. T. O. (Essex), b March 5, 1906

Smith, I. W. (Worcestershire), b Oct 26, 1880

Smith, J. C. (Worcestershire), b Sept 26, 1894

Smith, K. D. (Leicestershire), b April 29, 1922

Smith, Mr. M. J. K. (Leicestershire and Oxford Univ.), b June 30, 1933

Smith, Mr. R. (Lancashire), b May 1, 1868

Smith, R. (Essex), b Aug 10, 1914

Smith, R. (Somerset), b April 14, 1930

Smith, Mr. S. (Manager, Australian Teams, 1921 and 1926), b March 1, 1880

Smith, S. (Lancashire), b Jan 14, 1929

Smith, Mr. S. G. (West Indies, Northamptonshire and New Zealand), b Jan 15, 1881

Smith, Mr. T. M. (Hampshire), b June 15, 1899

Smith, T. P. B. (Essex), b Oct 30, 1908

Smith, Mr. V. I. (South Africa), b Feb 23, 1925

Smith, Mr. W. A. (Leicestershire), b Feb 23, 1913

Smith, W. C. (Oxfordshire and Surrey), b Oct 4. 1877, d July 15, 1946

Smithson, G. A. (Yorkshire and Leicestershire), b Nov 1, 1926

Smoker, H. G. (Hampshire and Cheshire), b March 1, 1881

Snary, H. C. (Leicestershire), b Sept 22, 1898

Snedden, Mr. N. C. (New Zealand), b April 3, 1892

Snell, Mr. A. P. (Essex), b March 17, 1870, d July 26, 1937

Snooke, Mr. S. D. (South Africa), b Nov. 11, 1878

Snooke, Mr. S. J. (South Africa), b Feb 1, 1881

Snowden, Mr. A. W. (Northamptonshire), b Aug 15, 1913

Soar, T. (Hampshire and Carmarthen), b Sept 3, 1865

Sohoni, S. W. (India), b March 5, 1918

Solbé, Mr. E. P. (Kent), b May 10, 1902

Somers, 6th Lord (Worcestershire, President, M.C.C., 1936), b March 19, 1887, d July 14, 1944

Somerset, Mr. A. P. F. C. (Sussex), b Sept 28, 1889

Southerton, Mr. S. J. (Editor of *Wisden* 1934–1935), b July 7, 1874, d March 12. 1935

Spanswick. J. (Kent), b Sept 30, 1933

Spence, L. A. (Leicestershire), b Jan 14, 1932

Spencer, C. T. (Leicestershire), b Aug 18, 1931

Spencer, Mr. R. (Camb. Univ. and Northumberland), b April 14, 1861, d Aug 23, 1926

Spencer, T. W. (Kent), b Mar 22, 1914

Spens, Major-Gen. James (Hampshire), b March 30, 1853, d June 19, 1934

Sperry, J. (Leicestershire), b March 19, 1910

Spiers, Mr. F. W. (Promoter of first English Team to Australia), d May 31, 1911, aged 79

Spiller, Mr. W. (Glamorgan), b July 8, 1886

Spiro, Mr. D. G. (Camb. Univ.), b Dec 21, 1863, d Jan 16, 1935

Spofforth, Mr. F. R. (New South Wales, Victoria and Derbyshire), b Sept 9, 1853, d June 4, 1926

Spooner, Mr. A. F. (Lancashire), b May 21, 1886

Spooner, Mr. R. H. (Lancashire), b Oct 21, 1880

Spooner, R. T. (Warwickshire), b Dec 30, 1919

Spring, A. W. (Surrey), b May 17, 1881

Spring, Major T. C. (Somerset and Northumberland), b Feb 6, 1882, d March 13, 1926

Sprinks, Mr. H. S. (Hampshire), b Aug 19, 1905

Sprot, Mr. E. M. (Hampshire), b Feb 4, 1872, d Oct 8, 1945

Spry, E. (Gloucestershire), b July 31, 1881

Squires, H. S. (Surrey), b Feb 22, 1909, d Jan 24, 1950

Stacey, F. C. (Surrey), b April 27, 1878

Stainton, Mr. R. G. (Oxford Univ. and Sussex), b May 23, 1910

Stanley, Mr. H. C. (Yorkshire), b Feb 16, 1888, d May 18, 1934

Stannard, G. (Sussex), b July 9, 1894

Stanning, Mr. H. D. (Lancashire), b Nov 14, 1881 d March 5, 1946

Stanning, Mr. J. (Camb. Univ. and Lancashire), b Oct. 10, 1877, d May 19, 1929

Stanton, Mr. H. V. L. ("Wanderer" of the *Sportsman*), b Nov 10, 1859, d May, 30, 1933

Stanyforth, Major R. T. (Army, Capt. of M.C.C. in South Africa, 1927–28, and Yorkshire). b May 30, 1892

Staples, A. (Nottinghamshire), b Feb 4, 1899

Staples, S. J. (Nottinghamshire), b Sept 18, 1892, d June 4, 1950

Stapleton, J. (Nottinghamshire and Derbyshire), b Aug 8, 1880, d July 10, 1944

Starkie, S. (Northamptonshire), b April 4, 1926

Statham, J. B. (Lancashire), b June 17, 1930

Steel, Mr. A. G. (Camb. Univ. and Lancashire, President, M.C.C., 1902), b Sept 24, 1858, d June 5, 1914

Steel, Mr. D. Q. (Camb. Univ. and Lancashire), b June 19, 1856, d Dec 2, 1933

Steel, Mr. E. E. (Lancashire), b June 25, 1864, d July 14, 1941

Steel, Mr. H. B. (Lancashire), b April 9, 1862, d June 29, 1911

Steele, Mr. D. A. (Hampshire), b June 3, 1869, d March 25, 1935

Steele, Dr. D. M. (South Australia), b Aug 17, 1893

Steele, Rev. J. W. J. (Hampshire), b July 30, 1905

Steeples, A. (Derbyshire), b July 28, 1870, d Aug 14, 1945

Steeples, R. (Derbyshire and Monmouthshire), b April 30, 1873, d Aug 2, 1946

Stephens, E. J. (Gloucestershire), b March 23, 1910

Stephens, Mr. F. G. (Warwickshire), b April 26, 1889

Stephens, Mr. G. W. (Warwickshire), b April 26, 1889, d 950

Stephenson, G. F. (Lancashire), b April 24, 1853, d July, 1927

Stephenson, H. W. (Somerset), b July 18, 1920

Stephenson, Mr. J. S. (Oxford Univ. and Yorkshire), b Nov 10, 1903

Stephenson, Lt.-Col. J. W. A. (Essex and Worcestershire), b Aug 1, 1907

Stevens, Mr. G. T. S. (Oxford Univ. and Middlesex), b Jan 7, 1901

Stevenson, Mr. M. H. (Camb. Univ. and Derbyshire), b June 13, 1927

Stewart, Mr. H. C. (Kent), b Feb 28, 1868, d June 16, 1942

Stewart, M. J. (Surrey), b Sept 16, 1932

Stewart-Brown, Mr. P. H. (Oxford Univ.), b April 30, 1904

Steyn, Mr. S. S. L. (South Africa), b March 11, 1905

Stirling, Mr. W. S. (South Australia and Australian Imperial Forces Team), b March 20, 1891

Stocks, Mr. F. W. (Leicestershire and Oxford Univ.), b Dec 10, 1873, d May 21, 1929

Stocks, F. W. (Nottinghamshire), b Nov 6, 1918

Stoddart, Mr. W. B. (Lancashire), b April 27, 1871, d Jan 8, 1935

Stogdon, Mr. J. H. (Camb. Univ. and Middlesex), b April 25, 1876, d Dec 17, 1944

Stokes, Mr. F. (Kent), b July 12, 1850, d Jan 7, 1929

Stollmeyer, Mr. J. B. (West Indies), b March 11, 1921

Stollmeyer, Mr. V. H. (West Indies), b Jan 24, 1916

Stone, Mr. C. C. (Leicestershire and Oxfordshire), b June 13, 1865, d Nov 11, 1951

Stone, James (Hampshire and Glamorgan), b Nov 29, 1878, d Nov 15, 1942

Storer, H. (Derbyshire), b Feb 2, 1898

Stork, Mr. J. B. (Northamptonshire), b March 21, 1867, d Aug 26, 1944

Straw, T. (Worcestershire), b Sept 2, 1872

Streatfeild, Mr. E. C. (Camb. Univ. and Surrey), b June 16, 1870, d Aug 22, 1932

Street, A. E. (Surrey), b July 7, 1871, d Feb 18, 1951

Street, Mr. F. E. (Kent), b Feb 16, 1851, d June, 1928

Stricker, Mr. L. A. (South Africa), b May 26, 1884

Strudwick, H. (Surrey), b Jan 28, 1880

Studd, Mr. A. H. (Hampshire), b Nov 19, 1863, d Jan 26, 1919

Studd, Mr. C. T. (Camb. Univ. and Middlesex), b Dec 2, 1860, d July 16, 1931

Studd, Mr. E. J. C. (Cheltenham and M.C.C.), b Feb 13, 1849, d March 9, 1909

Studd, Mr. G. B. (Camb. Univ. and Middlesex), b Oct 20, 1859, d Feb 13, 1945

Studd, Brig.-Gen. H. W. (Middlesex and Hampshire), b Dec 26, 1870, d Aug 8, 1947

Studd, Sir J. E. K., 1st Bart. (Camb. Univ. and Middlesex, President, M.C.C., 1930), b July 26, 1858, d Jan 14, 1944

Studd, Mr. P. M. (Camb. Univ.), b Sept 15, 1916

Studd, Mr. R. A. (Camb. Univ. and Hampshire), b Dec 18, 1873, d Feb 3, 1948

Sturman, W. (Leicestershire), b Aug 29, 1883

Sturt, Mr. M. A. S. (Somerset), b Nov 11, 1876

Styler, S. W. (Worcestershire), b Aug 26, 1908

Subba Row, Mr. R. (Camb. Univ., Surrey and Northamptonshire), b Jan 29, 1932

Sugg, F. H. (Yorkshire, Derbyshire and Lancashire), b Jan 11, 1862, d May 29, 1933

Sugg, W. (Yorkshire and Derbyshire), b May 21, 1860, d May 21, 1933

Sullivan, D. (Surrey and Glamorgan), b Jan 28, 1887

Summers, D. W. L. (Worcestershire), b Oct 12, 1911

Summers, F. T. (Worcestershire), b Jan 25, 1887

Sunnucks, P. R. (Kent), b June 22, 1916

Surridge, Mr. W. S. (Surrey), b Sept 3, 1917

Susskind, Mr. M. J. (Middlesex and South Africa), b June 8, 1891

Sutcliffe, Mr. B. (New Zealand), b Nov 17, 1923

Sutcliffe, H. (Yorkshire), b Nov 24, 1894

Sutcliffe, Mr. W. H. H. (Yorkshire), b Oct 10, 1926

Sutherland, T. (Hampshire), b Feb 17, 1880

Sutthery, Mr. A. M. (Camb. Univ. and Devon), b March 25, 1864, d May 15, 1937

Suttle, K. G. (Sussex), b Aug 25, 1928

Sutton, Mr. M. A. (Oxford Univ.), b March 29, 1921

Swalwell, Major R. S. (Worcestershire), b June 25, 1873, d Sept 20, 1930

Swan, Mr. H. D. (President, Essex C.C.), b July 28, 1879, d Dec 21, 1941

Swetman, R. (Surrey), b Oct 25, 1933

Swift, Mr. J. S. (Victoria), d Feb 28, 1926, aged 74

Symington, Mr. S. J. (Leicestershire), b Sept 16, 1926

Symonds, Mr. H. G. (Glamorgan), b June 24, 1889, d Jan 1, 1945

Tabart, Mr. T. A. (Tasmania), b Aug 10, 1879

Taberer, Mr. H. M. (Essex and South Africa), b Oct. 7, 1870, d June, 1932

Tabor, Mr. A. S. (Camb. Univ. and Middlesex), b Nov 9, 1852, d Oct 14, 1927

Tait, Mr. J. R. (Glamorgan), b Nov 20, 1886, d April 13, 1945

Talbot, Mr. R. O. (New Zealand), b Nov 26, 1904

Tallon, Mr. D. (Queensland), b Feb 17, 1916

Tancred, Mr. L. J. (South Africa), b Oct 7, 1876, d July 30, 1934

Tanner, Mr. A. R. (Middlesex), b Dec 25, 1889

Tapscott, Mr. G. L. (South Africa), b Nov 7, 1889, d Dec 13, 1940

Tapscott, Mr. L. E. (Griqualand West), b March 18, 1894, d July 7, 1934

Tarbox, C. V. (Worcestershire and Hertfordshire), b July 2, 1893

Tarrant, F. A. (Victoria and Middlesex), b Dec 11, 1881, d Jan 29, 1951

Tasker, Mr. J. (Yorkshire), b Feb 4, 1887

Tate, C. F. (Derbyshire and Warwickshire), b May 1, 1908

Tate, E. (Hampshire), b Aug 30, 1877, d Jan 4, 1953

Tate, F. W. (Sussex), b July 24, 1867, d Feb 24, 1943

Tate, M. W. (Sussex), b April 29, 1895

Tattersall, R. (Lancashire), b Aug 17, 1922

Tayfield, Mr. H. J. (South Africa), b Jan 30, 1929

Taylor, B. (Essex), b June 19, 1932

Taylor, B. (Nottinghamshire), b June 16, 1875

Taylor, Mr. C. H. (Oxford Univ., Leicestershire and Buckinghamshire), b Feb 6, 1904

Taylor, Mr. D. (Natal), b Sept 22, 1852, d Oct. 1927

Taylor, D. (Warwickshire), b 1918

Taylor, Don. (Warwickshire), b March 2, 1923

Taylor, Mr. E. J. (Gloucestershire), b Dec 31, 1854, d Dec 25, 1936

Taylor, Mr. Frank (Gloucestershire and Lancashire), b May 4, 1855, d Aug 16, 1936

Taylor, Mr. F. H. (Derbyshire), b June 14, 1890

Taylor, Mr. G. R. (Hampshire), b Nov 25, 1912

Taylor, H. (Kent), b April 5, 1908

Taylor, Mr. H. W. (South Africa), b May 5, 1889

Taylor, Mr. J. M. (New South Wales), b Oct 10, 1895

Taylor, K. A. (Warwickshire), b Sept 29, 1916

Taylor, M. L. (Lancashire and Dorset), b July 16, 1904

Taylor, Mr. R. A. (Nottinghamshire), b March 25, 1909

Taylor, R. M. (Essex), b Nov 30, 1909

Taylor, Mr. T. L. (Camb. Univ. and Yorkshire), b May 25, 1878

Taylor, Mr. W. H. (Worcestershire), b June 23, 1885

Taylor, Mr. W. T. (Derbyshire, Secretary, Derbyshire C.C.), b April 14, 1885

Teape, Mr. C. A. (Middlesex), b 1844, d Aug 1, 1925

Tebay, H. (Sussex), b Oct 5, 1866

Teece, Mr. R. (Sydney Univ. and N.S.W.C.A.). b April 27, 1847, d Dec 13, 1928

Teesdale, Mr. H. (Oxford Univ. and Surrey), b Feb 12, 1886

Tennyson, 3rd Lord (Hon. L. H.) (Hampshire), b Nov 7, 1889, d June 6, 1951

Thesiger, Hon. F. J. N. (1st Visct. Chelmsford) (Oxford Univ. and Middlesex, President, M.C.C., 1922), b Aug 12, 1868, d April 1, 1933

Thomas, A. E. (Northamptonshire), b June 7. 1893

Thomas, Mr. P. F. ("Hippo") (Cricket Writer), b May 27, 1866, d Oct 13, 1931

Thomas, R. (Lancashire), b July 15, 1871

Thompson, A. (Middlesex), b April 17, 1916

Thompson, Mr. A. R. (Northamptonshire), b Dec 1, 1876, d Feb 1951

Thompson, E. C. (Essex), b Feb 27, 1907

Thompson, Mr. F. C. (Queensland), b Aug 1, 1890

Thompson, G. J. (Northamptonshire), b Oct 27, 1877, d March 3, 1943

Thompson, H. (Surrey), b Dec 6, 1870

Thompson, Mr. H. (Leicestershire), b May 14, 1886, d Aug 8, 1941

Thompson, Mr. J. R. (Camb. Univ. and Warwickshire), b May 10, 1918

Thompson, R. G. (Warwickshire), b Sept 26, 1932

Thomson, N. I. (Sussex), b Jan 23, 1930

Thornton, Mr. A. J. (Sussex and Kent), b Jan 16, 1856, d June 14, 1931

Thornton, Mr. C. I. (Camb. Univ., Kent and Middlesex), b March 20, 1850, d Dec 10, 1929

Thornton, Dr. G. (Yorkshire, Middlesex and South Africa), b Dec 24, 1867, d Jan 31, 1939

Thorp, P. (Worcestershire), b May 6, 1911

Thorpe, Mr. C. (Northamptonshire), b Aug 11, 1882, d May 5, 1953

Thursting, L. D. (Leicestershire), b Sept 9, 1916

Tillard, Mr. C. (Camb. Univ., Surrey and Norfolk), b April 18, 1851, d March 7, 1944

Timms, J. E. (Northamptonshire), b Nov 3, 1907

Timms, Mr. W. W. (Northamptonshire), b Sept 28, 1902

Tindall, Mr. E. (New South Wales), b March 31, 1851, d Jan 15, 1926

Tindall, Mr. M. (Camb. Univ. and Middlesex), b March 31, 1914

Tindall, Capt. R. G. (Oxford Univ. and Dorset), b Feb 20, 1912, d Jan 29, 1942

Tindill, Mr. E. W. (New Zealand), b Dec 18, 1910

Tinsley, A. (Yorkshire, Lancashire and Staffordshire), b March 12, 1867, d 1933

Tinsley, H. J. (Yorkshire and Lancashire), b Feb 20, 1865

Titchmarsh, Mr. C. H. (Herts and M.C.C.), b Feb 18, 1881, d May 23, 1930

Titmus, F. J. (Middlesex), b Nov 24, 1932

Todd, L. J. (Kent), b June 19, 1907

Tomlinson, Mr. D. S. (South Africa), b Sept 4, 1910

Tomlinson, Mr. W. J. V. (Camb. Univ. and Derbyshire), b Aug 10, 1901

Tompkin, M. (Leicestershire), b Feb 17, 1919

Toone, Sir F. C. (Sec., Yorkshire C.C.C. 1903 to 1930, Sec., Leicestershire 1897 to 1902), b June 25, 1868, d June 10, 1930

Toppin, Mr. C. (Camb. Univ., Cumberland and Worcestershire), b Aug 9, 1864, d June 8, 1928

Toppin, Mr. C. G. (Worcestershire), b April 17, 1906

Tordoff, Mr. G. G. (Camb. Univ. and Somerset), b Dec 6, 1929

Toshack, Mr. E. R. H. (New South Wales), b Dec 15, 1917

Towell, Mr. E. F. (Northamptonshire), b July 5, 1901

Towler, W. (Yorkshire), b Nov 12, 186?

Townsend, A. F. (Derbyshire), b March 29, 1912

Townsend, A. (Warwickshire), b Aug 26, 1921

Townsend, Mr. A. F. M. (Gloucestershire and Essex), b Aug 1, 1885, d 1950

Townsend, Mr. C. L. (Gloucestershire), b Nov 7, 1876

Townsend, Mr. D. C. H. (Oxford Univ. and Durham), b April 20, 1912

Townsend, L. F. (Derbyshire and Northumberland), b June 8, 1903

Trapnell, Mr. B. M. W. (Camb. Univ. and Middlesex), b May 18, 1924

Trask, Mr. W. (Somerset), b July 15, 1859, d June 24, 1949

Travers, Mr. B. H. (Oxford Univ. and Oxfordshire), b July 7, 1919

Treglown, Mr. C. J. H. (Essex), b Feb 13, 1893

Tremlett, M. F. (Somerset), b July 5, 1923

Tremlin, B. (Essex), b Sept 18, 1877, d April 12, 1936

Trestrail, Mr. K. B. (West Indies), b Nov 26, 1927

Tribe, G. E. (Victoria and Northants), b Oct 4, 1920

Troughton, Lt.-Col. L. H. W. (Kent), b May 17, 1879, d Aug 31, 1933

Troup, Mr. W. (Gloucestershire), b Oct 16, 1869, d Jan 1941

Trueman, F. S. (Yorkshire), b Feb 6, 1931

Trumble, Mr. Hugh (Victoria), b May 12, 1867, d Aug 14, 1938

Trumble, Mr. J. W. (Victoria), b Sept 16, 1863, d Aug 17, 1944

Trumper, Mr. V. T. (New South Wales), b Nov 2, 1877, d June 28, 1915

Tuckett, Mr. L. (South Africa), b Feb 2, 1919

Tufnell, Mr. N. C. (Camb. Univ. and Surrey), b June 13, 1887, d Aug 3, 1951

Tufton, Hon. J. S. R., 2nd Lord Hothfield (Kent), b Nov 8, 1873, d Dec 21, 1952

Tuke, Dr. C. M. (Middlesex), b May 23, 1857, d Jan 24, 1925

Tumilty, Mr. L. R. (Tasmania), b June 12, 1884

Tunnicliffe, John (Yorkshire), b Aug 26, 1866, d July 11, 1948

Tuppin, A. G. (Sussex), b Dec 17, 1911

Turnbull, Major M. J. (Camb. Univ. and Glamorgan), b March 16, 1906, d Aug 5, 1944

Turner, A. (Yorkshire), b Sept 2, 1885, d Aug 29, 1951

Turner, Brig.-Gen. Arthur Jervois (Essex), b July 10, 1878, d Sept 8, 1952

Turner, C. (Yorkshire), b Jan 11, 1902

Turner, Mr. C. T. B. (New South Wales), b Nov 16, 1862, d Jan 1, 1944

Turner, Mr. N. V. C. (Nottinghamshire), b May 12, 1887, d June 13, 1941

Turner, R. E. (Worcestershire), b May 4, 1888

Turner, Mr. R. H. T. (Nottinghamshire), b Oct. 26, 1888 d Sept 13, 1947

Turner, Lt.-Col. W. M. F. (Essex), b April 4, 1881, d Feb 1, 1948

Twining, Mr. R. H. (Oxford Univ. and Middlesex), b Nov 3, 1889

Tyldesley, E. (Lancashire), b Feb 5, 1889

Tyldesley, Harry (Lancashire), b 1893, d Aug 30, 1935

Tyldesley, Jas. D. (Lancashire), b Aug 10, 1889, d Jan 31, 1923

Tyldesley, J. T. (Lancashire), b Nov 22, 1873, d Nov 27, 1930

Tyldesley, Richard Knowles (Lancashire), b March 11, 1898, d Sept 17, 1943

Tylecote, Mr. E. F. S. (Oxford Univ., Bedfordshire and Kent), b June 23, 1849, d March 15, 1938

Tylecote, Mr. H. G. (Oxford Univ., Bedfordshire and Hertfordshire), b July 24, 1853, d March 8, 1935

Tyler, Mr. C. (Gloucestershire), b Jan 26, 1911

Tyler, Mr. C. H. (Northamptonshire), b Sept 13, 1887

Tyson, C. (Yorkshire), b Jan 24, 1889, d April 4, 1940

Tyson, F. H. (Northamptonshire), b June 6, 1930

Udal, Mr. N. R. (Oxford Univ., Dorset and Devon), b Oct 16, 1883

Ufton, D. G. (Kent), b May 31, 1928

Ullswater, 1st Viscount (President M.C.C., 1923), b April 1, 1855, d March 27, 1949

Umrigar, Mr. P. R. (India), b March 28, 1926

Unwin, Mr. F. St. G. (Essex), b April 23, 1911

Upham, Mr. E. F. (New Zealand), b March 22, 1873, d Oct 23, 1935

Urquhart, Mr. J. R. (Camb. Univ. and Essex), b May 29, 1921

Utley, Pilot-Officer R. T. H. (R.A.F. and Hampshire), b Feb 11, 1906

Valentine, Mr A. L. (West Indies), b April 28, 1930

Valentine, Mr. B. H. (Camb. Univ. and Kent), b Jan 17, 1908

Valentine, V. A. (West Indies), b April 4, 1908

Van der Bijl, Mr. P. G. (Oxford Univ. and South Africa), b Oct 21, 1907

Van der Merwe, Mr. E. A. (South Africa), b Nov 9, 1904

Van Ryneveld, Mr. C. B. (Oxford Univ. and South Africa), b March 19, 1928

Vann, Mr. D. W. A. (Northamptonshire), b Nov 21, 1916

Vassall, Mr. G. C. (Somerset), b April 5, 1876, d Sept 19, 1941

Vaulkhard, Mr. P. (Nottinghamshire, Northumberland and Derbyshire), b Sept 15, 1911

Venn, W. H. (Warwickshire), b July 4, 1892, d Nov 23, 1953

HH

Vere Hodge, Mr. N. (Essex), b Oct 31, 1912

Verity, Capt. Hedley (Yorkshire), b May 18, 1905, d July 31, 1943

Vials, Mr. G. A. T. (Northamptonshire), b March 18, 1887

Vidler, Mr. J. L. S. (Oxford Univ., Sussex and Oxfordshire), b March 30, 1890

Vigar, F. H. (Essex), b July 7, 1917

Vigar, H. E. (Surrey), b Nov 29, 1883

Viljoen, Mr. K. G. (South Africa, Manager South Africa in England, 1955), b May 14, 1910

Vincent, Mr. C. L. (South Africa), b Feb 16, 1902

Vincent, Mr. H. G. (Camb. Univ.), b Nov 13, 1891

Vincett, J. H. (Sussex and Surrey), b May 24 1883

Vine, J. (Sussex), b May 15, 1875, d April 25, 1946

Vivian, Mr. H. G. (New Zealand), b Nov 4, 1912

Vizard, Mr. W. O. (Gloucestershire), b Nov 16, 1861, d Jan 10, 1929

Vizianagram, Maharaj Kumar, Sir Vijaya of (India), b Dec 28, 1905

Voce, W. (Nottinghamshire), b Aug 8, 1909

Vogler, A. E. E. (South Africa), b Nov 28, 1876, d Aug 10, 1946

Waddington, A. (Yorkshire), b Feb 4, 1893

Waddy, Rev. E. F. (New South Wales and Warwickshire), b Oct 5, 1880

Waddy, Mr. E. L. (New South Wales), b Dec 3, 1878

Waddy, Canon P. S. (New South Wales and Oxford Univ.), b Jan 8, 1875, d Feb 8, 1937

Wade, Mr. H. F. (South Africa), b Sept 14, 1905

Wade, S. (Yorkshire), b Feb 8, 1858, d Nov 5, 1931

Wade, T. H. (Essex), b Nov 24, 1911

Wade, Mr. W. W. (South Africa), b June 18, 1914

Wainwright, W. (Yorkshire), b Jan 9, 1882

Wait, Mr. O. J. (Camb. Univ. and Surrey), b Aug 2, 1926

Waite, Mr. J. H. B. (South Africa), b Jan 19, 1930

Waite, Mr. M. G. (South Australia), b Jan 7, 1911

Walcott, Mr. C. L. (West Indies), b Jan 17, 1926

Walden, F. (Northamptonshire), b March 1, 1888, d May 3, 1949

Waldock, Mr. F. A. (Oxford Univ. and Somerset), b March 16, 1898

Walford, Mr. M. M. (Oxford Univ., Durham and Somerset), b Nov 27, 1915

Walker, Mr. Ashley (Camb. Univ. and Yorkshire), b June 22, 1844, d May 26, 1927

Walker, C. (Yorkshire and Hampshire), b June 27, 1920

Walker, F/O C. W. (South Australia), b Feb 19, 1909, d Dec 21 1942

Walker, Flt.-Lt. D. F. (Oxford Univ. and Norfolk), b May 31, 1913, d Feb 6, 1942

Walker, Flt.-Lt. D. F. (Hampshire), b Aug 15, 1912, d June 18, 1941

Walker, G. A. (Nottinghamshire), b Jan 25, 1919

Walker, Mr. J. G. (Oxford Univ. and Middlesex), b Oct 9, 1859, d March 24, 1923

Walker, Mr. L. (Surrey), b June 13, 1879, d Oct 10, 1940

Walker, Mr. R. D. (Oxford Univ. and Middlesex), b Feb 13, 1842, d March 29, 1922

Walker, T. (Yorkshire), b April 3, 1854, d Aug 29, 1925

Walker, Willis (Nottinghamshire), b Nov 24, 1894

Wall, Mr. T. W. (South Australia), b May 13, 1904

Wallace, Col. N. W. (Hampshire and Gloucestershire), b April 20, 1839, d July 31, 1931

Wallace, Mr. W. M. (New Zealand), b Dec 19, 1916

Wallach, B. (Transvaal), b Sept 28, 1873, d May 25, 1935

Wallington, Sir E. W. (Oxford Univ. and Wiltshire), b Dec 7, 1854, d Dec 12, 1933

Wallroth, Mr. C. A. (Oxford Univ., Kent and Derbyshire), b May 17, 1851, d Feb 22, 1926

Walsh, J. E. (Leicestershire) b Dec 4, 1912

Walshe, Mr. A. P. (Oxford Univ.), b Jan 1, 1934

Walters, Mr. C. F. (Glamorgan and Worcestershire), b Aug 28, 1905

Walton, Mr. A. C. (Oxford Univ.), b Sept 26, 1933

Walton, Mr. H. (Yorkshire), b May 21, 1868

Waqar Hassan (Pakistan), b Sept 12, 1932

Ward, A. (Yorkshire and Lancashire), b Nov 21, 1865, d Jan 6, 1939

Ward, Rev. C. G. (Hampshire, Lincolnshire and Hertfordshire), b Sept 23, 1875, d June 27, 1954

Ward, D. J. (Glamorgan), b Aug 30, 1934

Ward, Rev. E. E. Harrison (Camb. Univ. and Suffolk), b July 16. 1847, d March 25, 1940

Ward, F. (Lancashire), b Jan 9, 1865

Ward, Mr. F. A. (South Australia), b Feb 23, 1909

Ward, Mr. H. P. (Oxford Univ.), b Jan 20, 1899, d Dec 16, 1946

Ward, Mr. T. A. (South Africa), b Aug 2, 1887, d Feb 16, 1936

Ward, W. (Warwickshire), b May 24, 1874

Wardall, T. (Yorkshire), b April 19, 1863, d Dec 20, 1932

Warden, Mr. J. S. (India), b Jan 13, 1885, d Jan 16, 1928

Wardle, J. H. (Yorkshire), b Jan 8, 1923

Warne, F. (Victoria and Worcestershire), b Oct 3, 1908

Warner, Sir Pelham F. (Oxford Univ. and Middlesex), b in West Indies, Oct 2, 1873

Warr, Mr. J. J. (Camb. Univ. and Middlesex), b July 16, 1927

Warren, A. R. (Derbyshire), b April 2, 1875, d Sept 3, 1951

Washbrook, C. (Lancashire), b Dec 6, 1914

Washington, I. (Yorkshire), b Dec 11, 1879, d Oct 20, 1927

Wass, T. (Nottinghamshire), b Dec 26, 1873, d Oct 27, 1953

Waterman, Mr. A. G. (Essex), b May 13, 1911

Waters, Mr. A. E. (Gloucestershire), b May 8, 1902

Wathen, Mr. A. C. (Kent), b March 27, 1841, d March 14, 1937

Watkin, D. (Nottinghamshire), b June 28, 1914

Watkins, A. J. (Glamorgan), b April 21, 1922

Watkins, B. T. L. (Gloucestershire), b June 25, 1907

Watson, Lt.-Col. A. C. (Essex and Sussex), b March 17, 1884, d Jan 16, 1952

Watson, Mr. A. K. (Oxford Univ., Middlesex, Suffolk and Norfolk), b March 23, 1867, d Jan 2, 1947

Watson, Mr. A. L. (Hampshire), b Aug 27, 1866

Watson, F. (Lancashire), b Sept 17, 1899

Watson, G. S. (Leicestershire and Kent), b April 10, 1909

Watson, H. (Yorkshire), b Sept 26, 1884

Watson, Mr. H. D. (Oxford Univ.), b Dec 31, 1869, d Oct 9, 1947

Watson, W. (Yorkshire), b March 7, 1920

Watt, A. E. (Kent), b June 19, 1907

Watt, Mr. K. E. (Tasmania), b Dec 12, 1891

Watts, E. A. (Surrey), b Aug 1, 1911

Watts, G. (Surrey and Cambridgeshire), b Feb 18, 1867, d April 22, 1949

Watts, Mr. H. E. (Somerset and Camb. Univ.), b March 4, 1922

Wauchope, Mr. A. R. Don (Scotland), b April 29, 1861, d Jan 16, 1948

Wazir Ali, S. (India), b Sept 15, 1903, d June 17, 1950

Wazir Mohammad (Pakistan), b Dec 12, 1929

Webb, A. (Hampshire), b Aug 6, 1869

Webb, R. T. (Sussex), b July 11, 1922

Webbe, Mr. A. J. (Oxford Univ. and Middlesex), b Jan 16, 1855, d Feb 19, 1941

Webster, Mr. H. (South Australia), b Feb 17, 1889, d Oct 7, 1949

Webster, Mr. J. (Camb. Univ. and Northamptonshire), b Oct 28, 1917

Webster, Mr. W. H. (Camb. Univ. and Middlesex), b Feb 22, 1910

Wedel, Mr. G. A. (Gloucestershire), b May 18, 1900

Weekes, Mr. E. (West Indies), b Feb 26 1925

Weekes, Mr. K. H. (West Indies), b Jan 24, 1912

Weeks, R. T. (Warwickshire), b April 30, 1930

Weigall, Mr. G. J. V. (Camb. Univ. and Kent), b Oct 19, 1870, d May 17, 1944

Weir, Mr. G. L. (New Zealand), b June 2, 1908

Welch, T. B. G. (Northamptonshire), b July 31, 1906

Welford, J. W. (Warwickshire), b March 27, 1869, d Jan 17, 1945

Wellard, A. W. (Somerset), b April 8, 1903

Welldon, Mr. J. T. (Essex and Kent), b Aug 3, 1847, d Feb 6, 1927

Wellings, Mr. E. M. (Oxford Univ. and Surrey), b April 6, 1909

Wells, B. D. (Gloucestershire), b July 27, 1930

Wells, Mr. C. M. (Camb. Univ., Surrey and Middlesex), b March 21, 1871

Wells, Mr. L. S. (Middlesex), b Feb 3, 1870, d April 26, 1928

Wells, Mr. T. U. (Cambridge Univ. and Sussex), b Feb 6, 1927

Wells, W. (Northamptonshire), b Mar 14, 1881, d March 18, 1939

Welman, Mr. F. T. (Somerset and Middlesex), b Feb 19, 1849, d Dec 30, 1931

Wensley, A. F. (Sussex), b May 24, 1898

West, W. A. J. (Northamptonshire and Warwickshire, Umpire), b Nov 17, 1862, d Feb 22, 1938

Westcott, A. H. (Somerset), b Nov 6, 1870

Weston, Mr. H. W. (Middlesex), b Jan 2, 1888, d 1914

Wetherall, Mr. C. R. (Northamptonshire), b Aug 24, 1878, d April 22, 1955

Wharmby, G. E. (Nottinghamshire, Lancashire and Bedfordshire), b Dec 7, 1870, d 1951

Wharton, A. (Lancashire), b April 30, 1923

Whately, Mr. E. G. (Somerset and Hertfordshire), b July 27, 1882

Wheat, A. B. (Nottinghamshire), b May 13, 1898

Wheatley, Mr. G. A. (Oxford Univ. and Surrey), b May 28, 1923

Whitby, Mr. H. O. (Oxford Univ. and Warwickshire), b April 12, 1864, d Oct 14, 1934

Whitcombe, Mr. P. A. (Oxford Univ. and Middlesex), b April 23, 1923

Whitcombe, Mr. P. J. (Oxford Univ. and Worcestershire), b Nov 11, 1928

White, Mr. A. F. T. (Camb. Univ., Warwickshire and Worcestershire), b Sept 5, 1915

White, Mr. A. H. (Camb. Univ.), b Oct 18, 1901

White, Sir A. W., 4th Bart. (Yorkshire), b Oct 11, 1877, d Dec 16, 1945

White, Mr. E. S. (New South Wales), b April 17, 1913

White, Rev. H. (Northumberland and Oxford Univ.), b June 16, 1876

White, Mr. J. C. (Somerset), b Feb 19, 1891

White, M. E. (Worcestershire), b Jan 21, 1908

White, Brig.-Gen. W. N. (Hampshire), b Sept 10, 1879, d Dec 27, 1951

Whitehead, H. (Leicestershire), b Sept 19, 1875, d Sept 16, 1944

Whitehead, J. P. (Yorkshire and Worcestershire), b Sept 3, 1925

Whitehead, Ralph (Lancashire), b Oct 16, 1883

Whiteside, J. P. (Lancashire and Leicestershire), b June 11, 1861, d March 8, 1946

Whitfield, E. W. (Surrey and Northamptonshire), b May 31, 1911

Whiting, Mr. A. O. (Oxford Univ.), b April 23, 1861, d Jan 23, 1931

Whiting, C. P. (Yorkshire), b April 19, 1890

Whiting, N. H. (Worcestershire), b Oct 2, 1920

Whitington, Mr. R. S. (Adelaide Univ. and South Australia), b June 30, 1912

Whittaker, G. J. (Surrey), b May 29, 1916

Whitting, Mr. E. J. (Somerset), b Sept 1, 1872, d March 8, 1938

Whittington, Mr. T. A. L. (Glamorgan), b July 29, 1881, d July 19, 1944

Whittle, A. E. (Warwickshire and Somerset), b Sept 16, 1877, dead

Whitty, Mr. W. J. (South Australia), b Aug 15, 1886

Whitwell, Mr. J. F. (Yorkshire and Durham), b Feb 22, 1869, d Nov 6, 1932

Whitwell, Mr. W. F. (Yorkshire and Durham), b Dec 12, 1867, d April 12, 1942

Whysall, W. W. (Nottinghamshire), b Oct 31, 1887, d Nov 11, 1930

Wickham, Preb. A. P. (Oxford Univ., Norfolk and Somerset), b Nov 9, 1855, d Oct 13, 1935

Wigginton, S. H. (Leicestershire), b March 26, 1909

Wight, Mr. C. V. (West Indies), b July 28, 1902

Wight, Mr. O. S. (West Indies), b Aug 10, 1906

Wight, P. B. (Somerset), b June 25, 1930

Wilcox, Mr. A. G. S. (Gloucestershire), b July 7, 1920

Wilcox, Mr. D. R. (Camb. Univ. and Essex), b June 4, 1910, d Feb 6, 1953

Wild, Mr. J. (Northamptonshire), b Feb 24, 1935

Wild, Mr. J. V. (Camb. Univ.), b April 26, 1915

Wiles, Mr. C. A. (West Indies), b Aug 11, 1892

Wiley, Mr. W. G. A. (Oxford Univ.), b Nov 7, 1931

Wilkinson, Mr. C. T. A. (London County and Surrey), b Oct 4, 1884

Wilkinson, F. (Yorkshire), b May 23, 1914

Wilkinson, Mr. H. (Yorkshire), b Dec 11, 1877

Wilkinson, John (Gloucestershire), b July 16, 1876, d 1948

Wilkinson, L. L. (Lancashire), b Nov 5, 1916

Wilkinson, W. (Nottinghamshire), b July 5, 1869

Wilkinson, Major W. A. C. (Oxford Univ.), b Dec 6, 1892

Wilkinson, W. H. (Yorkshire), b March 12, 1881

Willatt, Mr. G. L. (Camb. Univ., Nottinghamshire and Derbyshire), b May 7, 1918

Williams, Mr. A. B. (New Zealand), b Jan 6, 1870, d Aug 20, 1929

Williams, Mr. C. B. (West Indies), b March 8, 1926

Williams, Mr. C. C. P. (Oxford Univ. and Essex), b Feb 9, 1933

Williams, Mr. E. A. V. (West Indies), b April 10, 1914

Williams, Mr. Leo (Sussex), b May 15, 1900

Williams, Sir P. F. C., 2nd Bart. (Gloucestershire), b July 6, 1884

Williams, Mr. P. V. (Sussex), b July 10, 1897

Williams, Mr. R. A. (Oxford Univ., Oxfordshire and Berkshire), b Feb 2, 1879

Williams, Mr. R. H. (Worcestershire), b April 23, 1901

Williams, Mr. R. J. (South Africa), b April 12, 1912

Williams, Mr. W. (Middlesex), b April 12, 1861, d April 14, 1951

Willingdon, 1st Marquis of (*see* Freeman-Thomas), d Aug 12, 1941

Willis, Mr. C. B. (Victoria and Australian Imperial Forces Team), b March 23, 1893, d May 12, 1930

Willis, Mr. H. (Surrey), b March 17, 1841, d Sept 29, 1926

Willoughby, F. G. (Hampshire), b April 25, 1862

Wilmot, K. (Warwickshire), b April 3, 1911

Wilmot, W. (Derbyshire), b Dec 25, 1872

Wilson, A. (Lancashire), b April 24, 1921

Wilson, A. E. (Gloucestershire), b May 5, 1912

Wilson, B. B. (Yorkshire), b Dec 11, 1879

Wilson, Bishop C. (Kent), b Sept 9, 1860, d Jan 20, 1941

Wilson, Major C. (Somerset), b Aug 31, 1850, d Feb, 1927

Wilson, Prebendary C. E. M. (Camb. Univ. and Yorkshire), b May 15, 1875, d Feb 8, 1944

Wilson, Mr. C. P. (Camb. Univ. and Norfolk), b May 12, 1859, d March 9, 1938

Wilson, E. F. (Surrey), b June 24, 1907

Wilson, Mr. E. R. (Camb. Univ. and Yorkshire), b March 25, 1879

Wilson, Mr. F. B. (Camb. Univ.), b Sept 21, 1881, d Jan 19, 1932

Wilson, Mr. G. (Camb. Univ. and Yorkshire), b Aug 21, 1895

Wilson, Mr. G. (Worcestershire), b April 9, 1932

Wilson, Mr. G. A. (Yorkshire), b Feb 2, 1916

Wilson, G. A. (Worcestershire), b April 5, 1877

Wilson, Mr. H. L. (Suffolk and Sussex), b June 27, 1881, d March 14, 1937

Wilson, Mr. John (Yorkshire), b June 20, 1858, d Nov 13, 1931

Wilson, Mr. J. P. (Yorkshire), b April 3, 1889

Wilson, J. V. (Yorkshire), b Jan 17, 1921

Wilson, Mr. Leslie (Kent), b March 16, 1859, d April 15, 1944

Wilson, Canon R. A. (Rugby and M.C.C.; senior brother of C. E. M. and E. R.), b July 18, 1868

Wilson, R. C. (Kent), b Feb 18, 1928

Wilson, Mr. T. S. B. (Oxford Univ.), b Aug 15, 1870, d May 19, 1941

Winlaw, Sqdn.-Ldr. R. de W. K. (Camb. Univ., Bedfordshire and Surrey), b March 28, 1912, d Oct 31, 1942

Winn, Mr. C. E. (Oxford Univ. and Sussex), b Nov 13, 1926

Winning, Mr. C. S. (Australian Imperial Forces Team), b July 17, 1889

Winrow, H. (Nottinghamshire), b Jan 17, 1916

Winrow, R. (Nottinghamshire), b Dec 30, 1910

Winslow, Mr. P. L. (South Africa), b May 21, 1929

Winter, Rev. A. H. (Camb. Univ. and Middlesex), b Dec 4, 1844, d Dec 31, 1937

Winter, Mr. C. E. (Camb. Univ.), b Sept 1, 1879

Wisden, John (Sussex), Founder of John Wisden & Co. and *Wisden's Cricketers' Almanack*, b Sept 5, 1826, d April 5, 1884

Witherden, E. G. (Kent), b May 1, 1922

Wolton, A. V. G. (Berkshire and Warwickshire), b June 12, 1919

Womersley, Mr. D. (Essex), b July 28, 1860, d Aug 22, 1942

Wood, A. (Yorkshire), b Aug 25, 1898

Wood, Mr. A. M. (Nottinghamshire, Derbyshire and Philadelphia), b Feb 21, 1861, d Aug 25, 1947

Wood, Mr. C. J. B. (Leicestershire), b Nov 21, 1875

Wood, D. J. (Sussex), b May 19, 1914

Wood, Mr. G. E. C. (Camb. Univ. and Kent), b Aug 22, 1893

Wood, Rev. H. (Yorkshire and Camb. Univ.), b March 22, 1855, d July 31, 1941

Wood, Sir J. B. (Oxford Univ.), b April 27, 1870, d Feb 10, 1933

Woodfull, Mr. W. M. (Victoria), b Aug 22, 1897

Woodhead, Mr. F. E. (Yorkshire), b May 29, 1868, d Aug 25, 1943

Woodhead, F. G. (Nottinghamshire), b Oct 30, 1912

Woodhouse, Mr. G. E. S. (Somerset), b Feb 15, 1924

Woodhouse, Mr. W. H. (Yorkshire), b April 16, 1857, d March 4, 1938

Woods, Mr. S. M. J. (Somerset and Camb. Univ.), b April 14, 1868, d April 30, 1931

Woof, W. A. (Gloucestershire), b July 9, 1859, d April 4, 1937

Wooler, C. (Leicestershire), b June 30, 1930

Wooler, Mr. W. (Camb. Univ. and Glamorgan), b Nov 20, 1912

Woollett, A. F. (Kent), b Sept 20, 1927

Woolley, C. N. (Gloucestershire and Northamptonshire), b May 5, 1886

Woolley, F. E. (Kent), b May 27, 1887

Wootton, James (Kent and Hampshire), b Mar 9, 1860, d Feb 1941

Wormald, Mr. J (Middlesex), b Feb 23, 1882

Worrall, Mr. J. (Victoria), b May 12, 1863, d Nov 17, 1937

Worrell, Mr. F. M. (West Indies), b Aug 1, 1924

Worsley, Capt. Sir W. A., 4th Bart. (Yorkshire), b April 5, 1890

Worthington, Mr. C. R. (Camb. Univ. and Kent), b Feb 28, 1877, d Dec 7, 1950

Worthington, T. S. (Derbyshire), b Aug 21, 1905

Wrathall, H. (Gloucestershire and Northumberland), b Feb 1, 1869

Wreford-Brown, Mr. A. J. (Sussex), b Oct 26, 1912

Wreford-Brown, Mr. C. (Gloucestershire), b Oct 9, 1866, d Nov 26, 1951

Wright, A. C. (Kent), b April 6, 1896

Wright, Mr. C. C. G. (Camb. Univ.), b March 7, 1887

Wright, Mr. C. W. (Camb. Univ. and Nottinghamshire), b May 27, 1863, d Jan 10, 1936

Wright, D. V. P. (Kent), b Aug 21, 1914

Wright, Mr. E. C (Gloucestershire, Oxford Univ. and Kent), b April 23, 1874, d July 28, 1947

Wright, Mr. H. F. (Derbyshire), b Oct 9, 1870, d Feb 23, 1947

Wright, L. (Worcestershire), b Jan 20, 1903

Wright, Mr. L. G. (Derbyshire), b Jan 15, 1862, d Jan 11, 1953

Wright, Mr. P. A. (Camb. Univ. and Northamptonshire), b May 16, 1903

Wright, Walter (Nottinghamshire and Kent), b Feb 29, 1856, d March 22, 1940

Wrigley, Mr. M. H. (Oxford Univ.), b July 30, 1924

Wyatt, Mr. G. N. (Gloucestershire, Surrey and Sussex), b Aug 25, 1850, d Feb 16, 1926

Wyatt, Mr. R. E. S. (Warwickshire and Worcestershire), b May 2, 1901

Wykes, Mr. N. G. (Camb. Univ. and Essex), b March 19, 1906

Wyld, Mr. H. J. (Oxford Univ. and Middlesex), b April 16, 1880

Wynyard, Major E. G. (Hampshire), b April 1, 1861, d Oct 30, 1936

Yardley, Mr. N. W. D. (Camb. Univ. and Yorkshire), b March 19, 1915

Yarnold, H. (Worcestershire), b July 6, 1917

Yates, Major H. W. M. (Hampshire), b March 25, 1883

Yates, W. G. (Nottinghamshire), b June 18, 1919

Yawar Saeed (Somerset), b Jan 22, 1935

Young, A. (Somerset), b 1890, d April 2, 1936

Young, D. M. (Worcestershire and Gloucestershire), b April 15, 1924

Young, H. (Essex), b Feb 5, 1876

Young, J. A. (Middlesex), b Oct 14, 1912

Young, Mr. R. A. (Camb. Univ. and Sussex), b Sept 16, 1885

Zulch, Mr. J. W., jun. (South Africa), b June 20, 1886, d May 19, 1924

Zulfiqar Ahmed (Pakistan), b Nov 22, 1926

OBITUARY, 1955

ALEXANDER, MR. E. B., who died on March 21, aged 83, was in the Forest School XI before going up to Oxford where he gained his Blue as an Association football half-back in 1894 and 1895. He also played for the Corinthians. He spent much of his life in Ceylon, where he was at one time Acting-Governor. After serving in France during the First World War, he represented Ceylon at the 1927 Colonial Office Conference.

ALLEN, SIR RICHARD WILLIAM, who died at his London home on July 17, aged 88, was in 1899 one of the founders of Bedfordshire County C.C., of which he was Honorary Secretary until 1919 and President from 1953 till his death. At one time President of the Institution of Mechanical Engineers, he was awarded the C.B.E. in 1918 and knighted in 1942.

ARROWSMITH, MR. ISAAC FREDERICK, who died in Bristol on November 9 shortly before his 95th birthday, was a life-long cricket lover who at one time played as an all-rounder with Dr. W. G. Grace. For many years a Gloucestershire member, he was a founder-member of the Bohemian C.C.

ASHCROFT, DR. E. MAYNARD, who died suddenly at his home at Upton, near Chester, on February 26, aged 79, played for Derbyshire from 1897 to 1906. Shared the captaincy with A. E. Lawton in 1904 and 1905. Of his eight centuries, the highest was 162 against Leicestershire at Leicester in 1902 when he headed the Derbyshire batting figures with 843 runs, average 46.83. A free-scoring batsman, he drove and cut specially well.

BAISS, MR. REGINALD SIDNEY HABERSHON, who died on May 2, aged 82, played in seven matches for Kent between 1895 and 1901. A wicket-keeper, he was in the Tonbridge XI for four years from 1899 and played in trials at Oxford without gaining a Blue.

BALOO, MR. PALWANKAR, who died in India on July 4, aged 78, played for the Hindus from 1907 to 1920, doing much good work as a slow left-arm bowler. His death occurred on the day which for so long had been printed in *Wisden* Births and Deaths as the date of his birth, which actually was March 19. His best analysis for the Hindus was eight wickets for 43 runs in the second innings of the Parsees in the 1919 Quadrangular Tournament.

He toured England with the 1911 All-India Team, heading the bowling averages with 114 wickets, average 18.86, in all matches. During that tour his chief feats were eight wickets for 103 *v.* Cambridge University; seven for 83 *v.* Lancashire and eight for 15 in the two innings of Ulster at Belfast.

BARNES, DR. STANLEY, died in August, aged 80, four and a half months after his election to the Presidency of Warwickshire in which he was succeeded by Lord Bennett of Edgbaston. His cricket interest was of long standing, going back to the days when he captained the XI at Camp Hill Grammar School, Birmingham. A member of Warwickshire for many years, he gave £5,000 in 1954 to start the Pavilion West Wing development. Brother of the former Bishop of Birmingham, Dr. E. W. Barnes, and of Sir Sidney Barnes, for so long identified with the Admiralty, he possessed a European reputation as a neurologist. In 1931 he gave up his practice to become Dean of the Faculty of Medicine in Birmingham and was largely instrumental in the development and building of the huge Queen Elizabeth Hospital there.

BATTERSBY, MR. JAMES LARATT, whose body was washed up by the sea at Formby, Lancashire, on September 29, played as an all-rounder in the Malvern XI of 1925 and 1926, being captain in the second year. Aged 48, he had been missing since September 14.

BERKELEY, MR. GEORGE FITZ-HARDINGE, who died at Hanwell Castle, Banbury, on November 14, aged 85, accomplished many fine performances as a medium-paced left-arm bowler late last century. Born in Dublin, he was in the Wellington College XI for four years, heading the bowling averages from 1887 to 1889. In 1887 he took 63 wickets, average 10.31, and in 1889 took 47, average 8.10. He gained his Blue at Oxford as a Freshman in 1890 and played four times against

Cambridge, obtaining in the big matches 27 wickets for less than 13 runs each. His best performances in the University matches were five wickets for 20 runs in the second innings in 1891, when Cambridge, having compelled Oxford to follow on 102 behind, scrambled home by two wickets, and five for 38—including the wickets of K. S. Ranjitsinhji, E. C. Streatfield and C. M. Wells—and four for 56 in 1893. It was in the 1891 match that the Hon. F. J. N. Thesiger slipped when fielding during the opening hour, sprained his wrist and dropped out of the game. G. McGregor, the Cambridge captain, allowed T. B. Case to replace him in the Oxford team. In 1890, Berkeley distinguished himself for Oxford against the Australians by dismissing eight men for 70 runs. Two years later he appeared without success for Gentlemen against Players at The Oval. For some seasons from 1904 he played occasionally for Oxfordshire. He served in the Worcestershire Regiment from 1898 to 1901, afterwards became a barrister and author and saw service in the First World War as Brigade musketry officer in the 3rd Cavalry Reserve Regiment and on the Claims Commission in France and Italy.

BIRRELL, MR. W. S., who died in Bridge of Earn Hospital in January, aged 89, was the doyen of Scottish cricketers. He was knocked down by a motor-van five weeks before his death. For 42 years from 1884 he played for Cupar C.C., holding every office and becoming a life member.

BLACKIE, MR. DONALD J., who died in Melbourne on April 21, aged 73, played for Australia against the England team led by A. P. F. Chapman in Australia in 1928–29 when 46, being the oldest player to represent his country. He headed the Test averages with fourteen wickets in three Test appearances at a cost of 31.71 runs each, six for 94 in the first innings of the third game at Melbourne being his best analysis. An off-break bowler of wiry physique who flighted the ball and allied swerve to spin and accuracy of length, he varied his pace skilfully from medium to slow-medium. Not until a late age did he enter big cricket after three years with the St. Hilda C.C., Melbourne. Then he rendered good service to Victoria, taking 159 wickets, average 23.88. In 1926–27, he bowled more balls—2,495—than anybody else in Australian first-class cricket and took more wickets—33—conceding only 816 runs.

BLANDFORD, MR. J. A. R., who died in an Auckland hospital on December 24, aged 42, played for New Zealand in two "unofficial" Test matches against E. R. T. Holmes's M.C.C. Team of 1935–36, scoring 40 and 36. An aggressive right-handed batsman, specially strong in off-side strokes, he was also a capable wicket-keeper and represented Wellington. When at Victoria University College, he was prominent as a Rugby football full-back and a lawn-tennis player. During service with a field ambulance unit in the Middle East and Italy in the Second World War, he contracted a severe rheumatic disease, but, settling in Auckland, became a prominent member of Middlemore C.C. side for several seasons.

BRAUND, LEONARD CHARLES, who died at his home in Fulham on December 22, aged 80, was one of the best-known professional all-rounders of his time and between 1902 and 1907 played in twenty-three matches for England. He enjoyed a long and distinguished career. After appearing occasionally for Surrey during three seasons, and when qualifying for Somerset, he profited from the experience of playing for London County with W. G. Grace. In 1899 against the Australians he scored 63 for an England XI on a bad pitch at Truro; 125 for W. G. Grace's XI at the Crystal Palace, he and Alec Hearne putting on 242 for the third wicket in two hours and forty minutes, and 82 for Somerset at Taunton.

A fine bat on all kinds of pitches, a beautiful field in the slips and a clever leg-break bowler, Braund showed such form directly he appeared in Championship matches for Somerset that in 1901 he scored 1,064 runs for them, with three hundreds and an average of 35, besides taking 78 wickets. His bowling successes included ten Yorkshire wickets at Taunton, eleven Kent wickets at Catford—five for 23 runs in the first innings—and seven Gloucestershire wickets for 70 in the second innings at Bristol. In a memorable match at Leeds, 222 of 238 arrears were hit off by L. C. H. Palairet and Braund before a wicket fell and the Somerset total reached 630. Palairet made 173, Braund 107 and F. A. Phillips 122. Then Yorkshire, set to make 393, failed so completely that they were all out for 113 suffering by 279 runs their only Championship defeat of the summer. Sharing the bowling honours with B. Cranfield, Braund took four wickets for 41.

Braund played for Somerset until 1920, six times registering over 1,000 runs in a season and four times taking more than 100 wickets. On three occasions, from 1901 to 1903, he achieved the "cricketers' double." His bowling record in 1902 was 172 wickets for less than 20 runs each and in the following year 134 for just over 21 runs apiece, and each season he exceeded 1,400 runs. Altogether during his career he made 17,801 runs, average 25.61, took 1,101 wickets, average 27.45, and held no fewer than 508 catches.

His slip-catching was phenomenal. In the 1901 Gentlemen *v*. Players match at Lord's he dismissed C. B. Fry with the catch of the season and in the 1902 Test match at Birmingham he disposed of Clem Hill with a time talked-about effort which helped Rhodes and George Hirst dispose of Australia for 36—the smallest total for which they have been dismissed in a Test. Anticipating a leg-glance by the left-handed Hill off Hirst, the fast left-arm bowler, Braund darted across from slip to the leg-side and held an amazing catch. Braund played in all that series of five Test matches. At Manchester he joined F. S. Jackson when five wickets were down for 44 and shared in a partnership of 141, of which his share was 65. Wonderful bowling by W. H. Lockwood subsequently left England on the second evening with victory in sight, but following a heavy fall of rain during the night Australia snatched a win by three runs. Had F. W. Tate caught J. Darling, whose 37 was top score in a second innings total of 86, off Braund, the result must have been different, for four wickets would have been down for 16. By holding two catches at slip off S. F. Barnes, Braund was responsible for Darling getting a "pair" in the Test at Sheffield.

With the teams led by A. C. MacLaren in 1901-2, P. F. Warner in 1903-4 and A. O. Jones in 1907-8, Braund went to Australia three times and on his first visit, when he made 103 not out at Adelaide, his batting average for the Test matches was 36 and he took twenty-one wickets. During the next tour he scored 102 at Sydney when R. E. Foster, with 287, created a record, but on his third trip he fared moderately. Against the famous South African attack of 1907, Braund hit 104 at Lord's, this being one of the two centuries obtained in Test matches against the bowling combination which included Aubrey Faulkner, R. O. Schwarz, A. E. Vogler and Gordon White.

After giving up active cricket, Braund became a first-class umpire, discharging his duties with marked ability until the end of the 1938 season. In 1943 it became necessary for his right leg to be amputated and three years later he lost the other, but his cheerfulness and his enthusiasm for cricket remained undiminished and for some years he watched cricket at Lord's seated in a bath chair. He was one of the twenty-six retired professional cricketers who in 1949 were given honorary membership of M.C.C.

C. B. Fry, the former England captain, said of Braund: "He was one of the greatest all-round cricketers—and to think that Surrey let him go! The thing about Len Braund was that he was a big-match player. I have never seen a better slip fieldsman. He had such a delicate hand. He would push it out and the ball would stick. Archie MacLaren would never take the field without him. He was a most valuable member of the England team and as cool as a cucumber."

C. T. Bennett, captain of the 1925 Cambridge University team described by Sydney H. Pardon, then Editor of *Wisden*, as "probably the best sent up to Lord's by either University since the war," said: "Braund was the greatest gentleman in cricket, either amateur or professional, I ever met. His coaching made the 1925 side, four of whom played for the Gentlemen at Lord's that year, and K. S. Duleepsinhji would be the first to admit that he owed him a lot."

BROOKES, MR. WILFRED H., who died in a nursing home at Putney on May 28, aged 60, was Editor of *Wisden* from 1936 to 1939, and for several years until the outbreak of the Second World War a partner in the Cricket Reporting Agency.

BROOKMAN, MR. SIDNEY GEORGE, who died suddenly at Bristol on May 2, aged 80, was father-in-law of T. W. Graveney, the England and Gloucestershire cricketer, who left the match with the University at Oxford upon hearing the news of his death. One of the oldest active cricketers in the country, Brookman once played against Dr. W. G. Grace. He had been a member of the School-masters' C.C. since he was 18 and until 1954 played occasionally for Bristol Wayfarers C.C. of which he was a founder member. He also played Rugby football for Bristol, Saracens and United Services.

BROWNLEE, MR. L. D., who died on September 22, aged 72, represented Oxford in the 1904 University match in which J. F. Marsh (Cambridge) set up record for the highest individual innings in the big fixture by scoring 172 not out in the second innings. Brownlee also played golf for his University against Cambridge in 1905. In the Clifton XI from 1899 to 1901, he headed the batting average in 1900. From 1901 to 1909 he appeared occasionally for Gloucestershire for whom, against Kent at Canterbury in 1902, he hit 103, his only century in first class cricket.

BURN, MR. ROLAND CLIVE WALLACE, who died on May 8, aged 72, played as slow bowler for Oxford against Cambridge in four years from 1902 to 1905 without achieving much success. In the Winchester XI in 1901, he headed the bowling averages with 33 wickets, average 19.90. He visited the West Indies with Lord Brackley's Team in 1905, taking 37 wickets during the tour—eight of them for 1 runs against Eighteen of Jamaica in an innings of 165.

CARTWRIGHT, MR. PHILIP, who died in a sanatorium at Virginia Water on November 21, aged 75, appeared for Sussex between 1905 and 1922. Born at Gibraltar, he was a steady left-hand batsman who played many valuable defensive innings. His best season for the county was that of 1909, when he scored 730 runs, average 24.33, including an innings of 101, his only first-class century, against Leicestershire at Leicester, he and C. L. A. Smith, his captain, sharing in an eighth wicket partnership of 168. *Wisden* referring to Cartwright, said: "He is far better than his somewhat peculiar style might lead one to suppose."

COE, SAMUEL, who died at his home at Earl Shilton, Hinckley, on November 4, aged 82, was one of the best batsmen who ever played for Leicestershire. Between 1896 and 1923 he scored 17,438 runs, average 24.69, seven times passing 1,000 in a season. The highest of his nineteen centuries, 252 not out, hit without chance in four hours when he was 41 from the Northamptonshire bowling at Leicester in 1914, remains the biggest innings ever played for the county. He represented Players against Gentlemen at The Oval in 1908. An attractive left-hand batsman he was specially good in on-side strokes. Also a useful left-arm medium-pace bowler, he took 336 wickets.

COHEN, PILOT OFFICER ALEC, who was killed in a flying accident in May aged 21, joined the Glamorgan ground staff at the beginning of last summer A wicket-keeper and batsman, he represented the Welsh Secondary Schools a both cricket and Rugby football.

CREW, MR. A. E., who died at Bristol just before the start of last season aged 68, had been scorer for Gloucestershire. For over thirty years he was English and games master at Cotham Grammar School. He helped to bring to the notice of the County Club C. A. Milton and J. Mortimore, former pupils of his school A good club wicket-keeper, he also at one time captained Bristol R.F.C.

DORNING, MR. HERBERT, who died at Truro on February 2, aged 80, was well known for his activities in fostering cricket in the Argentine. Indeed, a Buenos Aires newspaper, in recording his death, referred to him as "the W. G Grace of Argentine cricket." He was a past President of the Argentine Cricket Association. Until 1935, he played in 33 of the annual North v. South matches, taking 210 wickets, average 13.45, and scoring 909 runs, highest innings 151. Of Lancashire birth, he first played for Rosario and captained Belgrano for many years. He turned out against Lord Hawke's M.C.C. Team in 1912 and for Argentine against P. F. Warner's side in 1927 he distinguished himself by taking 10 wickets for 67 runs—seven of them in the first innings for 38. Originally a fast left-arm bowler, he later turned to medium pace. In his youth he was a good Association and Rugby footballer. He returned to England after the Second World War. One of his sons, Noel Dorning, is captain of Cornwall C.C.C.

FAIRFAX, MR. ALAN G., who died in London on May 17, aged 48, played as an all-rounder in ten Test matches for Australia from 1929 to 1931. He had been in indifferent health following a serious injury received during the Second World War, after which he joined the staff of a London Sunday newspaper. Progressing through grade cricket, Fairfax reached Inter-State rank following an innings of 107 for New South Wales Colts against Queensland Colts in 1928–29 and he made his first appearance as a steady and somewhat restrained stroke-player for Australia in the fifth Test match against A. P. F. Chapman's team that season. In the first innings he scored 65, sharing in a stand of 183 with D. G. Bradman (123) which set up a record for the fifth Australian wicket. He visited England under W. M. Woodfull in 1930, taking part in four of the Test Matches. With 53 not out his best innings, he averaged 50 against England, and in all first class games during the tour scored 536 runs, average 25.52, and, with right-arm medium-pace bowling from a good height, took 41 wickets for 29.70 runs each. Next season in Australia he played in all five Test Matches against West Indies, being third in the batting averages with figures of 48.75 for six innings. He returned to England in 1932 as professional to Accrington in the Lancashire League and afterwards until the outbreak of War ran an indoor cricket school in London.

FLINT, WILLIAM A., who died in Nottingham on February 5, aged 64, was one of the most prominent all-round sportsmen of his time. From 1919 till 1928 he played cricket for Nottinghamshire, scoring 3,345 runs and taking 237 wickets; from 1908 to 1926 he appeared as a wing half-back for Notts County F.C., becoming captain. In his first game for Nottinghamshire he took six wickets for 53 and two for 34 against Middlesex at Lord's and in the return game he hit 98, sharing with John Gunn in a last wicket stand of 111. His best season as an all-rounder was that of 1924, when he scored 412 runs and was second in his county's bowling figures with 58 wickets, average 19.74. That summer against Surrey at The Oval he scored 103, the highest of his three-figure innings, he and W. Walker adding 178 for the seventh wicket. When scoring a hard-hit 100 not out from the Northamptonshire bowling at Trent Bridge in 1927, he helped W. Payton in an unfinished partnership of 247 in three hours.

GILES, MR. WALTER, who died at Bristol in June, aged 74, was Honorary Treasurer of Gloucestershire from 1937 till his death. He was a member of the County Committee for thirty years. In his youth he played for United Banks. For many years President of the Bristol and District Cricket Association and the Umpires' Association, he was also prominent in local Freemasonry.

GOLD, MR. PETER HENRY GRAHAM, who died on November 3, aged 54, was in the Harrow XI for three years from 1918, being captain in 1920. In the match with Eton in 1919, when Harrow twice collapsed against the bowling of W. W. Hill-Wood and C. H. Gibson, Gold was top-scorer in the second innings with 12 out of a total of 41. He did not get a cricket Blue at Cambridge, but played against Oxford at golf in 1923 and 1924. He was related to C. A. Gold, who played for Eton in 1905 and 1906, their fathers being "double-first cousins."

GOODWIN, MR. HARRY SMYTH, who died on November 13, aged 85, played 50 innings for Gloucestershire between 1896 and 1907, scoring 546 runs, average 12.40. His highest score was 46 against Somerset at Taunton in 1899. For some years he was President of Horsham C.C.

GREEN, MR. HERBERT, who died at Mitcham, Surrey, on November 27, played for some years for the East Lancashire C.C. and was a member of the team which won the Worsley Cup in 1925. He played hockey for Blackburn from 1919 to 1933.

HAIGH SMITH, MR. HAMILTON AUGUSTUS, who died in St. Mary's Hospital, London, following an operation on October 28, aged 71, made occasional appearances as batsman and slow bowler for Hampshire from 1909 to 1914. His highest score was 43 not out against Worcestershire at Worcester in his first season. He also represented the county at Rugby football and hockey. Educated at Marlborough, he was best known for his activities in football circles. As a forward he played for Trojans, Blackheath and the famous Barbarians before the First World War, and for some years was Hon. Secretary of the Barbarians, of which club he was also President at the time of his death. In 1938 he was Hon. Assistant-manager of the British Rugby team which toured South Africa and became Hon. Treasurer of the Four Home Unions Tours Committee. For a number of seasons he acted as touch-judge for England in international matches.

HARGREAVES, MR. TOM KNIGHT, who died in hospital at Rotherham on November 19, aged 61, was a prominent all-rounder in Yorkshire Council cricket from 1921 till 1951. He played for Wath till he was 57, scoring many runs and proving successful as a slow bowler. A forcing batsman, he scored 191 in ninety minutes against Brampton in 1935. He brought off one of the biggest hits in cricket on one occasion when playing at the Wath Athletic Ground. A mighty six sent the ball soaring out of the ground and into a wagon of a goods-train on the nearby railway line. The ball was carried on to Scunthorpe.

HARTIGAN, MR. GERALD PATRICK DESMOND, who died in a Durban hospital on January 7, aged 70, played for South Africa at both cricket and Association football. As a right-handed batsman and fast-medium bowler, he appeared for Border in the Currie Cup competition from 1903 to 1927, his highest innings being 176 not out against Eastern Province in 1910–11. In 1912 he was a member of the South African team who figured in the Triangular Tournament in England, but he played in only twelve matches, including two Tests, for, in returning a ball from the deep field, he fractured an arm. In 1913–14 he took part in the first three Tests matches against the England touring side led by J. W. H. T. Douglas and at Johannesburg in the second was top scorer in the first innings with 51.

HEARN, MR. WILLIAM HENRY, who died on November 19, was a well-known cricketer and umpire in the Tunbridge Wells area for many years. His father was at one time groundman at the Nevill Ground and his son is P. Hearn, the Kent left-handed batsman.

HUNTER, MR. CHARLES HERBERT, who died on April 2, aged nearly 88, played in two matches for Kent in 1895 when with Bickley Park C.C. One of these games was that in which Dr. W. G. Grace, hitting 257 and 73 not out for Gloucestershire at Gravesend, was on the field for the whole of the three days. In that season "W. G." became the first batsman in history to score 1,000 runs in May. A good wicket-keeper, Hunter played for Uppingham in 1885 and 1886, but did not get a Blue when going up to Cambridge, where he was overshadowed by Gregor MacGregor, of Middlesex and England fame.

HYLTON, MR. LESLIE G., died in Jamaica on May 17, aged 50. He played in six Test Matches for West Indies. A fast bowler for Jamaica, he helped in the winning of the rubber against R. E. S. Wyatt's team in the West Indies in 1934–35 when, in four Tests, he dismissed 13 batsmen at an average cost of 19.30. In 1939 he visited England under the captaincy of R. S. Grant, being chosen for two of the Test matches, but met with moderate success.

JESSOP, MR. GILBERT LAIRD, who died at St. George's Vicarage, Dorchester on May 11, aged 80, was famed as the most remarkable hitter cricket has ever produced. He had lived with the Rev. Gilbert Jessop, his only child, from 1936 till his death.

Born at Cheltenham on May 19, 1874, he enjoyed a memorable career in first-class cricket which, dating from 1894 to the start of the First World War extended over twenty years. There have been batsmen who hit the ball even harder than Jessop, notably C. I. Thornton and the two Australians, George Bonnor and Jack Lyons, but no one who did so more often or who, in match after match scored as rapidly. Where Jessop surpassed all other hitters was in the all-round nature of his scoring. At his best, he could make runs from any ball, however good it might be. Although only 5 ft. 7 ins. in height, he bent low as he shaped to play, a method which earned him the sobriquet of "The Croucher." Extraordinarily quick on his feet, he was ready to hit firm-footed if the ball were pitched well up and equally, when it was of shorter length, to dash down the pitch and drive. When executing leg-side strokes, he almost lay down and swept round with the bat practically horizontal, putting great power behind the ball as, thanks to strong, supple wrists, he also did when bringing off the square cut. Lightness of foot allied to wonderful sight made it possible for him to run out to the fastest bowlers of his time—Richardson and Mold—and at the peak of his form pull or straight-drive them with almost unerring certainty. No one ever approached him in this particular feat; indeed, nobody else could have attempted it with reasonable hope of success.

At times Jessop sacrificed his wicket through trying to hit before he got a true sight of the ball or judged the pace of the turf and, not unnaturally in view of the liberties he took with good length bowling, the ball which kept low often dismissed him. A batsman with such marvellous gifts that in half an hour he might win a game seemingly lost, he was a wonderful personality on the field and the idol of spectators who always love a fearless batsman.

Jessop's claims to distinction were not limited to the brilliancy of his run-getting. For a number of years he ranked high as a fast bowler and for a man of his pace he showed surprising stamina. Far more remarkable than his bowling, however, was his fielding, which might fairly be termed as phenomenal as his hitting and which was a matter of great pride to him. No hit proved too hard for him to stop and his gathering and returning of the ball approached perfection. In his early days he fielded at cover-point; later he specialised in the position of extra mid-off, standing so deep that with almost anyone else a run would have been a certainty. Jessop's presence deterred the boldest of batsmen from making any attempt. In short, such a fine bowler and such a superb fieldsman was he that, even without his batting ability, he would have been worth a place in almost any team. A man of engaging manners, he was a charming companion and, like most truly great men, modest to a degree.

First tried for Gloucestershire in 1894, Jessop established his reputation a year later when, among other performances, he hit 63 out of 65 in less than half an hour from the Yorkshire bowling at Cheltenham. He continued to assist Gloucestershire till the end of his first-class career and for thirteen years from 1900 he captained the side. By 1897 he had become one of the great players of the day, making 1,219 runs in first-class matches and taking 116 wickets for less than 18 runs each. In that summer he hit two particularly noteworthy innings—140 for Cambridge University against the Philadelphians in 95 minutes and 101 out of 118 in 40 minutes against Yorkshire at Harrogate. In the course of the latter display he hit the ball six times out of the ground and some dozen times over the ropes. Until 1907 a hit over the ropes counted four; only a hit out of the ground earned six. Except in 1898 he regularly made over 1,000 runs every season until 1909, when a bad back injury sustained while fielding in the Test Match at Leeds in early July kept him out of the game for the rest of the year. In 1900 he scored 2,210 runs and took 104 wickets and next summer his aggregate amounted to 2,323, including 157 out of 201 in an hour against West Indies at Bristol.

Among his 53 centuries were five of more than 200: 286 out of 335 in 175 minutes for Gloucestershire against Sussex at Brighton, 1903 (he and J. H. Board adding 320 for the sixth wicket); 240 out of 337 in 200 minutes for Gloucestershire *v.* Sussex at Bristol, 1907; 234 out of 346 in 155 minutes for Gloucestershire *v.* Somerset at Bristol, 1905; 233 out of 318 in 150 minutes for An England XI *v.* Yorkshire at Lord's, 1901; and 206 out of 317 in 150 minutes for Gloucestershire *v.* Nottinghamshire at Trent Bridge, 1904.

Four times for Gloucestershire he reached three figures in each innings of a match: 104 and 139 *v.* Yorkshire at Bradford, 1900, when the newspapers stated that, in the two innings he cleared the ropes more than twenty times; 143 and 133 not out *v.* Somerset at Bath, 1908; 161 and 129 *v.* Hampshire at Bristol, 1909; and 153 and 123 not out *v.* Hampshire at Southampton, 1911. He achieved the feat on another occasion, against Somerset in a friendly game organised for the opening of a new club pavilion. S. M. J. Woods termed this a remarkable performance on a pitch far from true and against professional bowling. Altogether in first-class cricket he hit 26,058 runs, average 32.60.

His bowling successes included 8 wickets for 34 runs *v.* Hampshire, 1898; 5 for 13 *v.* Lancashire, 1895; 8 for 54 *v.* Lancashire, 1898; 8 for 29 *v.* Essex, 1900; 8 for 58 *v.* Middlesex, 1902. All these were achieved for Gloucestershire except that against Hampshire, on which occasion he was playing for Cambridge. His wickets in first-class cricket totalled 851, average 22.91.

Jessop took part in eighteen Test matches between 1899 and 1909, thirteen against Australia and five against South Africa, and would probably have appeared in others but for the back strain he suffered in 1909. He disappointed in Australia except for his fielding, and in most of the contests in England met with moderate success; but he earned undying fame in The Oval Test of 1902. There, under conditions considerably helpful to bowlers, England, set 273 to make to win, lost their first five wickets for 48. Australia looked to have the match in hand, but Jessop joined F. S. Jackson and in marvellous fashion hit 104 out of 139 in an hour and a quarter, paving the way to victory by one wicket for England. Twice he sent the ball on to the roof of the Pavilion and from another big hit was caught on the Players' Balcony by H. K. Foster.

Jessop went to Cambridge in 1896 and played for the University for four seasons, being captain in 1899. He accomplished little of note against Oxford in the way of batting, two innings of over 40 being his best scores on the big occasion, but he bowled to good purpose in two of the games, taking six wickets for 65 in the first innings in 1897 and six for 126 in the first innings a year later.

Besides his cricketing ability, Jessop was an all-round athlete of note. He got his Blue as a hockey goalkeeper, but fell ill and could not play in the University match; came near getting an Association football Blue and played for The Casuals as half-back or goalkeeper. He also appeared as a wing threequarter for Gloucester R.F.C. He would have played billiards for Cambridge against Oxford, but was "gated" and could not take part. In one week he made two breaks of over 150. He could run the 100 yards in 10.2 seconds and frequently entered for sports meetings. A scratch golfer, he took part in the Amateur Championship in 1914, was Secretary of the Cricketers' Golfing Society and for some years Secretary of the Edgware Club.

In addition to the visit he paid to Australia in 1901–2 under A. C. MacLaren, he went to America with the team captained by P. F. Warner in 1897, and again in 1899 when K. S. Ranjitsinhji led the side.

For Beccles School in 1895, when a master there, Jessop scored 1,058 runs, average 132, and took 100 wickets at a cost of less than two and a half runs apiece.

He served as a captain in the Manchester Regiment during the First World War from 1914 till he was invalided out with a damaged heart in 1918. Married in October 1902, he first met his bride a few months earlier during his visit to Australia. She died in 1953.

Tributes paid to Jessop include:

Sir Pelham Warner: "He was a wonderful cricketer. It was a great pleasure to play with or against him. It has been said that he was unorthodox, but no one watched the ball more closely."

Sir John Hobbs: "He was undoubtedly the most consistently fast scorer I have seen. He was a big hitter, too, and it was difficult to bowl a ball from which he could not score. He made me glad that I was not a bowler. Gilbert Jessop certainly drew the crowds, too, even more than Bradman, I should say."

KINGSTON, MR. H. E., who died on June 9, aged 78, took part in the first match for Northamptonshire when they were accorded first-class status in 1905. In that game, against Hampshire at Southampton, he scored 33 and 68. He played in twelve matches altogether during 1905 and the following season.

KNIGHT, MR. ROBERT FRANCIS, who died on January 9, aged 75, was a member of the team which played against Hampshire at Southampton in Northamptonshire's opening game as a first-class county in 1905. He made occasional appearances for the county till 1921. He was in the Wellingborough School XI and though not very successful in county cricket, enjoyed considerable success in club matches. For Wellingborough Amateurs in 1910, he scored 98 and took ten Burton-on-Trent wickets for 62. He also achieved distinction at hockey, golf, Rugby and Association football.

LAWTON, MR. ALBERT E., who died in a Manchester nursing home on Christmas Day, aged 76, played for Derbyshire from 1900 to 1909. Very tall, he was a prodigious hitter. He captained Derbyshire in 1902 when he hit three of his ten first-class centuries—149 (in two and a quarter hours) against London County, captained by W. G. Grace; 146 *v.* Hampshire and 126 (in just over two hours) *v.* Warwickshire, all at Derby. In all matches that season he scored 1,044 runs, average 27.47. He continued to lead the county side the following season and for the next two shared the captaincy with E. M. Ashcroft. When his activities in the cotton industry took him to Manchester, he appeared for Lancashire from 1912 till the outbreak of the First World War in 1914. In all he scored 7,254 runs in first-class cricket, average 25.10, took 112 wickets, average 30.85, and held 118 catches.

McCAUGHEY, MR. S., who died at Deniliquin, N.S.W., on January 29, played as a fast bowler in two games for Cambridge University in 1913. In the first innings of Middlesex at Fenner's, he took seven wickets for 46 runs.

MORTIMER, SIR RALPH GEORGE ELPHINSTONE, who died at Ponteland, Northumberland, on May 3, aged 85, played in one match for Lancashire in 1891 and for some seasons from 1893 assisted Northumberland, for whom he scored three centuries. Educated at Harrow and Trinity College, Cambridge, he did not gain a place in either eleven. He had been President and Chairman of Northumberland. Always prominent in local affairs, he was High Sheriff of Northumberland in 1916–17. He received the O.B.E. in 1920 and was knighted in 1934.

NEALE, WILLIAM LEGGE, who after a long illness died in hospital at Gloucester on October 26, aged 51, played for Gloucestershire from 1923 till 1948, scoring 14,752 runs, average 23.75. Educated at Cirencester Grammar School, he appeared as an amateur for six years before becoming a professional. Of his fourteen centuries, the highest was 145 not out against Hampshire at Southampton in 1927. His best summer as a steady right-handed batsman was that of 1938 when, reaching three figures on five occasions, he scored 1,488 runs, average 29.76. Six times he exceeded 1,000 runs in a season. In 1937 he (121) and W. R. Hammond (217) set up a Gloucestershire fourth wicket record by adding 321 against Leicestershire at Gloucester. Though not often called upon to bowl, he occasionally broke a stubborn stand when the regular members of the attack had failed to do so, and at Bristol in 1937 he distinguished himself by dismissing six Somerset batsmen for nine runs. As a fieldsman he excelled near the boundary.

OXLADE, MR. ROBERT AUBREY, who died in Sydney on September 13, aged 69, was a former Chairman, Treasurer and Secretary of the Australian Board of Control for International Cricket. He joined Manly C.C. in 1910 and for many years was the club's delegate to the New South Wales Cricket Association, of which he became a life member. He was a solicitor.

PALAIRET, MR. RICHARD CAMERON NORTH, who died at his home at Budleigh Salterton, Devon, on February 11, aged 83, played, like his more famous brother, Lionel, for Repton, Oxford University and Somerset. Born at Grange-over-Sands, Lancashire, on June 25, 1871, Richard was the more consistent of the two brothers during three seasons in the Repton XI from 1888, hitting 172 against Malvern. An injury received while playing as inside forward at Association football at Oxford prevented him from rivalling Lionel in more important cricket, for he was a graceful batsman, strong in forward play and possessing a fluent drive. As it was, a damaged knee handicapped him in running and batting and ended his activities as an athlete at which he excelled at school. Even so, he gained his Blue in 1893 and 1894 as an opening batsman. Among his best performances was that against Lancashire when, with Briggs and Mold bowling for the county, he scored 70 out of 94 in sixty-five minutes. He also played in the Association football match against Cambridge in 1891.

From 1889 to 1902 he appeared frequently for Somerset, his highest innings being 156 against Sussex at Taunton in 1896. In the winter of 1896–97, he formed one of the team taken to the West Indies by Sir Arthur Priestley. Soon after the outbreak of the First World War in 1914 he took a commission in the Devonshire Regiment at the age of 43 and rose to the rank of Staff Captain, seeing much service in India. In 1920 he became Secretary of Surrey, a post he held till 1932, and in the winter of 1932–33 he and Sir Pelham Warner were joint managers of D. R. Jardine's M.C.C. Team in Australia on what became known as "The Bodyline Tour." From 1937 to 1946 he was President of Somerset. After service as an air raid warden in the Second World War, his health steadily failed.

PHILLIPS, MR. FRANK ASHLEY, who died on March 5, aged 81, played in three University matches for Oxford late in the last century. After being in the XI at Rossall for three years from 1889, he gained a Blue in 1892 and, though passed over in the following season, in 1894 and 1895. With the cut and the drive his best strokes, he was a free-scoring batsman, though not specially strong in defence, a fine deep fieldsman and useful medium-pace bowler. His best performance against Cambridge was in 1894 when, hitting 78, he helped C. B. Fry in a fifth wicket partnership of 137. In 1892 he played for Essex, then a second-class county, and from 1894 he assisted Monmouthshire, the county of his birth, until in 1897 he began an association with Somerset which lasted till 1911.

His highest innings for Somerset was 163 against Sussex at Taunton in 1899 when, in a game yielding 1,293 runs for the loss of twenty-six wickets, he and

C. A. Bernard put on 171 for the third wicket. Phillips bore a handsome part in the one defeat of Yorkshire on their way to the County Championship in 1901. Against the bowling of Hirst, Rhodes and Haigh, Somerset were dismissed at Leeds for 87 but, facing first innings arrears of 238, they built up a total of 630, of which Phillips's share was 122, and triumphed by 279 runs. In 1895, he was a member of Frank Mitchell's team which visited America. A schoolmaster by profession, he served in both the Boer War and the First World War, when he was awarded the D.S.O., and for a time was an assistant District Commissioner in Southern Nigeria.

PLATT, GEORGE J. W., who died at Old Hill, Birmingham, on April 14, aged 73, played occasionally as a medium-paced bowler for Surrey from 1906 to 1914. In 1909 at The Oval, he took five wickets for 40 in the Somerset second innings, the last four in 16 deliveries for 11 runs. His best season was that of 1910 when in thirteen county games he dismissed 43 batsmen for 19.65 runs each. After the First World War he became professional to Old Hill C.C., doing good work as off-break bowler, and later played for West Bromwich Dartmouth before taking up the position of head groundsman and coach at Worcester which he held till his retirement in 1952.

POYNTZ, COLONEL H. S., who died on June 22, aged 77, played occasionally for Somerset between 1904 and 1910. His best performance was at Beckenham in his first season when he scored 85 and 48. Kent won the match thanks to the all-round success of J. R. Mason, who, besides hitting 126, took ten wickets for 180 runs. Poyntz was also a good Association footballer and captained the Army in 1907. He fought in the Boer War and in the First World War in which he was awarded the D.S.O. and twice mentioned in despatches.

PREST, MR. HAROLD EDWARD WESTRAY, who died on January 5, aged 64, gained his Blue at Cambridge for cricket, golf and Association football early in the century. In the Malvern XI for three years before going to the University, he headed the batting averages in 1908 with 174 not out his best innings, and *Wisden* stated: "It is doubtful whether Prest had a superior as a batsman among the school boys of the year. He plays in excellent style, with a full quiver of fine forcing strokes anywhere except behind point. He is a fine field into the bargain."
He played against Oxford as a Freshman in 1909, when he scored 54 and shared in a sixth wicket partnership of 94 with J. F. Ireland. His other University match was that of 1911, when he made 6 and 16. In the second innings he fell to a magnificent wide return catch with the left hand by P. R. Le Couteur off a full-blooded drive. Le Couteur did much to win the match for the Dark Blues by taking in that innings eight wickets for 99 runs. Prest played a little for Kent between 1909 and 1911. In the last season he distinguished himself with an innings of 133 not out in two and a half hours against Somerset at Taunton, taking part in stands of 108 with F. H. Huish and 128 with D. W. Carr. This was his only century in first-class cricket.

RICE, FATHER WILLIAM IGNATIUS, O.S.B., M.A., who died at Douai Abbey on April 22, aged 72, was Headmaster of Douai School from 1915 to 1952. In his younger days he played for Warwickshire during the summer holidays and for some years enjoyed the distinction of being the only monk whose cricket performances were chronicled in *Wisden*.

RILEY, MR. WILLIAM NAIRN, who died at Hove on November 20, aged 62, gained a Blue as opening batsman for Cambridge in 1912 when the Light Blues, following a tie on the first innings, beat Oxford in an exciting struggle by three wickets. The result might have been even closer had not G. E. V. Crutchley, after reaching 99 not out in the first Oxford innings, been compelled to retire from the match owing to measles. From 1911 to the outbreak of the First World War in 1914, Riley, who was educated at Worcester Grammar School, appeared for Leicestershire with no special distinction except in 1913. That season he scored 521 runs, average 22.65, and registered a hard-hit century against Yorkshire at Leicester. Actually he obtained 100 out of 141, at one point 60 out of 72 in forty minutes, punishing G. H. Hirst for 24 in an over. In the same match he brought off a remarkable right-hand catch in the long field when dismissing M. W. Booth. He was a Vice-President of Sussex.

SHINDE, SADASHIV G., who died in Bombay on June 22, aged 31, played in seven Test Matches for India between 1946 and 1952. A slow leg-break and googly bowler, he toured England in 1946 and 1952 without much success. His best performance in a Test match was in the first England innings at New Delhi in 1951–52, when he took six wickets for 91 runs.

SORRIE, MR. JAMES WEBSTER, who died at Blackpool in August, aged 69, played twelve times for Scotland between 1912 and 1924. For many years he was a leading batsman for the Carlton Club, Edinburgh, being specially effective against fast bowling.

WETHERALL, MR. C. R., who died on April 22, aged 76, played as a batsman for Northamptonshire in the early part of the century before they became a first-class county.

WHITE, MR. FREDERICK CHARLES, who died in a Brighton hospital on June 2 following a road accident, was a Vice-President of Sussex and Chairman of the Sussex Cricket Club Welfare Association. Since the War, he helped to raise thousands of pounds for sporting charities.

WINSTON, MR. JOHN HENRY ERNEST, who died on December 15, aged 62, was a Vice-President of the Guy's Hospital and Old Whitgiftians cricket and Rugby football clubs. For many years he was fixtures secretary of Guy's R.F.C.

OBITUARY, 1954

BULLOCK, BURN W. who died suddenly on December 23, aged 58, scored many runs as a professional for Surrey II XI between 1921 and 1925, his highest innings being 153 in 1923. As Surrey were specially strong in batting at that time, he could rarely find a place in the first team and in 1926 he became coach and cricket organiser to the late Mr. Jimmy White, the millionaire financier. He later returned to the Mitcham Club, for whom he made his first appearance at the age of 15.

BUSHER, MR. S. E., who died in Australia, where he had lived for many years, played in a few matches for Worcestershire in 1908 and 1910. Educated at Lancing, he appeared for Surrey in the Easter-tide game at The Oval in 1908 against Gentlemen of England. He scored 52 and in the match took seven wickets for 92, twice bowling Dr. W. G. Grace, then close upon 60 and making his only first-class appearance of the season.

CHARLTON, MR. PERCY CHATER, who died at Sydney on September 30, aged 87, was a member of the Australian team which visited England under W. L. Murdoch in 1890, taking part in two Test Matches. During the tour he scored 534 runs, average 14.30, and with fast-medium bowling took 42 wickets, average 19.04. He played his early cricket for the Ivanhoe and Belvedere clubs in Sydney, N.S.W., and first achieved prominence when, for Eighteen Sydney Juniors in 1888, he took seven wickets, including that of Shrewsbury, against Shaw, Shrewsbury and James Lillywhite's English team. Ill-health limited his first-class career.

DOUGLAS, MR. CECIL HERBERT, who died at Frinton-on-Sea in September, aged 68, was the younger brother of J. W. H. T. Douglas, the Essex and England captain. Cecil, generally known as "Pickles," played for Essex in a few matches from 1912 to 1914, his highest innings being 78 against Lancashire at Old Trafford in 1919. He was a celebrated boxing referee.

FANE, MR. FREDERICK LUTHER, who died on December 9, aged 79, was a prominent figure in the cricket world for some twenty years before the First World War. Born at the Curragh Camp on April 27, 1875, he was educated at Charterhouse, where he was in the XI from 1892 to 1894, and Oxford and played a lot for Essex, whom he captained from 1904 to 1906. Though he did not quite realise expectations at the University, he gained a Blue in 1897 and the following year.

Meanwhile in 1905 he began his long association with Essex, for whom he exceeded 1,000 runs in each of five years. His best season was that of 1906, when he scored 1,572 runs, average 34. In 1899 he hit his highest innings, 207 against

Leicestershire, in which he showed all his attractive style and sound judgment. In 1905, when Essex beat the Australians by 19 runs, Fane finished the match with a truly remarkable catch, not for any exceptional excellence as a piece of fielding, but from the place where it was made. With a close finish clearly in sight and Buckenham bowling at great pace, Fane, to save a possible boundary from byes, took up a position practically in line with the wickets and just inside the Pavilion rails—in short, that of very deep long-stop. Frank Laver, sweeping the ball right round with a curious stiff-armed stroke from the shoulder, lifted it high and straight to where Fane was standing. Though not as a rule the safest of fieldsmen, Fane did not fail his side on that occasion.

In the winter of 1907–8, when going to Australia as a member of the side under A. O. Jones, Fane led the Englishmen in the first three Test Matches when his captain fell ill. During the tour he scored 774 runs, average 33, his first notable innings being 101 against New South Wales. In the four Test Matches in which he played, he averaged 24. Fane also visited South Africa twice, in 1905–6 and in 1909–10, New Zealand in 1902–3 and the West Indies in early 1902.

GODSELL, MR. R. T., who died in March, aged 74, played in the 1903 University match for Cambridge. Dismissed without scoring in the first innings, he was first in and last out for 59 in the second. In the Clifton XI in 1898, he assisted Gloucestershire on occasion from 1903 to 1910. His best season for the county was that of 1905, when he scored 356 runs, average 22.25. That year, against Nottinghamshire at Bristol, he carried his bat through an innings of 269 with 98 not out.

OSBORN, F., who died on October 12, aged 64, played in two matches for Leicestershire in 1911 and 1913.

THOMSON, MR. E. W. S., who died at Littlehampton in May, was for many years secretary to the Argentine Cricket Association and managed tours in South America and England.

WAUGH, MR. H. P., who died in a London hospital on December 13, aged 56, played occasionally as opening batsman for Essex. Specially good in cutting, he scored 128 against Glamorgan at Leyton in 1928, he and J. A. Cutmore sharing in an opening partnership of 161. From 1934 he appeared for Suffolk, being captain for five years till the start of the Second World War, scoring 1,515 runs and, with fast-medium bowling, taking 84 wickets. He played for Minor Counties and Club Cricket Conference in representative matches.

OBITUARY, 1953

GEHRS, MR. D. R. A., who died in June, aged 72, was a prominent batsman for South Australia in the early part of the century. In all he scored 3,387 runs for his State, average 39.38. He took part in one Test Match against England in 1903 and one when visiting this country with J. Darling's team in 1905, showing disappointing form. During the tour he scored 675 runs in all matches, average 21.77. In 1910, when South Africa went to Australia, "Algy" Gehrs did better, making four Test appearances and hitting 67 at Sydney and 58 at Melbourne.

CRICKETERS OF THE YEAR

Following is a complete alphabetical list of cricketers whose portraits and biographies have appeared in *Wisden* since, in the issue for 1889, the idea of publishing photographs of prominent players was first adopted. The number of cricketers selected for this feature has varied from time to time. Six bowlers of the year were chosen for the 1889 issue and in the following edition portraits of nine batsmen were given in the Almanack. A group of five representative wicket-keepers formed the subject of illustration for 1891 and photographs of five all-round cricketers were published in a subsequent issue.

Apart from a few exceptions, most recently during the war years in the issues from 1941 to 1946, each successive *Wisden* has included portraits and biographical details of five players who, in the opinion of the Editor, most deserved the honour by reason of their accomplishments, especially during the previous season.

Abel, R. (Surrey), 1890
Adams, P. W. (Cheltenham), 1919
Ames, L. E. G. (Kent), 1929
Appleyard, R. (Yorks.), 1952
Armstrong, W. W. (Aust.), 1903
Ashton, H. (Winchester, Camb. U. and Essex), 1922
Astill, W. E. (Leics.), 1933
Attewell, W. (Notts.), 1892

Bailey, T. E. (Dulwich, Camb. U. and Essex), 1950
Bakewell, A. H. (Northants), 1934
Bardsley, W. (Aust.), 1910
Barnes, S. F. (War., Lancs. and Staffs.), 1910
Barnes, William (Notts.), 1890
Barnett, C. J. (Glos.), 1937
Bartlett, H. T. (Dulwich, Camb. U., Surrey and Sussex), 1939
Bedser, A. V. (Surrey), 1947
Blackham, J. McC. (Aust.), 1891
Blunt, R. C. (N.Z.), 1928
Blythe, C. (Kent), 1904
Booth, M. W. (Yorks.), 1914
Bosanquet, B. J. T. (Middx.), 1905
Bowes, W. E. (Yorks.), 1932
Bowley, E. H. (Sussex), 1930
Bradman, Sir Donald G. (Aust.), 1931
Braund, L. C. (Surrey and Som.), 1902
Brearley, W. (Lancs.), 1909
Briggs, John (Lancs.), 1889
Brockwell, W. (Surrey), 1895
Brown, F. R. (Leys, Camb. U. and Surrey), 1933
Brown, J. T. (Yorks), 1895
Brown, W. A. (Aust.), 1939
Bryan, J. L. (Rugby, Camb. U. and Kent), 1922
Bull, F. G. (Essex), 1898
Burnup, C. J. (Malvern, Camb. U. and Kent), 1903

Calder, H. L. (Cranleigh School), 1918
Cameron, H. B. (S.A.), 1936
Carr, A. W. (Notts.), 1923
Carr, D. W. (Kent), 1910
Catterall, R. H. (S.A.), 1925
Chapman, A. P. F. (Uppingham), 1919
Compton, D. C. S. (Middx.) 1939
Constantine, L. N. (W.I.), 1940
Copson, W. H. (Derby.), 1937
Cowdrey, M. C. (Tonbridge, Oxford U. and Kent), 1956
Crawford, J. N. (Repton and Surrey), 1907
Cuttell, W. R. (Yorks. and Lancs.), 1898

Darling, J. (Aust.), 1900
Day, A. P. (Malvern and Kent), 1910
Dempster, C. S (N.Z.), 1932
Denton, David (Yorks.), 1906
Dollery, H. E. (War.), 1952
Donnelly, M. P. (N.Z. and Oxf. U.), 1948
Dooland, B. (Aust. and Notts), 1955
Douglas, J. W. H. T. (Felsted School and Essex), 1915
Druce, N. F. (Marlborough, Camb. U. and Surrey), 1898
Ducat, A. (Surrey), 1920
Duckworth, G. (Lancs.), 1929
Duleepsinhji, K. S. (Camb. U. and Sussex), 1930

Edrich, W. J. (Middx.), 1940
Evans, T. G. (Kent), 1951

Farnes, K. (Camb U. and Essex), 1939
Fazal Mahmood (Pakistan), 1955
Fender, P. G. H. (St. Paul's School, Sussex and Surrey), 1915
Ferris, J. J. (Aust. and Glos.), 1889
Fielder, A. (Kent), 1907
Firth, J. E. D'E. (Winchester), 1918

Fishlock, L. B. (Surrey), 1947
Foster, F. R. (War.), 1912
Foster, H. K. (Malvern, Oxf. U. and Worcs.), 1911
Foster, R. E. (Malvern, Oxf. U. and Worcs.), 1901
Freeman, A. P. (Kent), 1923
Fry, C. B. (Repton, Oxf. U., Surrey and Sussex), 1895

Geary, G. (Leics.), 1927
Gibson, C. H. (Eton), 1918
Giffen, George (Aust.), 1894
Gilligan, A. E. R. (Dulwich, Camb. U. and Sussex), 1924
Gimblett, H. (Somerset), 1953
Goddard, T. W. (Glos.), 1938
Gore, A.C. (Eton), 1919
Gover, A. R. (Surrey), 1937
Grace, W. G. (Glos.), 1896
Graveney, T. W. (Glos.), 1953
Gregory, J. M. (Aust.), 1922
Gregory, S. E. (Aust.), 1897
Grimmett, C. V. (Aust.), 1931
Gunn, George (Notts.), 1914
Gunn, John (Notts.), 1904
Gunn, William (Notts.), 1890

Haigh, S. (Yorks.), 1901
Hall, L. (Yorks.), 1890
Hallam, A. (Lancs. and Notts.), 1908
Halliwell, E. A. (S.A.), 1905
Hallows, C. (Lancs.), 1928
Hallows, J. (Lancs.) 1905
Hammond, W. R. (Glos.), 1928
Hardinge, H. T. W. (Kent), 1915
Hardstaff, J. (junr.) (Notts.), 1938
Hartley, A. (Lancs.), 1911
Harvey, R. N. (Aust.), 1954
Hassett, A. L. (Aust.), 1949
Hawke, Lord (Eton, Camb. U. and Yorks.), 1909
Hayes, E. G. (Surrey), 1907
Hayward, T. (Surrey), 1895
Headley, G. (W.I.), 1934
Hearne, Alec (Kent), 1894
Hearne, J. T. (Middx.), 1892
Hearne, J. W. (Middx.), 1912
Hedges, L. P. (Tonbridge), 1919
Henderson, R. (Surrey), 1890
Hendren, E. (Middx.), 1920
Hewett, H. T. (Harrow Oxf. U. and Som.), 1893
Hill, Clem (Aust.), 1900
Hirst, G. H. (Yorks.), 1901
Hitch, J. W. (Surrey), 1914
Hobbs, Sir J. B. (Surrey), 1909 and special portrait, 1926
Hollies, W. E. (War.), 1955
Holmes, E. R. T. (Oxf. U. and Surrey), 1936
Holmes, P. (Yorks.), 1920

Hutchings, K. L. (Tonbridge and Kent), 1907
Hutton, L. (Yorks.), 1938

Insole, D. J. (Camb. U. and Essex), 1956
Iremonger, J. (Notts.), 1903

Jackson, Hon. Sir F. Stanley (Harrow, Camb. U. and Yorks.), 1894
Jardine, D. R. (Winchester, Oxf. U. and Surrey), 1928
Jenkins, R. O. (Worcs.), 1950
Jessop, G. L. (Camb. U. and Glos.), 1898
Johnston, W. A. (Aust.), 1949
Jones, A. O. (Camb. U. and Notts.), 1900
Jupp, V. W. C. (Sussex and Northants), 1928

Keeton, W. W. (Notts.), 1940
Kelly, J. J. (Aust.), 1903
Kennedy, A. (Hants), 1933
Kilner, Roy (Yorks.), 1924
Kinneir, S. P. (War.), 1912
Knight, A. E. (Leics.), 1904
Knight, D. J. (Malvern, Oxf. U. and Surrey), 1915
Knox, N. A. (Dulwich College and Surrey), 1907

Laker, J. C. (Surrey), 1952
Langridge, James (Sussex), 1932
Langridge, John (Sussex), 1950
Larwood, H. (Notts.), 1927
Lees, Walter (Surrey), 1906
Leyland, M. (Yorks.), 1929
Lilley, A. A. (War.), 1897
Lindwall, R. R. (Aust.), 1949
Llewellyn, C. B. (S.A. and Hants) 1911
Lock, G. A. R. (Surrey), 1954
Lockwood, W. H. (Notts. and Surrey) 1899
Lohmann, George (Surrey), 1889
Lyon, B. H. (Rugby, Oxf. U. and Glos.), 1931

Macartney, C. G. (Aust.), 1922
Macaulay, G. G. (Yorks.), 1924
MacBryan, J. C. W. (Camb. U. and Som.), 1925
McCabe, S. J. (Aust.), 1935
McDonald, E. A. (Aust.), 1922
McGahey, C. P. (Essex), 1902
McGlew, D. J. (S.A.), 1956
MacGregor, G. (Uppingham, Camb U. and Middx.), 1891
MacLaren, A. C. (Harrow and Lancs.), 1895
Mankad, M. (India), 1947

Marshal, Alan (Queensland and Surrey), 1909

Martin, F. (Kent), 1892

Mason, J. R. (Winchester and Kent), 1898

May, P. B. H. (Charterhouse, Camb. U. and Surrey), 1952

Mead, C. P. (Hants), 1912

Mead, Walter (Essex), 1904

Melville, A. (Oxf. U., Sussex and S.A.), 1948

Mercer, J. (Glam.), 1927

Merchant, V. M. (India), 1937

Miller, K. R. (Aust.), 1954

Mitchell, B. (S.A.), 1936

Mitchell, Frank (Camb. U., Yorks. and S.A.), 1902

Mold, A. (Lancs.), 1892

Morris, A. R. (Aust.), 1949

Nayudu, C. K. (India), 1933

Newstead, J. T. (Yorks.), 1909

Nichols, M. S. (Essex), 1934

Noble, M. A. (Aust.), 1900

Nourse, A. D., junr. (S.A.), 1948

Oldfield, W. A. (Aust.), 1927

O'Reilly, W. J. (Aust.), 1935

Owen-Smith, H. G. (S.A.), 1930

Paine, G. A. E. (War.), 1935

Palairet, L. C. H. (Repton, Oxf. U. and Som.) 1893

Parker, C. (Glos.), 1923

Parkin, C. (Lancs.), 1924

Parks, J. H. (Sussex) 1938

Partridge, N. E. (Malvern), 1919

Pataudi, Nawab of (Chief's College, Lahore and Oxf. U.), 1932

Paynter, E. (Lancs.), 1938

Peebles, I. A. R. (Glasgow Academy and Middx.), 1931

Peel, R. (Yorks.), 1889

Perrin, P. A. (Essex), 1905

Pilling, R. (Lancs.), 1891

Ponsford, W. H. (Aust.), 1935

Poore, Major R. M. (Hants), 1900

Quaife, W. G. (Sussex and War.), 1902

Ramadhin, S. (W.I.), 1951

Ranjitsinhji, K. S. (Camb. U. and Sussex), 1897

Ransford, V. (Aust.), 1910

Read, M. (Surrey), 1890

Read, W. W. (Surrey), 1893

Relf, A. E (Sussex), 1914

Rhodes W. (Yorks.), 1899

Richardson, T. (Surrey), 1897

Robertson, J. D. (Middx.), 1948

Robins, R. W. V. (Camb. U. and Middx.), 1930

Rotherham, G. A. (Rugby), 1918

Rowan, E. A. B. (S.A.), 1952

Russell, A. C. (Essex), 1923

Sandham, A. (Surrey), 1923

Schwarz, R. O. (Middx. and S.A.), 1908

Scott, S. W. (Middx.), 1893

Sellers, A. B. (Yorks.), 1940

Sharpe, J. W. (Surrey and Notts.), 1892

Sheppard, D. S. (Sherborne, Camb. U. and Sussex), 1953

Sherwin, M. (Notts.), 1891

Shrewsbury, A. (Notts.), 1890

Simpson, R. T. (Notts.), 1950

Smith, C. I. J. (Middx.), 1935

Smith, D. (Derby.), 1936

Smith, S. G. (W.I. and Northants), 1915

Smith, T. P. B. (Essex), 1947

Smith, W. C. (Surrey), 1911

Spooner, R. H. (Marlborough and Lancs.), 1905

Staples, S. J. (Notts.), 1929

Statham, J. B. (Lancs.), 1955

Stevens, G. T. S. (University College School), 1918

Stoddart, A. E. (Middx.), 1893

Storer, William (Derby.), 1899

Strudwick, H. (Surrey), 1912

Sugg, F. H. (Yorks., Derby. and Lancs.), 1890

Surridge, W. S. (Emmanuel and Surrey), 1953

Sutcliffe, B. (N.Z.), 1950

Sutcliffe, H. (Yorks.), 1920

Tallon, D. (Aust.), 1949

Tarrant, F. A. (Victoria and Middx.), 1908

Tate, M. W. (Sussex), 1924

Tayfield, H. J. (S.A.), 1956

Taylor, H. W. (S.A.), 1925

Taylor, T. L. (Uppingham, Camb. U. and Yorks.), 1901

Tennyson, Lord (Eton and Hants), 1914

Thompson, G. J. (Northants), 1906

Townsend, C. L. (Clifton and Glos.), 1899

Townsend, L. (Derby.), 1934

Tribe, G. E. (Aust. and Northants.), 1955

Trott, A. E. (Aust. and Middx.), 1899

Trott, G. H. S. (Aust.), 1894

Trueman, F. S. (Yorkshire), 1953

Trumble, H. (Aust.), 1897

Trumper, V. (Aust.), 1903

Tunnicliffe, John (Yorks.), 1901

Turnbull, M. J. (Downside, Camb. U. and Glam.), 1931

Turner, C. T. B. (Aust.), 1889

Tyldesley, E. (Lancs.), 1920

Tyldesley, J. T. (Lancs.), 1902

Tyldesley, R. (Lancs.), 1925
Tyson, F. H. (Durham U. and Northants), 1956

Valentine, A. L. (W.I.), 1951
Verity, H. (Yorks.), 1932
Vine, J. (Sussex), 1906
Voce, W. (Notts.), 1933
Vogler, A. E. (S.A.), 1908

Wainwright, E. (Yorks.), 1894
Walters, C. F. (Glam. and Worcs.) 1934
Ward, A. (Yorks. and Lancs.), 1890
Wardle, J. H. (Yorks.), 1954
Warner, Sir Pelham (Rugby, Oxf. U. and Middx.), 1904 and special portrait, 1921
Washbrook, C. (Lancs.), 1947
Wass, T. (Notts.), 1908
Watson, W. (Yorks.), 1954

Weekes, E. D. (W.I.), 1951
Wellard, A. W. (Som.), 1936
White, J. C. (Som.), 1929
Whysall, W. (Notts.), 1925
Wisden, John (Sussex). Special memoir and portrait, 1913
Wood, A. (Yorks.), 1939
Wood, H. (Surrey), 1891
Woodfull, W. M. (Aust.), 1927
Woods, S. M. J. (Camb. U., Som. and Aust.), 1889
Woolley, F. E. (Kent), 1911
Worrell, F. M. (W.I.), 1951
Worthington, T. S. (Derby.), 1937
Wright, D. V. P. (Kent), 1940
Wright, L. G. (Derby.), 1906
Wyatt, R. E. S. (War.), 1930

Yardley, N. W. D. (St. Peter's, Camb. U. and Yorks.), 1948

ADDRESSES OF REPRESENTATIVE BODIES

ENGLAND: M.C.C., Lord's Cricket Ground, St. John's Wood, London, N.W.8.

AUSTRALIA: Australian Cricket Board of Control, V.C.A. Rooms, 1 Collins Place, Melbourne, C.1, Victoria.

SOUTH AFRICA: South African Cricket Association, P.O. Box 19, P.O. Northlands, Johannesburg.

WEST INDIES: West Indies Board of Control, P.O. Box 286, Port of Spain, Trinidad.

INDIA: India Cricket Board of Control, Ranji Stadium, Eden Gardens, Calcutta.

NEW ZEALAND: New Zealand Cricket Council, P.O. Box 958, Christchurch, N.Z.

PAKISTAN: Board of Control for Cricket in Pakistan, Group Capt. M. M. A. Cheema, R.P.A.F. Station, Drigh Road, Karachi, 8.

CANADA: Canadian Cricket Association, Donald King, 534A, Eglinton Avenue West, Toronto 12, Ontario.

The addresses of the First-Class Counties, Universities and Minor Counties are given at the head of each separate section.

THE LAWS OF CRICKET

(1947 Code—2nd Edition)

(Copyright of M.C.C. and reprinted by permission of M.C.C. Copies of the "Laws of Cricket" may be obtained from Lord's Cricket Ground, price 1/-.)

Preface by Col. R. S. Rait Kerr, D.S.O., M.C.
Secretary of M.C.C. 1936–52

During the last two hundred years the conduct of the game of Cricket has been governed by a series of Codes of Laws. These Codes were established as indicated below, subject to alterations by the governing authorities of the time. Since its formation in 1787 the Marylebone Cricket Club has been recognised as the sole authority for drawing up the Code and for all alterations.

There is little doubt that Cricket was subject to recognised rules as early as 1700, though the earliest known Code is that drawn up in 1744 by certain Noblemen and Gentlemen who used the Artillery Ground in London. These Laws were revised in 1755 by "Several Cricket-Clubs, particularly that of the Star and Garter in Pall-Mall."

The next arrangement, by "a Committee of Noblemen and Gentlemen of Kent, Hampshire, Surry, Sussex, Middlesex and London," at the Star and Garter on February 25th, 1774, was revised by a similar body in February, 1786.

From May 30th, 1788, the first M.C.C. Code remained in force until May 19th, 1835, when a new Code of Laws, amended from time to time, stood until April 21st, 1884. Then, after consultation with cricket clubs both at home and overseas, important alterations were incorporated and adopted at a Special General Meeting of the M.C.C.

By 1939 these Laws, supplemented as they had been by the inclusion of many definitions and interpretations in the form of notes, were in need of revision, and immediately on the conclusion of the World War the opinions of controlling Bodies and Clubs throughout the world were sought, with the result that the present code was adopted at a Special General Meeting of the M.C.C. on May 7th, 1947.

This revision in the main aimed at the clarification and better arrangement of the previous Laws and their interpretations, but did not exclude certain definite alterations designed firstly to provide greater latitude in the conduct of the game as required by the widely differing conditions in which it is played, and secondly to eliminate certain umpiring difficulties.

This, the second edition of the 1947 Code, contains no alterations to the Laws, but certain corrections and a few additions to the Notes have been made.

Under the Rules of the Marylebone Cricket Club the Laws of Cricket can only be changed by the vote of two-thirds of the members present and voting at a Special General Meeting, of which due notice is required to be given.

From time to time the Committee of the M.C.C. are required to give interpretations on points of difficulty arising from the Laws, and these are given in the form of notes to the Laws themselves.

The primary purpose of the book as expressed by the late Sir Francis Lacey (Secretary of the M.C.C. from 1898 to 1926) remains unchanged:—

"The aim of this publication is to remove difficulties, which are known to exist, although they are not always apparent. Hundreds of cases are sent to the M.C.C. for decision every year. It is from this source that the chief difficulties have become manifest. Saturday and League Matches are especially productive of disputes, and it is hoped that those who read these notes may find an answer to any doubt which may arise as to the proper interpretation of the Laws of Cricket."

Lord's Cricket Ground,   *1st July*, 1952.
London, N.W.8.

(A)—THE PLAYERS, UMPIRES, AND SCORERS

SIDES

1.—A match is played between two sides of eleven players each, unless otherwise agreed. Each side shall play under a Captain who before the toss for innings shall nominate his players who may not thereafter be changed without the consent of the opposing Captain.

NOTES

1.—If a Captain is not available at any time, a Deputy must act for him to deal promptly with any points arising from this and other laws.

2.—No match in which more than eleven players a side take part can be regarded as First-class, and in any case no side should field with more than eleven players.

SUBSTITUTES

2.—A Substitute shall be allowed to field or run between the wickets for any player who may during the match be incapacitated from illness or injury, but not for any other reason without the consent of the opposing Captain; no Substitute shall be allowed to bat or to bowl. Consent as to the person to act as substitute in the field shall be obtained from the opposing Captain, who may indicate positions in which the Substitute shall not field.

NOTES

1.—A player may bat, bowl or field even though a substitute has acted for him previously.

2.—An injured batsman may be "Out" should his runner infringe Laws 36, 40 or 41. As *Striker* he remains himself subject to the Laws: should he be out of his ground for any purpose he may be "Out" under Laws 41 and 42 at the wicket-keeper's end, irrespective of the position of the other batsman or the substitute when the wicket is put down. When *not the Striker* the injured batsman is out of the game and stands where he does not interfere with the play.

THE APPOINTMENT OF UMPIRES

3.—Before the toss for innings two Umpires shall be appointed; one for each end to control the game as required by the Laws with absolute impartiality. No Umpire shall be changed during a match without the consent of both Captains.

NOTE

1.—The umpires should report themselves to the executive of the ground 30 minutes before the start of each day's play.

THE SCORERS

4.—All runs scored shall be recorded by Scorers appointed for the purpose; the Scorers shall accept and acknowledge all instructions and signals given to them by the Umpires.

NOTE

1.—The umpires should wait until a signal has been answered by a scorer before allowing the game to proceed. Mutual consultation between the scorers and the umpires to clear up doubtful points is at all times permissible.

(B)—THE IMPLEMENTS OF THE GAME, AND THE GROUND

THE BALL

5.—The Ball shall weigh not less than $5\frac{1}{2}$ ounces, nor more than $5\frac{3}{4}$ ounces. It shall measure not less than 8 13/16 inches, nor more than 9 inches in circumference. Subject to agreement to the contrary, either Captain may demand a new ball at the start of each innings. In the event of a ball being lost or becoming unfit for play, the Umpires shall allow another ball to be taken into use. They shall inform the Batsmen whenever a ball is to be changed.

NOTES

1.—All cricket balls used in First-class matches should be approved before the start of a match by the umpires and captains. The latter may demand a new ball at the start of each innings.

2.—Except in the United Kingdom, or if local regulations provide otherwise, after 200 runs have been made off a ball in First-class matches, the captain of the fielding side may demand a new one. In First-class matches in the United Kingdom the fielding side may demand a new ball after 65 (6 ball) overs have been bowled with the old one. In other grades of cricket these regulations will not apply unless agreed before the toss for innings.

3.—Any ball substituted for one lost or becoming unfit for play should have had similar wear or use as that of the one discarded.

THE BAT

6.—The Bat shall not exceed $4\frac{1}{4}$ inches in the widest part. It shall not be more than 38 inches in length.

THE PITCH

7.—The Pitch is deemed to be the area of ground between the bowling creases, 5 feet in width on either side of the line joining the centre of the wickets. Before the toss for innings, the executive of the ground shall be responsible for the selection and preparation of the Pitch; thereafter the Umpires shall control its use and maintenance. The Pitch shall not be changed during a match unless it becomes unfit for play, and then only with the consent of both Captains.

THE WICKETS

8.—The Wickets shall be pitched opposite and parallel to each other at a distance of 22 yards from stump to stump. Each Wicket shall be 9 inches in width and consist of three stumps with two bails upon the top. The stumps shall be of equal and of sufficient size to prevent the ball from passing through, with their tops 28 inches above the ground. The bails shall be each 4 3/8 inches in length, and, when in position on the top of the stumps, shall not project more than $\frac{1}{2}$ inch above them.

NOTES

1.—Except for the bail grooves the tops of the stumps shall be dome-shaped

2.—In a high wind the captains may agree, with the approval of the umpires to dispense with the use of bails (*see* Law 31, Note 3).

THE BOWLING AND POPPING CREASES

9.—The Bowling crease shall be in line with the stumps; 8 feet 8 inches in length; the stumps in the centre; with a Return crease at each end at right angle behind the wicket. The Popping crease shall be marked 4 feet in front of and parallel with the Bowling crease. Both the Return and Popping creases shall be deemed unlimited in length.

NOTE

1.—The distance of the Popping Crease from the wicket is measured from line running through the centre of the stumps to the inside edge of the crease.

(C)—THE CARE AND MAINTENANCE OF THE PITCH

ROLLING, MOWING AND WATERING

10.—Unless permitted by special regulations, the Pitch shall not be rolled during a match except before the start of each innings and of each day's play, when if the Captain of the batting side so elect, it may be swept and rolled for not more than 7 minutes. The Pitch shall not be mown during a match unless special regulation so provide. Under no circumstances shall the Pitch be watered during a match.

NOTES

1.—"Special Regulations," within the framework of the Laws, referred to in this and subsequent Laws, are those authorised by M.C.C. in respect of County cricket, or by Overseas Governing Bodies in respect of cricket in the countries concerned. Such Regulations do not apply to matches played by touring teams unless included in these Notes and Interpretations of the Official Laws, or unless agreed to by both parties before the visiting team arrives.

2.—The umpires are responsible that any rolling permitted by this Law and carried out at the request of the captain of the batting side, is in accordance with the regulations laid down and that it is completed so as to allow play to start at the stipulated time. The normal rolling before the start of each day's play shall take place not earlier than half an hour before the start of play, but the captain of the batting side may delay such rolling until 10 minutes before the start of play should he so desire.

3.—The time allowed for rolling shall be taken out of the normal playing time if a captain declare an innings closed either, (*a*) before play starts on any day so late that the other captain is prevented from exercising his option in regard to rolling under this Law, or (*b*) during the luncheon interval later than 15 minutes after the start of such interval.

4.—In Australia, South Africa, the West Indies and New Zealand, if at any time a rain affected pitch is damaged by play thereon, it shall be swept and rolled for a period of not more than ten consecutive minutes at any time between the close of play on the day on which it was damaged and the next resumption of play, provided that:—

(i) The umpires shall instruct the groundsman to sweep and roll the pitch only after they have agreed that damage caused to it as a result of play after rain has fallen warrants such rolling additional to that provided for in Law 10.

(ii) Such rolling shall in all cases be done under the personal supervision of both umpires and shall take place at such time and with such roller as the groundsman shall consider best calculated to repair the damage to the pitch.

(iii) Not more than one such additional rolling shall be permitted as a result of rain on any particular day.

(iv) The rolling provided for in Law 10 to take place before the start of play shall not be permitted on any day on which the rolling herein provided for takes place within two hours of the time appointed for commencement of play on that day.

5.—The pitch shall be mown under the supervision of the umpires before play begins on alternate days after the start of a match, but should the pitch not be so mown on any day on account of play not taking place, it shall be mown on the first day on which the match is resumed and thereafter on alternate days. For the purpose of this rule a rest day counts as a day.)

COVERING THE PITCH

11.—The Pitch shall not be completely covered during a match unless special regulations so provide; covers used to protect the bowlers' run up shall not extend to a greater distance than 3½ feet in front of the Popping creases.

NOTE

1.—It is usual under this Law to protect the bowlers' run up, before and during a match both at night and, when necessary, during the day. The covers should be removed early each morning, if fine.

MAINTENANCE OF THE PITCH

12.—The Batsman may beat the Pitch with his bat, and Players may secure their footholds by the use of sawdust, provided Law 46 be not thereby contravened. In wet weather the Umpires shall see that the holes made by the Bowlers and Batsmen are cleaned out and dried whenever necessary to facilitate play.

(D)—THE CONDUCT OF THE GAME

INNINGS

13.—Each side has two innings, taken alternately, except in the case provided for in Law 14. The choice of innings shall be decided by tossing on the field of play.

NOTES

1.—The captains should toss for innings not later than 15 minutes before the time agreed upon for play to start. The winner of the toss may not alter his decision to bat or field once it has been notified to the opposing captain.

2.—This Law also governs a One-day match in which play continues after the completion of the first innings of both sides. (*See also* Law 22.)

FOLLOWING INNINGS

14.—The side which bats first and leads by 150 runs in a match of three days or more, by 100 runs in a two-day match, or by 75 runs in a one-day match, shall have the option of requiring the other side to follow their innings.

DECLARATIONS

15.—The Captain of the Batting side may declare an innings closed in a match of three days or more, at any time on the second and succeeding days; in a two-day match, at any time but on the first day not later than 1 hour and 40 minutes before the hour agreed on for drawing stumps; in a one-day match, at any time.

NOTE

1.—In a two-day match, after the initial innings, either side may declare at any time.

16.—When the start of play is delayed by weather, Laws 14 and 15 shall apply in accordance with the number of days' play remaining from the actual start of the match.

START AND CLOSE OF PLAY AND INTERVALS

17.—The Umpires shall allow such intervals as have been agreed upon fo meals, **10 minutes between each innings and not more than 2 minutes for each fresh** batsman to come in. At the start of each innings and of each day's play and at the end of any interval the Umpire at the Bowler's end shall call "Play," when the side refusing to play shall lose the match. After "Play" has been called no trial ball shall be allowed to any player, and when one of the Batsmen is out the use of the bat shall not be allowed to any player until the next Batsman shall come in.

NOTES

1.—The umpires shall not award a match under this Law unless (i) "Play" has been called in such a manner that both sides can clearly understand that play is to start, (ii) an appeal has been made, and (iii) they are satisfied that a side will not, or cannot, continue play.

2.—It is an essential duty of the captains to ensure that the "in-going" batsman passes the "out-going" one before the latter leaves the field of play. This is all the more important in view of the responsibility resting on the umpire for deciding whether or not the delay of the individual amounts to a refusal o the batting side to continue play.

3.—The interval for luncheon should not exceed 45 minutes unless otherwis agreed (but *see* Law 10, Note 3). In the event of the last wicket falling within 2 minutes of the time arranged for luncheon or tea, the game shall be resumed at the usual hour, no allowance being made for the 10 minutes between the innings

4.—Bowling practice *on the pitch* is forbidden at any time during the game

18.—The Umpires shall call "Time," and at the same time remove the bail from both wickets, on the cessation of play before any arranged interval, at the end of each day's play, and at the conclusion of the match. An "Over" shall alway be started if "Time" has not been reached, and shall be completed unless a batsma is "Out" or "Retires" within 2 minutes of the completion of any period of play but the "Over" in progress at the close of play on the final day of a match shal be completed at the request of either Captain even if a wicket fall after "Time" has been reached.

SCORING

19.—The score shall be reckoned by runs. A run is scored:—

1st.—So often as the Batsmen after a hit, or at any time while the ball is i play, shall have crossed and made good their ground from end to end; bu if either Batsman run a short run, the Umpire shall call and signal "On short" and that run shall not be scored. The Striker being caught, no ru shall be scored; a Batsman being run out, that run which was being attempte shall not be scored.

2nd.—For penalties under Laws 21, 27, 29, 44, and boundary allowance under Law 20.

NOTES

1.—If while the ball is in play, the batsmen have crossed in running, neithe returns to the wicket he has left except in the case of a boundary hit, or unde Laws 30, Note 1, and 46, Note 4 (vii). This rule applies even should a short ru have been called, or should no run be reckoned as in the case of a catch.

2.—A run is "short" if either, or both, batsmen fail to make good thei ground in turning for a further run. Although such a "short" run shortens th succeeding one, the latter, if completed, counts. Similarly a batsman taking stanc in front of his popping crease may run from that point without penalty.

3 (1).—One run only is deducted if both batsmen are short in one and th same run.

(2).—Only if three or more runs are attempted can more than one run b "short" and then subject to (1) above, all runs so called shall be disallowed.

4.—An umpire signals "short" runs when the ball becomes "Dead" by bending his arm upwards to touch the shoulder with the tips of his fingers. If there has been more than one "short" run, the umpires must instruct the scorers as to the number of runs disallowed. (See note 1 to Law 4.)

BOUNDARIES

20.—Before the toss for innings the Umpires shall agree with both sides on the Boundaries for play, and on the allowances to be made for them. An Umpire shall call or signal "Boundary" whenever, in his opinion, a ball in play hits, crosses or is carried over the Boundary. The runs completed at the instant the ball reaches the Boundary shall count only should they exceed the allowance, but if the "Boundary" result from an overthrow or from the wilful act of a fieldsman, any runs already made and the allowance shall be added to the score.

NOTES

1.—If flags or posts are used to mark a boundary, the real or imaginary line joining such points shall be regarded as the boundary, which should be marked by a white line if possible.

2.—In deciding on the allowances to be made for boundaries the umpires will be guided by the prevailing custom of the ground.

3.—It is a "Boundary" if the ball touches any boundary line or if a fieldsman with the ball in hand grounds any part of his person on or over that line. A fieldsman, however, standing within the playing area may lean against or touch a boundary fence in fielding a ball (*see also* Law 35, Note 5).

4.—An obstacle, or person, within the playing area is not regarded as a boundary unless so arranged by the umpires. The umpire is not a boundary, but sight screens within the playing area shall be so regarded.

5.—The customary allowance for a boundary is 4 runs, but it is usual to allow 6 runs for all hits pitching over and clear of the boundary line or fence (even though the ball has been previously touched by a fieldsman). It is not usual to allow 6 runs when a ball hits a sight screen full pitch, if the latter is on or inside the boundary.

6.—In the case of a boundary resulting from either an over-throw or the wilful act of a fieldsman, the run in progress counts provided that the batsmen have crossed at the instant of the throw or act.

7.—The umpire signals "Boundary" by waving an arm from side to side, or a boundary "6" by raising both arms above the head.

LOST BALL

21.—If a ball in play cannot be found or recovered any Fieldsman may call "Lost Ball," when 6 runs shall be added to the score; but if more than 6 have been run before "Lost Ball" be called, as many runs as have been run shall be scored.

THE RESULT

22.—A match is won by the side which shall have scored a total of runs in excess of that scored by the opposing side in its two completed innings, one-day matches, unless thus played out, shall be decided by the first innings. A match may also be determined by being given up as lost by one of the sides, or in the case governed by Law 17. A match not determined in any of these ways shall count as a "Draw."

NOTES

1.—It is the responsibility of the captains to satisfy themselves on the correctness of the scores on the conclusion of play.

2.—Neither side can be compelled to continue after a match is finished; a one-day match shall not be regarded as finished on the result of the first innings if the umpires consider there is a prospect of carrying the game to a further issue in the time remaining.

3.—The result of a finished match is stated as a win by runs, except in the case of a win by the side batting last, when it is by the number of wickets stil then to fall. In a one-day match which is not played out on the second innings this rule applies to the position at the time when a result on the first innings was reached.

4.—A "Draw" is regarded as a "Tie" when the scores are equal at the conclusion of play but only if the match has been played out. If the scores of the completed first innings of a one-day match are equal, it is a "Tie," but only if the match has not been played out to a further conclusion.

THE OVER

23.—The ball shall be bowled from each wicket alternately in Overs of either 8 or 6 balls according to the agreed conditions of play. When the agreed number have been bowled and it has become clear to the Umpire at the Bowler's wicket that both sides have ceased to regard the ball as in play, the Umpire shall call "Over" in a distinct manner before leaving the wicket. Neither a "No Ball" nor a "Wide Ball" shall be reckoned as one of the "Over."

NOTE

1.—In default of any agreement to the contrary, in the United Kingdom the "over" shall be 6 balls.

24.—A Bowler shall finish an "Over" in progress unless he be incapacitated or be suspended for unfair play. He shall be allowed to change ends as often as desired, provided only that he shall not bowl two "Overs" consecutively in one innings. A Bowler may require the Batsman at the wicket from which he is bowling to stand on whichever side of it he may direct.

DEAD BALL

25.—The ball shall be held to be "dead"—on being in the opinion of the Umpire finally settled in the hands of the Wicket-keeper or of the Bowler; or on reaching or pitching over the boundary; or, whether played or not, on lodging in the dress of either a Batsman or Umpire; or on the call of "Over" or "Time" by the Umpire; or on a Batsman being out from any cause; or on any penalty being awarded under Laws 21 or 44. The Umpire shall call "Dead Ball" should he decide to intervene under Law 46 in a case of unfair play or in the event of a serious injury to a player; or should he require to suspend play prior to the Striker receiving a delivery. The ball shall cease to be "Dead" on the Bowler starting his run or bowling action.

NOTES

1.—Whether the ball is "finally settled" is a question of fact for the umpire alone to decide.

2.—An umpire is justified in suspending play prior to the striker receiving a delivery in any of the following circumstances:—

(i) If satisfied that, for an *adequate* reason, the striker is not ready to receive the ball, and makes no attempt to play it.

(ii) If the bowler drops the ball accidentally before delivery, or if the ball does not leave his hand for any reason.

(iii) If one or both bails fall from the striker's wicket before he receives the delivery.

In such cases the ball is regarded as "Dead" from the time it last came into play.

3.—A ball does not become "Dead" when it strikes an umpire (unless it lodges in his dress), when the wicket is broken or struck down (unless a batsman is out thereby), or when an unsuccessful appeal is made.

4.—For the purpose of this and other Laws, the term "dress" includes the equipment and clothing of players and umpires as normally worn.

NO BALL

26.—For a delivery to be fair the ball must be bowled, not thrown or jerked: either Umpire be not entirely satisfied of the absolute fairness of a delivery in his respect, he shall call and signal "No Ball" instantly upon delivery. The Umpire at the Bowler's wicket shall call and signal "No Ball" if he is not satisfied that at he instant of delivery the Bowler has at least some part of one foot behind the owling crease and within the Return crease, and not touching or grounded over ther crease.

NOTES

1.—Subject to the provisions of the Law being complied with a bowler is ot debarred from delivering the ball with both feet behind the bowling crease.

2.—The striker is entitled to know whether the bowler intends to bowl over r round the wicket, overarm or underarm, right or left handed. An umpire ay regard any failure to notify a change in the mode of delivery as "unfair," if), he should call "No ball."

3.—It is a "No Ball" if the bowler before delivering a ball throws it at the riker's wicket even in an attempt to run him out (see Law 46, Note 4 (vii).)

4.—If a bowler break the near wicket with any part of his person during the elivery, such act in itself does not constitute a "No Ball."

5.—The umpire signals "No Ball" by extending one arm horizontally.

6.—An umpire should revoke the call "No Ball" if the ball does not leave he bowler's hand for any reason.

27.—The ball does not become "Dead" on the call of "No Ball." The Striker ay hit a "No Ball" and whatever runs result shall be added to his score, but runs ade otherwise from a "No Ball" shall be scored "No Balls," and if no runs be made ne run shall be so scored. The Striker shall be out from a "No Ball" if he break aw 37, and either Batsman may be run out, or given out if he break Laws 36 or 40.

NOTES

1.—The penalty for a "No Ball" is only scored if no runs result otherwise.

2.—Law 46, Note 4 (vii), covers attempts to run before the ball is delivered, ut should the non-striker unfairly leave his ground too soon, the fielding side ay run out the batsman at the bowler's end by any recognised method. If the owler throws at the near wicket, the umpire does not call "No Ball," though ny runs resulting are so scored. The throw does not count in the "Over."

WIDE BALL

28.—If the Bowler shall bowl the ball so high over or so wide of the wicket at in the opinion of the Umpire it passes out of reach of the Striker, and would ot have been within his reach when taking guard in the normal position, the Umpire all call and signal "Wide Ball" as soon as it shall have passed the Striker.

NOTES

1.—If a ball which the umpire considers to have been delivered comes to st in front of the striker "Wide" should not be called, and no runs should be dded to the score unless they result from the striker hitting the ball which he as a right to do without interference by the fielding side.

2.—The umpire signals "Wide" by extending both arms horizontally.

3.—An umpire should revoke the call if the striker hits a ball which has been alled "Wide."

29.—The ball does not become "Dead" on the call of "Wide Ball." All runs at are run from a "Wide Ball" shall be scored "Wide Balls," or if no runs be made ne run shall be so scored. The Striker may be out from a "Wide Ball" if he break aws 38 or 42, and either Batsman may be run out, or given out if he break Laws 6 or 40.

BYE AND LEG BYE

30.—If the ball, not having been called "Wide" or "No Ball," pass the Striker without touching his bat or person, and any runs be obtained, the Umpire shall call or signal "Bye"; but if the ball touch any part of the Striker's dress or person except his hand holding the bat, and any run be obtained, the Umpire shall call or signal "Leg Bye"; such runs to be scored "Byes" and "Leg Byes" respectively.

NOTES

1.—Leg byes which result from the unintentional deflection of the ball by any part of the striker's person, other than the hand holding the bat, whether he has played at the ball or not, are fair. If the umpire is not entirely satisfied that the act was unintentional he shall call "Dead Ball" as soon as he sees that the fielding side have no chance of dismissing either batsman as an immediate result of such deflection.

2.—The umpire signals "Bye" by raising an open hand above the head, and "Leg Bye" by touching a raised knee with the hand.

THE WICKET IS DOWN

31.—The wicket shall be held to be "Down" if either the ball or the Striker's bat or person completely removes either bail from the top of the stumps, or, if both bails be off, strikes a stump out of the ground. Any player may use his hand or arm to put the wicket down or, even should the bails be previously off, may pull up a stump, provided always that the ball is held in the hand or hands so used.

NOTES

1.—A wicket is not "down" merely on account of the disturbance of a bail, but it is "down" if a bail in falling from the wicket lodges between two of the stumps.

2.—If one bail is off, it is sufficient for the purpose of this Law to dislodge the remaining one in any of the ways stated or to strike any of the three stumps out of the ground.

3.—If, owing to the strength of the wind, the captains have agreed to dispense with the use of bails (see Law 8, Note 2), the decision as to when a wicket is "down" is one for the umpires to decide on the facts before them. In such circumstances the wicket would be held to be "down" even though a stump had not been struck out of the ground.

4.—If the wicket is broken while the ball is in play, it is not the umpire's duty to remake the wicket until the ball has become "dead." A fieldsman, however, may remake the wicket in such circumstances.

5.—For the purpose of this and other Laws, the term "person" includes a player's dress as defined in Law 25, Note 4.

OUT OF HIS GROUND

32.—A Batsman shall be held to be "Out of his ground" unless some part of his bat in hand or of his person be grounded behind the line of the Popping Crease.

BATSMAN RETIRING

33.—A Batsman may retire at any time, but may not resume his innings without the consent of the opposing Captain, and then only on the fall of a wicket.

NOTE

1.—When a batsman has retired owing to illness, injury, or some other unavoidable cause, his innings is recorded as "Retired, Not Out," but otherwise as a completed innings to be recorded as "Retired, Out."

BOWLED

34.—The Striker is out "Bowled"—If the wicket be bowled down, even if the ball first touch his bat or person.

NOTE

1.—The striker, after playing the ball, is out "Bowled" if he then kicks or hits it on to his wicket before the completion of his stroke.

2.—The striker is out "Bowled" under this Law when the ball is deflected on to his wicket off his person, even though a decision against him might be justified under Law 39 L.B.W.

CAUGHT

35.—The Striker is out "Caught"—If the ball, from a stroke of the bat or of the hand holding the bat, but not the wrist, be held by a Fieldsman before it touch the ground, although it be hugged to the body of the catcher, or be accidentally lodged in his dress. The Fieldsman must have both his feet entirely within the playing area at the instant the catch is completed.

NOTES

1.—Provided the ball does not touch the ground, the hand holding it may do so in effecting a catch.

2.—The umpire is justified in disregarding the fact that the ball has touched the ground, or has been carried over the boundary provided that a catch has in fact been completed prior to such occurrence.

3.—The fact that a ball has touched the striker's person before or after touching his bat does not invalidate a catch.

4.—The striker may be "Caught" even if the fieldsman has not touched the ball with his hands, including the case of a ball lodging in the wicket-keeper's pads.

5.—A fieldsman standing within the playing area may lean against the boundary to catch a ball, and this may be done even if the ball has passed over the boundary.

6.—If the striker lawfully plays the ball a second time he may be out under this Law, but only if the ball has not touched the ground since being first struck.

7.—The striker may be caught off any obstruction within the playing area provided it has not previously been decided on as a boundary.

HANDLED THE BALL

36.—Either Batsman is out "Handled the ball"—If he touch it while in play with his hands, unless it be done at the request of the opposite side.

NOTES

1.—A hand holding the bat is regarded as part of it for the purposes of Laws 6, 37 and 39.

2.—The correct entry in the score book when a batsman is given out under this Law is "Handled the Ball," and the bowler does not get credit for the wicket.

HIT THE BALL TWICE

37.—The Striker is out "Hit the ball twice"—If the ball be struck or be topped by any part of his person, and he wilfully strike it again, except for the sole purpose of guarding his wicket, which he may do with his bat or any part of his person, other than his hands. No runs except those which result from an overthrow shall be scored from a ball lawfully struck twice.

NOTES

1.—It is for the umpire to decide whether the ball has been so struck a second time legitimately or not. The umpire may regard the fact that a run is attempted as evidence of the batsmen's intention to take advantage of the second stroke, but it is not conclusive.

2.—A batsman may not attempt to hit the ball twice, if in so doing he baulk the wicket-keeper or any fieldsman attempting to make a catch.

3.—This Law is infringed if the striker, after playing the ball and without any request from the opposite side, uses his bat to return the ball to a fieldsman.

4.—The correct entry in the score book when the striker is given out under this Law is "Hit the ball twice," and the bowler does not get credit for the wicket.

HIT WICKET

38.—The Striker is out "Hit wicket"—If in playing at the ball he hit down his wicket with his bat or any part of his person.

NOTES

1.—The striker is "Out" under this Law if:—

(i) In making a second stroke to keep the ball out of his wicket he hits it down.

(ii) While playing at the ball, but not otherwise, his wicket is broken by his cap or hat falling, or by part of his bat.

2.—A batsman is not out for breaking the wicket with his bat or person while in the act of running.

L.B.W.

39.—The Striker is out "Leg before wicket"—If with any part of his person except his hand, which is in a straight line between wicket and wicket, even though the point of impact be above the level of the bails, he intercept a ball which has not first touched his bat or hand, and which, in the opinion of the Umpire, shall have, or would have, pitched on a straight line from the Bowler's wicket to the Striker's wicket, or shall have pitched on the off-side of the Striker's wicket, provided always that the ball would have hit the wicket.

NOTES

1.—The word "hand" used in this Law should be interpreted as the hand holding the bat.

2.—A batsman is only "Out" under this Law if *all* the four following questions are answered in the affirmative.

(i) Would the ball have hit the wicket?

(ii) Did the ball pitch on a straight line between wicket and wicket (and this case includes a ball intercepted full pitch by the striker), or did it pitch on the offside of the striker's wicket?

(iii) Was it part of the striker's person other than the hand which first intercepted the ball?

(iv) Was that part of the striker's person in a straight line between wicket and wicket at the moment of impact, irrespective of the height of the point of impact?

OBSTRUCTING THE FIELD

40.—Either Batsman is out "Obstructing the field"—If he wilfully obstruct the opposite side; should such wilful obstruction by either Batsman prevent a ball from being caught it is the Striker who is out.

NOTES

1.—The umpire must decide whether the obstruction was "wilful" or not. The involuntary interception by a batsman while running of a throw in is not in itself an offence.

2.—The correct entry in the score book when a batsman is given out under this Law is "Obstructing the field," and the bowler does not get credit for the wicket.

RUN OUT

41.—Either Batsman is out "Run out"—If in running or at any time, while the ball is in play, he be out of his ground, and his wicket be put down by the opposite side. If the batsmen have crossed each other, he that runs for the wicket which is put down is out; if they have not crossed, he that has left the wicket which is put down is out. But unless he attempt to run, the Striker shall not be given "Run out" in the circumstances stated in Law 42, even should "No Ball" have been called.

NOTE

1.—If the ball is played on to the opposite wicket, neither batsman is liable to be "Run out" unless the ball has been touched by a fieldsman before the wicket is put down.

STUMPED

42.—The Striker is out "Stumped"—If in receiving a ball, not being a "No Ball," delivered by the Bowler, he be out of his ground otherwise than in attempting a run, and the wicket be put down by the Wicket-keeper without the intervention of another fieldsman. Only when the ball has touched the bat or person of the Striker may the Wicket-keeper take it in front of the wicket for this purpose.

NOTE

1.—The striker may be "Stumped" if the wicket is broken by a ball rebounding from the wicket-keeper's person.

THE WICKET-KEEPER

43.—The Wicket-keeper shall remain wholly behind the wicket until a ball delivered by the Bowler touches the bat or person of the Striker, or passes the wicket, or until the Striker attempts a run. Should the Wicket-keeper contravene this Law, the Striker shall not be out except under Laws 36, 37, 40 and 41 and then only subject to Law 46.

NOTE

1.—This Law is provided to secure to the striker his right to play the ball and to guard his wicket without interference from the wicket-keeper. The striker may not be penalised if in the legitimate defence of his wicket he interferes with the wicket-keeper except as provided for in Law 37, Note 2.

THE FIELDSMAN

44.—The Fieldsman may stop the ball with any part of his person, but if he wilfully stop it otherwise five runs shall be added to the run or runs already made; if no run has been made five shall be scored. The penalty shall be added to the score of the Striker if the ball has been struck, but otherwise to the score of Byes, Leg Byes, No Balls or Wides as the case may be.

NOTES

1.—A fieldsman must not use his cap, etc., for the purpose of fielding a ball.

2.—The five runs are a penalty and the batsmen do not change ends.

E)—DUTIES OF THE UMPIRES

45.—Before the toss for innings, the Umpires shall acquaint themselves with any special regulations, and shall agree with both Captains on any other conditions affecting the conduct of the match; shall satisfy themselves that the wickets are properly pitched; and shall agree between themselves on the watch or clock to be followed during play.

NOTES

1.—Apart from "Special Regulations" (*see* Law 10, Note 1), other conditions of play within the framework of the Laws are frequently necessary, *e.g.* Hours of play, Intervals, etc.

2.—The captains are entitled to know which clock or watch will be followed during play.

46.—Before and during a match the Umpires shall ensure that the conduct of the game and the implements used are strictly in accordance with the Laws; they are the sole judges of fair and unfair play, and the final judges of the fitness of the ground, the weather and the light for play in the event of the decision being left to them; all disputes shall be determined by them, and if they disagree the actual state of things shall continue. The Umpires shall change ends after each side has had one innings.

NOTES

1.—An umpire should stand where he can best see any act upon which his decision may be required. Subject to this over-riding consideration the umpire at the bowler's end should stand where he does not interfere with either the bowler's run up or the striker's view. If the other umpire wishes to stand on the off instead of the leg side of the pitch, he should obtain the permission of the captain of the fielding side and inform the batsman.

2.—The umpires must not allow the attitude of the players or spectators to influence their decisions under the Laws.

3.—A code of signals for umpires is laid down in the Notes to the relevant Laws; but an umpire must call as well as signal, if necessary, to inform the players and scorers.

4.—FAIR AND UNFAIR PLAY.

(i) The umpires are entitled to intervene without appeal in the case of unfair play, but should not otherwise interfere with the progress of the game, except as required to do so by the Laws.

(ii) In the event of a player failing to comply with the instructions of an umpire or criticising his decisions, the umpires should in the first place request the captains to take action, and if this proves ineffective, report the incident forthwith to the executives of the teams taking part in the match.

(iii) It is illegal for a player to lift the seam of the ball in order to obtain a better hold. In such a case the umpire will if necessary change the ball for one which has had similar wear, and will warn the captain that the practice is unfair. The use of resin, wax, etc., by bowlers is also unfair, but a bowler may dry the ball when wet on a towel or with sawdust.

(iv) An umpire is justified in intervening under this Law should any player of the fielding side incommode the striker by any noise or motion while he is receiving a ball.

(v) The umpires are justified in preventing players from causing damage to the pitch which may assist the bowlers.

(vi) The persistent bowling of fast short-pitched balls at the batsman is unfair if, in the opinion of the umpire at the bowler's end, it constitutes a systematic attempt at intimidation. In such event it must adopt the following procedure:—

(a) When he decides that such bowling is becoming persistent he forthwith "cautions" the bowler.

(b) If this "caution" is ineffective, he informs the captain of the fielding side and the other umpire of what has occurred.

(c) Should the above prove ineffective, the umpire at the bowler's end must:—

(i) At the first repetition call "Dead Ball," when the over is regarded as completed.

(ii) Request the captain of the fielding side to take the bowler off forthwith.

(iii) Report the occurrence to the captain of the batting side as soon as an interval of play takes place.

A bowler who has been "taken off" as above may not bowl again during the same innings.

(vii) Any attempt by the batsmen to *steal a run* during the bowler's run up is unfair. Unless the bowler throws the ball at either wicket (*see* Laws 26 Note 3, and 27, Note 2), the umpire should call "Dead Ball" as soon as the batsmen cross in any such attempt to run, after which they return to their original wickets.

(viii) No player shall leave the field for the purpose of having a rub down or shower while play is actually in progress.

5.—GROUND, WEATHER AND LIGHT.

(i) Unless agreement to the contrary is made before the start of a match, the captains (during actual play the batsmen at the wickets may deputise for their captain) may elect to decide in regard to the fitness of the ground, weather or light for play; otherwise or in the event of disagreement, the Umpires are required to decide.

(ii) Play should only be suspended when the conditions are so bad that it is unreasonable or dangerous for it to continue. The ground is unfit for play when water stands on the surface or when it is so wet or slippery as to deprive the batsmen or bowlers of a reasonable foothold, or the fieldsmen of the power of free movement. Play should *not* be suspended merely because the grass is wet and the ball slippery.

(iii) After any suspension of play, the captains, or, if the decision has been left to them, the Umpires, unaccompanied by any of the players, will without further instruction carry out an inspection immediately the conditions improve, and will continue to inspect at intervals. Immediately the responsible parties decide that play is possible, they must call upon the players to resume the game.

APPEALS

47.—The Umpires shall not order a Batsman out unless appealed to by the other side which shall be done prior to the delivery of the next ball, and before "Time" is called under Law 18. The Umpire at the Bowler's wicket shall answer appeals before the other Umpire in all cases except those arising out of Laws 38 or 42 and out of Law 41 for run out at the Striker's wicket. In any case in which an Umpire is unable to give a decision, he shall appeal to the other Umpire whose decision shall be final.

NOTES

1.—An appeal, "How's that?" covers all ways of being out (within the jurisdiction of the umpire appealed to), unless a specific way of getting out is stated by the person asking. When either umpire has given a batsman "Not out" the other umpire may answer any appeal within his jurisdiction, provided it is made in time.

2.—The umpires signal "Out" by raising the index finger above the head. If the batsman is not out, the umpire calls "Not out."

3.—An umpire may alter his decision provided that such alteration is made promptly.

4.—Nothing in this Law prevents an umpire before giving a decision from consulting the other umpire on a point of fact which the latter may have been in a better position to observe. An umpire should not appeal to the other umpire in cases on which he could give a decision, merely because he is unwilling to give that decision. If after consultation he is still in any doubt, the principle laid down in Law 46 applies and the decision will be in favour of the batsman.

5.—The umpires should intervene if satisfied that a batsman, not having been given out, has left his wicket under a misapprehension.

6.—Under Law 25 the ball is "Dead" on "Over" being called; this does not invalidate an appeal made prior to the first ball of the following "Over," provided the bails have not been removed by both umpires after "Time" has been called.

NOTES FOR SCORERS AND UMPIRES

1. (a) Law 4 explains the status of the scorers in relation to the umpires.

(b) During the progress of the game, if two scorers have been appointed, they should frequently check the total to ensure that the score sheets agree.

(c) The following method of entering "No Balls" and "Wides" (Laws 27 and 29) in the score sheet is recommended:—

(i) If no run is scored from the bat off a "No Ball," the latter should be entered as an "Extra," and a dot placed in the bowling analysis with a circle round it to show that the ball does not count in the over.

(ii) If runs are scored from the bat off a "No Ball," they should be credited to the striker, and entered in the bowling analysis with a circle round the figure. Such runs count against the bowler in his analysis even though the ball does not count in the over.

(iii) All runs scored from "Wide Balls" are entered as "Extras," and inserted in the bowler's analysis with a cross to indicate that the ball does not count in the over.

2. The following code of signalling between the umpires and the scorers has been approved:—

> Boundaries—by waving the hand from side to side.
> A boundary six—by raising both arms above the head.
> Byes—by raising the open hand above the head.
> Leg Byes—by touching a raised knee with the hand.
> Wides—by extending both arms horizontally.
> No Balls—by extending one arm horizontally.
> The decision "Out"—by raising the index finger above the head.
> "One Short"—by bending the arm upwards and by touching the top of the nearest shoulder with the tips of the fingers of one hand.

3. If the above instructions are properly carried out, cases of disagreement as regards the scores and the results of matches should not occur.

It is, however, important that the captains should satisfy themselves of the correctness of the scores on the conclusion of play, as errors cannot subsequently be corrected.

It should be noted that, in general, by accepting the result notified by the scorers, the captain of the losing side has thereby acquiesced in the "playing out or giving up" of the match as stated in Law 22.

SPECIAL INSTRUCTIONS FOR UMPIRES IN FIRST-CLASS MATCHES, 1955

1. The conduct of the game will be governed by the Official Laws of Cricket, 1947 Code, 2nd Edition, 1952. The attention of Umpires is particularly drawn to the provisions of Law 46 and the Notes thereto. In addition to reporting as laid down in Note 4, they will make a report to the Secretary of the M.C.C. and to the Secretary of the Club to which the offending player belongs in the event of their having to intervene in any case of "unfair" play.

Any waste of time by either side, which in the opinion of both Umpires is unfair, and may affect the Championship table shall be dealt with under this Instruction.

2. APPEALS AGAINST THE LIGHT

(a) Law 46 will apply in respect of bad light in the following sense: Appeals against the light, in any form whatever, may not be made by the players of either side. If, however, either Umpire considers that the light is so bad that to continue play would be dangerous to the striker, he will consult his fellow Umpire, and, if both are agreed, the game will be suspended. Should conditions improve later the Umpires shall, without waiting for instructions, call upon the players to resume the game. Umpires will note that it is the light as it affects the striker which is the deciding factor, therefore it may sometimes be necessary for both of them to observe the conditions from each end of the pitch. The Umpires must make their decision and act upon it without conferring with the Captain of the fielding side or any of the players.

3. NEW BALL RULE—LAW 5, NOTE 2

Law 5, Note 2, as applicable to first-class matches in the United Kingdom, will be in abeyance and the captain of the fielding side may demand a new ball after 200 runs have been made off the old one.

4. DECLARATIONS

(*a*) In 1955, Law 15 shall be in abeyance only in so far as it refers to a declaration on the first day of a match lasting three days or more, or when such a match has become a two-day match owing to no play being possible on the first day.

The captain of the batting side may declare an innings closed at any time during a match subject to provision of sub-para. (*b*).

(*b*) If under Law 16 a match becomes a one-day one, the following words shall be added to that part of Law 15 which refers to such matches:—

"But no side shall declare its first innings closed until it has batted for at least sixty minutes."

(*c*) Law 15 provides an option to the captain of a batting side only, and it is not the intention that any declaration should become the subject of an agreement between the captains. If the umpires have grounds for thinking that any such agreement has taken place, they shall report accordingly to the M.C.C., and if the M.C.C. Committee is satisfied that agreement is proved, any points scored shall not be counted in the Championship table.

5. MOWING THE PITCH.   See Law 10, Note 5.

6. ROLLING OF THE PITCH.   See Law 10, Note 2.

7. DRYING OF THE PITCH

The attention of Umpires is drawn to the regulations on pp. 23 and 24 of the 1947—2nd Edition, 1952, code of the Official Laws of Cricket.

N.B.—*For* "wicket" *read* "pitch" in paras. 1, 2 (iv), (v) and (vi).

8. COVERING THE PITCH

Law 11 shall apply. The whole pitch may be covered only (i) not earlier than 11 a.m. on the day immediately preceding a match and until the first ball is bowled and (ii) in the case of a week-end match, provided it is the rule of the ground, when, if necessary, the pitch may be wholly covered from the cessation of play on Saturday until the re-start of play. Such covering, however, is permissible only if the pitch has already been wholly covered as provided in (i) above. (iii) If both captains and umpires are in agreement that, during the course of the match, the pitch has become so saturated that further rain will considerably delay the restart. In this event the umpires shall decide when the covers shall be removed. (The umpires may, if they consider it necessary, issue instructions to the groundsman overnight regarding the removal of covers early next day.)

9. ATTENDANCE OF UMPIRES

Umpires shall report themselves to the management of the ground half an hour before the commencement of play on the first day and at 9 a.m. on succeeding days. They must remain on the ground for half an hour after "Time" on each day, if required to do so by the management.

N.B.—Except where otherwise stated, these instructions apply in all First-class Matches with South Africa, including Test Matches, with the exception of Instruction No. 8.

REGULATIONS FOR DRYING THE PITCH AND GROUND IN FIRST-CLASS MATCHES IN THE UNITED KINGDOM

N.B.—*These regulations are primarily designed for First-class Cricket, and their application in whole or in part in other grades of Cricket in the United Kingdom is at the discretion of the ground, etc., authorities.*

1. Except as provided below, the existing regulations in regard to the rolling of the wicket and the fitness of the ground for play shall apply. (*See* Laws 10, 12 and 46.)

2. (i) To enable play to proceed with the least possible delay after rain, the groundsman shall adopt every practical means to protect or rid the surface of the ground, *other than the pitch*, of water or dampness at any time except while play is in progress.

(ii) Prior to tossing for choice of innings, the artificial drying of the pitch shall be at the discretion of the groundsman, but thereafter, and throughout the match, the drying process shall be carried out only on the instructions and under the supervision of the umpires, who shall be empowered to have the pitch dried, without reference to the captains, at any time they are of opinion that it is unfit for play.

(iii) In wet weather, the umpires shall see that the foot-holes made by the bowlers and batsmen are cleaned, dried and filled up with sawdust at any time during the match, although the game is not actually in progress.

The groundsman, without instructions from the umpires, may also clean out in this way foot-holes, provided they are not on any part of the pitch, more than 3 ft. 6 ins. in front of the Popping creases.

The *drying* of foot-holes on the pitch itself shall be supervised by the umpires, but, in the interval between close of play on any day and its further resumption, the groundsman may *protect* against further rain, marks made by the bowlers, even though they be more than 3 ft. 6 ins. in front of the Popping creases, provided they are not between wicket and wicket, with loose sawdust, which, however, shall be removed prior to the resumption of play.

(iv) The umpires shall ascertain from the groundsman before the commencement of a match what equipment is available for drying the pitch artificially.

Before drying the pitch the umpires shall have regard to the condition of the outfield and the prospects of its fitness for play. The drier shall be removed when they are satisfied that the pitch is fit for play, or as they may direct.

Any roller may be used, if the umpires think desirable but only (except as laid down in paragraph (2) (v)) for the purpose of drying the pitch and making it fit for play, and not otherwise. This would allow umpires to roll the pitch after drying it, say with a light roller, for a minute or two, should they consider it desirable.

(v) When the artificial drying of the pitch, under the supervision of the umpires, coincides with any interval during the match, after the toss for choice of innings, the umpires, and not the captain of the batting side, shall select the roller to be used.

(vi) The fact that the umpires may have dried the pitch artificially does not take the decision as regards the fitness of the pitch and ground for play out of the hands of the captains, even though the umpires may have selected the roller to be used for the drying process. Law 46, Note 5 (i) is applicable in such cases.

IMPERIAL CRICKET CONFERENCE

CONSTITUTION

The governing bodies of cricket in countries within the British Commonwealth, having been duly elected, shall be entitled to send not more than two representatives to a meeting of the Conference. The M.C.C., on its own initiative, may, or on the request of any two members, summon a meeting of the Imperial Cricket Conference.

RULES FOR TEST MATCHES

Test Matches are matches played between sides duly selected by Governing Bodies of cricket who are members of the Imperial Cricket Conference.

A cricketer can be qualified to play in a Test Match either by birth or residence.

(a) QUALIFICATION BY BIRTH.—A cricketer unless debarred by the Imperial Cricket Conference is always eligible to play for the country of his birth.

(b) QUALIFICATION BY RESIDENCE.—A cricketer unless debarred by the Imperial Cricket Conference shall be entitled to play for any country in which he is residing and has been residing during the four immediately preceding years provided that he has not played for the country of his birth during that period.

(c) Notwithstanding anything hereinbefore contained, any player who has once played in a Test Match for any country shall not afterwards be eligible to play in a Test Match against that country without the consent of its Governing Body.

(d) Members shall be responsible for submitting, in reasonable time for the approval of the Conference, the names of any cricketers whose qualifications are in doubt, and who are likely to be selected to play in any approaching series of Test Matches, furnishing their qualifications and stating if any player has during the four immediately preceding years played for the country of his birth. In the case of cricketers qualified by residence, they shall further state the periods of residence upon which such qualifications are founded.

RULES FOR APPOINTMENT OF TEST UMPIRES

The following rules for the selection and appointment of Test Match umpires shall be followed as far as it is practicable to do so:—

(a) The Home authority to nominate a group of umpires considered qualified to officiate in Test Matches.

(b) All umpires in this group should be considered as equally qualified for the purpose of appointment in accordance with the policy of the Home authority in this matter.

(c) While a captain is entitled to submit objections to a particular umpire being appointed for a Test Match, he may not ask for a particular umpire to be given precedence for appointment over any other umpire in the group.

(d) Previous to any Test Match the visiting captain whenever possible should be given an opportunity of judging the umpires being considered for appointment, and the names of the umpires to be appointed to officiate in a Test Match shall not be made public until the captains have had reasonable opportunity to submit objections.

(e) During each series of Test Matches a Committee should be appointed by the Home authority to adjudicate on matters arising from (c) and (d) and their decisions shall be regarded as final.

(f) The sole authority for handling Press enquiries shall be the official representative appointed by the Home authority for the purpose, and not the captains or any of the players.

FIRST-CLASS MATCH DEFINED

A match of three or more days duration between two sides of eleven players officially adjudged First-class shall be regarded as a First-class fixture.

The following matches by this definition shall not be regarded as First-class: If either team has more than 11 players. If the duration of the match is shorter than three days.

The Governing body in each country shall decide the status of teams.

Any question arising under these rules shall be submitted to the Imperial Cricket Conference, and their decision shall be final.

DURATION OF TEST MATCHES

Beginning with the M.C.C. 1946–47 tour, the duration of Test matches between England and Australia has been standardised at 30 hours' play spread over six days in Australia and five days in England, without prejudice to the final Test which may be played to a finish in certain circumstances.

FUTURE TOURS

Visits to U.K.		*Tours Abroad*	
1956	Australia.	1955–56	New Zealand to Pakistan and India.
1957	West Indies.		
1958	New Zealand.	1955–56	M.C.C. "A" to Pakistan.
1959	India.	1955–56	West Indies to New Zealand.
1960	South Africa.	1956–57	M.C.C. to South Africa.
1961	Australia.	1956–57	Australia to New Zealand.
1962	Pakistan.	1957–58	Australia to South Africa.
1963	West Indies.	1957–58	Pakistan to West Indies.
1964	Australia.	1958–59	M.C.C. to Australia and New Zealand.
		1959–60	M.C.C. to West Indies.
		1961–62	M.C.C. to India, Pakistan and Ceylon.
		1962–63	M.C.C. to Australia and New Zealand.
		1964–65	M.C.C. to South Africa.

BOARD OF CONTROL OF "TEST" MATCHES AT HOME

(Formed at the request of the Counties by the M.C.C., 1898)

To consist of the President of M.C.C. or his nominee, and not more than five of its Club Committee, one representative from each of the first ten Counties of the previous season's First-class Championship table, and one representative from each County on whose ground a Test Match is to be played subject to such County not already being represented, whenever matters affecting such Test Matches are to be discussed.

The Board shall be responsible for the organisation and administration of all Test and Trial matches in England.

N.B.1.—The Agenda for the Board of Control meetings will be issued to all Counties and the Minor Counties' Cricket Association.

N.B.2.—Counties not represented on the Board of Control may send one representative to the meetings of the Board. In addition, the Minor Counties Cricket Association may appoint one of their members to attend meetings of the Board. Such representatives shall not be entitled to vote on any resolution, but provided not less than three days' previous notice has been given to the Secretary of the M.C.C. of the wish of a County Committee, their representative shall be permitted to take part in the discussion upon specifically stated Agenda items.

Rules for 1955

(TEST MATCHES WITH SOUTH AFRICA)

FINANCIAL CONDITIONS

The Manager of the visiting team will receive on behalf of his Governing Body from each ground authority, 50 per cent of the net revenue, after deduction of Entertainment Tax, received in respect of admission of spectators at the outer gate.

The charge for admission at the outer gate in Test Matches at all grounds shall be 5/– per day.

No collections shall be allowed on the ground during any Test Match.

PLAYING CONDITIONS

Except as specially provided for, the current Official Laws of Cricket shall apply in all Test Matches.

The attention of umpires is called to the Special Instructions issued for 1955, which shall apply in all Test Matches, except so far as they are not varied by the following playing conditions.

UMPIRES

The Chairman of the Selection Committee and the Captain of the visiting team shall be notified confidentially in advance of Test Matches of the names of the umpires appointed to stand. Any objection lodged against either umpire must be received within three days of the notice being issued, and will be dealt with by the Umpires' Committee whose decision shall be final.

No member of either team will make any statement to the Press in connection with the appointment of umpires.

DURATION OF MATCHES AND HOURS OF PLAY

The Test Matches shall be of five days' duration. In all Test Matches play shall begin at 11.30 a.m. on each day. Stumps shall be drawn at 6.30 each day. Luncheon Interval 1.30–2.10. A Tea Interval shall be allowed as provided for in Match Regulation No. 3.

Drinks shall not be taken on the field to the same team more than once in each period of play.

EXCHANGING TEAMS

The two captains before tossing shall give each other a list of the eleven selected to play together with the emergency fieldsman. Afterwards no alteration shall be made in either eleven or emergency fieldsman without the consent of the opposing captain.

PLAYERS LEAVING THE FIELD

No player on the fielding side shall leave the field for the purpose of having a rub down or shower whilst a Test Match is actually in progress.

BOUNDARIES

The boundary lines shall be in accordance with the custom of the ground for Test Matches except when agreement to the contrary has been reached between the parties concerned not less that 14 days before the start of any match.

SCREENS

The matter of providing screens behind the bowler's arm at each end of the ground shall be left to the discretion of the ground authority on which a Test Match is played, the usual custom on such ground to prevail.

COVERING THE PITCH

The pitch shall be completely protected against rain if necessary and as far as practicable twenty-four hours before the time advertised for the start of a Test Match or until play begins. After the first ball has been bowled the covers shall not protect more than 3 ft. 6 in. in front of the popping crease at each end.

MOWING AND ROLLING THE PITCH

The grass on the pitch shall be mown as laid down in Law 10 Note 5 of the Official Laws of Cricket.

Except as provided for in the Regulations for drying the pitch, Law 10 of the Official Laws of Cricket shall govern the rolling of the pitch.

FITNESS OF PITCH AND GROUND

Except as provided for in the Official Laws of Cricket the two captains shall decide as to the fitness of the pitch and ground for play, unless they disagree or prefer to leave the decision to the umpires. If the decision is left to the umpires the captains shall forthwith advise them accordingly.

In wet weather the pitch may be dried artificially in accordance with the Regulations in the Official Laws of Cricket.

TRAVELLING EXPENSES

A player or umpire will be paid the cost of a first-class railway fare from the ground on which he was last engaged or from his home, if he has not been immediately engaged prior to the Test Match. He will similarly be paid the cost of a first-class railway fare to the ground on which he is next engaged or to his home if he is not so engaged.

Selectors may claim an allowance of 6d. per mile for the use of their private car in the course of their duties.

If a player or umpire travels by car he may claim the equivalent railway fare as stipulated above, but may not claim garage charges in addition.

HOTEL AND INCIDENTAL EXPENSES

The ground authority, when so requested, will arrange for hotel accommodation, and will pay the hotel account excluding expenses for guests, drinks, tobacco and other personal items.

Players who do not use the accommodation so provided will not be entitled to claim hotel or lodging charges. Umpires and Selectors may however do so.

All professionals and umpires will be allowed 10/– per day for the actual duration of any match for incidental expenses. This allowance does not apply to amateurs who will be entitled to claim an allowance of 10/– a meal for meals taken away from the hotel and during journeys to and from the match.

A match allowance of £7 10s. 0d. for a five-day Test Match (the allowance to be £6 and £4 10s. 0d. respectively for a four-day and three-day Test Match) to cover travelling expenses not otherwise provided for, fares to and from the ground and hotel, tips, upkeep of equipment and clothing and the cost of laundry.

REMUNERATION OF PLAYERS, ETC.

						Test Match
Professionals playing	..	..	..	..	..	£75 per match
12th man (if selected as Reserve)	..		..	..	..	£10 per day
Reserves	..	..	..	..	..	£22 per match
Umpires	..	..	..	..	..	£50 per match
Scorer for match of over 3 days' duration	..			..	..	£20 per match

An emergency fieldsman will be paid a fee to be agreed on by the Ground Authority and the Chairman of the Selection Committee.

INSURANCE OF PLAYERS

The Secretary M.C.C. will take out an insurance policy to cover the risk of accidents to professionals (including 12th man and reserves) playing in Test or Trial Matches.

DISTRIBUTION OF PROFITS

All monies taken at Stands and Enclosures at all Test Matches together with gate money in respect thereof, less the opponents' 50 per cent share for each person paying admission at the outer gate, less tax and expenses, shall be distributed as follows: 40 per cent between each first-class county on whose ground the Test Match is played; 50 per cent between the remaining first-class counties (Oxford and Cambridge Universities together to count as one first-class county) 10 per cent between each Minor County with Combined Services to receive one half of the amount given to a Minor County club. M.C.C. to rank as a first-class county for the purpose of the foregoing.

SELECTION COMMITTEE

The Selection Committee shall consist of a Chairman and three members with the power to call into consultation at any meeting any cricketer, past or present. The Committee shall select a captain who shall be an *ex-officio* member of the Committee. The Committee, with the captain, shall select the team. In the event of no majority agreement, the captain's wish in regard to the selection of a player shall prevail.

ADVISORY COUNTY CRICKET COMMITTEE

In 1904, with the approval of the Counties, the M.C.C. formed an Advisory County Cricket Committee to consider cases arising out of County and other Cricket.

RULES

1.—The Advisory County Cricket Committee shall consist of a representative of each First-Class County, appointed by his Committee, and three members representing and appointed by the Minor Counties' Cricket Association, and at least one member of the M.C.C.

2.—The Chairman of this Committee shall be the President of the M.C.C. or some other member of the Committee of the M.C.C. nominated by him or in default of such nomination, by the Committee of the M.C.C.

3.—All resolutions passed by this Committee shall be submitted to the M.C.C. Committee for confirmation.

4.—A meeting may be convened either by five or more First-Class Counties or by the Minor Counties' Cricket Association and two, or more, First-Class Counties or by the M.C.C., and notice shall be sent to all parties interested at least 21 days before the day of meeting.

5.—When submitting any item for inclusion in the Agenda, it shall be incumbent on the proposer to forward a memorandum on the subject.

6.—The notice shall contain an agenda of the meeting. Notice of an amendment to a resolution on the agenda must be given at least 14 days before the day of meeting.

THE COUNTY CRICKET COMPETITIONS AND CLASSIFICATION

1. Cricketing Counties may be classified either as First-class or Minor; included in the latter category are the second XI's of First-class Counties who have joined the Minor Counties' Cricket Association.

2. First-class Counties are as defined in Appendix III to the Rules of the Imperial Cricket Conference. Minor Counties are as defined in the Rules of the Minor Counties' Cricket Association.

3. There shall be no limit to the number of First-class Counties. The M.C.C. Committee may bring new Counties into the list, may remove existing Counties from it, or may do both.

4. That a meeting of County Secretaries be held annually at The Oval during the first week in March, for the purpose of revising the provisional lists referred to in paragraph 3, and to elect the fixtures Sub-Committee for the following year.

5. After the close of each cricket season, the Committee of the M.C.C. shall, if necessary, decide the First-class County Championship.

6. The Rules for the Minor County competition are laid down in the Minor Counties' Cricket Association's handbook.

REGULATIONS FOR A.C.C.C. FIXTURES SUB-COMMITTEE

1. That a Sub-Committee be appointed annually to arrange provisionally the County fixtures for the year next but one.

2. That the Sub-Committee shall consist of four members:—One County Secretary, who will be eligible for re-election; One member of the M.C.C., not a County Secretary, who shall be nominated annually by the M.C.C. The Secretaries of two Counties who shall be elected annually by ballot at the meeting referred to in paragraph 4, who shall serve for one year and shall not be eligible for re-election until all other Counties have (by their Secretaries) served on the Sub-Committee.

3. That the Secretary of each County shall submit before 1st January for the consideration of the Sub-Committee a draft programme of matches to be played by his County calling attention to particular dates, "weeks," etc. Provisional programmes shall then be arranged by the Sub-Committee and circulated to the Secretaries by the middle of February.

4. That a meeting of County Secretaries be held annually at The Oval during the first week in March, for the purpose of revising the provisional lists referred to in paragraph 3, and to elect the fixtures Sub-Committee for the following year.

5. That the Sub-Committee shall have power at the meeting of Secretaries referred to in paragraph 4 (March) to revise any list and that no alterations in the provisional lists shall be made before that meeting except with the approval of the Fixtures Sub-Committee and no alterations after that meeting except by mutual consent.

6. Every County shall play every other County each season; twelve of the opponents to be played twice and the remainder once.

Each County shall have eight opponents who will remain "Permanent" subject to alteration as is provided for below, and who will be played twice in each season. Not more than four of such permanent opponents may be selected by mutual agreement, and the remainder will be allotted by the Fixtures Sub-Committee.

Of the remaining Counties, four shall be played once each season (List A) for two consecutive seasons and the remaining four (List B) shall be played twice; at the end of the two-year cycle, Lists A and B shall be reversed.

In the case of the four Counties played once each season two matches shall be "Home" and two "Away"; these shall be reversed in the following season.

The division of the eight non-permanent opponents into List A and B shall be made by the Fixtures Sub-Committee on the principle of equalising as closely as possible the distribution of matches between the two lists.

Counties may, by mutual agreement, make changes in their permanent fixtures to take effect at the end of each four-year cycle; any changes must be made in time to conform to paragraph 3 of these Regulations.

7. That the Annual Meeting of Secretaries at Lord's be held in December.

8. No alteration in these rules shall be adopted for recommendation to the A.C.C.C. unless notice of such proposed alteration is given to the Chairman of the Fixtures Sub-Committee in time to be included by him in the notice convening the Annual Meeting of the County Secretaries at The Oval. (March.)

MATCH REGULATIONS
FIRST-CLASS MATCHES, 1955

REGULATION 1. HOURS OF PLAY.

The "Standard" hours of play in Inter-County Matches are as under:—

1st and 2nd days	11.30 a.m. to 6.30 p.m.
3rd day	11.30 a.m. to 6 p.m. with an extra 30 minutes on this day on the demand of either Captain for the purpose of securing a result in the match or on the first innings.

Alterations in the above "Standard" hours shall only be permitted in the following circumstances and within the limits stated:—

(a) The total hours (including all intervals, stoppages and extra time) shall not exceed 21 hours, or be less than 20 hours in any match, and shall not exceed 7 hours (including extra time) on the third day, or 8 hours (excluding extra time) on any other day.

(b) On no day shall play commence earlier than 11 a.m. or end later than 7.30 p.m. (including extra time) on either of the first two days, or 6.30 p.m. (including extra time) on the third day.

(c) Subject to (a) and (b) above, the executive of the Home County may modify the "Standard" hours of play in order to meet the requirements of evening play on the first and second days, and, if essential, to facilitate travelling on the third day in those cases only in which a team will be unable to reach its next destination before midnight.

The "Standard" hours of play shall be adhered to as closely as possible, and any departure from them, mutually agreed between the two Counties will be notified to all concerned including the Press, before the commencement of the season and thereafter no alternative will be permitted, except to meet exceptional travelling difficulties of either team or the umpires. In the latter case the County requiring departure from the "Standard" hours, shall notify its opponents within 7 days of the match, and the Home County will be responsible for giving notice of such alterations to the Umpires and the Press.

(d) If, in the opinion of both Captains, 30 minutes extra time at the end of the first and/or second day's play would bring about a definite result on that day the umpires shall order the same. If, however, the Captains disagree the decision shall be left to the umpires. Any time so claimed will not preclude either side demanding an extra 30 minutes on the third day for the purpose of securing a result in the match or on the first innings, provided the maximum of 21 hours allowed by sub-para. (a) is not exceeded.

REGULATION 2. INTERVALS.

The first bell shall be rung 15 minutes before the time appointed for the start of play on each day. The second bell shall be rung 10 minutes later, when the umpires shall go to the wickets. Luncheon shall take place at 1.30 p.m., or at such hour as may be mutually agreed in advance of the match, unless an alteration owing to the weather or the state of the ground has been agreed upon by the Captains or ordered by the umpires. The first bell shall be rung at 1.55 p.m. and the ground cleared. The second bell shall be rung 10 minutes later, when the umpires shall go to the wickets. Play shall commence at 2.10 p.m. unless the above-mentioned alteration has been made, when corresponding intervals shall be observed. Five minutes before the termination of an interval, between innings or for tea, the bell shall be rung, when the ground shall be cleared and the umpires shall go to the wickets.

REGULATION 3. TEA INTERVAL.

1. Subject to the provisions in sub-paras. (2) and (3)—

   (a) A tea interval of 20 minutes shall be taken to START not earlier than 3.45 p.m. or later than 4.45 p.m.

   (b) Tea shall be taken at 4.15 p.m. except in the following circumstances—

      (i) If nine wickets are then down, play shall continue for a period not exceeding 30 minutes after which tea will be taken.

      (ii) If at or after 3.45 p.m. an innings closes or play is suspended—this includes a suspension which may have begun before 3.45 p.m.—the tea interval of 20 minutes (to include the interval between innings) shall then be taken.

      (iii) If before 3.45 p.m. an innings closes or the game is resumed after a stoppage, tea shall be taken at 4.15 p.m. or after 50 minutes' play, whichever is the later.

2. There shall be no tea interval on any day—

(i) If both Captains agree to forgo it.

(ii) If the close of play on any day (excluding any extra time permitted by Regulation 1) has been fixed at or before 5.30 p.m.

(iii) If there has been no play at all between 2.45 p.m. and 3.45 p.m.

3. The above timings shall apply in all cases, except when the close of play on any day has been fixed for 7 p.m. or later (excluding any extra time permitted by Regulation 1). In such cases all the timings in this Regulation shall be 15 minutes later.

REGULATION 4. REPORT BY UMPIRES, ETC.

The umpires and the executive of the Home Ground shall report any breach of Regulations 1 to 3 inclusive to the Secretary of M.C.C. Before submitting a report the umpires will inform the Secretary of the Home County of the points on which they are reporting.

REGULATION 5. SCORING OF POINTS IN THE COUNTY CHAMPIONSHIP.

The scheme for scoring in the County Championship is as follows:—

(*a*) Should a match be finished the winning side to score 12 points.

(*b*) Should a match be finished and the scores be equal (a "Tie") each side to score 6 points.

(*c*) Should the scores be equal in a drawn match the side batting in the fourth innings to score 6 points in all (whether or not it has first innings lead) and the opponents to score no points, except they will retain such first innings points as they may already have gained.

(*d*) Should a match be finished, the side which leads on the first innings, if it loses the match, to score 4 points. If the scores on the first innings are equal, the side which loses the match to score 2 points.

(*e*) Should a match not be finished the side which leads on the first innings to score 4 points (subject to (*c*) above).

(*f*) Should a match not be finished and the scores of the first innings be equal each side to score 2 points (subject to (*c*) above).

(*g*) Even should there be no play for any reason, or no result obtained on the first innings, every match shall be included in the table of results as a "Match played"; in these cases neither side to score points.

(*h*) If there is no play on the first two days of a match, and it is not carried to a further conclusion than that of the first innings, the side which leads on the first innings shall score 8 points.

(*i*) The side which has the highest aggregate of points gained at the end of the season shall be the Champion County.

N.B.—Regulations No. 2, 3 and 4 shall apply in Test Matches. A special Board of Control rule provides for hours of play in Test Matches.

RULES OF COUNTY CRICKET
FIRST- AND SECOND-CLASS COUNTY COMPETITIONS
As amended by the Advisory County Cricket Committee on March 9, 1954, and to become operative as from April 1, 1954)

GENERAL ARRANGEMENT	RULES
General Rules	1 to 5.
Qualifications	6 to 7
Special Registration	8.
Engagement of Players	9.
Appeals and Decisions	10 to 11.

DEFINITIONS

(*a*) The term "Cricket Dominion" unless otherwise stated shall include only those countries, other than the United Kingdom, who are members or associate members of the Imperial Cricket Conference.

(*b*) An "Overseas First-Class Cricketer" is a cricketer not having been born in the United Kingdom who has played at any time in a first-class competition, organised by the Governing Body of a Cricket Dominion.

(*c*) The term "Residence" as used in these Rules shall mean a bona fide home, and not a mere acquirement or hiring of a tenement during a cricket season only.

(*d*) For the purpose of County Cricket, geographical County Boundaries are those applying at the time of a player's birth, or at the time of his qualification by residence or by any other means. The County of London is not to be regarded as a separate County.

GENERAL RULES

RULE 1. ALTERATIONS TO RULES

No alteration in, or addition to, the Rules of County Cricket shall be made except at a Meeting of the Advisory County Cricket Committee duly convened for the purpose; and no such alteration or addition shall be made except by a vote of two-thirds of the representatives present at such Meeting.

RULE 2. REGISTRATION OF PLAYERS

Before the beginning of each cricket season, each County Cricket Club shall send to the M.C.C. and to every other County Cricket Club, a list of the cricketers, with their respective qualifications, who are expected to play for the County during that season; and if, in the course of the season, a County wishes to play a cricketer not included in that list, his name and qualification shall be circulated in a similar manner forthwith.

Cricketers who have been specially registered for any County will continue to be shown as qualified under Rule 8, so long as they are on the playing strength of that County.

RULE 3. CRICKETER REFUSING RENEWAL OF ENGAGEMENT

A Cricketer who has refused the offer of a renewal of his engagement with a County by whom he has been previously employed, provided this offer did not involve pecuniary loss to the player, shall not be re-registered under any form of qualification.

RULE 4. CRICKETER NOT TO PLAY FOR MORE THAN ONE COUNTY IN A SEASON

A cricketer may not play for more than one County in either competition within the Calendar Year. The penalty for an infringement of this Rule shall be disqualification for two years. A Cricket Dominion shall for the purpose of this Rule be regarded as a County in respect of an Overseas First-class cricketer.

RULE 5. NOTICE TO COUNTIES

Correspondence on all matters which concerns a County Cricket Club will be addressed to the Secretary, and any notice sent to the Secretary of a County Cricket Club shall be regarded as notice to that County.

QUALIFICATIONS

RULE 6. BIRTH AND RESIDENCE

Subject to the provisions of Rules 4 and 9, a cricketer shall be qualified to play:—

(*a*) For the County of his birth.

(b) If born in the United Kingdom—for the County in which he is residing and has resided continually for not less than 12 months. The residence of a Master at a School shall count as a residence for this purpose.

(c) For the County in which his boarding School is situated:—
  (i) Whilst at School
  (ii) For the 12 months thereafter.
If a cricketer has so played and provided that, at any time during the period referred to in (ii) above, he elects to continue to play for that County, his qualification under this Rule shall remain unbroken until he plays for another County.

(d) If born out of the United Kingdom, but not having played previously as an Overseas First-class cricketer—for the County in which he has resided for the previous 24 consecutive months and in which he is still residing.

(e) If born out of the United Kingdom, and having played as an Overseas First-class cricketer—for the County in which he has resided for the previous 36 consecutive months, and in which he is still residing. During this residential qualifying period he shall not engage in a cricket contract outside the County for which he is qualifying.

NOTE.—The County for which an Overseas cricketer is qualifying by residence shall notify M.C.C. of the date on which this player starts his residential qualification.

(f) If he has no qualifications for any County and is resident or was born in a County in which no First or Second-class cricket is played—for the County, the capital of which is nearest to the place of his birth or residence.

(g) For the County for which he has been Specially Registered.

(h) For the County for which his father has played regularly for at least three years.

RULE 7. CONTINUANCE AND CESSATION

(a) A cricketer qualified by residence for one County who then plays for the County of his birth loses the residential qualification for the first named. If he wishes to play again for the County for which he originally played under a residential qualification, he must be re-qualified or be Specially Registered.

(b) A cricketer may play for the County for which he has played and for which he is qualified by residence or by Special Registration, or if he has so played under Rule 6, para. (c) (i) and (ii) above—always provided he has elected to continue to play for that County within one year of the date of his leaving School—for the rest of his cricketing career.

(c) A cricketer, in the course of qualifying by residence for a County, breaks his qualification for that County if he plays for another, or if he engages in a regular cricket contract outside the County for which he is qualifying.

(d) A cricketer acquiring residential qualification for a County does not interrupt that qualifying period by undertaking Government Service or occasional winter work for business reasons outside the County in which his bona fide residence is situated.

SPECIAL REGISTRATION

RULE 8. PROCEDURE

(a) Notwithstanding the provisions of Rule 6, a Registration Committee appointed by M.C.C. for the purpose, may specially register cricketers of the categories stated in this Rule, always provided that:—
  (i) The County applying for a Special Registration has not, during any cricket season, more than 10 players, of whom not more than 8 may be Professionals, shown as qualified under this Rule on their list of players circulated in accordance with Rule 2. (This number shall include any cricketers who, since their Special Registration, may have become qualified by residence under Rule 6.)

(ii) Not more than two applications for Special Registration for any County shall be approved in any Calendar Year, beginning on 1st January.

(iii) The County applying for a Special Registration shall offer a Professional cricketer an engagement for a minimum of 3 years, exclusive of any period of National Service.

(In the case of an amateur cricketer, the County shall undertake to make reasonable use of the player's services, as far as these may be available for at least 2 seasons.)

(*b*) A cricketer shall be eligible for Special Registration if he is not required by the County (or Counties) for which he is qualified, or in which he is residing.

(*c*) The following shall not be eligible for Special Registration:—

(i) A cricketer born outside the United Kingdom, unless he has been resident in the United Kingdom for 10 consecutive years.

(ii) A cricketer who has been specially registered for another County within the previous 5 years, unless the Registration has been cancelled. (Vide paragraph (*f*).)

(*d*) Applications for Special Registration shall be made to M.C.C. on the form provided for the purpose and shall contain a full statement of the case with the written consent of the County (or Counties), for which the cricketer is qualified, or in which he is residing. Each such County shall, in addition, certify that:—

(i) The formalities laid down in Rule 9 have been completely complied with by the applying County.

(ii) They have no evidence that valuable consideration of any nature has passed in order to bring about the engagement or move.

The County applying for the Special Registration shall further guarantee that reasonable use is to be made of the services of the cricketer, and it shall be the duty of the Registration Committee to withhold approval to any application unless absolutely satisfied that the engagement or move is in the interests of the cricketer.

In considering an application for Special Registration, it shall be open either to the County (or Counties) asked to release the cricketer or to the Registration Committee:—

(i) to withhold consent, or

(ii) to agree to qualification under Rule 6 (b), or

(iii) to defer agreement, or

(iv) to agree to the cricketer's immediate Special Registration for the County applying.

(*e*) Subject to Rule 4, a cricketer shall be eligible to play for a County as soon as, but not until the Special Registration has been approved, and on receipt of the approval of a registration by the Registration Committee, the County concerned shall immediately carry out the provisions of Rule 2.

(*f*) M.C.C. shall be empowered to cancel a Special Registration, in any case in which a County has failed to carry out its obligations to make reasonable use of a player, or has been prevented from doing so, but only if such a course is shown to be in the interests of the cricketer.

(*g*) *Infringement of Rule 8 (above)*.—Should the attention of the M.C.C. be called to any unreasonable advantage being taken of the provisions of Rule 8, they shall be empowered to cancel the Special Registration of any cricketer, granted under that Rule. The penalty in Rule 4 shall apply in such cases.

ENGAGEMENT OF PLAYERS

RULE 9. PROCEDURE

a) *Cricketer NOT previously engaged by, or having played for, any County*

A County wishing to offer a trial to, to engage or play a cricketer who has not previously been engaged by, Specially Registered for, or played for another County, must obtain the written consent of the County (or Counties) for which the cricketer is qualified, before starting negotiations with him. Such consent shall not be unreasonably withheld.

(b) Cricketers engaged by, or having played for, a County within the previous 24 months

Should a cricketer who has been engaged by, Specially Registered for, or played for a County within the previous 24 months, wish to qualify by residence for another County, he must obtain a written consent, which must not be antedated from the former County. His residential qualification shall not begin to run until he has obtained this consent, which shall not be unreasonably withheld.

A County wishing to engage or play a cricketer who is engaged by, Specially Registered for, or has played for another County within the previous 24 months, must give written notice to the latter County before starting negotiations with the cricketer.

(c) Overseas First-class Cricketers

The provisions of Paras. *(a)* and *(b)* above, apply to an Overseas First-class cricketer, except that in such cases written consent must be obtained from the State, Province, Colony, or other Cricket Authority concerned, before such a cricketer's residential qualification begins to run.

(d) Cricketer wishing to play for the County of his birth

A cricketer who wishes to play for the County of his birth (see Rule 6) must give written notice to any other County for which he has played within the previous 24 months.

(e) Infringement of Rule 9 (above)

In the event of the infringement of Rule 9, M.C.C. shall have special authority to fix the date when the cricketer shall become qualified by residence, or even bar him from qualifying.

APPEALS AND DECISIONS

Rule 10. Doubtful cases of Qualification

If required to do so, it is obligatory on the County for which a cricketer wishes to play to prove his qualifications to the satisfaction of M.C.C.

Rule 11. Appeals

Any question arising under these Rules shall be left to the decision of M.C.C. which shall be final.

MINOR COUNTIES' CRICKET ASSOCIATION RULES

1. The Association shall be called "The Minor Counties' Cricket Association."

2. All Counties not in the first-class (as classified by the M.C.C.) and the second elevens of first-class Counties shall be eligible to join the Association upon payment of an annual subscription of three guineas or such other sum as the Association shall from time to time determine, and shall be entitled to compete in the Second Division of the County Championship (the Minor Counties' Competition).

3. The Officers of the Association shall consist of President, Chairman, Hon. Secretary, Hon. Treasurer and the representatives of the Minor Counties on the Advisory County Cricket Committee, all of whom shall be *ex-officio* members of the Committee.

4. The Committee shall consist of the *ex-officio* members and one representative each from ten Counties, together with any duly elected Life Member.

5. The officers of the Association shall be elected and the Counties forming the Committee chosen annually at the Annual Meeting.

6. The Association shall have power to elect Life Members to the Committee.

7. The Annual Meeting shall be held at Lord's on the same day as the Annual Meeting of County Secretaries. A Special Meeting shall be called by the Hon. Secretary at the request of four or more Counties. One month's notice of every such Meeting shall be sent to each County, and the notice shall contain the agenda of the Meeting.

8. Only one representative from each County shall be entitled to vote at General Meetings of the Association.

9. Notices of motions to be brought forward at the Annual Meeting shall be sent to the Hon. Secretary before the end of October.

10. A County desirous of entering the Competition for the first time shall give notice to the Hon. Secretary before the end of the previous August.

11. Every County shall play out and home two-day matches with at least four other Counties. In cases of emergency and in order to enable all counties to obtain the necessary number of qualifying matches, prior to the Annual Meeting in each year, the Committee may, after consultation with County Secretaries, re-arrange fixtures for this purpose.

12. A County shall give twelve months' previous notice in writing to the Hon. Secretary and to their opponents of their intention to leave the Competition, such notice to expire on the 30th day of September in any one year.

13. The County which shall have obtained the greatest average points shall (in the absence of a challenge under Rule 16) be reckoned Champion County of the Second Division.

14. If two or more Counties shall have obtained the same average points, preference shall be given to that County which shall have won the greatest number of completed matches.

15. If two or more Counties shall have obtained the same average points and also won the same number of completed matches, their priority shall be decided according to the net batting averages.

* 16. If the two top Counties shall not have played each other, the second County shall have the right to challenge the first to a three-day match, which shall decide the Championship, and shall be played on a ground chosen by the challenged County. In the event of a challenge match, the winners shall be the Champion County, but in the event of a decision on the first innings only (the match not being played as a one-day match) the points for a result on the first innings shall be added in the table of results to those already gained by the respective Counties, and their average re-calculated accordingly. If no result shall have been attained in this match, the Championship shall be decided as if there had been no challenge.

17. In every challenge match under Rule 16 the hours of play shall be those in force for matches played in the First-Class Competition. Each County shall bear its own expenses and shall receive half the gross gate-money, after deducting the fees paid to the umpires and Entertainment Tax. Gross gate-money shall be regarded as the total sum paid for admission to the Ground by spectators as distinct from admission to Stands.

18. Points in the Competition shall be reckoned as follows:—Ten points shall be scored for a win in a completed two-day match and for a win on the first innings when there is no play on the first day of a two-day match, provided the match is not played out, when the match shall be played under the Rules of Cricket for one-day matches. Should a two-day match not be completed the side leading on the first innings shall score three points and its opponents one point. In the event of a tie on the first innings in an unfinished match each side shall be awarded two points. In matches in which no result shall have been attained each side

* See page 1014.

will be awarded two points. In the event of a tie,* the ten points shall be equally divided.

* A tied match is one in which the scores are equal at the conclusion of play, but only if the match has been played out.

First innings qualifying points (3) gained shall be retained irrespective of the final result of a match, provided that a county shall receive not more than ten points in such match.

In a one-day match, there having been no play on the first day, a tie is recorded if the scores of the completed first innings are equal, providing only if the match has not been played out to a further conclusion.

19. Neutral umpires shall be provided for all matches in the Competition, and the arrangements for the selection and appointment of such umpires shall be left to the Secretary of the M.C.C.

20. The normal hours of play in the Competition shall be from 11.30 a.m. to 7 p.m. on the first day, and from 11 a.m. to 6 p.m. on the second day except only that, by agreement between the captains and when it is necessary to leave the ground for luncheon, the luncheon interval may be extended and the additional time made up at the end of the day. The umpires shall be informed of such extension before the luncheon interval. The interval for luncheon shall not exceed 40 minutes, unless a captain shall declare an innings closed during the luncheon interval later than 15 minutes after the start of such interval, in which case the time allowed for rolling the wicket (viz. 7 minutes) shall be added to the 40 minutes interval. The time for the luncheon interval shall be left to the home captain to decide before the day's play commences. An extra half-hour shall be allowed on the second day of a match, if necessary, on the demand of either side.

21. Before and after the actual commencement of play the wicket may be protected when necessary, and shall be protected every night if possible during the continuance of a match, but the covering must not protect more than 3 ft. 6 ins. in front of the popping crease. In the case of matches played on First-Class County Grounds, the wicket shall be covered in accordance with the rules in force on that ground.

22. The result of each match in the Competition shall be telegraphed, and the full score (with bowling analysis) shall be posted to the Hon. Secretary by the home county immediately after its conclusion. This score shall for all purposes be deemed the official score.

23. All disputes arising out of the Laws of the Game shall be referred to the M.C.C., whose decision shall be final.

†24. Should any matter arise not provided for in these Rules, the Committee shall have power to deal with it.

25. Except where they are inconsistent with the foregoing, the Rules governing the matches of the First Division of the County Championship shall apply.

26. These Rules shall not be altered except at a General Meeting of the Association.

At their Annual Meeting at Lord's on December 7, 1954, the Minor Counties Cricket Association revised the following rules which take effect from the 1955 season:

*Rule 16. If the two top Counties shall not have played each other, the second County shall have the right to challenge the first to a three-day match which shall decide the Championship and shall be played on a ground chosen by the challenged County. If no result shall have been attained in this match, the Championship shall be decided as if there had been no challenge. A lead on the first innings or a tie shall not be a "result" within the meaning of this Rule.

†Rule 24. Should any matter arise not provided for in these rules or in the case of any dispute or difference as to the interpretation or application thereof, such questions shall be referred to the Committee whose decision on all matters shall be final and conclusive.

MEETINGS IN 1955

TEST SELECTORS

The Board of Control for Test Matches at Home met at Lord's on March 8 and appointed the following Selection Committee for 1955: G. O. Allen (Cambridge University and Middlesex) (chairman), L. E. G. Ames (Kent), A. B. Sellers (Yorkshire) and W. Wooller (Glamorgan).

EDGBASTON ON TEST MATCH ROTA

On the same day the Board of Control decided that the Warwickshire County Cricket Club's ground at Edgbaston should be added to the grounds on which Test Matches would be played from 1957.

Six venues, Lord's, The Oval, Old Trafford, Headingley, Trent Bridge and Edgbaston, will share the Test Matches.

Whenever the Australians tour England, Lord's, The Oval, Old Trafford and Headingley, will always be allocated a Test Match. The fifth venue will alternate between Trent Bridge and Edgbaston. Edgbaston will stage a Test when the Australians visit England in 1961. When any other touring side visits England, the arrangements will be slightly different. There will always be two Tests in London—at Lord's and The Oval, and the remaining four grounds will each drop out in turn.*

No application was received for playing Test Cricket in Wales.

* Old Trafford are the first to drop out in 1957. Then the sequence continues as follows:— 1958, Trent Bridge (New Zealand tour); 1959, Edgbaston (India tour); 1960, Headingley (South Africa); 1961, Trent Bridge (Australia).

FIVE-DAY TEST MATCHES

In future all members of the Imperial Cricket Conference visiting England will play five five-day Test Matches. This will bring India, West Indies, New Zealand and Pakistan into line for the first time with Australia snd South Africa.

"A" TEAM TOURS APPROVED

The Advisory County Cricket Committee also met at Lord's on March 8, and approved, in principle, the suggestion that M.C.C. should send "A" teams on tours abroad. (The first such tour was made to Pakistan in the winter of 1955–56.)

The Committee decided that the maximum duration of a county match shall be twenty-one hours, including intervals, and the minimum twenty hours. In the past the maximum has been twenty-one and the minimum nineteen.

NUMBER OF COUNTY MATCHES UNCHANGED

The Advisory County Cricket Committee, meeting on November 8, turned down by a considerable majority the Fixture Sub-Committee's recommendation to increase the number of matches for each county in the Championship from twenty-eight to thirty-two. They also rejected the idea of reducing the number of matches played by each county to twenty-four.

The Committee stated that the counties would not lose sight of the possibility of a knock-out tournament. The main problem was the drawn match.

DISTRIBUTION OF TEST PROFITS

The Board of Control announced on November 8 that the total receipts for the five Tests between England and South Africa were £97,000. The money, excepting £15,000 from Television, was distributed as follows:—

(i) £6,608 to each of the counties on whose ground a Test was played;
(ii) £2,950 to each of the other first-class counties;
(iii) £446 to each Minor County;
(iv) £223 to the Combined Services;
(v) £1,475 to each University.

TEST MATCH ARRANGEMENTS

The Board of Control announced the following provisional dates for the five Test Matches against West Indies in 1957—

First Test, at Edgbaston, May 30, 31, June 1, 3, 4.
Second Test, at Lord's, June 20, 21, 22, 24, 25.
Third Test, at Trent Bridge, July 4, 5, 6, 8, 9.
Fourth Test, at Leeds, July 25, 26, 27, 29, 30.
Fifth Test, at The Oval, August 22, 23, 24, 26, 27.

Admission to the Test Matches against West Indies will be five shillings.

TAKING OF NEW BALL

The counties agreed that in the season 1956 the new ball shall be optional after 200 runs or 75 overs.

Statistics kept by scorers in English first-class cricket showed that in 1955 the average number of overs bowled before a new ball was taken was 78. In 1954 the figure was 79.

APPEALS AGAINST THE LIGHT

The Counties and the Australians have agreed that in all first-class matches in 1956 there may be one appeal against the light by each batting side during each session of play. They also agreed to continue the experimental law that the captain of the batting side may declare at any time on the first day.

COVERING OF PITCH

In order to protect pitches from heavy rain, the counties decided that, providing no match is in progress, the pitch prepared for a match may be wholly covered at any time prior to the game and not only during the twenty-four hours before the time fixed for the start of play.

The counties decided to experiment with the renovation of holes caused by the bowlers. Groundsmen may now renovate overnight any holes close to the stumps.

CHAMPION COUNTY v. THE REST

The revived Champion County v. The Rest match at The Oval in September 1955, produced £850 for the Umpires' Testimonial Fund.

COUNTY SECRETARIES' MEETING

Mr. R. Aird, Secretary of M.C.C., in his speech at the annual meeting of County Secretaries at Lord's on December 6, wondered whether the whole system of first-class county cricket needed reorganising.

After referring to the fact that most county clubs were not self-supporting from their membership and match receipts, Mr. Aird said: "What I would like to see is some system which would enable some of the many potential first-class and even England cricketers playing in club cricket to be given the chance of taking part in the first-class game. In other words, to have a system which would bring more amateurs back into the game."

Problem Unsolved

Mr. Aird went on: "Beyond the obvious solution of playing over the week-end, I confess I have failed to think of a practical answer to this problem. I am afraid that one is not practical under existing legislation, apart from the natural dislike of making a working day of the first day of the week.

"One of the difficulties about the county programme is that the conditions vary in the counties and what suits one does not necessarily suit another. I cannot help thinking that if you cannot have a Championship in which each county plays the other twice, and in my view you cannot have that unless you reduce the number of first-class counties considerably or make two divisions, then I believe there should be a minimum number of matches laid down and each county should be allowed to arrange a programme to suit its own local conditions."

Too Much County Cricket

"This would mean returning to percentages, but I have never quite known why they are supposed to be so objectionable. It does not seem right to me that some counties should be forced to play matches which economically do them no good, while other counties should be forced to play fewer matches than they would like."

After admitting that the present system was a good compromise, Mr. Aird remarked: "My own view is that there is a good deal too much county cricket. Some of it is of poor quality. I feel it would be better for the game to improve the quality and diminish the quantity."

"Easy Money"

Mr. Aird pointed out that since 1947 attendances had fallen and that the majority of counties depended for survival on supporters' clubs, Test Match profits and television fees.

"These receipts seem to me to come under the heading of 'easy money' which I believe to be a dangerous thing. We must try to make cricket self-supporting without this outside help."

Television

Discussing television, the M.C.C. secretary said that there was no doubt that the screening of Test Matches was a menace to county cricket, and it was therefore necessary to demand high fees.

He added that the I.T.A. had suggested televising about four county matches next season. Mr. Aird considered that 1956 should be used experimentally to see what effect this screening might have on gates. "I think it is possible that the televising of county cricket, if the cricket is attractive, might help the game," he said.

Bowler's Drag

Dealing with the question of the bowler's drag, Mr. Aird said he preferred the front foot to be the deciding factor. As an alternative he suggested that the drag should be legalised, provided the back foot lands behind the bowling crease initially in the delivery stride.

Umpires

Mr. Aird declared that, in his view, the importance of the umpire in the game and the importance of maintaining a high standard of umpiring had not always been sufficiently realised. "I would like," he said, "to pay a high tribute to Frank Chester who is retiring after a brilliantly successful career in that department. Frank Chester set a very high standard in umpiring and has a record which is unlikely to be equalled. I am sure we all hope that his health will improve as the result of less exacting work."

Footnote. On November 21 M.C.C. announced that for reasons of health Chester had decided not to seek nomination to the first-class umpires list for 1956. He had been on the list for 28 seasons (excluding the war years) and stood in 48 Test Matches.

UMPIRES FOR 1956

Captains of the first-class counties chose these twenty-three umpires to stand in first-class matches in 1956:—

H. G. Baldwin (Surrey), T. J. Bartley (Cheshire), J. S. Buller (Worcestershire), E. Cooke (Nottinghamshire), P. Corrall (Leicestershire), D. Davies (Glamorgan), E. Davies (Glamorgan), C. S. Elliott (Derbyshire), Harry Elliott (Derbyshire), Harold Elliott (Lancashire), L. H. Gray (Middlesex), J. J. Hills (Glamorgan), John Langridge (Sussex), R. S. Lay (Northamptonshire), F. S. Lee (Somerset),

K. McCanlis (Bedfordshire), W. E. Phillipson (Lancashire), A. E. Pothecary (Hampshire), W. F. Price (Middlesex), E. A. Roberts (Hertfordshire), F. W Shipston (Nottinghamshire), A. Skelding (Leicestershire), T. Spencer (Kent).

Newcomers to the list are C. S. Elliott, Langridge, Lay, Phillipson and Shipston

MINOR COUNTIES' UMPIRES FOR 1956

Minor Counties' representatives chose the following thirty-three umpires to officiate in their Championship matches for 1956:—

J. W. Ashley, A. Barrett, F. Berry, J. B. Bowes, A. E. Bradford, W. V. Brown J. Buckingham, C. A. Cassie, W. D. Cory, A. Crawshaw, L. D'Arcy, C. E. Dunn J. H. Elliss, C. Fairservice, D. C. Field, L. Fisher, P. J. Franklin, G. E. Hart T. S. Jennings, L. W. K. Martin, T. McMurray, S. H. Moore, J. O'Connor, H. W Parks, G. W. F. Reeves, D. S. Richards, R. E. Rushworth, W. F. Simpson, A. E. D Smith, W. Stephens, H. C. Turner, J. Waddington, C. H. Welch.

Newcomers to the list are Crawshaw, Fisher, O'Connor and Parks.

MINOR COUNTIES' ASSOCIATION

The Minor Counties' Association at their 51st annual meeting at Lord's on December 6 re-elected all their officers and appointed W. B. Franklin (President and Chairman), Frank Crompton (Hon. Secretary) and L. Hancock as their representatives on the Advisory County Cricket Committee.

In addition to W. B. Franklin and Sir Pelham Warner, the following were elected Life Members in recognition of their long services to the Association H. R. Neate and Frank Crompton, of Bedfordshire, and R. A. C. Forrester, o Wiltshire.

Arising from the fact that Surrey had been unable to permit any of their players to be chosen for representative matches since 1950, the following resolution was passed: "That all member counties of the Association should co-operate with the Committee in connection with the choice of players for Representative Matches it being the desire of this Association not only to honour visiting teams from overseas by producing the best available team, but also to maintain a high standard of cricket." It was stated on behalf of Surrey that in recent years the Representative match had clashed with other fixtures and the county had not the players to spare

THE SMALLER BALL

During the 1955 season a smaller ball was tried in twenty-five non-competitive first-class matches. Its circumference was $8\frac{11}{16}$ inches–$8\frac{13}{16}$ inches against the normal ball's $8\frac{13}{16}$ inches–9 inches. It did not produce the results expected and as the large majority of players who used it showed no enthusiasm the Advisory County Cricket Committee decided to shelve the matter, at least for the time being

FOOT DRAG

M.C.C. have paid attention to the matter of foot-dragging by bowlers during the past year. Experiments were carried out at Lord's and among those who watched were the two M.C.C. officials, R. Aird and S. C. Griffith, K. G. Viljoen the South African manager, and two umpires, F. S. Lee and L. Gray. In the trials, a bowler was penalised when he went past the popping crease with his front foot and at other times the "dragger" was brought back to a line drawn eighteen inches to two feet behind the return crease. It was found easier to arbitrate on the front foot.

CRICKET BOOKS 1955

By John Arlott

The titles submitted for review since *Wisden's* last notice of cricket books represent an output greater than that of the preceding twelve months, but still smaller than those noted for several other post-war years. Since 1947, however, bulk has become a minor consideration in the field of cricket writing. The 1955 list does, indeed, contain items of authority which promise enduring importance. On the other hand, the issue of twenty-one books on five Test tours represents a degree of duplication which can profit no one.

The Game of Cricket (Batsford: 25s.) consists of 34 quarto pages of reproductions of pictures from the M.C.C.'s collection, with a substantial essay by Sir Norman Birkett and notes on the illustrations by Diana Rait Kerr, curator of the museum at Lord's. The book is a successor to—as distinct from a reissue of—*The Noble Game*, published by the same house in 1941 as, virtually, an illustrated catalogue of the collection of cricket pictures then belonging to Sir Jeremiah Colman. The edition was limited to 150 copies, of which 50 were "reserved for the collector," and it has since become, in the salerooms, the most expensive modern book on cricket. After Sir Jeremiah Colman's death, most of his pictures passed into the possession of M.C.C. and the plates in the present book are based, with a few exceptions, upon the former Colman collection.

The Game of Cricket is a finely produced book; its illustrations are both pleasing and of historic importance. Miss Rait Kerr's notes are scholarly and valuable, while Sir Norman Birkett has contributed an essay at once as learned and as delightful as his after-dinner speeches on the game had promised.

Cricket in Ireland (The Kerryman Ltd., Tralee, Eire: 15s.) is a well-written and authoritative history of a limited, but not unimportant, centre of the game. Patrick Hone, a member of Ireland's leading cricketing family, was himself captain of the All-Ireland eleven and is now President of the Irish Cricket Union. His book is the product of considerable research and is written with wit, grace and precision. Little more, for instance, could be asked of a critic than such a passage as "Completely self-taught, he [Kirwan] played in a style unadorned with any of the frills of the more sophisticated, and his watchfulness put him in a high class on a bowler's wicket." Every library which aims at historical soundness will include Mr. Hone's book.

Richmond's 100 *Years of Cricket* (Meehen & Co., South Melbourne, Victoria, Australia), by Percy Taylor, is the history, published to mark the centenary of the Melbourne "Grade" Cricket Club which produced D. Smith, E. L. McCormack, L. P. O'Brien,

V. Johnston and D. Ring, all Australian Test match players. Within its 126 pages it traces the successful history of this substantial club which has a membership of well over a thousand. Attractively produced in a black binding, it forms one of the minor histories which tend towards the filling in of Australia's rather scanty cricket history.

The Glad Season (Collins: 15s.)—published some months earlier in Australia under the title *Green Sprigs*—is the third book of Ray Robinson, one of the most accomplished essayists cricket as known. These studies are in Mr. Robinson's now familiar, substantial—four-thousand-word—essay form. His subjects include Harvey, Close, Tyson, Cowdrey, Hanif Mohammad, Archer, May, the New Zealand Sutcliffe, and the Bedser–Morris contest. As usual, Mr. Robinson's writing is well documented, fresh, informed and enthusiastic: no one has created more effective prose portraits of the players of contemporary cricket.

In *Batsman's Paradise* (Hollis and Carter: 12s. 6d.) Ronald Mason has attempted the not uncommon task of a book on the playing and watching life and impressions of an admittedly undistinguished cricketer. The result is an unusually pleasant and readable book. There are quotations from T. S. Eliot and Proust, but there is also "I was half-way to the wicket to begin my first innings, brimming over with confidence and anticipatory delight, when I had forcibly to be dragged back to remove my blazer, which in the excitement I had forgotten to take off." There is, too, this description of Sir John Hobbs as a batsman—"neat and unhurried and brilliant": many have used more words to less accurate effect.

J. P. W. Mallalieu, M.P., in *Sporting Days* (Phoenix House: 15s.), writes as a "Travelling Partisan" lightly and briefly. Forty-eight essays, each of about a thousand words in length, cover many sports. His dozen cricket studies have a conversational ease, and a lightness which is a valuable corrective to the ponderousness of some cricket writing: their main quality is diverting rather than memorable.

Cricketing Courtesy by Bobbie Burlton (from the Author: Whittenden, Hawkhurst, Kent: 5s. 6d. post free) is sub-titled "Manners, Customs and Etiquette." One hundred and forty-nine notes of varying length proffer to the player such advice as "A mild apology to your captain if a rank bad ball is treated with great discourtesy by the batsman and to your wicket-keeper if he allows byes because you quite unintentionally bowled a ball wide of the leg stump, are further occasions where 'manners maketh man'." Mr. Burlton's 66 pages combine cricket wisdom and good taste.

The 1954 edition of *The Playfair Book of Cricket Records* (Playfair: 25s.) by Roy Webber adds a 16-page appendix, covering 1951–53, to the edition of 1951. The mechanical problems involved in revising a book of such size are clearly so considerable that the addition of extra pages may well represent the only economic and practicable method of keeping up to date this considerable work of cricket reference.

Cricket: a Bicentenary in an Essex Setting by E. Montagu Williams (Maldon Cricket Club: 1s.) was produced to celebrate 200 years of cricket in the town. Messages of goodwill from Mr H. S. Altham and representatives of each of the first-class counties preface the nine pages of text and a reproduction of a Victorian engraving which comprise an historical sketch of the game in Maldon.

One Hundred Years at Raeburn Place 1854–1954 (The Edinburgh Academical Club) is "A Short History of the Edinburgh Academy's Playing Field." Apart from its place in the general history of the field, cricket is given seven separate pages and there is a reproduction of "Academy Cricketer, 1828," believed to be the earliest Scottish cricket picture.

The main weight of the year's publication lies in accounts of Test tours—twenty-one books on five series. The New Zealand tour of South Africa in 1953–54 was not, by world cricket standards important; it included, however, an extremely dramatic match in the second Test, at Johannesburg.

Silver Fern on the Veld by R. T. Brittenden (A. H. & A. W. Reed, Wellington, New Zealand: 17s. 6d.) is a soundly written account of the tour through South Africa, the three matches played in Australia on the return journey and the home-coming match.

---

gainst an eleven of the New Zealand players who had not made
ne tour.

The Pakistan team in England in 1954, by its success in drawing
ne Test rubber with England, aroused considerable enthusiasm
n Pakistan for cricket in general and for Kardar's team in par-
cular. It is not, therefore, surprising to find that four books on
ne tour were published in Pakistan. *Test Status on Trial* by
. H. Kardar (National Publications, Karachi: 6/8 rupees) is the
aptain's own account of the tour. It is slight—less than 40,000
vords long—and one could wish for more detail of the Tests, but
: remains important for the record it provides of an essay in team-
uilding.

Shabash! Pakistan by F. Sultan Husain (Modern Papers Ltd.,
ahore: 2/8 rupees) is frankly sub-titled "An 'Ear-witness' account
f the English tour 1954." Compiled in Pakistan by an experienced
ournalist from available broadcast commentaries, it makes intelli-
ent use of quotations from English Press comment on the play
nd players, but must inevitably lack the authority of actual
bservation. Paper-covered, *Shabash! Pakistan* includes scores and
eports of every match played by the touring team, statistics, and
welve illustrations, in its 150 pages.

Pakistan on Cricket Map by Quamaruddin Butt, a Southern
unjab and Delhi cricketer (published by the author, Ministry of
nterior, Government of Pakistan, Karachi: 4/8 rupees), is a larger

book, with 218 pages of text, board covers, and photographic illustrations. It also appears to have been compiled in Pakistan presumably from Press reports, and ends with substantial biographical sketches of each member of the party.

Pakistan vs. England by M. H. Maqsood and M. I. Merchant (Pakistan Printing Works, Karachi: 5/8 rupees), the most extensively illustrated of the three "edited" accounts, was also compiled from reports and research. It sets out to give a full account of the tour, and to provide background to the matches in terms of geography and cricket history. The illustrations are better, as well as more numerous, than those in the other books. Its 194 pages include full match scores, averages and statistics.

The M.C.C. tour of Australia, 1954–55, gave rise to ten books, three booklets and a pamphlet. It is important to note that no one of them reports the continuation of the tour into New Zealand. In reviewing these publications on a necessarily comparative basis Wisden's usual method will be adopted: the books will be arranged in alphabetical order of authors and, from each, the passage relating to a certain incident, chosen at random—in this case the dismissal of Harvey in the first innings of the second Test—will be quoted, together with scope, details of numbers of pages, illustrations and price. In the cases of the books which have looked beyond the cricket for their material, this must be regarded as a matter for further mention.

The Ashes Ablaze by Sidney Barnes (William Kimber: 12s. 6d.) 192 pages, 16 pp. of illustration) is a well-produced book dealing with the Tests and the matches surrounding them: it does not contain match scores. Its "sample" passage reads—"Harvey was positively strokeless, and he remained for 69 minutes to score only 12 runs, when he fell with a sheepishly indifferent stroke to his newly-discovered *bête noire*, Frank Tyson." Mr. Barnes writes with his usual, uninhibited, critical observation.

The Picture Post Book of the Tests by Denzil Batchelor (Hulton Press: 3s. 6d.) is of 48 pages: 23 of those pages are of pictures. The text is devoted to Tests only, and Harvey's dismissal is reported: "But now Harvey produced a tentative and ill-assumed poke at a leaping long-hop from Tyson that popped from the handle of his bat into the hip-bath hands of Colin Cowdrey in the gully."

Arthur Gilligan wrote *The Urn Returns* (André Deutsch: 12s. 6d.) in episodic form, covering all matches of the tour in Australia, and it was the first book on the series to be published. Its manner is terse and personal, with frequent use of headline technique. In the account of the second Test Match the relevant passage reads: "Hole appeared but with four added, Harvey was out—caught by Cowdrey off Tyson (a similar ball to the one Bill Edrich had the previous day). The ball kicked and Neil couldn't get his bat away. He had not been on good terms with himself and never looked comfortable." (207 pages, 16 pages of illustrations.)

Bruce Harris entitled the sixth of his books on England–Australia Test series *Ashes Triumphant 1954–55* (Hutchinson: 10s. 6d.) and, as usual, it was quickly and well produced, at economic price, with 204 pages—14 of illustrations. Major attention is devoted to the Test Matches with excursions to the Barrier Reef and to the Davis Cup final. On the Harvey dismissal, Mr. Harris wrote: "Now Tyson took over the taking of wickets. One run later a kicker from him, of the same sort that had Edrich out the previous day, caused Harvey to lift a catch into the gully."

The Long Hop (Stanley Paul: 12s. 6d.) by Margaret Hughes is an enthusiastic book. The author is interested in people, places and things that happen, so that the Australia of her book is not merely a setting for cricket but a place of interest, of fun and of new impressions, all of which share place with the cricket. All the Test Matches are covered but no scores are included. On the sample incident, Miss Hughes writes: "Now the Englishmen suddenly came to life. 4 runs later Harvey received a beast of a ball from Tyson which spat up at him and splashed off his bat to Cowdrey. 104 for four."

The partnership of the two Australian cricketer-journalists, Keith Miller and R. S. Whitington, produced a sixth title—*Cricket Typhoon* (Macdonald: 12s. 6d.)—divided, according to their usual formula, between essays and accounts of the Test Matches. It is a lively book which runs, at the chosen point: "Harvey played a most unnatural innings. Instead of hitting his way out of his usual early edginess, he played the way the England batsmen had shaped on the first day. When he had scored 12 in sixty-six minutes without threatening the boundary, Tyson found the spot at the Randwick end that had caused the blows to Hutton and May's hands, and caused the dismissal of Edrich and Morris." The book, which also contains an essay by C. B. Fry titled "Appointment with Speed," has 256 pages, seven of illustrations.

The Fight for the Ashes 1954–55 (Harrap: 18s. 9d.) is Mr. A. G. Moyes' second volume in that series. On the sample event, he writes, "Burke, as already recorded, was the first to go, and Neil Harvey followed him about fifteen minutes later, caught off one which lifted abruptly. He had not batted well—a nondescript type of innings which lasted for 69 minutes and left no memories." As usual in the series, all matches in Australia are fully reported. A well-produced book of 268 pages—16 of illustrations—it has a sound statistical appendix.

Ian Peebles on the Ashes (Hodder & Stoughton: 12s. 6d.: 196 pages, 15 pages of illustrations), is a well-made book, conversational in tone, and frequently concerned with the social side of the tour. The chosen passage reads "Neither batsman was quite happy against the enormous pace he [Tyson] generated, and it was no surprise when a ball of good length lifted and Harvey was caught

n the gully off the splice." Mr. Peebles deals with all the team's
matches in Australia.

In *Australia 55* (Michael Joseph: 21s.), Alan Ross goes often
outside the cricket to meet his social and topographical interests
which produced many of his photographs, arranged here in 32
pages of illustration. Of the cricket, he covers the entire tour.
On the fall of Harvey's wicket—"Harvey was an hour over six
runs, two of his scoring shots sending the ball skimming past the
heads of May and Cowdrey in the gully. He seemed, however, to
have settled down for the day when Tyson, whom Hutton had
brought on for Statham, made one kick sharply. Harvey, already
into his stroke, could not withdraw in time, and Cowdrey took as
simple a catch in the gully as Benaud had done to remove Edrich
from a similar ball." There are 271 pages of text, a sound index—
incidentally this is the only book on the tour which has an index at
all—and the standard of production is extremely good.

Victory in Australia (The *Daily Telegraph*: 2s. 6d.) by E. W.
Swanton is a piecing together of the author's reports to his paper
on the Test series. Presented in paper covers, it is well printed
and its 172 pages include a prologue and an epilogue by C. B. Fry
as well as statistics which extend to some revealing comparisons
between periods of Test play. Its sample report runs: "Next,
Harvey got a horrible ball from Tyson that he could only fend off
into gully's hands."

The Ashes Retained (Evans: 12s. 6d.) by E. M. Wellings, which deals with the Test Matches in detail, is clearly printed on 208 pages of large type and has 16 pages of illustrations. On the fall of Harvey's wicket, Mr. Wellings writes: "Harvey played a weak stroke at a shortish ball, which lifted more than he seemed to expect, and gave a simple catch in the gully."

England Keep the Ashes (*News Chronicle*: 2s. 6d.) by Crawford White and Roy Webber has 48 quarto pages between paper covers and includes Test accounts, a sketch of an outstanding player, and a full page from Mr. Webber's score book to each Test innings.

1954–55 "Ashes" Test Album (R. H. Baker, 2 Aynho Walk, Sunnyside, Kingsthorpe, Northampton: 1s.) is a 24-page pamphlet with Test scores, averages and four pages of illustrations. All proceeds of its sale go to the English Schools' Cricket Association.

The Kangaroo Conquers (Museum Press: 15s.) by Pat Landsberg is the only book presented for review on the 1955 Australian visit to the West Indies. Its 224 well-produced pages include 9 of illustrations and cover all the matches of a remarkable tour.

Behind the South African Tests (Putnam: 10s. 6d.) is Norman Cutler's second cricket book. In 222 pages—8 of illustrations—it deals with the background of the South African touring side in England in 1955, and treats of the Test Matches in detail.

England versus South Africa (Hutchinson: 10s. 6d.) by Bruce Harris, covers the same series, with particular attention to the Test Matches but providing much biographical information about the players on both sides and giving the scores and averages for all the matches of the tour. Once again good production makes the price of the book extremely reasonable.

I'll Spin You a Tale (Museum Press: 12s. 6d.) is the autobiography of Eric Hollies, the Warwickshire spin-bowler, and as befits that player's reputation as a raconteur, it contains many revealing and humorous cricket stories.

Instructions to Young Cricketers (Museum Press: 9s. 6d.) by Tom Graveney and Brian Statham is another cheaply priced book with 107 pages of text and plenty of photographs and diagrams. It provides sound basic instruction, its points constantly impressed by references to outstanding players.

Cricket—How to Play (Educational Productions Ltd.: 6s.) has been produced for the M.C.C. It is intended primarily for young cricketers, and represents most admirably the stage of study prior to that provided by the *M.C.C. Cricket Coaching Book.* Clearly much of the experience gained in preparing that book and in the development of the M.C.C.'s coaching schemes has gone into the present volume.

The Umpire's Decision (Phoenix House: 6s.) by Frank S. Lee, the famous county and Test umpire, is a fine reference book for his fellows in that office, who will find it of a size convenient to be carried in the pocket. It consists of the Laws of Cricket and the official notes upon them, amplified and illustrated by the expert comment of the author, and by diagrams.

Artificial Cricket Pitches (Contractors Record Ltd.: 9s. 6d.) by Reginald Wesley, Parks Superintendent of Southgate, is a most valuable book, and one likely to have a considerable, if unacknowledged, effect on British cricket. It is an examination of all types of artificial wickets, the methods of constructing them, and of the various mats suitable for use on them. Concrete pitches, of course, receive most attention, but the "Dutch," clinker-bitumen and asphalt types, are examined, as well as those prepared in sheets or slabs. The chapter headed "Where Pitches Can be Seen" provides an unusual and important guide for club officials who wish to see wickets of various kinds in use before making their own choice.

Wisden Cricketers' Almanack for 1955 (Sporting Handbooks: linen cover 12s. 6d., cloth boards 15s.), the 92nd edition, is once more edited by Norman Preston. Its 1030 pages provide reference to cricket throughout the world and on many levels. Once more, however, it is regrettable that the match scores in the domestic competitions of New Zealand, India, Pakistan and West Indies cannot be given in full: four overseas tours, however, are given extensive coverage, and that of the Canadians in England receives wise treatment. The "Five Cricketers of the Year" are Fazal Mahmood (Pakistan), E. Hollies (Warwickshire), B. Dooland (Notts), G. E. Tribe (Northants) and J. B. Statham (Lancs.). This is the first time for many years that all five have been bowlers, and it is noteworthy that two of them are spin bowlers who developed their craft in Australia before coming into English cricket, and who are ineligible for Test Matches. The special articles in this issue are by Neville Cardus, on the South African team cricket; Sir Pelham Warner—"Twilight Reflections"; and J. M. Kilburn, who writes on Yorkshire. Painstakingly indexed and well produced *Wisden* remains the authoritative reference book of the cricket world.

Playfair Cricket Annual, 1955 (Playfair Books Ltd.: 5s.) represents the eighth year of publication of an annual which has achieved considerable popularity through its attractive presentation, generous illustration and readable quality. Edited, once more, by Gordon Ross, it contains an admirably succinct account, by W. E. Bowes, of the Test series in Australia, 1954–55, and continues valuable reference sections in "Who's Who" and the "Career Records" of contemporary batsmen, bowlers and wicket-keepers.

The Sunday Chronicle Cricket Annual, 1955 (Kemsley Newspapers Ltd.: 1s. 6d.), edited by Ivan Sharpe, in its 58th year of publication, drops the golf section which it has included in post war years and reverts solely to cricket. It maintains its wide coverage of fixtures and statistics.

The News Chronicle Cricket Annual (*News Chronicle*: 1s.), by Crawford White, retains as its outstanding feature, the short biographies of the players of each county, and has reviews of major Test series of the preceding year.

M.C.C. Diary 1955–56 (Heinemann: 4s.) runs from April 1955 to April 1956 and contains much valuable and well-arranged information.

Cricket Fixtures 1955 (*The Times*: 1s.) is an annual booklet containing first-class and Minor Counties fixtures for the season and the major averages of 1954.

"Flagstaff" Cricket Annual 1955 (Flagstaff Press: 2s.) is a 50-page booklet of octavo size edited by Roy Lester. It contains feature articles, a study of each county side with notes on individual players, a note on women's cricket, and an intelligently condensed section of the chief records.

South African Cricket Annual, 1954 (obtainable in Britain from E. K. Brown, Bevois Mount, Liskeard, Cornwall: 6s. 3d.), edited by Geoffrey A. Chettle, continues happily into its third year. A foreword by the President of the South African Cricket Association calling upon the Unions to support it, indicates welcome official support for what is already the longest-lived of South African cricket annuals. 208 pages of text and 16 of illustration provide the only adequate reference to cricket in South Africa.

The South African Non-European Cricket Almanack, 1954–55 (obtainable in Britain from E. K. Brown, Bevois Mount, Liskeard, Cornwall: 4s. 3d.) is a soundly-produced, 86-page record of "non European" cricket in the Union, edited by S. J. Reddy and D. N. Bansda. Well arranged and fully informative within its own field, it also notices cricket in India, Fiji, West Indies, Pakistan, Ceylon, Uganda and Kenya.

The Cricket Almanack of New Zealand 1954 (obtainable in Britain from E. K. Brown, Bevois Mount, Liskeard, Cornwall: 7s. 9d. post free) edited by A. H. Carman and N. S. MacDonald has grown, in its seventh issue, to 176 pages and continues to provide a full record of the game in that country.

Indian Cricket: Almanack for 1953–54 (obtainable in Britain from *The Hindu*, 2 and 3, Salisbury Court, London, E.C.4: 5s.) in its eighth year, uses a method of dating different from that usually adopted so that, recording its publication date as December 1954, it contains results and records of the 1953–54 season in India and of the Pakistani tour in England, 1954. Under the continuing editorship of S. K. Gurunathan, it is 248 pages long and contains full statistics of cricket in India and a long and important appreciation of Vinoo Mankad by V. M. Merchant.

Cricket in Pakistan Annual (Universal Cricket Club, Karachi: 5 rupees) bears the colophon "First published in 1948 and Second in 1951." It is a board-covered volume of 100 octavo pages and is edited by Syed M. H. Maqsood with an Advisory Committee. It contains a number of feature articles, an account of the Quaid-i-Azam Trophy competition, the M.C.C. visit to Pakistan in 1951, and the Pakistan tour of India, 1952–53.

The Official Souvenir Cricket Brochure: New Zealand Tour of South Africa 1953–54 by G. A. Chettle (obtainable in Britain from E. K. Brown, Bevois Mount, Liskeard, Cornwall: 2s.) is in the now familiar format for these publications: it has 48 pages and contains portraits and biographical notes of the members of the touring party and the leading South African players.

Cricketers from South Africa (Playfair Books: 1s.), edited by Gordon Ross, consists of photographs and short biographies of the South African team of 1955 and statistics by Roy Webber within 24 pages.

1955 saw the publication of the fifth *Official Souvenir of the Scarborough Cricket Festival* (Secretary, Scarborough Cricket Festival, Cricket Ground, Scarborough: 1s.) a pleasantly illustrated and presented brochure of 24 pages.

Cricket Quiz (Joiner and Steele: 2s. 6d.) compiled by I. Norris and M. Jones has a foreword by Leslie Compton: it contains 308 questions and answers on cricket.

The Spring Annual, Winter Annual, and ten fortnightly numbers in 1955 comprised Volume 38 of *The Cricketer*.

Derbyshire County Cricket Year Book (Derbyshire County Cricket Supporters' Club: 1s.) appears for the second time from the Club, edited by F. G. Peach and H. F. Dawn. It has 148 pages, some good illustrations, interesting feature articles, a full record of the county's matches in 1954 and useful information regarding the clubs and associations within the county.

Essex County Cricket Club Annual 1955 (Essex C.C.C.: 2s.) edited by Trevor Bailey is 134 pages long and, attractively made up, forms a good record of the county team, second eleven and of cricket within Essex.

Glamorgan County Cricket Club Year Book, 1955 (Glamorgan C.C.C.: 1s.) has 68 pages and comprises an illustrated record of the county team's matches in 1954.

Hampshire County Cricket Club Handbook for 1955 (Hampshire C.C.C.: 1s.) contains, in its 120 pages, ten feature articles, eight illustrations, accounts of county matches in 1954, and numerous records.

Kent County Cricket Annual 1955 (Kent C.C.C.: 2s.) has 180 pages, eight pages of illustration, substantial accounts of the county's matches in 1954 and an extensive section of records.

Nottinghamshire County Cricket Club Handbook 1955 (Nottinghamshire C.C.C.: 1s. 6d.) contains within 76 pages five illustrations, some feature articles and accounts of the county's matches in 1954.

Somerset County Cricket Club Year Book 1954–55 (Somerset C.C.C.: 1s.) is 116 pages long, has nine illustrations, three feature articles and records of the county first team, second team and the Somerset Dragons' eleven.

The Warwickshire Cricket Annual 1955 (Warwickshire C.C.C.: 1s.) (116 pages, 8 pages of illustrations) is edited and compiled by W. G. Wanklyn and E. A. Davies. It is a well-made book with feature articles, the county's matches of 1954, records, statistics and a tabulated reference to the results of all the county's fixtures since 1894.

The Yorkshire County Cricket Club: Fifty-seventh annual report: 1955 (free to members) continues a sturdy volume, 392 pages long, including names and addresses of all members and exhaustive records of the county club and its players.

* * * * *

The normal dictates of literary criticism preclude Mr. Arlott from noticing his own books. During 1954 he had published *Australian Test Journal* (Phoenix House: 9s. 6d.) (pp. 160: 9 pp. illus.). On the dismissal of Harvey in the second Test, the "sample" incident selected in the notices of the other books quoted on the series, he wrote "Hole faced Bailey and Tyson with little comfort but it was Harvey who received from Tyson a ball which reared nastily from just short of a length so that it went, off a reflex backstroke, in a gentle arc to Cowdrey at gully: 104: 4: 12."

The Picture of Cricket (Penguin Books: 5s.) comprises sixteen pages of illustrations, most of them coloured, of cricket pictures between 1778 and 1948, together with an essay which traces the parallel between English social history, cricket history and the development of popular illustration.

FIXTURES FOR 1956

Saturday, April 28

Lord's	M.C.C. v. Yorkshire
Oxford	Univ. v. Gloucs.
Cambridge	Univ. v. Surrey
Arundel	Duke of Norfolk's XI v. Australians (1 day)

Monday, April 30

Southampton	Hants v. Sussex (2 days)

Wednesday, May 2

Lord's	M.C.C. v. Surrey
Birmingham	Warwick. v. Sussex
Worcester	Worcs. v. Australians
Oxford	Univ. v. Middlesex
Cambridge	Univ. v. Yorkshire
Bristol	Gloucs. v. Glam. (2 days)
Taunton	Somerset v. Hants (2 days)

Saturday, May 5

Leicester	Leics. v. Australians
Canterbury	Kent v. Glamorgan
Lord's	M.C.C. v. Hampshire
Northampton	Northants v. Notts.
Taunton	Somerset v. Essex
Oval	Surrey v. Derby.
Hove	Sussex v. Worcs.
Oxford	Univ. v. Yorkshire
Cambridge	Univ. v. Lancs.

Wednesday, May 9

Bradford	Yorkshire v. Australians
Ilford	Essex v. Glamorgan
Lord's	Middlesex v. Notts.
Taunton	Somerset v. Leics.
Oval	Surrey v. Northants
Oxford	Univ. v. Lancs.
Cambridge	Univ. v. Sussex
Southampton	Hants v. Worcs. (2 days)

Saturday, May 12

Nottingham	Notts. v. Australians
Ilford	Essex v. Leics.
Cardiff	Glamorgan v. Surrey
Portsmouth	Hants v. Sussex
Manchester	Lancs. v. Somerset
Lord's	Middlesex v. Gloucs.
Northampton	Northants v. Yorkshire
Worcester	Worcs. v. Warwick.
Cambridge	Univ. v. Kent
Ilkeston	Derby. v. R.A.F.

Wednesday, May 16

Oval	Surrey v. Australians
Bristol	Gloucs. v. Warwick.

Dartford	Kent v. Essex
Lord's	Middlesex v. Derby.
Hove	Sussex v. Glamorgan
Worcester	Worcs. v. Somerset
Oxford	Univ. v. Hampshire
Cambridge	Univ. v. Leics.
Hull	Yorkshire v. Scotland

Saturday, May 19

Cambridge	Univ. v. Australians
Derby	Derby. v. Warwick.
Romford	Essex v. Worcs.
Cardiff	Glam. v. Comb. Serv.
Bristol	Gloucs. v. Somerset
Southampton	Hants v. Kent
Leicester	Leics. v. Northants
Lord's	Middlesex v. Sussex
Nottingham	Notts. v. Surrey
Leeds	Yorkshire v. Lancs.
Oxford	Univ. v. Free Foresters

Wednesday, May 23

Manchester	Lancs. v. Australians
Chesterfield	Derby. v. Middlesex
Romford	Essex v. Gloucs.
Swansea	Glamorgan v. Kent
Leicester	Leics. v. Surrey
Northampton	Northants v. Worcs.
Taunton	Somerset v. Hants
Birmingham	Warwick. v. Yorkshire
Oxford	Univ. v. Notts.
Lord's	M.C.C. v. Club Ckt. Conf. (2 days)

Saturday, May 26

Lord's	M.C.C. v. Australians
Gloucester	Gloucs. v. Surrey
Cowes	Hants v. Worcs.
Manchester	Lancs. v. Glamorgan
Nottingham	Notts. v. Northants
Yeovil	Somerset v. Derby.
Worthing	Sussex v. Essex
Coventry	Warwick. v. Kent
Sheffield	Yorkshire v. Middlesex

Wednesday, May 30

Oxford	Univ. v. Australians
Gravesend	Kent v. Derby.
Liverpool	Lancs. v. Warwick.
Oval	Surrey v. Leics.
Worthing	Sussex v. Gloucs.
Sunderland	Durham v. Yorkshire
Cambridge	Univ. v. Middlesex
Lord's	M.C.C. v. Scotland
Taunton	Somerset v. R.A.F.

Friday, June 1

Lord's	M.C.C. v. R.M.A. (Sandhurst) (1 day)

Saturday, June 2

Hove	Sussex v. Australians
Chesterfield	Derby. v. Yorkshire
Brentwood	Essex v. Northants
Llanelly	Glamorgan v. Leics.
Southampton	Hants v. Gloucs.
Gravesend	Kent v. Notts.
Lord's	Middlesex v. Warwick.
Oval	Surrey v. Somerset
Dudley	Worcs. v. Lancs.
Cambridge	Univ. v. Cambridgeshire

Wednesday, June 6

Buxton	Derby. v. Lancs.
Brentwood	Essex v. Somerset
Cardiff	Glamorgan v. Notts.
Bristol	Gloucs. v. Northants
Leicester	Leics. v. Kent
Lord's	Middlesex v. Worcs.
Bradford	Yorkshire v. Sussex
Oxford	Univ. v. The Army
Cambridge	Univ. v. Warwick.

Thursday, June 7

Nottingham	ENGLAND v. AUS-TRALIA (First Test, 5 days)

Saturday, June 9

Swansea	Glamorgan v. Derby.
Stroud	Gloucs. v. Notts.
Portsmouth	Hants v. Surrey
Manchester	Lancs. v. Essex
Lord's	Middlesex v. Yorkshire
Bath	Somerset v. Kent
Birmingham	Warwick. v. Northants
Worcester	Worcs. v. Leics.
Oxford	Univ. v. Sussex
Cambridge	Univ. v. Free Foresters

Wednesday, June 13

Northampton	Northants v. Australians
Bournemouth	Hants v. Glamorgan
Manchester	Lancs. v. Middlesex
Bath	Somerset v. Notts.
Stourbridge	Worcs. v. Kent
Sheffield	Yorkshire v. Gloucs.
Oxford	Univ. v. Derbyshire
Lord's	M.C.C. v. Camb. Univ.
Birmingham	Warwick. v. Comb. Ser.

Saturday, June 16

Canterbury	Kent v. Australians
Chesterfield	Derby. v. Glamorgan
Chelmsford	Essex v. Camb. Univ.
Hinckley	Leics. v. Warwick.
Lord's	Middlesex v. Hants
Nottingham	Notts. v. Lancs.
Bath	Somerset v. Worcs.

Oval	Surrey v. Yorkshire (J. C. Laker's Benefit)
Horsham	Sussex v. Northants

Wednesday, June 20

Chelmsford	Essex v. Lancs.
Cardiff	Glamorgan v. Hants
Bristol	Gloucs. v. Northants
Tun. Wells	Kent v. Leics.
Nottingham	Notts. v. Middlesex
Oval	Surrey v. Oxford Univ
Horsham	Sussex v. Warwick.
Worcester	Worcs. v. Camb. Univ

Thursday, June 21

Lord's	ENGLAND v. AUSTRALIA (Second Test, 5 days)

Saturday, June 23

Swansea	Glamorgan v. Worcs.
Bristol	Gloucs. v. Oxford Un
Tun. Wells	Kent v. Sussex
Leicester	Leics. v. Notts.
Northampton	Northants v. Middles
Taunton	Somerset v. Camb.Un
Guildford	Surrey v. Hampshire
Birmingham	Warwick. v. Lancs.
Leeds	Yorkshire v. Derby.

Wednesday, June 27

Sheffield	Yorkshire v. Australia
Derby	Derby. v. Northants
Manchester	Lancs. v. Kent
Lord's	Middlesex v. Essex
Nottingham	Notts. v. Glamorgan
Guildford	Surrey v. Camb. Univ
Hove	Sussex v. Leics.
Birmingham	Warwick. v. Oxfor Univ.
Southampton	Hants v. The Army
Worcester	Worcs. v. R.A.F.

Saturday, June 30

Bristol	Gloucs. v. Australians
Burton	Derby. v. Leics.
Westcliff	Essex v. Hants
Lord's	Middlesex v. Lancs.
Kettering	Northants v. Glamorga
Nottingham	Notts. v. Somerset
Oval	Surrey v. Kent
Hove	Sussex v. Camb. Univ
Worcester	Worcs. v. Oxford Uni
Bradford	Yorkshire v. Warwick
Edinburgh	Scotland v. Ireland

Wednesday, July 4

Taunton	Somerset v. Australia
Westcliff	Essex v. Middlesex
Bristol	Gloucs. v. Leics.

Manchester	Lancs. v. Derby.
Northampton	Northants v. Surrey
Birmingham	Warwick. v. Notts.
Hull	Yorkshire v. Hants
Lord's	M.C.C. v. Oxford Univ.
Eastbourne	Col. L. C. Stevens' XI v. Camb. Univ.

Saturday, July 7

Southampton	Hants v. Australians
Lord's	Oxford v. Cambridge
Blackheath	Kent v. Surrey
Manchester	Lancs. v. Sussex
Ashby	Leics. v. Derby.
Peterborough	Northants v. Essex
Nottingham	Notts. v. Yorkshire (F. W. Stocks's Benefit)
Glastonbury	Somerset v. Middlesex (M. F. Tremlett's Benefit)
Birmingham	Warwick. v. Glamorgan
Worcester	Worcs. v. Gloucs.

Wednesday, July 11

Derby	Derby. v. Sussex
Portsmouth	Hants v. Warwick.
Northampton	Northants v. Somerset
Oval	Surrey v. Gloucs.
Kidderminster	Worcs. v. Yorkshire
Paisley	Scotland v. Lancs.

Thursday, July 12

Leeds	ENGLAND v. AUSTRALIA (Third Test, 5 days)

Friday, July 13

Lord's	Eton v. Harrow (2 days)

Saturday, July 14

Chesterfield	Derby. v. Hants
Cardiff	Glamorgan v. Essex
Gloucester	Gloucs. v. Middlesex
Maidstone	Kent v. Northants
Manchester	Lancs. v. Leics.
Nottingham	Notts. v. Sussex
Taunton	Somerset v. Yorkshire
Birmingham	Warwick. v. Worcs.
Oval	Surrey v. Comb. Serv.

Wednesday, July 18

Lord's	Gentlemen v. Players
Colchester	Essex v. Derby.
Swansea	Glamorgan v. Yorkshire
Gloucester	Gloucs. v. Hampshire
Maidstone	Kent v. Middlesex
Liverpool	Lancs. v. Notts.
Leicester	Leics. v. Somerset
Worcester	Worcs. v. Sussex
Northampton	Northants v. R.A.F.

Friday, July 20

Oval	Club Ckt. Conf. v. Australians (1 day)

Saturday, July 21

Lord's	Middlesex v. Australians
Derby	Derby. v. Somerset
Colchester	Essex v. Warwick.
Ebbw Vale	Glamorgan v. Northants
Bournemouth	Hants v. Leics.
Blackpool	Lancs. v. Gloucs.
Hastings	Sussex v. Kent
Worcester	Worcs. v. Notts.
Sheffield	Yorkshire v. Surrey (W. Watson's Benefit)

Wednesday, July 25

Bristol	Gloucs. v. Essex
Bournemouth	Hants v. Lancs.
Lord's	Middlesex v. Glamorgan
Northampton	Northants v. Kent
Hastings	Sussex v. Surrey
Dudley	Worcs. v. Derby.
Harrogate	Yorkshire v. Somerset
Nottingham	Notts. v. R.A.F.
Birmingham	Warwick. v. Scotland

Thursday, July 26

Manchester	ENGLAND v. AUSTRALIA (Fourth Test, 5 days)

Saturday, July 28

Ilkeston	Derby. v. Notts.
Bristol	Gloucs. v. Worcs.
Gillingham	Kent v. Somerset
Loughborough	Leics. v. Middlesex
Northampton	Northants v. Sussex
Oval	Surrey v. Essex
Birmingham	Warwick. v. Hants
Middlesbro.	Yorkshire v. Glamorgan
Lord's	Beaumont v. Oratory (1 day)

Monday, July 30

Lord's	Clifton v. Tonbridge (2 days)

Wednesday, August 1

Oval	Surrey v. Australians
Chesterfield	Derby. v. Worcs.
Southampton	Hants v. Middlesex
Blackpool	Lancs. v. Northants (K. Grieves's Benefit)
Leicester	Leics. v. Sussex
Nottingham	Notts. v. Essex
Coventry	Warwick. v. Gloucs.
Scarborough	Yorkshire v. Kent
Lord's	Rugby v. Marlborough (2 days)

Friday, August 3

| Lord's | Cheltenham v. Hailey-bury and I.S.C. (2 days) |

Saturday, August 4

Swansea	Glam. v. Australians
Canterbury	Kent v. Hampshire
Manchester	Lancs. v. Yorkshire
Northampton	Northants v. Leics.
Taunton	Somerset v. Gloucs.
Oval	Surrey v. Notts.
Hove	Sussex v. Middlesex
Birmingham	Warwick. v. Derby.
Worcester	Worcs. v. Essex

Monday, August 6

| Lord's | Southern Schools v. The Rest (2 days) |

Wednesday, August 8

Clacton	Essex v. Surrey
Birmingham	Warwick. v. Australians
Newport	Glamorgan v. Gloucs.
Canterbury	Kent v. Lancs.
Leicester	Leics. v. Yorkshire
Rushden	Northants v. Hants
Nottingham	Notts. v. Derby.
Hove	Sussex v. Somerset
Lord's	Comb. Serv. v. Public Schools (2 days)

Friday, August 10

| Lord's | Royal Navy v. R.A.F. (2 days) |

Saturday, August 11

Derby	Derby. v. Australians
Clacton	Essex v. Kent
Cardiff	Glamorgan v. Somerset
Cheltenham	Gloucs. v. Sussex
Leicester	Leics. v. Hants (V. E. Jackson's Benefit)
Wellingboro'	Northants v. Lancs.
Nottingham	Notts. v. Warwick.
Oval	Surrey v. Middlesex
Bradford	Yorkshire v. Worcs.

Monday, August 13

| Lord's | The Army v. R.A.F. (2 days) |

Wednesday, August 15

Manchester	Lancs. v. Australians
Cheltenham	Gloucs. v. Glamorgan
Portsmouth	Hants v. Essex
Lord's	Middlesex v. Kent
Wellingboro'	Northants v. Derby.
Nottingham	Notts. v. Worcs.
Weston	Somerset v. Warwick.
Oval	Surrey v. Sussex
Scarborough	Yorkshire v. Leics.

Saturday, August 18

Southend	Essex v. Australians
Cheltenham	Gloucs. v. Kent
Portsmouth	Hants v. Northants
Manchester	Lancs. v. Worcs.
Lord's	Middlesex v. Surrey
Weston	Somerset v. Glamorga
Eastbourne	Sussex v. Derby.
Birmingham	Warwick. v. Leics.
Leeds	Yorkshire v. Notts.

Wednesday, August 22

Derby	Derby. v. Surrey
Southend	Essex v. Yorkshire
Dover	Kent v. Warwick.
Leicester	Leics. v. Gloucs.
Lord's	Middlesex v. Northant
Weston	Somerset v. Lancs.
Eastbourne	Sussex v. Hants
Worcester	Worcs. v. Glamorgan

Thursday, August 23

| Oval | ENGLAND v. AUS TRALIA (Fifth Test, 5 days) |

Saturday, August 25

Chesterfield	Derby. v. Gloucs.
Neath	Glamorgan v. Lancs.
Dover	Kent v. Yorkshire
Leicester	Leics. v. Essex
Dublin	Ireland v. Susse (2 days)
Nottingham	Notts. v. Hants
Taunton	Somerset v. Northants
Birmingham	Warwick. v. Surrey
Worcester	Worcs. v. Middlesex

Tuesday, August 28

| Lord's | M.C.C. Young Pros. London Fed. of Boy Clubs (1 day) |

Wednesday, August 29

Lord's	Gents. of England Australians
Cardiff	Glamorgan v. Sussex
Bournemouth	Hants v. Somerset
Leicester	Leics. v. Worcs.
Nottingham	Notts. v. Gloucs.
Oval	Surrey v. Lancs.
Birmingham	Warwick. v. Essex
Scarborough	Yorkshire v. M.C.C.

Saturday, September 1

Hastings	An England XI Australians
Bournemouth	Hants v. Notts.
Hove	Sussex v. Lancs.
Worcester	Worcs. v. Surrey

arborough	Gentlemen v. Players
orquay	North v. South
ord's	M.C.C. Young Pros. v. Young Amateurs of Middlesex (1 day)

Monday, September 3

ord's	M.C.C. Young Pros. v. English Schools C.A. (1 day)

Wednesday, September 5

arborough	T. N. Pearce's XI v. Australians
val	Surrey v. Warwick.
orquay	An England XI v. A Commonwealth XI

Hastings	An England XI v. A Commonwealth XI

Saturday, September 8

Newcastle	Minor Co's. v. Australians (2 days)
Oval	Champion County v. The Rest (4 days)

Wednesday, September 12

Glasgow	Scotland v. Australians (2 days)

Friday, September 14

Aberdeen	Scotland v. Australians (2 days)

AUSTRALIAN TOUR 1956

APRIL

Arundel	v. Duke of Norfolk's XI (1 day)

MAY

Worcester	v. Worcestershire
Leicester	v. Leicestershire
Bradford	v. Yorkshire
Nottingham	v. Nottinghamshire
Oval	v. Surrey
Cambridge	v. Cambridge Univ.
Manchester	v. Lancashire
Lord's	v. M.C.C.
Oxford	v. Oxford Univ.

JUNE

Hove	v. Sussex
Nottingham	v. ENGLAND (First Test, 5 days)
Northampton	v. Northants
Canterbury	v. Kent
Lord's	v. ENGLAND (Second Test, 5 days)
Sheffield	v. Yorkshire
Bristol	v. Gloucestershire

JULY

4	Taunton	v. Somerset
7	Southampton	v. Hampshire
12	Leeds	v. ENGLAND (Third Test, 5 days)
20	Oval	v. Club Ckt. Conf. (1 day)
21	Lord's	v. Middlesex
26	Manchester	v. ENGLAND (Fourth Test, 5 days)

AUGUST

1	Oval	v. Surrey
4	Swansea	v. Glamorgan
8	Birmingham	v. Warwickshire
11	Derby	v. Derbyshire
15	Manchester	v. Lancashire
18	Southend	v. Essex
23	Oval	v. ENGLAND (Fifth Test, 5 days)
29	Lord's	v. Gentlemen of England

SEPTEMBER

1	Hastings	v. An England XI
5	Scarborough	v. T. N. Pearce's XI
8	Newcastle	v. Minor Counties (2 days)
12	Glasgow	v. Scotland (2 days)
14	Aberdeen	v. Scotland (2 days)

MINOR COUNTIES

Wednesday, May 9

ottingham	Notts. II v. Derby. II
anchester	Lancs. II v. Warwick. II

Tuesday, May 15

rmingham	Warwick. II v. Surrey II

Wednesday, May 16

Bath	Somerset II v. Kent II
Hornsey	Middx. II v. Northants II
Melton Mowbray	Leics. II v. Notts. II

Saturday, May 19

Oval	Surrey II v. Kent II

Monday, May 21

Chester-le-Street	Durham v. Northmbld.
Woodhall Spa	Lincs. v. Notts. II
Manchester	Lancs. II v. Yorks. II
Birmingham	Warwick. II v. Derby. II

Wednesday, May 23

Settle	Yorks. II v. Cumbld.

Friday, May 25

Oval	Surrey II v. Middx. II

Monday, May 28

Rothwell	Northants II v. Lancs. II
Beckenham	Kent II v. Surrey II
Birmingham (Mitchell & Butler's)	Warwick. II v. Staffs.
Newcastle	Northmbld. v. Cheshire

Wednesday, May 30

Leicester (Electricity Sports)	Leics. II v. Lincs.
Middlesbro.	Yorks. II v. Cheshire
Nottingham (Mansfield Road)	Notts. II v. Lancs. II
Hadleigh	Essex II v. Kent II

Monday, June 4

Workington	Cumbld. v. Yorks. II
Birmingham	Warwick. II v. Durham
Northampton	Northants II v. Leics. II

Wednesday, June 6

Bourne	Lincs. v. Beds.
Norton	Staffs. v. Durham
Gravesend	Kent II v. Essex II

Friday, June 8

Northampton	Northants II v. Middx. II

Monday, June 11

Sittingbourne	Kent II v. Somerset II
Huddersfield	Yorks. II v. Staffs.
Leicester (Electricity Sports)	Leics. II v. Northants II
Derby	Derby. II v. Notts. II

Wednesday, June 13

Purfleet	Essex II v. Surrey II
Stalybridge	Cheshire v. Lancs. II
Snibstone, Coalville	Leics. II v. Derby. II

Monday, June 18

Hull	Yorks. II v. Notts. II
Manchester	Lancs II v. Durham

Wednesday, June 20

Wisbech	Cambs. v. Beds.
Harrogate	Yorks. II v. Lincs.
Manchester	Lancs. II v. Derby. II

Thursday, June 21

Mitcham	Surrey II v. Warwick. II

Monday, June 25

B. Auckland	Durham v. Staffs.
Jesmond	Northmbld. v. Yorks. II
Southport	Lancs. II v. Cheshire

Tuesday, June 26

Grimsby	Lincs. v. Cambs.
Oval	Surrey II v. Wilts.

Wednesday, June 27

Newcastle	Northumbld. v. Staffs.
Northampton	Northants II v. Notts. II

Thursday, June 28

Folkestone	Kent II v. Wilts.

Wednesday, July 4

Hitchin	Herts. v. Beds.
Leicester (Electricity Sports)	Leics. II v. Warwick. II
Middlewich	Cheshire v. Yorks. II
March	Cambs. v. Essex II
Streetley	Notts. II v. Lincs.

Thursday, July 5

Oval	Surrey II v. Lancs. II

Monday, July 9

Carlisle	Cumbld. v. Northumble

Tuesday, July 10

Buckhurst Hill	Essex II v. Cambs.

Wednesday, July 11

Broadstairs	Kent II v. Middx. II
Worksop	Notts. II v. Yorks. II
Manchester	Lancs. II v. Northumbo
Coventry (G.E.C. Ground)	Warwick. II v. Leics. II

Friday, July 13

skeard	Cornwall v. Somerset II
stley	Essex II v. Suffolk

Monday, July 16

ling	Middx. II v. Norfolk
rthampton	Northants II v. Yorks. II
uth Shields	Durham v. Cumbld.

Wednesday, July 18

field	Middx. II v. Kent II
y	Cambs. v. Lincs.
acclesfield	Cheshire v. Staffs.
dcar	Yorks. II v. Durham
wcastle	Northmbld. v. Cumbld.
ollaton	Notts. II v. Warwick. II

Friday, July 20

andford	Dorset v. Somerset II

Monday, July 23

ardown Pk.,	Beds. v. Leics. II
Luton	
wcastle	Northmbld. v. Lancs. II
rmingham	Warwick. II v. North-
Mitchell	ants II
& Butler's)	

Wednesday, July 25

olverhamtn.	Staffs. v. Yorks. II
rlington	Durham v. Lancs. II
esterfield	Derby. II v. Leics. II

Thursday, July 26

nden Park	Kent II v. Norfolk

Monday, July 30

Wycombe	Bucks. v. Oxfordshire
wark	Notts. II v. Leics. II
rrow	Lancs. II v. Cumbld.

Wednesday, August 1

nstanton	Norfolk v. Bucks.
mborne	Cornwall v. Berks.
coln	Lincs. v. Yorks. II
ackhill	Durham v. Warwick. II
ndal	Cumbld. v. Lancs. II

Friday, August 3

owbridge	Wilts. v. Somerset II
kenham	Norfolk v. Middx. II
lmouth	Cornwall v. Dorset
orris Mtrs.,	Oxfordshire v. Bucks.
Oxford	
rquay	Devon v. Berks.

Monday, August 6

Bedford Sch.	Beds. v. Lincs.
Lakenham	Norfolk v. Herts.
Swindon	Wilts. v. Surrey II
Scarborough	Yorks. II v. Lancs. II
Newcastle	Northmbld. v. Durham
H. Wycombe	Bucks. v. Berks.
Instow	Devon v. Dorset
Nottingham	Notts. II v. Northants II
Derby	Derby. II v. Warwick. II
Felixstowe	Suffolk v. Essex II

Wednesday, August 8

Bedford Sch.	Beds. v. Cambs.
Slough	Bucks. v. Herts.
Winchmore Hill	Middx. II v. Essex II
Lakenham	Norfolk v. Suffolk
Plymouth	Devon v. Cornwall
Uttoxeter	Staffs. v. Cheshire
Reading Sch.	Berks. v. Oxfordshire
Bridlington	Yorks. II v. Northmbld.
Keswick	Cumbld. v. Durham
Poole	Dorset v. Wilts.

Friday, August 10

Bedford Sch.	Beds. v. Herts.
Taunton	Somerset II v. Cornwall
Lowestoft	Suffolk v. Middx. II
Lakenham	Norfolk v. Notts. II
Oxford, Sports Club ground	Oxfordshire v. Wilts.
Reading	Berks. v. Bucks.

Monday, August 13

Felixstowe	Suffolk v. Herts.
Beddington	Surrey II v. Essex II
Newbury	Berks. v. Cornwall
Chesham	Bucks. v. Kent II
Longton	Staffs. v. Northmbld.
Swindon	Wilts. v. Oxfordshire
Weymouth	Dorset v. Devon
Nuneaton	Warwick. II v. Notts. II

Wednesday, August 15

Fenner's	Cambs. v. Herts.
Frome	Somerset II v. Wilts.
Lakenham	Norfolk v. Kent II
Weymouth	Dorset v. Cornwall
Porthill	Staffs. v. Warwick. II
Oxford (Sports Club ground)	Oxfordshire v. Devon
Stockton	Durham v. Yorks. II
Buxton	Derby. II v. Lancs. II
Oxton	Cheshire v. Northmbld.

Thursday, August 16

Scunthorpe	Lincs. v. Leics. II

Friday, August 17

Felixstowe	Suffolk v. Norfolk
Canterbury	Kent II v. Bucks.
Reading	Berks. v. Devon
Chippenham	Wilts. v. Dorset

Monday, August 20

Wiggeston	Leics. II v. Beds.
Croxley Green	Herts. v. Bucks.
Oxford (Sports Club ground)	Oxfordshire v. Dorset
Marlborough College	Wilts. v. Kent II
St. Helens	Lancs. II v. Northants II

Wednesday, August 22

Hertford	Herts. v. Cambs.
Southgate	Middx. II v. Suffolk
Nottingham	Notts. II v. Norfolk
Birmingham	Warwick. II v. Lancs. II
York	Yorks. II v. Northants II
Reading	Berks. v. Dorset

Friday, August 24

St. Albans	Herts. v. Suffolk
Ascott Park	Bucks. v. Norfolk

Penzance	Cornwall v. Devon
	Somerset II v. Dorset
Oxford (Sports Club ground)	Oxfordshire v. Berks.

Saturday, August 25

Lord's	Middx. II v. Surrey II

Monday, August 27

B. Stortford	Herts. v. Norfolk
Exeter	Devon v. Oxfordshire
Corby	Northants II v. War.
Manchester	Lancs. II v. Notts. II
Blandford	Dorset v. Berks.

Wednesday, August 29

Sidmouth	Devon v. Somerset II
Braintree	Essex II v. Middx. II
Manchester	Lancs. II v. Surrey II
Dorchester	Dorset v. Oxfordshire

Wednesday, September 5

Chard	Somerset II v. Devon

Saturday, September 8

Newcastle	Minor Counties v. Australians (2 days)